# Contents

# Preface

This is a completely new work in the Oxford Mini-dictionary range and is designed primarily for English-speaking users. It provides a handy yet extremely comprehensive reference work for students of Russian, tourists, and business people.

Particular attention has been given to the provision of inflected forms where these cause difficulty, and to showing the stressed syllable of every Russian word as well as changes in stress where they occur. Perfective and imperfective aspects are distinguished and both are given wherever appropriate.

Thanks are due to Alexander and Nina Levtov for their editorial help and valuable advice on contemporary Russian usage, and to Helen McCurdy for help with proof-reading.

D.J.T.

*March 1995*

# Introduction

In order to save space, related words are often grouped together in paragraphs, as are cross-references and compound entries.

The swung dash (~) and the hyphen are also used to save space. The swung dash represents the headword preceding it in bold, or the preceding Russian word, e.g. **Georgian** *n* грузи́н, ~ка. The hyphen is mainly used, in giving grammatical forms, to stand for part of the preceding, or (less often) following, Russian word, e.g. **приходи́ть** (-ожу́, -о́дишь).

Russian headwords are followed by inflexional information where considered necessary. So-called regular inflexions for the purpose of this dictionary are listed in the Appendices.

Where a noun ending is given but not labelled in the singular, it is the genitive ending; other cases are named; in the plural, where cases are identifiable by their endings, they are not labelled, e.g. **сестра́** (*pl* сёстры, сестёр, сёстрам). The gender of Russian nouns can usually be deduced from their endings and it is indicated only in exceptional cases (e.g. for masculine nouns in **-а, -я,** and **-ь,** neuter nouns in **-мя,** and all indeclinable nouns).

Verbs are labelled *impf* or *pf* to show their aspect. Where a perfective verb is formed by the addition of a prefix to the imperfective, this is shown at the headword by a light vertical stroke, e.g. **про|лепета́ть.** When a verb requires the use of a case other than the accusative, this is indicated, e.g. **маха́ть** *impf,* **махну́ть** *pf* + *instr* wave, brandish.

Both the comma and the ampersand (&) are used to show alternatives, e.g. **хотéть** + *gen, acc* means that the Russian verb may govern either the genitive or accusative; **сиротá** *m* & *f* orphan means that the Russian noun is treated as masculine or feminine according to the sex of the person denoted; **Cossack** *n* казáк, -áчка represents the masculine and feminine translations of Cossack; **dilate** *vt* & *i* расширя́ть(ся) means that the Russian verb forms cover both the transitive and intransitive English verbs.

## Stress

The stress of Russian words is shown by an acute accent over the vowel of the stressed syllable. The vowel ё has no stress-mark since it is almost always stressed. The presence of two stress-marks indicates that either of the marked syllables may be stressed.

Changes of stress in inflexion are shown, e.g.

> i) **предложи́ть** (-жý, -жишь)

The absence of a stress-mark on the second person singular indicates that the stress is on the preceding syllable and that the rest of the conjugation is stressed in this way.

> ii) **нача́ть** (.............; нáчал, -á, -о)

The final form, нáчало, takes the stress of the first of the two preceding forms when these differ from each other. Forms that are not shown, here нáчали, are stressed like the last form given.

> iii) **дождь** (-дя́)

The single form given in brackets is the genitive singular and all other forms have the same stressed syllable.

> iv) **душá** (*acc* -у; *pl* -и)

If only one case-labelled form is given in the singular, it is an exception to the regular paradigm. If only one plural form is given (the nominative), the rest follow this. In other words, in this example, the accusative singular and all the plural forms have initial stress.

v) **скобá** (*pl* -ы, -áм)

In the plural, forms that are not shown (here instrumental and prepositional) are stressed like the last form given.

# Proprietary terms

This dictionary includes some words which are, or are asserted to be, proprietary names or trade marks. Their inclusion does not imply that they have acquired for legal purposes a non-proprietary or general significance, nor is any other judgement implied concerning their legal status. In cases where the editor has some evidence that a word is used as a proprietary name or trade mark this is indicated by the label *propr*, but no judgement concerning the legal status of such words is made or implied thereby.

# Abbreviations used in the Dictionary

| | | | |
|---|---|---|---|
| abbr | abbreviation | eccl | ecclesiastical |
| abs | absolute | econ | economics |
| acc | accusative | electr | electricity |
| adj, adjs | adjective(s) | electron | electronics |
| adv, advs | adverb(s) | emph | emphatic |
| aeron | aeronautics | esp | especially |
| agric | agriculture | etc. | etcetera |
| anat | anatomy | | |
| approx | approximate(ly) | f | feminine |
| archaeol | archaeology | fig | figurative |
| archit | architecture | fut | future (tense) |
| astron | astronomy | | |
| attrib | attributive | gen | genitive |
| aux | auxiliary | geog | geography |
| | | geol | geology |
| bibl | biblical | geom | geometry |
| biol | biology | gram | grammar |
| bot | botany | | |
| | | hist | historical |
| chem | chemistry | | |
| cin | cinema(tography) | imper | imperative |
| coll | colloquial | impers | impersonal |
| collect | collective(ly) | impf | imperfective |
| comb | combination | indecl | indeclinable |
| comm | commerce | indef | indefinite |
| comp | comparative | indet | indeterminate |
| comput | computing | inf | infinitive |
| conj, conjs | conjunction(s) | instr | instrumental |
| cul | culinary | int | interjection |
| | | interrog | interrogative |
| dat | dative | | |
| def | definite | ling | linguistics |
| derog | derogatory | loc | locative |
| det | determinate | | |
| dim | diminutive | m | masculine |

| | | | |
|---|---|---|---|
| math | mathematics | propr | proprietary term |
| med | medicine | psych | psychology |
| meteorol | meteorology | | |
| mil | military | refl | reflexive |
| mus | music | rel | relative |
| | | relig | religion; religious |
| n | noun | | |
| naut | nautical | rly | railway |
| neg | negative | | |
| neut | neuter | sb | substantive |
| nn | nouns | sg | singular |
| nom | nominative | sl | slang |
| | | s.o. | someone |
| o.s. | oneself | sth | something |
| | | superl | superlative |
| parl | parliamentary | | |
| part | participle | tech | technical |
| partl | particle | tel | telephony |
| pers | person | theat | theatre |
| pf | perfective | theol | theology |
| philos | philosophy | | |
| phon | phonetics | univ | university |
| phot | photography | usu | usually |
| phys | physics | | |
| pl | plural | v | verb |
| polit | political | v aux | auxiliary verb |
| poss | possessive | vbl | verbal |
| predic | predicate; predicative | vi | intransitive verb |
| | | voc | vocative |
| pref | prefix | vt | transitive verb |
| prep | preposition; prepositional | vulg | vulgar |
| | | vv | verbs |
| pres | present (tense) | | |
| pron, prons | pronoun(s) | zool | zoology |

# A

**a**[1] *conj* and, but; **а (не) то** or else, otherwise.

**а**[2] *int* oh, ah.

**абажу́р** lampshade.

**абба́тство** abbey.

**аббревиату́ра** abbreviation.

**абза́ц** indention; paragraph.

**абонеме́нт** subscription, season ticket. **абоне́нт** subscriber.

**абориге́н** aborigine.

**або́рт** abortion; **де́лать** *impf*, **с~** *pf* ~ have an abortion.

**абрико́с** apricot.

**абсолю́тно** *adv* absolutely. **абсолю́тный** absolute.

**абстра́ктный** abstract.

**абсу́рд** absurdity; the absurd. **абсу́рдный** absurd.

**абсце́сс** abscess.

**аванга́рд** advanced guard; vanguard; avant-garde. **аванга́рдный** avant-garde. **аванпо́ст** outpost; forward position.

**ава́нс** advance (*of money*); *pl* advances, overtures. **ава́нсом** *adv* in advance, on account.

**авансце́на** proscenium.

**авантю́ра** (*derog*) adventure; venture; escapade; shady enterprise. **авантюри́ст** (*derog*) adventurer. **авантюри́стка** (*derog*) adventuress. **авантю́рный** adventurous; adventure.

**авари́йный** breakdown; emergency. **ава́рия** accident, crash; breakdown.

**а́вгуст** August. **а́вгустовский** August.

**а́виа** *abbr* (*of* авиапо́чтой) by airmail.

**авиа-** *abbr in comb* (*of* авиацио́нный) air-, aero-; aviation. **авиакомпа́ния** airline. **~ли́ния** air-route, airway. **~но́сец** (-сца) aircraft carrier. **~по́чта** airmail. **авиацио́нный** aviation; flying; aircraft. **авиа́ция** aviation; aircraft; air-force.

**авока́до** *neut indecl* avocado (pear).

**аво́сь** *adv* perhaps; **на ~** at random, on the off-chance.

**австрали́ец** (-и́йца), **австрали́йка** Australian. **австрали́йский** Australian. **Австра́лия** Australia.

**австри́ец** (-и́йца), **австри́йка** Austrian. **австри́йский** Austrian. **А́встрия** Austria.

**авто-** *in comb* self-; auto-; automatic; motor-. **автоба́за** motor-transport depot. **~биографи́ческий** autobiographical. **~биогра́фия** autobiography; curriculum vitae. **автобус** bus. **~вокза́л** bus-station. **автогра́ф** autograph. **~запра́вочная ста́нция** petrol station. **~кра́т** autocrat. **~крати́ческий** autocratic. **~кра́тия** autocracy. **~магистра́ль** motorway. **~маши́на** motor vehicle. **~моби́ль** *m* car. **~но́мия**

autonomy. ~**но́мный** autonomous; self-contained. ~**пило́т** automatic pilot. ~**портре́т** self-portrait. ~**ру́чка** fountain-pen. ~**ста́нция** bus-station. ~**стра́да** motorway.

**автома́т** slot-machine; automatic device, weapon, etc.; sub-machine gun; robot; **(телефо́н-)~** public call-box.

**автоматиза́ция** automation.

**автоматизи́ровать** *impf & pf* automate; make automatic.

**автомати́ческий** automatic.

**а́втор** author; composer; inventor; *(fig)* architect.

**авторизо́ванный** authorized.

**авторите́т** authority. **авторите́тный** authoritative.

**а́вторск|ий** author's; ~**ий гонора́р** royalty; ~**ое пра́во** copyright. **а́вторство** authorship.

**ара́** *int* aha; yes.

**аге́нт** agent. **аге́нтство** agency. **агенту́ра** (network of) agents.

**агита́тор** agitator, propagandist; canvasser. **агитацио́нный** propaganda, agitation. **агита́ция** propaganda, agitation; campaign. **агити́ровать** *impf (pf* **с~)** agitate, campaign; (try to) persuade, win over. **агитпу́нкт** *abbr* agitation centre.

**аго́ния** agony.

**агра́рный** agrarian.

**агрега́т** aggregate; unit.

**агресси́вный** aggressive. **агре́ссия** aggression. **агре́ссор** aggressor.

**агроно́м** agronomist. **агроно́мия** agriculture.

**ад** *(loc -ý)* hell.

**ада́птер** adapter; *(mus)* pick-up.

**адвока́т** lawyer. **адвокату́ра** legal profession; lawyers.

**администрати́вный** administrative. **администра́тор** administrator; manager. **администра́ция** administration; management.

**адмира́л** admiral.

**а́дрес** *(pl -á)* address. **адреса́т** addressee. **а́дрес|ный** address; ~**ая кни́га** directory. **адресова́ть** *impf & pf* address, send.

**а́дский** infernal, hellish.

**адъюта́нт** aide-de-camp; **ста́рший** ~ adjutant.

**ажу́рн|ый** delicate, lacy; ~**ая рабо́та** openwork; tracery.

**аза́рт** heat; excitement; fervour, ardour, passion. **аза́ртн|ый** venturesome; heated; ~**ая игра́** game of chance.

**а́збука** alphabet; ABC.

**Азербайджа́н** Azerbaijan. **азербайджа́нец** (-нца), **азербайджа́нка** Azerbaijani. **азербайджа́нский** Azerbaijani.

**азиа́т, ~ка** Asian. **азиа́тский** Asian, Asiatic. **А́зия** Asia.

**азо́т** nitrogen.

**а́ист** stork.

**ай** *int* oh; oo.

**а́йсберг** iceberg.

**акаде́мик** academician. **академи́ческий** academic. **акаде́мия** academy.

**аквала́нг** aqualung.

**акваре́ль** water-colour.

**аква́риум** aquarium.

**акведу́к** aqueduct.

**акклиматизи́ровать** *impf & pf* acclimatize; ~**ся** become acclimatized.

**аккомпанеме́нт** accompaniment; **под** ~+*gen* to the accompaniment of. **аккомпаниа́тор**

accompanist. **аккомпани́ровать** *impf* +*dat* accompany.

**акко́рд** chord.

**аккордео́н** accordion.

**акко́рдный** by agreement; ~**ая рабо́та** piece-work.

**аккредити́в** letter of credit. **аккредитова́ть** *impf & pf* accredit.

**аккумуля́тор** accumulator.

**аккура́тный** neat, careful; punctual; exact, thorough.

**акри́л** acrylic. **акри́ловый** acrylic.

**акроба́т** acrobat.

**аксессуа́р** accessory; (stage) props.

**аксио́ма** axiom.

**акт** act; deed; document; **обвини́тельный** ~ indictment.

**актёр** actor.

**акти́в** (*comm*) asset(s).

**активиза́ция** stirring up, making (more) active. **активизи́ровать** *impf & pf* make (more) active, stir up. **акти́вный** active.

**активи́ровать** *impf & pf* (*pf also* **с~**) register, record, presence or absence of; (*sl*) write off.

**а́ктовый зал** assembly hall.

**актри́са** actress.

**актуа́льный** topical, urgent.

**аку́ла** shark.

**аку́стика** acoustics. **акусти́ческий** acoustic.

**акушёр** obstetrician. **акуше́рка** midwife.

**акце́нт** accent, stress. **акценти́ровать** *impf & pf* accent; accentuate.

**акционе́р** shareholder. **акционе́рный** joint-stock. **а́кция**[1] share; *pl* stock. **а́кция**[2] action.

**а́лгебра** algebra.

**а́либи** *neut indecl* alibi.

**алиме́нты** (*pl*; *gen* -**ов**) (*law*) maintenance.

**алкоголи́зм** alcoholism. **алкого́лик** alcoholic. **алкого́ль** *m* alcohol. **алкого́льный** alcoholic.

**аллего́рия** allegory.

**аллерги́я** allergy.

**алле́я** avenue; path, walk.

**аллига́тор** alligator.

**алло́** hello! (*on telephone*).

**алма́з** diamond.

**алта́рь** (-**я́**) *m* altar; chancel, sanctuary.

**алфави́т** alphabet. **алфави́тный** alphabetical.

**а́лчный** greedy, grasping.

**а́лый** scarlet.

**альбо́м** album; sketch-book.

**альмана́х** literary miscellany; almanac.

**альпи́йский** Alpine. **альпини́зм** mountaineering. **альпини́ст, альпини́стка** (mountain-)climber.

**альт** (-**а́**; *pl* -**ы́**) alto; viola.

**альтернати́ва** alternative. **альтернати́вный** alternative.

**альтруисти́ческий** altruistic.

**алюми́ний** aluminium.

**амазо́нка** Amazon; horsewoman; riding-habit.

**амба́р** barn; storehouse, warehouse.

**амби́ция** pride; arrogance.

**амбулато́рия** out-patients' department; surgery. **амбулато́рный больно́й** *sb* out-patient.

**Аме́рика** America. **америка́нец** (-**нца**), **америка́нка** American. **америка́нский** American; US.

**аминокислота́** amino acid.

**ами́нь** *m* amen.

аммиа́к ammonia.

амни́стия amnesty.

амора́льный amoral; immoral.

амортиза́тор shock-absorber.

амортиза́ция depreciation; shock-absorption.

ампе́р (gen pl ампе́р) ampere.

ампута́ция amputation. ампути́ровать impf & pf amputate.

амфетами́н amphetamine.

амфи́бия amphibian.

амфитеа́тр amphitheatre; circle.

ана́лиз analysis; ~ кро́ви blood test. анализи́ровать impf & pf analyse. анали́тик analyst. аналити́ческий analytic(al).

ана́лог analogue. аналоги́чный analogous. анало́гия analogy.

анана́с pineapple.

анархи́ст, ~ка anarchist. анархи́ческий anarchic. ана́рхия anarchy.

анатоми́ческий anatomical. анато́мия anatomy.

анахрони́зм anachronism. анахрони́ческий anachronistic.

анга́р hangar.

а́нгел angel. а́нгельский angelic.

ангина sore throat.

англи́йск|ий English; ~ая була́вка safety-pin. англича́нин (pl -ча́не, -ча́н) Englishman. англича́нка Englishwoman. А́нглия England, Britain.

анекдо́т anecdote; story; funny thing.

анеми́я anaemia.

анестезио́лог anaesthetist. анестези́ровать impf & pf anaesthetize. анестези́рующее сре́дство anaesthetic.

анестези́я anaesthesia.

анке́та questionnaire.

аннекси́ровать impf & pf annex. анне́ксия annexation.

аннули́ровать impf & pf annul; cancel, abolish.

анома́лия anomaly. анома́льный anomalous.

анони́мка anonymous letter. анони́мный anonymous.

анонси́ровать impf & pf announce.

анорекси́я anorexia.

анса́мбль m ensemble; company, troupe.

антагони́зм antagonism.

Анта́рктика the Antarctic.

анте́нна antenna; aerial.

антибио́тик antibiotic(s).

антидепресса́нт antidepressant.

антиква́р antiquary; antique-dealer. антиквариа́т antique-shop. антиква́рный antiquarian; antique.

антило́па antelope.

антипа́тия antipathy.

антисемити́зм anti-Semitism. антисеми́тский anti-Semitic.

антисе́птик antiseptic. антисепти́ческий antiseptic.

антите́зис (philos) antithesis.

антите́ло (pl -а́) antibody.

антифри́з antifreeze.

анти́чность f antiquity; classical. анти́чный ancient, classical.

антоло́гия anthology.

антра́кт interval.

антраци́т anthracite.

антреко́т entrecôte, steak.

антрепренёр impresario.

антресо́ли (pl; gen -ей) mezzanine; shelf.

антропо́лог anthropologist. антропологи́ческий anthropological. антрополо́гия anthropology.

**анфила́да** suite (of rooms).

**анчо́ус** anchovy.

**аншла́г** 'house full' notice.

**апарте́ид** apartheid.

**апати́чный** apathetic. **апа́тия** apathy.

**апелли́ровать** *impf & pf* appeal. **апелляцио́нный суд** Court of Appeal. **апелля́ция** appeal.

**апельси́н** orange; orange-tree. **апельси́нный**, **апельси́новый** orange.

**аплоди́ровать** *impf +dat* applaud. **аплодисме́нты** *m pl* applause.

**апло́мб** aplomb.

**Апока́липсис** Revelation. **апокалипти́ческий** apocalyptic.

**апо́стол** apostle.

**апостро́ф** apostrophe.

**аппара́т** apparatus; machinery, organs. **аппарату́ра** apparatus, gear; (*comput*) hardware. **аппара́тчик** operator; apparatchik.

**аппе́ндикс** appendix. **аппендици́т** appendicitis.

**аппети́т** appetite; прия́тного ~a! bon appétit! **аппети́тный** appetizing.

**апре́ль** *m* April. **апре́льский** April.

**апте́ка** chemist's. **апте́карь** *m* chemist. **апте́чка** medicine chest; first-aid kit.

**ара́б**, **ара́бка** Arab. **ара́бский** Arab, Arabic.

**арави́йский** Arabian.

**аранжи́ровать** *impf & pf* (*mus*) arrange. **аранжиро́вка** (*mus*) arrangement.

**ара́хис** peanut.

**арби́тр** arbitrator. **арбитра́ж** arbitration.

**арбу́з** water-melon.

**аргуме́нт** argument. **аргу-**

**мента́ция** reasoning; arguments. **аргументи́ровать** *impf & pf* argue, (try to) prove.

**аре́на** arena, ring.

**аре́нда** lease. **аренда́тор** tenant. **аре́ндная пла́та** rent. **арендова́ть** *impf & pf* rent.

**аре́ст** arrest. **арестова́ть** *pf*, **аресто́вывать** *impf* arrest; seize, sequestrate.

**аристокра́т**, ~ка aristocrat. **аристократи́ческий** aristocratic. **аристокра́тия** aristocracy.

**арифме́тика** arithmetic. **арифмети́ческий** arithmetical.

**а́рия** aria.

**а́рка** arch.

**А́рктика** the Arctic. **аркти́ческий** arctic.

**армату́ра** fittings; reinforcement; armature. **армату́рщик** fitter.

**арме́йский** army.

**Арме́ния** Armenia.

**а́рмия** army.

**армяни́н** (*pl* -я́не, -я́н), **армя́нка** Armenian. **армя́нский** Armenian.

**арома́т** scent, aroma. **арома́тный** aromatic, fragrant.

**арсена́л** arsenal.

**арте́ль** artel.

**арте́рия** artery.

**арти́куль** *m* (*gram*) article.

**артилле́рия** artillery.

**арти́ст**, ~ка artiste, artist; expert. **артисти́ческий** artistic.

**артри́т** arthritis.

**а́рфа** harp.

**архаи́ческий** archaic.

**арха́нгел** archangel.

**археоло́г** archaeologist. **археологи́ческий** archaeological. **археоло́гия** archaeology.

**архи́в** archives. **архиви́ст**

archivist. **архи́вный** archive, archival.

**архиепи́скоп** archbishop. **архиере́й** bishop.

**архипела́г** archipelago.

**архите́ктор** architect. **архитекту́ра** architecture. **архитекту́рный** architectural.

**арши́н** arshin (71 cm.).

**асбе́ст** asbestos.

**асимметри́чный** asymmetrical. **асимметри́я** asymmetry.

**аске́т** ascetic. **аске́тизм** asceticism. **аскети́ческий** ascetic.

**асоциа́льный** antisocial.

**аспира́нт, ~ка** post-graduate student. **аспиранту́ра** post-graduate course.

**аспири́н** aspirin.

**ассамбле́я** assembly.

**ассигна́ция** banknote.

**ассимиля́ция** assimilation.

**ассисте́нт** assistant; junior lecturer, research assistant.

**ассортиме́нт** assortment.

**ассоциа́ция** association. **ассоции́ровать** impf & pf associate.

**а́стма** asthma. **астмати́ческий** asthmatic.

**астро́лог** astrologer. **астроло́гия** astrology.

**астрона́вт** astronaut. **астроно́м** astronomer. **астрономи́ческий** astronomical. **астроно́мия** astronomy.

**асфа́льт** asphalt.

**ата́ка** attack. **атакова́ть** impf & pf attack.

**атама́н** ataman (Cossack chieftain); (gang-)leader.

**атеи́зм** atheism. **атеи́ст** atheist.

**ателье́** neut indecl studio; atelier.

**а́тлас**¹ atlas.

**атла́с**² satin. **атла́сный** satin.

**атле́т** athlete; strong man. **атле́тика** athletics. **атлети́ческий** athletic.

**атмосфе́ра** atmosphere. **атмосфе́рный** atmospheric.

**а́том** atom. **а́томный** atomic.

**атташе́** m indecl attaché.

**аттеста́т** testimonial; certificate; pedigree. **аттестова́ть** impf & pf attest; recommend.

**аттракцио́н** attraction; sideshow; star turn.

**ау́** int hi, cooee.

**аудито́рия** auditorium, lecture-room.

**аукцио́н** auction.

**аул** aul (Caucasian or Central Asian village).

**аутопсия** autopsy.

**афе́ра** speculation, trickery. **афери́ст** speculator, trickster.

**афи́ша** placard, poster.

**афори́зм** aphorism.

**А́фрика** Africa. **африка́нец** (-нца), **африка́нка** African. **африка́нский** African.

**аффе́кт** fit of passion; temporary insanity.

**ах** int ah, oh. **а́хать** impf (pf **а́хнуть**) sigh; exclaim; gasp.

**аэро|вокза́л** air terminal. **~дром** aerodynamics. **~дро́м** aerodrome, air-field. **~зо́ль** m aerosol. **~по́рт** (loc -ý) airport.

# Б

**б** partl: see **бы**

**ба́ба** (coll) (old) woman; **сне́жная** ~ snowman.

**ба́бочка** butterfly.

**ба́бушка** grandmother; grandma.

**бага́ж** (-á) luggage. **бага́жник**

carrier; luggage-rack; boot. **ба-га́жный ваго́н** luggage-van.

**баго́р** (-ра́) boat-hook.

**багро́вый** crimson, purple.

**бадминто́н** badminton.

**ба́за** base; depot; basis; ~ **да́нных** database.

**база́р** market; din.

**ба́зис** base; basis.

**байда́рка** canoe.

**ба́йка** flannelette.

**бак**[1] tank, cistern.

**бак**[2] forecastle.

**бакала́вр** (*univ*) bachelor.

**бакале́йный** grocery. **бакале́я** groceries.

**ба́кен** buoy.

**бакенба́рды** (*pl; gen* -ба́рд) side-whiskers.

**баклажа́н** (*gen pl* -ов *or* -жа́н) aubergine.

**бакте́рия** bacterium.

**бал** (*loc* -у́; *pl* -ы́) dance, ball.

**балага́н** farce.

**балала́йка** balalaika.

**бала́нс** (*econ*) balance.

**баланси́ровать** *impf* (*pf* с~) balance; keep one's balance.

**балбе́с** booby.

**балдахи́н** canopy.

**балери́на** ballerina. **бале́т** ballet.

**ба́лка**[1] beam, girder.

**ба́лка**[2] gully.

**балко́н** balcony.

**балл** mark (*in school*); degree; force; **ве́тер в пять ~ов** wind force 5.

**балла́да** ballad.

**балла́ст** ballast.

**балло́н** container, carboy, cylinder; balloon tyre.

**баллоти́ровать** *impf* vote; put to the vote; **~ся** be a candidate (**в** *or* **на**+*acc* for).

**балова́ть** *impf* (*pf* из~) spoil, pamper; **~ся** play about, get up to tricks; amuse o.s. **бало́вство** spoiling; mischief.

**Балти́йское мо́ре** Baltic (Sea).

**бальза́м** balsam; balm.

**балюстра́да** balustrade.

**бамбу́к** bamboo.

**ба́мпер** bumper.

**бана́льность** banality; platitude. **бана́льный** banal.

**бана́н** banana.

**ба́нда** band, gang.

**банда́ж** (-á) truss; belt, band.

**бандеро́ль** wrapper; printed matter, book-post.

**ба́нджо** *neut indecl* banjo.

**банди́т** bandit; gangster.

**банк** bank.

**ба́нка** jar; tin.

**банке́т** banquet.

**банки́р** banker. **банкно́та** banknote. **банкро́т** bankrupt. **банкро́тство** bankruptcy.

**бант** bow.

**ба́ня** bath; bath-house.

**бараба́н** drum. **бараба́нить** *impf* drum, thump. **бараба́нная перепо́нка** ear-drum. **бараба́нщик** drummer.

**бара́к** wooden barrack, hut.

**бара́н** ram; sheep. **бара́нина** mutton; lamb.

**бара́нка** ring-shaped roll; (steering-)wheel.

**барахло́** old clothes, jumble; odds and ends. **барахо́лка** flea market.

**бара́шек** (-шка) young ram; lamb; wing nut; catkin. **бара́шковый** lambskin.

**ба́ржа́** (*gen pl* барж(е́й)) barge.

**ба́рин** (*pl* -ре *or* -ры, бар) landowner; sir.

**баритóн** baritone.

**бáрка** barge.
**бáрмен** barman.
**барóкко** *neut indecl* baroque.
**барóметр** barometer.
**барóн** baron. **баронéсса** baroness.
**барóчный** baroque.
**баррикáда** barricade.
**барс** snow-leopard.
**бáрский** lordly; grand.
**барсýк** (-á) badger.
**бархáн** dune.
**бáрхат** (-у) velvet. **бáрхатный** velvet.
**бáрыня** landowner's wife; madam.
**барыш** (-á) profit. **барышник** dealer; (ticket) speculator.
**барышня** (*gen pl* -шень) young lady; miss.
**барьéр** barrier; hurdle.
**бас** (*pl* -ы́) bass.
**баскетбóл** basket-ball.
**баснослóвный** mythical, legendary; fabulous. **бáсня** (*gen pl* -сен) fable; fabrication.
**басóвый** bass.
**бассéйн** (*geog*) basin; pool; reservoir.
**бастовáть** *impf* be on strike.
**батальóн** battalion.
**батарéйка**, **батарéя** battery; radiator.
**батóн** long loaf; stick, bar.
**бáтька** *m*, **бáтюшка** *m* father; priest. **бáтюшки** *int* good gracious!
**бах** *int* bang!
**бахвáльство** bragging.
**бахромá** fringe.
**бац** *int* bang! crack!
**бацилла** bacillus. **бациллоноситель** *m* carrier.
**бачóк** (-чкá) cistern.
**бáшка** head.
**башлык** (-á) hood.
**башмáк** (-á) shoe; **под ~óм**

у+*gen* under the thumb of.
**бáшня** (*gen pl* -шен) tower, turret.
**баю́кать** *impf* (*pf* у~) sing lullabies (to). **баю́шки-баю́** *int* hushaby!
**баян** accordion.
**бдéние** vigil. **бди́тельность** vigilance. **бди́тельный** vigilant.
**бег** (*loc* -ý; *pl* -á) run, running; race. **бéгать** *indet* (*det* бежáть) *impf* run.
**бегемóт** hippopotamus.
**беглéц** (-á), **беглянка** fugitive. **бéглость** speed, fluency, dexterity. **бéглый** rapid, fluent; fleeting, cursory; *sb* fugitive, runaway. **беговóй** running; race. **бегóм** *adv* running, at the double. **беготня** running about; bustle. **бéгство** flight; escape. **бегýн** (-á), **бегýнья** (*gen pl* -ний) runner.
**бедá** (*pl* -ы) misfortune; disaster; trouble; ~ **в том, что** the trouble is (that). **беднéть** *impf* (*pf* о~) grow poor. **бéдность** poverty; the poor. **бéдный** (-ден, -днá, -дно) poor. **беднягá** *m*, **бедняжка** *m* & *f* poor thing. **бедня́к** (-á), **бедня́чка** poor peasant; poor man, poor woman.
**бедрó** (*pl* бёдра, -дер) thigh; hip.
**бéдственный** disastrous. **бéдствие** disaster. **бéдствовать** *impf* live in poverty.
**бежáть** (бегý *det*; *indet* бéгать) *impf* (*pf* по~) run; flow; fly; boil over; *impf* & *pf* escape. **бéженец** (-нца), **бéженка** refugee.
**без** *prep*+*gen* without; ~ **пяти́**

(мину́т) три five (minutes) to three; ~ че́тверти a quarter to.

**без-, безъ-, бес-** *in comb* in-, un-; non-; -less. **безалкого́льный** non-alcoholic. ~апелляцио́нный peremptory, categorical. ~бо́жие atheism. ~бо́жный godless; shameless, outrageous. ~боле́зненный painless. ~бра́чный celibate. ~бре́жный boundless. ~ве́стный unknown; obscure. ~вку́сие lack of taste, bad taste. ~вку́сный tasteless. ~вла́стие anarchy. ~во́дный arid. ~возвра́тный irrevocable; irrecoverable. ~возме́здный free, gratis. ~во́лие lack of will. ~во́льный weak-willed. ~вре́дный harmless. ~вре́менный untimely. ~вы́ходный hopeless; desperate; uninterrupted. ~гла́зый one-eyed; eyeless. ~гра́мотный illiterate. ~грани́чный boundless, infinite. ~да́рный untalented. ~де́йственный inactive. ~де́йствие inertia, idleness; negligence. ~де́йствовать *impf* be idle, be inactive; stand idle.

**безде́лица** trifle. **безделу́шка** knick-knack. **безде́льник** idler; ne'er-do-well. **безде́льничать** *impf* idle, loaf.

**бе́здна** abyss, chasm; a huge number, a multitude.

**без-.** **бездоказа́тельный** unsubstantial. ~до́мный homeless. ~до́нный bottomless; fathomless. ~доро́жье lack of (good) roads; season when roads are impassable. ~ду́мный unthinking. ~ду́шный heartless; inanimate; life-

less. ~жа́лостный pitiless, ruthless. ~жи́зненный lifeless. ~забо́тный carefree; careless. ~заве́тный selfless, wholehearted. ~зако́ние lawlessness; unlawful act. ~зако́нный illegal; lawless. ~засте́нчивый shameless, barefaced. ~защи́тный defenceless. ~зву́чный silent. ~зло́бный good-natured. ~ли́чный characterless; impersonal. ~лю́дный uninhabited; sparsely populated; lonely.

**безме́н** steelyard.

**без-. безме́рный** immense; excessive. ~мо́лвие silence. ~мо́лвный silent, mute. ~мяте́жный serene, placid. ~наде́жный hopeless. ~надзо́рный neglected. ~нака́занно *adv* with impunity. ~нака́занный unpunished. ~но́гий legless; one-legged. ~нра́вственный immoral.

**безо** *prep*+*gen* = без (*used before* весь *and* вся́кий).

**безобра́зие** ugliness; disgrace, scandal. **безобра́зничать** *impf* make a nuisance of o.s. **безобра́зный** ugly; disgraceful.

**без-. безогово́рочный** unconditional. ~опа́сность safety; security. ~опа́сный safe; secure. ~ору́жный unarmed. ~основа́тельный groundless. ~остано́вочный unceasing; non-stop. ~отве́тный meek, unanswering; dumb. ~отве́тственный irresponsible. ~отка́зно *adv* without a hitch. ~отка́зный trouble-free, smooth-(running). ~отлага́тельный urgent. ~относи́-

**тельно** *adv*+к+*dat* irrespective of. **~отчётный** uncountable. **~ошибочный** unerring; correct. **~рабо́тица** unemployment. **~рабо́тный** unemployed. **~разли́чие** indifference. **~разли́чно** *adv* indifferently; it is all the same. **~разли́чный** indifferent. **~рассу́дный** reckless, imprudent. **~ро́дный** alone in the world; without relatives. **~ро́потный** uncomplaining; meek. **~рука́вка** sleeveless pullover. **~ру́кий** armless; one-armed. **~уда́рный** unstressed. **~уде́ржный** unrestrained; impetuous. **~укори́зненный** irreproachable.

**безу́мец** (-мца) madman. **безу́мие** madness. **безу́мный** mad. **безу́мство** madness.

**без-**. **безупре́чный** irreproachable, faultless. **~усло́вно** *adv* unconditionally; of course, undoubtedly. **~усло́вный** unconditional, absolute; indisputable. **~успе́шный** unsuccessful. **~уста́нный** tireless. **~уте́шный** inconsolable. **~уча́стие** indifference, apathy. **~уча́стный** indifferent, apathetic. **~ымя́нный** nameless, anonymous; **~ымя́нный па́лец** ring-finger. **~ыску́сный** artless, ingenuous. **~ысхо́дный** irreparable; interminable.

**бейсбо́л** baseball.
**бека́р** (*mus*) natural.
**бека́с** snipe.
**беко́н** bacon.
**Белару́сь** Belarus.
**беле́ть** *impf* (*pf* по~) turn white; show white.
**белизна́** whiteness. **бели́ла**

(*pl*; *gen* -и́л) whitewash; Tippex (*propr*). **бели́ть** (белю́шь) *impf* (*pf* вы́-, на-, по-) whitewash; whiten; bleach.
**бе́лка** squirrel.
**беллетри́ст** writer of fiction. **беллетри́стика** fiction.
**бело-** *in comb* white-, leuco-. **белогварде́ец** (-е́йца) White Guard. **~кро́вие** leukaemia. **~ку́рый** fair, blonde. **~ру́с, ~ру́ска, ~ру́сский** Belorussian. **~сне́жный** snow-white.
**белови́к** (-а́) fair copy. **белово́й** clean, fair.
**бело́к** (-лка́) white (*of egg, eye*); protein.
**белоше́йка** seamstress. **белоше́йный** linen.
**белу́га** white sturgeon. **белу́ха** white whale.
**бе́л**|**ый** (бел, -а́, бе́ло) white; clean, blank; *sb* white person; **~ая берёза** silver birch; **~ое кале́ние** white heat; **~ый медве́дь** polar bear; **~ые но́чи** white nights, midnight sun.
**бельги́ец, -ги́йка** Belgian. **бельги́йский** Belgian. **Бе́льгия** Belgium.
**бельё** linen; bedclothes; underclothes; washing.
**бельмо́** (*pl* -а́) cataract.
**бельэта́ж** first floor; dress circle.
**бемо́ль** *m* (*mus*) flat.
**бенефи́с** benefit (performance).
**бензи́н** petrol.
**бензо-** *in comb* petrol. **бензоба́к** petrol-tank. **~во́з** petrol tanker. **~запра́вочная** *sb* filling-station. **~коло́нка** petrol pump. **~прово́д** petrol pipe, fuel line.

**берёг** etc.: see **беречь**.

**бéрег** (loc -ý; pl -á) bank, shore; coast; **на ~ý мóря** at the seaside. **береговóй** coast; coastal.

**бережёшь** etc.: see **беречь**.

**бережлúвый** thrifty. **бéрежный** careful.

**берёза** birch. **Берёзка** hard-currency shop.

**берéменеть** impf (pf за~) be(come) pregnant. **берéменная** pregnant (+instr with). **берéменность** pregnancy; gestation.

**берёт** etc.: see **брать**.

**беречь** (-регý, -режёшь; -рёг, -лá) impf take care of; keep; cherish; husband; be sparing of; **~ся** take care; beware (+gen of).

**берлóга** den, lair.

**берý** etc.: see **брать**.

**бес** devil, demon.

**бес-**: see **без-**.

**бесéда** talk, conversation.

**бесéдка** summer-house.

**бесéдовать** impf talk, converse.

**бесúть** (бешý, бéсишь) impf (pf вз~) enrage; **~ся** go mad; be furious.

**бес-. бесконéчность** infinity; endlessness. **~конéчный** endless. **~корыстие** disinterestedness. **~корыстный** disinterested; **~крáйний** boundless.

**бесóвский** devilish.

**бес-. беспáмятство** unconsciousness. **~партúйный** non-party **~перспектúвный** without prospects; hopeless. **~печность** carelessness, unconcern. **~плáтно** adv free. **~плáтный** free. **~плóдие** sterility, barren-

ness. **~плóдность** futility. **~плóдный** sterile, barren; futile. **~поворóтный** irrevocable. **~подóбный** incomparable. **~позвонóчный** invertebrate.

**беспокóить** impf (pf о~, по~) disturb, bother; trouble; **~ся** worry; trouble. **беспокóйный** anxious; troubled; fidgety. **беспокóйство** anxiety.

**бес-. бесполéзный** useless. **~помощный** helpless; feeble. **~порóдный** mongrel, not thoroughbred. **~порядок** (-дка) disorder; untidy state. **~порядочный** disorderly; untidy. **~посáдочный** non-stop. **~почвенный** groundless. **~пошлинный** duty-free. **~пощáдный** merciless. **~прáвный** without rights. **~предéльный** boundless. **~предмéтный** aimless; abstract. **~препятственный** unhindered; unimpeded. **~прерывный** continuous. **~престáнный** continual.

**беспризóрник, -ница** waif, homeless child. **беспризóрный** neglected; homeless; sb waif, homeless child.

**бес-. беспримéрный** unparalleled. **~принцúпный** unscrupulous. **~пристрáстие** impartiality. **~пристрáстный** impartial. **~просвéтный** pitch-dark; hopeless; unrelieved. **~пýтный** dissolute. **~связный** incoherent. **~сердéчный** heartless. **~сúлие** impotence; feebleness. **~сúльный** impotent, powerless. **~слáвный** inglorious. **~слéдно** adv without trace. ~**слове́сный** dumb; silent, meek; (*theat*) walk-on. ~**сме́нный** permanent, continuous. ~**сме́ртие** immortality. ~**сме́ртный** immortal. ~**смы́сленный** senseless; foolish; meaningless. ~**сли́ца** nonsense. ~**со́вестный** unscrupulous; shameless. ~**созна́тельный** unconscious; involuntary. ~**со́нница** insomnia. ~**спо́рный** indisputable. ~**сро́чный** indefinite; without a time limit. ~**стра́стный** impassive. ~**стра́шный** fearless. ~**стыдный** shameless. ~**та́ктный** tactless.

**бестолко́вщина** confusion, disorder. **бестолко́вый** muddle-headed, stupid; incoherent.

**бес**-. **бесфо́рменный** shapeless. ~**характе́рный** weak, spineless. ~**хи́тростный** artless; unsophisticated. ~**хозя́йственный** improvident. ~**цве́тный** colourless. ~**це́льный** aimless; pointless. ~**це́нный** priceless. ~**це́нок: за ~це́нок** very cheap, for a song. ~**церемо́нный** unceremonious. ~**челове́чный** inhuman. ~**че́стить** (-е́щу) *impf* (*pf* о~**че́стить**) dishonour. ~**че́стный** dishonourable. ~**чи́сленный** innumerable, countless.

**бесчу́вственный** insensible; insensitive. **бесчу́вствие** insensibility; insensitivity.

**бес**-. **бесшу́мный** noiseless.

**бето́н** concrete. **бето́нный** concrete. **бетономеша́лка** concrete-mixer. **бето́нщик** concrete-worker.

**бечева́** tow-rope; rope. **бечёвка** cord, string.

**бе́шенство** rabies; rage. **бе́-**

шеный rabid; furious.

**бешу́** etc.: *see* **беси́ть**

**библе́йский** biblical. **библиографи́ческий** bibliographical. **библиогра́фия** bibliography. **библиоте́ка** library. **библиоте́карь** *m*, -**те́карша** librarian. **би́блия** bible.

**бива́к** bivouac, camp.

**би́вень** (-вня) *m* tusk.

**бигуди́** *pl indecl* curlers.

**бидо́н** can; churn.

**бие́ние** beating; beat.

**бижуте́рия** costume jewellery.

**би́знес** business. **бизнесме́н** businessman.

**биле́т** ticket; card; pass. **биле́тный** ticket.

**биллио́н** billion.

**билья́рд** billiards.

**бино́кль** *m* binoculars.

**бинт** (-á) bandage. **бинтова́ть** *impf* (*pf* за~) bandage. **бинто́вка** bandaging.

**био́граф** biographer. **биографи́ческий** biographical. **биогра́фия** biography. **био́лог** biologist. **биологи́ческий** biological. **биоло́гия** biology. **биохи́мия** biochemistry.

**би́ржа** exchange.

**би́рка** name-plate; label.

**бирюза́** turquoise.

**бис** *int* encore.

**би́сер** (*no pl*) beads.

**бискви́т** sponge cake.

**би́та** bat.

**би́тва** battle.

**битко́м** *adv*: ~ **наби́т** packed.

**биту́м** bitumen.

**бить** (бью, бьёшь) *impf* (*pf* за~, по~, про~, уда́рить) beat; hit; defeat; sound; thump, bang; smash; ~ **в цель** hit the target; ~ **на**+*acc* strive for; ~ **отбо́й** beat a retreat;

~ по+dat damage, wound; ~ся fight; beat; struggle; break; +instr knock, hit, strike; +над+instr struggle with, rack one's brains over. **бифштекс** beefsteak.

**бич** (-á) whip, lash; scourge; homeless person. **бичевáть** (-чýю) impf flog; castigate.

**блáго** good; blessing.

**блáго-** in comb well-, good-. **Благовéщение** Annunciation. ~**вúдный** plausible, specious. ~**волéние** goodwill; favour. ~**воспúтанный** well-brought-up.

**благодарúть** (-рю) impf (pf по~) thank. **благодáрность** gratitude; не стóит ~ности don't mention it. **благодáрный** grateful. **благодаря́** prep+dat thanks to, owing to.

**благо-** **благодéтель** m benefactor. ~**дéтельница** benefactress. ~**дéтельный** beneficial. ~**дýшный** placid; good-humoured. ~**желáтель** m well-wisher. ~**желáтельный** well-disposed; benevolent. ~**звýчный** melodious, harmonious. ~**надёжный** reliable. ~**намéренный** well-intentioned. ~**получие** wellbeing; happiness. ~**получно** adv all right, well; happily; safely. ~**получный** happy, successful; safe. ~**прия́тный** favourable. ~**приятствовать** impf+dat favour. ~**разýмие** sense; prudence. ~**разýмный** sensible. ~**родие**: вáше ~**рóдие** Your Honour. ~**рóдный** noble. ~**рóдство** nobility. ~**склóнность** favour, good graces. ~**склóнный** favourable; gracious. ~**сло**-

**вúть** pf, **благословля́ть** impf bless. ~**состоя́ние** prosperity. ~**твори́тель** m, -**ница** philanthropist. ~**твори́тельный** charitable, charity. ~**твóрный** salutary; beneficial; wholesome. ~**устрóенный** well-equipped, well-planned; with all amenities.

**блажéнный** blissful; simpleminded. **блажéнство** bliss.

**бланк** form.

**блат** (sl) string-pulling; pull, influence. **блатнóй** criminal; soft, cushy.

**бледнéть** (-éю) impf (pf по~) (grow) pale. **блéдность** paleness, pallor. **блéдный** (-ден, -днá, -о) pale.

**блеск** brightness, brilliance, lustre; magnificence.

**блеснýть** (-нý, -нёшь) pf flash, gleam; shine. **блестéть** (-ещý, -стишь or блещешь) impf shine; glitter. **блёстка** sparkle; sequin. **блестя́щий** shining, bright; brilliant.

**блея́ть** (-éет) impf bleat.

**ближáйший** nearest, closest; next. **ближе** comp of **близкий, близко. ближний** near, close; neighbouring; sb neighbour. **близ** prep+gen near, by. **близкий** (-зок, -зкá, -о) near; close; imminent; ~**кие** sb pl one's nearest and dearest, close relatives. **близко** adv near (от+gen to). **близнéц** (-á) twin; pl Gemini. **близорýкий** short-sighted. **близость** closeness, proximity.

**блик** patch of light; highlight. **блин** (-á) pancake. **блиндáж** (-á) dug-out. **блистáть** impf shine; sparkle. **блок** block, pulley, sheave.

блока́да blockade. **блоки-**
**ровать** *impf & pf* blockade;
**~ся** form a bloc. **блокно́т**
writing-pad, note-book.

**блонди́н, блонди́нка** blond(e).

**блоха́** (*pl* -и, -а́м) flea.

**блуд** lechery. **блудни́ца** whore.
**блужда́ть** *impf* roam, wander.

**блу́за, блу́зка** blouse.

**блю́дечко** saucer; small dish.
**блю́до** dish; course. **блю́дце**
saucer.

**боб** (-а́) bean. **бо́бовый** bean.
**бобр** (-а́) beaver.

**Бог** (*voc* Бо́же) God; **дай ~**
God grant; **~ его́ зна́ет** who
knows? **не дай ~** God forbid;
**Бо́же (мой)!** my God! good
God!; **ра́ди ~а** for God's
sake; **сла́ва ~у** thank God.

**богате́ть** (*pf* раз~) grow
rich. **бога́тство** wealth. **бо-**
**га́тый** rich, wealthy; *sb* rich
man. **бога́ч** (-а́) rich man.

**богаты́рь** (-я́) *m* hero; strong
man.

**боги́ня** goddess. **Богома́терь**
Mother of God. **богомо́лец**
(-льца), **богомо́лка** devout
person; pilgrim. **богомо́лье**
pilgrimage. **богомо́льный**
religious, devout. **Богоро́-**
**дица** the Virgin Mary. **бого-**
**сло́в** theologian. **богосло́-**
**вие** theology. **богослуже́-**
**ние** divine service. **богото-**
**ри́ть** *impf* idolize; deify.
**богоху́льство** blasphemy.

**бодри́ть** *impf*. stimulate, invigorate; **~ся** try to keep up
one's spirits. **бо́дрость** cheer-
fulness, courage. **бо́дрство-**
**вать** be awake; stay awake;
keep vigil. **бо́дрый** (бодр, -а́,
-о) cheerful, bright.

**боеви́к** (-а́) smash hit. **бое-**
**во́й** fighting, battle. **бого-**

**ло́вка** warhead. **боепри-**
**па́сы** (*pl*; *gen* -ов) ammunition. **боеспосо́бный** battle-
worthy. **бое́ц** (бойца́) soldier;
fighter, warrior.

**Бо́же**: *see* Бог. **бо́жеский** divine; just. **боже́ственный** divine. **божество́** deity; divin-
ity. **бо́ж|ий** God's; **~ья ко-**
**ро́вка** ladybird. **божо́к** (-жка́)
idol.

**бой** (*loc* -ю́; *pl* -и́, -ёв) battle,
action, fight; fighting; slaugh-
tering; striking; breakage(s).

**бо́йкий** (бо́ек, бойка́, -о) smart,
sharp; glib; lively.

**бойко́т** boycott.

**бо́йня** (*gen pl* бо́ен) slaughterhouse; butchery.

**бок** (*loc* -у́; *pl* -а́) side; flank;
**~ о́ ~** side by side; **на́ ~** to
the side; **на ~у́** on one side;
**под ~ом** near by; **с ~у** from
the side, from the flank; **с ~у**
**на́ бок** from side to side.

**бока́л** glass, goblet.

**боково́й** side; lateral. **бо́ком**
*adv* sideways.

**бокс** boxing. **боксёр** boxer.

**болва́н** blockhead. **болва́н-**
**ка** pig (*of iron etc.*).

**болга́рин** (*pl* -га́ры), **болга́р-**
**ка** Bulgarian. **болга́рский**
Bulgarian. **Болга́рия** Bulgaria.

**бо́лее** *adv* more; **~ всего́**
most of all; **тем ~, что** especially as.

**боле́зненный** sickly; unhealthy; painful. **боле́знь** illness, disease; abnormality.

**боле́льщик, -щица** fan, supporter. **боле́ть**[1] (-е́ю) *impf*
be ill, suffer. **боле́ть**[2] (-ли́т)
*impf* ache, hurt.

**боло́тистый** marshy. **боло́то**
marsh, bog.

болтáть¹ *impf* stir; shake; dangle; ~ся dangle, swing; hang about.

болтáть² *impf* chat, natter. болтлúвый talkative; indiscreet. болтовня́ talk; chatter; gossip. болтýн (-á), болтýнья chatterbox.

боль pain; ache. больнúца hospital. больнúчный hospital; ~ листóк medical certificate. бóльно¹ *adv* painfully, badly; *predic*+*dat* it hurts. больнó² *adv* very, terribly. больнóй (-лен, -льнá) ill, sick; diseased; sore; *sb* patient, invalid.

бóльше *comp of* большóй, мнóго; bigger, larger; greater; more; ~ не not any more, no longer; ~ тогó and what is more; *adv* for the most part. большевúк Bolshevik. бóльший greater, larger; ~ей чáстью for the most part. большинствó majority. больш|óй big, large; great; grown-up; ~áя бýква capital letter; ~óй пáлец thumb; big toe; ~úе *sb pl* grown-ups.

бóмба bomb. бомбардировáть *impf* bombard; bomb. бомбардирóвка bombardment, bombing. бомбардирóвщик bomber. бомбёжка bombing. бомбúть (-блю) bomb. бомбоубéжище bomb shelter.

бор (*loc* -ý; *pl* -ы́) coniferous forest.

бордóвый wine-red.

бордюр border.

борéц (-рцá) fighter; wrestler.

бóрзый swift.

бормашúна (dentist's) drill.

бормотáть (-очý, -óчешь) *impf* (*pf* про~) mutter, mumble.

бородá (*acc* бóроду; *pl* бóроды, -рóд, -áм) beard. борóдавка wart. борóдатый bearded.

бороздá (*pl* бóрозды, -óзд, -áм) furrow. бороздúть (-зжý) *impf* (*pf* вз~) furrow.

боронá (*acc* бóрону; *pl* бóроны, -рóн, -áм) harrow. боронúть *impf* (*pf* вз~) harrow.

борóться (-рюсь, -рёшься) *impf* wrestle; struggle, fight.

борт (*loc* -ý; *pl* -á, -óв) side, ship's side; front; за ~, за ~ом overboard; на ~, на ~ý on board. бортпроводнúк air steward. бортпроводнúца air hostess.

борщ (-á) borshch (*beetroot soup*).

борьбá wrestling; struggle, fight.

босикóм *adv* barefoot.

боснúец (-úйца), боснúйка Bosnian. боснúйский Bosnian. Бóсния Bosnia.

босóй (бос, -á, -о) barefooted. босонóжка sandal.

бот, бóтик small boat. ботáник botanist. ботáника botany. ботанúческий botanical.

ботúнок (-нка; *gen pl* -нок) (*ankle-high*) boot.

бóцман boatswain.

бóчка barrel. бочóнок (-нка) keg, small barrel.

боязлúвый timid, timorous. боязнь fear, dread.

боя́рин (*pl* -я́ре, -я́р) boyar.

боя́рышник hawthorn.

боя́ться (бою́сь) *impf* +*gen* afraid of, fear; dislike.

брак¹ marriage.

брак² defective goods; flaw. браковáть *impf* (*pf* за~) reject.

**браконьёр** poacher.

**бракоразводный** divorce. **бракосочета́ние** wedding.

**брани́ть** *impf* (*pf* вы́~) scold; abuse, curse; ~ся swear, curse; quarrel. **бра́нный** abusive; ~ое сло́во swear-word.

**брань** bad language; abuse.

**брасле́т** bracelet.

**брасс** breast stroke.

**брат** (*pl* -тья, -тьев) brother; comrade; mate; lay brother, monk. **бра́таться** *impf* (*pf* по~) fraternize. **братоуби́йство** fratricide. **бра́тский** brotherly, fraternal. **бра́тство** brotherhood, fraternity.

**брать** (беру́, -рёшь; брал, -а́, -о) *impf* (*pf* взять) take; obtain; hire; seize; demand, require; surmount, clear; work; +*instr* succeed by means of; ~ся +за+*acc* touch; seize; get down to; +за+*acc or inf* undertake; appear, come.

**бра́чный** marriage; mating.

**бреве́нчатый** log. **бревно́** (*pl* брёвна, -вен) log, beam.

**бред** (*loc* -у́) delirium; raving(s). **бре́дить** (-е́жу) *impf* be delirious, rave; +*instr* rave about, be infatuated with. **бредо́вый** delirious; fantastic, nonsensical.

**бреду́** *etc.: see* **брести́. бре́жу** *etc.: see* **бре́дить**

**брезга́ть** *impf* (*pf* по~) +*inf or instr* be squeamish about. **брезгли́вый** squeamish.

**брезе́нт** tarpaulin.

**бре́зжить(ся** *impf* dawn; gleam faintly, glimmer.

**брёл** *etc.: see* **брести́**

**брело́к** charm, pendant.

**бремени́ть** *impf* (*pf* о~) bur- den. **бре́мя** (-мени) *neut*

burden; load.

**бренча́ть** (-чу́) *impf* strum; jingle.

**брести́** (-еду́, -едёшь; брёл, -а́) *impf* stroll; drag o.s. along.

**брете́ль, брете́лька** shoulder strap.

**брешь** breach; gap.

**брею́** *etc.: see* **брить**

**брига́да** brigade; crew, team. **бригади́р** brigadier; team-leader; foreman.

**бриллиа́нт, брилья́нт** diamond.

**брита́нец** (-нца), **брита́нка** Briton. **брита́нский** British; Б~ие острова́ the British Isles.

**бри́тва** razor. **бри́твенный** shaving. **бри́тый** shaved; clean-shaven. **брить** (бре́ю) *impf* (*pf* по~) shave; ~ся shave (o.s.).

**бровь** (*pl* -и, -е́й) eyebrow; brow.

**брод** ford.

**броди́ть** (-ожу́, -о́дишь) *impf* wander, roam, stroll; ferment. **бродя́га** *m* & *f* tramp, vagrant. **бродя́жничество** vagrancy. **бродя́чий** vagrant; wandering. **броже́ние** ferment, fermentation.

**броне-** *in comb* armoured, armour. **броневи́к** (-á) armoured car. **~во́й** armoured. **~но́сец** (-сца) battleship; armadillo.

**бро́нза** bronze; bronzes. **бро́нзовый** bronze; tanned.

**брониро́ванный** armoured. **брони́ровать** *impf & pf* (*pf also* за~) reserve, book.

**бронхи́т** bronchitis.

**броня́**[1] reservation; commandeering.

**броня́**[2] armour.

**броса́ть** *impf*, **бро́сить** (-о́шу) *pf* throw (down); leave, desert; give up, leave off; ~**ся** throw o.s., rush; +*inf* begin; +*instr* squander; pelt one another with; ~**ся в глаза́** be striking. **бро́ский** striking; garish, glaring. **бросо́к** (-ска́) throw; bound, spurt.

**бро́шка**, **брошь** brooch.

**брошю́ра** pamphlet, brochure.

**брус** (*pl* -сья, -сьев) squared beam, joist; (**паралле́льные**) ~**ья** parallel bars.

**брусни́ка** red whortleberry; red whortleberries.

**брусо́к** (-ска́) bar; ingot.

**бру́тто** *indecl adj* gross.

**бры́згать** (-зжу *or* -гаю) *impf*, **бры́знуть** (-ну) *pf* splash; sprinkle. **бры́зги** (брызг) *pl* spray, splashes; fragments.

**брыка́ть** *impf*, **брыкну́ть** (-ну́, -нёшь) *pf* kick.

**брюзга́** *m & f* grumbler. **брюзгли́вый** grumbling, peevish. **брюзжа́ть** (-жу́) *impf* grumble.

**брю́ква** swede.

**брю́ки** (*pl*; *gen* брюк) trousers.

**брюне́т** dark-haired man. **брюне́тка** brunette.

**брю́хо** (*pl* -и) belly; stomach. **брюшно́й** abdominal; ~ **тиф** typhoid.

**бряца́ть** *impf* rattle; clank, clang.

**бу́бен** (-бна) tambourine. **бубене́ц** (-нца́) small bell. **бу́бны** (*pl*; *gen* -бён, *dat* -бна́м) (*cards*) diamonds. **бубно́вый** diamond.

**буго́р** (-гра́) mound, hillock; bump, lump.

**будди́зм** Buddhism. **будди́йский** Buddhist. **будди́ст** Buddhist.

**бу́дет** that will do.

**буди́льник** alarm-clock. **буди́ть** (бужу́, бу́дишь) *impf* (*pf* про~, раз~) wake; arouse.

**бу́дка** box, booth; hut; stall.

**бу́дни** (*pl*; *gen* -ней) *pl* weekdays; working days; humdrum existence. **бу́дний**, **бу́дничный** weekday; everyday; humdrum.

**бу́дто** *conj* as if, as though; ~ (**бы**), (**как**) ~ apparently, ostensibly.

**бу́ду** *etc.*: *see* **быть**. **бу́дучи** being. **бу́дущий** future; next; ~**ее** *sb* future. **бу́дущность** future. **будь(те)**: *see* **быть**

**бужу́**: *see* **буди́ть**

**бузина́** (*bot*) elder.

**буй** (*pl* -и́, -ёв) buoy.

**буйвол** buffalo.

**бу́йный** (бу́ен, буйна́, -о) violent, turbulent; luxuriant, lush. **бу́йство** unruly behaviour; uproar. **бу́йствовать** *impf* create an uproar, behave violently.

**бук** beech.

**бука́шка** small insect.

**бу́ква** (*gen pl* букв) letter; ~ **в бу́кву** literally. **буква́льно** *adv* literally. **буква́льный** literal. **буква́рь** (-я́) *m* ABC. **букво́ед** pedant.

**буке́т** bouquet; aroma.

**букини́ст** second-hand bookseller.

**бу́кля** curl, ringlet.

**бу́ковый** beech.

**букси́р** tug-boat; tow-rope. **букси́ровать** *impf* tow.

**буксова́ть** *impf* spin, slip.

**була́вка** pin.

**бу́лка** roll; white loaf. **бу́лочка** roll, bun. **бу́лочная** *sb* baker's. **бу́лочник** baker.

**булы́жник** cobble-stone, cobbles.

бульва́р avenue; boulevard.

бульдо́г bulldog.

бульдо́зер bulldozer.

булька́ть *impf* gurgle.

бульо́н broth.

бум (*sport*) beam.

бума́га cotton; paper; document. бума́жка piece of paper; (bank)note. бума́жник wallet; paper-maker. бума́жный cotton; paper.

бу́нкер bunker.

бунт (*pl* -ы́) rebellion; riot; mutiny. бунта́рь (-я́) *m* rebel; insurgent. бунтова́ть(ся *impf* (*pf* вз~) rebel; riot. бунтовщи́к (-а́), -щи́ца rebel, insurgent.

бур auger.

бура́в (-а́; *pl* -а́) auger; gimlet. бура́вить (-влю) *impf* (*pf* про~) bore, drill.

бура́н snowstorm.

буреве́стник stormy petrel.

буре́ние boring, drilling.

буржуа́ *m indecl* bourgeois. буржуази́я bourgeoisie. буржуа́зный bourgeois.

бури́льщик borer, driller. бури́ть *impf* (*pf* про~) bore, drill.

бурли́ть *impf* seethe.

бу́рный (-рен, -рна́, -о) stormy; rapid; energetic.

бурово́|й boring; ~а́я вы́шка derrick; ~а́я (сква́жина) borehole; ~о́й стано́к drilling rig.

бу́рый (бур, -а́, -о) brown.

бурья́н tall weeds.

бу́ря storm.

бу́сина bead. бу́сы (*pl*; *gen* бус) beads.

бутафо́рия (*theat*) props.

бутербро́д open sandwich.

буто́н bud.

бу́тсы (*pl*; *gen* -ов) *pl* football boots.

буты́лка bottle. буты́ль large bottle; carboy.

буфе́т snack bar; sideboard; counter. буфе́тчик barman. буфе́тчица barmaid.

бух *int* bang, plonk. бу́хать *impf* (*pf* бу́хнуть) thump, bang; bang down; thunder, thud; blurt out.

буха́нка loaf.

бухга́лтер accountant. бухгалте́рия accountancy; accounts department.

бу́хнуть (-ну) *impf* swell.

бу́хта bay.

бушева́ть (-шу́ю) *impf* rage, storm.

буя́н rowdy. буя́нить *impf* create an uproar.

бы, б *partl* I. +past tense or *inf* indicates the conditional or subjunctive. II. (+ни) forms indef *prons* and *conjs*.

быва́лый experienced; former; habitual, familiar. быва́ть *impf* be; happen; be inclined to be; как ни в чём не быва́ло as if nothing had happened; быва́ло *partl* used to; would; мать быва́ло ча́сто пе́ла э́ту пе́сню my mother would often sing this song. бы́вший former, ex-.

бык (-а́) bull, ox; pier.

были́на ancient Russian epic.

бы́ло *partl* nearly, on the point of; (only) just. был|о́й past, bygone; ~о́е *sb* the past. быль true story; fact.

быстрота́ speed. бы́стрый (быстр, -а́, -о) fast, quick.

быт (*loc* -у́) way of life. бытие́ being, existence; objective reality; кни́га Бытия́ Genesis. бытово́й everyday; social.

быть (*pres 3rd sg* есть, *pl* суть; *fut* бу́ду; *past* был, -а́, -о;

бу́дь(те)) *impf* be; be situated; happen. **бытьё** way of life.
**бычо́к** (-чка́) steer.
**бью** *etc.: see* **бить**
**бюдже́т** budget.
**бюллете́нь** *m* bulletin; ballot-paper; doctor's certificate.
**бюро́** *neut indecl* bureau; office; writing-desk. **бюрокра́т** bureaucrat. **бюрократи́зм** bureaucracy. **бюрократи́ческий** bureaucratic. **бюрокра́тия** bureaucracy; bureaucrats.
**бюст** bust. **бюстга́льтер** bra.

# В

**в, во** *prep* **I.** +*acc* into; to; on; at; within; through; **быть в** take after; **в два ра́за бо́льше** twice as big; **в на́ши дни** in our day; **войти́ в дом** go into the house; **в понеде́льник** on Monday; **в тече́ние**+*gen* during; **в четы́ре часа́** at four o'clock **высото́й в три ме́тра** three metres high; **игра́ть в ша́хматы** play chess; **пое́хать в Москву́** go to Moscow; **сесть в ваго́н** get into the carriage; **смотре́ть в окно́** look out of the window. **II.** +*prep* in; at; **в двадцатом ве́ке** in the twentieth century; **в теа́тре** at the theatre; **в трёх киломе́трах от го́рода** three kilometres from the town; **в э́том году́** this year; **в январе́** in January.
**ваго́н** carriage, coach; ~**рестора́н** restaurant car. **ваго́нетка** truck, trolley. **ваго́новожа́тый** *sb* tram-driver.
**ва́жничать** *impf* give o.s. airs; +*instr* plume o.s., pride o.s.,

on. **ва́жность** importance; pomposity. **ва́жный** (-жен, -жна́, -о) important; weighty; pompous.
**ва́за** vase, bowl.
**вазели́н** Vaseline (*propr*).
**вака́нсия** vacancy. **вака́нтный** vacant.
**ва́кса** (shoe-)polish.
**ва́куум** vacuum.
**вакци́на** vaccine.
**вал**¹ (*loc* -у́; *pl* -ы́) bank; rampart; billow, roller; barrage.
**вал**² (*loc* -у́; *pl* -ы́) shaft.
**ва́ленок** (-нка; *gen pl* -нок) felt boot.
**вале́т** knave, Jack.
**ва́лик** roller, cylinder.
**вали́ть**¹ *impf* flock, throng.
**вали́ть**² (-лю́, -лишь) *impf* (*pf* по~, с~) throw down, bring down; pile up; ~**ся** fall, collapse.
**валли́ец** (-и́йца) Welshman. **валли́йка** Welshwoman.
**валово́й** gross; wholesale.
**валто́рна** French horn.
**валу́н** (-а́) boulder.
**вальс** waltz. **вальси́ровать** *impf* waltz.
**валю́та** currency; foreign currency.
**валя́ть** *impf* (*pf* на~, с~) drag; roll; shape; bungle; ~ **дурака́** play the fool; ~**ся** lie, lie about; roll, wallow.
**вам, ва́ми:** *see* **вы**
**вампи́р** vampire.
**вада́л** vandal. **вандали́зм** vandalism.
**вани́ль** vanilla.
**ва́нна** bath. **ва́нная** *sb* bathroom.
**ва́рвар** barbarian. **ва́рварский** barbaric. **ва́рварство** barbarity; vandalism.
**ва́режка** mitten.

варёный boiled. варе́нье jam. вари́ть (-рю́, -ришь) impf (pf c~) boil; cook; ~ся boil; cook.

вариа́нт version; option; scenario.

вас: see вы

василёк (-лька́) cornflower.

ва́та cotton wool; wadding.

ватерли́ния water-line. ватерпа́с (spirit-)level.

вати́н (sheet) wadding. ва́тник quilted jacket. ва́тный quilted, wadded.

ватру́шка cheese-cake.

ватт (gen pl ватт) watt.

ва́учер coupon (exchangeable for government-issued share).

ва́фля (gen pl -фель) wafer; waffle.

ва́хта (naut) watch. вахтёр janitor, porter.

ваш (-его) m, ва́ша (-ей) f, ва́ше (-его) neut, ва́ши (-их) pl, pron your, yours.

вбега́ть impf, вбежа́ть (вбегу́) pf run in.

вберу́ etc.: see вобра́ть

вбива́ть impf of вбить

вбира́ть impf of вобра́ть

вбить (вобью́, -бьёшь) pf (impf вбива́ть) drive in, hammer in.

вблизи́ adv (+от+gen) close (to), near by.

вбок adv sideways, to one side.

вброд adv: переходи́ть ~ ford, wade.

вва́ливать impf, ввали́ть (-лю́, -лишь) pf throw heavily, heave, bundle; ~ся heave heavily; sink, become sunken; burst in.

введе́ние introduction. введу́ etc.: see ввести́

ввезти́ (-зу́, -зёшь; ввёз, -ла́) pf (impf ввози́ть) import; bring in.

вве́рить pf (impf вверя́ть) entrust, confide; ~ся +dat trust in, put one's faith in.

ввернуть (-ну́, -нёшь) pf, ввёртывать impf screw in; insert.

вверх adv up, upward(s); ~дном upside down; ~ (по ле́стнице) upstairs. вверху́ adv above, overhead.

вверя́ть(ся) impf of вве́рить(ся)

ввести́ (-еду́, -едёшь; ввёл, -а́) pf (impf вводи́ть) bring in; introduce.

вви́ду prep+gen in view of.

ввинти́ть (-нчу́) pf, ввинчи́вать impf screw in.

ввод lead-in. вводи́ть (-ожу́, -о́дишь) impf of ввести́. вво́дный introductory; parenthetic.

ввожу́ see вводи́ть, ввози́ть

ввоз importation; import(s). ввози́ть (-ожу́, -о́зишь) impf of ввезти́

вво́лю adv to one's heart's content.

ввысь adv up, upward(s).

ввяза́ть (-яжу́, -я́жешь) pf, ввя́зывать impf knit in; involve; ~ся meddle, get or be mixed up (in).

вглубь adv & prep+gen deep (into), into the depths.

вгляде́ться (-яжу́сь) pf, вгля́дываться impf peer, look closely (в+acc at).

вгоня́ть impf of вогна́ть.

вдава́ться (вдаю́сь, -ёшься) impf of вда́ться.

вда́вить (-авлю́, -а́вишь) pf, вда́вливать impf press in.

вдалеке́, вдали́ adv in the distance, far away. вдаль

into the distance.

**вда́ться** (-а́мся, -а́шься, -а́стся, -ади́мся; -а́лся, -ла́сь) *pf* (*impf* **вдава́ться**) jut out; penetrate, go in.

**вдво́е** *adv* twice; double; ~ **бо́льше** twice as big, as much, as many. **вдвоём** *adv* (the) two together, both. **вдвойне́** *adv* twice as much, double; doubly.

**вдева́ть** *impf of* **вдеть**

**вде́лать** *pf*, **вде́лывать** *impf* set in, fit in.

**вдёргивать** *impf*, **вдёрнуть** (-ну) *pf* в+*acc* thread through, pull through.

**вдеть** (-е́ну) *pf* (*impf* **вдева́ть**) put in, thread.

**вдоба́вок** *adv* in addition; besides.

**вдова́** widow. **вдове́ц** (-вца́) widower.

**вдо́воль** *adv* enough; in abundance.

**вдого́нку** *adv* (за+*instr*) after, in pursuit (of).

**вдоль** *adv* lengthwise; ~ и **поперёк** far and wide; in detail; *prep*+*gen or* по+*dat* along.

**вдох** breath. **вдохнове́ние** inspiration. **вдохнове́нный** inspired. **вдохнови́ть** (-влю́) *pf*, **вдохновля́ть** *impf* inspire. **вдохну́ть** (-ну́, -нёшь) *pf* (*impf* **вдыха́ть**) breathe in.

**вдре́безги** *adv* to smithereens.

**вдруг** *adv* suddenly.

**вду́маться** *pf*, **вду́мываться** *impf* ponder, meditate; +в+*acc* think over. **вду́мчивый** thoughtful.

**вдыха́ние** inhalation. **вдыха́ть** *impf of* **вдохну́ть**

**вегетариа́нец** (-нца), -нка vegetarian. **вегетариа́нский** vegetarian.

**ве́дать** *impf* know; +*instr* manage, handle. **ве́дение**[1] authority, jurisdiction.

**ве́дение**[2] conducting, conduct; ~ **книг** book-keeping.

**ве́домость** (*gen pl* -е́й) list, register. **ве́домственный** departmental. **ве́домство** department.

**ведро́** (*pl* вёдра, -дер) bucket; vedro (*approx* 12 litres).

**веду́** *etc.: see* **вести́. веду́щий** leading.

**ведь** *partl & conj* you see, you know; isn't it? is it?

**ве́дьма** witch.

**ве́ер** (*pl* -а́) fan.

**ве́жливость** politeness. **ве́жливый** polite.

**везде́** *adv* everywhere.

**везе́ние** luck. **везу́чий** lucky. **везти́** (-зу́, -зёшь; вёз, -ла́) *impf* (*pf* по~) convey; bring, take; *impers*+*dat* be lucky; **ему́ не везло́** he had no luck.

**век** (*loc* -у́; *pl* -а́) century; age; life, lifetime. **век** *adv* for ages.

**ве́ко** (*pl* -и, век) eyelid.

**веково́й** ancient, age-old.

**ве́ксель** (*pl* -я́, -е́й) *m* promissory note, bill (of exchange).

**вёл** *etc.: see* **вести́**

**веле́ть** (-лю́) *impf & pf* order; не ~ forbid.

**велика́н** giant. **вели́кий** (вели́к, -а́ *or* -а́) great; big, large; too big; ~ **пост** Lent.

**велико-** *in comb* great. **Великобрита́ния** Great Britain. **великоду́шие** magnanimity. ~**ду́шный** magnanimous. ~**ле́пие** splendour. ~**ле́пный** splendid.

**велича́вый** stately, majestic. **велича́йший** greatest, supreme. **вели́чественный**

majestic, grand. **вели́чество** Majesty. **вели́чие** greatness, grandeur. **величина́** (*pl* -и́ны, -а́м) size; quantity, magnitude; value; great figure.

**велосипе́д** bicycle. **велосипеди́ст** cyclist.

**вельве́т** velveteen; ~ в ру́бчик corduroy.

**вельмо́жа** *m* grandee.

**ве́на** vein.

**венге́рец** (-рца), **венге́рка** Hungarian. **венге́рский** Hungarian. **Ве́нгрия** Hungary.

**венде́тта** vendetta.

**венери́ческий** venereal.

**вене́ц** (-нца́) crown; wreath.

**ве́ник** besom; birch twigs.

**вено́к** (-нка́) wreath, garland.

**ве́нтиль** *m* valve.

**вентиля́тор** ventilator; extractor (fan). **вентиля́ция** ventilation.

**венча́ние** wedding; coronation. **венча́ть** *impf* (*pf* об~, по~, у~) crown; marry; ~ся be married, marry. **ве́нчик** halo; corolla; rim; ring, bolt.

**ве́ра** faith, belief.

**вера́нда** veranda.

**ве́рба** willow; willow branch. **ве́рбн|ый**; ~ое воскресе́нье Palm Sunday.

**верблю́д** camel.

**вербова́ть** *impf* (*pf* за~) recruit; win over. **вербо́вка** recruitment.

**верёвка** rope; string; cord. **верёвочный** rope.

**верени́ца** row, file, line, string.

**ве́реск** heather.

**веретено́** (*pl* -тёна) spindle.

**вереща́ть** (-щу́) *impf* squeal; chirp.

**ве́рить** *impf* (*pf* по~) believe,

have faith; +*dat or* в+*acc* trust (in), believe in.

**вермише́ль** vermicelli.

**верне́е** *adv* rather. **ве́рно** *partl* probably, I suppose. **ве́рность** faithfulness, loyalty.

**верну́ть** (-ну́, -нёшь) *pf* (*impf* **возвраща́ть**) give back, return; ~ся return.

**ве́рный** (-рен, -рна́, -о) faithful, loyal; true; correct; reliable.

**ве́рование** belief. **ве́ровать** *impf* believe. **вероиспове́дание** religion; denomination. **вероло́мный** treacherous, perfidious. **вероотсту́пник** apostate. **веротерпи́мость** (religious) toleration. **вероя́тно** *adv* probably. **вероя́тность** probability. **вероя́тный** probable.

**ве́рсия** version.

**верста́** (*pl* вёрсты) verst (*1.06 km.*).

**верста́к** (-а́) work-bench.

**ве́ртел** (*pl* -а́) spit, skewer.

**верте́ть** (-чу́, -тишь) *impf* turn (round); twirl; ~ся turn (round), spin. **вертля́вый** fidgety; flighty.

**вертика́ль** vertical line. **вертика́льный** vertical.

**вертолёт** helicopter.

**ве́рующий** *sb* believer.

**верфь** shipyard.

**верх** (*loc* -у́; *pl* -и́) top; summit; height; *pl* upper crust, top brass; high notes. **ве́рхний** upper; top. **верхо́вный** supreme. **верхово́й** riding; *sb* rider. **верхо́вье** (*gen pl* -вьев) upper reaches. **верхола́з** steeple-jack. **верхо́м** *adv* on horseback; astride. **верху́шка** top, summit; apex; top brass.

верчу́ etc.: see верте́ть

верши́на top, summit; peak; apex. верши́ть *impf* +*instr* manage, control.

вершо́к vershok (*4.4 cm.*); smattering.

вес (*loc* -у́; *pl* -á) weight.

весели́ть *impf* (*pf* раз~) cheer, gladden; ~ся enjoy o.s.; amuse o.s. ве́село *adv* merrily. весёлый (ве́сел, -á, -о) merry; cheerful. весе́лье merriment.

весе́нний spring.

ве́сить (ве́шу) *impf* weigh. ве́ский weighty, solid.

весло́ (*pl* вёсла, -сел) oar.

весна́ (*pl* вёсны, -сен) spring. весно́й *adv* in (the) spring. весну́шка freckle.

вест (*naut*) west; west wind.

вести́ (веду́, -дёшь; вёл, -á) *impf* (*pf* по~) lead, take; conduct; drive; run; keep; ~ себя́ behave, conduct o.s.; ~сь be the custom.

вестибю́ль *m* (entrance) hall, lobby.

ве́стник herald; bulletin. весть¹ (*gen pl* -е́й) news; без вести without trace. весть²: Бог ~ God knows.

весы́ (*pl*; *gen* -о́в) scales, balance; Libra.

весь (вся *m*, вся, всей *f*, всё, всего́ *neut*, все, всех *pl*) *pron* all (the whole of; всего́ хоро́шего! all the best!; всё everything; без всего́ without anything; все everybody.

весьма́ *adv* very, highly.

ветвь (*gen pl* -е́й) branch; bough.

ве́тер (-тра, *loc* -у́) wind. ветеро́к (-рка́) breeze.

ветера́н veteran.

ветерина́р vet.

ве́тка branch; twig.

ве́то *neut indecl* veto.

ве́тошь old clothes, rags.

ве́треный windy; frivolous. ветрово́й wind; ~о́е стекло́ windscreen. ветря́к (-á) wind turbine; windmill.

ве́тхий (ветх, -á, -о) old; dilapidated; В~ заве́т Old Testament.

ветчина́ ham.

ветша́ть *impf* (*pf* об~) decay; become dilapidated.

ве́ха landmark.

ве́чер (*pl* -á) evening; party. вечери́нка party. вече́рний evening. вече́рня (*gen pl* -рен) vespers. ве́чером *adv* in the evening.

ве́чно *adv* for ever, eternally. вечнозелёный evergreen. ве́чность eternity; ages. ве́чный eternal.

ве́шалка peg, rack; tab, hanger. ве́шать *impf* (*pf* взве́сить, пове́сить, све́шать) hang; weigh (out); ~ся hang o.s.; weigh o.s.

ве́шу etc.: see ве́сить

веща́ние broadcasting. веща́ть *impf* broadcast.

веще́вой clothing; ~ мешо́к hold-all, kit-bag. ве́ществ-енный substantial, material, real. вещество́ substance; matter. вещь (*gen pl* -е́й) thing.

ве́ялка winnowing-machine. ве́яние winnowing; blowing; trend. ве́ять (ве́ю) *impf* (*pf* про~) winnow; blow; flutter.

взад *adv* backwards; ~ и вперёд back and forth.

взаи́мность reciprocity. взаи́мный mutual, reciprocal.

взаимо- *in comb* inter-. взаимоде́йствие interaction;

operation. **~действовать** *impf* interact; cooperate. **~отношение** interrelation; *pl* relations. **~помощь** mutual aid. **~понимание** mutual understanding. **~связь** interdependence, correlation.

**взаймы** *adv*: **взять** ~ borrow; **дать** ~ lend.

**взамен** *prep+gen* instead of; in return for.

**взаперти** *adv* under lock and key; in seclusion.

**взбалмошный** unbalanced, eccentric.

**взбегать** *impf*, **взбежать** (-егу) *pf* run up.

**взбесить** *etc.*: *see* **взбеситься**. **вз|бесить(ся** (-ешу(сь, -есишь(ся) *pf*. **взбивать** *impf of* **взбить**, **взбираться** *impf of* **взобраться**

**взбитый** whipped, beaten. **взбить** (взобью, -бьёшь) *pf* (*impf* **взбивать**) beat (up), whip; shake up.

**вз|бороздить** (-зжу) *pf*. **вз|бунтоваться** *pf*.

**взбухать** *impf*, **взбухнуть** (-нет; -ух) *pf* swell (out).

**взваливать** *impf*, **взвалить** (-лю, -лишь) *pf* load; +**на**+*acc* saddle with.

**взвесить** (-ешу) *pf* (*impf* **вешать**, **взвешивать**) weigh.

**взвести** (-еду, -едёшь; -ёл, -á) *pf* (*impf* **взводить**) lead up; raise; cock; +**на**+*acc* impute to.

**взвешивать** *impf of* **взвесить**

**взвивать(ся** *impf of* **взвить(ся**

**взвизг** scream; yelp. **взвизгивать** *impf*, **взвизгнуть** (-ну) *pf* scream; yelp.

**взвинтить** (-нчу) *pf*, **взвинчивать** *impf* excite, work up;

inflate. **взвинченный** worked up; nervy; inflated.

**взвить** (взовью, -ёшь; -ил, -á, -о) *pf* (*impf* **взвивать**) raise; ~**ся** rise, be hoisted; soar.

**взвод**[1] platoon, troop.

**взвод**[2] notch. **взводить** (-ожу, -одишь) *impf of* **взвести**

**взволнованный** agitated; worried. **вз|волновать(ся** (-ную(сь) *pf*.

**взгляд** look; glance; opinion. **взглядывать** *impf*, **взглянуть** (-яну, -янешь) *pf* look, glance.

**взгорье** hillock.

**вздёргивать** *impf*, **вздёрнуть** (-ну) *pf* hitch up; jerk up; turn up.

**вздор** nonsense. **вздорный** cantankerous; foolish.

**вздорожание** rise in price. **вз|дорожать** *pf*.

**вздох** sigh. **вздохнуть** (-ну, -нёшь) *pf* (*impf* **вздыхать**) sigh.

**вздрагивать** *impf* (*pf* **вздрогнуть**) shudder, quiver.

**вздремнуть** *pf* have a nap, doze.

**вздрогнуть** (-ну) *pf* (*impf* **вздрагивать**) start; wince.

**вздуваться** *impf of* **вздуть**[1](ся

**вздумать** *pf* take it into one's head; **не вздумай(те)**! don't you dare!

**вздутие** swelling. **вздутый** swollen. **вздуть**[1] *pf* (*impf* **вздувать**) inflate; ~**ся** swell.

**вздуть**[2] *pf* thrash.

**вздыхать** *impf* (*pf* **вздохнуть**) breathe; sigh.

**взимать** *impf* levy, collect.

**взламывать** *impf of* **взломать**. **вз|лелеять** *pf*.

**взлёт** flight; take-off. **взле-**

та́ть *impf*, **взлете́ть** (-лечу́) *pf* fly (up); take off. **взлёт-ный** take-off; **взлётно-поса́-дочная полоса́** runway.

**взлом** breaking open, break-ing in. **взлома́ть** *pf* (*impf* **взла́мывать**) break open; break up. **взло́мщик** burglar.

**взлохма́ченный** dishevelled.

**взмах** stroke, wave, flap. **взма́-хивать** *impf*, **взмахну́ть** (-ну́, -нёшь) *pf* +*instr* wave, flap.

**взмо́рье** seaside; coastal wa-ters.

**вз|мути́ть** (-учу́, -у́ти́шь) *pf*.

**взнос** fee, dues.

**взнузда́ть** *pf*, **взну́здывать** *impf* bridle.

**взобра́ться** (взберу́сь, -ёшься, -а́лся, -ла́сь, -а́ло́сь) *pf* (*impf* **взбира́ться**) climb (up).

**взобью́** *etc.*: *see* **взбить**. **взо-вью́** *etc.*: *see* **взвить**.

**взойти́** (-йду́, -йдёшь; -ошёл, -шла́) *pf* (*impf* **вос-**, **восхо-ди́ть**) rise, go up; на+*acc* mount.

**взор** look, glance.

**взорва́ть** (-ву́, -вёшь; -а́л, -а́, -о) *pf* (*impf* **взрыва́ть**) blow up; exasperate; **~ся** burst, ex-plode.

**взро́слый** *adj & sb* adult.

**взрыв** explosion; outburst. **взрыва́тель** *m* fuse. **взры-ва́ть** *impf*, **взрыть** (-ро́ю) *pf* (*pf also* **взорва́ть**) blow up; **~ся** explode. **взрывно́й** ex-plosive; blasting. **взрыва́т-ка** explosive. **взры́вчатый** explosive.

**взъеро́шенный** tousled, di-shevelled. **взъеро́шивать** *impf*, **взъеро́шить** (-шу) *pf* tousle, rumple.

**взыва́ть** *impf of* **воззва́ть**

**взыска́ние** penalty; exaction.

**взыска́тельный** exacting. **взыска́ть** (-ыщу́, -ы́щешь) *pf*, **взы́скивать** *impf* exact, re-cover; call to account.

**взя́тие** taking, capture. **взя́т-ка** bribe. **взя́точничество** bribery. **взя́ть(ся** (возьму́(сь, -мёшь(ся; -я́л(ся, -а́(сь, -о(сь) *pf of* **бра́ть(ся**

**вибра́ция** vibration. **вибри́-ровать** *impf* vibrate.

**вивисе́кция** vivisection.

**вид**[1] (*loc* -ý) look; appearance; shape, form; condition; view; prospect; sight; aspect; **де́лать вид** pretend; **име́ть в -ý** in-tend; mean; bear in mind.

**вид**[2] kind; species.

**вида́ть** *impf* (*pf* **по~**) meet. **виде́ние**[1] sight, vision. **виде́-ние**[2] vision, apparition.

**ви́део** *neut indecl* video (cas-sette) recorder; video film; video cassette. **видеоигра́** video game. **видеока́мера** video camera. **видеокассе́та** video cassette. **видеомагнитофо́н** video (cas-sette) recorder.

**ви́деть** (ви́жу) *impf* (*pf* **у~**) see; **во сне** dream (of); **~ся** see one another; appear. **ви́димо** *adv* evidently. **ви́ди-мость** visibility; appearance. **ви́димый** visible; apparent, evident. **ви́дный** (-ден, -дна́, -о) visible; distinguished.

**видоизмене́ние** modifica-tion. **видоизмени́ть** *pf*, **ви-доизменя́ть** *impf* modify.

**видоиска́тель** *m* view-finder.

**ви́жу** *see* **ви́деть**

**ви́за** visa.

**визг** squeal; yelp. **визжа́ть** (-жу́) *impf* squeal, yelp, squeak.

**визи́т** visit. **визи́тка** business card.

**виктори́на**[2] quiz.

ви́лка fork; plug. ви́лы (*pl*; *gen* вил) pitchfork.

вильну́ть (-ну́, -нёшь) *pf*, виля́ть *impf* twist and turn; prevaricate; +*instr* wag.

вина́ (*pl* ви́ны) fault, guilt; blame.

винегре́т Russian salad; medley.

вини́тельный accusative. вини́ть *impf* accuse; ~ся (*impf* по~) confess.

ви́нный wine; winy. вино́ (*pl* -а) wine.

винова́тый guilty. вино́вник initiator; culprit. вино́вный guilty.

виногра́д vine; grapes. виногра́дина grape. виногра́дник vineyard. виногра́дный grape; wine. винокуренный заво́д distillery.

винт (-а́) screw. винти́ть (-нчу́) *impf* screw up. винто́вка rifle. винтово́й screw; spiral.

виолонче́ль cello.

вира́ж (-а́) turn; bend.

виртуо́з virtuoso. виртуо́зный masterly.

ви́рус virus. ви́русный virus.

ви́селица gallows. висе́ть (вишу́) *impf* hang. ви́снуть (-ну; вис(нул)) *impf* hang; droop.

ви́ски *neut indecl* whisky.

висо́к (-ска́) temple.

високо́сный год leap-year.

вист whist.

вися́чий hanging; ~ замо́к padlock; ~ мост suspension bridge.

витами́н vitamin.

витиева́тый flowery, ornate. вито́й twisted, spiral. вито́к (-тка́) turn, coil.

витра́ж (-а́) stained-glass window. витри́на shop-window;

showcase.

вить (вью, вьёшь; вил, -а́, -о) *impf* (*pf* с~) twist, wind, weave; ~ся wind, twine; curl; twist; whirl.

вихо́р (-хра́) tuft. вихра́стый shaggy.

вихрь *m* whirlwind; vortex; снéжный ~ blizzard.

ви́це- *pref* vice-. ви́це-адмира́л vice-admiral. ~прези́дент vice-president.

ВИЧ (*abbr of* ви́рус иммунодефици́та челове́ка) HIV.

вишнёвый cherry. ви́шня (*gen pl* -шен) cherry, cherries; cherry-tree.

вишу́: *see* висе́ть

вишь *partl* look, just look!

вка́лывать *impf* (*sl*) work hard; *impf of* вколо́ть

вка́пывать *impf of* вкопа́ть

вкати́ть (-ачу́, -а́тишь) *pf*, вка́тывать *impf* roll in; administer.

вклад deposit; contribution. вкла́дка supplementary sheet. вкладно́й лист loose leaf, insert. вкла́дчик depositor.

вкла́дывать *impf of* вложи́ть

вкле́ивать *impf*, вкле́ить *pf* stick in.

вкли́ниваться *impf*, вкли́ниться *pf* edge one's way in.

включа́тель *m* switch. включа́ть *impf*, включи́ть (-чу́) *pf* include; switch on; plug in; ~ся в+*acc* join in, enter into. включа́я including. включе́ние inclusion, insertion; switching on. включи́тельно *adv* inclusive.

вкола́чивать *impf*, вколоти́ть (-очу́, -о́тишь) *pf* hammer, knock in.

**вколо́ть** (-олю́, -о́лешь) *pf* (*impf* вка́лывать) stick (in).

**вкопа́ть** *pf* (*impf* вка́пывать) dig in.

**вкось** *adv* obliquely.

**вкра́дчивый** ingratiating. **вкра́дываться** *impf*, **вкра́сться** (-аду́сь, -адёшься) *pf* creep in; insinuate o.s.

**вкра́тце** *adv* briefly, succinctly.

**вкривь** *adv* aslant; wrongly, perversely.

**вкруг** = вокру́г

**вкруту́ю** *adv* hard(-boiled).

**вкус** taste. **вкуси́ть** (-ушу́, -у́сишь) *pf*, **вкуша́ть** *impf* taste; partake of. **вку́сный** (-сен, -сна́, -о) tasty, nice.

**вла́га** moisture.

**влага́лище** vagina.

**владе́лец** (-льца) *-лица* owner. **владе́ние** ownership; possession; property. **владе́тель** *m*, **-ница** possessor; sovereign. **владе́ть** (-е́ю) *impf* +*instr* own, possess; control.

**влады́ка** *m* master, sovereign. **влады́чество** dominion, sway.

**вла́жность** humidity; moisture. **вла́жный** (-жен, -жна́, -о) damp, moist, humid.

**вла́мываться** *impf* of вломи́ться

**вла́ствовать** *impf* +(над+) *instr* rule, hold sway over. **власти́н** ruler; master. **вла́стный** imperious, commanding; empowered, competent. **власть** (*gen pl* -е́й) power; authority.

**вле́во** *adv* to the left (от+*gen* of).

**влеза́ть** *impf*, **влезть** (-зу; влез) *pf* climb in; get in; fit in.

**влёк** *etc.*: *see* влечь

**влета́ть** *impf*, **влете́ть** (-ечу́) *pf* fly in; rush in.

**влече́ние** attraction; inclination. **влечь** (-еку́, -ечёшь; влёк, -ла́) *impf* draw; attract; ~ за собо́й involve, entail.

**влива́ть** *impf*, **влить** (волью́, -ёшь; влил, -а́, -о) *pf* pour in; instil.

**влия́ние** influence. **влия́тельный** influential. **влия́ть** *impf* (*pf* по~) на+*acc* influence, affect.

**вложе́ние** enclosure; investment. **вложи́ть** (-ожу́, -о́жишь) *pf* (*impf* вкла́дывать) put in, insert; enclose; invest.

**вломи́ться** (-млю́сь, -мишься) *pf* (*impf* вла́мываться) break in.

**влюби́ть** (-блю́, -бишь) *pf*, **влюбля́ть** *impf* make fall in love (в+*acc* with); ~ся fall in love. **влюблённый** (-лён, -á) in love; *sb* lover.

**вма́зать** (-а́жу) *pf*, **вма́зывать** *impf* cement, putty in.

**вмени́ть** *pf*, **вменя́ть** *impf* impute; impose. **вменя́емый** (*law*) responsible; sane.

**вме́сте** *adv* together; ~ с тем at the same time, also.

**вмести́лище** receptacle. **вмести́мость** capacity; tonnage. **вмести́тельный** capacious. **вмести́ть** (-ещу́) *pf* (*impf* вмеща́ть) hold, accommodate; put; ~ся go in.

**вме́сто** *prep*+*gen* instead of.

**вмеша́тельство** interference; intervention. **вмеша́ть** *pf*, **вме́шивать** *impf* mix in; implicate; ~ся interfere, intervene.

**вмеща́ть(ся** *impf* of вмести́ть(ся

**вмиг** *adv* in an instant.

вмина́ть *impf*, вмять (вомну́, -нёшь) *pf* press in, dent. вмя́тина dent.

внаём, внаймы́ *adv* to let; for hire.

внача́ле *adv* at first.

вне *prep+gen* outside; ~ себя́ beside o.s.

вне- *pref* extra-; outside; -less. внебра́чный extra-marital; illegitimate. ~временный timeless. ~кла́ссный extra-curricular. ~очередно́й out of turn; extraordinary. ~шта́тный freelance, casual.

внедре́ние introduction; inculcation. внедри́ть *pf*, внедря́ть *impf* inculcate; introduce; ~ся take root.

внеза́пно *adv* suddenly. внеза́пный sudden.

вне́млю *etc.*: see внима́ть

внесе́ние bringing in; deposit. внести́ (-су́, -сёшь; внёс, -ла́) *pf* (*impf* вноси́ть) bring in; introduce; deposit; insert.

вне́шне *adv* outwardly. вне́шний outer; external; outside; foreign. вне́шность exterior; appearance.

вниз *adv* down(wards); ~ по+*dat* down. внизу́ *adv* below; downstairs.

вника́ть *impf*, вни́кнуть (-ну; вник) *pf* в+*acc* go carefully into, investigate thoroughly.

внима́ние attention. внима́тельный attentive. внима́ть *impf* (*pf* внять) listen to; heed.

вничью́ *adv*: око́нчиться ~ end in a draw; сыгра́ть ~ draw.

вновь *adv* anew, again.

вноси́ть (-ошу́, -о́сишь) *impf of* внести́

внук grandson; *pl* grandchildren, descendants.

вну́тренний inner; internal. вну́тренность interior; *pl* entrails; internal organs. внутри́ *adv* & *prep+gen* inside. внутрь *adv* & *prep+gen* inside, in; inwards.

вну́чата (*pl*; *gen* -ча́т) grand-children. внуча́тый second, great-; ~ брат second cousin; ~ племя́нник great-nephew. вну́чка grand-daughter.

внуша́ть *impf*, внуши́ть (-шу́) *pf* instil; +*dat* inspire with. внуше́ние suggestion; reproof. внуши́тельный inspiring; imposing.

вня́тный distinct. внять (*no fut*; -ял, -á, -о) *pf of* внима́ть

во: see в

вобра́ть (вберу́, -рёшь; -а́л, -а́, -о) *pf* (*impf* вбира́ть) absorb; inhale.

вобью́ *etc.*: see вбить

вовлека́ть *impf*, вовле́чь (-еку́, -ечёшь; -ёк, -екла́) *pf* draw in, involve.

во́время *adv* in time; on time.

во́все *adv* quite; ~ не not at all.

во-вторы́х *adv* secondly.

вогна́ть (вгоню́, -о́нишь; -гна́л, -á, -о) *pf* (*impf* вгоня́ть) drive in. во́гнутый concave. вогну́ть (-ну́, -нёшь) *pf* (*impf* вгиба́ть) bend or curve inwards.

вода́ (*acc* во́ду, *gen* -ы́; *pl* -ы) water; *pl* the waters; spa.

водвори́ть *pf*, водворя́ть *impf* settle, install; establish.

води́тель *m* driver. води́ть (вожу́, во́дишь) *impf* lead; conduct; take; drive; ~ся be found; associate (with); be the custom.

во́дка vodka. во́дн|ый water; ~ые лы́жи water-skiing; water-skis.

**водо-** *in comb* water, water-; hydraulic; hydro-. **водобоя́знь** hydrophobia. **~воро́т** whirlpool; maelstrom. **~ём** reservoir. **~измеще́ние** displacement. **~ка́чка** watertower, pumping station. **~ла́з** diver. **~ле́й** Aquarius. **~непроница́емый** waterproof. **~отво́дный** drainage. **~па́д** waterfall. **~по́й** wateringplace. **~прово́д** water-pipe, water-main; water supply. **~прово́дчик** plumber. **~разде́л** watershed. **~ро́д** hydrogen. **во́доросль** water-plant; seaweed. **~снабже́ние** water supply. **~сто́к** drain, gutter. **~храни́лище** reservoir.

**водружа́ть** *impf*, **водрузи́ть** (-ужу́) *pf* hoist; erect.

**водяни́стый** watery. **водяно́й** water.

**воева́ть** (вою́ю) *impf* wage war. **воево́да** *m* voivode; commander.

**воеди́но** *adv* together.

**военко́м** military commissar.

**военно-** *in comb* military; war-. **вое́нно-возду́шный** air-, air-force. **вое́нно-морско́й** naval. **~пле́нный** *sb* prisoner of war. **вое́нно-полево́й суд** court-martial. **~слу́жащий** *sb* serviceman.

**вое́нн|ый** military; war; *sb* serviceman; **~ое положе́ние** martial law; **~ый суд** courtmartial.

**вожа́к** (-á) guide; leader. **вожа́тый** *sb* guide; tram-driver.

**вожделе́ние** *neut* desire, lust.

**вождь** (-я́) *m* leader, chief.

**вожжа́** (*pl* -и, -е́й) rein.

**вожу́** *etc.: see* **води́ть, вози́ть**

**воз** (*loc* -у́; *pl* -ы́) cart; cartload.

**возбуди́мый** excitable. **возбуди́тель** *m* agent; instigator. **возбуди́ть** (-ужу́) *pf*, **возбужда́ть** *impf* excite, arouse; incite. **возбужда́ющ|ий**; **~ее сре́дство** stimulant. **возбужде́ние** excitement. **возбуждённый** excited.

**возвести́** (-еду́, -дёшь; -вёл, -лá) *pf* (*impf* **возводи́ть**) elevate; erect; level; +к+*dat* trace to.

**возвести́ть** (-ещу́) *pf*, **возвеща́ть** *impf* proclaim.

**возводи́ть** (-ожу́, -о́дишь) *impf of* **возвести́**

**возвра́т** return; repayment. **возврати́ть** (-ащу́) *pf*, **возвраща́ть** *impf* (*pf also* **верну́ть**) return, give back; **~ся** return; go back, come back. **возвра́тный** return; reflexive. **возвраще́ние** return.

**возвы́сить** *pf*, **возвыша́ть** *impf* raise; ennoble; **~ся** rise. **возвыше́ние** rise; raised place. **возвы́шенность** height; loftiness. **возвы́шенный** high; elevated.

**возгла́вить** (-влю) *pf*, **возглавля́ть** *impf* head.

**во́зглас** exclamation. **возгласи́ть** (-ашу́) *pf*, **возглаша́ть** *impf* proclaim.

**возгора́емый** inflammable. **возгора́ть** *impf*, **возгоре́ться** (-рю́сь) *pf* flare up; be seized (with).

**воздава́ть** (-даю́, -даёшь) *impf*, **возда́ть** (-áм, -áшь, -áст, -ади́м; -áл, -á, -о) *pf* render.

**воздвига́ть** *impf*, **воздви́гнуть** (-ну; -дви́г) *pf* raise.

**возде́йствие** influence. **возде́йствовать** *impf & pf* **~на**+*acc* influence.

**возде́лать** *pf*, **возде́лывать**

*impf* cultivate, till.

**воздержа́ние** abstinence; abstention. **возде́ржанный** abstemious. **воздержа́ться** (-жу́сь, -жи́шься) *pf*, **возде́рживаться** *impf* refrain; abstain.

**во́здух** air. **воздухонепроница́емый** air-tight. **возду́шный** air, aerial; airy; flimsy; ~ый змей kite; ~ый шар balloon.

**воззва́ние** appeal. **воззва́ть** (-зову́, -вёшь) *pf* (*impf* взыва́ть) appeal (o+*prep* for).

**воззре́ние** opinion, outlook.

**вози́ть** (вожу́, во́зишь) *impf* convey; carry; bring, take; ~ся romp, play noisily; busy o.s.; potter about.

**возлага́ть** *impf of* возложи́ть

**во́зле** *adv* & *prep*+*gen* by, near; near by; past.

**возложи́ть** (-жу́, -жишь) *pf* (*impf* возлага́ть) lay; place.

**возлю́бленный** beloved; *sb* sweetheart.

**возме́здие** retribution.

**возмести́ть** (-ещу́) *pf*, **возмеща́ть** *impf* compensate for; refund. **возмеще́ние** compensation; refund.

**возмо́жно** *adv* possibly; +*comp* as ... as possible. **возмо́жность** possibility; opportunity. **возмо́жный** possible.

**возмужа́лый** mature; grown up. **возмужа́ть** *pf* grow up; gain strength.

**возмути́тельный** disgraceful. **возмути́ть** (-ущу́) *pf*, **возмуща́ть** *impf* disturb; stir up; rouse to indignation; ~ся be indignant. **возмуще́ние** indignation. **возмущённый** (-щён, -щена́) indignant.

**вознагради́ть** (-ажу́) *pf*, воз-

**награжда́ть** *impf* reward. **вознагражде́ние** reward; fee.

**возненави́деть** (-и́жу) *pf* conceive a hatred for.

**вознесе́ние** Ascension. **вознести́** (-несу́, -несёшь; -нёс, -ла́) *pf* (*impf* возноси́ть) raise, lift up; ~сь rise; ascend.

**возника́ть** *impf*, **возни́кнуть** (-нет; -ни́к) *pf* arise, spring up. **возникнове́ние** rise, beginning, origin.

**возни́ца** *m* coachman.

**возноси́ть(ся** (-ошу́(сь, -о́сишь(ся) *impf of* вознести́(сь. **возноше́ние** raising, elevation.

**возня́** row, noise; bother.

**возобнови́ть** (-влю́) *pf*, **возобновля́ть** *impf* renew; restore; ~ся begin again. **возобновле́ние** renewal; revival.

**возража́ть** *impf*, **возрази́ть** (-ажу́) *pf* object. **возраже́ние** objection.

**во́зраст** age. **возраста́ние** growth, increase. **возраста́ть** *impf*, **возрасти́** (-тёт; -рос, -ла́) *pf* grow, increase.

**возроди́ть** (-ожу́) *pf*, **возрожда́ть** *impf* revive; ~ся revive. **возрожде́ние** revival; Renaissance.

**возро́с** *etc.: see* возрасти́. **возро́сший** increased.

**во́зчик** carter, carrier.

**возьму́** *etc.: see* взять

**во́ин** warrior; soldier. **во́инск|ий** military; ~ая пови́нность conscription. **во́инственный** warlike. **во́инствующий** militant.

**вой** howl(ing); wail(ing).

**войду́** *etc.: see* войти́

**во́йлок** felt. **во́йлочный** felt.

война́ (pl -ы) war.

во́йско (pl -á) army; pl troops, forces. войсково́й military.

войти́ (-йду́, -йдёшь; вошёл, -шла́) pf (impf входи́ть) go in, come in, enter; get in(to).

вокза́л (railway) station.

во́кмен Walkman (propr), personal stereo.

вокру́г adv & prep+gen round, around.

вол (-á) ox, bullock.

вола́н flounce; shuttlecock.

волды́рь (-я́) m blister; bump.

волево́й strong-willed.

волейбо́л volleyball.

во́лей-нево́лей adv willy-nilly.

волк (pl -и, -ов) wolf. волкода́в wolf-hound.

волна́ (pl -ы, волна́м) wave. волне́ние choppiness; agitation; emotion. волни́стый wavy. волнова́ть impf (pf вз~) disturb, agitate; excite; ~ся be disturbed; worry, be nervous. волноло́м, волноре́з breakwater. волну́ющий disturbing; exciting.

волоки́та red tape; rigmarole.

волокни́стый fibrous, stringy. волокно́ (pl -a) fibre, filament.

волоку́ etc.: see волочь

во́лос (pl -ы, -óс, -áм); pl hair. волоса́тый hairy. волосно́й capillary.

во́лость (pl -и, -éй) volost (administrative division).

волочи́ть (-очу́, -о́чишь) impf drag; ~ся drag, trail; +за+instr run after, court. воло́чь (-оку́, -очёшь; -о́к, -ла́) impf drag.

во́лчий wolf's; wolfish. волчи́ха, волчи́ца she-wolf.

волчо́к (-чка́) top; gyroscope.

волчо́нок (-нка; pl -ча́та, -ча́т) wolf cub.

волше́бник magician; wizard. волше́бница enchantress. волше́бный magic, magical; enchanting. волшебство́ magic, enchantment.

вольнонаёмный civilian. во́льность liberty; license. во́льный (-лен, -льна́, -о, во́льны́) free; free-style.

вольт¹ (gen pl вольт) volt.

вольт² (loc -ý) vault.

вольфра́м tungsten.

во́ля will; liberty.

во́мну etc.: see вмять

вон adv out; off, away.

вон partl there, over there.

вонза́ть impf, вонзи́ть (-нжу́) pf plunge, thrust.

вонь stench. воню́чий stinking. воня́ть stink.

вообража́емый imaginary. вообража́ть impf, вообрази́ть (-ажу́) pf imagine. воображе́ние imagination. вообрази́мый imaginable.

вообще́ adv in general; generally.

воодушевля́ть (-влю) pf, воодушевля́ть impf inspire. воодушевле́ние inspiration; fervour.

вооружа́ть impf, вооружи́ть (-жу́) pf arm, equip; ~ся arm o.s.; take up arms. вооруже́ние arming; arms; equipment. вооружённый (-жён, -á) armed; equipped.

воо́чию adv with one's own eyes.

во-пе́рвых adv first, first of all.

вопи́ть (-плю́) impf yell, howl. вопию́щий crying; scandalous.

воплоти́ть (-ощу́) pf, воплоща́ть impf embody. воплоще́ние embodiment.

**вопль** *m* cry, wail; howling.

**вопреки́** *prep+dat* in spite of.

**вопро́с** question; problem.

**вопроси́тельный** interrogative; questioning; ~ **знак** question-mark.

**вор** (*pl* -ы́, -о́в) thief; criminal.

**ворва́ться** (-ву́сь, -вёшься; -а́лся, -ла́сь, -а́ло́сь) *pf* (*impf* **врыва́ться**) burst in.

**воркотня́** grumbling.

**воробе́й** sparrow.

**ворова́тый** thievish; furtive.

**ворова́ть** *impf* (*pf* с~) steal.

**воро́вка** woman thief. **воро́вский** furtively. **воро́вство** stealing; theft.

**во́рон** raven. **воро́на** crow.

**воро́нка** funnel; crater.

**вороно́й** black.

**во́рот**[1] collar; neckband.

**во́рот**[2] winch; windlass.

**воро́та** (*pl*; *gen* -ро́т) gate(s); gateway; goal.

**вороти́ть** (-очу́, -о́тишь) *pf* bring back, get back; turn back; ~**ся** return.

**воротни́к** (-а́) collar.

**во́рох** (*pl* -а́) heap, pile; heaps.

**воро́чать** *impf* turn; move; +*instr* have control of; ~**ся** move, turn.

**ворочу́(сь** *etc.*: *see* **вороти́ть(ся**

**вороши́ть** (-шу́) *impf* stir up; turn (over).

**ворс** nap, pile.

**ворча́ть** (-чу́) *impf* grumble; growl. **ворчли́вый** peevish; grumpy.

**восвоя́си** *adv* home.

**восемна́дцатый** eighteenth. **восемна́дцать** eighteen.

**во́семь** (-сьми́, *instr* -семью́ *or* -семью́) eight. **во́семьдесят** (-сьми́десяти, -семью́десятью)

eighty. **восемьсо́т** (-сьми-со́т, -ста́ми) eight hundred.

**во́семью** *adv* eight times.

**воск** wax, beeswax.

**воскли́кнуть** (-ну) *pf*, **восклица́ть** *impf* exclaim. **восклица́ние** exclamation. **восклица́тельный** exclamatory; ~ **знак** exclamation mark.

**восково́й** wax; waxy; waxed.

**воскреса́ть** *impf*, **воскре́снуть** (-ну; -éc) *pf* rise from the dead; revive. **воскресе́ние** resurrection. **воскре-се́нье** Sunday. **воскреси́ть** (-ешу́) *pf*, **воскреша́ть** *impf* resurrect; revive. **воскреше́ние** resurrection; revival.

**воспале́ние** inflammation. **воспалённый** (-лён, -á) inflamed. **воспали́ть** *pf*, **воспаля́ть** *impf* inflame; ~**ся** become inflamed.

**воспита́ние** upbringing, education. **воспита́нник, -ница** pupil. **воспи́танный** well-brought-up. **воспита́тель** *m* tutor; educator. **воспита́тельный** educational. **воспита́ть** *pf*, **воспи́тывать** *impf* bring up; foster; educate.

**воспламени́ть** *pf*, **воспламеня́ть** *impf* ignite; fire; ~**ся** ignite; flare up. **воспламеня́емый** inflammable.

**вос|по́льзоваться** *pf*.

**воспомина́ние** recollection, memory; *pl* memoirs; reminiscences.

**вос|препя́тствовать** *pf*.

**воспрети́ть** (-ещу́) *pf*, **воспреща́ть** *impf* forbid. **воспреще́ние** prohibition. **воспрещённый** (-щён, -á) prohibited.

**восприи́мчивый** impressionable; susceptible. **восприни-**

**ма́ть** *impf*, **восприня́ть** (-иму́, -и́мешь; -и́нял, -а́, -о) *pf* perceive; grasp. **восприя́тие** perception.

**воспроизведе́ние** reproduction. **воспроизвести́** (-еду́, -едёшь; -вёл, -а́) *pf*, **воспроизводи́ть** (-ожу́, -о́дишь) *impf* reproduce. **воспроизводи́тельный** reproductive.

**вос**|**проти́виться** (-влюсь) *pf*.

**воссоедине́ние** reunification. **воссоедини́ть** *pf*, **воссоединя́ть** *impf* reunite.

**восстава́ть** (-таю́, -таёшь) *impf of* **восста́ть**.

**восста́ние** insurrection, uprising.

**восстанови́ть** (-влю́, -вишь) *pf* (*impf* **восстана́вливать**) restore; reinstate; recall; ~ **про́тив**+*gen* set against. **восстановле́ние** restoration.

**восста́ть** (-а́ну) *pf* (*impf* **восстава́ть**) rise (up).

**восто́к** east.

**восто́рг** delight, rapture. **восторга́ться**+*instr* be delighted with, go into raptures over. **восто́рженный** enthusiastic.

**восто́чный** east, eastern; easterly; oriental.

**востре́бование:** до востре́бования to be called for, poste restante.

**восхвали́ть** (-лю́, -лишь) *pf*, **восхваля́ть** *impf* praise, extol.

**восхити́тельный** entrancing; delightful. **восхити́ть** (-хищу́) *pf*, **восхища́ть** *impf* enrapture; ~**ся** +*instr* be enraptured by. **восхище́ние** delight; admiration.

**восхо́д** rising. **восходи́ть** (-ожу́, -о́дишь) *impf of* **взойти́**; ~ **к**+*dat* go back to, date

from. **восхожде́ние** ascent.

**восходя́щий** rising.

**восше́ствие** accession.

**восьма́я** *sb* eighth; octave. **восьмёрка** eight; figure eight; No. 8; figure of eight.

**восьми-** *in comb* eight-; octo-. **восьмигра́нник** octahedron. ~**деся́тый** eightieth. ~**ле́тний** eight-year; eight-year-old. ~**со́тый** eight-hundredth. ~**уго́льник** octagon. ~**уго́льный** octagonal.

**восьмо́й** eighth.

**вот** *partl* here (is), there (is); this (is); ~ **и всё** and that's all; ~ **как!** no! really? ~ **та́к!** that's right!; ~ **что!** no! not really? **вот-во́т** *adv* just, on the point of; *partl* that's right!

**воткну́ть** (-ну́, -нёшь) *pf* (*impf* **втыка́ть**) stick in, drive in.

**вотру́** *etc.: see* **втере́ть**

**воцари́ться** *pf*, **воцаря́ться** *impf* come to the throne; set in.

**вошёл** *etc.: see* **войти́**

**вошь** (вши; *gen pl* вше́й) louse.

**вошью́** *etc.: see* **вшить**

**во́ю** *etc.: see* **выть**

**вою́ю** *etc.: see* **воева́ть**

**впада́ть** *impf*, **впасть** (-аду́) *pf* flow; lapse; fall in; +**в**+*acc* verge on, approximate to. **впаде́ние** confluence, (river-)mouth. **впа́дина** cavity, hollow; socket. **впа́лый** sunken.

**впервы́е** *adv* for the first time.

**вперёд** *adv* forward(s), ahead; in future; in advance; **идти́** ~ (of clock) be fast. **впереди́** *adv* in front, ahead; in (the) future; *prep*+*gen* in front of, before.

**впечатле́ние** impression. **впечатли́тельный** impressionable.

вписа́ть (-ишу́, -и́шешь) *pf*, впи́сывать *impf* enter, insert; ~ся be enrolled, join.

впита́ть *pf*, впи́тывать *impf* absorb, take in; ~ся soak.

впи́хивать *impf*, впихну́ть (-ну́, -нёшь) *pf* cram in; shove.

вплавь *adv* (by) swimming.

вплести́ (-ету́, -етёшь; -ёл, -ёла́) *pf*, вплета́ть *impf* plait in, intertwine; involve.

вплотну́ю *adv* close; in earnest.

вплоть *adv*; ~ до+*gen* (right) up to.

вполго́лоса *adv* under one's breath.

вполне́ *adv* fully, entirely; quite.

впопыха́х *adv* hastily; in one's haste.

впо́ру *adv* at the right time; just right, exactly.

впосле́дствии *adv* subsequently.

впотьма́х *adv* in the dark.

впра́ве *adv*: быть ~ have a right.

впра́во *adv* to the right (от+*gen* of).

впредь *adv* in (the) future; ~ до+*gen* until.

впро́голодь *adv* half starving.

впро́чем *conj* however, but; though.

впры́скивание injection. впры́скивать *impf*, впры́снуть (-ну) *pf* inject.

впряга́ть *impf* впрячь (-ягу́, -яжёшь; -яг, -ла́) *pf* harness.

впуск admittance. впуска́ть *impf*, впусти́ть (-ущу́, -у́стишь) *pf* admit, let in.

впусту́ю *adv* to no purpose, in vain.

впущу́ *etc.*: see впусти́ть

враг (-á) enemy. вражда́ enmity. враждебный hostile. враждова́ть be at enmity.

вра́жеский enemy.

вразбро́д *adv* separately, disunitedly.

вразре́з *adv*: идти́ ~ с+*instr* go against.

вразуми́тельный intelligible, clear; persuasive.

врасплóх *adv* unawares.

враста́ть *impf*, врасти́ (-тёт; врос, -ла́) *pf* grow in; take root.

врата́рь (-я́) *m* goalkeeper.

врать (вру, врёшь; -ал, -á, -о) *impf* (*pf* на~, со~) lie, tell lies; talk nonsense.

врач (-á) doctor. враче́бный medical.

враща́ть *impf* rotate, revolve; ~ся revolve, rotate. враще́ние rotation, revolution.

вред (-á) harm; damage. вреди́тель *m* pest; wrecker; *pl* vermin. вреди́тельство wrecking, (act of) sabotage. вреди́ть (-ежу́) *impf* (*pf* по~) +*dat* harm; damage. вре́дный (-ден, -дна́, -о) harmful.

вре́зать (-е́жу) *pf*, вреза́ть *impf* cut in; set (in) (в; *sl*) +*dat* hit; ~ся cut (into); run (into); be engraved; fall in love.

времена́ми *adv* at times. вре́менно *adv* temporarily. временно́й temporal. вре́менный temporary; provisional. вре́мя (-мени; *pl* -мена́, -мён, -а́м) *neut* time; tense; ~ го́да season; ~ от вре́мени at times, from time to time; на ~ for a time; ско́лько вре́мени? what is the time?; тем вре́менем meanwhile.

у́ровень level, on a level.

вро́де *prep*+*gen* like; *partl* such as, like; apparently.

врождённый (-дён, -á) innate.

врозны, врозь *adv* separately, apart.

врос etc.: see врасти́. вру etc.: see врать

врун (-á), вру́нья liar.

вруча́ть impf, вручи́ть (-чу́) pf hand, deliver; entrust.

вручну́ю adv by hand.

врыва́ть(ся impf of во-рва́ться

вряд (ли) adv it's not likely; hardly, scarcely.

вса́дить (-ажу́, -а́дишь) pf, вса́живать impf thrust in; sink in. вса́дник rider, horseman. вса́дница rider, horsewoman.

вса́сывать impf of всоса́ть

всё, все pron: see весь. всё adv always, all the time; ~ (ещё) still; conj however, nevertheless; ~ же all the same.

все- in comb all-, omni-. всевозмо́жный of every kind; all possible. ~дозво́ленность permissiveness. ~ми́рный of every kind. ~ми́рный world, world-wide. ~могу́щий omnipotent. ~наро́дно publicly. ~наро́дный national; nation-wide. ~объе́млющий comprehensive, all-embracing. ~росси́йский All-Russian. ~си́льный omnipotent. ~сторо́нний all-round; comprehensive.

всегда́ always.

всего́ adv in all, all told; only.

вселе́нная sb universe.

вселя́ю pf, всели́ть impf install, lodge, inspire; ~ся move in, install o.s.; be implanted.

всено́щная sb night service.

всеобщий general, universal.

всерьёз adv seriously, in earnest.

всё-таки conj & partl all the same, still. всеце́ло adv completely.

вска́кивать impf of вскочи́ть

вскачь adv at a gallop.

вскипа́ть impf, вс|кипе́ть (-плю́) pf boil up; flare up.

вс|кипяти́ть(ся (-ячу́(сь) pf.

всколыхну́ть (-ну́, -нёшь) pf stir; stir up.

вскользь adv slightly; in passing.

вско́ре adv soon, shortly after.

вскочи́ть (-очу́, -о́чишь) pf (impf вска́кивать) jump up.

вскри́кивать impf, вскри́кнуть (-ну) pf shriek, scream. вскрича́ть (-чу́) pf exclaim.

вскрыва́ть impf, вскрыть (-ро́ю) pf open; reveal; dissect. вскры́тие opening; revelation; post-mortem.

вслед adv & prep+dat after; ~ за+instr after, following. всле́дствие prep+gen in consequence of.

вслепу́ю blindly; blindfold.

вслух adv aloud.

вслу́шаться pf, вслу́шиваться impf listen attentively.

всма́триваться impf, всмотре́ться (-рю́сь, -ришься) pf look closely.

всмя́тку adv soft(-boiled).

всо́вывать impf of всу́нуть

всоса́ть (-су́, -сёшь) pf (impf вса́сывать) suck in; absorb; imbibe.

вс|паха́ть (-ашу́, -а́шешь) pf, вспа́хивать impf plough up. вспа́шка ploughing.

вс|пени́ться pf.

всплеск splash. вспле́скивать impf, всплесну́ть (-ну́, -нёшь) pf splash; ~ рука́ми throw up one's hands.

всплыва́ть impf, всплыть

(-ыву, -ывёшь; -ыл, -а́, -о) pf
rise to the surface; come to
light.

вспомина́ть impf, вспо́мнить
pf remember; ~ся impers
+dat: мне вспо́мнилось I remembered.

вспомога́тельный auxiliary.

вс|поте́ть pf.

вспры́гивать impf, вспры́гнуть (-ну) pf jump up.

вспу́хивать impf, вс|пу́хнуть (-нет; -ух) pf swell up.

вспыли́ть pf flare up. вспы́льчивый hot-tempered.

вспы́хивать impf, вспы́хнуть (-ну) pf blaze up; flare up. вспы́шка flash; outburst; outbreak.

встава́ть (-таю́, -таёшь) impf of встать

вста́вить (-влю) pf, вставля́ть impf put in, insert. вста́вка insertion; framing; mounting; inset. вставн|о́й inserted; set in; ~ы́е зу́бы false teeth.

встать (-а́ну) pf (impf встава́ть) get up; stand up.

встрево́женный adj anxious. вс|трево́жить (-жу) pf.

встрепену́ться (-ну́сь, -нёшься) pf rouse o.s.; start (up); beat faster.

встре́тить (-е́чу) pf, встреча́ть impf meet (with); ~ся meet; be found. встре́ча meeting. встре́чный coming to meet; contrary, head; counter; sb person met with; пе́рвый ~ the first person you meet, anybody.

встря́ска shaking; shock. встря́хивать impf, встряхну́ть (-ну́, -нёшь) pf shake (up); rouse; ~ся shake o.s.; rouse o.s.

вступа́ть impf, вступи́ть (-плю́, -пишь) pf +в+acc enter (into); join (in); +на+acc go up, mount; ~ся intervene; +за+acc stand up for. вступи́тельный introductory; entrance. вступле́ние entry, joining; introduction.

всу́нуть (-ну) pf (impf всо́вывать) put in, stick in.

всхли́пнуть (-ну) pf, всхли́пывать impf sob.

всходи́ть (-ожу́, -о́дишь) impf of взойти́. всхо́ды (pl; gen -ов) (corn-)shoots.

всю: see ввесь

всю́ду adv everywhere.

вся: see весь

вся́к|ий any; every, all kinds of; ~ом слу́чае in any case; на ~ий слу́чай just in case; pron anyone. вся́чески adv in every possible way.

вта́йне adv secretly.

вта́лкивать impf of втолкну́ть. вта́птывать impf of втопта́ть. вта́скивать impf, втащи́ть (-щу́, -щишь) pf drag in.

втере́ть (вотру́, вотрёшь; втёр) pf (impf втира́ть) rub in; ~ся insinuate o.s., worm o.s.

втира́ть(ся impf of втере́ть(ся

втиски́вать impf, вти́снуть (-ну) pf squeeze in; ~ся squeeze (o.s.) in.

втихомо́лку adv surreptitiously.

втолкну́ть (-ну́, -нёшь) pf (impf вта́лкивать) push in.

втопта́ть (-пчу́, -пчешь) pf (impf вта́птывать) trample (in).

вторга́ться impf, вто́ргнуться (-нусь; вто́ргся, -ла́сь)

**вто́рить** *impf* play or sing second part; +*dat* repeat, echo. **вторже́ние** invasion; intrusion.

**вто́рить** *impf* play or sing second part; +*dat* repeat, echo. **втори́чный** second, secondary. **вто́рник** Tuesday. **втор-|о́й** second; ~о́е *sb* second course. **второстепе́нный** secondary, minor.

**второпя́х** *adv* in haste.

**в-тре́тьих** *adv* thirdly. **втро́е** *adv* three times. **втроём** *adv* three (together). **втройне́** *adv* three times as much.

**вту́лка** plug.

**втыка́ть** *impf of* воткну́ть

**втя́гивать** *impf*, **втяну́ть** (-ну́, -нешь) *pf* draw in; ~ся *в+acc* enter; get used to.

**вуа́ль** veil.

**вуз** *abbr (of* вы́сшее уче́бное заведе́ние) higher educational establishment; college.

**вулка́н** volcano.

**вульга́рный** vulgar.

**вундерки́нд** infant prodigy.

**вход** entrance; entry. **входи́ть** (-ожу́, -о́дишь) *impf of* войти́. **входно́й** entrance.

**вхолосту́ю** *adv* idle, free.

**вцепи́ться** (-плю́сь, -пишься) *pf*, **вцепля́ться** *impf* +*в+acc* clutch, catch hold of.

**вчера́** *adv* yesterday. **вчера́шний** yesterday's.

**вчерне́** in rough.

**вче́тверо** *adv* four times. **вчетверо́м** *adv* four (together).

**вши** *etc.*: *see* вошь

**вшива́ть** *impf of* вшить

**вши́вый** lousy.

**вширь** *adv* in breadth; widely.

**вшить** (вошью́, -ьёшь) *pf (impf* вшива́ть) sew in.

**въе́дливый** corrosive; caustic.

**въезд** entry; entrance. **въе-**

зжа́ть *impf*, **въе́хать** (-е́ду, -е́дешь) *pf (в+acc)* ride in(to); drive in(to); crash into.

**вы** (вас, вам, ва́ми, вас) *pron* you.

**выбега́ть** *impf*, **вы́бежать** (-егу, -ежишь) *pf* run out.

**вы́|белить** *pf*.

**вы́беру** *etc.*: *see* вы́брать. **выбива́ть(ся** *impf of* вы́бить(ся. **выбира́ть(ся** *impf of* вы́брать(ся

**вы́бить** (-бью) *pf (impf* выбива́ть) knock out; dislodge; ~ся get out; break loose; come out; ~ся из сил exhaust o.s.

**вы́бор** choice; selection; *pl* election(s). **вы́борный** elective; electoral. **вы́борочный** selective.

**вы́|бранить** *pf*. **выбра́сывать(ся** *impf of* вы́бросить(ся

**вы́брать** (-беру) *pf (impf* выбира́ть) choose; elect; take out; ~ся get out.

**выбрива́ть** *impf*, **вы́брить** (-рею) *pf* shave.

**вы́бросить** (-ошу) *pf (impf* выбра́сывать) throw out; throw away; ~ся throw o.s. out, leap out.

**выбыва́ть** *impf*, **вы́быть** (-буду) *pf* из+*gen* leave, quit.

**выва́ливать** *impf*, **вы́валить** *pf* throw out; pour out; ~ся tumble out.

**вы́везти** (-зу; -ез) *pf (impf* вывози́ть) take, bring, out; export; rescue.

**вы́верить** *pf (impf* выверя́ть) adjust, regulate.

**вы́вернуть** (-ну) *pf*, **вывёртывать** *impf* turn inside out; unscrew; wrench.

**выверя́ть** *impf of* вы́верить

**вы́весить** (-ешу) *pf* (*impf* вы-
ве́шивать) weigh; hang out.
**вы́веска** sign; pretext.
**вы́вести** (-еду; -ел) *pf* (*impf*
выводи́ть) lead, bring, take,
out; drive out; remove; exterminate; deduce; hatch; grow,
breed; erect; depict; draw;
~**сь** go out of use; become
extinct; come out; hatch out.
**выве́тривание** airing.
**выве́шивать** *impf of* вы́ве-
сить
**вы́вих** dislocation. **вывихи́-
вать** *impf*, **вы́вихнуть** (-ну)
*pf* dislocate.
**вы́вод** conclusion; withdrawal.
**выводи́ть(ся** (-ожу́(сь, -о́дишь-
(ся) *impf of* вы́вести(сь. вы́-
**водок** (-дка) brood; litter.
**вывожу́** *see* выводи́ть, вы-
возить
**вы́воз** export; removal. вы-
**вози́ть** (-ожу́, -о́зишь) *impf of*
вы́везти. вывозно́й export.
**вы́гадать** *pf*, выга́дывать
*impf* gain, save.
**вы́гиб** curve. выгиба́ть *impf
of* вы́гнуть
**вы́гладить** (-ажу) *pf*.
**вы́глядеть** (-яжу) *impf* look,
look like. выгля́дывать
*impf*, **вы́глянуть** (-ну) *pf*
look out; peep out.
**вы́гнать** (-гоню) *pf* (*impf*
выгоня́ть) drive out; distil.
**вы́гнутый** curved, convex.
**вы́гнуть** (-ну) *pf* (*impf* выги-
ба́ть) bend, arch.
**выгова́ривать** *impf*, вы́гово-
рить (-рю) *pf* pronounce, speak;
+*dat* reprimand; ~**ся** speak
out. вы́говор pronunciation;
reprimand.
**вы́года** advantage; gain. вы́-
**годный** advantageous; profitable.

**вы́гон** pasture; common. вы-
гоня́ть *impf of* вы́гнать
**выгора́ть** *impf*, вы́гореть
(-рит) *pf* burn down; fade.
**вы́гравировать** *pf*.
**выгружа́ть** *impf*, вы́грузить
(-ужу) *pf* unload; disembark.
**вы́грузка** unloading; disembarkation.
**выдава́ть** (-даю́, -даёшь)
*impf*, вы́дать (-ам, -ашь, -аст,
-адим) *pf* give (out); issue;
betray; extradite; +*за+acc*
pass off as; ~**ся** protrude;
stand out; present itself. вы́-
**дача** issue; payment; extradition. выдаю́щийся promi-
nent.
**выдвига́ть** *impf*, вы́дви-
**нуть** (-ну) *pf* move out; pull
out; put forward, nominate;
~**ся** move forward, move out;
come out; get on (in the
world). **выдвиже́ние** nomination; promotion.
**выделе́ние** secretion; excretion; isolation; apportionment.
**вы́делить** *pf*, выделя́ть
*impf* pick out; detach; allot;
secrete; excrete; isolate; ~
**курси́вом** italicize; ~**ся** stand
out, be noted (+*instr* for).
**выдёргивать** *impf of* вы́-
дернуть
**вы́держанный** consistent;
self-possessed; firm; matured,
seasoned. **выде́рживать** (-жу)
*pf*, вы́держать *impf* bear;
endure; contain o.s.; pass
(*exam*); sustain. вы́держка[1]
endurance; self-possession;
exposure.
**вы́держка[2]** excerpt.
**вы́дернуть** (-ну) *pf* (*impf* выдёргивать) pull out.
**вы́дохнуть** (-ну) *pf* (*impf*
выдыха́ть) breathe out; ~**ся**

have lost fragrance or smell; be past one's best.

**вы́дра** otter.

**вы́|драть** (-деру) *pf.* **вы́|дрессировать** *pf.*

**выдува́ть** *impf of* **вы́дуть**

**вы́думанный** made-up, fabricated. **вы́думать** *pf,* **вы́думывать** *impf* invent; fabricate. **вы́думка** invention; device; inventiveness.

**вы́дуть** *pf* (*impf* **выдува́ть**) blow; blow out.

**выдыха́ние** exhalation. **выдыха́ть(ся** *impf of* **вы́дохнуть(ся**

**вы́езд** departure; exit. **выездно́й** exit; ~**ая се́ссия** суда́ assizes. **выезжа́ть** *impf of* **вы́ехать**

**вы́емка** taking out; excavation; hollow.

**вы́ехать** (-еду) *pf* (*impf* **выезжа́ть**) go out, depart; drive out, ride out; move (house).

**вы́жать** (-жму, -жмешь) *pf* (*impf* **выжима́ть**) squeeze out; wring out.

**вы́жечь** (-жгу) *pf* (*impf* **выжига́ть**) burn out; cauterize.

**выжива́ние** survival. **выжива́ть** *impf of* **вы́жить**

**выжига́ть** *impf of* **вы́жечь**

**выжида́тельный** waiting; temporizing.

**выжима́ть** *impf of* **вы́жать**

**вы́жить** (-иву) *pf* (*impf* **выжива́ть**) survive; hound out; ~ **из ума́** become senile.

**вы́звать** (-зову) *pf* (*impf* **вызыва́ть**) call (out); send for; challenge; provoke; ~**ся** volunteer.

**выздора́вливать** *impf,* **вы́здороветь** (-ею) *pf* recover. **выздоровле́ние** recovery; convalescence.

**вы́зов** call; summons; challenge.

**вы́золоченный** gilt.

**вызубрива́ть** *impf,* **вы́|зубрить** *pf* learn by heart.

**вызыва́ть(ся** *impf of* **вы́звать(ся. вызыва́ющий** defiant; provocative.

**вы́играть** *pf,* **выи́грывать** *impf* win; gain. **вы́игрыш** win; gain; prize. **вы́игрышный** winning; lottery; advantageous.

**вы́йти** (-йду; -шел, -шла) *pf* (*impf* **выходи́ть**) go out; come out; get out; appear; turn out; be used up; have expired; ~ **в свет** appear; ~ **за́муж** (за+*acc*) marry; ~ **из себя́** lose one's temper.

**выка́лывать** *impf of* **вы́колоть. выка́пывать** *impf of* **вы́копать**

**выка́рмливать** *impf of* **вы́кормить**

**вы́качать** *pf,* **выка́чивать** *impf* pump out.

**выки́дывать** *impf,* **вы́кинуть** *pf* throw out, reject; put out; miscarry, abort; ~ **флаг** hoist a flag. **вы́кидыш** miscarriage, abortion.

**вы́кладка** laying out; lay-out; facing; kit; computation, calculation. **выкла́дывать** *impf of* **вы́ложить**

**выключа́тель** *m* switch. **выключа́ть** *impf,* **вы́ключить** (-чу) *pf* turn off, switch off; remove, exclude.

**выкола́чивать** *impf,* **вы́колотить** (-лочу) *pf* knock out, beat out; beat; extort, wring out.

**вы́колоть** (-лю) *pf* (*impf* **выка́лывать**) put out; gouge out; tattoo.

вы́|копать pf (impf also выка́пывать) dig; dig up, dig out; exhume; unearth.

вы́кормить (-млю) pf, выка́рмливать impf rear, bring up.

выкорчёвывать (-чую) pf, выкорчёвывать impf uproot, root out; eradicate.

выкра́ивать impf of вы́кроить

вы́|красить (-ашу) pf, выкра́шивать impf paint; dye.

выкри́кивать impf, вы́крикнуть (-ну) pf cry out; yell.

вы́кроить pf (impf выкра́ивать) cut out; find (time etc.). вы́кройка pattern.

вы́крутить (-учу) pf, выкру́чивать impf unscrew; twist; ~ся extricate o.s.

вы́куп ransom; redemption.

вы́|купать¹(ся pf.

выкупа́ть² impf, вы́купить (-плю) pf ransom, redeem.

вы́лазка sally, sortie; excursion.

выла́мывать impf of вы́ломать

вылеза́ть impf, вы́лезти (-зу; -лез) pf climb out; come out.

вы́|лепить (-плю) pf.

вы́лет flight; take-off. вылета́ть impf, вы́лететь (-ечу) pf fly out; take off.

вылечивать impf, вы́лечить (-чу) pf cure; ~ся recover, be cured.

вылива́ть(ся pf of вы́лить(ся

вы́|линять pf.

вы́лить (-лью) pf (impf вылива́ть) pour out; cast, found; ~ся flow (out); be expressed.

вы́ложить (-жу) pf (impf выкла́дывать) lay out.

вы́ломать pf, вы́ломить (-млю) pf выла́мы- вать) break open.

вы́лупиться (-плюсь) pf, вылупля́ться impf hatch (out).

вы́лью etc.: see вы́лить

вы́|мазать (-ажу) pf, выма́зывать impf smear, dirty.

выма́нивать impf, вы́манить pf entice, lure.

вы́мереть (-мрет; -мер) pf (impf вымира́ть) die out; become extinct. вы́мерший extinct.

вы́мести (-ету) pf, вымета́ть impf sweep out.

вымога́тельство blackmail, extortion. вымога́ть impf extort.

вымока́ть impf, вы́мокнуть (-ну; -ок) pf be drenched; soak; rot.

вы́молвить (-влю) pf say, utter.

вы́|мостить (-ощу) pf. вы́мою etc.: see вы́мыть

вы́мпел pennant.

вы́мрет see вы́мереть. вымыва́ть(ся impf of вы́мыть(ся

вы́мысел (-сла) invention, fabrication; fantasy.

вы́|мыть (-мою) pf (impf also вымыва́ть) wash; wash out, off; wash away; ~ся wash o.s.

вы́мышленный fictitious.

вы́мя (-мени) neut udder.

вына́шивать impf of выноси́ть²

вы́нести (-су; -нес) pf (impf выноси́ть¹) carry out, take out; carry away; endure.

вынима́ть (impf of вы́нуть

вы́нос carrying out. выноси́ть¹ (-ошу, -о́сишь) pf of вы́нести. выноси́ть² pf (impf вына́шивать) bear; nurture.

вы́носка carrying out; removal; footnote. **выно́сливость** endurance; hardiness.

**вы́нудить** (-ужу) *pf*, **вынужда́ть** *impf* force, compel. **вы́нужденный** forced.

**вы́нуть** (-ну) *pf* (*impf* **вынима́ть**) take out.

**вы́пад** attack; lunge. **выпада́ть** *impf of* **вы́пасть**

**вы́палывать** *impf of* **вы́полоть**

**выпа́ривать** *impf*, **вы́парить** evaporate; steam. **выпа́рывать** *impf of* **вы́пороть**[2]

**вы́пасть** (-аду; -ал) *pf* (*impf* **выпада́ть**) fall out; fall; occur, turn out; lunge.

**выпека́ть** *impf*, **вы́печь** (-еку; -ек) *pf* bake.

**выпива́ть** *impf of* **вы́пить**; enjoy a drink. **вы́пивка** drinking bout; drinks.

**выпи́ливать** *impf*, **вы́пилить** *pf* saw, cut out.

**вы́писать** (-ишу) *pf*, **выпи́сывать** *impf* copy out; write out; order; subscribe to; send for; discharge, release; ~ся be discharged; check out. **вы́писка** writing out; extract; ordering, subscription; discharge.

**вы́пить** (-пью) *pf* (*impf also* **выпива́ть**) drink; drink up.

**вы́плавить** (-влю) *pf*, **выплавля́ть** *impf* smelt. **вы́плавка** smelting; smelted metal.

**вы́плата** payment. **вы́платить** (-ачу) *pf*, **выпла́чивать** *impf* pay (out); pay off.

**выплёвывать** *impf of* **вы́плюнуть**

**выплыва́ть** *impf*, **вы́плыть** (-ыву) *pf* swim out, sail out; emerge; crop up.

**вы́плюнуть** (-ну) *pf* (*impf* **выплёвывать**) spit out.

**выполза́ть** *impf*, **вы́ползти** (-зу; -олз) *pf* crawl out.

**выполне́ние** execution, carrying out; fulfilment. **вы́полнить** *pf*, **выполня́ть** *impf* execute, carry out; fulfil.

**вы́полоскать** (-ощу) *pf*.

**вы́полоть** (-лю) *pf* (*impf also* **вы́палывать**) weed out; weed.

**вы́пороть**[1] (-рю) *pf*.

**вы́пороть**[2] (-рю) *pf* (*impf* **выпа́рывать**) rip out, rip up.

**вы́потрошить** (-шу) *pf*.

**вы́правка** bearing; correction.

**выпра́шивать** *impf of* **вы́просить**; solicit.

**выпрова́живать** *impf*, **вы́проводить** (-ожу) *pf* send packing.

**вы́просить** (-ошу) *pf* (*impf* **выпра́шивать**) (ask for and) get.

**выпряга́ть** *impf of* **вы́прячь**

**вы́прямить** (-млю) *pf*, **выпрямля́ть** *impf* straighten (out); rectify; ~ся become straight; draw o.s. up.

**вы́прячь** (-ягу; -яг) *pf* (*impf* **выпряга́ть**) unharness.

**вы́пуклый** protuberant; bulging; convex.

**вы́пуск** output; issue; discharge; part, instalment; final-year students; omission. **выпуска́ть** *impf*, **вы́пустить** (-ущу) *pf* let out; issue; produce; omit. **выпускни́к** (-а́), **-и́ца** final-year student. **выпускно́й** discharge; exhaust; ~о́й экза́мен finals, final examination.

**вы́путать** *pf*, **выпу́тывать** *impf* disentangle; ~ся extricate o.s.

**вы́пью** *etc.*: *see* **вы́пить**

**вырабáтывать** *impf*, **вырабóтать** *pf* work out; work up; draw up; produce; make; earn. **вырабóтка** manufacture; production; working out; drawing up; output; make.

**выравнивать(ся** *impf of* **выровнять(ся**

**выражáть** *impf*, **вырáзить** (-ажу) *pf* express; ~**ся** express o.s. **выражéние** expression. **вырази́тельный** expressive.

**вырастáть** *impf*, **вы́расти** (-ту; -рос) *pf* grow, grow up. **вы́растить** (-ащу) *pf*, **вырáщивать** *impf* bring up; breed; cultivate.

**вы́рвать**[1] (-ву) (*impf* **вырывáть**[2]) pull out, tear out; extort; ~**ся** break loose, break free; escape; shoot.

**вы́рвать**[2] (-ву) *pf*.

**вы́резать** cut; décolleté. **вы́резать** (-ежу) *pf*, **вырезáть** *impf*, **вырéзывать** *impf* cut (out); engrave. **вы́резка** cutting out, excision; fillet.

**вы́ровнять** *pf* (*impf* **вырáвнивать**) level; straighten (out); draw up; ~**ся** become level; equalize; catch up.

**вы́родиться** (-ится), **вырождáться** *impf* degenerate. **вы́родок** (-дка) degenerate; black sheep. **вырождéние** degeneration.

**вы́ронить** *pf* drop.

**вы́рос** *etc.*: *see* **вырасти**

**вы́рою** *etc.*: *see* **вырыть**

**вырубáть** *impf*, **вы́рубить** (-блю) *pf* cut down; cut (out); carve (out). **вы́рубка** cutting down; hewing out.

**вы́ругать(ся** *pf*.

**вырýливать** *impf*, **вы́рулить** *pf* taxi.

**выручáть** *impf*, **вы́ручить** (-чу) *pf* rescue; help out; gain; make. **вы́ручка** rescue; gain; proceeds; earnings.

**вырывáть**[1] *impf*, **вы́рыть** (-рою) *pf* dig up, unearth.

**вырывáть**[2](ся *impf of* **вы́рвать(ся**

**вы́садить** (-ажу) *pf*, **выса́живать** *impf* set down; put ashore; transplant; smash; ~**ся** alight; disembark. **вы́садка** disembarkation; landing; transplanting.

**выса́сывать** *impf of* **вы́сосать**

**вы́свободить** (-божу) *pf*, **высвобождáть** *impf* free; release.

**высекáть** *impf of* **вы́сечь**[2]

**выселéние** eviction. **вы́селить** *pf*, **выселя́ть** *impf* evict; evacuate; move; ~**ся** move, remove.

**вы́сечь**[1] (-еку; -сек) *pf*. **вы́сечь**[2] (-еку; -сек) (*impf* **секáть**) cut (out); carve.

**вы́сидеть** (-ижу) *pf*, **выси́живать** *impf* sit out; stay; hatch.

**вы́ситься** *impf* rise, tower.

**выскáбливать** *impf of* **вы́скоблить**

**вы́сказать** (-кажу) *pf*, **выскáзывать** *impf* express; state; ~**ся** speak out. **выскáзывание** utterance, pronouncement.

**выскáкивать** *impf of* **вы́скочить**

**вы́скоблить** *pf* (*impf* **выскáбливать**) scrape out; erase; remove.

**вы́скочить** (-чу) *pf* (*impf* **выскáкивать**) jump out; spring out; ~+*instr* come out with. **вы́скочка** upstart.

**вы́слать** (вышлю) *pf* (*impf*

высыла́ть) send (out); exile; deport.

вы́|следить (-ежу) pf, высле́живать impf trace; shadow.

выслу́живать impf, выслу́жить (-жу) pf qualify for; serve for; ~ся gain promotion; curry favour.

вы́слушать pf, выслу́шивать impf hear out; sound; listen to.

высме́ивать impf, вы́смеять (-ею) pf ridicule.

вы́|сморкать(ся pf. высма́рковывать(ся impf of вы́сморкнуть(ся

высо́кий (-о́к, -а́, -о́кó) high; tall; lofty; elevated.

высоко- in comb high-, highly. высокоблагоро́дие (your) Honour, Worship. ~во́льтный high-tension. ~го́рный mountain. ~ка́чественный high-quality. ~квалифици́рованный highly qualified. ~ме́рие haughtiness. ~ме́рный haughty. ~па́рный high-flown; bombastic. ~часто́тный high-frequency.

вы́сосать (-осу) pf (impf выса́сывать) suck out.

высота́ (pl -ы) height, altitude. высо́тный high-altitude; high-rise.

вы́|сохнуть (-ну; -ох) pf (impf also высыха́ть) dry (out); dry up; wither (away).

вы́спаться (-плюсь, -пишься) pf (impf высыпа́ться²) have a good sleep.

вы́ставить (-влю) pf, выставля́ть impf display, exhibit; post; put forward; set down; take out; +instr represent as; ~ся show off. вы́ставка exhibition.

выста́ивать impf of вы́стоять

вы́|стегать pf. вы́|стирать pf.

вы́стоять (-ою) pf (impf выста́ивать) stand; stand one's ground.

вы́страдать pf suffer; gain through suffering.

выстра́ивать(ся impf of вы́строить(ся

вы́стрел shot; report. вы́стрелить pf shoot, fire.

вы́|строгать pf.

вы́строить pf (impf выстра́ивать) build; draw up, order, arrange; form up. ~ся form up.

вы́ступ protuberance, projection. выступа́ть impf, вы́ступить (-плю) pf come forward; come out; perform; speak; +из+gen go beyond. выступле́ние appearance, performance; speech; setting out.

вы́сунуть (-ну) pf (impf высо́вывать) put out, thrust out; ~ся show o.s., thrust o.s. forward.

вы́|сушить(ся (-шу(сь) pf.

вы́сший highest; high; higher.

высыла́ть impf of вы́слать. вы́сылка sending, dispatch; expulsion, exile.

высыпа́ть (-плю) pf, высыпа́ть impf pour out; spill. ~ся¹ pour out; spill. высыпа́ться² impf of вы́спаться

высыха́ть impf of вы́сохнуть

высь height; summit.

выта́лкивать impf of вы́толкать, вы́толкнуть. выта́скивать impf of вы́тащить. выта́чивать impf of вы́точить

вы́|тащить (-щу) pf (impf also выта́скивать) drag out; pull out.

вы́|твердить (-ржу) pf.

**вытека́ть** *impf* (*pf* **вы́течь**); ~ **из**+*gen* flow from, out of; result from.

**вы́тереть** (-тру; -тер) *pf* (*impf* **вытира́ть**) wipe (up); dry; wear out.

**вы́терпеть** (-плю) *pf* endure.

**вы́тертый** threadbare.

**вы́теснить** *pf*, **вытесня́ть** *impf* force out; oust; displace.

**вы́течь** (-чет; -ек) *pf* (*impf* **вытека́ть**) flow out, run out.

**вытира́ть** *impf of* **вы́тереть**

**вы́толкать** *pf*, **вы́толкнуть** (-ну) *pf* (*impf* **выта́лкивать**) throw out; push out.

**вы́точенный** turned. **вы́|точить** (-чу; -чи) *pf* (*impf also* **выта́чивать**) turn; sharpen; gnaw through.

**вы́|травить** (-влю) *pf*, **вытра́вливать** *impf*, **вытравля́ть** *impf* exterminate, destroy; remove; etch; trample down, damage.

**вытрезви́тель** *m* detoxification centre. **вы́трезвить(ся** (-влю(сь) *pf*, **вытрезвля́ть(ся** *impf* sober up.

**вы́тру** *etc.: see* **вы́тереть**

**вы́|трясти** (-су; -яс) *pf* shake out.

**вытря́хивать** *impf*, **вы́тряхнуть** (-ну) *pf* shake out.

**выть** (во́ю) *impf* howl; wail.

**вытя́гивать** *impf*, **вы́тянуть** (-ну) *pf* stretch (out); extend; extract; endure; ~**ся** stretch, stretch out, stretch o.s.; shoot up; draw o.s. up. **вы́тяжка** drawing out, extraction; extract.

**вы́|утюжить** (-жу) *pf*.

**выу́чивать** *impf*, **вы́учить** (-чу) *pf* learn; teach; ~**ся** +*dat or* in learn.

**выха́живать** *impf of* **вы́ходить**[2]

**вы́хватить** (-ачу) *pf*, **выхва́тывать** *impf* snatch out, up, away; pull out.

**вы́хлоп** exhaust. **выхлопно́й** exhaust, discharge.

**вы́ход** going out; departure; way out, exit; vent; appearance; yield; ~ **за́муж** marriage. **вы́ходец** (-дца) emigrant; immigrant. **выходи́ть**[1] (-ожу, -о́дишь) *impf of* **вы́йти**; +**на**+*acc* look out on.

**вы́ходить**[2] (-ожу) *pf* (*impf* **выха́живать**) nurse; rear, bring up.

**вы́ходка** trick; prank.

**выходно́й** exit; going-out, outgoing; discharge; ~**о́й день** off; ~**о́й** *sb* person off duty; day off. **выхожу́** *etc.: see* **выходи́ть**[1]. **вы́хожу** *etc.: see* **вы́ходить**[2].

**вы́|цвести** (-ветет) *pf*, **выцвета́ть** *impf* fade. **вы́цветший** faded.

**вы́черкивать** *impf*, **вы́черкнуть** (-ну) *pf* cross out.

**вы́черпать** *pf*, **вычерпывать** *impf* bale out.

**вы́честь** (-чту; -чел, -чла) *pf* (*impf* **вычита́ть**) subtract. **вы́чет** deduction.

**вычисле́ние** calculation. **вычисли́тель** *m* calculator. **вычисли́тельный** calculating, computing; ~**ая маши́на** computer. **вы́числить** *pf*, **вычисля́ть** *impf* calculate, compute.

**вы́чистить** (-ищу) *pf* (*impf also* **вычища́ть**) clean, clean up.

**вычита́ние** subtraction. **вычита́ть** *impf of* **вы́честь** **вычища́ть** *impf of* **вы́чистить**. **вы́чту** *etc.: see* **вы́честь**

**вы́швырнуть** (-ну) *pf*, **вы-**

швы́ривать *impf* chuck out.
вы́ше higher, taller; *prep+gen* beyond; over; *adv* above.
вы́ше- in *comb* above-, afore-.
вышеизло́женный foregoing. ~на́званный aforenamed. ~ска́занный, ~ука́занный aforesaid. ~упомя́нутый afore-mentioned.
вы́шел *etc.: see* вы́йти
вышиба́ла *m* chucker-out. вышиба́ть *impf*, вы́шибить (-бу; -иб) *pf* knock out; chuck out.
вышива́ние embroidery, needlework. вышива́ть *impf of* вы́шить. вы́шивка embroidery.
вышина́ height.
вы́шить (-шью) *pf* (*impf* вышива́ть) embroider. вы́шитый embroidered.
вы́шка tower; (бурова́я) ~ derrick.
вы́шлю *etc.: see* вы́слать.
вы́шью *etc.: see* вы́шить
вы́явить (-влю) *pf*, выявля́ть *impf* reveal; make known; expose; ~ся come to light, be revealed.
выясне́ние elucidation; explanation. вы́яснить *pf*, выясня́ть *impf* elucidate; explain; ~ся become clear; turn out.
Вьетна́м Vietnam. вьетна́мец, -мка Vietnamese. вьетна́мский Vietnamese.
вью *etc: see* вить
вью́га snow-storm, blizzard.
вьюно́к (-нка́) bindweed.
вью́чн|ый pack; ~ое живо́тное beast of burden.
вью́щийся climbing; curly.
вяжу́ *etc.: see* вяза́ть. вя́жущий astringent.
вяз elm.
вяза́ние knitting, crocheting;

binding, tying. вя́занка[1] knitted garment. вяза́нка[2] bundle. вя́заный knitted, crocheted. вяза́нье knitting; crochet(-work). вяза́ть (вяжу́, вя́жешь) *impf* (*pf* c~) tie, bind; knit, crochet; be astringent; ~ся accord; tally. вя́зка tying; knitting, crocheting; bunch.
вя́зкий (-зок, -зка́, -о) viscous; sticky; boggy. вя́знуть (-ну; вяз(нул), -зла) *impf* (*pf* за~, у~) stick, get stuck.
вя́зовый elm.
вязь ligature; arabesque.
вя́леный dried; sun-cured.
вя́лый limp; sluggish; slack.
вя́нуть (-ну; вял) *impf* (*pf* за~, у~) fade, wither; flag.

# Г

г. *abbr* (*of* год) year; (*of* го́род) city; (*of* господи́н) Mr.
г *abbr* (*of* грамм) gram.
га *abbr* (*of* гекта́р) hectare.
га́вань harbour.
гага́чий пух eiderdown.
гад reptile; repulsive person; *pl.* vermin.
гада́лка fortune-teller. гада́ние fortune-telling; guess-work. гада́ть *impf* (*pf* по~) tell fortunes; guess.
га́дина reptile; repulsive person; *pl* vermin. га́дить (га́жу) *impf* (*pf* на~) +в+*prep*, на+*acc*, *prep* foul, dirty, defile. га́дкий (-док, -дка́, -о) nasty, vile repulsive. га́дость (-и) filth, muck; dirty trick; *pl* filthy expressions. гадю́ка adder, viper; repulsive person.
га́ечный ключ spanner, wrench.
газ[1] gauze.

**газ²** gas; wind; **дать ~** step on the gas; **сба́вить ~** reduce speed.

**газе́та** newspaper. **газе́тчик** journalist; newspaper-seller.

**газиро́ванный** aerated. **га́зовый** gas.

**газо́н** lawn. **газонокоси́лка** lawn-mower.

**газопрово́д** gas pipeline; gas-main.

**га́йка** nut; female screw.

**гала́ктика** galaxy.

**галантере́йный магази́н** haberdasher's. **галантере́я** haberdashery.

**гала́нтный** gallant.

**галере́я** gallery. **галёрка** gallery, gods.

**галифе́** indecl pl riding-breeches.

**га́лка** jackdaw.

**галлюцина́ция** hallucination.

**гало́п** gallop.

**га́лочка** tick.

**га́лстук** tie; neckerchief.

**галу́шка** dumpling.

**га́лька** pebbles; shingle.

**гам** din, uproar.

**гама́к** (-á) hammock.

**га́мма** scale; gamut; range.

**гангре́на** gangrene.

**га́нгстер** gangster.

**гара́ж** (-á) garage.

**гаранти́ровать** impf & pf guarantee. **гара́нтия** guarantee.

**гардеро́б** wardrobe; cloakroom. **гардеро́бщик, -щица** cloakroom attendant.

**гарди́на** curtain.

**гармонизи́ровать** impf & pf harmonize.

**гармо́ника** accordion, concertina. **гармони́ческий, гармони́чный** harmonious. **гармо́ния** harmony; concord. **гар-**

**мо́нь** accordion, concertina.

**гарнизо́н** garrison.

**гарни́р** garnish; vegetables. **гарниту́р** set; suite.

**гарь** burning; cinders.

**гаси́тель** m extinguisher; suppressor. **гаси́ть** (гашу́, га́сишь) impf (pf за~, по~) extinguish; suppress. **га́снуть** (-ну; гас) impf (pf за~, по~, у~) be extinguished, go out; grow feeble.

**гастро́ли** f pl tour; guest-appearance, performance. **гастроли́ровать** impf (be on) tour.

**гастроно́м** gourmet; provision shop. **гастрономи́ческий** gastronomic; provision. **гастроно́мия** gastronomy; provisions; delicatessen.

**гауптва́хта** guardroom.

**гаши́ш** hashish.

**гварде́ец** (-е́йца) guardsman. **гварде́йский** guards'. **гва́рдия** Guards.

**гво́здик** tack. **гвозди́ка** pink(s), carnation(s); cloves. **гво́здики** (-ов) pl stilettos. **гвоздь** (-я́; pl -и, -е́й) m nail; tack; crux; highlight, hit.

**гг.** abbr (of го́ды) years.

**где** adv where; **~ бы ни** wherever. **где́-либо** adv anywhere. **где́-нибудь** adv somewhere; anywhere. **где́-то** adv somewhere.

**гекта́р** hectare.

**ге́лий** helium.

**гемоглоби́н** haemoglobin. **геморро́й** haemorrhoids. **гемофили́я** haemophilia.

**ген** gene.

**ге́незис** origin, genesis.

**генера́л** general. **генера́льный** general; **~ая репети́ция** dress rehearsal.

**генера́тор** generator.

**генера́ция** generation; oscillation.

**гене́тика** genetics. **генети́ческий** genetic.

**гениа́льный** brilliant. **ге́ний** genius.

**гео-** *in comb* geo-. **гео́граф** geographer. **~графи́ческий** geographical. **~гра́фия** geography. **гео́лог** geologist. **~логи́ческий** geological. **~ло́гия** geology. **~метри́ческий** geometric. **~ме́трия** geometry.

**георги́н** dahlia.

**геофи́зика** geophysics.

**гепа́рд** cheetah.

**гепати́т** hepatitis.

**гера́нь** geranium.

**герб** arms, coat of arms. **ге́рбовый** heraldic; **~ая печа́ть** official stamp.

**геркуле́с** Hercules; rolled oats.

**герма́нец** (-нца) ancient German. **Герма́ния** Germany. **герма́нский** Germanic.

**гермафроди́т** hermaphrodite.

**гермети́чный** hermetic; hermetically sealed; air-tight.

**герои́зм** heroism. **герои́ня** heroine. **герои́ческий** heroic. **геро́й** hero. **геро́йский** heroic.

**герц** (*gen pl* герц) hertz.

**ге́рцог** duke. **герцоги́ня** duchess.

**г-жа́** *abbr* (*of* госпожа́) Mrs.; Miss.

**гиаци́нт** hyacinth.

**ги́бель** death; destruction; ruin; loss; wreck; downfall. **ги́бельный** disastrous, fatal.

**ги́бкий** (-бок, -бка́, -бко) flexible; supple, versatile; supple. **ги́бкость** flexibility; suppleness.

**ги́бнуть** (-ну; ги́б(нул)) *impf* (*pf* по~) perish.

**гибри́д** hybrid.

**гига́нт** giant. **гига́нтский** gigantic.

**гигие́на** hygiene. **гигиени́ческий, -и́чный** hygienic, sanitary.

**гид** guide.

**гидравли́ческий** hydraulic.

**гидро-** *pref* hydro-. **~электроста́нция** hydro-electric powerstation.

**гие́на** hyena.

**ги́льза** cartridge-case; sleeve; (cigarette-)wrapper.

**гимн** hymn.

**гимна́зия** grammar school, high school.

**гимна́ст** gymnast. **гимна́стика** gymnastics. **гимнасти́ческий** gymnastic.

**гинеко́лог** gynaecologist. **гинеколо́гия** gynaecology.

**гипе́рбола** hyperbole.

**гипно́з** hypnosis. **гипнотизёр** hypnotist. **гипнотизи́ровать** *impf* (*pf* за~) hypnotize. **гипноти́ческий** hypnotic.

**гипо́теза** hypothesis. **гипотети́ческий** hypothetical.

**гиппопота́м** hippopotamus.

**гипс** gypsum, plaster (of Paris); plaster cast. **ги́псовый** plaster.

**гирля́нда** garland.

**ги́ря** weight.

**гистерэктоми́я** hysterectomy.

**гита́ра** guitar.

**гл.** *abbr* (*of* глава́) chapter.

**глав-** *abbr in comb* head, chief, main.

**глава́** (*pl* -ы) head; chief; chapter; cupola. **глава́рь** (-я́) *m* leader, ring-leader. **главк** central directorate. **главнокома́ндующий** *sb* commander-in-chief. **гла́вный** chief, main;

**~ым о́бразом** chiefly, mainly, for the most part; **~ое** sb the main thing; the essentials. **глаго́л** verb.

**гла́дить** (-а́жу) impf (pf вы́-, по~) stroke; iron. **гла́дкий** smooth; plain. **гла́дко** adv smoothly. **гладь** smooth surface.

**глаз** (loc -ý; pl -á, глаз) eye; in **~á** to one's face; **за ~á**+gen behind the back of; **смотре́ть во все ~á** be all eyes. **глазиро́ванный** glazed; glossy; iced; glacé.

**глазни́ца** eye-socket. **глазно́й** eye; optic; **~ врач** oculist. **глазо́к** (-зка́) peephole. **глазу́рь** fried eggs.

**глазу́рь** glaze; syrup; icing. **гла́нды** (гланд) pl tonsils. **гла́сность** publicity; glasnost, openness. **гла́сный** public; vowel; sb vowel.

**гли́на** clay. **гли́нистый** clayey. **гли́няный** clay; earthenware; clayey.

**глиссе́р** speed-boat.

**глист** (intestinal) worm.

**глицери́н** glycerine.

**гло́бус** globe.

**глота́ть** impf swallow. **гло́тка** gullet; throat. **глото́к** (-тка́) gulp; mouthful.

**гло́хнуть** (-ну; глох) impf (pf за~, о~) become deaf; die away, subside; grow wild.

**глубина́** (pl -ы) depth; heart, interior. **глубо́кий** (-о́к, -á, -о́ко) deep; profound; late, advanced, extreme. **глубокомы́слие** profundity. **глубокоуважа́емый** (in formal letters) dear.

**глуми́ться** (-млю́сь) impf mock, jeer **+instr** at. **глумле́ние** mockery.

**глупе́ть** (-е́ю) impf (pf по~)

grow stupid. **глупе́ц** (-пца́) fool. **глу́пость** stupidity. **глу́пый** (глуп, -á, -о) stupid.

**глуха́рь** (-я́) m capercaillie. **глухо́й** (глух, -á, -о) deaf; muffled; obscure, vague; dense; wild; remote; deserted; sealed; blank; **~о́й, ~а́я** sb deaf man, woman. **глухонемо́й** deaf and dumb; sb deaf mute. **глухота́** deafness. **глуши́тель** m silencer. **глуши́ть** (-шу́) impf (pf за~, о~) stun; muffle; dull; jam; extinguish; stifle; suppress. **глушь** backwoods.

**глы́ба** clod; lump, block.

**глюко́за** glucose.

**гляде́ть** (-яжу́) impf (pf по~, гля́нуть) look, gaze, peer; **в о́ба** be on one's guard; **(того́ и) гляди́** it looks as if; I'm afraid; **гля́дя по**+dat depending on.

**гля́нец** (-нца) gloss, lustre; polish.

**гля́нуть** (-ну) pf (impf гляде́ть) glance.

**гм** int hm!

**г-н** abbr (of господи́н) Mr.

**гнать** (гоню́, го́нишь; гнал, -á, -о) impf drive; urge (on); hunt, chase; persecute; distil; **~ся за** pursue.

**гнев** anger, rage. **гне́ваться** impf (pf раз~) be angry. **гне́вный** angry.

**гнедо́й** bay.

**гнездо́** (pl гнёзда) nest.

**гнёт** weight; oppression. **гнету́щий** oppressive.

**гни́да** nit.

**гние́ние** decay, putrefaction, rot. **гнило́й** (-ил, -á, -о) rotten; muggy. **гнить** (-ию́, -иёшь; -ил, -á, -о) impf (pf с~) rot. **гное́ние** suppuration. **гно́и́ться** impf (pf с~) suppurate, discharge matter. **гной** pus. **гно́йник** abscess; ulcer. **гно́йный** purulent.

**гну́сный** (-сен, -сна́, -о) vile.

**гнуть** (гну, гнёшь) *impf* (*pf* co~) bend; aim at; ~**ся** bend; stoop.

**гнуша́ться** *impf* (*pf* по~) disdain; +*gen* or *instr* shun; abhor.

**гобеле́н** tapestry.

**гобо́й** oboe.

**гове́ть** (-е́ю) *impf* fast.

**говно́** (*vulg*) shit.

**говори́ть** *impf* (*pf* по~, сказа́ть) speak, talk; say; tell; ~**ся**: как говори́тся as they say.

**говя́дина** beef. **говя́жий** beef.

**го́гот** cackle; loud laughter. **гогота́ть** (-очу́, -о́чешь) *impf* cackle; roar with laughter.

**год** (*loc* -у́; *pl* -ы or -а́, *gen* -о́в *or* лет) year. **года́ми** *adv* for years (on end).

**годи́ться**, (-жу́сь) *impf* be fit, suitable; serve.

**годи́чный** a year's; annual.

**го́дный** (-ден, -дна́, -о, -ы *or* -ы́) fit, suitable; valid.

**годова́лый** one-year-old. **годово́й** annual. **годовщи́на** anniversary.

**гожу́сь** *etc.: see* годи́ться

**гол** goal.

**голени́ще** (boot-)top. **го́лень** shin.

**голла́ндец** (-дца) Dutchman. **Голла́ндия** Holland. **голла́ндка** Dutchwoman; tiled stove. **голла́ндский** Dutch.

**голова́** (*acc* го́лову; *pl* го́ловы, -о́в, -а́м) head. **голова́стик** tadpole. **голо́вка** head; cap, nose, tip. **головн|о́й** head; leading; ~**а́я боль** headache; ~**о́й мозг** brain, cerebrum; ~**о́й убо́р** headgear, head-

dress. **головокруже́ние** giddiness, dizziness. **головоло́мка** puzzle. **головоре́з** cut-throat; rascal.

**го́лод** hunger; famine; acute shortage. **голода́ние** starvation; fasting. **голода́ть** *impf* go hungry, starve; fast. **голо́дный** (го́лоден, -дна́, -о, -ы *or* -ы́) hungry. **голодо́вка** hunger-strike.

**голо́лёд, гололе́дица** (period of) black ice.

**го́лос** (*pl* -á) voice; part; vote. **голоси́ть** (-ошу́) *impf* sing loudly; cry; wail.

**голосло́вный** unsubstantiated, unfounded.

**голосова́ние** voting; poll. **голосова́ть** *impf* (*pf* про~) vote; vote on.

**голу́бка** pigeon; (my) dear, darling. **голубо́й** light blue. **голу́бчик** my dear (fellow); darling. **го́лубь** *m* pigeon, dove. **голубя́тня** (*gen pl* -тен) dovecot, pigeon-loft.

**го́лый** (гол, -ла́, -ло) naked, bare.

**гольф** golf.

**гомоге́нный** homogeneous.

**го́мон** hubbub.

**гомосексуали́ст** homosexual. **гомосексуа́льный** homosexual.

**гондо́ла** gondola.

**гоне́ние** persecution. **го́нка** race; dashing; haste.

**гонора́р** fee.

**го́ночный** racing.

**гонча́р** (-á) potter.

**го́нщик** racing driver *or* cyclist.

**гоню́** *etc.: see* гнать. **гоня́ть** *impf* drive; send on errands; ~**ся** +за+*instr* chase, hunt.

**гора́** (*acc* го́ру; *pl* го́ры, -а́м) mountain; hill; в го́ру uphill; по́д гору downhill.

гора́здо *adv* much, far, by far.
горб (-а́, *loc* -ý) hump; bulge.
горба́тый hunchbacked. горби́ть (-блю) *impf* (*pf* с~) arch, hunch; ~ся stoop. горбу́н (-а́) *m*, горбу́нья (*gen pl* -ний) hunchback. горбу́шка (*gen pl* -шек) crust (of loaf).
горди́ться (-ржу́сь) *impf* put on airs; +*instr* be proud of. го́рдость pride. го́рдый (горд, -а́, -о, го́рды) proud. горды́ня arrogance.
го́ре grief, sorrow; trouble. горева́ть (-рю́ю) *impf* grieve.
горе́лка burner. горе́лый burnt. горе́ние burning, combustion; enthusiasm.
го́рестный sad; mournful. го́ресть sorrow; *pl* misfortunes. горе́ть (-рю́) *impf* burn; be on fire.
горе́ц (-рца) mountain-dweller. го́речь bitterness; bitter taste.
горизо́нт horizon. горизонта́ль horizontal. горизонта́льный horizontal.
гори́стый mountainous, hilly. го́рка hill; hillock; steep climb.
го́рло throat; neck. горлово́й throat; guttural; raucous. го́рлышко neck.
гормо́н hormone.
горн¹ furnace, forge.
горн² bugle.
го́рничная *sb* maid, chambermaid.
горнорабо́чий *sb* miner.
горноста́й ermine.
го́рный mountain; mountainous; mineral; mining. горня́к (-а́) miner.
го́род (*pl* -а́) town; city. городо́к (-дка́) small town. городско́й urban; city; municipal. горожа́нин (*pl* -а́не, -а́н)

*m*, -жа́нка town-dweller.
гороско́п horoscope.
горо́х pea, peas. горо́шек (-шка) spots, spotted pattern; души́стый ~ sweet peas; зелёный ~ green peas. горо́шина pea.
горсове́т *abbr* (of городско́й сове́т) city soviet, town soviet.
горсть (*gen pl* -е́й) handful.
горта́нный guttural. горта́нь larynx.
горчи́ца mustard. горчи́чник mustard plaster.
горшо́к (-шка́) flowerpot; pot; potty; chamber-pot.
го́рький (-рек, -рька́, -о) bitter.
горю́ч|ий combustible; ~ee *sb* fuel. горя́чий (-ря́ч, -а́) hot; passionate; ardent. горячи́ться (-чу́сь) *impf* (*pf* раз~) get excited. горя́чка fever; feverish haste. горя́чность zeal.
гос- *abbr in comb* (of госуда́рственный) state.
го́спиталь *m* (military) hospital.
го́споди *int* good heavens! господи́н (*pl* -ода́, -о́д, -а́м) master; gentleman; Mr; *pl* ladies and gentlemen. госпо́дство supremacy. госпо́дствовать *impf* hold sway; prevail. Госпо́дь (Го́спода, *voc* Го́споди) *m* God, the Lord. госпожа́ lady; Mrs.
гостеприи́мный hospitable. гостеприи́мство hospitality. гости́ная *sb* sitting-room, living-room, drawing-room. гости́ница hotel. гости́ть (гощу́) *impf* stay, be on a visit. гость (*gen pl* -е́й) *m*, го́стья (*gen pl* -ий) guest, visitor.

госуда́рственный State, public. госуда́рство State. госуда́рыня, госуда́рь *m* sovereign; Your Majesty.

готи́ческий Gothic.

гото́вить (-влю) *impf* (*pf* с∼) prepare; ∼ся prepare (o.s.); be at hand. гото́вность readiness, willingness. гото́вый ready.

гофриро́ванный corrugated; waved; pleated.

грабёж robbery; pillage. граби́тель *m* robber. граби́тельский predatory; exorbitant. гра́бить (-блю) *impf* (*pf* o∼) rob, pillage.

гра́бли (-бель *or* -блей) *pl* rake.

гравёр, гравиро́вщик engraver.

гра́вий gravel. гравирова́ть *impf* (*pf* вы∼) engrave; etch. гравиро́вка engraving.

гравитацио́нный gravitational.

гравю́ра engraving, print; etching.

град¹ city, town.

град² hail; volley. гра́дина hailstone.

гра́дус degree. гра́дусник thermometer.

граждани́н (*pl* гра́ждане, -дан), гражда́нка citizen. гражда́нский civil; civic; civilian. гражда́нство citizenship.

грамза́пись (gramophone) recording.

грамм gram.

грамма́тика grammar. граммати́ческий grammatical.

гра́мота reading and writing; official document; deed. гра́мотность literacy. гра́мотный literate; competent.

грампласти́нка (gramo-phone) record.

грана́т pomegranate; garnet. грана́та shell, grenade.

грандио́зный grandiose.

гранёный cut, faceted; cut-glass.

грани́т granite.

грани́ца border; boundary; limit; за грани́цей, за грани́цу abroad. грани́чить *impf* border.

грань border, verge; side, facet.

граф count; earl.

графа́ column. гра́фик graph; chart; schedule; graphic artist. гра́фика drawing; graphics; script.

графи́н carafe; decanter.

графи́ня countess.

графи́т graphite.

графи́ческий graphic.

графлёный ruled.

гра́фство county.

грацио́зный graceful. гра́-ция grace.

грач (-á) rook.

гребёнка comb. гре́бень *m* comb; crest. гребе́ц (-бца́) rower, oarsman. гребно́й rowing. гребу́ *etc.*: *see* грести́

грёза day-dream, dream. гре́-зить (-éжу) *impf* dream.

грек Greek.

гре́лка hot-water bottle.

греме́ть *impf* (*pf* про∼) thunder, roar; rattle; resound. грему́чая змея́ rattlesnake.

грести́ (-ебу́, -ебёшь; грёб, -бла́) *impf* row; rake.

греть (-éю) *impf* warm, heat; ∼ся warm o.s., bask.

грех (-á) sin. грехо́вный sinful. грехопаде́ние the Fall; fall.

Гре́ция Greece. гре́цкий оре́х walnut. греча́нка Greek. гре́-ческий Greek, Grecian.

**гречи́ха** buckwheat. **гре́чневый** buckwheat.

**греши́ть** (-шу́) *impf* (*pf* по~, со~) sin. **гре́шник, -ница** sinner. **гре́шный** (-шен, -шна́, -о) sinful.

**гриб** (-а́) mushroom. **грибно́й** mushroom.

**гри́ва** mane.

**гри́венник** ten-copeck piece.

**грим** make-up; grease-paint. **гримирова́ть** (*pf* за~) make up; +*instr* make up as.

**грипп** flu.

**гриф** neck (*of violin etc.*).

**гри́фель** *m* pencil lead.

**гроб** (*loc* -у́; *pl* -ы́ *or* -а́) coffin; grave. **гро́бница** tomb. **гробово́й** coffin; deathly. **гробовщи́к** (-а́) coffin-maker; undertaker.

**гроза́** (*pl* -ы) (thunder-)storm.

**гроздь** *f* [*pl* -ди *or* -дья, -де́й *or* -дьев] cluster, bunch.

**грози́ть(ся** (-ожу́(сь) *impf* (*pf* по~, при~) threaten. **гро́зный** (-зен, -зна́, -о) menacing; terrible; severe.

**гром** (*pl* -ы, -о́в) thunder.

**грома́да** mass; bulk, pile. **грома́дный** huge, colossal.

**громи́ть** (-млю́) *impf* destroy; smash, rout.

**гро́мкий** (-мок, -мка́, -о) loud; famous; notorious; fine-sounding. **гро́мко** *adv* loud(ly); aloud. **громкоговори́тель** *m* loud-speaker. **громово́й** thunder; thunderous; crushing. **громогла́сный** loud; public.

**громозди́ть** (-зжу́) *impf* (*pf* на~) pile up; ~ся tower; clamber up. **громо́здкий** cumbersome.

**гро́мче** *comp of* гро́мкий, гро́мко

**гроссме́йстер** grand master.

**гроте́скный** grotesque.

**гро́хот** crash, din.

**грохота́ть** (-очу́, -о́чешь) *impf* (*pf* про~) crash; rumble; roar.

**грош** (-а́) half-copeck piece; farthing. **грошо́вый** cheap; trifling.

**грубе́ть** (-е́ю) *impf* (*pf* за~, о~, по~) grow coarse. **груби́ть** (-блю́) *impf* (*pf* на~) be rude. **грубия́н** boor. **гру́бость** rudeness; coarseness; rude remark. **гру́бый** (груб, -а́, -о) coarse; rude.

**гру́да** heap, pile. **груди́нка** brisket; breast. **грудно́й** breast, chest; pectoral. **грудь** (-й *or* -и́, *instr* -ю, *loc* -и́; *pl* -и, -е́й) breast; chest.

**груз** load; burden.

**грузи́н** (*gen pl* -и́н), **грузи́нка** Georgian. **грузи́нский** Georgian.

**грузи́ть** (-ужу́, -у́зишь) *impf* (*pf* за~, на~, по~) load; ~ся load, take on cargo.

**Гру́зия** Georgia.

**гру́зный** (-зен, -зна́, -о) weighty; bulky. **грузови́к** (*gen* -а́) lorry, truck. **грузово́й** goods, cargo. **гру́зчик** stevedore; loader.

**грунт** ground, soil; priming. **грунтова́ть** *impf* (*pf* за~) prime. **грунтово́й** soil, earth; priming.

**гру́ппа** group. **группирова́ть** *impf* (*pf* с~) group; ~ся group, form groups. **группиро́вка** grouping. **группово́й** group; team.

**грусти́ть** (-ущу́) *impf* grieve, mourn; +*по*+*dat* pine for. **гру́стный** (-тен, -тна́, -о) sad. **грусть** sadness.

гру́ша pear.

гры́жа hernia, rupture.

грызть (-зу́, -зёшь; грыз) *impf* (*pf* раз~) gnaw; nag; ~ся fight; squabble. грызу́н (-а́) rodent.

гряда́ (*pl* -ы, -ам) ridge; bed; row, series; bank. гря́дка (flower-)bed.

гряду́щий approaching; future.

грязни́ть (-зен, -зна́, -о) muddy; dirty. грязь (*loc* -и́) mud; dirt, filth; *pl* mud-cure.

гря́нуть (-ну) *pf* ring out, crash out; strike up.

губа́ (*pl* -ы, -а́м) lip; *pl* pincers.

губерна́тор governor. губе́рния province. губе́рнский provincial.

губи́тельный ruinous; pernicious. губи́ть (-блю́, -бишь) *impf* (*pf* по~) ruin; spoil.

гу́бка sponge.

губна́я пома́да lipstick.

гу́бчатый porous, spongy.

гуверна́нтка governess. гуверне́р tutor.

гуде́ть (гужу́) *impf* (*pf* про~) hum; drone; buzz; hoot. гудо́к (-дка́) hooter, siren, horn, whistle; hoot.

гудро́н tar. гудро́нный tar, tarred.

гул rumble. гу́лкий (-лок, -лка́, -о) resonant; booming.

гуля́нье (*gen pl* -ний) walk; fête; outdoor party. гуля́ть *impf* (*pf* по~) stroll; go for a walk; have a good time.

гуманита́рный of the humanities; humane. гума́нный humane.

гумно́ (*pl* -а, -мен *or* -мён, -ам) threshing-floor; barn.

гурт (-а́) herd; flock. гуртовщи́к (-а́) herdsman. гурто́м *adv* wholesale; en masse.

гуса́к (-а́) gander.

гу́сеница caterpillar; (caterpillar) track. гу́сеничный caterpillar.

гусёнок (-нка; *pl* -ся́та, -ся́т) gosling. гуси́ный goose; ~ая ко́жа goose-flesh.

густе́ть (-е́ет) *impf* (*pf* за~) thicken. густо́й (густ, -а́, -о) thick, dense; rich. густота́ thickness, density; richness.

гусы́ня goose. гусь (*pl* -и, -е́й) *m* goose. гусько́м *adv* in single file.

гутали́н shoe-polish.

гу́ща grounds, sediment; thicket; thick. гу́ще *comp* of густо́й.

ГЭС *abbr* (*of* гидроэлектроста́нция) hydro-electric power station.

# Д

д. *abbr* (*of* дере́вня) village; (*of* дом) house.

да *conj* and; but.

да *partl* yes; really? well? +*3rd pers of v*, may, let; да здра́вствует...! long live ...!

дава́ть (даю́, -ёшь) *impf of* дать; дава́й(те) let us, let's; come on; ~ся yield; come easy.

дави́ть (-влю́, -вишь) *impf* (*pf* за~, по~, раз~, у~) press; squeeze; crush; oppress; ~ся choke; hang o.s. да́вка crushing; crush. давле́ние pressure.

да́вний ancient; of long standing. давно́ *adv* long ago; for a long time. да́вность antiquity; remoteness; long standing. давны́м-давно́ *adv* long long ago.

дади́м etc.: see дать. даю́ etc.: see дава́ть.

да́же adv even.

да́лее adv further; и так ~ and so on, etc. далёкий (-ёк, -á, -ёко́) distant, remote; far (-away). далеко́ adv far; far off; by a long way; ~ за long after; ~ не far from. даль (loc -и́) distance. дальне́йший further. да́льний distant, remote; long; ~ Восто́к the Far East. дальнозо́ркий long-sighted. да́льность distance; range. да́льше adv further; then, next; longer.

дам etc.: see дать

да́ма lady; partner; queen.

да́мба dike; dam.

да́мский ladies'.

Да́ния Denmark.

да́нные sb pl data; facts. да́нный given, present. дань tribute; debt.

данти́ст dentist.

дар (pl -ы́) gift. дари́ть (-рю́, -ришь) impf (pf по~) +dat give, make a present.

дарова́ние talent. дарова́ть impf & pf grant, confer. дарови́тый gifted. даровой free (of charge). да́ром adv free, gratis; in vain.

да́та date.

да́тельный dative.

дати́ровать impf & pf date.

да́тский Danish. датча́нин (pl -áне, -áн), датча́нка Dane.

дать (дам, дашь, даст, дади́м, дади́те, даду́т; дал, -á, да́ло) pf (impf дава́ть) give; grant; let; ~ взаймы́ lend; ~ся pf of дава́ться

да́ча dacha; на да́че in the country. да́чник (holiday) visitor.

два m & neut, две f (двух, ум, -умя́, -ух) two. двадцати-ле́тний twenty-year; twenty-year-old. два́дцатый twentieth; ~ые го́ды the twenties. два́дцать (-и, instr -ью́) twenty. два́жды adv twice; double. двена́дцатый twelfth. двена́дцать twelve.

дверь (loc -и́; pl -и, -éй, instr -я́ми or -ьми́) door.

две́сти (двухсо́т, -умста́м, -умяста́ми, -ухста́х) two hundred.

дви́гатель m engine; motor; motive force. дви́гать (-аю or -и́жу) impf, дви́нуть (-ну) pf move; set in motion; advance; ~ся move; advance; get started. движе́ние movement; motion; exercise; traffic. дви́жимость chattels; personal property. дви́жимый movable; moved. дви́жущий motive.

дво́е (-и́х) two; two pairs. двое- in comb two-; double(-). двоебо́рье biathlon. ~жéнец (-нца) bigamist. ~жéнство bigamy. ~то́чие colon.

двои́ться impf divide in two; appear double; у него́ двои́лось в глаза́х he saw double. двойно́й double, twofold; binary. дво́йка two; figure 2; No. 2. двойни́к (-á) double. двойно́й double, twofold; binary. двойня́ (gen -óен) twins. дво́йственный two-faced; dual.

двор (-á) yard; courtyard; homestead; court. дворе́ц (-рца́) palace. дво́рник yard caretaker; windscreen-wiper. дво́рня servants. дворо́вый yard, courtyard; sb house-serf. дворяни́н (pl -я́не, -я́н), дворя́нка member of the nobility or gentry. дворя́нство nobility, gentry.

**двою́родн|ый;** ~ый брат, ~ая сестра (first) cousin; ~ый дя́дя, ~ая тётка first cousin once removed. **двоя́кий** double; two-fold.

**дву-, двух-** *in comb* two-; bi-; double. **двубо́ртный** double-breasted. ~ли́чный two-faced. ~но́гий two-legged. ~ру́чный two-handed; two-handled. ~ру́шник double-dealer. ~смы́сленный ambiguous. ~(х)спа́льный double. ~сторо́нний double-sided; two-way; bilateral. ~хгоди́чный two-year. ~хле́тний two-year; two-year-old; biennial. ~хме́стный two-seater; two-berth. ~хмото́рный twin-engined. ~хсотле́тие bicentenary. ~хсо́тый two-hundredth. ~хта́ктный two-stroke. ~хэта́жный two-storey. ~язы́чный bilingual.

**деба́ты** (-ов) *pl* debate.

**де́бет** debit. **дебетова́ть** *impf & pf* debit.

**дебит** yield, output.

**де́бри** (-ей) *pl* jungle; thickets; the wilds.

**дебю́т** début.

**де́ва** maid, maiden; Virgo.

**девальва́ция** devaluation.

**дева́ться** *impf of* **де́ться**

**деви́з** motto; device.

**деви́ца** spinster; girl. **де́вичий** girlish, maidenly; ~ья фами́лия maiden name. **де́вочка** wench; lass; tart. **де́вочка** (little) girl. **де́вственник, -ица** virgin. **де́вственный** virgin; innocent. **де́вушка** girl. **девчо́нка** girl.

**девяно́сто** ninety. **девяно́стый** ninetieth. **девя́тка** nine; figure 9; No. 9. **девятна́дца-**

тый nineteenth. **девятна́дцать** nineteen. **девя́тый** ninth. **девя́ть** (-и́, *instr* -ью) nine. **девятьсо́т** (-тисо́т, -тиста́м, -тьюста́ми, -тиста́х) nine hundred.

**дегенери́ровать** *impf & pf* degenerate.

**дёготь** (-гтя) tar.

**дегуста́ция** tasting.

**дед** grandfather; grandad. **де́душка** grandfather; grandad.

**дееприча́стие** adverbial participle.

**дежу́рить** *impf* be on duty. **дежу́рный** duty; on duty; *sb* person on duty. **дежу́рство** (being on) duty.

**дезерти́р** deserter. **дезерти́ровать** *impf & pf* desert.

**дезинфе́кция** disinfection. **дезинфици́ровать** *impf & pf* disinfect.

**дезодора́нт** deodorant; air-freshener.

**дезориента́ция** disorientation. **дезориенти́ровать** *impf & pf* disorient; ~ся lose one's bearings.

**де́йственный** efficacious; effective. **де́йствие** action; operation; effect; act. **действи́тельно** *adv* really; indeed. **действи́тельность** reality; validity; efficacy. **действи́тельный** actual; valid; efficacious; active. **де́йствовать** *impf* (*pf* по~) affect, have an effect; act; work. **де́йствующий** active; in force; working; ~ее лицо́ character; ~ие ли́ца cast.

**декабри́ст** Decembrist. **дека́брь** (-я́) *m* December. **дека́брьский** December.

**дека́да** ten-day period *or* festival.

дека́н dean. деканат office of dean.

деклама́ция recitation, declamation. деклами́ровать *impf* (*pf* про~) recite, declaim.

деклара́ция declaration.

декорати́вный decorative. декора́тор scene-painter. декора́ция scenery.

декре́т decree; maternity leave. декре́тный о́тпуск maternity leave.

де́ланный artificial, affected. де́лать *impf* (*pf* с~) make; do; ~ вид pretend; ~ся become; happen.

делега́т delegate. делега́ция delegation; group.

делёж (-á), делёжка sharing; partition. деле́ние division; point (*on a scale*).

деле́ц (-льца́) smart operator.

делика́тный delicate.

дели́мое *sb* dividend. дели́мость divisibility. дели́тель *m* divisor. дели́ть (-лю́, -лишь) *impf* (*pf* по~, раз~) divide; share; ~ шесть на три divide six by three; ~ся divide; be divisible; +*instr* share.

де́ло (*pl* -á) business; affair; matter; deed; thing; case; в са́мом де́ле really, indeed; ~ в том the point is; как (ва́ши) дела́? how are things?; на са́мом де́ле in actual fact; по де́лу, по дела́м on business. делови́тый business-like, efficient. делово́й business; business-like. де́льный efficient; sensible.

де́льта delta.

дельфи́н dolphin.

демаго́г demagogue.

демобилиза́ция demobilization. демобилизова́ть *impf* & *pf* demobilize.

демокра́т democrat. демократиза́ция democratization. демократизи́ровать *impf* & *pf* democratize. демократи́ческий democratic. демокра́тия democracy.

де́мон demon.

демонстра́ция demonstration. демонстри́ровать *impf* & *pf* demonstrate.

де́нежный monetary; money; ~ перево́д money order.

денусь *etc.*: *see* де́ться

день (дня) *m* day; afternoon; днём in the afternoon; на днях the other day; one of these days; че́рез ~ every other day.

де́ньги (-нег, -ньга́м) *pl* money.

департа́мент department.

депо́ *neut indecl* depot.

депорта́ция deportation. депорти́ровать *impf* & *pf* deport.

депута́т (*parl*) deputy; delegate.

дёргать *impf* (*pf* дёрнуть) pull, tug; pester; ~ся twitch; jerk.

дереве́нский village; rural. дере́вня (*pl* -и, -ве́нь, -вня́м) village; the country. де́рево (*pl* -е́вья, -ьев) tree; wood. деревя́нный wood; wooden.

держа́ва power. держа́ть (-жу́, -жишь) *impf* hold; support; keep; ~ пари́ bet; ~ себя́ behave; ~ся +*acc* hold on to; be held up; hold o.s.; hold out; +*gen* keep to.

дерза́ние daring. дерза́ть *impf*, дерзну́ть (-ну́, -нёшь) *pf* dare. де́рзкий impudent; daring. де́рзость impertinence; daring.

дёрн turf.

дёрнуть(ся (-ну(сь) *pf of* дёргать(ся

**деру́** *etc.: see* **драть**

**деса́нт** landing; landing force.

**десе́рт** dessert.

**де́скать** *partl indicating reported speech.*

**десна́** (*pl* дёсны, -сен) gum.

**де́спот** despot.

**десятиле́тие** decade; tenth anniversary. **десятиле́тка** ten-year (*secondary*) school. **десятиле́тний** ten-year; ten-year-old. **деся́тичный** decimal. **деся́тка** ten; figure 10; No. 10; tenner (*10-rouble note*). **деся́ток** (-тка) ten; decade. **деся́тый** tenth. **де́сять** (-и́, *instr* -ью) ten.

**дета́ль** detail; part, component. **дета́льный** detailed; minute.

**детдо́м** (*pl* -á) children's home.

**детекти́в** detective story.

**детёныш** young animal; *pl* young. **де́ти** (-те́й, -тям, -тьми́, -тях) *pl* children. **детса́д** (*pl* -ы́) kindergarten.

**де́тская** *sb* nursery. **де́тский** children's; childish. **де́тство** childhood.

**де́ться** (-денусь) *pf* (*impf* **дева́ться**) get to, disappear to.

**дефе́кт** defect.

**дефи́с** hyphen.

**дефици́т** deficit; shortage. **дефици́тный** scarce.

**дешеве́ть** (-е́ет) *impf* (*pf* **по∼**) fall in price. **деше́вле** *comp of* **дёшево, дешёвый**. **дёшево** *adv* cheap, cheaply. **дешёвый** (дёшев, -á, -о) cheap.

**де́ятель** *m*: **госуда́рственный ∼** statesman; **обще́ственный ∼** public figure. **де́ятельность** activity; work. **де́ятельный** active, energetic.

**джаз** jazz.

**дже́мпер** pullover.

**джентельме́н** gentleman.

**джи́нсовый** denim. **джи́нсы** (-ов) *pl* jeans.

**джо́йстик** joystick.

**джу́нгли** (-ей) *pl* jungle.

**диабе́т** diabetes. **диабе́тик** diabetic.

**диа́гноз** diagnosis.

**диагона́ль** diagonal.

**диагра́мма** diagram.

**диале́кт** dialect. **диале́ктика** dialectics.

**диало́г** dialogue.

**диа́метр** diameter.

**диапазо́н** range; band.

**диапозити́в** slide.

**диафра́гма** diaphragm.

**дива́н** sofa; divan.

**диверса́нт** saboteur. **диве́рсия** sabotage.

**диви́зия** division.

**ди́вный** marvellous. **ди́во** wonder, marvel.

**дида́ктика** didactics.

**дие́з** (*mus*) sharp.

**дие́та** diet. **диети́ческий** dietetic.

**дизайн** design. **дизайнер** designer.

**ди́зель** *m* diesel; diesel engine. **ди́зельный** diesel.

**дизентери́я** dysentery.

**дика́рь** (-я́) *m*, **дика́рка** savage. **ди́кий** wild; savage; queer; preposterous. **дикобра́з** porcupine. **дикорасту́щий** wild. **ди́кость** wildness, savagery; absurdity.

**дикта́нт** dictation. **дикта́тор** dictator. **диктату́ра** dictatorship.

**диктова́ть** *impf* (*pf* **про∼**) dictate. **ди́ктор** announcer. **ди́кция** diction.

**диле́мма** dilemma.

**дилета́нт** dilettante.

**дина́мика** dynamics.

**динами́т** dynamite.

**динами́ческий** dynamic.

**дина́стия** dynasty.

**диноза́вр** dinosaur.

**дипло́м** diploma; degree; degree work. **диплома́т** diplomat. **дипломати́ческий** diplomatic.

**директи́ва** instructions; directives. **дире́ктор** (pl ~á) director; principal. **дире́кция** management.

**дирижа́бль** m airship, dirigible.

**дирижёр** conductor. **дирижи́ровать** impf +instr conduct.

**диск** disc, disk; dial; discus.

**ди́скант** treble.

**дискоте́ка** discotheque.

**дискре́тный** discrete; digital.

**дискримина́ция** discrimination.

**диску́ссия** discussion, debate.

**диспансе́р** clinic.

**диспе́тчер** controller.

**ди́спут** public debate.

**диссерта́ция** dissertation, thesis.

**дистанцио́нный** distance, distant, remote; remote-control. **диста́нция** distance; range; region.

**дисципли́на** discipline.

**дитя́** (-я́ти; pl де́ти, -е́й) neut child; baby.

**дифтери́т** diphtheria.

**дифто́нг** diphthong.

**диффама́ция** libel.

**ди́чь** game.

**длина́** length. **дли́нный** (-нен, -нна́, -о) long. **дли́тельность** duration. **дли́тельный** long, protracted. **дли́ться** (pf про~) last.

**для** prep+gen for; for the sake of; ~ того́, что́бы... in order to.

**дне́ва́льный** sb orderly, man on duty. **дне́вни́к** (-á) diary, journal. **дневно́й** day; daily. **днём** adv in the day time; in the afternoon. **дни** etc.: see **день**

**дни́ще** bottom.

**ДНК** abbr (of дезоксирибонуклеи́новая кислота́) DNA.

**дно** (дна; pl до́нья, -ьев) bottom.

**до** prep+gen (up) to; as far as; until; before; to the point of; до на́шей э́ры BC; до сих пор till now; до тех пор till then, before; до того́, как before; до того́, что to such an extent that, to the point where; мне не до I'm not in the mood for.

**доба́вить** (-влю) pf, **добавля́ть** impf (+acc or gen) add. **доба́вка** addition; second helping. **добавле́ние** addition; supplement; extra. **доба́вочный** additional.

**добега́ть** impf, **добежа́ть** (-егу́) pf +до+gen run to, as far as; reach.

**добива́ть** impf, **доби́ть** (-бью, -бьёшь) pf finish (off); ~ся +gen get, obtain; ~ся своего́ get one's way.

**добира́ться** impf of **добра́ться**

**до́блесть** valour.

**добра́ться** (-беру́сь, -ёшься; -а́лся, -ла́сь, -а́лось) pf (impf **добира́ться**) +до+gen get to, reach.

**добро́** good; э́то не к добру́ it is a bad sign.

**добро-** in comb good-, well-. **доброво́лец** (-льца) volunteer. ~**во́льно** adv voluntarily. ~**во́льный** voluntary. ~**де́тель** virtue. ~**де́тель-**

ный virtuous. **~ду́шие** good nature. **~ду́шный** good-natured. **~жела́тельный** benevolent. **~ка́чественный** of good quality: benign. **~со́вестный** conscientious.

**доброта́** goodness, kindness. **добро́тный** of good quality. **до́брый** (добр, -а́, -о, до́бры) good; kind; **бу́дьте добры́** +imper please; would you be kind enough to.

**добыва́ть** impf, **добы́ть** (-бу́ду; до́бы́л, -а́, -о) pf get, obtain, procure; mine. **добы́ча** output; mining; booty.

**добью́** etc.: see **доби́ть**. **доведу́** etc.: see **довести́**.

**довезти́** (-зу́, -зёшь; -вёз, -ла́) pf (impf **довози́ть**) take (to), carry (to), drive (to).

**дове́ренность** warrant; power of attorney. **дове́ренный** trusted; sb agent, proxy. **дове́рие** trust, confidence. **дове́рить** (impf **доверя́ть**) entrust; **~ся** +dat trust in; confide in.

**до́верху** adv to the top.

**дове́рчивый** trustful, credulous. **доверя́ть** impf of **дове́рить** (+dat) to trust.

**дове́сок** (-ска) makeweight.

**довести́** (-еду́, -едёшь; -вёл, -а́) pf, **доводи́ть** (-ожу́, -о́дишь) impf lead, take (to); bring, drive (to). **до́вод** argument, reason.

**дово́енный** pre-war.

**довози́ть** (-ожу́, -о́зишь) impf of **довезти́**

**дово́льно** adv enough; quite, fairly. **дово́льный** satisfied; pleased. **дово́льствие** contentment. **дово́льствоваться** impf (pf у**~**) be content.

**догада́ться** pf, **дога́дываться** impf guess; suspect. **дога́дка** surmise, conjecture. **дога́дливый** quick-witted.

**до́гма** dogma.

**догна́ть** (-гоню́, -го́нишь; -гна́л, -а́, -о) pf (impf **догоня́ть**) catch up (with).

**догова́риваться** impf, **договори́ться** pf come to an agreement; arrange. **до́говор** (pl -ы or -а́, -о́в) agreement; contract; treaty. **догово́рный** contractual; agreed.

**догоня́ть** impf of **догна́ть**

**догора́ть** impf, **догоре́ть** (-ри́т) pf burn out, burn down.

**дое́ду** etc.: see **дое́хать**. **доезжа́ть** impf of **дое́хать**

**дое́хать** (-е́ду) pf (impf **доезжа́ть**) +**до**+gen reach, arrive at.

**дожда́ться** (-ду́сь, -дёшься; -а́лся, -ала́сь, -ало́сь) pf +gen wait for, wait until.

**дождеви́к** (-а́) raincoat. **дождево́й** rain(y). **дождли́вый** rainy. **дождь** (-я́) m rain; **идёт ~** it is raining.

**дожива́ть** impf, **дожи́ть** (-иву́, -ивёшь; до́жи́л, -а́, -о) pf live out; spend. **дожида́ться** impf +gen wait for.

**до́за** dose.

**дозво́лить** pf, **дозволя́ть** impf permit.

**дозвони́ться** pf get through, reach by telephone.

**дозо́р** patrol.

**дозрева́ть** impf, **дозре́ть** (-е́ет) pf ripen.

**доистори́ческий** prehistoric.

**дои́ть** impf (pf по**~**) milk.

**дойти́** (дойду́, -дёшь; дошёл, -шла́) pf (impf **доходи́ть**) +**до**+gen reach; get through to.

**док** dock.

доказа́тельный conclusive. доказа́тельство proof, evidence. доказа́ть (-ажу́, -а́жешь) *pf*, дока́зывать *impf* demonstrate, prove.

докати́ться (-ачу́сь, -а́тишься) *pf*, дока́тываться *impf* roll; boom; ~до+*gen* sink into.

докла́д report; lecture. докладна́я (запи́ска) report; memo. докла́дчик speaker, lecturer. докла́дывать *impf* of доложи́ть

до́красна *adv* to red heat; to redness.

до́ктор (*pl* -а́) doctor. до́кторский doctoral. до́кторша woman doctor; doctor's wife.

доктри́на doctrine.

докуме́нт document; deed. документа́льный documentary. документа́ция documentation; documents.

долби́ть (-блю́) *impf* hollow; chisel; repeat; swot up.

долг (*loc* -у́; *pl* -и́) duty; debt; взять в ~ borrow; дать в ~ lend.

до́лгий (до́лог, -гга́, -о) long. до́лго *adv* long, (for) a long time. долгове́чный lasting, durable. долгожда́нный long-awaited. долгоигра́ющая пласти́нка LP.

долголе́тие longevity. долголе́тний of many years; longstanding. долгосро́чный long-term.

долгота́ (*pl* -ы) length; longitude.

долево́й lengthwise. до́лее *adv* longer.

должа́ть *impf* (*pf* за~) borrow.

до́лжен (-жна́) *predic*+*dat* in debt to; +*inf* obliged, bound, likely; must, have to, ought to.

должно́ быть probably. до́лжник (-а́), -ница debtor. до́лжное *sb* due. должностно́й official. до́лжность (*gen pl* -е́й) post, office; duties. до́лжный due, fitting.

доли́на valley.

до́ллар dollar.

доложи́ть¹ (-ожу́, -о́жишь) *pf* (*impf* докла́дывать) add. доложи́ть² (-ожу́, -о́жишь) *pf* (*impf* докла́дывать) +*acc* or о+*prep* report; announce.

доло́й *adv* away, off; +*acc* down with!

долото́ (*pl* -а́) chisel.

до́лька segment; clove.

до́льше *adv* longer.

до́ля (*gen pl* -е́й) portion; share; lot, fate.

дом (*pl* -а́) house; home. до́ма *adv* at home. дома́шн|ий house; home; domestic; home-made; ~яя хозя́йка housewife.

до́менн|ый blast-furnace; ~ая печь blast-furnace.

домини́ровать *impf* dominate, predominate.

домкра́т jack.

до́мна blast-furnace.

домовладе́лец (-льца), -лица house-owner; landlord. домово́дство housekeeping; domestic science. домо́вый house; household; housing.

домога́тельство solicitation; bid. домога́ться *impf* +*gen* solicit, bid for.

домо́й *adv* home, homewards. домохозя́йка housewife. домрабо́тница domestic servant, maid.

доне́льзя *adv* in the extreme.

донесе́ние dispatch, report. донести́ (-су́, -сёшь; -нёс, -сла́) *pf* (*impf* доноси́ть) report, an-

**дóнизу** adv to the bottom; **свéрху ~** from top to bottom.

nounce; +dat inform; +**нá**+acc inform against; **~сь** be heard; **+дó**+gen reach.

**дóнор** donor.

**донóс** denunciation, information. **доносúть(ся** (-ношý(сь), -нóсишь(ся) impf of **донестú(сь**

**донóсчик** informer.

**донскóй** Don.

**доны́не** adv hitherto.

**дóнья** etc.: see **днo**

**до н.э.** abbr (of **до нáшей э́ры**) BC.

**доплáта** additional payment, excess fare. **доплатúть** (-ачý, -áтишь) pf, **доплáчивать** impf pay in addition; pay the rest.

**доподлинно** adv for certain. **доподлинный** authentic, genuine.

**дополнéние** supplement, addition; (gram) object. **дополнúтельно** adv in addition. **дополнúтельный** supplementary, additional. **дополнить** pf, **дополнять** impf supplement.

**допрáшивать** impf, **допросúть** (-ошý, -óсишь) pf interrogate. **допрóс** interrogation.

**дóпуск** right of entry, admittance. **допускáть** impf, **допустúть** (-ущý, -ýстишь) pf admit; permit; tolerate; suppose. **допустúмый** permissible, acceptable. **допущéние** assumption.

**дореволюциóнный** pre-revolutionary.

**дорóга** road; way; journey; route; **по дорóге** on the way.

**дóрого** adv dear, dearly. **дороговúзна** high prices.

**дорогóй** (дóрог, -á, -о) dear.

**дорóдный** portly.

**дорожáть** impf (pf вз~, по~) rise in price, go up. **дорóже** comp of **дорогó**, **дóрого**.

**дорожúть** (-жý) impf +instr value.

**дорóжка** path; track; lane; runway; strip, runner, stair-carpet. **дорóжный** road; highway; travelling.

**досáда** annoyance. **досадúть** (-ажý) pf, **досаждáть** impf dat annoy. **досáдный** annoying. **досáдовать** be annoyed (**на**+acc with).

**доскá** (acc дóску; pl -и, -сóк, -скáм) board; slab; plaque.

**дослóвный** literal; word-for-word.

**досмóтр** inspection.

**доспéхи** pl armour.

**досрóчный** ahead of time, early.

**доставáть(ся** (-таю́(сь, -ёшь(ся) impf of **достáть(ся**

**достáвить** (-влю) pf, **доставлять** impf deliver; supply; cause, give. **достáвка** delivery.

**достáну** etc.: see **достáть**

**достáток** (-тка) sufficiency; prosperity. **достáточно** adv enough, sufficiently. **достáточный** sufficient; adequate. **достáть** (-áну) pf (impf доставáть) take (out); get, obtain; +gen or дo+gen touch; reach; impers suffice; **~ся** +dat be inherited by; fall to the lot of; **емý достáнется** he'll catch it.

**достигáть** impf, **достúгнуть, достúчь** (-úгну; -стúг) pf +gen reach, achieve; +gen or дo+gen reach. **достижéние** achievement.

**достове́рный** reliable, trustworthy; authentic.

**досто́инство** dignity; merit; value. **досто́йный** deserved; suitable; worthy; +gen worthy of.

**достопримеча́тельность** sight, notable place.

**достоя́ние** property.

**до́ступ** access. **досту́пный** accessible; approachable; reasonable; available.

**досу́г** leisure, (spare) time. **досу́жий** leisure; idle.

**до́сыта** adv to satiety.

**досье́** neut indecl dossier.

**досяга́емый** attainable.

**дота́ция** grant, subsidy.

**дотла́** utterly; to the ground.

**дотра́гиваться** impf, **дотро́нуться** (-нусь) pf +до+gen touch.

**дотя́гивать** impf, **дотяну́ть** (-яну́, -я́нешь) pf draw, drag, stretch out; hold out; live; put off; ~**ся** stretch, reach; drag on.

**до́хлый** dead; sickly. **до́хнуть**[1] (-нет, дох) pf (pf из~, по~, с~) die; kick the bucket. **дохну́ть**[2] (-ну́, -нёшь) pf draw a breath.

**дохо́д** income; revenue. **доходи́ть** (-ожу́, -о́дишь) impf of **дойти́**. **дохо́дный** profitable. **дохо́дчивый** intelligible.

**доце́нт** reader, senior lecturer.

**до́чиста** adv clean; completely.

**до́чка** daughter. **дочь** (-чери, instr -черью; pl -чери, -чере́й, instr -черьми́) daughter.

**дошёл** etc.: see **дойти́**

**дошко́льник**, **-ница** child under school age. **дошко́льный** pre-school.

**доща́тый** plank, board. **дощ́ечка** small plank, board; plaque.

**доя́рка** milkmaid.

**драгоце́нность** jewel; treasure; pl jewellery; valuables. **драгоце́нный** precious.

**дразни́ть** (-ню́, -нишь) impf tease.

**дра́ка** fight.

**драко́н** dragon.

**дра́ма** drama. **драмати́ческий** dramatic. **драмату́рг** playwright. **драматурги́я** dramatic art; plays.

**драп** thick woollen cloth.

**драпиро́вка** draping; curtain; hangings. **драпиро́вщик** upholsterer.

**драть** (деру́, -рёшь; драл, -а́, -о) impf (pf вы~, за~, со~) tear (up); irritate; make off; flog; ~**ся** fight.

**дребезги́** pl; в ~ to smithereens. **дребезжа́ть** (-жи́т) impf jingle, tinkle.

**древеси́на** wood; timber. **древе́сный** wood; ~ у́голь charcoal.

**дре́вко** (pl -и, -ов) pole, staff; shaft.

**древнегре́ческий** ancient Greek. **древнееврейский** Hebrew. **древнеру́сский** Old Russian. **дре́вний** ancient; aged. **дре́вность** antiquity.

**дрейф** drift; leeway. **дрейфова́ть** impf drift.

**дрема́ть** (-млю́ -млешь) impf doze; slumber. **дремо́та** drowsiness.

**дрему́чий** dense.

**дрессиро́ванный** trained; performing. **дрессирова́ть** impf (pf вы~) train; school. **дрессиро́вка** training. **дрессиро́вщик** trainer.

**дроби́ть** (-блю́) impf (pf раз~) break up, smash; crush;

~ся break to pieces, smash.
**дробови́к** (-á) shot-gun.
**дробь** (small) shot; drumming; fraction. **дро́бный** fractional.

**дрова́** (дров) *pl* firewood.
**дро́гнуть** (-ну) *pf*, **дрожа́ть** (-жу́) *impf* tremble; shiver; quiver.

**дро́жжи** (-éй) *pl* yeast.
**дрожь** shivering, trembling.
**дрозд** (-á) thrush.
**дро́ссель** *m* throttle, choke.
**дро́тик** javelin, dart.

**друг**[1] (*pl* -узья́, -зéй) friend.
**друг**[2]: ~ дру́га (дру́гу) each other, one another. **друго́й** other, another; ~ на ~ день (the) next day. **дру́жба** friendship. **дружелю́бный**, **дру́жеский**, **дру́жественный** friendly. **дружи́ть** (-жу́, -у́жишь) *impf* be friends; ~ся (*pf* по~ся) make friends. **дру́жный** (-жен, -жна́, -о) amicable; harmonious; simultaneous, concerted.

**дря́блый** (дрябл, -á, -о) flabby.
**дря́зги** (-зг) *pl* squabbles.
**дрянно́й** worthless; good-for-nothing. **дрянь** rubbish.
**дряхле́ть** (-éю) *impf* (*pf* о~) become decrepit. **дря́хлый** (-хл, -лá, -о) decrepit, senile.

**дуб** (*pl* -ы́) oak; blockhead. **дуби́на** club, cudgel; blockhead. **дуби́нка** truncheon, baton.

**дублёнка** sheepskin coat.
**дублёр** understudy. **дублика́т** duplicate. **дубли́ровать** duplicate; understudy; dub.

**дубо́вый** oak; coarse; clumsy.
**дуга́** (*pl* -и) arc; arch.
**ду́дка** pipe, fife.
**ду́ло** muzzle; barrel.
**ду́ма** thought; Duma; council.

**ду́мать** *impf* (*pf* по~) think; +*inf* think of, intend. **ду́маться** *impf* (*impers* +*dat*) seem.

**дунове́ние** puff, breath. **ду́нуть** (-ну) *pf* of **дуть**

**дупло́** (*pl* -á, -пел) hollow; hole; cavity.

**ду́ра, дура́к** (-á) fool. **дура́чить** (-чу) *impf* (*pf* о~) fool, dupe; ~ся play the fool. **дуре́ть** (-éю) *impf* (*pf* о~) grow stupid.

**дурма́н** narcotic; intoxicant. **дурма́нить** *impf* (*pf* о~) stupefy.

**дурно́й** (-рен, -рнá, -о) bad, evil; ugly; **мне ду́рно** I feel faint, sick. **дурнота́** faintness; nausea.

**ду́тый** hollow; inflated. **дуть** (ду́ю) *impf* (*pf* вы́~, по~), **ду́нуть** (-ну) blow; **ду́ет** there is a draught. **дутьё** glass-blowing. **ду́ться** (ду́юсь) *impf* pout; sulk.

**дух** spirit; spirits; heart; mind; breath; ghost; smell; **в ~е** in a good mood; **не в моём ~е** not to my taste; **ни слу́ху ни ~у** no news, not a word. **духи́** (-о́в) *pl* scent, perfume. **Ду́хов день** Whit Monday. **духове́нство** clergy. **духови́дец** (-дца) clairvoyant; medium. **духо́вка** oven. **духо́вный** spiritual; ecclesiastical. **духово́й** wind. **духота́** stuffiness, closeness.

**душ** shower(-bath).
**душа́** (*acc* -у, *pl* -и) soul; heart; feeling; spirit; inspiration; **в душе́** inwardly; at heart; **от всей души́** with all one's heart. **душева́я** *sb* shower-room. **душевнобольно́й** mentally ill, insane; *sb* mental patient.

lunatic. **душе́вный** mental;
sincere, cordial.

**души́стый** fragrant; ~ горо́-
шек sweet pea(s).

**души́ть** (-шу́, -шишь) *impf* (*pf*
за~) strangle; stifle, smother.

**души́ться** (-шу́сь, -шишься)
*impf* (*pf* на~) use, put on,
perfume.

**ду́шный** (-шен, -шна́, -о) stuffy,
close.

**дуэ́ль** duel.

**дуэ́т** duet.

**ды́бом** *adv* on end; у меня́
во́лосы вста́ли ~ my hair
stood on end. **ды́бы:** станови́ться на ~ rear; resist.

**дым** (loc -у́; *pl* -ы́) smoke. **дыми́ть** (-млю́) *impf* (*pf* на~)
smoke; ~ся smoke, steam;
billow. **ды́мка** haze. **ды́мный**
smoky. **дымово́й** smoke; ~а́я
труба́ flue, chimney. **дымо́к**
(-мка́) puff of smoke. **дымохо́д** flue.

**ды́ня** melon.

**дыра́** (*pl* -ы), **ды́рка** (*gen pl*
-рок) hole; gap.

**дыха́ние** breathing; breath.
**дыха́тельный** respiratory;
breathing; ~ое го́рло windpipe. **дыша́ть** (-шу́, -шишь)
*impf* breathe.

**дья́вол** devil. **дья́вольский**
devilish, diabolical.

**дья́кон** (*pl* -а́) deacon.

**дю́жина** dozen.

**дюйм** inch.

**дю́на** dune.

**дя́дя** (*gen pl* -ей) *m* uncle.

**дя́тел** (-тла) woodpecker.

# Е

**ева́нгелие** gospel; the Gospels.
**евангели́ческий** evangelical.

**евре́й, евре́йка** Jew; Hebrew. **евре́йский** Jewish.

**Евро́па** Europe. **европе́ец**
(-е́йца) European. **европе́йский** European.

**Еги́пет** Egypt. **египтя́нин** (*pl* -я́не,
-я́н), **египтя́нка** Egyptian.

**его́** *see* он, оно́; *pron* his; its.

**еда́** food; meal.

**едва́** *adv & conj* hardly; just;
scarcely; ~ ли hardly; ~ (ли)
не almost, all but.

**еди́м** *etc.*: *see* есть[1]

**едине́ние** unity. **едини́ца**
(figure) one; unity; unit; individual. **едини́чный** single;
individual.

**едино-** *in comb* mono-, uni-;
one; со-. **единобра́чие** monogamy. ~вла́стие autocracy. ~вре́менно *adv* only
once; simultaneously. ~гла́сие unanimity. ~гла́сный,
~ду́шный unanimous.
~кро́вный брат half-brother.
~мы́слие like-mindedness;
agreement. ~мы́шленник
like-minded person. ~утро́бный брат half-brother.

**еди́нственно** *adv* only, solely.
**еди́нственный** only, sole.
**еди́нство** unity. **еди́ный**
one; single; united.

**е́дкий** (е́док, едка́, -о) caustic; pungent.

**едо́к** (-а́) mouth, head; eater.

**е́ду** *etc.*: *see* е́хать

**её** *see* она́; *pron* her, hers; its.

**ёж** (ежа́) hedgehog.

**еже-** *in comb* every; -ly. **ежего́дник** annual, year-book.
~го́дный annual. ~дне́вный daily. ~ме́сячник,
~ме́сячный monthly. ~неде́льник, ~неде́льный weekly.

**ежеви́ка** (*no pl*; *usu collect*)

blackberry; blackberries; blackberry bush.

**ёжели** *conj* if.

**ёжиться** (ёжусь) *impf* (*pf* съ~) huddle up; shrink away.

**езда́** ride, riding; drive, driving; journey. **е́здить** (е́зжу) *impf* go; ride, drive; ~ **верхо́м** ride. **ездо́к** (-á) rider.

**ей** *see* **она́**

**ей-бо́гу** *int* really! truly!

**ел** *etc.: see* **есть**[1]

**е́ле** *adv* scarcely; only just.

**е́ле-е́ле** *emphatic variant of* **е́ле**

**ёлка** fir-tree, spruce; Christmas tree. **ёлочка** herringbone pattern. **ёлочный** Christmas-tree. **ель** fir-tree; spruce.

**ем** *etc.: see* **есть**[1]

**ёмкий** capacious. **ёмкость** capacity.

**ему́** *see* **он**, **оно́**

**епи́скоп** bishop.

**е́ресь** heresy. **ерети́к** (-á) heretic. **ерети́ческий** heretical.

**ёрзать** *impf* fidget.

**еро́шить** (-шу) *impf* (*pf* взъ~) ruffle, rumple.

**ерунда́** nonsense.

**е́сли** *conj* if; ~ **бы** if only; ~ **бы не** but for, if it were not for; ~ **не** unless.

**ест** *see* **есть**[1]

**есте́ственно** *adv* naturally. **есте́ственный** natural. **естество́** nature; essence. **естествозна́ние** (natural) science.

**есть**[1] (ем, ешь, ест, еди́м; ел) *impf* (*pf* съ~) eat; corrode, eat away.

**есть**[2] *see* **быть**; is, are; there is, there are; **у меня́ ~ I** have.

**ефре́йтор** lance-corporal.

**е́хать** (е́ду) *impf* (*pf* по~) go; ride, drive; travel; ~ **верхо́м** ride.

**ехи́дный** malicious, spiteful.

**ешь** *see* **есть**[1]

**ещё** *adv* still; yet; (some) more; any more; yet, further; again; +*comp* still, yet even; **всё ~** still; ~ **бы!** of course! oh yes! can you ask?; ~ **не**, **нет ~** not yet; ~ **раз** once more, again; **пока́ ~** for the present, for the time being.

**е́ю** *see* **она́**

# Ж

**ж** *conj: see* **же**

**жа́ба** toad.

**жа́бра** (*gen pl* -бр) gill.

**жа́воронок** (-нка) lark.

**жа́дничать** *impf* be greedy; be mean. **жа́дность** greed; meanness. **жа́дный** (-ден, -дна́, -о) greedy; avid; mean.

**жа́жда** thirst; +*gen* thirst, craving for. **жа́ждать** (-ду) *impf* thirst, yearn.

**жаке́т, жаке́тка** jacket.

**жале́ть** (-е́ю) *impf* (*pf* по~) pity, feel sorry for; regret; +*acc or gen* grudge.

**жа́лить** (*pf* у~) sting, bite.

**жа́лкий** (-лок, -лка́, -о) pitiful. **жа́лко** *predic: see* **жаль**

**жа́ло** sting.

**жа́лоба** complaint. **жа́лобный** plaintive.

**жа́лованье** salary. **жа́ловать** *impf* (*pf* по~) +*acc* or *dat* of person, *instr or acc* of thing grant, bestow on; ~**ся** complain (на+*acc* of, about).

**жа́лостливый** compassionate. **жа́лостный** piteous; compassionate. **жа́лость** pity. **жаль, жа́лко** *predic, impers* (it is) a pity; +*dat* it grieves;

+*gen* grudge; **как ~** what a pity; **мне ~ его** I'm sorry for him.

**жалюзи** *neut indecl* Venetian blind.

**жанр** genre.

**жар** (*loc* -ý) heat; heat of the day; fever; (high) temperature; ardour. **жара́** heat; hot weather.

**жарго́н** slang.

**жа́реный** roast; grilled; fried. **жа́рить** *impf* (*pf* за~, из~) roast; grill; fry; scorch, burn; ~**ся** roast, fry. **жа́рк|ий** (-рок, -рка́, -о) hot; passionate; ~**ое** *sb* roast (meat). **жаро́вня** (*gen pl* -вен) brazier. **жар-пти́ца** Firebird. **жа́рче** *comp of* жа́ркий.

**жа́тва** harvest. **жать**[1] (жну, жнёшь) *impf* (*pf* с~) reap, cut.

**жать**[2] (жму, жмёшь) *impf* press, squeeze; pinch; oppress.

**жва́чка** chewing, rumination; cud; chewing-gum. **жва́чн|ый** ~**ое** *sb* ruminant.

**жгу** *etc.: see* жечь

**жгут** (-á) plait; tourniquet.

**жгу́чий** burning. **жёг** *etc.: see* жечь

**ждать** (жду, ждёшь; -ал, -á, -о) *impf* +*gen* wait (for); expect.

**же, ж** but; and; however; also; *partl* giving emphasis or expressing identity; **мне же ка́жется** it seems to me, however; **сего́дня же** this very day; **что же ты де́лаешь?** what on earth are you doing?

**жева́тельная рези́нка** chewing-gum. **жева́ть** (жую, жуёшь) *impf* chew; ruminate.

**жезл** (-á) rod; staff.

**жела́ние** wish, desire. **жела́нный** longed-for; beloved.

**жела́тельный** desirable; advisable. **жела́ть** *impf* (*pf* по~) +*gen* wish for, desire; want.

**желе́** *neut indecl* jelly.

**железа́** (*pl* же́лезы, -лёз, -за́м) gland; *pl* tonsils.

**железнодоро́жник** railwayman. **железнодоро́жный** railway; **желе́зн|ый** railway; ~**ая доро́га** railway. **желе́зо** iron.

**железобето́н** reinforced concrete.

**жёлоб** (*pl* -á) gutter. **желобо́к** (-бка́) groove, channel, flute.

**желте́ть** (-е́ю) *impf* (*pf* по~) turn yellow; be yellow. **желто́к** (-тка́) yolk. **желту́ха** jaundice. **жёлтый** (желт, -á, желто́) yellow.

**желу́док** (-дка) stomach. **желу́дочный** stomach; gastric.

**жёлудь** (*gen pl* -е́й) *m* acorn.

**жёлчный** bilious; gall; irritable. **жёлчь** bile, gall.

**жема́ниться** *impf* mince, put on airs. **жема́нный** mincing, affected. **жема́нство** affectedness.

**жемчуг** (*pl* -á) pearl(s). **жемчу́жина** pearl. **жемчу́жный** pearl(y).

**жена́** (*pl* жёны) wife. **жена́тый** married.

**жени́ть** (-ню́, -нишь) *impf & pf* (*pf also* по~) marry. **жени́тьба** marriage. **жени́ться** (-ню́сь, -нишься) *impf & pf* (+**на**+*prep*) marry, get married (to). **жени́х** (-á) fiancé; bridegroom.

**же́нский** woman's; feminine; female. **же́нственный** womanly, feminine. **же́нщина** woman.

**жердь** (*gen pl* -е́й) pole; stake.

**жеребёнок** (-нка; *pl* -бя́та)

-бя́т) foal. **жеребе́ц** (-бца́) stallion.

**жеребьёвка** casting of lots.

**жерло́** (*pl* -а) muzzle; crater.

**жёрнов** (*pl* -а́, -о́в) millstone.

**же́ртва** sacrifice; victim. **же́ртвенный** sacrificial. **же́ртвовать** *impf* (*pf* по~) present, make a donation (of); +*instr* sacrifice.

**жест** gesture. **жестикули́ровать** *impf* gesticulate.

**жёсткий** (-ток, -тка́, -о) hard, tough; rigid, strict.

**жесто́кий** (-то́к, -а́, -о) cruel; severe. **жесто́кость** cruelty.

**жесть** tin(-plate). **жестяно́й** tin.

**жето́н** medal; counter; token.

**жечь** (жгу, жжёшь; жёг, жгла) *impf* (*pf* с~) burn; ~**ся** burn, sting; burn o.s.

**живи́тельный** invigorating. **жи́вность** poultry, fowl. **живо́й** (жив, -а́, -о) living, alive; lively; vivid; brisk; animated; poignant; bright; **на ~ую ни́тку** hastily, anyhow; **шить на ~ую ни́тку** tack. **живопи́сец** (-сца) painter. **живопи́сный** picturesque. **жи́вопись** painting. **жи́вость** liveliness.

**живо́т** (-а́) abdomen; stomach. **животново́дство** animal husbandry. **живо́тное** *sb* animal. **живо́тный** animal.

**живу́** *etc.*: *see* жить. **живу́чий** hardy. **живьём** *adv* alive.

**жи́дк|ий** (-док, -дка́, -о) liquid; watery; weak; sparse; ~**ий криста́лл** liquid crystal. **жи́дкость** liquid; fluid; wateriness, weakness. **жи́же** sludge; slush; liquid. **жи́же** *comp of* жи́дкий

**жи́зненный** life, of life; vital;

living; ~ **у́ровень** standard of living. **жизнеописа́ние** biography. **жизнера́достный** cheerful. **жизнеспосо́бный** capable of living; viable. **жизнь** life.

**жи́ла** vein; tendon, sinew.

**жиле́т, жиле́тка** waistcoat.

**жиле́ц** (-льца́), **жили́ца** lodger; tenant; inhabitant.

**жили́ще** dwelling, abode. **жили́щный** housing; living.

**жи́лка** vein; fibre; streak.

**жил|о́й** dwelling; habitable; ~**о́й дом** dwelling house; block of flats; ~**а́я пло́щадь, жилпло́щадь** floor-space; housing, accommodation. **жильё** habitation; dwelling.

**жир** (*loc* -у́; *pl* -ы́) fat; grease. **жире́ть** (-ре́ю) *impf* (*pf* о~, раз~) grow fat. **жи́рный** (-рен, -рна́, -о) fatty; greasy; rich. **жирово́й** fatty; fat.

**жира́ф** giraffe.

**жите́йский** worldly; everyday. **жи́тель** *m* inhabitant; dweller. **жи́тельство** residence. **жи́тница** granary. **жи́то** corn, cereal. **жить** (живу́, -вёшь; жил, -а́, -о) *impf* live. **житьё** life; existence; habitation.

**жму** *etc.*: *see* жать[2]

**жму́риться** *impf* (*pf* за~) screw up one's eyes, frown.

**жни́вье** (*pl* -ья, -ьев) stubble (-field). **жну** *etc.*: *see* жать[1]

**жоке́й** jockey.

**жонглёр** juggler.

**жрать** (жру, жрёшь; -ал, -а́, -о) guzzle.

**жре́бий** lot; fate; destiny; ~ **бро́шен** the die is cast.

**жрец** priest. **жри́ца** priestess.

**жужжа́ть** (-жжу́) hum, buzz, drone; whiz(z).

**жук** (-á) beetle.

**жу́лик** petty thief; cheat. **жу́льничать** *impf* (*pf* с~) cheat.

**жура́вль** (-я́) *m* crane.

**жури́ть** *impf* reprove.

**журна́л** magazine, periodical. **журнали́ст** journalist. **журнали́стика** journalism.

**журча́ние** babble; murmur. **журча́ть** (-чи́т) *impf* babble, murmur.

**жу́ткий** (-ток, -тка́, -о) uncanny; terrible, terrifying. **жу́тко** *adv* terrifyingly; terribly, awfully.

**жую́** *etc.*: see **жева́ть**

**жюри́** *neut indecl* judges.

## З

**за** *prep* I. +*acc* (*indicating motion or action*) *or instr* (*indicating rest or state*) behind; beyond; across, the other side of; at; to; **за́ город, за́ городом** out of town; **за рубежо́м** abroad; **сесть за роя́ль** sit down at the piano; **сиде́ть за роя́лем** be at the piano; **за́ угол, за угло́м** round the corner. II. +*acc* after; over; during, in the space of; by; for; to; **за ва́ше здоро́вье!** your health!; **вести́ за́ руку** lead by the hand; **далеко́ за́ полночь** long after midnight; **за два дня до**+*gen* two days before; **за три киломе́тра от дере́вни** three kilometres from the village; **плати́ть за биле́т** pay for a ticket; **за после́днее вре́мя** lately. III. +*instr* after; for; because of; at, during; **год за го́дом** year after year; **идти́ за молоко́м**

go for milk; **за обе́дом** at dinner.

**заба́ва** amusement; game; fun. **забавля́ть** *impf* amuse; ~**ся** amuse o.s. **заба́вный** amusing, funny.

**забастова́ть** *pf* strike; go on strike. **забасто́вка** strike. **забасто́вщик** striker.

**забве́ние** oblivion.

**забе́г** heat, race. **забега́ть** *impf*, **забежа́ть** (-егу́) *pf* run up; +к+*dat* drop in on; ~ **вперёд** run ahead; anticipate.

**за|бере́менеть** (-ею) *pf* become pregnant.

**заберу́** *etc.*: see **забра́ть**

**забива́ние** jamming. **забива́ть(ся** *impf* of **заби́ть(ся¹**

**забинтова́ть** *pf*, **забинто́вывать** *impf* bandage.

**забира́ть(ся** *impf* of **забра́ть(ся**

**заби́тый** downtrodden. **заби́ть¹** (-бью́, -бьёшь) *pf* (*impf* **забива́ть**) drive in, hammer in; score; seal, block up; obstruct; choke; jam; cram; beat up; beat; ~**ся** hide, take refuge; become cluttered or clogged; +в+*acc* get into, penetrate. **за|би́ть(ся²** *pf* begin to beat. **заби́яка** *m & f* squabbler; bully.

**заблаговре́менно** *adv* in good time; well in advance. **заблаговре́менный** timely.

**заблесте́ть** (-ещу́, -ести́шь *or* -е́щешь) *pf* begin to shine, glitter, glow.

**заблуди́ться** (-ужу́сь, -у́дишься) *pf* get lost. **заблу́дший** lost, stray. **заблужда́ться** *impf* be mistaken. **заблужде́ние** error; delusion.

**забо́й** (pit-)face.

**заболева́емость** sickness

rate. **заболева́ние** sickness, illness; falling ill. **заболева́ть**[1] *impf*, **заболе́ть**[1] (-е́ю) *pf* fall ill; +*instr* go down with. **заболева́ть**[2] *impf*, **заболе́ть**[2] (-ли́т) *pf* (begin to) ache, hurt.

**забо́р**[1] fence.

**забо́р**[2] taking away; obtaining on credit.

**забо́та** concern; care; trouble(s). **забо́тить** (-о́чу) *impf* (*pf* **о∼**) trouble, worry; **∼ся** *impf* (*pf* **по∼**) worry; take care (**o**+*prep* of); take trouble; care. **забо́тливый** solicitous, thoughtful.

**за|бракова́ть** *pf*.

**забра́сывать** *impf of* **заброса́ть**, **забро́сить**.

**забра́ть** (-беру́, -берёшь; -а́л, -а́, -о) *pf* (*impf* **забира́ть**) take; take away; seize; appropriate; **∼ся** climb; get to, into.

**забреда́ть** *impf*, **забрести́** (-еду́, -едёшь; -ёл, -а́) *pf* stray, wander; drop in.

**за|брони́ровать** *pf*.

**заброса́ть** *pf* (*impf* **забра́сывать**) fill up; bespatter, deluge. **забро́сить** (-о́шу) *pf* (*impf* **забра́сывать**) throw; abandon; neglect. **забро́-шенный** neglected; deserted.

**забры́згать** *pf*, **забры́згивать** *impf* splash, bespatter.

**забыва́ть** *impf*, **забы́ть** (-бу́ду) *pf* forget; **∼ся** doze off; lose consciousness; forget o.s. **забы́вчивый** forgetful. **забытьё** oblivion; drowsiness.

**забью́** *etc.*: *see* **забить**

**зава́ливать** *impf*, **завали́ть** (-лю́, -лишь) *pf* block up; pile; cram; overload; knock down; make a mess of; **∼ся** fall; collapse; tip up.

**зава́ривать** *impf*, **завари́ть**

(-арю́, -а́ришь) *pf* make; brew; weld. **зава́рка** brewing; brew; welding.

**заведе́ние** establishment. **заве́довать** *impf* +*instr* manage.

**заве́домо** *adv* wittingly. **заве́домый** notorious, undoubted.

**заведу́** *etc.*: *see* **завести́**

**заве́дующий** *sb* (+*instr*) manager; head.

**завезти́** (-зу́, -зёшь; -ёз, -ла́) *pf* (*impf* **завози́ть**) convey, deliver.

**за|вербова́ть** *pf*.

**завери́тель** *m* witness. **заве́-рить** *pf* (*impf* **заверя́ть**) assure; certify; witness.

**заверну́ть** (-ну́, -нёшь) *pf* (*impf* **завёртывать**, **заве́р-чивать**) wrap, wrap up; roll up; screw tight, screw up; turn (off); drop in, call in.

**заверте́ться** (-рчу́сь, -ртишь-ся) *pf* begin to turn *or* spin; lose one's head.

**завёртывать** *impf of* **заверну́ть**

**заверша́ть** *impf*, **заверши́ть** (-шу́) *pf* complete, conclude. **заверше́ние** completion; end. **заверша́ть** *impf of* **заве́сить**

**заве́са** veil, screen. **заве́сить** (-е́шу) *pf* (*impf* **заве́шивать**) curtain (off).

**завести́** (-еду́, -ёшь; -вёл, -а́) *pf* (*impf* **заводи́ть**) take, bring; drop off; start up; acquire; introduce; wind (up), crank; **∼сь** be; appear; be established; start.

**заве́т** behest, bidding, ordinance; Testament. **заве́тный** cherished; secret.

**заве́шивать** *impf of* **заве́сить**

**завеща́ние** will, testament.

**завеща́ть** bequeath.

**завзя́тый** inveterate, out-and-out.

**завива́т(ся** impf of завить(ся. **зави́вка** waving; curling; wave.

**зави́дно** impers+dat: мне ~ I feel envious. **зави́дный** enviable. **зави́довать** impf (pf по~) +dat envy.

**завинти́ть** (-нчу́) pf, **зави́нчивать** impf screw up.

**зави́сеть** (-ишу) impf +от+gen depend on. **зави́симость** dependence; в зави́симости от depending on, subject to. **зави́симый** dependent.

**зави́стливый** envious. **за́висть** envy.

**завито́й** (за́вит, -а́, -о) curled, waved. **завито́к** (-тка́) curl, lock; flourish. **завить** (-вью, -вьёшь; -и́л, -а́, -о) pf (impf **завива́ть**) curl, wave; ~ся curl, wave, twine; have one's hair curled.

**завладева́ть** impf, **завладе́ть** (-е́ю) pf +instr take possession of; seize.

**завлека́тельный** alluring, fascinating. **завлека́ть** impf, **завле́чь** (-еку́, -ечёшь; -лёк, -ла́) pf lure; fascinate.

**заво́д**¹ factory; works; stud-farm.

**заво́д**² winding mechanism. **заводи́ть(ся** (-ожу́(сь, -о́дишь(ся) impf of завести́(сь. **заводно́й** clockwork; winding; cranking.

**заводско́й** factory; sb factory worker. **заво́дчик** factory owner.

**заво́дь** backwater.

**завоева́ние** winning; conquest; achievement. **завоева́тель** m conqueror. **завое-**

**ва́ть** (-ою́ю) pf, **завоёвывать** impf conquer; win, gain; try to get.

**завожу́** etc.: see заводи́ть, завози́ть

**заво́з** delivery; carriage. **завози́ть** (-ожу́, -о́зишь) impf of завезти́

**завора́чивать** impf of заверну́ть. **заворо́т** turn, turning; sharp bend.

**завою́** etc.: see завы́ть

**завсегда́** adv always. **завсегда́тай** habitué, frequenter.

**за́втра** tomorrow. **за́втрак** breakfast; lunch. **за́втракать** impf (pf по~) have breakfast; have lunch. **за́втрашний** tomorrow's; ~ день tomorrow.

**завыва́ть** impf, **завы́ть** (-во́ю) pf (begin to) howl.

**завяза́ть** (-яжу́, -я́жешь) pf (impf **завя́зывать**) tie, tie up; start; ~ся start; arise; (of fruit) set. **завя́зка** string; lace; start; opening.

**за|вя́знуть** (-ну; -я́з) pf. **завя́зывать(ся** impf of завяза́ть(ся

**за|вя́нуть** (-ну; -я́л) pf.

**загада́ть** pf, **зага́дывать** impf think of; plan ahead; guess at the future; ~ зага́дку ask a riddle. **зага́дка** riddle; enigma. **зага́дочный** enigmatic, mysterious.

**зага́р** sunburn, tan.

**за|гаси́ть** (-ашу́, -а́сишь) pf. **за|га́снуть** (-ну) pf.

**загво́здка** snag; difficulty.

**заги́б** fold; exaggeration. **загиба́ть** impf of загну́ть

**за|гипнотизи́ровать** pf.

**загла́вие** title; heading. **загла́вн|ый** title; ~ая бу́ква capital letter.

**загла́дить** (-а́жу) pf, **загла́-**

живáть *impf* iron, iron out; make up for expiate; ~ся iron out, become smooth; fade.

за|глóхнуть (-ну; -глóх) *pf*.

заглушáть *impf*, за|глушить (-шý) *pf* drown, muffle; jam; suppress, stifle; alleviate.

заглядéнье lovely sight. за-глядéться (-яжýсь) *pf*, за-глядываться *impf* на+*acc* stare at; be lost in admiration of. загля́дывать *impf*, заглянýть (-нý, -нешь) *pf* peep; drop in.

загнáть (-гоню́, -гóнишь; -áл, -á, -о) *pf* (*impf* загонять) drive in, drive home; drive; exhaust.

загнивáние decay; suppuration. загнивáть *impf*, загнить (-ию́, -иёшь; -ил, -á, -о) *pf* rot; decay; fester.

загнýть (-ну́, -нёшь) *pf* (*impf* загибáть) turn up, turn down; bend.

заговáривать *impf*, заговорить *pf* begin to speak; tire out with talk; cast a spell over; protect with a charm (от+*gen* against). зáговор plot; spell. заговóрщик conspirator.

заголóвок (-вка) title; heading; headline.

загóн enclosure, pen; driving in. загоня́ть¹ *impf* of за-гнáть. загоня́ть² *pf* tire out; work to death.

загорáживать *impf* of за-городить

загорáть *impf*, загорéть (-рю́) *pf* become sunburnt; ~ся catch fire; blaze; impers+*dat* want very much. загорéлый sunburnt.

загородить (-рожý, -рóдишь) *pf* (*impf* загорáживать) enclose, fence in; obstruct. зá-горóдка fence, enclosure.

зáгородный suburban; country.

заготáвливать *impf*, загото́влять *impf*, заготóвить (-влю) *pf* lay in (a stock of); store; prepare. заготóвка (State) procurement, purchase; laying in.

заградить (-ажý) *pf*, заграждáть *impf* block, obstruct; bar. заграждéние obstruction; barrier.

заграница abroad, foreign parts. заграничный foreign.

загребáть *impf*, загрести (-ебý, -ебёшь; -ёб, -лá) *pf* rake up, gather; rake in.

загривок (-вка) withers; nape (of the neck).

за|гримировáть *pf*.

загромождáть *impf*, загромоздить (-зжý) *pf* block up, encumber; cram.

загружáть *impf*, за|грузить (-ужý, -ýзишь) *pf* load; feed; ~ся +*instr* load up with, take on. загрýзка loading, feeding; charge, load, capacity.

за|грунтовáть *pf*.

загрустить (-ущý) *pf* grow sad.

загрязнéние pollution. за|грязнить *pf*, загрязня́ть *impf* soil; pollute; ~ся become dirty.

загс *abbr* (*of* отдéл) зáписи áктов граждáнского состоя́ния) registry office.

загубить (-блю́, -бишь) *pf* ruin; squander, waste.

загýливать *pf*, загýливать *impf* take to drink.

за|густéть *pf*.

зад (loc -ý; pl -ы́) back; hind-quarters; buttocks; ~ом наперёд back to front.

задавáть(ся (-даю́(сь) *impf of* задáть(ся

**задави́ть** (-влю́, -вишь) *pf* crush; run over.

**задади́м** *etc.*, **зада́м** *etc.*: *see* **зада́ть**

**зада́ние** task, job.

**зада́тки** (-тков) *pl* abilities, promise.

**зада́ток** (-тка) deposit, advance.

**зада́ть** (-а́м, -а́шь, -а́ст, -ади́м; за́дал, -а́, -о) *pf* (*impf* **задава́ть**) set; give; ~ **вопро́с** ask a question; ~**ся** turn out well; succeed; ~**ся мы́слью, це́лью** make up one's mind. **зада́ча** problem; task.

**задвига́ть** *impf*, **задви́нуть** (-ну) *pf* bolt; bar; push; ~**ся** shut; slide. **задви́жка** bolt; catch.

**задво́рки** (-рок) *pl* back yard; backwoods.

**задева́ть** *impf of* **заде́ть**

**заде́лать** *impf*, **заде́лывать** *impf* do up; block up, close up.

**заде́ну** *etc.*: *see* **заде́ть**. **заде́ргивать** *impf of* **задёрнуть**

**задержа́ние** detention. **задержа́ть** (-жу́, -жишь) *pf*, **заде́рживать** *impf* delay; withhold; arrest; ~**ся** stay too long; be delayed. **заде́ржка** delay.

**задёрнуть** (-ну) *pf* (*impf* **заде́ргивать**) pull; draw.

**заде́ру** *etc.*: *see* **задра́ть**

**заде́ть** (-е́ну) *pf* (*impf* **задева́ть**) brush (against); graze; offend; catch (against).

**задира́** *m & f* bully; troublemaker. **задира́ть** *impf of* **задра́ть**

**за́дний** back, rear; **дать ~ий ход** reverse; **~яя мысль** ulterior motive; **~ий план** background; **~ий прохо́д** anus.

**за́дник** back; backdrop.

**задо́лго** *adv* +**до**+*gen* long before.

**за|должа́ть** *pf*. **задо́лженность** debts.

**задо́р** fervour. **задо́рный** provocative; fervent.

**задохну́ться** (-ну́сь, -нёшься; -о́хся *or* -у́лся) *pf* (*impf* **задыха́ться**) suffocate; choke; pant.

**за|дра́ть** (-деру́, -дерёшь; -а́л, -а́, -о) *pf* (*impf also* **задира́ть**) tear to pieces, kill; lift up; break; provoke, insult.

**задрема́ть** (-млю́, -млешь) *pf* doze off.

**задрожа́ть** (-жу́) *pf* begin to tremble.

**задува́ть** *impf of* **заду́ть**

**заду́мать** *pf*, **заду́мывать** *impf* plan; intend; think of; ~**ся** become thoughtful; meditate. **заду́мчивость** reverie. **заду́мчивый** pensive.

**заду́ть** (-у́ю) *pf* (*impf* **задува́ть**) blow out; begin to blow.

**заду́шевный** sincere; intimate.

**за|души́ть** (-ушу́, -у́шишь) *pf*.

**задыха́ться** *impf of* **задохну́ться**

**заеда́ть** *impf of* **зае́сть**

**зае́зд** calling in; lap, heat.

**зае́здить** (-зжу) *pf* override; wear out. **заезжа́ть** *impf of* **зае́хать**. **зае́зженный** hackneyed; worn out. **зае́зжий** visiting.

**заём** (за́йма) loan.

**зае́сть** (-е́м, -е́шь, -е́ст, -еди́м) *pf* (*impf* **заеда́ть**) torment; jam; entangle.

**зае́хать** (-е́ду) *pf* (*impf* **заезжа́ть**) call in; enter, ride in, drive in; reach; +**за**+*acc* go past; +**за**+*instr* call for, fetch.

**за|жа́рить(ся** *pf*.

**зажа́ть** (-жму́, -жмёшь)

(*impf* **зажимáть**) squeeze;
grip; suppress.
**зажéчь** (-жгý, -жжёшь; -жёг,
-жглá) *pf* (*impf* **зажигáть**)
set fire to; kindle; light; ~**ся**
catch fire.
**заживáть** *impf of* **зажи́ть**. **зажи-
ви́ть** (-влю́) *pf*, **зажи-
вля́ть** *impf* heal. **зáживо**
*adv* alive.
**зажигáлка** lighter. **зажигá-
ние** ignition. **зажигáтель-
ный** inflammatory; incendiary. **зажигáть(ся** *impf of* **за-
жéчь(ся**
**зажи́м** clamp; terminal; suppression. **зажимáть** *impf of*
**зажáть**. **зажимнóй** tight-
fisted.
**зажи́точный** prosperous. **за-
жи́ть** (-ивý, -ивёшь; -и́л, -á, -о)
*pf* (*impf* **заживáть**) heal; begin to live.
**зажмý** *etc.: see* **зажáть**. **за|жмý-
риться** *pf.*
**звенéть** (-и́т) *pf* begin to
ring.
**зазеленéть** (-éет) *pf* turn
green.
**заземлéние** earthing; earth.
**заземли́ть** *pf*, **заземля́ть**
*impf* earth.
**зазнавáться** (-наю́сь, -наёшь-
ся) *impf*, **зазнáться** *pf* give
o.s. airs.
**зазу́брина** notch.
**за|зубри́ть** (-рю́, -у́бри́шь) *pf.*
**заи́грывать** *impf* flirt.
**зáйка** *m & f* stammerer. **заикá-
ние** stammer. **заикáться** *impf*,
**заикнýться** (-нýсь, -нёшься)
*pf* stammer, stutter; +**о**+*prep*
mention.
**заи́мствование** borrowing.
**заи́мствовать** *impf & pf* (*pf
also* **по~**) borrow.
**заинтересóванный** inter-

ested. **заинтересовáть** *pf*,
**заинтересóвывать** *impf* interest; ~**ся** +*instr* become interested in.
**заи́скивать** *impf* ingratiate o.s.
**зайдý** *etc.: see* **зайти́**. **займý**
*etc.: see* **заня́ть**.
**зайти́** (-йдý, -йдёшь; зашёл,
-шлá) *pf* (*impf* **заходи́ть**) call;
drop in; set; +**в**+*acc* reach;
+**за**+*acc* go behind, turn; +**за**
+*instr* call for, fetch.
**зáйчик** little hare (*esp. as endearment*); reflection of sunlight. **зайчи́ха** doe hare.
**закабали́ть** *pf*, **закабаля́ть**
*impf* enslave.
**закады́чный** intimate, bosom.
**закáз** order; **на** ~ to order.
**заказáть** (-ажý, -áжешь) *pf*,
**закáзывать** *impf* order; book.
**заказнóй** made to order;
~**óе** (**письмó**) registered letter. **закáзчик** customer, client.
**закáл** temper; cast. **закáли-
вать** *impf*, **закали́ть** (-лю́)
*pf* (*impf also* **закаля́ть**) temper; harden. **закáлка** tem-
pering, hardening.
**закáлывать** *impf of* **зако-
лóть**. **закаля́ть** *impf of* **за-
кали́ть**. **закáнчивать(ся**
*impf of* **закóнчить(ся**
**закáпать** *pf*, **закáпывать**[1]
*impf* begin to drip; rain; spot.
**закáпывать**[2] *impf of* **за-
копáть**
**закáт** sunset. **закатáть** *pf*, **за-
кáтывать**[1] begin to roll;
roll up; roll out. **закати́ть**
(-ачý, -áтишь) *pf*, **закáты-
вать**[2] *impf* roll; ~**ся** roll; set.
**заквáска** ferment; leaven.
**закидáть** *pf*, **заки́дывать**[1]
*impf* shower; bespatter.
**заки́дывать**[2] *impf*, **заки́нуть**
(-ну) *pf* throw (out, away).

закипа́ть *impf*, закипе́ть (-пи́т) *pf* begin to boil.

закиса́ть *impf*, заки́снуть (-ну; -ис, -ла) *pf* turn sour; become apathetic. за́кись oxide.

закла́д pawn; pledge; bet; би́ться об ~ bet; в ~е in pawn. закла́дка laying; bookmark. закладно́й pawn. закла́дывать *impf of* заложи́ть

закле́ивать *impf*, закле́ить *pf* glue up.

заклепа́ть *pf*, заклёпывать *impf* rivet. заклёпка rivet; riveting.

заклина́ние incantation; spell. заклина́ть *impf* invoke; entreat.

заключа́ть *impf*, заключи́ть (-чу́) *pf* conclude; enter into; contain; confine. заключа́ться consist; lie, be. заключе́ние conclusion; decision; confinement. заключённый *sb* prisoner. заключи́тельный final, concluding.

закля́тие pledge. закля́тый sworn.

закова́ть (-кую́, -куёшь) *pf*, зако́вывать *impf* chain; shackle.

закола́чивать *impf of* заколоти́ть

заколдо́ванный bewitched; ~ круг vicious circle. заколдова́ть *pf* bewitch; lay a spell on.

зако́лка hair-grip; hair-slide.

заколоти́ть (-лочу́, -ло́тишь) *pf* (*impf* закола́чивать) board up; knock in; knock insensible.

за|коло́ть (-олю́, -о́лешь) *pf* (*impf also* зака́лывать) stab;

pin up; (*impers*) у меня́ заколо́ло в боку́ I have a stitch.

зако́н law. законнорождённый legitimate. зако́нность legality. зако́нный legal; legitimate.

зако́но- *in comb* law, legal. законове́дение law, jurisprudence. ~да́тельный legislative. ~да́тельство legislation. ~ме́рность regularity, normality. ~ме́рный regular, natural. ~прое́кт bill.

за|консерви́ровать *pf*. за|конспекти́ровать *pf*.

зако́нченность completeness. зако́нченный finished; accomplished. зако́нчить (-чу) *pf* (*impf* зака́нчивать) end, finish; ~ся end, finish.

закопа́ть *pf* (*impf* зака́пывать²) begin to dig; bury.

закопте́лый sooty, smutty. за|копте́ть (-ти́т) *pf* за|копти́ть (-пчу́) *pf*.

закорене́лый deep-rooted; inveterate.

закосне́лый incorrigible.

закоу́лок (-лка) alley; nook.

закочене́лый numb with cold. за|коченёть (-е́ю) *pf*.

закра́дываться *impf of* закра́сться

закра́сить (-а́шу) *pf* (*impf* закра́шивать) paint over.

закра́сться (-аду́сь, -адёшься) *pf* (*impf* закра́дываться) steal in, creep in.

закра́шивать *impf of* закра́сить

закрепи́тель *m* fixative. закрепи́ть (-плю́) *pf*, закрепля́ть *impf* fasten; fix; consolidate; +*за*+*instr* assign to; ~ за собо́й secure.

за|крепости́ть (-ощу́) *pf*, закрепоща́ть *impf* enslave.

**закрепоще́ние** enslavement; slavery; serfdom.
**закрича́ть** (-чу́) *pf* cry out; begin to shout.
**закро́йщик** cutter.
**закро́ю** *etc.: see* **закры́ть**
**закругле́ние** rounding; curve.
**закругли́ть** (-лю́) *pf*, **закругля́ть** *impf* make round; round off; **~ся** become round; round off.
**закружи́ться** (-ужу́сь, -у́жи́шься) *pf* begin to whirl *or* go round.
**за|крути́ть** (-учу́, -у́тишь) *pf*, **закру́чивать** *impf* twist, twirl; wind round; turn; screw in; turn the head of; **~ся** twist, twirl, whirl; wind round.
**закрыва́ть** *impf*, **закры́ть** (-ро́ю) *pf* close, shut; turn off; close down; cover; **~ся** close, shut; end; close down; cover o.s.; shelter. **закры́тие** closing; shutting; closing down; shelter. **закры́тый** closed, shut; private.
**закули́сный** behind the scenes; backstage.
**закупа́ть** *impf*, **закупи́ть** (-плю́, -пишь) *pf* buy up; stock up with. **заку́пка** purchase.
**заку́поривать** *impf*, **заку́порить** *pf* cork; stop up; coop up. **заку́порка** corking; thrombosis.
**заку́почный** purchase. **заку́пщик** buyer.
**заку́ривать** *impf*, **закури́ть** (-рю́, -ришь) *pf* light up; begin to smoke.
**закуси́ть** (-ушу́, -у́сишь) *pf*, **заку́сывать** *impf* have a snack; bite. **заку́ска** hors-d'oeuvre; snack. **заку́сочная** *sb* snackbar.
**за|ку́тать** *pf*, **заку́тывать** *impf*

wrap up; **~ся** wrap o.s. up.
**зал** hall; **~** ожида́ния waiting-room.
**залега́ть** *impf see* **зале́чь**
**за|ледене́ть** (-е́ю) *pf*.
**залежа́лый** stale, long unused. **залежа́ться** (-жу́сь) *pf*, **зале́живаться** *impf* lie too long; find no market; become stale. **за́лежь** deposit, seam; stale goods.
**залеза́ть** *impf*, **зале́зть** (-зу; -ез) *pf* climb, climb up; get in; creep in.
**за|лепи́ть** (-плю́, -пишь) *pf*, **залепля́ть** *impf* paste over; glue up.
**залета́ть** *impf*, **залете́ть** (-ечу́) *pf* fly; **~в +acc** fly into.
**залеча́ть** *impf*, **залечи́ть** (-чу́, -чишь) *pf* heal, cure; **~ся** heal (up).
**зале́чь** (-ля́гу, -ля́жешь; залёг, -ла́) *pf* (*impf* **залега́ть**) lie down; lie low; lie, be deposited.
**зали́в** bay; gulf. **залива́ть** *impf*, **зали́ть** (-лью́, -льёшь; за́лил, -а́, -о) *pf* flood, inundate; spill on; extinguish; spread; **~ся** be flooded; pour, spill; **+instr** break into.
**зало́г** deposit; pledge; security, mortgage; token; voice. **заложи́ть** (-жу́, -жишь) *pf* (*impf* **закла́дывать**) lay; put; mislay; pile up; pawn, mortgage; harness; lay in. **зало́жник** hostage.
**залп** volley, salvo; **~ом** without pausing for breath.
**залью́** *etc.: see* **зали́ть**. **заля́гу** *etc.: see* **зале́чь**
**зам** *abbr* (*of* **замести́тель**) assistant, deputy. **зам-** *abbr in comb* (*of* **замести́тель**) assistant, deputy, vice-.
**за|ма́зать** (-а́жу) *pf*, **зама́зывать** *impf* paint over; putty;

smear; soil; **~ся** get dirty.

**зама́зка** putty; puttying.

**зама́лчивать** impf of **замолча́ть**

**зама́нивать** impf, **замани́ть** (-ню́, -нишь) pf entice; decoy. **зама́нчивый** tempting.

**за|маринова́ть** pf.

**за|маскирова́ть** pf, **зама-скиро́вывать** impf mask; disguise; **~ся** disguise o.s.

**зама́хиваться** impf, **замах-ну́ться** (-ну́сь, -нёшься) pf +instr raise threateningly.

**зама́чивать** impf of **замочи́ть**

**замедле́ние** slowing down, deceleration; delay. **заме́д-лить** pf, **замедля́ть** impf slow down; slacken; delay; **~ся** slow down.

**замёл** etc.: see **замести́**

**заме́на** substitution; substitute. **замени́мый** replaceable. **за-мени́тель** m (+gen) substitute (for). **замени́ть** (-ню́, -нишь) pf, **заменя́ть** impf replace; be a substitute for.

**замере́ть** (-мру́, -мрёшь; за́мер, -ла́, -о) pf (impf **замира́ть**) stand still; freeze; die away.

**замерза́ние** freezing. **замер-за́ть** impf, **за|мёрзнуть** (-ну; замёрз) pf freeze (up); freeze to death.

**заме́рить** pf (impf **замеря́ть**) measure, gauge.

**замеси́ть** (-ешу́, -е́сишь) pf (impf **заме́шивать²**) knead.

**замести́** (-ету́, -етёшь; мёл, -а́) pf (impf **замета́ть**) sweep up; cover.

**замести́тель** m substitute; as-sistant, deputy, vice-. **заме-сти́ть** (-ещу́) pf (impf **заме-ща́ть**) replace; deputize for.

**замета́ть** impf of **замести́**

**заме́тить** (-е́чу) pf (impf **заме-**

**ча́ть**) notice; note; remark. **заме́тка** mark; note. **заме́т-ный** noticeable; outstanding.

**замеча́ние** remark; repri-mand. **замеча́тельный** re-markable; splendid. **заме-ча́ть** impf of **заме́тить**

**замеша́тельство** confusion; embarrassment. **замеша́ть** pf, **заме́шивать¹** impf mix up, entangle. **заме́шивать²** impf of **замеси́ть**

**замеща́ть** impf of **замести́ть**. **замеще́ние** substitution; fill-ing.

**зами́нка** hitch; hesitation.

**замира́ть** impf of **замере́ть**

**за́мкнутый** reserved; closed, exclusive. **замкну́ть** (-ну́, -нёшь) pf (impf **замыка́ть**) lock; close; **~ся** close; shut o.s. up; be-come reserved.

**за́мок¹** (-мка) castle.

**замо́к²** (-мка́) lock; padlock; clasp.

**замолка́ть** impf, **замо́лкнуть** (-ну; -мо́лк) pf fall silent; stop.

**замолча́ть** (-чу́) pf (impf **за-ма́лчивать**) fall silent; cease corresponding; hush up.

**замора́живать** impf, **заморо́-зить** (-о́жу) pf freeze. **заморо́женный** frozen; iced. **за́морозки** (-ов) pl (slight) frost.

**замо́рский** overseas.

**за|мочи́ть** (-чу́, -чишь) pf (impf also **зама́чивать**) wet; soak; ret.

**замо́чная сква́жина** keyhole.

**замру́** etc.: see **замере́ть**

**за́муж** adv: **вы́йти ~** (за+acc) marry. **за́мужем** adv married (за+instr to).

**за|му́чить** (-чу) pf torment; wear out; bore to tears. **за|му́читься** (-чусь) pf.

за́мша suede.

замыка́ние locking; short circuit. замыка́ть(ся *impf of* замкну́ть(ся

за́мысел (-сла) project, plan. замы́слить *pf*, замышля́ть *impf* plan; contemplate.

за́навес, занаве́ска curtain.

занести́ (-су́, -сёшь; -ёс, -ла́) *pf* (*impf* заноси́ть) bring; note down; (*impers*) cover with snow etc.; (*impers*) skid.

занима́ть *impf* (*pf* заня́ть) occupy; interest; engage; borrow; ~ся +*instr* be occupied with; work at; study.

зано́за splinter. занози́ть (-ожу́) *pf* get a splinter in.

зано́с snow-drift; skid. заноси́ть (-ошу́, -о́сишь) *impf of* занести́. зано́счивый arrogant.

заня́тие occupation; *pl* studies. за́нятый busy. за́нятый (-нят, -а́, -о) occupied; taken; engaged. заня́ть(ся (займу́(сь, -мёшь(ся; за́нял(ся, -а́(сь, -о(сь) *pf of* занима́ть(ся

заодно́ *adv* in concert; at one; at the same time.

заостри́ть *pf*, заостря́ть *impf* sharpen; emphasize.

зао́чник, -ница student taking correspondence course; external student. зао́чно *adv* in one's absence; by correspondence course. зао́чный курс correspondence course.

за́пад west. за́падный west, western; westerly.

западня́ (*gen pl* -не́й) trap; pitfall, snare.

за|пакова́ть *pf*, запако́вывать *impf* pack; wrap up.

запа́л ignition; fuse. запа́льная свеча́ (spark-)plug.

запа́с reserve; supply; hem.

запаса́ть *impf*, запасти́ (-су́, -сёшь; -а́с, -ла́) *pf* lay in a stock of; ~ся +*instr* stock up with. запасно́й, запа́сный spare; reserve; ~ вы́ход emergency exit.

за́пах smell.

запа́хивать *impf*, запахну́ть2 (-ну́, -нёшь) *pf* wrap up. запа́хнуть1 (-ну; -ах) *pf* begin to smell.

за|па́чкать *pf*.

запева́ть *impf of* запе́ть; lead the singing.

запека́ть(ся *impf of* запе́чь(ся. запеку́ etc.: see запе́чь

за|пелена́ть *pf*.

запере́ть (-пру́, -прёшь; за́пер, -ла́, -ло) *pf* (*impf* запира́ть) lock; lock in; bar; ~ся lock o.s. in.

запе́ть (-пою́, -поёшь) *pf* (*impf* запева́ть) begin to sing.

запеча́тать *pf*, запеча́тывать *impf* seal. запечатлева́ть *impf*, запечатле́ть (-е́ю) *pf* imprint, engrave.

запе́чь (-еку́, -ечёшь; -пёк, -ла́) *pf* (*impf* запека́ть) bake; ~ся bake; become parched; clot, coagulate.

запива́ть *impf of* запи́ть

запина́ться *impf of* запну́ться. запи́нка hesitation.

запира́ть *impf of* запере́ть(ся

записа́ть (-ишу́, -и́шешь) *pf*, запи́сывать *impf* note; take down; record; enter; enrol; ~ся register, enrol (в+*acc* at, in). запи́ска note. записн|о́й note; inveterate; ~а́я кни́жка notebook. за́пись recording; registration; record.

запи́ть (-пью́, -пьёшь; за́пил, -а́, -о) *pf* (*impf* запива́ть) begin drinking; wash down (with).

запиха́ть *pf*, запи́хивать *impf*, запихну́ть (-ну́, -нёшь) *pf* push in, cram in.

запишу́ *etc*.: *see* записа́ть

запла́кать (-а́чу) *pf* begin to cry.

запла́та patch.

за|плати́ть (-ачу́, -а́тишь) *pf* pay (за+*acc* for).

заплачу́ *etc*.: *see* запла́кать.

заплачу́ *see* заплати́ть

заплести́ (-ету́, -етёшь; -ёл, -а́) *pf*, заплета́ть *impf* plait.

за|пломбирова́ть *pf*.

заплы́в heat, round. заплыва́ть *impf*, заплы́ть (-ыву́, -ывёшь; -ы́л, -а́, -о) *pf* swim in, sail in; swim out, sail out; be bloated.

запну́ться (-ну́сь, -нёшься) *pf* (*impf* запина́ться) hesitate, stumble.

запове́дник reserve; preserve; госуда́рственный ~ national park. запове́дный prohibited. за́поведь *pre*cept; commandment.

заподо́зривать *impf*, за|подо́зрить *pf* suspect (в+*prep* of).

запозда́лый belated; delayed. запозда́ть *pf* (*impf* запа́здывать) be late.

запо́й hard drinking.

заполза́ть *impf*, заползти́ (-зу́, -зёшь; -о́лз, -зла́) *pf* creep, crawl.

запо́лнить *pf*, заполня́ть *impf* fill (in, up).

запомина́ть *impf*, запо́мнить *pf* remember; memorize; ~ся stay in one's mind.

запо́нка cuff-link; stud.

запо́р bolt; lock; constipation.

за|поте́ть (-е́ет) *pf* mist over.

запою́ *etc*.: *see* запе́ть

запра́вить (-влю) *pf*, за|правля́ть *impf* tuck in; prepare; refuel; season, dress; mix in; ~ся refuel. запра́вка refuelling; seasoning, dressing.

запра́шивать *impf* of запроси́ть

запре́т prohibition, ban. запрети́ть (-ещу́) *pf*, запреща́ть *impf* prohibit, ban. запре́тный forbidden. запреще́ние prohibition.

за|программи́ровать *pf*.

запро́с inquiry; overcharging; *pl* needs. запроси́ть (-ошу́, -о́сишь) *pf* (*impf* запра́шивать) inquire.

за́просто *adv* without ceremony.

запрошу́ *etc*.: *see* запроси́ть.

запру́ *etc*.: *see* запере́ть

запру́да dam, weir; mill-pond.

запряга́ть *impf*, запря́чь (-ягу́, -яжёшь; -я́г, -ла́) *pf* harness; yoke.

запуга́ть *pf*, запу́гивать *impf* cow, intimidate.

за́пуск launching. запуска́ть *impf*, запусти́ть (-ущу́, -у́стишь) *pf* thrust (in); start; launch; (+*acc or instr*) fling; neglect. запусте́лый neglected; desolate. запусте́ние neglect; desolation.

за|пу́тать *pf*, запу́тывать *impf* tangle; confuse; ~ся get tangled; get involved.

запущу́ *etc*.: *see* запусти́ть

запча́сть (*gen pl* -éй) *abbr* (of запасна́я часть) spare part.

запыха́ться *pf* be out of breath.

запью́ *etc*.: *see* запи́ть

запя́стье wrist.

запята́я *sb* comma.

за|пятна́ть *pf*.

зараба́тывать *impf*, зарабо́тать *pf* earn; start (up). за́ра-

**ботн|ый;** ~**ая пла́та** wages; pay. **за́работок** (-тка) earnings.

**заража́ть** impf, **зарази́ть** (-ажу́) pf infect; ~**ся** +instr be infected with, catch. **зара́за** infection. **зарази́тельный** infectious. **зара́зный** infectious.

**зара́нее** adv in good time; in advance.

**зараста́ть** impf, **зарасти́** (-ту́, -тёшь; -ро́с, -ла́) pf be overgrown; heal.

**за́рево** glow.

**за|регистри́ровать(ся** pf.

**за|ре́зать** (-е́жу) pf kill, knife; slaughter.

**зарека́ться** impf of **заре́чься**

**зарекомендова́ть** pf: ~ **себя́** +instr show o.s. to be.

**заре́чься** (-еку́сь, -ечёшься, -ёкся, -екла́сь) pf (impf **зарека́ться)** +inf renounce.

**за|ржа́веть** (-еет) pf.

**зарисо́вка** sketching; sketch.

**зароди́ть** (-ожу́) pf, **зарожда́ть** impf generate; ~**ся** be born; arise. **заро́дыш** foetus; embryo. **зарожде́ние** conception; origin.

**заро́к** vow, pledge.

**заро́с** etc.: see **зарасти́**

**зарою́** etc.: see **зары́ть**

**зарпла́та** abbr (of **за́работная пла́та**) wages; pay.

**заруба́ть** impf of **заруби́ть**

**зарубе́жный** foreign.

**заруби́ть** (-блю́, -бишь) pf (impf **заруба́ть)** kill, cut down; notch. **зару́бка** notch.

**заруча́ться** impf, **заручи́ться** (-учу́сь) pf +instr secure.

**зарыва́ть** impf, **зары́ть** (-ро́ю) pf bury.

**заря́** (pl зо́ри, зорь) dawn; sunset.

**заря́д** charge; supply. **заряди́ть** (-яжу́, -я́ди́шь) pf, **заряжа́ть** impf load; charge; stoke; ~**ся** be loaded; be charged. **заря́дка** loading; charging; exercises.

**заса́да** ambush. **засади́ть** (-ажу́, -а́дишь) pf, **заса́живать** impf plant; drive; set (за+acc) to; ~ **(в тюрьму́)** put in prison. **заса́живаться** impf of **засе́сть**

**заса́ливать** impf of **засоли́ть**

**засвети́ть** (-ечу́, -е́тишь) pf light; ~**ся** light up.

**за|свиде́тельствовать** pf.

**засе́в** sowing; seed; sown area. **засева́ть** impf of **засе́ять**

**заседа́ние** meeting; session. **заседа́ть** impf sit, be in session.

**засе́ивать** impf of **засе́ять**. **засе́к** etc.: see **засе́чь**. **засека́ть** impf of **засе́чь**

**засекре́тить** (-ре́чу) pf, **засекре́чивать** impf classify as secret; clear, give access to secret material.

**засеку́** etc.: see **засе́чь**. **засе́л** etc.: see **засе́сть**

**заселе́ние** settlement. **засели́ть** pf, **заселя́ть** impf settle; colonize; populate.

**засе́сть** (-ся́ду; -се́л) pf (impf **заса́живаться)** sit down; sit tight; settle; lodge in.

**засе́чь** (-еку́, -ечёшь; -ёк, -ла́) pf (impf **засека́ть)** flog to death; notch.

**засе́ять** (-е́ю) pf (impf **засева́ть, засе́ивать)** sow.

**заси́лье** dominance, sway.

**заслони́ть** pf, **заслоня́ть** impf cover, screen; push into the background. **засло́нка** (furnace, oven) door.

**заслу́га** merit, desert; service.

**заслу́женный** deserved, merited; Honoured; time-honoured. **заслу́живать** impf, **заслужи́ть** (-ужу́, -у́жишь) pf deserve; earn; +gen deserve.

**засмея́ться** (-ею́сь, -еёшься) begin to laugh.

**заснима́ть** impf of **засня́ть**

**засну́ть** (-ну́, -нёшь) pf (impf **засыпа́ть**) fall asleep.

**засня́ть** (-ниму́, -и́мешь; -я́л, -á, -о) pf (impf **заснима́ть**) photograph.

**засо́в** bolt, bar.

**засо́вывать** impf of **засу́нуть**

**засо́л** salting, pickling. **засоли́ть** (-олю́, -о́лишь) pf (impf **заса́ливать**) salt, pickle.

**засоре́ние** littering; contamination; obstruction. **засори́ть** (-рю́) pf, **засоря́ть** impf litter; get dirt into; clog.

**за|со́хнуть** (-ну; -со́х) pf (impf also **засыха́ть**) dry (up); wither.

**заста́ва** gate; outpost.

**застава́ть** (-таю́, -таёшь) impf of **заста́ть**

**заста́вить** (-влю) pf, **заставля́ть** impf make; compel.

**заста́иваться** impf of **застоя́ться. заста́ну** etc.: see **заста́ть**

**заста́ть** (-а́ну) pf (impf **застава́ть**) find; catch.

**застёгивать** impf, **застегну́ть** (-ну́, -нёшь) pf fasten, do up. **застёжка** fastening; clasp, buckle; ~-**мо́лния** zip.

**застекли́ть** pf, **застекля́ть** impf glaze.

**засте́нок** (-нка) torture chamber.

**засте́нчивый** shy.

**застига́ть** impf, **засти́гнуть, засти́чь** (-и́гну; -сти́г) pf catch; take unawares.

**засти́чь** see **засти́гнуть**

**засто́й** stagnation. **засто́йный** stagnant.

**за|сто́пориться** pf.

**застоя́ться** (-и́тся) pf (impf **заста́иваться**) stagnate; stand too long.

**застра́ивать** impf of **застро́ить**

**застрахо́ванный** insured. **за|страхова́ть** (-ху́ю) pf, **застрахо́вывать** impf insure.

**застрева́ть** impf of **застря́ть**

**застрели́ть** (-елю́, -е́лишь) pf shoot (dead); **~ся** shoot o.s.

**застро́ить** (-о́ю) pf (impf **застра́ивать**) build over, on, up. **застро́йка** building.

**застря́ть** (-я́ну) pf (impf **застрева́ть**) stick; get stuck.

**за́ступ** spade.

**заступа́ться** impf, **заступи́ться** (-плю́сь, -пишься) pf +за+acc stand up for. **засту́пник** defender. **засту́пничество** protection; intercession.

**застыва́ть** impf, **засты́ть** (-ы́ну) pf harden, set; become stiff; freeze; be petrified.

**засу́нуть** (-ну) pf (impf **засо́вывать**) thrust in, push in.

**за́суха** drought.

**засыпа́ть¹** (-плю) pf, **засыпа́ть** (-а́ю) impf fill up; strew.

**засыпа́ть²** impf of **засну́ть**

**засыха́ть** impf of **засо́хнуть**

**засяду** etc.: see **засе́сть**

**зата́ённый** (-ён, -ена́) secret; repressed. **зата́ивать** impf, **затаи́ть** pf suppress; conceal; harbour; ~ **дыха́ние** hold one's breath.

**зата́пливать** impf of **затопи́ть. зата́птывать** impf of **затопта́ть**

**зата́скивать** (-щу́, -щишь) pf drag in; drag off; drag away.

**затвердева́ть** *impf*, **за|тверде́ть** (-е́ет) *pf* become hard; set. **затвердение** hardening; callus.

**затво́р** bolt; lock; shutter; flood-gate. **затвори́ть** (-рю́, -ришь) *pf*, **затворя́ть** *impf* shut, close; ~ся shut o.s. up, lock o.s. in. **затво́рник** hermit, recluse.

**затева́ть** *impf of* **зате́ять**

**затёк** *etc.*: *see* **зате́чь**. **зате- ка́ть** *impf of* **зате́чь**

**зате́м** *adv* then, next; ~ что because.

**затемне́ние** darkening, obscuring; blacking out; blackout. **затемни́ть** *pf*, **затемня́ть** *impf* darken, obscure; black out.

**зате́ривать** *impf*, **затеря́ть** *pf* lose, mislay; ~ся be lost; be mislaid; be forgotten.

**зате́чь** (-ечёт, -еку́т; -тёк, -кла́) *pf* (*impf* **затека́ть**) pour, flow; swell up; become numb.

**зате́я** undertaking, venture; escapade; joke. **зате́ять** *pf* (*impf* **затева́ть**) undertake, venture.

**затиха́ть** *impf*, **зати́хнуть** (-ну; -тих) *pf* die down, abate; fade. **зати́шье** calm; lull.

**заткну́ть** (-ну́, -нёшь) *pf* (*impf* **затыка́ть**) stop up; stick, thrust.

**затмева́ть** *impf*, **затми́ть** (-мишь) *pf* darken; eclipse; overshadow. **затме́ние** eclipse.

**зато́** *conj* but then, but on the other hand.

**затону́ть** (-о́нет) *pf* sink, be submerged.

**затопи́ть**[1] (-плю, -пишь) *pf* (*impf* **зата́пливать**) light; turn on the heating.

**затопи́ть**[2] (-плю, -пишь) *pf*,

**затопля́ть** *impf* flood, submerge; sink.

**затопта́ть** (-пчу́, -пчешь) *pf* (*impf* **зата́птывать**) trample (down).

**зато́р** obstruction, jam; congestion.

**за|тормози́ть** (-ожу́) *pf*.

**зато́чить** *impf*, **заточи́ть** (-чу́) *pf* incarcerate. **заточе́ние** incarceration.

**затра́гивать** *impf of* **затро́- нуть**

**затра́та** expense; outlay. **за- тра́тить** (-а́чу) *pf*, **затра́- чивать** *impf* spend.

**затре́бовать** *pf* request, require; ask for.

**затро́нуть** (-ну) *pf* (*impf* **затра́гивать**) affect; touch (on).

**затрудне́ние** difficulty. **за- трудни́тельный** difficult. **затрудни́ть** *pf*, **затрудня́ть** *impf* trouble; make difficult; hamper; ~ся *+inf or instr* find difficulty in.

**за|туши́ться** (-пится) *pf*.

**за|туши́ть** (-шу́, -шишь) *pf* extinguish; suppress.

**за́тхлый** musty, mouldy; stuffy.

**затыка́ть** *impf of* **заткну́ть**

**заты́лок** (-лка) back of the head; scrag-end.

**затя́гивать** *impf*, **затяну́ть** (-ну́, -нешь) *pf* tighten; cover; close, heal; spin out; ~ся be covered; close; be delayed; drag on; inhale. **затя́жка** inhaling; prolongation; delaying; putting off; lagging. **затяж- но́й** long-drawn-out.

**заура́дный** ordinary; mediocre.

**зау́треня** morning service.

**зау́чивать** *impf*, **заучи́ть** (-чу́, -чишь) *pf* learn by heart.

**за|фарширова́ть** pf. **за|фик-**
**си́ровать** pf. **за|фрахто́-**
**ва́ть** pf.

**захва́т** seizure, capture. **за-**
**хвати́ть** (-ачу́, -а́тишь) pf,
**захва́тывать** impf take;
seize; thrill. **захва́тниче-**
**ский** aggressive. **захва́тчик**
aggressor. **захва́тывающий**
gripping.

**захлебну́ть** (-ну́сь, -нёшь-**
ся) pf, **захлёбываться** impf
choke (**от**+gen with).

**захлестну́ть** (-ну́, -нёшь) pf,
**захлёстывать** impf flow
over, swamp, overwhelm.

**захло́пнуть** (-ну) pf, **захло́-**
**пывать** impf slam, bang;
**~ся** slam (to).

**захо́д** sunset; calling in. **за-**
**ходи́ть** (-ожу́, -о́дишь) impf
of **зайти́**

**захолу́стный** remote, provincial. **захолу́стье** backwoods.

**за|хорони́ть** (-ню́, -нишь) pf.
**за|хоте́ть(ся** (-очу́(сь, -о́чешь-
(ся, -оти́м(ся) pf.

**зацвести́** (-етёт; -вёл, -а́) pf,
**зацвета́ть** impf come into
bloom.

**зацепи́ть** (-плю́, -пишь) pf,
**зацепля́ть** impf hook; engage; sting; catch (**за**+acc on);
**~ся за**+acc catch on; catch
hold of.

**зачасту́ю** adv often.

**зача́тие** conception. **зача́ток**
(-тка) embryo; rudiment;
germ. **зача́точный** rudimentary. **зача́ть** (-чну́, -чнёшь;
-ча́л, -а́, -о) pf (impf **зачи-**
**на́ть**) conceive.

**зачёл** etc.: see **заче́сть**

**заче́м** adv why; what for.
**заче́м-то** adv for some reason.

**зачёркивать** impf, **зачерк-**

**ну́ть** (-ну́, -нёшь) pf cross out.

**зачерпну́ть** (-ну́, -нёшь) pf,
**заче́рпывать** impf scoop up;
draw up.

**за|черстве́ть** (-е́ет) pf.

**заче́сть** (-чту́, -чтёшь; -чёл,
-чла́) pf (impf **зачи́тывать**)
take into account, reckon as
credit. **зачёт** test; **получи́ть,**
**сдать ~ по**+dat pass a test in;
**поста́вить ~ по**+dat pass in.
**зачётная кни́жка** (student's)
record book.

**зачина́ть** impf of **зача́ть**.
**зачи́нщик** instigator.

**зачи́слить, зачисля́ть** impf
include; enter; enlist; **~ся**
join, enter.

**зачи́тывать** impf of **заче́сть**.
**зачту́** etc.: see **заче́сть**. **за-**
**шёл** etc.: see **зайти́**

**зашива́ть** impf, **заши́ть** (-шью́,
-шьёшь) pf sew up.

**за|шифрова́ть** pf, **зашифро́-**
**вывать** impf encipher, encode.

**за|шнурова́ть** pf, **зашнуро́-**
**вывать** impf lace up.

**за|шпаклева́ть** (-лю́ю) pf.
**за|штопать** pf. **за|штукату́-**
**рить** pf. **заши́ю** etc.: see **заши́-**
**ть**

**защи́та** defence; protection.
**защити́ть** (-ищу́) pf, **защи-**
**ща́ть** impf defend, protect.
**защи́тник** defender. **защи́т-**
**ный** protective.

**заяви́ть** (-влю́, -вишь) pf, **за-**
**явля́ть** impf announce, declare; **~ся** turn up. **зая́вка**
claim; demand. **заявле́ние**
statement; application.

**за́яц** (за́йца) hare; stowaway;
**е́хать за́йцем** travel without
a ticket.

**зва́ние** rank; title. **зва́ный** in-
vited; **~ обе́д** banquet, dinner.

зва́тельный vocative. **звать** (зову́, -вёшь; звал, -á, -о) *impf* (*pf* по~) call; ask, invite; **как вас зову́т?** what is your name?; ~**ся** be called.

звезда́ (*pl* звёзды) star. **звёздный** star; starry; star-lit; stellar. **звёздочка** little star; asterisk.

звене́ть (-ню́) *impf* ring; +*instr* jingle, clink.

звено́ (*pl* зве́нья, -ьев) link; team, section; unit; component. **звеньево́й** *sb* section leader.

звери́нец (-нца) menagerie. **зверово́дство** fur farming. **зве́рский** brutal; terrific. **зве́рство** atrocity. **зве́рствовать** *impf* commit atrocities. **зверь** (*pl* -и, -éй) *m* wild animal.

звон ringing (sound); peal, chink, clink. **звони́ть** *impf* (*pf* по~) ring; ring up; ~ **кому́-нибудь (по телефо́ну)** ring s.o. up. **зво́нкий** (-нок, -нка́, -о) ringing, clear. **звоно́к** (-нка́) bell; (*telephone*) call.

звук sound. **звуко-** *in comb* sound. **звукоза́пись** (sound) recording. ~**изоля́ция** sound-proofing. ~**непроница́емый** sound-proof. ~**снима́тель** *m* pick-up. **звуково́й** sound; audio; acoustic. **звуча́ние** sound(ing); vibration. **звуча́ть** (-чи́т) *impf* (*pf* про~) be heard; sound. **зву́чный** (-чен, -чна́, -о) sonorous.

зда́ние building.

здесь *adv* here. **зде́шний** local; **я не зде́шний** I am no a stranger here.

здоро́ваться *impf* (*pf* по~) exchange greetings. **здо́рово** *adv* splendidly; very (much);

well done!; great! **здоро́вый** healthy, strong; well; wholesome, sound. **здоро́вье** health; **за ва́ше** ~! your health! **как ва́ше** ~? how are you? **здра́вница** sanatorium. **здравомы́слящий** sensible, judicious. **здравоохране́ние** public health.

здра́вствовать *impf* be healthy; prosper. **здра́вствуй(те)** how do you do?; hello! **да здра́вствует!** long live! **здра́вый** sensible; ~ **смысл** common sense.

зе́бра zebra.

зева́ть *impf*, **зевну́ть** (-ну́, -нёшь) *pf* yawn; gape; (*pf also* про~) miss, let slip, lose. **зево́к** (-вка́), **зево́та** yawn.

зелене́ть (-éет) *impf* (*pf* по~) turn green; show green. **зелёный** (зе́лен, -á, -о) green; ~ **лук** spring onions. **зе́лень** green; greenery; greens.

земе́льный land.

земле- *in comb* land; earth. **землевладе́лец** (-льца) landowner. ~**де́лец** (-льца) farmer. ~**де́лие** farming, agriculture. ~**де́льческий** agricultural. ~**ко́п** navvy. ~**ро́йный** excavating. ~**трясе́ние** earthquake.

земля́ (*acc* -ю; *pl* -и, земе́ль, -ям) earth; ground; land; soil. **земля́к** (-á) fellow-countryman. **земляни́ка** (*no pl; usu collect*) wild strawberry; wild strawberries. **земля́нка** dugout; mud hut. **земляно́й** earthen; earth. **земля́чка** country-woman. **земно́й** earthly; terrestrial; ground; mundane; ~ **шар** the globe.

зени́т zenith. **зени́тный** zenith; anti-aircraft.

**зéркало** (*pl* -á) mirror. **зеркáльный** mirror; smooth; plate-glass.

**зернúстый** grainy. **зернó** (*pl* зёрна, зёрен) grain; seed; kernel, core; **кóфе в зёрнах** coffee beans. **зерновóй** grain. **зерновы́е** *sb pl* cereals. **зернохранúлище** granary.

**зигзáг** zigzag.

**зимá** (*acc* -у; *pl* -ы) winter. **зúмний** winter, wintry. **зимовáть** *impf* (*pf* пере~, про~) spend the winter; hibernate. **зимóвка** wintering; hibernation. **зúмовье** winter quarters. **зимóй** *adv* in winter.

**зия́ть** *impf* gape, yawn.

**злак** grass; cereal.

**злить** (злю) *impf* (*pf* обо~, о~, разо~) anger; irritate; ~ся be angry, be in a bad temper; rage. **зло** (*gen pl* зол) evil; harm; misfortune; malice. **зло-** *in comb* evil, harm, malice. **зловéщий** ominous. ~**вóние** stink. ~**вóнный** stinking. ~**кáчественный** malignant; pernicious. ~**пáмятный** rancorous, unforgiving. ~**рáдный** malevolent, gloating. ~**слóвие** malicious gossip. ~**умышленник** malefactor; plotter. ~**язы́чный** slanderous.

**злóба** spite; anger; ~ **дня** topic of the day, latest news. **злóбный** malicious. **злободнéвный** topical. **злодéй** villain. **злодéйский** villainous. **злодéйство** villainy; crime, evil deed. **злодея́ние** crime, evil deed. **злой** (зол, зла) evil; wicked; malicious; vicious; bad-tempered; severe. **злóстный** malicious; inten-

tional. **злость** malice; fury.

**злоупотребúть** (-блю) *pf*, **злоупотребля́ть** *impf* +*instr* abuse. **злоупотреблéние** +*instr* abuse of.

**змейный** snake; cunning. **змей** snake; dragon; kite. **змея́** (*pl* -и) snake.

**знак** sign; mark; symbol.

**знакóмить** (-млю) *impf* (*pf* о~, по~) acquaint; introduce; ~**ся** become acquainted; get to know; +*c*+*instr* meet, make the acquaintance of. **знакóмство** acquaintance; (circle of) acquaintances. **знакóмый** familiar; **быть** ~**ым** *c*+*instr* be acquainted with, know; ~**ый**, ~**ая** *sb* acquaintance.

**знаменáтель** *m* denominator. **знаменáтельный** significant. **знáмение** sign. **знаменúтость** celebrity. **знаменúтый** celebrated, famous. **знáмя** (-мени; *pl* -мёна) *neut* banner; flag.

**знáние** knowledge.

**знáтный** (-тен, -тná, -о) distinguished; aristocratic; splendid.

**знатóк** (-á) expert; connoisseur. **знать** *impf* know; **дать** ~ inform, let know.

**значéние** meaning; significance; importance. **знáчит** so then; that means. **значúтельный** considerable; important; significant. **знáчить** (-чу) *impf* mean; signify; be of importance; ~**ся** be; be mentioned, appear. **значóк** (-чкá) badge; mark.

**знáющий** expert; learned.

**знобúть** *impf*, *impers*+*acc*: **меня́**, *etc.*, **знобúт** I feel shivery.

**зной** intense heat. **зно́йный** hot; burning.

**зов** call, summons. **зову́** *etc.*: *see* **звать**

**зо́дчество** architecture. **зо́дчий** *sb* architect.

**зол** *see* **зло, злой**

**зола́** ashes, cinders.

**золо́вка** sister-in-law (*husband's sister*).

**золоти́стый** golden. **зо́лото** gold. **золото́й** gold; golden.

**золочёный** gilt, gilded.

**зо́на** zone; region.

**зонд** probe. **зонди́ровать** *impf* sound, probe.

**зонт** (-а́) **зо́нтик** umbrella.

**зоо́лог** zoologist. **зоологи́ческий** zoological. **зооло́гия** zoology. **зоопа́рк** zoo. **зоотéхник** livestock specialist.

**зо́ри** *etc.*: *see* **заря́**

**зо́ркий** (-рок, -рка́, -о) sharp-sighted; perspicacious.

**зрачо́к** (-чка́) pupil (*of the eye*).

**зре́лище** sight; spectacle.

**зре́лость** ripeness; maturity; **аттеста́т зре́лости** school-leaving certificate. **зре́лый** (зрел, -а́, -о) ripe, mature.

**зре́ние** (eye)sight, vision; **то́чка зре́ния** point of view.

**зреть** (-е́ю) *impf* (*pf* **со~**) ripen; mature.

**зри́мый** visible.

**зри́тель** *m* spectator, observer; *pl* audience. **зри́тельный** visual; optic; **~ зал** hall, auditorium.

**зря** *adv* in vain.

**зуб** (*pl* -ы *or* -бья, -о́в *or* -бьев) tooth; cog. **зуби́ло** chisel. **зубно́й** dental; tooth; **~ врач** dentist. **зубовраче́бный** dentists', dental; **~ кабине́т** dental surgery. **зубочи́стка** toothpick.

**зубр** (European) bison; die-hard.

**зубри́ть** (-рю́, зу́бри́шь) *impf* (*pf* **вы~, за~**) cram.

**зубча́тый** toothed; serrated.

**зуд** itch. **зуде́ть** (-и́т) itch.

**зы́бкий** (-бок, -бка́, -о) unsteady, shaky; vacillating. **зыбь** (*gen pl* -е́й) ripple, rippling.

**зюйд** (*naut*) south; south wind.

**зя́блик** chaffinch.

**зя́бнуть** (-ну; зяб) *impf* suffer from cold, feel the cold.

**зябь** land ploughed in autumn for spring sowing.

**зять** (*pl* -тья́, -тьёв) son-in-law; brother-in-law (*sister's husband or husband's sister's husband*).

# И, Й

**и** *conj* and; even; too; (*with neg*) either; **и... и** both ... and.

**и́бо** *conj* for.

**и́ва** willow.

**игла́** (*pl* -ы) needle; thorn; spine; quill. **иглоука́лывание** acupuncture.

**игнори́ровать** *impf & pf* ignore.

**и́го** yoke.

**иго́лка** needle.

**иго́рный** gaming, gambling.

**игра́** (*pl* -ы) play, playing; game; hand; turn; **~ слов** pun. **игра́льный** playing; **~ые ко́сти** dice. **игра́ть** *impf* (*pf* **сыгра́ть**) play; act; **~ в**+*acc* play (*game*); **~ на**+*prep* play (*an instrument*). **игри́вый** playful. **игро́к** (-а́) player; gambler. **игру́шка** toy.

**идеа́л** ideal. **идеали́зм** idealism. **идеа́льный** ideal.

**иде́йный** high-principled; acting on principle; ideological.

**идеологи́ческий** ideological. **идеоло́гия** ideology.

**идёт** *etc.*: *see* **идти́**

**иде́я** idea; concept.

**иди́ллия** idyll.

**идио́т** idiot.

**и́дол** idol.

**идти́** (иду́, идёшь; шёл, шла) *impf* (*pf* пойти́) go; come; run, work; pass; go on, be in progress; be on; fall; +(к+)*dat* suit.

**иере́й** priest.

**иждиве́нец** (-нца), **-ве́нка** dependant. **иждиве́ние** maintenance; **на иждиве́нии** at the expense of.

**из, изо** *prep*+*gen* from, out of, of.

**изба́** (*pl* -ы) izba (*hut*).

**изба́вить** (-влю) *pf*, **избавля́ть** *impf* save, deliver; **~ся** be saved, escape; **~ся от** get rid of; get out of.

**избало́ванный** spoilt. **из**|**балова́ть** *pf*.

**избега́ть** *impf*, **избе́гнуть** (-ну; -бе́г(нул)) *pf*, **избежа́ть** (-егу́) *pf*+*gen or inf* avoid; escape.

**изберу́** *etc.*: *see* **избра́ть**

**избива́ть** *impf of* **изби́ть. изби́ние** slaughter; massacre; beating, beating-up.

**избира́тель** *m*, **~ница** elector, voter. **избира́тельный** electoral; election. **избира́ть** *impf of* **избра́ть**

**изби́тый** trite, hackneyed. **изби́ть** (изобью́, -бьёшь) *pf* (*impf* **избива́ть**) beat unmercifully, beat up; massacre.

**и́збранн**|**ый** selected; select; **~ые** *sb pl* the élite. **избра́ть** (-беру́, -берёшь; -а́л, -а́, -о) *pf* (*impf* **избира́ть**) elect; choose.

**избы́ток** (-тка) surplus; abundance. **избы́точный** surplus; abundant.

**и́зверг** monster. **изверже́ние** eruption; expulsion; excretion.

**изверну́ться** (-ну́сь, -нёшься) *pf* (*impf* **извора́чиваться**) dodge, be evasive.

**изве́стие** news; information; *pl* proceedings. **извести́ть** (-ещу́) *pf* (*impf* **извеща́ть**) inform, notify.

**изве́стка** lime.

**изве́стно** it is (well) known; of course, certainly. **изве́стность** fame, reputation. **изве́стный** known; well-known, famous; notorious; certain.

**известня́к** (-а́) limestone. **и́звесть** lime.

**извеща́ть** *impf of* **извести́ть. извеще́ние** notification; advice.

**извива́ться** *impf* coil; writhe; twist, wind; meander. **изви́лина** bend, twist. **изви́листый** winding; meandering.

**извине́ние** excuse; apology. **извини́ть**, **извиня́ть** *impf* excuse; **извини́те (меня́)** excuse me, (I'm) sorry; **~ся** apologize; excuse o.s.

**изви́ться** (изовью́сь, -вьёшься; -и́лся, -а́сь, -ось) *pf* coil; writhe.

**извлека́ть** *impf*, **извле́чь** (-еку́, -ечёшь; -ёк, -ла́) *pf* extract; derive; elicit.

**извне́** *adv* from outside.

**изво́зчик** cabman; carrier.

**извора́чиваться** *impf of* **изверну́ться. изворо́т** bend, twist; *pl* tricks, wiles. **изворо́тливый** resourceful; shrewd.

**изврати́ть** (-ащу́) *pf*, **извраща́ть** *impf* distort; pervert. **извраще́ние** perversion; distortion. **извращённый** perverted; unnatural.

**изги́б** bend, twist. **изгиба́ть(ся** *impf of* **изогну́ть(ся**

**изгна́ние** banishment; exile. **изгна́нник** exile. **изгоню́** (-гоню́, -го́нишь; -а́л, -а́, -о) *pf* (*impf* **изгоня́ть**) banish; exile.

**изголо́вье** bed-head.

**изголода́ться** be famished, starve; +**по**+*dat* yearn for.

**изгоню́** *etc.: see* **изгна́ть. изгоня́ть** *impf of* **изгна́ть**

**и́згородь** fence, hedge.

**изгота́вливать** *impf*, **изгото́вить** (-влю) *pf*, **изготовля́ть** *impf* make, manufacture; ~**ся** get ready. **изготовле́ние** making, manufacture.

**издава́ть** (-даю́, -даёшь) *impf of* **изда́ть**

**и́здавна** *adv* from time immemorial; for a very long time.

**издади́м** *etc.: see* **изда́ть издалека́, и́здали** *advs* from afar.

**изда́ние** publication; edition; promulgation. **изда́тель** *m* publisher. **изда́тельство** publishing house. **изда́ть** (-а́м, -а́шь, -а́ст, -ади́м; -а́л, -а́, -о) *pf* (*impf* **издава́ть**) publish; promulgate; produce; emit; ~**ся** be published.

**издева́тельство** mockery; taunt. **издева́ться** *impf* (+**над**+*instr* mock (at).

**изде́лие** work; make; article; *pl* wares.

**изде́ржки** (-жек) *pl* expenses; costs; cost.

**из**|**до́хнуть** *pf.* **из**|**жа́рить(ся** *pf.*

**изжо́га** heartburn.

**из-за** *prep*+*gen* from behind; because of.

**излага́ть** *impf of* **изложи́ть**

**излече́ние** treatment; recovery;

cure. **излечи́ть** (-чу́, -чишь) cure; ~**ся** be cured; +**от**+*gen* rid o.s. of.

**изли́шек** (-шка) surplus; excess. **изли́шество** excess; over-indulgence. **изли́шний** (-шен, -шня) superfluous.

**изложе́ние** exposition; account. **изложи́ть** (-жу́, -жишь) *pf* (*impf* **излага́ть**) expound; set forth; word.

**изло́м** break, fracture; sharp bend. **излома́ть** *pf* break; smash; wear out; warp.

**излуча́ть** *impf* radiate, emit. **излуче́ние** radiation; emanation.

**из**|**ма́зать** (-а́жу) *pf* dirty, smear all over; use up; ~**ся** get dirty, smear o.s. all over.

**изме́на** betrayal; treason; infidelity.

**измене́ние** change, alteration; inflection. **измени́ть**[1] (-ню́, -нишь) *pf* (*impf* **изменя́ть**[1]) change, alter; ~**ся** change.

**измени́ть**[2] (-ню́, -нишь) *pf* (*impf* **изменя́ть**[2]) +*dat* betray; be unfaithful to. **изме́нник, -ица** traitor.

**изменя́емый** variable. **изменя́ть**[1,2](**ся** *impf of* **измени́ть**[1,2](**ся**

**измере́ние** measurement, measuring. **изме́рить, из**|**ме́рять** *impf* measure, gauge.

**измождённый** (-ён, -а́) worn out.

**из**|**му́чить** (-чу) *pf* torment; tire out, exhaust; ~**ся** be exhausted. **изму́ченный** worn out.

**измышле́ние** fabrication, invention.

**измя́тый** crumpled, creased; haggard, jaded. **из**|**мя́ть(ся** (изомну́(сь, -нёшь(ся) *pf.*

**изна́нка** wrong side; seamy side.

**из|наси́ловать** pf rape, assault.

**изна́шивание** wear (and tear). **изна́шивать(ся** impf of **износи́ть(ся**

**изне́женный** pampered; delicate; effeminate.

**изнемога́ть** impf, **изнемо́чь** (-огу́, -о́жешь; -о́г, -ла́) pf be exhausted. **изнеможе́ние** exhaustion.

**изно́с** wear; wear and tear; deterioration. **износи́ть** (-ошу́, -о́сишь) pf (impf **изна́шивать**) wear out; ~ся wear out; be used up. **изно́шенный** worn out; threadbare.

**изнуре́ние** exhaustion. **изнуре́нный** (-ён, -ена́) exhausted, worn out; jaded. **изнури́тельный** exhausting.

**изнутри́** adv from inside, from within.

**изо** see **из**

**изоби́лие** abundance, plenty. **изоби́ловать** impf +instr abound in, be rich in. **изоби́льный** abundant.

**изоблича́ть** impf, **изобличи́ть** (-чу́) pf expose; show. **изобличе́ние** exposure; conviction.

**изобража́ть** impf, **изобрази́ть** (-ажу́) pf represent, depict, portray (+instr as); ~ся себя́+acc make o.s. out to be. **изображе́ние** image; representation; portrayal. **изобрази́тельный** graphic; decorative; ~ые иску́сства fine arts.

**изобрести́** (-ету́, -ете́шь; -ёл, -а́) pf, **изобрета́ть** impf invent; devise. **изобрета́тель** m inventor. **изобрета́тельный** inventive. **изобрете́ние**

invention.

**изобью́** etc.: see **изби́ть**. **изовью́сь** etc.: see **извить́ся**

**изо́гнутый** bent, curved; winding. **изогну́ть(ся** -ну́(сь, -не́шь(ся) pf (impf **изгиба́ть(ся**) bend, curve.

**изоли́ровать** impf & pf isolate; insulate. **изоля́тор** insulator; isolation ward; solitary confinement cell. **изоля́ция** isolation; quarantine; insulation.

**изомну́(сь** etc.: see **измя́ть**

**изо́рванный** tattered, torn. **изорва́ть** (-ву́, -вёшь; -а́л, -а́, -о) pf tear, tear to pieces; ~ся be in tatters.

**изощрённый** (-рён, -а́) refined; keen. **изощри́ться** pf, **изощря́ться** impf acquire refinement; excel.

**из-под** prep+gen from under.

**Изра́иль** m Israel. **изра́ильский** Israeli.

**из|расхо́довать(ся** pf.

**и́зредка** adv now and then.

**изреза́ть** (-е́жу) pf cut up.

**изрече́ние** dictum, saying.

**изры́ть** (-ро́ю) pf dig up, plough up. **изры́тый** pitted.

**изря́дно** adv fairly, pretty. **изря́дный** fair, handsome; fairly large.

**изуве́чить** (-чу) pf maim, mutilate.

**изуми́тельный** amazing. **изуми́ть** (-млю́) pf, **изумля́ть** impf amaze; ~ся be amazed. **изумле́ние** amazement.

**изумру́д** emerald.

**изуро́дованный** maimed; disfigured. **из|уро́довать** pf.

**изуча́ть** impf, **изучи́ть** (-чу́, -чишь) pf learn, study. **изуче́ние** study.

**изъе́здить** (-зжу) pf travel all

over; wear out.

**изъяви́ть** (-влю́, -вишь) *pf*, **изъявля́ть** *impf* express.

**изъя́н** defect, flaw.

**изъя́тие** withdrawal; removal; exception. **изъя́ть** (изыму́, -мешь) *pf* изыма́ть *impf* withdraw.

**изыска́ние** investigation, research; prospecting; survey. **изы́сканный** refined. **изыска́ть** (-ыщу́, -ыщешь) *pf*, **изы́скивать** *impf* search out; (try to) find.

**изю́м** raisins.

**изя́щество** elegance, grace. **изя́щный** elegant, graceful.

**ика́ть** *impf*, **икну́ть** (-ну́, -нёшь) *pf* hiccup.

**ико́на** icon.

**ико́та** hiccup, hiccups.

**икра́**[1] (hard) roe; caviare.

**икра́**[2] (*pl* -ы) calf (*of leg*).

**ил** silt; sludge.

**и́ли** *conj* or; ~... ~ either ... or.

**и́листый** muddy, silty.

**иллюзиони́ст** conjurer. **иллю́зия** illusion.

**иллюмина́тор** porthole. **иллюмина́ция** illumination.

**иллюстра́ция** illustration. **иллюстри́ровать** *impf & pf* illustrate.

**им** *see* он, они́, оно́

**им.** *abbr* (*of* и́мени) named after.

**и́мени** *etc.*: *see* и́мя

**име́ние** estate.

**имени́ны** (-и́н) *pl* name-day (party). **имени́тельный** nominative. **и́менно** *adv* namely; exactly, precisely; вот ~! exactly!

**име́ть** (-е́ю) *impf* have; ~ де́ло с+*instr* have dealings with; ~ ме́сто take place;

~ся be; be available.

**и́мик** *see* они́

**имита́ция** imitation. **имити́ровать** *impf* imitate.

**иммигра́нт**, **-ка** immigrant. **иммигра́ция** immigration.

**импера́тор** emperor. **импера́торский** imperial. **императри́ца** empress. **империали́зм** imperialism. **империали́ст** imperialist. **империалисти́ческий** imperialist(ic). **импе́рия** empire.

**и́мпорт** import. **импорти́ровать** *impf & pf* import. **и́мпортный** import(ed).

**импровиза́ция** improvisation. **импровизи́ровать** *impf & pf* improvise.

**и́мпульс** impulse.

**иму́щество** property.

**и́мя** (и́мени; *pl* имена́, -ён) *neut* name; first name; noun; ~ прилага́тельное adjective; ~ существи́тельное noun; ~ числи́тельное numeral.

**и́наче** *adv* differently, otherwise; так и́ли ~ in any event; *conj* otherwise, or else.

**инвали́д** disabled person; invalid. **инвали́дность** disablement, disability.

**инвента́рь** (-я́) *m* stock; equipment; inventory.

**инде́ец** (-е́йца) (American) Indian. **инде́йка** (*gen pl* -е́ек) turkey(-hen). **инде́йский** (American) Indian.

**и́ндекс** index; code.

**индиа́нка** Indian; American Indian. **инди́ец** (-и́йца) Indian.

**индивидуали́зм** individualism. **индивидуа́льность** individuality. **индивидуа́льный** individual. **индиви́дуум** individual.

инди́йский Indian. И́ндия India. инду́с, инду́ска Hindu. инду́сский Hindu.

индустриализа́ция industrialization. индустриализи́ровать impf & pf industrialize. индустриа́льный industrial. инду́стрия industry.

индю́к, индю́шка turkey.

и́ней hoar-frost.

ине́ртность inertia; sluggishness. ине́рция inertia.

инжене́р engineer; ~-меха́ник mechanical engineer; ~-стро́итель m civil engineer.

инжи́р fig.

инициа́л initial.

инициати́ва initiative. инициа́тор initiator.

инквизи́ция inquisition.

инкруста́ция inlaid work, inlay.

инкуба́тор incubator.

ино- in comb other, different; hetero-. иногоро́дний of, from, another town. ~ро́дец (-дца) non-Russian. ~ро́дный foreign. ~сказа́тельный allegorical. ~стра́нец (-нца), ~стра́нка (gen pl -нок) foreigner. ~стра́нный foreign. ~язы́чный speaking, of, another language; foreign.

иногда́ adv sometimes.

ино́й different; other; some; ~ раз sometimes.

и́нок monk. и́нокиня nun.

иноотде́л foreign department.

инсектици́д insecticide.

инспе́ктор inspector. инспе́кция inspection; inspectorate.

инста́нция instance.

инсти́нкт instinct. инсти́нкти́вный instinctive.

институ́т institute.

инстру́ктор instructor. инстру́кция instructions.

инструме́нт instrument; tool.

инсули́н insulin.

инсцениро́вка dramatization, adaptation; pretence.

интегра́ция integration.

интелле́кт intellect. интеллектуа́льный intellectual.

интеллиге́нт intellectual. интеллиге́нтный cultured, educated. интеллиге́нция intelligentsia.

интенси́вность intensity. интенси́вный intensive.

интерва́л interval.

интерве́нция intervention.

интервью́ neut indecl interview.

интере́с interest. интере́сный interesting. интересова́ть impf interest; ~ся be interested (+instr in).

интерна́т boarding-school.

интернациона́льный international.

интерни́ровать impf & pf intern.

интерпрета́ция interpretation. интерпрети́ровать impf & pf interpret.

интерье́р interior.

инти́мный intimate.

интона́ция intonation.

интри́га intrigue; plot. интриго́вать impf, (pf за~) intrigue.

интуи́ция intuition.

инфа́ркт infarct; coronary (thrombosis); heart attack.

инфекцио́нный infectious. инфе́кция infection.

инфля́ция inflation.

информа́ция information.

инфракра́сный infra-red.

ио́д etc.: see йод

ио́н ion.

ипохо́ндрик hypochondriac. ипохо́ндрия hypochondria.

ипподро́м racecourse.

**Ира́к** Iraq. **ира́кец** (-кца) Iraqi. **ира́кский** Iraqi.

**Ира́н** Iran. **ира́нец** (-нца), **ира́нка** Iranian. **ира́нский** Iranian.

**ирла́ндец** (-дца) Irishman. **Ирла́ндия** Ireland. **ирла́ндка** Irishwoman. **ирла́ндский** Irish.

**ирони́ческий** ironic. **иро́ния** irony.

**иррига́ция** irrigation.

**иск** suit, action.

**искажа́ть** impf, **исказить** (-ажу́) pf distort, pervert; misrepresent. **искаже́ние** distortion, perversion.

**искале́ченный** crippled, maimed. **искале́чить** (-чу) pf cripple, maim; break.

**иска́ть** (ищу́, и́щешь) impf (+acc or gen) seek, look for.

**исключа́ть** impf, **исключи́ть** (-чу́) pf exclude; eliminate; expel. **исключа́я** prep+gen except. **исключе́ние** exception; exclusion; expulsion; elimination; **за исключе́нием** +gen with the exception of. **исключи́тельно** adv exceptionally; exclusively. **исключи́тельный** exceptional; exclusive.

**иско́нный** primordial.

**ископа́емое** sb mineral; fossil. **ископа́емый** fossilized, fossil.

**искорени́ть** pf, **искореня́ть** impf eradicate.

**и́скоса** adv askance; sidelong.

**и́скра** spark.

**и́скренний** sincere. **и́скренность** sincerity.

**искривле́ние** bend; distortion, warping.

**ис|купа́ть**[1]**(ся** pf.

**искупа́ть**[2] impf, **искупи́ть**

(-плю́, -пишь) pf atone for; make up for. **искупле́ние** redemption, atonement.

**искуси́ть** (-ушу́) pf of **искуша́ть**

**иску́сный** skilful; expert. **иску́сственный** artificial; feigned. **иску́сство** art; skill. **искусствове́д** art historian. **искуша́ть** impf (pf **искуси́ть**) tempt; seduce. **искуше́ние** temptation, seduction.

**испа́нец** (-нца) Spaniard. **Испа́ния** Spain. **испа́нка** Spanish woman. **испа́нский** Spanish.

**испаре́ние** evaporation; pl fumes. **испари́ться** pf, **испаря́ться** impf evaporate.

**ис|па́чкать** pf. **ис|пе́чь** (-еку́, -ечёшь) pf.

**испове́довать** impf & pf confess; profess; **~ся** confess; make one's confession; +в+prep unburden o.s. of. **и́споведь** confession.

**исподти́шка** adv in an underhand way; on the quiet.

**исполи́н** giant. **исполи́нский** gigantic.

**исполко́м** abbr (of **исполни́тельный комите́т**) executive committee.

**исполне́ние** fulfilment, execution. **исполни́тель** m, **~ница** executor; performer. **исполни́тельный** executive. **испо́лнить** pf, **исполня́ть** impf carry out, execute; fulfil; perform; **~ся** be fulfilled.

**испо́льзование** utilization. **испо́льзовать** impf & pf make (good) use of, utilize.

**ис|по́ртить(ся** (-рчу(сь) pf. **испо́рченный** depraved; spoiled; rotten.

**исправи́тельный** correctional; corrective. **испра́вить** (-влю) pf, **исправля́ть** impf rectify, correct; mend; reform; **~ся** improve, reform. **исправле́ние** repairing; improvement; correction. **испра́вленный** improved, corrected; revised; reformed. **испра́вный** in good order; punctual; meticulous.

**ис|про́бовать** pf.

**испу́г** fright. **ис|пуга́ть(ся** pf.

**испуска́ть** impf, **испусти́ть** (-ущу́, -у́стишь) pf emit, let out.

**испыта́ние** test, trial; ordeal. **испыта́ть** pf, **испы́тывать** impf test; try; experience.

**иссле́дование** investigation; research. **иссле́дователь** m researcher; investigator. **иссле́довательский** research. **иссле́довать** impf & pf investigate, examine; research into.

**истаска́ться** pf, **иста́скиваться** impf wear out; be worn out.

**истека́ть** impf of **исте́чь**. **исте́кший** past.

**исте́рика** hysterics. **истери́ческий** hysterical. **истери́я** hysteria.

**истече́ние** outflow; expiry. **исте́чь** (-ечёт; -тёк, -ла́) pf (impf **истека́ть**) elapse; expire.

**и́стина** truth. **и́стинный** true.

**истлева́ть** impf, **истле́ть** (-е́ю) pf rot, decay; be reduced to ashes.

**исто́к** source.

**истолкова́ть** pf, **истолко́вывать** impf interpret; comment on.

**ис|толо́чь** (-лку́, -лчёшь; -ло́к, -лкла́) pf.

**исто́ма** languor.

**исторга́ть** impf, **исто́ргнуть** (-ну; -о́рг) pf throw out.

**исто́рик** historian. **истори́ческий** historical; historic. **исто́рия** history; story; incident.

**исто́чник** spring; source.

**истоща́ть** impf, **истощи́ть** (-щу́) pf exhaust; emaciate. **истоще́ние** emaciation; exhaustion.

**ис|тра́тить** (-а́чу) pf.

**истреби́тель** m destroyer; fighter. **истреби́ть** (-блю́) pf, **истребля́ть** impf destroy; exterminate.

**ис|тупи́ться** (-пится) pf.

**истяза́ние** torture. **истяза́ть** impf torture.

**исхо́д** outcome; end; Exodus. **исходи́ть** (-ожу́, -о́дишь) impf (+из or от+gen) issue (from), come (from); proceed (from). **исхо́дный** initial; departure.

**исхуда́лый** undernourished, emaciated.

**исцеле́ние** healing; recovery. **исцели́ть** pf, **исцеля́ть** impf heal, cure.

**исчеза́ть** impf, **исче́знуть** (-ну; -е́з) pf disappear, vanish. **исчезнове́ние** disappearance.

**исче́рпать** pf, **исче́рпывать** impf exhaust; conclude. **исче́рпывающий** exhaustive.

**исчисле́ние** calculation; calculus.

**ита́к** conj thus; so then.

**Ита́лия** Italy. **италья́нец** (-нца), **италья́нка** Italian. **италья́нский** Italian.

**ИТАР-ТАСС** abbr (of Информацио́нное телегра́фное аге́нтство Росси́и; see **ТАСС**) ITAR-Tass.

**и т.д.** abbr (of **и так да́лее**) etc., and so on.

**ито́г** sum; total; result. **ито́го**

*adv* in all, altogether.

**и т.п.** *abbr* (*of* и тому подобное) etc., and so on.

**иуде́й, иуде́йка** Jew. **иуде́йский** Judaic.

**их** their, theirs; *see* они́.

**иша́к** (-а́) donkey.

**ище́йка** bloodhound; police dog.

**ищу́** etc.: *see* иска́ть

**июль** *m* July. **ию́льский** July.

**ию́нь** *m* June. **ию́ньский** June.

**йо́га** yoga.

**йод** iodine.

**йо́та** iota.

# К

**к, ко** *prep+dat* to, towards; by; for; on; on the occasion of; **к пе́рвому января́** by the first of January; **к тому́ вре́мени** by then; **к тому́ же** besides, moreover; **к чему́?** what for?

**-ка** *partl* modifying force of *imper* or *expressing decision or intention*; да́йте-ка пройти́ let me pass, please; скажи́-ка мне do tell me.

**каба́к** (-а́) tavern.

**кабала́** servitude.

**каба́н** (-а́) wild boar.

**кабаре́** *neut indecl* cabaret.

**кабачо́к** (-чка́) marrow.

**ка́бель** *m* cable. **ка́бельтов** cable, hawser.

**каби́на** cabin; booth; cockpit; cubicle; cab. **кабине́т** study; surgery; room; office; Cabinet.

**каблу́к** (-а́) heel.

**кабота́ж** coastal shipping. **кабота́жный** coastal.

**кабы́** if.

**кавале́р** knight; partner, gentleman. **кавалери́йский** cavalry. **кавалери́ст** cavalryman.

**кавале́рия** cavalry.

**ка́верзный** tricky.

**Кавка́з** the Caucasus. **кавка́зец** (-зца) **кавка́зка** Caucasian. **кавка́зский** Caucasian.

**кавы́чки** (-чек) *pl* inverted commas, quotation marks.

**каде́т** cadet. **каде́тский ко́рпус** military school.

**ка́дка** tub, vat.

**кадр** frame, still; close-up; cadre; *pl* establishment; staff; personnel; specialists. **ка́дровый** (*mil*) regular; skilled, trained.

**кады́к** (-а́) Adam's apple.

**каждодне́вный** daily, everyday. **ка́ждый** each, every; *sb* everybody.

**ка́жется** etc.: *see* каза́ться

**каза́к** (-а́; *pl* -áки, -áко́в), **каза́чка** Cossack.

**каза́рма** barracks.

**каза́ться** (кажу́сь, ка́жешься) *impf* (*pf* по~) seem, appear; *impers* ка́жется, каза́лось apparently; каза́лось бы it would seem; +*dat*: мне ка́жется it seems to me; I think.

**Казахста́н** Kazakhstan. **каза́чий** Cossack.

**казема́т** casemate.

**казённый** State; government; fiscal; public; formal; banal, conventional. **казна́** Exchequer, Treasury; public purse; the State. **казначе́й** treasurer, bursar; paymaster.

**казино́** *neut indecl* casino.

**казни́ть** *impf* & *pf* execute; punish; castigate. **казнь** execution.

**кайма́** (*gen pl* каём) border, edging.

**как** *adv* how; what; **вот ~!** you don't say!; **~ вы ду́маете?**

what do you think?; ~ **его зову́т?** what is his name?; ~ **же** naturally, of course; ~ **же так?** how is that?; ~ **ни** however. **как** *conj* as; like; when; since; +*neg* but, except, than; **в то вре́мя** ~ while, whereas; ~ **мо́жно**, ~ **нельзя**+*comp* as ... as possible; ~ **мо́жно скоре́е** as soon as possible; **нельзя́ лу́чше** as well as possible; ~ **то́лько** as soon as, when; **ме́жду тем** ~ while, whereas. **как бу́дто** *conj* as if; *partl* apparently. **как бы** how; as if; **как бы... не** what if, supposing; **как бы... ни** however. **как-либо** somehow. **ка́к-нибудь** *adv* somehow; anyhow. **как раз** *adv* just, exactly. **как-то** *adv* somehow; once.

**кака́о** *neut indecl* cocoa.

**како́в** (-á, -ó, -ы́) *pron* what, what sort of?; ~ **он?** what is he like?; ~ **он собо́й?** what does he look like?; **пого́да-то какова́!** what weather! **каково́** *adv* how. **како́й** *pron* what; (such) as; which; ~... **ни** whatever, whichever. **како́й-либо**, **како́й-нибудь** *prons* some; any; only. **како́й-то** *pron* some; a; a kind of.

**как раз**, **ка́к-то** *see* **как**

**ка́ктус** cactus.

**кал** faeces, excrement.

**каламбу́р** pun.

**кале́ка** *m & f* cripple.

**календа́рь** (-я́) *m* calendar.

**кале́ние** incandescence.

**кале́чить** (-чу) *impf* (*pf* **ис-**, **по-**) cripple, maim; ~**ся** become a cripple.

**кали́бр** calibre; bore; gauge.

**ка́лий** potassium.

**кали́тка** (wicket-)gate.

**каллигра́фия** calligraphy.

**кало́рия** calorie.

**кало́ша** galosh.

**ка́лька** tracing-paper; tracing.

**калькуля́ция** calculation.

**кальсо́ны** (-н) *pl* long johns.

**ка́льций** calcium.

**ка́мбала** flat-fish; plaice; flounder.

**камени́стый** stony, rocky. **каменноуго́льный** coal; ~ **бассе́йн** coal-field. **ка́менный** stone; rock; stony; hard, immovable; ~ **век** Stone Age; ~ **у́голь** coal. **каменоло́мня** (*gen pl* -мен) quarry. **ка́менщик** (stone)mason; bricklayer. **ка́мень** (-мня; *pl* -мни, -мне́й) *m* stone.

**ка́мера** chamber; cell; camera; inner tube, (football) bladder; ~ **хране́ния** cloak-room, left-luggage office. **ка́мерный** chamber. **камерто́н** tuning-fork.

**ками́н** fireplace; fire.

**камко́рдер** camcorder.

**камо́рка** closet, very small room.

**кампа́ния** campaign; cruise.

**камы́ш** (-á) reed, rush; cane.

**кана́ва** ditch; gutter.

**Кана́да** Canada. **кана́дец** (-дца), **кана́дка** Canadian. **кана́дский** Canadian.

**кана́л** canal; channel. **канализа́ция** sewerage (system).

**канаре́йка** canary.

**кана́т** rope; cable.

**канва́** canvas; groundwork; outline, design.

**канда́лы** (-о́в) *pl* shackles.

**кандида́т** candidate; ~ **нау́к** person with higher degree. **кандидату́ра** candidature.

**кани́кулы** (-ул) *pl* vacation; holidays.

**кани́стра** can, canister.

**канони́ческий** canon(ical).

**кано́э** *neut indecl* canoe.

**кант** edging; mount. **канто-ва́ть** *impf*; «не ~» 'this way up'.

**кану́н** eve.

**ка́нуть** (-ну) *pf* drop, sink; **как в во́ду ~** vanish into thin air.

**канцеля́рия** office. **канцеля́рский** office; clerical. **канцеля́рщина** red-tape.

**ка́нцлер** chancellor.

**ка́пать** (-аю *or* -плю) *impf* (*pf* **ка́пнуть**, **на~**) drip, drop; trickle; +*instr* spill.

**капе́лла** choir; chapel.

**ка́пелька** small drop; a little; **~ росы́** dew-drop.

**капельме́йстер** conductor; bandmaster.

**капилля́р** capillary.

**капита́л** capital. **капитали́зм** capitalism. **капитали́ст** capitalist. **капиталисти́ческий** capitalist. **капита́льный** capital; main, fundamental; major.

**капита́н** captain; skipper.

**капитули́ровать** *impf & pf* capitulate. **капитуля́ция** capitulation.

**капка́н** trap.

**ка́пля** (*gen pl* -пель) drop; bit, scrap. **ка́пнуть** (-ну) *pf* of **ка́пать**.

**капо́т** hood, cowl, cowling; bonnet; house-coat.

**капри́з** caprice. **капри́зничать** *impf* play up. **капри́зный** capricious.

**капу́ста** cabbage.

**капюшо́н** hood.

**ка́ра** punishment.

**кара́бкаться** *impf* (*pf* вс~) clamber.

**карава́н** caravan; convoy.

**кара́кули** *f pl* scribble.

**караме́ль** caramel; caramels.

**каранда́ш** (-á) pencil.

**каранти́н** quarantine.

**кара́т** carat.

**кара́тельный** punitive. **кара́ть** *impf* (*pf* по~) punish.

**карау́л** guard; watch; ~! help! **карау́лить** *impf* guard; lie in wait for. **карау́льный** guard; *sb* sentry, sentinel, guard.

**карбюра́тор** carburettor.

**каре́та** carriage, coach.

**ка́рий** brown; hazel.

**карикату́ра** caricature; cartoon.

**карка́с** frame; framework.

**ка́ркать** *impf*, **ка́ркнуть** (-ну) *pf* caw, croak.

**ка́рлик**, **ка́рлица** dwarf; pygmy. **ка́рликовый** dwarf; pygmy.

**карма́н** pocket. **карма́нник** pickpocket. **карма́нный** *adj* pocket.

**карни́з** cornice; ledge.

**карп** carp.

**ка́рта** map; (playing-)card. **карта́вить** (-влю) *impf* burr.

**картёжник** gambler.

**карте́чь** case-shot, grape-shot.

**карти́на** picture; scene. **карти́нка** picture; illustration. **карти́нный** picturesque; picture.

**карто́н** cardboard. **карто́нка** cardboard box.

**картоте́ка** card-index.

**карто́фель** *m* potatoes; potato(-plant). **карто́фельн|ый** potato; ~ое пюре́ mashed potatoes.

**ка́рточка** card; season ticket; photo. **ка́рточный** card.

**карто́шка** potatoes; potato.

**карусе́ль** merry-go-round.

**ка́рцер** cell, lock-up.

**карье́р**[1] full gallop.

**карьёр**[2] quarry; sand-pit.

**карьери́ст** careerist.

**касáние** contact. **касáтельная** *sb* tangent. **касáться** *impf* (*pf* **косну́ться**) +*gen or* до+*gen* touch; touch on; concern; **что касáется** as regards.

**кáска** helmet.

**каскáд** cascade.

**каспи́йский** Caspian.

**кáсса** till; cash-box; booking-office; box-office; cash-desk; cash.

**кассéта** cassette. **кассéтный магнитофóн** cassette recorder.

**касси́р, касси́рша** cashier.

**кастрáт** eunuch. **кастрáция** castration. **кастри́ровать** *impf & pf* castrate, geld.

**кастрю́ля** saucepan.

**каталóг** catalogue.

**катáние** rolling; driving; ~ **верхóм** riding; ~ **на конькáх** skating.

**катапу́льта** catapult. **катапульти́ровать(ся** *impf & pf* catapult.

**катáр** catarrh.

**катарáкта** cataract.

**катастрóфа** catastrophe. **катастрофи́ческий** catastrophic.

**катáть** *impf* roll; (take for a) drive; ~**ся** (*pf* **по**~) roll, roll about; go for a drive; ~**ся верхóм** ride, go riding; ~**ся на конькáх** skate, go skating. **категори́ческий** categorical. **категóрия** category.

**кáтер** (*pl* -á) cutter; launch.

**кати́ть** (-ачу́, -áтишь) *impf* bowl along, rip, tear; ~**ся** rush, tear; flow, stream, roll; **кати́сь, кати́тесь** get out! clear off! **катóк** (-ткá) skating-rink; roller.

**катóлик, католи́чка** Catho- lic. **католи́ческий** Catholic.

**кáторга** penal servitude, hard labour. **кáторжник** convict. **кáторжный** penal; ~**ые рабóты** hard labour; drudgery.

**кату́шка** reel, bobbin; spool; coil.

**каучу́к** rubber.

**кафé** *neut indecl* café.

**кáфедра** pulpit; rostrum; chair; department.

**кáфель** *m* Dutch tile.

**качáлка** rocking-chair. **качáние** rocking, swinging; pumping. **качáть** *impf* (*pf* **качну́ть**) +*acc or instr* rock, swing; shake; ~**ся** rock, swing; roll; reel. **качéли** (-ей) *pl* swing.

**кáчественный** qualitative; high-quality. **кáчество** quality; **в кáчестве**+*gen* as, in the capacity of.

**кáчка** rocking; tossing.

**качну́ть(ся** (-ну́(сь, -нёшь(ся) *pf of* качáть(ся. **качу́** *etc.*: *see* кати́ть

**кáша** gruel, porridge; **завари́ть кáшу** stir up trouble.

**кáшель** (-шля) cough. **кáшлянуть** (-ну) *pf*, **кáшлять** *impf* (have a) cough.

**каштáн** chestnut. **каштáновый** chestnut.

**каю́та** cabin, stateroom.

**кáющийся** penitent. **кáяться** (кáюсь) *impf* (*pf* **по**~, **рас**~) repent; confess; **кáюсь** I (must) confess.

**кв.** *abbr* (*of* квадрáтный) square; (*of* квартéра) flat.

**квадрáт** square; quad; **в квадрáте** squared; **возвести́ в** ~ square. **квадрáтный** square; quadratic.

**квáкать** *impf*, **квáкнуть** (-ну) *pf* croak.

квалифика́ция qualification.
квалифици́рованный qualified, skilled.

квант, ква́нта quantum. ква́нтовый quantum.

кварта́л block; quarter. кварта́льный quarterly.

кварти́ра flat; apartment(s); quarters. квартира́нт, -ра́нтка lodger; tenant. кварти́рная пла́та, квартпла́та rent.

кварц quartz.

квас (pl ~ы́) kvass. ква́сить (-а́шу) impf sour; pickle. ква́шеная капу́ста sauerkraut.

кве́рху adv up, upwards.

квит, кви́ты quits.

квита́нция receipt. квито́к (-тка́) ticket, check.

КГБ abbr (of Комите́т госуда́рственной безопа́сности) KGB.

ке́гля skittle.

кедр cedar.

ке́ды (-ов) pl trainers.

кекс (fruit-)cake.

ке́лья (gen pl -лий) cell.

кем see кто

ке́мпинг campsite.

кенгуру́ m indecl kangaroo.

ке́пка cloth cap.

кера́мика ceramics.

керога́з stove. кероси́н paraffin. кероси́нка paraffin stove.

ке́та Siberian salmon. ке́товый: ~ая икра́ red caviare.

кефи́р kefir, yoghurt.

киберне́тика cybernetics.

кива́ть impf (кивну́ть (-ну́, -нёшь) pf (голово́й) nod (one's head); (+на+acc) motion (to). киво́к (-вка́) nod.

кида́ть impf (кину́ть throw, fling; ~ся fling o.s.

rush; +instr throw.

кий (-я; pl -и́, -ёв) (billiard) cue.

киле́в|о́й keel; ~я́я ка́чка pitching.

кило́ neut indecl kilo. кило-ва́тт kilowatt. килогра́мм kilogram. киломе́тр kilometre.

киль m keel; fin. кильва́тер wake.

ки́лька sprat.

кинжа́л dagger.

кино́ neut indecl cinema.
кино- in comb film-, cine-. киноаппара́т cinecamera. ~арти́ст, ~арти́стка film actor, actress. ~журна́л newsreel. ~за́л cinema; auditorium. ~звезда́ film-star. ~зри́тель m film-goer. ~карти́на film. ~опера́тор camera-man. ~плёнка film. ~режиссёр film director. ~теа́тр cinema. ~хро́ника news-reel.

ки́нуть(ся (-ну(сь) pf of ки-да́ть(ся

кио́ск kiosk, stall.

ки́па pile, stack; bale.

кипари́с cypress.

кипе́ние boiling. кипе́ть (-плю́) impf (pf вс~) boil, seethe.

кипу́чий boiling, seething; ebullient. кипяти́льник kettle, boiler. кипяти́ть (-ячу́) impf (pf вс~) boil; ~ся boil; get excited. кипято́к (-тка́) boiling water. кипячёный boiled.

Кирги́зия Kirghizia.

кирка́ pick(axe).

кирпи́ч (-а́) brick; bricks. кирпи́чный brick; brick-red.

кисе́ль m kissel, blancmange.

кисе́т tobacco-pouch.

кисея́ muslin.

кислоро́д oxygen. кислота́

(*pl* -ы) acid; acidity. **кисло́т-ный** acid. **ки́слый** sour; acid.
**ки́снуть** (-ну; кис) *impf* (*pf* про~) turn sour.

**ки́сточка** brush; tassel. **кисть** (*gen pl* -е́й) cluster, bunch; brush; tassel; hand.

**кит** (-а́) whale.

**кита́ец** (-а́йца; *pl* -цы, -цев) Chinese. **Кита́й** China. **кита́йский** Chinese. **китая́нка** Chinese (woman).

**китобо́й** whaler. **кито́вый** whale.

**кичи́ться** (-чу́сь) *impf* plume o.s.; strut. **кичли́вость** conceit. **кичли́вый** conceited.

**кише́ть** (-ши́т) *impf* swarm, teem.

**кише́чник** bowels, intestines. **кише́чный** intestinal. **кишка́** gut, intestine; hose.

**клавеси́н** harpsichord. **клавиату́ра** keyboard. **кла́виша, кла́виш** key. **кла́вишный:** ~ **инструме́нт** keyboard instrument.

**клад** treasure.

**кла́дбище** cemetery, graveyard.

**кла́дка** laying; masonry. **кладова́я** *sb* pantry; store-room. **кладовщи́к** (-а́) storeman. **кладу́** *etc.: see* **класть**

**кла́няться** *impf* (*pf* **поклони́ться**) +*dat* bow to; greet.

**кла́пан** valve; vent.

**кларне́т** clarinet.

**класс** class; class-room. **кла́ссик** classic. **кла́ссика** the classics. **классифици́ровать** *impf* & *pf* classify. **класси́ческий** classical. **кла́ссный** class; first-class. **кла́ссовый** class.

**класть** (-аду́, -аде́шь; -ал) *impf* (*pf* **положи́ть, сложи́ть**) lay; put.

**клева́ть** (клюю́, клюёшь) *impf* (*pf* **клю́нуть**) peck; bite.

**кле́вер** (*pl* -а́) clover.

**клевета́** slander; libel. **клевета́ть** (-ещу́, -е́щешь) *impf* (*pf* на~) +на+*acc* slander; libel. **клеветни́к** (-а́), **-ни́ца** slanderer. **клеветни́ческий** slanderous; libellous.

**клеёнка** oilcloth. **кле́ить** *impf* (*pf* с~) glue; stick; ~**ся** stick; become sticky. **клей** (*loc* -ю́; *pl* -и́) glue, adhesive. **кле́йкий** sticky.

**клейми́ть** (-млю́) *impf* (*pf* за~) brand; stamp; stigmatize. **клеймо́** (*pl* -а) brand; stamp; mark.

**кле́йстер** paste.

**клён** maple.

**клепа́ть** *impf* rivet.

**кле́тка** cage; check; cell. **кле́точка** cellule. **кле́точный** cellular. **клетча́тка** cellulose. **кле́тчатый** checked.

**клёш** flare.

**клешня́** (*gen pl* -е́й) claw.

**кле́щи** (-е́й) *pl* pincers, tongs.

**клие́нт** client. **клиенте́ла** clientèle.

**кли́зма** enema.

**клик** cry, call. **кли́кать** (-и́чу) *impf*, **кли́кнуть** (-ну) *pf* call.

**кли́макс** menopause.

**кли́мат** climate. **климати́ческий** climatic.

**клин** (*pl* -нья, -ньев) wedge. **клино́к** (-нка́) blade.

**кли́ника** clinic. **клини́ческий** clinical.

**клипс** clip-on ear-ring.

**клич** call. **кли́чка** name; nickname. **кли́чу** *etc.: see* **кли́кать**

**клок** (-а́; *pl* -о́чья, -ьев *or* -и́, -о́в) rag, shred; tuft.

**кло́кот** bubbling; gurgling.

**клокота́ть** (-о́чет) *impf* bubble; gurgle; boil up.

**клони́ть** (-ню́, -нишь) *impf* bend; incline; +к+*dat* drive at; **~ся** bow, bend; +к+*dat* near, approach.

**клоп** (-а́) bug.

**кло́ун** clown.

**клочо́к** (-чка́) scrap, shred. **кло́чья** *etc.: see* клок

**клуб**[1] club.

**клуб**[2] (*pl* -ы́) puff; cloud.

**клу́бень** (-бня) *m* tuber.

**клуби́ться** *impf* swirl; curl.

**клубни́ка** (*no pl; usu collect*) strawberry; strawberries.

**клубо́к** (-бка́) ball; tangle.

**клу́мба** (flower-)bed.

**клык** (-а́) fang; tusk; canine (*tooth*).

**клюв** beak.

**клю́ква** cranberry; cranberries.

**клю́нуть** (-ну) *pf of* клева́ть

**ключ**[1] (-а́) key; clue; keystone; clef; wrench, spanner.

**ключ**[2] (-а́) spring; source.

**ключево́й** key. **ключи́ца** collarbone.

**клю́шка** (hockey) stick; (golf-) club.

**клюю́** *etc.: see* клева́ть

**кля́кса** blot, smudge.

**кляну́** *etc.: see* клясть

**кля́нчить** (-чу) *impf* (*pf* вы́~) beg.

**кляп** gag.

**клясть** (-яну́, -янёшь; -ял, -а́, -о) *impf* curse; **~ся** (*pf* по~ся) swear, vow. **кля́тва** oath, vow. **кля́твенный** on oath.

**кни́га** book.

**книго-** *in comb* book, biblio-. **книгове́дение**[1] bibliography. **~веде́ние**[2] book-keeping. **~изда́тель** *m* publisher. **~лю́б** bibliophile, book-lover. **~храни́лище** library;

book-stack.

**кни́жечка** booklet. **кни́жка** book; note-book; bank-book. **кни́жный** book; bookish.

**кни́зу** *adv* downwards.

**кно́пка** drawing-pin; press-stud; (push-)button, knob.

**кнут** (-а́) whip.

**княги́ня** princess. **кня́жество** principality. **княжна́** (*gen pl* -жо́н) princess. **князь** (*pl* -зья́, -зе́й) *m* prince.

**ко** *see* к *prep*.

**коали́ция** coalition.

**кобура́** holster.

**кобы́ла** mare; (vaulting-)horse.

**ко́ваный** forged; wrought; terse.

**кова́рный** insidious, crafty; perfidious. **кова́рство** insidiousness, craftiness; perfidy.

**кова́ть** (кую́, -ёшь) *impf* (*pf* под~) forge; hammer; shoe.

**ковёр** (-вра́) carpet; mat.

**кове́ркать** *impf* (*pf* ис~) distort, mangle, ruin.

**ко́вка** forging; shoeing.

**коври́жка** honeycake, gingerbread.

**ко́врик** rug; mat.

**ковче́г** ark.

**ковш** (-а́) scoop, ladle.

**ковы́ль** *m* feather-grass.

**ковыля́ть** *impf* hobble.

**ковырну́ть** (-ну́, -нёшь) *pf*, **ковыря́ть** *impf* dig into; tinker; +в+*prep* pick (at); **~ся** rummage; tinker.

**когда́** *adv* when; ~ (бы) ни whenever; *conj* when; while; as; if. **когда́-либо, когда́-нибудь** *advs* some time; ever. **когда́-то** *adv* once; formerly; some time.

**кого́** *see* кто

**ко́готь** (-гтя; *pl* -гти, -гте́й) *m* claw; talon.

**код** code.

**коде́йн** codeine.

**ко́декс** code.

**ко́е-где́** *adv* here and there. **ко́е-ка́к** *adv* anyhow; somehow (or other). **ко́е-како́й** *pron* some. **ко́е-кто́** *pron* somebody; some people. **ко́е-что́** (-чего́) *pron* something; a little.

**ко́жа** skin; leather; peel. **ко́жанка** leather jacket. **ко́жаный** leather. **коже́венный** leather; tanning. **ко́жный** skin. **кожура́** rind, peel, skin.

**коза́** (*pl* -ы) goat, nanny-goat. **козёл** (-зла́) billy-goat. **Козеро́г** Capricorn. **ко́зий** goat; ~ **пух** angora. **козлё-нок** (-нка; *pl* -ля́та, -ля́т) kid. **ко́злы** (-зел) *pl* coach driver's seat; trestle(s); saw-horse. **ко́зни** (-ей) *pl* machinations. **козырёк** (-рька́) peak. **козырно́й** trump. **козырну́ть** (-ну́, -нёшь) *pf*, **козыря́ть** *impf* lead trumps; trump; play one's trump card; salute. **ко́зырь** (*pl* -и, -ей) *m* trump.

**ко́йка** (*gen pl* ко́ек) berth, bunk; bed.

**кока́ин** cocaine.

**ко́ка-ко́ла** Coca-Cola (*propr*).

**коке́тка** coquette. **коке́тство** coquetry.

**коклю́ш** whooping-cough.

**ко́кон** cocoon.

**коко́с** coconut.

**кокс** coke.

**кокте́йль** *m* cocktail.

**кол** (-á; *pl* -лья, -ьев) stake, picket.

**ко́лба** retort.

**колбаса́** (*pl* -ы) sausage.

**колго́тки** (-ток) *pl* tights.

**колдова́ть** *impf* practise witchcraft. **колдовство́** sorcery. **колду́н** (-á) sorcerer,

wizard. **колду́нья** (*gen pl* -ний) witch, sorceress.

**колеба́ние** oscillation; variation; hesitation. **колеба́ть** (pf по~) shake; ~**ся** oscillate; fluctuate; hesitate.

**коле́но** (*pl* -и, -ей, -ям) knee; (*in pl*) lap. **коле́нчатый** crank, cranked; bent; ~ **вал** crankshaft.

**колесни́ца** chariot. **колесо́** (*pl* -ёса) wheel.

**колея́** rut; track, gauge.

**ко́лика** (*usu pl*) colic; stitch.

**коли́чественный** quantitative; ~**ое числи́тельное** cardinal number. **коли́чество** quantity; number.

**колле́га** *m & f* colleague. **колле́гия** board; college.

**коллекти́в** collective. **коллективиза́ция** collectivization. **коллекти́вный** collective. **коллекционе́р** collector. **колле́кция** collection.

**колли́зия** clash, conflict.

**коло́да** block; pack (*of cards*).

**коло́дец** (-дца) well.

**ко́локол** (*pl* -á, -о́в) bell. **колоко́льный** bell. **колоко́льня** bell-tower. **колоко́ль-чик** small bell; bluebell.

**колониали́зм** colonialism. **колониа́льный** colonial. **колониза́тор** colonizer. **колониза́ция** colonization. **колонизова́ть** *impf & pf* colonize. **коло́ния** colony.

**коло́нка** geyser; (*street*) water fountain; stand-pipe; column; **бензи́новая ~** petrol pump. **коло́нна** column.

**колори́т** colouring, colour. **колори́тный** colourful, vivid.

**ко́лос** (*pl* -о́сья, -ьев) ear. **коло-си́ться** *impf* form ears.

**колосса́льный** huge; terrific.

**колоти́ть** (-очу́, -о́тишь) *impf* (*pf* по~) beat; pound; thrash; smash; ~ся pound, thump; shake.

**колоть**¹ (-лю́, -лешь) *impf* (*pf* рас~) break, chop.

**колоть**² (-лю́, -лешь) *impf* (*pf* за~, кольну́ть) prick; stab; sting; slaughter; ~ся prick.

**колпа́к** (-а́) cap; hood, cowl.

**колхо́з** *abbr* (*of* **колле-кти́вное хозя́йство**) kolkhoz, collective farm. **колхо́зник**, ~ица kolkhoz member. **колхо́зный** kolkhoz.

**колыбе́ль** cradle.

**колыха́ть** (-ы́шу) *impf*, **колыхну́ть** (-ну́, -нёшь) *pf* sway, rock; ~ся sway; flutter.

**кольну́ть** (-ну́, -нёшь) *pf of* **коло́ть**

**кольцо́** (*pl* -а, -ле́ц, -льцам) ring.

**колю́ч|ий** prickly; sharp; ~ая про́волока barbed wire. **колю́чка** prickle; thorn.

**коля́ска** carriage; pram; side-car.

**ком** (*pl* -мья, -мьев) lump; ball.

**ком** *see* **кто**

**кома́нда** command; order; detachment; crew; team. **команди́р** commander. **командирова́ть** *impf* & *pf* post, send on a mission. **командиро́вка** posting, mission, business trip. **командиро́вочные** *sb pl* travelling expenses. **кома́ндование** command. **кома́ндовать** *impf* (*pf* с~) give orders; be in command; +*instr* command. **кома́ндующий** *sb* commander.

**кома́р** (-а́) mosquito.

**комба́йн** combine harvester.

**комбина́т** industrial complex.

**комбина́ция** combination; manoeuvre; slip. **комбине-зо́н** overalls, boiler suit; dungarees. **комбини́ровать** *impf* (*pf* с~) combine.

**коме́дия** comedy.

**коменда́нт** commandant; manager; warden. **комендату́ра** commandant's office.

**коме́та** comet.

**ко́мик** comic actor; comedian. **ко́микс** comic, comic strip.

**комисса́р** commissar.

**комиссио́нер** (commission-) agent, broker. **комиссио́н-ный** commission; ~ый мага-зи́н second-hand shop; ~ые *sb pl* commission. **коми́ссия** commission; committee.

**комите́т** committee.

**коми́ческий** comic; comical. **коми́чный** comical, funny.

**ко́мкать** *impf* (*pf* с~) crumple.

**коммента́рий** commentary; *pl* comment. **коммента́тор** commentator. **комменти́ро-вать** *impf* & *pf* comment (on).

**коммерса́нт** merchant; businessman **комме́рция** commerce. **комме́рческий** commercial.

**коммивояжёр** commercial traveller.

**комму́на** commune. **комму-на́льный** communal; municipal. **коммуни́зм** communism. **коммуника́ция** communication.

**коммуни́ст**, ~ка communist. **коммунисти́ческий** communist.

**коммута́тор** switchboard.

**коммюнике́** *neut indecl* communiqué.

**ко́мната** room. **ко́мнатный** room; indoor.

**комо́д** chest of drawers.

комо́к (-мка́) lump.

компа́кт-ди́ск compact disc. компа́ктный compact.

компа́ния company. компаньо́н, ~ка companion; partner.

компа́ртия Communist Party.

ко́мпас compass.

компенса́ция compensation. компенси́ровать *impf & pf* compensate.

ко́мплекс complex. ко́мплексный complex, compound, composite; combined.

компле́кт (complete) set; complement; kit. комплектова́ть (*pf* c~, y~) complete; bring up to strength. компле́кция build; constitution.

комплиме́нт compliment.

компози́тор composer. компози́ция composition.

компоне́нт component.

компо́ст compost.

компо́стер punch. компости́ровать *impf* (*pf* про~) punch.

компо́т stewed fruit.

компре́ссор compressor.

компромети́ровать *impf* (*pf* c~) compromise. компроми́сс compromise.

компью́тер computer.

комсомо́л Komsomol. комсомо́лец (-льца), -лка Komsomol member. комсомо́льский Komsomol.

кому́ *see* кто

комфо́рт comfort.

конве́йер conveyor.

конве́рт envelope; sleeve.

конвои́р escort. конвои́ровать *impf* escort. конво́й escort, convoy.

конгре́сс congress.

конденса́тор condenser.

конди́терская *sb* confectioner's, cake shop.

кондиционе́р air-conditioner. кондицио́нный air-conditioning.

кондýктор (*pl* -á), -торша conductor; guard.

конево́дство horse-breeding.

конёк (-нька́) *dim of* конь; hobby(-horse).

коне́ц (-нца́) end; в конце́ концо́в in the end, after all. коне́чно *adv* of course. коне́чность extremity. коне́чный final, last; ultimate; finite.

кони́ческий conic, conical.

конкре́тный concrete.

конкуре́нт competitor. конкуре́нция competition. конкури́ровать *impf* compete. ко́нкурс competition; contest.

ко́нница cavalry. ко́нный horse; mounted; equestrian; ~ заво́д stud.

конопля́ hemp.

консервати́вный conservative. консерва́тор Conservative.

консервато́рия conservatoire.

консерви́ровать *impf & pf* (*pf also* за~) preserve; can, bottle. консе́рвн|ый preserving; ~ая ба́нка tin; ~ый нож tin-opener. консерво́открыва́тель *m* tin-opener. консе́рвы (-ов) *pl* tinned goods.

конси́лиум consultation.

конспе́кт synopsis, summary. конспекти́ровать *impf* (*pf* за~, про~) make an abstract of.

конспирати́вный secret, clandestine. конспира́ция security.

констата́ция ascertaining; establishment. констати́ровать

*impf* & *pf* ascertain; establish.

**конституцио́нный** constitutional. **конститу́ция** constitution.

**констру́и́ровать** *impf* & *pf* (*pf also* c~) construct; design. **конструкти́вный** structural; constructional; constructive. **констру́ктор** designer, constructor. **констру́кция** construction; design.

**ко́нсул** consul. **ко́нсульство** consulate.

**консульта́ция** consultation; advice; clinic; tutorial. **консульти́ровать** *impf* (*pf* про~) advise; +c+*instr* consult; ~ся obtain advice; +c+*instr* consult.

**конта́кт** contact. **конта́ктные ли́нзы** *f pl* contact lenses.

**конте́йнер** container.

**конте́кст** context.

**контине́нт** continent.

**конто́ра** office. **конто́рский** office.

**контраба́нда** contraband. **контрабанди́ст** smuggler.

**контраба́с** double-bass.

**контра́кт** contract.

**контра́льто** *neut/fem indecl* contralto (*voice/person*).

**контрама́рка** complimentary ticket.

**контрапу́нкт** counterpoint.

**контра́ст** contrast.

**контрибу́ция** indemnity.

**контрнаступле́ние** counteroffensive.

**контролёр** inspector; ticket-collector. **контроли́ровать** *impf* (*pf* про~) check; inspect. **контро́ль** *m* control; check; inspection. **контро́льн|ый** control; ~ая рабо́та test.

**контрразве́дка** counter-intelligence; security service.

**контрреволю́ция** counter-revolution.

**конту́зия** bruising; shell-shock.

**ко́нтур** contour, outline; circuit.

**конура́** kennel.

**ко́нус** cone.

**конфедера́ция** confederation.

**конфере́нция** conference.

**конфе́та** sweet.

**конфискова́ть** *impf* & *pf* confiscate.

**конфли́кт** conflict.

**конфо́рка** ring (*on stove*).

**конфу́з** discomfort, embarrassment. **конфу́зить** (-у́жу) *impf* (*pf* c~) confuse, embarrass; ~ся feel embarrassed.

**концентра́т** concentrate. **концентрацио́нный** concentration. **концентра́ция** concentration. **концентри́ровать(ся)** *impf* (*pf* c~) concentrate.

**конце́пция** conception.

**конце́рт** concert; concerto. **концертме́йстер** leader. **конце́ртный** concert.

**концла́герь** *abbr* (*of* концентрацио́нный ла́герь) concentration camp.

**конча́ть** *impf*, **ко́нчить** *pf* finish; end; +*inf* stop; ~ся end, finish; expire. **ко́нчик** tip. **кончи́на** decease.

**конь** (-я́; *pl* -и, -е́й) *m* horse; knight. **коньки́** (-о́в) *pl* skates; ~ на ро́ликах roller skates. **конькобе́жец** (-жца) skater.

**конья́к** (-а́) cognac.

**ко́нюх** groom, stable-boy. **коню́шня** (*gen pl* -шен) stable.

**кооперати́в** cooperative. **кооперати́вный** cooperative. **коопера́ция** cooperation.

**координа́та** coordinate. **координа́ция** coordination.

**копа́ть** *impf* (*pf* **копну́ть, вы́~**) dig; dig up, dig out; **~ся** rummage.

**копе́йка** copeck.

**ко́пи** (-ей) *pl* mines.

**копи́лка** money-box.

**копирова́льный** carbon paper. **копирова́ние** copying. **копи́ровать** *impf* (*pf* **с~**) copy; imitate.

**копи́ть** (-плю́, -пишь) *impf* (*pf* **на~**) save (up); accumulate; **~ся** accumulate.

**ко́пия** copy.

**копна́** (*pl* -ы, -пён) shock, stook.

**копну́ть** (-ну́, -нёшь) *pf of* **копа́ть**

**ко́поть** soot.

**копте́ть** (-пчу́) *impf* swot; vegetate. **копти́ть** (-пчу́) *impf* (*pf* **за~, на~**) smoke, cure; blacken with smoke. **копче́ние** smoking; smoked foods. **копчёный** smoked.

**копы́то** hoof.

**копьё** (*pl* -я, -пий) spear, lance.

**кора́** bark; cortex; crust.

**кора́бельный** ship; naval. **кораблевожде́ние** navigation. **кораблекруше́ние** shipwreck. **кораблестрое́ние** shipbuilding. **кора́бль** (-я́) *m* ship, vessel; nave.

**кора́лл** coral.

**коре́йский** Korean. **Коре́я** Korea.

**корена́стый** thickset. **корени́ться** *impf* be rooted. **коренно́й** radical, fundamental; native. **ко́рень** (-рня; *pl* -и, -ей) *m* root. **корешо́к** (-шка́) root(let); spine; counterfoil.

**корзи́на, корзи́нка** basket.

**коридо́р** corridor.

**кори́ца** cinnamon.

**кори́чневый** brown.

**ко́рка** crust; rind, peel.

**корм** (*loc* -ý; *pl* -á) fodder.

**корма́** stern.

**корми́лец** (-льца) bread-winner. **корми́ть** (-млю́, -мишь) *impf* (*pf* **на~, по~, про~**) feed; +*instr* live on, make a living by. **кормле́ние** feeding. **кормово́й**[1] fodder.

**кормово́й**[2] stern.

**корнево́й** root; radical. **корнепло́ды** (-ов) root-crops.

**коро́бить** (-блю) *impf* (*pf* **по~**) warp; jar upon; **~ся** (*pf also* **с~ся**) warp.

**коро́бка** box.

**коро́ва** cow.

**короле́ва** queen. **короле́вский** royal. **короле́вство** kingdom. **коро́ль** (-я́) *m* king.

**коромы́сло** yoke; beam; rocking shaft.

**коро́на** crown.

**коронаротромбо́з** coronary (thrombosis).

**коро́нка** crown. **коронова́ть** *impf & pf* crown.

**коро́ткий** (ко́роток, -тка́, ко́ро́тко́, ко́ро́тки) short; intimate. **ко́ротко** *adv* briefly; intimately. **коротково́лновый** short-wave. **коро́че** *comp of* **коро́ткий, ко́ро́тко**

**корпора́ция** corporation.

**ко́рпус** (*pl* -ы, -ов *or* -á, -ов) corps; services; building; hull; housing, case; body.

**корректи́ровать** *impf* (*pf* **про~, с~**) correct, edit. **корре́ктный** correct, proper. **корре́ктор** (*pl* -á) proof-reader. **корректу́ра** proof-reading; proof.

**корреспонде́нт** correspondent. **корреспонде́нция** correspondence.

**корро́зия** corrosion.

**корру́пция** corruption.

**корт** (-tennis-)court.

**корте́ж** cortège; motorcade.

**ко́ртик** dirk.

**ко́рточки** (-чек) *pl*: **сиде́ть на ко́рточках** squat.

**корчева́ть** (-чу́ю) *impf* root out.

**ко́рчить** (-чу) *impf* (*pf* с~) contort; *impers* convulse; ~ **из себя́** pose as; ~**ся** writhe.

**ко́ршун** kite.

**коры́стный** mercenary. **коры́сть** avarice; profit.

**коры́то** trough; wash-tub.

**корь** measles.

**коса́**[1] (*acc* -у; *pl* -ы) plait, tress.

**коса́**[2] (*acc* ко́су; *pl* -ы) spit.

**коса́**[3] (*acc* ко́су; *pl* -ы) scythe.

**ко́свенный** indirect.

**коси́лка** mowing-machine, mower. **коси́ть**[1] (кошу́, ко́сишь) *impf* (*pf* с~) cut; mow (down).

**коси́ть**[2] (кошу́) *impf* (*pf* по~, с~) squint; be crooked; ~**ся** slant; look sideways; look askance.

**косме́тика** cosmetics, make-up. **косми́ческий** cosmic; space. **космодро́м** spacecraft launching-site. **космона́вт, -на́втка** cosmonaut, astronaut. **ко́смос** cosmos; (outer) space.

**косноязы́чный** tongue-tied.

**косну́ться** (-ну́сь, -нёшься) *pf of* каса́ться

**косогла́зие** squint. **косо́й** (кос, -а́, -о) slanting; oblique; sidelong; squinting, cross-eyed.

**костёр** (-тра́) bonfire; camp-fire.

**костля́вый** bony. **ко́стный** bone. **ко́сточка** (small) bone; stone.

**косты́ль** (-я́) *m* crutch.

**кость** (*loc* и́; *pl* -и, -е́й) bone; die.

**костю́м** clothes; suit. **костю́ми́рованный** fancy-dress.

**костяно́й** bone; ivory.

**коси́нка** (*triangular*) head-scarf, shawl.

**кот** (-а́) tom-cat.

**котёл** (-тла́) boiler; copper, cauldron. **котело́к** (-лка́) pot; mess-tin; bowler (hat). **коте́льная** *sb* boiler-room, -house.

**котёнок** (-нка; *pl* -тя́та, -тя́т) kitten. **ко́тик** fur-seal; sealskin.

**котле́та** rissole; burger; **отбивна́я** ~ chop.

**котлова́н** foundation pit, trench.

**кото́мка** knapsack.

**кото́рый** *pron* which, what; who; that; ~ **час?** what time is it?

**котя́та** *etc.*: *see* котёнок

**ко́фе** *m indecl* coffee. **кофева́рка** percolator. **кофеи́н** caffeine.

**ко́фта, ко́фточка** blouse, top.

**коча́н** (-а́ *or* -чна́) (cabbage-) head.

**кочева́ть** (-чу́ю) *impf* be a nomad; wander; migrate. **коче́вник** nomad. **кочево́й** nomadic.

**кочега́р** stoker, fireman. **кочега́рка** stokehold, stokehole.

**кочене́ть** *impf* (*pf* за~, о~) grow numb.

**кочерга́** (*gen pl* -рёг) poker.

**ко́чка** hummock.

**кошелёк** (-лька́) purse.

**ко́шка** cat.

**кошма́р** nightmare. **кошма́рный** nightmarish.

**кошу́** *etc.*: *see* коси́ть

**кощу́нство** blasphemy.

**коэффицие́нт** coefficient.

**КП** *abbr* (*of* **Коммунисти́ческая па́ртия**) Communist

Party. **КПСС** *abbr (of* **Коммунисти́ческая па́ртия Сове́тского Сою́за)** Communist Party of the Soviet Union, CPSU.

**краб** crab.

**кра́деный** stolen. **краду́** *etc.: see* **красть**

**кра́жа** theft; ~ **со взло́мом** burglary.

**край** (*loc* -ю́; *pl* -я́, -ёв) edge; brink; land; region. **кра́йне** *adv* extremely. **кра́йний** extreme; last; outside; wing; **по кра́йней ме́ре** at least. **кра́йность** extreme; extremity.

**крал** *etc.: see* **красть**

**кран** tap; crane.

**крапи́ва** nettle.

**краса́вец** (-вца) handsome man. **краса́вица** beauty. **краси́вый** beautiful; handsome.

**краси́тель** *m* dye. **кра́сить** (-а́шу) *impf (pf* вы́~, о~, по~) paint; colour; dye; stain; ~**ся** (*pf* на~) make-up. **кра́ска** paint, dye; colour.

**красне́ть** (-е́ю) *impf (pf* по~) blush; redden; show red.

**красноарме́ец** (-е́йца) Red Army man. **красноарме́йский** Red Army. **красноречи́вый** eloquent.

**краснота́** redness. **кра́сн|ый** (-сен, -сна́, -о) red; beautiful; fine; ~**ое де́рево** mahogany; ~**ая сморо́дина** (*no pl; usu collect*) redcurrant; redcurrants; ~**ая строка́** (first line of) new paragraph.

**красова́ться** *impf* impress by one's beauty; show off. **красота́** (*pl* -ы) beauty. **кра́сочный** paint; ink; colourful.

**красть** (-аду́, -адёшь; крал)

*impf (pf* у~) steal; ~**ся** creep.

**кра́тер** crater.

**кра́ткий** (-ток, -тка́, -о) short; brief. **кратковре́менный** brief; transitory. **кратко-сро́чный** short-term.

**кра́тное** *sb* multiple.

**кратча́йший** *superl of* **кра́ткий**. **кра́тче** *comp of* **кра́ткий**, **кра́тко**

**крах** crash; failure.

**крахма́л** starch. **крахма́лить** *impf (pf* на~) starch.

**кра́ше** *comp of* **краси́вый**, **краси́во**

**кра́шеный** painted; coloured; dyed; made up. **кра́шу** *etc.: see* **кра́сить**

**креве́тка** shrimp; prawn.

**креди́т** credit. **креди́тный** credit. **кредитоспосо́бный** solvent.

**кре́йсер** (*pl* -а́, -ов) cruiser.

**крем** cream.

**кремато́рий** crematorium.

**креме́нь** (-мня́) *m* flint.

**кремль** (-я́) *m* citadel; Kremlin.

**кре́мниевый** silicon.

**кре́мовый** cream.

**крен** list, heel; bank. **кре-ни́ться** *impf (pf* на~) heel over, list; bank.

**крепи́ть** (-плю́) *impf* strengthen; support; make fast; constipate; ~**ся** hold out. **креп|кий** (-пок, -пка́, -о) strong; firm; ~**ие напи́тки** spirits. **крепле́ние** strengthening; fastening.

**кре́пнуть** (-ну; -еп) *impf (pf* о~) get stronger.

**крепостни́чество** serfdom. **крепостн|о́й** serf; ~**ое пра́во** serfdom; ~**о́й** *sb* serf. **кре́пость** fortress. **кре́пче** *comp of* **кре́пкий**, **кре́пко**

**кре́сло** (gen pl -сел) armchair; stall.

**крест** (-á) cross. **кре́стины** (-и́н) pl christening. **крести́ть** (крещу́, -е́стишь) impf & pf (pf also о~, пере~) christen; make sign of the cross over; ~ся cross o.s.; be christened. **крест-на́крест** adv crosswise. **кре́стник, кре́стница** god-child. **крёстн|ый;** ~ая (мать) godmother; ~ый оте́ц godfather. **кресто́вый похо́д** crusade. **крестоно́сец** (-сца) crusader.

**крестья́нин** (pl -я́не, -я́н), **крестья́нка** peasant. **крестья́нский** peasant. **крестья́нство** peasantry.

**креще́ние** christening; Epiphany. **крещён|ый** (-ён, -ена́) baptized; sb Christian. **крещу́** etc.: see **крести́ть**

**крива́я** sb curve. **кривизна́** crookedness; curvature. **криви́ть** (-влю́) impf (pf по~, с~) bend, distort; ~ душо́й go against one's conscience; ~ся become crooked or bent; make a wry face. **криви́ться** impf give o.s. airs. **криво́й** (крив, -á, -o) crooked; curved; one-eyed.

**кри́зис** crisis.

**крик** cry, shout. **кри́кет** cricket. **кри́кнуть** (-ну) pf of **крича́ть**

**криминáльный** criminal.

**криста́лл** crystal. **криста́лли́ческий** crystal.

**крите́рий** criterion.

**кри́тик** critic. **кри́тика** criticism; critique. **критикова́ть** impf criticize. **крити́ческий** critical.

**крича́ть** (-чу́) impf (pf кри́кнуть) cry, shout.

**кров** roof; shelter. **крова́вый** bloody.

**крова́тка, крова́ть** bed.

**кровено́сный** blood-; circulatory.

**кро́вля** (gen pl -вель) roof.

**кро́вный** blood; thoroughbred; vital, intimate.

**крово-** in comb blood. **кровожа́дный** bloodthirsty. ~**излия́ние** haemorrhage. ~**обраще́ние** circulation. ~**проли́тие** bloodshed. ~**проли́тный** bloody. ~**смеше́ние** incest. ~**тече́ние** bleeding; haemorrhage. ~**точи́ть** (-чи́т) impf bleed.

**кровь** (loc -и́) blood. **кровяно́й** blood.

**крои́ть** (крою́) impf (pf с~) cut (out). **кро́йка** cutting out.

**крокоди́л** crocodile.

**кро́лик** rabbit.

**кроль** m crawl(-stroke).

**кроль́иха** she-rabbit, doe.

**кро́ме** prep+gen except; besides; ~ того́ besides, moreover.

**кро́мка** edge.

**кро́на** crown; top.

**кронште́йн** bracket; corbel.

**кропотли́вый** painstaking; laborious.

**кросс** cross-country race.

**кроссво́рд** crossword (puzzle).

**крот** (-á) mole.

**кро́ткий** (-ток, -тка́, -тко) meek, gentle. **кро́тость** gentleness; mildness.

**кро́хотный, кро́шечный** tiny.

**кро́шка** crumb; a bit.

**круг** (loc -ý; pl -и́) circle; circuit; sphere. **круглосу́точный** round-the-clock. **кру́глый** (кругл, -á, -o) round; complete; ~ год all the year round. **кругово́й** circular;

all-round. **кругозо́р** prospect; outlook. **круго́м** *adv* around; *prep+gen* round. **кругосве́тный** round-the-world.

**кружевно́й** lace; lacy. **кру́жево** (*pl* -á, -ев, -áм) lace.

**кружи́ть** (-ужу́, -у́жи́шь) *impf* whirl, spin round; **~ся** whirl, spin round.

**кру́жка** mug.

**кружо́к** (-жка́) circle, group.

**круи́з** cruise.

**крупа́** (*pl* -ы) groats; sleet. **крупи́ца** grain.

**кру́пный** large, big; great; coarse; **~ый план** close-up.

**крутизна́** steepness.

**крути́ть** (-учу́, -у́тишь) *impf* (*pf* за-, с~) twist, twirl; roll; turn, wind; **~ся** turn, spin; whirl.

**круто́й** (крут, -á, -о) steep; sudden; sharp; severe; drastic. **кру́ча** steep slope. **кру́че** *comp* of **круто́й**, **кру́то**

**кручу́** *etc.*: see **крути́ть**

**круше́ние** crash; ruin; collapse.

**крыжо́вник** gooseberries; gooseberry bush.

**крыла́тый** winged. **крыло́** (*pl* -лья, -льев) wing; vane; mudguard.

**крыльцо́** (*pl* -а, -ле́ц, -ца́м) porch; (front, back) steps.

Крым the Crimea. **кры́мский** Crimean.

**кры́са** rat.

**крыть** (кро́ю) *impf* cover; roof; trump; **~ся** be, lie; be concealed. **кры́ша** roof. **кры́шка** lid.

**крюк** (-á; *pl* -ки́, -ко́в *or* -ючья, -чьев) hook; detour. **крючо́к** (-чка́) hook.

**кря́ду** *adv* in succession.

**кряж** ridge.

**кря́кать** *impf*, **кря́кнуть** (-ну) *pf* quack.

**кряхте́ть** (-хчу́) *impf* groan.

**кста́ти** *adv* to the point; opportunely; at the same time; by the way.

**кто** (кого́, кому́, кем, ком) *pron* who; anyone; **~ (бы) ни** whoever. **кто́-либо**, **кто́-нибудь** *prons* anyone; someone. **кто́-то** *pron* someone.

**куб** (*pl* -ы́) cube; boiler; **в ~е** cubed.

**куби́к** brick, block.

**куби́нский** Cuban.

**куби́ческий** cubic; cube.

**ку́бок** (-бка) goblet; cup.

**кубо́метр** cubic metre.

**кувши́н** jug; pitcher. **кувши́нка** water-lily.

**кувырка́ться** *impf*, **кувырну́ться** (-ну́сь) *pf* turn somersaults. **кувырко́м** *adv* head over heels; topsy-turvy.

**куда́** *adv* where (to); what for; +*comp* much, far; **~ (бы) ни** wherever. **куда́-либо**, **куда́-нибудь** *adv* anywhere, somewhere. **куда́-то** *adv* somewhere.

**ку́дри** (-е́й) *pl* curls. **кудря́вый** curly; florid.

**кузне́ц** (-á) blacksmith. **кузне́чик** grasshopper. **ку́зница** forge, smithy.

**ку́зов** (*pl* -á) basket; body.

**ку́кла** doll; puppet. **ку́колка** dolly; chrysalis. **ку́кольный** doll's; puppet.

**кукуру́за** maize.

**куку́шка** cuckoo.

**кула́к** (-á) fist; kulak. **кула́цкий** kulak. **кула́чный** fist.

**кулёк** (-лька́) bag.

**кули́к** (-á) sandpiper.

**кулина́рия** cookery. **кулина́рный** culinary.

**кули́сы** (-ис) wings; **за кули́сами** behind the scenes.

**кули́ч** (-á) Easter cake.

**кулуа́ры** (-ов) *pl* lobby.

**кульмина́ция** culmination.

**культ** cult. **культиви́ровать** *impf* cultivate.

**культу́ра** culture; standard; cultivation. **культури́зм** body-building. **культу́рно** *adv* in a civilized manner. **культу́рный** cultured; cultivated; cultural.

**куми́р** idol.

**кумы́с** koumiss (*fermented mare's milk*).

**куни́ца** marten.

**купа́льный** bathing. **купа́льня** bathing-place. **купа́ть** *impf* (*pf* вы́~, ис~) bathe; bath; ~ся bathe; take a bath.

**купе́** *neut indecl* compartment.

**купе́ц** (-пца́) merchant. **купе́ческий** merchant. **купи́ть** (-плю́, -пишь) *pf* (*impf* покупа́ть) buy.

**ку́пол** (*pl* -á) cupola, dome.

**купо́н** coupon.

**купоро́с** vitriol.

**купчи́ха** merchant's wife; female merchant.

**кура́нты** (-ов) *pl* chiming clock; chimes.

**курга́н** barrow; tumulus.

**куре́ние** smoking. **кури́льщик, -щица** smoker.

**кури́ный** hen's; chicken's.

**кури́ть** (-рю́, -ришь) *impf* (*pf* по~) smoke; ~ся burn; smoke.

**ку́рица** (*pl* ку́ры, кур) hen, chicken.

**куро́к** (-рка́) cocking-piece; взвести́ ~ cock a gun; спусти́ть ~ pull the trigger.

**куропа́тка** partridge.

**куро́рт** health-resort; spa.

**курс** course; policy; year; exchange rate. **курса́нт** student.

**курси́в** italics.

**курси́ровать** *impf* ply.

**ку́ртка** jacket.

**курча́вый** curly(-headed).

**ку́ры** *etc.: see* ку́рица

**курье́р** a funny thing. **курье́зный** curious.

**курье́р** messenger; courier. **курье́рский** express.

**куря́тник** hen-house.

**куря́щий** *sb* smoker.

**куса́ть** *impf* bite; sting; ~ся bite.

**кусо́к** (-ска́) piece; lump. **кусо́чек** (-чка) piece.

**куст** (-á) bush, shrub. **куста́рник** bush(es), shrub(s).

**куста́рный** hand-made; handicrafts; primitive; ~ая промы́шленность cottage industry. **куста́рь** (-я́) *m* craftsman.

**кута́ть** *impf* (*pf* за~) wrap up; ~ся muffle o.s. up.

**кути́ть** (кучу́, ку́тишь) *impf*, **кутну́ть** (-ну́, -нёшь) *pf* carouse; go on a binge.

**ку́харка** cook. **ку́хня** (*gen pl* -хонь) kitchen; cuisine. **ку́хонный** kitchen.

**ку́ча** heap; heaps.

**ку́чер** (*pl* -á) coachman.

**ку́чка** small heap *or* group.

**кучу́** *see* кути́ть

**куша́к** (-á) sash; girdle.

**ку́шанье** food; dish. **ку́шать** *impf* (*pf* по~, с~) eat.

**куше́тка** couch.

**кую́** *etc.: see* кова́ть

# Л

**лабора́нт, -а́нтка** laboratory assistant. **лаборато́рия** laboratory.

**ла́ва** lava.

**лави́на** avalanche.

**ла́вка** bench; shop. **ла́вочка**

small shop.
**лавр** bay tree, laurel.
**ла́герный** camp. **ла́герь** (pl -я or -и, -ей or -ей) m camp; campsite.
**лад** (loc -ý; pl -ы́, -о́в) harmony; manner, way; stop, fret.
**ла́дан** incense.
**ла́дить** (ла́жу) impf get on, be on good terms. **ла́дно** adv all right; very well! **ла́дный** fine, excellent; harmonious.
**ладо́нь** palm.
**ладья́** rook, castle; boat.
**ла́жу** etc.: see **ла́дить, ла́зить**.
**лазаре́т** field hospital; sick-bay.
**ла́зить** see **ла́зить. лазе́йка** hole; loop-hole.
**ла́зер** laser.
**ла́зить** (ла́жу), **ла́зать** impf climb, clamber.
**лазу́рный** sky-blue, azure. **лазу́рь** azure.
**лазу́тчик** scout; spy.
**лай** bark, barking. **ла́йка**[1] (Siberian) husky, laika.
**ла́йка**[2] kid. **ла́йковый** kid; kidskin.
**ла́йнер** liner; airliner.
**лак** varnish, lacquer.
**лака́ть** impf (pf вы́~) lap.
**лаке́й** footman, man-servant; lackey.
**лакирова́ть** impf (pf от~) varnish; lacquer.
**ла́кмус** litmus.
**ла́ковый** varnished, lacquered.
**ла́комиться** (-млюсь) impf (pf по~) +instr treat o.s. to.
**ла́комка** m & f gourmand. **ла́комство** delicacy. **ла́комый** dainty, tasty; +до fond of.
**лакони́чный** laconic.
**ла́мпа** lamp; valve, tube. **лампа́да** icon-lamp. **ла́мпочка**

lamp; bulb.
**ландша́фт** landscape.
**ла́ндыш** lily of the valley.
**лань** fallow deer; doe.
**ла́па** paw; tenon.
**ла́поть** (-птя; pl -и, -ей) m bast shoe.
**ла́почка** pet, sweetie.
**лапша́** noodles; noodle soup.
**ларёк** (-рька́) stall. **ларь** (-я́) m chest; bin.
**ла́ска**[1] caress.
**ла́ска**[2] weasel.
**ласка́ть** impf caress, fondle; ~ся +к+dat make up to; fawn upon. **ла́сковый** affectionate, tender.
**ла́сточка** swallow.
**латви́ец** (-и́йца), **-и́йка** Latvian. **латви́йский** Latvian. **Ла́твия** Latvia.
**лати́нский** Latin.
**лату́нь** brass.
**ла́ты** (лат) pl armour.
**латы́нь** Latin.
**латы́ш, латы́шка** Latvian. Lett. **латы́шский** Latvian, Lettish.
**лауреа́т** prize-winner.
**ла́цкан** lapel.
**лачу́га** hovel, shack.
**ла́ять** (ла́ю) impf bark.
**лба** etc.: see **лоб**
**лгать** (лгу, лжёшь; лгал, -á, -о) impf (pf на~, со~) lie; tell lies; +на+acc slander. **лгун** (-á), **лгу́нья** liar.
**лебеди́ный** swan. **лебёдка**[1] swan, pen; winch. **лебёдь** (pl -и, -е́й) m swan, cob.
**лев** (льва) lion.
**левобере́жный** left-bank.
**левша́** (gen pl -е́й) m & f left-hander. **ле́вый** adj left; left-hand; left-wing.
**лёг** etc.: see **лечь**
**лега́льный** legal.

**леге́нда** legend. **легенда́рный** legendary.

**лёгк|ий** (-гок, -гка́, лёгки́) light; easy; slight, mild; ~**ая атле́тика** field and track events. **легко́** *adv* easily, lightly, slightly.

**легко-** *in comb* light; easy, easily. **легкове́рный** credulous. ~**вес** light-weight. ~**мы́сленный** thoughtless; flippant, frivolous; superficial. ~**мы́слие** flippancy, frivolity.

**легков|о́й**: ~**а́я маши́на** (private) car. **лёгкое** *sb* lung. **лёгкость** lightness; easiness.

**ле́гче** *comp of* **лёгкий, легко́**

**лёд** (льда, *loc* -у́; *pl* -ы́) ice. **леде́ть** (-е́ю) *impf* (*pf* за~, о~) freeze; grow numb with cold. **ледене́ц** (-нца́) fruit-drop. **леденя́щий** chilling, icy.

**ле́ди** *f indecl* lady.

**ле́дник**[1] ice-box; refrigerator van. **ледни́к**[2] (-а́) glacier. **леднико́вый** glacial; ~ **пери́од** Ice Age. **ледо́вый** ice. **ледоко́л** ice-breaker. **ледяно́й** icy.

**лежа́ть** (-жу́) *impf* lie; be, be situated. **лежа́чий** lying (down).

**ле́звие** (cutting) edge; razor-blade.

**лезть** (-зу; лез) *impf* (*pf* по~) climb; clamber, crawl; get, go; fall out.

**лейбори́ст** Labourite.

**ле́йка** watering-can.

**лейтена́нт** lieutenant.

**лека́рство** medicine.

**ле́ксика** vocabulary. **лексико́н** lexicon; vocabulary.

**ле́ктор** lecturer. **ле́кция** lecture.

**леле́ять** (-е́ю) *impf* (*pf* вз~)

cherish, foster.

**лён** (льна) flax.

**лени́вый** lazy.

**ленингра́дский** (of) Leningrad. **ле́нинский** (of) Lenin; Leninist.

**лени́ться** (-ню́сь, -нишься) *impf* (*pf* по~) be lazy; +*inf* be too lazy to.

**ле́нта** ribbon; band; tape.

**лентя́й, -я́йка** lazy-bones. **лень** laziness.

**лепесто́к** (-тка́) petal. **лепета́ть** (-ечу́, -е́чешь) *impf* (*pf* про~) babble, prattle. **лепёшка** scone; tablet, pastille.

**лепи́ть** (-плю́, -пишь) *impf* (*pf* вы~, за~, с~) model, fashion; mould; ~**ся** cling; crawl. **ле́пка** modelling. **лепно́й** modelled, moulded.

**лес** (*loc* -у́; *pl* -а́) forest, wood; *pl* scaffolding.

**леса́** (*pl* ле́сы) fishing-line.

**лесни́к** (-а́) forester. **лесни́чий** *sb* forestry officer; forest warden. **лесно́й** forest.

**лесо-** *in comb* forest, forestry; timber wood. **лесово́дство** forestry. ~**загото́вка** logging. ~**пи́лка**, ~**пи́льня** (*gen pl* -лен) sawmill. ~**ру́б** woodcutter.

**ле́стница** stairs, staircase; ladder.

**ле́стный** flattering. **лесть** flattery.

**лёт** (*loc* -у́) flight, flying.

**лета́** (лет) *pl* years; age; **ско́лько вам лет?** how old are you?

**лета́тельный** flying. **лета́ть** *impf*, **лете́ть** (лечу́) *impf* (*pf* полете́ть) fly; rush; fall.

**ле́тний** summer.

**лётный** flying, flight.

**ле́то** (pl -á) summer; pl years. **ле́том** adv in summer.

**ле́топись** chronicle.

**летосчисле́ние** chronology.

**летуч|ий** flying; passing; brief; volatile; ~ая мышь bat. **лётчик**, -чица pilot.

**лече́бница** clinic. **лече́бный** medical; medicinal. **лече́ние** (medical) treatment. **лечи́ть** (-чу́, -чишь) impf treat (от for); ~ся be given, have treatment (от for).

**лечу́** etc.: see **лете́ть**, **лечи́ть**

**лечь** (ля́гу, ля́жешь; лёг, -лá) pf (impf **ложи́ться**) lie, lie down; go to bed.

**лещ** (-á) bream.

**лжесвиде́тельство** false witness.

**лжец** (-á) liar. **лжи́вый** lying; deceitful.

**ли**, **ль** interrog partl & conj whether, if; **ли,... ли** whether ... or; **ра́но ли**, **по́здно ли** sooner or later.

**либера́л** liberal. **либера́льный** liberal.

**ли́бо** conj or; ~... ~ either ... or.

**ли́вень** (-вня) m heavy shower, downpour.

**ливре́я** livery.

**ли́га** league.

**ли́дер** leader. **лиди́ровать** impf & pf be in the lead.

**лиза́ть** (лижу́, -ешь) impf, **лизну́ть** (-ну́, -нёшь) pf lick.

**ликвида́ция** liquidation; abolition. **ликвиди́ровать** impf & pf liquidate; abolish.

**ликёр** liqueur.

**ликова́ние** rejoicing. **ликова́ть** impf rejoice.

**ли́лия** lily.

**лило́вый** lilac, violet.

**лима́н** estuary.

**лими́т** limit.

**лимо́н** lemon. **лимона́д** lemonade; squash. **лимо́нный** lemon.

**ли́мфа** lymph.

**лингви́ст** linguist. **лингви́стика** linguistics. **лингвисти́ческий** linguistic.

**лине́йка** ruler; line. **лине́йный** linear; ~ кора́бль battleship.

**ли́нза** lens.

**ли́ния** line.

**лино́леум** lino(leum).

**линя́ть** impf (pf вы́~, по~, с~) fade; moult.

**ли́па** lime tree.

**ли́пкий** (-пок, -пкá, -о) sticky. **ли́пнуть** (-ну; лип) impf stick.

**ли́повый** lime.

**ли́ра** lyre. **ли́рик** lyric poet. **ли́рика** lyric poetry. **лири́ческий** lyric; lyrical.

**лиса́** (pl -ы), -си́ца fox.

**лист** (-á; pl -ы́ or -ья, -óв or -ьев) leaf; sheet; page; form; **игра́ть с ~á** play at sight. **листа́ть** impf leaf through. **листва́** foliage. **ли́ственница** larch **ли́ственный** deciduous. **листо́вка** leaflet. **листово́й** sheet, plate; leaf. **листо́к** (-тка́) dim of лист; leaflet; form, pro-forma.

**Литва́** Lithuania.

**лите́йный** founding, casting.

**литера́тор** man of letters. **литерату́ра** literature. **литерату́рный** literary.

**лито́вец** (-вца), **лито́вка** Lithuanian. **лито́вский** Lithuanian.

**лито́й** cast.

**литр** litre.

**лить** (лью, льёшь; лил, -á, -о) impf (pf с~) pour; shed; cast;

mould. **литьё** founding, casting, moulding; castings, mouldings. **ли́ться** (льётся, ли́лся, -ась, ли́лось) *impf* flow; pour.

**лиф** bodice. **ли́фчик** bra.

**лифт** lift.

**лихо́й**[1] (лих, -á, -о) dashing, spirited.

**лихо́й**[2] (лих, -á, -о, ли́хи) evil. **лихора́дка** fever. **лихора́дочный** feverish.

**лицево́й** facial; exterior; front. **лицеме́р** hypocrite. **лицеме́рие** hypocrisy. **лицеме́рный** hypocritical.

**лицо́** (*pl* -a) face; exterior; right side; person; **быть к лицу́** +*dat* suit, befit. **личи́нка** larva, grub; maggot. **ли́чно** *adv* personally, in person. **ли́чность** personality; person. **ли́чный** personal; private; ~ **соста́в** staff, personnel.

**лиша́й** lichen; herpes; shingles. **лиша́йник** lichen.

**лиша́ть(ся** *impf of* **лиши́ть(ся лише́ние** deprivation; privation. **лишённый** (-ён, -ена́) +*gen* lacking in, devoid of. **лиши́ть** (-шу́) *impf* (*impf* **лиша́ть**) +*gen* deprive of; ~**ся** +*gen* lose, be deprived of. **ли́шн|ий** superfluous; unnecessary; spare; ~ **раз** once more; **с ~им** odd, and more.

**лишь** *adv* only; *conj* as soon as; ~ **бы** if only, provided that.

**лоб** (лба, *loc* лбу) forehead.

**ло́бзик** fret-saw.

**лови́ть** (-влю́, -вишь) *impf* (*pf* **пойма́ть**) catch, try to catch. **ло́вкий** (-вок, -вка́, -о) adroit; cunning. **ло́вкость** adroitness; cunning.

**ло́вля** (*gen pl* -вель) catching, hunting; fishing-ground. **лову́шка** trap.

**ло́вче** *comp of* **ло́вкий**

**логари́фм** logarithm.

**ло́гика** logic. **логи́ческий, логи́чный** logical.

**ло́говище, ло́гово** den, lair.

**ло́дка** boat.

**ло́дырничать** *impf* loaf, idle about. **ло́дырь** *m* loafer, idler.

**ло́жа** box; (masonic) lodge.

**ложби́на** hollow.

**ло́же** couch; bed.

**ложи́ться** (-жу́сь) *impf of* **печь**

**ло́жка** spoon.

**ло́жный** false. **ложь** (лжи) lie, falsehood.

**лоза́** (*pl* -ы) vine.

**ло́зунг** slogan, catchword.

**лока́тор** radar *or* sonar apparatus.

**локомоти́в** locomotive.

**ло́кон** lock, curl.

**ло́коть** (-ктя; *pl* -и, -éй) *m* elbow.

**лом** (*pl* -ы, -óв) crowbar; scrap, waste. **ло́маный** broken. **лома́ть** *impf* (*pf* по~, с~) break; cause to ache; ~**ся** break; crack; put on airs; be obstinate.

**ломба́рд** pawnshop.

**ло́мберный стол** card-table.

**ломи́ть** (ло́мит) *impf* break; break through, rush; *impers* cause to ache; ~**ся** be (near to) breaking. **ло́мка** breaking; *pl* quarry. **ло́мкий** (-мок, -мка́, о) fragile, brittle.

**ломо́ть** (-мтя́; *pl* -мти́) *m* large slice; hunk; chunk. **ло́мтик** slice.

**ло́но** bosom, lap.

**ло́пасть** (*pl* -и, -éй) blade; fan, vane; paddle.

**лопа́та** spade; shovel. **лопа́тка** shoulder-blade; shovel; trowel.

ло́паться *impf*, ло́пнуть (-ну) *pf* burst; split; break; fail; crash.

лопу́х (-á) burdock.

лорд lord.

лоси́на elk-skin, chamois leather; elk-meat.

лоск lustre, shine.

лоску́т (-á; *pl* -ы́ *or* -ья, -óв *or* -ьéв) rag, shred, scrap.

лосни́ться *impf* be glossy, shine.

ло́со́сь *m* salmon.

лось (*pl* -и, -éй) *m* elk.

лосьо́н lotion; aftershave; cream.

лот lead, plummet.

лотере́я lottery, raffle.

лото́к (-тка́) hawker's stand *or* tray; chute; gutter; trough.

лохма́тый shaggy; dishevelled.

лохмо́тья (-ьéв) *pl* rags.

ло́цман pilot.

лошади́ный horse; equine. ло́шадь (*pl* -и, -éй, *instr* -дьми́ *or* -дя́ми) horse.

лощёный glossy, polished.

лощи́на hollow, depression.

лоя́льный fair, honest; loyal.

лубо́к (-бка́) splint; popular print.

луг (*loc* -ý; *pl* -á) meadow.

лу́жа puddle.

лужа́йка lawn, glade.

лужёный tin-plated.

лук[1] onions.

лук[2] bow.

лука́вить (-влю) *impf* (*pf* с~) be cunning. лука́вство craftiness. лука́вый crafty, cunning.

лу́ковица onion; bulb

луна́ (*pl* -ы) moon. луна́тик sleep-walker.

лу́нка hole; socket.

лу́нный moon; lunar.

лупа́ magnifying-glass.

лупи́ть (-плю́, -пишь) *impf* (*pf*

от~) flog.

луч (-á) ray; beam. лучево́й ray, beam; radial; radiation. лучеза́рный radiant.

лучи́на splinter.

лу́чше better; ~ всего́, ~ всех best of all. лу́чший better; best; в ~ем слу́чае at best; всего́ ~его! all the best!

лы́жа ski. лы́жник skier. лы́жный спорт skiing. лы́жня ski-track.

лы́ко bast.

лысе́ть (-éю) *impf* (*pf* об~, по~) grow bald. лы́сина bald spot; blaze. лы́сый (лыс, -á, -о) bald.

ль *see* ли

льва *etc.*: *see* лев. льви́ный lion, lion's. льви́ца lioness.

льго́та privilege; advantage. льго́тный privileged; favourable.

льда *etc.*: *see* лёд. льди́на block of ice; ice-floe.

льна *etc.*: *see* лён. льново́дство flax-growing.

льнуть (-ну, -нёшь) *impf* (*pf* при~) +к+*dat* cling to; have a weakness for; make up to.

льняно́й flax, flaxen; linen; linseed.

льсте́ц (-á) flatterer. льсти́вый flattering; smooth-tongued. льсти́ть (льщу) *impf* (*pf* по~) +*dat* flatter.

лью *etc.*: *see* пить

любе́зность courtesy; kindness; compliment. любе́зный courteous; obliging; kind; бу́дьте ~ы be so kind (as to).

люби́мец (-мца), -мица pet, favourite. люби́мый beloved; favourite. люби́тель *m*, -ница lover; amateur. люби́тельский amateur. люби́ть (-блю́, -бишь) *impf* love; like.

**любова́ться** *impf* (*pf* по~) +*instr or* на+*acc* admire.

**любо́вник** lover. **любо́вница** mistress. **любо́вный** love-; loving. **любо́вь** (-бви́, *instr* -бо́вью) love.

**любозна́тельный** inquisitive.

**любо́й** any; either; *sb* anyone.

**любопы́тный** curious; inquisitive. **любопы́тство** curiosity.

**любя́щий** loving.

**лю́ди** (-е́й, -ям, -дьми́, -ях) *pl* people. **лю́дный** populous; crowded. **людое́д** cannibal; ogre. **людско́й** human.

**люк** hatch(way); trap; manhole.

**лю́лька** cradle.

**люминесце́нтный** luminescent. **люминесце́нция** luminescence.

**лю́стра** chandelier.

**лю́тня** (*gen pl* -тен) lute.

**лю́тый** (лют, -а́, -о) ferocious.

**ляга́ть** *impf*, **лягну́ть** (-ну́, -нёшь) *pf* kick; ~ся kick.

**ля́гу** *etc.: see* лечь

**лягу́шка** frog.

**ля́жка** thigh, haunch.

**ля́згать** *impf* clank; +*instr* rattle.

**ля́мка** strap; тяну́ть ля́мку toil.

# M

**мавзоле́й** mausoleum.

**мавр, маврита́нка** Moor. **маврита́нский** Moorish.

**магази́н** shop.

**маги́стр** (holder of) master's degree.

**магистра́ль** main; main line; main road.

**маги́ческий** magic(al). **ма́гия** magic.

**магнети́зм** magnetism.

**ма́гний** magnesium.

**магни́т** magnet. **магни́тный** magnetic. **магнитофо́н** tape-recorder.

**мада́м** *f indecl* madam, madame.

**мажо́р** major (key); cheerful mood. **мажо́рный** major; cheerful.

**ма́зать** (ма́жу) *impf* (*pf* вы́~, за~, из~, на~, по~, про~) oil, grease; smear, spread; soil; ~ся get dirty; make up. **мазо́к** (-зка́) touch, dab; smear. **мазу́т** fuel oil. **мазь** ointment; grease.

**ма́ис** maize.

**май** May. **ма́йский** May.

**ма́йка** T-shirt.

**майо́р** major.

**мак** poppy, poppy-seeds.

**макаро́ны** (-н) *pl* macaroni.

**мака́ть** (*impf* макну́ть) dip.

**маке́т** model; dummy.

**макну́ть** (-ну́, -нёшь) *pf of* мака́ть

**макре́ль** mackerel.

**максима́льный** maximum. **ма́ксимум** maximum; at most.

**макулату́ра** waste paper; pulp literature.

**маку́шка** top; crown.

**мал** *etc.: see* ма́лый

**малахи́т** malachite.

**мале́йший** least, slightest. **ма́ленький** little; small.

**мали́на** (*no pl*; *usu collect*) raspberry; raspberries; raspberry-bush. **мали́новый** raspberry.

**ма́ло** *adv* little, few; not enough; ~ того́ moreover; ~ того́ что... not only ...

**мало-** *in comb* (too) little. **малова́жный** of little importance. ~вероя́тный unlikely; ~гра́мотный semi-literate;

crude. ~**ду́шный** faint-hearted. ~**иму́щий** needy. ~**кро́вие** anaemia. ~**ле́тний** young; juvenile; minor. ~**о́пытный** inexperienced. ~**чи́сленный** small (in number), few.

**мало-ма́льски** adv in the slightest degree; at all. **мало-пома́лу** adv little by little.

**ма́л**|**ый** (мал, -а́) little, (too) small; **са́мое** ~**ое** at the least; sb fellow; lad. **малы́ш** m kiddy; little boy. **ма́льчик** boy. **ма́льчишка** m urchin, boy. **мальчуга́н** little boy. **малю́тка** m & f baby, little one.

**маля́р** (-а́) painter, decorator.

**маля́рия** malaria.

**ма́ма** mother, mummy. **ма́маша** mummy. **ма́мин** mother's.

**ма́монт** mammoth.

**мандари́н** mandarin, tangerine.

**манда́т** warrant; mandate.

**маневр** manoeuvre; shunting. **маневри́ровать** impf (pf c~) manoeuvre; shunt; +instr make good use of.

**мане́ж** riding-school.

**манеке́н** dummy; mannequin. **манеке́нщик**, **-щица** model.

**мане́ра** manner; style. **мане́рный** affected.

**манже́та** cuff.

**маникю́р** manicure.

**манипули́ровать** impf manipulate. **манипуля́ция** manipulation; machination.

**мани́ть** (-ню́, -нишь) impf (pf по~) beckon; attract; lure.

**манифе́ст** manifesto. **манифеста́ция** demonstration.

**мани́шка** (false) shirt-front.

**ма́ния** mania; ~ **вели́чия** megalomania.

**ма́нная ка́ша** semolina.

**мано́метр** pressure-gauge.

**ма́нтия** cloak; robe, gown.

**мануфакту́ра** manufacture; textiles.

**манья́к** maniac.

**марафо́нский бег** marathon.

**марга́нец** (-нца) manganese.

**маргари́н** margarine.

**маргари́тка** daisy.

**марино́ванный** pickled. **маринова́ть** impf (pf за~) pickle; put off.

**марионе́тка** puppet.

**ма́рка** stamp; counter; brand; trade-mark; grade; reputation.

**ма́ркий** easily soiled.

**маркси́зм** Marxism. **маркси́ст** Marxist. **маркси́стский** Marxist.

**ма́рлевый** gauze. **ма́рля** gauze; cheesecloth.

**мармела́д** fruit jellies.

**ма́рочный** high-quality.

**Марс** Mars.

**март** March. **ма́ртовский** March.

**марты́шка** marmoset; monkey.

**марш** march.

**марша́л** marshal.

**марширова́ть** impf march.

**маршру́т** route, itinerary.

**ма́ска** mask. **маскара́д** masked ball; masquerade. **маскирова́ть** impf (pf за~) disguise; camouflage. **маскиро́вка** disguise; camouflage.

**Ма́сленица** Shrovetide. **маслёнка** butter-dish; oil-can. **масли́на** olive. **ма́сло** (pl -а́, ма́сел, -сла́м) butter; oil; oil paints. **маслобо́йка** churn. **маслобо́йня** (gen pl -о́ен), **маслозаво́д** dairy. **масляни́стый** oily. **ма́сляный** oil.

**ма́сса** mass; a lot, lots.

**масса́ж** massage. **масси́ровать** impf & pf massage.

**масси́в** massif; expanse, tract.
**масси́вный** massive.
**ма́ссовый** mass.
**ма́стер** (pl -á), **мастери́ца** foreman, forewoman; (master) craftsman; expert. **мастери́ть** impf (pf c~) make, build. **мастерска́я** sb workshop. **мастерско́й** masterly. **мастерство́** craft; skill.
**масти́ка** mastic; putty; floor-polish.
**масти́тый** venerable.
**масть** (pl -и, -е́й) colour; suit.
**масшта́б** scale.
**мат¹** checkmate.
**мат²** mat.
**мат³** foul language.
**матема́тик** mathematician. **матема́тика** mathematics. **математи́ческий** mathematical.
**материа́л** material. **материали́зм** materialism. **материалисти́ческий** materialist. **материа́льный** material.
**матери́к** (-á) continent; mainland. **материко́вый** continental.
**матери́нский** maternal, motherly. **матери́нство** maternity.
**мате́рия** material; pus; topic.
**ма́тка** womb; female.
**ма́товый** matt; frosted.
**матра́с, матра́ц** mattress.
**матрёшка** Russian doll.
**ма́трица** matrix; die, mould.
**матро́с** sailor, seaman.
**матч** match.
**мать** (ма́тери, instr -рью; pl -тери, -ре́й) mother.
**ма́фия** Mafia.
**мах** swing, stroke. **маха́ть** (машу́, ма́шешь) impf, **махну́ть** (-ну́, -нёшь) pf +instr wave; brandish; wag; flap; go; rush.

**махина́ция** machinations.
**маховико́** (-á) fly-wheel.
**махро́вый** dyed-in-the-wool; terry.
**ма́ча** stepmother.
**ма́чта** mast.
**маши́на** machine; car. **маши́нальный** mechanical. **машини́ст** operator; engine-driver; scene-shifter. **машини́стка** typist; **~стенографи́стка** shorthand-typist. **маши́нка** machine; typewriter; sewing-machine. **машинопи́сный** typewritten. **машинопись** typing; typescript. **машиностроение** mechanical engineering.
**мая́к** (-á) lighthouse; beacon.
**ма́ятник** pendulum. **ма́яться** impf toil; suffer; languish.
**мгла** haze; gloom.
**мгнове́ние** instant, moment. **мгнове́нный** instantaneous, momentary.
**ме́бель** furniture. **меблиро́ванный** furnished. **меблиро́вка** furnishing; furniture.
**мегава́тт** (gen pl -а́тт) megawatt. **мего́м** megohm. **мега́тонна** megaton.
**мёд** (loc -у́; pl -ы́) honey.
**меда́ль** medal. **медальо́н** medallion.
**медве́дица** she-bear. **медве́дь** m bear. **медве́жий** bear('s). **медвежо́нок** (-нка; pl -жа́та, -жа́т) bear cub.
**ме́дик** medical student; doctor. **медикаме́нты** (-ов) pl medicines.
**медици́на** medicine. **медици́нский** medical.
**ме́дленный** slow. **ме́длительный** sluggish; slow. **ме́длить** impf linger; be slow.
**ме́дный** copper; brass.

**медо́вый** honey; ~ ме́сяц honeymoon.

**медосмо́тр** medical examination, check-up. **медпу́нкт** first aid post. **медсестра́** (pl -сёстры, -сестёр, -сёстрам) nurse.

**меду́за** jellyfish.

**медь** copper.

**меж** prep+instr between.

**меж-** in comb inter-.

**межа́** (pl -и, меж, -ám) boundary.

**междоме́тие** interjection.

**ме́жду** prep+instr between; among; ~ про́чим incidentally, by the way; ~ тем meanwhile; ~ тем, как while.

**между-** in comb inter-. **междугоро́дный** inter-city. **наро́дный** international.

**межконтинента́льный** intercontinental. **межплане́тный** interplanetary.

**мезони́н** attic (storey); mezzanine (floor).

**Ме́ксика** Mexico.

**мел** (loc -ý) chalk.

**мёл** etc.: see **мести́**

**меланхо́лия** melancholy.

**меле́ть** (-е́ет) impf (pf об~) grow shallow.

**мелиора́ция** land improvement.

**ме́лкий** (-лок, -лка́, -о) small; shallow; fine; petty. **ме́лко** adv fine, small. **мелкобуржуа́зный** petty bourgeois. **мелково́дный** shallow.

**мелоди́чный** melodious, melodic. **мело́дия** melody.

**ме́лочный** petty. **ме́лочь** (pl -и, -éй) small items; (small) change; pl trifles, trivialities.

**мель** (loc -ý) shoal; bank; на ме́ли aground.

**мелька́ть** impf, **мелькну́ть**

(-ну́, -нёшь) pf be glimpsed fleetingly; flash in passing; fleetingly. **ме́льком** adv in passing; fleetingly.

**ме́льник** miller. **ме́льница** mill.

**мельча́йший** superl of **ме́лкий**. **ме́льче** comp of **ме́лкий**, **ме́лко**. **мелюзга́** small fry.

**мелю́** etc.: see **моло́ть**

**мембра́на** membrane; diaphragm.

**мемора́ндум** memorandum.

**мемуа́ры** (-ов) pl memoirs.

**ме́на** exchange, barter.

**ме́неджер** manager.

**ме́нее** adv less; тем не ~ none the less.

**мензу́рка** measuring-glass.

**меново́й** exchange; barter.

**менуэ́т** minuet.

**ме́ньше** smaller; less. **меньшеви́к** (-á) Menshevik. **ме́ньший** lesser, smaller; younger. **меньшинство́** minority.

**меню́** neut indecl menu.

**меня́** see **я** pron

**меня́ть** impf (pf об~, по~) change; exchange; **~ся** change; +instr exchange.

**ме́ра** measure.

**мере́щиться** (-щусь) impf (pf по~) seem, appear.

**мерза́вец** (-вца) swine, bastard. **ме́рзкий** (-зок, -зка́, -о) disgusting.

**мерзлота́: ве́чная ~** permafrost. **мёрзнуть** (-ну; мёрз) impf (pf за~) freeze.

**ме́рзость** vileness; abomination.

**меридиа́н** meridian.

**мери́ло** standard, criterion.

**ме́рин** gelding.

**ме́рить** impf (pf по~, с~) measure; try on. **ме́рка** measure.

**ме́рный** measured; rhythmi-

cal. **мероприя́тие** measure.
**мертве́ть** (-е́ю) *impf* (*pf* о~,
по~) grow numb; be be-
numbed. **мертве́ц** (-á) corpse,
dead man. **мёртвый** (мёртв,
-á, мёртво) dead.
**мерца́ть** *impf* twinkle; flicker.
**меси́ть** (мешу́, ме́сишь) *impf*
(*pf* с~) knead.
**ме́сса** Mass.
**места́ми** *adv* here and there.
**месте́чко** (*pl* -и, -чек) small
town.
**мести́** (мету́, -тёшь; мёл, -á)
*impf* sweep; whirl.
**ме́стность** locality; area. **ме́ст-
ный** local; locative. **ме́ст-
ный** *in comb* -berth, -seater.
**ме́сто** (*pl* -á) place; site; seat;
room; job. **местожи́тельство**
(place of) residence. **место-
име́ние** pronoun. **местона-
хожде́ние** location, whereabouts. **месторожде́ние** deposit; layer.
**месть** vengeance, revenge.
**ме́сяц** month; moon. **ме́сяч-
ный** monthly; *sb pl* period.
**мета́лл** metal. **металли́че-
ский** metal, metallic. **метал-
лу́ргия** metallurgy.
**мета́н** methane.
**мета́ние** throwing, flinging.
**мета́ть**[1] (мечу́, ме́чешь) *impf*
(*pf* метну́ть) throw, fling; ~ся
rush about; toss (and turn).
**мета́ть**[2] *impf* (*pf* на~, с~)
tack.
**метафи́зика** metaphysics.
**мета́фора** metaphor.
**метёлка** panicle.
**мете́ль** snow-storm.
**метео́р** meteor. **метеори́т** meteorite. **метеоро́лог** meteoro-
logist. **метеорологи́ческий**
meteorological. **метеороло́-
гия** meteorology.

**метеосво́дка** weather report.
**метеоста́нция** weather-sta-
tion.
**ме́тить**[1] (ме́чу) *impf* (*pf* на~,
по~) mark.
**ме́тить**[2] (ме́чу) *impf* (*pf* на~)
aim; mean.
**ме́тка** marking, mark.
**ме́ткий** (-ток, -ткá, -о) well-
aimed, accurate.
**метла́** (*pl* мётлы, -тел) broom.
**метну́ть** (-ну́, -нёшь) *pf of*
**мета́ть**[1]
**ме́тод** method. **мето́дика**
method(s); methodology. **ме-
тоди́чный** methodical. **мето-
доло́гия** methodology.
**метр** metre.
**ме́трика** birth certificate. **мет-
ри́ческ|ий**[1]: ~ое свиде́-
тельство birth certificate.
**метри́ческий**[2] metric; metrical.
**метро́** *neut indecl*, **метропо-
лите́н** Metro; underground.
**мету́** *etc.: see* **мести́**
**мех**[1] (*loc* -ý; *pl* -á) fur.
**мех**[2] (*pl* -и́) wine-skin, water-
skin; *pl* bellows.
**механиза́ция** mechanization.
**механи́зм** mechanism; gear-
(ing). **меха́ник** mechanic.
**меха́ника** mechanics; trick;
knack. **механи́ческий** mechanical; mechanistic.
**мехово́й** fur.
**меч** (-á) sword.
**ме́ченый** marked.
**мече́ть** mosque.
**мечта́** (day-)dream. **мечта́-
тельный** dreamy. **мечта́ть**
*impf* dream.
**мечу́** *etc.: see* **ме́тить**. **мечу́**
*etc.: see* **мета́ть**
**меша́лка** mixer.
**меша́ть**[1] *impf* (*pf* по~) +*dat*
hinder; prevent; disturb.
**меша́ть**[2] *impf* (*pf* по~, с~)

stir; mix; mix up; ~**ся** (в+*acc*) interfere (in), meddle (with).

**мешо́к** (-шка́) bag; sack. **мешкови́на** sacking, hessian.

**мещани́н** (*pl* -а́не, -а́н) petty bourgeois; Philistine. **меща́нский** bourgeois, narrow-minded; Philistine. **меща́нство** petty bourgeoisie; philistinism, narrow-mindedness.

**миг** moment, instant.

**мига́ть** *impf*, **мигну́ть** (-ну́, -нёшь) *pf* blink; wink; twinkle.

**ми́гом** *adv* in a flash.

**мигра́ция** migration.

**мигре́нь** migraine.

**мизантро́п** misanthrope.

**мизи́нец** (-нца) little finger; little toe.

**микро́б** microbe.

**микроволно́вая печь** microwave oven.

**микро́н** micron.

**микроорганизм** microorganism.

**микроско́п** microscope. **микроскопи́ческий** microscopic.

**микросхе́ма** microchip.

**микрофо́н** (*gen pl* -н) microphone.

**ми́ксер** (*cul*) mixer, blender.

**миксту́ра** medicine, mixture.

**ми́ленький** pretty; sweet; dear.

**милитари́зм** militarism.

**милиционе́р** militiaman, policeman. **мили́ция** militia, police force.

**миллиа́рд** billion, a thousand million. **миллиме́тр** millimetre. **миллио́н** million. **миллионе́р** millionaire.

**милосе́рдие** mercy, charity. **милосе́рдный** merciful, charitable.

**ми́лостивый** gracious, kind. **ми́лостыня** alms. **ми́лость**

favour, grace. **ми́лый** (мил, -а́, -о) nice; kind; sweet; dear.

**ми́ля** mile.

**ми́мика** (facial) expression; mimicry.

**ми́мо** *adv* & *prep* +*gen* by, past. **мимолётный** fleeting. **мимохо́дом** *adv* in passing.

**ми́на**[1] mine; bomb.

**ми́на**[2] expression, mien.

**минда́ль** (-я́) *m* almond(-tree); almonds.

**минера́л** mineral. **минерало́гия** mineralogy. **минера́льный** mineral.

**миниатю́ра** miniature. **миниатю́рный** miniature; tiny.

**минима́льный** minimum. **ми́нимум** minimum.

**министе́рство** ministry. **мини́стр** minister.

**минова́ть** *impf* & *pf* pass; *impers*+*dat* escape.

**миноме́т** mortar. **миноно́сец** (-сца) torpedo-boat.

**мино́р** minor (key); melancholy.

**мину́вш|ий** past; ~**ee** *sb* the past.

**ми́нус** minus.

**мину́та** minute. **мину́тный** minute; momentary.

**мину́ть** (-нешь; ми́нул) *pf* pass.

**мир**[1] (*pl* -ы́) world.

**мир**[2] peace.

**мира́ж** mirage.

**мири́ть** *impf* (*pf* по~, при~) reconcile; ~**ся** be reconciled.

**ми́рный** peace; peaceful.

**мировоззре́ние** (world-)outlook; philosophy. **мирово́й** world. **мирозда́ние** universe.

**миролюби́вый** peace-loving.

**ми́ска** basin, bowl.

**мисс** *f indecl* Miss.

**миссионе́р** missionary.

**ми́ссис** *f indecl* Mrs.

**ми́ссия** mission.

**ми́стер** Mr.

**ми́стика** mysticism.

**мистифика́ция** hoax, leg-pull.

**ми́тинг** mass meeting; rally.

**митрополи́т** metropolitan.

**миф** myth. **мифи́ческий** mythical. **мифологи́ческий** mythological. **мифоло́гия** mythology.

**ми́чман** warrant officer.

**мише́нь** target.

**ми́шка** (Teddy) bear.

**младе́нец** (-нца) baby; infant. **мла́дший** younger; youngest; junior.

**млекопита́ющие** *sb pl* mammals. **Мле́чный Путь** Milky Way.

**мне** *see* я *pron*

**мне́ние** opinion.

**мни́мый** imaginary; sham. **мни́тельный** hypochondriac; mistrustful. **мнить** (мню) *impf* think.

**мно́гие** *sb pl* many (people); ~ое *sb* much, a great deal. **мно́го** *adv+gen* much; many; на ~ by much.

**много-** *in comb* many-, poly-, multi-, multiple-. **многобо́рье** combined event. **~гра́нный** polyhedral; many-sided. **~де́тный** having many children. **~же́нство** polygamy. **~значи́тельный** significant. **~кра́тный** repeated; frequentative. **~ле́тний** lasting, living, many years; of many years' standing; perennial. **~лю́дный** crowded. **~национа́льный** multi-national. **~обеща́ющий** promising. **~обра́зие** diversity. **~сло́вный** verbose. **~сторо́нний** multi-lateral; many-sided; versatile.

**~то́чие** dots, omission points.

**~уважа́емый** respected; Dear. **~уго́льный** polygonal. **~цве́тный** multi-coloured; multiflorous. **~чи́сленный** numerous. **~эта́жный** many-storeyed. **~язы́чный** polyglot.

**мно́жественный** plural. **мно́жество** great number. **мно́жить** (-жу) *impf* (*pf* у~) multiply; increase.

**мной** *etc.: see* я *pron.* **мну** *etc.: see* мять

**мобилиза́ция** mobilization. **мобилизова́ть** *impf & pf* mobilize.

**мог** *etc.: see* мочь

**моги́ла** grave. **моги́льный** (of the) grave; sepulchral.

**могу́** *etc.: see* мочь. **могу́чий** mighty. **могуще́ственный** powerful. **могу́щество** power, might.

**мо́да** fashion.

**модели́ровать** *impf & pf* design. **моде́ль** model; pattern. **моделье́р** fashion designer. **моде́льный** model; fashionable.

**модернизи́ровать** *impf & pf* modernize.

**моди́стка** milliner.

**модифика́ция** modification. **модифици́ровать** *impf & pf* modify.

**мо́дный** (-ден, -дна́, -о) fashionable; fashion.

**мо́жет** *see* мочь

**можжеве́льник** juniper.

**мо́жно** one may, one can; it is permissible; it is possible; как +*comp* as ... as possible; как ~ скоре́е as soon as possible.

**мозаи́ка** mosaic; jigsaw.

**мозг** (*loc* -у́, *pl* -и́) brain; marrow. **мозгово́й** cerebral.

**мозо́ль** corn; callus.

**мой** (моего́) *m*, **моя́** (мое́й) *f*, **моё** (моего́) *neut*, **мои́** (-и́х) *pl pron* my; mine; **по-мо́ему** in my opinion; in my way.

**мо́йка** washing.

**мо́кнуть** (-ну; мок) *impf* get wet; soak. **мокро́та** phlegm. **мо́крый** wet, damp.

**мол** (*loc* -у́) mole, pier.

**молва́** rumour, talk.

**моле́бен** (-бна) church service.

**моле́кула** molecule. **молекуля́рный** molecular.

**моли́тва** prayer. **моли́ть** (-лю́, -лишь) *impf* pray; beg; **~ся** (*pf* по**~**) pray.

**моллю́ск** mollusc.

**молниено́сный** lightning. **мо́лния** lightning; zip(-fastener).

**молодёжь** youth, young people. **молоде́ть** (-е́ю) *impf* (*pf* по**~**) get younger, look younger. **молоде́ц** (-дца́) fine fellow *or* girl; **~!** well done! **молодожёны** (-ов) *pl* newly-weds. **молодо́й** (мо́лод, -а́, -о) young. **мо́лодость** youth. **моло́же** *comp* of **молодо́й**

**молоко́** milk.

**мо́лот** hammer. **молоти́ть** (-очу́, -о́тишь) *impf* (*pf* с**~**) thresh; hammer. **молото́к** (-тка́) hammer. **мо́лотый** ground. **моло́ть** (мелю́, ме́лешь) *impf* (*pf* с**~**) grind, mill.

**моло́чная** *sb* dairy. **моло́чный** milk; dairy; milky.

**мо́лча** *adv* silently, in silence. **молчали́вый** silent, taciturn; tacit. **молча́ние** silence. **молча́ть** (-чу́) *impf* be or keep silent.

**моль** moth.

**мольба́** entreaty.

**мольбе́рт** easel.

**моме́нт** moment; feature. **момента́льно** *adv* instantly. **момента́льный** instantaneous.

**мона́рх** monarch. **монархи́ст** monarchist.

**монасты́рь** (-я́) *m* monastery; convent. **мона́х** monk. **мона́хиня** nun.

**монго́л**, **~ка** Mongol.

**моне́та** coin.

**моногра́фия** monograph.

**моноли́тный** monolithic.

**моноло́г** monologue.

**монопо́лия** monopoly.

**моното́нный** monotonous.

**монта́ж** (-а́) assembling, mounting; editing. **монта́жник** rigger, fitter. **монтёр** fitter, mechanic. **монти́ровать** *impf* (*pf* с**~**) mount; install; fit; edit.

**монуме́нт** monument. **монумента́льный** monumental.

**мора́ль** moral; morals, ethics. **мора́льный** moral; ethical.

**морг** morgue.

**морга́ть** *impf*, **моргну́ть** (-ну́, -нёшь) *pf* blink; wink.

**мо́рда** snout, muzzle; (ugly) mug.

**мо́ре** (*pl* -я́, -е́й) sea.

**морепла́вание** navigation. **морепла́ватель** *m* seafarer. **морехо́дный** nautical.

**морж** (-а́), **моржи́ха** walrus.

**Мо́рзе** *indecl* Morse; **а́збука ~** Morse code.

**мори́ть** *impf* (*pf* у**~**) exhaust; **~ го́лодом** starve.

**морко́вка** carrot. **морко́вь** carrots.

**моро́женое** *sb* ice-cream. **моро́женый** frozen, chilled. **моро́з** frost; *pl* intensely cold weather. **моро́зилка** freezer compartment; freezer. **морози́льник** deep-freeze.

**моро́зить** (-о́жу) freeze. **моро́зный** frosty.

**моро́сить** impf drizzle.

**морск|о́й** sea; maritime; marine, nautical; ~а́я свинка guinea-pig; ~о́й флот navy, fleet.

**мо́рфий** morphine.

**морщи́на** wrinkle; crease. **мо́рщить** (-щу) impf (pf на~, по~, с~) wrinkle; pucker; ~ся knit one's brow; wince; crease, wrinkle.

**моря́к** (-а́) sailor, seaman.

**москви́ч** (-а́), ~ка Muscovite. **моско́вский** (of) Moscow.

**мост** (мо́ста́, loc -у́; pl -ы́) bridge. **мо́стик** bridge. **мости́ть** (-ощу́) impf (pf вы́~) pave. **мостки́** (-о́в) pl planked footway. **мостова́я** sb roadway; pavement. **мостово́й** bridge.

**мота́ть**[1] impf (pf мотну́ть, на~) wind, reel.

**мота́ть**[2] impf (pf про~) squander.

**мота́ться** impf dangle; wander; rush about.

**моти́в** motive; reason; tune, motif. **мотиви́ровать** impf & pf give reasons for, justify. **мотивиро́вка** reason(s); justification.

**мотну́ть** (-ну́, -нёшь) pf of мота́ть

**мото-** in comb motor-, engine-. **мотого́нки** (-нок) pl motorcycle races. ~пе́д moped. ~пехо́та motorized infantry. ~ро́ллер (motor-)scooter. ~ци́кл motor cycle.

**мото́к** (-тка́) skein, hank.

**мото́р** motor, engine. **моторист** motor-mechanic. **мото́рный** motor; engine.

**моты́га** hoe, mattock.

**мотылёк** (-лька́) butterfly, moth.

**мох** (мха or мо́ха, loc мху; pl мхи, мхов) moss. **мохна́тый** hairy, shaggy.

**моча́** urine.

**моча́лка** loofah.

**мочи́ть** (-чу́, -чишь) impf (pf за~, на~) wet, moisten; soak; ~ся (pf по~ся) urinate.

**мо́чка** ear lobe.

**мочь** (могу́, мо́жешь; мог, -ла́) impf (pf с~) be able; мо́жет (быть) perhaps.

**моше́нник** rogue. **моше́нничать** impf (pf с~) cheat, swindle. **моше́ннический** rascally.

**мо́шка** midge. **мошкара́** (swarm of) midges.

**мо́щность** power; capacity. **мо́щный** (-щен, -щна́, -о) powerful.

**мощу́** etc.: see мости́ть

**мощь** power.

**мо́ю** etc.: see мыть. **мо́ющий** washing; detergent.

**мрак** darkness, gloom. **мрако́бес** obscurantist.

**мра́мор** marble. **мра́морный** marble.

**мра́чный** dark; gloomy.

**мсти́тельный** vindictive. **мстить** (мщу) impf (pf ото~) take vengeance on; +за+acc avenge.

**муж** (pl -жья́ or -и́) husband. **мужа́ть** impf grow up; mature; ~ся take courage. **мужеподо́бный** mannish; masculine. **му́жественный** manly, steadfast. **му́жество** courage.

**мужи́к** (-á) peasant; fellow.

**мужско́й** masculine; male. **мужчи́на** *m* man.

**му́за** muse.

**музе́й** museum.

**му́зыка** music. **музыка́льный** musical. **музыка́нт** musician.

**му́ка**¹ torment.

**мука́**² flour.

**мультиплика́ция, мульти-фи́льм** cartoon film.

**му́мия** mummy.

**мунди́р** (full-dress) uniform.

**мундшту́к** (-á) mouthpiece; cigarette-holder.

**муниципа́льный** municipal.

**мураве́й** (-вья́) ant. **мура-ве́йник** ant-hill.

**мурлы́кать** (-ы́чу *or* -каю) *impf* purr.

**муска́т** nutmeg.

**му́скул** muscle. **му́скульный** muscular.

**му́сор** refuse; rubbish. **му́сор-ный я́щик** dustbin.

**мусульма́нин** (*pl* -ма́не, -ма́н), -а́нка Muslim.

**мути́ть** (мучу́, му́ти́шь) *impf* (*pf* вз~) make muddy; stir up, upset. **му́тный** (-тен, -тна́, -о) turbid, troubled; dull. **муть** sediment; murk.

**му́ха** fly.

**муче́ние** torment, torture. **му́ченик, му́ченица** martyr. **мучи́тельный** agonizing. **му́-чить** (-чу) *impf* (*pf* за~, из~) torment; harass; **~ся** torment o.s.; suffer agonies.

**мучно́й** flour, meal; starchy.

**мха** *etc.*: *see* **мох**

**мчать** (-чу) *impf* rush along, whirl along; **~ся** rush.

**мщу** *etc.*: *see* **мстить**

**мы** (нас, нам, на́ми, нас) *pron* we; **мы с ва́ми** you and I.

**мы́лить** *impf* (*pf* на~) soap;

**~ся** wash o.s. **мы́ло** (*pl* -á) soap. **мы́льница** soap-dish. **мы́льный** soap, soapy.

**мыс** cape, promontory.

**мы́сленный** mental. **мысли́-мый** conceivable. **мысли́тель** *m* thinker. **мы́слить** *impf* think; conceive. **мысль** thought; idea. **мы́слящий** thinking.

**мыть** (мо́ю) *impf* (*pf* вы́~, по~) wash; **~ся** wash (о.s.).

**мыча́ть** (-чу́) *impf* (*pf* про~) low, moo; bellow; mumble.

**мышело́вка** mousetrap.

**мы́шечный** muscular.

**мышле́ние** thinking, thought.

**мы́шца** muscle.

**мышь** (*gen pl* -е́й) mouse.

**мэр** mayor. **мэ́рия** town hall.

**мя́гкий** (-гок, -гка́, -о) soft; mild; **~ знак** soft sign, the letter ь. **мя́гче** *comp of* **мя́гкий, мя́гко. мя́коть** fleshy part, flesh; pulp.

**мяси́стый** fleshy; meaty. **мяс-ни́к** (-á) butcher. **мясно́й** meat. **мя́со** meat; flesh. **мясо-ру́бка** mincer.

**мя́та** mint; peppermint.

**мяте́ж** (-á) mutiny, revolt. **мя-те́жник** mutineer, rebel. **мя-те́жный** rebellious; restless.

**мя́тный** mint, peppermint.

**мять** (мну, мнёшь) *impf* (*pf* из~, раз~, с~) work up; knead; crumple; **~ся** become crumpled; crush (easily).

**мяу́кать** *impf* miaow.

**мяч** (-á), **мя́чик** ball.

# Н

**на**¹ *prep* I. +*acc* on; on to, to; into; at; till, until; for; by. II. +*prep* on, upon; in; at.

**на²** *partl* here; here you are.

**наба́вить** (-влю) *pf*, **набавля́ть** *impf* add (to), increase.

**наба́т** alarm-bell.

**набе́г** raid, foray.

**набекре́нь** *adv* aslant.

**на|бели́ть** (-е́лишь) *pf*. **на́бело** *adv* with corrections.

**на́бережная** *sb* embankment, quay.

**наберу́** *etc.*: *see* набра́ть

**набива́ть(ся** *impf of* наби́ть(ся. **наби́вка** stuffing, padding; (textile) printing.

**набира́ть(ся** *impf of* набра́ть(ся

**наби́тый** packed, stuffed; crowded. **наби́ть** (-бью, -бьёшь) *pf* (*impf* набива́ть) stuff, pack, fill; print; smash; hammer, drive; **~ся** crowd in.

**наблюда́тель** *m* observer. **наблюда́тельный** observant; observation. **наблюда́ть** *impf* observe, watch; **+за**+*instr* look after; supervise. **наблюде́ние** observation; supervision.

**на́божный** devout, pious.

**на́бок** *adv* on one side, crooked.

**наболе́вший** sore, painful.

**набо́р** recruiting; collection, set; type-setting. **набра́сывать(ся** *impf of* наброса́ть, набро́сить(ся

**набра́ть** (-беру́, -берёшь; -а́л, -а́, -о) *pf* (*impf* набира́ть) gather; enlist; compose, set up; **~** но́мер dial a number; **~ся** assemble, collect; +*gen* find, acquire, pick up; **~ся** сме́лости pluck up courage.

**набрести́** (-еду́, -дёшь; -ёл, -ела́) *pf* **+на**+*acc* come across.

**наброса́ть** *pf* (*impf* набра́сывать) throw (down); sketch; jot down. **набро́сить** (-о́шу) *pf*

(*impf* набра́сывать) throw; **~ся** throw o.s.; **~ся на** attack.

**набро́сок** (-ска) sketch, draft.

**набуха́ть** *impf*, **набу́хнуть** (-нет; -ух) *pf* swell.

**набью́** *etc.*: *see* наби́ть

**наважде́ние** delusion.

**нава́ливать** *impf*, **навали́ть** (-лю́, -лишь) *pf* heap, pile up; load; **~ся** lean; **+на**+*acc* fall (up)on.

**наведе́ние** laying (on); placing.

**наведу́** *etc.*: *see* навести́

**наве́к, наве́ки** *adv* for ever.

**навёл** *etc.*: *see* навести́

**наве́рно, наве́рное** *adv* probably. **наверняка́** *adv* certainly, for sure.

**наверста́ть** *pf* (*impf* навёрстывать** *impf* make up for.

**наве́рх** *adv* up(wards); upstairs. **наверху́** *adv* above; upstairs.

**наве́с** awning.

**наве́сить** (-е́шу) *pf* (*impf* наве́шивать) hang (up). **навесно́й** hanging.

**навести́** (-еду́, -едёшь; -вёл, -á) *pf* (*impf* наводи́ть) direct; aim; cover (with), spread; introduce; bring; make.

**навести́ть** (-ещу́) *pf* (*impf* навеща́ть) visit.

**навеша́ть** *pf*, **наве́шивать¹** *impf* hang (out); weigh out.

**наве́шивать²** *impf of* наве́сить. **навеща́ть** *impf of* навести́ть

**на́взничь** *adv* backwards, on one's back.

**навзры́д** *adv*: пла́кать **~** sob.

**навига́ция** navigation.

**нависа́ть** *impf*, **нави́снуть** (-нет; -ви́с) *pf* overhang, hang (over); threaten. **нави́сший** beetling.

навлека́ть *impf*, навле́чь (-еку́, -ечёшь; -ёк, -ла́) *pf* bring, draw; incur.

наводи́ть (-ожу́, -о́дишь) *impf of* навести́; наводя́щий вопро́с leading question. наво́дка aiming; applying.

наводне́ние flood. наводни́ть *pf*, наводня́ть *impf* flood; inundate.

наво́з dung, manure.

на́волочка pillowcase.

на|вра́ть (-ру́, -рёшь; -а́л, -а́, -о) *pf* tell lies, romance; talk nonsense; +в+*prep* make mistake(s) in.

навреди́ть (-ежу́) *pf*+*dat* harm.

навсегда́ *adv* for ever.

навстре́чу *adv* to meet; идти́ ~ to meet; meet halfway.

навы́ворот *adv* inside out; back to front.

на́вык experience, skill.

навы́нос *adv* to take away.

навы́пуск *adv* worn outside.

навью́чивать *impf*, на|вью́чить (-чу) *pf* load.

навяза́ть (-яжу́, -я́жешь) *pf*, навя́зывать *impf* tie, fasten; thrust, foist; ~ся thrust o.s.

навя́зчивый importunate; obsessive.

на|га́дить (-а́жу) *pf*.

нага́н revolver.

нагиба́ть(ся *impf of* нагну́ть(ся

нагишо́м *adv* stark naked.

нагле́ц (-а́) impudent fellow. на́глость impudence. на́глый (нагл, -а́, -о) impudent.

нагля́дный clear, graphic; visual.

нагна́ть (-гоню́, -го́нишь; -а́л, -а́, -о) *pf* (*impf* нагоня́ть) overtake, catch up (with); inspire, arouse.

нагнести́ (-ету́, -етёшь) *pf*,

нагнета́ть *impf* compress; supercharge.

нагное́ние suppuration. нагнои́ться *pf* suppurate.

нагну́ть (-ну́, -нёшь) *pf* (*impf* нагиба́ть) bend; ~ся bend, stoop.

нагова́ривать *impf*, наговори́ть *pf* slander; talk a lot (of); record.

наго́й (наг, -а́, -о) naked, bare.

на́голо *adv* naked, bare.

нагоня́ть *impf of* нагна́ть

нагора́ть *impf*, нагоре́ть (-ри́т) *pf* be consumed; *impers*+*dat* be scolded.

наго́рный upland, mountain; mountainous.

нагота́ nakedness, nudity.

награ́бить (-блю) *pf* amass by dishonest means.

награ́да reward; decoration; prize. награди́ть (-ажу́) *pf*, награжда́ть *impf* reward; decorate; award prize to.

нагрева́тельный heating. нагрева́ть *impf*, нагре́ть (-е́ю) *pf* warm, heat; ~ся get hot, warm up.

нагроможда́ть *impf*, на|громозди́ть (-зжу́) *pf* heap up, pile up. нагроможде́ние heaping up; conglomeration.

на|грубить (-блю́) *pf*.

нагружа́ть *impf*, на|грузи́ть (-ужу́, -у́зишь) *pf* load; ~ся load o.s. нагру́зка loading; load; work; commitments.

нагря́нуть (-ну) *pf* appear unexpectedly.

над, надо *prep*+*instr* over, above; on, at.

надави́ть (-влю́, -вишь) *pf*, нада́вливать *impf* press; squeeze out; crush.

надба́вка addition, increase.

надбавля́ть *impf*, надви́нуть

(-ну) *pf* move, pull, push; ~**ся** approach.

**на́двое** *adv* in two.

**надгро́бие** *epitaph*. **надгро́бный** (*on or over a*) grave.

**надева́ть** *impf of* наде́ть

**наде́жда** hope. **надёжность** reliability. **надёжный** reliable.

**наде́л** allotment.

**наде́лать** *pf* make; cause; do. **надели́ть** (-лю́, -ли́шь) *pf*, **наде́лять** *impf* endow, provide.

**наде́ть** (-е́ну) *pf* (*impf* **надева́ть**) put on.

**наде́яться** (-е́юсь) *impf* (*pf* по~) hope; rely.

**надзира́тель** *m* overseer, supervisor. **надзира́ть** *impf* +*за*+*instr* supervise, oversee. **надзо́р** supervision; surveillance.

**надла́мывать(ся** *impf of* надломи́ть(ся

**надлежа́щий** fitting, proper, appropriate. **надлежи́т** (-жа́ло) *impers* (+*dat*) it is necessary, required.

**надло́м** break; crack; breakdown. **надломи́ть** (-млю́, -мишь) *pf* (*impf* **надла́мывать**) break; crack; breakdown. ~**ся** break, crack, breakdown. **надло́мленный** broken.

**надме́нный** haughty, arrogant.

**на́до**[1] (+*dat*) it is necessary; I (*etc.*) must, ought to; I (*etc.*) need. **на́добность** necessity, need.

**на́до**[2]: *see* над.

**надоеда́ть** *impf*, **надое́сть** (-е́м, -е́шь, -е́ст, -еди́м) *pf* +*dat* bore, pester. **надое́дливый** boring, tiresome.

**надо́лго** *adv* for a long time.

**надорва́ть** (-ву́, -вёшь; -а́л, -а́, -о) *pf* (*impf* **надрыва́ть**) tear;

strain; ~**ся** tear; overstrain o.s.

**на́дпись** inscription.

**надре́з** cut, incision. **надре́зать** (-е́жу) *pf*, **надреза́ть** *impf* make an incision in.

**надруга́тельство** outrage. **надруга́ться** *pf* +*над*+*instr* outrage, insult.

**надры́в** tear; strain; breakdown; outburst. **надрыва́ть(ся** *impf of* надорва́ть(ся. **надры́вный** hysterical; heartrending.

**надста́вить** (-влю) *pf*, **надставля́ть** *impf* lengthen.

**надстра́ивать** *impf*, **надстро́ить** (-о́ю) *pf* build on top; extend upwards. **надстро́йка** building upwards; superstructure.

**надува́тельство** swindle. **надува́ть(ся** *impf of* наду́ть(ся. **надувно́й** pneumatic, inflatable.

**наду́манный** far-fetched.

**наду́тый** swollen; haughty; sulky. **наду́ть** (-у́ю) *pf* (*impf* **надува́ть**) inflate; swindle; ~**ся** swell out; sulk.

**на**|**души́ть(ся** (-шу́(сь, -ши́шь(ся) *pf*

**наеда́ться** *impf of* нае́сться

**наедине́** *adv* privately, alone.

**нае́зд** flying visit; raid. **нае́здник, -ица** rider. **наезжа́ть** *impf of* нае́здить, нае́хать; pay occasional visits.

**наём** (на́йма) hire; renting; взять в ~ rent; сдать в ~ let. **наёмник** hireling; mercenary. **наёмный** hired, rented.

**нае́сться** (-е́мся, -е́шься, -е́стся, -еди́мся) *pf* (*impf* **наеда́ться**) eat one's fill; stuff o.s.

**нае́хать** (-е́ду) *pf* (*impf* **наезжа́ть**) arrive unexpectedly;

**+на**+*acc* run into, collide with.
**нажа́ть** (-жму́, -жмёшь) *pf* (*impf* **нажима́ть**) press; put pressure (on).
**наждáк** (-á) emery. **наждáчная бумáга** emery paper.
**нажи́ва** profit, gain.
**наживáть(ся** *impf of* **нажи́ть(ся**
**нажи́м** pressure; clamp. **нажимáть** *impf of* **нажáть**.
**нажи́ть** (-иву́, -ивёшь; нáжил, -á, -о) *pf* (*impf* **нажива́ть**) acquire; contract, incur; **~ся** (-жи́лся, -áсь) get rich.
**нажму́** *etc.: see* **нажáть**
**назáвтра** *adv* (the) next day.
**назáд** *adv* back(wards); (тому́) ~ ago.
**назвáние** name; title. **назвáть** (-зову́, -зовёшь; -áл, -á, -о) *pf* (*impf* **называ́ть**) call, name; **~ся** be called.
**назéмный** ground, surface.
**нáзло́** *adv* out of spite; to spite.
**назначáть** *impf*, **назна́чить** (-чу) *pf* appoint; fix, set; prescribe. **назначéние** appointment; fixing, setting; prescription.
**назову́** *etc.: see* **назвáть**
**назо́йливый** importunate.
**назревáть** *impf*, **назре́ть** (-éет) *pf* ripen, mature; become imminent.
**называ́емый:** так ~ so-called. **называ́ть(ся** *impf of* **назвáть(ся**
**наибо́лее** *adv* (the) most. **наибóльший** greatest, biggest.
**наи́вный** naive.
**наивы́сший** highest.
**наигрáть** *pf*, **наи́грывать** *impf* win; play, pick out.
**наизнáнку** *adv* inside out.
**наизу́сть** *adv* by heart.
**наилу́чший** best.

**наименовáние** name; title.
**нáискось** *adv* obliquely.
**найму́** *etc.: see* **наня́ть**
**найти́** (-йду́, -йдёшь; нашёл, -шлá, -шло́) *pf* (*impf* **находи́ть**) find; **~сь** be found; be, be situated.
**наказáние** punishment. **наказáть** (-ажу́, -áжешь) *pf*, **нака́зывать** *impf* punish.
**накáл** incandescence. **накáливать** *impf*, **накали́ть** *pf*, **накаля́ть** *impf* heat; make red-hot; strain, make tense; **~ся** glow, become incandescent; become strained.
**накáливать(ся** *impf of* **наколо́ть(ся**
**накану́не** *adv* the day before.
**накáпливать(ся** *impf of* **накопи́ть(ся**
**накáчать** *pf*, **накáчивать** *impf* pump (up).
**наки́дка** cloak, cape; extra charge. **наки́нуть** (-ну) *pf*, **наки́дывать** *impf* throw; throw on; **~ся** throw o.s.; **~ся на** attack.
**нáкипь** scum; scale.
**накладнáя** *sb* invoice. **накладнóй** laid on; false; **~ые расхóды** overheads. **наклáдывать** *impf of* **наложи́ть** *pf.*
**наклéивать** *impf*, **наклéить** *pf* stick on. **наклéйка** sticking (on, up); label.
**наклóн** slope, incline. **наклонéние** inclination; mood. **наклони́ть** (-ню́, -нишь) *pf*, **наклоня́ть** *impf* incline, bend; **~ся** stoop, bend. **наклóнный** inclined, sloping.
**нако́лка** pinning; (*pinned-on*) ornament for hair; tattoo.
**наколо́ть**[1] (-лю́, -лешь) *pf*

(*impf* **нака́лывать**) prick;
pin; ~ся prick o.s.
**наколо́ть**[2] (-лю́, -лешь) *pf*
(*impf* **нака́лывать**) chop.
**наконе́ц** *adv* at last. **нако-
не́чник** tip, point.
**на|копи́ть** (-плю́, -пишь) *pf*,
**накопля́ть** *impf* (*impf also*
**нака́пливать**) accumulate;
~ся accumulate. **нако-
пле́ние** accumulation.
**на|копти́ть** (-пчу́) *pf*. **на|кор-
ми́ть** (-млю́, -мишь) *pf*.
**накра́сить** (-а́шу) *pf* paint;
make up. **на|кра́ситься**
(-а́шусь) *pf*.
**на|крахма́лить** *pf*.
**на|крени́ть** *pf*. **накрени́ться**
(-ни́тся) *pf*, **накреня́ться**
*impf* list.
**накрича́ть** (-чу́) *pf* (+**на**+*acc*)
shout (at).
**накро́ю** *etc.*: *see* **накры́ть**
**накрыва́ть** *impf*, **накры́ть**
(-ро́ю) *pf* cover; catch; ~ (на)
**стол** lay the table; ~ся cover
o.s.
**накури́ть** (-рю́, -ришь) *pf* fill
with smoke.
**налага́ть** *impf of* **наложи́ть**
**нала́дить** (-а́жу) *pf*, **нала́-
живать** *impf* regulate, put
right; organize; ~ся come
right; get going.
**на|лга́ть** (-лгу́, -лжёшь; -а́л,
-а́, -о) *pf*.
**нале́во** *adv* to the left.
**налёг** *etc.*: *see* **нале́чь. нале-
га́ть** *impf of* **нале́чь**
**налегке́** *adv* lightly dressed;
without luggage.
**налёт** raid; flight; thin coating.
**налета́ть**[1] *pf* have flown.
**налета́ть**[2] *impf*, **налете́ть**
(-лечу́) *pf* swoop down; come
flying; spring up.
**нале́чь** (-ля́гу, -ля́жешь; -лёг,

-ла́) *pf* (*impf* **налега́ть**) lean,
apply one's weight; lie; apply
o.s.
**налжёшь** *etc.*: *see* **налга́ть**
**налива́ть(ся** *impf of* **нали́ть-
(ся. нали́вка** fruit liqueur.
**нали́ть** (-лью́, -льёшь; на́лил,
-а́, -о) *pf* (*impf* **налива́ть**) pour
(out), fill; ~ся (-и́лся, -ась,
-ило́сь) pour in; ripen.
**налицо́** *adv* present; available.
**нали́чие** presence. **нали́чн|ый**
on hand; cash; ~ые (де́ньги)
ready money.
**нало́г** tax. **налогоплате́ль-
щик** taxpayer. **нало́женн|ый**:
~ым платежо́м C.O.D. на-
ложи́ть (-жу́, -жишь) *pf*
(*impf* **накла́дывать**, **нала-
га́ть**) lay (in, on), put (in, on);
apply; impose.
**налью́** *etc.*: *see* **нали́ть**
**наля́гу** *etc.*: *see* **нале́чь**
**нам** *etc.*: *see* **мы**
**на|ма́зать** (-а́жу) *pf*, **нама́-
зывать** *impf* oil, grease;
smear, spread.
**нама́тывать** *impf of* **намо-
та́ть. нама́чивать** *impf of*
**намочи́ть**
**намёк** hint. **намека́ть** *impf*,
**намекну́ть** (-ну́, -нёшь) *pf*
hint.
**намерева́ться** *impf* +*inf* intend to. **наме́рен** *predic*: я
~(а)+*inf* I intend to. **наме́-
рение** intention. **наме́рен-
ный** intentional.
**на|мета́ть**[1] *pf*. **на|ме́тить**[1] (-е́чу)
*pf*.
**наме́тить**[2] (-е́чу) *pf* (*impf* **на-
меча́ть**) plan; outline; nomi-
nate; ~ся be outlined, take
shape.
**намно́го** *adv* much, far.
**намока́ть** *impf*, **намо́кнуть**
(-ну) *pf* get wet.

**намо́рдник** muzzle.

**на|мо́рщить(ся** (-щу(сь) *pf.*

**на|мота́ть** *pf* (*impf also* нама́тывать) wind, reel.

**на|мочи́ть** (-очу́, -о́чишь) *pf* (*impf also* нама́чивать) wet; soak; splash, spill.

**намы́ливать** *impf,* **на|мы́лить** *pf* soap.

**нанести́** (-су́, -сёшь; -ёс, -ла́) *pf* (*impf* наноси́ть) carry, bring; draw, plot; inflict.

**на|низа́ть** (-ижу́, -и́жешь) *pf,* **нани́зывать** *impf* string, thread.

**нанима́тель** *m* tenant; employer. **нанима́ть(ся** *impf of* наня́ть(ся

**наноси́ть** (-ошу́, -о́сишь) *impf of* нанести́

**наня́ть** (найму́, -мёшь; на́нял, -а́, -о) *pf* (*impf* нанима́ть) hire; rent; **~ся** get a job.

**наоборо́т** *adv* on the contrary; back to front; the other, the wrong, way (round); vice versa.

**наотма́шь** *adv* violently.

**наотре́з** *adv* flatly, point-blank.

**напада́ть** *impf of* напа́сть. **напада́ющий** *sb* forward. **нападе́ние** attack; forwards. **напа́рник** co-driver, (work)-mate.

**напа́сть** (-аду́, -адёшь; -а́л) *pf* (*impf* напада́ть) на+*acc* attack; descend on; seize; come upon. **напа́сть** misfortune.

**напе́в** tune. **напева́ть** *impf of* напе́ть

**наперебо́й** *adv* interrupting, vying with, one another.

**наперёд** *adv* in advance.

**напереко́р** *adv+dat* in defiance of, counter to.

**напёрсток** (-тка) thimble.

**напе́ть** (-по́ю, -по́ешь) *pf* (*impf* напева́ть) sing; hum, croon.

**на|печа́тать(ся** *pf.* **напива́ться** *impf of* напи́ться

**напи́льник** file.

**на|писа́ть** (-ишу́, -и́шешь) *pf*

**напи́ток** (-тка) drink. **напи́ться** (-пью́сь, -пьёшься; -и́лся, -а́сь, -и́лось) *pf* (*impf* напива́ться) quench one's thirst, drink; get drunk.

**напиха́ть** *pf,* **напи́хивать** *impf* cram, stuff.

**на|плева́ть** (-лю́ю, -лю́ешь) *pf,* **~!** to hell with it! who cares?

**наплы́в** influx; accumulation; canker.

**наплыю́** *etc.: see* наплева́ть

**напова́л** *adv* outright.

**наподо́бие** *prep+gen* like, not unlike.

**на|пои́ть** (-ою́, -о́ишь) *pf.*

**напока́з** *adv* for show.

**наполни́тель** *m* filler. **наполни́ть(ся** *pf,* наполня́ть(ся *impf)* fill.

**наполови́ну** *adv* half.

**напомина́ние** reminder. **напомина́ть** *impf,* **напо́мнить** *pf* (+*dat*) remind.

**напо́р** pressure. **напо́ристый** energetic, pushing.

**напосле́док** *adv* in the end; after all.

**напою́** *etc.: see* напе́ть, напои́ть

**напр.** *abbr* (*of* наприме́р) e.g., for example.

**напра́вить** (-влю) *pf,* **направля́ть** *impf* direct; send; sharpen; **~ся** make (for), go (towards). **направле́ние** direction; trend; warrant; order. **напра́вленный** purposeful.

**напра́во** *adv* to the right.

**напра́сно** *adv* in vain, for nothing; unjustly, mistakenly.

**напра́шиваться** *impf of* напроси́ться

**наприме́р** for example.
**на|прока́зничать** *pf*.
**напрока́т** *adv* for, on, hire.
**напролёт** *adv* through, without a break.
**напроло́м** *adv* straight, regardless of obstacles.
**напроси́ться** (-ошу́сь, -о́сишься) *pf* (*impf* **напра́шиваться**) thrust o.s.; suggest itself; ~ **на** ask for, invite.
**напро́тив** *adv* opposite; on the contrary. **напро́тив** *prep+gen* opposite.
**напряга́ть(ся** *impf of* **напря́чь(ся. напряже́ние** tension; exertion; voltage. **напряжённый** tense; intense; intensive.
**напрями́к** *adv* straight (out).
**напря́чь** (-ягу́, -яжёшь; -яг, -ла́) *pf* (*impf* **напряга́ть**) strain; ~**ся** strain o.s.
**на|пуга́ть(ся** *pf*. **на|пу́дриться** *pf*.
**напуска́ть** *impf*, **напусти́ть** (-ущу́, -у́стишь) *pf* let in; let loose; ~**ся** +**на**+*acc* fly at, go for.
**напу́тать** *pf* +**в**+*prep* make a mess of.
**на|пыли́ть** *pf*.
**напью́сь** *etc*.: *see* **напи́ться**
**наравне́** *adv* level; equally.
**нараспа́шку** *adv* unbuttoned.
**нараста́ние** growth, accumulation. **нараста́ть** *impf*, **нарасти́** (-тёт; -ро́с, -ла́) *pf* grow; increase.
**нарасхва́т** *adv* very quickly, like hot cakes.
**нарва́ть¹** (-рву́, -рвёшь; -а́л, -а́, -о) *pf* (*impf* **нарыва́ть**) pick; tear off.
**нарва́ть²** (-вёт; -а́л, -а́, -о) *pf* (*impf* **нарыва́ть**) gather.
**нарва́ться** (-ву́сь, -вёшься;

-а́лся, -ала́сь, -а́ло́сь) *pf* (*impf* **нарыва́ться**) +**на**+*acc* run into, run up against.
**наре́зать** (-е́жу) *pf*, **нареза́ть** *impf* cut (up), slice, carve; thread, rifle.
**наре́чие¹** dialect.
**наре́чие²** adverb.
**на|рисова́ть** *pf*.
**нарко́з** narcosis. **наркома́н, -ма́нка** drug addict. **наркома́ния** drug addiction. **нарко́тик** narcotic.
**наро́д** people. **наро́дность** nationality; national character. **наро́дный** national; folk; popular; people's.
**наро́ст** *etc*.: *see* **нарасти́**
**наро́чно** *adv* on purpose, deliberately. **на́рочный** *sb* courier.
**нару́жность** exterior. **нару́жный** external, outward. **нару́жу** *adv* outside.
**нару́чник** handcuff. **нару́чный** wrist.
**наруше́ние** breach; infringement. **наруши́тель** *m* transgressor. **нару́шить** (-шу) *pf*, **наруша́ть** *impf* break; disturb, infringe, violate.
**нарци́сс** narcissus; daffodil.
**на́ры** (нар) *pl* plank-bed.
**нары́в** abscess, boil. **нарыва́ть(ся** *impf of* **нарва́ть(ся**
**наря́д¹** order, warrant.
**наря́д²** attire; dress. **наряди́ть** (-яжу́) *pf* (*impf* **наряжа́ть**) dress (up); ~**ся** dress up. **наря́дный** well-dressed.
**наряду́** *adv* alike, equally; side by side.
**наряжа́ть(ся** *impf of* **наряди́ть(ся. нас** *see* **мы**
**насади́ть** (-ажу́, -а́дишь) *pf*, **насажда́ть** *impf* (*impf also* **наса́живать**) plant; propa-

gate; implant. **наса́дка** setting, fixing. **насажде́ние** planting; plantation; propagation. **наса́живать** *impf of* **насади́ть**

**насеко́мое** *sb* insect.

**населе́ние** population. **населённость** density of population. **населённый** populated; ~ **пункт** settlement; built-up area. **насели́ть**, **население** *impf* settle, people.

**наси́лие** violence, force. **наси́ловать** *impf* (*pf* **из**~) coerce; rape. **наси́льно** *adv* with difficulty. **наси́льник** aggressor; rapist; violator. **наси́льно** *adv* by force. **наси́льственный** violent, forcible.

**наска́кивать** *impf of* **наскочи́ть**

**насквозь** *adv* through, throughout.

**наско́лько** *adv* how much?, how far?; as far as.

**наско́ро** *adv* hastily.

**наскочи́ть** (**-очу́**, **-о́чишь**) (*impf* **наска́кивать**) +**на**+*acc* run into, against, collide with; fly at.

**наску́чить** (**-чу**) *pf* bore.

**наслади́ться** (**-ажу́сь**) *pf*, **наслажда́ться** *impf* (+*instr*) enjoy, take pleasure. **наслажде́ние** pleasure, enjoyment.

**насле́дие** legacy; heritage. **насле́дить** (**-ежу́**) *pf*, **сле́дник** heir; successor. **насле́дница** heiress. **насле́дный** next in succession. **насле́довать** *impf* & *pf* (*pf also* **у**~) inherit, succeed to. **насле́дственность** heredity. **насле́дственный** hereditary, inherited. **насле́дство** inheritance; heritage.

**на́смерть** *adv* to (the) death. **на|смеши́ть** (**-шу́**) *pf* **насме́шка** mockery; gibe. **на-**

**смешли́вый** mocking.

**на́сморк** runny nose; cold.

**на|сори́ть** *pf*.

**насо́с** pump.

**на́спех** *adv* hastily.

**на|спле́тничать** *pf*. **наставля́ть** (**-таёт**) *impf of* **наста́ть**

**наставле́ние** exhortation; directions, manual.

**наста́вник** tutor, mentor.

**настава́ть**[1] *impf of* **настоя́ть**[1]. **наста́ивать**[2](**ся** *impf of* **настоя́ть**[2](**ся**

**наста́ть** (**-а́нет**) *pf* (*impf* **наставля́ть**) come, begin, set in.

**на́стежь** *adv* wide (open).

**настелю́** *etc.: see* **настла́ть**

**настига́ть** *impf of* **насти́гнуть**, **насти́чь** (**-и́гну**; **-и́г**) *pf* catch up with, overtake.

**насти́л** flooring, planking.

**настила́ть** *impf of* **настла́ть**

**насти́чь** *see* **настига́ть**

**настла́ть** (**-телю́**, **-те́лешь**) *pf* (*impf* **настила́ть**) lay, spread.

**насто́йка** liqueur, cordial.

**насто́йчивый** persistent; urgent.

**насто́лько** *adv* so, so much.

**насто́льный** table, desk; reference.

**настора́живать** *impf*, **насторожи́ть** (**-жу́**) *pf* set; prick up; ~**ся** prick up one's ears.

**насторо́женный** (**-ен**, **-енна**) guarded; alert.

**настоя́тельный** insistent; urgent. **настоя́ть**[1] (**-ою́**) *pf* (*impf* **наста́ивать**[1]) insist.

**настоя́ть**[2] (**-ою́**) *pf* (*impf* **наста́ивать**[2]) brew; ~**ся** draw, stand.

**настоя́щее** *sb* the present. **настоя́щий** (the) present, this; real, genuine.

**настра́ивать(ся** *impf of* **настро́ить(ся**

настри́чь (-игу́, -ижёшь; -и́г) pf shear, clip.

настрое́ние mood. настро́ить (-о́ю) pf (impf настра́ивать) tune (in); dispose; ~ся dispose o.s. настро́йка tuning. настро́йщик tuner.

на|строчи́ть (-чу́) pf.

наступа́тельный offensive. наступа́ть¹ impf of наступи́ть¹

наступа́ть² impf of наступи́ть². наступа́ющий¹ coming.

наступа́ющий² sb attacker.

наступи́ть¹ (-плю́, -пишь) pf (impf наступа́ть¹) tread; attack; advance.

наступи́ть² (-у́пит) pf (impf наступа́ть²) come, set in. наступле́ние¹ coming.

наступле́ние² offensive, attack.

насу́питься (-плюсь) pf, насу́пливаться impf frown.

на́сухо adv dry. насуши́ть (-шу́, -шишь) pf dry.

насу́щный urgent, vital; хлеб ~ daily bread.

насчёт prep+gen about, concerning; as regards. насчита́ть pf, насчи́тывать impf count; hold; ~ся +gen number.

насыпа́ть (-плю) pf, насыпа́ть impf pour in, on; fill; spread; heap up. на́сыпь embankment.

насы́тить (-ы́щу) pf, насыща́ть impf satiate; saturate; ~ся be full; be saturated.

ната́лкивать(ся impf of натолкну́ть(ся. ната́лпивать impf of натопи́ть

натаска́ть pf, ната́скивать impf train; coach, cram; bring in, lay in.

натвори́ть pf do, get up to.

натере́ть (-тру́, -трёшь; -тёр) pf (impf натира́ть) rub on, in; polish; chafe; grate; ~ся rub o.s.

на́тиск onslaught.

наткну́ться (-ну́сь, -нёшься) pf (impf натыка́ться) +на+acc run into; strike, stumble on.

натолкну́ть (-ну́, -нёшь) pf (impf ната́лкивать) push; lead; ~ся run against, across.

натопи́ть (-плю́, -пишь) pf (impf ната́лпивать) heat (up); stoke up; melt.

на|точи́ть (-чу́, -чишь) pf.

натоща́к adv on an empty stomach.

натра́вить (-влю́, -вишь) pf, натра́вливать impf, натравля́ть impf set on; stir up.

на|тренирова́ть(ся pf.

на́трий sodium.

нату́ра nature. натура́льный natural; genuine. нату́рщик, -щица artist's model.

натыка́ть(ся impf of наткну́ть(ся

натюрмо́рт still life.

натя́гивать impf, натяну́ть (-ну́, -нешь) pf stretch; draw; pull (on); ~ся stretch. натя́нутость tension. натя́нутый tight; strained.

науга́д adv at random.

нау́ка science; learning.

нау́тро adv (the) next morning.

на|учи́ть(ся (-чу́(сь, -чишь(ся) pf.

нау́чн|ый scientific; ~ая фанта́стика science fiction.

нау́шник ear-flap; ear-phone.

нафтали́н naphthalene.

наха́л, -ха́лка impudent creature. наха́льный impudent. наха́льство impudence.

нахвата́ть pf, нахва́тывать

*impf* pick up, get hold of; **~ся** +*gen* pick up.

**нахлёбник** hanger-on.

**нахлы́нуть** (-нет) *pf* well up; surge; gush.

**на|хму́рить(ся** *pf.*

**находи́ть(ся** (-ожу́(сь, -о́дишь(ся) *impf of* найти́(сь. **нахо́дка** find. **нахо́дчивый** resourceful, quick-witted.

**наце́ливать** *impf*, **наце́лить** *pf* aim; **~ся** (take) aim.

**наце́нка** surcharge, mark-up.

**наци́зм** Nazism. **национализа́ция** nationalization. **национализи́ровать** *impf & pf* nationalize. **национали́зм** nationalism. **националисти́ческий** nationalist(ic). **национа́льность** nationality; ethnic group. **национа́льный** national. **наци́ст**, **-и́стка** Nazi. **наци́стский** Nazi. **на́ция** nation. **нацме́н, -ме́нка** *abbr* member of national minority.

**нача́ло** beginning; origin; principle, basis. **нача́льник** head, chief; boss. **нача́льный** initial; primary. **нача́льство** the authorities; command. **нача́ть** (-чну́, -чнёшь; на́чал, -а́, -о) *pf* (*impf* **начина́ть**) begin; **~ся** begin.

**начерта́ть** *pf* trace, inscribe. **на|черти́ть** (-рчу́, -ртишь) *pf.*

**начина́ние** undertaking. **начина́ть(ся** *impf of* нача́ть(ся. **начина́ющий** *sb* beginner.

**начини́ть** *pf*, **начиня́ть** *impf* stuff, fill. **начи́нка** stuffing, filling.

**начи́стить** (-и́щу) *pf* (*impf* **начища́ть**) clean. **на́чисто** *adv* clean; flatly, decidedly; openly, frankly. **начистоту́**

*adv* openly, frankly.

**начи́танность** learning; wide reading. **начи́танный** well-read.

**начища́ть** *impf of* начи́стить

**наш** (-его) *m*, **на́ша** (-ей) *f*, **на́ше** (-его) *neut*, **на́ши** (-их) *pl*, *pron* our, ours.

**нашаты́рный спирт** ammonia. **нашаты́рь** (-я́) *m* salammoniac; ammonia.

**нашёл** *etc.: see* найти́

**наше́ствие** invasion.

**нашива́ть** *impf*, **наши́ть** (-шью, -шьёшь) *pf* sew on. **наши́вка** stripe, chevron; tab.

**нашлёпать** *impf* slap.

**нашуме́ть** (-млю) *pf* make a din; cause a sensation.

**нашью́** *etc.: see* наши́ть

**нащу́пать** *pf*, **нащу́пывать** *impf* grope for.

**на|электризова́ть** *pf.*

**наяву́** *adv* awake; in reality.

**не** *partl* not.

**не-** *pref* un-, in-, non-, mis-, dis-; -less; not. **неаккура́тный** careless; untidy; unpunctual. **небезразли́чный** not indifferent. **небезызве́стный** not unknown; notorious; well-known.

**небеса́** *etc.: see* не́бо². **небе́сный** heavenly; celestial.

**не-. неблагода́рный** ungrateful; thankless. **неблагонадёжный** unreliable. **неблагополу́чный** unsuccessful, bad, unfavourable. **неблагоприя́тный** unfavourable. **неблагоразу́мный** imprudent. **неблагоро́дный** ignoble, base.

**не́бо¹** palate.

**не́бо²** (*pl* -беса́, -бе́с) sky; heaven.

**не-. небога́тый** of modest

means, modest. **небольшо́й** small, not great; **с небольши́м** a little over.

**небосво́д** firmament. **небоскло́н** horizon. **небоскрёб** skyscraper.

**небо́сь** adv I dare say; probably.

**не-. небре́жный** careless. **небыва́лый** unprecedented; fantastic. **небыли́ца** fable, cock-and-bull story. **небытие́** non-existence. **небью́щийся** unbreakable. **нева́жно** adv not too well, indifferently. **нева́жный** unimportant; indifferent. **невдалеке́** adv not far away. **неве́дение** ignorance. **неве́домый** unknown; mysterious. **неве́жа** m & f boor, lout. **неве́жда** m & f ignoramus. **неве́жественный** ignorant. **неве́жество** ignorance. **неве́жливый** rude. **невели́кий** (-и́к, -á, -и́ко) small. **неве́рие** unbelief, atheism; scepticism. **неве́рный** (-рен, -рнá, -о) incorrect, wrong; inaccurate, unsteady; unfaithful. **невероя́тный** improbable; incredible. **неве́рующий** sb unbeliever. **невесёлый** joyless, sad. **невесо́мый** weightless; imponderable.

**неве́ста** fiancée; bride. **неве́стка** daughter-in-law; brother's wife, sister-in-law.

**не-. невзго́да** adversity. **невзира́я на** prep+acc regardless of. **невзнача́й** adv by chance. **невзра́чный** unattractive, plain. **неви́данный** unprecedented, unheard-of. **неви́димый** invisible. **неви́нность** innocence. **неви́нный** innocent. **неви-**

**вменя́емый** irresponsible. **невмеша́тельство** non-intervention; non-interference. **невмоготу́, невмо́чь** advs unbearable, too much (for). **невнима́тельный** inattentive, thoughtless.

**не́вод** seine(-net).

**не-. невозврати́мый, невозвра́тный** irrevocable, irrecoverable. **невозмо́жный** impossible. **невозмути́мый** imperturbable.

**нево́льник, -ница** slave. **нево́льный** involuntary; unintentional; forced. **нево́ля** captivity; necessity.

**не-. невообрази́мый** unimaginable, inconceivable. **невооружённый** unarmed; **~ым гла́зом** with the naked eye. **невоспи́танный** ill-bred, bad-mannered. **невоспламеня́ющийся** non-flammable. **невосприи́мчивый** unreceptive; immune.

**невралги́я** neuralgia. **невреди́мый** safe, unharmed. **невро́з** neurosis. **невроло́гический** neurological. **невроти́ческий** neurotic.

**не-. невы́годный** disadvantageous; unprofitable. **невы́держанный** lacking self-control; unmatured. **невыноси́мый** unbearable. **невыполни́мый** impracticable. **невысо́кий** (-о́к, -á, -о́ко) low; short.

**не́га** luxury; bliss.

**негати́в** negative.

**не́где** adv (there is) nowhere.

**не-. неги́бкий** (-бок, -бкá, -о) inflexible, stiff. **негла́сный** secret. **неглубо́кий** (-о́к, -á, -о) shallow. **неглу́пый** (-у́п, -á, -о) sensible, quite intelligent. **него́дный** (-ден, -днá, -о) un-

fit, unsuitable; worthless. не-
года́ние indignation. не-
года́ть *impf* be indignant.
него́дяй *scoundrel.* него-
степрии́мный inhospitable.
**негр** Negro, black man.
**негра́мотность** illiteracy. не-
**гра́мотный** illiterate.
**негритя́нка** Negress, black
woman. **негритя́нский** Negro.

не-. **негро́мкий** (-мок, -мка́,
-о) quiet. **неда́вний** recent.
**неда́вно** *adv* recently. **неда-**
**лёкий** (-ёк, -á, -ёкó) near;
short; not bright, dull-witted.
**недалеко́** *adv* not far, near.
**неда́ром** *adv* not for nothing, not without reason. **не-**
**дви́жимость** real estate. **не-**
**дви́жимый** immovable. **не-**
**двусмы́сленный** unequivocal. **неде́йствительный**
ineffective; invalid. **недели́-**
**мый** indivisible.

**неде́льный** of a week, week's.
**неде́ля** week.

не-. **недёшево** *adv* dear(ly).
**недоброжела́тель** *m* ill-
wisher. **недоброжела́тель-**
**ность** hostility. **недоброка́-**
**чественный** of poor quality.
**недобросо́вестный** unscrupulous; careless. **недо́брый**
(-бр, -бра́, -о) unkind; bad.
**недове́рие** distrust. **недо-**
**ве́рчивый** distrustful **недо-**
**во́льный** dissatisfied. **недо-**
**во́льствие** dissatisfaction. **недо-**
**едáние** malnutrition. **не-**
**доедáть** *impf* be undernourished.

не-. **недо́лгий** (-лог, -лга́, -о)
short, brief. **недо́лго** *adv* not
long. **недолгове́чный** short-
lived. **недомогáние** indispo-
sition. **недомогáть** *impf* be

unwell. **недомы́слие** thought-
lessness. **недоно́шенный** premature. **недооце́нивать** *impf,*
**недооцени́ть** (-ню́, -нишь) *pf*
underestimate; underrate. **не-**
**дооце́нка** underestimation.
**недопусти́мый** inadmissible, intolerable. **недоразу-**
**ме́ние** misunderstanding. **не-**
**дорого́й** (-до́рог, -á, -о) inexpensive. **недосмотре́ть**
(-рю́,-ришь) *pf* overlook. **не-**
**доспа́ть** (-плю́ -пи́шь, -á, -о) *pf*
(*impf* **недосыпа́ть**) not have
enough sleep.

**недоставáть** (-таёт) *impf,*
**недостáть** (-áнет) *pf impers*
be missing, be lacking. **не-**
**достáток** (-тка) shortage,
deficiency. **недостáточный**
insufficient, inadequate. **недо-**
**стáча** lack, shortage.

не-. **недостижи́мый** unattainable. **недосто́йный** unworthy, недосту́пный inaccessible. **недосчита́ться** *pf,*
**недосчи́тываться** *impf*
miss, find missing, be short
(of). **недосыпáть** *impf of*
**недоспáть**. **недосяга́емый**
unattainable.

**недоумевáть** *impf* be at a
loss, be bewildered. **недо-**
**уме́ние** bewilderment.

не-. **недоу́чка** *m & f* half-
educated person. **недочёт**
deficit; defect.

**не́дра** (недр) *pl* depths, heart,
bowels.

не-. **не́друг** enemy. **недружe-**
**любный** unfriendly.

**неду́г** illness, disease.

**недурно́й** not bad; not bad-
looking.

не-. **неесте́ственный** unnatural. **нежда́нный** unexpected. **нежелáние** unwill-

ingness. **нежела́тельный** undesirable.

**не́жели** than.

**женена́тый** unmarried.

**не́женка** m & f mollycoddle.

**нежило́й** uninhabited; uninhabitable.

**не́житься** (-жусь) impf luxuriate, bask. **не́жность** tenderness; pl endearments. **не́жный** tender; affectionate.

**не-. незабве́нный** unforgettable. **незабу́дка** forget-me-not. **незабыва́емый** unforgettable. **незави́симость** independence. **незави́симый** independent. **незадо́лго** adv not long. **незаконнорождённый** illegitimate. **незако́нный** illegal, illicit; illegitimate. **незако́нченный** unfinished. **незамени́мый** irreplaceable. **незамерза́ющий** ice-free; anti-freeze. **незаме́тный** imperceptible. **незаму́жняя** unmarried. **незапа́мятный** immemorial. **незаслу́женный** unmerited. **незауря́дный** uncommon, outstanding.

**не́зачем** adv there is no need.

**не-. незащищённый** unprotected. **незва́ный** uninvited. **нездоро́виться** impf, impers +dat: мне **нездоро́вится** I don't feel well. **нездоро́вый** unhealthy. **нездоро́вье** ill health. **незнако́мец** (-мца), **незнако́мка** stranger. **незнако́мый** unknown, unfamiliar. **незна́ние** ignorance. **незначи́тельный** insignificant. **незре́лый** unripe, immature. **незри́мый** invisible. **незы́блемый** unshakable, firm. **неизбе́жность** inevitability. **неизбе́жный** inevitable. **не-**

**изве́данный** unknown. **неизве́стность** uncertainty; ignorance; obscurity. **неизве́стный** unknown; sb stranger.

**не-. неизлечи́мый** incurable. **неизме́нный** unchanged, unchanging; devoted. **неизмери́мый** unalterable. **неизмери́мый** immeasurable, immense. **неизу́ченный** unexplored. **неиму́щий** poor. **неинтере́сный** uninteresting. **неи́скренний** insincere. **неиску́шённый** inexperienced, unsophisticated. **неисполни́мый** impracticable. **неисправи́мый** incorrigible; irreparable. **неиспра́вный** out of order, defective; careless. **неиссле́дованный** unexplored. **неисся́каемый** inexhaustible. **неи́стовство** fury, frenzy; atrocity. **неи́стовый** furious, frenzied, uncontrolled. **неистощи́мый**, **неисчерпа́емый** inexhaustible. **неисчисли́мый** innumerable.

**нейло́н**, **нейло́новый** nylon. **нейро́н** neuron.

**нейтрализа́ция** neutralization. **нейтрализова́ть** impf & pf neutralize. **нейтралите́т** neutrality. **нейтра́льный** neutral. **нейтро́н** neutron.

**неквалифици́рованный** unskilled.

**не́кий** pron a certain, some.

**не́когда**[1] adv once, formerly.

**не́когда**[2] there is no time; мне ~ I have no time.

**не́кого** (не́кому, не́кого, не́ о ком) pron there is nobody.

**некомпете́нтный** not competent, unqualified.

**не́котор|ый** *pron* some; **~ые** *sb pl* some (people).

**некраси́вый** plain, ugly; not nice.

**некроло́г** obituary.

**некста́ти** *adv* at the wrong time, out of place.

**не́кто** *pron* somebody; a certain.

**не́куда** *adv* there is nowhere. **не-. некульту́рный** uncivilized, uncultured. **некуря́щий** *sb* non-smoker. **нела́дный** wrong. **нелега́льный** illegal. **нелёгкий** not easy; heavy. **неле́пость** absurdity, nonsense. **неле́пый** absurd. **нело́вкий** awkward. **нело́вкость** awkwardness.

**нельзя́** *adv* it is impossible; it is not allowed.

**не-. нелюби́мый** unloved. **нелюди́мый** unsociable. **нема́ло** *adv* quite a lot (of). **нема́лый** considerable. **неме́дленно** *adv* immediately. **неме́дленный** immediate.

**неме́ть** (-е́ю) *impf* (*pf* о~) become dumb. **не́мец** (-мца) German. **неме́цкий** German.

**немину́емый** inevitable.

**не́мка** German woman.

**немно́гие** *sb pl* (a) few. **немно́го** *adv* a little; some; a few. **немно́жко** *adv* a little.

**немо́й** (нем, -а́, -о) dumb, mute, silent. **немота́** dumbness.

**не́мощный** feeble.

**немы́слимый** unthinkable.

**ненави́деть** (-и́жу) *impf* hate. **ненави́стный** hated; hateful. **не́нависть** hatred.

**не-. ненагля́дный** beloved. **ненадёжный** unreliable. **ненадо́лго** *adv* for a short time. **нена́стье** bad weather. **ненасы́тный** insatiable. **ненор-**

**ма́льный** abnormal. **нену́жный** unnecessary, unneeded. **необду́манный** thoughtless, hasty. **необеспе́ченный** without means, unprovided for. **необита́емый** uninhabited. **необозри́мый** boundless, immense. **необосно́ванный** unfounded, groundless. **необрабо́танный** uncultivated; crude; unpolished. **необразо́ванный** uneducated.

**необходи́мость** necessity. **необходи́мый** necessary.

**не-. необъясни́мый** inexplicable. **необъя́тный** immense. **необыкнове́нный** unusual. **необыча́йный** extraordinary. **необы́чный** unusual. **необяза́тельный** optional. **неограни́ченный** unlimited. **неоднокра́тный** repeated. **неодобри́тельный** disapproving. **неодушевлённый** inanimate.

**неожи́данность** unexpectedness. **неожи́данный** unexpected, sudden.

**неокласси́цизм** neoclassicism. **не-. неоко́нченный** unfinished. **неопла́ченный** unpaid. **неопра́вданный** unjustified. **неопределённый** indefinite; infinitive; vague. **неопровержи́мый** irrefutable. **неопублико́ванный** unpublished. **нео́пытный** inexperienced. **неоргани́ческий** inorganic. **неоспори́мый** incontestable. **неосторо́жный** careless. **неосуществи́мый** impracticable. **неотврати́мый** inevitable.

**нео́ткуда** *adv* there is nowhere.

**не-. неотло́жный** urgent. **неотрази́мый** irresistible. **неот-**

**сту́пный** persistent. **неотъ-** **е́млемый** inalienable. **не-** **официа́льный** unofficial. **неохо́та** reluctance. **неохо́т-** **но** adv reluctantly. **неоцени́мый** inestimable, invaluable. **непарти́йный** non-party; unbefitting a member of the (Communist) Party. **не-** **переводи́мый** untranslatable. **непереходный** intransitive. **неплатёжеспосо́б-** **ный** insolvent.

**не-. неплохо** adv not badly, quite well. **неплохо́й** not bad, quite good. **неповинове́ние** insubordination. **неповоро́т-** **ливый** clumsy. **неповтори́-** **мый** inimitable, unique. **непого́да** bad weather. **непо-** **греши́мый** infallible. **непо-** **далёку** adv not far (away). **неподви́жный** motionless, immovable; fixed. **непод-** **де́льный** genuine; sincere. **неподку́пный** incorruptible. **неподража́емый** inimitable. **неподходя́щий** unsuitable, inappropriate. **непоколеби́-** **мый** unshakable, steadfast. **непоко́рный** recalcitrant, unruly.

**не-. неполадки** (-док) pl defects. **неполноце́нность**; **ко́мплекс неполноце́нности** inferiority complex. **неполно-** **це́нный** defective; inadequate. **непо́лный** incomplete; not (a) full. **непоме́рный** excessive. **непонима́ние** incomprehension, lack of understanding. **непоня́тный** incomprehensible. **непопра́вимый** irreparable. **непоря́док** (-дка) disorder. **непоря́дочный** dishonourable. **непосе́да** m &

f fidget. **непоси́льный** beyond one's strength. **непо-** **сле́довательный** inconsistent. **непослуша́ние** disobedience. **непослу́шный** disobedient. **непосре́дствен-** **ный** immediate; spontaneous. **непостижи́мый** incomprehensible. **непостоя́нный** inconstant, changeable. **непо-** **хо́жий** unlike; different.

**не-. непра́вда** untruth. **не-** **правдоподо́бный** improbable. **непра́вильно** adv wrong. **непра́вильный** irregular; wrong. **непра́вый** wrong. **непракти́чный** unpractical. **непревзойдён-** **ный** unsurpassed. **непред-** **ви́денный** unforeseen. **не-** **предубеждённый** unprejudiced. **непредусмо́тренный** unforeseen. **непредусмо-** **три́тельный** short-sighted. **непрекло́нный** inflexible; adamant. **непрело́жный** immutable.

**не-. непреме́нно** adv without fail. **непреме́нный** indispensable. **непреодоли́мый** insuperable. **непререка́емый** unquestionable. **непреры́в-** **но** adv continuously. **непре-** **ры́вный** continuous. **непре-** **ста́нный** incessant. **непри-** **ве́тливый** unfriendly; bleak. **непривлека́тельный** unattractive. **непривы́чный** unaccustomed. **непригля́дный** unattractive. **неприго́дный** unfit, useless. **неприе́мле-** **мый** unacceptable. **непри-** **коснове́нность** inviolability, immunity. **неприкосно-** **ве́нный** inviolable; reserve. **неприли́чный** indecent. **не-** **примири́мый** irreconcilable.

uble. **неразры́вный** indissoluble. **неразу́мный** unwise; unreasonable. **нераствори́мый** insoluble.

**непринуждённый** unconstrained; relaxed. **неприспосо́бленный** unadapted; maladjusted. **непристо́йный** obscene. **непристу́пный** inaccessible. **непритяза́тельный**, **неприхотли́вый** unpretentious, simple. **неприя́зненный** hostile, inimical. **неприя́знь** hostility. **неприя́тель** *m* enemy. **неприя́тельский** enemy. **неприя́тность** unpleasantness; trouble. **неприя́тный** unpleasant.

**нерв** nerve. **не́рвничать** *impf* fret, be nervous. **нервнобольно́й** *sb* neurotic. **не́рвный** (-вен, -вна́, -о) nervous; nerve; irritable. **нервозный** nervy, irritable.

**не-. непрове́ренный** unverified. **непрогля́дный** pitch-dark. **непроезжа́й** impassable. **непрозра́чный** opaque. **непроизводи́тельный** unproductive. **непроизво́льный** involuntary. **непромока́емый** waterproof. **непроница́емый** impenetrable. **прости́тельный** unforgivable. **непроходи́мый** impassable. **непро́чный** (-чен, -чна́, -о) fragile, flimsy.

**не-. нереа́льный** unreal; unrealistic. **нере́дкий** (-док, -дка́, -о) not infrequent, not uncommon. **нереши́тельность** indecision. **нереши́тельный** indecisive, irresolute. **нержаве́ющая сталь** stainless steel. **неро́вный** (-вен, -вна́, -о) uneven, rough; irregular. **неруши́мый** inviolable.

**не прочь** *predic* not averse.

**неря́ха** *m & f* sloven. **неря́шливый** slovenly.

**не-. непро́шеный** uninvited, unsolicited. **неработоспосо́бный** disabled. **нерабо́чий**: ~ **день** day off. **нера́венство** inequality. **неравноме́рный** uneven. **нера́вный** (-вен, -вна́, -о) unequal. **нерадивый** lackadaisical. **неразбери́ха** muddle. **неразбо́рчивый** not fastidious; illegible. **неразвито́й** (-ра́звит, -а́, -о) undeveloped; backward. **неразгово́рчивый** taciturn. **неразделённый**: **~ая любо́вь** unrequited love. **неразличи́мый** indistinguishable. **неразлу́чный** inseparable. **неразрешённый** unsolved; forbidden. **неразреши́мый** insol-

**не-. несбы́точный** unrealizable. **несваре́ние желудка** indigestion. **несве́жий** (-ж, -á) not fresh; tainted; weary. **несвоевре́менный** ill-timed; overdue. **несво́йственный** not characteristic. **несгора́емый** fireproof. **несерьёзный** not serious.

**несессе́р** case.

**несимметри́чный** asymmetrical.

**нескла́дный** incoherent; awkward.

**несклоня́емый** indeclinable. **не́сколько** (-их) *pron* some, several; *adv* somewhat.

**не-. несконча́емый** interminable. **нескро́мный** (-мен, -мна́, -о) immodest; indiscreet. **несло́жный** simple. **неслы́ханный** unprecedented. **неслы́шный** inaudible. **несме́тный** countless, incalculable. **несмолка́емый** ceaseless.

**несмотря́ на** *prep*+*acc* in spite of.

**не-. несно́сный** intolerable. **несоблюде́ние** non-observance. **несовершенноле́тний** under-age; *sb* minor. **несоверше́нный** imperfect, incomplete; imperfective. **несоверше́нство** imperfection. **несовмести́мый** incompatible. **несогла́сие** disagreement. **несогласо́ванный** uncoordinated. **незазна́тельный** irresponsible. **несоизмери́мый** incommensurable. **несокруши́мый** indestructible. **несомне́нный** undoubted, unquestionable. **несообра́зный** incongruous. **несоотве́тствие** disparity. **несостоя́тельный** insolvent; of modest means; untenable. **неспе́лый** unripe. **неспоко́йный** restless; uneasy. **неспосо́бный** not bright; incapable. **несправедли́вость** injustice. **несправедли́вый** unjust, unfair; incorrect. **несравне́нный** (-нен, -нна) incomparable. **несравни́мый** incomparable. **нестерпи́мый** unbearable.

**нести́** (-су́, -сёшь; нёс, -ла́) *impf* (*pf* понести́, с~) carry; bring, take; suffer; incur; lay; ~сь rush, fly; float, be carried

**не-. несто́йкий** unstable. **несуще́ственный** immaterial, inessential.

**несу́** *etc.*: *see* **нести́**

**несхо́дный** unlike, dissimilar. **несчастли́вый** unfortunate, unlucky; unhappy. **несча́стный** unhappy, unfortunate; ~ слу́чай accident. **несча́стье** misfortune; к несча́стью un-

fortunately. **несчётный** innumerable.

**нет** *partl* no, not; nothing. **нет**, **не́ту** there is not, there are not.

**не-. нетакти́чный** tactless. **нетвёрдый** (-ёрд, -а́, -о) unsteady, shaky. **нетерпели́вый** impatient. **нетерпе́ние** impatience. **нетерпи́мый** intolerable, intolerant. **нетороп-ли́вый** leisurely. **нето́чный** (-чен, -чна́, -о) inaccurate, inexact. **нетре́звый** drunk. **нетро́нутый** untouched; chaste, virginal. **нетрудово́й дохо́д** unearned income. **нетрудоспосо́бность** disability.

**не́тто** *indecl adj* & *adv* net(t).

**не́ту** *see* **нет**

**не-. неубеди́тельный** unconvincing. **неуваже́ние** disrespect. **неуве́ренность** uncertainty. **неуве́ренный** uncertain. **неувяда́ющий**, **неувяда́емый**, unfading. **неугомо́нный** indefatigable. **неуда́ча** failure. **неуда́чливый** unlucky. **неуда́чник**, -ница unlucky person, failure. **неуда́чный** unsuccessful, unfortunate. **неудержи́мый** irrepressible. **неудо́бный** uncomfortable; inconvenient; embarrassing. **неудо́бство** discomfort; inconvenience; embarrassment. **неудовлетворе́ние** dissatisfaction. **неудовлетворённый** dissatisfied. **неудовлетвори́тельный** unsatisfactory. **неудово́льствие** displeasure.

**неуже́ли?** *partl* really?

**не-. неузнава́емый** unrecognizable. **неукло́нный** steady; undeviating. **неуклю́жий**

clumsy. **неулови́мый** elusive; subtle. **неуме́лый** inept; clumsy. **неуме́ренный** immoderate. **неуме́стный** inappropriate; irrelevant. **неумоли́мый** implacable, inexorable. **неумы́шленный** unintentional.

**не-**. **неупла́та** non-payment. **неуравнове́шенный** unbalanced. **неурожа́й** bad harvest. **неуро́чный** untimely, inopportune. **неуря́дица** disorder, mess. **неуспева́емость** poor progress. **неусто́йка** forfeit. **неусто́йчивый** unstable; unsteady. **неусту́пчивый** unyielding. **неуте́шный** inconsolable. **неутоли́мый** unquenchable. **неутоми́мый** tireless. **неу́ч** ignoramus. **неучти́вый** discourteous. **неуязви́мый** invulnerable.

**нефри́т** jade.

**нефте-** in comb oil, petroleum. **нефтено́сный** oilbearing. **~перего́нный заво́д** (oil) refinery. **~прово́д** (oil) pipeline. **~проду́кты** (-ов) pl petroleum products.

**нефть** oil, petroleum. **нефтяно́й** oil, petroleum.

**не-**. **нехва́тка** shortage. **нехорошо́** adv badly. **нехоро́ший** (-о́ш, -а́) bad; **~о́** it is bad, it is wrong. **не́хотя** adv unwillingly; unintentionally. **нецелесообра́зный** inexpedient; pointless. **нецензу́рный** unprintable. **неча́янный** unexpected; accidental.

**не́чего** (не́чему, не́чем, не́ о чем) pron (with separable pref) (there is) nothing.

**нечелове́ческий** inhuman, superhuman.

**нече́стный** dishonest, unfair. **нечётный** odd.

**нечистопло́тный** dirty; slovenly; unscrupulous. **нечистота́** (pl -о́ты, -о́т) dirtiness, filth; pl sewage. **нечи́стый** (-и́ст, -а́, -о) dirty, unclean; impure; unclear. **не́чисть** evil spirits; scum.

**нечленоразде́льный** inarticulate.

**не́что** pron something.

**не-**. **неэконо́мный** uneconomical. **неэффекти́вный** ineffective; inefficient. **неявка** failure to appear. **нея́ркий** dim, faint; dull, subdued. **нея́сный** (-сен, -сна́, -о) not clear; vague.

**ни** partl not a; **ни оди́н** (одна́, одно́) not a single; (with prons and pronominal advs) ever; **кто...** **ни** whoever. **ни** conj: **ни... ни** neither ... nor; **ни то** **ни сё** neither one thing nor the other.

**ни́ва** cornfield, field.

**нивели́р** level.

**нигде́** adv nowhere.

**нидерла́ндец** (-дца; gen -дцев) Dutchman. **нидерла́ндка** Dutchwoman. **нидерла́ндский** Dutch. **Нидерла́нды** (-ов) pl the Netherlands.

**ни́же** adj lower, humbler; adv below; prep+gen below, beneath. **нижесле́дующий** following. **ни́жний** lower, under-; **~ее белье́** underclothes; **~ий эта́ж** ground floor. **низ** (loc -у́; pl -ы́) bottom; pl lower classes; low notes.

**низа́ть** (нижу́, ни́жешь) impf (pf на~) string, thread.

**низверга́ть** impf, **низверг-**

ну́ть (-ну́; -ёрг) *pf* throw down, overthrow; **~ся** crash down; be overthrown. **низве́ржение** overthrow.

**низи́на** low-lying place. **ни́зкий** (-зок, -зка́, -о) low; base. **низкопокло́нство** servility. **низкопро́бный** low-grade. **низкоро́слый** undersized. **низкосо́ртный** low-grade. **ни́зменность** lowland; baseness. **ни́зменный** low-lying; base.

**низо́вье** (*gen pl* -ьев) the lower reaches. **ни́зость** baseness, meanness. **ни́зш|ий** lower, lowest; **~ее образова́ние** primary education.

**ника́к** *adv* in no way. **никако́й** *pron* no; no ... whatever

**ни́кель** *m* nickel.

**нике́м** *see* никто́. **никогда́** *adv* never. **никто́** (-кого́, -кому́, -ке́м, ни о ком) *pron* (*with separable pref*) nobody, no one. **никуда́** nowhere. **никче́мный** useless. **нима́ло** *adv* not in the least.

**нимб** halo, nimbus.

**ни́мфа** nymph; pupa.

**ниотку́да** *adv* from nowhere. **нипочём** *adv* it is nothing; dirt cheap; in no circumstances.

**ниско́лько** *adv* not at all.

**ниспроверга́ть** *impf*, **ниспрове́ргнуть** (-ну; -ёрг) *pf* overthrow. **ниспроверже́ние** overthrow.

**нисходя́щий** descending.

**ни́тка** thread; string; **до ни́тки** to the skin; **на живу́ю ни́тку** hastily, anyhow. **ни́точка** thread. **нить** thread; filament.

**ничего́** *etc.*: *see* ничто́. **ничего́** *adv* all right; it doesn't matter, never mind; *as indecl adj*

not bad, pretty good. **ниче́й** (-чья́, -чьё) *pron* nobody's; **ничья́ земля́** no man's land. **ничья́** *sb* draw; tie.

**ничко́м** *adv* face down, prone. **ничто́** (-чего́, -чему́, -че́м, ни о чём) *pron* (*with separable pref*) nothing. **ничто́жество** nonentity, nobody. **ничто́жный** insignificant; worthless.

**ничу́ть** *adv* not a bit.

**ничье́, ничья́:** *see* ниче́й.

**ни́ша** niche, recess.

**ни́щенка** beggar-woman. **ни́щенский** beggarly. **нищета́** poverty. **ни́щий** (нищ, -а́, -е) destitute, poor; *sb* beggar.

**но** *conj* but; still.

**нова́тор** innovator. **нова́торский** innovative. **нова́торство** innovation.

**Но́вая Зела́ндия** New Zealand.

**нове́йший** newest, latest. **нове́лла** short story. **но́венький** brand-new. **новизна́** novelty; newness. **нови́нка** novelty. **новичо́к** (-чка́) novice.

**ново-** *in comb* new(ly). **новобра́нец** (-нца) new recruit. **~бра́чный** *sb* newly-wed. **~введе́ние** innovation. **~го́дний** new year's. **~зела́ндец** (-дца; *gen pl* -дцев), **~зела́ндка** New-Zealander. **~зела́ндский** New Zealand. **~лу́ние** new moon. **~прибы́вший** newly-arrived; *sb* newcomer. **~рождённый** newborn. **~сёл** new settler. **~се́лье** new home; house-warming. **новостро́йка** new building.

**но́вость** (*gen pl* -е́й) news; novelty. **но́вшество** innovation, novelty. **но́вый** (нов, -а́, -о)

но́вый (нов, -а́, -о) new; modern; ~ год New Year's Day.

нога́ (acc но́гу; pl но́ги, ног, нога́м) foot, leg.

но́готь (-гтя; pl -и) m fingernail, toe-nail.

нож (-а́) knife.

но́жка small foot or leg; leg; stem, stalk.

но́жницы (-иц) pl scissors, shears.

но́жны (-жен) pl sheath, scabbard.

ножо́вка saw, hacksaw.

ноздря́ (pl -и, -е́й) nostril.

нока́ут knock-out. нокаути́ровать impf & pf knock out.

нолево́й, нулево́й zero. ноль (-я́), нуль (-я́) m nought, zero, nil.

номенклату́ра nomenclature; top positions in government.

но́мер (pl -а́) number; size; (hotel-)room; item; trick. номеро́к (-рка́) tag; label, ticket.

номина́л face value. номина́льный nominal.

нора́ (pl -ы) burrow, hole.

Норве́гия Norway. норве́жец (-жца), норве́жка Norwegian. норве́жский Norwegian.

норд (naut) north; north wind.

но́рка mink.

но́рма standard, norm; rate. нормализа́ция standardization. норма́льно all right, OK. норма́льный normal; standard. нормирова́ние, нормиро́вка regulation; rate-fixing; rationing. нормирова́ть impf & pf regulate, standardize; ration.

нос (loc -у́; pl -ы́) nose; beak; bow, prow. но́сик (small) nose; spout.

носи́лки (-лок) pl stretcher; litter. носи́льщик m porter. носи́тель m, ~ница (fig) bearer; (med) carrier. носи́ть (-ошу́ -о́сишь) impf carry, bear; wear; ~ся rush, tear along, fly; float, be carried; wear. но́ска carrying, wearing. но́ский hard-wearing.

носово́й nose; nasal; ~ плато́к (pocket) handkerchief.

носо́к (-ска́) little nose; toe; sock. носоро́г rhinoceros.

но́та note; pl music. нота́ция notation; lecture, reprimand.

нота́риус notary.

ночева́ть (-чу́ю) impf (pf пере~) spend the night. ночёвка spending the night. ночле́г place to spend the night; passing the night. ночле́жка doss-house. ночни́к (-а́) night-light. ночн|о́й night, nocturnal; ~а́я руба́шка nightdress; ~о́й горшо́к potty; chamber-pot. ночь (loc -и́; gen pl -е́й) night. но́чью adv at night.

но́ша burden. но́шеный worn; second-hand.

ною́ etc.: see ныть.

ноя́брь (-я́) m November. ноя́брьский November.

нрав disposition; temper; pl customs, ways. нра́виться (-влюсь) impf (pf по~) please; мне нра́вится I like. нра́вственность morality, morals. нра́вственный moral.

ну int & partl well, well then.

ну́дный tedious.

нужда́ (pl -ы) need. нужда́ться impf be in need; +в+prep need, require. ну́жн|ый (-жен, -жна́, -о, нужны́) necessary; ~о it is necessary; +dat I, etc., must, ought to, need.

**нулево́й, нуль** see **нолево́й, ноль**

**нумера́ция** numeration; numbering. **нумерова́ть** impf (pf **про~**) number.

**нутро́** inside, interior; instinct(s).

**ны́не** adv now; today. **ны́нешний** present; today's. **ны́нче** adv today; now.

**нырну́ть** (-ну́, -нёшь) pf, **ныря́ть** impf dive.

**ныть** (но́ю) impf ache; whine. **нытьё** whining.

**н.э.** abbr (of **на́шей э́ры**) AD.

**нюх** scent; flair. **ню́хать** impf (pf **по~**) smell, sniff.

**ня́нчить** (-чу) impf nurse, look after; **~ся** c+instr nurse; fuss over. **ня́нька** nanny. **ня́ня** (children's) nurse, nanny.

# О

**о, об, о́бо** prep I. +prep of, about, concerning. II. +acc against; on, upon.

**о** int oh!

**оа́зис** oasis.

**об** see **о** prep.

**о́ба** (обо́их) m & neut, **о́бе** (обе́их) f both.

**обалдева́ть** impf, **обалде́ть** (-е́ю) pf go crazy; become dulled; be stunned.

**обанкро́титься** (-о́чусь) pf go bankrupt.

**обая́ние** fascination, charm. **обая́тельный** fascinating, charming.

**обва́л** fall(ing); crumbling; collapse; caving-in; landslide; (сне́жный) ~ avalanche. **обвали́ть** (-лю́, -лишь) pf (impf **обва́ливать**) cause to fall or collapse; crumble; heap round;

**~ся** collapse, cave in; crumble.

**обва́ливать** impf of **обвали́ть**) roll.

**обва́ривать** impf, **обвари́ть** (-рю́, -ришь) pf pour boiling water over; scald; **~ся** scald o.s.

**обведу́** etc.: see **обвести́**. **обвёл** etc.: see **обвести́**. **об|венча́ть(ся** pf.

**обверну́ть** (-ну́, -нёшь) pf, **обвёртывать** impf wrap, wrap up.

**обве́с** short weight. **обве́сить** (-е́шу) pf (impf **обве́шивать**) cheat in weighing.

**обвести́** (-еду́, -еде́шь; -ёл, -ела́) pf (impf **обводи́ть**) lead round, take round; encircle; surround; outline; dodge.

**обве́тренный** weather-beaten.

**обветша́лый** decrepit. **об|ветша́ть** pf.

**обве́шивать** impf of **обве́сить**. **обвива́ть(ся** impf of **обви́ть(ся**

**обвине́ние** charge, accusation; prosecution. **обвини́тель** m accuser; prosecutor. **обвини́тельный** accusatory; ~ **акт** indictment; ~ **пригово́р** verdict of guilty. **обвини́ть** pf, **обвиня́ть** impf prosecute, indict; +в+prep accuse of, charge with. **обвиня́емый** sb the accused; defendant.

**обви́ть** (обовью́, обовьёшь; обви́л, -а́, -о) pf (impf **обвива́ть**) wind round; **~ся** wind round.

**обводи́ть** (-ожу́, -о́дишь) impf of **обвести́**

**обвора́живать** impf, **обворожи́ть** (-жу́) pf charm, enchant. **обворожи́тельный** charming, enchanting.

обвяза́ть (-яжу́, -я́жешь) *pf*, обвя́зывать *impf* tie round; ~ся +*instr* tie round o.s.

обго́н passing. обгоня́ть *impf of* обогна́ть

обгора́ть *impf*, обгоре́ть (-рю́) *pf* be burnt, be scorched. обгоре́лый burnt, charred, scorched.

обде́лать *pf* (*impf* обде́лывать) finish; polish; set; manage, arrange.

обдели́ть (-лю́, -лишь) *pf* (*impf* обделя́ть) do out of one's (fair) share of.

обде́лывать *impf of* обде́лать. обделя́ть *impf of* обдели́ть

обдеру́ *etc.: see* ободра́ть. обдира́ть *impf of* ободра́ть

обду́манный deliberate, well-considered. обду́мать *pf*, обду́мывать *impf* consider, think over.

о́бе: *see* о́ба. обега́ть *impf of* обежа́ть. обегу́ *etc.: see* обежа́ть

обе́д dinner, lunch. обе́дать *impf* (*pf* по~) have dinner, dine. обе́денный dinner.

обедне́вший impoverished. обедне́ние impoverishment. о|бедне́ть (-е́ю) *pf*.

обе́дня (*gen pl* -ден) mass.

обежа́ть (-егу́) *pf* (*impf* обега́ть) run round; run past; outrun.

обезбо́ливание anaesthetization. обезбо́ливать *impf*, обезбо́лить *pf* anaesthetize.

обезвре́дить (-е́жу) *pf*, обезвре́живать *impf* render harmless.

обездо́ленный unfortunate, hapless.

обеззара́живающий disinfectant.

обезли́ченный depersonalized; robbed of individuality. обезобра́живать *impf*, о|безобра́зить (-а́жу) *pf* disfigure.

обезопа́сить (-а́шу) *pf* secure.

обезору́живать *impf*, обезору́жить (-жу) *pf* disarm.

обезу́меть (-ею) *pf* lose one's senses, lose one's head.

обезья́на monkey; ape.

обели́ть *pf*, обеля́ть *impf* vindicate; clear of blame.

оберега́ть *impf*, обере́чь (-егу́, -ежёшь; -рёг, -ла́) *pf* guard; protect.

оберну́ть (-ну́, -нёшь) *pf* (*impf also* обора́чивать) twist; wrap up; turn; ~ся turn (round); turn out; +*instr or* в+*acc* turn into. обёртка wrapper; (dust-) jacket, cover. обёрточный wrapping.

оберу́ *etc.: see* обобра́ть

обескура́живать *impf*, обескура́жить (-жу) *pf* discourage; dishearten.

обескро́вить (-влю) *pf*, обескро́вливать *impf* drain of blood, bleed white; render lifeless.

обеспе́чение securing, guaranteeing; ensuring; provision; guarantee; security. обеспе́ченность security; +*instr* provision of. обеспе́ченный well-to-do; well provided for. обеспе́чивать *impf*, обеспе́чить (-чу) *pf* provide for; secure; ensure; protect; +*instr* provide with.

о|беспоко́ить(ся *pf*.

обесси́леть (-ею) *pf* grow weak, lose one's strength. обесси́ливать *impf*, обесси́лить *pf* weaken. о|бессла́вить (-влю) *pf*. обессме́ртить (-рчу) *pf* immortalize.

обесцене́ние depreciation. обесце́нивать *impf*, обесце́нить *pf* depreciate; cheapen; ~ся depreciate.

о|бесче́стить (-е́щу) *pf*.

обе́т vow, promise. обето́ванный promised. обеща́ние promise. обеща́ть *impf* & *pf* (*pf also* по~) promise.

обжа́лование appeal. обжа́ловать *pf* appeal against.

обже́чь обожгу́, обожжёшь; обжёг, обожгла́) *pf*, обжига́ть *impf* burn; scorch; bake; ~ся burn o.s.; burn one's fingers.

обжо́ра *m* & *f* glutton. обжо́рство gluttony.

обзавести́сь (-еду́сь, -едёшься; -вёлся, -ла́сь) *pf*, обзаводи́ться (-ожу́сь, -о́дишься) *impf* +*instr* provide o.s. with; acquire.

обзову́ *etc.*: *see* обозва́ть обзо́р survey, review.

обзыва́ть *impf of* обозва́ть обива́ть *impf of* оби́ть. оби́вка upholstering; upholstery.

оби́да offence, insult; nuisance. оби́деть (-и́жу) *pf*, обижа́ть *impf* offend; hurt; wound; ~ся take offence; feel hurt. оби́дный offensive; annoying. оби́дчивый touchy. оби́женный offended.

оби́лие abundance. оби́льный abundant.

обира́ть *impf of* обобра́ть обита́емый inhabited. оби́татель *m* inhabitant. обита́ть *impf* live.

оби́ть (обобью́, -ьёшь) *pf* (*impf* обива́ть) upholster; knock off.

обихо́д custom, (general) use, practice. обихо́дный everyday.

обкла́дывать(ся *impf of* обложи́ть(ся

обкра́дывать *impf of* обокра́сть

обла́ва raid; cordon, cordoning off.

облага́емый taxable. облага́ть(ся *impf of* обложи́ть (-ся: ~ся нало́гом be liable to tax.

облада́ние possession. облада́тель *m* possessor. облада́ть *impf* +*instr* possess.

о́блако (*pl* -á, -óв) cloud.

обла́мывать(ся *impf of* обло́мать(ся, обломи́ться

областно́й regional. о́бласть (*gen pl* -е́й) region; field, sphere.

о́блачность cloudiness. о́блачный cloudy.

облёг *etc.*: *see* обле́чь. облега́ть *impf of* обле́чь

облегча́ть *impf*, облегчи́ть (-чу́) *pf* lighten; relieve; alleviate; facilitate. облегче́ние relief.

обледене́лый ice-covered. обледене́ние icing over. обледене́ть (-е́ет) *pf* become covered with ice.

обле́злый shabby; mangy.

облека́ть(ся *impf of* обле́чь²(ся. облеку́ *etc.*: *see* обле́чь²

облепи́ть (-плю́, -пишь) *pf*, облепля́ть *impf* stick to, cling to; throng round; plaster.

облета́ть *impf*, облете́ть (-печу́) *pf* fly (round); spread (all over); fall.

обле́чь¹ (-ля́жет; -лёг, -ла́) *pf* (*impf* облега́ть) cover, envelop; fit tightly.

**обле́чь²** (-еку́, -ечёшь; -ёк, -кла́) *pf* (*impf* облека́ть) clothe, invest; **~ся** clothe o.s. +*gen* take the form of.

**облива́ть(ся** *impf of* обли́ть(ся

**облига́ция** bond.

**облиза́ть** (-ижу́, -и́жешь) *pf*, **обли́зывать** *impf* lick (all over); **~ся** smack one's lips.

**о́блик** look, appearance.

**о́блитый** (о́бли́т, -á, -о) covered, enveloped. **обли́ть** (оболью́, -льёшь; о́бли́л, -ила́, -о) *pf* (*impf* облива́ть) pour, sluice, spill; **~ся** sponge down, take a shower; pour over o.s.

**облицева́ть** (-цу́ю) *pf*, **облицо́вывать** *impf* face. **облицо́вка** facing; lining.

**облича́ть** *impf*, **обличи́ть** (-чу́) *pf* expose; reveal; point to. **обличе́ние** exposure, denunciation. **обличи́тельный** denunciatory.

**обложе́ние** taxation; assessment. **обложи́ть** (-жу́, -жишь) *pf* (*impf* обкла́дывать, облага́ть) edge; face; cover; surround; assess; **круго́м обложи́ло (не́бо)** the sky is completely overcast; **~ нало́гом** tax; **~ся** +*instr* surround o.s. with. **обло́жка** (dust-)cover; folder.

**облока́чиваться** *impf*, **облокоти́ться** (-очу́сь, -о́ти́шься) *pf* на+*acc* lean one's elbows on.

**обломáть** *pf* (*impf* обла́мывать) break off; **~ся** break off. **обломи́ться** (-ло́мится) *pf* (*impf* обла́мываться) break off. **обло́мок** (-мка) fragment.

**облу́пленный** chipped.

**облучи́ть** (-чу́) *pf*, **облуча́ть** *impf* irradiate. **облуче́ние** ir-radiation.

**об|лысе́ть** (-е́ю) *pf*.

**обля́жет** *etc.*: *see* обле́чь¹

**обма́зать** (-а́жу) *pf*, **обма́зывать** *impf* coat; putty; besmear; **~ся** +*instr* get covered with.

**обма́кивать** *impf*, **обмак-ну́ть** (-ну́, -нёшь) *pf* dip.

**обма́н** deceit; illusion; **~ зре́ния** optical illusion. **обма́нный** deceitful. **обману́ть** (-ну́, -нешь) *pf*, **обма́нывать** *impf* deceive; cheat; **~ся** be deceived. **обма́нчивый** deceptive. **обма́нщик** deceiver; fraud.

**обма́тывать(ся** *impf of* об-мота́ть(ся

**обма́хивать** *impf*, **обмах-ну́ть** (-ну́, -нёшь) *pf* brush off; fan; **~ся** fan o.s.

**обмёл** *etc.*: *see* обмести́

**обмеле́ние** shallowing. **об|меле́ть** (-е́ет) *pf* become shallow.

**обме́н** exchange; barter; **в ~ за**+*acc* in exchange for; **~ веще́ств** metabolism. **обме́нивать** *impf*, **обмени́ть** (-ню́, -нишь) *pf*, **обменя́ть** *pf* exchange; **~ся** +*instr* exchange. **обме́нный** exchange.

**обме́р** measurement; false measure.

**обмере́ть** (обомру́, -рёшь; о́бмер, -ла́, -ло) *pf* (*impf* обмира́ть) faint; **~ от у́жаса** be horror-struck.

**обме́ривать** *impf*, **обме́рить** *pf* measure; cheat in measuring.

**обмести́** (-ету́, -етёшь; -мёл, -а́) *pf*, **обмета́ть¹** *impf* sweep off, dust.

**обмета́ть²** (-ечу́ *or* -а́ю, -е́чешь

*or* -а́ешь) *pf* (*impf* обмёты-
вать) oversew.

обмету́ *etc.*: *see* обмести́. об-
мётывать *impf of* обмета́ть.
обмира́ть *impf of* обмере́ть.

обмо́лвиться (-влю́сь) *pf*
make a slip of the tongue;
+*instr* say, utter. обмо́лвка
slip of the tongue.

обморо́женный frost-bitten.
о́бморок fainting-fit, swoon.

обмота́ть (-а́ю) *pf* (*impf* обма́ты-
вать) wind round; ~ся +*instr*
wrap o.s. in. обмо́тка winding; *pl* puttees.

обмо́ю *etc.*: *see* обмы́ть.
обмундирова́ние fitting out
(with uniform); uniform. об-
мундирова́ть *pf*, обмунди-
ро́вывать *impf* fit out
(with uniform).

обмыва́ть *impf*, обмы́ть (-мо́ю)
*pf* bathe, wash; ~ся wash,
bathe.

обмяка́ть *impf*, обмя́кнуть
(-ну; -мя́к) *pf* become soft *or*
flabby.

обнадёживать *impf*, обна-
дёжить (-жу) *pf* reassure.

обнажа́ть *impf*, обнажи́ть
(-жу́) *pf* bare, uncover; reveal.
обнажённый (-ён, -ена́) naked, bare; nude.

обнаро́довать *impf & pf*
promulgate.

обнаруже́ние revealing; discovery; detection. обнару́-
живать *impf*, обнару́жить
(-жу) *pf* display; reveal; discover; ~ся come to light.

обнести́ (-су́, -сёшь; -нёс, -ла́)
*pf* (*impf* обноси́ть) enclose;
+*instr* serve round; pass over,
leave out.

обнима́ть(ся *impf of* обня́ть-
(ся. обниму́ *etc.*: *see* обня́ть
обнища́ние impoverishment.

обнови́ть (-влю́) *pf*, обно-
вля́ть *impf* renovate; renew.
обно́вка new acquisition;
new garment. обновле́ние
renovation, renewal.

обноси́ть (-ошу́, -о́сишь) *impf*
of обнести́; ~ся *pf* have
worn out one's clothes.

обня́ть (-ниму́, -ни́мешь; о́бнял,
-а́, -о) *pf* (*impf* обнима́ть)
embrace; span; ~ся embrace;
hug one another.

обо *see o prep*.

обобра́ть (оберу́, -рёшь; обо-
бра́л, -а́, -о) *pf* (*impf* оби-
ра́ть) rob; pick.

обобща́ть *impf*, обобщи́ть
(-щу́) *pf* generalize. обоб-
ще́ние generalization. обоб-
ществи́ть (-влю́) *pf*, обоб-
ществля́ть *impf* socialize;
collectivize. обобществле́-
ние socialization; collectivization.

обобью́ *etc.*: *see* оби́ть.
обовью́ *etc.*: *see* обви́ть.

обогати́ть (-ащу́) *pf*, обо-
гаща́ть *impf* enrich; ~ся become rich; enrich o.s. обо-
гаще́ние enrichment.

обогна́ть (обгоню́, -о́нишь;
обогна́л, -а́, -о) *pf* (*impf*
обгоня́ть) pass; outstrip.

обогну́ть (-ну́, -нёшь) *pf* (*impf*
огиба́ть) round, skirt; bend
round.

обогрева́тель *m* heater.
обогрева́ть *impf*, обогре́ть
(-е́ю) *pf* heat, warm; ~ся
warm up.

обо́д (*pl* -о́дья, -ьев) rim.
ободо́к (-дка́) thin rim, narrow border.

обо́дранный ragged. обо-
дра́ть (обдеру́, -рёшь; -а́л,
-а́, -о) *pf* (*impf* обдира́ть)
skin, flay; peel; fleece.

ободре́ние encouragement, reassurance. ободри́тельный encouraging, reassuring. ободри́ть pf, ободря́ть impf encourage, reassure; ~ся cheer up, take heart.

обожа́ть impf adore.

обожгу́ etc.: see обже́чь

обожестви́ть (-влю́) pf, обожествля́ть impf deify.

обожжённый (-ён, -ена́) burnt, scorched.

обо́з string of vehicles; transport.

обозва́ть (обзову́, -вёшь; -а́л, -а́, -о) pf (impf обзыва́ть) call; call names.

обозлённый (-ён, -а́) angered; embittered. обо|зли́ть pf, о|зли́ть pf anger; embitter; ~ся get angry.

обознача́ть impf, обозна́чить (-чу) pf mean; mark; ~ся appear, reveal o.s. обозначе́ние sign, symbol.

обозрева́тель m reviewer; columnist. обозрева́ть impf, обозре́ть (-рю́) pf survey. обозре́ние survey; review; revue. обозри́мый visible.

обо́и (-ев) pl wallpaper.

обо́йма (gen pl -о́йм) cartridge clip.

обойти́ (-йду́, -йдёшь; -ошёл, -ошла́) pf (impf обходи́ть) go round; pass; avoid; pass over; ~сь manage, make do; +c+instr treat.

обокра́сть (обкраду́, -дёшь) pf (impf обкра́дывать) rob.

оболо́чка casing; membrane; cover, envelope, jacket; shell.

обольсти́тель m seducer. обольсти́тельный seductive. обольсти́ть (-льщу́) pf,

обольща́ть impf seduce. обольще́ние seduction; delusion.

оболью́ etc.: see обли́ть

обомру́ etc.: see обмере́ть

обоня́ние (sense of) smell. обоня́тельный olfactory.

обопру́ etc.: see опере́ть

обора́чивать(ся impf of оберну́ть(ся, оборо́ти́ть(ся

обо́рванный torn, ragged. оборва́ть (-ву́, -вёшь; -а́л, -а́, -о) pf (impf обрыва́ть) tear off; break; snap; cut short; ~ся break; snap; fall; stop suddenly.

обо́рка frill, flounce.

оборо́на defence. оборони́тельный defensive. обороня́ть(ся defend o.s. оборо́нный defence, defensive.

оборо́т turn; revolution; circulation; turnover; back; ~ ре́чи (turn of) phrase; смотри́ на ~ P.T.O. обороти́ть (-рочу́, -ро́тишь) pf (impf обора́чивать) turn; ~ся turn (round); +instr or в+acc turn into. оборо́тный circulating; reverse; ~ капита́л working capital.

обоснова́ние basing; basis, ground. обосно́ванный well-founded. обоснова́ть pf, обосно́вывать impf ground, base; substantiate; ~ся settle down.

обосо́бленный isolated, solitary.

обостре́ние aggravation. обострённый keen; strained; sharp, pointed. обостри́ть pf, обостря́ть impf sharpen.

strain; aggravate; **~ся** become strained; be aggravated; become acute.

**оботру́** *etc.: see* **оберете́ть**

**обо́чина** verge; shoulder, edge.

**обошёл** *etc.: see* **обойти́. обо́шью** *etc.: see* **обши́ть**

**обою́дный** mutual, reciprocal.

**обраба́тывать** *impf*, **обрабо́тать** *pf* till, cultivate; work, work up; treat, process. **обрабо́тка** working (up); processing; cultivation.

**об|ра́довать(ся** *pf*.

**о́браз** shape, form; image; manner; way; icon; **гла́вным ~ом** mainly; **таки́м ~ом** thus. **образе́ц** (-зца́) model; pattern; sample. **о́бразный** graphic, figurative. **образова́ние** formation; education. **образо́ванный** educated. **образова́тельный** educational. **образова́ть** *impf* & *pf*, **образо́вывать** *impf* form; **~ся** form; arise; turn out well.

**образу́мить** (-млю) *pf* bring to reason; **~ся** see reason.

**образцо́вый** model. **образцо́вый специме́н** specimen, sample.

**обра́мить** (-млю) *pf*, **обрамля́ть** *impf* frame.

**обраста́ть** *impf*, **обрасти́** (-ту́, -тёшь; -ро́с, -ла́) *pf* be overgrown.

**обрати́мый** reversible, convertible. **обрати́ть** (-ащу́) *pf*, **обраща́ть** *impf* turn; convert; **~ внима́ние на**+*acc* pay or draw attention to; **~ся** turn; appeal; apply; address; +**в**+*acc* turn into; +**с**+*instr* treat; handle. **обра́тно** *adv* back; backwards; conversely; **~ пропорциона́льный** inversely proportional. **обра́тный** re-

verse; return; opposite; inverse. **обраще́ние** appeal, address; conversion; (+**с**+*instr*) treatment (of); handling (of); use (of).

**обре́з** edge; sawn-off gun; **в ~**+*gen* only just enough. **об|ре́зать** (-е́жу) *pf*, **обреза́ть** *impf* cut (off); clip, trim; pare; prune; circumcise; **~ся** cut o.s. **обре́зок** (-зка) scrap; *pl* ends; clippings.

**обрека́ть** *impf of* **обре́чь. обреку́** *etc.: see* **обре́чь. обрёл** *etc.: see* **обрести́**

**обремени́тельный** onerous. **о|бремени́ть** *pf*, **обременя́ть** *impf* burden.

**обрести́** (-ету́, -етёшь; -рёл, -а́) *pf*, **обрета́ть** *impf* find.

**обрече́ние** doom. **обречённый** doomed. **обре́чь** (-еку́ -ечёшь; -ёк, -ла́) *pf* (*impf* **обрека́ть**) doom.

**обрисова́ть** *pf*, **обрисо́вывать** *impf* outline, depict; **~ся** appear (in outline).

**оброни́ть** (-ню́, -нишь) *pf* drop; let drop.

**обро́с** *etc.: see* **обрасти́.**

**обруба́ть** *impf*, **обруби́ть** (-блю́, -бишь) *pf* chop or cut off. **обру́бок** (-бка) stump.

**об|руга́ть** *pf*.

**о́бруч** (*pl* -и, -е́й) hoop. **обруча́льный** engagement; **~ое кольцо́** betrothal ring, wedding ring. **обруча́ть** *impf*, **обручи́ть** (-чу́) betroth; **~ся** +**с**+*instr* become engaged to. **обруче́ние** engagement.

**обру́шивать** *impf*, **об|ру́шить** (-шу) *pf* bring down; **~ся** come down, collapse.

**обры́в** precipice. **обрыва́ть(ся** *impf of* **оборва́ть(ся. обры́вок** (-вка) scrap; snatch.

**обры́згать** *pf*, **обры́згивать** *impf* splash; sprinkle.

**обрю́зглый** flabby.

**обря́д** rite, ceremony.

**обсервато́рия** observatory.

**обсле́дование** inspection. **обсле́дователь** *m* inspector. **обсле́довать** *impf & pf* inspect.

**обслу́живание** service; maintenance. **обслу́живать** *impf*, **обслужи́ть** (-жу́, -жишь) *pf* serve; operate.

**обсо́хнуть** (-ну; -о́х) *pf* (*impf* **обсыха́ть**) dry (off).

**обста́вить** (-влю) *pf*, **обставля́ть** *impf* surround; furnish; arrange. **обстано́вка** furniture; situation, conditions; set.

**обстоя́тельный** thorough, reliable; detailed. **обстоя́тельство** circumstance. **обстоя́ть** (-ои́т) *impf* be; go; **как обстои́т де́ло?** how is it going?

**обстре́л** firing, fire; **под ~ом** under fire. **обстре́ливать** *impf*, **обстреля́ть** *pf* fire at; bombard.

**обступа́ть** *impf*, **обступи́ть** (-у́пит) *pf* surround.

**обсуди́ть** (-ужу́, -у́дишь) *pf*, **обсужда́ть** *impf* discuss. **обсужде́ние** discussion.

**обсчита́ть** *pf*, **обсчи́тывать** *impf* shortchange; **~ся** miscount, miscalculate.

**обсы́пать** (-плю) *pf*, **обсыпа́ть** *impf* strew; sprinkle.

**обсыха́ть** *impf of* **обсо́хнуть**. **обта́чивать** *impf of* **обточи́ть**

**обтека́емый** streamlined.

**обтере́ть** (оботру́, -трёшь; обтёр) *pf* (*impf* **обтира́ть**) wipe; rub; **~ся** dry o.s.; sponge down.

**о(б)теса́ть** (-ешу́, -е́шешь) *pf*, **о(б)тёсывать** *impf* roughhew; teach good manners to; trim.

**обтира́ние** sponge-down. **обтира́ть(ся** *impf of* **обтере́ть(ся**

**обточи́ть** (-чу́, -чишь) *pf* (*impf* **обта́чивать**) grind; machine.

**обтрёпанный** frayed; shabby.

**обтяну́ть** *impf*, **обтяну́ть** (-ну́, -нешь) *pf* cover; fit close. **обтя́жка** cover; skin; **в обтя́жку** close-fitting.

**обува́ть(ся** *impf of* **обу́ть(ся. обувь** footwear; boots, shoes.

**обу́гливать** *impf*, **обу́глить** *pf* char; carbonize; **~ся** char, become charred.

**обу́за** burden.

**обузда́ть** *pf*, **обу́здывать** *impf* bridle, curb.

**обурева́ть** *impf* grip; possess.

**обусло́вить** (-влю) *pf*, **обусло́вливать** *impf* cause; +*instr* make conditional on; **~ся** +*instr* be conditional on; depend on.

**обу́тый** shod. **обу́ть** (-у́ю) *pf* (*impf* **обува́ть**) put shoes on; **~ся** put on one's shoes.

**обу́х** butt, back.

**обуча́ть** *impf*, **об|учи́ть** (-чу́, -чишь) *pf* teach; train; **~ся** +*dat or inf* learn. **обуче́ние** teaching; training.

**обхва́т** girth; **в ~е** in circumference. **обхвати́ть** (-ачу́, -а́тишь) *pf*, **обхва́тывать** *impf* embrace; clasp.

**обхо́д** round(s); roundabout way; bypass. **обходи́тельный** courteous; pleasant. **обходи́ть(ся** (-ожу́(сь, -о́дишь(ся) *impf of* **обойти́(сь. обхо́дный** roundabout.

**обша́ривать** *impf*, **обша́рить** *pf* rummage through, ransack.

**обшива́ть** *impf of* **обши́ть.** **обши́вка** edging; trimming; boarding, panelling; plating.

**обши́рный** extensive; vast.

**обши́ть** (обошью́, -шьёшь) *pf* (*impf* **обшива́ть**) edge; trim; make outfit(s) for; plank.

**обшла́г** (-á; *pl* -á, -óв) cuff.

**обща́ться** *impf* associate.

**обще-** *in comb* common(ly), general(ly). **общедосту́пный** moderate in price; popular. **~жи́тие** hostel. **~изве́стный** generally known. **~наро́дный** national, public. **~образова́тельный** of general education. **~при́нятый** generally accepted. **~сою́зный** All-Union. **~челове́ческий** common to all mankind; universal.

**обще́ние** contact; social intercourse. **обще́ственность** public; public opinion; community. **обще́ственный** social, public; voluntary. **о́бщество** society; company.

**о́бщий** general; common; в **~ем** on the whole, in general. **о́бщина** community; commune.

**об|щипа́ть** (-плю́, -плешь) *pf.* **общи́тельный** sociable. **о́бщность** community.

**объеда́|ть(ся** *impf of* **объе́сть(ся**

**объедине́ние** unification; merger; union, association. **объединённый** (-ён, -á) united. **объедини́тельный** unifying. **объедини́ть** *pf,* **объединя́ть** unite; join; combine; **~ся** unite.

**объе́дки** (-ов) *pl* leftovers, scraps.

**объе́зд** riding round; detour. **объе́здить** (-зжу, -здишь) *pf*

(*impf* **объезжа́ть**) travel over; break in.

**объезжа́ть** *impf of* **объе́здить, объе́хать**

**объе́кт** object; objective; establishment, works. **объекти́в** lens. **объекти́вность** objectivity. **объекти́вный** objective.

**объём** volume; scope. **объёмный** by volume, volumetric.

**объе́сть** (-е́м, -е́шь, -е́ст, -еди́м) *pf* (*impf* **объеда́ть**) gnaw (round), nibble; **~ся** overeat.

**объе́хать** (-е́ду) *pf* (*impf* **объезжа́ть**) drive or go round; go past; travel over.

**объяви́ть** (-влю́, -вишь) *pf,* **объявля́ть** *impf* declare, announce; **~ся** turn up; +*instr* declare o.s. **объявле́ние** declaration, announcement; advertisement.

**объясне́ние** explanation. **объясни́мый** explainable. **объясни́ть** *pf,* **объясня́ть** *impf* explain; **~ся** be explained; make o.s. understood; +*c+instr* have it out with.

**объя́тие** embrace.

**обыва́тель** *m* Philistine. **обыва́тельский** narrow-minded.

**обыгра́ть** *pf,* **обы́грывать** *impf* beat (*in a game*).

**обы́денный** ordinary; everyday.

**обыкнове́ние** habit. **обыкнове́нно** *adv* usually. **обыкнове́нный** usual; ordinary.

**о́быск** search. **обыска́ть** (-ыщу́, -ыщешь) *pf,* **обы́скивать** *impf* search.

**обы́чай** custom; usage. **обы́чно** *adv* usually. **обы́чный** usual.

**обя́занность** duty; responsibility. **обя́занный** (+*inf*) obliged; +*dat* indebted to (+*instr* for). **обяза́тельно** *adv* without fail. **обяза́тельный** obligatory. **обяза́тельство** obligation; commitment. **обяза́ть** (-яжу́, -я́жешь) *pf*, **обя́зывать** *impf* bind; commit; oblige; ~**ся** pledge o.s., undertake.

**ова́л** oval. **ова́льный** oval.

**ова́ция** ovation.

**овдове́ть** (-е́ю) *pf* become a widow, widower.

**овёс** (овса́) oats.

**ове́чка** *dim of* **овца́**; harmless person.

**овладева́ть** *impf*, **овладе́ть** (-е́ю) *pf* +*instr* seize; capture; master.

**о́вод** (*pl* -ы *or* -а́) gadfly.

**о́вощ** (*pl* -и, -е́й) vegetable. **овощно́й** vegetable.

**овра́г** ravine, gully.

**овся́нка** oatmeal; porridge. **овся́ный** oat, oatmeal.

**овца́** (*pl* -ы, ове́ц, о́вцам) sheep; ewe. **овча́рка** sheepdog. **овчи́на** sheepskin.

**ога́рок** (-рка) candle-end.

**огиба́ть** *impf of* **обогну́ть**

**оглавле́ние** table of contents.

**огласи́ть** (-ашу́) *pf*, **оглаша́ть** *impf* announce; fill (with sound); ~**ся** resound. **огла́ска** publicity. **оглаше́ние** publication.

**огло́бля** (*gen pl* -бель) shaft.

**о|гло́хнуть** (-ну, -ох) *pf*.

**оглуша́ть** *impf*, **о|глуши́ть** (-шу́) *pf* deafen; stun. **оглуши́тельный** deafening.

**огляде́ть** (-яжу́) *pf*, **огля́дывать** *impf*, **огляну́ть** (-ну́, -нешь) *pf* look round; look over; ~**ся** look round; look back. **огля́дка** looking back.

**огнево́й** fire; fiery. **о́гненный** fiery. **огнеопа́сный** inflammable. **огнеприпа́сы** (-ов) *pl* ammunition. **огнесто́йкий** fire-proof. **огнестре́льный**: ~**ое ору́жие** firearm(s). **огнетуши́тель** *m* fire-extinguisher. **огнеупо́рный** fire-resistant.

**ого́** *int* oho!

**огова́ривать** *impf*, **оговори́ть** *pf* slander; stipulate (for); ~**ся** make a proviso; make a slip (of the tongue). **огово́р** slander. **огово́рка** reservation, proviso; slip of the tongue.

**оголённый** bare, nude. **оголи́ть** *pf* (*impf* **оголя́ть**) bare; strip; ~**ся** strip o.s.; become exposed.

**оголя́ть(ся** *impf of* **оголи́ть(ся**

**огонёк** (-нька́) (*small*) light; zest. **ого́нь** (огня́) *m* fire; light.

**огора́живать** *impf*, **огороди́ть** (-рожу́, -ро́дишь) *pf* fence in, enclose; ~**ся** fence o.s. in. **огоро́д** kitchen-garden. **огоро́дный** kitchengarden.

**огорча́ть** *impf*, **огорчи́ть** (-чу́) *pf* grieve, pain; ~**ся** be distressed. **огорче́ние** grief; chagrin.

**о|гра́бить** (-блю) *pf*. **ограбле́ние** robbery; burglary.

**огра́да** fence. **огради́ть** (-ажу́) *pf*, **огражда́ть** *impf* guard, protect.

**ограниче́ние** limitation, restriction. **ограни́ченный** limited. **ограни́чивать** *impf*, **ограни́чить** (-чу) *pf* limit, restrict; ~**ся** +*instr* limit or confine o.s. to; be limited to.

**огро́мный** huge; enormous.

**о|грубе́ть** (-е́ю) *pf*.

**огры́зок** (-зка) bit, end; stub.

**огуре́ц** (-рца́) cucumber.

**ода́лживать** *impf of* **одолжи́ть**

**одарённый** gifted. **ода́ривать** *impf*, **одари́ть**, **одаря́ть** *impf* give presents (to); +*instr* endow with.

**одева́ть(ся** *impf of* **оде́ть(ся**

**оде́жда** clothes; clothing.

**одеколо́н** eau-de-Cologne.

**одели́ть** *pf*, **оделя́ть** *impf* (+*instr*) present (with); endow (with).

**оде́ну** *etc.: see* **оде́ть. одёргивать** *impf of* **одёрнуть**

**о|деревене́ть** (-е́ю) *pf*.

**одержа́ть** (-жу́, -жишь) *pf*, **оде́рживать** *impf* gain. **одержи́мый** possessed.

**одёрнуть** (-ну) *pf* (*impf* **одёргивать**) pull down, straighten.

**оде́тый** dressed; clothed. **оде́ть** (-е́ну) *pf* (*impf* **одева́ть**) dress; clothe; **~ся** dress (o.s.). **одея́ло** blanket. **одея́ние** garb, attire.

**оди́н** (одного́), **одна́** (одно́й), **одно́** (одного́); *pl* **одни́** (одни́х) one; a, an; a certain; alone; only; nothing but; same; **одно́ и то же** the same thing; **оди́н на оди́н** in private; **оди́н за други́м** one after another; **одни́м сло́вом** in a word; **по одному́** one by one.

**одина́ковый** identical, the same, equal.

**одиннадцатый** eleventh. **оди́ннадцать** eleven.

**одино́кий** solitary; lonely; single. **одино́чество** solitude; loneliness. **одино́чка** *m & f* (one) person alone. **одино́чный** individual; one-man; single; **~ое заключе́ние** solitary confinement.

**одича́лый** wild.

**одна́жды** *adv* once; one day; once upon a time.

**одна́ко** *conj* however.

**одно-** *in comb* single, one; uni-, mono-, homo-. **однобо́кий** one-sided. **~вре́менно** *adv* simultaneously, at the same time. **~вре́менный** simultaneous. **~зву́чный** monotonous. **~знача́щий** synonymous. **~зна́чный** synonymous; one-digit. **~именный** of the same name. **~кла́ссник** classmate. **~кле́точный** unicellular. **~кра́тный** single. **~ле́тний** one-year; annual. **~ме́стный** single-seater. **~обра́зие** monotony. **~обра́зный** monotonous. **~ро́дность** homogeneity, uniformity. **~ро́дный** homogeneous; similar. **~сторо́нний** one-sided; unilateral; one-way. **~фами́лец** (-льца) person of the same surname. **~цве́тный** one-colour; monochrome. **~эта́жный** one-storeyed.

**одобре́ние** approval. **одобри́тельный** approving. **одо́брить** *pf*, **одобря́ть** *impf* approve (of).

**одолева́ть** *impf*, **одоле́ть** (-е́ю) *pf* overcome.

**одолжа́ть** *impf*, **одолжи́ть** (-жу́) *pf* lend; +*у*+*gen* borrow from. **одолже́ние** favour.

**о|дряхле́ть** (-е́ю) *pf*.

**одува́нчик** dandelion.

**одума́ться**, **одумываться** *impf* change one's mind.

**одуре́лый** stupid. **о|дуре́ть** (-е́ю) *pf*.

**одурма́нивать** *impf*, **о|дурма́нить** *pf* stupefy. **одуря́ть** *impf* stupefy.

одухотворённый inspired; spiritual. одухотворить pf, одухотворять impf inspire.

одушевить (-влю) pf, одушевлять impf animate. одушевление animation.

одышка shortness of breath.

ожерелье necklace.

ожесточать impf, ожесточить (-чу) pf embitter, harden. ожесточение bitterness. ожесточённый bitter; hard.

оживать impf of ожить

оживить (-влю) pf, оживлять impf revive; enliven; ~ся become animated. оживление animation; reviving; enlivening. оживлённый animated, lively.

ожидание expectation; waiting. ожидать impf + gen or acc wait for; expect.

ожирение obesity. о|жиреть (-ею) pf.

ожить (-иву, -ивёшь; ожил, -á, -о) pf (impf оживать) come to life, revive.

ожог burn, scald.

озабоченность preoccupation; anxiety. озабоченный preoccupied; anxious.

озаглавить (-лю) pf, озаглавливать impf entitle; head.

озадачивать impf, озадачить (-чу) pf perplex, puzzle.

озарить pf, озарять impf light up, illuminate; ~ся light up.

оздоровительный бег jogging. оздоровление sanitation.

озеленить pf, озеленять impf plant (with trees etc.).

озеро (pl озёра) lake.

озимые sb winter crops. озимый winter. озимь winter crop.

озираться impf look round; look back.

о|злить(ся: see обозлить(ся

озлобить (-блю) pf, озлоблять impf embitter; ~ся grow bitter. озлобление bitterness, animosity. озлобленный embittered.

о|знакомить (-млю) pf, ознакомлять impf c+instr acquaint with; ~ся c+instr familiarize o.s. with.

ознаменовать pf, ознаменовывать impf mark; celebrate.

означать impf mean, signify.

озноб shivering, chill.

озон ozone.

озорник (-á) mischief-maker. озорной naughty, mischievous. озорство mischief.

озябнуть (-ну; озяб) pf be cold, be freezing.

ой int oh.

оказать (-ажу, -ажешь) pf (impf оказывать) render, provide, show; ~ся turn out, prove; find o.s., be found.

оказия unexpected event, funny thing.

оказывать(ся impf of оказать(ся

окаменелость fossil. окаменелый fossilized; petrified. о|каменеть (-ею) pf.

окантовка mount.

оканчивать(ся impf of окончить(ся. окапывать(ся impf of окопать(ся

окаянный damned, cursed.

океан ocean. океанский ocean; oceanic.

окидывать impf, окинуть (-ну) pf; ~ взглядом take in at a glance, glance over.

óкисел (-сла) oxide. окисление oxidation. óкись oxide.

**оккупа́нт** invader. **оккупа́ция** occupation. **оккупи́ровать** impf & pf occupy.

**окла́д** salary scale; (basic) pay.

**оклевета́ть** (-ещу́, -е́щешь) pf slander.

**окле́ивать** impf, **окле́ить** pf cover; paste over; ~ **обо́ями** paper.

**окно́** (pl о́кна) window.

**о́ко** (pl о́чи, оче́й) eye.

**око́вы** (око́в) pl fetters.

**околдова́ть** pf, **околдо́вывать** impf bewitch.

**о́коло** adv & prep+gen by; close (to), near; around; about.

**око́льный** roundabout. **око́льным** window.

**оконча́ние** end; conclusion, termination; ending. **оконча́тельный** final. **око́нчить** (-чу) pf (impf **ока́нчивать**) finish, end; ~**ся** finish, end.

**око́п** trench. **окопа́ть** (impf **ока́пывать**) dig round; ~**ся** entrench o.s., dig in. **око́пный** trench.

**о́корок** (pl -á, -о́в) ham, gammon.

**окочене́лый** stiff with cold. **о|кочене́ть** (-ю) pf.

**око́шечко, око́шко** (small) window.

**окра́ина** outskirts, outlying districts.

**о|кра́сить** (-а́шу) pf, **окра́шивать** impf paint, colour; dye. **окра́ска** painting; colouring; dyeing; colouration.

**о|кре́пнуть** (-ну) pf. **о|крести́ть(ся** (-ещу́(сь, -е́стишь(ся) pf.

**окре́стность** environs. **окре́стный** neighbouring.

**о́крик** hail; shout. **окри́кивать** impf, **окри́кнуть** (-ну) pf hail, call, shout to.

**окрова́вленный** bloodstained.

**о́круг** (pl -á) district. **окру́га** neighbourhood. **округли́ть** pf, **округля́ть** impf round; round off. **окру́глый** rounded. **окружа́ть** impf, **окружи́ть** (-жу́) pf surround; encircle. **окружа́ющий** surrounding; ~**ее** sb environment; ~**ие** sb pl associates. **окруже́ние** encirclement; environment. **окружно́й** district. **окру́жность** circumference.

**окрыли́ть** pf, **окрыля́ть** impf inspire, encourage.

**окта́ва** octave.

**окта́н** octane.

**октя́брь** (-я́) m October. **октя́брьский** October.

**окули́ст** oculist.

**окуна́ть** impf, **окуну́ть** (-ну́, -нёшь) pf dip; ~**ся** dip; plunge; become absorbed.

**о́кунь** (pl -и, -е́й) m perch.

**окупа́ть** impf, **окупи́ть** (-плю́, -пишь) pf compensate, repay; ~**ся** be repaid, pay for itself.

**оку́рок** (-рка) cigarette-end.

**оку́тать** pf, **оку́тывать** impf wrap up; shroud, cloak.

**оку́чивать** impf, **оку́чить** (-чу) pf earth up.

**ола́дья** (gen pl -ий) fritter; drop-scone.

**оледене́лый** frozen. **о|ледене́ть** (-ю) pf.

**оле́ний** deer, deer's; reindeer. **олени́на** venison. **оле́нь** m deer; reindeer.

**оли́ва** olive. **оли́вковый** olive; olive-coloured.

**олига́рхия** oligarchy.

**олимпиа́да** olympiad; Olympics. **олимпи́йск|ий** Olympic; Olympian; ~**ие и́гры** Olympic games.

**оли́фа** drying oil (*e.g. linseed oil*).

**олицетворе́ние** personification; embodiment. **олицетвори́ть** *pf*, **олицетворя́ть** *impf* personify, embody.

**о́лово** tin. **оловя́нный** tin.

**ом** ohm.

**ома́р** lobster.

**омерзе́ние** loathing. **омерзи́тельный** loathsome.

**омертве́лый** stiff, numb; necrotic. **о|мертве́ть** (-е́ю) *pf*.

**омле́т** omelette.

**омоложе́ние** rejuvenation.

**омо́ним** homonym.

**омо́ю** *etc.: see* **омы́ть**

**омрача́ть** *impf*, **омрачи́ть** (-чу́) *pf* darken, cloud.

**о́мут** whirlpool; maelstrom.

**омыва́ть** *impf*, **омы́ть** (омо́ю) *pf* wash; **~ся** be washed.

**он** (его́, ему́, им, о нём) *pron* he. **она́** (её, ей, ей (е́ю), о ней) *pron* she.

**онда́тра** musk-rat.

**онеме́лый** numb. **о|неме́ть** (-е́ю) *pf*.

**они́** (их, им, и́ми, о них) *pron* they. **оно́** (его́, ему́, им, о нём) *pron* it; this, that.

**опада́ть** *impf of* **опа́сть**

**опа́здывать** *impf of* **опозда́ть**

**опа́ла** disgrace.

**о|пали́ть** *pf*.

**опа́ловый** opal.

**опа́лубка** casing.

**опаса́ться** *impf* +*gen* fear; avoid, keep off. **опасе́ние** fear; apprehension.

**опа́сность** danger; peril. **опа́сный** dangerous.

**опа́сть** (-адёт) *pf* (*impf* опада́ть) fall, fall off; subside.

**опе́ка** guardianship; trusteeship. **опека́емый** *sb* ward. **опе-**

**ка́ть** *impf* be guardian of; take care of. **опеку́н** (-á), **-у́нша** guardian; tutor; trustee.

**о́пера** opera.

**операти́вный** efficient; operative, surgical; operation(s), operational. **опера́тор** operator; cameraman. **операцио́нный** operating; **~ая** *sb* operating theatre. **опера́ция** operation.

**опереди́ть** (-режу́) *pf*, **опережа́ть** *impf* outstrip, leave behind.

**опере́ние** plumage.

**опере́тта, -е́тка** operetta.

**опере́ть** (обопру́, -прёшь; опёр, -ла́) *pf* (*impf* опира́ть) +о+*acc* lean against; **~ся** на *or* о+*acc* lean on, lean against.

**опери́ровать** *impf* & *pf* operate on; operate, act; +*instr* use.

**о́перный** opera; operatic.

**о|печа́лить(ся** *pf*.

**опеча́тать** *pf* (*impf* опеча́тывать) seal up.

**опеча́тка** misprint.

**опеча́тывать** *impf of* **опеча́тать**

**опеши́ть** (-шу) *pf* be taken aback.

**опи́лки** (-лок) *pl* sawdust; filings.

**опира́ть(ся** *impf of* **опере́ть(ся**

**описа́ние** description. **описа́тельный** descriptive. **описа́ть** (-ишу́, -и́шешь) *pf*, **опи́сывать** *impf* describe; **~ся** make a slip of the pen. **опи́ска** slip of the pen. **о́пись** inventory.

**о́пиум** opium.

**опла́кать** (-а́чу) *pf*, **опла́кивать** *impf* mourn for; bewail.

**опла́та** payment. **оплати́ть** (-ачу́, -а́тишь) *pf*, **оплачи-**

вать *impf* pay (for).
опла́чу *etc.: see* опла́кать. оплачу́ *etc.: see* оплати́ть.
оплёуха slap in the face.
оплодотвори́ть *pf*, оплодотворя́ть *impf* impregnate; fertilize.
о|пломбирова́ть *pf*.
опло́т stronghold, bulwark.
опло́шность blunder, mistake.
оповести́ть (-ещу́) *pf*, оповеща́ть *impf* notify. оповеще́ние notification.
опозда́вший *sb* late-comer. опозда́ние lateness; delay. опозда́ть *pf (impf* опа́здывать) be late; +на+*acc* be late for.
опознава́тельный distinguishing; ~ знак landmark. опознава́ть (-наю́, -наёшь) *impf*, опозна́ть *pf* identify. опозна́ние identification.
о|позо́рить(ся *pf*.
оползти́ *impf*, оползти́ (-зёт; -о́лз, -ла́) *pf* slip, slide. о́ползень (-зня) *m* landslide.
ополче́ние militia.
опо́мниться *pf* come to one's senses.
опо́р: во весь ~ at full speed. опо́ра support; pier; то́чка опо́ры fulcrum, foothold.
опора́жнивать *impf of* опоро́жнить
опо́рный support, supporting, supported; bearing.
опоро́жни́ть *pf*, опорожня́ть *impf (impf also* опора́жнивать) empty.
о|поро́чить (-чу) *pf*.
опохмели́ться *pf*, опохмеля́ться *impf* take a hair of the dog that bit you.
опо́шлить *pf*, опошля́ть *impf* vulgarize, debase.
опоя́сать (-я́шу) *pf*, опоя́-

сывать *impf* gird; girdle.
оппозицио́нный opposition. оппози́ция opposition.
оппортуни́зм opportunism.
опра́ва setting, mounting; spectacle frames.
оправда́ние justification; excuse; acquittal. оправда́тельный пригово́р verdict of not guilty. оправда́ть *pf*, опра́вдывать *impf* justify; excuse; acquit; ~ся justify o.s.; be justified.
опра́вить (-влю) *pf*, оправля́ть *impf* set right, adjust; mount; ~ся put one's dress in order; recover; +от+*gen* get over.
опра́шивать *impf of* опроси́ть
определе́ние definition; determination; decision. определённый definite; certain. определи́мый definable. определи́ть *pf*, определя́ть *impf* define; determine; appoint; ~ся be formed; be determined; find one's position.
опроверга́ть *impf*, опрове́ргнуть (-ну; -ве́рг) *pf* refute, disprove. опроверже́ние refutation; denial.
опроки́дывать *impf*, опроки́нуть (-ну) *pf* overturn; topple; ~ся overturn; capsize.
опроме́тчивый rash, hasty.
опро́с (cross-)examination; (opinion) poll. опроси́ть (-ошу́, -о́сишь) *pf (impf* опра́шивать) question; (cross-)examine. опро́сный лист questionnaire.
опры́скать *pf*, опры́скивать *impf* sprinkle; spray.
опря́тный neat, tidy.
о́птик optician. о́птика op-

tics. **опти́ческий** optic, optical.

**оптима́льный** optimal. **оптими́зм** optimism. **оптими́ст** optimist. **оптимисти́ческий** optimistic.

**опто́вый** wholesale. **о́птом** *adv* wholesale.

**опубликова́ние** publication; promulgation. **о|публикова́ть** *pf*, **опублико́вывать** *impf* publish; promulgate.

**опуска́ть(ся** *impf of* **опусти́ть(ся**

**опусте́лый** deserted. **о|пусте́ть** (-е́ет) *pf*.

**опусти́ть** (-ущу́, -у́стишь) *pf* (*impf* **опуска́ть**) lower; let down; turn down; omit; post; ~**ся** lower o.s.; sink; fall; go down; go to pieces.

**опустоша́ть** *impf*, **опустоши́ть** (-шу́) *pf* devastate. **опустоше́ние** devastation. **опустоши́тельный** devastating.

**опу́тать** *pf*, **опу́тывать** *impf* entangle; ensnare.

**опуха́ть** *impf*, **опу́хнуть** (-ну; онух) *pf* swell, swell up. **опу́холь** swelling; tumour.

**опу́шка** edge of a forest; trimming.

**опущу́** *etc.: see* **опусти́ть**

**опыле́ние** pollination. **опыли́ть** *pf*, **опыля́ть** *impf* pollinate.

**о́пыт** experience; experiment. **о́пытный** experienced; experimental.

**опьяне́ние** intoxication. **о|пьяне́ть** (-е́ю) *pf*, **о|пьяни́ть** *pf*, **опьяня́ть** *impf* intoxicate, make drunk.

**опя́ть** *adv* again.

**ора́ва** crowd, horde.

**ора́кул** oracle.

**орангута́нг** orangutan.

**ора́нжевый** orange. **оранжере́я** greenhouse, conservatory.

**ора́тор** orator. **орато́рия** oratorio.

**ора́ть** (ору́, орёшь) *impf* yell.

**орби́та** orbit; (eye-)socket.

**о́рган**[1] organ; body. **орга́н**[2] (*mus*) organ. **организа́тор** organizer. **организацио́нный** organization(al). **организа́ция** organization. **органи́зм** organism. **организо́ванный** organized. **организова́ть** *impf & pf* (*pf also* **с~**) organize; ~**ся** be organized; organize. **органи́ческий** organic.

**о́ргия** orgy.

**орда́** (*pl* -ы) horde.

**о́рден** (*pl* -á) order.

**о́рдер** (*pl* -á) order; warrant; writ.

**ордина́та** ordinate.

**ордина́тор** house-surgeon.

**орёл** (орла́) eagle; ~ **и́ли ре́шка?** heads or tails?

**орео́л** halo.

**оре́х** nut, nuts; walnut. **оре́ховый** nut; walnut. **оре́шник** hazel; hazel-thicket.

**оригина́л** original; eccentric. **оригина́льный** original.

**ориента́ция** orientation. **ориенти́р** landmark; reference point. **ориенти́роваться** *impf & pf* orient o.s.; +**на**+*acc* head for; aim at. **ориентиро́вка** orientation. **ориентиро́вочный** reference; tentative; approximate.

**орке́стр** orchestra.

**орли́ный** eagle; aquiline.

**орна́мент** ornament; ornamental design.

**о|робе́ть** (-е́ю) *pf*.

**ороси́тельный** irrigation.

ороси́ть (-ошу́) *pf*, ороша́ть *impf* irrigate. ороше́ние irrigation; поля́ ороше́ния sewage farm.

ору́ *etc.: see* ора́ть

ору́дие instrument; tool; gun. оруди́йный gun. ору́довать *impf* +*instr* handle; use. оруже́йный arms; gun. ору́жие arm, arms; weapons.

орфографи́ческий orthographic(al). орфогра́фия orthography, spelling.

оса́ (*pl* -ы) wasp.

оса́да siege. осади́ть[1] (-ажу́) *pf* (*impf* осажда́ть) besiege.

осади́ть[2] (-ажу́, -а́дишь) *pf* (*impf* оса́живать) check; force back; rein in; take down a peg.

оса́дный siege.

оса́док (-дка) sediment; fall-out; after-taste; *pl* precipitation, fall-out. оса́дочный sedimentary.

осажда́ть *impf of* осади́ть[1]

оса́живать *impf of* осади́ть[2]. осажу́ *see* осади́ть[1,2]

оса́нка carriage, bearing.

осва́ивать(ся *impf of* освои́ть(ся

осведоми́тельный informative; information. осве́домить (-млю) *pf*, осведомля́ть *impf* inform; ~ся о+*prep* inquire about, ask after. осве-домле́ние notification. осве-домлённый well-informed, knowledgeable.

освежа́ть *impf*, освежи́ть (-жу́) *pf* refresh; air. освежи́тельный refreshing.

освети́тельный illuminating. освети́ть (-ещу́) *pf*, освеща́ть *pf* light up; illuminate; throw light on; ~ся light up. освеще́ние lighting, illumi-

nation. освещённый (-ён, -á) lit.

освиде́тельствовать *pf*.

освиста́ть (-ищу́, -и́щешь) *pf*, освисты́вать *impf* hiss (off); boo.

освободи́тель *m* liberator. освободи́тельный liberation, emancipation. освобо-ди́ть (-ожу́) *pf*, освобо-жда́ть *impf* liberate; emancipate; dismiss; vacate; empty; ~ся free о.s.; become free. освобожде́ние liberation; release; emancipation; vacation. освобождённый (-ён, -á) freed, free; exempt.

освое́ние mastery; opening up. освои́ть *pf* (*impf* осва́ивать) master; become familiar with; ~ся familiarize о.s.

освящённый (-ён, -ена́) consecrated; sanctified; ~ ве-ка́ми time-honoured.

оседа́ть *impf of* осе́сть

оседла́ть *pf*, осёдлывать *impf* saddle. осёдлый settled.

осека́ться *impf of* осе́чься

осёл (-сла́) donkey; ass.

осело́к (-лка́) touchstone; whetstone.

осени́ть *pf* (*impf* осеня́ть) overshadow; dawn upon.

осе́нний autumn(al). о́сень autumn. о́сенью *adv* in autumn.

осеня́ть *impf of* осени́ть

осе́сть (ося́ду; осёл) *pf* (*impf* оседа́ть) settle; subside.

осётр (-á) sturgeon. осе-три́на sturgeon.

осе́чка misfire. осе́чься (-еку́сь, -ечёшься; -ёкся, -екла́сь) *pf* (*impf* осека́ться) stop short.

оси́ливать *impf*, оси́лить *pf* overpower; master.

оси́на aspen.

о|си́пнуть (-ну; оси́п) get hoarse.

осироте́лый orphaned. осироте́ть (-е́ю) pf be orphaned.

оска́ливать impf, о|ска́лить pf; ~ зу́бы, ~ся bare one's teeth.

о|сканда́лить(ся pf.

оскверни́ть pf, оскверня́ть impf profane; defile.

оско́лок (-лка) splinter; fragment.

оско́мина bitter taste (in the mouth); наби́ть оско́мину set the teeth on edge.

оскорби́тельный insulting, abusive. оскорби́ть (-блю́) pf, оскорбля́ть impf insult; offend; ~ся take offence. оскорбле́ние insult. оскорблённый (-ён, -á) insulted.

ослабева́ть impf, о|слабе́ть (-е́ю) pf weaken; slacken. осла́бить (-блю) pf, ослабля́ть impf weaken; slacken. ослабле́ние weakening; slackening, relaxation.

ослепи́тельный blinding, dazzling. ослепи́ть (-плю́) pf, ослепля́ть impf blind, dazzle. ослепле́ние blinding; dazzling; blindness. о|слепну́ть (-ну; -éп) pf.

осли́ный donkey; asinine. осли́ца she-ass.

осложне́ние complication. осложни́ть pf, осложня́ть impf complicate; ~ся become complicated.

ослы́шаться (-шусь) pf mishear.

осма́тривать(ся impf of осмотре́ть(ся. осме́ивать impf of осмея́ть

о|смеле́ть (-е́ю) pf. осме́ли-

ва́ться impf, осме́литься pf dare; venture.

осмея́ть (-ею́, -еёшь) pf (impf осме́ивать) ridicule.

осмо́тр examination, inspection. осмотре́ть (-рю́, -ришь) pf (impf осма́тривать) examine, inspect; look round; ~ся look round. осмотри́тельный circumspect.

осмы́сленный sensible, intelligent. осмы́сливать impf, осмы́слить pf, осмысля́ть impf interpret; comprehend.

оснасти́ть (-ащу́) pf, оснаща́ть impf fit out, equip. осна́стка rigging. оснаще́ние fitting out; equipment.

осно́ва base, basis, foundation; pl framework; stem (of a word). основа́ние founding, foundation; base; basis; reason; на како́м основа́нии? on what grounds? основа́тель m founder. основа́тельный well-founded; solid; thorough. основа́ть (-ную́, -нуёшь) pf, осно́вывать impf found; base; ~ся settle; be founded, be based. основно́й fundamental, basic; main; в основно́м in the main, on the whole. основополо́жник founder.

осо́ба person. осо́бенно especially. осо́бенность peculiarity; в осо́бенности in particular. осо́бенный special, particular, peculiar. особня́к (-á) private residence; detached house. особняко́м adv by o.s. осо́бо adv apart; especially. осо́бый special; particular.

осознава́ть (-наю́, -наёшь) impf, осозна́ть pf realize.

осо́ка sedge.

о́спа smallpox; pock-marks.

оспа́рива|ть *impf*, оспо́рить *pf* dispute; contest.

о|срами́ть(ся (-млю(сь) *pf*.

остава́ться (-таю́сь, -таёшься *impf of* оста́ться

ост (*naut*) east; east wind.

оста́вить (-влю) *pf*, оставля́ть *impf* leave; abandon; reserve.

остальн|о́й the rest of; ~о́е *sb* the rest; ~ые *sb pl* the others.

остана́влива|ть(ся *impf of* останови́ть(ся

оста́нки (-ов) *pl* remains.

останови́ть (-влю́, -вишь) *pf* (*impf* остана́вливать) stop; restrain; ~ся stop, halt; stay; +на+*prep* dwell on; settle on. остано́вка stop.

оста́ток (-тка) remainder; rest; residue; *pl* remains; leftovers. оста́ться (-а́нусь) *pf* (*impf* остава́ться) remain; stay; *impers* it remains, it is necessary; нам не остаётся ничего́ друго́го, как мы have no choice but.

остекли́ть *pf*, остекля́ть *impf* glaze.

остервене́ть *pf* become enraged.

остерега́ть *impf*, остере́чь (-регу́, -режёшь; -рёг, -ла́) *pf* warn; ~ся (+*gen*) beware (of).

о́стов frame, framework; skeleton.

о|столбене́ть (-е́ю) *pf*.

осторо́жно *adv* carefully; ~! look out! осторо́жность care, caution. осторо́жный careful, cautious.

острига́ть(ся *impf of* остри́чь(ся

острие́ point; spike; (cutting) edge. остри́ть[1] *impf* sharpen.

остри́ть[2] *impf* c~) be witty.

о|стри́чь (-игу́, -ижёшь; -и́г) (*impf also* острига́ть) cut, clip; ~ся have one's hair cut.

о́стров (*pl* -á) island. острово́к (-вка́) islet; ~ безопа́сности (traffic) island.

острота́[1] witticism, joke. острота́[2] sharpness; keenness; pungency.

остроу́мие wit. остроу́мный witty.

о́стрый (остр, -á, -о) sharp; pointed; acute; keen. остря́к (-á) wit.

о|студи́ть (-ужу́, -у́дишь) *pf*, остужа́ть *impf* cool.

оступа́ться *impf*, оступи́ться (-плю́сь, -пишься) *pf* stumble.

остыва́ть *impf*, осты́ть (-ы́ну) *pf* get cold; cool down.

осуди́ть (-ужу́, -у́дишь) *pf*, осужда́ть *impf* condemn; convict. осужде́ние condemnation; conviction. осуждён|ный (-ён, -á) condemned, convicted; *sb* convict.

осу́нуться (-нусь) *pf* grow thin, become drawn.

осуша́ть *impf*, осуши́ть (-шу́, -шишь) *pf* drain; dry. осуше́ние drainage.

осуществи́мый feasible. осуществи́ть (-влю) *pf*, осуществля́ть *impf* realize, bring about; accomplish; ~ся be fulfilled; come true. осуществле́ние realization; accomplishment.

осчастли́вить (-влю) *pf*, осчастли́вливать *impf* make happy.

осыпа́ть (-плю) *pf*, осыпа́ть *impf* strew; shower; ~ся crumble; fall. о́сыпь scree.

ось (*gen pl* -е́й) axis; axle.

**осьмино́г** octopus.

**ося́ду** etc.: see **осе́сть**

**осяза́емый** tangible. **осяза́ние** touch. **осяза́тельный** tactile; tangible. **осяза́ть** impf feel.

**от, о́то** prep+gen from; of; against.

**ота́пливать** impf of **отопи́ть**

**ота́ра** flock (of sheep).

**отба́вить** (-влю) pf, **отбавля́ть** impf pour off; **хоть отбавля́й** more than enough.

**отбега́ть** impf, **отбежа́ть** (-егу́) pf run off.

**отберу́** etc.: see **отобра́ть**

**отбива́ть(ся** impf of **отби́ть(ся**

**отбивна́я котле́та** cutlet, chop.

**отбира́ть** impf of **отобра́ть**

**отби́ть** (отобью́, -ёшь) pf (impf **отбива́ть**) beat (off), repel; win over; break off; **~ся** break off; drop behind; **+от**+gen defend o.s. against.

**о́тблеск** reflection.

**отбо́й** repelling; retreat; ringing off; **бить ~** beat a retreat; **дать ~** ring off.

**отбо́йный молото́к** (-тка́) pneumatic drill.

**отбо́р** selection. **отбо́рный** choice, select(ed).

**отбра́сывать** impf, **отбро́сить** (-о́шу) pf throw off or away; hurl back; reject; **~ тень** cast a shadow. **отбро́сы** (-ов) pf garbage.

**отбыва́ть** impf, **отбы́ть** (-бу́ду; о́тбыл, -а́, -о) pf depart; serve (a sentence).

**отва́га** courage, bravery.

**отва́живаться** impf, **отва́житься** (-жусь) pf dare. **отва́жный** courageous.

**отва́л** dump, slag-heap; cast-

ing off; **до ~а** to satiety.

**отва́ливать** impf, **отвали́ть** (-лю́, -лишь) pf push aside.

**отва́р** broth; decoction. **отва́ривать** impf, **отвари́ть** (-рю́, -ришь) pf boil. **отварно́й** boiled.

**отве́дать** pf (impf **отве́дывать**) taste, try.

**отведу́** etc.: see **отвести́**

**отве́дывать** impf of **отве́дать**

**отвезти́** (-зу́, -зёшь; -вёз, -ла́) pf (impf **отвози́ть**) take or cart away.

**отвёл** etc.: see **отвести́**

**отверга́ть** impf, **отве́ргнуть** (-ну; -ве́рг) pf reject; repudiate.

**отве́рженный** outcast.

**отверну́ть** (-ну́, -нёшь) pf (impf **отвёртывать, отвора́чивать**) turn aside; turn down; turn on; unscrew; screw off; **~ся** turn away; come unscrewed.

**отве́рстие** opening; hole.

**отверте́ть** (-рчу́, -ртишь) pf (impf **отвёртывать**) unscrew; twist off; **~ся** come unscrewed; get off. **отвёртка** screwdriver.

**отвёртывать(ся** impf of **отверну́ть(ся, отверте́ть(ся**

**отве́с** plumb; vertical slope. **отве́сить** (-е́шу) pf (impf **отве́шивать**) weigh out. **отве́сный** perpendicular, sheer.

**отвести́** (-еду́, -едёшь; -вёл, -а́) pf (impf **отводи́ть**) lead, take; draw or take aside; deflect; draw off; reject; allot.

**отве́т** answer.

**ответви́ться** pf, **ответвля́ться** impf branch off. **ответвле́ние** branch, offshoot.

**отве́тить** (-е́чу) *pf*, **отвеча́ть** *impf* answer; +**на**+*acc* answer to; +**за**+*acc* answer for. **отве́тить** in reply, return. **отве́тственность** responsibility. **отве́тственный** responsible. **отве́тчик** defendant.

**отве́шивать** *impf of* **отве́сить. отве́шу** *etc.: see* **отве́сить**

**отвинти́ть** (-нчу́) *pf*, **отви́нчивать** *impf* unscrew.

**отвиса́ть** *impf*, **отви́снуть** (-нет; -ис) *pf* hang down, sag. **отви́слый** hanging, baggy.

**отвлека́ть** *impf*, **отвле́чь** (-еку́, -ечёшь; -влёк, -ла́) *pf* distract, divert; **~ся** be distracted. **отвлечённый** abstract.

**отво́д** taking aside; diversion; leading, taking; rejection; allotment. **отводи́ть** (-ожу́, -о́дишь) *impf of* **отвести́**

**отвоева́ть** (-ою́ю) *pf*, **отвоёвывать** *impf* win back; spend in fighting.

**отвози́ть** (-ожу́, -о́зишь) *impf of* **отвезти́. отвора́чивать(ся** *impf of* **отверну́ть(ся**

**отвори́ть** (-рю́, -ришь) *pf* (*impf* **отворя́ть**) open; **~ся** open. **отворя́ть(ся** *impf of* **отвори́ть(ся. отворю́** *etc.: see* **отвоева́ть**

**отврати́тельный** disgusting. **отвраще́ние** disgust, repugnance.

**отвыка́ть** *impf*, **отвы́кнуть** (-ну; -ык) *pf* +**от** *or inf* lose the habit of; grow out of.

**отвяза́ть** (-яжу́, -я́жешь) *pf*, **отвя́зывать** *impf* untie, unfasten; **~ся** come untied, come loose; +**от**+*gen* get rid of; leave alone.

**отгада́ть** *pf*, · **отга́дывать** *impf* guess. **отга́дка** answer.

**отгиба́ть(ся** *impf of* **отогну́ть(ся**

**отгла́дить** (-а́жу) *pf*, **отгла́живать** *impf* iron (out).

**отгова́ривать** *impf*, **отговори́ть** *pf* dissuade; **~ся** +*instr* plead. **отгово́рка** excuse, pretext.

**отголо́сок** (-ска) echo.

**отгоня́ть** *impf of* **отогна́ть**

**отгора́живать** *impf*, **отгороди́ть** (-ожу́, -о́дишь) *pf* fence off; partition off; **~ся** shut o.s. off.

**отдава́ть**[1] (-даю́(сь) *impf of* **отда́ть(ся. отдава́ть**[2] (-аёт) *impf impers*+*instr* taste of; smell of; smack of; **от него́** **отдаёт во́дкой** he reeks of vodka.

**отдале́ние** removal; distance. **отдалённый** remote. **отдали́ть** *pf*, **отдаля́ть** *impf* remove; estrange; postpone; **~ся** move away; digress.

**отда́ть** (-а́м, -а́шь, -а́ст, -ади́м; о́тдал, -а́, -о) *pf* (*impf* **отдава́ть**[1]) give back, return; give; give up; give away; recoil; cast off; **~ся** give o.s. (up); resound. **отда́ча** return; payment; casting off; efficiency; output; recoil.

**отде́л** department; section. **отде́лать** *pf* (*impf* **отде́лывать**) finish, put the finishing touches to; trim; **~ся** +**от**+*gen* get rid of; +*instr* get off with.

**отделе́ние** separation; department; compartment; section. **отдели́ть** (-елю́, -е́лишь) *pf* (*impf* **отделя́ть**) separate; detach; **~ся** separate; detach o.s.; get detached.

**отде́лка** finishing; finish,

decoration. **отде́лывать(ся**
*impf of* **отде́лать(ся**

**отде́льно** separately; apart.
**отде́льный** separate. **отделя́-
ть(ся** *impf of* **отдели́ть(ся**

**отдёргивать** *impf*, **отдёрнуть** (-ну) *pf* draw *or* pull
aside *or* back.

**отдеру́** *etc.: see* **отодра́ть**.
**отдира́ть** *impf of* **отодра́ть**

**отдохну́ть** (-ну́, -нёшь) *pf*
(*impf* **отдыха́ть**) rest.

**отду́шина** air-hole, vent.

**о́тдых** rest. **отдыха́ть** *impf*
(*pf* **отдохну́ть**) rest; be on
holiday.

**отдыша́ться** (-шу́сь, -шишься)
*pf* recover one's breath.

**отека́ть** *impf of* **оте́чь**. **о|те-
ли́ться** (-е́лится) *pf*.

**оте́ль** *m* hotel.

**отеса́ть** *etc.: see* **обтеса́ть**

**оте́ц** (отца́) father. **оте́че-
ский** fatherly, paternal. **оте́-
чественный** home, native.
**оте́чество** native land, fatherland.

**оте́чь** (-еку́, -ечёшь; отёк, -ла́)
*pf* (*impf* **отека́ть**) swell (up).

**отжива́ть** *impf*, **отжи́ть** (-иву́,
-ивёшь; о́тжил, -а́, -о) *pf* become obsolete *or* outmoded.
**отжи́вший** obsolete; outmoded.

**о́тзвук** echo.

**о́тзыв**[1] opinion; reference; review; response. **отзы́в**[2] recall. **отзыва́ть(ся** *impf of*
**отозва́ть(ся**. **отзы́вчивый**
responsive.

**отка́з** refusal; repudiation; failure; natural. **отказа́ть** (-ажу́,
-а́жешь) *pf*, **отка́зывать** *impf*
break down (+*dat* *s.o.'s*)
refuse, deny (*s.o. sth*); **~ся**
(+*от*+*gen* *or* +*inf*) refuse; turn
down; renounce, give up.

**отка́лывать(ся** *impf of* **от-
коло́ть(ся**. **отка́пывать** *impf
of* **откопа́ть**. **отка́рмливать**
*impf of* **откорми́ть**

**откати́ть** (-ачу́, -а́тишь) *pf*,
**отка́тывать** *impf* roll away;
**~ся** roll away *or* back; be
forced back.

**отка́чивать** *impf*, **отка́чать** *pf*
pump out; give artificial respiration to.

**отка́шливаться** *impf*, **от-
ка́шляться** *pf* clear one's
throat.

**откидно́й** folding, collapsible.
**отки́дывать** *impf*, **отки́нуть**
(-ну) *pf* fold back; throw aside.

**откла́дывать** *impf of* **отло-
жи́ть**

**откле́ивать** *impf*, **откле́ить**
(-е́ю) *pf* unstick; **~ся** come
unstuck.

**о́тклик** response; comment;
echo. **отклика́ться** *impf*,
**откли́кнуться** (-нусь) *pf* answer, respond.

**отклоне́ние** deviation; declining; refusal; deflection.
**отклони́ть** (-ню́, -нишь) *pf*,
**отклоня́ть** *impf* deflect; decline; **~ся** deviate; diverge.

**отключа́ть** *impf*, **отключи́ть**
(-чу́) *pf* cut off, disconnect.

**отколоти́ть** (-очу́, -о́тишь) *pf*
knock off; beat up.

**отколо́ть** (-лю́, -лешь) *pf*
(*impf* **отка́лывать**) break off;
chop off; unpin; **~ся** break
off; come unpinned; break
away.

**откопа́ть** *pf* (*impf* **отка́пы-
вать**) dig up; exhume.

**откорми́ть** (-млю́, -мишь) *pf*
(*impf* **отка́рмливать**) fatten.

**отко́с** slope.

**открепи́ть** (-плю́) *pf*, **откре-
пля́ть** *impf* unfasten; **~ся**

become unfastened.

**откровéние** revelation. **открове́нный** frank; outspoken; unconcealed. **откро́ю** *etc.*: *see* **откры́ть**

**открути́ть** (-учу́, -у́тишь) *pf*, **откру́чивать** *impf* untwist, unscrew.

**открыва́ть** *impf*, **откры́ть** (-ро́ю) *pf* open; reveal; discover; turn on; ~ся open; come to light, be revealed. **откры́тие** discovery; revelation; opening. **откры́тка** postcard, card. **откры́то** openly. **откры́тый** open.

**откуда** *adv* from where; from which; how; ~ ни возьми́сь from out of nowhere. **откуда-либо**, **-нибудь** from somewhere or other. **откуда-то** from somewhere.

**отку́поривать** *impf*, **отку́порить** *pf* uncork.

**откуси́ть** (-ушу́, -у́сишь) *pf*, **отку́сывать** *impf* bite off.

**отлага́тельство** delay. **отлага́ть** *impf of* **отложи́ть**

**от|лакирова́ть** *pf*. **отла́мывать** *impf of* **отлома́ть**, **отломи́ть**

**отлепи́ть** (-плю́, -пишь) *pf* unstick, take off; ~ся come unstuck, come off.

**отлёт** flying away; departure. **отлета́ть** *impf*, **отлете́ть** (-лечу́) *pf*, fly, fly away, fly off; rebound.

**отли́в** ebb, ebb-tide; tint; play of colours. **отлива́ть** *impf*, **отли́ть** (отолью́; о́тлил, -á, -о) *pf* pour off; pump out; cast, found; (*no pf*) +*instr* be shot with. **отли́вка** casting; moulding.

**отлича́ть** *impf*, **отличи́ть** (-чу́) *pf* distinguish; ~ся distin-

guish o.s.; differ; +*instr* be notable for. **отли́чие** difference; distinction; **знак отли́чия** order, decoration; **с отли́чием** with honours. **отли́чник** outstanding student, worker, etc. **отличи́тельный** distinctive; distinguishing. **отли́чный** different; excellent.

**отло́гий** sloping.

**отложе́ние** sediment; deposit. **отложи́ть** (-ожу́, -о́жишь) *pf* (*impf* откла́дывать, отлага́ть) put aside; postpone; deposit.

**отлома́ть** (-млю́, -мишь) *pf* (*impf* отла́мывать) break off.

**отлу́пить** *pf*.

**отлуча́ть** *impf*, **отлучи́ть** (-чу́) *pf* (**от це́ркви**) excommunicate; ~ся absent o.s. **отлу́чка** absence.

**отлы́нивать** *impf* +**от**+*gen* shirk.

**отма́хиваться** *impf*, **отмахну́ться** (-ну́сь, -нёшься) *pf* **от**+*gen* brush off; brush aside.

**отмежева́ться** (-жу́юсь) *pf*, **отмежёвываться** *impf* **от**+*gen* dissociate o.s. from.

**о́тмель** (sand-)bank.

**отме́на** abolition; cancellation. **отмени́ть** (-ню́, -нишь) *pf*, **отменя́ть** *impf* repeal; abolish; cancel.

**отмере́ть** (отомрёт; о́тмер, -лá, -ло) *pf* (*impf* отмира́ть) die off; die out.

**отме́ривать** *impf*, **отме́рить** *pf*, **отмеря́ть** *impf* measure off.

**отмести́** (-ету́, -ете́шь; -ёл, -á) *pf* (*impf* отмета́ть) sweep aside.

**отмета́ть** *impf of* отмести́

**отме́тить** (-е́чу) *pf*, **отмеча́ть**

*impf* mark, note; celebrate; **~ся** sign one's name; sign out. **отме́тка** note; mark.

**отмира́ть** *impf of* **отмере́ть**

**отмора́живать** *impf*, **отморо́зить** (-о́жу) *pf* injure by frost-bite. **отморо́жение** frost-bite. **отморо́женный** frost-bitten.

**отмо́ю** *etc.: see* **отмы́ть**

**отмыва́ть** *impf*, **отмы́ть** (-мо́ю) *pf* wash clean; wash off; **~ся** wash o.s. clean; come out.

**отмыка́ть** *impf of* **отомкну́ть** **отмы́чка** master key.

**отнести́** (-су́, -сёшь; -нёс, -ла́) *pf* (*impf* **относи́ть**) take; carry away; ascribe, attribute; **~сь к**+*dat* treat; regard; apply to; concern, have to do with.

**отнима́ть(ся** *impf of* **отня́ть(ся**

**относи́тельно** *adv* relatively; *prep*+*gen* concerning. **относи́тельность** relativity. **относи́тельный** relative. **относи́ть(ся** (-ошу́(сь, -о́сишь(ся) *impf of* **отнести́(сь.** **отноше́ние** attitude; relation; respect; ratio; **в отноше́нии**+*gen*, **по отноше́нию к**+*dat* with regard to; **в прямо́м (обра́тном) отноше́нии** in direct (inverse) ratio.

**отны́не** *adv* henceforth.

**отню́дь** not at all.

**отня́тие** taking away; amputation. **отня́ть** (-ниму́, -ни́мешь; о́тнял, -а́, -о) *pf* (*impf* **отнима́ть**) take (away); amputate; **~ от груди** wean; **~ся** be paralysed.

**ото́:** *see* **от**

**отобража́ть** *impf*, **отобрази́ть** (-ажу́) *pf* reflect; represent. **отображе́ние** reflec-

tion; representation.

**отобра́ть** (отберу́, -рёшь; отобра́л, -а́, -о) *pf* (*impf* **отбира́ть**) take (away); select.

**отобью́** *etc.: see* **отби́ть**

**отовсю́ду** *adv* from everywhere.

**отогна́ть** (отгоню́, -о́нишь; отогна́л, -а́, -о) *pf* (*impf* **отгоня́ть**) drive away, off.

**отогну́ть** (-ну́, -нёшь) *pf* (*impf* **отгиба́ть**) bend back; **~ся** bend.

**отогрева́ть** *impf*, **отогре́ть** (-е́ю) *pf* warm.

**отодвига́ть** *impf*, **отодви́нуть** (-ну) *pf* move aside; put off.

**отодра́ть** (отдеру́, -рёшь; отодра́л, -а́, -о) *pf* (*impf* **отдира́ть**) tear off, rip off.

**отож(д)естви́ть** (-влю́) *pf*, **отож(д)ествля́ть** *pf* identify.

**отозва́ть** (отзову́, -вёшь; отозва́л, -а́, -о) *pf* (*impf* **отзыва́ть**) take aside; recall; **~ся на**+*acc* answer; **на**+*acc or prep* tell on; have an affect on.

**отойти́** (-йду́, -йдёшь; отошёл, -шла́) *pf* (*impf* **отходи́ть**) move away; depart; withdraw; digress; come out; recover.

**отолью́** *etc.: see* **отли́ть.** **отомрёт** *etc.: see* **отмере́ть.** **ото|мсти́ть** (-мщу́) *pf*.

**отомкну́ть** (-ну́, -нёшь) *pf* (*impf* **отмыка́ть**) unlock, unbolt.

**отопи́тельный** heating. **отопи́ть** (-плю́, -пишь) *pf* (*impf* **ота́пливать**) heat. **отопле́ние** heating.

**отопру́** *etc.: see* **отпере́ть.** **отопью́** *etc.: see* **отпи́ть.**

**ото́рванный** cut off, isolated. **оторва́ть** (-ву́, -вёшь) (*impf* **отрыва́ть**) tear off; tear away; **~ся** come off, be torn off; be cut off, lose touch; break away; tear o.s. away; **~ся от земли́** take off.

**оторопе́ть** (-е́ю) *pf* be struck dumb.

**отосла́ть** (-ошлю́, -ошлёшь) *pf* (*impf* **отсыла́ть**) send (off); send back; **+к+**dat refer to.

**отоспа́ться** (-сплю́сь; -а́лся, -ала́сь, -ось) *pf* (*impf* **отсыпа́ться**) catch up on one's sleep.

**отошёл** *etc.*: *see* **отойти́. отошлю́** *etc.*: *see* **отосла́ть**

**отпада́ть** *impf of* **отпа́сть**

**от|пари́ровать** *impf*, **отпа́рывать** *impf of* **отпоро́ть**

**отпа́сть** (-адёт) *pf* (*impf* **отпада́ть**) fall off; fall away; pass.

**отпева́ние** funeral service.

**отпере́ть** (отопру́, -прёшь; о́тпер, -ла́, -ло) *pf* (*impf* **отпира́ть**) unlock; **~ся** open; **+от+**gen deny; disown.

**от|печа́тать** *pf*, **отпеча́тывать** *impf* print (off); type (out); imprint. **отпеча́ток** (-тка) imprint, print.

**отпива́ть** *impf of* **отпи́ть**

**отпи́ливать** *impf*, **отпили́ть** (-лю́, -лишь) *pf* saw off.

**от|пира́тельство** denial. **отпира́ть(ся** *impf of* **отпере́ть(ся**

**отпи́ть** (отопью́, -пьёшь; о́тпил, -а́, -о) *pf* (*impf* **отпива́ть**) take a sip of.

**отпи́хивать** *impf*, **отпихну́ть** (-ну́, -нёшь) *pf* push off; shove aside.

**отплати́ть** (-ачу́, -а́тишь) *pf*, **отпла́чивать** *impf* +dat pay back.

**отплыва́ть** *impf*, **отплы́ть**

(-ыву́, -ывёшь; -ы́л, -а́, -о) *pf* (set) sail; swim off. **отплы́тие** sailing, departure.

**о́тповедь** rebuke.

**отполза́ть** *impf*, **отползти́** (-зу́, -зёшь; -о́лз, -ла́) *pf* crawl away.

**от|полирова́ть** *pf*. **от|полоска́ть** (-ощу́) *pf*.

**отпо́р** repulse; rebuff.

**отпоро́ть** (-рю́, -решь) *pf* (*impf* **отпа́рывать**) rip off.

**отправи́тель** *m* sender. **отпра́вить** (-влю) *pf*, **отправля́ть** *impf* send, dispatch; **~ся** set off, start. **отпра́вка** dispatch. **отправле́ние** sending; departure; performance. **отправн|о́й**: **~о́й пункт, ~а́я то́чка** starting-point.

**от|пра́здновать** *pf*.

**отпра́шиваться** *impf*, **отпроси́ться** (-ошу́сь, -о́сишься) *pf* ask for leave, get leave.

**отпры́гивать** *impf*, **отпры́гнуть** (-ну) *pf* jump *or* spring back *or* aside.

**о́тпрыск** offshoot, scion.

**отпряга́ть** *impf of* **отпря́чь**

**отпряну́ть** (-ну) *pf* recoil, start back.

**отпря́чь** (-ягу́, -яжёшь; -я́г, -ла́) *pf* (*impf* **отпряга́ть**) unharness.

**отпу́гивать** *impf*, **отпугну́ть** (-ну́, -нёшь) *pf* frighten off.

**о́тпуск** (*pl* -а́) leave, holiday(s).

**отпуска́ть** *impf*, **отпусти́ть** (-ущу́, -у́стишь) *pf* let go, let off; set free; release; slacken; (let) grow; allot; remit. **отпускни́к** (-а́) person on leave. **отпускно́й** holiday; leave. **отпуще́ние** remission; **козёл отпуще́ния** scapegoat.

**отраба́тывать** *impf*, **отрабо́тать** *pf* work off; master.

**отрабо́танный** worked out; waste, spent, exhaust.

**отра́ва** poison. **отрави́ть** (-влю́, -вишь) pf, **отравля́ть** impf poison.

**отра́да** joy, delight. **отра́дный** gratifying, pleasing.

**отража́тель** m reflector; scanner. **отража́ть** impf, **отрази́ть** (-ажу́) pf reflect; repulse; +на+prep affect. **отраже́ние** reflection; repulse.

**о́трасль** branch.

**отраста́ть** impf, **отрасти́** (-тёт; отро́с, -ла́) pf grow. **отрасти́ть** (-ащу́) pf, **отра́щивать** impf (let) grow.

**от|реаги́ровать** pf. **от|регули́ровать** pf. **от|редакти́ровать** pf.

**отре́з** cut; length. **отреза́ть** (-е́жу) pf, **отреза́ть** impf cut off; snap.

**о|трезве́ть** (-е́ю) pf. **отрезви́ть** (-влю́, -вишь) pf, **отрезвля́ть** impf sober; ~ся sober up.

**отре́зок** (-зка) piece; section; segment.

**отрека́ться** impf of **отре́чься**

**от|рекомендова́ть(ся** pf.

**отрёкся** etc.: see **отре́чься**. **от|ремонти́ровать** pf. **от|репети́ровать** pf.

**отре́пье, отре́пья** (-ьев) pl rags.

**от|реставри́ровать** pf.

**отрече́ние** renunciation; ~ от престо́ла abdication. **отре́чься** (-еку́сь, -ечёшься) pf (impf **отрека́ться**) renounce.

**отреша́ться** impf, **отреши́ться** (-шу́сь) pf renounce; get rid of.

**отрица́ние** denial; negation. **отрица́тельный** negative.

---

**отрица́ть** impf deny.

**отро́с** etc.: see **отрасти́**. **отро́сток** (-тка) shoot, sprout; appendix.

**о́трочество** adolescence.

**отруби́ть** (-бю́) pf **отруби́ть**

**о́труби** (-е́й) pl bran.

**отруба́ть** (-блю́, -бишь) pf (impf **отруба́ть**) chop off; snap back.

**от|руга́ть** pf.

**отры́в** tearing off; alienation; isolation; в ~e от+gen out of touch with; ~ (от земли́) take-off. **отрыва́ть(ся** impf of **оторва́ть(ся. отры́вистый** staccato; disjointed. **отрывно́й** tear-off. **отры́вок** (-вка) fragment, excerpt. **отры́вочный** fragmentary, scrappy.

**отры́жка** belch; throw-back.

**от|ры́ть** (-ро́ю) pf.

**отря́д** detachment; order.

**отря́хивать** impf, **отряхну́ть** (-ну́, -нёшь) pf shake down or off.

**от|салютова́ть** pf.

**отса́сывание** suction. **отса́сывать** impf of **отсоса́ть**

**отсве́чивать** impf be reflected; +instr shine with.

**отсе́в** sifting, selection; dropping out. **отсева́ть(ся, отсе́ивать(ся** impf of **отсе́ять(ся**

**отсе́к** compartment. **отсека́ть** impf, **отсе́чь** (-еку́, -ечёшь, -се́к, -ла́) pf chop off.

**отсе́ять** (-е́ю) pf (impf **отсева́ть, отсе́ивать**) sift; screen; eliminate; ~ся drop out.

**отсиде́ть** (-ижу́) pf, **отси́живать** impf make numb by sitting; sit through; serve out.

**отска́кивать** impf, **отскочи́ть** (-чу́, -чишь) pf jump aside or away; rebound; come off.

отслу́живать *impf*, отслужи́ть (-жу́, -жишь) *pf* serve one's time; be worn out.

отсоса́ть (-осу́, -осёшь) *pf* (*impf* отса́сывать) suck off, draw off.

отсо́хнуть (-ну) *pf* (*impf* отсыха́ть) wither.

отсро́чивать *impf*, отсро́чить *pf* postpone, defer. отсро́чка postponement, deferment.

отстава́ние lag; lagging behind. отстава́ть (-таю́, -аёшь) *impf of* отста́ть

отста́вить (-влю) *pf*, отставля́ть *impf* set or put aside. отста́вка resignation; retirement; в отста́вке retired; вы́йти в отста́вку resign, retire. отставно́й retired.

отста́ивать(ся *impf of* отстоя́ть(ся

отста́лость backwardness. отста́лый backward. отста́ть (-а́ну) *pf* (*impf* отстава́ть) fall behind; lag behind; become detached; lose touch; break off; be slow. отста́ющий *sb* backward pupil.

от|стега́ть *pf*.

отстёгивать *impf*, отстегну́ть (-ну́, -нёшь) *pf* unfasten, undo; ~ся come unfastened *or* undone.

отстоя́ть[1] (-ою́) *pf* (*impf* отста́ивать) defend; stand up for. отстоя́ть[2] (-ою́т) *impf* на+*acc* be ... distant (от+*gen* from). отстоя́ться *pf* (*impf* отста́иваться) settle; become stabilized.

отстра́ивать(ся *impf of* отстро́ить(ся

отстране́ние pushing aside; dismissal. отстрани́ть *pf*, отстраня́ть *impf* push aside;

remove; suspend; ~ся move away; keep aloof; ~ся от dodge.

отстре́ливаться *impf*, отстреля́ться *pf* fire back.

отстрига́ть *impf*, отстри́чь (-игу́, -ижёшь; -риг) *pf* cut off.

отстро́ить (-о́ю) *pf* (*impf* отстра́ивать) finish building; build up.

отступа́ть *impf*, отступи́ть (-плю́, -пишь) *pf* step back; recede; retreat; back down; ~ от+*gen* give up; deviate from; ~ся от+*gen* give up; go back on. отступле́ние retreat; deviation; digression. отступн|о́й: ~ые де́ньги, ~о́е *sb* indemnity, compensation. отступя́ *adv* (farther) off, away (от+*gen* from).

отсу́тствие absence; lack. отсу́тствовать *impf* be absent. отсу́тствующий absent; *sb* absentee.

отсчита́ть *pf*, отсчи́тывать *impf* count off.

отсыла́ть *impf of* отосла́ть

отсыпа́ть (-плю) *pf*, отсыпа́ть *impf* pour out; measure off.

отсыпа́ться *impf of* отоспа́ться

отсыре́лый damp. от|сыре́ть (-е́ет) *pf*.

отсыха́ть *impf of* отсо́хнуть

отсю́да *adv* from here; hence.

отта́ивать *impf of* отта́ять

отта́лкивать *impf of* оттолкну́ть. отта́лкивающий repulsive, repellent.

отта́чивать *impf of* отточи́ть

отта́ять (-а́ю) *pf* (*impf* отта́ивать) thaw out.

отте́нок (-нка) shade, nuance; tint.

о́ттепель thaw.

оттесни́ть *pf*, оттесня́ть

*impf* drive back; push aside.

**óттиск** impression; off-print, reprint.

**оттогó** *adv* that is why; ~, **что** because.

**оттолкнýть** (-нý, -нёшь) *pf* (*impf* **оттáлкивать**) push away; antagonize; ~**ся** push off.

**оттопы́ренный** protruding. **оттопы́ривать** *impf*, **оттопы́рить** *pf* stick out; ~**ся** protrude; bulge.

**отточи́ть** (-чý, -чишь) *pf* (*impf* **оттáчивать**) sharpen.

**оттýда** *adv* from there.

**оття́гивать** *impf*, **оттянýть** (-нý, -нешь) *pf* draw out; draw off; delay. **оття́жка** delay.

**отупéние** stupefaction. **о|тупéть** (-éю) *pf* sink into torpor.

**от|утю́жить** (-жу) *pf*.

**отучáть** *impf*, **отучи́ть** (-чý, -чишь) *pf* break (of); ~**ся** break o.s. (of).

**отхáркать** *pf*, **отхáркивать** *impf* expectorate.

**отхвати́ть** (-чý, -тишь) *pf*, **отхвáтывать** *impf* snip or chop off.

**отхлебнýть** (-нý, -нёшь) *pf*, **отхлёбывать** *impf* sip, take a sip of.

**отхлы́нуть** (-нет) *pf* flood or rush back.

**отхóд** departure; withdrawal. **отходи́ть** (-ожý, -óдишь) *impf* of **отойти́**. **отхóды** (-ов) *pl* waste.

**отцвести́** (-етý, -етёшь; -ёл, -á) *pf*, **отцветáть** *impf* finish blossoming, fade.

**отцепи́ть** (-плю́, -пишь) *pf*, **отцепля́ть** *impf* unhook; uncouple.

**отцóвский** father's; paternal.

**отчáиваться** *impf* of **отчáяться**

**отчáливать** *impf*, **отчáлить** *pf* cast off.

**отчáсти** *adv* partly.

**отчáяние** despair. **отчáянный** desperate. **отчáяться** (-áюсь) *pf* (*impf* **отчáиваться**) despair.

**отчегó** *adv* why. **отчегó-либо, -нибудь** *adv* for some reason or other. **отчего-то** *adv* for some reason.

**от|чекáнить** *pf*.

**óтчество** patronymic.

**отчёт** account; **отдáть себé в+**prep be aware of, realize. **отчётливый** distinct; clear. **отчётность** book-keeping; accounts. **отчётный** *adj*: ~ **год** financial year, current year; ~ **доклáд** report.

**отчи́зна** native land. **óтчий** paternal. **óтчим** step-father.

**отчислéние** deduction; dismissal. **отчи́слить** *pf*, **отчисля́ть** *impf* deduct; dismiss.

**отчи́тывать** *impf* tell off; ~**ся** report back.

**отчуждéние** alienation; estrangement.

**отшатнýться** (-нýсь, -нёшься) *pf*, **отшáтываться** *impf* start back, recoil; **+от+**gen give up, forsake.

**отшвы́ривать** *impf*, **отшвырнýть** (-нý, -нёшь) *pf* fling away; throw off.

**отшéльник** hermit; recluse.

**от|шлифовáть** *pf*. **от|штукатýрить** *pf*.

**отщепéнец** (-нца) renegade.

**отъéзд** departure. **отъезжáть** *impf*, **отъéхать** (-éду) *pf* drive off, go off.

**отъя́вленный** inveterate.

**отыгрáть** *pf*, **оты́грывать** *impf* win back; ~**ся** win back what one has lost.

отыска́ть (-ыщу́, -ы́щешь) pf, оты́скивать impf find; look for; ~ся turn up, appear.

отяготи́ть (-ощу́) pf, отягоща́ть impf burden.

офице́р officer. офице́рский officer's, officers'.

официа́льный official.

официа́нт waiter. официа́нтка waitress.

официо́з semi-official organ. официо́зный semi-official.

оформи́тель m designer; stage-painter. офо́рмить (-млю) pf, оформля́ть impf design; put into shape; make official; process; ~ся take shape; go through the formalities. оформле́ние design; mounting; staging; processing.

ох int oh! ah!

оха́пка armful.

о|характеризова́ть pf.

о́хать impf (pf о́хнуть) moan; sigh.

охва́т scope; inclusion; outflanking. охвати́ть (-ачу́, -а́тишь) pf, охва́тывать impf envelop; seize; comprehend.

охладева́ть, impf, охладе́ть (-е́ю) pf grow cold. охлади́ть (-ажу́) pf, охлажда́ть impf cool; ~ся become cool, cool down. охлажде́ние cooling; coolness.

о|хмеле́ть (-е́ю) pf. о́хнуть (-ну) pf of о́хать

охо́та¹ hunt, hunting; chase.

охо́та² wish, desire.

охо́титься (-о́чусь) impf hunt.

охо́тник¹ hunter.

охо́тник² volunteer; enthusiast.

охо́тничий hunting.

охо́тно adv willingly, gladly.

о́хра ochre.

охра́на guarding; protection; guard. охрани́ть pf, охра-

ня́ть impf guard, protect.

о|хри́плый, охри́пший hoarse.

о|хри́пнуть (-ну; охри́п) pf become hoarse.

о|цара́пать(ся pf.

оце́нивать impf, оцени́ть (-ню́, -нишь) pf estimate; appraise. оце́нка estimation; appraisal; estimate. оце́нщик valuer.

о|цепене́ть (-е́ю) pf.

оцепи́ть (-плю́, -пишь) pf, оцепля́ть impf surround; cordon off.

оча́г (-а́) hearth; centre; breeding ground; hotbed.

очарова́ние charm, fascination. очарова́тельный charming. очарова́ть pf, очаро́вывать impf charm, fascinate.

очеви́дец (-дца) eye-witness. очеви́дно adv obviously, evidently. очеви́дный obvious.

о́чень adv very; very much.

очередно́й next in turn; usual; regular; routine. о́чередь (gen pl -е́й) turn; queue.

о́черк essay, sketch.

о|черстве́ть (-е́ю) pf.

очерта́ние outline(s), contour(s). очерти́ть (-рчу́, -ртишь) pf, оче́рчивать impf outline.

о́чи etc.: see о́ко

очисти́тельный cleansing. о|чи́стить (-и́щу) pf, очища́ть impf clean; refine; clear; peel; ~ся become clear (от+gen of). очи́стка cleaning; purification; clearance. очи́стки (-ов) pl peelings. очище́ние cleansing; purification.

очки́ (-о́в) pl spectacles. очко́ (gen pl -о́в) pip; point. очко́вая змея́ cobra.

очну́ться (-ну́сь, -нёшься) pf wake up; regain consciousness.

**óчн|ый:** ~ое обучéние classroom instruction; ~ая стáвка confrontation.

**очути́ться** (-ти́шься) *pf* find o.s.

**оше́йник** collar.

**ошеломи́тельный** stunning. **ошеломи́ть** (-млю́) *pf,* **ошеломля́ть** *impf* stun.

**ошиба́ться** *impf,* **ошиби́ться** (-бу́сь, -бёшься, -и́бся) *pf* be mistaken, make a mistake; be wrong. **оши́бка** mistake; error. **оши́бочный** erroneous.

**ошпа́ривать** *impf,* о|шпа́рить *pf* scald.

о|штрафова́ть *pf.* о|штукату́рить *pf.*

**ощети́ниваться** *impf,* о|щети́ниться *pf* bristle (up).

о|щипа́ть (-плю́, -плешь) *pf,* **ощи́пывать** *impf* pluck.

**ощу́пать** *impf,* **ощу́пывать** *impf* feel; grope about. **óщупь: на** ~ to the touch; by touch. **óщупью** *adv* gropingly; by touch.

**ощути́мый, ощути́тельный** perceptible; appreciable. **ощути́ть** (-ущу́) *pf,* **ощуща́ть** *impf* feel, sense. **ощуще́ние** feeling.

# П

**па** *neut indecl* dance step.

**павильо́н** pavilion; film studio.

**павли́н** peacock.

**па́водок** (-дка) (sudden) flood.

**па́вший** fallen.

**па́губный** pernicious, ruinous.

**па́даль** carrion.

**па́дать** *impf (pf* **пасть, упа́сть)** fall; ~ **ду́хом** lose heart. **падёж** (-á) case. **паде́ние** fall; degradation; incidence. **па́дкий на**+*acc or* до+*gen* having a weakness for.

**па́дчерица** step-daughter.

**паёк** (пайка́) ration.

**па́зуха** bosom; sinus; axil.

**пай** (*pl* -и́, -ёв) share. **па́йщик** shareholder.

**паке́т** package; packet; paper bag.

**Пакиста́н** Pakistan. **пакиста́нец** (-нца), **-а́нка** Pakistani. **пакиста́нский** Pakistani.

**па́кля** tow; oakum.

**пакова́ть** *impf (pf* за~, у~) pack.

**па́костный** dirty, mean. **па́кость** dirty trick; obscenity.

**пакт** pact.

**пала́та** chamber, house. **пала́тка** tent; stall, booth.

**пала́ч** (-á) executioner.

**па́лец** (-льца) finger; toe.

**палиса́дник** (*small*) front garden.

**палиса́ндр** rosewood.

**пали́тра** palette.

**пали́ть**[1] *impf (pf* о~, с~) burn; scorch.

**пали́ть**[2] *impf (pf* вы́~, пальну́ть) fire, shoot.

**па́лка** stick; walking-stick.

**пало́мник** pilgrim. **пало́мничество** pilgrimage.

**па́лочка** stick; bacillus; wand; baton.

**па́луба** deck.

**пальба́** fire.

**па́льма** palm(-tree). **па́льмовый** palm.

**пальну́ть** (-ну́, -нёшь) *pf of* пали́ть.

**пальто́** *neut indecl* (over)coat.

**паля́щий** burning, scorching.

**па́мятник** monument; memorial. **па́мятный** memorable; memorial. **па́мять** memory; consciousness; **на** ~ as a keepsake.

**панаце́я** panacea.

**пане́ль** footpath; panel(ling), wainscot(ing). **пане́льный** panelling.

**па́ника** panic. **паникёр** alarmist.

**панихи́да** requiem.

**пани́ческий** panic; panicky.

**панно́** neut indecl panel.

**панора́ма** panorama.

**пансио́н** boarding-house; board and lodging. **пансиона́т** holiday hotel. **пансионе́р** boarder; guest.

**пантало́ны** (-о́н) pl knickers.

**панте́ра** panther.

**пантоми́ма** mime.

**па́нцирь** m armour, coat of mail.

**па́па**[1] m pope.

**па́па**[2] m, **папа́ша** m daddy.

**папа́ха** m fur cap.

**папиро́са** (Russian) cigarette.

**па́пка** file; folder.

**па́поротник** fern.

**пар**[1] (loc -у́; pl -ы́) steam.

**пар**[2] (loc -у́; pl -ы́) fallow.

**па́ра** pair; couple; (two-piece) suit.

**пара́граф** paragraph.

**пара́д** parade; review. **пара́дный** parade; gala; main, front; **~ая фо́рма** full dress (uniform).

**парадо́кс** paradox. **парадокса́льный** paradoxical.

**парази́т** parasite.

**парализова́ть** impf & pf paralyse. **парали́ч** (-а́) paralysis.

**паралле́ль** parallel. **паралле́льный** parallel.

**пара́метр** parameter.

**парано́йя** paranoia.

**парашю́т** parachute.

**паре́ние** steaming.

**па́рень** (-рня; gen pl -рне́й) m lad; fellow.

**пари́** neut indecl bet; **держа́ть**

~ bet, lay a bet.

**пари́к** (-а́) wig. **парикма́хер** hairdresser. **парикма́херская** sb hairdresser's.

**пари́ровать** impf & pf (pf also от~) parry, counter.

**парите́т** parity.

**пари́ть**[1] impf soar, hover.

**па́рить**[2] impf steam; stew; impers па́рит it is sultry; **~ся** (pf по~ся) steam, sweat; stew.

**парк** park; depot; stock.

**парке́т** parquet.

**парла́мент** parliament. **парла́ментарий** parliamentarian. **парламентёр** envoy; bearer of flag of truce. **парла́ментский** parliamentary; **~ зако́н** Act of Parliament.

**парни́к** (-а́) hotbed; seed-bed. **парнико́вый** adj: **~ые расте́ния** hothouse plants.

**парни́шка** m boy, lad.

**парно́й** fresh; steamy.

**па́рный** (forming a) pair; twin.

**паро-** in comb steam-. **парово́з** (steam-)engine, locomotive. **~обра́зный** vaporous. **~хо́д** steamer; steamship. **~хо́дство** steamship-line.

**парово́й** steam; steamed.

**паро́дия** parody.

**паро́ль** m password.

**паро́м** ferry(-boat).

**парт-** abbr in comb Party. **партбиле́т** Party (membership) card. **~ко́м** Party committee. **~организа́ция** Party organization.

**па́рта** (school) desk.

**парте́р** stalls; pit.

**партиза́н** (gen pl -а́н) partisan; guerilla. **партиза́нский** partisan, guerilla; unplanned.

**парти́йный** party; Party; sb Party member.

партиту́ра (*mus*) score.

па́ртия party; group; batch; game, set; part.

партнёр partner.

па́рус (*pl* -á, -óв) sail. паруси́на canvas. па́русник sailing vessel. па́русный sail; ~ спорт sailing.

парфюме́рия perfumes.

парча́ (*gen pl* -éй) brocade.

па́сека apiary, beehive.

пасётся *see* пасти́сь

па́сквиль *m* lampoon; libel.

па́смурный overcast; gloomy.

па́спорт (*pl* -á) passport.

пасса́ж passage; arcade.

пассажи́р passenger.

пасси́вный passive.

па́ста paste.

па́стбище pasture.

па́ства flock.

пасте́ль pastel.

пастерна́к parsnip.

пасти́ (-су́, -сёшь; пас, -ла́) *impf* graze; tend.

пасти́сь (-сётся; па́сся, -ла́сь) *impf* graze. пасту́х (-á) shepherd. па́стырь *m* pastor.

пасть[1] mouth; jaws.

пасть[2] (паду́, -дёшь; пал) *pf of* па́дать

Па́сха Easter; Passover.

па́сынок (-нка) stepson, stepchild.

пат stalemate.

пате́нт patent.

патети́ческий passionate.

па́тока treacle; syrup.

патоло́гия pathology.

патриа́рх patriarch.

патрио́т, ~ка patriot. патриоти́зм patriotism. патриоти́ческий patriotic.

патро́н cartridge; chuck; lampsocket.

патру́ль (-я́) *m* patrol.

па́уза pause; (*also mus*) rest.

пау́к (-á) spider. паути́на cobweb; gossamer; web.

па́фос zeal, enthusiasm.

пах (*loc* -у́) groin.

па́харь *m* ploughman. паха́ть (пашу́, па́шешь) *impf* (*pf* вс~) plough.

па́хнуть[1] (-ну; пах) *impf* smell (+*instr of*).

пахну́ть[2] (-нёт) *pf* puff, blow.

па́хота ploughing. па́хотный arable.

паху́чий odorous, strongsmelling.

пацие́нт, ~ка patient.

пацифи́зм pacificism. пацифи́ст pacifist.

па́чка bundle; packet, pack; tutu.

па́чкать *impf* (*pf* за~, ис~) dirty, soil, stain.

пашу́ *etc.*: *see* паха́ть. па́шня (*gen pl* -шен) ploughed field.

паште́т pâté.

пая́льная ла́мпа blow-lamp. пая́льник soldering iron. пая́ть (-я́ю) *impf* solder.

пая́ц clown, buffoon.

певе́ц (-вца́), певи́ца singer. певу́чий melodious. певчий singing; *sb* chorister.

пе́гий piebald.

педаго́г teacher; pedagogue. педаго́гика pedagogy. педагоги́ческий pedagogical; educational; ~ институ́т (teachers') training college.

педа́ль pedal.

педиа́тр paediatrician. педиатри́ческий paediatric.

педикю́р chiropody.

пейза́ж landscape; scenery.

пёк *see* печь. пека́рный baking. пека́рня (*gen pl* -рен) bakery. пе́карь (*pl* -я́, -ей) *m* baker. пе́кло scorching heat; hell-fire. пеку́ *etc.*: *see* печь

**пелена́** (*gen pl* -ле́н) shroud. **пелена́ть** *impf* (*pf* за~) swaddle; put a nappy on.

**пе́ленг** bearing. **пеленгова́ть** *impf* & *pf* take the bearings of.

**пелёнка** nappy.

**пельме́нь** *m* meat dumpling.

**пе́на** foam; scum; froth.

**пена́л** pencil-case.

**пе́ние** singing.

**пе́нистый** foamy; frothy. **пе́ниться** *impf* (*pf* вс~) foam.

**пе́нка** skin. **пенопла́ст** plastic foam.

**пеницилли́н** penicillin.

**пенсионе́р, пенсионе́рка** pensioner. **пенсио́нный** pensionable. **пе́нсия** pension.

**пень** (пня) *m* stump, stub.

**пенька́** hemp.

**пе́пел** (-пла) ash, ashes. **пе́пельница** ashtray.

**перве́йший** the first; first-class. **пе́рвенец** (-нца) first-born. **пе́рвенство** first place; championship. **пе́рвенствовать** *impf* take first place; take priority. **перви́чный** primary.

**перво-** *in comb* first; prime. **первобы́тный** primitive; primeval. **~исто́чник** source; origin. **~кла́ссный** first-class. **~ку́рсник** first-year student. **~нача́льный** original; primary. **~со́ртный** best-quality; first-class. **~степе́нный** paramount.

**пе́рвое** *sb* first course. **пе́рвый** first; former.

**перга́мент** parchment.

**перебега́ть** *impf*, **перебежа́ть** (-бегу́) *pf* cross, run across; desert. **перебе́жчик** deserter; turncoat.

**переберу́** *etc.*: *see* перебра́ть

**перебива́ть(ся** *impf of* переби́ть(ся

**перебира́ть(ся** *impf of* перебра́ть(ся

**переби́ть** (-бью́, -бьёшь) *pf* (*impf* **перебива́ть**) interrupt; slaughter; beat; break; reupholster; **~ся** break; make ends meet. **перебо́й** interruption; stoppage; irregularity.

**перебо́рка** sorting out; partition; bulkhead.

**переборо́ть** (-рю́, -решь) *pf* overcome.

**переборщи́ть** (-щу́) *pf* go too far; overdo it.

**перебра́сывать(ся** *impf of* перебро́сить(ся

**перебра́ть** (-беру́, -берёшь; -а́л, -а́, -о) *pf* (*impf* **перебира́ть**) sort out; look through; turn over in one's mind; finger; **~ся** get over; cross; move.

**перебро́сить** (-о́шу) *pf* (*impf* **перебра́сывать**) throw over; transfer; **~ся** fling o.s.; spread. **перебро́ска** transfer.

**перебью́** *etc.*: *see* переби́ть

**перева́л** crossing; pass. **перева́ливать** *impf*, **перевали́ть** (-лю́, -лишь) *pf* transfer, shift; cross, pass.

**перева́ривать** *impf*, **перевари́ть** (-рю́, -ришь) *pf* reheat; overcook; digest; tolerate.

**переведу́** *etc.*: *see* перевести́

**перевезти́** (-зу́, -зёшь; -вёз, -ла́) *pf* (*impf* **перевози́ть**) take across; transport; (re)move.

**переверну́ть** (-ну́, -нёшь) *pf*, **переверте́ть** *impf* (*impf also* **перевора́чивать**) turn (over); upset; turn inside out; **~ся** turn (over).

**переве́с** preponderance; advantage. **переве́сить** (-е́шу) *pf* (*impf* **переве́шивать**) re-weigh; outweigh; tip the scales; hang elsewhere.

**перевести́** (-веду́, -веде́шь; -ве́л, -а́) *pf* (*impf* **переводи́ть**) take across; transfer, move, shift; translate; convert; **~сь** be transferred; run out; become extinct.

**переве́шивать** *impf of* **переве́сить**. **перевира́ть** *impf of* **перевра́ть**

**перево́д** transfer, move, shift; translation; conversion; waste. **переводи́ть(ся** (-ожу́(сь, -о́дишь(ся) *impf of* **перевести́(сь**. **переводно́й**: **~я́я бума́га** carbon paper; **~я́я карти́нка** transfer. **переводно́й** transfer; translated. **перево́дчик**, **~ица** translator; interpreter.

**перево́з** transporting; ferry. **перевози́ть** (-ожу́, -о́зишь) *impf of* **перевезти́**. **перево́зка** conveyance. **перево́зчик** ferryman; removal man.

**перевооружа́ть** *impf*, **перевооружи́ть** (-жу́) *pf* rearm; **~ся** rearm. **перевооруже́ние** rearmament.

**перевоплоти́ть** (-лощу́) *pf*, **перевоплоща́ть** *impf* re-incarnate; **~ся** be reincarnated. **перевоплоще́ние** re-incarnation.

**перевора́чивать(ся** *impf of* **переверну́ть(ся. переворо́т** revolution; overturn; cata-clysm; **госуда́рственный ~** coup d'état.

**перевоспита́ние** re-education. **перевоспита́ть** *pf*, **перевоспи́тывать** *impf* re-educate.

**перевра́ть** (-ру́, -рёшь; -а́л,

-á, -о) *pf* (*impf* **перевира́ть**) garble; misquote.

**перевыполне́ние** over-fulfilment. **перевы́полнить** *pf*, **перевыполня́ть** *impf* over-fulfil.

**перевяза́ть** (-яжу́, -я́жешь) *pf*, **перевя́зывать** *impf* bandage; tie up; re-tie. **перевя́зка** dressing, bandage.

**переги́б** bend; excess, ex-treme. **перегиба́ть(ся** *impf of* **перегну́ть(ся**

**перегля́дываться** *impf*, **перегляну́ться** (-ну́сь, -не́шь-ся) *pf* exchange glances.

**перегна́ть** (-гоню́, -го́нишь; -а́л, -а́, -о) *pf* (*impf* **перегоня́ть**) outdistance; surpass; drive; distil.

**перегно́й** humus.

**перегну́ть** (-ну́, -нёшь) *pf* (*impf* **перегиба́ть**) bend; **~ па́лку** go too far; **~ся** bend; lean over.

**перегова́ривать** *impf*, **переговори́ть** (-рю́) *pf* talk; out-talk; **~ся** (с+*instr*) exchange remarks (with). **перегово́ры** (- ов) *pl* negotiations, parley.

**перегово́рный** *adj*: **~ пункт** public call-boxes; trunk-call of-fice.

**перего́н** driving; stage. **перего́нка** distillation. **перего́нный** distilling, distillation. **перегоню́** *etc.*: *see* **перегна́ть**. **перегоня́ть** *impf of* **перегна́ть**

**перегора́живать** *impf of* **перегороди́ть**

**перегора́ть** *impf*, **перегоре́ть** (-ри́т) *pf* burn out, fuse.

**перегороди́ть** (-рожу́, -ро́дишь) *pf* (*impf* **перегора́живать**) partition off; block. **перего-ро́дка** partition.

перегрёв overheating. **пере-
грева́ть** *impf,* **перегре́ть**
(-е́ю) *pf* overheat; **~ся** overheat.

**перегружа́ть** *impf,* **перегру-
зи́ть** (-ужу́, -у́зишь) *pf* overload; transfer. **перегру́зка**
overload; transfer.

**перегрыза́ть** *impf,* **пере-
гры́зть** (-зу́, -зёшь; -гры́з) *pf*
gnaw through.

**перёд, пёредо, пред, пре́до**
*prep+instr* before; in front of;
compared to. **перёд** (пе́реда;
*pl* -а́) front, forepart.

**передава́ть** (-даю́, -даёшь)
*impf,* **переда́ть** (-а́м, -а́шь,
-а́ст, -ади́м; пе́редал, -а́, -о)
*pf* pass, hand, hand over;
transfer; hand down; make
over; tell; communicate; convey; give too much; **~ся** pass;
be transmitted; be communi-
cated; be inherited. **переда́т-
чик** transmitter. **переда́ча**
passing; transmission; communication; transfer; broadcast;
drive; gear, gearing.

**передвига́ть** *impf,* **передви́-
нуть** (-ну) *pf* move, shift; **~ся**
move, shift. **передвиже́ние**
movement; transportation.
**передви́жка** movement; *in
comb* travelling; itinerant.
**передвижно́й** movable, mobile.

**переде́лать** *pf,* **переде́лы-
вать** *impf* alter; refashion.
**переде́лка** alteration.

**передёргивать(ся** *impf of*
**передёрнуть(ся**

**передержа́ть** (-жу́, -жишь) *pf,*
**переде́рживать** *impf* overdo;
overcook; overexpose.

**передёрнуть** (-ну) *pf* (*impf*
**передёргивать**) pull aside
*or* across; cheat; distort;

**~ся** wince.

**пере́дний** front; **~ план** foreground. **пере́дник** apron.
**пере́дняя** *sb* (entrance) hall,
lobby. **пе́редо:** *see* **перёд.
передови́к** (-а́) exemplary
worker. **передови́ца** leading
article. **передово́й** advanced; foremost; leading.

**передохну́ть** (-ну́, -нёшь) *pf*
pause for breath.

**передра́знивать** *impf,* **пере-
дразни́ть** (-ню́, -нишь) *pf*
mimic.

**переду́мать** *pf,* **переду́мы-
вать** *impf* change one's mind.
**переды́шка** respite.

**перее́зд** crossing; move. **пере-
езжа́ть** *impf,* **перее́хать**
(-е́ду) *pf* cross; run over,
knock down; move (house).

**пережа́ривать** *impf,* **пере-
жа́рить** *pf* overdo, overcook.

**пережда́ть** (-жду́, -ждёшь; -а́л,
-а́, -о) *pf* (*impf* **пережида́ть**)
wait for the end of.

**пережёвывать** *impf* chew;
repeat over and over again.

**пережива́ние** experience.
**пережива́ть** *impf of* **пере-
жи́ть**

**пережида́ть** *impf of* **пере-
жда́ть**

**пережито́е** *sb* the past. **пере-
жи́ток** (-тка) survival; vestige.
**пережи́ть** (-иву́, -ивёшь; пе́ре-
жи́л, -а́, -о) *pf* (*impf* **пережи-
ва́ть**) experience; go through;
endure; outlive.

**перезаряди́ть** (-яжу́, -я́дишь)
*pf,* **перезаряжа́ть** *impf* re-
charge, reload.

**перезва́нивать** *impf,* **пере-
звони́ть** *pf +dat* ring back.

**пере**|**зимова́ть** *pf*

**перезре́лый** overripe.

**переигра́ть** *pf,* **переигры-**

вать *impf* play again; overact.
**переизбира́ть** *impf*, **переизбра́ть** (-беру́, -берёшь; -бра́л, -а́, -о) *pf* re-elect. **переизбра́ние** re-election.
**переиздава́ть** (-даю́, -даёшь) *impf*, **переизда́ть** (-а́м, -а́шь, -а́ст, -ади́м; -а́л, -а́, -о) *pf* republish, reprint. **переизда́ние** republication; new edition.
**переименова́ть** *pf*, **переимено́вывать** *impf* rename.
**перейму́** *etc.: see* **перенять́**
**перейти́** (-йду́, -йдёшь; перешёл, -шла́) *pf* (*impf* **переходи́ть**) cross; go, walk, pass; move, change, switch; turn (в+*acc* into).
**перека́пывать** *impf of* **перекопа́ть**
**перекати́ть** (-чу́, -тишь) *pf*, **перека́тывать** *impf* roll; ~ся roll.
**перекача́ть** *pf*, **перека́чивать** *impf* pump (across).
**переквалифици́роваться** *impf & pf* retrain.
**переки́дывать** *impf*, **переки́нуть** (-ну) *pf* throw over; ~ся leap.
**пе́рекись** peroxide.
**перекла́дина** cross-beam; joist; horizontal bar.
**перекла́дывать** *impf of* **переложи́ть**
**перекли́чка** roll-call.
**переключа́тель** *m* switch. **переключа́ть** *impf*, **переключи́ть** (-чу́) *pf* switch (over); ~ся switch (over) (на+*acc* to).
**перекова́ть** (-кую́, -куёшь) *pf*, **переко́вывать** *impf* re-shoe; re-forge.
**перекопа́ть** *pf* (*impf* **перека́пывать**) dig (all of); dig again.

**перекоси́ть** (-ошу́, -о́сишь) *pf* warp; distort; ~ся warp; become distorted.
**перекочева́ть** (-чу́ю) *pf*, **перекочёвывать** *impf* migrate.
**переко́шенный** distorted, twisted.
**перекра́ивать** *impf of* **перекрои́ть**
**перекра́сить** (-а́шу) *pf*, **перекра́шивать** *impf* (re-)paint; (re-)dye; ~ся change colour; turn one's coat.
**пере|крести́ть** (-ещу́, -е́стишь) *pf*, **перекре́щивать** *impf* cross; ~ся cross, intersect; cross o.s. **перекрёстн**|**ый** cross; ~ый допро́с cross-examination; ~ый ого́нь cross-fire; ~ая ссы́лка cross-reference. **перекрёсток** (-тка) cross-roads, crossing.
**перекри́кивать** *impf*, **перекрича́ть** (-чу́) *pf* shout down.
**перекрои́ть** (-ою́) *pf* (*impf* **перекра́ивать**) cut out again; reshape.
**перекрыва́ть** *impf*, **перекры́ть** (-ро́ю) *pf* re-cover; exceed. **перекры́тие** ceiling.
**перекупаю́** *etc.: see* **перекупа́ть**
**перекупа́ть** *impf*, **перекупи́ть** (-плю́, -пишь) *pf* buy up; buy by outbidding s.o. **переку́пщик** second-hand dealer.
**перекуси́ть** (-ушу́, -у́сишь) *pf*, **переку́сывать** *impf* bite through; have a snack.
**перелага́ть** *impf of* **переложи́ть**
**перела́мывать** *impf of* **переломи́ть**
**перелеза́ть** *impf*, **переле́зть** (-зу; -ёз) *pf* climb over.
**переле́сок** (-ска) copse.
**перелёт** migration; flight.

перелета́ть *impf*, перелете́ть (-лечу́) *pf* fly over. перелётный migratory.

перелива́ние decanting; transfusion. перелива́ть *impf* of перели́ть. перелива́ться *impf* of перели́ться; gleam; modulate.

перелиста́ть *pf*, перели́стывать *impf* leaf through.

перели́ть (-лью́, -льёшь; -и́л, -а́, -о) *pf* (*impf* перелива́ть) pour; decant; let overflow; transfuse. перели́ться (-льётся; -ли́лся, -липа́сь, -ли́ло́сь) *pf* (*impf* перелива́ться) flow; overflow.

перелицева́ть (-цу́ю) *pf*, перелицо́вывать *impf* turn; have turned.

переложе́ние arrangement. переложи́ть (-жу́, -жишь) *pf* (*impf* переклада́дывать, перелага́ть) put elsewhere; shift; transfer; interlay; put in too much; set; arrange; transpose.

перело́м breaking; fracture; turning-point, crisis; sudden change. переломáть *pf* break; ~ся break, be broken. переломи́ть (-млю́, -мишь) *pf* (*impf* перела́мывать) break in two; master. перело́мный critical.

перелью́ *etc.: see* перели́ть

перема́нивать *impf*, перемани́ть (-ню́, -нишь) *pf* win over; entice.

перемежа́ться *impf* alternate.

переме́на change; break. перемени́ть (-ню́, -нишь) *pf*, переменя́ть *impf* change; ~ся change. переме́нный variable; ~ ток alternating current. переме́нчивый changeable.

перемести́ть (-мещу́) *pf* (*impf* перемеща́ть) move; transfer; ~ся move.

переме́шивать *pf*, переме́шивать *impf* mix; mix up; shuffle; ~ся get mixed (up).

перемеща́ть(ся *impf* of перемести́ть(ся. перемеще́ние transference; displacement. перемещённый displaced; ~ые ли́ца displaced persons.

переми́рие armistice, truce.

перемыва́ть *impf*, перемы́ть (-мо́ю) *pf* wash (up) again.

перенапряга́ть *impf*, перенапря́чь (-ягу́, -яжёшь: -я́г, -ла́) *pf* overstrain.

переселе́ние overpopulation. переселённый (-лён, -а́) overpopulated; overcrowded.

перенести́ (-су́, -сёшь; -нёс, -ла́) *pf* (*impf* переноси́ть) carry, move, take; transfer; take over; postpone; endure, bear; ~сь be carried; be carried away.

перенима́ть *impf* of переня́ть

перено́с transfer; word division; знак ~a end-of-line hyphen. перено́сный endurable. переноси́ть(ся (-ошу́(сь, -о́сишь(ся *impf* of перенести́(сь

перено́сица bridge (*of the* nose).

перено́ска carrying over; transporting; carriage. перено́сный portable; figurative.

перено́счик carrier.

пере|ночева́ть (-чу́ю) *pf*. переношу́ *etc.: see* переноси́ть

переня́ть (-ейму́, -еймёшь; пе́реня́л, -а́, -о) *pf* (*impf* перенима́ть) imitate; adopt.

**переобору́довать** *impf & pf* re-equip.

**переобува́ться** *impf*, **переобу́ться** (-у́юсь, -у́ешься) *pf* change one's shoes.

**переодева́ться** *impf*, **переоде́ться** (-е́нусь) *pf* change (one's clothes).

**переосвиде́тельствовать** *impf & pf* re-examine.

**переоце́нивать** *impf*, **переоцени́ть** (-ню́, -нишь) *pf* overestimate; revalue. **переоце́нка** overestimation; revaluation.

**перепа́чкать** *pf* make dirty; **~ся** get dirty.

**пе́репел** (*pl* -á) *pf* quail.

**перепелена́ть** *pf* change (a baby).

**перепеча́тать** *pf*, **перепеча́тывать** *impf* reprint. **перепеча́тка** reprint.

**перепи́ливать** *impf*, **перепили́ть** (-лю́, -лишь) *pf* saw in two.

**переписа́ть** (-ишу́, -и́шешь) *pf*, **перепи́сывать** *impf* copy; re-write; make a list of. **перепи́ска** copying; correspondence. **перепи́сываться** *impf* correspond. **пе́репись** census.

**переплави́ть** (-влю) *pf*, **переплавля́ть** *impf* smelt.

**переплати́ть** (-ачу́, -а́тишь) *pf*, **перепла́чивать** *impf* overpay.

**переплести́** (-лету́, -лете́шь; -лёл, -á) *pf*, **переплета́ть** *impf* bind; interlace, intertwine; re-plait; **~ся** interlace, interweave; get mixed up. **переплёт** binding. **переплётчик** bookbinder.

**переплыва́ть** *impf*, **переплы́ть** (-ыву́, -ыве́шь; -ы́л, -á, -о) *pf* swim or sail across.

**переподгото́вка** further training; refresher course.

**переполза́ть** *impf*, **переползти́** (-зу́, -зёшь; -блз, -лá) *pf* crawl or creep across.

**переполне́ние** overfilling; overcrowding. **перепо́лненный** overcrowded; too full. **перепо́лнить** *pf*, **переполня́ть** *impf* overfill; overcrowd.

**переполо́х** commotion.

**перепо́нка** membrane; web.

**перепра́ва** crossing; ford. **перепра́вить** (-влю) *pf*, **переправля́ть** *impf* convey; forward; **~ся** cross, get across.

**перепродава́ть** (-даю́, -даёшь) *impf*, **перепрода́ть** (-ám, -áшь, -áст, -ади́м; -про́дал, -á, -о) *pf* re-sell. **перепрода́жа** re-sale.

**перепроизво́дство** overproduction.

**перепры́гивать** *impf*, **перепры́гнуть** (-ну) *pf* jump (over).

**перепуга́ть** *pf* frighten; scare; **~ся** get a fright.

**перепу́тать** *pf*, **перепу́тывать** *impf* tangle; confuse, mix up.

**перепу́тье** cross-roads.

**перераба́тывать** *impf*, **перерабо́тать** *pf* convert; treat; re-make; re-cast; process; work overtime; overwork; **~ся** overwork. **перерабо́тка** processing; reworking; overtime work.

**перераспределе́ние** redistribution. **перераспредели́ть** *pf*, **перераспределя́ть** *impf* redistribute.

**перераста́ние** outgrowing; escalation; development (into).

**перераста́ть** *impf*, **пере-**

расти́ (-ту́, -тёшь; -ро́с, -ла́) pf outgrow; develop.

перерасхо́д over-expenditure; overdraft. перерасхо́довать impf & pf expend too much of.

перерасчёт recalculation.

перерва́ть (-ву́, -вёшь; -а́л, -а́, -о) pf (impf перерыва́ть) break, tear asunder; ~ся break, come apart.

перере́зать (-е́жу) pf, перере́зать impf, перере́зывать impf cut off; kill.

перероди́ть (-ожу́) pf, перерожда́ть impf regenerate; ~ся be reborn; be regenerated; degenerate. перерожде́ние regeneration; degeneration.

перерос etc.: see перерасти́. перерою etc.: see перерыть.

переруби́ть impf, переруби́ть (-блю́, -бишь) pf chop in two.

переры́в break; interruption; interval.

перерыва́ть¹(ся impf of перерва́ть(ся

перерыва́ть² impf, переры́ть (-ро́ю) pf dig up; rummage through.

пересади́ть (-ажу́, -а́дишь) pf, переса́живать impf transplant; graft; seat someone else. переса́дка transplantation; grafting; change.

переса́живаться impf of пересе́сть. переса́ливать impf of пересоли́ть

пересдава́ть (-даю́сь) impf, пересда́ть (-а́м, -а́шь, -а́ст, -ади́м; -да́л, -а́, -о) pf sublet; re-sit.

пересека́ть(ся impf of пересе́чь(ся

пересе́ленец (-нца) settler;

immigrant. переселе́ние migration; immigration, resettlement; moving. пересели́ть pf, переселя́ть impf move; ~ся move; migrate.

пересе́сть (-ся́ду) pf (impf переса́живаться) change one's seat; change (trains etc.).

пересече́ние crossing, intersection. пересе́чь (-еку́, -ечёшь; -сёк, -ла́) pf (impf пересека́ть) cross; intersect; ~ся cross, intersect.

переси́ливать impf, переси́лить pf overpower.

переска́з (re)telling; exposition. пересказа́ть (-ажу́, -а́жешь) pf, переска́зывать impf retell.

переска́кивать impf, перескочи́ть (-чу́, -чишь) pf jump or skip (over).

пересла́ть (-ешлю́, -шлёшь) pf (impf пересыла́ть) send; forward.

пересма́тривать impf, пересмотре́ть (-трю́, -тришь) pf look over; reconsider. пересмо́тр revision; reconsideration; review.

пересоли́ть (-олю́, -о́ли́шь) pf (impf переса́ливать) oversalt; overdo it.

пересо́хнуть (-нет; -о́х) pf (impf пересыха́ть) dry up; become parched.

переспа́ть (-плю́; -а́л, -а́, -о) pf oversleep; spend the night.

переспе́лый overripe.

переспра́шивать impf, переспроси́ть (-ошу́, -о́сишь) pf ask again.

переставать (-таю́, -таёшь) impf of переста́ть

переста́вить (-влю) pf, переставля́ть impf move; rearrange; transpose. переста-

**нóвка** rearrangement; transposition.

**перестáть** (-áну) pf (impf **перестáвать**) stop, cease.

**перестрадáть** pf have suffered.

**перестрáивать(ся** impf of **перестрóить(ся**

**перестрахóвка** re-insurance; overcautiousness.

**перестрéлка** exchange of fire. **перестреля́ть** pf shoot (down).

**перестрóить** pf (impf **перестрáивать**) rebuild; reorganize; retune; **~ся** re-form; reorganize o.s.; switch over (**на**+acc to). **перестрóйка** reconstruction; reorganization; retuning; perestroika.

**переступáть** impf, **переступи́ть** (-плю́, -пишь) pf step over; cross; overstep.

**пересчитáть** pf, **пересчи́тывать** impf (pf also **пересчéсть**) re-count; count.

**пересылáть** impf of **переслáть**. **пересы́лка** sending, forwarding.

**пересыпáть** impf, **пересы́пать** (-плю, -плешь) pf pour; sprinkle; pour too much.

**пересыхáть** impf of **пересóхнуть**. **перся́ду** etc.: see **пересéсть**. **перетáпливать** impf of **перетопи́ть**

**перетáскивать** impf, **перетащи́ть** (-щу́, -щишь) pf drag (over, through); move.

**перетерéть** (-тру́, -трёшь, -тёр) pf, **перетирáть** impf wear out, wear down; grind; wipe; **~ся** wear out or through.

**перетопи́ть** (-плю́, -пишь) pf (impf **перетáпливать**) melt.

**перетру́** etc.: see **перетерéть**

**перетьб** (пру, прёшь; пёр, -ла)

impf go; make or force one's way; haul; come out.

**перетя́гивать** impf, **перетяну́ть** (-ну́, -нешь) pf pull, draw; win over; outweigh.

**переубеди́ть** pf, **переубеждáть** impf make change one's mind.

**переу́лок** (-лка) side street, alley, lane.

**переустрóйство** reconstruction, reorganization.

**переутоми́ть** (-млю́) pf, **переутомля́ть** impf overtire; **~ся** overtire o.s. **переутомлéние** overwork.

**переучёт** stock-taking.

**переу́чивать** impf, **переучи́ть** (-чу́, -чишь) pf teach again.

**перефрази́ровать** impf & pf paraphrase.

**перехвати́ть** (-ачу́, -áтишь) pf, **перехвáтывать** impf intercept; snatch a bite (of); borrow.

**перехитри́ть** pf outwit.

**перехóд** transition; crossing; conversion. **переходи́ть** (-ожу́, -óдишь) impf of **перейти́**. **перехóдный** transitional; transitive. **переходя́щий** transient; intermittent; brought forward.

**пéрец** (-рца) pepper.

**перечéл** etc.: see **перечéсть**

**пéречень** (-чня) m list, enumeration.

**перечёркивать** impf, **перечеркну́ть** (-ну́, -нёшь) pf cross out, cancel.

**перечéсть** (-чту́, -чтёшь; -чёл, -чла) pf: see **перечитáть**, **перечи́слить**

**перечислéние** enumeration; transfer. **перечи́слить** pf, **перечисля́ть** impf enumerate; transfer.

перечита́ть pf, перечи́тывать impf (pf also перече́сть) re-read.

пере́чить (-чу) impf contradict; cross, go against.

пе́речница pepper-pot.

перечту́ etc.: see перече́сть. пере́чу etc.: see пере́чить.

перешага́ть impf, перешагну́ть (-ну́, -нёшь) pf step over.

перешеёк (-е́йка) isthmus, neck.

перешёл etc.: see перейти́.

перешива́ть impf, переши́ть (-шью́, -шьёшь) pf alter; have altered.

перешлю́ etc.: see пересла́ть.

переэкзамено́вывать impf re-examine; retake an exam.

пери́ла (-и́л) pl railing(s); banisters.

пери́на feather-bed.

пери́од period. перио́дика periodicals. периоди́ческий periodical; recurring.

пери́стый feathery; cirrus.

перифери́я periphery.

перламу́тр mother-of-pearl. перламу́тровый mother-of-pearl. перло́в|ый: ~ая крупа́ pearl barley.

пермане́нт perm. пермане́нтный permanent.

перна́тый feathered. перна́тые sb pl birds. перо́ (pl пе́рья, -ьев) feather; nib. перочи́нный нож, но́жик penknife.

перпендикуля́рный perpendicular.

перро́н platform.

перс Persian. перси́дский Persian.

пе́рсик peach.

персия́нка Persian woman.

персо́на person; со́бственной персо́ной in person. персона́ж character; personage. персона́л personnel, staff. персона́льный personal.

перспекти́ва perspective; vista; prospect. перспекти́вный perspective; long-term; promising.

пе́рстень (-тня) m ring.

перфока́рта punched card.

пе́рхоть dandruff.

перча́тка glove.

пе́рчить (-чу) impf (pf по~) pepper.

пёс (пса) dog.

пе́сенник song-book; (choral) singer; song-writer. пе́сенный song; of songs.

песе́ц (-сца́) (polar) fox.

песнь (gen pl -ей) song; canto. пе́сня (gen pl -сен) song.

песо́к (-ска́) sand. песо́чный sand; sandy.

пессими́зм pessimism. пессими́ст pessimist. пессимисти́ческий pessimistic.

пестрота́ diversity of colours; diversity. пёстрый variegated; diverse; colourful.

песча́ник sandstone. песча́ный sandy. песчи́нка grain of sand.

петербу́ргский (of) St Petersburg.

пети́ция petition.

петли́ца buttonhole; tab. пе́тля (gen pl -тель) loop; noose; stitch; hinge.

петру́шка[1] parsley.

петру́шка[2] m Punch; f Punch-and-Judy show.

пету́х (-а́) cock. петушо́к (-шка́) cockerel.

петь (пою́, поёшь) impf (pf про~, с~) sing.

пехо́та infantry, foot. **пехо-
ти́нец** (-нца) infantryman.
**пехо́тный** infantry.

**печа́лить** *impf* (*pf* о~) sadden; **~ся** grieve, be sad.
**печа́ль** sorrow. **печа́льный** sad.

**печа́тать** *impf* (*pf* на~, от~)
print; **~ся** write, be published; be at the printer's.
**печа́тный** printing; printer's; printed; **~ые бу́квы**
block capitals; **~ый стано́к**
printing-press. **печа́ть** seal,
stamp; print; printing; press.

**пече́ние** baking.
**печёнка** liver.
**печёный** baked.
**пе́чень** liver.

**пече́нье** pastry; biscuit. **пе́ч-
ка** stove. **печно́й** stove; oven;
kiln. **печь** (*loc* -и́, *gen pl* -е́й)
stove; oven; kiln. **печь** (пеку́,
-чёшь; пёк, -ла́) *impf* (*pf* ис~)
bake; **~ся** bake.

**пешехо́д** pedestrian. **пеше-
хо́дный** pedestrian; foot-.
**пе́ший** pedestrian; foot. **пе́ш-
ка** pawn. **пешко́м** *adv* on foot.

**пеще́ра** cave. **пеще́рный** cave;
~ **челове́к** cave-dweller.

**пиани́но** *neut indecl* (upright)
piano. **пиани́ст, ~ка** pianist.

**пивна́я** *sb* pub. **пивно́й** beer.
**пи́во** beer. **пивова́р** brewer.

**пигме́й** pygmy.
**пиджа́к** (-а́) jacket.
**пижа́ма** pyjamas.
**пижо́н** dandy.
**пик** peak; **часы́ пик** rush-hour.
**пи́ка** lance.
**пика́нтный** piquant; spicy.
**пика́п** pick-up (van).
**пике́** *neut indecl* dive.
**пике́т** picket. **пике́тчик** picket.
**пи́ки** (пик) *pl* (cards) spades.
**пики́ровать** *impf* & *pf* (*pf*
*also* с~) dive.

**пикиро́вщик, пики́рующий
бомбардиро́вщик** dive-
bomber.

**пикни́к** (-а́) picnic.
**пи́кнуть** (-ну) *pf* squeak; make
a sound.

**пи́ковый** of spades.

**пила́** (*pl* -ы) saw; nagger. **пи-
лёный** sawed, sawn. **пили́ть**
(-лю́, -лишь) *impf* saw; nag
(at). **пи́лка** sawing; fret-saw;
nail-file.

**пило́т** pilot.
**пило́тка** forage-cap.
**пилоти́ровать** *impf* pilot.
**пилю́ля** pill.
**пина́ть** *impf* (*pf* пнуть) kick.
**пино́к** (-нка́) kick.
**пингви́н** penguin.
**пинце́т** tweezers.
**пио́н** peony.
**пионе́р** pioneer. **пионе́рский**
pioneer.

**пипе́тка** pipette.
**пир** (*loc* -у́, *pl* -ы́) feast, banquet. **пирова́ть** *impf* feast.
**пирами́да** pyramid.
**пира́т** pirate.
**пиро́г** (-а́) pie. **пиро́жное** *sb*
cake, pastry. **пирожо́к** (-жка́)
pasty.

**пирс** pier.
**пируэ́т** pirouette.
**пи́ршество** feast; celebration.
**пи́саный** handwritten. **пи́сарь**
(*pl* -я́) *m* clerk. **писа́тель** *m*,
**писа́тельница** writer, author. **писа́ть** (пишу́, пи́шешь)
*impf* (*pf* на~) write; paint; ~
**ма́слом** paint in oils; **~ся** be
spelt.

**писк** squeak, chirp. **пискли́-
вый** squeaky. **пи́скнуть** (-ну)
*pf of* пища́ть

**пистоле́т** pistol; gun; **~-пуле-
мёт** sub-machine gun.

**пистóн** (percussion-)cap; piston.

писчебума́жный stationery. пи́счая бума́га writing paper. пи́сьменность literature. пи́сьменный writing, written. письмо́ (*pl* -а, -ем) letter.

пита́ние nourishment; feeding. пита́тельный nutritious; alimentary; feed. пита́ть *impf* feed; nourish; supply; ~ся be fed, eat; +*instr* feed on.

пито́мец (-мца) charge; pupil; alumnus. пито́мник nursery.

пить (пью, пьёшь; пил, -а́, -о) *impf* (*pf* вы́~) drink. питьё (*pl* -тья́, -те́й, -тьям) drinking, drink. питьево́й drinkable; drinking.

пиха́ть *impf*, пихну́ть (-ну́, -нёшь) *pf* push, shove.

пи́хта (silver) fir.

пи́чкать *impf* (*pf* на~) stuff.

пи́шущий writing; ~ая маши́нка typewriter.

пи́ща food.

пища́ть (-щу́) *impf* (*pf* пи́скнуть) squeak; cheep.

пищеваре́ние digestion. пищево́д oesophagus, gullet. пищево́й food.

пия́вка leech.

пла́вание swimming; sailing; voyage. пла́вательный swimming; ~ бассе́йн swimming-pool. пла́вать *impf* swim; float; sail. плавба́за depot ship, factory ship.

пла́вкий melting, smelting. пла́вильня foundry.

пла́вить (-влю) *impf* (*pf* рас~) melt, smelt; ~ся melt. пла́вка fusing; melting.

пла́вки (-вок) *pl* bathing trunks.

пла́вкий fusible; fuse. плавле́ние melting.

плавни́к (-а́) fin; flipper. пла́вный smooth, flowing; liquid. плаву́чий floating.

плагиа́т plagiarism. плагиа́тор plagiarist.

пла́зма plasma.

плака́т poster; placard.

пла́кать (-а́чу) *impf* cry, weep; ~ся complain, lament; +на+*acc* complain of; bemoan.

пла́кса cry-baby. плакси́вый whining. плаку́чий weeping; blaze.

пла́менный flaming; ardent. пла́мя (-мени) *neut* flame; blaze.

план plan.

планёр glider. планери́зм gliding. планери́ст glider-pilot.

плане́та planet. плане́тный planetary.

плани́рование[1] planning.

плани́рование[2] gliding; glide.

плани́ровать[1] *impf* (*pf* за~) plan.

плани́ровать[2] *impf* (*pf* с~) glide (down).

пла́нка lath, slat.

пла́новый planned, systematic; planning. планоме́рный systematic, planned.

планта́ция plantation.

пласт (-а́) layer; stratum. пласти́на plate. пласти́нка plate; (*gramophone*) record. пласти́ческий, пласти́чный plastic. пластма́сса plastic. пластма́ссовый plastic.

пла́стырь *m* plaster.

пла́та pay; charge; fee. платёж (-а́) payment. платёжеспосо́бный solvent. платёжный pay.

пла́тина platinum. пла́тиновый platinum.

плати́ть (-ачу́, -а́тишь) *impf* (*pf* за~, у~) pay; ~ся (*pf* по~ся) за+acc pay for. **плáтный** paid; requiring payment.

**платóк** (-ткá) shawl; head-scarf; handkerchief.

**платонúческий** platonic.

**платфóрма** platform; truck.

**плáтье** (gen pl -ьев) clothes, clothing; dress; gown. **платянóй** clothes.

**плафóн** ceiling; lamp shade.

**плацдáрм** bridgehead, beach-head; base; springboard.

**плацкáрта** reserved-seat ticket.

**плач** weeping. **плачéвный** lamentable. **плáчу** etc.: see **плáкать**

**плачý** etc.: see **платúть**

**плашмя́** adv flat, prone.

**плащ** (-á) cloak; raincoat.

**плебéй** plebeian.

**плевáтельница**    spittoon. **плевáть** (плюю́, плюёшь) impf (pf на~, плю́нуть) spit; inf+dat: мне ~ I don't give a damn (на+acc about); ~ся spit.

**плевóк** (-вкá) spit, spittle.

**плеврúт** pleurisy.

**плед** rug; plaid.

**плёл** etc.: see **плестú**

**племеннóй** tribal; pedigree. **плéмя** (gen pl -мя́н, -мён) neut tribe. **племя́нник** nephew. **племя́нница** niece.

**плен** (loc -ý) captivity.

**пленáрный** plenary.

**пленúтельный** captivating. **пленúть** pf (impf **пленя́ть**) captivate; ~ся be captivated.

**плёнка** film; tape; pellicle.

**плéнник** prisoner. **плéнный** captive.

**плéнум** plenary session.

**пленя́ть(ся** impf of **пленúть(ся**

**плéсень** f mould.

**плеск** splash, lapping. **плескáть** (-ещý, -éщешь) impf

(pf **плеснýть**) splash; lap; ~ся splash; lap.

**плéсневеть** (-еет) impf (pf за~) go mouldy, grow musty.

**плеснýть** (-нý, -нёшь) pf of **плескáть**

**плестú** (-етý, -етёшь; плёл, -á) impf (pf с~) plait; weave; ~сь trudge along. **плетéние** plaiting; wickerwork. **плетёный** wattled; wicker. **плетéнь** (-тня́) m wattle fencing. **плётка, плеть** (gen pl -éй) lash.

**плéчико** (pl -и, -ов) shoulder-strap; pl coat-hanger. **плечúстый** broad-shouldered. **плечó** (pl -и, -áм) shoulder.

**плешúвый** bald. **плешúна, плешь** bald patch.

**плещý** etc.: see **плескáть**

**плúнтус** plinth; skirting-board.

**плис** velveteen.

**плиссирóванный** impf pleat.

**плитá** (pl -ы) slab; flag(stone); stove, cooker; могúльная ~ gravestone. **плúтка** tile; (thin) slab; stove, cooker; ~ шоколáда bar of chocolate. **плúточный** tiled.

**пловéц** (-вцá), **пловчúха** swimmer. **пловýчий** floating; buoyant.

**плод** (-á) fruit. **плодúть** (-ожý) impf (pf рас~) produce, procreate; ~ся propagate.

**плодо-** in comb fruit-. **плодовúтый** fruitful; prolific; fertile. ~вóдство fruit-growing. ~нóсный fruit-bearing, fruitful. ~овощнóй fruit and vegetable. ~рóдный fertile. ~твóрный fruitful.

**плóмба** seal; filling. **плóмбировáть** impf (pf за~, о~) fill; seal.

**плóский** (-сок, -скá, -о) flat; trivial.

**плóско-** in comb flat. **плоскогóрье** plateau. **~гýбцы** (-ев) pl pliers. **~дóнный** flat-bottomed.

**плóскость** (gen pl -éй) flatness; plane; platitude.

**плот** (-á) raft.

**плотúна** dam; weir; dyke.

**плóтник** carpenter.

**плóтность** solidity; density. **плóтный** (-тен, -тнá, -о) thick; compact; dense; solid, strong; tight.

**плотоя́дный** carnivorous. **плоть** flesh.

**плохóй** bad; poor.

**площáдка** area, (sports) ground, court, playground; site; landing; platform. **плóщадь** (gen pl -éй) area; space; square.

**плуг** (pl -и) plough.

**плут** (-á) cheat, swindler; rogue. **плутовáтый** cunning. **плутовскóй** roguish; picaresque.

**плутóний** plutonium.

**плыть** (-ывý, -ывёшь; плыл, -á, -о) impf swim; float; sail.

**плю́нуть** (-ну) pf of **плевáть**

**плюс** plus; advantage.

**плющ** (-á) ivy.

**плюю́** etc.: see **плевáть**

**пляж** beach.

**плясáть** (-яшý, -я́шешь) impf (pf c~) dance. **пля́ска** dance; dancing.

**пневматúческий** pneumatic.

**пневмонúя** pneumonia.

**пнуть** (пну, пнёшь) pf of **пинáть**

**пня** etc.: see **пень**

**по** prep I. +dat on; along; round, about; by; over; according; in accordance with; for; in; at; by (reason of); on account of; from; **по понедéльникам** on Mondays; **по профéссии** by profession; **по рáдио** over the radio. II. +dat or acc of cardinal number, forms distributive number: **пó два, пó двое** in twos, two by two; **по пять рублéй штýка** at five roubles each. III. +acc to, up to; for, to get; **идтú по вóду** go to get water; **по пéрвое сентября́** up to (and including) 1st September. IV. +prep on, (immediately) after; **по прибы́тии** on arrival.

**по-** pref I. in comb +dat of adjs, or with advs in -и, indicates manner, use of a named language, or accordance with the opinion or wish of: **говорúть по-рýсски** speak Russian; **жить по-стáрому** live in the old style; **по-мóему** in my opinion. II. in comb with adjs and nn, indicates situation along or near a thing: **помóрье** seaboard, coastal region. III. in comb with comp of adjs indicates a smaller degree of comparison: **помéньше** a little less.

**побáиваться** impf be rather afraid.

**побéг**[1] flight; escape.

**побéг**[2] shoot; sucker.

**побегýшки: быть на побегýшках** run errands.

**побéда** victory. **победúтель** m victor; winner. **победúть** pf (impf **побеждáть**) conquer; win. **побéдный, победонóсный** victorious, triumphant.

**по|бежáть** pf.

**побеждáть** impf of **победúть**

**по|белéть** (-éю) pf. **по|белúть** pf. **побéлка** whitewashing.

побере́жный coastal. побе́-
ре́жье (sea-)coast.

по|беспоко́ить(ся *pf*.

побира́ть *impf* beg; live by
begging.

по|би́ть(ся (-бью́(сь, -бьёшь-
(ся) *pf*. по|благодари́ть *pf*.

побла́жка indulgence.

по|бледне́ть (-е́ю) *pf*.

поблёскивать *impf* gleam.

поблизости *adv* nearby.

побо́и (-ев) *pl* beating. побо́и-
ще slaughter; bloody battle.

побо́рник champion, advo-
cate. поборо́ть (-рю́, -решь)
*pf* overcome.

побо́чный secondary; done
on the side; ~ проду́кт by-
product.

по|брани́ться *pf*.

по|брата́ться *pf*. побрати́м
twin brother.

по|брезгать *pf*. по|бри́ть(ся
(-бре́ю(сь) *pf*.

побуди́тельный stimulating.
побуди́ть (-ужу́) *pf*, побу-
жда́ть *impf* induce, prompt.
побужде́ние motive; inducement.

побыва́ть *pf* have been, have
visited; look in, visit. побы́в-
ка leave. побы́ть (-бу́ду, -дешь;
по́бы́л, -а́, -о) *pf* stay (for a
short time).

побью́(сь *etc.*: *see* поби́ть(ся

повади́ться (-а́жусь) *pf* get into
the habit (of). пова́дка habit.

по|вали́ть(ся (-лю́(сь, -лишь-
(ся) *pf*.

пова́льно *adv* without exception. пова́льный general,
mass.

по́вар (*pl* -а́) cook, chef. пова́-
ренный culinary; cookery,
cooking.

по-ва́шему *adv* in your opinion.

пове́дать *pf* disclose; relate.

поведе́ние behaviour.

поведу́ *etc.*: *see* повести́

по|везти́ (-зу́, -зёшь; -вёз,
-ла́) *pf* повёл *etc.*: *see* пове-
сти́

повелева́ть *impf* +*instr* rule
(over); +*dat* command. пове-
ле́ние command. повели́-
тельный imperious; imperative.

по|венча́ть(ся *pf*.

поверга́ть *impf*, пове́ргнуть
(-ну; -ве́рг) *pf* throw down;
plunge.

пове́ренная *sb* confidante.
пове́ренный *sb* attorney;
confidant; ~ в дела́х chargé
d'affaires. пове́рить[1], пове́-
рить[2] *pf* (*impf* поверя́ть)
check; confide. пове́рка
check; roll-call.

поверну́ть (-ну́, -нёшь) *pf*,
повёртывать *impf* (*impf
also* повора́чивать) turn; ~ся
turn.

пове́рх *prep*+*gen* over. по-
ве́рхностный surface, superficial. пове́рхность surface.

пове́рье (*gen pl* -ий) popular
belief, superstition. пове-
ря́ть *impf* of пове́рить[2]

пове́са playboy.

по|веселе́ть (-е́ю) *pf*.

повесели́ть *pf* cheer (up),
amuse; ~ся have fun.

пове́сить(ся (-ве́шу(сь) *pf of*
ве́шать(ся

повествова́ние narrative, narration. повествова́тельный
narrative. повествова́ть *impf*
+о+*prep* narrate, relate.

по|вести́ (-еду́, -едёшь; -вёл,
-а́) *pf* (*impf* поводи́ть) +*instr*
move.

пове́стка notice; summons; ~
(дня) agenda.

**по́весть** (gen pl -éй) story, tale.
**пове́трие** epidemic; craze.
**пове́шу** etc.: see **пове́сить.**
**по|вздо́рить** pf.
**повзросле́ть** (-éю) pf grow up.
**по-ви|да́ть(ся** pf.
**по-ви́димому** apparently.
**пови́дло** jam.
**по|вини́ться** pf.
**пови́нность** duty, obligation;
во́инская ~ conscription. **пови́нный** guilty.
**повинова́ться** impf & pf obey.
**повинове́ние** obedience.
**повиса́ть** impf, **по|ви́снуть** (-ну; -вис) pf hang (on); hang down, droop.
**повле́чь** (-еку́, -ечёшь; -ёк, -ла́) pf (**за собо́й**) entail, bring in its train.
**по|влия́ть** pf.
**по́вод**[1] occasion, cause; по ~у+gen as regards, concerning.
**по́вод**[2] (loc -у́, pl -о́дья, -ьев) rein; **быть на ~у** +gen be under the thumb of. **поводи́ть** (-ожу́, -о́дишь) impf of **повести́. поводо́к** (-дка́) leash. **поводы́рь** (-я́) m guide.
**пово́зка** cart; vehicle.
**повора́чивать(ся** impf of **поверну́ть(ся, повороти́ть(ся; повора́ивайся, -а́йтесь!** get a move on!
**поворо́т** turn, turning; bend; turning-point. **повороти́ть(ся** (-рочу́(сь, -ро́тишь(ся) pf (impf **повора́чивать(ся)** turn. **повооро́тливый** agile, nimble; manoeuvrable. **пово́ротный** turning; rotary; revolving.
**по|вреди́ть** (-ежу́) pf, **по-врежда́ть** impf damage, injure; **~ся** be damaged; be injured. **поврежде́ние** damage, injury.

**повремени́ть** pf wait a little; +c+instr delay over.
**повседне́вный** daily; everyday.
**повсеме́стно** adv everywhere. **повсеме́стный** universal, general.
**повста́нец** (-нца) rebel, insurgent. **повста́нческий** rebel; insurgent.
**повсю́ду** adv everywhere.
**повторе́ние** repetition. **по-втори́ть** pf, **повторя́ть** impf repeat; **~ся** repeat o.s.; be repeated; recur. **повто́рный** repeated.
**повы́сить** (-ы́шу) pf, **повы-ша́ть** impf raise, heighten; **~ся** rise. **повыше́ние** rise; promotion. **повы́шенный** heightened, high.
**повяза́ть** (-яжу́, -я́жешь) pf, **повя́зывать** impf tie. **по-вя́зка** band; bandage.
**по|гада́ть** pf.
**пога́нка** toadstool. **пога́ный** foul; unclean.
**погаса́ть** impf, **по|га́снуть** (-ну) pf go out, be extinguished. **по|гаси́ть** (-ашу́, -а́сишь) pf. **погаша́ть** impf liquidate, cancel. **пога́шенный** used, cancelled, cashed.
**погиба́ть** impf, **по|ги́бнуть** (-ну; -ги́б) pf perish; be lost. **поги́бель** ruin. **поги́бший** lost; ruined; killed.
**по|глади́ть** (-а́жу) pf.
**поглоти́ть** (-ощу́, -о́тишь) pf, **поглоща́ть** impf swallow up; absorb. **поглоще́ние** absorption.
**по|глупе́ть** (-е́ю) pf.
**по|гляде́ть** (-яжу́) pf. **погля́-дывать** impf glance (from time to time); **+за**+instr keep an eye on.

**погна́ть** (-гоню́, -го́нишь; -гна́л, -а́, -о) *pf* drive; ~ся за+*instr* run after; start in pursuit of.

**по|гну́ть(ся** (-ну́(сь, -нёшь(ся) *pf.* по|гну́шаться *pf.*

**поговори́ть** *pf* have a talk.

**погово́рка** saying, proverb.

**пого́да** weather.

**погоди́ть** (-ожу́) *pf* wait a little; **немно́го погодя́** a little later.

**поголо́вный** *adv* one and all. **поголо́вно** general; capitation. **поголо́вье** number.

**пого́н** (*gen pl* -о́н) shoulder-strap.

**пого́нщик** driver. **погоню́** *etc.*: *see* **погна́ть. пого́ня** pursuit, chase. **погоня́ть** *impf* urge on, drive.

**погорячи́ться** (-чу́сь) *pf* get worked up.

**пого́ст** graveyard.

**пограни́чник** frontier guard. **пограни́чный** frontier.

**по́греб** (*pl* -а́) cellar. **погреба́льный** funeral. **погреба́ть** *impf of* **погрести́. погребе́ние** burial.

**погрему́шка** rattle.

**погрести́**[1] (-ебу́, -ебёшь; -рёб, -ла́) *pf* (*impf* **погреба́ть**) bury. **погрести́**[2] (-ебу́, -ебёшь; -рёб, -ла́) *pf* row for a while.

**погре́ть** (-е́ю) *pf* warm; ~ся warm o.s.

**по|греши́ть**[1] (-шу́) *pf* sin; err. **погре́шность** error, mistake. **по|грози́ть(ся** (-ожу́(сь) *pf.* **по|грубе́ть** (-е́ю) *pf.*

**погружа́ть** *impf,* **по|грузи́ть** (-ужу́, -у́зи́шь) *pf* load; ship; dip, plunge, immerse; ~ся sink, plunge; dive; be plunged, absorbed. **погруже́ние** submergence; immersion; dive. **погру́зка** loading; shipment.

**погряза́ть** *impf,* **по|гря́знуть** (-ну; -яз) *pf* be bogged down; wallow.

**по|губи́ть** (-блю́, -бишь) *pf.* **по|гуля́ть** *pf.*

**под, подо** *prep* **I.** +*acc or instr* under; near, close to; **взять под ру́ку**+*acc* take the arm of; ~ **ви́дом**+*gen* under the guise of; **под го́ру** downhill; ~ **Москво́й** in the environs of Moscow. **II.** +*instr* occupied by, used as; (meant, implied) by; in, with; **говя́дина** ~ **хре́ном** beef with horse-radish. **III.** +*acc* towards; to (the accompaniment of); in imitation of; on; for, to serve as; **ему́** ~ **пятьдеся́т (лет)** he is getting on for fifty.

**подава́ть(ся** (-даю́(сь, -даёшь(ся) *impf of* **пода́ть(ся**

**подави́ть** (-влю́, -вишь) *pf,* **подавля́ть** *impf* suppress; depress; overwhelm. **по|дави́ться** (-влю́сь, -вишься) *pf.* **подавле́ние** suppression; repression. **пода́вленность** depression. **пода́вленный** suppressed; depressed. **подавля́ющий** overwhelming.

**пода́вно** *adv* all the more.

**пода́гра** gout.

**пода́льше** *adv* a little further.

**по|дари́ть** (-рю́, -ришь) *pf.* **пода́рок** (-рка) present.

**пода́тливый** pliant, pliable.

**пода́ть** (*gen pl* -е́й) tax. **по|да́ть** (-а́м, -а́шь, -а́ст, -ади́м; по́дал, -а́, -о) *pf* (*impf* **подава́ть**) serve; give; put, move, turn; put forward, present, hand in; ~ся give way; yield; +на+*acc* set out for. **пода́ча** giving, presenting; serve; feed, supply. **пода́чка** handout, crumb. **подаю́** *etc.*

*see* подава́ть. подая́ние alms.

подбега́ть *impf*, подбежа́ть (-егу́) *pf* come running (up).

подбива́ть *impf of* подби́ть

подберу́ *etc.*: *see* подобра́ть.

подбира́ть(ся *impf of* подобра́ть(ся

подби́ть (-добью́, -добьёшь) *pf* (*impf* подбива́ть) line; re-sole; bruise; put out of action; incite.

подбодри́ть *pf*, подбодря́ть *impf* cheer up, encourage; ~ся cheer up, take heart.

подбо́р selection, assortment.

подборо́док (-дка) chin.

подбоче́нившись *adv* with hands on hips.

подбра́сывать *impf*, подбро́сить (-о́шу) *pf* throw up.

подва́л cellar; basement. подва́льный basement, cellar.

подведу́ *etc.*: *see* подвести́

подвезти́ (-зу́, -зёшь; -вёз, -ла́) *pf* (*impf* подвози́ть) bring, take; give a lift.

подвене́чный wedding.

подверга́ть *impf*, подве́ргнуть (-ну; -вёрг) *pf* subject; expose; ~ся +*dat* undergo. подве́рженный subject, liable.

подверну́ть (-ну́, -нёшь) *pf*, подвёртывать *impf* turn up; tuck under; sprain; tighten; ~ся be sprained; be turned up; be tucked under.

подве́сить (-е́шу) *pf* (*impf* подве́шивать) hang up, suspend. подвесно́й hanging, suspended.

подвести́ (-еду́, -едёшь; -вёл, -а́) *pf* (*impf* подводи́ть) lead up, bring up; place (under); bring under, subsume; let down; ~ ито́ги reckon up; sum up.

подве́шивать *impf of* подве́сить

по́двиг exploit, feat.

подвига́ть(ся *impf of* подви́нуть(ся

подви́жник religious ascetic; champion.

подвижно́й mobile; ~ соста́в rolling-stock. подви́жность mobility. подви́жный mobile; lively; agile.

подвиза́ться *impf* (в *or* на+*prep*) work (in).

подви́нуть (-ну) *pf* (*impf* подвига́ть) move; push; advance; ~ся move; advance.

подвла́стный +*dat* subject to; under the control of.

подво́да cart. подводи́ть (-ожу́, -о́дишь) *impf of* подвести́

подво́дн|ый submarine; underwater; ~ая скала́ reef.

подво́з transport; supply. подвози́ть (-ожу́, -о́зишь) *impf of* подвезти́

подворо́тня (*gen pl* -тен) gateway.

подво́х trick.

подвы́пивший tipsy.

подвяза́ть (-яжу́, -я́жешь) *pf*, подвя́зывать *impf* tie up. подвя́зка garter; suspender.

подгиба́ть *impf of* подогну́ть подгля́деть (-яжу́) *pf*, подгля́дывать *impf* peep; spy.

подгова́ривать *impf*, подговори́ть *pf* incite.

подгоню́ *etc.*: *see* подогна́ть.

подгоня́ть *impf of* подогна́ть

подгора́ть *impf*, подгоре́ть (-ри́т) *pf* get a bit burnt. подгоре́лый slightly burnt.

подготови́тельный preparatory. подгото́вить (-влю) *pf*, подготовля́ть *impf* prepare; ~ся prepare, get ready. подгото́вка preparation, training.

поддава́ться (-даю́сь, -даёшься) *impf of* подда́ться

подда́кивать *impf* agree, assent.

по́дданный *sb* subject; citizen. по́дданство citizenship.

подда́ть (-а́мся, -а́шься, -а́стся, -ади́мся, -а́лся, -ла́сь) *pf* (*impf* поддава́ться) yield, give way.

подде́лать *pf*, подде́лывать *impf* counterfeit; forge. подде́лка falsification; forgery; imitation. подде́льный false, counterfeit.

поддержа́ть (-жу́, -жишь) *pf*, подде́рживать *impf* support; maintain. подде́ржка support.

по|де́йствовать *pf*.

поде́лать *pf* do; ничего́ не поде́лаешь it can't be helped. по|дели́ть(ся (-лю́(сь, -лишь(ся) *pf*.

поде́лка *pl* small (handmade) articles.

подело́м *adv*: ~ ему́ (etc.) it serves him (etc.) right.

подённый by the day. подёнщик, -ица day-labourer.

подёргиваться twitch.

поде́ржанный second-hand.

подёрнуть (-нет) *pf* cover.

по|дешеве́ть (-е́ет) *pf*.

подеру́ etc.: see подра́ть.

поджа́ривать(ся *impf*, поджа́рить(ся *pf* fry, roast, grill; toast. поджа́ристый brown(ed).

поджа́рый lean, wiry.

поджа́ть (-жму́, -жмёшь) *pf* (*impf* поджима́ть) draw in, draw under; ~ гу́бы purse one's lips.

подже́чь (-дожгу́, -ожжёшь; -жёг, -дожгла́) *pf*, поджига́ть *impf* set fire to; burn. поджига́тель *m* arsonist;

instigator.

поджида́ть *impf* (+*gen*) wait (for).

поджима́ть *impf of* поджа́ть.

поджо́г arson.

подзаголо́вок (-вка) sub-title, sub-heading.

подзащи́тный *sb* client.

подземе́лье (*gen pl* -лий) cave; dungeon. подзе́мный underground.

подзову́ *etc.: see* подозва́ть

подзо́рная труба́ telescope.

подзыва́ть *impf of* подозва́ть

по|диви́ться (-влю́сь) *pf*.

подка́пывать(ся *impf of* подкопа́ть(ся

подкара́уливать *impf*, подкара́улить *pf* be on the watch (for).

подкати́ть (-ачу́, -а́тишь) *pf*, подка́тывать *impf* roll up, drive up; roll.

подка́шивать(ся *impf of* подкоси́ть(ся

подки́дывать *impf*, подки́нуть (-ну) *pf* throw up. подки́дыш foundling.

подкла́дка lining. подкла́дывать *impf of* подложи́ть

подкле́ивать *impf*, подкле́ить *pf* glue (up); mend.

подко́ва (horse-)shoe. подко|ва́ть (-кую́, -куёшь) *pf*, подко́вывать *impf* shoe.

подко́жный hypodermic.

подкоми́ссия, подкомите́т sub-committee.

подко́п undermining; underground passage. подкопа́ть *pf* (*impf* подка́пывать) undermine; ~ся под+*acc* undermine; burrow under.

подкоси́ть (-ошу́, -о́сишь) *pf* (*impf* подка́шивать) cut down; ~ся give way.

подкра́дываться *impf of* подкра́сться

подкра́сить (-а́шу) *pf* (*impf* подкра́шивать) touch up; ~ся make up lightly.

подкра́сться (-аду́сь, -адёшься) *pf* (*impf* подкра́дываться) sneak up.

подкра́шивать(ся *impf of* подкра́сить(ся. подкра́шу *etc.*: *see* подкра́сить

подкрепи́ть (-плю́) *pf* (*impf* подкрепля́ть) reinforce; support; corroborate; fortify; ~ся fortify o.s. подкрепле́ние confirmation; sustenance; reinforcement.

подкрути́ть (-учу́, -у́тишь) *pf* (*impf* подкру́чивать) tighten up.

по́дкуп bribery. подкупи́ть (-плю́, -пишь) *pf* bribe; win over.

подла́диться (-а́жусь) *pf*, подла́живаться *impf* +*к*+*dat* adapt o.s. to; make up to.

подла́мываться *impf of* подломи́ться

по́дле *prep*+*gen* by the side of, beside.

подлежа́ть (-жу́) *impf* +*dat* be subject to; не подлежи́т сомне́нию it is beyond doubt. подлежа́щее *sb* subject. подлежа́щий+*dat* subject to.

подлеза́ть *impf*, подле́зть (-зу, -ез) *pf* crawl (under).

подле́сок (-ска) undergrowth.

подле́ц (-а́) scoundrel.

подлива́ть *impf of* подли́ть. подли́вка sauce, dressing; gravy.

подли́за *m* & *f* toady. подли́за́ться (-ижу́сь, -и́жешься) *pf*, подли́зываться *impf* +*к*+*dat* suck up to.

по́длинник original. по́длин-

но *adv* really. по́длинный genuine; authentic; original; real.

подли́ть (-долью́, -дольёшь; по́дли́л, -а́, -о) *pf* (*impf* подлива́ть) pour; add.

подло́г forgery.

подло́дка submarine.

подложи́ть (-жу́, -жишь) *pf* (*impf* подкла́дывать) add; +*под*+*acc* lay under; line.

подло́жный false, spurious; counterfeit, forged.

подлоко́тник arm (of chair).

подломи́ться (-о́мится) *pf* (*impf* подла́мываться) break; give way.

по́длость meanness, baseness; mean trick. по́длый (подл, -а́, -о) mean, base.

подма́зать (-а́жу) *pf*, подма́зывать *impf* grease; bribe.

подмасте́рье (*gen pl* -ьев) *m* apprentice.

подме́н, подме́на replacement. подме́нивать *impf*, подмени́ть (-ню́, -нишь) *pf*, подменя́ть *impf* replace.

подмести́ (-ету́, -етёшь; -мёл, -а́) *pf*, подмета́ть¹ *impf* sweep.

подмета́ть² *pf* (*impf* подмётывать) tack.

подме́тить (-е́чу) *pf* (*impf* подмеча́ть) notice.

подмётка sole.

подмётывать *impf of* подмета́ть². подмеча́ть *impf of* подме́тить

подмеша́ть *pf*, подме́шивать *impf* mix in, stir in.

подми́гивать *impf*, подмигну́ть (-ну́, -нёшь) *pf* +*dat* wink at.

подмо́га help.

подмока́ть *impf*, подмо́кнуть (-нет; -мо́к) *pf* get damp, get wet.

**подмора́живать** *impf,* **подморо́зить** *pf* freeze.

**подмоско́вный** (situated) near Moscow.

**подмо́стки** (-ов) *pl* scaffolding; stage.

**подмо́ченный** damp; tarnished.

**подмыва́ть** *impf,* **подмы́ть** (-о́ю) *pf* wash; wash away; его́ так и подмыва́ет he feels an urge (to).

**подмы́шка** armpit.

**поднево́льный** dependent; forced.

**поднести́** (-су́, -сёшь; -ёс, -ла́) *pf* (*impf* **подноси́ть**) present; take, bring.

**поднима́ть(ся** *impf of* **подня́ть(ся**

**поднови́ть** (-влю́) *pf,* **подновля́ть** *impf* renew, renovate.

**подного́тная** *sb* ins and outs.

**подно́жие** foot; pedestal. **подно́жка** running-board. **подно́жный корм** pasture.

**подно́с** tray. **подноси́ть** (-ошу́, -о́сишь) *impf of* **поднести́.** **подноше́ние** giving; present.

**подня́тие** raising. **подня́ть** (-ниму́, -ни́мешь; по́днял, -а́, -о) *pf* (*impf* **поднима́ть, поды́мать**) raise; lift (up); rouse; ~ся rise; go up.

**подо** *see* **под**

**подоба́ть** *impf* befit, become. **подоба́ющий** proper.

**подо́бие** likeness; similarity. **подо́бный** like, similar; и тому́ ~ое and so on, and such like; ничего́ ~ого! nothing of the sort!

**подобостра́стие** servility. **подобостра́стный** servile.

**подобра́ть** (-деру́, -дерёшь; -брал, -а́, -о) *pf* (*impf* **подбира́ть**) pick up; tuck up,

put up; pick; ~ся steal up.

**подобью́** *etc.: see* **подби́ть**

**подогна́ть** (-гоню́, -го́нишь; -а́л, -а́, -о) *pf* (*impf* **подгоня́ть**) drive; urge on; adjust.

**подогну́ть** (-ну́, -нёшь) *pf* (*impf* **подгиба́ть**) tuck in; bend under.

**подогрева́ть** *impf,* **подогре́ть** (-е́ю) *pf* warm up.

**пододвига́ть** *impf,* **пододви́нуть** (-ну) *pf* move up.

**пододея́льник** blanket cover; top sheet.

**подожгу́** *etc.: see* **подже́чь**

**подожда́ть** (-ду́, -дёшь; -а́л, -а́, -о) *pf* wait (+*gen or acc* for).

**подожму́** *etc.: see* **поджа́ть**

**подозва́ть** (-дзову́, -дзовёшь; -а́л, -а́, -о) *pf* (*impf* **подзыва́ть**) call to; beckon.

**подозрева́емый** suspected; suspect. **подозрева́ть** *impf* suspect. **подозре́ние** suspicion. **подозри́тельный** suspicious.

**по|до́ить** (-ою́, -о́ишь) *pf.*

**подойти́** (-йду́, -йдёшь; -ошёл, -шла́) *pf* (*impf* **подходи́ть**) approach; come up; +*dat* suit, fit.

**подоко́нник** window-sill.

**подо́л** hem.

**подо́лгу** *adv* for ages; for hours (*etc.*) on end.

**подолью́** *etc.: see* **подли́ть**

**подо́нки** (-ов) *pl* dregs; scum.

**подоплёка** underlying cause.

**подопру́** *etc.: see* **подпере́ть**

**подо́пытный** experimental.

**подорва́ть** (-рву́, -рвёшь; -а́л, -а́, -о) *pf* (*impf* **подрыва́ть**) undermine; blow up.

**по|дорожа́ть** *pf.*

**подоро́жник** plantain. **подоро́жный** roadside.

**подосла́ть** (-ошлю́, -ошлёшь) *pf* (*impf* **подсыла́ть**) send (secretly).

**подоспева́ть** *impf*, **подоспе́ть** (-е́ю) *pf* arrive, appear (in time).

**подостла́ть** (-дстелю́, -о́стелешь) *pf* (*impf* **подстила́ть**) lay under.

**подотде́л** section, subdivision.

**подотру́** *etc.*: *see* **подтере́ть**

**подотчётный** accountable.

**по|до́хнуть** (-ну) *pf* (*impf also* **подыха́ть**)

**подохо́дный нало́г** income-tax.

**подо́шва** sole; foot.

**подошёл** *etc.*: *see* **подойти́. подошлю́** *etc.*: *see* **подосла́ть подошью́** *etc.*: *see* **подши́ть.**

**подпада́ть** *impf*, **подпа́сть** (-аду́, -адёшь; -а́л) *pf* **под+**acc fall under.

**подпева́ть** *impf* (+dat) sing along (with).

**подпере́ть** (-допру́; -пёр) *pf* (*impf* **подпира́ть**) prop up.

**подпи́ливать** *impf*, **подпили́ть** (-лю́, -лишь) *pf* saw; saw a little off.

**подпира́ть** *impf of* **подпере́ть**

**подписа́ние** signing. **подписа́ть** (-ишу́, -и́шешь) *pf*, **подпи́сывать** *impf* sign; ~**ся** sign; subscribe. **подпи́ска** subscription. **подписно́й** subscription. **подпи́счик** subscriber. **по́дпись** signature.

**подплыва́ть** *impf*, **подплы́ть** (-ыву́, -ывёшь; -плы́л, -а́, -о) *pf* **к+**dat swim *or* sail up to.

**подполза́ть** *impf*, **подползти́** (-зу́, -зёшь; -по́лз, -ла́) *pf* creep up (**к+**dat to); **+под+**acc crawl under.

**подполко́вник** lieutenant-colonel.

**подпо́лье** cellar; underground. **подпо́льный** underfloor; underground.

**подпо́ра, подпо́рка** prop, support.

**подпо́чва** subsoil.

**подпра́вить** (-влю) *pf*, **подправля́ть** *impf* touch up, adjust.

**подпры́гивать** *impf*, **подпры́гнуть** (-ну) *pf* jump up (and down).

**подпуска́ть** *impf*, **подпусти́ть** (-ущу́, -у́стишь) *pf* allow to approach.

**подраба́тывать** *impf*, **подрабо́тать** *pf* earn on the side; work up.

**подра́внивать** *impf of* **подровня́ть**

**подража́ние** imitation. **подража́ть** *impf* imitate.

**подразделе́ние** subdivision. **подраздели́ть** *pf*, **подразделя́ть** *impf* subdivide.

**подразумева́ть** *impf* imply, mean; ~**ся** be meant, be understood.

**подраста́ть** *impf*, **подрасти́** (-ту́, -тёшь; -ро́с, -ла́) *pf* grow.

**по|дра́ть(ся** (-деру́(сь, -дерёшь(ся, -а́л(ся, -ла́(сь, -о́(сь) *pf*: *see* **драть(ся**

**подре́зать** (-е́жу) *pf*, **подреза́ть** *impf* cut; clip, trim.

**подро́бно** *adv* in detail. **подро́бность** detail. **подро́бный** detailed.

**подровня́ть** *pf* (*impf* **подра́внивать**) level, even; trim.

**подро́с** *etc.*: *see* **подрасти́. подро́сток** (-тка) adolescent; youth.

**подро́ю** *etc.*: *see* **подры́ть**

подрубáть¹ *impf*, подрубить (-блю, -бишь) *pf* chop down; cut short(er).

подрубáть² *impf*, подрубить (-блю, -бишь) *pf* hem.

подрýга friend; girlfriend. подрýжески *adv* in a friendly way. подружиться (-жýсь) *pf* make friends.

по-другóму *adv* differently.

подрýчный at hand; improvised; *sb* assistant.

подрыв undermining; injury.

подрывáть¹ *impf of* подорвáть

подрывáть² *impf*, подрыть (-рóю) *pf* undermine, sap. подрывнóй blasting, demolition; subversive.

подряд¹ *adv* in succession.

подряд² contract. подрядчик contractor.

подсáживаться *impf of* подсéсть

подсáливать *impf of* подсолить

подсвéчник candlestick.

подсéсть (-сяду, -сядешь; -сéл) *pf* (*impf* подсáживаться) sit down (к+*dat* near).

подсказáть (-ажý, -áжешь) *pf*, подскáзывать *impf* prompt; suggest. подскáзка prompting.

подскáкивать *impf*, подскочить (-чý, -чишь) *pf* jump (up); soar; come running.

подсластить (-ащý) *pf*, подслáщивать *impf* sweeten.

подслéдственный under investigation.

подслýшать *pf*, подслýшивать *impf* overhear; eavesdrop, listen.

подсмáтривать *impf*, подсмотрéть (-рю, -ришь) *pf* spy (on).

подснéжник snowdrop.

подсóбный subsidiary; auxiliary.

подсóвывать *impf of* подсýнуть

подсознáние subconscious (mind). подсознáтельный subconscious.

подсолить (-сóлишь) *pf* (*impf* подсáливать) add salt to.

подсóлнечник sunflower. подсóлнечный sunflower.

подсóхнуть (-ну) *pf* (*impf* подсыхáть) dry out a little.

подспóрье help.

подстáвить (-влю) *pf*, подставлять *impf* put (under); bring up; expose; ~ нóжку +*dat* trip up. подстáвка stand; support. подставнóй false.

подстакáнник glass-holder.

подстелю *etc.*: *see* подостлáть

подстерегáть *impf*, подстерéчь (-егý, -ежёшь; -рёг, -лá) *pf* lie in wait for.

подстилáть *impf of* подостлáть. подстилка litter.

подстрáивать *impf of* подстрóить

подстрекáтель *m* instigator. подстрекáтельство instigation. подстрекáть *impf*, подстрекнýть (-нý, -нёшь) *pf* instigate, incite.

подстрéливать *impf*, подстрелить (-лю, -лишь) *pf* wound.

подстригáть *impf*, подстричь (-игý, -ижёшь; -иг) *pf* cut; clip, trim; ~ся have a hair-cut.

подстрóить *pf* (*impf* подстрáивать) build on; cook up.

подстрóчный literal; ~ примечáние footnote.

**по́дступ** approach. **подступа́ть** *impf*, **подступи́ть** (-плю́, -пишь) *pf* approach; **~ся** к+*dat* approach.

**подсуди́мый** *sb* defendant; the accused. **подсу́дный**+*dat* under the jurisdiction of.

**подсу́нуть** (-ну) *pf* (*impf* подсо́вывать) put, shove; palm off.

**подсчёт** calculation; count. **подсчита́ть** *pf*, **подсчи́тывать** count (up); calculate.

**подсыла́ть** *impf of* подосла́ть. **подсыха́ть** (*impf of* подсо́хнуть. **подся́ду** *etc.*: *see* подсе́сть. **подта́лкивать** *impf of* подтолкну́ть

**подта́скивать** *impf of* подта́щить

**подтасова́ть** *pf*, **подтасо́вывать** *impf* shuffle unfairly; juggle with.

**подта́чивать** *impf of* подточи́ть

**подта́щить** (-щу́, -щишь) *pf* (*impf* подта́скивать) drag up.

**подтверди́ть** (-ржу́) *pf*, **подтвержда́ть** *impf* confirm; corroborate. **подтвержде́ние** confirmation, corroboration.

**подтёк** bruise. **подтека́ть** *impf of* подте́чь; leak.

**подтере́ть** (-дотру́, -дотрёшь; подтёр) *pf* (*impf* подтира́ть) wipe (up).

**подте́чь** (-ечёт; -тёк, -ла́) *pf* (*impf* подтека́ть) под+*acc* flow under.

**подтира́ть** *impf of* подтере́ть

**подтолкну́ть** (-ну́, -нёшь) *pf* (*impf* подта́лкивать) push; urge on.

**подточи́ть** (-чу́, -чишь) *pf* (*impf* подта́чивать) sharpen; eat away; undermine.

**подтру́нивать** *impf*, **подтруни́ть** *pf* над+*instr* tease.

**подтя́гивать** *impf*, **подтяну́ть** (-ну́, -нешь) *pf* tighten; pull up; move up; **~ся** tighten one's belt *etc.*; move up; pull o.s. together. **подтя́жки** (-жек) *pl* braces, suspenders. **подтя́нутый** smart.

**по|ду́мать** *pf* think (for a while). **поду́мывать** *impf*+*inf* or o+*prep* think about.

**по|ду́ть** (-у́ю) *pf*.

**поду́шка** pillow; cushion.

**подхали́м** *m* toady. **подхали́мство** grovelling.

**подхвати́ть** (-ачу́, -а́тишь) *pf*, **подхва́тывать** *impf* catch (up), pick up, take up.

**подхлестну́ть** (-ну́, -нёшь) *pf*, **подхлёстывать** *impf* whip up.

**подхо́д** approach. **подходи́ть** (-ожу́, -о́дишь) *impf of* подойти́. **подходя́щий** suitable.

**подцепи́ть** (-плю́, -пишь) *pf*, **подцепля́ть** *impf* hook on; pick up.

**подча́с** *adv* sometimes.

**подчёркивать** *impf*, **подчеркну́ть** (-ну́, -нёшь) *pf* underline; emphasize.

**подчине́ние** subordination; submission. **подчинённый** subordinate. **подчини́ть** (-ню́) *pf*, **подчиня́ть** *impf* subordinate, subject; **~ся** +*dat* submit to.

**подшива́ть** *impf of* подши́ть. **подши́вка** hemming; lining; soling.

**подши́пник** bearing.

**подши́ть** (-дошью́, -дошьёшь) *pf* (*impf* подшива́ть) hem, line; sole.

**подшути́ть** (-учу́, -у́тишь) *pf*,

подшу́чивать *impf* над+*instr* mock; play a trick on.

подъе́ду *etc.: see* подъе́хать

подъе́зд entrance, doorway; approach. подъезжа́ть *impf of* подъе́хать

подъём lifting; raising; ascent; climb; enthusiasm; instep; reveille. подъёмник lift, elevator, hoist. подъёмный lifting; ~ кран crane; ~ мост drawbridge.

подъе́хать (-е́ду) *pf* (*impf* подъезжа́ть) drive up.

подыма́ть(ся *impf of* подня́ть(ся

подыска́ть (-ыщу́, -ы́щешь) *pf*, подыскивать *impf* seek (out).

подыто́живать *impf*, подыто́жить (-жу) *pf* sum up.

подыха́ть *impf of* подо́хнуть

подыша́ть (-шу́, -шишь) *pf* breathe.

поеда́ть *impf of* пое́сть

поеди́нок (-нка) duel.

по́езд (*pl* -а́) train. пое́здка trip.

пое́сть (-е́м, -е́шь, -е́ст, -еди́м; -е́л) *pf* (*impf* поеда́ть) eat, eat up; have a bite to eat.

пое́хать (-е́ду) *pf* go; set off.

по|жале́ть (-е́ю) *pf*.

по|жа́ловать(ся *pf*. пожа́луй *adv* perhaps. пожа́луйста *partl* please; you're welcome.

пожа́р fire. пожа́рище scene of a fire. пожа́рник, пожа́рный *sb* fireman. пожа́рный fire; ~ая кома́нда fire-brigade; ~ая ле́стница fire-escape; ~ая маши́на fire-engine.

пожа́тие handshake. пожа́ть[1] (-жму́, -жмёшь) *pf* (*impf* пожима́ть) press; ~ ру́ку+*dat*

shake hands with; ~ плеча́ми shrug one's shoulders.

пожа́ть[2] (-жну́, -жнёшь) *pf* (*impf* пожина́ть) reap.

пожела́ть wish, desire. по|жела́ть *pf*.

по|желте́ть (-е́ю) *pf*.

по|жени́ть (-ню́, -нишь) *pf*. по|жени́ться (-женимся) *pf* get married.

поже́ртвование donation. по|же́ртвовать *pf*.

пожива́ть *impf* live; как (вы) пожива́ете? how are you (getting on)? поживи́тельный life(long). пожило́й elderly.

пожима́ть *impf of* пожа́ть[1].

пожина́ть *impf of* пожа́ть[2].

пожира́ть *impf of* пожра́ть

пожи́тки (-ов) *pl* belongings.

пожи́ть (-иву́, -ивёшь; по́жил, -а́, -о) *pf*. live for a while; stay.

пожму́ *etc.: see* пожа́ть[1].

пожну́ *etc.: see* пожа́ть[2]

пожра́ть (-ру́, -рёшь; -а́л, -а́, -о) *pf* (*impf* пожира́ть) devour.

по́за pose.

по|забо́титься (-о́чусь) *pf*.

позаба́вить *impf*, позабы́ть (-у́ду) *pf* forget all about.

по|зави́довать *pf*. по|за́втракать *pf*.

позавчера́ *adv* the day before yesterday.

позади́ *adv & prep*+*gen* behind.

по|заимствовать *pf*.

позапро́шлый before last.

по|зва́ть (-зову́, -зовёшь; -а́л, -а́, -о) *pf*.

позволе́ние permission. позволи́тельный permissible. позво́лить *pf*, позволя́ть *impf* + *dat* allow, permit, позво́ль(те) allow me; excuse me.

**по|звони́ть** pf.

**позвоно́к** (-нка́) vertebra. **позвоно́чник** spine. **позвоно́чн|ый** spinal; vertebrate; **~ые** sb pl vertebrates.

**поздне́е** adv later. **по́здний** late; **по́здно** it is late.

**по|здоро́ваться** pf. **поздра́вить** (-влю) pf, **поздравля́ть** impf c+instr congratulate on. **поздравле́ние** congratulation.

**по|зелене́ть** (-е́ет) pf.

**по́зже** adv later (on).

**пози́ровать** impf pose.

**позити́в** positive. **позити́вный** positive.

**пози́ция** position.

**познава́тельный** cognitive. **познава́ть** (-наю́, -наёшь) impf of **позна́ть**

**по|знако́мить(ся** (-млю(сь)) pf.

**позна́ние** cognition. **позна́ть** pf (impf **познава́ть**) get to know.

**позоло́та** gilding. **по|золоти́ть** (-лочу́) pf.

**позо́р** shame, disgrace. **позо́рить** impf (pf o~) disgrace; **~ся** disgrace o.s. **позо́рный** shameful.

**поигра́ть** pf play (for a while).

**поимённо** adv by name.

**по́имка** capture.

**поинтересова́ться** pf be curious.

**поиска́ть** (-ищу́, -и́щешь) pf look for. **по́иски** (-ов) pl search.

**пои́стине** adv indeed.

**пои́ть** (пою́, по́ишь) impf (pf на~) give someone to drink; water.

**пойду́** etc.: see **пойти́**

**по́йло** swill.

**пойма́ть** pf of **лови́ть**. **пойму́** etc.: see **поня́ть**

**пойти́** (-йду́, -йдёшь; пошёл, -шла́) pf of **идти́**, **ходи́ть**; go, walk; begin to walk; +inf begin; **пошёл!** off you go! I'm off; **пошёл вон!** be off!

**пока́** adv for the present; cheerio; **~ что** in the meanwhile. **пока́** conj while; **~ не** until.

**пока́з** showing, demonstration. **пока́зание** testimony, evidence; reading. **показа́тель** m index. **показа́тельный** significant; model; demonstration. **показа́ть** (-ажу́, -а́жешь), **пока́зывать** impf show. **показа́ться** (-ажу́сь, -а́жешься) pf, **пока́зываться** impf show o.s.; appear. **показно́й** for show; ostentatious. **показу́ха** show.

**по|кале́чить(ся** (-чу(сь)) pf.

**пока́мест** adv & conj for the present; while; meanwhile.

**по|кара́ть** pf.

**по|ката́ться** pf.

**покати́ть** (-чу́, -тишь) pf start (rolling); **~ся** start rolling.

**пока́тый** sloping; slanting.

**покача́ть** (-чу́) pf rock, swing; **~ голово́й** shake one's head. **пока́чивать** rock slightly; **~ся** rock; stagger. **покачну́ть** (-ну́, -нёшь) pf shake; rock; **~ся** sway, totter, lurch.

**пока́шливать** impf have a slight cough.

**покая́ние** confession; repentance. **по|ка́яться** pf.

**поквита́ться** pf be quits; get even.

**покида́ть** impf, **поки́нуть** (-ну) pf leave; abandon. **поки́нутый** deserted.

**покладя́** : не **~ рук** untiringly.

**покла́дистый** complaisant, obliging.

поклóн bow; greeting; regards. поклонéние worship. поклони́ться (-ню́сь -ни́шься) pf of кла́няться. поклóнник admirer; worshipper. поклоня́ться impf +dat worship.

по|кля́сться (-яну́сь, -нёшься; -я́лся, -ла́сь) pf.

покóиться impf rest, repose. покóй rest, peace; room. покóйник, -ица the deceased. покóйный calm, quiet; deceased.

по|колеба́ть(ся (-éблю(сь) pf.

поколéние generation.

по|колоти́ть(ся (-очу́(сь, -óтишь(ся) pf.

покóнчить (-чу) pf c+instr finish; put an end to; ~ с собóй commit suicide.

покорéние conquest. покори́ть pf (impf покоря́ть) subdue; conquer; ~ся submit.

по|корми́ть(ся (-млю́(сь, (ся) pf.

покóрный humble; submissive, obedient.

по|коробить(ся (-блю(сь) pf.

покоря́ть(ся impf of покори́ть(ся

покóс mowing; meadow(-land).

покоси́вшийся rickety, ramshackle. по|коси́ть(ся (-ошу́(сь) pf.

по|кра́сить (-áшу) pf. покра́ска painting, colouring.

по|красне́ть (-éю) pf. по|криви́ть(ся (-влю́(сь) pf.

покрóв cover. покрови́тель m, покрови́тельница patron; sponsor. покрови́тельственный protective; patronizing. покрови́тельство protection, patronage. покрови́тельствовать impf +dat protect, patronize.

покрóй cut.

покроши́ть (-шу́, -шишь) pf crumble; chop.

покрути́ть (-учу́, -у́тишь) pf twist.

покрыва́ло cover; bedspread; veil. покрыва́ть impf, по|кры́ть (-рóю) pf cover; ~ся cover o.s.; get covered. покры́тие covering; surfacing; payment. покры́шка cover; tyre.

покупа́тель m buyer; customer. покупа́ть impf of купи́ть. покýпка purchase. покупнóй bought, purchased; purchase.

по|кури́ть (-рю́, -ришь) pf have a smoke.

по|кýшать(ся pf.

покушéние +на+acc attempted assassination of.

пол¹ (loc -ý; pl -ы́) floor.

пол² sex.

пол- in comb with n in gen, in oblique cases usu полу-, half.

пола́ (pl -ы) flap; из-под полы́ on the sly.

полага́ть impf suppose, think. полага́ться impf of положи́ться; полага́ется impers one is supposed to; +dat it is due to.

по|ла́комить(ся (-млю(сь) pf.

полгóда (полугóда) m half a year.

пóлдень (-дня or -лýдня) m noon. пóлдневный adj.

пóле (pl -я́, -éй) field; ground; margin; brim. полевóй field; ~ые цветы́ wild flowers.

полежа́ть (-жу́) pf lie down for a while.

полéзный useful; helpful; good, wholesome; ~ая нагрýзка payload.

по|лéзть (-зу; -лéз) pf.

полемизи́ровать impf debate, engage in controversy. **полемика** controversy; polemics. **полемический** polemical.

**полениться** (-ню́сь, -нишься) pf.

**полено** (pl -е́нья, -ьев) log.

**полёт** flight. **по|лете́ть** (-лечу́) pf.

**ползать** indet impf, **ползти́** (-зу́, -зёшь; полз, -ла́) det impf crawl, creep; ooze; fray. **ползу́чий** creeping.

**поли-** in comb poly-.

**полива́ть(ся** impf of **поли́ть(ся. поли́вка** watering.

**полига́мия** polygamy.

**полигло́т** polyglot.

**полиграфи́ческий** printing. **полиграфи́я** printing.

**полиго́н** range.

**поликли́ника** polyclinic.

**полиме́р** polymer.

**полиня́лый** faded. **по|линя́ть** pf.

**полиомиели́т** poliomyelitis

**полирова́льный** polishing. **полирова́ть** impf (pf от~) polish. **полиро́вка** polishing; polish. **полиро́вщик** polisher.

**полит-** abbr in comb (of **полити́ческий**) political. **политбюро́** neut indecl Politburo. ~**заключённый** sb political prisoner.

**политехни́ческий** polytechnic.

**поли́тик** politician. **поли́тика** policy; politics. **полити́ческий** political.

**поли́ть** (-лью́, -льёшь; по́ли́л, -а́, -о) pf (impf **полива́ть**) pour over; water; ~**ся** +instr pour over o.s.

**полице́йский** police; sb policeman. **поли́ция** police.

**поли́чн|ое** sb: с ~ым redhanded.

**полк** (-á, loc -ý) regiment.

**по́лка** shelf; berth.

**полко́вник** colonel. **полково́дец** (-дца) commander; general. **полково́й** regimental.

**пол-ли́тра** half a litre.

**полне́ть** (-е́ю) impf (pf по~) put on weight.

**по́лно** adv that's enough! stop it!

**полно-** in comb full; completely. **полнолу́ние** full moon. ~**метра́жный** full-length. ~**пра́вный** enjoying full rights; competent. ~**це́нный** of full value.

**полномо́чие** (usu pl) authority, power. **полномо́чный** plenipotentiary.

**по́лностью** adv in full; completely. **полнота́** completeness; corpulence.

**по́лночь** (-л(у)ночи) midnight. **по́лный** (-лон, -лна́, по́лно́) full; complete; plump.

**полови́к** (-á) mat, matting.

**полови́на** half; два с полови́ной two and a half; ~ шесто́го half-past five. **полови́нка** half.

**полови́ца** floor-board.

**полово́дье** high water.

**полово́й**[1] floor.

**полово́й**[2] sexual.

**поло́гий** gently sloping.

**положе́ние** position; situation; status; regulations; thesis; provisions. **поло́женный** agreed; determined. **поло́жим** let us assume; suppose. **положи́тельный** positive. **положи́ть** (-жу́, -жишь) pf (impf **класть**) put; lay (down); ~**ся** (impf **полага́ться**) rely.

по́лоз (pl -о́зья, -ьев) runner.
по|лома́ть(ся pf. поло́мка breakage.
полоса́ (acc по́лосу; pl поло́сы, -ло́с, -а́м) stripe; band; region; belt; period. полоса́тый striped.
полоска́ть (-ощу́, -о́щешь impf (pf вы́~, от~, про~) rinse; ~ го́рло gargle; ~ся paddle; flap.
по́лость¹ (gen pl -е́й) cavity.
по́лость² (gen pl -е́й) travelling rug.
полоте́нце (gen pl -нец) towel.
полотёр floor-polisher.
полоти́ще width; panel. полотно́ (pl -а, -тен) linen; canvas. полотня́ный linen.
поло́ть (-лю́, -лешь) impf (pf вы́~) weed.
полощу́ etc.: see полоска́ть
полти́нник fifty copecks.
полтора́ (-у́тора) m & neut, полторы́ (-у́тора) f one and a half. полтора́ста (полу́т-) a hundred and fifty.
полу-¹ see полон
полу-² in comb half-, semi-, demi-. полуботи́нок (-нка; gen pl -нок) shoe. ~го́дие half a year. ~годи́чный six months', lasting six months. ~годово́й six-month-old. ~годово́й half-yearly, six-monthly. ~гра́мотный semi-literate. ~защи́тник half-back. ~круг semicircle. ~кру́глый semicircular. ~ме́сяц crescent (moon). ~мра́к semi-darkness. ~но́чный midnight. ~о́стров peninsula. ~откры́тый ajar. ~прово́дни́к (-а́) semi-conductor, transistor. ~стано́к (-нка) halt. ~тьма́ semi-darkness. ~фабрика́т semi-finished

product, convenience food. ~фина́л semi-final. ~часово́й half-hourly. ~ша́рие hemisphere. ~шу́бок (-бка) sheepskin coat.
полу́денный midday.
получа́тель m recipient. получа́ть impf, получи́ть (-чу́, -чишь) pf get, receive, obtain; ~ся come, turn up; turn out; из э́того ничего́ не получи́лось nothing came of it. получе́ние receipt. полу́чка receipt; pay(-packet).
полу́чше adv a little better.
полчаса́ (получа́са) m half an hour.
по́лчище horde.
по́лый hollow; flood.
по|лысе́ть (-е́ю) pf.
по́льза use; benefit, profit; в по́льзу+gen in favour of, on behalf of. по́льзование use. по́льзоваться impf (pf вос~) +instr make use of, utilize; profit by; enjoy.
по́лька Pole; polka. по́льский Polish; sb polonaise.
по|льсти́ть(ся (-льщу́(сь) pf.
полью́ etc. see поли́ть
По́льша Poland.
полюби́ть (-блю́, -бишь) pf come to like; fall in love with.
по|любова́ться (-бу́юсь) pf.
полюбо́вный amicable.
по|любопы́тствовать pf.
по́люс pole.
поля́к Pole.
поля́на glade, clearing.
поляриза́ция polarization.
поля́рник polar explorer. поля́рн|ый polar; ~ая звезда́ pole-star.
пом- abbr in comb (of помо́щник) assistant. ~на́ч assistant chief, assistant head.
пома́да pomade; lipstick.

помаза́ние anointment. по|ма́-зать(ся (-а́жу(сь) pf. пома-зо́к (-зка́) small brush.

помале́ньку adv gradually; gently; modestly; so-so.

пома́лкивать impf hold one's tongue.

по|мани́ть (-ню́, -нишь) pf.

пома́рка blot; pencil mark; correction.

по|ма́слить (-ашу, -а́шешь) pf.

помаха́ть (-машу́, -ма́шешь), пома́хивать impf +instr wave; wag.

поме́длить pf +c+instr delay.

поме́ньше a little smaller; a little less.

по|меня́ть(ся pf.

помере́ть (-мру́, -мрёшь; -мер, -ла́, -ло) pf (impf помира́ть) die.

по|мере́щиться (-щусь) pf. по|ме́рить pf.

помертве́лый deathly pale. по|мертве́ть (-е́ю) pf.

помести́ть (-ещу́) pf (impf помеща́ть) accommodate; place, locate; invest; ~ся lodge; find room. поме́стье (gen pl -тий, -тьям) estate.

по́месь cross(-breed), hybrid.

помёт dung; droppings; litter, brood.

поме́та, поме́тка mark, note. по|ме́тить (-е́чу) pf (impf also помеча́ть) mark; date; ~ га́лочкой tick.

поме́ха hindrance; obstacle; pl interference.

помеча́ть impf of поме́тить

поме́шанный mad; sb lunatic. помеша́тельство madness; craze. по|меша́ть pf. поме-ша́ться pf go mad.

помеща́ть impf of помести́ть помеща́ться impf of помести́ться; be (situated); be ac-

commodated, find room. помеще́ние premises; apartment, room, lodging; location; investment. поме́щик land-owner.

помидо́р tomato.

поми́лование forgiveness. поми́ловать pf forgive.

поми́мо prep+gen apart from; besides; without the knowledge of.

помина́ть impf of помяну́ть; не ~ ли́хом remember kindly. поми́нки (-нок) pl funeral repast.

помира́ть impf of помере́ть по|мири́ть(ся pf.

по́мнить impf remember.

помога́ть impf of помо́чь

по-мо́ему adv in my opinion.

помо́и (-ев) pl slops. помо́й-ка (gen pl -о́ек) rubbish dump. помо́йный slop.

помо́л grinding.

помо́лвка betrothal.

по|моли́ться (-люсь, -лишься) pf. по|молоде́ть (-е́ю) pf.

помолча́ть (-чу́) pf be silent for a time.

помо́рье: see по- II.

по|мо́рщиться (-щусь) pf.

помо́ст dais; rostrum.

по|мочи́ться (-чу́сь, -чишься pf.

помо́чь (-огу́, -о́жешь; -о́г, -ла́) pf (impf помога́ть) (+dat) help. помо́щник, помо́щница assistant. по́мощь help; на ~! help!

помо́ю etc.: see помы́ть

по́мпа pump.

помутне́ние dimness, clouding.

помча́ться (-чу́сь) pf rush; dart off.

помыка́ть impf +instr order about.

по́мысел (-сла) intention; thought.

по|мы́ть(ся (-мо́ю(сь) pf.

помяну́ть (-ну́, -нешь) pf (impf помина́ть) mention; pray for.

помя́тый crumpled. по|мя́ть|ся (-мнётся) pf.

по|наде́яться (-е́юсь) pf count, rely.

понадо́биться (-блюсь) pf be or become necessary; е́сли пона́добится if necessary.

понапра́сну adv in vain.

понаслы́шке adv by hearsay.

по-настоя́щему adv properly, truly.

понача́лу adv at first.

понево́ле adv willynilly; against one's will.

понеде́льник Monday.

понемно́гу, понемно́жку adv little by little.

по|нести́(сь (-су́(сь, -сёшь(ся; -нёс(ся, -ла́(сь) pf.

понижа́ть impf, пони́зить (-и́жу) pf lower; reduce; ~ся fall, drop, go down. пониже́ние fall; lowering; reduction.

поника́ть impf, по|ни́кнуть (-ну; -ни́к) pf droop, wilt.

понима́ние understanding. понима́ть impf of поня́ть

по-но́вому adv in a new fashion.

поно́с diarrhoea.

поноси́ть[1] (-ошу́, -о́сишь) pf carry; wear.

поноси́ть[2] (-ошу́, -о́сишь) impf abuse (verbally).

поно́шенный worn; threadbare.

по|нра́виться (-влюсь) pf.

понто́н pontoon.

понуди́ть (-у́жу) pf, понужда́ть impf compel.

понука́ть impf urge on.

пону́рить pf: ~ го́лову hang

one's head. пону́рый downcast.

по|ню́хать pf. поню́шка: ~ табаку́ pinch of snuff.

поня́тие concept; notion, idea. поня́тливый bright, quick. поня́тный understandable, comprehensible; clear; ~о naturally; ~о? (do you) see? поня́ть (пойму́, -мёшь; по́нял, -á, -о) pf (impf понима́ть) understand; realize.

по|обе́дать pf. по|обеща́ть pf.

поо́даль adv at some distance.

поодино́чке adv one by one.

поочерёдно adv in turn.

поощре́ние encouragement. поощри́ть pf, поощря́ть impf encourage.

поп (-á) priest.

попада́ние hit. попада́ть(ся impf of попа́сть(ся

попадья́ priest's wife.

попа́ло: see попа́сть. по|па́риться pf.

попа́рно adv in pairs, two by two.

попа́сть (-аду́, -адёшь; -а́л) pf (impf попада́ть) +в+acc hit; get (in)to, find o.s. in; +на+acc turn up, come on; не туда́ ~ get the wrong number; ~ся be caught; find o.s.; turn up; что попадётся anything. попа́ло with prons & advs: где ~ anywhere; как ~ anyhow; что ~ the first thing to hand.

поперёк adv & prep+gen across.

попереме́нно adv in turns.

попере́чник diameter. попере́чный transverse, diametrical, cross; ~ый разре́з, ~ое сече́ние cross-section.

попёрхну́ться (-ну́сь, -нёшь-
ся) pf choke.
по|пе́рчить (-чу) pf.
попече́ние care; charge; на
попече́нии+gen in the care of.
попечи́тель m guardian,
trustee.
попира́ть impf (pf попра́ть)
trample on; flout.
попи́ть (-пью́, -пьёшь; по́пил,
-ла́, по́пило) pf have a drink.
поплаво́к (-вка́) float.
попла́кать (-а́чу) pf cry a little.
по|плати́ться (-чу́сь, -ти́шь-
ся) pf.
поплы́ть (-ыву́, -ывёшь; -ы́л,
-ыла́, -о) pf. start swimming.
попо́йка drinking-bout.
попола́м adv in two, in half;
half-and-half.
поползнове́ние half a mind;
pretension(s).
пополне́ние replenishment;
reinforcement. по|полне́ть
(-е́ю) pf. попо́лнить (-ню), по-
полня́ть impf replenish; re-
stock; reinforce.
пополу́дни adv in the afternoon; p.m.
попо́на horse-cloth.
по|по́тчевать (-чую) pf.
поправи́мый rectifiable. по-
пра́вить (-влю) pf, поправ-
ля́ть impf repair; correct, put
right; set straight; ~ся correct
o.s.; get better, recover; improve. попра́вка correction;
repair; adjustment; recovery.
попра́ть pf of попира́ть
по-пре́жнему adv as before.
попрёк reproach. попрека́ть
impf, попрекну́ть (-ну́, -нёшь)
pf reproach.
по́прище field; walk of life.
по|про́бовать pf. по|проси́ть
(-ся (-ошу́(сь), -о́сишь(ся)) pf.

по́просту adv simply; without
ceremony.
попроша́йка m & f cadger. по-
проша́йничать impf cadge.
попроща́ться pf (+c+instr)
say goodbye (to).
попры́гать pf jump, hop.
попуга́й parrot.
популя́рность popularity.
популя́рный popular.
попусти́тельство conniv-
ance.
по-пусто́му, по́пусту adv in
vain.
попу́тно adv at the same time;
in passing. попу́тный passing.
попу́тчик fellow-traveller.
по|пыта́ться pf. попы́тка
attempt.
по|пя́титься (-я́чусь) pf. по-
пя́тный backward; идти́ на
~ go back on one's word.
по́ра¹ pore.
пора́² (acc -у; pl -ы, пор, -а́м)
time; it is time; до каки́х пор?
till when?; до сих пор till now;
с каки́х пор? since when?
порабо́тать pf do some work.
порабо́тить (-ощу́) pf, пора-
боща́ть impf enslave. пора-
боще́ние enslavement.
поравня́ться pf come alongside.
по|ра́довать(ся) pf.
поража́ть impf, по|рази́ть
(-ажу́) pf hit; strike; defeat;
affect; astonish; ~ся be as-
tounded. пораже́ние defeat.
порази́тельный striking; astonishing.
по-ра́зному adv differently.
по|ра́нить pf wound; injure.
порва́ть (-ву́, -вёшь; -ва́л, -а́,
-о) pf (impf порыва́ть) tear
(up); break, break off; ~ся
tear; break (off).
по|реде́ть (-е́ет) pf.

поре́з cut. поре́зать (-е́жу) *pf* cut; ~ся cut o.s.

поре́й leek.

по|рекомендова́ть *pf.* по|ржа́веть (-еет) *pf.*

по́ристый porous.

порица́ние censure; blame. порица́ть *impf* blame; censure.

по́рка flogging.

по́ровну *adv* equally.

поро́г threshold; rapids.

поро́да breed, race, species; (*also* го́рная поро́да) rock. поро́дистый thoroughbred. породи́ть (-ожу́) *pf* (*impf* рожда́ть) give birth to; give rise to.

по|родни́ть(ся *pf.* поро́дный pedigree.

порожда́ть *impf of* породи́ть

поро́жний *adv* separately, apart.

поро́й, поро́ю *adv* at times.

поро́к vice; defect.

поросёнок (-нка; *pl* -ся́та, -ся́т) piglet.

по́росль shoots; young wood.

поро́ть¹ (-рю́, -решь) *impf* (*pf* вы~) thrash; whip.

поро́ть² (-рю́, -решь) *impf* (*pf* рас~) undo, unpick; ~ся come unstitched.

по́рох (*pl* ~а́) gunpowder, powder. порохово́й powder.

поро́чить (-чу) *impf* (*pf* о~) discredit; smear. поро́чный vicious, depraved; faulty.

пороши́ть (-ши́т) *impf* snow slightly.

порошо́к (-шка́) powder.

порт (*loc* -у́; *pl* -ы́, -о́в) port.

портати́вный portable; ~ телефо́н mobile phone.

портве́йн port (wine).

по́ртить (-чу) *impf* (*pf* ис~) spoil; corrupt; ~ся deteriorate; go bad.

портни́ха dressmaker. порт-

но́вский tailor's. портно́й *sb* tailor.

порто́вый port.

портре́т portrait.

портсига́р cigarette-case.

португа́лец (-льца), -лка Portuguese. Португа́лия Portugal. португа́льский Portuguese.

портфе́ль *m* brief-case; portfolio.

портье́ра curtain(s), portière.

портя́нка foot-binding.

поруга́ние desecration; humiliation.

пору́ганный desecrated; outraged. поруга́ть *pf* scold, swear at; ~ся swear; fall out.

пору́ка bail; guarantee; surety; на пору́ки on bail.

по-ру́сски *adv* (in) Russian.

поруча́ть *impf of* поручи́ть. поруче́ние assignment; errand; message.

по́ручень (-чня) *m* handrail.

поручи́тельство guarantee; bail.

поручи́ть (-чу́, -чишь) *pf* (*impf* поруча́ть) entrust; instruct. поручи́ться (-чу́сь, -чишься) *pf of* руча́ться

порха́ть *impf*, порхну́ть (-ну́, -нёшь) *pf* flutter, flit.

по́рция portion; helping.

по́рча spoiling; damage; curse.

по́ршень (-шня) *m* piston.

порыв¹ gust; rush; fit.

порыв² breaking. порыва́ть(ся¹ *impf of* порва́ть(ся

порыва́ться² *impf* make jerky movements; endeavour. поры́вистый gusty; jerky; impetuous; fitful.

поря́дковый ordinal. поря́док (-дка) order; sequence; manner, way; procedure; всё в поря́дке everything is alright; ~ дня agenda, order of the day. поря́дочный decent; honest; respectable; fair, considerable.

посади́ть (-ажу́, -а́дишь) pf of сади́ть, сажа́ть. поса́дка planting; embarkation; boarding; landing. поса́дочный planting; landing.

посажу́ etc.: see посади́ть.

по|сва́тать(ся pf. по|све|же́ть (-е́ет) pf. по|светли́ть (-ечу́, -е́тишь) pf. по|светле́ть (-е́ет) pf.

посви́стывать impf whistle.

по-сво́ему adv (in) one's own way.

посвяти́ть (-ящу́) pf, посвяща́ть impf devote; dedicate; let in; ordain. посвяще́ние dedication; initiation; ordination.

посе́в sowing; crops. посевн|о́й sowing; ~а́я пло́щадь area under crops.

по|седе́ть (-е́ю) pf.

поселе́нец (-нца) settler; exile. поселе́ние settlement; exile. по|сели́ть pf, поселя́ть impf settle; lodge; arouse; ~ся settle, take up residence. посёлок (-лка) settlement; housing estate.

посеребрённый (-рён, -а́) silver-plated. по|серебри́ть pf.

посереди́не adv & prep+gen in the middle (of).

посети́тель m visitor. посети́ть (-ещу́) pf (impf посеща́ть) visit; attend.

по|се́товать pf.

посеща́емость attendance. посеща́ть impf of посети́ть. посеще́ние visit.

по|се́ять (-е́ю) pf.

посиде́ть (-ижу́) pf sit (for a while).

поси́льный within one's power; feasible.

посине́лый gone blue. по|сине́ть (-е́ю) pf.

по|скака́ть (-ачу́, -а́чешь) pf.

поскользну́ться (-ну́сь, -нёшься) pf slip.

поско́льку conj as far as, (in) so far as.

по|скро́мничать pf. по|скупи́ться (-плю́сь) pf.

посла́нец (-нца) messenger, envoy. посла́ние message; epistle. посла́нник envoy, minister. посла́ть (-шлю́, -шлёшь) pf (impf посыла́ть) send.

по́сле adv & prep+gen after; afterwards.

по́сле- in comb post-; after-. послевое́нный post-war. ~за́втра adv the day after tomorrow. ~родово́й postnatal. ~сло́вие epilogue; concluding remarks.

после́дний last; recent; latest; latter. после́дователь m follower. после́довательность sequence; consistency. после́довательный consecutive; consistent. по|сле́довать pf. после́дствие consequence. после́дующий subsequent; consequent.

посло́вица proverb, saying.

по|слу́шать(ся pf. послу́шный obedient.

послужн|о́й service.

послуша́ние obedience. по|слу́шать(ся pf. послу́шный obedient.

по|слы́шаться (-шится) pf.

посма́тривать impf look from time to time.

посме́иваться impf chuckle.

посме́ртный posthumous.

по|сме́ть (-е́ю) pf.

посмея́ние ridicule. посме́яться (-ею́сь, -еёшься) pf

laugh; +над+*instr* laugh at.
по|смотре́ть(ся (-рю́сь, -ри́шь(ся) *pf*.

посо́бие aid; allowance, benefit; textbook. посо́бник accomplice.

по|сове́товать(ся *pf*. по|содействовать *pf*.

посо́л (-сла́) ambassador.

по|соли́ть (-олю́, -о́лишь) *pf*.

посо́льство embassy.

поспа́ть² (-сплю́; -а́л, -а́, -о) *pf* sleep; have a nap.

поспева́ть¹ *impf*, по|спе́ть¹ (-е́ет) *pf* ripen.

поспева́ть² *impf*, по|спе́ть² (-е́ю) *pf* have time; be in time (к+*dat*, на+*acc* for); +за+*instr* keep up with.

по|спеши́ть (-шу́) *pf*. поспе́шный hasty, hurried.

по|спо́рить *pf*. по|спосо́бствовать *pf*.

посрами́ть (-млю́) *pf*, посрамля́ть *impf* disgrace.

посреди́, посреди́не *adv* & *prep*+*gen* in the middle (of). посре́дник mediator. посре́дничество mediation. посре́дственный mediocre. посре́дством *prep*+*gen* by means of.

по|ссо́рить(ся *pf*.

пост¹ (-á, *loc* -ý) post.

пост² (-á, *loc* -ý) fast(ing).

по|ста́вить¹ (-влю) *pf*.

по|ста́вить² (-влю) *pf*, ставля́ть *impf* supply. поста́вка delivery. поставщи́к (-á) supplier.

постаме́нт pedestal.

постанови́ть (-влю́, -вишь) *pf* (*impf* постановля́ть) decree; decide.

постано́вка production; arrangement; putting, placing. постановле́ние decree; decision. постановля́ть *impf* of

постанови́ть

постано́вщик producer; (film) director.

по|стара́ться *pf*.

по|старе́ть (-е́ю) *pf*. по-ста́рому *adv* as before.

посте́ль bed. посте́лю *etc.*: *see* постла́ть

постепе́нный gradual.

по|стесня́ться *pf*.

постига́ть *impf* of пости́чь.

пости́гнуть (-ну): *see* пости́чь.

постиже́ние comprehension, grasp. постижи́мый comprehensible.

постила́ть *impf* of постла́ть

постира́ть *pf* do some washing.

пости́ться (-щу́сь) *impf* fast.

пости́чь, пости́гнуть (-и́гну; -и́г(нул)) *pf* (*impf* постига́ть) comprehend, grasp; befall.

по|стла́ть (-стелю́, -сте́лешь) *pf* (*impf also* постила́ть) spread; make (*bed*).

по́стный lenten; lean; glum; ~ое ма́сло vegetable oil.

постово́й on point duty.

посто́й billeting.

посто́льку: ~, поско́льку *conj* to that extent, insofar as.

по|сторони́ться (-ню́сь, -ни́шься) *pf*. посторо́нний strange; foreign; extraneous; *sb* stranger, outsider.

постоя́нный permanent; constant; continual; ~ый ток di-rect current. постоя́нство constancy.

по|стоя́ть (-ою́) *pf* stand (for a while); +за+*acc* stand up for.

пострада́вший *sb* victim. по|страда́ть *pf*.

пострига́ться *impf*, по-стри́чься (-игу́сь, -иже́шься; -и́гся) *pf* take monastic vows; get one's hair cut.

**построе́ние** construction; building; formation. **по|стро́|ить(ся** (-ро́ю(сь)) pf. **постро́йка** building.

**постскри́птум** postscript.

**постули́ровать** impf & pf. postulate.

**постула́тельный** forward. **поступа́ть** impf, **поступи́ть** (-плю́, -пишь) pf act; do; be received; +в or на+acc enter, join; +c+instr treat; ~ся +instr waive, forgo. **поступле́ние** entering, joining; receipt. **посту́пок** (-пка) act, deed. **по́ступь** gait; step.

**по|стуча́ть(ся** (-чу́(сь)) pf.

**по|стыди́ться** (-ыжу́сь) pf. **постыдный** shameful.

**посу́да** crockery; dishes. **посу́дный** china; dish.

**по|сули́ть** pf.

**посчастли́виться** pf impers (+dat) be lucky; **ей посчастли́вилось** +inf she had the luck to.

**по|счита́ть** pf count (up). **по|счита́ться** pf.

**посыла́ть** impf of **посла́ть**. **посы́лка** sending; parcel; errand; premise. **посы́льный** sb messenger.

**посы́пать** (-плю, -плешь) pf, **посыпа́ть** impf strew. **посы́паться** (-плется) pf begin to fall; rain down.

**посяга́тельство** encroachment; infringement. **посяга́ть** impf, **посягну́ть** (-ну́, -нёшь) pf encroach, infringe.

**пот** (loc -у́; pl -ы́) sweat.

**потайно́й** secret.

**потака́ть** impf +dat indulge.

**потасо́вка** brawl.

**пота́ш** (-а́) potash.

**по-тво́ему** adv in your opinion.

**потво́рствовать** impf (+dat) be indulgent (towards), pander (to).

**потёк** damp patch.

**потёмки** (-мок) pl darkness. **по|темне́ть** (-е́ет) pf.

**потенциа́л** potential. **потенциа́льный** potential.

**по|тепле́ть** (-е́ет) pf.

**потерпе́вший** sb victim. **по|терпе́ть** (-плю́, -пишь) pf.

**поте́ря** loss; waste; pl casualties. **по|теря́ть(ся** pf.

**по|тесни́ть** pf. **по|тесни́ться** pf sit closer, squeeze up.

**поте́ть** (-е́ю) impf (pf вс~, за~) sweat; mist over.

**поте́ха** fun. **по|те́шить(ся** (-шу(сь)) pf. **поте́шный** amusing.

**поте́чь** (-чёт, -тёк, -ла́) pf begin to flow.

**потира́ть** impf rub.

**потихо́ньку** adv softly; secretly; slowly.

**по́тный** (-тен, -тна́, -тно) sweaty.

**пото́к** stream; torrent; flood.

**потоло́к** (-лка́) ceiling.

**по|толсте́ть** (-е́ю) pf.

**пото́м** adv later (on); then. **пото́мок** (-мка) descendant. **пото́мство** posterity.

**потому́** adv that is why; ~ что conj because.

**по|тону́ть** (-ну́, -нешь) pf. **по|то́п** flood, deluge. **по|топи́ть** (-плю́, -пишь) pf, **потопля́ть** impf sink.

**по|топта́ть** (-пчу́, -пчешь) pf. **по|торопи́ть(ся** (-плю́(сь, -пишь(ся) pf.

**пото́чный** continuous; production-line.

**по|тра́тить** (-а́чу) pf.

**потреби́тель** m consumer, user. **потреби́тельский** consumer; consumers'. **потреби́ть** (-блю́) pf, **потребля́ть**

*impf* consume. **потребле́ние** consumption. **потре́бность** need, requirement. **потре́бовать(ся)** *pf*.

**по|трево́жить(ся** (-жу(сь))) *pf*.

**потрёпанный** shabby; tattered. **по|трепа́ть(ся** (-плю́, -плешь(ся))) *pf*.

**по|тре́скаться** *pf*. **потре́скивать** *impf* crackle.

**потро́гать** *pf* touch, feel, finger.

**потроха́** (-о́в) *pl* giblets. **потроши́ть** (-шу́) *impf* (*pf* вы́-) disembowel, clean.

**потруди́ться** (-ужу́сь, -у́дишься) *pf* do some work; take the trouble.

**потряса́ть** *impf*, **потрясти́** (-су́, -сёшь; -я́с, -ла́) *pf* shake; rock; stagger; +*acc or instr* brandish, shake. **потряса́ющий** staggering, tremendous. **потрясе́ние** shock.

**поту́ги** *f pl* vain attempts; **ро́довые** ~ labour.

**поту́пить** (-плю) *pf*, **потупля́ть** *impf* lower; ~**ся** look down.

**по|тускне́ть** (-е́ет) *pf*.

**потусторо́нний мир** the next world.

**потуха́ть** *impf*, **по|ту́хнуть** (-нет, -у́х) *pf* go out; die out. **поту́хший** extinct; lifeless.

**по|туши́ть** (-шу́, -шишь) *pf*.

**по́тчевать** (-чую) *impf* (*pf* по~) +*instr* treat to.

**потя́гиваться** *impf*, **по|тяну́ться** (-ну́сь, -нешься) *pf* stretch o.s. **по|тяну́ть** (-ну́, -нешь) *pf*.

**по|у́жинать** *pf*. **по|умне́ть** (-е́ю) *pf*.

**поуча́ть** *impf* preach at. **поучи́тельный** instructive.

**поха́бный** obscene.

**похвала́** praise. **по|хва-**

**ли́ть(ся** (-лю́(сь), -лишь(ся))) *pf*. **похва́льный** laudable; laudatory.

**похити́тель** *m* kidnapper; abductor; thief. **похи́тить** (-хи́щу) *pf*, **похища́ть** *impf* kidnap; abduct; steal. **похище́ние** theft; kidnapping; abduction.

**похлёбка** broth, soup.

**похло́пать** *pf* slap; clap.

**по|хлопота́ть** (-очу́, -о́чешь) *pf*.

**похме́лье** hangover.

**похо́д** campaign; march; hike; excursion.

**по|хода́тайствовать** *pf*.

**походи́ть** (-ожу́, -о́дишь) *impf* на+*acc* resemble.

**похо́дка** gait, walk. **похо́дный** mobile, field; marching. **похожде́ние** adventure.

**похо́жий** alike; ~ **на** like.

**похолода́ние** drop in temperature.

**по|хорони́ть** (-ню́, -нишь) *pf*. **похоро́нный** funeral. **похо́роны** (-ро́н, -рона́м) *pl* funeral.

**по|хороше́ть** (-е́ю) *pf*.

**по́хоть** lust.

**по|худе́ть** (-е́ю) *pf*.

**по|целова́ть(ся** *pf*. **поцелу́й** kiss.

**поча́ток** (-тка) ear; (corn) cob.

**по́чва** soil; ground; basis. **по́чвенный** soil; ~ **покро́в** topsoil.

**почём** *adv* how much; how; ~ **знать?** who can tell? ~ **я зна́ю?** how should I know?

**почему́** *adv* why. **почему́-либо**, **-нибудь** *advs* for some reason or other. **почему́-то** *adv* for some reason.

**по́черк** hand(writing).

**почерне́лый** blackened, darkened. **по|черне́ть** (-е́ю) *pf*.

**почерпну́ть** (-ну́, -нёшь) *pf*.

draw, scoop up; glean.
**по|черстве́ть** (-е́ю) pf. **по|чеса́ть(ся** (-ешу́(сь, -е́шешь(ся) pf.
**по́честь** honour. **почёт** honour; respect. **почётный** of honour; honourable; honorary.
**по́чечный** renal; kidney.
**почива́ть** impf of **почи́ть**
**почи́н** initiative.
**по|чини́ть** (-ню́, -нишь) pf, **починя́ть** impf repair, mend. **почи́нка** repair.
**по|чи́стить(ся** (-и́щу(сь) pf.
**почита́ть**[1] impf honour; revere.
**почита́ть**[2] pf read for a while.
**почи́ть** (-и́ю, -и́ешь) pf (impf **почива́ть**) rest; pass away; **~ на ла́врах** rest on one's laurels.
**по́чка**[1] bud.
**по́чка**[2] kidney.
**по́чта** post, mail; post-office. **почтальо́н** postman. **почта́мт** (main) post-office.
**почте́ние** respect. **почте́нный** venerable; considerable.
**почти́** adv almost.
**почти́тельный** respectful.
**почти́ть** (-чту́) pf honour.
**почто́в|ый** postal; **~ая ка́рточка** postcard; **~ый перево́д** postal order; **~ый я́щик** letter-box.
**по|чу́вствовать** pf.
**по|чу́диться** (-ишься) pf.
**пошатну́ть** (-ну́, -нёшь) pf shake; **~ся** shake; stagger.
**по|шевели́ть(ся** (-елю́(сь, -е́ли̲шь(ся) pf. **пошёл** etc.: see **пойти́**
**поши́вочный** sewing.
**по́шлина** duty.
**по́шлость** vulgarity; banality. **по́шлый** vulgar; banal.
**поштучный** by the piece.

**по|шути́ть** (-учу́, -у́тишь) pf.
**поща́да** mercy. **по|щади́ть** (-ажу́) pf.
**по|щекота́ть** (-очу́, -о́чешь) pf.
**пощёчина** slap in the face.
**по|щу́пать** pf.
**поэ́зия** poetry. **поэ́ма** poem. **поэ́т** poet. **поэти́ческий** poetic.
**поэ́тому** adv therefore.
**пою́** etc.: see **петь, пои́ть**
**появи́ться** (-влю́сь, -вишься) pf, **появля́ться** impf appear. **появле́ние** appearance.
**по́яс** (pl -а́) belt; girdle; waistband; waist; zone.
**поясне́ние** explanation. **поясни́тельный** explanatory. **поясни́ть** pf (impf **поясня́ть**) explain; elucidate.
**поясни́ца** small of the back. **поясно́й** waist; to the waist; zonal.
**поясня́ть** impf of **поясни́ть**
**пра-** pref first; great-. **праба́бушка** great-grandmother.
**пра́вда** (the) truth. **правди́вый** true; truthful. **правдоподо́бный** likely; plausible.
**пра́ведный** righteous; just.
**пра́вило** rule; principle.
**пра́вильн|ый** right, correct; regular; **~о!** that's right!
**прави́тель** m ruler. **прави́тельственный** government(al). **прави́тельство** government.
**пра́вить**[1] (-влю) +instr rule, govern; drive.
**пра́вить**[2] (-влю) impf correct. **пра́вка** correcting.
**правле́ние** board; administration; government.
**пра́в|внук, -вну́чка** great-grandson, -granddaughter.
**пра́во**[1] (pl -а́) law; right; **(води́тельские) права́** driving licence; **на права́х**+gen in the

capacity of, as.
**пра́во²** *adv* really.
**пра́во-¹** *in comb* law; right. **пра-
воверный** orthodox. **~мер-
ный** lawful, rightful. **~моч-
ный** competent. **~наруше-
ние** infringement of the law,
offence. **~наруши́тель** *m*
offender, delinquent. **~пи-
са́ние** spelling, orthography.
**~сла́вный** orthodox; *sb*
member of the Orthodox
Church. **~су́дие** justice.
**пра́во-²** *in comb* right, right-
hand. **правосторо́нний** right;
right-hand.
**правово́й** legal.
**правота́** rightness; innocence.
**пра́вый¹** right; right-hand;
right-wing.
**пра́вый²** (прав, -а́, -о) right,
correct; just.
**пра́вящий** ruling.
**пра́дед** great-grandfather; *pl*
ancestors. **праде́душка** *m*
great-grandfather.
**пра́здник** (public) holiday.
**пра́здничный** festive. **пра́зд-
нование** celebration. **пра́зд-
новать** *impf* (*pf* **от~**) celebrate. **пра́здность** idleness.
**пра́здный** idle; useless.
**пра́ктика** practice; practical
work. **практикова́ть** *impf*
practise; **~ся** (*pf* **на~ся**) be
practised; **+в+**prep practise.
**практи́ческий**, **практи́ч-
ный** practical.
**пра́отец** (-тца) forefather.
**пра́порщик** ensign.
**прапраде́д** great-great-grand-
father. **прароди́тель** *m* forefather.
**прах** dust; remains.
**пра́чечная** *sb* laundry. **пра́ч-
ка** laundress.
**пребыва́ние** stay. **пребы-**

**ва́ть** *impf* be; reside.
**превзойти́** (-йду́, -йдёшь; -ошёл,
-шла́) *pf* (*impf* **превосхо-
ди́ть**) surpass; excel.
**превозмога́ть** *impf*, **пре-
возмо́чь** (-огу́, -о́жешь; -ог,
-ла́) *pf* overcome.
**превозноси́ть** (-су́, -сёшь; -ёс,
-ла́) *pf*, **превозноси́ть** (-ошу́,
-осишь) *impf* extol, praise.
**превосходи́тельство** Excellency. **превосходи́ть** (-ожу́,
-одишь) *impf* of **превзойти́**.
**превосхо́дный** superlative;
superb, excellent. **превос-
хо́дство** superiority. **превос-
ходя́щий** superior.
**преврати́ть** (-ащу́) *pf*, **пре-
враща́ть** *impf* convert, turn,
reduce; **~ся** turn, change.
**превра́тный** wrong; change-
ful. **превраще́ние** transformation.
**превы́сить** (-ы́шу) *pf*, **пре-
выша́ть** *impf* exceed. **пре-
выше́ние** exceeding, excess.
**прегра́да** obstacle; barrier.
**прегради́ть** (-ажу́) *pf*, **пре-
гражда́ть** *impf* bar, block.
**пред** *prep+instr*: *see* **пе́ред**
**предава́ть** (-даю́(сь, -да-
ёшь(ся) *impf* of **преда́ть**(ся
**преда́ние** legend; tradition;
handing over, committal. **пре́-
данность** devotion. **пре́дан-
ный** devoted. **преда́тель** *m*,
**~ница** betrayer, traitor. **пре-
да́тельский** treacherous.
**преда́тельство** treachery.
**преда́ть** (-а́м, -а́шь, -а́ст,
-ади́м; пре́дал, -а́, -о)
(*impf* **предава́ть**) hand over,
commit; betray; **~ся** abandon
o.s.; give way, indulge.
**предаю́** *etc.*: *see* **предава́ть**
**предвари́тельный** preliminary; prior. **предвари́ть**

**предваря́ть** *impf* forestall, anticipate.

**предвéстник** forerunner; harbinger. **предвеща́ть** *impf* portend; augur.

**предвзя́тый** preconceived; biased.

**предви́деть** (-и́жу) *impf* foresee.

**предвкуси́ть** (-ушу́, -у́сишь) *pf*, **предвкуша́ть** *impf* look forward to.

**предводи́тель** *m* leader. **предводи́тельствовать** *impf* +*instr* lead.

**предвоéнный** pre-war.

**предвосхити́ть** (-и́щу) *pf*, **предвосхища́ть** *impf* anticipate.

**предвы́борный** (pre-)election.

**предго́рье** foothills.

**преддвéрие** threshold.

**предéл** limit; bound. **предéльный** boundary; maximum; utmost.

**предзнаменова́ние** omen, augury.

**предисло́вие** preface.

**предлага́ть** *impf of* **предложи́ть. предло́г**[1] pretext. **предло́г**[2] preposition.

**предложéние**[1] sentence; clause.

**предложéние**[2] offer; proposition; proposal; motion; suggestion; supply. **предложи́ть** (-жу́, -жишь) *pf* (*impf* **предлага́ть**) offer; propose; suggest; order.

**предло́жный** prepositional.

**предмéстье** suburb.

**предмéт** object; subject.

**предназнача́ть** *impf*, **предназна́чить** (-чу) *pf* destine; earmark.

**преднамéренный** premeditated.

**прéдо:** *see* **перед**

**прéдок** (-дка) ancestor.

**предопределéние** predetermination. **предопредели́ть** *pf*, **предопределя́ть** *impf* predetermine, predestine.

**предоста́вить** (-влю) *pf*, **предоставля́ть** *impf* grant; leave; give.

**предостерега́ть** *impf*, **предостерéчь** (-егу́, -ежёшь; -ёг, -ла́) *pf* warn. **предостережéние** warning. **предосторо́жность** precaution.

**предосуди́тельный** reprehensible.

**предотврати́ть** (-ащу́) *pf*, **предотвраща́ть** *impf* avert, prevent.

**предохранéние** protection; preservation. **предохрани́тель** *m* guard; safety device, safety-catch; fuse. **предохрани́тельный** preservative; preventive; safety. **предохрани́ть** *pf*, **предохраня́ть** *impf* preserve, protect.

**предписáние** order; *pl* directions, instructions. **предписáть** (-ишу́, -и́шешь) *pf*, **предпи́сывать** *impf* order, direct; prescribe.

**предплéчье** forearm.

**предполага́емый** supposed. **предполага́ется** *impers* it is proposed. **предполага́ть** *impf*, **предположи́ть** (-жу́, -óжишь) *pf* suppose, assume. **предположéние** supposition, assumption. **предположи́тельный** conjectural; hypothetical.

**предпослéдний** penultimate, last-but-one.

**предпосы́лка** precondition; premise.

**предпочéсть** (-чту́, -чтёшь; -чёл,

-чла́) *pf* предпочита́ть *impf* prefer. **предпочте́ние** preference. **предпочти́тельный** preferable.

**предприи́мчивый** enterprising.

**предпринима́тель** *m* owner; entrepreneur; employer. **предпринима́тельство**: свобо́дное ~ free enterprise. **предпринима́ть** *impf*, **предприня́ть** (-иму́, -и́мешь; -и́нял, -а́, -о) *pf* undertake. **предприя́тие** undertaking, enterprise.

**предрасположе́ние** predisposition.

**предрассу́док** (-дка) prejudice.

**предрека́ть** *impf*, **предре́чь** (-еку́, -ече́шь; -ёк, -ла́) *pf* foretell.

**предреша́ть** *impf*, **предреши́ть** (-шу́) *pf* decide beforehand; predetermine.

**председа́тель** *m* chairman.

**предсказа́ние** prediction. **предсказа́ть** (-ажу́, -а́жешь) *pf*, **предска́зывать** *impf* predict; prophesy.

**предсме́ртный** dying.

**представи́тель** *m* representative. **представи́тельный** representative; imposing. **представи́тельство** representation; representatives.

**представля́ть** (-влю) *pf*, **представля́ть** *impf* present; submit; introduce; represent; ~ себе́ imagine. **представля́ть собо́й** represent, be; ~ся present itself, occur; seem; introduce o.s.; +*instr* pretend to be. **представле́ние** presentation; performance; idea, notion.

**предста́ть** (-а́ну) *pf* (*impf*

представа́ть) appear.

**предстоя́ть** (-ои́т) *impf* be in prospect, lie ahead. **предстоя́щий** forthcoming; imminent.

**предте́ча** *m & f* forerunner, precursor.

**предубежде́ние** prejudice.

**предугада́ть** *pf*, **предуга́дывать** *impf* guess; foresee.

**предупреди́тельный** preventive; warning; courteous, obliging. **предупреди́ть** (-ежу́) *pf*, **предупрежда́ть** *impf* warn; give notice; prevent; anticipate. **предупрежде́ние** notice; warning; prevention.

**предусма́тривать** *impf*, **предусмотре́ть** (-рю́, -ришь) *pf* envisage, foresee; provide for. **предусмотри́тельный** prudent; far-sighted.

**предчу́вствие** presentiment; foreboding. **предчу́вствовать** *impf* have a presentiment (about).

**предше́ственник** predecessor. **предше́ствовать** *impf* +*dat* precede.

**предъяви́тель** *m* bearer. **предъяви́ть** (-влю́, -вишь) *pf*, **предъявля́ть** *impf* show, produce; bring (lawsuit); ~ пра́во на+*acc* lay claim to.

**предыду́щий** previous.

**прее́мник** successor. **прее́мственность** succession; continuity.

**пре́жде** *adv* first; formerly; *prep*+*gen* before; ~ всего́ first of all; first and foremost; ~ чем *conj* before. **преждевре́менный** premature. **пре́жний** previous, former.

**презерва́тив** condom.

**президе́нт** president. **президе́нтский** presidential. **прези́диум** presidium.

презира́ть *impf* despise. **пре-зре́ние** contempt. **презре́нный** contemptible. **презри́-тельный** scornful.

**преиму́щественно** *adv* mainly, chiefly, principally. **пре-иму́щество** main, primary; preferential. **преиму́щество** advantage; preference; **по преиму́ществу** for the most part.

**преиспо́дняя** *sb* the underworld.

**прейскура́нт** price list, catalogue.

**преклоне́ние** admiration. **преклони́ть** *pf*, **преклоня́ть** *impf* bow, bend; **~ся** bow down; **+dat or перед+instr** admire, worship. **прекло́нный**: **~ во́зраст** old age.

**прекра́сный** beautiful; fine; excellent.

**прекрати́ть** (-ащу́) *pf*, **прекраща́ть** *impf* stop, discontinue; **~ся** cease, end. **прекраще́ние** halt; cessation.

**преле́стный** delightful. **пре́лесть** charm, delight.

**преломи́ть** (-млю́, -мишь) *pf*, **преломля́ть** *impf* refract. **преломле́ние** refraction.

**прельсти́ть** (-льщу́) *pf*, **прельща́ть** *impf* attract; entice; **~ся** be attracted; fall (+instr for).

**прелюбодея́ние** adultery.

**прелю́дия** prelude.

**премину́ть** (-ну) *pf with neg* not fail.

**премирова́ть** *impf & pf* award a prize for; give a bonus. **пре́мия** prize; bonus; premium.

**премье́р** prime minister; lead(ing actor). **премье́ра** première. **премье́р-мини́стр** prime minister. **премье́рша** leading lady.

**пренебрега́ть** *impf*, **пренебре́чь** (-егу́, -ежёшь; -ёг, -ла́) *pf* +instr scorn; neglect. **пренебреже́ние** scorn; neglect. **пренебрежи́тельный** scornful.

**пре́ния** (-ий) *pl* debate.

**преоблада́ние** predominance. **преоблада́ть** *impf* predominate; prevail.

**преобража́ть** *impf*, **преобрази́ть** (-ажу́) *pf* transform. **преображе́ние** transformation; Transfiguration. **пре-образова́ние** transformation; reform. **преобразова́ть** *pf*, **преобразо́вывать** *impf* transform; reform, reorganize.

**преодолева́ть** *impf*, **преодоле́ть** (-е́ю) *pf* overcome.

**препара́т** preparation.

**препина́ние**: зна́ки препина́-ния punctuation marks.

**препира́тельство** altercation, wrangling.

**преподава́ние** teaching. **преподава́тель** *m*, **~ница** teacher. **преподава́тель-ский** teaching. **преподава́ть** (-даю́, -даёшь) *impf* teach.

**преподнести́** (-су́, -сёшь; -ёс, -ла́) *pf*, **преподноси́ть** (-ошу́, -о́сишь) present with, give.

**препроводи́ть** (-вожу́, -во́-дишь) *pf*, **препровожда́ть** *impf* send, forward.

**препя́тствие** obstacle; hurdle. **препя́тствовать** *impf* (*pf* вос~) +dat hinder.

**прерва́ть** (-ву́, -вёшь; -а́л, -á, -о) *pf* (*impf* прерыва́ть) interrupt; break off; **~ся** be interrupted, break off.

**препрека́ние** argument. **пререка́ться** *impf* argue.

**прерыва́ть(ся** *impf of* пре-рва́ть(ся

**пресека́ть** *impf*, **пресе́чь** (-еку́, -ечёшь; -ёк, -екла́) *pf* stop; put an end to; ~ся stop; break.

**пресле́дование** pursuit; persecution; prosecution. **пресле́довать** *impf* pursue; haunt; persecute; prosecute.

**пресловутый** notorious.

**пресмыка́ться** *impf* grovel. **пресмыка́ющееся** *sb* reptile.

**пресново́дный** freshwater. **пре́сный** fresh; unleavened; insipid; bland.

**пресс** press. **пре́сса** the press. **пресс-конфере́нция** press-conference.

**преста́релый** aged. **прести́ж** prestige. **престо́л** throne.

**преступле́ние** crime. **престу́пник** criminal. **престу́пность** criminality; crime, delinquency. **престу́пный** criminal.

**пресы́титься** (-ы́щусь) *pf*, **пресыща́ться** *impf* be satiated. **пресыще́ние** surfeit, satiety.

**претвори́ть** *pf*, **претворя́ть** *impf* (в+*acc*) turn, change, convert; ~ в жизнь realize, carry out.

**претенде́нт** claimant; candidate; pretender. **претендова́ть** *impf* на+*acc* lay claim to; have pretensions to. **прете́нзия** claim; pretension; быть в прете́нзии на+*acc* have a grudge, a grievance, against.

**претерпева́ть** *impf*, **претерпе́ть** (-плю́, -пишь) *pf* undergo; suffer.

**преть** (пре́ет) *impf* (*pf* со~) rot.

**преувеличе́ние** exaggeration. **преувели́чивать** *impf*, **преувели́чить** (-чу) *pf* exaggerate.

**преуменьша́ть** *impf*, **преуме́ньшить** (-е́ньшу) *pf* underestimate; understate.

**преуспева́ть** *impf*, **преуспе́ть** (-е́ю) *pf* be successful; thrive.

**преходя́щий** transient.

**прецеде́нт** precedent.

**при** *prep* +*prep* by, at; in the presence of; attached to; with; about; on; in the time of; under; during; when, in case of; ~ всём том for all that.

**приба́вить** (-влю) *pf*, **прибавля́ть** *impf* add; increase; ~ся increase; rise; wax; день прибавился the days are getting longer. **приба́вка** addition; increase. **прибавле́ние** addition; supplement, appendix. **приба́вочный** additional; surplus.

**Приба́лтика** the Baltic States.

**прибау́тка** humorous saying.

**прибега́ть[1]** *impf of* **прибежа́ть**

**прибега́ть[2]** *impf*, **прибе́гнуть** (-ну; -бе́г) *pf* к+*dat* resort to.

**прибежа́ть** (-егу́) *pf* (*impf* **прибега́ть**) come running.

**прибе́жище** refuge.

**приберега́ть** *impf*, **прибере́чь** (-егу́, -ежёшь; -ёг, -ла́) *pf* save (up); reserve.

**приберу́** *etc.*: *see* **прибра́ть**.

**прибива́ть** *impf of* **приби́ть**. **прибира́ть** *impf of* **прибра́ть**

**приби́ть** (-бью, -бьёшь) *pf* (*impf* **прибива́ть**) nail; flatten; drive.

**приближа́ть** *impf*, **прибли́зить** (-и́жу) *pf* bring *or* move nearer; ~ся approach; come nearer. **приближе́ние** approach. **приблизи́тельный**

approximate.
**прибо́й** surf, breakers.
**прибо́р** instrument, device, apparatus; set. **прибо́рная доска́** instrument panel; dashboard.
**прибра́ть** (-беру́, -берёшь; -а́л, -а́, -о) pf (impf **прибира́ть**) tidy (up); put away.
**прибре́жный** coastal; offshore.
**прибыва́ть** impf, **прибы́ть** (-бу́ду; при́был, -а́, -о) pf arrive; increase, grow; rise; wax. **при́быль** profit, gain; increase, rise. **при́быльный** profitable. **прибы́тие** arrival.
**прибью́** etc.: see **прибы́ть**
**прива́л** halt.
**прива́ривать** impf, **привари́ть** (-рю́, -ришь) pf weld on.
**приватиза́ция** privatization. **приватизи́ровать** impf & pf privatize.
**приведу́** etc.: see **привести́**
**привезти́** (-зу́, -зёшь; -ёз, -ла́) (impf **привози́ть**) bring.
**привере́дливый** pernickety.
**приве́рженец** (-нца) adherent. **приве́рженный** devoted.
**приве́сить** (-е́шу) pf (impf **приве́шивать**) hang up, suspend.
**привести́** (-еду́, -едёшь; -ёл, -а́) pf (impf **приводи́ть**) bring; lead; take; reduce; cite; put in(to), set.
**приве́т** greeting(s); regards; hi! **приве́тливый** friendly; affable. **приве́тствие** greeting; speech of welcome. **приве́тствовать** impf & pf greet, salute; welcome.
**приве́шивать** impf of **приве́сить**
**привива́ть(ся** impf of **приви́ть(ся. приви́вка** inoculation.

привиде́ние ghost; apparition. **при|ви́деться** (-дится) pf.
**привилегиро́ванный** privileged. **привиле́гия** privilege.
**привинти́ть** (-нчу́) pf, **приви́нчивать** impf screw on.
**приви́ть** (-вью́, -вьёшь; -и́л, -а́, -о) pf (impf **привива́ть**) inoculate; graft; inculcate; foster; ~ся take; become established.
**при́вкус** after-taste; smack.
**привлека́тельный** attractive. **привлека́ть** impf, **привле́чь** (-еку́, -ечёшь; -ёк, -ла́) pf attract; draw; draw in, win over; (law) have up; ~ к суду́ sue. **привлече́ние** attraction.
**приво́д** drive, gear. **приводи́ть** (-ожу́, -о́дишь) impf of **привести́. приводно́й** driving.
**привожу́** etc.: see **приводи́ть, привози́ть**
**приво́з** bringing; importation; load. **привози́ть** (-ожу́, -о́зишь) impf of **привезти́. привозно́й, приво́зный** imported.
**приво́льный** free.
**привстава́ть** (-таю́, -таёшь) impf, **привста́ть** (-а́ну) pf half-rise; rise.
**привыка́ть** impf, **привы́кнуть** (-ну; -ык) pf get accustomed. **привы́чка** habit. **привы́чный** habitual, usual.
**привью́** etc.: see **приви́ть**
**привя́занность** attachment; affection. **привяза́ть** (-яжу́, -я́жешь) pf, **привя́зывать** impf attach; tie, bind; ~ся become attached; attach o.s.; +к+dat pester. **привя́зчивый** annoying; affectionate. **при́вязь** tie; lead, leash; tether.

пригиба́ть *impf of* пригну́ть

пригласи́ть (-ашу́) *pf*, приглаша́ть *impf* invite. приглаше́ние invitation.

пригляде́ться (-яжу́сь) *pf*, пригля́дываться *impf* look closely; +к+*dat* scrutinize; get used to.

пригна́ть (-гоню́, -го́нишь; -а́л, -а́, -о) *pf* (*impf* пригоня́ть) bring in; fit, adjust.

пригну́ть (-ну́, -нёшь) *pf* (*impf* пригиба́ть) bend down.

пригова́ривать[1] *impf* keep saying.

пригова́ривать[2] *impf*, приговори́ть *pf* sentence, condemn. пригово́р verdict, sentence.

пригоди́ться (-ожу́сь) *pf* prove useful. приго́дный fit, suitable.

пригоня́ть *impf of* пригна́ть

пригора́ть *impf*, пригоре́ть (-ри́т) *pf* be burnt.

при́город suburb. при́городный suburban.

приго́рок (-рка) hillock.

при́горшня (*gen pl* -ей) handful.

приготови́тельный preparatory. пригото́вить (-влю) *pf*, приготовля́ть *impf* prepare; ~ся prepare. приготовле́ние preparation.

пригрева́ть *impf*, пригре́ть (-е́ю) *pf* warm; cherish.

пригрози́ть (-ожу́) *pf*.

придава́ть (-даю́, -даёшь) *impf*, прида́ть (-а́м, -а́шь, -а́ст, -ади́м; при́дал, -а́, -о) *pf* add; give; attach. прида́ча adding; addition; в прида́чу into the bargain.

придави́ть (-влю́, -вишь) *pf*, прида́вливать *impf* press (down).

прида́ное *sb* dowry. прида-

ток (-тка) appendage.

придвига́ть *impf*, придви́нуть (-ну) *pf* move up, draw up; ~ся move up, draw near. придво́рный court.

приде́лать *pf*, приде́лывать *impf* attach.

приде́рживаться *impf* hold on, hold; +*gen* keep to.

придеру́сь *etc.*: *see* придра́ться. придира́ться *impf of* придра́ться. приди́рка quibble; fault-finding. приди́рчивый fault-finding.

придоро́жный roadside.

придра́ться (-деру́сь, -дерёшься; -а́лся, -а́сь, -а́лось) *pf* (*impf* придира́ться) find fault.

приду́ *etc.*: *see* прийти́

приду́мать *pf*, приду́мывать *impf* think up, invent.

прие́ду *etc.*: *see* прие́хать. прие́зд arrival. приезжа́ть *impf of* прие́хать. прие́зжий newly arrived; *sb* newcomer.

приём receiving; reception; surgery; welcome; admittance; dose; go; movement; welcome, way; trick. прие́млемый acceptable. приёмная *sb* waiting-room; reception room. приёмник (radio) receiver. приёмный receiving; reception; entrance; foster, adopted.

прие́хать (-е́ду) *pf* (*impf* приезжа́ть) arrive, come.

прижа́ть (-жму́, -жмёшь) *pf* (*impf* прижима́ть) press; clasp; ~ся nestle up.

приже́чь (-жгу́, -жжёшь; -жёг, -жгла́) *pf* (*impf* прижига́ть) cauterize.

прижива́ться *impf of* прижи́ться

прижига́ние cauterization. прижига́ть *impf of* приже́чь

прижима́ть(ся *impf of*

прижáть(ся

прижи́ться (-ивýсь, -ивёшься; -жи́лся, -áсь) pf (impf прижива́ться) become acclimatized.

прижмý etc.: see прижáть

приз (pl -ы́) prize.

призвáние vocation. призва́ть (-зовý, -зовёшь; -а́л, -á, -о) pf (impf призыва́ть) call; call upon; call up.

призе́мистый stocky, squat.

приземле́ние landing. приземли́ться pf, приземля́ться impf land.

призёр prizewinner.

при́зма prism.

признава́ть (-наю́, -наёшь) impf, призна́ть pf recognize; admit; ~ся confess. при́знак sign, symptom; indication. призна́ние confession, declaration; acknowledgement; recognition. при́знанный acknowledged, recognized. призна́тельный grateful.

призову́ etc.: see призва́ть при́зрак spectre, ghost. при́зрачный ghostly; illusory, imagined.

призы́в call, appeal; slogan; call-up. призыва́ть impf of призва́ть. призывно́й conscription.

при́иск mine.

прийти́ (придý, -дёшь; пришёл, -шла́) pf (impf приходи́ть) come; arrive; ~ в себя́ regain consciousness; ~сь +по+dat fit; suit; +на+acc fall on; impers+dat have to; happen (to), fall to the lot (of).

прика́з order, command. прика́за́ние order, command. приказа́ть (-ажý, -а́жешь) pf, прика́зывать impf order, command.

прика́лывать impf of приколо́ть. прикаса́ться impf of прикосну́ться

прика́нчивать impf of прико́нчить

прикати́ть (-ачý, -а́тишь) pf, прика́тывать impf roll up.

прики́дывать impf, прики́нуть (-ну) pf throw in; add; weigh; estimate; ~ся +instr pretend (to be).

прикла́д¹ butt.

прикла́д² trimmings. прикладно́й applied. прикла́дывать(ся impf of приложи́ть(ся

прикле́ивать impf, прикле́ить pf stick; glue.

приключа́ться impf, приключи́ться pf happen, occur. приключе́ние adventure. приключе́нческий adventure.

прикова́ть (-кую́, -куёшь) pf, прико́вывать impf chain; rivet.

прикола́чивать impf, приколоти́ть (-очý, -о́тишь) pf nail. приколо́ть (-лю́, -лешь) pf (impf прика́лывать) pin; stab.

прикомандирова́ть pf, прикомандиро́вывать impf attach.

прико́нчить (-чу) pf (impf прика́нчивать) use up; finish off.

прикоснове́ние touch; concern. прикосну́ться (-нýсь, -нёшься) pf (impf прикаса́ться) к+dat touch.

прикрепи́ть (-плю́) pf, прикрепля́ть impf fasten, attach. прикрепле́ние fastening; registration.

прикрыва́ть impf, прикры́ть (-ро́ю) pf cover; screen; shelter. прикры́тие cover; escort.

прикýривать impf, прикý-

**ри́ть** (-рю́, -ришь) *pf* get a light.

**прикуси́ть** (-ушу́, -у́сишь) *pf*, **прику́сывать** *impf* bite.

**прила́вок** (-вка) counter.

**прилага́тельное** *sb* adjective. **прилага́ть** *impf of* приложи́ть

**прила́дить** (-а́жу) *pf*, **прила́живать** *impf* fit, adjust.

**приласка́ть** *pf* caress, pet; ~**ся** snuggle up.

**прилега́ть** *impf* (*pf* приле́чь) к+*dat* fit; adjoin. **прилега́ющий** close-fitting; adjoining, adjacent.

**приле́жный** diligent.

**прилепи́ть(ся** (-плю́(сь, -пишь(ся) *pf*, **прилепля́ть(ся** *impf* stick.

**прилёт** arrival. **прилета́ть** *impf*, **прилете́ть** (-ечу́) *pf* arrive, fly in; come flying.

**приле́чь** (-ля́гу, -ля́жешь; -ёг, -гла́) *pf* (*impf* прилега́ть) lie down.

**прили́в** flow, flood; rising tide; surge. **прилива́ть** *impf of* прили́ть. **прили́вный** tidal.

**прилипа́ть** *impf*, **прили́пнуть** (-нет; -ли́п) *pf* stick.

**прили́ть** (-льёт; -и́л, -а́, -о) *pf* (*impf* прилива́ть) flow; rush.

**прили́чие** decency. **прили́чный** decent.

**приложе́ние** application; enclosure; supplement; appendix. **приложи́ть** (-жу́, -жишь) *pf* (*impf* прикла́дывать, прилага́ть) *pf* apply; affix; add; enclose; ~**ся** take aim; +*instr* put, apply; +к+*dat* kiss.

**прилёт** *etc.: see* прили́ть. **при|льну́ть** (-ну́, -нёшь) *pf*. **прилягу́** *etc.: see* приле́чь

**прима́нивать** *impf*, **примани́ть** (-ню́, -нишь) *pf* lure; en-

tice. **прима́нка** bait, lure.

**примене́ние** application; use. **примени́ть** (-ню́, -нишь) *pf*, **применя́ть** *impf* apply; use; ~**ся** adapt o.s., conform.

**приме́р** example. **приме́рить** *pf* (*impf also* примеря́ть) try on. **приме́рка** fitting.

**приме́рно** *adv* approximately. **приме́рный** exemplary; approximate.

**примеря́ть** *impf of* приме́рить

**при́месь** admixture.

**приме́та** sign, token. **приме́тный** perceptible; conspicuous.

**примеча́ние** note, footnote; *pl* comments. **примеча́тельный** notable.

**примеша́ть** *pf*, **приме́шивать** *impf* add, mix in.

**примина́ть** *impf of* примя́ть

**примире́ние** reconciliation. **примири́тельный** conciliatory. **при|мири́ть** *pf*, **примиря́ть** *impf* reconcile; conciliate; ~**ся** be reconciled.

**примити́вный** primitive.

**примкну́ть** (-ну́, -нёшь) *pf* (*impf* примыка́ть) join; fix, attach.

**приму́** *etc.: see* принять

**примо́рский** seaside; maritime. **примо́рье** seaside.

**примо́чка** wash, lotion.

**приму́** *etc.: see* приня́ть

**примча́ться** (-чу́сь) *pf* come tearing along.

**примыка́ть** *impf of* примкну́ть; +к+*dat* adjoin. **примыка́ющий** affiliated.

**примя́ть** (-мну́, -мнёшь) *pf* (*impf* примина́ть) crush; trample down.

**принадлежа́ть** (-жу́) *impf* belong. **принадле́жность** belonging; membership; *pl* accessories; equipment.

**принести́** (-су́, -сёшь; -нёс, -ла́) *pf* (*impf* **приноси́ть**) bring; fetch.

**принижа́ть** *impf*, **прини́зить** (-и́жу) *pf* humiliate; belittle.

**принима́ть(ся** *impf of* **приня́ть(ся**

**приноси́ть** (-ошу́, -о́сишь) *impf of* **принести́. приноше́ние** gift, offering.

**при́нтер** (*comput*) printer.

**принуди́тельный** compulsory. **прину́дить** (-у́жу) *pf*, **принужда́ть** *impf* compel. **принужде́ние** compulsion, coercion. **принуждённый** constrained, forced.

**принц** prince. **принце́сса** princess.

**при́нцип** principle. **принципиа́льно** *adv* on principle; in principle. **принципиа́льный** of principle; general.

**приня́тие** taking; acceptance; admission. **при́нято** it is accepted, it is usual; **не ~** it is not done. **приня́ть** (-иму́, -и́мешь; при́нял, -а́, -о) *pf* (*impf* **принима́ть**) take; take over; receive; **+за**+*acc* take for; **~ уча́стье** take part; **~ся** begin; take; take root; **~ за рабо́ту** set to work.

**приободри́ть** *pf*, **приободря́ть** *impf* cheer up; **~ся** cheer up.

**приобрести́** (-ету́, -ете́шь; -рёл, -а́) *pf*, **приобрета́ть** *impf* acquire. **приобрете́ние** acquisition.

**приобща́ть** *impf*, **приобщи́ть** (-щу́) *pf* join, attach, unite; **~ся к**+*dat* join in.

**приорите́т** priority.

**приостана́вливать** *impf*, **приостанови́ть** (-влю́ -вишь) *pf* stop, suspend; **~ся** stop. **приостано́вка** halt, suspension.

**приоткрыва́ть** *impf*, **приоткры́ть** (-ро́ю) *pf* open slightly.

**припа́док** (-дка) fit; attack.

**припа́сы** (-ов) *pl* supplies.

**припе́в** refrain.

**приписа́ть** (-ишу́ -и́шешь) *pf*, **припи́сывать** *impf* add; attribute. **припи́ска** postscript; codicil.

**припло́д** offspring; increase.

**приплыва́ть** *impf*, **приплы́ть** (-ыву́, -ыве́шь; -ы́л, -а́, -о) *pf* swim up; sail up.

**приплю́снуть** (-ну) *pf*, **приплю́щивать** *impf* flatten.

**приподнима́ть** *impf*, **приподня́ть** (-ниму́, -ни́мешь; -о́днял, -а́, -о) *pf* raise (a little); **~ся** raise o.s. (a little).

**припо́й** solder.

**приполза́ть** *impf*, **приползти́** (-зу́, -зёшь; -по́лз, -ла́) *pf* creep up, crawl up.

**припомина́ть** *impf*, **припо́мнить** (-ню) *pf* recollect.

**припра́ва** seasoning, flavouring. **припра́вить** (-влю) *pf*, **приправля́ть** *impf* season, flavour.

**припря́тать** (-я́чу) *pf*, **припря́тывать** *impf* secrete, put by.

**припу́гивать** *impf*, **припугну́ть** (-ну́, -нёшь) *pf* scare.

**прираба́тывать** *impf*, **прирабо́тать** *pf* earn ... extra. **при́работок** (-тка) additional earnings.

**прира́внивать** *impf*, **приравня́ть** *pf* equate (with **к**+*dat*).

**прираста́ть** *impf*, **прирасти́** (-тёт; -ро́с, -ла́) *pf* adhere; take; increase; accrue.

приро́да nature. приро́дный natural; by birth; innate. при‌рождённый innate; born.

приро́с etc.: see прирасти́. приро́ст increase.

прируча́ть impf, приручи́ть (-чу́) pf tame; domesticate.

приса́живаться impf of прис‌е́сть

присва́ивать impf, присво‌ить pf appropriate; award.

приседа́ть impf, присе́сть (-ся́ду) pf (impf also приса́жи‌ваться) sit down, take a seat.

прискака́ть (-ачу́, -а́чешь) pf come galloping.

прискорбный sorrowful.

присла́ть (-ишлю́, -ишлёшь) pf (impf присыла́ть) send.

прислони́ть(ся (-оню́(сь, -о́нишь‌(ся) pf, прислоня́ть(ся impf lean, rest.

прислу́га servant; crew. при‌слу́живать impf (к+dat) wait (on), attend.

прислу́шаться pf, прислу́‌шиваться impf listen; +к+dat listen to; heed.

присма́тривать impf, при‌смотре́ть (-рю́, -ришь) pf +за+instr look after, keep an eye on; ~ся (к+dat) look closely (at). присмо́тр supervision.

при|сни́ться pf.

присоедине́ние joining; addition; annexation. присоеди‌ни́ть pf, присоединя́ть impf join; add; annex; ~ся к+dat join; subscribe to (an opinion).

приспосо́бить (-блю) pf, при‌спосо́блять impf fit, adjust, adapt; ~ся adapt to. при‌способле́ние adaptation; device; appliance. приспосо‌бля́емость adaptability.

пристава́ть (-таю́, -таёшь)

impf of приста́ть

приста́вить (-влю) pf (impf приставля́ть) к+dat place, set, or lean against; add; ap‌point to look after.

приста́вка prefix.

приставля́ть impf of при‌ста́вить

приста́льный intent.

приста́нище refuge, shelter.

при́стань (gen pl -е́й) land‌ing-stage; pier; wharf.

приста́ть (-а́ну) pf (impf при‌става́ть) stick, adhere (к+dat to); pester.

пристёгивать impf, пристег‌ну́ть (-ну́, -нёшь) pf fasten.

присто́йный decent, proper.

пристра́ивать impf of при‌стро́ить(ся

пристра́стие predilection, passion; bias. пристра́стный biased.

пристре́ливать impf, при‌стрели́ть pf shoot (down).

пристро́ить (-о́ю) pf (impf пристра́ивать) add, build on; fix up; ~ся be fixed up; get a place. пристро́йка annexe, extension.

при́ступ assault; fit, attack. приступа́ть impf, присту‌пи́ть (-плю́, -пишь) pf к+dat set about, start.

при|стыди́ть (-ыжу́) pf.

при|стыкова́ться pf.

присуди́ть (-ужу́, -у́дишь) pf, присужда́ть impf sentence, condemn; award; confer. при‌сужде́ние awarding; conferment.

прису́тствие presence. при‌су́тствовать impf be present, attend. прису́тствующие sb pl those present.

прису́щий inherent; charac‌teristic.

**присыла́ть** *impf of* **присла́ть**

**прися́га** oath. **присяга́ть** *impf*, **присягну́ть** (**-ну́**, **-нёшь**) *pf* swear.

**прися́ду** *etc.: see* **присе́сть**

**прися́жный** *sb* juror.

**притаи́ться** *pf* hide.

**прита́птывать** *impf of* **притопта́ть**

**прита́скивать** *impf*, **притащи́ть** (**-ащу́**, **-а́щишь**) *pf* bring, drag, haul; **~ся** drag o.s.

**притвори́ться** *pf*, **притворя́ться** *impf* +*instr* pretend to be. **притво́рный** pretended, feigned. **притво́рство** pretence, sham. **притво́рщик** sham; hypocrite.

**притека́ть** *impf of* **прите́чь**

**притесне́ние** oppression. **притесни́ть** *pf*, **притесня́ть** *impf* oppress.

**прите́чь** (**-ечёт**, **-еку́т**; **-ёк**, **-ла́**) *pf* (*impf* **притека́ть**) pour in.

**притиха́ть** *impf*, **притихну́ть** (**-ну**; **-и́х**) *pf* quiet down.

**прито́к** tributary; influx.

**прито́лока** lintel.

**прито́м** *conj* (and) besides.

**прито́н** den, haunt.

**притопта́ть** (**-чу́**, **-пчешь**) *pf* (*impf* **прита́птывать**) trample down.

**прито́рный** sickly-sweet, luscious, cloying.

**притра́гиваться** *impf*, **притро́нуться** (**-нусь**) *pf* touch.

**притупи́ть** (**-плю́**, **-пишь**) *pf*, **притупля́ть** *impf* blunt, dull; deaden; **~ся** become blunt *or* dull.

**при́тча** parable.

**притяга́тельный** attractive, magnetic. **притя́гивать** *impf of* **притяну́ть**

**притяжа́тельный** possessive. **притяже́ние** attraction.

**притяза́ние** claim, pretension. **притяза́тельный** demanding.

**притя́нутый** far-fetched. **притяну́ть** (**-ну́**, **-нешь**) *pf* (*impf* **притя́гивать**) attract; drag (up).

**приуро́чивать** *impf*, **приуро́чить** (**-чу**) *pf* +*dat* time for.

**приуса́дебный**: **~ уча́сток** individual plot (*in kolkhoz*).

**приуча́ть** *impf*, **приучи́ть** (**-чу́**, **-чишь**) *pf* train, school.

**прихлеба́тель** *m* sponger.

**прихо́д** coming; arrival; receipts; parish. **приходи́ть(ся** (**-ожу́(сь**, **-о́дишь(ся**) *impf of* **прийти́(сь. прихо́дный** receipt; **прихо́дящий** non-resident. **приходя́щий больно́й** outpatient.

**прихожа́нин** (*pl* **-а́не**, **-а́н**), **-а́нка** parishioner.

**прихо́жая** *sb* hall, lobby.

**прихотли́вый** capricious; fanciful; intricate. **при́хоть** whim, caprice.

**прихра́мывать** limp (slightly).

**прице́л** sight; aiming. **прице́ливаться** *impf*, **прице́литься** *pf* take aim.

**прице́ниваться** *impf*, **прицени́ться** (**-ню́сь**, **-нишься**) *pf* (к+*dat*) ask the price (of).

**прице́п** trailer. **прицепи́ть** (**-плю́**, **-пишь**) *pf*, **прицепля́ть** *impf* hitch, hook on; **~ся** к+*dat* stick to, cling to. **прице́пка** hitching, hooking on; quibble. **прицепно́й**: **~ ваго́н** trailer.

**прича́л** mooring; mooring line. **прича́ливать** *impf*, **прича́лить** *pf* moor.

**прича́стие**[1] participle. **прича́стие**[2] communion. **причасти́ть** (**-ащу́**) *pf* (*impf* **причаща́ть**) give communion to; **~ся** receive communion.

**прича́стный**[1] participial. **при-**

**чáстный**[2] concerned; privy.

**причащáть** *impf of* **причаститься**

**причём** *conj* moreover, and.

**причесáть** (-ешý, -ешешь) *pf*, **причёсывать** *impf* comb; do the hair (of); **~ся** do one's hair, have one's hair done. **причёска** hair-do; haircut.

**причина** cause; reason. **причинить** *pf*, **причинять** *impf* cause.

**причислить** *pf*, **причислять** *impf* number, rank (к+*dat* among); add on.

**причитáние** lamentation. **причитáть** *impf* lament.

**причитáться** *impf* be due.

**причмóкивать** *impf*, **причмóкнуть** (-ну) *pf* smack one's lips.

**причуда** caprice, whim. **причудиться** *pf*.

**причудливый** odd; fantastic; whimsical.

**пришвартовáть** *pf*. **пришёл** *etc.: see* **прийти**

**пришелец** (-ьца) newcomer. **пришествие** coming; advent.

**пришивáть** *impf*, **пришить** (-шью, -шьёшь) *pf* sew on.

**пришлю** *etc.: see* **прислáть**

**пришпиливать** *impf*, **пришпилить** *pf* pin on.

**пришпоривать** *impf*, **пришпорить** *pf* spur (on).

**прищемить** (-млю) *pf*, **прищемлять** *impf* pinch.

**прищепка** clothes-peg.

**прищуривать** *impf*, **прищуриться** *pf* screw up one's eyes.

**приют** shelter, refuge. **приютить** (-ючу) *pf* shelter; **~ся** take shelter.

**приятель** *m*, **приятельница** friend. **приятельский** friendly. **приятный** nice, pleasant.

**про** *prep*+*acc* about; for; **~ себя** to o.s.

**проанализировать** *pf*.

**прóба** test; hallmark; sample.

**пробег** run; race. **пробегáть** *impf*, **пробежáть** (-егý) *pf* run; cover; run past. **пробéжка** run.

**пробел** blank, gap; flaw.

**проберý** *etc.: see* **пробрáть**.

**пробивáть(ся** *impf of* **пробить(ся**. **пробирáть(ся** *impf of* **пробрáть(ся**

**пробирка** test-tube. **пробировáть** *impf* test, assay.

**про|бить** (-бью, -бьёшь) *pf* (*impf also* **пробивáть**) make a hole in; pierce; punch; **~ся** force, make, one's way.

**пробка** cork; stopper; fuse; (traffic) jam, congestion. **пробковый** cork.

**проблéма** problem.

**проблеск** flash; gleam, ray.

**прóбный** trial, test; **~ кáмень** touchstone. **прóбовать** *impf* (*pf* **ис~, по~**) try; attempt.

**пробоина** hole.

**пробóр** parting.

**про|бормотáть** (-очý, -очешь) *pf*.

**пробрáть** (-берý, -берёшь; -áл, -á, -о) *pf* (*impf* **пробирáть**) penetrate; scold; **~ся** make or force one's way.

**пробýду** *etc.: see* **пробыть**

**про|будить** (-ужý, -удишь) *pf* **пробуждáть** *impf* wake (up); arouse; **~ся** wake up. **пробуждéние** awakening.

**про|бурáвить** (-влю) *pf*, **пробурáвливать** *impf* bore (through), drill.

**про|бурить** *pf*.

**пробыть** (-бýду; прóбыл, -á, -о) *pf* stay; be.

**пробью** *etc.: see* **пробить**

прова́л failure; downfall; gap.
прова́ливать *impf*, провали́ть (-лю́, -лишь) *pf* bring down; ruin; reject, fail; ~ся collapse; fall in; fail; disappear.
прове́дать *pf*, прове́дывать *impf* call on; learn.
проведе́ние conducting; construction; installation.
провезти́ (-зу́, -зёшь; -ёз, -ла́) *pf* (*impf* провози́ть) convey, transport.
прове́рить *pf*, проверя́ть *impf* check; test. прове́рка checking, check; testing.
про|вести́ (-еду́, -еде́шь; -ёл, -а́) *pf* (*impf also* проводи́ть) lead, take; build; install; carry out; conduct; pass; draw; spend; +*instr* pass over.
прове́тривать *impf*, прове́трить *pf* air.
про|ве́ять (-е́ю) *pf*.
провиде́ние Providence.
прови́зия provisions.
провини́ться *pf* be guilty; do wrong.
провинциа́льный provincial. прови́нция province; the provinces.
про́вод (*pl* -а́) wire, lead, line. проводи́мость conductivity. проводи́ть (-ожу́, -о́дишь) *impf of* провести́; conduct.
проводи́ть (-ожу́, -о́дишь) *pf* (*impf* провожа́ть) accompany; see off.
прово́дка leading, taking; building; installation; wiring, wires.
проводни́к¹ (-а́) guide; conductor.
проводни́к² (-а́) conductor; bearer; transmitter.
про́воды (-ов) *pl* send-off. провожа́тый *sb* guide, escort. провожа́ть *impf of*

проводи́ть
прово́з conveyance, transport.
провозгласи́ть (-ашу́) *pf*, провозглаша́ть *impf* proclaim; propose. провозглаше́ние proclamation.
провози́ть (-ожу́, -о́зишь) *impf of* провезти́
провока́тор agent provocateur. провока́ция provocation.
про́волока wire. про́волочный wire.
прово́рный quick; agile. прово́рство quickness; agility.
провоци́ровать *impf & pf* (*pf* с~) provoke.
прогада́ть *pf*, прога́дывать *impf* miscalculate.
прога́лина glade; space.
прогиба́ть(ся *impf of* прогну́ть(ся
прогла́тывать *impf*, проглоти́ть (-очу́, -о́тишь) *pf* swallow.
прогляде́ть (-яжу́) *pf*, прогля́дывать¹ *impf* overlook; look through. прогляну́ть (-я́нет) *pf*, прогля́дывать² *impf* show, peep through, appear.
прогна́ть (-гоню́, -го́нишь; -а́л, -а́, -о) *pf* (*impf* прогоня́ть) drive away; banish; drive; sack.
прогни́ть (-иёт; -и́л, -а́, -о) *pf* rot through.
прогно́з prognosis; (weather) forecast.
прогну́ть (-ну́, -нёшь) *pf* (*impf* прогиба́ть) cause to sag; ~ся sag, bend.
прогова́ривать *impf*, проговори́ть *pf* say, utter; talk; ~ся let the cat out of the bag.
проголода́ться *pf* get hungry.
про|голосова́ть *pf*
прого́н purlin; girder; stairwell.

прогоня́ть *impf of* прогна́ть

прогора́ть *impf*, прогоре́ть (-рю́) *pf* burn (through); burn out; go bankrupt.

прого́рклый rancid, rank.

програ́мма programme; syllabus. программи́ровать *impf* (*pf* за~) programme.

прогрева́ть *impf*, прогре́ть (-е́ю) *pf* heat; warm up; ~ся warm up.

про|греме́ть (-млю́) *pf.* про|грохота́ть (-очу́, -о́чешь) *pf.*

прогре́сс progress. прогресси́вный progressive. прогресси́ровать *impf* progress.

прогрыза́ть *impf*, прогры́зть (-зу́, -зёшь; -ы́з) *pf* gnaw through.

про|гуде́ть (-гужу́) *pf.*

прогу́л truancy; absenteeism. прогу́ливать *impf*, прогуля́ть *impf* play truant, be absent, (from); miss; take for a walk; ~ся take a walk. прогу́лка walk, stroll; outing. прогу́льщик absentee, truant.

продава́ть (-даю́, -даёшь) *impf*, прода́ть (-а́м, -а́шь, -а́ст, -ади́м; про́дал, -а́, -о) *pf* sell. продава́ться (-да́юсь) *impf* be for sale; sell. продаве́ц (-вца́) seller, vendor; salesman. продавщи́ца seller, vendor; saleswoman. прода́жа sale. прода́жный for sale; corrupt.

продвига́ть *impf*, продви́нуть (-ну) *pf* move on, push forward; advance; ~ся advance; move forward; push on. продвиже́ние advancement.

продева́ть *impf of* проде́ть

про|деклами́ровать *pf.*

проде́лать *pf*, проде́лывать *impf* do, perform, make. проде́лка trick; prank.

продемонстри́ровать *pf* demonstrate, show.

продёргивать *impf of* продёрнуть

продержа́ть (-жу́, -жишь) *pf* hold; keep; ~ся hold out.

продёрнуть (-ну, -нешь) *pf* (*impf* продёргивать) pass, run; criticize severely.

проде́ть (-е́ну) *pf* (*impf* продева́ть) pass; ~ ни́тку в иго́лку thread a needle.

продешеви́ть (-влю́) *pf* sell too cheap.

про|диктова́ть *pf.*

продлева́ть *impf*, продли́ть *pf* prolong. продле́ние extension. продли́ться *pf.*

прода́г grocery. продово́льственный food. продово́льствие food; provisions.

продолгова́тый oblong.

продолжа́тель *m* continuer. продолжа́ть *impf*, продо́лжить (-жу) *pf* continue; prolong; ~ся continue, last, go on. продолже́ние continuation; sequel; в ~+*gen* in the course of. продолжи́тельность duration. продолжи́тельный long; prolonged.

продо́льный longitudinal.

продро́гнуть (-ну; -о́г) *pf* be chilled to the bone.

продтова́ры (-ов) *pl* food products.

продува́ть *impf* проду́ть

проду́кт product; *pl* food-stuffs. продукти́вность productivity. продукти́вный productive. продукто́вый food. проду́кция production.

проду́манный well thought-out; considered. проду́мать *pf*, проду́мывать *impf* think over; think out.

проду́ть (-у́ю, -у́ешь) *pf* (*impf* продува́ть) blow through.

**продыря́вить** (-влю) *pf* make a hole in.

**проеда́ть** *impf of* проесть. **прое́ду** *etc.: see* прое́хать

**прое́зд** passage, thoroughfare; trip. **прое́здить** (-зжу) *pf* (*impf* проезжа́ть) spend travelling. **проездно́й** travelling; ~**о́й биле́т** ticket; ~**а́я пла́та** fare; ~**ы́е** *sb pl* travelling expenses. **проезжа́ть** *impf of* прое́здить, прое́хать. **прое́зжий** passing (by); *sb* passer-by.

**прое́кт** project, plan, design; draft. **проекти́ровать** *impf* (*pf* с~) project; plan. **прое́ктный** planning; planned. **прое́ктор** projector.

**проекцио́нный фона́рь** projector. **прое́кция** projection.

**прое́сть** (-е́м, -е́шь, -е́ст, -еди́м; -е́л) *pf* (*impf* проеда́ть) eat through, corrode; spend on food.

**прое́хать** (-е́ду) *pf* (*impf* прое́зжа́ть) pass, ride, drive (by, through); cover.

**прожа́ренный** (*cul*) well-done.

**прожева́ть** (-жую́, -жуёшь) *pf*, **прожёвывать** *impf* chew well.

**проже́ктор** (*pl* -ы *or* -а́) searchlight.

**проже́чь** (-жгу́, -жжёшь; -жёг, -жгла́) *pf* (*impf* прожига́ть) burn (through).

**прожива́ть** *impf of* прожи́ть.

**прожига́ть** *impf of* проже́чь

**прожи́точный ми́нимум** living wage. **прожи́ть** (-иву́, -ивёшь; -о́жи́л, -а́, -о) *pf* (*impf* прожива́ть) live; spend.

**прожо́рливый** gluttonous.

**про́за** prose. **прозаи́ческий** prose; prosaic.

**проза́ние, про́звище** nickname. **прозва́ть** (-зову́, -зо-
вёшь; -а́л, -а́, -о) *pf* (*impf* прозыва́ть) nickname, name.

**прозвуча́ть** *pf*.

**прозева́ть** *pf*. **прозимова́ть** *pf*. **прозову́** *etc.: see* прозва́ть

**прозорли́вый** perspicacious.

**прозра́чный** transparent.

**прозрева́ть** *impf*, **прозре́ть** *pf* regain one's sight; see clearly. **прозре́ние** recovery of sight; insight.

**прозыва́ть** *impf of* прозва́ть

**прозяба́ние** vegetation. **прозяба́ть** *impf* vegetate.

**проигра́ть** *pf*, **прои́грывать** *impf* lose; play; ~**ся** gamble away all one's money. **прои́грыватель** *m* record-player. **про́игрыш** loss.

**произведе́ние** work; production; product. **произвести́** (-еду́, -едёшь; -ёл, -а́) *pf*, **производи́ть** (-ожу́, -о́дишь) *impf* make; carry out; produce; +**в**+*acc/nom pl* promote to (the rank of). **производи́тель** *m* producer. **производи́тельность** productivity. **производи́тельный** productive. **произво́дный** derivative. **произво́дственный** industrial; production. **произво́дство** production.

**произво́л** arbitrariness; arbitrary rule. **произво́льный** arbitrary.

**произнести́** (-су́, -сёшь; -ёс, -ла́) *pf*, **произноси́ть** (-ошу́, -о́сишь) *impf* pronounce; utter. **произноше́ние** pronunciation.

**произойти́** (-ойдёт; -ошёл, -шла́) *pf* (*impf* происходи́ть) happen, occur; result; be descended.

**произраста́ть** *impf*, **произрасти́** (-ту́; -тёшь; -рос, -ла́) *pf* sprout; grow.

**про́иски** (-ов) *pl* intrigues.

**проистека́ть** *impf*, **происте́чь** (-ечёт; -ёк, -ла́) *pf* spring, result.

**происходи́ть** (-ожу́, -о́дишь) *impf of* произойти́. **происхожде́ние** origin; birth.

**происше́ствие** event, incident.

**пройдо́ха** *m & f* sly person.

**пройти́** (-йду́, -йдёшь; -ошёл, -шла́) *pf* (*impf* **проходи́ть**) pass; go; go past; cover; study; get through; ~сь (*impf* **проха́живаться**) take a stroll.

**прок** use, benefit.

**прокажённый** *sb* leper. **прока́за**[1] leprosy.

**прока́за**[2] mischief, prank. **прока́зничать** *impf* (*pf* на~) be up to mischief. **прока́зник** prankster.

**прока́лывать** *impf of* проколо́ть

**прока́пывать** *impf of* прокопа́ть

**прока́т** hire.

**прокати́ться** (-ачу́сь, -а́тишься) *pf* roll; go for a drive.

**прока́тный** rolling; rolled.

**прокипяти́ть** (-ячу́) *pf* boil (thoroughly).

**прокиса́ть** *impf*, **про|ки́снуть** (-нет) *pf* turn (sour).

**прокла́дка** laying; construction; washer; packing. **прокла́дывать** *impf of* проложи́ть

**проклама́ция** leaflet.

**проклина́ть** *impf*, **прокля́сть** (-яну́, -янёшь; -о́клял, -а́, -о) *pf* curse; damn. **прокля́тие** curse; damnation. **прокля́тый** (-я́т, -а́, -о) damned.

**проко́л** puncture.

**проколо́ть** (-лю́, -лешь) *pf* (*impf* **прока́лывать**) prick, pierce.

**прокомменти́ровать** *pf* comment (upon).

**про|компости́ровать** *pf*. **про|конспекти́ровать** *pf*. **про|консульти́ровать(ся** *pf*. **про|контроли́ровать** *pf*.

**прокопа́ть** *pf* (*impf* **прока́пывать**) dig, dig through.

**проко́рм** nourishment, sustenance. **про|корми́ть(ся** (-млю́(сь, -мишь(ся) *pf*.

**про|корректи́ровать** *pf*.

**прокра́дываться** *impf*, **прокра́сться** (-аду́сь, -адёшься) *pf* steal in.

**прокурату́ра** office of public prosecutor. **прокуро́р** public prosecutor.

**прокуси́ть** (-ушу́, -у́сишь) *pf*, **проку́сывать** *impf* bite through.

**прокути́ть** (-учу́, -у́тишь) *pf*, **проку́чивать** *impf* squander; go on a binge.

**пролага́ть** *impf of* проложи́ть **прола́мывать** *impf of* проломи́ть

**пролега́ть** *impf* lie, run.

**пролеза́ть** *impf*, **проле́зть** (-зу; -ле́з) *pf* get through, climb through.

**про|лепета́ть** (-ечу́, -е́чешь) *pf*.

**пролёт** span; stairwell; bay.

**пролетариа́т** proletariat. **пролета́рий** proletarian. **пролета́рский** proletarian.

**пролета́ть** *impf*, **пролете́ть** (-ечу́) *pf* fly; cover; fly by, past, through.

**проли́в** strait. **пролива́ть** *impf*, **проли́ть** (-лью, -льёшь; -о́лил, -а́, -о) *pf* spill, shed; ~ся be spilt.

**проло́г** prologue.

**проложи́ть** (-жу́, -жишь) *pf* (*impf* **прокла́дывать**, **прола-**

га́ть) lay; build; interlay.
**проло́м** breach, break. **про-ло́ма́ть, проломи́ть** (-млю́, -мишь) pf (impf **прола́мывать**) break (through).
**пролью́** etc.: see **проли́ть**
**про|ма́зать** (-а́жу) pf. **прома́тывать(ся** impf of **промота́ть(ся**
**про́мах** miss; slip, blunder.
**прома́хиваться** impf, **промахну́ться** (-ну́сь, -нёшься) pf miss; make a blunder.
**прома́чивать** impf of **промочи́ть**
**промедле́ние** delay. **промедли́ть** pf delay; procrastinate.
**промежу́ток** (-тка) interval; space. **промежу́точный** intermediate
**промелькну́ть** (-ну́, -нёшь) pf flash (past, by).
**проме́нивать** impf, **променя́ть** pf exchange.
**промерза́ть** impf, **промёрзнуть** (-ну; -ёрз) pf freeze through. **промёрзлый** frozen.
**промока́ть** impf, **промо́кнуть** (-ну; -мо́к) pf get soaked; let water in.
**промо́лвить** (-влю) pf say, utter.
**промолча́ть** (-чу́) pf keep silent.
**про|мота́ть** pf (impf also **прома́тывать**) squander.
**промочи́ть** (-чу́, -чишь) pf (impf **прома́чивать**) soak, drench.
**промо́ю** etc.: see **промы́ть**
**промтова́ры** (-ов) pl manufactured goods.
**промча́ться** (-чу́сь) pf rush by.
**промыва́ть** impf of **промы́ть**
**про́мысел** (-сла) trade, business; pl works. **промысло́вый** producers'; business; game.
**промы́ть** (-мо́ю) pf (impf **про-**

**мыва́ть**) wash (thoroughly); bathe; ~ **мозги́**+dat brain-wash.
**про|мыча́ть** (-чу́) pf.
**промы́шленник** industrialist.
**промы́шленность** industry.
**промы́шленный** industrial.
**пронести́** (-су́, -сёшь; -ёс, -ла́) pf (impf **проноси́ть**) carry (past, through); pass (over); ~**сь** rush past, through; scud (past); fly; spread.
**пронза́ть** impf, **пронзи́ть** (-нжу́) pf pierce, transfix.
**пронзи́тельный** piercing.
**прониза́ть** (-ижу́, -и́жешь) pf, **прони́зывать** impf pierce; permeate.
**проника́ть** impf, **прони́к-нуть** (-ну; -и́к) pf penetrate; percolate; ~**ся** be imbued. **проникнове́ние** penetration; feeling. **проникнове́н-ный** heartfelt.
**проница́емый** permeable. **проница́тельный** perspicacious.
**проноси́ть(ся** (-ошу́(сь, -о́сишь(ся) impf of **пронести́(сь.**
**про|нумерова́ть** pf.
**проню́хать** pf, **проню́хивать** impf smell out, get wind of.
**прообраз** prototype.
**пропага́нда** propaganda.
**пропаганди́ст** propagandist.
**пропада́ть** impf of **пропа́сть.**
**пропа́жа** loss.
**пропа́лывать** impf of **про-поло́ть**
**про́пасть** precipice; abyss; lots of.
**пропа́сть** (-аду́, -адёшь) pf (impf **пропада́ть**) be missing; be lost; disappear; be done for, die; be wasted. **пропа́-щий** lost; hopeless.
**пропека́ть(ся** impf of **пропе́чь-(ся. про|пе́ть** (-пою́, -поёшь) pf.

пропе́чь (-еку́, -ечёшь; -ёк, -ла́) *pf* (*impf* пропека́ть) bake thoroughly; ~ся get baked through.

пропива́ть *impf* of пропи́ть

прописа́ть (-ишу́, -и́шешь) *pf*, прописывать *impf* prescribe; register; ~ся register. пропи́ска registration; residence permit. прописн|о́й: ~а́я бу́ква capital letter; ~а́я и́стина truism. про́писью *adv* in words.

пропита́ние subsistence, sustenance. пропита́ть *pf*, пропи́тывать *impf* impregnate, saturate.

пропи́ть (-пью́, -пьёшь; -о́пи́л, -а́, -о) *pf* (*impf* пропива́ть) spend on drink.

проплыва́ть *impf*, проплы́ть (-ыву́, -ывёшь; -ы́л, -а́, -о) *pf* swim, sail, *or* float past *or* through.

пропове́дник preacher; advocate. пропове́довать *impf* preach; advocate. про́поведь sermon; advocacy.

проползти́ *impf*, проползти́ (-зу́, -зёшь; -по́лз, -ла́) *pf* crawl, creep.

пропо́лка weeding. пропо́ло́ть (-лю́, -лешь) *pf* (*impf* пропа́лывать) weed.

пропорциона́льный proportional, proportionate. пропо́рция proportion.

про́пуск (*pl* -а́ *or* -и, -о́в *or* -ов) pass, permit; password; admission; omission; non-attendance; blank, gap. пропуска́ть *impf*, пропусти́ть (-ущу́, -у́стишь) *pf* let pass; let in; pass; leave out; miss. пропускно́й admission.

про|пылесо́сить *pf*.

пропью́ *etc.*: see пропи́ть

прораб works superintendent.

пораба́тывать *impf*, прорабо́тать *pf* work (through, at); study; pick holes in.

прораста́ние germination; sprouting. прораста́ть *impf*, прорасти́ (-тёт; -ро́с, -ла́) *pf* germinate, sprout.

прорва́ть (-ву́, -вёшь; -а́л, -а́, -о) *pf* (*impf* прорыва́ть) break through; ~ся burst open; break through.

про|реаги́ровать *pf*.

проре́дить (-ежу́) *pf*, проре́живать *impf* thin out.

про́рез cut; slit, notch. проре́зать (-е́жу) *pf*, прореза́ть *impf* (*impf also* проре́зывать) cut through; ~ся be cut, come through.

проре́зывать(ся *impf* of проре́зать(ся. про|репети́ровать *pf*.

проре́ха tear, slit; flies; deficiency.

про|рецензи́ровать *pf*.

проро́к prophet.

пророни́ть *pf* utter.

проро́с *etc.*: see прорасти́

проро́ческий prophetic. проро́чество prophecy.

проро́ю *etc.*: see проры́ть

проруба́ть *impf*, проруби́ть (-блю́, -бишь) *pf* cut *or* hack through. про́рубь ice-hole.

проры́в break; break-through; hitch. прорыва́ть[1](ся *impf* of прорва́ть(ся

прорыва́ть[2] *impf*, проры́ть (-ро́ю) *pf* dig through; ~ся dig one's way through.

проса́чиваться *impf* of просочи́ться

просве́рливать *impf*, просверли́ть *pf* drill, bore.

perforate.

**просве́т** (clear) space; shaft of light; ray of hope; opening. **просвети́тельный** educational. **просвети́ть**[1] (-ещу́) pf (impf **просвеща́ть**) enlighten.

**просвети́ть**[2] (-ечу́, -е́тишь) pf (impf **просве́чивать**) X-ray.

**просветле́ние** brightening (up); lucidity. **про|светле́ть** (-е́ет) pf.

**просве́чивание** radioscopy. **просве́чивать** impf of **просвети́ть**; be translucent; be visible.

**просвеща́ть** impf of **просвети́ть**. **просвеще́ние** enlightenment.

**просви́ра** communion bread.

**про́седь** streak(s) of grey.

**просе́ивать** impf of **просе́ять**

**про́сека** cutting, ride.

**просёлок** (-лка) country road.

**просе́ять** (-е́ю) pf (impf **просе́ивать**) sift.

**про|сигнализи́ровать** pf.

**просиде́ть** (-ижу́) pf, **проси́живать** impf sit.

**проси́тельный** pleading. **проси́ть** (-ошу́, -о́сишь) impf (pf **по~**) ask; beg; invite; **~ся** ask; apply.

**проскака́вать** impf of **проскочи́ть**

**проска́льзывать** impf, **проскользну́ть** (-ну́, -нёшь) pf slip, creep.

**проскочи́ть** (-чу́, -чишь) pf (impf **проска́кивать**) rush by; slip through; creep in.

**просла́вить** (-влю) pf, **прославля́ть** impf glorify; make famous; **~ся** become famous.

**просла́вленный** renowned.

**проследи́ть** (-ежу́) pf, **просле́живать** impf track

(down); trace.

**прослези́ться** (-ежу́сь) pf shed a few tears.

**просло́йка** layer, stratum.

**прослужи́ть** (-жу́, -жишь) pf serve (for a certain time).

**про|слу́шать** pf, **прослу́шивать** impf hear; listen to; miss, not catch.

**про|слы́ть** (-ыву́, -ывёшь; -ы́л, -á, -о) pf.

**просма́тривать** impf, **просмотре́ть** (-рю́, -ришь) pf look over; overlook. **просмо́тр** survey; view, viewing; examination.

**просну́ться** (-ну́сь, -нёшься) pf (impf **просыпа́ться**) wake up.

**про́со** millet.

**просо́вывать(ся** impf of **просу́нуть(ся**

**про|со́хнуть** (-ну; - óх) pf (impf also **просыха́ть**) dry out.

**просочи́ться** (-и́тся) pf (impf **проса́чиваться**) percolate; seep (out); leak (out).

**проспа́ть** (-плю́; -а́л, -á, -о) pf (impf **просыпа́ть**) sleep (through); oversleep.

**проспе́кт** avenue.

**про|спряга́ть** pf.

**просро́ченный** overdue; expired. **просро́чить** (-чу) pf allow to run out; be behind with; overstay. **просро́чка** delay; expiry of time limit.

**проста́ивать** impf of **простоя́ть**

**проста́к** (-á) simpleton.

**просте́нок** (-нка) pier (between windows).

**простере́ться** (-трётся, -тёрся) pf, **простира́ться** impf extend.

**прости́тельный** pardonable, excusable. **прости́ть** (-ощу́) pf (impf **проща́ть**) forgive;

excuse; ~ся (c+*instr*) say goodbye (to).

проститу́тка prostitute. проститу́ция prostitution. про́сто *adv* simply.

простоволо́сый bare-headed.

простоду́шный simple-hearted; ingenuous.

просто́й[1] downtime.

просто́й[2] simple; plain; mere; ~ым гла́зом with the naked eye; ~о́е число́ prime number.

простоква́ша thick sour milk.

про́сто-на́просто *adv* simply.

простонаро́дный of the common people.

просто́р spaciousness; space.

просто́рный spacious.

просторе́чие popular speech.

простосерде́чный simple-hearted.

простота́ simplicity.

простоя́ть (-ою́) *pf* (*impf* проста́ивать) stand (idle).

простра́нный extensive, vast.

простра́нственный spatial. простра́нство space.

простре́л lumbago. простре́ливать *impf*, прострели́ть (-лю́, -лишь) *pf* shoot through. про|стро́чить (-очу́, -о́чишь) *pf*.

просту́да cold. простуди́ться (-ужу́сь, -у́дишься) *pf*, простужа́ться *impf* catch (a) cold.

проступа́ть *impf*, проступи́ть (-ит) *pf* appear.

просту́пок (-пка) misdemeanour.

простыня́ (*pl* про́стыни, -ы́нь, -ня́м) sheet.

просты́ть (-ы́ну) *pf* get cold.

просу́нуть (-ну) *pf* (*impf* просо́вывать) push, thrust.

просу́шивать *impf*, просу-ши́ть (-шу́, -шишь) *pf* dry out;

~ся (get) dry.

просуществова́ть *pf* exist; endure.

просчёт error. просчита́ть-ся *pf*, просчи́тываться *impf* miscalculate.

просы́пать (-плю) *pf*, сыпа́ть[1] *impf* spill; ~ся get spilt.

просыпа́ть[2] *impf of* проспа́ть. просыпа́ться *impf of* просну́ться. просыха́ть *impf of* просо́хнуть.

про́сьба request.

прота́лкивать *impf of* протолкну́ть(ся. прота́пливать *impf of* протопи́ть.

прота́птывать *impf of* протопта́ть.

прота́скивать *impf*, протащи́ть (-щу́, -щишь) *pf* drag, push (through).

проте́з artificial limb, prosthesis; зубно́й ~ denture.

протеи́н protein.

протека́ть *impf of* проте́чь.

проте́кция patronage.

протере́ть (-тру́, -трёшь; -тёр) *pf* (*impf* протира́ть) wipe (over); wear (through).

проте́ст protest. протеста́нт, ~ка Protestant. протестова́ть *impf* & *pf* protest.

проте́чь (-ечёт, -тёк, -ла́) *pf* (*impf* протека́ть) flow; leak; seep; pass; take its course.

про́тив *prep*+*gen* against; opposite; contrary to, as against.

проти́вень (-вня) *m* baking-tray; meat-pan.

проти́виться (-влюсь) *impf* (*pf* вос~) +*dat* oppose; resist.

проти́вник opponent; the enemy. проти́вный[1] opposite; contrary. проти́вный[2] nasty, disgusting.

противо- *in comb* anti-, contra-,

counter-. **противове́с** counterbalance. **~возду́шный** anti-aircraft. **~га́з** gas-mask. **~де́йствие** opposition. **~де́йствовать** *impf* +*dat* oppose, counteract. **~есте́ственный** unnatural. **~зако́нный** illegal. **~зача́точный** contraceptive. **~поло́жность** opposite; opposition, contrast. **~поло́жный** opposite; contrary. **~поста́вить** (**-влю**) *pf*, **~поставля́ть** *impf* oppose; contrast. **~речи́вый** contradictory; conflicting. **~ре́чие** contradiction. **~ре́чить** (**-чу**) *impf* +*dat* contradict. **~сто́ять** (**-ою**) *impf* +*dat* resist, withstand. **~та́нковый** anti-tank. **~я́дие** antidote.

**протира́ть** *impf of* **протере́ть**
**проти́скивать** *impf*, **проти́снуть** (**-ну**) *pf* force, squeeze (through, in).
**проткну́ть** (**-ну́, -нёшь**) *pf* (*impf* **протыка́ть**) pierce.
**протоко́л** minutes; report; protocol.
**протолкну́ть** (**-ну́, -нёшь**) *pf* (*impf* **прота́лкивать**) push through; **~ся** push one's way through.
**прото́н** proton.
**протопи́ть** (**-плю́, -пишь**) *pf* (*impf* **прота́пливать**) heat (thoroughly).
**протопта́ть** (**-пчу́, -пчешь**) *pf* (*impf* **прота́птывать**) tread; wear out.
**проторённый** beaten, well-trodden.
**прототи́п** prototype.
**прото́чный** flowing, running.
**про|тра́ливать** *pf.* **протру́** *etc.: see* **протере́ть. про|труби́ть** (**-блю**) *pf.*
**протрезви́ться** (**-влю́сь**) *pf,*

**протрезвля́ться** *impf* sober up.
**протуха́ть** *impf*, **проту́хнуть** (**-нет, -ух**) *pf* become rotten; go bad.
**протыка́ть** *impf of* **проткну́ть**
**протя́гивать** *impf*, **протяну́ть** (**-ну́, -нешь**) *pf* stretch; extend; hold out; reach out; extend; last. **~ся** protя-же́ние extent, stretch; period.
**протя́жный** long-drawn-out; drawling.
**проу́чивать** *impf*, **проучи́ть** (**-чу́, -чишь**) *pf* study; teach a lesson.
**профа́н** ignoramus.
**профана́ция** profanation.
**профессиона́л** professional. **профессиона́льный** professional; occupational. **профе́ссия** profession. **профе́ссор** (*pl* **-а́**) professor.
**профила́ктика** prophylaxis; preventive measures.
**про́филь** *m* profile; type.
**про|фильтрова́ть** *pf.*
**профсою́з** trade-union.
**проха́живаться** *impf of* **пройти́сь**
**прохво́ст** scoundrel.
**прохла́да** coolness. **прохлади́тельный** refreshing, cooling. **прохла́дный** cool, chilly.
**прохо́д** passage; gangway, aisle; duct. **проходи́мец** (**-мца**) rogue. **проходи́мый** passable. **проходи́ть** (**-ожу́, -о́дишь**) *impf of* **пройти́. проходно́й** entrance; communicating. **проходя́щий** passing. **прохо́жий** passing, in transit; *sb* passer-by.
**процвета́ние** prosperity. **процвета́ть** *impf* prosper, flourish.

**процеди́ть** (-ежу́, -е́дишь) *pf* (*impf* **проце́живать**) filter, strain.

**процеду́ра** procedure; (*usu in pl*) treatment.

**проце́живать** *pf of* **процеди́ть**

**проце́нт** percentage; per cent; interest.

**проце́сс** process; trial; legal proceedings. **проце́ссия** procession.

**про|цити́ровать** *pf*.

**прочёска** screening; combing.

**проче́сть** (-чту́, -чтёшь; -чёл, -чла́) *pf of* **чита́ть**

**про́чий** other.

**прочи́стить** (-и́щу) *pf* (*impf* **прочища́ть**) clean; clear.

**про|чита́ть** *pf*, **прочи́тывать** *impf* read (through).

**прочища́ть** *impf of* **прочи́стить**

**про́чность** firmness, stability, durability. **про́чный** (-чен, -чна́, -о) firm, sound, solid; durable.

**прочте́ние** reading. **прочту́** *etc.*: *see* **проче́сть**

**прочу́вствовать** *pf* feel deeply; experience, go through.

**прочь** *adv* away, off; averse to.

**проше́дший** past; last. **прошёл** *etc.*: *see* **пройти́**

**проше́ние** application, petition.

**прошепта́ть** (-пчу́, -пчешь) *pf* whisper.

**проше́ствие**: **по проше́ствии** +*gen* after.

**прошива́ть** *impf*, **проши́ть** (-шью́, -шьёшь) *pf* sew, stitch.

**прошлого́дний** last year's. **про́шл|ый** past; last; ~**ое** *sb* the past.

**про|шнурова́ть** *pf*. **прошью́** *etc.*: *see* **проши́ть**

**проща́й(те)** goodbye. **проща́льный** parting; farewell. **проща́ние** farewell; parting. **проща́ть(ся** *impf of* **прости́ть(ся**

**про́ще** simpler, plainer. **проще́ние** forgiveness, pardon.

**прощу́пать** *pf*, **прощу́пывать** *impf* feel out.

**про|экзаменова́ть** *pf*.

**проявитель** *m* developer. **прояви́ть** (-влю́, -вишь) *pf*, **проявля́ть** *impf* show, display; develop; ~**ся** reveal itself. **проявле́ние** display; manifestation; developing.

**проясни́ться** *pf*, **проясня́ться** (*of sky*) *impf* clear, clear up.

**пруд** (-а́, *loc* -у́) pond. **пруди́ть** (-ужу́, -у́дишь) *impf* (*pf* **за~**) dam.

**пружи́на** spring. **пружи́нистый** springy. **пружи́нный** spring.

**пру́сский** Prussian.

**прут** (-а *or* -а́; *pl* -тья) twig.

**пры́гать** *impf*, **пры́гнуть** (-ну) *pf* jump, leap; bounce; ~ **с шесто́м** pole-vault. **прыгу́н** (-а́), **прыгу́нья** (*gen pl* -ний) jumper. **прыжо́к** (-жка́) jump; leap; прыжки́ jumping; прыжки́ в во́ду diving; ~ **в высоту́** high jump; ~ **в длину́** long jump.

**пры́скать** *impf*, **пры́снуть** (-ну) *pf* spurt; sprinkle; burst out laughing.

**прыть** speed; energy.

**прыщ** (-а́), **прыщик** pimple.

**пряди́льный** spinning. **пряди́льня** (*gen pl* -лен) spinning) mill. **пряди́льщик** spinner. **пряду́** *etc.*: *see* **прясть**. **прядь** lock; strand. **пря́жа** yarn, thread.

**пря́жка** buckle, clasp.

**пря́лка** distaff; spinning-wheel.

**прям|а́я** *sb* straight line. **~о́** *adv* straight; straight on; frankly; really. **прямоду́шие** directness, straightforwardness. **~ду́шный** direct, straightforward. **прям|о́й** (-я́м, -а́, -о) straight; upright, erect; through; direct; straightforward; real. **прямолине́йный** rectilinear; straightforward. **прямоуго́льник** rectangle. **прямоуго́льный** rectangular.

**пря́ник** spice cake. **пря́ность** spice. **пря́ный** spicy; heady.

**пряс|ть** (-яду́, -ядёшь; -ял, -я́ла, -о) *impf* (*pf* c~) spin.

**пря́т|ать** (-я́чу) *impf* (*pf* c~) hide; **~ся** hide. **пря́тки** (-ток) *pl* hide-and-seek.

**пса** *etc.*: *see* **пёс**

**псало́м** (-лма́) psalm. **псалты́рь** Psalter.

**псевдони́м** pseudonym.

**псих** madman, lunatic. **психиатри́я** psychiatry. **пси́хика** psyche; psychology. **психи́ческий** mental, psychical. **психоана́лиз** psychoanalysis. **психо́з** psychosis. **психо́лог** psychologist. **психологи́ческий** psychological. **психоло́гия** psychology. **психопа́т** psychopath. **психопати́ческий** psychopathic. **психосомати́ческий** psychosomatic. **психотерапе́вт** psychotherapist. **психотерапи́я** psychotherapy. **психоти́ческий** psychotic.

**птен|е́ц** (-нца́) nestling; fledgling. **пти́ца** bird. **птицефе́рма** poultry-farm. **пти́чий** bird, bird's. **пти́чка** bird; tick.

**пу́блика** public; audience. **публика́ция** publication; notice, advertisement. **публикова́ть** *impf* (*pf* o~) publish. **публици́стика** writing on current affairs. **публи́чность** publicity. **публи́чный** public; **~ дом** brothel.

**пу́гало** scarecrow. **пуга́ть** *impf* (*pf* ис~, на~) frighten, scare; **~ся** (+*gen*) be frightened (of). **пуга́ч** (-а́) toy pistol. **пугли́вый** fearful.

**пу́говица** button.

**пуд** (*pl* -ы́) pood (= 16.38 kg). **пудово́й**, **пудо́вый** one pood in weight.

**пу́дель** *m* poodle.

**пу́динг** blancmange.

**пу́дра** powder. **пу́дреница** powder compact. **пу́дреный** powdered. **пу́дриться** *impf* (*pf* на~) powder one's face.

**пуза́тый** pot-bellied.

**пузыр|ёк** (-рька́) vial; bubble. **пузы́рь** (-я́) *m* bubble; blister; bladder.

**пук** (*pl* -и́) bunch, bundle; tuft. **пу́к|ать** *impf*, **~нуть** *pf* fart.

**пулемёт** machine-gun. **пулемётчик** machine-gunner. **пуленепробива́емый** bullet-proof.

**пульвериза́тор** atomizer; spray.

**пульс** pulse. **пульса́р** pulsar. **пульси́ровать** *impf* pulsate.

**пульт** desk, stand; control panel.

**пу́ля** bullet.

**пункт** point; post; item. **пункти́р** dotted line. **пункти́рный** dotted, broken. **пунктуа́льный** punctual. **пунктуа́ция** punctuation.

**пунцо́вый** crimson.

**пуп** (-а́) navel. **пупови́на** umbilical cord. **пупо́к** (-пка́) navel; gizzard.

**пурга́** blizzard.

**пурита́нин** (pl -та́не, -та́н), **-а́нка** Puritan.

**пу́рпур** purple, crimson. **пурпу́р|ный**, **~овый** purple.

**пуск** starting (up). **пуска́й** see **пусть**. **пуска́ть(ся** impf of **пусти́ть(ся. пусково́й** starting.

**пусте́ть** (-е́ет) impf (pf o~) empty; become deserted.

**пусти́ть** (пущу́, пу́стишь) pf (impf **пуска́ть**) let go; let in; let; start; send; set in motion; throw; put forth; **~ся** set out; start.

**пустова́ть** impf be or stand empty. **пусто́й** (-ст, -а́, -о) empty; uninhabited; idle; shallow. **пустота́** (pl -ы) emptiness; void; vacuum; futility. **пустоте́лый** hollow.

**пусты́нный** uninhabited; deserted; desert. **пусты́ня** desert. **пусты́рь** (-я́) m waste land; vacant plot.

**пусты́шка** blank; hollow object; dummy.

**пусть, пуска́й** partl let; all right; though, even if.

**пустя́к** (-а́) trifle. **пустяко́вый** trivial.

**пу́таница** muddle, confusion. **пу́таный** muddled, confused. **пу́тать** impf (pf за~, пере~, с~) tangle; confuse; mix up; **~ся** get confused or mixed up.

**путёвка** pass; place on a group tour. **путеводи́тель** m guide, guide-book. **путево́й** travelling; road. **путём** prep+gen by means of. **путеше́ственник** traveller. **путеше́ствие** journey; voyage. **путеше́ствовать** impf travel; voyage.

**пу́ты** (пут) pl shackles.

**путь** (-и́, instr -ём, prep -и́) way; track; path; course; journey; voyage; means; **в пути́** en route, on one's way.

**пух** (loc -ý) down; fluff.

**пу́хлый** (-хл, -а́, -о) plump. **пу́хнуть** (-ну; пух) impf (pf вс~, о~) swell.

**пухови́к** (-а́) feather-bed. **пухо́вка** powder-puff. **пухо́вый** downy.

**пучи́на** abyss; the deep.

**пучо́к** (-чка́) bunch, bundle.

**пу́шечный** gun, cannon.

**пуши́нка** bit of fluff. **пуши́стый** fluffy.

**пу́шка** gun, cannon.

**пушни́на** furs, pelts. **пушно́й** fur; fur-bearing.

**пу́ще** adv more; **~ всего́** most of all.

**пущу́** etc.: see **пусти́ть**

**пчела́** (pl -ёлы) bee. **пчели́ный** bee, bees'. **пчелово́д** bee-keeper. **пче́льник** apiary.

**пшени́ца** wheat. **пшени́чный** wheat(en).

**пшённый** millet. **пшено́** millet.

**пыл** (loc -ý) heat, ardour. **пыла́ть** impf blaze; burn.

**пылесо́с** vacuum cleaner. **пылесо́сить** impf (pf про~) vacuum(-clean).

**пыли́нка** speck of dust. **пыли́ть** impf (pf за~, на~) raise a dust; cover with dust; **~ся** get dusty.

**пы́лкий** ardent; fervent.

**пыль** (loc -и́) dust. **пы́льный** (-лен, -льна́, -о) dusty. **пыльца́** pollen.

**пыре́й** couch grass.

**пырну́ть** (-ну́, -нёшь) pf jab.

**пыта́ть** impf torture. **пыта́ться** impf (pf по~) try. **пы́тка** torture, torment. **пытли́вый** inquisitive.

пыхте́ть (-хчу́) *impf* puff, pant.

пы́шка bun.

пы́шность splendour. пы́шный (-шен, шна́, шно) splendid; lush.

пьедеста́л pedestal.

пье́са play; piece.

пью *etc.: see* пить

пьяне́ть (-е́ю) *impf* (*pf* о~) get drunk. пьяни́ть *impf* (*pf* о~) intoxicate, make drunk. пья́ница *m & f* drunkard. пья́нство drunkenness. пья́нствовать *impf* drink heavily. пья́ный drunk.

пюпи́тр lectern; stand.

пюре́ *neut indecl* purée.

пядь (*gen pl* -е́й) span; ни пя́ди not an inch.

пя́льцы (-лец) *pl* embroidery frame.

пята́ (*pl* -ы, -а́м) heel.

пята́к (-а́), пятачо́к (-чка́) five-copeck piece. пятёрка five; figure 5; No. 5; fiver (5-rouble note).

пяти- *in comb* five; penta-. пятибо́рье pentathlon. ~десятиле́тие fifty years; fiftieth anniversary, birthday. П~деся́тница Pentecost. ~деся́тый fiftieth. ~деся́тые го́ды the fifties. ~коне́чный five-pointed. ~ле́тие five years; fifth anniversary. ~ле́тка five-year plan. ~со́тый five-hundredth. ~уго́льник pentagon. ~уго́льный pentagonal.

пя́титься (пя́чусь) *impf* (*pf* по~) move backwards; back.

пя́тка heel.

пятна́дцатый fifteenth. пятна́дцать fifteen.

пятна́ть *impf* (*pf* за~) spot, stain. пятна́шки (-шек) *pl* tag. пятни́стый spotted.

пя́тница Friday.

пятно́ (*pl* -а, -тен) stain; spot; blot; роди́мое ~ birth-mark.

пя́тый fifth. пять (-и́, *instr* -ью) five. пятьдеся́т (-и́десяти, *instr* -ью́десятью) fifty. пятьсо́т (-тисо́т, -тиста́м) five hundred. пя́тью *adv* five times.

# Р

раб (-а́), раба́ slave. рабовладе́лец (-льца) slave-owner. раболе́пие servility. раболе́пный servile. раболе́пствовать cringe, fawn.

рабо́та work; job; functioning. рабо́тать *impf* work; function; be open; ~ над+*instr* work on. рабо́тник, -ица worker. работоспосо́бность capacity for work, efficiency. работоспосо́бный able-bodied, hardworking. рабо́тящий hardworking. рабо́чий *sb* worker. рабо́чий worker's; working; ~ая си́ла manpower.

ра́бский slave; servile. ра́бство slavery. рабы́ня female slave.

равви́н rabbi.

ра́венство equality. равне́ние alignment. равни́на plain. равно́ *adv* alike; equally; ~ как well as. равно́ *predic: see* ра́вный

равно- *in comb* equi-, iso-. равнобе́дренный isosceles. ~ве́сие equilibrium; balance. ~де́нствие equinox. ~ду́шие indifference. ~ду́шный indifferent. ~ме́рный even; uniform. ~пра́вие equality of rights. ~пра́вный having equal rights. ~си́льный of equal strength; equal, equivalent, tantamount. ~сторо́нний equilateral. ~це́нный of equal value; equivalent.

ра́вный (-вен, -вна́) equal. равно́ predic make(s), equals; всё ~о (it is) all the same. равня́ть impf (pf c~) make even; treat equally; +c+instr compare with, treat as equal to; ~ся compete, compare; be equal; be tantamount.

рад (-а, -о) predic glad.

рада́р radar.

ра́ди prep+gen for the sake of.

радиа́тор radiator. радиа́ция radiation.

ра́дий radium.

радика́льный radical.

ра́дио neut indecl radio.

ра́дио- in comb radio-; radioactive. радиоакти́вный radioactive. ~веща́ние broadcasting. ~волна́ radio-wave. ~гра́мма radio-telegram. ра́диолог radiologist. ~ло́гия radiology. ~лока́тор radar (set). ~люби́тель m radio amateur, ham. ~мая́к (-а́) radio beacon. ~переда́тчик radio transmitter. ~переда́ча broadcast. ~приёмник radio (set). ~связь radio communication. ~слу́шатель m listener. ~ста́нция radio station. ~электро́ника radio-electronics.

радио́ла radiogram.

ради́ровать impf & pf radio.

ради́ст radio operator.

ра́диус radius.

ра́довать impf (pf об~, по~) gladden, make happy; ~ся be glad, rejoice. ра́достный joyful, glad. ра́дость gladness, joy.

ра́дуга rainbow. ра́дужн|ый iridescent; cheerful; ~ая обо-ло́чка iris.

раду́шие cordiality. раду́шный cordial.

ражу́ etc.: see рази́ть

раз (pl -ы́, раз) time, occasion; one; ещё ~ (once) again; как ~ just, exactly; не ~ more than once; ни ~у not once. раз adv once, one day. раз conj if; since.

разба́вить (-влю) pf, разбавля́ть pf dilute.

разба́заривать impf, разбаза́рить pf squander.

разба́лтывать(ся impf of разболта́ть(ся

разбе́г running start. разбега́ться impf, разбежа́ться (-егу́сь) pf take a run, run up; scatter.

разберу́ etc.: see разобра́ть

разбива́ть(ся impf of разби́ть(ся. разби́вка laying out; spacing (out).

разбинтова́ть pf, разбинто́вывать impf unbandage.

разбира́тельство investigation. разбира́ть impf of разобра́ть; ~ся impf of разобра́ться

разби́ть (-зобью́, -зобьёшь) pf (impf разбива́ть) break; smash; divide (up); damage; defeat; mark out; space (out); ~ся break, get broken; hurt o.s. разби́тый broken; jaded. разбога́теть (-е́ю) pf.

разбо́й robbery. разбо́йник robber. разбо́йничий robber.

разболе́ться[1] (-ли́тся) pf begin to ache badly.

разболе́ться[2] (-е́юсь) pf become ill.

разболта́ть[1] pf (impf разба́лтывать) divulge, give away.

разболта́ть[2] pf (impf раз-

**ба́лтывать**) shake up; loosen; **~ся** work loose; get out of hand.

**разбомби́ть** (-блю́) *pf* bomb, destroy by bombing.

**разбо́р** analysis; critique; discrimination; investigation. **разбо́рка** sorting out; dismantling. **разбо́рный** collapsible. **разбо́рчивый** legible; discriminating.

**разбра́сывать** *impf of* **разброса́ть**

**разбреда́ться** *impf*, **разбрести́сь** (-еде́тся; -ёлся, -ла́сь) *pf* disperse; straggle. **разбро́д** disorder.

**разбро́санный** scattered; disconnected; incoherent. **разброса́ть** (*pf* (*impf* **разбра́сывать**) throw about; scatter.

**раз|буди́ть** (-ужу́, -у́дишь) *pf*.

**разбуха́ть** *impf*, **разбу́хнуть** (-нет; -бу́х) *pf* swell.

**разбушева́ться** (-шу́юсь) *pf* fly into a rage; blow up; rage.

**развал** breakdown, collapse. **разва́ливать** *impf*, **развали́ть** (-лю́, -лишь) *pf* pull down; mess up; **~ся** collapse; go to pieces; tumble down; sprawl. **разва́лина** ruin; wreck.

**ра́зве** *partl* really?; **~ (то́лько)**, **~ (что)** except that, only.

**развева́ться** *impf* fly, flutter.

**разве́дать** *pf* (*impf* **разве́дывать**) find out; reconnoitre.

**разведе́ние** breeding; cultivation.

**разведённ|ый** divorced; **~ый**, **~ая** *sb* divorcee.

**разве́дка** intelligence (service); reconnaissance; prospecting. **разве́дочный** prospecting, exploratory.

**разве́ду** *etc.*: *see* **развести́**

**разве́дчик** intelligence officer; scout; prospector. **разве́дывать** *impf of* **разве́дать**

**развезти́** (-зу́, -зёшь; -ёз, -ла́) *pf* (*impf* **развози́ть**) convey; transport; deliver.

**разве́ивать(ся** *impf of* **разве́ять(ся. развёл** *etc.*: *see* **развести́**

**развенча́ть** *pf*, **развенчи́вать** *impf* dethrone; debunk.

**развёрнутый** extensive, all-out; detailed. **разверну́ть** (-ну́, -нёшь) *pf* (*impf* **развёртывать**, **развора́чивать**) unfold, unwrap; unroll; unfurl; deploy; expand; develop; turn; scan; display; **~ся** unfold, unroll, come unwrapped; deploy; develop; spread; turn.

**развёрстка** allotment, apportionment.

**развёртывать(ся** *impf of* **разверну́ть(ся**

**раз|весели́ть** *pf* cheer up, amuse; **~ся** cheer up.

**разве́сить**[1] (-е́шу) *pf* (*impf* **разве́шивать**) spread; hang (out).

**разве́сить**[2] (-е́шу) *pf* (*impf* **разве́шивать**) weigh out. **разве́ска** weighing. **развесно́й** sold by weight.

**развести́** (-еду́, -едёшь; -ёл, -а́) *pf* (*impf* **разводи́ть**) take; separate; divorce; dilute; dissolve; start; breed; cultivate; **~сь** get divorced; breed, multiply.

**разветви́ться** (-ви́тся) *pf*, **разветвля́ться** *impf* branch; fork. **разветвле́ние** branching, forking; branch; fork.

**разве́шать** *pf*, **разве́шивать** *impf* hang

**развешивать** *impf of* **развесить, развешать. развешу** *etc.: see* **развесить**

**развеять** (-ею) *pf* (*impf* **развевать**) scatter, disperse; dispel; **~ся** disperse; be dispelled.

**развивать(ся** *impf of* **развить(ся**

**развилка** fork.

**развинтить** (-нчу) *pf*, **развинчивать** *impf* unscrew.

**развитие** development. **развитой** (развит, -á, -о) developed; mature. **развить** (-зовью; -зовьёшь; -ил, -á, -о) *pf* (*impf* **развивать**) develop; unwind; **~ся** develop.

**развлекать** (-еку, -ечёшь; -ёк, -ла) *pf* entertain, amuse; **~ся** have a good time; amuse o.s. **развлечение** entertainment, amusement.

**развод** divorce. **разводить(ся** (-ожу(сь, -одишь(ся *impf of* **развести(сь. разводка** separation. **разводной:** **~ ключ** adjustable spanner; **~ мост** drawbridge.

**развозить** (-ожу, -озишь) *impf of* **развезти**

**разволновать(ся** *pf* get excited, be agitated.

**разворачивать(ся** *impf of* **развернуть(ся**

**разворовать** *pf*, **разворовывать** *impf* loot; steal.

**разворот** U-turn; turn; development.

**разврат** depravity, corruption. **развратить** (-ащу) *pf*. **развращать** *impf* corrupt; deprave. **развратник** lead a depraved life. **развратный** (-тен, -тна) debauched, corrupt. **развращённый** (-ён, -á) corrupt.

**развязать** (-яжу, -яжешь) *pf*, **развязывать** *impf* untie; unleash; **~ся** come untied; **~ся** c+*instr* rid o.s. of. **развязка** dénouement; outcome. **развязный** overfamiliar.

**разгадать** *pf*, **разгадывать** *impf* solve, guess, interpret. **разгадка** solution.

**разгар** height, climax.

**разгибать(ся** *impf of* **разогнуть(ся**

**разглагольствовать** *impf* hold forth.

**разгладить** (-áжу) *pf*, **разглаживать** *impf* smooth out; iron (out).

**разгласить** (-ашу) *pf*, **разглашать** *impf* divulge; +о+*prep* trumpet. **разглашение** disclosure.

**разглядеть** (-яжу) *pf*, **разглядывать** *impf* make out, discern.

**разгневать** *pf* anger. **раз|гневаться** *pf*.

**разговаривать** *impf* talk, converse. **разговор** conversation. **разговорник** phrase-book. **разговорный** colloquial. **разговорчивый** talkative.

**разгон** dispersal; running start; distance. **разгонять(ся** *impf of* **разогнать(ся**

**разгораживать** *impf of* **разгородить(ся**

**разгораться** *impf*, **разгореться** (-рюсь) *pf* flare up.

**разгородить** (-ожу, -одишь) *pf* (*impf* **разгораживать**) partition off.

**раз|горячить(ся** (-чу(сь) *pf*.

**разграбить** (-блю) *pf* plunder, loot. **разграбление** plunder, looting.

**разграничение** demarcation; differentiation. **разграничи-**

чива́ть *impf*, разграни́чить (-чу) *pf* delimit; differentiate.

разгреба́ть *impf*, разгрести́ (-ебу́, -ебёшь; -ёб, -ла́) *pf* rake *or* shovel (away).

разгро́м crushing defeat; devastation; havoc. разгроми́ть (-млю́) *pf* rout, defeat.

разгружа́ть *impf*, разгрузи́ть (-ужу́, -у́зи́шь) *pf* unload; relieve; ~ся unload; be relieved. разгру́зка unloading; relief.

разгрыза́ть *impf*, раз|гры́зть (-зу́, -зёшь; -ы́з) *pf* crack.

разгу́л revelry; outburst. разгу́ливать *pf* stroll about. разгу́ливаться *impf*, разгуля́ться *pf* spread o.s.; become wide awake; clear up. разгу́льный wild, rakish.

раздава́ть(ся (-даю́(сь, -даёшь(ся) *impf of* разда́ть(ся

раз|дави́ть (-влю́, -вишь) *pf*. разда́вливать *impf* crush; run over.

разда́ть (-а́м, -а́шь, -а́ст, -ади́м; ро́з- *or* разда́л, -а́, -о) *pf* (*impf* раздава́ть) distribute, give out; ~ся be heard; resound; ring out; make way; expand; put on weight. разда́ча distribution. раздаю́ *etc.: see* раздава́ть

раздва́ивать(ся *impf of* раздво́ить(ся

раздвига́ть *impf*, раздви́нуть (-ну) *pf* move apart; ~ся move apart. раздвижно́й expanding; sliding.

раздвое́ние division; split; ~ ли́чности split personality. раздво́енный forked; cloven; split. раздво́ить *pf* (*impf* раздва́ивать) divide into two; bisect; ~ся fork; split.

раздева́лка cloakroom. раз

дева́ть(ся *impf of* разде́ть(ся

разде́л division; section.

разде́латься *pf* +*c*+*instr* finish with; settle accounts with.

разделе́ние division. раздели́мый divisible. раз|дели́ть (-лю́, -лишь) *pf*, разделя́ть *impf* divide; separate; share; ~ся divide; be divided; be divisible; separate. разде́льный separate.

разде́ну *etc.: see* разде́ть. раздеру́ *etc.: see* разодра́ть

разде́ть (-де́ну) *pf* (*impf* раздева́ть) undress; ~ся undress; take off one's coat.

раздира́ть *impf of* разодра́ть

раздобыва́ть *impf*, раздобы́ть (-бу́ду) *pf* get, get hold of.

раздо́лье expanse; liberty. раздо́льный free.

раздо́р discord.

раздоса́довать *pf* vex.

раздража́ть *impf*, раздражи́ть (-жу́) *pf* irritate; annoy; ~ся get annoyed. раздраже́ние irritation. раздражи́тельный irritable.

раз|дроби́ть (-блю́) *pf*, раздробля́ть *impf* break; smash to pieces.

раздува́ть(ся *impf of* разду́ть(ся

разду́мать *pf*, разду́мывать *impf* change one's mind; ponder. разду́мье meditation; thought.

разду́ть (-у́ю) *pf* (*impf* раздува́ть) blow; fan; exaggerate; whip up; swell; ~ся swell.

разжа́лобить (-блю) *pf* move (to pity).

разжа́ловать *pf* demote.

разжа́ть (-зожму́, -мёшь) *pf*

(*impf* **разжима́ть**) unclasp, open; release.

**разжева́ть** (-жую́, -жуёшь) *pf*, **разжёвывать** *impf* chew.

**разже́чь** (-зожгу́, -зожжёшь; -жёг, -зожгла́) *pf*, **разжига́ть** *impf* kindle; rouse.

**разжима́ть** *impf of* **разжа́ть**

**раз|жире́ть** (-е́ю) *pf*.

**рази́нуть** (-ну) *pf* (*impf* **разева́ть**) open; **~ рот** gape. **рази́ня** *m* & *f* scatter-brain.

**рази́тельный** striking. **рази́ть** (ражу́) *impf* (*pf* **по~**) strike.

**разлага́ть(ся** *impf of* **разложи́ть(ся**

**разла́д** discord; disorder. **разла́мывать(ся** *impf of* **разлома́ть(ся, разломи́ть(ся.**

**разлёгся** *etc.: see* **разле́чься**

**разлеза́ться** *impf*, **разле́зться** (-зется; -ле́зся) *pf* come to pieces; fall apart.

**разлета́ться** *impf*, **разлете́ться** (-лечу́сь) *pf* fly away; scatter; shatter; rush.

**разле́чься** (-ля́гусь; -лёгся, -гла́сь) *pf* stretch out.

**разли́в** bottling; flood; overflow. **разлива́ть** *impf*, **разли́ть** (-золью́, -зольёшь; -ли́л, -а́, -о) *pf* pour out; spill; flood (with); **~ся** spill; overflow; spread. **разливно́й** draught.

**различа́ть** *impf*, **различи́ть** (-чу́) *pf* distinguish; discern; **~ся** differ. **разли́чие** distinction; difference. **различи́тельный** distinctive, distinguishing. **разли́чный** different.

**разложе́ние** decomposition; decay; disintegration. **разложи́ть** (-жу́, -жишь) *pf* (*impf* **разлага́ть, раскла́дывать**) put away; spread (out); distribute; break down; decom-

pose; resolve; corrupt; **~ся** decompose; become demoralized; be corrupted; disintegrate, go to pieces.

**разло́м** breaking; break. **разлома́ть, разломи́ть** (-млю́, -мишь) *pf* (*impf* **разла́мывать**) break to pieces; pull down; **~ся** break to pieces.

**разлу́ка** separation. **разлуча́ть** *impf*, **разлучи́ть** (-чу́) *pf* separate, part; **~ся** separate, part.

**разлюби́ть** (-блю́, -бишь) *pf* stop loving or liking.

**разля́гусь** *etc.: see* **разле́чься**

**разма́зать** (-а́жу) *pf*, **разма́зывать** *impf* spread, smear.

**разма́лывать** *impf of* **размоло́ть**

**разма́тывать** *impf of* **размота́ть**

**разма́х** sweep; swing; span; scope. **разма́хивать** *impf* +*instr* swing; brandish. **разма́хиваться** *impf*, **размахну́ться** (-ну́сь, -нёшься) *pf* swing one's arm. **разма́шистый** sweeping.

**размежева́ние** demarcation, delimitation. **размежева́ть** (-жу́ю) *pf*, **размежёвывать** *impf* delimit.

**размёл** *etc.: see* **размести́**

**размельча́ть** *impf*, **раз|мельчи́ть** *pf* crush, pulverize.

**размелю́** *etc.: see* **размоло́ть**

**разме́н** exchange. **разме́нивать** *impf*, **разменя́ть** *pf* change; **~ся** +*instr* exchange; dissipate. **разме́нная моне́та** (small) change.

**разме́р** size; measurement; amount; scale; extent; *pl* proportions. **разме́ренный** measured. **разме́рить** *pf*, **размеря́ть** *impf* measure.

**размести́** (-ету́, -ете́шь; -мёл, -а́) pf (impf **размета́ть**) sweep clear; sweep away.

**размести́ть** (-ещу́) pf (impf **размеща́ть**) place, accommodate; distribute; **~ся** take one's seat.

**размета́ть** impf of **размести́**

**разме́тить** (-е́чу) pf, **размеча́ть** impf mark.

**размеша́ть** pf, **разме́шивать** impf stir (in).

**размеща́ть(ся** impf of **размести́ть(ся. размеще́ние** placing; accommodation; distribution. **размещу́** etc.: see **размести́ть**

**размина́ть(ся** impf of **размя́ть(ся**

**разми́нка** limbering up.

**размину́ться** (-ну́сь, -нёшься) pf pass; +c+instr pass; miss.

**размножа́ть** impf, **размно́жить** (-жу) pf multiply, duplicate; breed; **~ся** multiply, breed.

**размозжи́ть** (-жу́) pf smash.

**размо́лвка** tiff.

**размоло́ть** (-мелю́, -ме́лешь) pf (impf **разма́лывать**) grind.

**размора́живать** impf, **разморо́зить** (-о́жу) pf unfreeze, defrost; **~ся** unfreeze; defrost.

**размота́ть** pf (impf **разма́тывать**) unwind.

**размыва́ть** impf, **размы́ть** (-о́ет) pf wash away; erode.

**размыка́ть** pf of **размокну́ть**

**размышле́ние** reflection; meditation. **размышля́ть** impf reflect, ponder.

**размягча́ть** impf, **размягчи́ть** (-чу́) pf soften; **~ся** soften.

**размяка́ть** impf, **размя́к-**

**нуть** (-ну; -мя́к) pf soften.

**разммя́ть** (-зомну́, -зомнёшь) pf (impf also **размина́ть**) knead; mash; **~ся** stretch one's legs; limber up.

**разна́шивать** impf of **разноси́ть**

**разнести́** (-су́, -сёшь; -ёс, -ла́) pf (impf **разноси́ть**) carry; deliver; spread; note down; smash; scold; scatter; impers make puffy, swell.

**разнима́ть** impf of **разня́ть**

**ра́зниться** impf differ. **ра́зница** difference.

**разно-** in comb different, vari-, hetero-. **разнобо́й** lack of co-ordination; difference. **~ви́дность** variety. **~гла́сие** disagreement; discrepancy. **~обра́зие** variety, diversity. **~обра́зный** various, diverse. **~речи́вый** contradictory. **~ро́дный** heterogeneous. **~сторо́нний** many-sided; versatile. **~цве́тный** variegated. **~шёрстный** of different colours; ill-assorted.

**разноси́ть¹** (-ошу́, -о́сишь) pf (impf **разна́шивать**) wear in.

**разноси́ть²** (-ошу́, -о́сишь) impf of **разнести́. разно́ска** delivery.

**ра́зность** difference.

**разно́счик** pedlar.

**разношу́** etc.: see **разноси́ть**

**разну́зданный** unbridled.

**ра́зный** different; various; **~ое** sb various things.

**разню́хать** pf, **разню́хивать** impf smell out.

**разня́ть** (-ниму́, -ни́мешь; ро́з or разня́л, -а́, -о) pf (impf **разнима́ть**) take to pieces; separate.

**разоблача́ть** impf, **разо-блачи́ть** (-чу́) pf expose.

**разоблаче́ние** exposure.

**разобра́ть** (-зберу́, -рёшь; -а́л, -а́, -о) *pf* (*impf* **разбира́ть**) take to pieces; buy up; sort out; investigate; analyse; understand; **~ся** sort things out; +*в+prep* investigate, look into; understand.

**разобща́ть** *impf*, **разобщи́ть** (-щу́) *pf* separate; estrange, alienate.

**разобью́** *etc.: see* **разби́ть. разовью́** *etc.: see* **разви́ть.**

**ра́зовый** single.

**разогна́ть** (-згоню́, -о́нишь; -гна́л, -а́, -о) *pf* (*impf* **разгоня́ть**) scatter; disperse; dispel; drive fast; **~ся** gather speed.

**разогну́ть** (-ну́, -нёшь) *pf* (*impf* **разгиба́ть**) unbend, straighten; **~ся** straighten up.

**разогрева́ть** *impf*, **разогре́ть** (-е́ю) *pf* warm up.

**разоде́ть(ся** (-е́ну(сь) *pf* dress up.

**разодра́ть** (-здеру́, -рёшь; -а́л, -а́, -о) *pf* (*impf* **раздира́ть**) tear (up); lacerate.

**разожгу́** *etc.: see* **разже́чь. разожму́** *etc.: see* **разжа́ть разо|зли́ть** *pf*.

**разойти́сь** (-йду́сь, -йдёшься; -ошёлся, -ошла́сь) *pf* (*impf* **расходи́ться**) disperse; diverge; radiate; differ; conflict; part; be spent; be sold out.

**разолью́** *etc.: see* **разли́ть.**

**ра́зом** *adv* at once, at one go.

**разомкну́ть** (-ну́, -нёшь) *pf* (*impf* **размыка́ть**) open; break.

**разомну́** *etc.: see* **размя́ть.**

**разорва́ть** (-ву́, -вёшь; -а́л, -а́, -о) *pf* (*impf* **разрыва́ть**) tear; break (off); blow up; **~ся** tear; break; explode.

**разоре́ние** ruin; destruction.

**разори́тельный** ruinous; wasteful. **разори́ть** *pf* (*impf* **разоря́ть**) ruin; destroy; **~ся** ruin o.s.

**разоружа́ть** *impf*, **разоружи́ть** (-жу́) *pf* disarm; **~ся** disarm. **разоруже́ние** disarmament.

**разоря́ть(ся** *impf of* **разори́ть(ся**

**разосла́ть** (-ошлю́, -ошлёшь) *pf* (*impf* **рассыла́ть**) distribute, circulate.

**разостла́ть, расстели́ть** (-сстелю́, -те́лешь) *pf* (*impf* **расстила́ть**) spread (out); lay; **~ся** spread.

**разотру́** *etc.: see* **растере́ть. разочарова́ние** disappointment.

**разочарова́ть** *pf*, **разочаро́вывать** *impf* disappoint; **~ся** be disappointed.

**разочту́** *etc.: see* **расче́сть. разошёлся** *etc.: see* **разойти́сь. разошлю́** *etc.: see* **разосла́ть. разошью́** *etc.: see* **расши́ть**

**разраба́тывать** *impf*, **разрабо́тать** *pf* cultivate; work, exploit; work out; develop. **разрабо́тка** cultivation; exploitation; working out; mining; quarry.

**разража́ться** *impf*, **разрази́ться** (-ажу́сь) *pf* break out; burst out.

**разраста́ться** *impf*, **разрасти́сь** (-тётся; -ро́сся, -ла́сь) *pf* grow; spread.

**разрежённый** (-ён, -а́) rarefied.

**разре́з** cut; section; point of view. **разре́зать** (-е́жу) *pf*, **разреза́ть** *impf* cut; slit.

**разреша́ть** *impf*, **разреши́ть** (-шу́) *pf* (+*dat*) allow; solve;

settle; ~ся be allowed; be solved; be settled. разреше́ние permission; permit; solution; settlement. разреши́мый solvable.

разро́зненный uncoordinated; odd; incomplete.

разро́сся etc.: see разрасти́сь. разро́ю etc.: see разры́ть

разруба́ть impf, разруби́ть (-блю́, -бишь) pf cut; chop up.

разру́ха ruin, collapse. разруша́ть impf, разру́шить (-шу) pf destroy; demolish; ruin; ~ся go to ruin, collapse. разруше́ние destruction. разруши́тельный destructive.

разры́в break; gap; rupture; burst. разрыва́ть¹(ся impf of разорва́ть(ся

разрыва́ть² impf of разры́ть

разрывно́й explosive.

разрыда́ться pf burst into tears.

разры́ть (-ро́ю) pf (impf разрыва́ть) dig (up).

раз|рыхли́ть pf, разрыхля́ть impf loosen; hoe.

разря́д¹ category; class.

разря́д² discharge. разряди́ть (-яжу́, -яди́шь) pf (impf разряжа́ть) unload; discharge; space out; ~ся run down; clear, ease. разря́дка spacing (out); discharging; unloading; relieving.

разряжа́ть(ся impf of разряди́ть(ся

разубеди́ть (-ежу́) pf, разубежда́ть impf dissuade; ~ся change one's mind.

разуваться pf of разуться разуве́рить pf, разуверя́ть impf dissuade, undeceive; ~ся (в+prep) lose faith (in).

разузнава́ть (-наю́, -наёшь)

impf, разузна́ть pf (try to) find out.

разукра́сить (-а́шу) pf, разукра́шивать impf adorn, embellish.

ра́зум reason; intellect. разуме́ться (-е́ется) impf be understood; be meant; (само́ собо́й) разуме́ется of course; it goes without saying. разу́мный rational, intelligent; sensible; reasonable; wise.

разу́ться (-у́юсь) pf (impf разува́ться) take off one's shoes.

разу́чивать impf, разучи́ть (-чу́, -чишь) pf learn (up). разу́чиваться impf, разучи́ться (-чу́сь, -чишься) pf forget (how to).

разъеда́ть impf of разъе́сть

разъедини́ть pf, разъединя́ть impf separate; disconnect.

разъе́дусь etc.: see разъе́хаться

разъе́зд departure; siding (track); mounted patrol; pl travel; journeys. разъездно́й travelling. разъезжа́ть impf drive or ride about; travel; ~ся impf of разъе́хаться

разъе́сть (-е́ст, -едя́т; -е́л) pf (impf разъеда́ть) eat away; corrode.

разъе́хаться (-е́дусь) pf (impf разъезжа́ться) depart; separate; pass (one another); miss (one another).

разъярённый (-ён, -а́) furious. разъяри́ть pf, разъяря́ть impf infuriate; ~ся get furious.

разъясне́ние explanation; interpretation. разъясни́тельный explanatory.

разъясни́ть pf, разъясня́ть impf explain; interpret; ~ся

become clear, be cleared up.

**разыгра́ть** pf, **разы́грывать** impf perform; draw; raffle; play a trick on; **~ся** get up; run high.

**разыска́ть** (-ыщу́, -ы́щешь) pf find. **разы́скивать** impf search for.

**рай** (loc -ю́) paradise; garden of Eden.

**райко́м** district committee.

**райо́н** region. **райо́нный** district.

**ра́йский** heavenly.

**рак** crayfish; cancer; Cancer.

**раке́та¹** racket.

**раке́та²** rocket; missile; flare.

**ра́ковина** shell; sink.

**ра́ковый** cancer; cancerous.

**раку́шка** cockle-shell, mussel.

**ра́ма** frame. **ра́мка** frame; pl framework.

**ра́мпа** footlights.

**ра́на** wound. **ране́ние** wounding; wound. **ра́неный** wounded; injured.

**ранг** rank.

**ра́нец** (-нца) knapsack; satchel.

**ра́нить** impf & pf wound; injure.

**ра́нний** early. **ра́но** adv early. **ра́ньше** adv earlier; before; formerly.

**рапи́ра** foil.

**ра́порт** report. **рапортова́ть** impf & pf report.

**ра́са** race. **раси́зм** racism. **раси́стский** racist.

**раска́иваться** impf of **раска́яться**

**раскалённый** (-ён, -а́) scorching; incandescent. **раскали́ть** pf (impf **раскаля́ть**) make red-hot; **~ся** become red-hot. **раска́лывать(ся** impf of **расколо́ть(ся. раскаля́ть(ся** impf of **раскали́ть(ся. рас-**

**ка́пывать** impf of **раскопа́ть**

**раска́т** roll, peal. **раската́ть** pf, **раска́тывать** impf roll (out), smooth out; level; drive or ride (about). **раска́тистый** rolling, booming. **раскати́ться** (-ачу́сь, -а́тишься) pf, **раска́тываться** impf gather speed; roll away; peal, boom.

**раскача́ть** pf, **раска́чивать** impf swing; rock; **~ся** swing, rock.

**раска́яние** repentance. **рас|ка́яться** pf (impf also **раска́иваться**) repent.

**расквита́ться** pf settle accounts.

**раски́дывать** impf, **раски́нуть** (-ну) pf stretch (out); spread; pitch; **~ся** spread out; sprawl.

**раскладно́й** folding. **раскла-ду́шка** camp-bed. **раскла́-дывать** impf of **разложи́ть**

**раскла́няться** pf bow; take leave.

**раскле́ивать** impf, **раскле́-ить** (-е́ю) pf unstick; stick (up); **~ся** come unstuck.

**раско́л** split; schism. **рас|коло́ть** (-лю́, -лешь) pf (impf also **раска́лывать**) split; break; disrupt; **~ся** split. **раско́ль-ник** dissenter.

**раскопа́ть** pf (impf **раска́-пывать**) dig up, unearth, excavate. **раско́пки** (-пок) pl excavations.

**раско́сый** slanting.

**раскра́ивать** impf of **рас-кро́ить**

**раскра́сить** (-а́шу) pf, impf **раскра́шивать** paint, colour.

**раскрепости́ть** (-ощу́) pf, **раскрепоща́ть** impf liberate. **раскрепоще́ние** emancipation.

раскритикова́ть *pf* criticize harshly.

раскро́ить *pf* (*impf* раскра́ивать) cut out.

раскро́ю *etc.: see* раскры́ть

раскрути́ть (-учу́, -у́тишь) *pf*, раскру́чивать *impf* untwist; ~ся come untwisted.

раскрыва́ть *impf*, раскры́ть (-бю) *pf* open; expose; reveal; discover; ~ся open; uncover o.s.; come to light.

раскупа́ть *impf*, раскупи́ть (-у́пит) *pf* buy up.

раску́поривать *impf*, раску́порить *pf* uncork, open.

раскуси́ть (-ушу́, -у́сишь) *pf*, раску́сывать *impf* bite through; see through.

ра́совый racial.

распа́д disintegration; collapse. распада́ться *impf of* распа́сться

распакова́ть *pf*, распако́вывать *impf* unpack.

распа́рывать(ся *impf of* распоро́ть(ся

распа́сться (-адётся) *pf* (*impf* распада́ться) disintegrate, fall to pieces.

распаха́ть (-ашу́, -а́шешь) *pf*, распа́хивать¹ *impf* plough up.

распа́хивать² *impf*, распахну́ть (-ну́, -нёшь) *pf* throw open; fling open, swing open; ~ся fly open, swing open.

распашо́нка baby's vest.

распева́ть *impf* sing.

распеча́тать *pf*, распеча́тывать *impf* open; unseal.

распи́ливать *impf*, распили́ть (-лю́, -лишь) *pf* saw up.

распина́ть *impf of* распя́ть

расписа́ние time-table. расписа́ть (-ишу́, -и́шешь) *pf*, распи́сывать *impf* enter; assign; paint; ~ся sign; register

one's marriage; +в+*prep* sign for; acknowledge. распи́ска receipt. расписно́й painted, decorated.

распиха́ть *pf*, распи́хивать *impf* push, shove, stuff.

рас|пла́вить (-влю) *pf*, распла́вля́ть *impf* melt, fuse. распла́вленный molten.

распла́каться (-а́чусь) *pf* burst into tears.

распласта́ть *pf*, распла́стывать *impf* spread; flatten; split; ~ся sprawl.

распла́та payment; retribution. расплати́ться (-ачу́сь, -а́тишься) *pf*, распла́чиваться *impf* (+с+*instr*) pay off; get even; +за+*acc* pay for.

расплеска́ть(ся (-ещу́(сь, -е́щешь(ся) *pf*, расплёскивать(ся *impf* spill.

расплести́ (-ету́, -етёшь; -ёл, -а́) *pf* расплета́ть *impf* unplait; untwist.

рас|плоди́ть(ся (-ожу́(сь) *pf*.

расплыва́ться *impf*, расплы́ться (-ывётся; -ылся, -ась) *pf* run. расплы́вчатый indistinct; vague.

расплю́щивать *impf*, расплю́щить (-щу) *pf* flatten out, hammer out.

распну́ *etc.: see* распя́ть

распознава́ть (-наю́, -наёшь) *impf*, распозна́ть *pf* recognize, identify; diagnose.

располага́ть *impf* +*instr* have at one's disposal. располага́ться *impf of* расположи́ться

располза́ться *impf*, располсти́сь (-зётся; -о́лзся, -зла́сь) *pf* crawl (away); give at the seams.

расположе́ние disposition; arrangement; situation; tendency; liking; mood. **расположе́нный** disposed, inclined. **расположи́ть** (-жу́, -жишь) *pf* (*impf* **располага́ть**) dispose; set out; win over; **~ся** settle down.

**распо́рка** cross-bar, strut.

**рас|поро́ть** (-рю́, -решь) *pf* (*impf also* **распа́рывать**) unpick, rip; **~ся** rip, come undone.

**распоряди́тель** *m* manager. **распоряди́тельный** capable; efficient. **распоряди́ться** (-яжу́сь) *pf*, **распоряжа́ться** *impf* order, give orders; see; +*instr* manage, deal with. **распоря́док** (-дка) order; routine. **распоряже́ние** order; instruction; disposal, command.

**распра́ва** violence; reprisal.

**распра́вить** (-влю) *pf*, **расправля́ть** *impf* straighten; smooth out; spread.

**распра́виться** (-влюсь) *pf*, **расправля́ться** *impf* c+*instr* deal with severely; make short work of.

**распределе́ние** distribution; allocation. **распредели́тель** *m* distributor. **распредели́тельный** distributive, distributing; **~ щит** switchboard. **распредели́ть** *pf*, **распределя́ть** *impf* distribute; allocate.

**распродава́ть** (-даю́, -даёшь) *impf*, **распрода́ть** (-а́м, -а́шь, -а́ст, -ади́м; -о́дал, -а́, -о) *pf* sell off; sell out of. **распрода́жа** (clearance) sale.

**распростёртый** outstretched; prostrate.

**распростране́ние** spreading; dissemination. **распространё́нный** (-ён, -а́) widespread,

prevalent. **распространи́ть** *pf*, **распространя́ть** *impf* spread; **~ся** spread.

**ра́спря** (*gen pl* -ей) quarrel.

**распряга́ть** *impf*, **распря́чь** (-яту́, -яжёшь; -я́г, -ла́) *pf* unharness.

**распрями́ться** *pf*, **распрямля́ться** *impf* straighten up.

**распуска́ть** *impf*, **распусти́ть** (-ущу́, -у́стишь) *pf* dismiss; dissolve; let out; relax; let get out of hand; melt; spread; **~ся** open; come loose; dissolve; melt; get out of hand; let o.s. go.

**распу́тать** *pf* (*impf* **распу́тывать**) untangle; unravel.

**распу́тица** season of bad roads.

**распу́тный** dissolute. **распу́тство** debauchery.

**распу́тывать** *impf of* **распу́тать**

**распу́тье** crossroads.

**распуха́ть** *impf*, **распу́хнуть** (-ну; -ух) *pf* swell (up).

**распу́щенный** undisciplined; spoilt; dissolute.

**распыли́тель** *m* spray, atomizer. **распыли́ть** *pf*, **распыля́ть** *impf* spray; pulverize; disperse.

**распя́тие** crucifixion; crucifix. **распя́ть** (-пну́, -пнёшь) *pf* (*impf* **распина́ть**) crucify.

**расса́да** seedlings. **расса́ди́ть** (-ажу́, -а́дишь) *pf*, **расса́живать** *impf* plant out; seat; separate, seat separately.

**расса́живаться** *impf of* **рассе́сться**. **рассасыва́ться** *impf of* **рассоса́ться**

**рассвести́** (-етёт; -ело́) *pf*, **рассвета́ть** *impf* dawn. **рассве́т** dawn.

**рас|свирипе́ть** (-е́ю) *pf*.

**расседла́ть** *pf* unsaddle.

**рассе́ивание** dispersal, scattering. **рассе́ивать(ся** *impf of* **рассе́ять(ся**

**рассека́ть** *impf of* **рассе́чь**

**расселе́ние** settling, resettlement; separation.

**рассе́лина** cleft, fissure.

**рассели́ть** *pf*, **расселя́ть** *impf* settle, resettle; separate.

**рас|серди́ть(ся** (-жу́(сь, -рди́шь(ся) *pf.*

**рассе́сться** (-ся́дусь) *pf* (*impf* **расса́живаться**) take seats.

**рассе́чь** (-еку́, -ече́шь; -е́к, -ла́) *pf* (*impf* **рассека́ть**) cut (through); cleave.

**рассе́янность** absent-mindedness; dispersion. **рассе́янный** absent-minded; diffused; scattered. **рассе́ять** (-е́ю) *pf* (*impf* **рассе́ивать**) disperse, scatter; dispel; ~**ся** disperse, scatter; clear; divert o.s.

**расска́з** story; account. **рассказа́ть** (-ажу́, -а́жешь) *pf*, **расска́зывать** *impf* tell, recount. **расска́зчик** storyteller, narrator.

**рассла́бить** (-блю) *pf*, **расслабля́ть** *impf* weaken; ~**ся** relax.

**рассла́ивать(ся** *impf of* **расслои́ть(ся**

**рассле́дование** investigation, examination; inquiry; **произвести́** ~+*gen* hold an inquiry into. **рассле́довать** *impf & pf* investigate, look into, hold an inquiry into.

**расслои́ть** *pf* (*impf* **рассла́ивать**) divide into layers; ~**ся** become stratified; flake off.

**расслы́шать** (-шу) *pf* catch.

**рассма́тривать** *impf of* **рассмотре́ть**; examine; consider.

**рас|смеши́ть** (-шу́) *pf.*

**рассмея́ться** (-ею́сь, -ёёшься) *pf* burst out laughing.

**рассмотре́ние** examination; consideration. **рассмотре́ть** (-рю́, -ришь) *pf* (*impf* **рассма́тривать**) examine, consider; discern, make out.

**рассова́ть** (-сую́, -суёшь) *pf*, **рассо́вывать** *impf* по+*dat* shove into.

**рассо́л** brine; pickle.

**рассо́риться** *pf* с+*instr* fall out with.

**рас|сортирова́ть** *pf*, **рассортиро́вывать** *impf* sort out.

**рассоса́ться** (-сётся) *pf* (*impf* **расса́сываться**) resolve.

**рассо́хнуться** (-нется; -о́хся) *pf* (*impf* **рассыха́ться**) crack.

**расспра́шивать** *impf*, **расспроси́ть** (-ошу́, -о́сишь) *pf* question; make inquiries of.

**рассро́чить** (-чу) *pf* spread (over a period). **рассро́чка** instalment.

**расстава́ние** parting. **расстава́ться** (-таю́сь, -таёшься) *impf of* **расста́ться**

**расста́вить** (-влю) *pf*, **расставля́ть** *impf* place, arrange; move apart. **расстано́вка** arrangement; pause.

**расста́ться** (-а́нусь) *pf* (*impf* **расстава́ться**) part, separate.

**расстёгивать** *impf*, **расстегну́ть** (-ну́, -нёшь) *pf* undo, unfasten; ~**ся** come undone; undo one's coat.

**расстели́ть(ся**, *etc.*: *see* **разостла́ть(ся. расстила́ть(ся, -а́ю(сь** *impf of* **разостла́ть(ся**

**расстоя́ние** distance.

**расстра́ивать(ся** *impf of* **расстро́ить(ся**

**расстре́л** execution by firing squad. **расстре́ливать** *impf*, расстреля́ть *pf* shoot.

расстро́енный disordered; upset; out of tune. расстро́ить *pf* (*impf* расстра́ивать) upset; thwart; disturb; throw into confusion; put out of tune; ~ся be upset; get out of tune; fall into confusion; fall through.

расстро́йство upset; disarray; confusion; frustration.

расступа́ться *impf*, расступи́ться (-у́пится) *pf* part, make way.

рассуди́тельный reasonable; sensible. рассуди́ть (-ужу́, -у́дишь) *pf* judge; think; decide. рассу́док (-дка) reason; intellect. рассужда́ть *impf* reason; +о+*prep* discuss. рассужде́ние reasoning; discussion; argument.

рассую́ *etc.*: *see* рассова́ть

рассчи́танный deliberate; intended. рассчита́ть *pf*, рассчи́тывать *impf*, расче́сть (разочту́, -тёшь; расчёл, -чла́) *pf* calculate; count; depend; ~ся settle accounts.

рассыла́ть *impf of* разосла́ть. рассы́лка distribution. рассы́льный *sb* delivery man.

рассы́пать (-плю) *pf*, рассыпа́ть *impf* spill; scatter; ~ся spill, scatter; spread out; crumble. рассы́пчатый friable; crumbly.

рассыха́ться *impf of* рассо́хнуться. рассяду́сь *etc.*: *see* рассе́сться. раста́лкивать *impf of* растолка́ть. раста́пливать(ся *impf of* растопи́ть(ся

раста́скивать *impf*, раста́щить (-щу́, -щишь) *pf* pilfer, filch.

растащи́ть *see* растаска́ть.

рас|та́ять (-а́ю) *pf*.

раство́р[2] opening, span. раство́р[1] solution; mortar. раствори́мый soluble. раствори́тель *m* solvent. раствори́ть[1] *pf* (*impf* растворя́ть) dissolve; ~ся dissolve.

раствори́ть[2] (-рю́, -ри́шь) *pf* (*impf* растворя́ть) open; ~ся open.

растворя́ть(ся *impf of* раствори́ть(ся. растека́ться *impf of* расте́чься

расте́ние plant.

растере́ть (разотру́, -трёшь; растёр) *pf* (*impf* растира́ть) grind; spread; rub; massage.

растерза́ть *pf*, расте́рзывать *impf* tear to pieces.

расте́рянность confusion, dismay. расте́рянный confused, dismayed. растеря́ть *pf* lose; ~ся get lost; lose one's head.

расте́чься (-ечётся, -еку́тся; -тёкся, -ла́сь) *pf* (*impf* растека́ться) run; spread.

расти́ (-ту́, -тёшь; рос, -ла́) *impf* grow; grow up.

растира́ние grinding; rubbing, massage. растира́ть(ся *impf of* растере́ть(ся

расти́тельность vegetation; hair. расти́тельный vegetable. расти́ть (ращу́) *impf* bring up; train; grow.

растлева́ть *impf*, растли́ть *pf* seduce; corrupt.

растолка́ть *pf* (*impf* раста́лкивать) push apart; shake.

растолкова́ть *pf*, растолко́вывать *impf* explain.

рас|толо́чь (-лку́, -лчёшь; -лóк, -лкла́) *pf*.

растолсте́ть (-е́ю) *pf* put on weight.

растопи́ть[1] (-плю́, -пишь) *pf*

(impf растапливать) melt; thaw; ~ся melt.

растопить[2] (-плю, -пишь) pf (impf растапливать) light, kindle; ~ся begin to burn.

растоптать (-пчу, -пчешь) pf trample, trample on.

расторгать impf, расторгнуть (-ну; -орг) pf annul, dissolve. расторжение annulment, dissolution.

расторопный quick; efficient.

расточать impf, расточить (-чу) pf squander, dissipate. расточительный extravagant, wasteful.

растравить (-влю, -вишь) pf, растравлять impf irritate.

растрата spending; waste; embezzlement. растратить (-ачу) pf, растрачивать impf spend; waste; embezzle.

растрёпанный dishevelled; tattered. рас|трепать (-плю, -плешь) pf disarrange; tatter.

растрескаться pf, растрескиваться impf crack, chap.

растрогать pf move, touch; ~ся be moved.

растущий growing.

растягивать impf, растянуть (-ну, -нешь) pf stretch (out); strain, sprain; drag out; ~ся stretch; drag on; sprawl. растяжение tension; strain, sprain. растяжимый tensile; stretchable. растянутый stretched; long-winded.

рас|фасовать pf. расформировывать impf break up; disband.

расхаживать impf walk about; pace up and down.

расхваливать impf, расхвалить (-лю, -лишь) pf lavish praises on.

расхватать pf, расхватывать impf seize on, buy up.

расхититель m embezzler.

расхитить (-ищу) pf, расхищать impf steal, misappropriate. расхищение misappropriation.

расхлябанный loose; lax.

расход expenditure; consumption; pl expenses, outlay. расходиться (-ожусь, -одишься) impf of разойтись. расходование expense, expenditure. расходовать impf (pf из~) spend; consume. расхождение divergence.

расхолаживать impf, расхолодить (-ожу) pf damp the ardour of.

расхотеть (-очу, -очешь, -отим) pf no longer want.

расхохотаться (-очусь, -очешься) pf burst out laughing.

расцарапать pf scratch (all over).

расцвести (-ету, -етёшь; -ёл, -а) pf, расцветать impf blossom; flourish. расцвет blossoming (out); flowering, heyday.

расцветка colours; colouring.

расценивать impf, расценить (-ню, -нишь) pf estimate, value; consider. расценка valuation; price; (wage-)rate.

расцепить (-плю, -пишь) pf, расцеплять impf uncouple, unhook.

расчесать (-ешу, -ешешь) pf (impf расчёсывать) comb; scratch. расчёска comb.

расчесть etc.: see рассчитать.

расчёсывать impf of расчёсать.

расчёт[1] calculation; estimate; gain; settlement. расчётливый thrifty; careful. расчётный calculation; pay; accounts; calculated.

расчи́стить (-и́щу) pf, расчища́ть impf clear; ~ся clear. расчи́стка clearing.

рас|члени́ть pf, расчленя́ть impf dismember; divide.

расшата́ть pf, расша́тывать impf shake loose, make rickety; impair.

расшевели́ть (-лю́, -ели́шь) pf stir; rouse.

расшиба́ть impf, расшиби́ть (-бу́, -бёшь; -и́б) pf smash to pieces; hurt; stub; ~ся hurt o.s.

расшива́ть impf of расши́ть

расшире́ние widening; expansion; dilation, dilatation.

расши́рить pf, расширя́ть impf widen; enlarge; expand; ~ся broaden, widen; expand, dilate.

расши́ть (разошью́, -шьёшь) pf (impf расшива́ть) embroider; unpick.

расшифрова́ть pf, расшифро́вывать impf decipher.

расшнурова́ть pf, расшнуро́вывать impf unlace.

расще́лина crevice.

расщепи́ть (-плю́) pf, расщепля́ть impf split; ~ся split. расщепле́ние splitting; fission.

ратифици́ровать impf & pf ratify.

рать army, battle.

ра́унд round.

рафини́рованный refined.

рацио́н ration.

рационализа́ция rationalization. рационализи́ровать impf & pf rationalize. рациона́льный rational; efficient. ра́ция walkie-talkie.

рвану́ться (-ну́сь, -нёшься) pf dart, dash.

рва́ный torn; lacerated. рвать[1] (рву, рвёшь; рвал, -а́, -о) impf tear (out); pull out; pick; blow up; break off; ~ся break; burst, bursting; be bursting.

рвать[2] (рвёт; рва́ло) impf (pf вы~) impers+acc vomit.

рвач (-а́) self-seeker.

рве́ние zeal.

рво́та vomiting.

реабилита́ция rehabilitation. реабилити́ровать impf & pf rehabilitate.

реаги́ровать impf (pf от~, про~) react.

реакти́в reagent. реакти́вный reactive; jet-propelled. реа́ктор reactor.

реакционе́р reactionary. реакцио́нный reactionary. реа́кция reaction.

реализа́ция realization. реали́зм realism. реализова́ть impf & pf realize. реали́ст realist. реалисти́ческий realistic.

реа́льность reality; practicability. реа́льный real; practicable.

ребёнок (-нка; pl ребя́та, -я́т and де́ти, -е́й) child; infant.

ребро́ (pl рёбра, -бер) rib; edge.

ребя́та (-я́т) pl children; guys; lads. ребя́ческий child's; childish. ребя́чество childishness. ребя́читься (-чусь) impf be childish.

рёв roar; howl.

рева́нш revenge; return match.

реве́ранс curtsey.

реве́ть (-ву́, -вёшь) impf roar; bellow; howl.

ревизио́нный inspection; auditing. реви́зия inspection; audit; revision. ревизо́р inspector.

**ревмати́зм** rheumatism.

**ревни́вый** jealous. **ревнова́ть** *impf (pf* при~) be jealous. **ре́вностный** zealous. **ре́вность** jealousy.

**револьве́р** revolver.

**революционе́р** revolutionary. **революцио́нный** revolutionary. **револю́ция** revolution.

**рега́та** regatta.

**ре́гби** *neut indecl* rugby.

**ре́гент** regent.

**регио́н** region. **региона́льный** regional.

**регистра́тор** registrar. **регистрату́ра** registry. **регистра́ция** registration. **регистри́ровать** *impf & pf (pf also* за~) register, record; ~**ся** register; register one's marriage.

**регла́мент** standing orders; time-limit. **регламента́ция** regulation. **регламенти́ровать** *impf & pf* regulate.

**регресси́ровать** *impf* regress.

**регули́ровать** *impf (pf* от~, у~) regulate; adjust. **регулиро́вщик** traffic controller. **регуля́рный** regular. **регуля́тор** regulator.

**редакти́ровать** *impf (pf* от~) edit. **реда́ктор** editor. **реда́кторский** editorial. **редакцио́нный** editorial, editing. **реда́кция** editorial staff; editorial office; editing.

**реде́ть** (-е́ет) *impf (pf* по~) thin (out).

**реди́с** radishes. **реди́ска** radish.

**ре́дкий** (-док, -дка́, -о) thin; sparse; rare. **ре́дко** *adv* sparsely; rarely, seldom. **ре́дкость** rarity.

**редколе́гия** editorial board.

**рее́стр** register.

**режи́м** régime; routine; procedure; regimen; conditions.

**режиссёр-(постано́вщик)** producer; director.

**ре́жущий** cutting, sharp. **ре́зать** (ре́жу) *impf (pf* за~, про~, с~) cut; engrave; kill, slaughter.

**резви́ться** (-влю́сь) *impf* gambol, play. **ре́звый** frisky, playful.

**резе́рв** reserve. **резе́рвный** reserve; back-up.

**резервуа́р** reservoir.

**резе́ц** (-зца́) cutter; chisel; incisor.

**резиде́нция** residence.

**рези́на** rubber. **рези́нка** rubber; elastic band. **рези́новый** rubber.

**ре́зкий** sharp; harsh; abrupt; shrill. **резно́й** carved. **резня́** carnage.

**резолю́ция** resolution.

**резона́нс** resonance; response.

**результа́т** result.

**резьба́** carving, fretwork.

**резюме́** *neut indecl* résumé.

**рейд**[1] roads, roadstead.

**рейд**[2] raid.

**ре́йка** lath, rod.

**рейс** trip; voyage; flight.

**рейту́зы** (-уз) *pl* leggings; riding breeches.

**река́** (*acc* ре́ку; *pl* -и, ре́кам) river.

**ре́квием** requiem.

**реквизи́т** props.

**рекла́ма** advertising, advertisement. **реклами́ровать** *impf & pf* advertise. **рекла́мный** publicity.

**рекоменда́тельный** of recommendation. **рекоменда́ция** recommendation; reference. **рекомендова́ть** *impf* & *pf* (*pf also* **от~**, **по~**) recommend; **~ся** introduce o.s.; be advisable.

**реконструи́ровать** *impf* & *pf* reconstruct. **реконстру́кция** reconstruction.

**реко́рд** record. **реко́рдный** record, record-breaking. **реко́рдсме́н**, **-е́нка** record-holder.

**ре́ктор** principal (*of university*).

**реле́** (*electr*) *neut indecl* relay.

**религио́зный** religious. **рели́гия** religion.

**рели́квия** relic.

**релье́ф** relief. **релье́фный** relief; raised, bold.

**рельс** rail.

**рема́рка** stage direction.

**реме́нь** (**-мня́**) *m* strap; belt.

**реме́сленник** artisan, craftsman. **реме́сленный** handicraft; mechanical. **ремесло́** (*pl* **-ёсла**, **-ёсел**) craft; trade.

**ремо́нт** repair(s); maintenance. **ремонти́ровать** *impf* & *pf* (*pf also* **от~**) repair; recondition. **ремо́нтный** repair.

**ре́нта** rent; income. **ре́нтабельный** paying, profitable.

**рентге́н** X-rays. **рентге́новский** X-ray. **рентгено́лог** radiologist. **рентгеноло́гия** radiology.

**реоргани́за́ция** reorganization. **реорганизова́ть** *impf* & *pf* reorganize.

**ре́па** turnip.

**репатрии́ровать** *impf* & *pf* repatriate.

**репертуа́р** repertoire.

**репети́ровать** *impf* (*pf* **от~**, **про~**, **с~**) rehearse; coach. **репети́тор** coach. **репети́ция** rehearsal.

**ре́плика** retort; cue.

**репорта́ж** report; reporting. **репортёр** reporter.

**репре́ссия** repression.

**репроду́ктор** loud-speaker. **репроду́кция** reproduction.

**репута́ция** reputation.

**ресни́ца** eyelash.

**респу́блика** republic. **республика́нский** republican.

**рессо́ра** spring.

**реставра́ция** restoration. **реставри́ровать** *impf* & *pf* (*pf also* **от~**) restore.

**рестора́н** restaurant.

**ресу́рс** resort; *pl* resources.

**ретрансля́тор** (*radio*)relay.

**рефера́т** synopsis, abstract; paper, essay.

**рефере́ндум** referendum.

**рефле́кс** reflex. **рефле́ктор** reflector.

**рефо́рма** reform. **реформи́ровать** *impf* & *pf* reform.

**рефрижера́тор** refrigerator.

**рецензи́ровать** *impf* (*pf* **про~**) review. **реце́нзия** review.

**реце́пт** prescription; recipe.

**рециди́в** relapse. **рецидиви́ст** recidivist.

**речево́й** speech; vocal.

**ре́чка** river. **речно́й** river.

**речь** (*gen pl* **-е́й**) speech.

**реша́ть(ся** *impf of* **реши́ть**(**ся**. **реша́ющий** decisive, deciding. **реше́ние** decision; solution.

**решётка** grating; grille, railing; lattice, trellis; fender, (fire)guard; (fire)grate; tail. **решето́** (*pl* **-ёта**) sieve. **решётчатый** lattice, latticed.

**реши́мость** resoluteness; resolve. **реши́тельно** *adv* resolutely; definitely; absolutely. **реши́тельность** determination. **реши́тельный** definite.

decisive. **реши́ть** (-шу́) *pf* (*impf* **реша́ть**) decide; solve; ~**ся** make up one's mind.

**ржа́веть** (-еет) *impf* (*pf* **за-**, **по**~) rust. **ржа́вчина** rust. **ржа́вый** rusty.

**ржано́й** rye.

**ржать** (ржу, ржёшь) *impf* neigh.

**ри́млянин** (*pl* -яне, -ян), **ри́млянка** Roman. **ри́мский** Roman.

**ринг** boxing ring.

**ри́нуться** (-нусь) *pf* rush, dart.

**рис** rice.

**риск** risk. **риско́ванный** risky; risqué. **рискова́ть** *impf*, **рискну́ть** *pf* run risks; +*instr* or *inf* risk.

**рисова́ние** drawing. **рисова́ть** *impf* (*pf* **на**~) draw; paint, depict; ~**ся** be silhouetted; appear; pose.

**ри́совый** rice.

**рису́нок** (-нка) drawing; figure; pattern, design.

**ритм** rhythm. **ритми́ческий**, **ритми́чный** rhythmic.

**ритуа́л** ritual.

**риф** reef.

**ри́фма** rhyme. **рифмова́ть** *impf* rhyme; ~**ся** rhyme.

**робе́ть** (-е́ю) *impf* (*pf* **о**~) be timid. **ро́бкий** (-бок, -бка́, -о) timid, shy. **ро́бость** shyness.

**ро́бот** robot.

**ров** (рва, *loc* -у́) ditch.

**рове́сник** coeval. **ро́вно** *adv* evenly; exactly; absolutely. **ро́вный** flat; even; level; equable; exact; equal. **ровня́ть** *impf* (*pf* **с**~) even, level.

**рог** (*pl* -а́, -о́в) horn; antler. **рога́тка** catapult. **рога́тый** horned. **рогови́ца** cornea. **роговой** horn; horny; hornrimmed.

**род** (*loc* -у́; *pl* -ы́) family, kin, clan; birth, origin, stock; generation; genus; sort, kind. **роди́льный** maternity. **ро́дина** native land; homeland. **роди́нка** birth-mark. **роди́тели** (-ей) *pl* parents. **роди́тельный** genitive. **роди́ть** (рожу́, -и́л, -ила́, -о) *impf* & *pf* (*impf also* **рожа́ть**, **рожда́ть**) give birth to; ~**ся** be born.

**родни́к** (-а́) spring.

**родни́ть** *impf* (*pf* **по**~) make related, link; ~**ся** become related. **родн|о́й** own; native; home; ~**о́й брат** brother; ~**ы́е** *sb pl* relatives. **родня́** relative(s); kinsfolk. **родово́й** tribal; ancestral; generic; gender. **родонача́льник** ancestor; father. **родосло́вн|ый** genealogical; ~**ая** *sb* genealogy, pedigree. **ро́дственник** relative. **ро́дственный** related. **родство́** relationship, kinship. **ро́ды** (-ов) *pl* childbirth; labour.

**ро́жа** (ugly) mug.

**рожа́ть**, **рожда́ть(ся** *impf of* **роди́ть(ся**. **рожда́емость** birth-rate. **рожде́ние** birth. **рожде́ственский** Christmas. **Рождество́** Christmas.

**рожь** (ржи) rye.

**ро́за** rose.

**ро́зга** (*gen pl* -зог) birch.

**ро́здал** *etc.*: *see* **разда́ть**

**розе́тка** electric socket, power point; rosette.

**ро́зница** retail; в ~у retail. **ро́зничный** retail. **рознь** difference; dissension.

**ро́знял** *etc.*: *see* **разня́ть**

**ро́зовый** pink.

**ро́зыгрыш** draw; drawn game.

**ро́зыск** search; inquiry.

**ро́ться** swarm. **рой** (loc -ю́; pl -и́, -ёв) swarm.

**рок** fate.

**рокиро́вка** castling.

**рок-му́зыка** rock music.

**роково́й** fateful; fatal.

**ро́кот** roar, rumble. **рокота́ть** (-о́чет) impf roar, rumble.

**ро́лик** roller; castor; pl roller skates.

**роль** (gen pl -е́й) role.

**ром** rum.

**рома́н** novel; romance. **рома-ни́ст** novelist.

**рома́нс** (mus) romance.

**рома́нтик** romantic. **рома́нти-ка** romance. **романти́ческий, романти́чный** romantic.

**рома́шка** camomile.

**ромб** rhombus.

**роня́ть** impf (pf урони́ть) drop.

**ро́пот** murmur, grumble. **ропта́ть** (-пщу́, -пщешь) impf murmur, grumble.

**рос** etc.: see расти́

**роса́** (pl -ы) dew. **роси́стый** dewy.

**роско́шный** luxurious; luxuriant. **ро́скошь** luxury; luxuriance.

**ро́слый** strapping.

**ро́спись** painting(s), mural(s).

**ро́спуск** dismissal; disbandment.

**росси́йский** Russian. **Росси́я** Russia.

**ро́ссыпи** f pl deposit.

**рост** growth; increase; height, stature.

**ро́стбиф** roast beef.

**ростовщи́к** (-а́) usurer, money-lender.

**росто́к** (-тка́) sprout, shoot.

**ро́счерк** flourish.

**рот** (рта, loc рту) mouth.

**ро́та** company.

**рота́тор** duplicator.

**ро́тный** company; sb company commander.

**ротозе́й, -зе́йка** gaper, rubberneck; scatter-brain.

**ро́ща** grove.

**ро́ю** etc.: see рыть

**роя́ль** m (grand) piano.

**ртуть** f mercury.

**руба́нок** (-нка) plane.

**руба́ха, руба́шка** shirt.

**рубе́ж** (-а́) boundary, border-(line); line; за ~о́м abroad.

**рубе́ц** (-бца́) scar; weal; hem; tripe.

**руби́н** ruby. **руби́новый** ruby-coloured.

**руби́ть** (-блю́, -бишь) impf (pf с~) fell; hew, chop; mince; build (of logs).

**руби́ще** rags.

**ру́бка**[1] felling; chopping; mincing.

**ру́бка**[2] deck house; **боева́я ~** conning-tower; **рулева́я ~** wheelhouse.

**рублёвка** one-rouble note. **рублёвый** (one-)rouble.

**ру́бленый** minced, chopped; of logs.

**рубль** (-я́) m rouble.

**ру́брика** rubric, heading.

**ру́бчатый** ribbed. **ру́бчик** scar; rib.

**руга́нь** f abuse, swearing. **руга́-тельный** abusive. **руга́тель-ство** oath, swear-word. **руга́ть** impf (pf вы~, об~, от~) curse, swear at; abuse; ~ся curse, swear; swear at one another.

**руда́** (pl -ы) ore. **рудни́к** (-а́) mine, pit. **рудни́чный** mine, pit; ~ **газ** fire-damp. **рудоко́п** miner.

**руже́йный** rifle, gun. **ружьё** (pl -ья, -жей, -жьям) gun, rifle.

**руи́на** *usu pl* ruin.

**рука́** (*acc* -y, *pl* -и, рук, -а́м) hand; arm; **идти́ по́д руку** c+*instr* walk arm in arm with; **под руко́й** at hand; **руко́й пода́ть** a stone's throw away; **э́то мне на́ руку** that suits me.

**рука́в** (-а́; *pl* -а́, -о́в) sleeve.

**рука́вица** mitten; gauntlet.

**руководи́тель** *m* leader; manager; instructor; guide. **руководи́ть** (-ожу́) *impf* +*instr* lead; guide; direct, manage. **руково́дство** leadership; guidance; direction; guide; handbook, manual; leaders. **руково́дствоваться**+*instr* follow; be guided by. **руководя́щий** leading; guiding.

**рукоде́лие** needlework.

**рукомо́йник** washstand.

**рукопа́шный** hand-to-hand.

**рукопи́сный** manuscript. **ру́копись** manuscript.

**рукоплеска́ние** applause. **рукоплеска́ть** (-ещу́, -е́щешь) *impf* +*dat* applaud.

**рукопожа́тие** handshake.

**рукоя́тка** handle.

**рулево́й** steering; *sb* helmsman.

**руле́тка** tape-measure; roulette.

**рули́ть** *impf* (*pf* вы́~) taxi.

**руль** (-я́) *m* rudder; helm; (steering-)wheel; handlebar.

**румы́н** (*gen pl* -ы́н), **~ка** Romanian. **Румы́ния** Romania. **румы́нский** Romanian.

**румя́на** (-я́н) *pl* rouge. **румя́нец** (-нца) flush, high colour; blush. **румя́ный** rosy, ruddy.

**ру́пор** megaphone; mouthpiece.

**руса́к** (-а́) hare.

**руса́лка** mermaid.

**русифици́ровать** *impf & pf* Russify.

**ру́сло** river-bed, channel; course.

**ру́сский** Russian; *sb* Russian.

**ру́сый** light brown.

**Русь** (*hist*) Russia.

**рути́на** routine.

**рухля́дь** junk.

**ру́хнуть** (-ну) *pf* crash down.

**руча́тельство** guarantee. **руча́ться** *impf* (*pf* поручи́ться) +за+*acc* vouch for, guarantee.

**руче́й** (-чья́) brook.

**ру́чка** handle; (door-)knob; (chair-)arm; pen. **ручн|о́й** hand; arm; manual; tame; **~ые часы́** wrist-watch.

**ру́шить** (-у) *impf* (*pf* об~) pull down; **~ся** collapse.

**ры́ба** fish. **рыба́к** (-а́) fisherman. **рыба́лка** fishing. **рыба́цкий**, **рыба́чий** fishing. **ры́бий** fish; fishy; **~ жир** cod-liver oil. **ры́бный** fish. **рыболо́в** fisherman. **рыболо́вный** fishing.

**рыво́к** (-вка́) jerk.

**рыда́ние** sobbing. **рыда́ть** *impf* sob.

**ры́жий** (рыж, -а́, -е) red, red-haired; chestnut.

**ры́ло** snout; mug.

**ры́нок** (-нка) market; market-place. **ры́ночный** market.

**рыса́к** (-а́) trotter.

**рысь¹** (*loc* -и́) trot; **~ю, на рыся́х** at a trot.

**рысь²** lynx.

**ры́твина** rut, groove. **рыть(ся** (ро́ю(сь) *impf* (*pf* вы́~, от~) dig; rummage.

**рыхли́ть** *impf* (*pf* вз~, раз~) loosen. **ры́хлый** (-л, -а́, -о) friable; loose.

**ры́царский** chivalrous. **ры́царь** *m* knight.

**рыча́г** (-а́) lever.

**рыча́ть** (-чу́) *impf* growl, snarl.

рья́ный zealous.

рюкза́к (gen -á) rucksack.

рю́мка wineglass.

ряби́на¹ rowan, mountain ash.

ряби́на² pit, pock. ряби́ть (-и́т) impf ripple; impers: у меня́ ряби́т в глаза́х I am dazzled. рябо́й pock-marked.

ря́бчик hazel hen, hazel grouse. рябь ripples; dazzle.

ря́вкать impf, ря́вкнуть (-ну) pf bellow, roar.

ряд (loc -у́, pl -ы́) row; line; file, rank; series; number. рядово́й ordinary; common; ~ соста́в rank and file; sb private. ря́дом adv alongside; close by; +c+instr next to.

ря́са cassock.

# С

с, со prep I. +gen from; since; off; for, with; on; by; с ра́дости for joy; с утра́ since morning. II. +acc about; the size of; с неде́лю for about a week. III. +instr with; and; мы с ва́ми you and I; что с ва́ми? what is the matter?

са́бля (gen pl -бель) sabre.

сабота́ж sabotage. саботи́ровать impf & pf sabotage.

са́ван shroud; blanket.

с|агити́ровать pf.

сад (loc -у́, pl -ы́) garden. сади́ть (сажу́, са́дишь) impf (pf по~) plant. сади́ться (сажу́сь) impf of сесть. садо́вник, -ница gardener. садово́дство gardening; horticulture. садо́вый garden; cultivated.

сади́зм sadism. сади́ст sadist. сади́стский sadistic.

са́жа soot.

сажа́ть impf (pf посади́ть) plant; seat; set, put. саже́нец (-нца) seedling; sapling.

са́жень (pl -и, -жен or -же́ней) sazhen (2.13 metres).

сажу́ etc.: see сади́ть

са́йка roll.

саксофо́н saxophone.

с|акти́ровать pf.

сала́зки (-зок) pl toboggan.

сала́т lettuce; salad.

са́ло fat, lard; suet; tallow.

сало́н salon; saloon.

салфе́тка napkin.

са́льный greasy; tallow; obscene.

салю́т salute. салютова́ть impf & pf (pf also от~) +dat salute.

сам (-ого́) m, сама́ (-о́й, acc -о́ё) f, само́ (-ого́) neut, са́ми (-и́х) pl, pron self, -self, -selves; myself, etc., ourselves, etc.; ~ по себе́ in itself; by o.s.; ~ собо́й of itself, of its own accord; ~о собо́й (разуме́ется) of course; it goes without saying.

са́мбо neut indecl abbr (of самозащи́та без ору́жия) unarmed combat.

саме́ц (-мца́) male. са́мка female.

само- in comb self-, auto-. самобы́тный original, distinctive. ~возгора́ние spontaneous combustion. ~во́льный wilful; unauthorized. ~де́льный home-made. ~держа́вие autocracy. ~держа́вный autocratic. ~де́ятельность amateur work, amateur performance; initiative. ~дово́льный self-satisfied. ~ду́р petty tyrant. ~ду́рство highhandedness. ~забве́ние selflessness. ~забве́нный self-less. ~защи́та self-defence. ~зва́нец (-нца) impostor.

pretender. ~ка́т scooter.
~кри́тика self-criticism.
~люби́вый proud; touchy.
~лю́бие pride, self-esteem.
~мне́ние conceit, self-importance. ~надѣ́янный presumptuous. ~облада́ние self-control. ~обма́н self-deception. ~оборо́на self-defence. ~образова́ние self-education. ~обслу́живание self-service. ~определе́ние self-determination. ~отве́рженность selflessness. ~отве́рженный selfless. ~поже́ртвование self-sacrifice. ~ро́док (-дка) nugget; person with natural talent. ~сва́л tip-up lorry. ~созна́ние (self-)consciousness. ~сохране́ние self-preservation. ~стоя́тельность independence. ~стоя́тельный independent. ~су́д lynch law, mob law. ~тёк drift. ~тёком adv by gravity; of its own accord. ~уби́йственный suicidal. ~уби́йство suicide. ~уби́йца m & f suicide. ~уваже́ние self-respect. ~уве́ренность self-confidence. ~уве́ренный self-confident. ~униже́ние self-abasement. ~управле́ние self-government. ~управля́ющийся self-governing. ~упра́вный arbitrary. ~учи́тель m self-instructor, manual. ~у́чка m & f self-taught person. ~хо́дный self-propelled. ~чу́вствие general state; как ва́ше ~чу́вствие? how do you feel?

самова́р samovar.
самого́н home-made vodka.
самолёт aeroplane.
самоцве́т semi-precious stone.

са́мый pron (the) very, (the) right; (the) same; (the) most.
сан dignity, office.
санато́рий sanatorium.
санда́лия sandal.
са́ни (-е́й) pl sledge, sleigh.
санита́р medical orderly; stretcher-bearer. санита́рия sanitation. санита́рка nurse. санита́рн|ый medical; health; sanitary; ~ая маши́на ambulance; ~ый у́зел = санузе́л.
са́нки (-нок) pl sledge; toboggan.
санкциони́ровать impf & pf sanction. са́нкция sanction.
сано́вник dignitary.
санпу́нкт medical centre.
санскри́т Sanskrit.
санте́хник plumber.
сантиме́тр centimetre; tape-measure.
сану́зел (-зла́) sanitary arrangements; WC.
санча́сть (gen pl -е́й) medical unit.
сапёр sapper.
сапо́г (-а́; gen pl -о́г) boot.
сапо́жник shoemaker; cobbler. сапо́жный shoe.
сапфи́р sapphire.
сара́й shed; barn.
саранча́ locust(s).
сарафа́н sarafan; pinafore dress.
сарде́лька small fat sausage.
сарди́на sardine.
сарка́зм sarcasm. саркасти́ческий sarcastic.
сатана́ m Satan. сатани́нский satanic.
сателли́т satellite.
сати́н sateen.
сати́ра satire. сати́рик satirist. сатири́ческий satirical.
Сау́довская Ара́вия Saudi Arabia.
сафья́н morocco. сафья́новый morocco.

**сахар** sugar. **сахарин** saccharine. **сахаристый** sugary. **сахарница** sugar-basin. **сахарн|ый** sugar; sugary; ~ый завод sugar-refinery; ~ый песок granulated sugar; ~ая пудра castor sugar; ~ая свёкла sugar-beet.

**сачок** (-чка́) net.

**сбавить** (-влю) pf, **сбавлять** impf take off; reduce.

**сбалансировать** pf.

**сбегать¹** pf run; ~за+instr run for. **сбегать²** impf, **сбежать** (-егу́) pf run down (from); run away; disappear; ~ся come running.

**сберегательная касса** savings bank. **сберегать** impf, **сберечь** (-егу́, -ежёшь; -ёг, -ла́) pf save; save up; preserve. **сбережение** economy; saving; savings. **сберкасса** savings bank.

**сбивать** impf, **с|бить** (собью, -бьёшь) pf bring down, knock down; knock off; distract; wear down; knock together; churn; whip, whisk; ~ся be dislodged; slip; go wrong; be confused; ~ся с пути lose one's way; ~ся с ног be run off one's feet. **сбивчивый** confused; inconsistent.

**сближать** impf, **сблизить** (-ижу) pf bring (closer) together, draw together; ~ся draw closer; become good friends. **сближение** rapprochement; closing in.

**сбоку** adv from one side; on one side.

**сбор** collection; duty; fee, toll; takings; gathering. **сборище** crowd, mob. **сборка** assembling, assembly; gather. **сборн|ик** collection. **сборный** assembly; mixed, combined; prefabricated; detachable. **сборочный** assembly. **сборщик** collector; assembler.

**сбрасывать(ся** impf of **сбросить(ся**

**сбривать** impf, **сбрить** (сбрею) pf shave off.

**сброд** riff-raff.

**сброс** fault, break. **сбросить** (-ошу) pf (impf **сбрасывать**) throw down, drop; throw off; shed; discard.

**сбруя** (collect) (riding) tack.

**сбывать** impf, **сбыть** (сбуду, сбыл, -а́, -о) pf sell, market; get rid of; ~ся come true, be realized. **сбыт** (no pl) sale; market.

**св.** abbr (of **святой**) Saint.

**свадебный** wedding. **свадьба** (gen pl -деб) wedding.

**сваливать** impf, **с|валить** (-лю, -лишь) pf throw down; overthrow; pile up; ~ся fall (down), collapse. **свалка** dump; scuffle.

**свалять** pf.

**сваривать** impf, **с|варить** (-рю, -ришь) pf boil; cook; weld. **сварка** welding.

**сварливый** cantankerous.

**сварной** welded. **сварочный** welding. **сварщик** welder.

**свастика** swastika.

**сватать** impf (pf по~, со~) propose as a husband or wife; propose to; ~ся к+dat or за+acc propose to.

**свая** pile.

**сведение** piece of information; knowledge; pl information, intelligence; knowledge. **сведущий** knowledgeable; versed.

**сведу́** etc.: see **свести**

**свежезаморо́женный** fresh-frozen; chilled. **свежесть**

freshness. **свеже́ть** (-е́ет) *impf* (*pf* **по~**) become cooler; freshen. **све́жий** (-еж, -а́, -о́, -и) fresh; new.

**свезти́** (-зу́, -зёшь; свёз, -ла́) *pf* (*impf* **свози́ть**) take; bring or take down *or* away.

**свёкла** beet, beetroot.

**свёкор** (-кра) father-in-law. **свекро́вь** mother-in-law.

**свёл** *etc.: see* **свести́**

**сверга́ть** *impf*, **све́ргнуть** (-ну; сверг) *pf* throw down, overthrow. **сверже́ние** overthrow.

**све́рить** *pf* (*impf* **сверя́ть**) collate.

**сверка́ть** *impf* sparkle, twinkle; glitter; gleam. **сверкну́ть** (-ну́, -нёшь) *pf* flash.

**сверли́льный** drill, drilling; boring. **сверли́ть** *impf* (*pf* **про~**) drill; bore (through); nag. **сверло́** drill. **сверля́щий** gnawing, piercing.

**сверну́ть** (-ну́, -нёшь) *pf* (*impf* **свёртывать, свора́чивать**) roll up; turn; curtail, cut down; ~ **ше́ю**+*dat* wring the neck of; ~ **ся** roll up, curl up; curdle, coagulate; contract.

**све́рстник** contemporary.

**свёрток** (-тка) package, bundle. **свёртывание** rolling (up); curdling, coagulation; curtailment, cuts. **свёртывать**(**ся**) *impf of* **сверну́ть**(**ся**)

**сверх** *prep*+*gen* over, above, on top of; beyond; in addition to; ~ **того́** moreover.

**сверх-** *in comb* super-, over-, hyper-. **сверхзвуково́й** supersonic. ~**пла́новый** over and above the plan. ~**при́быль** excess profit. ~**проводни́к** (-а́) superconductor. ~**секре́тный** top secret. ~**урочный**

overtime. ~**уро́чные** *sb pl* overtime. ~**челове́к** superman. ~**челове́ческий** superhuman. ~**ъесте́ственный** supernatural.

**све́рху** *adv* from above; ~ **до́низу** from top to bottom.

**сверчо́к** (-чка́) cricket.

**сверше́ние** achievement.

**сверя́ть** *impf of* **све́рить**

**све́сить** (-е́шу) *pf* (*impf* **све́шивать**) let down, lower; ~**ся** hang over, lean over.

**свести́** (-еду́, -еде́шь; -ёл, -а́) *pf* (*impf* **своди́ть**) take; take down; take away; remove; bring together; reduce; bring; cramp.

**свет**[1] light; daybreak.

**свет**[2] world; society.

**света́ть** *impf impers* dawn. **светло́** luminary. **свети́ть** (-чу́, -е́тишь) *impf* (*pf* **по~**) shine; +*dat* light; light the way for; ~**ся** shine, gleam. **светле́ть** (-е́ет) *impf* (*pf* **по~, про~**) brighten (up); grow lighter. **светлость** brightness; Grace. **све́тлый** light; bright; joyous. **светлячо́к** (-чка́) glow-worm.

**свето-** *in comb* light, photo-. **светонепроница́емый** lightproof. ~**фи́льтр** light filter. ~**фо́р** traffic light(s).

**светово́й** light; luminous; ~ **день** daylight hours.

**светопреставле́ние** end of the world.

**све́тский** fashionable; refined; secular.

**светя́щийся** luminous, fluorescent. **свеча́** (*pl* -и, -е́й) candle; (spark-)plug. **свече́ние** luminescence, fluorescence. **све́чка** candle. **свечу́** *etc.: see* **свети́ть**

с|вѐшать *pf.* свѐшивать(ся *impf* of свѐсить(ся. свива́ть *impf of* свить

свида́ние meeting; appointment; до свида́ния! goodbye!

свидѐтель *m.* -ница witness. свидѐтельство evidence; testimony; certificate. свидѐтельствовать *impf (pf* за~, о~) give evidence, testify; be evidence (of); witness.

свина́рник pigsty.

свинѐц (-нца́) lead.

свини́на pork. сви́нка mumps. свино́й pig; pork. сви́нство despicable act; outrage; squalor.

свинцо́вый lead; leaden.

свинья́ (*pl* -ньи, -нѐй, -ньям) pig, swine.

свирѐль (reed-)pipe.

свирепѐть (-ѐю) *impf (pf* рас~) grow savage; become violent. свирѐпствовать *impf* rage; be rife. свирѐпый fierce, ferocious.

свиса́ть *impf*, сви́снуть (-ну; -ис) *pf* hang down, dangle; trail.

свист whistle; whistling. свиста́ть (-ищу́, -и́щешь) *impf* whistle. свистѐть (-ищу́) *impf*, сви́стнуть (-ну) *pf* whistle; hiss. свисто́к (-тка́) whistle.

сви́та suite; retinue.

сви́тер sweater.

сви́ток (-тка) roll, scroll. с|вить (совью́, совьёшь; -и́л, -а́, -о) *pf* (*impf also* свива́ть) twist, wind; ~ся roll up.

свихну́ться (-ну́сь, -нёшься) *impf* go mad; go astray.

свищ (-а́) flaw; (knot-)hole; fistula.

свищу́ *etc.: see* свиста́ть, свистѐть

свобо́да freedom. свобо́дно *adv* freely; easily; fluently; loose(ly). свобо́дный free; easy; vacant; spare; loose; flowing. свободолюби́вый freedom-loving. свободомы́слие free-thinking.

свод code; collection; arch, vault.

сводить (-ожу́, -о́дишь) *impf of* свести́

сво́дка summary; report. сво́дный composite; step-.

сво́дчатый arched, vaulted.

своево́лие self-will, wilfulness. своево́льный wilful.

своевремѐнно *adv* in good time; opportunely. своеврѐменный timely, opportune.

своенра́вие capriciousness. своенра́вный wilful, capricious.

своеобра́зие originality; peculiarity. своеобра́зный original; peculiar.

свожу́ *etc.: see* сводить, свози́ть. свози́ть (-ожу́, -о́зишь) *impf of* свезти́

свой (своего́) *m*, своя́ (своѐй) *f*, своё (своего́) *neut*, свои́ (свои́х) *pl*, *pron* one's (own); my, his, her, its; our, your, their. сво́йственный peculiar, characteristic. сво́йство property, attribute, characteristic.

сво́лочь swine; riff-raff.

сво́ра leash; pack.

свора́чивать *impf of* сверну́ть, свороти́ть. с|ворова́ть *pf.*

свороти́ть (-очу́, -о́тишь) *pf* (*impf* свора́чивать) dislodge; shift; turn; twist.

своя́к brother-in-law (*husband of wife's sister*). своя́ченица sister-in-law (*wife's sister*)-

свыка́ться *impf*, свыкну́ться (-нусь, -ыкся) *pf* get used.

**свысока́** *adv* haughtily. **свы́ше** *adv* from above. **свы́ше** *prep*+*gen* over; beyond.

**свя́занный** constrained; combined; bound; coupled. **c|вя-за́ть** (-жу́, -жешь) *pf*, **свя́-зывать** *impf* tie, bind; connect; ~**ся** get in touch; get involved. **связи́ст, -и́стка** signaller; worker in communication services. **свя́зка** sheaf, bundle; ligament. **свя́зный** connected, coherent. **связь** (*loc* -и́) connection; link; bond; liaison; communication(s).

**святи́лище** sanctuary. **свя́т-ки** (-ток) *pl* Christmas-tide. **свя́то** *adv* piously; religiously. **свят|о́й** (-ят, -а́, -о) holy; ~**о́й, ~а́я** *sb* saint. **святы́ня** sacred object or place. **свя-ще́нник** priest. **свяще́нный** sacred.

**гиб** bend. **сгиба́ть** *impf of* **согну́ть**

**сгла́дить** (-а́жу) *pf*, **сгла́жи-вать** *impf* smooth out; smooth over, soften.

**сгла́зить** (-а́жу) *pf* put the evil eye on.

**сгнива́ть** *impf*, **c|гнить** (-ию́, -иёшь; -ил, -а́, -о) *pf* rot.

**c|гно́иться** *pf*.

**сгова́риваться** *impf*, **сгово-ри́ться** *pf* come to an arrangement; arrange. **сго́вор** agreement. **сгово́рчивый** compliant.

**сгоня́ть** *impf of* **согна́ть**

**сгора́ние** combustion; дви́га-тель вну́треннего сгора́ния internal-combustion engine. **сгора́ть** *impf of* **сгоре́ть**

**c|горбить(ся** (-блю(сь) *pf*.

**c|горе́ть** (-рю́) *pf* (*impf also* **сгора́ть**) burn down; be burnt

down; be used up; burn; burn o.s. out. **сгоряча́** *adv* in the heat of the moment.

**c|гото́вить(ся** (-влю(сь) *pf*.

**сгреба́ть** *impf*, **сгрести́** (-ебу́, -ебёшь; -ёб, -па́) *pf* rake up, rake together.

**сгружа́ть** *impf*, **сгрузи́ть** (-ужу́, -у́зишь) *pf* unload.

**c|группирова́ть(ся** *pf*.

**сгусти́ть** (-ущу́) *pf*, **сгуща́ть** *impf* thicken; condense; ~**ся** thicken; condense; clot. **сгу́-сток** (-тка) clot. **сгуще́ние** thickening, condensation; clotting.

**сдава́ть** (сдаю́, сдаёшь) *impf of* **сдать**; ~ **экза́мен** take an examination; ~**ся** *impf of* **сда́ться**

**сда́вить** (-влю́, -вишь) *pf*, **сда́вливать** *impf* squeeze.

**сдать** (-ам, -ашь, -аст, -ади́м; -ал, -а́, -о) *pf* (*impf* **сдава́ть**) hand over; pass; let, hire out; surrender, give up; deal; ~**ся** surrender, yield. **сда́ча** hand-ing over; hiring out; surrender; change; deal.

**сдвиг** displacement; fault; change, improvement. **сдви-га́ть** *impf*, **сдви́нуть** (-ну) *pf* shift, move; move together; ~**ся** move, budge; come together.

**c|де́лать(ся** *pf*. **сде́лка** trans-action; deal, bargain. **сде́ль-н|ый** piece-work; ~**ая рабо́та** piece-work. **сде́льщина** piece-work.

**сде́ргивать** *impf of* **сдёрнуть**

**сде́ржанный** restrained; reserved. **сдержа́ть** (-жу́, -жишь) *pf*, **сде́рживать** *impf* hold back; restrain; keep.

**сдёрнуть** (-ну) *pf* (*impf* **сдёр-гивать**) pull off.

сдеру́ etc.: see содра́ть.

сдира́ть impf of содра́ть.

сдо́ба shortening; fancy bread, bun(s). сдо́бный (-бен, -бна́, -о) rich, short.

с|до́хнуть (-нет; сдох) pf die; kick the bucket.

сдружи́ться (-жу́сь) pf become friends.

сдува́ть impf, сду́нуть (-ну) pf, сдуть (-у́ю) pf blow away or off.

сеа́нс performance; showing; sitting.

себесто́имость prime cost; cost (price).

себя́ (dat & prep себе́, instr собо́й or собо́ю) refl pron oneself; myself, yourself, himself, etc.; ничего́ себе́ not bad; собо́й -looking, in appearance.

себялю́бие selfishness.

сев sowing.

се́вер north. се́верный north, northern; northerly. се́веро-восто́к north-east. се́веро-восто́чный north-east(ern). се́веро-за́пад north-west. се́веро-за́падный northwest(ern). северя́нин (pl -я́не, -я́н) northerner.

севооборо́т crop rotation.

сего́ see сей. сего́дня adv today. сего́дняшний of today, today's.

седе́ть (-е́ю) impf (pf по~) turn grey. седина́ (pl -ы) grey hair(s).

седла́ть impf (pf о~) saddle. седло́ (pl сёдла, -дел) saddle.

седоборо́дый grey-bearded. седоволо́сый grey-haired. седо́й (сед, -а́, -о) grey(-haired).

седо́к (-а́) passenger; rider.

седьмо́й seventh.

сезо́н season. сезо́нный seasonal.

сей (сего́) m, сия́ (сей) f, сие́ (сего́) neut, сий (сих) pl, pron this; these; сию́ мину́ту at once, instantly.

сейсми́ческий seismic.

сейф safe.

сейча́с adv (just) now; soon; immediately.

сёк etc.: see сечь

секрет secret.

секретариа́т secretariat.

секрета́рский secretarial. секрета́рша, секрета́рь (-я́) m secretary.

секре́тный secret.

секс sex. сексуа́льный sexual; sexy.

секстет sextet.

се́кта sect. секта́нт sectarian.

се́ктор sector.

секу́ etc.: see сечь

секуляриза́ция secularization.

секу́нда second. секунда́нт second. секу́ндный second. секундоме́р stop-watch.

секцио́нный sectional. се́кция section.

селёдка herring.

селезёнка spleen.

се́лезень (-зня) m drake.

селе́кция breeding.

селе́ние settlement, village.

сели́тра saltpetre, nitre.

сели́ть(ся impf (pf по~) settle. село́ (pl сёла) village.

сельдере́й celery.

сельдь (pl -и, -е́й) herring.

се́льск|ий rural; village; ~ое хозя́йство agriculture. сельскохозя́йственный agricultural.

сельсове́т village soviet.

сема́нтика semantics. семанти́ческий semantic.

семафо́р semaphore; signal.

сёмга (smoked) salmon.

семе́йный family; domestic.

семе́йство family.

се́мени *etc.: see* се́мя

семени́ть *impf* mince.

семени́ться *impf* seed. семенни́к (-á) testicle; seed-vessel. семенно́й seed; seminal.

семёрка seven; figure 7; No. 7. се́меро (-ы́х) seven.

семе́стр term, semester.

се́мечко (*pl* -и) seed; *pl* sunflower seeds.

семидесятиле́тие seventy years; seventieth anniversary, birthday. семидеся́тый seventieth; ~ые го́ды the seventies. семиле́тка seven-year school. семиле́тний seven-year; seven-year-old.

семина́р seminar. семина́рия seminary.

семисо́тый seven-hundredth. семна́дцатый seventeenth. семна́дцать seventeen. семь (-ми́, -мью) seven. се́мьдесят (-мидесяти, -мьюдесятью) seventy. семьсо́т (-мисо́т, *instr* -мьюста́ми) seven hundred. се́мью *adv* seven times.

семья́ (*pl* -мьи, -ме́й, -мьям) family. семьяни́н family man.

се́мя (-мени; *pl* -мена́, -мя́н, -мена́м) seed; semen, sperm.

сена́т senate. сена́тор senator.

се́ни (-е́й) *pl* (entrance-)hall.

се́но hay. сенова́л hayloft.

сеноко́с haymaking; hayfield. сенокоси́лка mowing-machine.

сенсацио́нный sensational. сенса́ция sensation.

сенте́нция maxim.

сентимента́льный sentimental.

сентя́брь (-я́) *m* September. сентя́брьский September.

се́псис sepsis.

се́ра sulphur; ear-wax.

серб, ~ка Serb. Се́рбия Serbia. се́рбский Serb(ian). сербскохорва́тский Serbo-Croat(ian).

серва́нт sideboard.

серви́з service, set. сервирова́ть *impf & pf* serve; lay (a table). сервиро́вка laying; table lay-out.

серде́чник core. серде́чность cordiality; warmth. серде́чный heart; cardiac; cordial; warm(-hearted). серди́тый angry. серди́ть (-ржу́, -рдишь) *impf* (*pf* рас~) anger; ~ся be angry. сердобо́льный tender-hearted. се́рдце (*pl* -á, -де́ц) heart; в се́рдцах in anger; от всего́ се́рдца from the bottom of one's heart. сердцебие́ние palpitation. сердцеви́дный heart-shaped. сердцеви́на core, pith, heart.

серебри́стый silver-plated. серебри́стый silvery. серебри́ть *impf* (*pf* по~) silver, silver-plate; ~ся become silvery. серебро́ silver. сере́бряный silver.

середи́на middle.

серёжка earring; catkin.

серена́да serenade.

се́ренький grey; dull.

сержа́нт sergeant.

сери́йный serial; mass. се́рия series; part.

се́рный sulphur; sulphuric.

серогла́зый grey-eyed.

се́рость uncouthness; ignorance.

серп (-á) sickle; ~ луны́ crescent moon.

серпанти́н streamer.

сертифика́т certificate.

се́рый (сер, -á, -о) grey; dull; uneducated.

серьга́ (*pl* -и, -рёг) earring.

серьёзность seriousness. серьёзный serious.

се́ссия session.

сестра́ (*pl* сёстры, сестёр, сёстрам) sister.

сесть (ся́ду) *pf* (*impf* сади́ться) sit down; land; set; shrink; +на+*acc* board, get on.

се́тка net, netting; (luggage-) rack; string bag; grid.

се́товать *impf* (*pf* по~) complain.

сетча́тка retina. сеть (*loc* -и́, *pl* -и, -е́й) net; network.

сече́ние section. сечь (сечёшь, сёк) *impf* (*pf* вы́~) cut to pieces; flog; ~ся split.

се́ялка seed drill. се́ять (се́ю) *impf* (*pf* по~) sow.

сжа́литься *pf* take pity (над+*instr*) on.

сжа́тие pressure; grasp, grip; compression. сжа́тый compressed; compact; concise.

с|жа́ть¹ (сожму́, -нёшь) *pf*.

сжа́ть² (сожму́, -мёшь) *pf* (*impf* сжима́ть) squeeze; compress; grip; clench; ~ся tighten; shrink, contract.

с|же́чь (сожгу́, сожжёшь; сжёг, сожгла́) *pf* (*impf* сжига́ть) burn (down); cremate.

сжива́ть *impf* of сжи́ться

сжига́ть *impf* of сжечь

сжима́ть(ся *impf* of сжать²(ся

сжи́ться (-иву́сь, -ивёшься; -и́лся, -ась) *pf* (*impf* сжива́ться) с+*instr* get used to.

с|жу́льничать *pf*.

сза́ди *adv* from behind; behind. сза́ди *prep*+*gen* behind.

сзыва́ть *impf* of созва́ть

сиби́рский Siberian. Сиби́рь Siberia. сибиря́к (-а́), сибиря́чка Siberian.

сига́ра cigar. сигаре́та cigarette.

сигна́л signal. сигнализа́ция signalling. сигнализи́ровать *impf* & *pf* (*pf also* про~) signal. сигна́льный signal. сигна́льщик signalman.

сиде́лка sick-nurse. сиде́ние sitting. сиде́нье seat. сиде́ть (сижу́) *impf* sit; be; fit. сидя́чий sitting; sedentary.

сие́ *etc*.: *see* сей

си́зый (сиз, -а́, -о) (blue-)grey.

сий *see* сей

си́ла strength; force; power; в си́лу +*gen* on the strength of, because of; не по ~ам beyond one's powers; си́лой by force. сила́ч (-а́) strong man. си́литься *impf* try, make efforts. силово́й power; of force.

сило́к (-лка́) noose, snare.

си́лос silo; silage.

силуэ́т silhouette.

си́льно *adv* strongly, violently; very much, greatly. си́льный (-лен *or* -лён, -льна́, -о) strong; powerful; intense, hard.

симбио́з symbiosis.

си́мвол symbol. символизи́ровать *impf* symbolize. символи́зм symbolism. символи́ческий symbolic.

симме́трия symmetry.

симпатизи́ровать *impf* +*dat* like, sympathize with. симпати́чный likeable, nice. симпа́тия liking; sympathy.

симпо́зиум symposium.

симпто́м symptom.

симули́ровать *impf* & *pf* simulate, feign. симуля́нт malingerer, sham. симуля́ция simulation, pretence.

симфо́ния symphony.

синаго́га synagogue.

синева́ blue. синева́тый bluish. синегла́зый blue-eyed.

синеть (-éю) *impf* (*pf* по~) turn blue; show blue. синий (синь, -ня, -не) (dark) blue.

синица titmouse.

синод synod. синоним synonym. синтаксис syntax.

синтез synthesis. синтезировать *impf* & *pf* synthesize. синтетический synthetic.

синус sine; sinus.

синхронизировать *impf* & *pf* synchronize.

синь[1] blue. синь[2] *see* синий.

синька blueing; blue-print.

синяк (-á) bruise.

сионизм Zionism.

сиплый hoarse, husky. сипнуть (-ну; сип) *impf* (*pf* о~) become hoarse, husky.

сирена siren; hooter.

сиреневый lilac(-coloured). сирень lilac.

Сирия Syria.

сироп syrup.

сирота (*pl* -ы) *m* & *f* orphan. сиротливый lonely. сиротский orphan's, orphans'.

система system. систематизировать *impf* & *pf* systematize. систематический, систематичный systematic.

ситец (-тца) (printed) cotton; chintz.

сито sieve.

ситуация situation.

ситцевый print, chintz.

сифилис syphilis.

сифон siphon.

сия *see* сей

сияние radiance. сиять *impf* shine, beam.

сказ tale. сказание story, legend. сказать (-ажу, -ажешь) *pf* (*impf* говорить) say; speak; tell. сказаться (-ажусь, -ажешься) *pf*, сказываться *impf* tell (on); declare o.s. сказитель *m* story-teller. сказка (fairy)tale; fib. сказочный fairy-tale; fantastic. сказуемое *sb* predicate.

скакалка skipping-rope. скакать (-ачу, -ачешь) *impf* (*pf* по~) skip, jump; gallop. скаковой race, racing.

скала (*pl* -ы) rock; cliff. скалистый rocky.

скалить *impf* (*pf* о~); ~ зубы bare one's teeth; grin; ~ся bare one's teeth.

скалка rolling-pin.

скалолаз rock-climber.

скалывать *impf of* сколоть

скальп scalp.

скальпель *m* scalpel.

скамеечка footstool; small bench. скамейка bench. скамья (*pl* скамьи, -ей) bench; ~ подсудимых dock.

скандал scandal; brawl, rowdy scene. скандалист trouble-maker. скандалиться *impf* (*pf* о~) disgrace o.s. скандальный scandalous.

скандинавский Scandinavian. скандировать *impf* & *pf* declaim.

скапливать(ся *impf of* скопить(ся

скарб goods and chattels.

скаредный stingy.

скарлатина scarlet fever.

скат slope; pitch.

скатать *pf* (*impf* скатывать) roll (up).

скатерть (*pl* -и, -ей) table-cloth.

скатить (-ачу, -атишь) *pf*, скатывать[1] *impf* roll down; ~ся roll down; slip, slide. скатывать[2] *impf of* скатать

скафандр diving-suit; space-suit.

скачка gallop, galloping. скачки (-чек) *pl* horse-race; races.

скачóк (-чкá) jump, leap.

скáшивать *impf of* скоси́ть

сквáжина slit, chink; well.

сквер public garden.

скверно badly; bad. скверно-слóвить (-влю) *impf* use foul language. сквéрный foul; bad.

сквози́ть *impf* be transparent; show through; сквози́т *impers* there is a draught. сквознóй through; transparent. сквозня́к (-á) draught. сквозь *prep+acc* through.

скворéц (-рцá) starling.

скелéт skeleton.

скéптик sceptic. скептици́зм scepticism. скепти́ческий sceptical.

скетч sketch.

ски́дка reduction. ски́дывать *impf*, ски́нуть (-ну) *pf* throw off *or* down; knock off.

ски́петр sceptre.

скипидáр turpentine.

скирд (-á; *pl* -ы́), скирдá (*pl* -ы, -áм) stack, rick.

скисáть *impf*, ски́снуть (-ну; скис) *pf* go sour.

скитáлец (-льца) wanderer. скитáться *impf* wander.

скиф Scythian.

склад[1] depot; store.

склад[2] mould; turn; logical connection; ~ умá mentality.

склáдка fold; pleat; crease; wrinkle.

склáдно *adv* smoothly.

складнóй folding, collapsible.

склáдный (-ден, -днá, -о) well-knit, well-built; smooth, coherent.

склáдчина: в склáдчину by clubbing together. склáдывать(ся *impf of* сложи́ть(ся

склéивать *impf*, с|клéить *pf* stick together; ~ся stick together.

склеп (burial) vault, crypt.

склепáть *pf*, склёпывать *impf* rivet. склёпка riveting.

склерóз sclerosis.

склóка squabble.

склон slope; на ~е лет in one's declining years. склонéние inclination; declension. склони́ть (-ню́, -ни́шь), склоня́ть *impf* incline; bow; win over; decline; ~ся bend, bow; yield; be declined. склóнность inclination; tendency. склóнный (-нен, -ннá, -нно) inclined, disposed. склоня́емый declinable.

скля́нка phial; bottle; (*naut*) bell.

скобá (*pl* -ы, -áм) cramp, clamp; staple.

скóбка *dim of* скобá; bracket; *pl* parentheses, parentheses.

скобли́ть (-облю́, -óблишь) *impf* scrape, plane.

скóванность constraint. скóванный constrained; bound. сковáть (скую́, скуёшь) *pf* (*impf* скóвывать) forge; chain; fetter; pin down, hold, contain.

сковородá (*pl* сковóроды, -рóд, -áм), сковорóдка frying-pan.

скóвывать *impf of* сковáть

сколáчивать *impf*, сколоти́ть (-очу́, -óтишь) *pf* knock together.

сколóть (-лю́, -лешь) *pf* (*impf* скáлывать) chop off; pin together.

скольжéние sliding, slipping; glide. скользи́ть (-льжу́) *impf*, скользну́ть (-ну́, -нёшь) *pf* slide; glide. скóльзкий (-зок, -зкá, -о) slippery. скользя́щий sliding.

скóлько *adv* how much; how many; as far as.

с|командовáть *pf*. с|комби-

ни́ровать *pf.* с|ко́мкать *pf.*
с|комплектова́ть *pf.*
с|компромети́ровать *pf.*
с|конструи́ровать *pf.*
**сконфу́женный** embarrassed, confused, disconcerted. **с|конфу́зить(ся** (-у́жу(сь)) *pf.*
с|концентри́ровать *pf.*
**сконча́ться** *pf* pass away, die.
с|копи́ровать *pf.*
**скопи́ть** (-плю́, -пишь) *pf* (*impf* **ска́пливать**) save (up); amass; **~ся** accumulate. **скопле́ние** accumulation; crowd.
**ско́пом** *adv* in a crowd, en masse.
**скорбе́ть** (-блю́) *impf* grieve. **ско́рбный** sorrowful. **скорбь** (*pl* -и, -е́й) sorrow.
**скоре́е, скоре́й** *comp of* ско́ро, ско́рый; *adv* rather, sooner; **как мо́жно ~** as soon as possible; **~ всего́** most likely.
**скорлупа́** (*pl* -ы) shell.
**скорня́к** (-а́) furrier.
**ско́ро** *adv* quickly; soon.
**скоро-** *in comb* quick-, fast-. **скорова́рка** pressure-cooker. **~гово́рка** patter; tongue-twister. **ско́ропись** cursive; shorthand. **~по́ртящийся** perishable. **~пости́жный** sudden; **~спе́лый** early; fast-ripening; premature; **~сшива́тель** *m* binder, file. **~те́чный** transient, short-lived.
**скоростно́й** high-speed. **ско́рость** (*gen pl* -е́й) speed; gear.
**скорпио́н** scorpion; Scorpio.
с|корректи́ровать *pf.* с|ко́рчить(ся (-чу(сь)) *pf.*
**ско́рый** (скор, -а́, -о) quick, near; forthcoming; **~ая по́мощь** first-aid; ambulance.
с|коси́ть¹ (-ошу́, -о́сишь) *pf*

(*impf also* **ска́шивать**) mow.
с|коси́ть² (-ошу́) *pf* (*impf also* **ска́шивать**) squint; cut on the cross.
**скот** (-а́), **скоти́на** cattle; live-stock; beast. **ско́тный** cattle.
**ското-** *in comb* cattle. **ското-бо́йня** (*gen pl* -бен) slaugh-ter-house. **~во́д** cattle-breeder. **~во́дство** cattle-raising.
**ско́тский** cattle; brutish. **ско́тство** brutish condition; brutality.
**скра́сить** (-а́шу) *pf*, **скра́ши-вать** *impf* smooth over; re-lieve.
**скребо́к** (-бка́) scraper. **скребу́** *etc.: see* **скрести́**
**скре́жет** grating; gnashing. **скрежета́ть** (-ещу́, -е́щешь) *impf* grate; +*instr* gnash.
**скре́па** clamp, brace; counter-signature.
**скрепи́ть** (-плю́) *pf*, **скре-пля́ть** *impf* fasten (together); make fast; clamp; countersign, ratify; **скрепя́ се́рдце** reluc-tantly. **скре́пка** paper-clip. **скрепле́ние** fastening; clamp-ing; tie, clamp.
**скрести́** (-ебу́, -ебёшь; -ёб, -ла́) *impf* scrape; scratch; **~сь** scratch.
**скрести́ть** (-ещу́) *pf*, **скре́-щивать** *impf* cross; inter-breed. **скреще́ние** crossing. **скре́щивание** crossing; in-terbreeding.
с|криви́ть(ся (-влю́(сь)) *pf.*
**скрип** squeak, creak. **скри-па́ч** (-а́) violinist. **скрипе́ть** (-плю́) *impf*, **скри́пнуть** (-ну) *pf* squeak, creak; scratch. **скри́пичный** violin; **~ ключ** treble clef. **скри́пка** violin. **скрипу́чий** squeaky, creaking.

с|кро́йть *pf.*

скро́мничать *impf* (*pf* по~) be (too) modest. скро́мность modesty. скро́мный (-мен, -мна́, -о) modest.

скро́ю *etc.: see* скрыть.

скро́ю *etc.: see* скро́ить

скрупулёзный scrupulous.

с|крути́ть (-учу́, -у́тишь) *pf*, скру́чивать *impf* twist; roll; tie up.

скрыва́ть *impf*, скрыть (-о́ю) *pf* hide, conceal; ~ся hide, go into hiding, be hidden; steal away; disappear. скры́тничать *impf* be secretive. скры́тный secretive. скры́тый secret, hidden; latent.

скря́га *m & f* miser.

ску́дный (-ден, -дна́, -о) scanty; meagre. ску́дость scarcity, paucity.

ску́ка boredom.

скула́ (*pl* -ы) cheek-bone. скула́стый with high cheek-bones.

скули́ть *impf* whine, whimper.

скульпто́р sculptor. скульпту́ра sculpture.

ску́мбрия mackerel.

ску́нс skunk.

скупа́ть *impf of* скупи́ть

скупе́ц (-пца́) miser.

скупи́ть (-плю́, -пишь) *pf* (*impf* скупа́ть) buy (up).

скупи́ться (-плю́сь) *impf* (*pf* по~) be stingy; skimp; be sparing (of +на+*acc*).

ску́пка buying (up).

ску́по *adv* sparingly. скупо́й (-п, -а́, -о) stingy, meagre. ску́пость stinginess.

скупщи́к buyer(-up).

ску́тер (*pl* -а́) outboard speed-boat.

скуча́ть *impf* be bored; +по +*dat* miss, yearn for.

ску́ченность density, over-

crowding. ску́ченный dense, overcrowded. ску́чить (-чу) *pf* crowd (together); ~ся cluster; crowd together.

ску́чный (-чен, -чна́, -о) boring; мне ску́чно I'm bored.

с|ку́шать *pf.* скую́ *etc.: see* ско-ва́ть

слабе́ть (-е́ю) *impf* (*pf* о~) weaken, grow weak. слаби́тельный laxative; ~ое *sb* laxative. слаби́ть *impf* impers: его́ сла́бит he has diarrhoea.

сла́бо- *in comb* weak, feeble, slight. слабово́лие weakness of will. ~во́льный weak-willed. ~не́рвный nervy, nervous. ~ра́звитый under-developed. ~у́мие feeble-mindedness. ~у́мный feeble-minded.

сла́бость weakness. сла́бый (-б, -а́, -о) weak.

сла́ва glory; fame; на сла́ву wonderfully well. сла́вить (-влю) *impf* celebrate, sing the praises of; ~ся (+*instr*) be famous (for). сла́вный glorious, renowned; nice.

славяни́н (*pl* -я́не, -я́н), славя́нка Slav. славяно-фи́л Slavophil(e). славя́нский Slav, Slavonic.

слага́емое *sb* component, term, member. слага́ть *impf of* сложи́ть

сла́дить (-а́жу) *pf* c+*instr* cope with; handle; arrange.

сла́дкий (-док, -дка́, -о) sweet; ~ое *sb* sweet course. сладостра́стник voluptuary. сладостра́стный voluptuous. сла́дость joy; sweetness; *pl* sweets.

сла́женность harmony. сла́женный co-ordinated, harmonious.

сла́мывать *impf of* сломи́ть
сла́нец (-нца) *m* shale, slate.
сластёна *m & f* person with a sweet tooth. сласть (*pl* -и, -е́й) delight; *pl* sweets, sweet things.
слать (шлю, шлёшь) *impf* send.
слаща́вый sugary, sickly-sweet. сла́ще *comp of* сла́дкий
сле́ва *adv* to *or* on the left; ~ напра́во from left to right.
слёг *etc.*: *see* слечь
слегка́ *adv* slightly; lightly.
след (следа́, *dat* -у, *loc* -у́; *pl* -ы́) track; footprint; trace.
следи́ть[1] (-ежу́) *impf* +за+*instr* watch; follow; keep up with; look after; keep an eye on. следи́ть[2] (-ежу́) *impf* (*pf* на~) leave footprints. сле́дование movement. сле́дователь *m* investigator. сле́довательно *adv* consequently. сле́довать *impf* (*pf* по~) I. +*dat or* за+*instr* follow; go, be bound; II. *impers* ought; be owing, be owed; вам сле́дует +*inf* you ought to; как сле́дует properly; as it should be; ско́лько с меня́ сле́дует? how much do I owe (you)? сле́дом *adv* (за+*instr*) immediately after, close behind. сле́дственный investigation, inquiry. сле́дствие[1] consequence. сле́дствие[2] investigation. сле́дующий following, next.
слёжка shadowing.
слеза́ (*pl* -ёзы, -ам) tear.
слеза́ть *impf of* слезть
слези́ться (-и́тся) *impf* water. слезли́вый tearful. слёзный tear; tearful. слезоточи́вый watering; ~ газ tear-gas.
слезть (-зу; слез) *pf* (*impf*

слеза́ть) climb *or* get down; dismount; get off; come off.
слепе́нь (-пня́) *m* horse-fly.
слепе́ц (-пца́) blind man.
слепи́ть[1] *impf* blind; dazzle.
с|лепи́ть[2] (-плю́, -пишь) *pf* stick together.
слепну́ть (-ну; слеп) *impf* (*pf* о~) go blind. сле́по *adv* blindly. слеп|о́й (-п, -а́, -о) blind; *as sb* blind man; ~ы́е *sb pl* the blind. слепо́к (-пка) cast.
слепота́ blindness.
сле́сарь (*pl* -я́ *or* -и) *m* metalworker; locksmith.
слёт gathering; rally. слета́ть *impf*, слете́ть (-ечу́) *pf* fly down *or* away; fall down *or* off; ~ся fly together; congregate.
слечь (сля́гу, -я́жешь; слёг, -ла́) *pf* take to one's bed.
сли́ва plum; plum-tree.
слива́ть(ся *impf of* слить(ся.
сли́вки (-вок) *pl* cream. сли́вочн|ый cream; creamy; ~ое ма́сло butter; ~ое моро́женое dairy ice-cream.
слизи́стый slimy. слизня́к (-а́) slug. слизь mucus; slime.
с|линя́ть *pf*.
слипа́ться *impf*, сли́пнуться (-нется; -ипся) *pf* stick together.
сли́тно together, as one word.
сли́ток (-тка) ingot, bar.
с|лить (солью́, -ьёшь; -ил, -а́, -о) *pf* (*impf also* слива́ть) pour, pour out *or* off; fuse, amalgamate; ~ся flow together; blend; merge.
слича́ть *impf*, сличи́ть (-чу́) *pf* collate; check. сличе́ние collation, checking.
сли́шком *adv* too; too much.
слия́ние confluence; merging; merger.

**словáк, -áчка** Slovak. **словáцкий** Slovak.

**словáрный** lexical; dictionary. **словáрь (-я́)** *m* dictionary; vocabulary. **словéсность** literature; philology. **словéсный** verbal, oral. **слóвно** *conj* as if; like, as. **слóво** (*pl* **-á**) word; **одни́м ~м** in a word. **слóвом** *adv* in a word. **словообразовáние** word-formation. **словоохóтливый** talkative. **словосочетáние** word combination, phrase. **словоупотреблéние** usage.

**слог¹** style.

**слог²** (*pl* **-и́, -óв**) syllable.

**слоёный** flaky.

**сложéние** composition; addition; build, constitution. **сложи́ть** (**-жу́, -жишь**) *pf* (*impf* **класть, склáдывать, слагáть**) put *or* lay (together); pile, stack; add, add up; fold (up); compose; take off, put down; lay down; **~ся** turn out; take shape; arise; club together. **слóжность** complication; complexity. **слóжный** (**-жен, -жнá, -о**) complicated; complex; compound.

**слои́стый** stratified; flaky. **слой** (*pl* **-й, -ёв**) layer; stratum.

**слом** demolition, pulling down. **с|ломáть(ся** *pf.* **сломи́ть** (**-млю́, -мишь**) *pf* (*impf* **слáмывать**) break (off); overcome; **сломя́ гóлову** at breakneck speed; **~ся** break.

**слон** (**-á**) elephant; bishop. **слони́ха** she-elephant. **слонóвый** elephant; **~ая кость** ivory.

**слоня́ться** *impf* loiter, mooch (about).

**слугá** (*pl* **-и**) *m* (man) serv-

ant. **служáнка** servant, maid. **служáщий** *sb* employee. **слу́жба** service; work. **служéбный** office; official; auxiliary; secondary. **служéние** service, serving. **служи́ть** (**-жу́, -жишь**) *impf* (*pf* **по~**) serve; work.

**с|лукáвить** (**-влю**) *pf.*

**слух** hearing; ear; rumour; по **~у** by ear. **слухов|óй** acoustic, auditory; aural; **~óй аппарáт** hearing aid; **~óе окнó** dormer (window).

**слу́чай** incident, event; case; opportunity; chance; **ни в кóем случае** in no circumstances. **случáйно** *adv* by chance, accidentally; by any chance. **случáйность** chance. **случáйный** accidental; chance; incidental. **случáться** *impf*, **случи́ться** *pf* happen.

**слу́шание** listening; hearing. **слу́шатель** *m* listener; student; *pl* audience. **слу́шать** *impf* (*pf* **по~, про~**) listen (to); hear; attend lectures on; **(я) слу́шаю!** hello!; very well; **~ся** +*gen* obey, +*gen* heed.

**слыть** (**-ыву́, -ывёшь; -ыл, -á, -о**) *impf* (*pf* **про~**) have the reputation (+*instr or* **за**+*acc* for).

**слыхáть** *impf*, **слы́шать** (**-шу**) *impf* (*pf* **у~**) hear; sense. **слы́шаться** (**-шится**) *impf* (*pf* **по~**) be heard. **слы́шимость** audibility. **слы́шимый** audible. **слы́шный** (**-шен, -шнá, -шно**) audible.

**слюдá** mica.

**слюнá** (*pl* **-и, -éй**) saliva; spit; *pl* spittle. **слюня́вый** dribbling.

**слягу** *etc.: see* **слечь**

**сля́коть** slush.

**см.** *abbr* (*of* **смотри́**) see, *vide*.

**сма́зать** (-а́жу) *pf*, **сма́зывать** *impf* lubricate; grease; slur over. **сма́зка** lubrication; greasing; grease. **сма́зочный** lubricating.

**смак** relish. **смакова́ть** *impf* relish; savour.

**сманеври́ровать** *pf*.

**сма́нивать** *impf*, **смани́ть** (-ню́, -нишь) *pf* entice.

**смастери́ть** *pf*. **сма́тывать** *impf of* **смота́ть**

**сма́хивать** *impf*, **смахну́ть** (-ну́, -нёшь) *pf* brush away *or* off.

**сма́чивать** *impf of* **смочи́ть**

**сме́жный** adjacent.

**смека́лка** native wit.

**смёл** *etc.: see* **смести́**

**смеле́ть** (-е́ю) *impf* (*pf* о~) grow bolder. **сме́лость** boldness, courage. **сме́лый** (-л, -ла́, -ло) bold, courageous. **смельча́к** (-а́) daredevil.

**смелю́** *etc.: see* **смоло́ть**

**сме́на** changing; change; replacement(s); relief; shift. **смени́ть** (-ню́, -нишь) *pf*, **сменя́ть**[1] *impf* change; replace; relieve; ~**ся** hand over; be relieved; take turns; +*instr* give place to. **сме́нный** shift; changeable. **сме́нщик** relief; *pl* new shift. **сменя́ть**[2] *pf* exchange.

**сме́рить** *pf*.

**смерка́ться** *impf*, **смёркнуться** (-нется) *pf* get dark.

**смерте́льный** mortal, fatal, death; extreme. **сме́ртность** mortality. **сме́ртный** mortal; death; deadly, extreme. **смерть** (*gen pl* -е́й) death.

**смерч** whirlwind; waterspout.

**смеси́тельный** mixing. **сме́сить** (-ешу́, -е́сишь) *pf* (*impf* **сме́шивать**) sweep off, away.

**смести́ть** (-ещу́) *pf* (*impf* **смеща́ть**) displace; remove.

**смесь** mixture; medley.

**сме́та** estimate.

**смета́на** sour cream.

**смета́ть**[1] *pf* (*impf also* **смётывать**) tack (together).

**смета́ть**[2] *impf of* **смести́**

**сметли́вый** quick, sharp.

**смету́** *etc.: see* **смести́**. **смётывать** *impf of* **смета́ть**

**сметь** (-е́ю) *impf* (*pf* по~) dare.

**смех** laughter; laugh. **смехотво́рный** laughable.

**сме́шанный** mixed; combined. **сме́шать** *pf*, **сме́шивать** *impf* mix, blend; confuse; ~**ся** mix (inter)blend; get mixed up. **смеше́ние** mixture; mixing up.

**смеши́ть** (-шу́) *impf* (*pf* на~, рас~) make laugh. **смешли́вый** given to laughing. **смешно́й** (-шо́н, -шна́) funny; ridiculous.

**смешу́** *etc.: see* **смеси́ть**, **смеши́ть**

**смеща́ть(ся** *impf of* **смести́ть**(ся. **смеще́ние** displacement, removal. **смещу́** *etc.: see* **смести́ть**

**смея́ться** (-ею́сь, -ёшься) *impf* laugh (at +над+*instr*).

**смире́ние** humility, meekness. **смире́нный** humble, meek. **смири́тельный**: ~**ая руба́шка** straitjacket. **смири́ть** *pf*, **смиря́ть** *impf* restrain, subdue; ~**ся** submit; resign o.s. **сми́рно** *adv* quietly; ~**!** attention! **сми́рный** quiet; submissive.

**смогу́** *etc.: see* **смочь**

смола́ (*pl* -ы) resin; pitch, tar; rosin. смоли́стый resinous.

смолка́ть *impf*, смо́лкнуть (-ну; -олк) *pf* fall silent.

с́молоду *adv* from one's youth.

с́молоти́ть (-очу́, -о́тишь) *pf.* с́моло́ть (смелю́, сме́лешь) *pf.*

смоляно́й pitch, tar, resin.

с́монти́ровать *pf.*

сморка́ть *impf* (*pf* вы́~) blow; ~ся blow one's nose.

сморо́дина (*no pl*; *usu collect*) currant; currants; currant-bush.

смо́рщенный wrinkled. с́мо́рщить(ся) (-щу(сь)) *pf.*

смота́ть *pf* (*impf* сма́тывать) wind, reel.

смотр (*loc* -у́; *pl* -о́тры) review, inspection. смотре́ть (-рю́, -ришь) *impf* (*pf* по~) look (at на+*acc*); see; watch; look through; examine; +за+*instr* look after; +в+*acc*, на+*acc* look on to; +*instr* look (like); смотри́(те)! take care!; смотря́ it depends; смотря́ по+*dat* depending on; ~ся look at o.s. смотрово́й observation, inspection.

смочи́ть (-чу́, -чишь) *pf* (*impf* сма́чивать) moisten.

с́мочь (-огу́, -о́жешь; смог, -ла́) *pf.*

с́моше́нничать *pf.* смо́ю *etc.*: *see* смы́ть

смрад stench. смра́дный stinking.

сму́глый (-гл, -а́, -о) dark-complexioned, swarthy.

смути́ть (-ущу́) *pf*, смуща́ть *impf* be embarrass, confuse; ~ся be embarrassed; be confused. сму́тный vague; dim; troubled.

смуще́ние embarrassment,

confusion. смущённый (-ён, -а́) embarrassed, confused.

смыва́ть *impf* of смыть

смыка́ть(ся) *impf of* сомкну́ть(ся)

смысл sense; meaning. смы́слить (смы́слю) understand. смыслово́й semantic.

смыть (смо́ю) *pf* (*impf* смыва́ть) wash off, away.

смычо́к (-чка́) bow.

смышлёный clever.

смягча́ть *impf*, смягчи́ть (-чу́) *pf* soften; alleviate; ~ся soften; relent; grow mild.

смягче́ние confusion; commotion. с́мя́ть(ся (сомну́(сь, -нёшь(ся)) *pf.*

снабди́ть (-бжу́) *pf*, снабжа́ть *impf* +*instr* supply with.

снабже́ние supply, supplying.

сна́йпер sniper.

снару́жи *adv* on *or* from (the) outside.

снаря́д projectile, missile; shell; contrivance; tackle, gear. снаряди́ть (-яжу́) *pf*, снаряжа́ть *impf* equip, fit out. снаряже́ние equipment, outfit.

снасть (*gen pl* -е́й) tackle; *pl* rigging.

снача́ла *adv* at first; all over again.

сна́шивать *impf* of сноси́ть

СНГ *abbr* (*of* Содру́жество незави́симых госуда́рств) CIS.

снег (*loc* -у́; *pl* -а́) snow.

снеги́рь (-я́) bullfinch.

снегово́й snow. снегопа́д snowfall. Снегу́рочка Snow Maiden. снежи́нка snowflake. сне́жный snow(y); ~ая ба́ба snowman. снежо́к (-жка́) light snow; snowball.

снести́[1] (-су́, -сёшь; -ёс, -ла́) *pf* (*impf* сноси́ть) take;

together; bring or fetch down; carry away; blow off; demolish; endure; **~сь** communicate (+*instr* with).

**с|нести́²(сь** (-су́(сь, -сёшь(ся, снёс(ся, -сла́(сь) *pf*.

**снижа́ть** *impf*, **сни́зить (-и́жу)** *pf* lower; bring down; reduce; **~ся** come down; fall. **сниже́ние** lowering; loss of height.

**снизойти́ (-йду́, -йдёшь; -ошёл, -шла́)** *pf* (*impf* **снисходи́ть**) condescend.

**сни́зу** *adv* from below.

**снима́ть(ся** *impf of* **снять(ся. сни́мок (-мка)** photograph. **сниму́** *etc.*: *see* **снять**

**сниска́ть (-ищу́, -и́щешь)** *pf*, **сни́скивать** *impf* gain, win.

**снисходи́тельность** condescension; leniency. **снисходи́тельный** condescending; lenient. **снисходи́ть (-ожу́, -о́дишь)** *impf of* **снизойти́. снисхожде́ние** indulgence, leniency.

**сни́ться** *impf* (*pf* **при~**) *impers*+*dat* dream.

**сноби́зм** snobbery.

**сно́ва** *adv* again, anew.

**снова́ть (сную́, снуёшь)** *impf* rush about.

**сновиде́ние** dream.

**сноп (-á)** sheaf.

**сноро́вка** knack, skill.

**снос** demolition; drift; wear.

**сноси́ть¹ (-ошу́, -о́сишь)** *pf* (*impf* **сна́шивать**) wear out.

**сноси́ть²(ся (-ошу́(сь, -о́сишь(ся** *impf of* **снести́(сь. сно́ска** footnote. **сно́сно** *adv* tolerably, so-so. **сно́сный** tolerable; fair.

**снотво́рный** soporific.

**сноха́ (*pl* -и)** daughter-in-law.

**сноше́ние** intercourse; relations, dealings.

**сношу́** *etc.*: *see* **сноси́ть**

**сня́тие** taking down; removal; making. **снять (сниму́, -и́мешь; -я́л, -á, -о)** *pf* (*impf* **снима́ть**) take off; take down; gather in; remove; rent; take; make; photograph; **~ся** come off; move off; be photographed.

**со** *see* **с** *prep*.

**со-** *pref* co-, joint. **соа́втор** co-author.

**соба́ка** dog. **соба́чий** dog's; canine. **соба́чка** little dog; trigger.

**соберу́** *etc.*: *see* **собра́ть**

**собе́с** *abbr* (*of* **социа́льное обеспе́чение**) social security (department).

**собесе́дник** interlocutor, companion. **собесе́дование** conversation.

**собира́тель** *m* collector. **собира́ть(ся** *impf of* **собра́ть(ся**

**собла́зн** temptation. **собла́знитель** *m*, **~ница** tempter; seducer. **соблазни́тельный** tempting; seductive. **соблазни́ть** *pf*, **соблазня́ть** *impf* tempt; seduce.

**соблюда́ть** *impf*, **со|блюсти́ (-юду́, -дёшь; -ю́л, -á)** *pf* observe; keep (to). **соблюде́ние** observance; maintenance.

**собо́й, собо́ю** *see* **себя́**

**соболе́знование** sympathy, condolence(s). **соболе́зновать** *impf* +*dat* sympathize or commiserate with.

**со́боль (*pl* -и *or* -я́)** *m* sable.

**собо́р** cathedral; council, synod. **собо́рный** cathedral.

**собра́ние** meeting; assembly; collection. **со́бранный** collected; concentrated. **собра́т (*pl* -ья, -ьев)** colleague.

собра́ть (-беру́, -берёшь; -а́л, -а́, -о) pf (impf собира́ть) gather; collect; ~ся gather; prepare; intend, be going; +c+instr collect.

со́бственник owner, proprietor. со́бственнический proprietary; proprietorial. со́бственно adv: ~ (говоря́) strictly speaking, as a matter of fact. со́бственнору́чно adv personally, with one's own hand. со́бственность property; ownership. со́бственн|ый (one's) own; proper; true; и́мя ~ое proper name; ~ой персо́ной in person.

собы́тие event.

собью́ etc.: see сбить

сова́ (pl -ы) owl.

сова́ть (сую́, -ёшь) impf (pf су́нуть) thrust, shove; ~ся push, push in; butt in.

соверша́ть impf, соверши́ть (-шу́) pf accomplish; carry out; commit; complete; ~ся happen; be accomplished. соверше́ние accomplishment; perpetration. соверше́нно adv perfectly; absolutely, completely. совершенноле́тие majority. совершенноле́тний of age. соверше́нный[1] perfect; absolute, complete. соверше́нный[2] perfective. соверше́нство perfection. соверше́нствование perfecting; improvement. соверше́нствовать impf (pf y~) perfect; improve; ~ся в+instr perfect o.s. in; improve.

со́вестливый conscientious. со́вестно impers+dat be ashamed. со́весть conscience.

сове́т advice, counsel, opinion; council; soviet, Soviet. сове́тник adviser. сове́то-

вать impf (pf по~) advise; ~ся c+instr consult, ask advice of. сове́толог Kremlinologist. сове́тск|ий Soviet; ~ая власть the Soviet regime; ~ий Сою́з the Soviet Union. сове́тчик adviser.

совеща́ние conference. совеща́тельный consultative, deliberative. совеща́ться impf deliberate; consult.

совлада́ть pf c+instr control, cope with.

совмести́мый compatible. совмести́тель m person holding more than one office. совмести́ть (-ещу́) pf, совмеща́ть impf combine; ~ся coincide; be combined, combine. совме́стно jointly. совме́стный joint, combined.

сово́к (-вка́) shovel; scoop; dust-pan.

совокупи́ться (-плю́сь) pf, совокупля́ться impf copulate. совокупле́ние copulation. совоку́пно adv jointly. совоку́пность aggregate, sum total.

совпада́ть impf, совпа́сть (-адёт) pf coincide; agree; tally. совпаде́ние coincidence.

совраща́ть impf, соврати́ть (-ащу́) pf (impf совраща́ть) pervert, seduce. со|вра́ть (-вру́, -врёшь; -а́л, -а́, -о) pf.

совраща́ть(ся impf of соврати́ть(ся. совраще́ние perverting, seduction.

совреме́нник contemporary. совреме́нность the present (time); contemporaneity. совреме́нный contemporary; modern.

совру́ etc.: see соврать

совсе́м adv quite; entirely.

совхо́з State farm.

совью́ etc.: see свить

согла́сие consent; assent; agreement; harmony. согласи́ться (-ашу́сь) pf (impf соглаша́ться) consent; agree. согла́сно adv in accord, in harmony; prep+dat in accordance with. согла́сн|ый¹ agreeable (to); in agreement; harmonious. согла́сный² consonant(al); sb consonant.

согласова́ние co-ordination; agreement. согласо́ванность co-ordination. согласова́ть pf, согласо́вывать impf coordinate; make agree; ~ся conform; agree.

соглаша́ться impf of согласи́ться. соглаше́ние agreement. соглашу́ etc.: see согласи́ть

согна́ть (сгоню́, сго́нишь; -а́л, -а́, -о) pf (impf сгоня́ть) drive away; drive together.

со|гну́ть (-ну́, -нёшь) pf (impf also сгиба́ть) bend, curve; ~ся bend (down).

согрева́ть impf, согре́ть (-е́ю) pf warm, heat; ~ся get warm; warm o.s.

со|греши́ть (-шу́) pf.

со́да soda.

соде́йствие assistance. соде́йствовать impf & pf (pf also по~) +dat assist; promote; contribute to.

содержа́ние maintenance, upkeep; pay. содержа́тельный rich in content; pithy. содержа́ть (-жу́, -жишь) impf maintain; contain; ~ся be kept; be maintained; be; be contained. содержи́мое sb contents.

со|дра́ть (сдеру́, -рёшь; -а́л, -а́, -о) pf (impf also сдира́ть) tear off, strip off; fleece.

содрога́ние shudder. содро-

га́ться impf, содрогну́ться (-ну́сь, -нёшься) pf shudder.

содру́жество concord; commonwealth.

соедине́ние joining, combination; joint; compound; formation. Соединённое Короле́вство United Kingdom. Соединённые Шта́ты (Аме́рики) m pl United States (of America). соединённый (-ён, -á) united, joint. соедини́тельный connective, connecting. соедини́ть pf, соединя́ть impf join, unite; connect; combine; ~ся join, unite; combine.

сожале́ние regret; pity; к сожале́нию unfortunately. сожале́ть (-е́ю) impf regret, deplore.

сожгу́ etc.: see сжечь. сожже́ние burning; cremation.

сожи́тель m, ~ница roommate, flat-mate; lover. сожи́тельство co-habitation.

сожму́ etc.: see сжать². сожну́ etc.: see сжать¹. созва́ниваться impf of созвони́ться

созва́ть (-зову́, -зовёшь; -а́л, -á, -о) pf (impf сзыва́ть, созыва́ть) call together; call; invite.

созве́здие constellation.

созвони́ться pf (impf созва́ниваться) ring up; speak on the telephone.

созву́чие accord; assonance. созву́чный harmonious; +dat in keeping with.

создава́ть (-даю́, -даёшь) impf, созда́ть (-а́м, -а́шь, -а́ст, -ади́м; -о́зда́л, -а́, -о) pf create; establish; ~ся be created; arise, spring up. созда́ние creation; work; creature. созда́тель m creator; originator.

**созерца́ние** contemplation. **созерца́тельный** contemplative. **созерца́ть** *impf* contemplate.

**созида́ние** creation. **созида́тельный** creative.

**сознава́ть** (-наю́, -наёшь) *impf*, **созна́ть** *pf* be conscious of, realize; acknowledge; **~ся** confess. **созна́ние** consciousness; acknowledgement; confession. **созна́тельность** awareness, consciousness. **созна́тельный** conscious; deliberate.

**созову́** *etc.*: *see* **созва́ть**

**созрева́ть** *impf*, **со|зре́ть** (-е́ю) *pf* ripen, mature.

**созы́в** summoning, calling. **созыва́ть** *impf of* **созва́ть**

**соизмери́мый** commensurable.

**соиска́ние** competition. **соиска́тель** *m*, **~ница** competitor, candidate.

**сойти́** (-йду́, -йдёшь; сошёл, -шла́) *pf* (*impf* **сходи́ть**) go *or* come down; get off; leave; come off; pass, go off; **~ с ума́** go mad, go out of one's mind; **~сь** meet; gather; become friends; become intimate; agree.

**сок** (*loc* -у́) juice.

**со́кол** falcon.

**сократи́ть** (-ащу́) *pf*, **сокраща́ть** *impf* shorten; abbreviate; reduce; **~ся** grow shorter; decrease; contract. **сокраще́ние** shortening; abridgement; abbreviation; reduction.

**сокрове́нный** secret; innermost. **сокро́вище** treasure. **сокро́вищница** treasure-house.

**сокруша́ть** *impf*, **сокруши́ть** (-шу́) *pf* shatter; smash; distress; **~ся** grieve, be distressed. **сокруше́ние** smash-ing; grief. **сокрушённый** (-ён, -á) grief-stricken. **сокруши́тельный** shattering.

**скры́тие** concealment.

**со|лга́ть** (-лгу́, -лжёшь; -а́л, -á, -о) *pf*.

**солда́т** (*gen pl* -а́т) soldier. **солда́тский** soldier's.

**соле́ние** salting; pickling. **солёный** (со́лон, -á, -о) salt(y); salted; pickled. **соле́нье** salted food(s); pickles.

**солида́рность** solidarity. **соли́дный** solid; strong; reliable; respectable; sizeable.

**соли́ст, соли́стка** soloist.

**соли́ть** (-лю́, со́ли́шь) *impf* (*pf* по~) salt; pickle.

**со́лнечный** sun; solar; sunny; **~ свет** sunlight; sunshine; **~ уда́р** sunstroke. **со́лнце** sun. **солнцепёк: на ~е** in the sun. **солнцестоя́ние** solstice.

**со́ло** *neut indecl* solo; *adv* solo.

**солове́й** (-вья́) nightingale.

**со́лод** malt.

**соло́дковый** liquorice.

**соло́ма** straw; thatch. **соло́менный** straw; thatch. **соло́минка** straw.

**со́лон** *etc.*: *see* **солёный. солони́на** corned beef. **соло́нка** salt-cellar. **солонча́к** (-á) saline soil; *pl* salt marshes. **соль** (*pl* -и, -е́й) salt.

**со́льный** solo.

**солью́** *etc.*: *see* **слить**

**соляно́й, соля́ный** salt, saline; **соля́ная кислота́** hydrochloric acid.

**со́мкнутый** close. **сомкну́ть** (-ну́, -нёшь) *pf* (*impf* **смыка́ть**) close; **~ся** close.

**сомнева́ться** *impf* doubt, have doubts. **сомне́ние** doubt. **сомни́тельный** doubtful.

**сомну́** etc.: see **смять**

**сон** (сна) sleep; dream. **сонли́вость** sleepiness; somnolence. **сонли́вый** sleepy. **со́нный** sleepy; sleeping.

**сона́та** sonata.

**соне́т** sonnet.

**соображ́ать** impf, **сообрази́ть** (-ажу́) pf consider, think out; weigh; understand. **соображе́ние** consideration; understanding; notion. **сообрази́тельный** quick-witted.

**сообра́зный** c+instr conforming to, in keeping with.

**сообща́** adv together. **сообща́ть** impf, **сообщи́ть** (-щу́) pf communicate, report, announce; impart; +dat inform. **сообще́ние** communication, report; announcement. **сообще́ство** association. **соо́бщник** accomplice.

**сооруди́ть** (-ужу́) pf, **сооружа́ть** impf build, erect. **сооруже́ние** building; structure.

**соотве́тственно** adv accordingly, correspondingly; prep +dat according to, in accordance with. **соотве́тственный** corresponding. **соотве́тствие** accordance, correspondence. **соотве́тствовать** impf correspond, conform. **соотве́тствующий** corresponding; suitable.

**соотéчественник** fellow-countryman.

**соотноше́ние** correlation.

**сопéрник** rival. **сопéрничать** impf compete, vie. **сопéрничество** rivalry.

**сопéть** (-плю́) impf wheeze; snuffle.

**со́пка** hill, mound.

**сопли́вый** snotty.

**сопоста́вить** (-влю) pf, **со-** **поставля́ть** impf compare. **сопоставле́ние** comparison.

**сопредéльный** contiguous.

**со|прéть** pf.

**соприкаса́ться** impf, **соприкосну́ться** (-ну́сь, -нёшься) pf adjoin; come into contact. **соприкоснове́ние** contact.

**сопроводи́тельный** accompanying. **сопроводи́ть** (-ожу́) pf, **сопровожда́ть** impf accompany; escort. **сопровожде́ние** accompaniment; escort.

**сопротивле́ние** resistance. **сопротивля́ться** impf +dat resist, oppose.

**сопу́тствовать** impf +dat accompany.

**сопью́сь** etc.: see **спи́ться**

**сор** litter, rubbish.

**соразме́рить** pf, **соразмеря́ть** impf balance, match. **соразме́рный** proportionate, commensurate.

**сора́тник** comrade-in-arms.

**сорва́ть** (-ву́, -вёшь; -а́л, -а́, -о) pf (impf **срыва́ть**) tear off, away, down; break off; pick; get; break; ruin, spoil; vent; **~ся** break away, break loose; fall, come down; fall through.

**с|организова́ть** pf.

**соревнова́ние** competition; contest. **соревнова́ться** impf compete.

**сори́ть** impf (pf **на~**) +acc or instr litter; throw about. **со́рный** rubbish, refuse; **~ая трава́** weed(s). **сорня́к** (-а́) weed.

**со́рок** (-а́) forty.

**соро́ка** magpie.

**сороков́|ой** fortieth; **~ые го́ды** the forties.

**соро́чка** shirt; blouse; shift.

**сорт** (pl -á) grade, quality; sort. **сортировáть** impf (pf рас~) sort, grade. **сортировка** sorting. **сортиро́вочн|ый** sorting; ~ая sb marshalling-yard. **сортиро́вщик** sorter. **со́ртный** high quality.

**сосáть** (-су́, -сёшь) impf suck.

**со|свáтать** pf.

**сосéд** (pl -и, -ей, -ям), **сосéд|ка** neighbour. **сосéдний** neighbouring; adjacent, next. **сосéдский** neighbours'. **сосéдство** neighbourhood. **сосíска** frankfurter, sausage.

**со́ска** (baby's) dummy.

**соскáкивать** impf of **соскочи́ть**

**соскáльзывать** impf, **соскользну́ть** (-ну́, -нёшь) pf slide down, slide off.

**соскочи́ть** (-чу́, -чишь) pf (impf **соскáкивать**) jump off or down; come off.

**соску́читься** (-чусь) pf get bored; ~ по+dat miss.

**сослагáтельный** subjunctive.

**сослáть** (сошлю́, -лёшь) pf (impf **ссылáть**) exile, deport; ~ся на+acc refer to; cite; plead, allege.

**сосло́вие** estate; class.

**сослужи́вец** (-вца) colleague.

**соснá** (pl -ы, -сен) pine(-tree). **сосно́вый** pine; deal.

**сосо́к** (-ска́) nipple, teat.

**сосредото́ченный** concentrated. **сосредото́чивать** impf, **сосредото́чить** (-чу) pf concentrate; focus; ~ся concentrate.

**состáв** composition; structure; compound; staff; strength; train; в ~е +gen consisting of. **состáв|итель** m compiler. **состáвить** (-влю) pf, **составля́ть** impf put together;

make (up); draw up; compile; be, constitute; total; ~ся form, be formed. **составно́й** compound; component, constituent.

**со|стáрить(ся** pf.

**состоя́ние** state, condition; fortune. **состоя́тельный** well-to-do; well-grounded. **состоя́ть** (-ою́) impf be; +из+gen consist of; +в+prep consist in, be. **состоя́ться** (-ойтся) pf take place.

**сострадáние** compassion. **сострадáтельный** compassionate.

**с|острúть** pf. **со|стря́пать** pf.

**со|стыко́вывать** pf, **состыко́вывать** impf dock; ~ся dock.

**состязáние** competition, contest. **состязáться** impf compete.

**сосу́д** vessel.

**сосу́лька** icicle.

**сосущество́вание** co-existence.

**со|счита́ть** pf. **сот** see **сто**.

**сотворéние** creation. **со|твори́ть** pf.

**со|ткáть** (-ку́, -кёшь; -áл, -áла, -о) pf.

**со́тня** (gen pl -тен) a hundred.

**сотру́** etc.: see **стерéть**

**сотру́дник** collaborator; colleague; employee. **сотру́дничать** impf collaborate; +в+prep contribute to. **сотру́дничество** collaboration.

**сотрясáть** impf, **сотрясти́** (-су́, -сёшь; -яс, -ла́) pf shake; ~ся tremble. **сотрясéние** shaking; concussion.

**со́ты** (-ов) pl honeycomb.

**со́тый** hundredth.

**соумы́шленник** accomplice.

**со́ус** sauce; gravy; dressing.

**соучáстие** participation; complicity. **соуча́стник** participant; accomplice.

**софа́** (pl -ы) sofa.

**соха́** (pl -и) (wooden) plough.

**со́хнуть** (-ну; сох) impf (pf вы~, за~, про~) (get) dry; wither.

**сохране́ние** preservation; conservation; (safe)keeping; retention. **сохрани́ть** pf, **сохраня́ть** impf preserve, keep; ~**ся** remain (intact); last out; be well preserved. **сохра́нный** safe.

**социа́л-демокра́т** Social Democrat. **социа́л-демократи́ческий** Social Democratic. **социали́зм** socialism. **социали́ст** socialist. **социалисти́ческий** socialist. **социа́льн|ый** social; ~**ое обеспе́чение** social security. **социо́лог** sociologist. **социоло́гия** sociology.

**соцреали́зм** socialist realism. **сочета́ние** combination. **сочета́ть** impf & pf combine; ~**ся** combine; harmonize; match.

**сочине́ние** composition; work. **сочини́ть** pf, **сочиня́ть** impf compose; write; make up.

**сочи́ться** (-и́тся) impf ooze (out); trickle; ~ **кро́вью** bleed.

**со́чный** (-чен, -чна́, -о) juicy; rich.

**сочту́** etc.: see **счесть**

**сочу́вствие** sympathy. **сочу́вствовать** impf +dat sympathize with.

**сошёл** etc.: see **сойти́. сошло́** etc.: see **сосла́ть. сошью́** etc.: see **сшить**

**сощу́ривать** impf, **со|щу́рить** pf screw up, narrow; ~**ся** screw up one's eyes; narrow.

**сою́з**[1] union; alliance; league.

**сою́з**[2] conjunction. **сою́зник**

ally. **сою́зный** allied; Union.

**спад** recession; abatement. **спада́ть** impf of **спасть**

**спазм** spasm.

**спа́ивать** impf of **спая́ть**, **споить**

**спа́йка** soldered joint; solidarity, unity.

**с|пали́ть** pf.

**спа́льн|ый** sleeping; ~**ый ваго́н** sleeping car; ~**ое ме́сто** berth. **спа́льня** (gen pl -лен) bedroom.

**спа́ржа** asparagus.

**спартакиа́да** sports meeting.

**спаса́тельный** жи-ле́т life jacket; ~ **круг** lifebuoy; ~ **по́яс** lifebelt. **спаса́ть(ся** impf of **спасти́**(**сь. спасе́ние** rescue, escape; salvation. **спаси́бо** thank you. **спаси́тель** m rescuer; saviour. **спаси́тельный** saving; salutary.

**спасти́** (-су́, -сёшь; спас, -ла́) pf (impf **спаса́ть**) save; rescue; ~**сь** escape; be saved.

**спасть** (-адёт) pf (impf **спада́ть**) fall (down); abate.

**спать** (сплю; -ал, -а́, -о) impf sleep; **лечь** ~ go to bed.

**спа́янность** cohesion, unity. **спа́янный** united. **спая́ть** pf (impf **спа́ивать**) solder, weld; unite.

**спекта́кль** m performance; show.

**спектр** spectrum.

**спекули́ровать** impf speculate. **спекуля́нт** speculator, profiteer. **спекуля́ция** speculation; profiteering.

**спе́лый** ripe.

**сперва́** adv at first; first.

**спе́реди** adv in front, from the front; prep+gen (from) in front of.

**спёртый** close, stuffy.

спеси́вый arrogant, haughty. спесь arrogance, haughtiness.

спеть¹ (-е́ет) impf (pf по~) ripen.

с|петь² (спою́, споёшь) pf.

спец- abbr in comb (of специа́льный) special. спецко́р special correspondent. ~оде́жда protective clothing; overalls.

специализа́ция specialization. специализи́роваться impf & pf specialize. специали́ст, ~ка specialist, expert. специа́льность speciality; profession. специа́льный special; specialist.

специ́фика specific character. специфи́ческий specific.

спе́ция spice.

спецо́вка protective clothing; overall(s).

спеши́ть (-шу́) impf (pf по~) hurry, be in a hurry; be fast. спе́шка hurry, haste. спе́шный urgent.

спива́ться impf of спи́ться

СПИД abbr (of синдро́м приобретённого иммуноде-фици́та) Aids.

с|пики́ровать pf.

спи́ливать impf, спили́ть (-лю́, -лишь) pf saw down, off.

спина́ (acc -у, pl -ы) back. спи́нка back. спинно́й spinal; ~ мозг spinal cord.

спира́ль spiral.

спирт alcohol, spirit(s). спирт-н|о́й alcoholic; ~о́е sb alcohol. спирто́вка spirit-stove. спиртово́й spirit, alcoholic.

спи́сывать (-ишу́, -и́шешь) pf, спи́сывать impf copy; ~ся exchange letters. спи́сок (-ска) list; record.

спи́ться (сопьюсь, -ьёшься; -и́лся, -а́сь) pf (impf спива́ться)

take to drink.

спи́хивать impf, спихну́ть (-ну́, -нёшь) pf push aside, down.

спи́ца knitting-needle; spoke.

спи́чечн|ый match; ~ая коро́бка match-box. спи́чка match.

спишу́ etc.: see списа́ть

сплав¹ floating. сплав² alloy.

спла́вить¹ (-влю) pf, сплавля́ть¹ (impf float; raft; get rid of. спла́вить² (-влю) pf, сплавля́ть² impf alloy; ~ся fuse.

с|плани́ровать pf. спла́чивать(ся impf of сплоти́ть(ся сплёвывать impf of сплю́нуть

с|плести́ (-ету́, -етёшь; -ёл, -а́) pf, сплета́ть impf weave; plait; interlace. сплете́ние interlacing; plexus.

спле́тник, -ница gossip, scandalmonger. спле́тничать impf (pf на~) gossip. спле́тня (gen pl -тен) gossip, scandal.

сплоти́ть (-очу́) pf (impf спла́чивать) join; unite, rally; ~ся unite, rally; close ranks. сплоче́ние uniting. сплочённость cohesion, unity. сплочённый (-ён, -а́) united; firm; unbroken.

сплошн|о́й solid; complete; continuous; utter. сплошь adv all over; completely; ~ да ря́дом pretty often.

сплю see спать

сплю́нуть (-ну) pf (impf сплёвывать) spit; spit out.

сплю́щивать impf, сплю́-щить (-щу) pf flatten; ~ся become flat.

с|пляса́ть (-яшу́, -я́шешь) pf.

сподви́жник comrade-in-arms.

спои́ть (-ою́, -о́ишь) pf (impf спа́ивать) make a drunkard of.

споко́йн|ый quiet; calm; ~о ok

ночи good night! **спокойствие** quiet; calm, serenity.
**спола́скивать** *impf of* **сполос-
ну́ть**
**сползти́** (-зу́,
-зёшь; -о́лз, -ла́) *pf* climb
down; slip (down); fall away.
**сполна́** *adv* in full.
**сполосну́ть** (-ну́, -нёшь) *pf*
(*impf* **спола́скивать**) rinse.
**спо́нсор** sponsor, backer.
**спор** argument; controversy;
dispute. **спо́рить** *impf* (*pf*
по-) argue; dispute; debate.
**спо́рный** debatable, questionable; disputed; moot.
**спо́ра** spore.
**спорт** sport. **спорти́вный**
sports; ~ зал gymnasium.
**спортсме́н**, **~ка** athlete,
player.
**спо́соб** way, method; таки́м
~ом in this way. **спо́соб-
ность** ability, aptitude; capacity. **спосо́бный** able;
clever; capable. **спосо́бство-
вать** *impf* (*pf* по-) +*dat* assist; further.
**споткну́ться** (-ну́сь, -нёшься)
*pf*, **спотыка́ться** *impf* stumble.
**спохвати́ться** (-ачу́сь, -а́тишь-
ся) *pf*, **спохва́тываться** *impf*
remember suddenly.
**спою́** *etc.: see* **спеть**, **спо́ть**
**спра́ва** *adv* to or on the right.
**справедли́вость** justice; fairness; truth. **справедли́вый**
just; fair; justified.
**спра́вить** (-влю) *pf*, **справ-
ля́ть** *impf* celebrate. **спра́-
виться**[1] (-влюсь) *pf*, **справ-
ля́ться** *impf* c+*instr* cope
with, manage. **спра́виться**[2]
(-влюсь) *pf*, **справля́ться**
*impf* inquire; +в+*prep* consult.
**спра́вка** information; refer-

ence; certificate; **наводи́ть
спра́вки** make inquiries. **спра́-
вочник** reference-book, directory. **спра́вочный** inquiry, information, reference.
**спринт** sprint. **спри́нтер**
sprinter.
**с|провоци́ровать** *pf*. **с|прое-
кти́ровать** *pf*.
**спрос** demand; asking; без ~у
without permission. **спро-
си́ть** (-ошу́, -о́сишь) *pf* (*impf*
**спра́шивать**) ask (for); inquire; ~ся ask permission.
**спрут** octopus.
**спры́гивать** *impf*, **спры́гнуть**
(-ну) *pf* jump off, jump down.
**спры́скивать** *impf*, **спры́с-
нуть** (-ну) *pf* sprinkle.
**спряга́ть** *impf* (*pf* про-) conjugate. **спряже́ние** conjugation.
**с|прясть** (-яду́, -ядёшь; -ял,
-яла́, -о) *pf*. **с|пря́тать(ся**
(-я́чу(сь) *pf*.
**спу́гивать** *impf*, **спугну́ть**
(-ну́, -нёшь) *pf* frighten off.
**спуск** lowering; descent; slope.
**спуска́ть** *impf*, **спусти́ть**
(-ущу́, -у́стишь) *pf* let down,
lower; release; let out; send
out; go down; forgive; squander; ~ куро́к pull the trigger; ~
петлю́ drop a stitch; ~ся go
down, descend. **спуско́й**
drain. **спусково́й** trigger.
**спустя́** *prep*+*acc* after; *adv*
later.
**с|пу́тать(ся** *pf*.
**спу́тник** satellite, sputnik;
(travelling) companion.
**спущу́** *etc.: see* **спусти́ть**
**спя́чка** hibernation; sleepiness.

**ср.** *abbr (of* сравни́) cf.

**сраба́тывать** *impf*, **срабо́тать** *pf* make; work, operate.

**сравне́ние** comparison; simile. **сра́внивать** *impf of* сравни́ть, сравня́ть. **сравни́мый** comparable. **сравни́тельно** *adv* comparatively. **сравни́тельный** comparative. **сравни́ть** *pf (impf* сра́внивать) compare; ~ся с+*instr* compare with. **с|равня́ть** *pf (impf also* сра́внивать) make even, equal; level.

**сража́ть** *impf*, **срази́ть** (-ажу́) *pf* strike down; overwhelm, crush; ~ся fight. **сраже́ние** battle.

**сра́зу** *adv* at once.

**срам** shame. **срами́ть** (-млю́) *impf (pf* o~) shame; ~ся cover o.s. with shame. **срамота́** shame.

**сраста́ние** growing together. **сраста́ться** *impf*, **срасти́сь** (-тётся; сро́сся, -ла́сь) *pf* grow together; knit.

**среда́**[1] *(pl* -ы) environment, surroundings; medium. **среда́**[2] *(acc* -у; *pl* -ы, -а́м *or* -ам) Wednesday. **среди́** *prep+gen* among; in the middle of; ~ бе́ла дня in broad daylight. **средиземномо́рский** Mediterranean. **сре́дне** *adv* so-so. **средневеко́вый** medieval. **средневеко́вье** the Middle Ages. **сре́дний** middle; medium; mean; average; middling; secondary; neuter; ~ее *sb* mean, average. **средото́чие** focus. **сре́дство** means; remedy.

**срез** cut; section; slice. **с|ре́зать** (-е́жу) *pf*, **среза́ть** *impf* cut off; slice; fail; ~ся fail.

**с|репети́ровать** *pf*.

**срисова́ть** *pf*, **срисо́вывать** *impf* copy.

**с|ровня́ть** *pf*.

**сродство́** affinity.

**срок** date; term; time, period; в ~, к ~у in time, to time.

**сро́сся** *etc.: see* срасти́сь

**сро́чно** *adv* urgently. **сро́чность** urgency. **сро́чный** urgent; for a fixed period.

**сро́ю** *etc.: see* срыть

**сруб** felling; framework. **сруба́ть** *impf*, **с|руби́ть** (-блю́, -бишь) *pf* cut down; build (*of* logs).

**срыв** disruption; breakdown; ruining. **срыва́ть**[1]**(ся** *impf of* сорва́ть(ся

**срыва́ть**[2] *impf*, **срыть** (сро́ю) *pf* raze to the ground.

**сря́ду** *adv* running.

**сса́дина** scratch. **ссади́ть** (-ажу́, -а́дишь) *pf*, **сса́живать** *impf* set down; help down; turn off.

**ссо́ра** quarrel. **ссо́рить** *impf (pf* по~) cause to quarrel; ~ся quarrel.

**СССР** *abbr (of* Сою́з Сове́тских Социалисти́ческих Респу́блик) USSR.

**ссу́да** loan. **ссуди́ть** (-ужу́, -у́дишь) *pf*, **ссужа́ть** *impf* lend, loan.

**ссыла́ть** *impf of* сосла́ть(ся. **ссы́лка**[1] exile. **ссы́лка**[2] reference. **ссы́льный, ссы́льная** *sb* exile.

**ссыпа́ть** (-плю) *pf*, **ссыпа́ть** *impf* pour.

**стабилиза́тор** stabilizer; tailplane. **стабилизи́ровать(ся** *impf & pf* stabilize. **стаби́льность** stability. **стаби́льный** stable, firm.

**ста́вень** (-вня; *gen pl* -вней) *m*, **ста́вня** (*gen pl* -вен) shutter.

**ста́вить** (-влю) *impf* (*pf* по~) put, place, set; stand; station; erect; install; apply; present, stage. **ста́вка**[1] rate; stake.
**ста́вка**[2] headquarters.

**ста́вня** *see* ста́вень

**стадио́н** stadium.

**ста́дия** stage.

**ста́дность** herd instinct. **ста́дный** gregarious. **ста́до** (*pl* -а́) herd, flock.

**стаж** length of service; probation. **стажёр** probationer; student on a special non-degree course. **стажиро́вка** period of training.

**стака́н** glass.

**сталелите́йный** steel-founding; ~ заво́д steel foundry. **сталепла́вильный** steel-making; ~ заво́д steel works. **сталепрока́тный** (steel-)rolling; ~ стан rolling-mill.

**ста́лкивать(ся** *impf of* столкну́ть(ся

**ста́ло быть** *conj* consequently.

**сталь** steel. **стально́й** steel.

**стаме́ска** chisel.

**стан**[1] torso.

**стан**[2] camp.

**стан**[3] mill.

**станда́рт** standard. **станда́ртный** standard.

**стани́ца** Cossack village.

**станкострое́ние** machine-tool engineering.

**станови́ться** (-влюсь, -вишься) *impf of* стать[1]

**стано́к** (-нка́) machine tool, machine.

**ста́ну** *etc.*: *see* стать[2]

**станцио́нный** station. **ста́нция** station.

**ста́пель** (*pl* -я́) *m* stocks.

**ста́птывать(ся** *impf of* стопта́ть(ся

**стара́ние** effort. **стара́тель-**

**ность** diligence. **стара́тельный** diligent. **стара́ться** *impf* (*pf* по~) try.

**старе́ть** *impf* (*pf* по~, у~) grow old. **ста́рец** (-рца) elder, (*venerable*) old man. **стари́к** (-а́) old man. **старина́** antiquity, olden times; antique(s); old fellow. **стари́нный** ancient; old; antique. **ста́рить** *impf* (*pf* co~) age, make old; ~ся age, grow old.

**старо-** *in comb* old. **старове́р** Old Believer. ~жи́л old resident. ~мо́дный old-fashioned. ~славя́нский Old Slavonic.

**ста́роста** head; monitor; churchwarden. **ста́рость** old age.

**старт** start; на ~! on your marks! **стартёр** starter. **стартова́ть** *impf & pf* start. **ста́ртовый** starting.

**стару́ха**, **стару́шка** old woman. **ста́рческий** old man's; senile. **ста́рше** *comp of* ста́рый. **ста́рш|ий** oldest, eldest; older, elder; senior; head; ~ие *sb pl* (one's) elders; ~ий *sb* chief; man in charge. **старшина́** *m* sergeant-major; petty officer; leader. **ста́рый** (-ар, -а́, -о) old. **старьё** old things, junk.

**ста́скивать** *impf of* стащи́ть

**стасова́ть** *pf*.

**стати́ст** extra.

**стати́стика** statistics. **стати́стический** statistical.

**ста́тный** stately.

**ста́тский** civil, civilian.

**ста́тус** status. **ста́тус-кво́** *neut indecl* status quo.

**статуэ́тка** statuette.

**ста́туя** statue.

**стать**[1] (-а́ну) pf (impf станови́ться) stand; take up position; stop; cost; begin; +instr become; +c+instr become of; не ~ impers+gen cease to be; disappear; его́ не ста́ло he is no more; ~ на коле́ни kneel.

**стать**[2] physique, build.

**ста́ться** (-а́нется) pf happen.

**статья́** (gen pl -е́й) article; clause; item; matter.

**стациона́р** permanent establishment; hospital. **стациона́рный** stationary; permanent; ~ больно́й in-patient.

**ста́чечник** striker. **ста́чка** strike.

**с|тащи́ть** (-щу́, -щишь) pf (impf also ста́скивать) drag off, pull off

**ста́я** flock; school, shoal; pack.

**ствол** (-а́) trunk; barrel.

**ство́рка** leaf, fold.

**сте́бель** (-бля; gen pl -бле́й) m stem, stalk.

**стёган|ый** quilted; ~ое одея́ло quilt, duvet. **стега́ть**[1] impf (pf вы́~) quilt.

**стега́ть**[2] impf, **стегну́ть** (-ну́) pf (pf also от~) whip, lash.

**стежо́к** (-жка́) stitch.

**стезя́** path, way.

**стёк** etc.: see стечь. **стека́ть(ся** impf of сте́чь(ся

**стекло́** (pl -ёкла, -кол) glass; lens; (window-)pane.

**стекло́**- in comb glass. **стекло-воло́но́** glass fibre. ~очисти́тель m windscreen-wiper. ~ре́з glass-cutter. ~тка́нь fibreglass.

**стекля́нный** glass; glassy. **стеко́льщик** glazier.

**стели́ть** see стлать

**стелла́ж** (-а́) shelves, shelving.

**сте́лька** insole.

**стелю́** etc.: see стлать

**с|темне́ть** (-е́ет) pf.

**стена́** (acc -у; pl -ы, -а́м) wall.

**стенгазе́та** wall newspaper.

**стенд** stand.

**сте́нка** wall; side. **стенно́й** wall.

**стеногра́мма** shorthand record. **стено́граф, стено-графи́ст, ~ка** stenographer. **стенографи́ровать** impf & pf take down in shorthand. **стенографи́ческий** shorthand. **стеногра́фия** shorthand.

**стенока́рдия** angina.

**степе́нный** staid; middle-aged. **сте́пень** (gen pl -е́й) degree; extent; power.

**степно́й** steppe. **степь** (loc -и́; gen pl -е́й) steppe.

**стервя́тник** vulture.

**стерегу́** etc.: see стере́чь

**сте́рео** indecl adj stereo. **сте́-рео**- in comb stereo. **стерео-ти́п** stereotype. **стереоти́п-ный** stereotype(d). **стерео-фони́ческий** stereo(phonic). ~фо́ния stereo(phony).

**стере́ть** (сотру́, сотрёшь; стёр) pf (impf стира́ть[1]) wipe off; rub out, rub sore; ~ся rub off; wear down; be effaced.

**стере́чь** (-регу́, -режёшь; -ёг, -ла́) impf guard; watch for.

**сте́ржень** (-жня) m pivot; rod; core.

**стерилизова́ть** impf & pf sterilize. **стери́льный** sterile.

**сте́рлинг** sterling.

**сте́рлядь** (gen pl -е́й) sterlet.

**стерпе́ть** (-плю́, -пишь) pf bear, endure.

**стёртый** worn, effaced.

**стесне́ние** constraint. **стесни́-тельный** shy; inconvenient. **с|тесни́ть** pf, **стесня́ть** impf constrain; hamper; restrict.

с|тесни́ться *pf*, стесня́ться *impf* (*pf also* по~) +*inf* feel too shy (to), be ashamed to.

стече́ние confluence; gathering; combination. сте́чь (-чёт, -ёк, -ла́) *pf* (*impf* стека́ть) flow down; ~ся flow together; gather.

стилисти́ческий stylistic. стиль *m* style. сти́льный stylish; period.

сти́мул stimulus, incentive. стимули́ровать *impf* & *pf* stimulate.

стипе́ндия grant.

стира́льный washing. стира́ть¹(ся *impf of* стере́ть(ся

стира́ть² *impf* (*pf* вы́~) wash, launder; ~ся wash. сти́рка washing, wash, laundering.

сти́скивать *impf*, сти́снуть (-ну) *pf* squeeze; clench; hug.

стих (-а́) verse; line; *pl* poetry.

стиха́ть *impf of* сти́хнуть

стихи́йный elemental; spontaneous. стихи́я element.

сти́хнуть (-ну; стих) *pf* (*impf* стиха́ть) subside; calm down.

стихотворе́ние poem. стихотво́рный in verse form.

стлать, стели́ть (стелю́, сте́лешь) *impf* (*pf* по~) spread; ~ посте́ль make a bed; ~ся spread; creep.

сто (ста, *gen pl* сот) a hundred.

стог (*loc* -е & -у́; *pl* -а́) stack, rick.

сто́имость cost; value. сто́ить *impf* cost; be worth(while); deserve.

стой *see* стоя́ть

сто́йка counter, bar; prop; upright; strut. сто́йкий firm; stable; steadfast. сто́йкость firmness, stability; steadfastness. сто́йло stall. стойма́

*adv* upright.

сток flow; drainage; drain, gutter; sewer.

стол (-а́) table; desk; cuisine.

столб (-а́) post, pole, pillar, column. столбене́ть (-е́ю) *impf* (*pf* о~) be rooted to the ground. столбня́к (-а́) stupor; tetanus.

столе́тие century; centenary. столе́тний hundred-year-old; of a hundred years.

столи́ца capital; metropolis. столи́чный (of the) capital.

столкнове́ние collision; clash. столкну́ть (-ну́, -нёшь) *pf* (*impf* ста́лкивать) push off, away; cause to collide; bring +с+*instr* run into.

столо́вая *sb* dining-room; canteen. столо́вый table.

столп (-а́) pillar.

столпи́ться *pf* crowd.

столь *adv* so. сто́лько *adv* so much, so many.

столя́р (-а́) joiner, carpenter. столя́рный joiner's.

стомато́лог dentist.

стометро́вка (the) hundred metres.

стон groan. стона́ть (-ну́, -нешь) *impf* groan.

стоп! *int* stop!

стопа́¹ foot.

стопа́² (*pl* -ы) ream; pile.

сто́пка¹ pile.

сто́пка² small glass.

сто́пор stop, catch. стопо́риться *impf* (*pf* за~) come to a stop.

стопроце́нтный hundred-per-cent.

стоп-сигна́л brake-light.

стопта́ть (-пчу́, -пчешь) *pf* (*impf* ста́птывать) wear down; ~ся wear down.

с|торгова́ть(ся pf.

сто́рож (pl -а́) watchman, guard. сторожево́й watch; patrol-. сторожи́ть (-жу́) impf guard, watch (over).

сторона́ (acc сто́рону; pl сто́роны, -ро́н, -а́м) side; direction; hand; feature; part; land; в сто́рону aside; с мое́й стороны́ for my part; с одно́й стороны́ on the one hand. сторони́ться (-ню́сь, -ни́шься) impf (pf по∼) stand aside; +gen avoid. сторо́нник supporter, advocate.

сто́чный sewage, drainage.

стоя́нка stop; parking; stopping place, parking space; stand; rank. стоя́ть (-ою́) impf (pf по∼) stand; be; stay; stop; have stopped; +за+acc stand up for; ∼ на коле́нях kneel. стоя́чий standing; upright; stagnant.

стоя́щий deserving; worthwhile.

стр. abbr (of страни́ца) page.

страда́ (pl -ды) (hard work at) harvest time.

страда́лец (-льца) sufferer. страда́ние suffering. страда́тельный passive. страда́ть (-а́ю or -а́жду) impf (pf по∼) suffer; ∼ за +gen feel for.

стра́жа guard, watch; под стра́жей under arrest, in custody; стоя́ть на стра́же +gen guard.

страна́ (pl -ны) country; land; ∼ све́та cardinal point.

страни́ца page.

стра́нник, стра́нница wanderer.

стра́нно adv strangely. стра́нность strangeness; eccentricity. стра́нн|ый (-нен, -нна́, -о) strange.

стра́нствие wandering. стра́-

нствовать impf wander.

Страстно́й of Holy Week; ∼а́я пя́тница Good Friday. стра́стный (-тен, -тна́, -о) passionate. страсть[1] (gen pl -е́й) passion. страсть[2] adv awfully, frightfully.

стратеги́ческий strategic(al). страте́гия strategy. стратосфе́ра stratosphere.

стра́ус ostrich.

страх fear.

страхова́ние insurance; ∼ хова́ть impf (pf за∼) insure (от+gen against); ∼ся insure o.s. страхо́вка insurance.

страши́ться (-шу́сь) impf+gen be afraid of. стра́шно adv awfully. стра́шный (-шен, -шна́, -о) terrible, awful.

стрекоза́ (pl -ы) dragonfly. стрекота́ть (-очу́, -о́чешь) impf chirr.

стрела́ (pl -ы) arrow; boom. стреле́ц (-льца́) Sagittarius. стре́лка pointer; hand; needle; arrow; spit; points. стрелко́вый rifle; shooting; infantry. стрело́к (-лка́) shot; rifleman, gunner. стре́лочник pointsman. стрельба́ (pl -ы) shooting, firing. стре́льчатый pointed; arched. стреля́ть impf shoot; fire; ∼ся shoot o.s.; fight a duel.

стремгла́в adv headlong.

стреми́тельный swift; impetuous. стреми́ться (-млю́сь) impf strive, strive, aspiration. стремни́на rapid(s).

стре́мя (-мени, pl -мена́, -мя́н, -а́м) neut stirrup. стремя́нка step-ladder.

стресс stress. стре́ссовый stressful, stressed.

**стри́женый** short; short-haired, cropped; shorn. **стри́жка** hair-cut; shearing. **стричь** (-игу́, -ижёшь; -иг) *impf* (*pf* о~) cut, clip; cut the hair of; shear; ~ся have one's hair cut.

**строга́ть** *impf* (*pf* вы́~) plane, shave.

**стро́гий** strict; severe. **стро́гость** strictness.

**строево́й** combatant; line; drill. **строе́ние** building; structure; composition.

**строжа́йший, стро́же** *superl* & *comp of* **стро́гий**

**строи́тель** *m* builder. **строи́тельный** building, construction. **строи́тельство** building, construction; building site. **стро́ить** *impf* (*pf* по~) build; construct; make; base; draw up; ~ся be built, be under construction; draw up; **стро́йся!** fall in! **строй** (*loc* -ю́; *pl* -и́ *or* -и́, -ев *or* -ёв) system; régime; structure; pitch; formation. **стро́йка** building; building-site. **стро́йность** proportion; harmony; balance, order. **стро́йный** (-о́ен, -ойна́, -о) harmonious, orderly, well-proportioned, shapely.

**строка́** (*acc* -о́ку; *pl* -и, -а́м) line; **кра́сная** ~ new paragraph.

**строп, стро́па** sling; shroud line.

**стропи́ло** rafter, beam.

**стропти́вый** refractory.

**строфа́** (*pl* -ы, -а́м) stanza.

**строчи́ть** (-чу́, -о́чи́шь) *impf* (*pf* на~, про~) stitch; scribble, dash off. **стро́чка** stitch; line.

**стро́ю** *etc.*: *see* **стро́ить**

**струга́ть** *impf* (*pf* вы́~) plane. **стру́жка** shaving.

**струи́ться** *impf* stream.

**структу́ра** structure.

**струна́** (*pl* -ы) string. **стру́нный** stringed.

**струп** (*pl* -пья, -пьев) scab.

**с|тру́сить** (-ущу) *pf*.

**стручо́к** (-чка́) *pf*.

**струя́** (*pl* -и, -уй) jet, spurt, stream.

**стря́пать** *impf* (*pf* со~) cook; concoct. **стряпня́** cooking.

**стря́хивать** *impf*, **стряхну́ть** (-ну́, -нёшь) *pf* shake off.

**студени́стый** jelly-like.

**студе́нт, студе́нтка** student. **студе́нческий** student.

**сту́день** (-дня) *m* jelly; aspic.

**студи́ть** (-ужу́, -у́дишь) *impf* (*pf* о~) cool.

**сту́дия** studio.

**стужа** severe cold, hard frost.

**стук** knock; clatter. **сту́кать** *impf*, **сту́кнуть** (-ну) *pf* knock; bang; strike; ~ся knock (o.s.), bang. **стука́ч** (-а́) informer.

**стул** (*pl* -лья, -льев) chair. **стульча́к** (-а́) (*lavatory*) seat. **сту́льчик** stool.

**сту́па** mortar.

**ступа́ть** *impf*, **ступи́ть** (-плю́, -пишь) *pf* step; tread. **ступе́нчатый** stepped, graded. **ступе́нь** (*gen pl* -е́ней) step, rung; stage, grade. **ступе́нька** step. **ступня́** foot; sole.

**стуча́ть** (-чу́) *impf* (*pf* по~) knock; chatter; pound; ~ся в+*acc* knock at.

**стушёвываться** (-шу́юсь) *pf*, **стушёвываться** *impf* efface o.s.

**с|туши́ть** (-шу́, -шишь) *pf*.

**стыд** (-а́) shame. **стыди́ть** (-ижу́) *impf* (*pf* при~) put to shame; ~ся (*pf* по~ся) be ashamed. **стыдли́вый** bashful. **сты́дный** shameful; ~о! shame! ~о *impers+dat* ему́

~о he is ashamed; **как тебе́ не ~о!** you ought to be ashamed of yourself!

**стык** joint; junction. **стыко-ва́ть** *impf* (*pf* **с~**) join end to end; (*pf* **при~ся**) dock. **стыко́вка** docking.

**сты́нуть, стыть** (-ы́ну; стыл) *impf* cool; get cold.

**сты́чка** skirmish; squabble.

**стюарде́сса** stewardess.

**стя́гивать** *impf*, **стяну́ть** (-ну́, -нешь) *pf* tighten; pull together; assemble; pull off; steal; **~ся** tighten; assemble.

**стяжа́тель** (-я) *m* money-grubber. **стяжа́ть** *impf & pf* gain, win.

**суббо́та** Saturday.

**субсиди́ровать** *impf & pf* subsidize. **субси́дия** subsidy.

**субъе́кт** subject; ego; person; character, type. **субъекти́вный** subjective.

**сувени́р** souvenir.

**суверените́т** sovereignty. **сувере́нный** sovereign.

**сугли́нок** (-нка) loam.

**сугро́б** snowdrift.

**сугу́бо** *adv* especially.

**суд** (-а́) court; trial; verdict.

**суда́** *etc.*: *see* **суд**, **су́дно**[1]

**суда́к** (-а́) pike-perch.

**суде́бный** judicial; legal; forensic. **суде́йский** judge's; referee's, umpire's. **суди́мость** previous convictions.

**суди́ть** (сужу́, су́дишь) *impf* judge; try; referee, umpire; foreordain; **~ся** go to law.

**су́дно**[1] (*pl* -да́, -о́в) vessel, craft.

**су́дно**[2] (*gen pl* -ден) bed-pan.

**судово́й** ship's; marine.

**судомо́йка** kitchen-maid; scullery.

**судопроизво́дство** legal proceedings.

**су́дорога** cramp, convulsion. **судоро́жный** convulsive.

**судострое́ние** shipbuilding. **судострои́тельный** ship-building. **судохо́дный** navigable; shipping.

**судьба́** (*pl* -ы, -де́б) fate, destiny.

**судья́** (*pl* -дьи, -де́й, -дьям) *m* judge; referee; umpire.

**суеве́рие** superstition. **суеве́рный** superstitious.

**суета́** bustle, fuss. **суети́ться** (-ечу́сь) *impf* bustle, fuss. **суетли́вый** fussy, bustling.

**сужде́ние** opinion; judgement.

**суже́ние** narrowing; constriction. **су́живать** *impf*, **су́зить** (-у́жу) *pf* narrow, contract; **~ся** narrow; taper.

**сук** (-а́, *loc* -у́; *pl* су́чья, -ьев *or* -и́, -о́в) bough.

**су́ка** bitch. **су́кин** *adj*: **~ сын** son of a bitch.

**сукно́** (*pl* -а, -ко́н) cloth; **поло-жи́ть под ~** shelve. **суко́нный** cloth; clumsy, crude.

**сули́ть** *impf* (*pf* **по~**) promise.

**султа́н**[1] plume.

**сумасбро́д, сумасбро́дка** nutcase. **сумасбро́дный** wild, mad. **сумасбро́дство** wild behaviour. **сумасше́дш|ий** mad; *sб* madman; **~ая** *sб* lunatic. **сумасше́ствие** madness.

**сумато́ха** turmoil; bustle.

**сумбу́р** confusion. **сумбу́рный** confused.

**су́меречный** twilight. **су́мер-ки** (-рек) *pl* twilight, dusk.

**суме́ть** (-е́ю) *pf* +*inf* be able to, manage to.

**су́мка** bag.

**су́мма** sum. **сумма́рный** summary; total. **сумми́ровать** *impf & pf* add up; summarize.

**су́мрак** twilight; murk. **су́мрачный** gloomy.

**су́мчатый** marsupial.

**сунду́к** (-á) trunk, chest.

**су́нуть(ся** (-ну(сь) *pf of* **сова́ть(ся**

**суп** (*pl* -ы́) soup.

**суперма́ркет** supermarket.

**суперобло́жка** dust-jacket.

**супру́г** husband, spouse; *pl* husband and wife, (*married*) couple. **супру́га** wife, spouse. **супру́жеский** conjugal. **супру́жество** matrimony.

**сургу́ч** (-á) sealing-wax.

**сурди́нка** mute; **под сурди́нку** on the sly.

**суро́вость** severity, sternness. **суро́вый** severe, stern; bleak; unbleached.

**суро́к** (-рка́) marmot.

**суррога́т** substitute.

**су́слик** ground-squirrel.

**суста́в** joint, articulation.

**су́тки** (-ток) *pl* twenty-four hours; a day.

**су́толока** commotion.

**су́точн|ый** daily; round-the-clock; **~ые** *sb pl* per diem allowance.

**суту́литься** *impf* stoop. **суту́лый** round-shouldered.

**суть** essence, main point.

**суфлёр** prompter. **суфли́ровать** *impf* +*dat* prompt.

**су́ффикс** suffix.

**суха́рь** (-я́) *m* rusk; *pl* bread-crumbs. **су́хо** *adv* drily; coldly.

**сухожи́лие** tendon.

**сухо́й** (сух, -á, -о) dry; cold. **сухопу́тный** land. **су́хость** dryness; coldness. **сухоща́вый** lean, skinny.

**сучкова́тый** knotty; gnarled. **сучо́к** (-чка́) twig; knot.

**су́ша** (dry) land. **су́ше** *comp of* **сухо́й**. **сушёный** dried.

**суши́лка** dryer; drying-room.

**суши́ть** (-шу́, -шишь) *impf* (*pf* **вы́~**) dry, dry out, up; **~ся** (get) dry.

**суще́ственный** essential, vital. **существи́тельное** *sb* noun. **существо́** being, creature; essence. **существова́ние** existence. **существова́ть** *impf* exist. **су́щий** absolute, downright. **су́щность** essence.

**сую́** *etc.: see* **сова́ть**. **с|фабрикова́ть** *pf.* **с|фальши́вить** (-влю) *pf.*

**с|фантази́ровать** *pf.*

**сфе́ра** sphere. **сфери́ческий** spherical.

**сфинкс** sphinx.

**с|формирова́ть(ся** *pf.* **с|формова́ть** *pf.* **с|формули́ровать** *pf.* **с|фотографи́ровать(ся** *pf.*

**схвати́ть** (-ачу́, -а́тишь) *pf,* **схва́тывать** *impf* (*impf also* **хвата́ть**) seize; catch; grasp; **~ся** snatch, catch; grapple. **схва́тка** skirmish; *pl* contractions.

**схе́ма** diagram; outline, plan; circuit. **схемати́ческий** schematic; sketchy. **схемати́чный** sketchy.

**с|хитри́ть** *pf.*

**схлы́нуть** (-нет) *pf* (break and) flow back; subside.

**сход** coming off; descent; gathering. **сходи́ть**[1]**(ся** (-ожу́(сь, -о́дишь(ся *impf of* **сойти́(сь**. **сходи́ть**[2] (-ожу́, -о́дишь) *pf* go; +*за*+*instr* go to fetch. **схо́дка** gathering, meeting. **схо́дный** (-ден, -дна́, -о) similar; reasonable. **схо́дня** (*gen pl* -ей) (*usu pl*) gang-plank. **схо́дство** similarity.

**с|хорони́ть(ся** (-ню́(сь, -нишь(ся) *pf.*

сцеди́ть (-ежу́, -е́дишь) *pf*, сце́живать *impf* strain off, decant.

сце́на stage; scene. сцена́рий scenario; script. сцена́рист script-writer. сцени́ческий stage.

сцепи́ть (-плю́, -пишь) *pf*, сцепля́ть *impf* couple; ~ся be coupled; grapple. сце́пка coupling. сцепле́ние coupling; clutch.

счастли́вец (-вца), счастли́вчик lucky man. счастли́вица lucky woman. счастли́в|ый (счастли́в) happy; lucky; ~o! all the best!; ~ого пути́ bon voyage. сча́стье happiness; good fortune.

счесть(ся (сочту́(сь, -тёшь(ся; счёл(ся, сочла́(сь) *pf of* счита́ть(ся. счёт (*loc* -у́, *pl* -á) bill; account; counting, calculation; score; expense. счётный calculating; accounts. счетово́д book-keeper, accountant. счётчик counter; meter. счёты (-ов) *pl* abacus.

счи́стить (-и́щу) *pf* счища́ть) clean off; clear away.

счита́ть *impf* (*pf* с~, счесть) count; reckon; consider; ~ся (*pf also* по~ся) settle accounts; be considered; +с+*instr* take into consideration; reckon with.

счища́ть *impf of* счи́стить

США *pl indecl abbr* (*of* Соединённые Штаты Америки) USA.

сшиба́ть *impf*, сшиби́ть (-бу́, -бёшь; сшиб) *pf* strike, hit, knock (off); ~ с ног knock down; ~ся collide; come to blows.

сшива́ть *impf*, с|шить (сошью́, -ьёшь) *pf* sew (together).

до́бный edible; nice.

съе́ду *etc*.: *see* съе́хать

съёживаться *impf*, съёжиться (-жусь) *pf* shrivel, shrink.

съезд congress; conference; arrival. съе́здить (-зжу) *pf* go, drive, travel.

съезжа́ть(ся *impf of* съе́хать(ся. съе́ду *etc*.: *see* съесть

съёмка removal; survey, surveying; shooting. съёмный detachable, removable. съёмщик, съёмщица tenant; surveyor.

съестно́й food; ~о́е *sb* food (supplies). съе|сть (-ем, -ешь, -ест, -еди́м; съел) *pf* (*impf also* съеда́ть)

съе́хать (-е́ду) *pf* (*impf* съезжа́ть) go down; come down; move; ~ся meet; assemble.

съязви́ть (-влю́) *pf*.

сы́воротка whey; serum.

сыгра́ть *pf of* игра́ть; ~ся play (well) together.

сын (*pl* сыновья́, -ве́й, -вья́м *or* -ы́, -ов) son. сыно́вний filial. сыно́к (-нка́) little son; sonny.

сы́пать (-плю) *impf* pour; pour forth; ~ся fall; pour out; rain down; fray. сыпно́й тиф typhus. сыпу́чий friable; free-flowing; shifting. сыпь rash, eruption.

сыр (*loc* -у́; *pl* -ы́) cheese.

сыре́ть (-е́ю) *impf* (*pf* от~) become damp.

сыре́ц (-рца́) raw product.

сыро́|й (сыр, -а́, -о) damp; raw; uncooked; unboiled; unfinished; unripe. сы́рость dampness. сырьё raw material(s).

сыска́ть (сыщу́, сы́щешь) *pf*

сы́тный (-тен, -тна́, -о) filling. сы́тость satiety. сы́тый (сыт, -а́, -о) full.

**сыч** (-á) little owl.

**сы́щик** detective.

**с|эконóмить** (-млю) pf.

**сэр** sir.

**сюдá** adv here, hither.

**сюжéт** subject; plot; topic. **сюжéтный** subject; having a theme.

**сюи́та** suite.

**сюрпри́з** surprise.

**сюрреали́зм** surrealism. **сюрреалисти́ческий** surrealist.

**сюртýк** (-á) frock-coat.

**сяк** adv: see **так. сям** adv: see **там**

# Т

**та** see **тот**

**табáк** (-á) tobacco. **табакéрка** snuff-box. **табáчный** tobacco.

**тáбель** (-я; pl -и, -ей or -я́, -éй) m table, list. **тáбельный** table; time.

**таблéтка** tablet.

**таблúца** table; ~ умножéния multiplication table.

**тáбор** (gipsy) camp.

**табýн** (-á) herd.

**табурéт, табурéтка** stool.

**таврó** (pl -а, -áм) brand.

**тавтолóгия** tautology.

**таджи́к, -и́чка** Tadzhik.

**Таджикистáн** Tadzhikistan.

**таёжный** taiga.

**таз** (loc -ý; pl -ы́) basin; pelvis. **тазобéдренный** hip. **тáзовый** pelvic.

**таи́нственный** mysterious; secret. **таи́ть** impf hide, harbour; ~ся hide; lurk.

**Тайвáнь** m Taiwan.

**тайгá** taiga.

**тайкóм** adv secretly, surreptitiously; ~ от+gen behind the back of.

**тайм** half; period of play.

**тáйна** secret; mystery. **тайни́к** (-á) hiding-place; pl recesses. **тáйный** secret; privy.

**тайфýн** typhoon.

**так** adv so; like this; as it should be; just like that; и ~ even so; as it is; и ~ дáлее and so on; ~ и сяк this way and that; не ~ wrong; ~ же in the same way; ~ же... как as ... as; ~ и есть I thought so!; ~ ему́ и нáдо serves him right; ~ и́ли инáче one way or another; ~ себé so-so. так conj then; so; ~ как as, since; ~ что so.

**такелáж** rigging.

**тáкже** adv also, too, as well.

**такóв** m (-á f, -ó neut, -ы́ pl) pron such.

**так|óй** pron such (a); в ~óм слýчае in that case; кто он ~óй? who is he?; ~óй же the same; ~и́м óбразом in this way; что э́то ~óе? what is this? **такóй-то** pron so-and-so; such-and-such.

**тáкса** fixed rate; tariff.

**таксёр** taxi-driver. **такси́** neut indecl taxi. **такси́ст** taxi-driver. **таксопáрк** taxi depot.

**такт** time; beat; tact. **тáк-таки** after all, really.

**тáктика** tactics. **такти́ческий** tactical.

**такти́чность** tact. **такти́чный** tactful.

**тáктов|ый** time, timing; ~ая чертá bar-line.

**талáнт** talent. **талáнтливый** talented.

**талисмáн** talisman.

**тáлия** waist.

**талóн, талóнчик** coupon.

**тáлый** thawed, melted.

**тальк** talc; talcum powder.

**там** adv there; ~ и сям here and there; ~ же in the same place; ibid.

**тамада́** m toast-master.

**та́мбур**[1] tambour; lobby; platform. **та́мбур**[2] chain-stitch.

**тамо́женник** customs official. **тамо́женный** customs. **тамо́жня** custom-house.

**та́мошний** of that place, local.

**тампо́н** tampon.

**та́нгенс** tangent.

**та́нго** neut indecl tango.

**та́нец** (-нца) dance; dancing.

**тани́н** tannin.

**танк** tank. **та́нкер** tanker. **танки́ст** member of a tank crew. **та́нковый** tank, armoured.

**танцева́льный** dancing; ~ ве́чер dance. **танцева́ть** (-цу́ю) impf dance. **танцо́вщик**, **танцо́вщица** (ballet) dancer. **танцо́р**, **танцо́рка** dancer.

**та́пка**, **та́почка** slipper.

**та́ра** packing; tare.

**тарака́н** cockroach.

**тара́н** battering-ram.

**тара́нтул** tarantula.

**таре́лка** plate; cymbal; satellite dish.

**тари́ф** tariff.

**таска́ть** impf drag, lug; carry; pull; take; pull out; swipe; wear; ~ся drag; hang about.

**тасова́ть** (pf с~) shuffle.

**ТАСС** abbr (of Телегра́фное аге́нтство Сове́тского Сою́за) Tass (Telegraph Agency of the Soviet Union).

**тата́рин**, **тата́рка** Tatar.

**татуиро́вка** tattooing, tattoo.

**тафта́** taffeta.

**тахта́** ottoman.

**та́чка** wheelbarrow.

**тащи́ть** (-щу́, -щишь) impf (pf вы́~, с~) pull; drag, lug; carry; take; pull out; swipe; ~ся drag o.s. along; drag.

**та́ять** (та́ю) impf (pf рас~) melt; thaw; dwindle.

**тварь** creature(s); wretch.

**тверде́ть** (-е́ет) impf (pf за~) harden, become hard. **тверди́ть** (-ржу́) impf (pf вы́~) repeat, say again and again; memorize. **твёрдо** adv hard; firmly, firm. **твердоло́бый** thick-skulled; diehard. **твёрдый** hard; firm; solid; steadfast; ~ знак hard sign, ъ; ~ое те́ло solid. **тверды́ня** stronghold.

**твой** (-его́) m, **твоя́** (-е́й) f, **твоё** (-его́) neut, **твои́** (-и́х) pl your, yours.

**творе́ние** creation, work; creature. **творе́ц** (-рца́) creator. **твори́тельный** instrumental. **твори́ть** (pf со~) create; do; make; ~ся happen.

**творо́г** (-а́) curds; cottage cheese.

**тво́рческий** creative. **тво́рчество** creation; creative work; works.

**те** see **тот**

**т.е.** abbr (of то есть) that is, i.e.

**теа́тр** theatre. **театра́льный** theatre; theatrical.

**тебя́** etc.: see **ты**

**те́зис** thesis.

**тёзка** m & f namesake.

**тёк** see **течь**

**текст** text; libretto; lyrics.

**тексти́ль** m textiles. **тексти́льный** textile.

**текстура́** texture.

**теку́чий** fluid; unstable. **теку́щий** current; routine.

**теле-** in comb tele-; television. **телеателье́** neut indecl television maintenance workshop.

~ви́дение television. ~визио́нный television. ~ви́зор television (set). ~гра́мма telegram. ~гра́ф telegraph (office). ~графи́ровать *impf & pf* telegraph. ~гра́фный telegraph(ic). ~зри́тель *m* (television) viewer. ~объекти́в telephoto lens. ~патический telepathic. ~па́тия telepathy. ~ско́п telescope. ~ста́нция television station. ~сту́дия television studio. ~фо́н telephone; (telephone) number; (по)звони́ть по ~фо́ну *+dat* ring up. ~фон-автома́т public telephone, call-box. ~фони́ст, -и́стка (telephone) operator. ~фо́нный telephone; ~фо́нная кни́га telephone directory; ~фо́нная ста́нция telephone exchange; ~фо́нная тру́бка receiver. ~фон-отве́тчик answering machine. ~центр television centre.
**теле́га** cart, wagon. **теле́жка** small cart; trolley.
**те́лекс** telex.
**телёнок** (-нка; *pl* -я́та, -я́т) calf.
**теле́сн|ый** bodily; corporal; ~ого цве́та flesh-coloured.
**Теле́ц** (-льца́) Taurus.
**тели́ться** *impf* (*pf* o~) calve. **тёлка** heifer.
**те́ло** (*pl* -а́) body. **телогре́йка** padded jacket. **телосложе́ние** build. **телохрани́тель** *m* bodyguard.
**теля́та** *etc.: see* **телёнок. теля́тина** veal. **теля́чий** calf; veal.
**тем** *conj* (so much) the; ~ лу́чше so much the better; ~ не ме́нее nevertheless.
**тем** *see* **тот, тьма**

**те́ма** subject; theme. **тема́тика** subject-matter; themes. **темати́ческий** subject; thematic.
**тембр** timbre.
**темне́ть** (-е́ет) *impf* (*pf* по~, с~) become dark. **темни́ца** dungeon. **темно́** *predic* it is dark. **темноко́жий** dark-skinned, swarthy. **тёмно-си́ний** dark blue. **темнота́** darkness. **тёмный** dark.
**темп** tempo; rate.
**темпера́мент** temperament. **темпера́ментный** temperamental.
**температу́ра** temperature.
**те́мя** (-мени) *neut* crown, top of the head.
**тенде́нция** tendency; bias.
**теневой, тени́стый** shady.
**те́ннис** tennis. **тенниси́ст, -и́стка** tennis-player. **тенни́сн|ый** tennis; ~ая площа́дка tennis-court.
**те́нор** (*pl* -а́) tenor.
**тент** awning.
**тень** (*loc* -и́; *pl* -и, -е́й) shade; shadow; phantom; ghost; particle, vestige, atom; suspicion; те́ни для век *pl* eyeshadow.
**тео́лог** theologian. **теологи́ческий** theological. **теоло́гия** theology.
**теоре́ма** theorem. **теоре́тик** theoretician. **теорети́ческий** theoretical. **тео́рия** theory.
**тепе́решн|ий** present. **тепе́рь** *adv* now; today.
**тепле́ть** (-е́ет) *impf* (*pf* по~) get warm. **те́плиться** (-ится) *impf* flicker; glimmer. **тепли́ца** greenhouse, conservatory. **тепли́чный** hothouse. **тепло́** heat; warmth. **тепло́** *adv* warmly; *predic* it is warm.
**тепло-** *in comb* heat; thermal;

thermo-. **теплово́з** diesel locomotive. **~ёмкость** thermal capacity. **~кро́вный** warm-blooded. **~обме́н** heat exchange. **~проводя́щий** heat-conducting. **~сто́йкий** heat-resistant. **~хо́д** motor ship. **~центра́ль** heat and power station.

**теплово́й** heat; thermal. **теплота́** heat; warmth. **тёплый** (-пел, -пла́, тепло́) warm.

**терапе́вт** therapeutist. **терапи́я** therapy.

**тереби́ть** (-блю́) *impf* pull (at); pester.

**тере́ть** (тру, трёшь; тёр) *impf* rub; grate; **~ся** rub o.s.; **~ся о́коло**+*gen* hang about, hang around; **~ся среди́** +*gen* mix with.

**терза́ть** *impf* tear to pieces; torment; **~ся** +*instr* suffer; be a prey to.

**тёрка** grater.

**те́рмин** term. **терминоло́гия** terminology.

**терми́ческий** thermic, thermal. **термо́метр** thermometer. **те́рмос** thermos (flask). **термоста́т** thermostat. **термоя́дерный** thermonuclear.

**терно́вник** sloe, blackthorn. **терни́стый** thorny.

**терпели́вый** patient. **терпе́ние** patience. **терпе́ть** (-плю́, -пишь) *impf* (*pf* по~) suffer; bear, endure. **терпе́ться** (-пится) *impf impers*+*dat*: ему́ не те́рпится +*inf* he is impatient to. **терпи́мость** tolerance. **терпи́мый** tolerant; tolerable.

**те́рпкий** (-пок, -пка́, -о) astringent; tart.

**терра́са** terrace.

**территориа́льный** territorial.

**террито́рия** territory.

**терро́р** terror. **терроризи́ровать** *impf* & *pf* terrorize. **террори́ст** terrorist.

**тёртый** grated; experienced.

**терье́р** terrier.

**теря́ть** *impf* (*pf* по~, у~) lose; shed; **~ся** get lost; disappear; fail, decline; become flustered.

**тёс** boards, planks. **теса́ть** (тешу́, те́шешь) *impf* cut, hew.

**тесёмка** ribbon, braid.

**тесни́ть** *impf* (*pf* по~, с~) crowd; squeeze, constrict; be too tight; **~ся** press through; move up; crowd, jostle. **теснота́** crowded state; crush. **те́сный** crowded; (too) tight; close; compact; **~о** it is crowded.

**тесо́вый** board, plank.

**тест** test.

**те́сто** dough; pastry.

**тесть** *m* father-in-law.

**тесьма́** ribbon, braid.

**те́терев** (*pl* -а́) black grouse. **тете́рка** grey hen.

**тётка** aunt.

**тетра́дка, тетра́дь** exercise book.

**тётя** (*gen pl* -ей) aunt.

**тех-** *abbr in comb* (*of* техни́ческий) technical.

**те́хник** technician. **те́хника** technical equipment; technology; technique. **техни́кум** technical college. **техни́ческий** technical; **~ие усло́вия** specifications. **техно́лог** technologist. **технологи́ческий** technological. **техноло́гия** technology. **техперсона́л** technical personnel.

**тече́ние** flow; course; current, stream; trend.

**течь**[1] (-чёт; тёк, -ла́) *impf* flow; stream; leak. **течь**[2] leak.

**те́шить** (-шу) *impf* (*pf* по~)

amuse; gratify; **~ся** (+*instr*) amuse o.s. (with).

**тешу́** *etc.*: see **теса́ть**

**тёща** mother-in-law.

**тигр** tiger. **тигри́ца** tigress.

**тик**[1] tic.

**тик**[2] teak.

**ти́на** slime, mud.

**тип** type. **типи́чный** typical. **типово́й** standard; model. **типогра́фия** printing-house, press. **типогра́фский** typographical.

**тир** shooting-range, -gallery.

**тира́ж** (-á) draw; circulation; edition.

**тира́н** tyrant. **тира́нить** *impf* tyrannize. **тирани́ческий** tyrannical. **тира́ния** tyranny.

**тире́** *neut indecl* dash.

**ти́скать** *impf*, **ти́снуть** (-ну) *pf* press, squeeze. **тиски́** (-óв) *pl* vice; **в тиска́х** +*gen* in the grip of. **тисне́ние** stamping; imprint; design. **тиснёный** stamped.

**тита́н**[1] titanian.

**тита́н**[2] boiler.

**тита́н**[3] titan.

**титр** title, sub-title.

**ти́тул** title; title-page. **ти́тульный** title.

**тиф** (*loc* -ý) typhus.

**ти́хий** (тих, -á, -о) quiet; silent; calm; slow. **тихоокеа́нский** Pacific. **ти́ше** *comp of* **ти́хий**, **ти́хо**; *int* **ти́ше!** quiet! **тишина́** quiet, silence.

**т. к.** *abbr* (*of* **так как**) as, since.

**тка́ный** woven. **ткань** fabric, cloth; tissue. **ткать** (тку, ткёшь; -ал, -ала́, -о) *impf* (*pf* **со~**) weave. **тка́цкий** weaving; **~ стано́к** loom. **ткач**, **ткачи́ха** weaver.

**ткну́ть(ся** (-у(сь, -ёшь(ся) *pf of* **ты́кать(ся**

**тле́ние** decay; smouldering.

**тлеть** (-éет) *impf* rot, decay; smoulder; **~ся** smoulder.

**тля** aphis.

**тмин** caraway(-seeds).

**то** *pron* that; **а не то́** or else, otherwise; **(да) и то́** and even then, and that; **то́ есть** that is (to say); **то и де́ло** every now and then. **то** *conj* then; **не то...**, **не то** either ... or; half ..., half; **то..., то** now ..., now; **то ли...**, **то ли** whether ... or. **-то** *partl* just, exactly; **в то́м-то и де́ло** that's just it.

**тобо́й** *see* **ты**

**това́р** goods; commodity.

**това́рищ** comrade; friend; colleague. **това́рищеский** comradely; friendly.

**това́рищество** comradeship; company; association.

**това́рный** goods; commodity.

**това́ро-** *in comb* commodity; goods. **товарообме́н** barter. **~оборо́т** (sales) turnover. **~отправи́тель** *m* consignor. **~получа́тель** *m* consignee.

**тогда́** *adv* then; **~ как** whereas. **тогда́шний** of that time.

**того́** *see* **тот**

**тожде́ственный** identical. **тожде́ство** identity.

**то́же** *adv* also, too.

**ток** (*pl* -и) current.

**тока́рный** turning; **~ стано́к** lathe. **то́карь** (*pl* -я́, -е́й *or* -и, -ей) *m* turner, lathe operator.

**токси́ческий** toxic.

**толк** sense; use; **бе́з** *adv* senselessly; **знать ~ в**+*prep* know well; **сбить с ~у** confuse; **с ~ом** intelligently.

**толка́ть** *impf* (*pf* **толкну́ть**) push, shove; jog; **~ся** jostle.

**толки́** (-óв) *pl* rumours, gossip.

ТОЛКНУ́ТЬ(СЯ (-ну́(сь, -нёшь(ся) pf of ТОЛКА́ТЬ(СЯ

ТОЛКОВА́НИЕ interpretation; pl commentary. ТОЛКОВА́ТЬ impf interpret; explain; talk. ТОЛКО́ВЫЙ intelligent; clear; ~ слова́рь defining dictionary. ТО́ЛКОМ adv plainly; seriously.

ТОЛКОТНЯ́ crush, squash.

ТОЛКУ́ etc.: see ТОЛО́ЧЬ

ТОЛКУ́ЧКА crush, squash; second-hand market.

ТОЛОКНО́ oatmeal.

ТОЛО́ЧЬ (-лку́, -лчёшь; -лок, -лкла́) impf (pf ис~, рас~) pound, crush.

ТОЛПА́ (pl -ы) crowd. ТОЛПИ́ТЬСЯ impf crowd; throng.

ТОЛСТЕ́ТЬ (-е́ю) impf (pf по~) grow fat; put on weight. ТОЛСТОКО́ЖИЙ thick-skinned; pachydermatous. ТО́ЛСТЫЙ (-á, -о) fat; thick. ТОЛСТЯ́К (-á) fat man or boy.

ТОЛЧЁНЫЙ crushed; ground. ТОЛЧЁТ etc.: see ТОЛО́ЧЬ

ТОЛЧЕЯ́ crush; squash.

ТОЛЧО́К (-чка́) push, shove; (sport) put; jolt; shock, tremor.

ТО́ЛЩА thickness; thick. ТО́ЛЩЕ comp of ТО́ЛСТЫЙ. ТОЛЩИНА́ thickness; fatness.

ТОЛЬ m roofing felt.

ТО́ЛЬКО adv only, merely; ~ что (only) just; conj only, but; (как) ~, (лишь) ~ as soon as; ~ бы if only.

ТОМ (pl -á) volume. ТО́МИК small volume.

ТОМА́Т tomato. ТОМА́ТНЫЙ tomato.

ТОМИ́ТЕЛЬНЫЙ tedious, wearing; agonizing. ТОМИ́ТЬ (-млю́) impf (pf ис~) tire; torment; ~ся languish; be tormented. ТОМЛЕ́НИЕ languor. ТО́МНЫЙ

(-мен, -мна́, -о) languid, languorous.

ТОН (pl -á or -ы, -о́в) tone; note; shade; form. ТОНА́ЛЬНОСТЬ key.

ТО́НЕНЬКИЙ thin; slim. ТО́НКИЙ (-нок, -нка́, -о) thin; slim; fine; refined; subtle; keen. ТО́НКОСТЬ thinness; slimness; fineness; subtlety.

ТО́ННА ton.

ТОННЕ́ЛЬ see ТУННЕ́ЛЬ

ТО́НУС tone.

ТОНУ́ТЬ (-ну́, -нешь) impf (pf по~, у~) sink; drown.

ТО́НЬШЕ comp of ТО́НКИЙ

ТО́ПАТЬ impf (pf ТО́ПНУТЬ) stamp.

ТОПИ́ТЬ¹ (-плю́, -пишь) impf (pf по~, у~) sink; drown; ruin; ~ся drown o.s.

ТОПИ́ТЬ² (-плю́, -пишь) impf stoke; heat; melt (down); ~ся burn; melt. ТО́ПКА stoking; heating; melting (down); furnace.

ТО́ПКИЙ boggy, marshy.

ТО́ПЛИВНЫЙ fuel. ТО́ПЛИВО fuel.

ТО́ПНУТЬ (-ну) pf of ТО́ПАТЬ

ТОПОГРАФИ́ЧЕСКИЙ topographical. ТОПОГРА́ФИЯ topography.

ТО́ПОЛЬ (pl -я́ or -и) m poplar.

ТОПО́Р (-á) axe. ТОПО́РИК hatchet. ТОПО́РИЩЕ axe-handle. ТОПО́РНЫЙ axe; clumsy, crude.

ТО́ПОТ tramp; clatter. ТОПТА́ТЬ (-пчу́, -пчешь) impf (pf ис~) trample (down); ~ся stamp; ~ся на ме́сте mark time.

ТОПЧА́Н (-á) trestle-bed.

ТОПЬ bog, marsh.

ТОРГ (loc -у́; pl -и́) trading; bargaining; pl auction. ТОРГОВА́ТЬ impf (pf с~) trade; ~ся bargain, haggle. ТОРГО́ВЕЦ (-вца) merchant; tradesman. ТОРГО́ВКА market-woman; stall-holder. **торго́вля** trade. **торго́вый** trade, commercial; merchant. **торгпре́д** *abbr* trade representative.

**торе́ц** (-рца́) butt-end; wooden paving-block.

**торже́ственный** solemn; ceremonial; triumph. **торжество́** celebration; triumph. **торжествова́ть** *impf* celebrate; triumph.

**торможе́ние** braking. **тормоз** (*pl* -а́ *or* -ы) brake. **тормози́ть** (-ожу́) *impf* (*pf* за~) brake; hamper.

**тормоши́ть** (-шу́) *impf* pester; bother.

**торопи́ть** (-плю́, -пишь) *impf* (*pf* по~) hurry; hasten; ~ся hurry. **торопли́вый** hasty.

**торпе́да** torpedo.

**торс** torso.

**торт** cake.

**торф** peat. **торфяно́й** peat.

**торча́ть** (-чу́) *impf* stick out; protrude; hang about.

**торше́р** standard lamp.

**тоска́** melancholy; boredom; nostalgia; ~ по+*dat* longing for. **тоскли́вый** melancholy; depressed; dreary. **тоскова́ть** *impf* be melancholy, depressed; long; ~ по+*dat* miss.

**тост** toast.

**тот** *m* (та *f*, то *neut*, те *pl*) *pron* that; the former; the other; the one; the same; the right; и ~ и друго́й both; к тому́ же moreover; не ~ the wrong; ни ~ ни друго́й neither; тот, кто the one who, the person who. **то́тчас** *adv* immediately.

**тоталитари́зм** totalitarianism. **тоталита́рный** totalitarian. **тота́льный** total.

**точи́лка** sharpener; pencil-sharpener. **точи́ло** whetstone, grindstone. **точи́льный** grind-

ing; sharpening; ~ ка́мень whetstone, grindstone. **точи́льщик** (knife-)grinder. **точи́ть** (-чу́, -чишь) *impf* (*pf* вы~, на~) sharpen; hone; turn; eat away; gnaw at.

**то́чка** spot; dot; full stop; point; ~ зре́ния point of view; ~ с запято́й semicolon. **то́чно**[1] *adv* exactly, precisely; punctually. **то́чно**[2] *conj* as though, as if. **то́чность** punctuality; precision; accuracy; в то́чности exactly, precisely. **то́чный** (-чен, -чна́, -о) exact, precise; accurate; punctual. **точь-в-то́чь** *adv* exactly; word for word.

**тошни́ть** *impf impers*: меня́ тошни́т I feel sick. **тошнота́** nausea. **тошнотво́рный** sickening, nauseating.

**то́щий** (тощ, -á, -е) gaunt, emaciated; skinny; empty; poor.

**трава́** (*pl* -ы) grass; herb. **трави́нка** blade of grass.

**трави́ть** (-влю́, -вишь) *impf* (*pf* вы~, за~) poison; exterminate, destroy; etch; hunt; torment; badger. **травле́ние** extermination; etching. **тра́вля** hunting; persecution; badgering.

**тра́вма** trauma, injury.

**травоя́дный** herbivorous. **травяни́стый, травяно́й** grass; herbaceous; grassy.

**траге́дия** tragedy. **тра́гик** tragedian. **траги́ческий, траги́чный** tragic.

**традицио́нный** traditional. **тради́ция** tradition.

**траекто́рия** trajectory.

**тракта́т** treatise; treaty.

**тракти́р** inn, tavern.

**трактова́ть** *impf* interpret; treat, discuss. **тракто́вка**

treatment; interpretation.
**трáктор** tractor. **тракторúст** tractor driver.
**трал** trawl. **трáлить** *impf* (*pf* про~) trawl; sweep. **трáльщик** trawler; mine-sweeper.
**трамбовáть** *impf* (*pf* у~) ram, tamp.
**трамвáй** tram. **трамвáйный** tram.
**трамплúн** spring-board; ski-jump.
**транзúстор** transistor; transistor radio.
**транзúтный** transit.
**транс** trance.
**трансатлантúческий** transatlantic.
**транслúровать** *impf* & *pf* broadcast, transmit. **трансляцио́нный** transmission; broadcasting. **трансля́ция** broadcast, transmission.
**трáнспорт** transport; consignment. **транспортёр** conveyor. **транспортúр** protractor. **транспортúровать** *impf* & *pf* transport. **трáнспортный** transport.
**трансформáтор** transformer.
**траншéя** trench.
**трап** ladder.
**трáпеза** meal.
**трапéция** trapezium; trapeze.
**трáсса** line, course, direction; route, road.
**трáта** expenditure; waste. **трáтить** (-áчу) *impf* (*pf* ис~, по~) spend, expend; waste.
**трáулер** trawler.
**трáур** mourning. **трáурный** mourning; funeral; mournful.
**трафарéт** stencil; stereotype; cliché. **трафарéтный** stencilled; conventional, stereotyped.
**трáчу** *etc.*: see **трáтить**

**трéбование** demand; request; requirement; requisition, order; *pl* needs. **трéбовательный** demanding. **трéбовать** *impf* (*pf* по~) summon; +*gen* demand, require; need; ~ся be needed, be required.
**тревóга** alarm; anxiety. **тревóжить** (-жу) *impf* (*pf* вс~, по~) alarm; disturb; worry; ~ся worry, be anxious; trouble o.s. **тревóжный** worried, anxious; alarming; alarm.
**трéзвенник** teetotaller. **трезвéть** (-éю) *impf* (*pf* о~) sober up.
**трезвóн** peal (*of bells*); rumours; row.
**трéзвость** sobriety. **трéзвый** (-зв, -á, -о) sober; teetotal.
**трéйлер** trailer.
**трель** trill; warble.
**трéнер** trainer, coach.
**трéние** friction.
**тренировáть** *impf* (*pf* на~) train, coach; ~ся be in training. **тренирóвка** training, coaching. **тренирóвочный** training.
**трепáть** (-плю, -плешь) *impf* (*pf* ис~, по~, рас~) blow about; dishevel; wear out; pat; ~ся fray; wear out; flutter.
**трéпет** trembling; trepidation.
**трепетáть** (-ещу, -éщешь) *impf* tremble; flicker; palpitate. **трéпетный** trembling; flickering; palpitating; timid.
**треск** crack; crackle; fuss.
**трескá** cod.
**трéскаться¹** *impf* (*pf* по~) crack; chap.
**трéскаться²** *impf* of **трéснуться**
**трéснуть** (-нет) *pf* snap, crackle; crack; chap; bang; ~ся (*impf* **трéскаться**) +*instr* bang.

**трест** trust.

**тре́т|ий** (-ья, -ье) third; ~**ье** *sb* sweet (course).

**трети́ровать** *impf* slight.

**треть** (*gen pl* -**е́й**) third.

**тре́тье** *etc.*: *see* **тре́тий**.

**треуго́льник** triangle. **треуго́льный** triangular.

**тре́фы** (треф) *pl* clubs.

**трёх-** *in comb* three-, tri-. **трёхгоди́чный** three-year. ~**голо́сный** three-part. ~**гра́нный** three-edged; trihedral. ~**колёсный** three-wheeled. ~**ле́тний** three-year; three-year old. ~**ме́рный** three-dimensional. ~**ме́сячный** three-month; quarterly; three-month-old. ~**по́лье** three-field system. ~**со́тый** three-hundredth. ~**сторо́нний** three-sided; trilateral; tripartite. ~**эта́жный** three-storeyed.

**треща́ть** (-щу́) *impf* crack; crackle; creak; chirr; crack up; chatter. **тре́щина** crack, split; fissure; chap.

**три** (трёх, -ём, -емя́, -ёх) three.

**трибу́на** platform, rostrum; stand. **трибуна́л** tribunal.

**тригономе́трия** trigonometry.

**тридцатиле́тний** thirty-year; thirty-year old. **тридца́тый** thirtieth. **три́дцать** (-и́, *instr* -ью́) thirty. **три́жды** *adv* three times; thrice.

**трико́** *neut indecl* tricot; tights; knickers. **трикота́ж** knitted fabric; knitwear. **трикота́жный** jersey, tricot; knitted.

**трина́дцатый** thirteenth. **трина́дцать** thirteen. **трио́ль** triplet.

**три́ппер** gonorrhoea.

**три́ста** (трёхсо́т, -ёмста́м, -емяста́ми, -ёхста́х) three hundred.

**трито́н** *zool* triton.

**триу́мф** triumph.

**тро́гательный** touching, moving. **тро́гать(ся** *impf of* **тро́нуть(ся**

**тро́е** (-и́х) *pl* three. **троебо́рье** triathlon. **трёхкра́тный** thrice-repeated. **Тро́ица** Trinity; **тро́ица** trio. **Тро́ицын день** Whit Sunday. **тро́йка** figure 3; troika; No. 3; three-piece suit. **тройно́й** triple, treble; three-ply. **тро́йственный** triple; tripartite.

**тролле́йбус** trolley-bus.

**тромб** blood clot.

**тромбо́н** trombone.

**трон** throne.

**тро́нуть** (-ну) *pf* (*impf* **тро́гать**) touch; disturb; affect; ~**ся** start, set out; be touched; be moved.

**тропа́** path.

**тро́пик** tropic.

**тропи́нка** path.

**тропи́ческий** tropical.

**трос** rope, cable.

**тростни́к** (-а́) reed, rush. **тро́сточка, трость** (*gen pl* ~**е́й**) cane, walking-stick.

**тротуа́р** pavement.

**трофе́й** trophy; *pl* spoils (*of war*), booty.

**трою́родн|ый**: ~**ый брат**, ~**ая сестра́** second cousin.

**тру** *etc.*: *see* **тере́ть**

**труба́** (*pl* -ы) pipe; chimney; funnel; trumpet; tube. **труба́ч** (-а́) trumpeter; trumpet-player. **труби́ть** (-блю́) *impf* (*pf* **про~**) blow, sound; blare. **тру́бка** tube; pipe; (*telephone*) receiver. **трубопрово́д** pipe-line; piping; manifold. **трубочи́ст** chimney-sweep. **тру́бочный** pipe. **тру́бчатый** tubular.

**труд** (-á) labour; work; effort; **с ~óм** with difficulty. **тру-дúться** (-ужýсь, -ýдишься) *impf* toil, labour, work; trouble. **трýдно** *predic* it is difficult. **трýдность** difficulty. **трýдный** (-ден, -днá, -о) difficult; hard.

**трудо-** *in comb* labour, work. **трудодéнь** (-дня) *m* work-day (*unit*). **~ёмкий** labour-intensive. **~любúвый** industrious. **~любие** industry. **~спосóбность** ability to work. **~спосóбный** able-bodied; capable of working.

**трудовóй** work; working; earned; hard-earned. **трудя-щийся** working; **~иеся** *sb pl* the workers. **трýженик, трýженица** toiler.

**труп** corpse; carcass.

**трýппа** troupe, company.

**трус** coward.

**трýсики** (-ов) *pl* shorts; trunks; pants.

**трусúть¹** (-ушý) *impf* trot, jog along.

**трусúть²** (-ушý) *impf* (*pf* с~) be a coward; lose one's nerve; be afraid. **трусúха** coward. **труслúвый** cowardly. **трýсость** cowardice.

**трусы́** (-óв) *pl* shorts; trunks; pants.

**трухá** dust; trash.

**трушý** *etc.*: *see* **трусúть¹**, **трýсить**.

**трущóба** slum; godforsaken hole.

**трюк** stunt; trick.

**трюм** hold.

**трюмó** *neut indecl* pier-glass.

**трюфель** (*gen pl* -лéй) *m* truffle.

**тря́пка** rag; spineless creature; *pl* clothes. **тря́пьё** rags; clothes.

**тряси́на** quagmire. **тря́ска** shaking, jolting. **трясти́** (-сý, -сёшь; -яс, -лá) *impf*, **тряхнýть** (-нý, -нёшь) *pf* (*pf also* вы~) shake; shake out; jolt; **~сь** tremble; shiver; jolt.

**тсс** *int* sh! hush!

**туалéт** dress; toilet. **туалéт-ный** toilet.

**туберкулёз** tuberculosis.

**тугóй** *adv* tight(ly), taut; with difficulty. **тугóй** (туг, -á, -о) tight; taut; tightly filled; difficult.

**тудá** *adv* there, thither; that way; to the right place; **ни ~ ни сюдá** neither one way nor the other; **~ и обрáтно** there and back.

**тýже** *comp of* **тýго, тугóй**.

**тужýрка** (double-breasted) jacket.

**туз** (-á *acc* -á) ace; bigwig.

**тузéмец** (-мца), **-мка** native.

**тýловище** trunk; torso.

**тулýп** sheepskin coat.

**тумáн** fog; mist; haze. **тумá-нить** *impf* (*pf* за~) dim, cloud, obscure; **~ся** grow misty; be befogged. **тумáн-ность** fog, mist; nebula; obscurity. **тумáнный** foggy; misty; hazy; obscure, vague.

**тýмба** post; bollard; pedestal. **тýмбочка** bedside table.

**тýндра** tundra.

**тунея́дец** (-дца) sponger.

**тунúка** tunic.

**туннéль** *m*, **тоннéль** *m* tunnel.

**тупéть** (-éю) *impf* (*pf* о~) become blunt; grow dull. **тупúк** (-á) cul-de-sac, dead end; *im-passe*; **поставить в ~** stump, nonplus. **тупúться** (-пится) *impf* (*pf* за~, ис~) become blunt. **тýпица** *m* & *f* blockhead, dimwit. тупо́й (туп, -á, -о) blunt; obtuse; dull; vacant, stupid. ту́пость bluntness; vacancy; dullness, slowness.

тур turn; round.

тура́ rook, castle.

турба́за holiday village, camp-site.

турби́на turbine.

туре́цкий Turkish; ~ бара-ба́н bass drum.

тури́зм tourism. тури́ст, -и́стка tourist. тури́ст(и́че)ский tour-ist.

туркме́н (gen pl -ме́н), ~ка Turkmen. Туркмениста́н Turkmenistan.

турне́ neut indecl tour.

турне́пс swede.

турни́р tournament.

ту́рок (-рка) Turk. турча́нка Turkish woman. Ту́рция Tur-key.

ту́склый dim, dull; lacklustre. тускне́ть (-е́ет) impf (pf по~) grow dim.

тут adv here; now; ~ же there and then.

ту́фля shoe.

ту́хлый (-хл, -á, -о) rotten, bad. ту́хнуть¹ (-нет; тух) go bad.

ту́хнуть² (-нет; тух) impf (pf по~) go out.

ту́ча cloud; storm-cloud.

ту́чный (-чен, -чна́, -чно) fat; rich, fertile.

туш flourish.

ту́ша carcass.

тушева́ть (-шу́ю) impf (pf за~) shade.

тушёный stewed. туши́ть¹ (-шу́, -шишь) impf (pf с~) stew.

туши́ть² (-шу́, -шишь) impf (pf за~, по~) extinguish.

тушь gen: see тушева́ть. тушь Indian ink; ~ (для ресни́ц) mascara.

щта́тельность care. тща́-тельный careful; painstaking.

тщеду́шный feeble, frail.

тщесла́вие vanity, vainglory. тщесла́вный vain. тщета́ vanity. тщётный vain, futile.

ты (тебя́, тебе́, тобо́й, тебе́) you; thou; быть на ты c+instr be on intimate terms with.

ты́кать (ты́чу) impf (pf ткнуть) poke; prod; stick.

ты́ква pumpkin; gourd.

тыл (loc -ý, pl -ы́) back; rear. ты́льный back; rear.

тын paling; palisade.

ты́сяча (instr -ей or -ью) thou-sand. тысячеле́тие millen-nium; thousandth anniversary. ты́сячный thousandth; of (many) thousands.

тычи́нка stamen.

тьма¹ dark, darkness.

тьма² host, multitude.

тюбете́йка skull-cap.

тю́бик tube.

тюк (-á) bale, package.

тюле́нь m seal.

тюльпа́н tulip.

тюре́мный prison. тюре́мщик gaoler. тюрьма́ (pl -ы, -рем) prison, gaol.

тюфя́к (-á) mattress.

тя́га traction; thrust; draught; attraction; craving. тяга́ться impf vie, contend. тяга́ч (-á) tractor.

тя́гостный burdensome; pain-ful. тя́гость burden. тяготе́-ние gravity, gravitation; bent, inclination. тяготе́ть (-е́ю) impf gravitate; be attracted; ~ над hang over. тяготи́ть (-ощу́) impf be a burden on; oppress.

тягу́чий malleable, ductile; viscous; slow.

тя́жба lawsuit; competition.

**тяжело́** adv heavily; seriously. **тяжело́** predic it is hard; it is painful. **тяжелоатле́т** weight-lifter. **тяжелове́с** heavyweight. **тяжелове́сный** weighty; ponderous. **тяжёлый** (-ёл, -а́) heavy; hard; serious; painful. **тя́жесть** gravity; weight; heaviness; severity. **тя́жкий** heavy; severe; grave.

**тяну́ть** (-ну́, -нешь) impf (pf по~) pull; draw; drag; drag out; weigh; impers attract; be tight; ~ся stretch; extend; stretch out; stretch o.s.; drag on; crawl; drift; move along one after another; last out; reach.

**тяну́чка** toffee.

# У

**у** prep+gen by; at; with; from; of; belonging to; **у меня́ (есть)** I have; **у нас** at our place; in our country.

**уба́вить** (-влю) pf, **убавля́ть** impf reduce, diminish.

**у|баю́кать** pf, **убаю́кивать** impf lull (to sleep).

**убега́ть** impf of убежа́ть

**убеди́тельный** convincing; earnest. **убеди́ть** (-и́шь) pf (impf убежда́ть) convince; persuade; ~ся be convinced; make certain.

**убежа́ть** (-егу́) pf (impf убега́ть) run away; escape; boil over.

**убежда́ть(ся** impf of убеди́ть(ся. **убежде́ние** persuasion; conviction; belief. **убеждённость** conviction. **убеждённый** (-ён, -а́) convinced; staunch.

**убе́жище** refuge, asylum; shelter.

**уберега́ть** impf, **убере́чь** (-регу́, -режёшь; -рёг, -гла́) pf protect; preserve; ~ся от+gen protect o.s. against.

**убере́ц** etc.: see убра́ть

**убива́ть(ся** impf of уби́ть(ся. **уби́йственный** deadly; murderous; killing. **уби́йство** murder. **уби́йца** m & f murderer.

**убира́ть(ся** impf of убра́ть-(ся; убира́йся! clear off!

**уби́тый** killed; crushed; sb dead man. **уби́ть** (убью́, -ьёшь) pf (impf убива́ть) kill; murder; ~ся hurt o.s.

**убо́гий** wretched. **убо́жество** poverty; squalor.

**убо́й** slaughter.

**убо́р** dress, attire.

**убо́рка** harvesting; clearing up. **убо́рная** sb lavatory; dressing-room. **убо́рочный** harvesting; ~ая маши́на harvester. **убо́рщик, убо́рщица** cleaner. **убра́нство** furniture.

**убра́ть** (уберу́, -рёшь; -а́л, -ала́, -о) pf (impf убира́ть) remove; take away; put away; harvest; clear up; decorate; ~ посте́ль make a bed; ~ со стола́ clear the table; ~ся tidy up, clean up; clear off.

**убыва́ть** impf, **убы́ть** (убу́ду; убыл, -а́, -о) pf diminish; subside; wane; leave. **убыль** diminution; casualties. **убы́ток** (-тка) loss; pl damages. **убы́точный** unprofitable.

**убью́** etc.: see уби́ть

**уважа́емый** respected; dear. **уважа́ть** impf respect. **уваже́ние** respect; **с ~м** yours sincerely. **уважи́тельный** valid; respectful.

**уве́домить** (-млю) pf, **уведомля́ть** impf inform. **уведомле́ние** notification.

**уведу́** *etc.*: *see* **увести́**
**увезти́** (-зу́, -зёшь; увёз, -ла́) *pf* (*impf* **увози́ть**) take (away); steal; abduct.
**увекове́чивать** *impf*, **увекове́чить** (-чу) *pf* immortalize; perpetuate.
**увёл** *etc.*: *see* **увести́**
**увеличе́ние** increase; magnification; enlargement. **увели́чивать** *impf*, **увели́чить** (-чу) *pf* increase; magnify; enlarge; **~ся** increase, grow. **увеличи́тель** *m* enlarger. **увеличи́тельн|ый** magnifying; enlarging; **~ое стекло́** magnifying glass.
**у|венча́ть** *pf*, **уве́нчивать** *impf* crown; **~ся** be crowned.
**уве́ренность** confidence; certainty. **уве́ренный** confident; sure; certain. **уве́рить** *pf* (*impf* **уверя́ть**) assure; convince; **~ся** satisfy o.s.; be convinced.
**уверну́ться** (-ну́сь, -нёшься) *pf*, **увёртываться** *impf* **от**+*gen* evade. **увёртка** dodge, evasion; subterfuge; *pl* wiles. **увёртливый** evasive, shifty.
**увертю́ра** overture.
**уверя́ть(ся** *impf of* **уве́рить(ся**
**увеселе́ние** amusement, entertainment. **увесели́тельный** entertainment; pleasure. **увеселя́ть** *impf* amuse, entertain.
**уве́систый** weighty.
**увести́** (-еду́, -едёшь; -ёл, -а́) *pf* (*impf* **уводи́ть**) take (away); walk off with.
**уве́чить** (-чу) *impf* maim, cripple. **уве́чный** maimed, crippled; *sb* cripple. **уве́чье** maiming; injury.
**уве́шать** *pf*, **уве́шивать** *impf* hang (+*instr* with).
**увеща́ть** *impf*, **увещева́ть** *impf* exhort, admonish.
**у|вида́ть** *pf* see. **у|ви́деть(ся** (-и́жу(сь) *pf*.
**уви́ливать** *impf*, **увильну́ть** (-ну́, -нёшь) *pf* **от**+*gen* dodge; evade.
**увлажни́ть** *pf*, **увлажня́ть** *impf* moisten.
**увлека́тельный** fascinating. **увлека́ть** *impf*, **увле́чь** (-еку́, -ечёшь; -ёк, -ла́) *pf* carry away; fascinate; **~ся** be carried away; become mad (+*instr* about). **увлече́ние** animation; passion; crush.
**уво́д** withdrawal; stealing. **уводи́ть** (-ожу́, -о́дишь) *impf of* **увести́**
**увози́ть** (-ожу́, -о́дишь) *impf of* **увезти́**
**уво́лить** *pf*, **увольня́ть** *impf* discharge, dismiss; retire; **~ся** be discharged, retire. **увольне́ние** discharge, dismissal.
**увы́** *int* alas!
**увяда́ть** *impf of* **увя́нуть**. **увя́дший** withered.
**увяза́ть**[1] *impf of* **увя́знуть**
**увяза́ть**[2] (-яжу́, -я́жешь) *pf* (*impf* **увя́зывать**) tie up; pack up; co-ordinate; **~ся** pack; tag along. **увя́зка** tying up; co-ordination.
**у|вя́знуть** (-ну; -я́з) *pf* (*impf also* **увяза́ть**) get bogged down.
**увя́зывать(ся** *impf of* **увяза́ть(ся**
**у|вя́нуть** (-ну) *pf* (*impf also* **увяда́ть**) fade, wither.
**угада́ть** *pf*, **уга́дывать** *impf* guess.
**уга́р** carbon monoxide (poisoning); ecstasy. **уга́рный газ** carbon monoxide.
**угаса́ть** *impf*, **у|га́снуть** (-нет;

-а́с) *pf* go out; die down.
**угле-** *in comb* coal; charcoal; carbon. **~лево́д** carbohydrate. **~водоро́д** hydrocarbon. **~добы́ча** coal extraction. **~кислота́** carbonic acid; carbon dioxide. **~ки́слый** carbonate (of). **~ро́д** carbon.

**углово́й** corner; angular.

**углуби́ть** (-блю́) *pf*, **углубля́ть** *impf* deepen; **~ся** deepen; delve deeply; become absorbed. **углубле́ние** depression, dip; deepening. **углублённый** deepened; profound; absorbed.

**угна́ть** (угоню́, -о́нишь; -а́л, -а́, -о) *pf* (*impf* **угоня́ть**) drive away; despatch; steal; **~ся за**+*instr* keep pace with.

**угнета́тель** *m* oppressor. **угнета́ть** *impf* oppress; depress. **угнете́ние** oppression; depression. **угнетённый** oppressed; depressed.

**угова́ривать** *impf*, **уговори́ть** *pf* persuade; **~ся** arrange, agree. **угово́р** persuasion; agreement.

**уго́да:** в уго́ду +*dat* to please. **угоди́ть** (-ожу́) *pf*, **угожда́ть** *impf* fall, get; bang; (+*dat*) hit; +*dat or* на+*acc* please. **уго́дливый** obsequious. **уго́дно** *predic+dat:* как вам ~ as you wish; что вам ~? what would you like?; *partl* кто ~ anyone (you like); что ~ anything (you like).

**уго́дье** (*gen pl* -ий) land.

**у́гол** (угла́, *loc* -ý) corner; angle.

**уголо́вник** criminal. **уголо́вный** criminal.

**уголо́к** (-лка́, *loc* -ý) corner.

**у́голь** (у́гля, *pl* у́гли, -ей *or* -е́й) *m* coal; charcoal.

**уго́льник** set square.

**у́гольный** coal; carbon(ic).

**угомони́ть** *pf* calm down; **~ся** calm down.

**уго́н** driving away; stealing. **угоня́ть** *impf of* **угна́ть**

**угора́ть** *impf*, **угоре́ть** (-рю́) *pf* get carbon monoxide poisoning; be mad. **угоре́лый** mad; possessed.

**у́горь**[1] (угря́) *m* eel.

**у́горь**[2] (угря́) *m* blackhead.

**угости́ть** (-ощу́) *pf*, **угоща́ть** *impf* entertain; treat. **угоще́ние** entertaining, treating; refreshments.

**угрожа́ть** *impf* threaten. **угро́за** threat, menace.

**угро́зыск** *abbr* criminal investigation department.

**угрызе́ние** pangs.

**угрю́мый** sullen, morose.

**удава́ться** (удаётся) *impf of* **уда́ться**

**у|дави́ть(ся** (-влю́(сь, -вишь(ся) *pf*. **уда́вка** running-knot, half hitch.

**удале́ние** removal; sending away; moving off. **удали́ть** *pf* (*impf* **удаля́ть**) remove; send away; move away; **~ся** move off, away; retire.

**удало́й, уда́лый** (-а́л, -а́, -о) daring, bold. **у́даль, удальство́** daring, boldness.

**удаля́ть(ся** *impf of* **удали́ть(ся**

**уда́р** blow; stroke; attack; kick; thrust; seizure; bolt. **ударе́ние** accent; stress; emphasis. **уда́рить** (*impf also* **бить**) strike; hit; beat; **~ся** strike, hit; +в+*acc* break into; burst into. **уда́рник, -ница** shock-worker. **уда́рный** percussion; shock; stressed; urgent.

**уда́ться** (-а́стся, -аду́тся; -а́лся, -ла́сь) *pf* (*impf* **удава́ться**) succeed, be a success; *impers* +*dat* +*inf* succeed; manage; **мне удало́сь найти́ рабо́ту** I managed to find a job. **уда́ча** good luck; success. **уда́чный** successful; felicitous.

**удва́ивать** *impf*, **удво́ить** (-о́ю) *pf* double, redouble. **удвое́ние** (re)doubling.

**уде́л** lot, destiny.

**удели́ть** *pf* (*impf* **уделя́ть**) spare, give.

**уделя́ть** *impf of* **удели́ть**

**удержа́ние** deduction; retention, keeping. **удержа́ть** (-жу́, -жишь) *pf*, **уде́рживать** *impf* hold (on to); retain; restrain; suppress; deduct; **~ся** hold out; stand firm; refrain (from).

**удеру́** *etc.: see* **удра́ть**

**удешеви́ть** (-влю́) *pf*, **удешевля́ть** *impf* reduce the price of.

**удиви́тельный** surprising, amazing; wonderful. **удиви́ть** (-влю́) *pf*, **удивля́ть** *impf* surprise, amaze; **~ся** be surprised, be amazed. **удивле́ние** surprise, amazement.

**удила́** (-и́л) *pl* bit.

**удили́ще** fishing-rod.

**удира́ть** *impf of* **удра́ть**

**уди́ть** (ужу́, у́дишь) *impf* fish for; **~ ры́бу** fish; **~ся** bite.

**удлине́ние** lengthening; extension. **удлини́ть** *pf*, **удлиня́ть** *impf* lengthen; extend; **~ся** become longer; be extended.

**удо́бно** *adv* comfortably; conveniently. **удо́бный** comfortable; convenient.

**удобовари́мый** digestible.

**удобре́ние** fertilization; fertilizer. **удо́брить** *pf*, **удобря́ть** *impf* fertilize.

**удо́бство** comfort; convenience.

**удовлетворе́ние** satisfaction; gratification. **удовлетворё́нный** (-рё́н, -á) satisfied. **удовлетвори́тельный** satisfactory. **удовлетворя́ть** *impf* satisfy; +*dat* meet; +*instr* supply with; **~ся** be satisfied.

**удово́льствие** pleasure. **у|дово́льствоваться** *pf*.

**удо́й** milk-yield; milking.

**удоста́ивать(ся** *impf of* **удосто́ить(ся**

**удостовере́ние** certification; certificate; **~ ли́чности** identity card. **удостове́рить** *pf*, **удостоверя́ть** *impf* certify, witness; **~ся** make sure (в+*prep* of), assure o.s.

**удосто́ить** *pf* (*impf* **удоста́ивать**) make an award; +*gen* award; +*instr* favour with; **~ся** +*gen* be awarded; be favoured with.

**у́дочка** (fishing-)rod.

**удра́ть** (удеру́, -ёшь; удра́л, -á, -о) *pf* (*impf* **удира́ть**) make off.

**удруча́ть** *impf*, **удручи́ть** (-чу́) *pf* depress. **удручё́нный** (-чё́н, -á) depressed.

**удуша́ть** *impf*, **удуши́ть** (-шу́, -шишь) *pf* stifle, suffocate. **удуше́ние** suffocation. **уду́шливый** stifling. **уду́шье** asthma; asphyxia.

**уедине́ние** solitude; seclusion. **уединё́нный** secluded; lonely. **уедини́ть** *pf*, **уединя́ться** *impf* seclude o.s.

**уе́зд** uyezd, District.

**уезжа́ть** *impf*, **уе́хать** (уе́ду) *pf* go away, depart.

**уж**[1] (-á) grass-snake.

**уж**[2]: *see* **уже́**[2]. **уж**[3], **уже́**[3] *partl* indeed; really.

310

у|жа́лить *pf.*

**у́жас** horror, terror; *predic* it is awful. **ужаса́ть** *impf*, **ужасну́ть** (-ну́, -нёшь) *pf* horrify; ~**ся** be horrified; be terrified. **ужа́сно** *adv* terribly; awfully. **ужа́сный** awful, terrible.

**у́же**[1] *comp of* у́зкий

**уже́**[2], **уж**[2] *adv* already; ~ **не** no longer. **уж**[3]: *see* уж[3]

**уже́ние** fishing.

**ужива́ться** *impf of* ужи́ться. **ужи́вчивый** easy to get on with.

**ужи́мка** grimace.

**у́жин** supper. **у́жинать** *impf* (*pf* по~) have supper.

**ужи́ться** (-иву́сь, -ивёшься, -и́лся, -ла́сь) *pf* (*impf* ужива́ться) get on.

**ужу́** *see* уди́ть

**узако́нивать** *impf*, **узако́нить** *pf* legalize.

**узбе́к**, **-е́чка** Uzbek. **Узбекиста́н** Uzbekistan.

**узда́** (*pl* -ы) bridle.

**у́зел** (узла́) knot; junction; centre; node; bundle.

**у́зкий** (у́зок, узка́, -о) narrow; tight; narrow-minded. **узкоколе́йка** narrow-gauge railway.

**узлова́тый** knotty. **узлов|о́й** junction; main, key; ~**а́я ста́нция** junction.

**узнава́ть** (-наю́, -наёшь) *impf*, **узна́ть** *pf* recognize; get to know; find out.

**у́зник**, **у́зница** prisoner.

**узо́р** pattern, design. **узо́рчатый** patterned.

**у́зость** narrowness; tightness.

**узурпа́тор** usurper. **узурпи́ровать** *impf & pf* usurp.

**у́зы** (уз) *pl* bonds, ties.

**уйду́** *etc.*: *see* уйти́.

**у́йма** lots (of).

**уйму́** *etc.*: *see* уня́ть.

у|йти́ (уйду́, -дёшь; ушёл, ушла́) *pf* (*impf* уходи́ть) go away, leave, depart; escape; retire; bury o.s.; be used up; pass away.

**ука́з** decree; edict. **указа́ние** indication; instruction. **ука́занный** appointed, stated. **указа́тель** *m* indicator; gauge; index; directory. **указа́тельный** indicating; demonstrative; ~ **па́лец** index finger. **указа́ть** (-ажу́, -а́жешь) *pf*, **ука́зывать** *impf* show; indicate; point; point out. **ука́зка** pointer; orders.

**ука́лывать** *impf of* уколо́ть

**ука́тать**, **ука́тывать**[1] *impf* roll; flatten; wear out. **ука́тывать**[2] *impf* roll away; drive off; ~**ся** roll away.

**укача́ть**, **ука́чивать** *impf* rock to sleep; make sick.

**укла́д** structure; style; organization. **укла́дка** packing; stacking; laying; setting. **укла́дчик** packer; layer. **укла́дывать(ся)**[1] *impf of* уложи́ть(ся

**укла́дываться**[2] *impf of* уле́чься

**укло́н** slope; incline; gradient; bias; deviation. **уклоне́ние** deviation; digression. **уклони́ться** *pf*, **уклоня́ться** *impf* deviate; **+от**+*gen* turn (off, aside); avoid; evade. **укло́нчивый** evasive.

**уклю́чина** rowlock.

**уко́л** prick; injection; thrust. **уколо́ть** (-лю́, -лешь) *pf* (*impf* ука́лывать) prick; wound.

у|комплектова́ть *pf*, **укомплекто́вывать** *impf* complete; bring up to (full) strength; man; **+**instr equip with.

**укóр** reproach.

**укорáчивать** *impf of* **укорóтить**

**укорени́ть** *pf,* **укореня́ть** *impf* implant, inculcate; **~ся** take root.

**укори́зна** reproach. **укори́зненный** reproachful. **укори́ть** *pf (impf* **укоря́ть)** reproach (**в**+*prep* with).

**укороти́ть** (-очý) *pf (impf* **укорáчивать)** shorten.

**укоря́ть** *impf of* **укори́ть**

**укóс** (hay-)crop.

**украдкой** *adv* stealthily. **украдý** *etc.: see* **украсть**

**Украи́на** Ukraine. **украи́нец** (-нца), **украи́нка** Ukrainian. **украи́нский** Ukrainian.

**украси́ть** (-áшу) *pf (impf* **украшáть)** adorn, decorate; **~ся** be decorated; adorn o.s.

**у|красть** (-адý, -дёшь) *pf.*

**украшáть** *impf of* **украси́ть(ся. украшéние** decoration; adornment.

**укрепи́ть** (-плю́) *pf,* **укрепля́ть** *impf* strengthen; fix; fortify; **~ся** become stronger; fortify one's position. **укреплéние** strengthening; reinforcement; fortification.

**укрóмный** secluded, cosy.

**укрóп** dill.

**укроти́тель** *m* (animal-)tamer. **укроти́ть** (-ощý) *pf,* **укрощáть** *impf* tame; curb; **~ся** become tame; calm down. **укрощéние** taming.

**укрóю** *etc.: see* **укрыть**

**укрупнéние** enlargement; amalgamation. **укрупни́ть** *pf,* **укрупня́ть** *impf* enlarge; amalgamate.

**укрыва́тель** *m* harbourer. **укрыва́тельство** harbouring; receiving. **укрыва́ть** *impf*

**укрыть** (-рóю) *pf* cover; conceal, harbour; shelter; receive; **~ся** cover o.s.; take cover. **укры́тие** cover; shelter.

**ýксус** vinegar.

**укýс** bite; sting. **укуси́ть** (-ушý, -ýсишь) *pf* bite; sting.

**укýтать** *pf,* **укýтывать** *impf* wrap up; **~ся** wrap o.s. up.

**укушý** *etc.: see* **укуси́ть**

**ул.** *abbr (of* **ýлица**) street, road.

**улáвливать** *impf of* **улови́ть**

**улáдить** (-áжу) *pf,* **улáживать** *impf* settle, arrange.

**ýлей** (ýлья) (bee)hive.

**улетáть** *impf,* **улетéть** (улечý) *pf* fly (away). **улетýчиваться,** *impf,* **улетýчиться** (-чусь) *pf* evaporate; vanish.

**улéчься** (уля́гусь, -я́жешься; улёгся, -глась) *pf (impf* **укла́дываться)** lie down; settle; subside.

**ули́ка** clue; evidence.

**ули́тка** snail.

**ýлица** street; **на ýлице** in the street; outside.

**уличи́ть** *impf,* **уличи́ть** (-чý) *pf* establish the guilt of.

**ýличный** street.

**улóв** catch. **улови́мый** perceptible; audible. **улови́ть** (-влю́, -вишь) *pf (impf* **улáвливать)** catch; seize. **улóвка** trick, ruse.

**уложéние** code. **уложи́ть** (-жý, -жишь) *pf (impf* **укла́дывать)** lay; pack; pile; **~ спать** put to bed; **~ся** pack (up); fit in.

**улучáть** *impf,* **улучи́ть** (-чý) *pf* find, seize.

**улучшáть** *impf,* **улýчшить** (-шу) *pf* improve; better; **~ся** improve; get better. **улучшéние** improvement.

**улыбáться** *impf,* **улыбнýть-**

**ся** (-ну́сь, -нёшься) pf smile. **улыбка** smile.

**ультима́тум** ultimatum.

**ультра-** in comb ultra-. **ультразвуково́й** supersonic. **~фиоле́товый** ultra-violet.

**уля́гусь** etc.: see **уле́чься**

**ум** (-а́) mind, intellect; head; **сойти́ с ~а́** go mad.

**умали́ть** pf (impf **умаля́ть**) belittle.

**умалишённый** mad; sb lunatic.

**ума́лчивать** impf of **умолча́ть**

**умаля́ть** impf of **умали́ть**

**уме́лец** (-льца) skilled craftsman. **уме́лый** able, skilful. **уме́ние** ability, skill.

**уменьша́ть** impf, **уме́ньшить** (-шу) pf reduce, diminish, decrease; **~ся** diminish, decrease, abate. **уменьше́ние** decrease, reduction; abatement. **уменьши́тельный** diminutive.

**уме́ренность** moderation. **уме́ренный** moderate; temperate.

**умере́ть** (умру́, -рёшь; у́мер, -ла́, -о) pf (impf **умира́ть**) die.

**уме́рить** pf (impf **умеря́ть**) moderate; restrain.

**умертви́ть** (-рщвлю́, -ртви́шь) pf, **умерщвля́ть** impf kill, destroy; mortify. **у́мерший** dead; sb the deceased. **умерщвле́ние** killing, destruction; mortification.

**умеря́ть** impf of **уме́рить**

**умести́ть** (-ещу́) pf (impf **умеща́ть**) fit in, find room for; **~ся** fit in. **уме́стный** appropriate; pertinent; timely.

**уме́ть** (-е́ю) impf be able, know how.

**умеща́ть(ся** impf of **умести́ть(ся**

**умиле́ние** tenderness; emotion. **умили́ть** pf, **умиля́ть** impf move, touch; **~ся** be moved.

**умира́ние** dying. **умира́ть** impf of **умере́ть**. **умира́ющий** dying; sb dying person.

**умиротворе́ние** pacification; appeasement. **умиротвори́ть** pf, **умиротворя́ть** impf pacify; appease.

**умне́ть** (-е́ю) impf (pf по~) grow wiser. **у́мница** good girl; m & f clever person.

**умножа́ть** impf, **у|мно́жить** (-жу) pf multiply; increase; **~ся** increase, multiply. **умноже́ние** multiplication; increase. **умножи́тель** m multiplier.

**у́мный** (умён, умна́, у́мно) clever, wise, intelligent. **умозаключе́ние** deduction; conclusion.

**умоли́ть** pf (impf **умоля́ть**) move by entreaties.

**умолка́ть** impf, **умо́лкнуть** (-ну; -о́лк) pf fall silent; stop. **умолча́ть** (-чу́) pf (impf **ума́лчивать**) fail to mention; hush up.

**умоля́ть** impf of **умоли́ть**; beg, entreat.

**умопомеша́тельство** derangement.

**умори́тельный** incredibly funny, killing. **у|мори́ть** pf; exhaust.

**умо́ю** etc.: see **умы́ть**. **умру́** etc.: see **умере́ть**

**у́мственный** mental, intellectual.

**умудри́ть** pf, **умудря́ть** impf make wiser; **~ся** contrive.

**умыва́льная** sb wash-room. **умыва́льник** wash-stand, wash-basin. **умыва́ть(ся** impf of **умы́ть(ся**

**у́мысел** (-сла) design, intention.

**умы́ть** (умо́ю) *pf* (*impf* **умыва́ть**) wash; **~ся** wash (o.s.).

**умы́шленный** intentional.

**у|насле́довать** *pf*.

**унести́** (-су́, -сёшь; -ёс, -ла́) *pf* (*impf* **уноси́ть**) take away; carry off, make off with; **~сь** speed away; fly by; be carried (away).

**универма́г** *abbr* department store. **универса́льн|ый** universal; all-round; versatile; all-purpose; **~ магази́н** department store; **~ое сре́дство** panacea. **универса́м** *abbr* supermarket. **университе́т** university. **университе́тский** university.

**унижа́ть** *impf*, **уни́зить** (-и́жу) *pf* humiliate; **~ся** humble o.s.; stoop. **униже́ние** humiliation. **уни́женный** humble. **унизи́тельный** humiliating.

**уника́льный** unique.

**унима́ть(ся** *impf of* **уня́ть(ся**

**унисо́н** unison.

**унита́з** lavatory pan.

**унифици́ровать** *impf & pf* standardize.

**уничижи́тельный** pejorative.

**уничтожа́ть** *impf*, **уничто́жить** (-жу) *pf* destroy, annihilate; abolish; do away with. **уничтоже́ние** destruction, annihilation; abolition.

**уноси́ть(ся** (-ошу́(сь, -о́сишь(ся) *impf of* **унести́(сь**

**у́нция** ounce.

**уныва́ть** *impf* be dejected. **уны́лый** dejected; doleful, cheerless. **уны́ние** dejection, despondency.

**уня́ть** (уйму́, -мёшь; -я́л, -á, -о) *pf* (*impf* **унима́ть**) calm, soothe; **~ся** calm down.

**упа́док** (-дка) decline; decay; **~ ду́ха** depression. **упа́дочнический** decadent. **упа́дочный** decadent; decadent. **упаду́** *etc.*: *see* **упа́сть**

**у|пакова́ть** *pf*, **упако́вывать** *impf* pack (up). **упако́вка** packing; wrapping. **упако́вщик** packer.

**упа́сть** (-аду́, -адёшь) *pf of* **па́дать**

**упере́ть** (упру́, -рёшь; -ёр) *pf*, **упира́ть** *impf* rest, lean; **~ на+***acc* stress; **~ся** rest, lean; resist; **+в+***acc* come up against.

**упи́танный** well-fed; fatted.

**упла́та** payment. **у|плати́ть** (-ачу́, -а́тишь) *pf*, **упла́чивать** *impf* pay.

**уплотне́ние** compression; condensation; consolidation; sealing. **уплотни́ть** *pf*, **уплотня́ть** *impf* condense; compress; pack more into.

**уплыва́ть** *impf*, **уплы́ть** (-ыву́, -ывёшь; -ы́л, -á, -о) *pf* swim or sail away; pass.

**упова́ть** *impf* **+на+***acc* put one's trust in.

**уподобля́ть** *impf* (-блюсь) *pf*, **уподо́биться** *impf* **+***dat* become like.

**упое́ние** ecstasy, rapture. **упои́тельный** intoxicating, ravishing.

**уполза́ть** *impf*, **уползти́** (-зу́, -зёшь; -о́лз, -зла́) *pf* creep away, crawl away.

**уполномо́ченный** *sb* (authorized) agent, representative; proxy. **уполномо́чивать**, **уполномо́чивать** *impf*, **уполномо́чить** (-чу) *pf* authorize, empower.

**упомина́ние** mention. **упомина́ть** *impf*, **упомяну́ть** (-ну́, -нешь) *pf* mention, refer to.

упо́р prop, support; в ~ point-blank; сде́лать ~ на+acc or prep lay stress on. упо́рный stubborn; persistent. упо́рство stubbornness; persistence. упо́рствовать impf be stubborn; persist (в+prep in).

упоря́дочивать impf, упоря́дочить (-чу) pf regulate, put in order.

употреби́тельный (widely-)used; common. употребля́ть (-блю́) pf, употребля́ть impf use. употребле́ние use; usage.

упра́ва justice.

управдо́м abbr manager (of block of flats). упра́виться (-влюсь) pf, управля́ться impf cope, manage; +c+instr deal with. управле́ние management; administration; direction; control; driving, steering; government. управля́емый снаря́д guided missile. управля́ть impf +instr manage, direct, run; govern; be in charge of; operate; drive. управля́ющий sb manager.

упражне́ние exercise. упражня́ть impf exercise, train; ~ся practise, train.

упраздни́ть pf, упраздня́ть impf abolish.

упра́шивать impf of упроси́ть

упрёк reproach. упрека́ть impf, упрекну́ть (-ну́, -нёшь) pf reproach.

упроси́ть (-ошу́, -о́сишь) pf (impf упра́шивать) entreat; prevail upon.

упрости́ть (-ощу́) pf (impf упроща́ть) (over-)simplify.

упро́чивать impf, упро́чить (-чу) pf strengthen, consolidate; ~ся be firmly established.

упрошу́ etc.: see упроси́ть

упроща́ть impf of упрости́ть. упрощённый (-щён, -а́) (over-)simplified.

упру́ etc.: see упере́ть.

упру́гий elastic; springy. упру́гость elasticity; spring. упру́же comp of упру́гий

упря́жка harness; team. упряжно́й draught. у́пряжь harness.

упря́миться (-млюсь) impf be obstinate; persist. упря́мство obstinacy. упря́мый obstinate; persistent.

упуска́ть impf, упусти́ть (-ущу́, -у́стишь) pf let go, let slip; miss. упуще́ние omission; slip; negligence.

ура́ int hurrah!

уравне́ние equalization; equation. ура́внивать impf, уравня́ть pf equalize. уравни́тельный equalizing, levelling. уравнове́сить (-е́шу) pf, уравнове́шивать impf balance; counterbalance. уравнове́шенность composure. уравнове́шенный balanced, composed.

урага́н hurricane; storm.

ура́льский Ural.

ура́н uranium; Uranus. ура́новый uranium.

урва́ть (-ву́, -вёшь; -а́л, -а́, -о) pf (impf урыва́ть) snatch.

урегули́рование regulation; settlement. у|регули́ровать pf.

уре́зать (-е́жу) pf, уреза́ть, уре́зывать impf cut off; shorten; reduce.

у́рка m & f (sl) lag, convict.

у́рна urn; ballot-box; litter-bin.

у́ровень (-вня) m level; standard.

уро́д freak, monster.

**уроди́ться** (-ожу́сь) *pf* ripen; grow.

**уро́дливость** deformity; ugliness. **уро́дливый** deformed; ugly; bad. **уро́довать** *impf* (*pf* из~) disfigure; distort. **уро́дство** disfigurement; ugliness.

**урожа́й** harvest; crop; abundance. **урожа́йность** yield; productivity. **урожа́йный** productive, high-yield.

**урождённый** *née.* **уроже́нец** (-нца), **уроже́нка** native. **урожу́сь** *see* уроди́ться

**уро́к** lesson.

**уро́н** losses; damage. **урони́ть** (-ню́, -нишь) *pf of* роня́ть

**урча́ть** (-чу́) *impf* rumble.

**урыва́ть** *impf of* урва́ть. **урывками** *adv* in snatches, by fits and starts.

**ус** (*pl* -ы́) whisker; tendril; moustache.

**усади́ть** (-ажу́, -а́дишь) *pf*, **уса́живать** *impf* seat, offer a seat; plant. **уса́дьба** (*gen pl* -деб *or* -дьб) country estate; farmstead. **уса́живаться** *impf of* усе́сться

**уса́тый** moustached; whiskered.

**усва́ивать** *impf*, **усво́ить** *pf* master; assimilate; adopt. **усвое́ние** mastering; assimilation; adoption.

**усе́рдие** zeal; diligence. **усе́рдный** zealous; diligent.

**усе́сться** (уся́дусь; -е́лся) *pf* (*impf* уса́живаться) take a seat; settle down (to).

**усиде́ть** (-ижу́) *pf* remain seated; hold down a job. **усѝдчивый** assiduous.

**у́сик** tendril; runner; antenna; *pl* small moustache.

**усиле́ние** strengthening; reinforcement; intensification; amplification. **уси́ленный** intensified, increased; earnest. **уси́ливать** *impf*, **уси́лить** *pf* intensify, increase; amplify; strengthen, reinforce; ~ся increase, intensify; become stronger. **уси́лие** effort. **уси́литель** *m* amplifier; booster.

**ускака́ть** (-ачу́, -а́чешь) *pf* skip off; gallop off.

**ускольза́ть** *impf*, **ускользну́ть** (-ну́, -нёшь) *pf* slip off; steal away; escape.

**ускоре́ние** acceleration. **ускоренный** accelerated; rapid; crash. **ускори́тель** accelerator. **уско́рить**, **ускоря́ть** *impf* quicken; accelerate; hasten; ~ся accelerate, be accelerated; quicken.

**усло́вие** condition. **усло́виться** (-влюсь) *pf*, **усло́вливаться**, **усла́вливаться** *impf* agree; arrange. **усло́вленный** agreed, fixed. **усло́вность** convention. **усло́вный** conditional; conditioned; conventional; agreed; relative.

**усложне́ние** complication. **усложни́ть** *pf*, **усложня́ть** *impf* complicate; ~ся become complicated.

**услу́га** service; good turn. **услу́жливый** obliging.

**услыха́ть** (-шу́) *pf*, **у́слышать** (-шу) *pf* hear; sense; scent.

**усма́тривать** *impf of* усмотре́ть

**усмеха́ться** *impf*, **усмехну́ться** (-ну́сь, -нёшься) *pf* smile; grin; smirk. **усме́шка** smile; grin; sneer.

**усмире́ние** pacification; suppression. **усмири́ть** *pf*, **усмиря́ть** *impf* pacify; calm; suppress.

усмотрéние discretion, judgement. *pf* (*impf* усмáтривать) perceive; see; regard; +за+*instr* keep an eye on.

уснýть (-нý, -нёшь) *pf* go to sleep.

усовершéнствование advanced studies; improvement, refinement. у|совершéнствовать(ся *pf*.

усомнúться *pf* doubt.

успевáемость *f* progress. успевáть *impf*, успéть (-éю) *pf* have time; manage; succeed. успéх success; progress. успéшный successful.

успокáивать *impf*, успокóить *pf* calm, quiet, soothe; ∼ся calm down; abate. успокáивающий calming, sedative. успокоéние calming, soothing; calm; peace. успокóительн|ый calming; reassuring; ∼ое *sb* sedative, tranquillizer.

устá (-т, -тáм) *pl* mouth.

устáв regulations, statutes; charter.

уставáть (-таю, -ёшь) *impf* of устáть; не уставáя incessantly.

устáвить (-влю) *pf*, уставлять *impf* set, arrange; cover, fill; direct; ∼ся find room, go in; stare.

устáлость tiredness. устáлый tired.

устанáвливать *impf*, установúть (-влю, -вишь) *pf* put, set up; install; set; establish; fix; ∼ся dispose o.s.; be established; set in. устанóвка putting, setting up; installation; setting; plant, unit; directions. установлéние establishment. устанóвленный

established, prescribed.

устáну *etc.: see* устáть

устаревáть *impf*, у|старéть (-éю) *pf* become obsolete; become antiquated. устарéлый obsolete; antiquated, out-of-date.

устáть (-áну) *pf* (*impf* уставáть) get tired.

устилáть *impf*, устлáть (-телю, -телешь) *pf* cover; pave.

ýстный oral, verbal.

устóй abutment; foundation, support. устóйчивость stability, steadiness. устóйчивый stable, steady. устоять (-оýю) *pf* keep one's balance; stand firm; ∼ся settle; become fixed.

устрáивать(ся *impf of* устрóить(ся

устранéние removal, elimination. устранúть *pf*, устранять *impf* remove; eliminate; ∼ся resign, retire.

устрашáть *impf*, устрашúть (-шý) *pf* frighten; ∼ся be frightened.

устремúть (-млю) *pf*, устремлять *impf* direct, fix; ∼ся rush; be directed; concentrate. устремлéние rush; aspiration.

ýстрица oyster.

устроúтель *m*, ∼ница organizer. устрóить *pf* (*impf* устрáивать) arrange, organize; make; cause; settle, put in order; place, fix up; get; suit; ∼ся work out; manage; settle down; be found, get fixed up. устрóйство arrangement; construction; mechanism; device; system.

устýп shelf, ledge. уступáть *impf*, уступúть (-плю, -пишь) *pf* yield; give up; ∼ дорóгу make way. **усту́пка** concession. **усту́пчивый** pliable; compliant.

**устыди́ться** (-ыжу́сь) *pf* (+*gen*) be ashamed (of).

**у́стье** (*gen pl* -ьев) mouth; estuary.

**усугуби́ть** (-у́блю) *pf*, **усугубля́ть** *impf* increase; aggravate.

**усы́** *see* ус

**усынови́ть** (-влю́) *pf*, **усыновля́ть** *impf* adopt. **усыновле́ние** adoption.

**усы́пать** (-плю) *pf*, **усыпа́ть** *impf* strew, scatter.

**усыпи́тельный** soporific. **усыпи́ть** (-плю́) *pf*, **усыпля́ть** *impf* put to sleep; lull; weaken.

**уся́дусь** *etc.*: *see* **усе́сться**

**ута́ивать** *impf*, **утаи́ть** *pf* conceal; keep secret.

**ута́птывать** *impf* of **утопта́ть**

**ута́скивать** *impf*, **утащи́ть** (-щу́, -щишь) *pf* drag off.

**у́тварь** utensils.

**утверди́тельный** affirmative. **утверди́ть** (-ржу́) *pf*, **утвержда́ть** *impf* confirm; approve; ratify; establish; assert; ~**ся** gain a foothold; become established; be confirmed. **утвержде́ние** approval; confirmation; ratification; assertion; establishment.

**утека́ть** *impf* of **уте́чь**

**утёнок** (-нка; *pl* утя́та, -я́т) duckling.

**утепли́ть** *pf*, **утепля́ть** *impf* warm.

**утере́ть** (утру́, -рёшь; утёр) *pf* (*impf* **утира́ть**) wipe (off, dry).

**утерпе́ть** (-плю́, -пишь) *pf* restrain o.s.

**утёс** cliff, crag.

**уте́чка** leak, leakage; escape;

loss. **уте́чь** (-еку́, -ечёшь; утёк, -ла́) *pf* (*impf* **утека́ть**) leak, escape; pass.

**утеша́ть** *impf*, **уте́шить** (-шу) *pf*; ~**ся** console o.s. **утеше́ние** consolation. **утеши́тельный** comforting.

**утилизи́ровать** *impf* & *pf* utilize.

**ути́ль** *m*, **утильсырьё** scrap.

**ути́ный** duck, duck's.

**утира́ть(ся)** *impf* of **утере́ть(ся)**

**утиха́ть** *impf*, **ути́хнуть** (-ну; -их) *pf* abate, subside; calm down.

**у́тка** duck; canard.

**уткну́ть** (-ну́, -нёшь) *pf* bury; fix; ~**ся** bury o.s.

**утоли́ть** *pf* (*impf* **утоля́ть**) quench; satisfy; relieve.

**утолще́ние** thickening; bulge.

**утоля́ть** *impf* of **утоли́ть**

**утоми́тельный** tedious; tiring. **утоми́ть** (-млю́) *pf*, **утомля́ть** *impf* tire, fatigue; ~**ся** get tired. **утомле́ние** weariness. **утомлённый** weary.

**у|тону́ть** (-ну́, -нешь) *pf* drown, be drowned; sink.

**утонче́нный** refined.

**у|топи́ть(ся** (-плю́(сь, -пишь(ся) *pf*. **уто́пленник** drowned man.

**утопи́ческий** utopian. **уто́пия** Utopia.

**утопта́ть** (-пчу́, -пчешь) *pf* (*impf* **ута́птывать**) trample down.

**уточне́ние** more precise definition; amplification. **уточни́ть** *pf*, **уточня́ть** *impf* define more precisely; amplify.

**утра́ивать** *impf* of **утро́ить**

**у|трамбова́ть** *pf*, **утрамбо́вывать** *impf* ram, tamp; ~**ся** become flat.

**утра́та** loss. **утра́тить** (-а́чу) *pf,* **утра́чивать** *impf* lose.

**у́тренний** morning. **у́тренник** morning performance; early-morning frost.

**утри́ровать** *impf & pf* exaggerate.

**у́тро** (-а *or* -á, -y *or* -ý, *pl* -á, -ам *or* -áм) morning.

**утро́ба** womb; belly.

**утро́ить** *pf* (*impf* **утра́ивать**) triple, treble.

**утру́** *etc.: see* **утере́ть, у́тро**

**утружда́ть** *impf* trouble, tire.

**утю́г** (-á) iron. **утю́жить** (-жу) *impf* (*pf* **вы~, от~**) iron.

**ух** *int* oh, ooh, ah.

**уха́** fish soup.

**уха́б** pot-hole. **уха́бистый** bumpy.

**уха́живать** *impf* за+*instr* tend; look after; court.

**ухвати́ть** (-а́чу, -а́тишь) *pf,* **ухва́тывать** *impf* seize; grasp; **~ся** за+*acc* grasp, lay hold of; set to; seize; jump at. **ухва́тка** grip; skill; trick; manner.

**ухитри́ться** *pf,* **ухитря́ться** *impf* manage, contrive. **ухищре́ние** device, trick.

**ухмы́лка** smirk. **ухмыльну́ться** (-ну́сь, -нёшься) *pf,* **ухмыля́ться** *impf* smirk.

**у́хо** (*pl* у́ши, уше́й) ear; earflap.

**ухо́д**[1] +за+*instr* care of; tending, looking after.

**ухо́д**[2] leaving, departure. **уходи́ть** (-ожу́, -о́дишь) *impf of* **уйти́**

**ухудша́ть** *impf,* **ухудши́ть** (-шу) *pf* make worse; **~ся** get worse. **ухудше́ние** deterioration.

**уцеле́ть** (-е́ю) *pf* remain intact; survive.

**уце́нивать** *impf,* **уцени́ть** (-ню́, -нишь) *pf* reduce the price of.

**уцепи́ть** (-плю́, -пишь) *pf* catch hold of, seize; **~ся** за+*acc* catch hold of, seize; jump at.

**уча́ствовать** *impf* take part; hold shares. **уча́ствующий** *sb* participant. **уча́стие** participation; share; sympathy.

**участи́ть** (-ащу́) *pf* (*impf* **учаща́ть**) make more frequent; **~ся** become more frequent, quicken.

**уча́стливый** sympathetic. **уча́стник** participant. **уча́сток** (-тка) plot; part, section; sector; district; field, sphere.

**у́часть** lot, fate.

**учаща́ть(ся** *impf of* **участи́ть(ся**

**уча́щийся** *sb* student; pupil.

**учёба** studies; course; training. **уче́бник** text-book. **уче́бный** educational; school; training. **уче́ние** learning; studies; apprenticeship; teaching; doctrine; exercise.

**учени́к** (-á), **учени́ца** pupil; apprentice; disciple. **учени́ческий** pupil's(s); apprentice('s); unskilled; crude. **учёность** learning, erudition. **учёный** learned; scholarly; academic; scientific; **~ая сте́пень** (*university*) degree; **~ый** *sb* scholar; scientist.

**уче́сть** (учту́, -тёшь; учёл, учла́) *pf* (*impf* **учи́тывать**) take stock of; take into account; discount. **учёт** stock-taking; calculation; taking into account; registration; discount; **без ~а** +*gen* disregarding; **взять на ~** register. **учётный** registration; discount.

**учи́лище** (*specialist*) school.

**у|чинить** pf, **учинять** impf make; commit.

**учитель** (pl -я) m, **учительница** teacher. **учительский** teacher's, teachers'; **~ая** sb staff-room.

**учитывать** impf of **учесть**

**учить** (учу, учишь) impf (pf вы-, на-, об-) teach; be a teacher; learn; **~ся** be a student; +dat or inf learn, study.

**учредительный** constituent. **учредить** (-ежу) pf, **учреждать** impf found, establish. **учреждение** founding; establishment; institution.

**учтивый** civil, courteous. **учту** etc.: see **учесть**

**ушанка** hat with ear-flaps.

**ушёл** etc.: see **уйти**. **уши** etc.: see **ухо**

**ушиб** injury; bruise. **ушибать** impf, **ушибить** (-бу, -бёшь; ушиб) pf injure; bruise; hurt; **~ся** hurt o.s.

**ушко** (pl -и, -ов) eye; tab.

**ушной** ear, aural.

**ущелье** ravine, gorge, canyon.

**ущемить** (-млю) pf, **ущемлять** impf pinch, jam; limit; encroach on; hurt. **ущемление** pinching, jamming; limitation; hurting.

**ущерб** detriment; loss; damage; prejudice. **ущербный** waning.

**ущипнуть** (-ну, -нёшь) pf of **щипать**

**Уэльс** Wales. **уэльский** Welsh.

**уют** coziness, comfort. **уютный** cosy, comfortable.

**уязвимый** vulnerable. **уязвить** (-влю) pf, **уязвлять** impf wound, hurt.

**уяснить** pf, **уяснять** impf understand, make out.

# Ф

**фабрика** factory. **фабрикант** manufacturer. **фабрикат** finished product, manufactured product. **фабриковать** impf (pf с-) fabricate, forge. **фабричный** factory; manufacturing; factory-made; **~ая марка**, **~ое клеймо** trade-mark.

**фабула** plot, story.

**фагот** bassoon.

**фаза** phase; stage. **фазан** pheasant.

**фазис** phase.

**файл** (comput) file.

**факел** torch, flare.

**факс** fax.

**факсимиле** neut indecl facsimile.

**факт** fact; **совершившийся ~** fait accompli. **фактически** adv in fact; virtually. **фактический** actual; real; virtual.

**фактор** factor.

**фактура** texture; style, execution.

**факультативный** optional. **факультет** faculty, department.

**фалда** tail (of coat).

**фальсификатор** falsifier, forger. **фальсификация** falsification; adulteration; forgery. **фальсифицировать** impf & pf falsify; forge; adulterate. **фальшивить** (-влю) impf (pf с~) be a hypocrite; sing or play out of tune. **фальшивка** forged document. **фальшивый** false; spurious; forged; artificial; out of tune. **фальшь** deception; falseness.

**фами́лия** surname. **фамилья́рничать** be over-familiar. **фамилья́рность** (over-)familiarity. **фамилья́рный** (over-) familiar; unceremonious.

**фанати́зм** fanaticism. **фана́тик** fanatic.

**фане́ра** veneer; plywood.

**фантазёр** dreamer, visionary. **фантази́ровать** impf (pf c~) dream; make up, dream up; improvise. **фанта́зия** fantasy; fancy; imagination; whim. **фанта́стика** fiction, fantasy. **фантасти́ческий, фантасти́чный** fantastic.

**фа́ра** headlight.

**фарао́н** pharaoh; faro.

**фарва́тер** fairway, channel.

**фармазо́н** freemason.

**фармаце́вт** pharmacist.

**фарс** farce.

**фа́ртук** apron.

**фарфо́р** china; porcelain. **фарфо́ровый** china.

**фарцо́вщик** currency speculator.

**фарш** stuffing; minced meat. **фарширова́ть** impf (pf за~) stuff.

**фаса́д** façade.

**фасова́ть** impf (pf рас~) package.

**фасо́ль** kidney bean(s), French bean(s); haricot beans.

**фасо́н** cut; fashion; style; manner. **фасо́нный** shaped.

**фата́** veil.

**фатали́зм** fatalism. **фата́льный** fatal.

**фаши́зм** Fascism. **фаши́ст** Fascist. **фаши́стский** Fascist.

**фая́нс** faience, pottery.

**февра́ль** (-я́) m February. **февра́льский** February.

**федера́льный** federal. **федера́ция** federation.

**фееери́ческий** fairy-tale.

**фейерве́рк** firework(s).

**фе́льдшер** (pl -á), -шери́ца (partly-qualified) medical assistant.

**фельето́н** feuilleton, feature.

**фемини́зм** feminism. **феминисти́ческий, feminистский** feminist.

**фен** (hair-)dryer.

**феноме́н** phenomenon. **феномена́льный** phenomenal.

**феода́л** feudal lord. **феодали́зм** feudalism. **феода́льный** feudal.

**ферзь** (-я́) m queen.

**фе́рма**[1] farm.

**фе́рма**[2] girder, truss.

**ферма́та** (mus) pause.

**ферме́нт** ferment.

**фе́рмер** farmer.

**фестива́ль** m festival.

**фетр** felt. **фе́тровый** felt.

**фехтова́льщик, -щица** fencer. **фехтова́ние** fencing. **фехтова́ть** impf fence.

**фе́я** fairy.

**фиа́лка** violet.

**фиа́ско** neut indecl fiasco.

**фи́бра** fibre.

**фигля́р** buffoon.

**фигу́ра** figure; court-card; (chess-)piece. **фигура́льный** figurative, metaphorical. **фигури́ровать** impf figure, appear. **фигури́ст, -и́стка** figure-skater. **фигу́рка** figurine, statuette; figure. **фигу́рный** figured; ~ое ката́ние figure-skating.

**фи́зик** physicist. **фи́зика** physics. **физио́лог** physiologist. **физиологи́ческий** physiological. **физиоло́гия** physiology. **физионо́мия** physiognomy; face, expression. **физиотерапе́вт** physiotherapist. **физи́ческий** physical; physics.

**физкульту́ра** abbr P.E., gymnastics. **физкульту́рный** *abbr* gymnastic; athletic; **~ зал** gymnasium.

**фикса́ж** fixer. **фикса́ция** fixing. **фикси́ровать** *impf & pf* (*pf also* **за~**) fix; record.

**фикти́вный** fictitious. **~ брак** marriage of convenience. **фи́кция** fiction.

**филантро́п** philanthropist. **филантро́пия** philanthropy.

**филармо́ния** philharmonic society; concert hall.

**филатели́ст** philatelist.

**филе́** *neut indecl* sirloin; fillet.

**филиа́л** branch.

**фили́стер** philistine.

**фило́лог** philologist. **филологи́ческий** philological. **филоло́гия** philology.

**филосо́ф** philosopher. **филосо́фия** philosophy. **филосо́фский** philosophical.

**фильм** film. **фильмоско́п** projector.

**фильтр** filter. **фильтрова́ть** *impf* (*pf* **про~**) filter.

**фина́л** finale; final. **фина́льный** final.

**финанси́ровать** *impf & pf* finance. **фина́нсовый** financial. **фина́нсы** (**-ов**) *pl* finance, finances.

**фи́ник** date.

**фи́ниш** finish; finishing post.

**фи́нка** Finn. **Финля́ндия** Finland. **финля́ндский** Finnish. **финн** Finn. **фи́нский** Finnish.

**фиоле́товый** violet.

**фи́рма** firm; company. **фи́рменное блю́до** speciality of the house.

**фисгармо́ния** harmonium.

**фити́ль** (**-я́**) *m* wick; fuse.

**флаг** flag. **фла́гман** flagship.

**флако́н** bottle, flask.

**фланг** flank; wing.

**флане́ль** flannel.

**флегмати́чный** phlegmatic.

**фле́йта** flute.

**фле́ксия** inflexion. **флекти́вный** inflected.

**фли́гель** (*pl* **-я́**) *m* wing; annexe.

**флирт** flirtation. **флиртова́ть** *impf* flirt.

**фломастер** felt-tip pen.

**фло́ра** flora.

**флот** fleet. **фло́тский** naval.

**флю́гер** (*pl* **-а́**) weather-vane.

**флюоресце́нтный** fluorescent.

**флюс**[1] gumboil, abscess.

**флюс**[2] (*pl* **-ы**) flux.

**фля́га** flask; churn. **фля́жка** flask.

**фойе́** *neut indecl* foyer.

**фо́кус**[1] trick.

**фо́кус**[2] focus. **фокуси́ровать** *impf* focus.

**фо́кусник** conjurer, juggler.

**фолиа́нт** folio.

**фольга́** foil.

**фолькло́р** folklore.

**фон** background.

**фона́рик** small lamp; torch. **фона́рный** lamp; **~ столб** lamp-post. **фона́рь** (**-я́**) *m* lantern; lamp; light.

**фонд** fund; stock; reserves.

**фоне́тика** phonetics. **фонети́ческий** phonetic.

**фонта́н** fountain.

**форе́ль** trout.

**фо́рма** form; shape; mould; cast; uniform. **форма́льность** formality. **форма́льный** formal. **форма́т** format. **форма́ция** structure; stage; formation; mentality. **фо́рменный** uniform; proper, regular. **формирова́ние** forming; unit, formation. **формирова́ть** *impf* (*pf* **с~**) form; organize; **~ся** form, develop.

**формова́ть** *impf* (*pf* **с~**)

form, shape; mould, cast.
**фо́рмула** formula. **формули́ровать** *impf* & *pf* (*pf also* с~) formulate. **формули́ро́вка** formulation; wording; formula. **формуля́р** logbook; library card.
**форси́ровать** *impf* & *pf* force; speed up.
**форсу́нка** sprayer; injector.
**фортепья́но** *neut indecl* piano.
**фо́рточка** small hinged (window-)pane.
**форту́на** fortune.
**фо́рум** forum.
**фо́сфор** phosphorus.
**фо́то** *neut indecl* photo(graph).
**фото-** *in comb* photo-, photoelectric. **фотоаппара́т** camera. **~бума́га** photographic paper. **~гени́чный** photogenic. **фото́граф** photographer. **~графи́ровать** *impf* (*pf* с~) photograph. **~графи́роваться** be photographed, have one's photograph taken. **~графи́ческий** photographic. **~гра́фия** photography; photograph; photographer's studio. **~ко́пия** photocopy. **~люби́тель** *m* amateur photographer. **~объекти́в** (camera) lens. **~репортёр** press photographer. **~хро́ника** news in pictures. **~элеме́нт** photoelectric cell.
**фрагме́нт** fragment.
**фра́за** sentence; phrase. **фразеоло́гия** phraseology.
**фрак** tail-coat, tails.
**фракцио́нный** fractional; factional. **фра́кция** fraction; faction.
**франк** franc.
**франкмасо́н** Freemason.
**франт** dandy.
**Фра́нция** France. **францу́-**

**женка** Frenchwoman. **францу́з** Frenchman. **францу́зский** French.
**фрахт** freight. **фрахтова́ть** *impf* (*pf* за~) charter.
**фрега́т** frigate.
**фрезеро́вщик** milling machine operator.
**фре́ска** fresco.
**фронт** (*pl* -ы́, -о́в) front. **фронтови́к** (-а́) front-line soldier. **фронтово́й** front(-line).
**фронто́н** pediment.
**фрукт** fruit. **фрукто́вый** fruit; ~ **сад** orchard.
**фтор** fluorine. **фто́ристый** fluorine; fluoride. ~ **ка́льций** calcium fluoride.
**фу** *int* ugh! oh!
**фуга́нок** (-нка) smoothing-plane.
**фуга́с** landmine. **фуга́сный** high-explosive.
**фундаме́нт** foundation. **фундамента́льный** solid, sound; main; basic.
**функциона́льный** functional. **функциони́ровать** *impf* function. **фу́нкция** function.
**фунт** pound.
**фура́ж** (-а́) forage, fodder. **фура́жка** peaked cap, forage-cap.
**фурго́н** van; caravan.
**фут** foot; foot-rule. **футбо́л** football. **футболи́ст** footballer. **футбо́лка** T-shirt, sports shirt. **футбо́льный** football; ~ **мяч** football.
**футля́р** case, container.
**футури́зм** futurism.
**фуфа́йка** jersey; sweater.
**фы́ркать** *impf*, **фы́ркнуть** (-ну) *pf* snort.
**фюзеля́ж** fuselage.

# X

**хала́т** dressing-gown. **хала́тный** careless, negligent.

**халту́ра** pot-boiler; hackwork; money made on the side. **халту́рщик** hack.

**хам** boor, lout. **ха́мский** boorish, loutish. **ха́мство** boorishness, loutishness.

**хамелео́н** chameleon.

**хан** khan.

**хандра́** depression. **хандри́ть** *impf* be depressed.

**ханжа́** hypocrite. **ха́нжеский** sanctimonious, hypocritical.

**хао́с** chaos. **хаоти́чный** chaotic.

**хара́ктер** character. **характеризова́ть** *impf & pf* (*pf also* o~) describe; characterize; ~ся be characterized. **характери́стика** reference; description. **характе́рный** characteristic; distinctive; character.

**ха́ркать** *impf*, **ха́ркнуть** (-ну) *pf* spit.

**ха́ртия** charter.

**ха́та** peasant hut.

**хвала́** praise. **хвале́бный** laudatory. **хвалёный** highly-praised. **хвали́ть** (-лю́, -лишь) *impf* (*pf* по~) praise; ~ся boast.

**хва́стать(ся** *impf* (*pf* по~) boast. **хвастли́вый** boastful. **хвастовство́** boasting. **хвасту́н** (-á) boaster.

**хвата́ть**[1] **хвати́ть** (-ачу́, -а́тишь) *pf* (*pf also* **схвати́ть**) snatch, seize; grab; ~ся snatch at; *+gen* remember; realize the absence of; *+за+acc* snatch at, clutch at; take up.

**хвата́ть**[2] *impf*, **хвати́ть** (-а́тит) *pf, impers* (*+gen*) suffice, be

enough; last out; **вре́мени не хвата́ло** there was not enough time; **у нас не хвата́ет де́нег** we haven't enough money; **хва́тит!** that will do!; **э́того ещё не хвата́ло!** that's all we needed! **хва́тка** grasp, grip; method; skill.

**хво́йн|ый** coniferous; ~ые *sb pl* conifers.

**хвора́ть** *impf* be ill.

**хво́рост** brushwood; (*pastry*) straws. **хвороста́ина** stick, switch.

**хвост** (-á) tail; tail-end. **хво́стик** tail. **хвостово́й** tail.

**хво́я** needle(s); (*coniferous*) branch(es).

**херуви́м** cherub.

**хиба́р(к)а** shack, hovel.

**хи́жина** shack, hut.

**хи́лый** (-л, -á, -о) sickly.

**химе́ра** chimera.

**хи́мик** chemist. **химика́т** chemical. **хими́ческий** chemical. **хи́мия** chemistry.

**химчи́стка** dry-cleaning; dry-cleaner's.

**хи́на, хини́н** quinine.

**хиру́рг** surgeon. **хирурги́ческий** surgical. **хирурги́я** surgery.

**хитре́ц** (-á) cunning person. **хитри́ть** *impf* (*pf* c~) use cunning, be crafty. **хи́трость** cunning; ruse; skill; intricacy. **хи́трый** cunning; skilful; intricate.

**хихи́кать** *impf*, **хихи́кнуть** (-ну) *pf* giggle, snigger.

**хище́ние** theft; embezzlement. **хи́щник** predator, bird *or* beast of prey. **хи́щнический** predatory. **хи́щн|ый** predatory; rapacious; ~ые пти́цы birds of prey.

**хладнокро́вие** coolness, composure. **хладнокро́вный** cool, composed.

**хлам** rubbish.

**хлеб** (pl -ы, -ов or -á, -óв) bread; loaf; grain. **хлеба́ть** impf, **хлебну́ть** (-ну́, -нёшь) pf gulp down. **хле́бный** bread; baker's; grain. **хлебозаво́д** bakery. **хлебопека́рня** (gen pl -рен) bakery.

**хлев** (loc -у́; pl -á) cow-shed.

**хлеста́ть** (-ещу́, -е́щешь) impf, **хлестну́ть** (-ну́, -нёшь) pf lash; whip.

**хлоп** int bang! **хло́пать** impf (pf **хло́пнуть**) bang; slap; ~ **(в ладо́ши)** clap.

**хлопково́дство** cotton-growing. **хло́пковый** cotton.

**хло́пнуть** (-ну) pf of **хло́пать**

**хлопо́к**[1] (-пка́) clap.

**хло́пок**[2] (-пка) cotton.

**хлопота́ть** (-очу́, -о́чешь) impf (pf **по~**) busy o.s.; bustle about; take trouble; ~**о**+prep or **за**+acc petition for. **хлопотли́вый** troublesome; exacting; busy, bustling. **хло́поты** (-о́т) pl trouble; efforts.

**хлопчатобума́жный** cotton.

**хло́пья** (-ьев) pl flakes.

**хлор** chlorine. **хло́ристый**, **хло́рный** chloride; chloride. **хло́рка** bleach. **хлорофи́лл** chlorophyll. **хлорофо́рм** chloroform.

**хлы́нуть** (-нет) pf gush, pour.

**хлыст** (-á) whip, switch.

**хмеле́ть** (-е́ю) impf (pf **за~**, **о~**) get tipsy. **хмель** (loc -ю́) m hop, hops; drunkenness; **во хмелю́** tipsy. **хмельно́й** (-лён, -льна́) drunk; intoxicating.

**хму́рить** impf (pf **на~**): ~ **бро́ви** knit one's brows; ~**ся** frown; become gloomy; be overcast. **хму́рый** gloomy; overcast.

**хны́кать** (-ы́чу or -аю) impf whimper, snivel.

**хо́бби** neut indecl hobby.

**хо́бот** trunk. **хобото́к** (-тка́) proboscis.

**ход** (loc -у́; pl -ы, -ов or -á, -óв) motion; going; speed; course; operation; stroke; move; manoeuvre; entrance; passage; **в** ~**у́** in demand; **дать за́дний** ~ reverse; **дать** ~ set in motion; **на** ~**у́** in transit, on the move; in action; in operation; **по́лным** ~**ом** at full speed; **пусти́ть в** ~ start, set in motion; **три часа́** ~**у** three hours' journey.

**хода́тайство** petitioning; application. **хода́тайствовать** impf (pf **по~**) petition, apply.

**ходи́ть** (хожу́, хо́дишь) impf walk; go; run; pass, go round; lead, play; move; +**в**+prep wear; +**за**+instr look after. **хо́дкий** (-док, -дка́, -о) fast; marketable; popular. **ходьба́** walking; walk. **ходя́чий** walking; able to walk; popular; current.

**хозрасчёт** abbr (of **хозя́йственный расчёт**) self-financing system.

**хозя́ин** (pl -я́ева, -я́ев) owner, proprietor; master; boss; landlord; host; **хозя́ева по́ля** home team. **хозя́йка** owner; mistress; hostess; landlady. **хозя́йничать** impf keep house; be in charge; lord it. **хозя́йственник** financial manager. **хозя́йственный** economic; household; economical. **хозя́йство** economy; housekeeping; equipment; farm; **дома́шнее** ~ housekeeping; **се́льское** ~ agriculture.

**хоккеи́ст** (ice-)hockey-player. **хокке́й** hockey, ice-hockey.

**холе́ра** cholera.

**холестери́н** cholesterol.

**холл** hall, vestibule.

**холм** (-á) hill. **холми́стый** hilly.

**хо́лод** (pl -á, -óв) cold; coldness; cold weather. **холоди́льник** refrigerator. **хо́лодно** adv coldly. **холо́дный** (хо́лоден, -дна́, -о) cold; inadequate, thin; **~ое ору́жие** cold steel.

**холо́п** serf.

**холосто́й** (хо́лост, -á) unmarried, single; bachelor; idle; blank. **холостя́к** (-á) bachelor.

**холст** (-á) canvas; linen.

**холу́й** (-луя́) m lackey.

**хому́т** (-á) (horse-)collar; burden.

**хомя́к** (-á) hamster.

**хор** (pl хо́ры) choir; chorus.

**хорва́т** (-ка Croat. **Хорва́тия** Croatia. **хорва́тский** Croatian.

**хорёк** (-рька́) polecat.

**хореографи́ческий** choreographic. **хореогра́фия** choreography.

**хори́ст** member of a choir or chorus.

**хорони́ть** (-ню́, -нишь) impf (pf за~, по~, с~) bury.

**хоро́шенький** pretty; nice. **хоро́шенько** adv properly, thoroughly. **хороше́ть** (-е́ю) impf (pf по~) grow prettier. **хоро́ший** (-о́ш, -á, -о) good; nice; pretty, nice-looking; **хорошо́** predic it is good; it is nice. **хорошо́** adv well; nicely; all right! good.

**хо́ры** (хор or -ов) pl gallery.

**хоте́ть** (хочу́, хо́чешь, хоти́м) impf (pf за~) wish; +gen, or acc want; **~ пить** be thirsty; **~ сказа́ть** mean; **~ся** impers +dat want; **мне хо́телось бы** I should like; **мне хо́чется** I want.

**хоть** conj although; even if; partl at least, if only; for example; **~ бы** if only. **хотя́** conj although; **~ бы** even if; if only.

**хо́хот** loud laugh(ter). **хохота́ть** (-очу́, -о́чешь) impf laugh loudly.

**хочу́** etc.: see **хоте́ть**

**храбре́ц** (-á) brave man. **храбри́ться** make a show of bravery; pluck up courage. **хра́брость** bravery. **хра́брый** brave.

**храм** temple, church.

**хране́ние** keeping; storage; **ка́мера хране́ния** cloakroom, left-luggage office. **храни́лище** storehouse, depository. **храни́тель** m keeper, custodian; curator. **храни́ть** impf keep; preserve; **~ся** be, be kept.

**храпе́ть** (-плю́) impf snore; snort.

**хребе́т** (-бта́) spine; (mountain) range; ridge.

**хрен** horseradish.

**хрестома́тия** reader.

**хрип** wheeze. **хрипе́ть** (-плю́) impf wheeze. **хри́плый** (-пл, -á, -о) hoarse. **хри́пнуть** (-ну; хрип) impf (pf о~) become hoarse. **хрипота́** hoarseness.

**христиани́н** (pl -а́не, -а́н) **христиа́нка** Christian. **христиа́нский** Christian. **христиа́нство** Christianity. **Христо́с** (-иста́) Christ.

**хром** chromium; chrome. **хромати́ческий** chromatic. **хрома́ть** impf limp; be poor. **хромо́й** (хром, -á, -о) lame; sb lame person.

**хромосо́ма** chromosome.

**хромота́** lameness.

**хро́ник** chronic invalid. **хро́ника** chronicle; news items; news-

reel. **хрони́ческий** chronic.
**хронологи́ческий** chronological. **хроноло́гия** chronology.
**хру́пкий** (-пок, -пка́, -о) fragile; frail. **хру́пкость** fragility; frailness.
**хруст** crunch; crackle.
**хруста́ль** (-я́) m cut glass; crystal. **хруста́льный** cut-glass; crystal; crystal-clear.
**хрусте́ть** (-ущу́) impf, **хру́стнуть** (-ну) pf crunch; crackle.
**хрю́кать** impf, **хрю́кнуть** (-ну) pf grunt.
**хрящ** (-á) cartilage, gristle. **хрящево́й** cartilaginous, gristly.
**худе́ть** (-éю) impf (pf по~) grow thin.
**ху́до** harm; evil. **ху́до** adv ill, badly.
**худоба́** thinness.
**худо́жественный** art, arts; artistic; ~ фильм feature film. **худо́жник** artist.
**худо́й**[1] (худ, -á, -о) thin, lean.
**худо́й**[2] (худ, -á, -о) bad; full of holes; worn; **ему́ ху́до** he feels bad.
**худоща́вый** thin, lean.
**ху́дший** superl of **худо́й**, **плохо́й** (the) worst. **ху́же** comp of **худо́й**, **ху́до**, **плохо́й**, **пло́хо** worse.
**хула́** abuse, criticism.
**хулига́н** hooligan. **хулига́нить** impf behave like a hooligan. **хулига́нство** hooliganism.
**ху́нта** junta.
**ху́тор** (pl -á) farm; small village.

# Ц

**ца́пля** (gen pl -пель). heron.
**цара́пать** impf, **цара́пнуть** (-ну) pf (pf also **на~**) scratch; scribble; ~ся scratch; scratch one another. **цара́-**
**пина** scratch.
**цари́зм** tsarism. **цари́ть** impf reign, prevail. **цари́ца** tsarina; queen. **ца́рский** tsar's; royal; tsarist; regal. **ца́рство** kingdom, realm; reign. **ца́рствование** reign. **ца́рствовать** impf reign. **царь** (-я́) m tsar; king.
**цвести́** (-ету́, -етёшь; -ёл, -á) impf flower, blossom; flourish.
**цвет**[1] (pl -á) colour; ~ лица́ complexion.
**цвет**[2] (loc -ý; pl -ы́) flower; prime; **в цвету́** in blossom.
**цветни́к** (-á) flower-bed, flower-garden.
**цветно́й** coloured; colour; non-ferrous; ~ая капу́ста cauliflower; ~ое стекло́ stained glass.
**цветово́й** colour; ~ая слепота́ colour-blindness.
**цвето́к** (-тка́; pl цветы́ or цветки́, -óв) flower. **цвето́чный** flower. **цвету́щий** flowering; prosperous.
**цеди́ть** (цежу́, це́дишь) impf strain, filter.
**целе́бный** curative; healing.
**целево́й** earmarked for a specific purpose. **целенапра́вленный** purposeful. **целесообра́зный** expedient. **целеустремлённый** (-ён, -ённа or -ена́) purposeful.
**целико́м** adv whole; entirely.
**целина́** virgin lands, virgin soil. **цели́нный** virgin; ~ые зе́мли virgin lands.
**цели́тельный** healing, medicinal.
**це́лить(ся** impf (pf на~) aim, take aim.
**целлофа́н** cellophane.
**целова́ть** impf (pf по~) kiss; ~ся kiss.
**це́лое** sb whole; integer. **целому́дренный** chaste. **цело-**

му́дрие chastity. **це́лост-
ность** integrity. **це́лый** (цел,
-á, -о) whole; safe; intact.

**цель** target; aim, object, goal.

**це́льный** (-лен, -льнá, -о) of
one piece, solid; whole; integral; single. **це́льность** whole-
ness.

**цеме́нт** cement. **цементи́ро-
вать** *impf* & *pf* cement.
**цеме́нтный** cement.

**цена́** (*acc* -у; *pl* -ы) price, cost;
worth.

**ценз** qualification. **це́нзор**
censor. **цензу́ра** censorship.

**цени́тель** *m* judge, connoisseur.
**цени́ть** (-ню́, -нишь) *impf*
value; appreciate. **це́нность**
value; price; *pl* valuables; val-
ues. **це́нный** valuable.

**цент** cent. **це́нтнер** centner
(*100kg*).

**центр** centre. **централиза́-
ция** centralization. **центра-
лизовáть** *impf* & *pf* centralize. **центра́льный** central.
**центробéжный** centrifugal.

**цепенéть** (-éю) *impf* (*pf* о∼)
freeze; become rigid. **це́пкий**
tenacious; prehensile; sticky;
obstinate. **це́пкость** tenacity.

**цепля́ться** (-я́юсь) *impf* за+*acc*
clutch at; cling to.

**цепно́й** chain. **цепóчка** chain;
file. **цепь** (*loc* -и́; *gen pl* -éй)
chain; series; circuit.

**церемóниться** *impf* (*pf* по∼)
stand on ceremony. **церемó-
ния** ceremony.

**церковнославя́нский** Church
Slavonic. **церкóвный** Church;
ecclesiastical. **цéрковь** (-кви;
*pl* -и, -éй, *instr pl* -áми) church.

**цех** (*loc* -у́; *pl* -и or -á) shop;
section; guild.

**цивилизáция** civilization.
**цивилизóванный** civilized.
**цивилизовáть** *impf* & *pf*

civilize.

**цигéйка** beaver lamb.

**цикл** cycle.

**цикóрий** chicory.

**цили́ндр** cylinder; top hat. **ци-
линдри́ческий** cylindrical.

**цимбáлы** (-áл) *pl* cymbals.

**цингá** scurvy.

**цини́зм** cynicism. **ци́ник** cynic.
**цини́чный** cynical.

**цинк** zinc. **ци́нковый** zinc.

**цинóвка** mat.

**цирк** circus.

**циркули́ровать** *impf* circulate. **ци́ркуль** *m* (pair of)
compasses; dividers. **цирку-
ля́р** circular. **циркуля́ция**
circulation.

**цисте́рна** cistern, tank.

**цитадéль** *f* citadel.

**цитáта** quotation. **цити́ро-
вать** *impf* (*pf* про∼) quote.

**ци́трус** citrus. **ци́трусов|ый**
citrous; ∼ые *sb pl* citrus
plants.

**циферблáт** dial, face.

**ци́фра** figure; number, numeral.
**цифровóй** numerical, digital.

**цóколь** *m* socle, plinth.

**цыгáн** (*pl* -е, -áн or -ы, -ов), **цы-
гáнка** gipsy. **цыгáнский** gipsy.

**цыплёнок** (*pl* -ля́та, -ля́т)
chicken; chick.

**цы́почки**: на ∼, на цы́почках
on tip-toe.

# Ч

**чабáн** (-á) shepherd.

**чад** (*loc* -у́) fumes, smoke.

**чадрá** yashmak.

**чай** (-я (-ю); *pl* -и́, -ёв) tea. **чаевы́е**
(-ы́х) *sb pl* tip.

**чáйка** (*gen pl* чáек) (sea-)gull.

**чáйная** *sb* tea-shop. **чáйник**
teapot; kettle. **чáйный** tea.
**чайханá** tea-house.

чалма́ turban.

чан (*loc* -ý, *pl* -ы́) vat, tub.

чарова́ть *impf* bewitch; charm.

час (*with numerals* -á, *loc* -ý, *pl* -ы́) hour; *pl* guard-duty; кото́рый час? what's the time?; ~ one o'clock; в два ~á at two o'clock; стоя́ть на ~áх stand guard; ~ы́ пик rush-hour. часо́вня (*gen pl* -вен) chapel. часово́й *sb* sentry. часово́й clock, watch; of one hour, hour-long. часовщи́к (-á) watchmaker.

части́ца small part; particle. части́чно *adv* partly, partially. части́чный partial.

ча́стник private trader.

ча́стность detail; в ча́стности in particular. ча́стный private; personal; particular, individual.

ча́сто *adv* often; close, thickly. частоко́л paling, palisade. частота́ (*pl* -ы) frequency. частотный frequency. часту́шка ditty. ча́стый (част, -á, -о) frequent; close (together); dense; close-woven; rapid.

часть (*gen pl* -е́й) part; department; field; unit.

часы́ (-о́в) *pl* clock, watch.

ча́хлый stunted; sickly, puny. чахо́тка consumption.

ча́ша bowl; chalice; ~ весо́в scale, pan. ча́шка cup; scale, pan.

ча́ща thicket.

ча́ще *comp* of ча́сто, ча́стый; ~ всего́ most often, mostly.

ча́яние expectation; hope. ча́ять (ча́ю) *impf* hope, expect.

чва́нство conceit, arrogance.

чего́ *see* что

чей *m*, чья *f*, чьё *neut*, чьи *pl* *pron* whose. че́й-либо, че́й-нибудь anyone's. че́й-то someone's.

чек cheque; bill; receipt.

чека́нить *impf* (*pf* вы́~, от~) mint, coin; stamp, engrave; enunciate. чека́нка coinage, minting. чека́нный stamping, engraving; stamped, engraved; precise, expressive.

чёлка fringe; forelock.

чёлн (-á; *pl* чёлны) dug-out (canoe); boat. челно́к (-á) dug-out (canoe); shuttle.

челове́к (*pl* лю́ди; with numerals, *gen* -ве́к, -ам) man, person.

челове́ко- *in comb* man-, anthropo-. человеколюби́вый philanthropic. ~лю́бие philanthropy. ~ненави́стнический misanthropic. челове́ко-час (*pl* -ы́) man-hour.

челове́чек (-чка) little man. челове́ческий human; humane. челове́чество mankind. челове́чность humaneness. челове́чный humane.

че́люсть jaw(-bone); dentures; false teeth.

чем, чём *see* что. чем *conj* than; ~..., тем...+*comp* the more..., the more.

чемода́н suitcase.

чемпио́н, ~ка champion, title-holder. чемпиона́т championship.

чему́ *see* что

чепуха́ nonsense; trifle.

чепчик cap; bonnet.

че́рви (-е́й), че́рвы (черв) *pl* hearts. черво́нный of hearts; ~ое зо́лото pure gold.

червь (-я́; *pl* -и, -е́й) *m* worm; bug. червя́к (-á) worm.

черда́к (-á) attic, loft.

черёд (-á, *loc* -ý) turn; идти́

свои́м ~о́м take its course.
**чередова́ние** alternation.
**чередова́ть** *impf* alternate;
~**ся** alternate, take turns.
**че́рез, чрез** *prep+acc* across;
over; through; via; in; after;
every other.
**черёмуха** bird cherry.
**черено́к** (-нка́) handle; graft,
cutting.
**че́реп** (*pl* -а́) skull.
**черепа́ха** tortoise; turtle; tortoiseshell. **черепа́ховый** tortoise; turtle; tortoiseshell. **чере-
па́ший** tortoise, turtle; very
slow.
**черепи́ца** tile. **черепи́чный**
tile; tiled.
**черепо́к** (-пка́) potsherd, fragment of pottery.
**чересчу́р** *adv* too; too much.
**чере́шневый** cherry. **чере́шня**
(*gen pl* -шен) cherry(-tree).
**черке́с, черке́шенка** Circas-
sian.
**черкну́ть** (-ну́, -нёшь) *pf* scrape;
leave a mark on; scribble.
**черне́ть** (-е́ю) *impf* (*pf* по~)
turn black; show black. **чер-
ни́ка** (*no pl; usu collect*) bilberry; bilberries. **черни́ла**
(-и́л) *pl* ink. **черни́льница**
ink. **черни́ть** *impf* (*pf* о~)
blacken; slander.
**черно-** in comb black; unskilled; rough. **чёрно-бе́лый**
black-and-white. ~**бу́рый**
dark-brown; ~**бу́рая лиса́**
silver fox. ~**воло́сый** black-
haired. ~**гла́зый** black-eyed.
~**зём** chernozem, black earth.
~**ко́жий** black; *sb* black. ~
**мо́рский** Black-Sea. ~**рабо́-
чий** *sb* unskilled worker,
labourer. ~**сли́в** prunes. ~**смо-
ро́динный** blackcurrant.
**чернови́к** (-а́) rough copy,
draft. **черново́й** rough; draft.

**чернота́** blackness; darkness.
**чёрн|ый** (-рен, -рна́) black;
back; unskilled; ferrous;
gloomy; *sb* (*derog*) black person; ~**ая сморо́дина** (*no pl;
usu collect*) blackcurrant(s.
**черпа́к** (-а́) scoop. **черпа́ть**
*impf*, **черпну́ть** (-ну́, -нёшь)
*pf* draw; scoop; extract.
**черстве́ть** (-е́ю) *impf* (*pf* за~,
о~, по~) get stale; become
hardened. **чёрствый** (чёрств,
-á, -o) stale; hard.
**чёрт** (*pl* че́рти, -е́й) devil.
**черта́** line; boundary; trait,
characteristic. **чертёж** (-а́)
drawing; blueprint, plan. **чертёжник** draughtsman. **чертё-
жный** drawing. **черти́ть** (-рчу́,
-ртишь) *impf* (*pf* на~) draw.
**чёртов** *adj* devil's; devilish.
**чёрто́вский** devilish.
**чертополо́х** thistle.
**чёрточка** line; hyphen. **черче́-
ние** drawing. **черчу́** *etc.*:
*see* черти́ть
**чеса́ть** (чешу́, -шешь) *impf* (*pf*
по~) scratch; comb; card;
~**ся** scratch o.s.; itch; comb
one's hair.
**чесно́к** (-а́) garlic.
**че́ствование** celebration.
**че́ствовать** *impf* celebrate;
honour. **че́стность** honesty.
**че́стный** (-тен, -тна́, -о) honest. **честолюби́вый** ambitious. **честолю́бие** ambition.
**честь** (*loc* -и́) honour; от-
да́ть ~ *+dat* salute.
**чета́** pair, couple.
**четве́рг** (-а́) Thursday. **четве-
ре́ньки: на ~, на четве-
ре́ньках** on hands and knees.
**четвёрка** four; figure 4;
No. 4; (*figures*) four. **четве-
ро** (-ы́х) four. **четвероно́г|ий** four-legged;
~**ое** *sb* quadruped. **четверо-
сти́шие** quatrain. **четвёр-**

**тый** fourth. **че́тверть** (*gen pl* -е́й*) quarter; quarter of an hour; **без че́тверти час** a quarter to one. **че́тверть-фина́л** quarter-final.

**чёткий** (-ток, -тка́, -о) precise; clear-cut; clear; distinct. **чёткость** precision; clarity.

**чётный** even.

**четы́ре** (-рёх, -рьмя́, -рёх) four. **четы́реста** (-рёхсо́т, -ьмя-ста́ми, -ёхста́х) four hundred. **четырёх-** *in comb* four-, tetra-. **четырёхкра́тный** fourfold. ~**ме́стный** four-seater. ~**со́-тый** four-hundredth. ~**уго́ль-ник** quadrangle. ~**уго́ль-ный** quadrangular.

**четы́рнадцатый** fourteenth. **четы́рнадцать** fourteen.

**чех** Czech.

**чехо́л** (-хла́) cover, case.

**чечеви́ца** lentil; lens.

**чешка** (-shek; Czech. **че́шский** Czech.

**чешу́** *etc.: see* **чеса́ть**

**чешу́йка** scale. **чешуя́** scales.

**чи́бис** lapwing.

**чиж** (-а́) siskin.

**чин** (*pl* -ы́) rank.

**чини́ть** (-ню́, -нишь) *impf* (*pf* по~) repair, mend.

**чини́ть**[2] *impf* (*pf* y~) carry out; cause; ~ **препя́тствия** +*dat* put obstacles in the way of.

**чино́вник** civil servant; official.

**чип** (micro)chip.

**чи́псы** (-ов) *pl* (potato) crisps.

**чири́кать** *impf*, **чири́кнуть** (-ну) *pf* chirp.

**чи́ркать** *impf*, **чи́ркнуть** (-ну) *pf* +*instr* strike.

**чи́сленность** numbers; strength. **чи́сленный** numerical. **чи-сли́тель** *m* numerator. **чи-сли́тельное** *sb* numeral. **чи-сли́ть** *impf* count, reckon; ~**ся** be; be reckoned. **число́**

(*pl* -а, -сел) number; date; day; **в числе́** +*gen* among; **в числе́** including; **еди́нствен-ное ~** singular; **мно́жествен-ное ~** plural. **числово́й** nu-meral.

**чи́стилище** purgatory.

**чи́стильщик** cleaner. **чи́стить** (чи́щу) *impf* (*pf* вы́~, о~, по~) clean; peel; clear. **чи́ст-ка** cleaning; purge. **чи́сто** *adv* cleanly, clean; purely; com-pletely. **чистови́ть** fair, clean. **чистокро́вный** thoroughbred. **чистописа́ние** calligraphy. **чистопло́тный** clean; neat; decent. **чистосерде́чный** frank, sincere. **чистота́** clean-ness; neatness; purity. **чи́стый** clean; neat; pure; complete.

**чита́емый** widely-read, popu-lar. **чита́льный** reading. **чита́-тель** *m* reader. **чита́ть** *impf* (*pf* про~, прочте́сть) read; re-cite; ~ **ле́кции** lecture; ~**ся** be legible; be discernible. **чи́т-ка** reading.

**чиха́ть** *impf*, **чихну́ть** (-ну́, -нёшь) *pf* sneeze.

**чи́ще** *comp of* **чи́сто, чи́стый**

**чи́щу** *etc.: see* **чи́стить**

**член** member; limb; term; part; article. **члени́ть** *impf* (*pf* рас~) divide; articulate. **член-корреспонде́нт** cor-responding member, associ-ate. **членоразде́льный** ar-ticulate. **чле́нский** member-ship. **чле́нство** membership.

**чмо́кать** *impf*, **чмо́кнуть** (-ну) *pf* smack; squelch; kiss nois-ily; ~ **губа́ми** smack one's lips.

**чо́каться** *impf*, **чо́кнуться** (-нусь) *pf* clink glasses.

**чо́порный** prim; stand-offish.

**чрева́тый** +*instr* fraught with. **чре́во** belly, womb. **чрево-веща́тель** *m* ventriloquist.

чрез *see* че́рез. чрезвыча́й-
ный extraordinary; extreme;
~ое положе́ние state of emergency. чрезме́рный excessive.

чте́ние reading. чтец (-á)
reader; reciter.

чтить (чту) *impf* honour.

что, чего́, чему́, чем, о чём
*pron* what?; why?; why?; how
much?; which, what, who; anything?; в чём де́ло? what is
the matter? для чего́? what
... for? why?; ~ ему́ до э́то-
го? what does it matter to
him?; ~ с тобо́й? what's the
matter (with you)?; ~ за
what? what sort of?; what (a
..!; что conj that. что (бы) ни
*pron* whatever, no matter what.

чтоб, что́бы *conj* in order
(to), so as; that; to. что́-либо,
что́-нибудь *prons* anything.
что́-то¹ *pron* something. что́-
то² *adv* somewhat, slightly;
somehow, for some reason.

чу́вственность sensuality.
чувстви́тельность sensitivity; perceptibility; sentimentality. чувстви́тельный sensitive; perceptible; sentimental. чу́вство feeling; sense;
senses; прийти́ в ~ come
round. чу́вствовать *impf* (*pf*
по~) feel; realize; appreciate;
~ себя́ +*adv or instr* feel a
certain way; ~ся be perceptible; make itself felt.

чугу́н (-á) cast iron. чугу́н-
ный cast-iron.

чуда́к (-á), чуда́чка eccentric, crank. чуда́чество ec-
centricity.

чуде́са *etc.: see* чу́до. чуде́с-
ный miraculous; wonderful.

чуди́ться (-ишься) *impf* (*pf*
по~, при~) seem.

чу́дно *adv* wonderfully; wonderful! чудно́й (-дён, -дна́)

odd, strange. чу́дный wonderful; magical. чу́до (*pl* -деса́)
miracle; wonder. чудо́вище
monster. чудо́вищный mon-
strous. чудоде́йственный
miracle-working; miraculous.
чу́дом *adv* miraculously.
чудотво́рный miraculous,
miracle-working.

чужби́на foreign land. чуж-
да́ться *impf* +*gen* avoid;
stand aloof from. чу́ждый
(-жд, -á, -о) alien (to); +*gen*
free from, devoid of. чуже-
земец (-мца), -земка for-
eigner. чужезе́мный foreign.
чужо́й someone else's, others'; strange, alien; foreign.

чула́н store-room; larder.

чуло́к (-лка́; *gen pl* -ло́к) stocking.

чума́ plague.

чума́зый dirty.

чурба́н block. чу́рка block,
lump.

чу́ткий (-ток, -тка́, -о) keen;
sensitive; sympathetic; delicate.
чу́ткость keenness; delicacy.

чу́точка: ни чу́точки not in the
least; чу́точку a little (bit).

чу́тче *comp of* чу́ткий

чуть *adv* hardly; just; very
slightly; ~ не almost; ~-чуть a
tiny bit.

чутьё scent; flair.

чу́чело stuffed animal, stuffed
bird; scarecrow.

чушь nonsense.

чу́ять (чу́ю) *impf* scent; sense.

чьё *etc.: see* чей

# Ш

ша́баш sabbath.

шабло́н template; mould, stencil; cliché. шабло́нный stencil; trite; stereotyped.

шаг (with numerals -á, *loc* -ý; *pl* -и) step; footstep; pace. шага́ть *impf*, шагну́ть (-ну́, -нёшь) *pf* step; stride; pace; make progress. ша́гом *adv* at walking pace.

ша́йба washer; puck.

ша́йка[1] tub.

ша́йка[2] gang, band.

шака́л jackal.

шала́ш (-á) cabin, hut.

шали́ть *impf* be naughty; play up. шаловли́вый mischievous, playful. ша́лость prank; *pl* mischief. шалу́н (-á), шалу́нья (*gen pl* -ний) naughty child.

шаль shawl.

шально́й mad, crazy.

ша́мкать *impf* mumble.

шампа́нское *sb* champagne.

шампиньо́н field mushroom.

шампу́нь *m* shampoo.

шанс chance.

шанта́ж (-á) blackmail. шантажи́ровать *impf* blackmail.

ша́пка hat; banner headline. ша́почка hat.

шар (with numerals -á; *pl* -ы́) sphere; ball; balloon.

шара́хать *impf*, шара́хнуть (-ну) hit; ~ся dash; shy.

шарж caricature.

ша́рик ball; corpuscle. ша́риковый: ~ая (а́вто)ру́чка ball-point pen; ~ый подши́пник ball-bearing. шарикоподши́пник ball-bearing.

ша́рить *impf* grope; sweep.

ша́ркать *impf*, ша́ркнуть (-ну) *pf* shuffle; scrape.

шарлата́н charlatan.

шарма́нка barrel-organ. шарма́нщик organ-grinder.

шарни́р hinge, joint.

шарова́ры (-áр) *pl* (*wide*) trousers.

шарови́дный spherical. шаро-

во́й ball; globular. шарообра́зный spherical.

шарф scarf.

шасси́ *neut indecl* chassis.

шата́ть *impf* rock; shake; *impers* +acc его́ шата́ет he is reeling; ~ся sway; reel, stagger; come loose, be loose; be unsteady; loaf about.

шатёр (-трá) tent; marquee.

ша́ткий unsteady; shaky.

шату́н (-á) connecting-rod.

ша́фер (*pl* -á) best man.

шах check; ~ и мат checkmate. шахмати́ст chess-player. ша́хматы (-ат) *pl* chess; chessmen.

ша́хта mine, pit; shaft. шахтёр miner. шахтёрский miner's; mining.

ша́шка[1] draught; *pl* draughts.

ша́шка[2] sabre.

шашлы́к (-á) kebab; barbecue.

шва *etc.*: see шов

шва́бра mop.

шваль rubbish; riff-raff.

шварто́в mooring-line; *pl* moorings. швартова́ть (*pf* при-) moor; ~ся moor.

швед, ~ка Swede. шве́дский Swedish.

шве́йный sewing; ~ая маши́на sewing-machine.

швейца́р porter, doorman. швейца́рец (-рца), ~ка́рка Swiss. Швейца́рия Switzerland. швейца́рский Swiss.

Шве́ция Sweden.

швея́ seamstress.

швырну́ть (-ну́, -нёшь) *pf*, швыря́ть *impf* throw, fling; ~ся +*instr* throw (about); treat carelessly.

шевели́ть (-елю́, -е́ли́шь) *impf*, шевельну́ть (-ну́, -нёшь) (*pf* also по-) (+*instr*) move, stir; ~ся move, stir.

шеде́вр masterpiece.

ше́йка (*gen pl* ше́ек) neck.

шёл *see* идти́

ше́лест rustle. **шелесте́ть**
(-сти́шь) *impf* rustle.

шёлк (*loc* -ý; *pl* -á) silk. **шелко-
ви́стый** silky. **шелкови́ца**
mulberry(-tree). **шелкови́ч-
ный** mulberry; ~ **червь** silk-
worm. **шёлковый** silk.

шелохну́ть (-ну́, -нёшь) *pf*
stir, agitate; ~**ся** stir, move.

шелуха́ skin; peelings; peel.
**шелуши́ть** (-шу́) peel; shell;
~**ся** peel (off), flake off.

шепеля́вить (-влю) *impf* lisp.
**шепеля́вый** lisping.

шепну́ть (-ну́, -нёшь) *pf*, **шеп-
та́ть** (-пчу́, -пчешь) *impf* whisper; ~**ся** whisper (together).
**шёпот** whisper. **шёпотом**
*adv* in a whisper.

шере́нга rank; file.

шерохова́тый rough; uneven.

шерсть wool; hair, coat. **шер-
стяно́й** wool(len).

шерша́вый rough.

шест (-á) pole; staff.

ше́ствие procession. **ше́ст-
вовать** *impf* process; march.

шестёрка six; figure 6; No. 6.
**шестерня́** (*gen pl* -рён) gear-
wheel, cogwheel.

ше́стеро (-ы́х) six.

шести- *in comb* six-, hexa-,
sex(i)-. **шестигра́нник** hexa-
hedron. ~**дне́вка** six-day
(working) week. ~**деся́тый**
sixtieth. ~**ме́сячный** six-
month; six-month-old. ~**со́-
тый** six-hundredth. ~**уго́ль-
ник** hexagon.

шестнадцатиле́тний sixteen-
year; sixteen-year-old. **шест-
на́дцатый** sixteenth. **шест-
на́дцать** sixteen. **шесто́й**
sixth. **шесть** (-и́, *instr* -ью́) six.
**шестьдеся́т** (-и́деся́ти, *instr*
-ью́деся́тью) sixty. **шестьсо́т**
(-исо́т, -иста́м, -ьюста́ми, -иста́х)

six hundred. **ше́стью** *adv* six
times.

шеф boss, chief; patron, sponsor. **шеф-по́вар** chef. **ше́ф-
ство** patronage, adoption.
**ше́фствовать** *impf* +**над**+
*instr* adopt; sponsor.

ше́я neck.

шиворот collar.

шика́рный chic, smart; splendid.

ши́ло (*pl* -ья, -ьев) awl.

шимпанзе́ *m indecl* chimpanzee.

ши́на tyre; splint.

шине́ль overcoat.

шинкова́ть *impf* shred, chop.

ши́нный tyre.

шип (-á) thorn, spike, cram-
pon; pin; tenon.

шипе́ние hissing; sizzling. **ши-
пе́ть** (-плю́) *impf* hiss; sizzle;
fizz.

шипо́вник dog-rose.

шипу́чий sparkling; fizzy. **ши-
пу́чка** fizzy drink. **шипя́щий**
sibilant.

ши́ре *comp of* широ́кий, ши-
ро́. **ширина́** width; gauge.
**ши́рить** *impf* extend, expand;
~**ся** spread, extend.

ши́рма screen.

широ́к|ий (-о́к, -á, -о́ко) wide,
broad; **това́ры** ~**ого** потре-
бле́ния consumer goods.
**широ́ко** *adv* wide, widely,
broadly.

широко- *in comb* wide-, broadly. **широковеща́ние** broadcasting. ~**веща́тельный** broadcasting. ~**экра́нный** wide-
screen.

широта́ (*pl* -ты) width, breadth;
latitude. **широ́тный** of latitude; latitudinal. **широча́й-
ший** *superl of* широ́кий.
**ширпотре́б** *abbr* consumption; consumer goods. **ширь**

(wide) expanse.

**шить** (шью, шьёшь) *impf* (*pf* с~) sew; make; embroider. **шитьё** sewing; embroidery.

**шифер** slate.

**шифр** cipher, code; shelf-mark. **шифрованный** in cipher, coded. **шифровать** *impf* (*pf* за~) encipher. **шифровка** enciphering; coded communication.

**шишка** cone; bump; lump; (*sl*) big shot.

**шкала** (*pl* -ы) scale; dial.

**шкатулка** box, casket, case.

**шкаф** (*loc* -ý; *pl* -ы́) cupboard; wardrobe. **шкафчик** cupboard, locker.

**шквал** squall.

**шкив** (*pl* -ы́) pulley.

**школа** school. **школьник** schoolboy. **школьница** schoolgirl. **школьный** school.

**шкура** skin, hide, pelt. **шкурка** skin; rind; emery paper, sandpaper.

**шла** *see* **идти**

**шлагбаум** barrier.

**шлак** slag; dross; clinker. **шлакоблок** breeze-block.

**шланг** hose.

**шлейф** train.

**шлем** helmet.

**шлёпать** *impf*, **шлёпнуть** (-ну) *pf* smack, spank; shuffle; tramp; ~**ся** fall flat, plop down.

**шли** *see* **идти**

**шлифовальный** polishing; grinding. **шлифовать** *impf* (*pf* от~) polish; grind. **шлифовка** polishing.

**шло** *see* **идти**. **шлю** *etc*.: *see* **слать**

**шлюз** lock, sluice.

**шлюпка** boat.

**шляпа** hat. **шляпка** hat; head.

**шмель** (-я́) *m* bumble-bee.

**шмон** *sl* search, frisking.

**шмыгать** *impf*, **шмыгнуть** (-гнý, -гнёшь) *pf* dart, rush; +*instr* rub, brush; ~ **носом** sniff.

**шницель** *m* schnitzel.

**шнур** (-á) cord; lace; cable. **шнуровать** *impf* (*pf* за~, про~) lace up; tie. **шнурок** (-рка́) lace.

**шов** (шва) seam; stitch; joint.

**шовинизм** chauvinism. **шовинист** chauvinist. **шовинистический** chauvinistic.

**шок** shock. **шокировать** *impf* shock.

**шоколад** chocolate. **шоколадка** chocolate, bar of chocolate. **шоколадный** chocolate.

**шорох** rustle.

**шорты** (шорт) *pl* shorts.

**шоры** (шор) *pl* blinkers.

**шоссе** *neut indecl* highway.

**шотландец** (-дца) Scotsman, Scot. **Шотландия** Scotland. **шотландка**[1] Scotswoman. **шотландка**[2] tartan. **шотландский** Scottish, Scots.

**шофёр** driver; chauffeur. **шофёрский** driver's; driving.

**шпага** sword.

**шпагат** cord; twine; string; splits.

**шпаклевать** (-люю) *impf* (*pf* за~) caulk; fill, putty. **шпаклёвка** filling, puttying; putty.

**шпала** sleeper.

**шпана** (*sl*) hooligan(s); riff-raff.

**шпаргалка** crib.

**шпарить** *impf* (*pf* о~) scald.

**шпат** spar.

**шпиль** *m* spire; capstan. **шпилька** hairpin; hat-pin; tack; stiletto heel.

**шпинат** spinach.

**шпингалет** (vertical) bolt; catch, latch.

**шпион** spy. **шпионаж** espionage. **шпионить** *impf*

(за+*instr* on). шпио́нский
spy's; espionage.

шпо́ра spur.

шприц syringe.

шпро́та sprat.

шпу́лька spool, bobbin.

шрам scar.

шрапне́ль shrapnel.

шрифт (*pl* -ы́) type, print.

шт. *abbr* (*of* штука) item, piece.

штаб (*pl* -ы́) staff; headquarters.

шта́бель (*pl* -я́) *m* stack.

штабно́й staff; headquarters.

штамп die, punch; stamp; cliché. штампо́ванный punched, stamped, pressed; trite; stock.

шта́нга bar, rod, beam; weight. штанги́ст weight-lifter.

штани́шки (-шек) *pl* (*child's*) shorts. штаны́ (-о́в) trousers.

штат¹ State.

штат² , шта́ты (-ов) *pl* staff, establishment.

штати́в tripod, base, stand.

шта́тный staff; established.

штатск|ий civilian; ~ое (пла́тье) civilian clothes; ~ий *sb* civilian.

штемпель (*pl* -я́) *m* stamp; почто́вый ~ postmark.

ште́псель (*pl* -я́) *m* plug, socket.

штиль *m* calm.

штифт (-а́) pin, dowel.

што́льня (*gen pl* -лен) gallery.

што́пать *impf* (*pf* за~) darn. што́пка darning; darning wool.

што́пор corkscrew; spin.

што́ра blind.

шторм gale.

штраф fine. штрафно́й penal; penalty. штрафова́ть *impf* (*pf* о~) fine.

штрих (-а́) stroke; feature. штрихова́ть *impf* (*pf* за~) shade, hatch.

штуди́ровать *impf* (*pf* про~) study.

шту́ка item, one; piece; trick.

штукату́р plasterer. штукату́рить *impf* (*pf* от~, о~) plaster. штукату́рка plastering; plaster.

штурва́л (steering-)wheel, helm.

штурм storm, assault.

штурман (*pl* -ы or -а́) navigator.

штурмова́ть *impf* storm, assault. штурмов|о́й assault; storming; ~а́я авиа́ция ground-attack aircraft. штурмови́на rushed work.

шту́чный piece, by the piece.

штык (-а́) bayonet.

штырь (-я́) pintle, pin.

шу́ба fur coat.

шу́лер (*pl* -а́) card-sharper.

шум noise; uproar, racket; stir. шуме́ть (-млю́) *impf* make a noise; row; make a fuss. шу́мный (-мен, -мна́, -о) noisy; loud; sensational.

шумов|о́й sound; ~ы́е эффе́кты sound effects. шумо́к (-мка́) noise; под ~ on the quiet.

шу́рин brother-in-law (*wife's brother*).

шурф prospecting shaft.

шурша́ть (-шу́) *impf* rustle.

шу́стрый (-тёр, -тра́, -о) smart, bright, sharp.

шут (-а́) fool; jester. шути́ть (-чу́, -тишь) *impf* (*pf* по~) joke; play, trifle; +над+*instr* make fun of. шу́тка joke, jest. шутли́вый humorous; joking, light-hearted. шу́точный comic; joking. шутя́ *adv* for fun, in jest; easily.

шушу́каться *impf* whisper together.

шху́на schooner.

шью *etc.*: *see* шить

# Щ

**щаве́ль** (-я́) *m* sorrel.

**щади́ть** (щажу́) *impf* (*pf* по~) spare.

**щебёнка**, **ще́бень** (-бня) *m* crushed stone, ballast; road-metal.

**щебет** twitter, chirp. **щебета́ть** (-ечу́, -е́чешь) *impf* twitter, chirp.

**щего́л** (-гла́) goldfinch.

**ще́голь** *m* dandy, fop. **щегольну́ть** (-ну́, -нёшь) *pf*, **щеголя́ть** *impf* dress fashionably; strut about; +*instr* show off, flaunt. **щегольско́й** foppish.

**ще́дрость** generosity. **ще́дрый** (-др, -á, -o) generous; liberal.

**щека́** (*acc* щёку; *pl* щёки, -áм) cheek.

**щеко́лда** latch, catch.

**щекота́ть** (-очу́, -о́чешь) *impf* (*pf* по~) tickle. **щеко́тка** tickling, tickle. **щекотли́вый** ticklish, delicate.

**щёлкать** *impf*, **щёлкнуть** (-ну) *pf* crack; flick; trill; +*instr* click, snap, pop.

**щёлок** bleach. **щелочно́й** alkaline. **щёлочь** (*gen pl* -éй) alkali.

**щелчо́к** (-чка́) flick; slight; blow.

**щель** (*gen pl* -éй) crack; chink; slit; crevice; slit trench.

**щеми́ть** (-млю́) *impf* constrict; ache; oppress.

**щено́к** (-нка́; *pl* -нки́, -о́в *or* -ня́та, -я́т) pup; cub.

**щепа́** (*pl* -ы, -áм), **ще́пка** splinter, chip; kindling.

**щепети́льный** punctilious.

**ще́пка** *see* щепа́

**щепо́тка**, **щепо́ть** pinch.

**щети́на** bristle; stubble. **щети́нистый** bristly. **щети́ниться** *impf* (*pf* o~) bristle. **щётка** brush; fetlock.

**щи** (щей *or* щец, щам, щáми) *pl* shchi, cabbage soup.

**щи́колотка** ankle.

**щипа́ть** (-плю́, -плешь) *impf*, **щипну́ть** (-ну́, -нёшь) *pf* (*pf* also o6~, o~, ущипну́ть) pinch, nip; sting, bite; burn; pluck; nibble; ~ся pinch. **щипко́м** *adv* pizzicato. **щипо́к** (-пка́) pinch, nip. **щипцы́** (-о́в) *pl* tongs, pincers, pliers; forceps.

**щит** (-á) shield; screen; sluice-gate; (tortoise)-shell; board; panel. **щитови́дный** thyroid. **щито́к** (-тка́) dashboard.

**щу́ка** pike.

**щуп** probe. **щу́пальце** (*gen pl* -лец) tentacle; antenna. **щу́пать** *impf* (*pf* по~) feel, touch.

**щу́плый** (-пл, -á, -o) weak, puny.

**щу́рить** *impf* (*pf* co~) screw up, narrow; ~ся screw up one's eyes; narrow.

# Э

**эбе́новый** ebony.

**эвакуа́ция** evacuation. **эвакую́рованный** *sb* evacuee. **эвакуи́ровать** *impf* & *pf* evacuate.

**эвкали́пт** eucalyptus.

**эволюциони́ровать** *impf* & *pf* evolve. **эволюцио́нный** evolutionary. **эволю́ция** evolution.

**эги́да** aegis.

**эгои́зм** egoism, selfishness. **эгои́ст**, ~ка egoist. **эгоисти́ческий**, **эгоисти́чный** egoistic, selfish.

**эй** *int* hi! hey!

**эйфори́я** euphoria.

**эква́тор** equator.

**эквивале́нт** equivalent.

**экзальта́ция** exaltation.

**экза́мен** examination; **выде́ржать, сдать** (pf ~) pass an examination. **экзамена́тор** examiner. **экзаменова́ть** impf (pf **про~**) examine; **~ся** take an examination.

**экзеку́ция** (corporal) punishment.

**экзе́ма** eczema.

**экземпля́р** specimen; copy.

**экзистенциали́зм** existentialism.

**экзоти́ческий** exotic.

**э́кий** what (a).

**экипа́ж**[1] carriage.

**экипа́ж**[2] crew. **экипирова́ть** impf & pf equip. **экипиро́вка** equipping; equipment.

**эклекти́зм** eclecticism.

**экле́р** éclair.

**экологи́ческий** ecological. **эколо́гия** ecology.

**эконо́мика** economics; economy. **экономи́ст** economist. **эконо́мить** (**-млю**) impf (pf **с~**) use sparingly; save; economize. **экономи́ческий** economic; economical. **экономи́чный** economical. **эконо́мия** economy; saving. **эконо́мка** housekeeper. **эконо́мный** economical; thrifty.

**экра́н** screen. **экраниза́ция** filming; film version.

**экскава́тор** excavator.

**экскурса́нт** tourist. **экскурсио́нный** excursion. **экску́рсия** (conducted) tour; excursion. **экскурсово́д** guide.

**экспанси́вный** effusive.

**экспатриа́нт** expatriate. **экспатри́ровать** impf & pf expatriate.

**экспеди́ция** expedition; dispatch; forwarding office.

**экспериме́нт** experiment. **эксперимента́льный** experimental. **эксперименти́ровать** impf experiment.

**экспе́рт** expert. **эксперти́за** (expert) examination; commission of experts.

**эксплуата́тор** exploiter. **эксплуатацио́нный** operating. **эксплуата́ция** exploitation; operation. **эксплуати́ровать** impf exploit; operate, run.

**экспози́ция** lay-out; exposition; exposure. **экспона́т** exhibit. **экспоно́метр** exposure meter.

**э́кспорт** export. **экспорти́ровать** impf & pf export. **э́кспортный** export.

**экспре́сс** express (train etc.).

**экспро́мт** impromptu. **экспро́мтом** adv impromptu.

**экспроприа́ция** expropriation. **экспроприи́ровать** impf & pf expropriate.

**экста́з** ecstasy.

**экстравага́нтный** eccentric, bizarre.

**экстра́кт** extract.

**экстреми́ст** extremist. **экстреми́стский** extremist.

**э́кстренный** urgent; emergency; special.

**эксцентри́чный** eccentric.

**эксце́сс** excess.

**эласти́чный** elastic; supple.

**элева́тор** grain elevator; hoist.

**элега́нтный** elegant, smart.

**эле́гия** elegy.

**электризова́ть** impf (pf **на~**) electrify. **эле́ктрик** electrician. **электрифика́ция** electrification. **электрифици́ровать** impf & pf electrify. **электри́ческий** electric(al). **электри́чество** electricity. **электри́чка** electric train.

**электро-** in comb electro-, electric, electrical. **электробытовой** electrical. **~воз** electric locomotive. **~двигатель** m electric motor. **электролиз** electrolysis. **~магнитный** electromagnetic. **~монтёр** electrician. **~одеяло** electric blanket. **~поезд** electric train. **~прибор** electrical appliance. **~провод** (pl -á) electric cable. **~проводка** electric wiring. **~станция** power-station. **~техник** electrical engineer. **~техника** electrical engineering. **~шок** electric shock, electric-shock treatment. **~энергия** electrical energy.

**электрод** electrode.

**электрон** electron. **электроника** electronics.

**электронный** electron; electronic.

**элемент** element; cell; character. **элементарный** elementary.

**элита** élite.

**эллипс** elipse.

**эмалевый** enamel. **эмалировать** impf enamel. **эмаль** enamel.

**эмансипация** emancipation.

**эмбарго** neut indecl embargo.

**эмблема** emblem.

**эмбрион** embryo.

**эмигрант** emigrant, émigré. **эмиграция** emigration. **эмигрировать** impf & pf emigrate.

**эмоциональный** emotional. **эмоция** emotion.

**эмпирический** empirical.

**эмульсия** emulsion.

**эндшпиль** m end-game.

**энергетика** power engineering. **энергетический** energy. **энергичный** energetic.

**энергия** energy.

**энтомология** entomology.

**энтузиазм** enthusiasm. **энтузиаст** enthusiast.

**энциклопедический** encyclopaedic. **энциклопедия** encyclopaedia.

**эпиграмма** epigram. **эпиграф** epigraph.

**эпидемия** epidemic.

**эпизод** episode. **эпизодический** episodic; sporadic.

**эпилепсия** epilepsy. **эпилептик** epileptic.

**эпилог** epilogue. **эпитафия** epitaph. **эпитет** epithet. **эпицентр** epicentre.

**эпопея** epic.

**эпоха** epoch, era.

**эра** era; **до нашей эры** BC; **нашей эры** AD.

**эрекция** erection.

**эрозия** erosion.

**эротизм** eroticism. **эротика** sensuality. **эротический**, **эротичный** erotic, sensual.

**эрудиция** erudition.

**эскадра** (naut) squadron. **эскадрилья** (gen pl -лий) (aeron) squadron. **эскадрон** (mil) squadron. **эскадронный** squadron.

**эскалатор** escalator. **эскалация** escalation.

**эскиз** sketch; draft. **эскизный** sketch; draft.

**эскимос**, **эскимоска** Eskimo.

**эскорт** escort.

**эсминец** (-нца) abbr (of **эскадренный миноносец**) destroyer.

**эссенция** essence.

**эстакада** trestle bridge; overpass; pier, boom.

**эстамп** print, engraving, plate.

**эстафета** relay race; baton.

**эстетика** aesthetics. **эстетический** aesthetic.

**эстонец** (-нца), **эстонка** Estonian. **Эсто́ния** Estonia. **эсто́нский** Estonian.

**эстра́да** stage, platform; variety. **эстра́дный** stage; variety; ~ **конце́рт** variety show.

**эта́ж** (-á) storey, floor. **этажёрка** shelves.

**э́так** adv so, thus; about. **э́такий** such (a), what (a).

**этало́н** standard.

**эта́п** stage; halting-place.

**э́тика** ethics.

**этике́т** etiquette. **этике́тка** label.

**эти́л** ethyl.

**этимоло́гия** etymology.

**эти́ческий, эти́чный** ethical. **этни́ческий** ethnic. **этногра́фия** ethnography.

**э́то** partl this (is), that (is), it (is). **э́тот** m, **э́та** f, **э́то** neut, **э́ти** pl pron this, these.

**этю́д** study, sketch; étude.

**эфеме́рный** ephemeral.

**эфио́п**, ~**ка** Ethiopian. **эфио́пский** Ethiopian.

**эфи́р** ether; air. **эфи́рный** ethereal; ether, ester.

**эффе́кт** effect. **эффекти́вность** effectiveness. **эффекти́вный** effective. **эффе́ктный** effective; striking.

**эх** int eh! oh!

**э́хо** echo.

**эшафо́т** scaffold.

**эшело́н** echelon; special train.

# Ю

**юбиле́й** anniversary; jubilee. **юбиле́йный** jubilee.

**ю́бка** skirt. **ю́бочка** short skirt.

**ювели́р** jeweller. **ювели́рный** jeweller's, jewellery; fine, intricate.

**юг** south; **на** ~**е** in the south. **ю́го-восто́к** south-east. **ю́го-**

**за́пад** south-west. **югосла́в**, ~**ка** Yugoslav. **Югосла́вия** Yugoslavia. **югосла́вский** Yugoslav.

**юдофо́б** anti-Semite. **юдофо́бство** anti-Semitism.

**южа́нин** (pl -а́не, -а́н), **южа́нка** southerner. **ю́жный** south, southern; southerly.

**юла́** top; fidget. **юли́ть** impf fidget.

**ю́мор** humour. **юмори́ст** humourist. **юмористи́ческий** humorous.

**ю́ность** youth. **ю́ноша** (gen pl -шей) m youth. **ю́ношеский** youthful. **ю́ношество** youth; young people. **ю́ный** (юн, -á, -о) young; youthful.

**юпи́тер** floodlight.

**юриди́ческий** legal, juridical. **юрисконсу́льт** legal adviser. **юри́ст** lawyer.

**ю́ркий** (-рок, -рка́, -рко) quick-moving, brisk; smart.

**юро́дивый** crazy.

**ю́рта** yurt, nomad's tent.

**юсти́ция** justice.

**юти́ться** (ючу́сь) impf huddle (together).

# Я

**я** (меня́, мне, мной (-ю), (обо) мне) pron I.

**я́беда** m & f, tell-tale; informer.

**я́блоко** (pl -и, -ок) apple; глазно́е ~ eyeball. **я́блоневый, я́блочный** apple. **я́блоня** apple-tree.

**яви́ться** (явлю́сь, я́вишься) pf, **явля́ться** impf appear; arise; +instr be, serve as. **я́вка** appearance, attendance; secret rendez-vous. **явле́ние** phenomenon; appearance; осcurrence; scene. **я́вный** obvious; overt. **явственный** clear. **я́вствовать** be clear, be obvious.

**ягнёнок** (-нка; *pl* -ня́та, -я́т) lamb.

**я́года** berry; berries.

**я́годица** buttock(s).

**ягуа́р** jaguar.

**яд** poison; venom.

**я́дерный** nuclear.

**ядови́тый** poisonous; venomous.

**ядрёный** healthy; bracing; juicy. **ядро́** (*pl* -а, я́дер) kernel, core; nucleus; (cannon-) ball; shot.

**я́зва** ulcer, sore. **я́звенн|ый** ulcerous; ~ая боле́знь ulcers. **язви́тельный** caustic, sarcastic. **язви́ть** (-влю́) *impf* (*pf* съ~) be sarcastic.

**язы́к** (-á) tongue; clapper; language. **языкове́д** linguist. **языкове́дение, языкозна́-ние** linguistics. **языково́й** linguistic. **языко́вый** tongue; lingual. **язычко́вый** reed. **язы́чник** heathen, pagan. **язычо́к** (-чка́) tongue; reed; catch.

**яйчко** (*pl* -и, -чек) egg; testicle. **яйчник** ovary. **яйчница** fried eggs. **яйцо́** (*pl* яйца, яиц) egg; ovum.

**я́кобы** *conj* as if; *partl* supposedly.

**я́корн|ый** anchor; ~ая сто́я́нка anchorage. **я́корь** (*pl* -я́) *m* anchor.

**я́лик** skiff.

**я́ма** pit, hole.

**ямщи́к** (-á) coachman.

**янва́рский** January. **янва́рь** (-я́) *m* January.

**янта́рный** amber. **янта́рь** (-я́) *m* amber.

**япо́нец** (-нца), **япо́нка** Japanese. **Япо́ния** Japan. **япо́н-ский** Japanese.

**ярд** yard.

**я́ркий** (-рок, ярка́, -о) bright; colourful, striking.

**ярлы́к** (-á) label; tag.

**я́рмарка** fair.

**ярмо́** (*pl* -а) yoke.

**ярово́й** spring.

**я́ростный** furious, fierce. **я́рость** fury.

**я́рус** circle; tier; layer.

**я́рче** *comp of* **я́ркий**

**я́рый** fervent; furious; violent.

**я́сень** *m* ash(-tree).

**я́сли** (-ей) *pl* manger; crèche; day nursery.

**ясне́ть** (-е́ет) *impf* become clear, clear. **я́сно** *adv* clearly. **ясновиде́ние** clairvoyance. **ясновиде́ц** (-дца), **яснови́-дица** clairvoyant. **я́сность** clarity; clearness. **я́сный** (я́сен, -сна́, -о) clear; bright; fine.

**я́ства** (яств) *pl* victuals.

**я́стреб** (*pl* -á) hawk.

**я́хта** yacht.

**яче́йка** cell.

**ячме́нь**[1] (-я́) *m* barley.

**ячме́нь**[2] (-я́) *m* stye.

**я́щерица** lizard.

**я́щик** box; drawer.

# A

**a, an** *indef article*, *not usu translated*; **twice a week** два раза в неделю.
**aback** *adv*: **take ~** озадачивать *impf*, озадачить *pf*.
**abacus** *n* счёты *m pl*.
**abandon** *vt* покидать *impf*, покинуть *pf*; (*give up*) отказываться *impf*, отказаться *pf* от+*gen*; **~ o.s. to** предаваться *impf*, предаться *pf* +*dat*. **abandoned** *adj* покинутый; (*profligate*) распутный.
**abase** *vt* унижать *impf*, унизить *pf*. **abasement** *n* унижение.
**abate** *vi* затихать *impf*, затихнуть *pf*.
**abattoir** *n* скотобойня.
**abbey** *n* аббатство.
**abbreviate** *vt* сокращать *impf*, сократить *pf*. **abbreviation** *n* сокращение.
**abdicate** *vi* отрекаться *impf*, отречься *pf* от престола. **abdication** *n* отречение (от престола).
**abdomen** *n* брюшная полость. **abdominal** *adj* брюшной.
**abduct** *vt* похищать *impf*, похитить *pf*. **abduction** *n* похищение.
**aberration** *n* (*mental*) помутнение рассудка.
**abet** *vi* подстрекать *impf*, подстрекнуть *pf* (к совершению преступления *etc.*).
**abhor** *vt* ненавидеть *impf*. **abhorrence** *n* отвращение.

**abhorrent** *adj* отвратительный.
**abide** *vt* (*tolerate*) выносить *impf*, вынести *pf*; **~ by** (*rules etc.*) следовать *impf*, по~ *pf*. **ability** *n* способность.
**abject** *adj* (*wretched*) жалкий; (*humble*) униженный; **~ poverty** крайняя нищета.
**ablaze** *predic* охваченный огнём.
**able** *adj* способный, умелый; **be ~ to** мочь *impf*, с~ *pf*; (*know how to*) уметь *impf*, с~ *pf*.
**abnormal** *adj* ненормальный. **abnormality** *n* ненормальность.
**aboard** *adv* на борт(у́); (*train*) в поезд(е).
**abode** *n* жилище; **of no fixed ~** без постоянного местожительства.
**abolish** *vt* отменять *impf*, отменить *pf*. **abolition** *n* отмена.
**abominable** *adj* отвратительный. **abomination** *n* мерзость.
**aboriginal** *adj* коренной; *n* абориген, коренной житель *m*. **aborigine** *n* абориген, коренной житель *m*.
**abort** *vi* (*med*) выкидывать *impf*, выкинуть *pf*; *vt* (*terminate*) прекращать *impf*, прекратить *pf*. **abortion** *n* аборт; **have an ~** делать *impf*, с~ *pf* аборт. **abortive**

*adj* безуспе́шный.

**abound** *vi* быть в изоби́лии; ~ **in** изоби́ловать *impf* +*instr.*

**about** *adv & prep* (*approximately*) о́коло+*gen*; (*concerning*) о+*prep*, насчёт+*gen*; (*up and down*) по+*dat*; (*in the vicinity*) круго́м; **be ~ to** собира́ться *impf*, собра́ться *pf* +*inf.*

**above** *adv* наверху́; (*higher up*) вы́ше; **from ~** све́рху; *prep* над+*instr*; (*more than*) свы́ше+*gen*. **aboveboard** *adj* че́стный. **above-mentioned** *adj* вышеупомя́нутый.

**abrasion** *n* истира́ние; (*wound*) сса́дина. **abrasive** *adj* абрази́вный; (*manner*) колю́чий; *n* абрази́вный материа́л.

**abreast** *adv* в ряд; **keep ~ of** идти́ в но́гу с+*instr.*

**abridge** *vt* сокраща́ть *impf*, сократи́ть *pf*. **abridgement** *n* сокраще́ние.

**abroad** *adv* за грани́цей, за грани́цу; **from ~** из-за грани́цы.

**abrupt** *adj* (*steep*) круто́й; (*sudden*) внеза́пный; (*curt*) ре́зкий.

**abscess** *n* абсце́сс.

**abscond** *vi* скрыва́ться *impf*, скры́ться *pf*.

**absence** *n* отсу́тствие. **absent** *adj* отсу́тствующий; **be ~** отсу́тствовать *impf*; *vt*: **~ o.s.** отлуча́ться *impf*, отлучи́ться *pf*. **absentee** *n* отсу́тствующий *sb*. **absenteeism** *n* прогу́л. **absent-minded** *adj* рассе́янный.

**absolute** *adj* абсолю́тный; (*complete*) по́лный, соверше́нный.

**absolution** *n* отпуще́ние гре-

хо́в. **absolve** *vt* проща́ть *impf*, прости́ть *pf*.

**absorb** *vt* впи́тывать *impf*, впита́ть *pf*. **absorbed** *adj* поглощённый. **absorbent** *adj* вса́сывающий. **absorption** *n* впи́тывание; (*mental*) погружённость.

**abstain** *vi* возде́рживаться *impf*, воздержа́ться *pf* (**from** от+*gen*). **abstemious** *adj* возде́ржанный. **abstention** *n* воздержа́ние; (*person*) воздержа́вшийся *sb*. **abstinence** *n* воздержа́ние.

**abstract** *adj* абстра́ктный, отвлечённый; *n* рефера́т.

**absurd** *adj* абсу́рдный. **absurdity** *n* абсу́рд.

**abundance** *n* оби́лие. **abundant** *adj* оби́льный.

**abuse** *vt* (*insult*) руга́ть *impf*, вы́-, от-~ *pf*; (*misuse*) злоупотребля́ть *impf*, злоупотреби́ть *pf*; *n* (*curses*) ру́гань, руга́тельства *neut pl*; (*misuse*) злоупотребле́ние. **abusive** *adj* оскорби́тельный, руга́тельный.

**abut** *vi* примыка́ть *impf* (**on** к+*dat*).

**abysmal** *adj* (*extreme*) безграни́чный; (*bad*) ужа́сный. **abyss** *n* бе́здна.

**academic** *adj* академи́ческий. **academician** *n* акаде́мик. **academy** *n* акаде́мия.

**accede** *vi* вступа́ть *impf*, вступи́ть *pf* (**to** в, на+*acc*); (*assent*) соглаша́ться *impf*, согласи́ться *pf*.

**accelerate** *vt & i* ускоря́ть(ся) *impf*, уско́рить(ся) *pf*; (*motoring*) дава́ть *impf*, дать *pf* газ. **acceleration** *n* ускоре́ние. **accelerator** *n* ускори́тель *m*; (*pedal*) акселера́тор.

**accent** n акце́нт; (*stress*) ударе́ние; vt де́лать impf, c~ pf ударе́ние на+acc. **accentuate** vt акценти́ровать impf & pf.

**accept** vt принима́ть impf, приня́ть pf. **acceptable** adj прие́млемый. **acceptance** n приня́тие.

**access** n до́ступ. **accessible** adj досту́пный. **accession** n вступле́ние (на престо́л). **accessories** n принадле́жности f pl. **accessory** (*accomplice*) соуча́стник, **accident** n (*chance*) случа́йность; (*mishap*) несча́стный случай; (*crash*) ава́рия; **by** ~ случа́йно. **accidental** adj случа́йный.

**acclaim** vt (*praise*) восхваля́ть impf, восхвали́ть pf; n восхвале́ние.

**acclimatization** n акклиматиза́ция. **acclimatize** vt акклиматизи́ровать impf & pf.

**accommodate** vt помеща́ть impf, помести́ть pf; (*hold*) вмеща́ть impf, вмести́ть pf. **accommodating** adj услужли́вый. **accommodation** n (*hotel*) но́мер; (*home*) жильё.

**accompaniment** n сопровожде́ние; (*mus*) аккомпанеме́нт. **accompanist** n аккомпаниа́тор. **accompany** vt сопровожда́ть impf, сопроводи́ть pf; (*escort*) провожа́ть impf, проводи́ть pf; (*mus*) аккомпани́ровать impf +dat.

**accomplice** n соуча́стник, -ица.

**accomplish** vt соверша́ть impf, соверши́ть pf. **accomplished** adj зако́нченный. **accomplishment** n выполне́ние; (*skill*) соверше́нство.

**accord** n согла́сие; **of one's own** ~ доброво́льно; **of its own** ~ сам собо́й, сам по себе́. **accordance** n: **in** ~ **with** в соотве́тствии c+instr, согла́сно+dat. **according** adv: ~ **to** по+dat, ~ **to him** по его́ слова́м. **accordingly** adv соотве́тственно.

**accordion** n аккордео́н.

**accost** vt пристава́ть impf, приста́ть pf к+dat.

**account** n (*comm*) счёт; (*report*) отчёт; (*description*) описа́ние; **on no** ~ ни в ко́ем слу́чае; **on** ~ в счёт причита́ющейся су́ммы; **on** ~ **of** из-за+gen, по причи́не+gen; **take into** ~ принима́ть impf, приня́ть pf в расчёт; vi: ~ **for** объясня́ть impf, объясни́ть pf. **accountable** adj отве́тственный.

**accountancy** n бухгалте́рия. **accountant** n бухга́лтер.

**accrue** vi нараста́ть impf, нарасти́ pf.

**accumulate** vt & i нака́пливать(ся) impf, копи́ть(ся) impf, на~ pf. **accumulation** n накопле́ние. **accumulator** n аккумуля́тор.

**accuracy** n то́чность. **accurate** adj то́чный.

**accusation** n обвине́ние. **accusative** adj (n) вини́тельный (паде́ж). **accuse** vt обвиня́ть impf, обвини́ть pf (**of** в+prep); **the** ~**d** обвиня́емый sb.

**accustom** vt приуча́ть impf, приучи́ть pf (**to** к+dat). **accustomed** adj привы́чный; **be, get** ~ привыка́ть impf, привы́кнуть pf (**to** к+dat).

**ace** n туз; (*pilot*) ас.

**ache** n боль; vi боле́ть impf.

**achieve** vt достига́ть impf,

**achievement** n достижение.

**acid** n кислота; adj кислый; ~ **rain** кислотный дождь.

**acidity** n кислота.

**acknowledge** vt признавать impf, признать pf; (~ receipt of) подтверждать impf, подтвердить pf получение +gen.

**acknowledgement** n признание; подтверждение.

**acne** n прыщи m pl.

**acorn** n жёлудь m.

**acoustic** adj акустический. **acoustics** n pl акустика.

**acquaint** vt знакомить impf, по~ pf. **acquaintance** n знакомство; (person) знакомый sb. **acquainted** adj знакомый.

**acquiesce** vi соглашаться impf, согласиться pf. **acquiescence** n согласие.

**acquire** vt приобретать impf, приобрести pf. **acquisition** n приобретение. **acquisitive** adj стяжательский.

**acquit** vt оправдывать impf, оправдать pf; (~ o.s.) вести impf себя. **acquittal** n оправдание.

**acre** n акр.

**acrid** adj едкий.

**acrimonious** adj язвительный.

**acrobat** n акробат. **acrobatic** adj акробатический.

**across** adv & prep через+acc; (athwart) поперёк (+gen); (to, on, other side) на ту сторону (+gen), на той стороне (+gen); (crosswise) крест-накрест.

**acrylic** n акрил; adj акриловый.

**act** n (deed) акт, поступок; (law) акт, закон; (of play) действие; (item) номер; vi поступать impf, поступить pf; действовать impf, по~ pf; vt играть impf, сыграть pf. **acting** n игра; (profession) актёрство; adj исполняющий обязанности+gen.

**action** n действие, поступок; (law) иск, процесс; (battle) бой; ~ **replay** повтор; **be out of** ~ не работать impf.

**activate** vt приводить impf, привести pf в действие. **active** adj активный; ~ **service** действительная служба; ~ **voice** действительный залог. **activity** n деятельность.

**actor** n актёр. **actress** n актриса.

**actual** adj действительный. **actuality** n действительность. **actually** adv на самом деле, фактически.

**acumen** n проницательность.

**acupuncture** n иглоукалывание.

**acute** adj острый.

**AD** abbr н.э. (нашей эры).

**adamant** adj непреклонный.

**adapt** vt приспособлять impf, приспособить pf; (theat) инсценировать impf & pf; ~ **o.s.** приспособляться impf, приспособиться pf. **adaptable** adj приспособляющийся. **adaptation** n приспособление; (theat) инсценировка. **adapter** n адаптер.

**add** vt прибавлять impf, прибавить pf; (say) добавлять impf, добавить pf; ~ **together** складывать impf, сложить pf; ~ **up** суммировать impf & pf; ~ **up to** составлять impf, составить pf; (fig) сводиться impf, свестись pf к+dat. **addenda** n приложения pl.

**adder** n гадюка.

addict *n* наркома́н, ~ка. addicted *adj*: be ~ to быть рабо́м+*gen*; become ~ to пристрасти́ться *pf* к+*dat*. addiction *n* (*passion*) пристра́стие; (*to drugs*) наркома́ния

addition *n* прибавле́ние; дополне́ние; (*math*) сложе́ние; in ~ вдоба́вок, кро́ме того́. additional *adj* доба́вочный. additive *n* доба́вка.

address *n* а́дрес; (*speech*) речь; ~ book записна́я кни́жка; *vt* адресова́ть *impf* & *pf*; (*speak to*) обраща́ться *impf*, обрати́ться *pf* к+*dat*; ~ a meeting выступа́ть *impf*, вы́ступить *pf* на собра́нии. addressee *n* адреса́т.

adept *adj* све́дущий; *n* ма́стер.

adequate *adj* доста́точный.

adhere *vi* прилипа́ть *impf*, прили́пнуть *pf* (to к+*dat*); ~ to приде́рживаться *impf* +*gen*. adherence *n* приве́рженность. adherent *n* приве́рженец. adhesive *adj* ли́пкий; *n* кле́йкое вещество́.

ad hoc *adj* специа́льный.

ad infinitum *adv* до бесконе́чности.

adjacent *adj* сме́жный.

adjective *n* (и́мя) прилага́тельное.

adjoin *vt* прилега́ть *impf* к+*dat*.

adjourn *vt* откла́дывать *impf*, отложи́ть *pf*; *vi* объявля́ть *impf*, объяви́ть *pf* переры́в; (*move*) переходи́ть *impf*, перейти́ *pf*.

adjudicate *vi* выноси́ть *impf*, вы́нести *pf* реше́ние (in по+*dat*); суди́ть *impf*.

adjust *vt* & *i* приспособля́ть(ся) *impf*, приспособи́ть(ся) *pf*; *vt* пригоня́ть *impf*, пригна́ть *pf*; (*regulate*) регули́ровать *impf*, от~ *pf*. adjustable *adj* регули́руемый. adjustment *n* регули́рование, подго́нка.

ad lib *vt* & *i* импровизи́ровать *impf*, сымпровизи́ровать *pf*.

administer *vt* (*manage*) управля́ть *impf* +*instr*; (*give*) дава́ть *impf*, дать *pf*. administration *n* управле́ние; (*government*) прави́тельство. administrative *adj* администрати́вный. administrator *n* администра́тор.

admirable *adj* похва́льный.

admiral *n* адмира́л.

admiration *n* восхище́ние.

admire *vt* (*look at*) любова́ться *impf*, по~ *pf* +*instr*, на+*acc*; (*respect*) восхища́ться *impf*, восхити́ться *pf* +*instr*. admirer *n* покло́нник.

admissible *adj* допусти́мый.

admission *n* (*access*) до́ступ; (*entry*) вход; (*confession*) призна́ние. admit *vt* (*allow in*) впуска́ть *impf*, впусти́ть *pf*; (*confess*) признава́ть *impf*, призна́ть *pf*. admittance *n* до́ступ. admittedly *adv* призна́ться.

admixture *n* при́месь.

adolescence *n* о́трочество. adolescent *adj* подро́стко́вый; *n* подро́сток.

adopt *vt* (*child*) усыновля́ть *impf*, усынови́ть *pf*; (*thing*) усва́ивать *impf*, усво́ить *pf*; (*accept*) принима́ть *impf*, приня́ть *pf*. adoptive *adj* приёмный. adoption *n* усыновле́ние; приня́тие.

adorable *adj* преле́стный. adoration *n* обожа́ние. adore *vt* обожа́ть *impf*.

**adorn** vt украша́ть impf, укра́сить pf. **adornment** n украше́ние.

**adrenalin** n адренали́н.

**adroit** adj ло́вкий.

**adulation** n преклоне́ние.

**adult** adj & n взро́слый (sb).

**adulterate** vt фальсифици́ровать impf & pf.

**adultery** n супру́жеская изме́на.

**advance** n (going forward) продвиже́ние (вперёд); (progress) прогре́сс; (mil) наступле́ние; (of pay etc.) ава́нс; **in ~** зара́нее; pl (overtures) ава́нсы m pl; vi (go forward) продвига́ться impf, продви́нуться pf вперёд; идти́ impf вперёд; (mil) наступа́ть impf; vt продви́нуть impf, продви́нуть pf; (put forward) выдвига́ть impf, вы́двинуть pf. **advanced** adj (modern) передово́й. **advancement** n продвиже́ние.

**advantage** n преиму́щество; (profit) вы́года, по́льза; **take ~ of** по́льзоваться impf, вос~ pf +instr. **advantageous** adj вы́годный.

**adventure** n приключе́ние. **adventurer** n иска́тель m приключе́ний. **adventurous** adj предприи́мчивый.

**adverb** n наре́чие.

**adversary** n проти́вник. **adverse** adj неблагоприя́тный. **adversity** n несча́стье.

**advertise** vt (publicize) реклами́ровать impf & pf; vt & i (~ for) дава́ть impf, дать pf объявле́ние o+prep. **advertisement** n объявле́ние, рекла́ма.

**advice** n сове́т. **advisable** adj жела́тельный. **advise** vt со-

ве́товать impf, по~ pf +dat & inf; (notify) уведомля́ть impf, уве́домить pf. **advisedly** adv наме́ренно. **adviser** n сове́тник. **advisory** adj совеща́тельный.

**advocate** n (supporter) сторо́нник; vt выступа́ть impf, вы́ступить pf за+acc; (advise) сове́товать impf, по~ pf.

**aegis** n эги́да.

**aerial** n анте́нна; adj возду́шный.

**aerobics** n аэро́бика.

**aerodrome** n аэродро́м. **aerodynamics** n аэродина́мика. **aeroplane** n самолёт. **aerosol** n аэрозо́ль m.

**aesthetic** adj эстети́ческий. **aesthetics** n pl эсте́тика.

**afar** adv: **from ~** издалека́.

**affable** adj приве́тливый.

**affair** n (business) де́ло; (love) рома́н.

**affect** vt влия́ть impf, по~ pf на+acc; (touch) тро́гать impf, тро́нуть pf; (concern) затра́гивать impf, затро́нуть pf; **affectation** n жема́нство. **affected** adj жема́нный. **affection** n привя́занность. **affectionate** adj не́жный.

**affiliated** adj свя́занный (**to** c+instr).

**affinity** n (relationship) родство́; (resemblance) схо́дство; (attraction) влече́ние.

**affirm** vt утвержда́ть impf. **affirmation** n утвержде́ние. **affirmative** adj утверди́тельный.

**affix** vt прикрепля́ть impf, прикрепи́ть pf.

**afflict** vt постига́ть impf, пости́чь pf; **be afflicted with** страда́ть impf +instr. **affliction** n боле́знь.

**affluence** *n* бога́тство. **affluent** *adj* бога́тый.

**afford** *vt* позволя́ть *impf*, позво́лить *pf* себе́; (*supply*) предоставля́ть *impf*, предоста́вить *pf*.

**affront** *n* оскорбле́ние; *vt* оскорбля́ть *impf*, оскорби́ть *pf*.

**afield** *adv*: **far ~** далеко́; **farther ~** да́льше.

**afloat** *adv & predic* на воде́.

**afoot** *predic*: **be ~** гото́виться *impf*.

**aforesaid** *adj* вышеупомя́нутый.

**afraid** *predic*: **be ~** боя́ться *impf*.

**afresh** *adv* сно́ва.

**Africa** *n* А́фрика. **African** *n* африка́нец, -ка́нка; *adj* африка́нский.

**after** *adv* пото́м; *prep* по́сле +*gen*; (*time*) че́рез+*acc*; (*behind*) за+*acc*, *instr*; **~ all** в конце́ концо́в; *conj* по́сле того́, как.

**aftermath** *n* после́дствия *neut pl*. **afternoon** *n* втора́я полови́на дня; **in the ~** днём. **aftershave** *n* лосьо́н по́сле бритья́. **afterthought** *n* запозда́лая мысль.

**afterwards** *adv* впосле́дствии.

**again** *adv* опя́ть; (*once more*) ещё раз; (*anew*) сно́ва.

**against** *prep* (*opposing*) про́тив+*gen*; (*touching*) к+*dat*; (*hitting*) о+*acc*.

**age** *n* во́зраст; (*era*) век, эпо́ха; *vt* ста́рить *impf*, со~ *pf*; *vi* старе́ть *impf*, по~ *pf*. **aged** *adj* престаре́лый.

**agency** *n* аге́нтство. **agenda** *n* пове́стка дня. **agent** *n* аге́нт.

**aggravate** *vt* ухудша́ть *impf*,

уху́дшить *pf*; (*annoy*) раздража́ть *impf*, раздражи́ть *pf*.

**aggregate** *adj* совоку́пный; *n* совоку́пность.

**aggression** *n* агре́ссия. **aggressive** *adj* агресси́вный. **aggressor** *n* агре́ссор.

**aggrieved** *adj* оби́женный.

**aghast** *predic* в у́жасе (**at** от +*gen*).

**agile** *adj* прово́рный. **agility** *n* прово́рство.

**agitate** *vt* волнова́ть *impf*, вз~ *pf*; *vi* агити́ровать *impf*. **agitation** *n* волне́ние; агита́ция.

**agnostic** *n* агно́стик. **agnosticism** *n* агностици́зм.

**ago** *adv* (тому́) наза́д; **long ~** давно́.

**agonize** *vi* мучи́ться *impf*. **agonizing** *adj* мучи́тельный. **agony** *n* аго́ния.

**agrarian** *adj* агра́рный.

**agree** *vi* соглаша́ться *impf*, согласи́ться *pf*; (*arrange*) догова́риваться *impf*, договори́ться *pf*. **agreeable** *adj* (*pleasant*) прия́тный. **agreement** *n* согла́сие; (*treaty*) соглаше́ние; **in ~** согла́сен (-сна).

**agricultural** *adj* сельскохозя́йственный. **agriculture** *n* се́льское хозя́йство.

**aground** *predic* на мели́; *adv*: **run ~** сади́ться *impf*, сесть *pf* на мель.

**ahead** *adv* (*forward*) вперёд; (*in front*) впереди́; **~ of time** досро́чно.

**aid** *vt* помога́ть *impf*, помо́чь *pf* +*dat*; *n* по́мощь; (*teaching*) посо́бие; **in ~ of** в по́льзу +*gen*.

**Aids** *n* СПИД.

**ailing** *adj* (*ill*) больно́й.

**ailment** *n* неду́г.

**aim** n цель, наме́рение; **take ~** прице́ливаться *impf*, прице́литься *pf* (at в+*acc*); *vi* це́литься *impf*, на~ *pf* (at в+*acc*); (*also fig*) ме́тить *impf*, на~ *pf* (at в+*acc*); *vt* наце́ливать *impf*, наце́лить *pf*; (*also fig*) наводи́ть *impf*, навести́ *pf*. **aimless** *adj* бесце́льный.

**air** n (*look*) вид; by ~ самолётом; **on the ~** в эфи́ре; *attrib* возду́шный; *vt* (*ventilate*) прове́тривать *impf*, прове́трить *pf*; (*make known*) выставля́ть *impf*, вы́ставить *pf* напока́з. **air-conditioning** n кондициони́рование во́здуха. **aircraft** n самолёт. **aircraft-carrier** n авиано́сец. **airfield** n аэродро́м. **air force** n ВВС (вое́нно-возду́шные си́лы) f pl. **air hostess** n стюарде́сса. **airless** *adj* ду́шный. **airlift** n возду́шные перево́зки f pl; *vt* перевози́ть *impf*, перевезти́ *pf* по во́здуху. **airline** n авиакомпа́ния. **airlock** n возду́шная про́бка. **airmail** n а́виа(по́чта). **airman** n лётчик. **airport** n аэропо́рт. **air raid** n возду́шный налёт. **airship** n дирижа́бль n. **airstrip** n взлётно-поса́дочная полоса́. **airtight** *adj* гермети́чный. **air traffic controller** n диспе́тчер. **airwaves** n pl радиово́лны f pl. **aisle** n боково́й неф; (*passage*) прохо́д.

**ajar** *predic* приоткры́тый.

**akin** *predic* (*similar*) похо́жий; **be ~** to быть сродни́ к+*dat*.

**alabaster** n алеба́стр.

**alacrity** n быстрота́.

**alarm** n трево́га; *vt* трево́жить *impf*, вс~ *pf*; **~ clock**

**alarming** *adj* трево́жный. **alarmist** n паникёр; *adj* паникёрский.

**alas** *int* увы́!

**album** n альбо́м.

**alcohol** n алкого́ль m, спирт; спиртны́е напи́тки m pl. **alcoholic** *adj* алкого́льный; n алкого́лик, -и́чка.

**alcove** n алько́в.

**alert** *adj* бди́тельный; n трево́га; *vt* предупрежда́ть *impf*, предупреди́ть *pf*.

**algebra** n а́лгебра.

**alias** *adv* ина́че (называ́емый); n кли́чка, вы́мышленное и́мя *neut*.

**alibi** n али́би *indecl*.

**alien** n иностра́нец, -нка; *adj* чужо́й; **~ to** чу́ждый +*dat*. **alienate** *vt* отчужда́ть *impf*. **alienation** n отчужде́ние.

**alight**[1] *vi* сходи́ть *impf*, сойти́ *pf*; (*bird*) сади́ться *impf*, сесть *pf*.

**alight**[2] *predic* **be ~** горе́ть *impf*; (*shine*) сия́ть *impf*.

**align** *vt* выра́внивать *impf*, вы́ровнять *pf*. **alignment** n выра́внивание.

**alike** *predic* похо́ж; *adv* одина́ково.

**alimentary** *adj*: **~ canal** пищевари́тельный кана́л.

**alimony** n алиме́нты m pl.

**alive** *predic* жив, в живы́х.

**alkali** n щёлочь. **alkaline** *adj* щелочно́й.

**all** *adj* весь; n всё, pl все; *adv* совсе́м, соверше́нно; **~ along** всё вре́мя; **~ right** хорошо́, ла́дно; (*not bad*) та́к себе́; непло́хо; **~ the same** всё равно́; **in ~** всего́; **two ~** по́ два; **not at ~** ниско́лько.

**allay** *vt* успока́ивать *impf*

успоко́ить *pf.*

**allegation** *n* утвержде́ние. **allege** *vt* утвержда́ть *impf.* **allegedly** *adv* я́кобы.

**allegiance** *adv* ве́рность.

**allegorical** *adj* аллегори́ческий. **allegory** *n* аллего́рия.

**allergic** *adj* аллерги́ческий; **be ~ to** име́ть аллерги́ю к+*dat.* **allergy** *n* аллерги́я.

**alleviate** *vt* облегча́ть *impf,* облегчи́ть *pf.* **alleviation** *n* облегче́ние.

**alley** *n* переу́лок.

**alliance** *n* сою́з. **allied** *adj* сою́зный.

**alligator** *n* аллига́тор.

**allocate** *vt* (*distribute*) распределя́ть *impf,* распредели́ть *pf;* (*allot*) выделя́ть *impf,* вы́делить *pf.* **allocation** *n* распределе́ние; выделе́ние.

**allot** *vt* выделя́ть *impf,* вы́делить *pf;* (*distribute*) распределя́ть *impf,* распредели́ть *pf.* **allotment** *n* выделе́ние; (*land*) уча́сток.

**allow** *vt* разреша́ть *impf,* разреши́ть *pf;* (*let happen; concede*) допуска́ть *impf,* допусти́ть *pf;* **~ for** учи́тывать *impf,* уче́сть *pf.* **allowance** *n* (*financial*) посо́бие; (*deduction, also fig*) ски́дка; **make ~(s) for** учи́тывать *impf,* уче́сть *pf.*

**alloy** *n* сплав.

**all-round** *adj* разносторо́нний.

**allude** *vi* ссыла́ться *impf,* сосла́ться *pf* (**to** на+*acc*).

**allure** *vt* зама́нивать *impf,* замани́ть *pf.* **allure(ment)** *n* прима́нка. **alluring** *adj* зама́нчивый.

**allusion** *n* ссы́лка.

**ally** *n* сою́зник; *vt* соединя́ть *impf,* соедини́ть *pf;* **~ one-** self with вступа́ть *impf,* вступи́ть *pf* в сою́з с+*instr.*

**almighty** *adj* всемогу́щий.

**almond** *n* (*tree; pl collect*) минда́ль *m;* (*nut*) минда́льный оре́х.

**almost** *adv* почти́, едва́ не.

**alms** *n pl* ми́лостыня.

**aloft** *adv* наве́рх(-у́).

**alone** *predic* оди́н; (*lonely*) одино́к; *adv* то́лько; **leave ~** оставля́ть *impf,* оста́вить *pf* в поко́е; **let ~** не говоря́ уже́ о+*prep.*

**along** *prep* по+*dat,* (*position*) вдоль+*gen;* (*onward*) да́льше; **all ~** всё вре́мя; **~ with** вме́сте с+*instr.* **alongside** *adv* & *prep* ря́дом (с +*instr*).

**aloof** *predic* & *adv* (*distant*) сде́ржанный; (*apart*) в стороне́.

**aloud** *adv* вслух.

**alphabet** *n* алфави́т. **alphabetical** *adj* алфави́тный.

**alpine** *adj* альпи́йский.

**already** *adv* уже́.

**also** *adv* та́кже, то́же.

**altar** *n* алта́рь *m.*

**alter** *vt* (*modify*) переде́лывать *impf,* переде́лать *pf;* *vt & i* (*change*) изменя́ть(ся) *impf,* измени́ть(ся) *pf.* **alteration** *n* переде́лка; измене́ние.

**alternate** *adj* череду́ющийся; *vt & i* чередова́ть(ся) *impf;* **alternating current** переме́нный ток; **on ~ days** че́рез день. **alternation** *n* чередова́ние. **alternative** *n* альтернати́ва; *adj* альтернати́вный.

**although** *conj* хотя́.

**altitude** *n* высота́.

**alto** *n* альт.

**altogether** *adv* (*fully*) совсе́м;

*(in total)* всего́.

**altruistic** *adj* альтруисти́ческий.

**aluminium** *n* алюми́ний.

**always** *adv* всегда́; *(constantly)* постоя́нно.

**Alzheimer's disease** *n* боле́знь Альцге́ймера.

**a.m.** *abbr (morning)* утра́; *(night)* но́чи.

**amalgamate** *vt & i* слива́ть(ся) *impf*, сли́ть(ся) *pf*; *(chem)* амальгами́ровать(ся) *impf & pf*. **amalgamation** *n* слия́ние; *(chem)* амальгами́рование.

**amass** *vt* копи́ть *impf*, на~ *pf*.

**amateur** *n* люби́тель *m*, ~ница; *adj* люби́тельский. **amateurish** *adj* дилета́нтский.

**amaze** *vt* изумля́ть *impf*, изуми́ть *pf*. **amazement** *n* изумле́ние. **amazing** *adj* изуми́тельный.

**ambassador** *n* посо́л.

**amber** *n* янта́рь *m*.

**ambience** *n* среда́; атмосфе́ра.

**ambiguity** *n* двусмы́сленность. **ambiguous** *adj* двусмы́сленный.

**ambition** *n (quality)* честолю́бие; *(aim)* мечта́. **ambitious** *adj* честолюби́вый.

**amble** *vi* ходи́ть *indet*, идти́ *det* нетороп́ли́вым ша́гом.

**ambulance** *n* маши́на ско́рой по́мощи.

**ambush** *n* заса́да; *vt* напада́ть *impf*, напа́сть *pf* из заса́ды на+*acc*.

**ameliorate** *vt & i* улучша́ть(ся) *impf*, улу́чшить(ся) *pf*. **amelioration** *n* улучше́ние.

**amen** *int* ами́нь!

**amenable** *adj* сгово́рчивый

*(to +dat)*.

**amend** *vt (correct)* исправля́ть *impf*, испра́вить *pf*; *(change)* вноси́ть *impf*, внести́ *pf* попра́вки в+*acc*. **amendment** *n* попра́вка, исправле́ние. **amends** *n pl*: make ~ for загла́живать *impf*, загла́дить *pf*.

**amenities** *n pl* удо́бства *neut pl*.

**America** *n* Аме́рика. **American** *adj* америка́нский; *n* америка́нец, -нка. **Americanism** *n* американи́зм.

**amiable** *adj* любе́зный. **amicable** *adj* дружелю́бный.

**amid(st)** *prep* среди́+*gen*.

**amino acid** *n* аминокислота́.

**amiss** *adv* нела́дный; take ~ обижа́ться *impf*, оби́деться *pf* на+*acc*.

**ammonia** *n* аммиа́к; *(liquid* ~) нашаты́рный спирт.

**ammunition** *n* боеприпа́сы *m pl*.

**amnesia** *n* амнези́я.

**amnesty** *n* амни́стия.

**among(st)** *prep (amidst)* среди́+*gen*, *(between)* ме́жду+*instr*.

**amoral** *adj* амора́льный.

**amorous** *adj* влюблённый.

**amorphous** *adj* бесфо́рменный.

**amortization** *n* амортиза́ция.

**amount** *n* коли́чество; *vi*: ~ to составля́ть *impf*, соста́вить *pf*; *(be equivalent to)* быть равноси́льным+*dat*.

**ampere** *n* ампе́р.

**amphetamine** *n* амфетами́н.

**amphibian** *n* амфи́бия. **amphibious** *adj* земново́дный; *(mil)* плаваю́щий.

**amphitheatre** *n* амфитеа́тр.

**ample** *adj* доста́точный. **amplification** *n* усиле́ние.

**plifier** *n* усили́тель *m.* **amp-**
**lify** *vt* уси́ливать *impf*, уси́-
ли́ть *pf.* **amply** *adv* доста́-
точно.

**amputate** *vt* ампути́ровать
*impf* & *pf.* **amputation** *n*
ампута́ция.

**amuse** *vt* забавля́ть *impf*;
развлека́ть *impf*, развле́чь
*pf.* **amusement** *n* заба́ва,
развлече́ние; *pl* аттракцио́-
ны *m pl.* **amusing** *adj* за-
ба́вный; (*funny*) смешно́й.

**anachronism** *n* анахрони́зм.
**anachronistic** *adj* анахро-
ни́ческий.

**anaemia** *n* анеми́я. **anaemic**
*adj* анеми́чный.

**anaesthesia** *n* анестези́я. **an-**
**aesthetic** *n* обезбо́ливаю-
щее сре́дство. **anaesthetist**
*n* анестезио́лог. **anaesthet-**
**ize** *vt* анестези́ровать *impf*
& *pf.*

**anagram** *n* анагра́мма.

**analogous** *adj* аналоги́чный.
**analogue** *n* ана́лог. **analogy**
*n* анало́гия.

**analyse** *vt* анализи́ровать
*impf* & *pf.* **analysis** *n* ана́лиз.
**analyst** *n* анали́тик, психо-
анали́тик. **analytical** *adj* ана-
лити́ческий.

**anarchic** *adj* анархи́ческий.
**anarchist** *n* анархи́ст, ~ка,
*adj* анархи́стский. **anarchy**
*n* ана́рхия.

**anathema** *n* ана́фема.

**anatomical** *adj* анатоми́че-
ский. **anatomy** *n* анато́мия.

**ancestor** *n* пре́док. **ancestry**
*n* происхожде́ние.

**anchor** *n* я́корь *m*; *vt* ста́вить
*impf*, по~ *pf* на я́корь; *vi*
станови́ться *impf*, стать *pf*
на я́корь. **anchorage** *n* я́кор-
ная стоя́нка.

**anchovy** *n* анчо́ус.

**ancient** *adj* дре́вний, стари́н-
ный.

**and** *conj* и, (*but*) а; с+*instr*;
you ~ I мы с ва́ми; **my wife**
~ I мы с жено́й.

**anecdote** *n* анекдо́т.

**anew** *adv* сно́ва.

**angel** *n* а́нгел. **angelic** *adj*
а́нгельский.

**anger** *n* гнев; *vt* серди́ть *impf*,
рас~ *pf.*

**angina** *n* стенокарди́я.

**angle**[1] *n* у́гол; (*fig*) то́чка
зре́ния.

**angle**[2] *vi* уди́ть *impf* ры́бу.
**angler** *n* рыболо́в.

**angry** *adj* серди́тый.

**anguish** *n* страда́ние, му́ка.
**anguished** *adj* отча́янный.

**angular** *adj* углово́й; (*sharp*)
углова́тый.

**animal** *n* живо́тное *sb*; *adj*
живо́тный. **animate** *adj* жи-
во́й. **animated** *adj* оживлённый; ~ **cartoon** мульт-
фи́льм. **animation** *n* оживле́-
ние.

**animosity** *n* вражде́бность.

**ankle** *n* лоды́жка.

**annals** *n pl* ле́топись.

**annex** *vt* аннекси́ровать *impf*
& *pf.* **annexation** *n* анне́к-
сия. **annexe** *n* пристро́йка.

**annihilate** *vt* уничтожа́ть
*impf*, уничто́жить *pf.* **anni-**
**hilation** *n* уничтоже́ние.

**anniversary** *n* годовщи́на.

**annotate** *vt* комменти́ровать
*impf* & *pf.* **annotated** *adj* сна-
бжённый коммента́риями.
**annotation** *n* аннота́ция.

**announce** *vt* объявля́ть *impf*,
объяви́ть *pf*; заявля́ть *impf*,
заяви́ть *pf*; (*radio*) сообща́ть
*impf*, сообщи́ть *pf.* **announce-**
**ment** *n* объявле́ние; сообще́-

ние. **announcer** *n* ди́ктор.

**annoy** *vt* досажда́ть *impf*, досади́ть *pf*; раздража́ть *impf*, раздражи́ть *pf*. **annoyance** *n* доса́да. **annoying** *adj* доса́дный.

**annual** *adj* ежего́дный, (*of a given year*) годово́й; *n* (*book*) ежего́дник, (*bot*) одноле́тник. **annually** *adv* ежего́дно. **annuity** *n* (ежего́дная) ре́нта.

**annul** *vt* аннули́ровать *impf* & *pf*. **annulment** *n* аннули́рование.

**anoint** *vt* пома́зывать *impf*, пома́зать *pf*.

**anomalous** *adj* анома́льный. **anomaly** *n* анома́лия.

**anonymous** *adj* анони́мный. **anonymity** *n* анони́мность.

**anorak** *n* ку́ртка.

**anorexia** *n* анорекси́я.

**another** *adj*, *pron* друго́й; ~ **one** ещё (оди́н); **in ~ ten years** ещё че́рез де́сять лет.

**answer** *n* отве́т; *vt* отвеча́ть *impf*, отве́тить *pf* (*person*) +*dat*, (*question*) на+*acc*; ~ **the door** отворя́ть *impf*, отвори́ть *pf* дверь; ~ **the phone** подходи́ть *impf*, подойти́ *pf* к телефо́ну. **answerable** *adj* отве́тственный. **answering machine** *n* телефо́н-отве́тчик.

**ant** *n* мураве́й.

**antagonism** *n* антагони́зм. **antagonistic** *adj* антагонисти́ческий. **antagonize** *vt* настра́ивать *impf*, настро́ить *pf* про́тив себя́.

**Antarctic** *n* Анта́рктика.

**antelope** *n* антило́па.

**antenna** *n* у́сик, (*also radio*) анте́нна.

**anthem** *n* гимн.

**anthology** *n* антоло́гия.

**anthracite** *n* антраци́т.

**anthropological** *adj* антрополо́гический. **anthropologist** *n* антропо́лог. **anthropology** *n* антрополо́гия.

**anti-aircraft** *adj* зени́тный. **antibiotic** *n* антибио́тик. **antibody** *n* антите́ло. **anticlimax** *n* разочарова́ние. **anticlockwise** *adj* & *adv* про́тив часово́й стре́лки. **antidepressant** *n* антидепресса́нт. **antidote** *n* противоя́дие. **antifreeze** *n* антифри́з. **antipathy** *n* антипа́тия. **anti-Semitic** *adj* антисеми́тский. **anti-Semitism** *n* антисемити́зм. **antiseptic** *adj* антисепти́ческий; *n* антисе́птик. **antisocial** *adj* асоциа́льный. **anti-tank** *adj* противота́нковый. **antithesis** *n* противополо́жность; (*philos*) антите́зис.

**anticipate** *vt* ожида́ть *impf* +*gen*; (*with pleasure*) предвкуша́ть *impf*, предвкуси́ть *pf*; (*forestall*) предупрежда́ть *impf*, предупреди́ть *pf*. **anticipation** *n* ожида́ние; предвкуше́ние; предупрежде́ние.

**antics** *n* вы́ходки *f pl*.

**antiquarian** *adj* антиква́рный. **antiquated** *adj* устаре́лый. **antique** *adj* стари́нный; *n* антиква́рная вещь; ~ **shop** антиква́рный магази́н. **antiquity** *n* дре́вность.

**antler** *n* оле́ний рог.

**anus** *n* за́дний прохо́д.

**anvil** *n* накова́льня.

**anxiety** *n* беспоко́йство. **anxious** *adj* беспоко́йный; **be ~** беспоко́иться *impf*; трево́житься *impf*.

**any** *adj*, *pron* (*some*) како́й-

нибудь; ско́лько-нибудь; (every) вся́кий, любо́й; (anybody) кто́-нибудь, (anything) что́-нибудь; (with neg) никако́й, ни оди́н; ниско́лько; никто́, ничто́; adv ско́лько-нибудь; (with neg) ниско́лько, ничу́ть.
**anybody, anyone** pron кто́-нибудь; (everybody) вся́кий, любо́й; (with neg) никто́. **anyhow** adv ка́к-нибудь; ко́е-как; (with neg) ника́к; во вся́ком слу́чае; всё равно́. **anyone** see anybody. **anything** pron что́-нибудь, всё (что уго́дно); (with neg) ничего́. **anyway** adv во вся́ком слу́чае; как бы то ни́ бы́ло. **anywhere** adv где́-куда́ уго́дно; (with neg, interrog) где́-нибудь, куда́-нибудь.
**apart** adv (aside) в стороне́, в сто́рону; (separately) врозь; (distant) друг от дру́га; (into pieces) на ча́сти; ~ **from** кро́ме+gen.
**apartheid** n апарте́й.
**apartment** n (flat) кварти́ра.
**apathetic** adj апати́чный. **apathy** n апа́тия.
**ape** n обезья́на; vt обезья́нничать impf, с~ pf c+gen.
**aperture** n отве́рстие.
**apex** n верши́на.
**aphorism** n афори́зм.
**apiece** adv (per person) на ка́ждого; (per thing) за шту́ку; (amount) по+dat or acc with numbers.
**aplomb** n апло́мб.
**Apocalypse** n Апока́липсис. **apocalyptic** adj апокалипти́ческий.
**apologetic** adj извиня́ющийся; be ~ извиня́ться impf.
**apologize** vi извиня́ться impf, извини́ться pf (to пе́ред +instr;

for за+acc). **apology** n извине́ние.
**apostle** n апо́стол.
**apostrophe** n апостро́ф.
**appal** vt ужаса́ть impf, ужасну́ть pf. **appalling** adj ужа́сный.
**apparatus** аппара́т; прибо́р; (gymnastic) гимнасти́ческие снаря́ды m pl.
**apparel** n оде́яние.
**apparent** adj (seeming) ви́димый; (manifest) очеви́дный. **apparently** adv ка́жется, по-ви́димому.
**apparition** n виде́ние.
**appeal** n (request) призы́в, обраще́ние; (law) апелля́ция, обжа́лование; (attraction) привлека́тельность; ~ **court** апелляцио́нный суд; vi (request) взыва́ть impf, воззва́ть pf (**to** к+dat; **for** о+prep); обраща́ться impf, обрати́ться pf (с призы́вом); (law) апелли́ровать impf & pf; ~ **to** (attract) привлека́ть impf, привле́чь pf.
**appear** vi появля́ться impf, появи́ться pf; (in public) выступа́ть impf, вы́ступить pf; (seem) каза́ться impf, по-pf. **appearance** n появле́ние; (aspect) вид.
**appease** vt умиротворя́ть impf, умиротвори́ть pf.
**append** vt прилага́ть impf, приложи́ть pf. **appendicitis** n аппендици́т. **appendix** n приложе́ние; (anat) аппе́ндикс.
**appertain** vi: ~ **to** относи́ться impf +dat.
**appetite** n аппети́т. **appetizing** adj аппети́тный.
**applaud** vt аплоди́ровать impf +dat. **applause** n апло-

дисме́нты *m pl.

**apple** *n* я́блоко; *adj* я́блочный; ~ **tree** я́блоня.

**appliance** *n* прибо́р. **applicable** *adj* примени́мый. **applicant** *n* кандида́т. **application** *n* (*use*) примене́ние; (*putting on*) наложе́ние; (*request*) заявле́ние. **applied** *adj* прикладно́й. **apply** *vt* (*use*) применя́ть *impf*, примени́ть *pf*; (*put on*) накла́дывать *impf*, наложи́ть *pf*; *vi* (*request*) обраща́ться *impf*, обрати́ться *pf* (**to** k+*dat*; **for** +*acc*); ~ **for** (*job*) подава́ть *impf*, пода́ть *pf* заявле́ние на+*acc*; ~ **to** относи́ться *impf* k+*dat*.

**appoint** *vt* назнача́ть *impf*, назна́чить *pf*. **appointment** *n* назначе́ние; (*job*) до́лжность; (*meeting*) свида́ние.

**apposite** *adj* уме́стный.

**appraise** *vt* оце́нивать *impf*, оцени́ть *pf*.

**appreciable** *adj* заме́тный; (*considerable*) значи́тельный. **appreciate** *vt* цени́ть *impf*; (*understand*) понима́ть *impf*, поня́ть *pf*; *vi* повыша́ться *impf*, повыситься *pf* в цене́. **appreciation** *n* (*estimation*) оце́нка; (*gratitude*) призна́тельность; (*rise in value*) повыше́ние цены́. **appreciative** *adj* призна́тельный (**of** за+*acc*).

**apprehension** *n* (*fear*) опасе́ние. **apprehensive** *adj* опаса́ющийся.

**apprentice** *n* учени́к; *vt* отдава́ть *impf*, отда́ть *pf* в уче́ние. **apprenticeship** *n* уче́ничество.

**approach** *vt & i* подходи́ть *impf*, подойти́ *pf* (k+*dat*); приближа́ться *impf*, прибли́зить-

ся *pf* (k+*dat*); *vt* (*apply to*) обраща́ться *impf*, обрати́ться *pf* k+*dat*; *n* приближе́ние; подхо́д; подъе́зд; (*access*) до́ступ.

**approbation** *n* одобре́ние.

**appropriate** *adj* подходя́щий; *vt* присва́ивать *impf*, присво́ить *pf*. **appropriation** *n* присвое́ние.

**approval** *n* одобре́ние; **on** ~ на про́бу. **approve** *vt* утвержда́ть *impf*, утверди́ть *pf*; *vt & i* (~ **of**) одобря́ть *impf*, одо́брить *pf*.

**approximate** *adj* приблизи́тельный; *vi* приближа́ться *impf* (**to** k+*dat*). **approximation** *n* приближе́ние.

**apricot** *n* абрико́с.

**April** *n* апре́ль *m*; *adj* апре́льский.

**apron** *n* пере́дник.

**apropos** *adv*: ~ **of** по по́воду+*gen*.

**apt** *adj* (*suitable*) уда́чный; (*inclined*) скло́нный. **aptitude** *n* спосо́бность.

**aqualung** *n* аквала́нг. **aquarium** *n* аква́риум. **Aquarius** *n* Водоле́й. **aquatic** *adj* водяно́й; (*of sport*) во́дный. **aqueduct** *n* акведу́к.

**aquiline** *adj* орли́ный.

**Arab** *n* ара́б, ~ка; *adj* ара́бский. **Arabian** *adj* арави́йский. **Arabic** *adj* ара́бский.

**arable** *adj* па́хотный.

**arbitrary** *adj* произво́льный. **arbitrate** *vi* де́йствовать *impf* в ка́честве трете́йского судьи́. **arbitration** *n* арбитра́ж, трете́йское реше́ние. **arbitrator** *n* арби́тр, трете́йский судья́ *m*.

**arc** *n* дуга́. **arcade** *n* арка́да, (*shops*) пасса́ж.

**arch**[1] *n* а́рка, свод; (*of foot*) свод стопы́; *vt* & *i* выгиба́ть(ся) *impf*, вы́гнуть(ся) *pf*.

**arch**[2] *adj* игри́вый.

**archaeological** *adj* археологи́ческий. **archaeologist** *n* архео́лог. **archaeology** *n* археоло́гия.

**archaic** *adj* архаи́ческий.

**archangel** *n* арха́нгел.

**archbishop** *n* архиепи́скоп.

**arched** *adj* сво́дчатый.

**arch-enemy** *n* закля́тый враг.

**archer** *n* стрело́к из лу́ка. **archery** *n* стрельба́ из лу́ка.

**archipelago** *n* архипела́г.

**architect** *n* архите́ктор. **architectural** *adj* архитекту́рный. **architecture** *n* архитекту́ра.

**archive(s)** *n* архи́в.

**archway** *n* сво́дчатый прохо́д.

**Arctic** *adj* аркти́ческий; *n* А́рктика.

**ardent** *adj* горя́чий. **ardour** *n* пыл.

**arduous** *adj* тру́дный.

**area** *n* (*extent*) пло́щадь; (*region*) райо́н; (*sphere*) о́бласть.

**arena** *n* аре́на.

**argue** *vt* (*maintain*) утвержда́ть *impf*; доказывать *impf*; *vi* спо́рить *impf*, по~ *pf*. **argument** *n* (*dispute*) спор; (*reason*) до́вод. **argumentative** *adj* любящий спо́рить.

**aria** *n* а́рия.

**arid** *adj* сухо́й.

**Aries** *n* Ове́н.

**arise** *vi* возника́ть *impf*, возни́кнуть *pf*.

**aristocracy** *n* аристокра́тия. **aristocrat** *n* аристокра́т, ~ка. **aristocratic** *adj* аристократи́ческий.

**arithmetic** *n* арифме́тика. ar-

ithmetical *adj* арифмети́ческий.

**ark** *n* (Но́ев) ковче́г.

**arm**[1] *n* (*of body*) рука́; (*of chair*) ру́чка; ~ in ~ по́д руку; at ~'s length (*fig*) на почти́тельном расстоя́нии; with open ~s с распростёртыми объя́тиями.

**arm**[2] *n pl* (*weapons*) ору́жие; *pl* (*coat of ~s*) герб; *vt* вооружа́ть *impf*, вооружи́ть *pf*. **armaments** *n pl* вооруже́ние.

**armchair** *n* кре́сло.

**Armenia** *n* Арме́ния. **Armenian** *n* армяни́н, армя́нка; *adj* армя́нский.

**armistice** *n* переми́рие.

**armour** *n* (*for body*) доспе́хи *m pl*; (*for vehicles*) броня́. **armoured** *adj* брониро́ванный; (*vehicles only*) бронета́нковый, броне-; ~ car броневи́к. **armoury** *n* арсена́л.

**armpit** *n* подмы́шка.

**army** *n* а́рмия; *adj* арме́йский.

**aroma** *n* арома́т. **aromatic** *adj* аромати́ческий.

**around** *adv* круго́м; *prep* вокру́г+*gen*; all ~ повсю́ду.

**arouse** *vt* (*wake up*) буди́ть *impf*, раз~ *pf*; (*stimulate*) возбужда́ть *impf*, возбуди́ть *pf*.

**arrange** *vt* расставля́ть *impf*, расста́вить *pf*; (*plan*) устра́ивать *impf*, устро́ить *pf*; (*mus*) аранжи́ровать *impf* & *pf*; *vi*: ~ to догова́риваться *impf*, договори́ться *pf* +*inf*. **arrangement** *n* расположе́ние; устро́йство; (*agreement*) соглаше́ние; (*mus*) аранжиро́вка; *pl* приготовле́ния *neut pl*.

**array** *vt* выставля́ть *impf*, вы́ставить *pf*; *n* (*dress*) на-

ряд; (*display*) колле́кция.
**arrears** n pl задо́лженность.
**arrest** vt аресто́вывать impf, арестова́ть pf; n аре́ст.
**arrival** n прибы́тие, прие́зд; (*new ~*) вновь прибы́вший sb. **arrive** vi прибыва́ть impf, прибы́ть pf; приезжа́ть impf, прие́хать pf.
**arrogance** n высокоме́рие. **arrogant** adj высокоме́рный.
**arrow** n стрела́; (*pointer*) стре́лка.
**arsenal** n арсена́л.
**arsenic** n мышья́к.
**arson** n поджо́г.
**art** n иску́сство; pl гуманита́рные нау́ки f pl; adj худо́жественный.
**arterial** adj: ~ **road** магистра́ль. **artery** n арте́рия.
**artful** adj хи́трый.
**arthritis** n артри́т.
**article** n (*literary*) статья́; (*clause*) пункт; (*thing*) предме́т; (*gram*) арти́кль m.
**articulate** vt произноси́ть impf, произнести́ pf; (*express*) выража́ть impf, вы́разить pf; adj (*of speech*) членоразде́льный; **be ~** чётко выража́ть impf свои́ мы́сли. **articulated lorry** n грузово́й автомоби́ль с прице́пом.
**artifice** n хи́трость. **artificial** adj иску́сственный.
**artillery** n артилле́рия.
**artisan** n реме́сленник.
**artist** n худо́жник. **artiste** n арти́ст, ~ка. **artistic** adj худо́жественный.
**artless** adj простоду́шный.
**as** adv как; conj (*when*) когда́, в то вре́мя как; (*because*) так как; (*manner*) как; (*though, however*) как ни; rel pron ка

кой; кото́рый; что; **as ... as** так (же)... как; **as for, to** относи́тельно+gen; что каса́ется+gen; что бу́дто; **as it were** как бы; так сказа́ть; **as soon as** как то́лько; **as well** та́кже; то́же.
**asbestos** n асбе́ст.
**ascend** vt (*go up*) поднима́ться impf, подня́ться pf +dat; (*throne*) восходи́ть impf, взойти́ pf на+acc; vi возноси́ться impf, вознести́сь pf в власть. **Ascension** n (*eccl*) Вознесе́ние. **ascent** n восхожде́ние (**of** на+acc).
**ascertain** vt устана́вливать impf, установи́ть pf.
**ascetic** adj аскети́ческий; n аске́т. **asceticism** n аскети́зм.
**ascribe** vt припи́сывать impf, приписа́ть pf (**to** +dat).
**ash**[1] n (*tree*) я́сень m.
**ash**[2], **ashes** n зола́, пе́пел; (*human remains*) прах. **ashtray** n пе́пельница.
**ashamed** predic: **he is ~** ему́ сты́дно; **be, feel, ~ of** стыди́ться impf +gen; po~ pf +gen.
**ashen** adj (*pale*) ме́ртвенно-бле́дный.
**ashore** adv на бе́рег(у́).
**Asia** n А́зия. **Asian, Asiatic** adj азиа́тский; n азиа́т, ~ка.
**aside** adv в сто́рону.
**ask** vt & i (*enquire of*) спра́шивать impf, спроси́ть pf; (*request*) проси́ть impf, по~ pf (**for** acc, gen, o+prep); (*invite*) приглаша́ть impf, пригласи́ть pf; (*demand*) тре́бовать impf +gen (**of** от+gen); **~ after** осведомля́ться impf, осве́домиться pf o+prep; **~ a question** задава́ть impf,

задáть *pf* вопрóс.
**askance** *adv* кóсо.
**askew** *adv* кри́во.
**asleep** *predic & adv*: be ~ спать *impf*; fall ~ засыпáть *impf*, заснýть *pf*.
**asparagus** *n* спáржа.
**aspect** *n* вид; (*side*) сторонá.
**aspersion** *n* клеветá.
**asphalt** *n* асфáльт.
**asphyxiate** *vt* удушáть *impf*, удуши́ть.
**aspiration** *n* стремлéние. **aspire** *vi* стреми́ться *impf* (to к+*dat*).
**aspirin** *n* аспири́н; (*tablet*) таблéтка аспири́на.
**ass** *n* осёл.
**assail** *vt* нападáть *impf*, напáсть *pf* на+*acc*; (*with questions*) забрáсывать *impf*, забросáть *pf* вопрóсами. **assailant** *n* нападáющий *sb*.
**assassin** *n* уби́йца *m & f*. **assassinate** *vt* убивáть *impf*, уби́ть *pf*. **assassination** *n* уби́йство.
**assault** *n* нападéние; (*mil*) штурм; ~ and battery оскорблéние дéйствием; *vt* нападáть *impf*, напáсть *pf* на+*acc*.
**assemblage** *n* сбóрка. **assemble** *vt & i* собирáть(ся) *impf*, собрáть(ся) *pf* (*of machine*) сбóрка.
**assent** *vi* соглашáться *impf*, согласи́ться *pf* (to на+*acc*) *n* соглáсие.
**assert** *vt* утверждáть *impf*; ~ o.s. отстáивать *impf*, отстоя́ть *pf* свои́ правá. **assertion** *n* утверждéние. **assertive** *adj* насто́йчивый.
**assess** *vt* (*amount*) определя́ть *impf*, определи́ть *pf*; (*value*) оцéнивать *impf*, оце-

ни́ть *pf*. **assessment** *n* определéние; оцéнка.
**asset** *n* цéнное кáчество; (*comm*; *also pl*) акти́в.
**assiduous** *adj* приле́жный.
**assign** *vt* (*appoint*) назначáть *impf*, назнáчить *pf*; (*allot*) отводи́ть *impf*, отвести́ *pf*. **assignation** *n* свидáние. **assignment** *n* (*task*) задáние; (*mission*) командирóвка.
**assimilate** *vt* усвáивать *impf*, усвóить *pf*. **assimilation** *n* усвоéние.
**assist** *vt* помогáть *impf*, помóчь *pf* +*dat*. **assistance** *n* пóмощь. **assistant** *n* помóщник, ассистéнт.
**associate** *vt* ассоции́ровать *impf & pf*; *vi* общáться *impf* (with c+*instr*) *n* колле́га *m & f*. **association** *n* óбщество, ассоциáция.
**assorted** *adj* рáзный. **assortment** *n* ассортимéнт.
**assuage** *vt* (*calm*) успокáивать *impf*, успокóить *pf*; (*alleviate*) смягчáть *impf*, смягчи́ть *pf*.
**assume** *vt* (*take on*) принимáть *impf*, приня́ть *pf*; (*suppose*) предполагáть *impf*, предположи́ть *pf*; ~d name вымышленное и́мя *neut*; let us ~ допýстим. **assumption** *n* (*taking on*) приня́тие на себя́; (*supposition*) предположéние.
**assurance** *n* заверéние; (*self-* ~) самоуве́ренность; (*insurance*) страховáние. **assure** *vt* уверя́ть *impf*, уве́рить *pf*.
**asterisk** *n* звёздочка.
**asthma** *n* áстма. **asthmatic** *adj* астмати́ческий.
**astonish** *vt* удивля́ть *impf*, удиви́ть *pf*. **astonishing** *adj*

удиви́тельный. **astonishment** *n* удивле́ние.

**astound** *vt* изумля́ть *impf*, изуми́ть *pf*. **astounding** *adj* изуми́тельный.

**astray** *adv*: go ~ сбива́ться *impf*, сби́ться *pf* с пути́; lead ~ сбива́ть *impf*, сбить *pf* с пути́.

**astride** *prep* верхо́м на+*prep*.

**astringent** *adj* вя́жущий; те́рпкий.

**astrologer** *n* астро́лог. **astrology** *n* астроло́гия. **astronaut** *n* астрона́вт. **astronomer** *n* астроно́м. **astronomical** *adj* астрономи́ческий. **astronomy** *n* астроно́мия.

**astute** *adj* проница́тельный.

**asunder** *adv* (*apart*) врозь; (*in pieces*) на ча́сти.

**asylum** *n* сумасше́дший дом; (*refuge*) убе́жище.

**asymmetrical** *adj* асимметри́чный. **asymmetry** *n* асимме́трия.

**at** *prep* (*position*) на+*prep*, в+*prep*, у+*gen*: at a concert на конце́рте; at the cinema в кино́; at the window у окна́; (*time*) в+*acc*: at two o'clock в два часа́; at Easter на Па́сху; (*price*) по+*dat*: at 5p a pound по пяти́ пе́нсов за фунт; (*speed*): at 60 mph со ско́ростью шестьдеся́т миль в час; ~ first снача́ла, сперва́; ~ home до́ма; ~ last наконе́ц; ~ least по кра́йней ме́ре; ~ that на том; (*moreover*) к тому́ же.

**atheism** *n* атеи́зм. **atheist** *n* атеи́ст, ~ка.

**athlete** *n* спортсме́н, ~ка. **athletic** *adj* атлети́ческий. **athletics** *n* (лёгкая) атле́тика.

**atlas** *n* а́тлас.

**atmosphere** *n* атмосфе́ра. **atmospheric** *adj* атмосфе́рный.

**atom** *n* а́том; ~ bomb а́томная бо́мба. **atomic** *adj* а́томный.

**atone** *vi* искупа́ть *impf*, искупи́ть *pf* (for +*acc*). **atonement** *n* искупле́ние.

**atrocious** *adj* ужа́сный. **atrocity** *n* зве́рство.

**attach** *vt* (*fasten*) прикрепля́ть *impf*, прикрепи́ть *pf*; (*append*) прилага́ть *impf*, приложи́ть *pf*; (*attribute*) придава́ть *impf*, прида́ть *pf*; **~ed to** (*devoted*) привя́занный к+*dat*. **attaché** *n* атташе́ *m indecl*. **attachment** *n* прикрепле́ние; привя́занность; (*tech*) принадле́жность.

**attack** *vt* напада́ть *impf*, напа́сть *pf* на+*acc*; *n* нападе́ние; (*of illness*) припа́док.

**attain** *vt* достига́ть *impf*, дости́чь & дости́гнуть *pf* +*gen*. **attainment** *n* достиже́ние.

**attempt** *vt* пыта́ться *impf*, по~ *pf* +*inf*; *n* попы́тка.

**attend** *vt & i* (*be present at*) прису́тствовать *impf* (на+*prep*); *vt* (*accompany*) сопровожда́ть *impf*, сопроводи́ть *pf*; (*go to regularly*) посеща́ть *impf*, посети́ть *pf*; ~ to занима́ться *impf*, заня́ться *pf*. **attendance** *n* (*presence*) прису́тствие; (*number*) посеща́емость. **attendant** *adj* сопровожда́ющий; *n* дежу́рный *sb*; (*escort*) провожа́тый *sb*.

**attention** *n* внима́ние; **pay** ~ обраща́ть *impf*, обрати́ть *pf* внима́ние (to на+*acc*); *int* (*mil*) сми́рно! **attentive**

вни́ма́тельный; (*solicitous*) забо́тливый.

**attest** vt & i (*also* ~ **to**) заверя́ть *impf*, заве́рить *pf*; свиде́тельствовать *impf*, за~ *pf* (o+*prep*).

**attic** n черда́к.

**attire** vt наряжа́ть *impf*, наряди́ть *pf*; n наря́д.

**attitude** n (*posture*) по́за; (*opinion*) отноше́ние (*towards* к+*dat*).

**attorney** n пове́ренный *sb*; **power of** ~ дове́ренность.

**attract** vt привлека́ть *impf*, привле́чь *pf*. **attraction** n привлека́тельность; (*entertainment*) аттракцио́н. **attractive** *adj* привлека́тельный.

**attribute** vt припи́сывать *impf*, приписа́ть *pf*; n (*quality*) сво́йство. **attribution** n припи́сывание. **attributive** *adj* атрибути́вный.

**attrition** n: **war of** ~ война́ на истоще́ние.

**aubergine** n баклажа́н.

**auburn** *adj* тёмно-ры́жий.

**auction** n аукцио́н; vt продава́ть *impf*, прода́ть *pf* с аукцио́на. **auctioneer** n аукциони́ст.

**audacious** *adj* (*bold*) сме́лый; (*impudent*) де́рзкий. **audacity** n сме́лость; де́рзость.

**audible** *adj* слы́шный. **audience** n пу́блика, аудито́рия; (*listeners*) слу́шатели *m pl*; (*viewers, spectators*) зри́тели *m pl*; (*interview*) аудие́нция.

**audit** n прове́рка счето́в, реви́зия; vt проверя́ть *impf*, прове́рить *pf* (счета́+*gen*). **audition** n про́ба; vt устра́ивать *impf*, устро́ить *pf* про́бу +*gen*. **auditor** n ревизо́р. **auditorium** n зри́тельный зал.

**augment** vt увели́чивать *impf*, увели́чить *pf*.

**augur** vt & i предвеща́ть *impf*.

**August** n а́вгуст; *adj* а́вгустовский. **august** *adj* вели́чественный.

**aunt** n тётя, тётка.

**au pair** n домрабо́тница иностра́нного происхожде́ния.

**aura** n орео́л.

**auspices** n pl покрови́тельство. **auspicious** *adj* благоприя́тный.

**austere** *adj* стро́гий. **austerity** n стро́гость.

**Australia** n Австра́лия. **Australian** n австрали́ец, -и́йка; *adj* австрали́йский.

**Austria** n А́встрия. **Austrian** n австри́ец, -и́йка; *adj* австри́йский.

**authentic** *adj* по́длинный. **authenticate** vt устана́вливать *impf*, установи́ть *pf* по́длинность+*gen*. **authenticity** n по́длинность.

**author, authoress** n а́втор.

**authoritarian** *adj* авторита́рный. **authoritative** *adj* авторите́тный. **authority** n (*power*) власть, полномо́чие; (*weight, expert*) авторите́т; (*source*) авторите́тный исто́чник. **authorization** n уполномо́чивание; (*permission*) разреше́ние. **authorize** vt (*action*) разреша́ть *impf*, разреши́ть *pf*; (*person*) уполномо́чивать *impf*, уполномо́чить *pf*. **authorship** n а́вторство.

**autobiographical** *adj* автобиографи́ческий. **autobiography** n автобиогра́фия. **autocracy** n автокра́тия. **autocrat** n автокра́т. **autocratic** *adj* автократи́ческий. **autograph** n авто́граф. **automatic** *adj* автомати́ческий. **automation** n автоматиза́ция. **automaton** n автома́т. **automobile** n автомоби́ль m. **autonomous** adj автоно́мный. **autonomy** n автоно́мия. **autopilot** n автопило́т. **autopsy** n вскры́тие; ауто́псия.

**autumn** n о́сень. **autumn(al)** adj осе́нний.

**auxiliary** adj вспомога́тельный; n помо́щник, -ица.

**avail** n: to no ~ напра́сно; vt: ~ o.s. of по́льзоваться impf, вос~ pf +instr. **available** adj досту́пный, нали́чный.

**avalanche** n лави́на.

**avant-garde** n аванга́рд; adj аванга́рдный.

**avarice** n жа́дность. **avaricious** adj жа́дный.

**avenge** vt мстить impf, ото~ pf за+acc. **avenger** n мсти́тель m.

**avenue** n (of trees) алле́я; (wide street) проспе́кт; (means) путь m.

**average** n сре́днее число́, сре́днее sb; on ~ в сре́днем; adj сре́дний; vt де́лать impf в сре́днем; vt & i: ~ (out at) составля́ть impf, соста́вить pf в сре́днем.

**averse** adj: not ~ to не прочь +inf; не про́тив+gen. **aversion** n отвраще́ние. **avert** vt (ward off) предотвраща́ть impf, предотврати́ть pf; (turn away) отводи́ть impf, отвести́ pf.

**aviary** n пти́чник.

**aviation** n авиа́ция.

**avid** adj жа́дный; (keen) стра́стный.

**avocado** n авока́до neut indecl.

**avoid** vt избега́ть impf, избежа́ть pf +gen; (evade) укло-

ня́ться impf, уклони́ться pf от+gen. **avoidance** n избежа́ние, уклоне́ние.

**avowal** n призна́ние. **avowed** adj при́знанный.

**await** vt ждать impf +gen.

**awake** predic: be ~ не спать impf. **awake(n)** vt пробужда́ть impf, пробуди́ть pf; vi просыпа́ться impf, просну́ться pf.

**award** vt присужда́ть impf, присуди́ть pf (person dat, thing acc); награжда́ть impf, награди́ть pf (person acc, thing instr); n награ́да.

**aware** predic: be ~ of созна́вать impf; знать impf. **awareness** n созна́ние.

**away** adv прочь; be ~ отсу́тствовать impf; far ~ (from) далеко́ (от+gen); 5 miles ~ в пяти́ ми́лях отсю́да; ~ game игра́ на чужо́м по́ле.

**awe** n благогове́йный страх. **awful** adj ужа́сный. **awfully** adv ужа́сно.

**awhile** adv не́которое вре́мя.

**awkward** adj нело́вкий. **awkwardness** n нело́вкость.

**awning** n наве́с, тент.

**awry** adv ко́со.

**axe** n топо́р; vt уре́зывать, уреза́ть impf, уре́зать pf.

**axiom** n аксио́ма. **axiomatic** adj аксиомати́ческий.

**axis, axle** n ось.

**ay** int да!; n (in vote) го́лос "за".

**Azerbaijan** n Азербайджа́н. **Azerbaijani** n азербайджа́нец (-нца), -а́нка; adj азербайджа́нский.

**azure** n лазу́рь; adj лазу́рный.

# B

**BA** abbr (univ) бакала́вр.
**babble** n (voices) болтовня́; (water) журча́ние; vi болта́ть impf; (water) журча́ть impf.
**baboon** n павиа́н.
**baby** n ребёнок; ~-sit присма́тривать за детьми́ в отсу́тствие роди́телей; ~-sitter приходя́щая ня́ня.
**babyish** adj ребя́ческий.
**bachelor** n холостя́к; (univ) бакала́вр.
**bacillus** n баци́лла.
**back** n (of body) спина́; (rear) за́дняя часть; (reverse) оборо́т; (of seat) спи́нка; (sport) защи́тник; adj за́дний; vt (support) подде́рживать impf, поддержа́ть pf; (car) отодвига́ть impf, отодви́нуть pf; (horse) ста́вить impf, по~ pf на+acc; (finance) финанси́ровать impf & pf; vi отодвига́ться impf, отодви́нуться pf наза́д; **backed out of the garage** вы́ехал за́дом из гара́жа; ~ **down** уступа́ть impf, уступи́ть pf; ~ **out** уклоня́ться impf, уклони́ться pf (of от+gen); ~ **up** (support) подде́рживать impf, поддержа́ть pf; (confirm) подкрепля́ть impf, подкрепи́ть pf. **backbiting** n спле́тня. **backbone** n позвоно́чник; (support) гла́вная опо́ра; (firmness) твёрдость хара́ктера. **backcloth, backdrop** n за́дник; (fig) фон. **backer** n спо́нсор; (supporter) сторо́нник. **backfire** vi дава́ть impf, дать pf отсе́чку. **background**

n фон, за́дний план; (person's) происхожде́ние. **backhand(er)** n уда́р сле́ва. **backhanded** adj (fig) сомни́тельный. **backhander** n (bribe) взя́тка. **backing** n подде́ржка. **backlash** n реа́кция. **backlog** n задо́лженность. **backside** n зад. **backstage** adv за кули́сами; adj закули́сный. **backstroke** n пла́вание на спине́. **back-up** n подде́ржка; (copy) резе́рвная ко́пия; adj вспомога́тельный. **backward** adj отста́лый. **backward(s)** adv наза́д. **backwater** n заво́дь. **back yard** n за́дний двор.
**bacon** n беко́н.
**bacterium** n бакте́рия.
**bad** adj плохо́й; (food etc.) испо́рченный; (language) гру́бый; ~-mannered невоспи́танный; ~ **taste** безвку́сица; ~-tempered раздражи́тельный.
**badge** n значо́к.
**badger** n барсу́к; vt трави́ть impf, за~ pf.
**badly** adv пло́хо; (very much) о́чень.
**badminton** n бадминто́н.
**baffle** vt озада́чивать impf, озада́чить pf.
**bag** n (handbag) су́мка; (plastic ~, sack, under eyes) мешо́к; (paper ~) бума́жный паке́т; pl (luggage) бага́ж.
**baggage** n бага́ж.
**baggy** adj мешкова́тый.
**bagpipe** n волы́нка.
**bail[1]** n (security) поручи́тельство; **release on** ~ отпуска́ть impf, отпусти́ть pf на пору́ки; vt (~ out) брать impf, взять pf на пору́ки; (help) выруча́ть impf, вы́ручить pf.

**bail²**, **bale²** vt вычёрпывать impf, вычерпнуть pf (вóду из+gen); ~ **out** vi выбрасываться impf, выброситься pf с парашютом.

**bailiff** n судéбный исполнитель.

**bait** n нажива; примáнка (also fig); vt (torment) травить impf, за~ pf.

**bake** vt & i пéчь(ся) impf, ис~ pf. **baker** n пéкарь m, бýлочник. **bakery** n пекáрня; (shop) бýлочная sb.

**balalaika** n балалáйка.

**balance** n (scales) весы́ m pl; (equilibrium) равновéсие; (econ) балáнс; (remainder) остáток; ~ **sheet** балáнс; vt (make equal) уравновéшивать impf, уравновéсить pf; vt & i (econ; hold steady) балансировать impf, c~ pf.

**balcony** n балкóн.

**bald** adj лы́сый; ~ **patch** лы́сина. **balding** adj лысéющий. **baldness** n плешивость.

**bale¹** n (bundle) кипá.

**bale²** see **bail²**

**balk** vi артáчиться impf, за~ pf; **she balked at the price** ценá её испугáла.

**ball¹** n (in games) мяч; (sphere; billiards) шар; (wool) клубóк; ~**bearing** шарикоподшипник; ~**point (pen)** шáриковая рýчка.

**ball²** n (dance) бал.

**ballad** n баллáда.

**ballast** n баллáст.

**ballerina** n балери́на.

**ballet** n балéт. **ballet-dancer** n арти́ст, ~ка, балéта.

**balloon** n воздýшный шар.

**ballot** n голосовáние. **ballot-paper** n избирáтельный бюл-

летéнь m; vt держáть impf голосовáние между+instr.

**balm** n бальзáм. **balmy** adj (soft) мя́гкий.

**Baltic** n Балти́йское мóре; ~ **States** прибалти́йские госудáрства, Прибáлтика.

**balustrade** n балюстрáда.

**bamboo** n бамбýк.

**bamboozle** vt надувáть impf, надýть pf.

**ban** n запрéт; vt запрещáть impf, запрети́ть pf.

**banal** adj банáльный. **banality** n банáльность.

**banana** n банáн.

**band** n (stripe, strip) полосá; (braid, tape) тесьмá; (category) категóрия; (of people) грýппа; (gang) бáнда; (mus) оркéстр; (radio) диапазóн; vi: ~ **together** объединя́ться impf, объедини́ться pf.

**bandage** n бинт; vt бинтовáть impf, за~ pf.

**bandit** n банди́т.

**bandstand** n эстрáда для оркéстра.

**bandwagon** n: **jump on the** ~ по́льзоваться impf, вос~ pf благоприя́тными обстоя́тельствами.

**bandy-legged** adj кривоно́гий.

**bane** n отрáва.

**bang** n (blow) удáр; (noise) стук; (of gun) вы́стрел; vt (strike) ударя́ть impf, удáрить pf; vi хло́пать impf, хло́пнуть pf; (slam shut) захло́пываться impf, за~ хло́пнуться pf; ~ **one's head** ударя́ться impf, удáриться pf головóй; ~ **the door** хло́пать impf, хло́пнуть pf двéрью.

**bangle** n браслéт.

**banish** vt изгоня́ть impf, изгна́ть pf.

**banister** n пери́ла neut pl.

**banjo** n ба́нджо neut indecl.

**bank**¹ n (of river) бе́рег m; (of earth) вал; vt сгреба́ть impf, сгрести́ pf в ку́чу; vi (aeron) накреня́ться impf, накрени́ться pf.

**bank**² n (econ) банк; ~ **account** счёт в ба́нке; ~ **holiday** устано́вленный пра́здник; vi (keep money) держа́ть impf де́ньги (в ба́нке); vt (put in ~) класть impf, положи́ть pf в банк; ~ **on** полага́ться impf, положи́ться pf на+acc. **banker** n банки́р. **banknote** n банкно́та.

**bankrupt** n банкро́т; adj обанкро́тившийся; vt доводи́ть impf, довести́ pf до банкро́тства. **bankruptcy** n банкро́тство.

**banner** n зна́мя neut.

**banquet** n банке́т, пир.

**banter** n подшу́чивание.

**baptism** n креще́ние. **baptize** vt крести́ть impf, о~ pf.

**bar** n (beam) брусо́к; (of cage) решётка; (of chocolate) пли́тка; (of soap) кусо́к; (barrier) прегра́да; (law) адвокату́ра; (counter) сто́йка; (room) бар; (mus) такт; vt (obstruct) прегражда́ть impf, прегради́ть pf; (prohibit) запреща́ть impf, запрети́ть pf.

**barbarian** n ва́рвар. **barbaric**, **barbarous** adj ва́рварский.

**barbecue** n (party) шашлы́к; vt жа́рить impf, за~ pf на ве́ртеле.

**barbed wire** n колю́чая про́волока.

**barber** n парикма́хер; ~'s **shop** парикма́херская sb.

**bar code** n маркиро́вка.

**bard** n бард.

**bare** adj (naked) го́лый; (empty) пусто́й; (small) мини-ма́льный; vt обнажа́ть impf, обнажи́ть pf; ~ **one's teeth** ска́лить impf, о~ pf зу́бы. **barefaced** adj на́глый. **barefoot** adj босо́й. **barely** adv едва́.

**bargain** n (deal) сде́лка; (good buy) вы́годная сде́лка; vi торгова́ться impf, с~ pf; ~ **for, on** (expect) ожида́ть impf +gen.

**barge** n ба́ржа; vi: ~ **into** (room etc.) вырыва́ться impf, ворва́ться pf в+acc.

**baritone** n барито́н.

**bark**¹ n (of dog) лай; vi ла́ять impf.

**bark**² n (of tree) кора́.

**barley** n ячме́нь m.

**barmaid** n буфе́тчица. **barman** n буфе́тчик.

**barmy** adj тро́нутый.

**barn** n амба́р.

**barometer** n баро́метр.

**baron** n баро́н. **baroness** n бароне́сса.

**baroque** n баро́кко neut indecl; adj баро́чный.

**barrack**¹ n каза́рма.

**barrack**² vt освисты́вать impf, освиста́ть pf.

**barrage** n (in river) запру́да; (gunfire) огнево́й вал; (fig) град.

**barrel** n бо́чка; (of gun) дуло́.

**barren** adj беспло́дный.

**barricade** n баррика́да; vt баррикади́ровать impf, за~ pf.

**barrier** n барье́р.

**barring** prep исключа́я.

**barrister** n адвока́т.

**barrow** n теле́жка.

**barter** n товарообме́н; vi обме́ниваться impf, обменя́ться pf това́рами.

**base**[1] adj ни́зкий; (metal) неблагоро́дный.

**base**[2] n осно́ва; (also mil) ба́за; vt осно́вывать impf, основа́ть pf. **baseball** n бейсбо́л.

**baseless** adj необоснова́нный. **basement** n подва́л.

**bash** v тре́снуть pf; n: have a ~! попро́буй(те)!

**bashful** adj засте́нчивый.

**basic** adj основно́й. **basically** adv в основно́м.

**basin** n таз; (geog) бассе́йн.

**basis** n осно́ва, ба́зис.

**bask** vi гре́ться impf; (fig) наслажда́ться impf, насла-ди́ться pf (in +instr).

**basket** n корзи́на. **basketball** n баскетбо́л.

**bass** n, adj басо́вый.

**bassoon** n фаго́т.

**bastard** n (sl) негодя́й.

**baste** vt (cul) полива́ть impf, поли́ть pf жи́ром.

**bastion** n бастио́н.

**bat**[1] n (zool) лету́чая мышь.

**bat**[2] n (sport) бита́; vi бить impf, по~ pf по мячу́.

**bat**[3] vt: he didn't ~ an eyelid он и гла́зом не моргну́л.

**batch** n па́чка; (of loaves) вы́печка.

**bated** adj: with ~ breath зата́ив дыха́ние.

**bath** n (vessel) ва́нна; pl пла́вательный бассе́йн; have a bath принима́ть impf, приня́ть pf ва́нну; vt купа́ть impf, вы́~, ис~ pf. **bathe** vi купа́ться impf, вы́~, ис~ pf; vt омыва́ть impf, омы́ть pf. **bather** n купа́льщик, -ица. **bath-house** n ба́ня. **bathing** n: ~ cap купа́льная ша́поч-

ка; ~ costume купа́льный костю́м. **bathroom** n ва́нная sb.

**baton** n (staff of office) жезл; (sport) эстафе́та; (mus) (дирижёрская) па́лочка.

**battalion** n батальо́н.

**batten** n ре́йка.

**batter** n взби́тое те́сто; vt колоти́ть impf, по~ pf.

**battery** n батаре́я.

**battle** n би́тва; (fig) борьба́; vi боро́ться impf. **battlefield** n по́ле би́твы. **battlement** n зубча́тая стена́. **battleship** n лине́йный кора́бль m.

**bawdy** adj непристо́йный.

**bawl** v ора́ть impf.

**bay**[1] n (bot) лавр; adj лавро́вый.

**bay**[2] n (geog) зали́в.

**bay**[3] n (recess) пролёт; ~ window фона́рь m.

**bay**[4] vi (bark) ла́ять impf; (howl) выть impf.

**bay**[5] adj (colour) гнедо́й.

**bayonet** n штык.

**bazaar** n база́р.

**BC** abbr до н.э. (до на́шей э́ры).

**be**[1] v 1. быть: usually omitted in pres: he is a teacher он учи́тель. 2. (exist) существова́ть impf. 3. (frequentative) быва́ть impf. 4. (~ situated) находи́ться impf; (stand) стоя́ть impf; (lie) лежа́ть impf. 5. (in general definitions) явля́ться impf +instr: **Moscow is the capital of Russia** столи́цей Росси́и явля́ется го́род Москва́. 6.: **there is, are** име́ются, (emph) есть.

**be**[2] v aux 1. be+inf, expressing duty, plan: до́лжен+inf. 2. be+past participle passive, expressing passive: быть+past *participle passive in short form:* it was done бы́ло сде́лано; *impers construction of 3 pl+acc:* **I was beaten** меня́ би́ли; *reflexive construction:* **music was heard** слы́шалась му́зыка. 3. *be+pres participle active, expressing continuous tenses:* *imperfective aspect:* **I am reading** я чита́ю.

**beach** *n* пляж.

**beacon** *n* мая́к, сигна́льный ого́нь *m.*

**bead** *n* бу́сина; (*drop*) ка́пля; *pl* бу́сы *f pl.*

**beak** *n* клюв.

**beaker** *n* (*child's*) ча́шка с но́сиком; (*chem*) ме́нзурка.

**beam** *n* ба́лка; (*ray*) луч; *vi* (*shine*) сия́ть *impf.*

**bean** *n* фасо́ль, боб.

**bear¹** *n* медве́дь *m.*

**bear²** *vt* (*carry*) носи́ть *indet*, нести́ *det*, по~ *pf*; (*endure*) терпе́ть *impf*; (*child*) роди́ть *impf & pf*; ~ **out** подтвержда́ть *impf*, подтверди́ть *pf*; ~ **up** держа́ться *impf*. **bearable** *adj* терпи́мый.

**beard** *n* борода́. **bearded** *adj* борода́тый.

**bearer** *n* носи́тель *m*; (*of cheque*) предъяви́тель *m*; (*of letter*) пода́тель *m.*

**bearing** *n* (*deportment*) оса́нка; (*relation*) отноше́ние; (*position*) пе́ленг; (*tech*) подши́пник; **get one's ~s** ориенти́роваться *impf & pf*; **lose one's ~s** потеря́ть *pf* ориенти́ровку.

**beast** *n* живо́тное *sb*; (*fig*) скоти́на *m & f.* **beastly** *adj* (*coll*) проти́вный.

**beat** *n* бой; (*round*) обхо́д; (*mus*) такт; *vt* бить *impf*, по~ *pf*; (*sport*) выи́грывать

*impf*, вы́играть *pf* у+*gen*; (*cul*) взбива́ть *impf*, взбить *pf*; *vi* би́ться *impf*, ~ **off** отбива́ть *impf*, отби́ть *pf*; ~ **up** избива́ть *impf*, изби́ть *pf.*

**beating** *n* (*defeat*) пораже́ние; (*of heart*) бие́ние.

**beautiful** *adj* краси́вый. **beautify** *vt* украша́ть *impf*, укра́сить *pf.* **beauty** *n* красота́; (*person*) краса́вица.

**beaver** *n* бобр.

**because** *conj* потому́, что; так как; *adv:* ~ **of** из-за+*gen.*

**beckon** *vt* мани́ть *impf*, по~ *pf* к себе́.

**become** *vi* станови́ться *impf*, стать *pf* +*instr*; ~ *of* ста́ться *pf* c+*instr*. **becoming** *adj* (*dress*) иду́щий к лицу́+*dat.*

**bed** *n* крова́ть, посте́ль; (*garden*) гря́дка; (*sea*) дно; (*river*) ру́сло; (*geol*) пласт; **go to** ~ ложи́ться *impf*, лечь *pf* спать; **make the** ~ стели́ть *impf*, по~ *pf* посте́ль. **bed and breakfast** *n* (*hotel*) ма́ленькая гости́ница. **bedclothes** *n pl*, **bedding** *n* посте́льное бельё. **bedridden** *adj* прико́ванный к посте́ли. **bedroom** *n* спа́льня. **bedside table** *n* ту́мбочка. **bedsitter** *n* однокомнатная кварти́ра. **bedspread** *n* покрыва́ло. **bedtime** *n* вре́мя *neut* ложи́ться спать.

**bedlam** *n* бедла́м.

**bedraggled** *adj* растрёпанный.

**bee** *n* пчела́. **beehive** *n* у́лей.

**beech** *n* бук.

**beef** *n* говя́дина. **beefburger** *n* котле́та.

**beer** *n* пи́во.

**beetle** *n* жук.

**beetroot** *n* свёкла.

**befall** vt & i случа́ться impf, случи́ться pf (+dat).

**befit** vt подходи́ть impf, подойти́ pf +dat.

**before** adv ра́ньше; prep пе́ред+instr, до+gen; conj до того́ как; пре́жде чем; (rather than) скоре́е чем; **the day ~ yesterday** позавчера́. **beforehand** adv зара́нее.

**befriend** vt дружи́ться impf, по~ pf c+instr.

**beg** vt (ask) о́чень проси́ть impf, по~ pf (person+acc; thing+acc or gen); vi ни́щенствовать impf; (of dog) служи́ть impf; **~ for** проси́ть impf, по~ pf +acc or gen; **~ pardon** проси́ть impf проще́ния.

**beggar** n ни́щий sb.

**begin** vt (& i) начина́ть(ся) impf, нача́ть(ся) pf. **beginner** n начина́ющий sb. **beginning** n нача́ло.

**begrudge** vt (give reluctantly) жале́ть impf, по~ pf o+prep.

**beguile** vt (charm) очаро́вывать impf, очарова́ть pf; (seduce, delude) обольща́ть impf, обольсти́ть pf.

**behalf** n: **on ~ of** от и́мени +gen; (in interest of) в по́льзу +gen.

**behave** vi вести́ impf себя́. **behaviour** n поведе́ние.

**behest** n заве́т.

**behind** adv, prep сза́ди (+gen), позади́ (+gen), за (+gen, instr); n зад; **be, fall, ~** отстава́ть impf, отста́ть pf.

**behold** vt смотре́ть impf, по~ pf. **beholden** predic: **~ to** обя́зан+dat.

**beige** adj бе́жевый.

**being** n (existence) бытие́; (creature) существо́.

**Belarus** n Белару́сь.

**belated** adj запозда́лый.

**belch** vi рыга́ть impf, рыгну́ть pf; vt изверга́ть impf, изве́ргнуть pf.

**beleaguer** vt осажда́ть impf, осади́ть pf.

**belfry** n колоко́льня.

**Belgian** n бельги́ец, -ги́йка; adj бельги́йский. **Belgium** n Бе́льгия.

**belie** vt противоре́чить impf +dat.

**belief** n (faith) ве́ра; (confidence) убежде́ние. **believable** adj правдоподо́бный. **believe** vt ве́рить impf, по~ pf +dat; **~ in** ве́рить impf в+acc. **believer** n ве́рующий sb.

**belittle** vt умаля́ть impf, умали́ть pf.

**bell** n ко́локол; (doorbell) звоно́к; **~ tower** колоко́льня.

**bellicose** adj вои́нственный. **belligerence** n вои́нственность. **belligerent** adj вою́ющий; (aggressive) вои́нственный.

**bellow** vt & i реве́ть impf.

**bellows** n pl мехи́ m pl.

**belly** n живо́т.

**belong** vi принадлежа́ть impf (to (к)+dat). **belongings** n pl пожи́тки (-ков) pl.

**Belorussian** n белору́с, ~ка; adj белору́сский.

**beloved** adj & sb возлю́бленный.

**below** adv (position) внизу́; prep (position) под+instr; (less than) ни́же+gen.

**belt** n (strap) по́яс, (also tech) реме́нь; (zone) зо́на, полоса́.

**bench** n скаме́йка; (for work) стано́к.

**bend** n изги́б; vt (& i, also **~ down**) сгиба́ть(ся) impf, со~

гну́ть(ся) *pf*; ~ **over** склоня́ться *impf*, склони́ться *pf* над+*instr*.

**beneath** *prep* под+*instr*.

**benediction** *n* благослове́ние.

**benefactor** *n* благоде́тель *m*.

**benefactress** *n* благоде́тельница.

**beneficial** *adj* поле́зный. **beneficiary** *n* получа́тель *m*; (*law*) насле́дник. **benefit** *n* по́льза; (*allowance*) посо́бие; (*theat*) бенефи́с; *vt* приноси́ть *impf*, принести́ *pf* по́льзу +*dat*; *vi* извлека́ть *impf*, извле́чь *pf* вы́году.

**benevolence** *n* благожела́тельность. **benevolent** *adj* благожела́тельный.

**benign** *adj* до́брый, мя́гкий; (*tumour*) доброка́чественный.

**bent** *n* скло́нность.

**bequeath** *vt* завеща́ть *impf* & *pf* (**to**+*dat*). **bequest** *n* посме́ртный дар.

**berate** *vt* руга́ть *impf*, вы́~ *pf*.

**bereave** *vt* лиша́ть *impf*, лиши́ть *pf* (**of** +*gen*). **bereavement** *n* тяжёлая утра́та.

**berry** *n* я́года.

**berserk** *adj*: **go** ~ взбеси́ться *pf*.

**berth** *n* (*bunk*) ко́йка; (*naut*) стоя́нка; *vi* прича́ливать *impf*, прича́лить *pf*.

**beseech** *vt* умоля́ть *impf*, умоли́ть *pf*.

**beset** *vt* осажда́ть *impf*, осади́ть *pf*.

**beside** *prep* о́коло+*gen*, ря́дом с+*instr*; ~ **the point** некста́ти; ~ **o.s.** вне себя́. **besides** *adv* кро́ме того́; *prep* кро́ме+*gen*.

**besiege** *vt* осажда́ть *impf*, осади́ть *pf*.

**besotted** *adj* одурма́ненный.

**bespoke** *adj* сде́ланный на зака́з.

**best** *adj* лу́чший, са́мый лу́чший; *adv* лу́чше всего́, бо́льше всего́; **all the** ~! всего́ наилу́чшего! **at** ~ в лу́чшем слу́чае; **do one's** ~ де́лать *impf*, с~ *pf* всё возмо́жное; ~ **man** ша́фер.

**bestial** *adj* зве́рский. **bestiality** *n* зве́рство.

**bestow** *vt* дарова́ть *impf* & *pf*.

**bestseller** *n* бестсе́ллер.

**bet** *n* пари́ *neut indecl*; (*stake*) ста́вка; *vi* держа́ть *impf* пари́ (**on** на+*acc*); *vt* (*stake*) ста́вить *impf*, по~ *pf*; **he bet me £5** он поспо́рил со мной 5 фу́нтов.

**betray** *vt* изменя́ть *impf*, измени́ть *pf*+*dat*. **betrayal** *n* изме́на.

**better** *adj* лу́чший; *adv* лу́чше; (*more*) бо́льше; *vt* улучша́ть *impf*, улу́чшить *pf*; **all the** ~ тем лу́чше; ~ **off** бо́лее состоя́тельный; ~ **o.s.** выдвига́ться *impf*, вы́двинуться *pf*; **get** ~ (*health*) поправля́ться *impf*, попра́виться *pf*; **get the** ~ **of** брать *impf*, взять *pf* верх над+*instr*; **had** ~: **you had** ~ **go** вам (*dat*) лу́чше бы пойти́; **think** ~ **of** переду́мывать *impf*, переду́мать *pf*. **betterment** *n* улучше́ние.

**between** *prep* ме́жду+*instr*.

**bevel** *vt* ска́шивать *impf*, скоси́ть *pf*.

**beverage** *n* напи́ток.

**bevy** *n* ста́йка.

**beware** *vi* остерега́ться *impf*, остере́чься *pf* (**of** +*gen*).

**bewilder** *vt* сбива́ть *impf*, сбить *pf* с то́лку. **bewildered** *adj* озада́ченный. **bewilder-**

ment *n* замеша́тельство.

**bewitch** *vt* заколдо́вывать *impf*, заколдова́ть *pf*; (*fig*) очаро́вывать *impf*, очарова́ть *pf*. **bewitching** *adj* очарова́тельный.

**beyond** *prep* за+*acc* & *instr*; по ту сто́рону+*gen*; (*above*) сверх+*gen*; (*outside*) вне+*gen*; **the back of ~** край све́та.

**bias** *n* (*inclination*) укло́н; (*prejudice*) предубежде́ние. **biased** *adj* предубеждённый.

**bib** *n* нагру́дник.

**Bible** *n* Би́блия. **biblical** *adj* библе́йский.

**bibliographical** *n* библиографи́ческий. **bibliography** *n* библиогра́фия.

**bicarbonate (of soda)** *n* питьева́я со́да.

**biceps** *n* би́цепс.

**bicker** *vi* пререка́ться *impf*.

**bicycle** *n* велосипе́д.

**bid** *n* предложе́ние цены́; (*attempt*) попы́тка; *vt* & *i* предлага́ть *impf*, предложи́ть *pf* (це́ну) (**for** за+*acc*); *vt* (*command*) прика́зывать *impf*, приказа́ть *pf* +*dat*. **bidding** *n* предложе́ние цены́; (*command*) приказа́ние.

**bide** *vt*: **~ one's time** ожида́ть *impf* благоприя́тного слу́чая.

**biennial** *adj* двухле́тний; *n* двухле́тник.

**bier** *n* катафа́лк.

**bifocals** *n pl* бифока́льные очки́ *pl*.

**big** *adj* большо́й; (*also important*) кру́пный.

**bigamist** *n* (*man*) двоеже́нец; (*woman*) двуму́жница. **bigamy** *n* двубра́чие.

**bigwig** *n* ши́шка.

**bike** *n* велосипе́д. **biker** *n*

мотоцикли́ст.

**bikini** *n* бики́ни *neut indecl*.

**bilateral** *adj* двусторо́нний.

**bilberry** *n* черни́ка (*no pl; usu collect*).

**bile** *n* жёлчь. **bilious** *adj* жёлчный.

**bilingual** *adj* двуязы́чный.

**bill**[1] *n* счёт; (*parl*) законопрое́кт; (**~ of exchange**) ве́ксель; (*poster*) афи́ша; *vt* (*announce*) объявля́ть *impf*, объяви́ть *pf* в афи́шах; (*charge*) присыла́ть *impf*, присла́ть *pf* счёт+*dat*.

**bill**[2] *n* (*beak*) клюв.

**billet** *vt* расквартиро́вывать *impf*, расквартирова́ть *pf*.

**billiards** *n* билья́рд.

**billion** *n* биллио́н.

**billow** *n* вал; *vi* вздыма́ться *impf*.

**bin** *n* му́сорное ведро́; (*corn*) за́кром.

**bind** *vt* (*tie*) свя́зывать *impf*, связа́ть *pf*; (*oblige*) обя́зывать *impf*, обяза́ть *pf*; (*book*) переплета́ть *impf*, переплести́ *pf*. **binder** *n* (*person*) переплётчик; (*agric*) вяза́льщик; (*for papers*) па́пка. **binding** *n* переплёт.

**binge** *n* кутёж.

**binoculars** *n pl* бино́кль *n*.

**biochemistry** *n* биохи́мия. **biographer** *n* био́граф. **biographical** *adj* биографи́ческий. **biography** *n* биогра́фия. **biological** *adj* биологи́ческий. **biologist** *n* био́лог. **biology** *n* биоло́гия.

**bipartisan** *adj* двухпарти́йный.

**birch** *n* берёза; (*rod*) ро́зга.

**bird** *n* пти́ца; **~ of prey** хи́щная пти́ца.

**birth** *n* рожде́ние; (*descent*)

происхожде́ние; ~ certificate ме́трика; ~ control противозача́точные ме́ры *f pl.*
birthday *n* день *m* рожде́ния; fourth ~ четырёхле́тие.
birthplace *n* ме́сто рожде́ния. birthright *n* пра́во по рожде́нию.
biscuit *n* пече́нье.
bisect *vt* разреза́ть *impf*, разре́зать *pf* попола́м.
bisexual *adj* бисексуа́льный.
bishop *n* епи́скоп; (*chess*) слон.
bit¹ *n* (*piece*) кусо́чек; a ~ немно́го; not a ~ ничу́ть.
bit² *n* (*tech*) сверло́; (*bridle*) удила́ (-л) *pl.*
bitch *n* (*coll*) сте́рва. bitchy *adj* стерво́зный.
bite *n* уку́с; (*snack*) заку́ска; (*fishing*) клёв; *vt* куса́ть *impf*, укуси́ть *pf*; *vi* (*fish*) клева́ть *impf*, клю́нуть *pf.* biting *adj* е́дкий.
bitter *adj* го́рький. bitterness *n* го́речь.
bitumen *n* би́тум.
bivouac *n* бива́к.
bizarre *adj* стра́нный.
black *adj* чёрный; ~ eye подби́тый глаз; ~ market чёрный ры́нок; *v*: ~ out (*vt*) затемня́ть *impf*, затемни́ть *pf*; (*vi*) теря́ть *impf*, по-~ *pf* созна́ние; *n* (*colour*) чёрный цвет; (~ person) чёрный, ~и́тянка; (*mourning*) тра́ур. blackberry *n* ежеви́ка (*no pl; usu collect*). blackbird *n* чёрный дрозд. blackboard *n* доска́. blackcurrant *n* чёрная сморо́дина (*no pl; usu collect*). blacken *vt* (*fig*) черни́ть *impf*, о-~ *pf.* blackleg *n* штрейкбре́хер. blacklist *n* вноси́ть *impf*, внести́ *pf*

в чёрный спи́сок. blackmail *n* шанта́ж; *vt* шантажи́ровать *impf*. blackout *n* затемне́ние; (*faint*) поте́ря созна́ния. blacksmith *n* кузне́ц.
bladder *n* пузы́рь *m.*
blade *n* (*knife*) ле́звие; (*oar*) ло́пасть; (*grass*) были́нка.
blame *n* вина́, порица́ние; *vt* вини́ть *impf* (for в+*prep*); be to ~ быть винова́тым. blameless *adj* безупре́чный.
blanch *vt* (*vegetables*) ошпа́ривать *impf*, ошпа́рить *pf*; *vi* бледне́ть *impf*, по-~ *pf.*
bland *adj* мя́гкий; (*dull*) пре́сный.
blandishments *n pl* лесть.
blank *adj* (*look*) отсу́тствующий; (*paper*) чи́стый; *n* (*space*) про́пуск; (*form*) бланк; (*cartridge*) холосто́й патро́н; ~ cheque незапо́лненный чек.
blanket *n* одея́ло.
blare *vi* труби́ть *impf*, про-~ *pf.*
blasé *adj* пресы́щенный.
blasphemous *adj* богоху́льный. blasphemy *n* богоху́льство.
blast *n* (*wind*) поры́в ве́тра; (*explosion*) взрыв; *vt* взрыва́ть *impf*, взорва́ть *pf*; ~ off стартова́ть *impf & pf.* blastfurnace *n* до́мна.
blatant *adj* я́вный.
blaze *n* (*flame*) пла́мя *neut*; (*fire*) пожа́р; *vi* пыла́ть *impf.*
blazer *n* лёгкий пиджа́к.
bleach *n* хло́рка, отбе́ливатель *m*; *vt* отбе́ливать *impf*, отбели́ть *pf.*
bleak *adj* пусты́нный; (*dreary*) уны́лый.
bleary-eyed *adj* с затума́ненными глаза́ми.
bleat *vi* бле́ять *impf.*

**bleed** vi кровоточи́ть impf.

**bleeper** n персона́льный сигнализа́тор.

**blemish** n пятно́.

**blend** n смесь; vt сме́шивать impf, смеша́ть pf; vi гармони́ровать impf. **blender** n ми́ксер.

**bless** vt благословля́ть impf, благослови́ть pf. **blessed** adj благослове́нный. **blessing** n (action) благослове́ние; (object) бла́го.

**blight** vt губи́ть impf, по~ pf.

**blind** adj слепо́й; ~ **alley** тупи́к; n што́ра; vt ослепля́ть impf, ослепи́ть pf. **blindfold** vt завя́зывать impf, завяза́ть pf глаза́+dat. **blindness** n слепота́.

**blink** vi мига́ть impf, мигну́ть pf. **blinkers** n pl шо́ры (-p) pl.

**bliss** n блаже́нство. **blissful** adj блаже́нный.

**blister** n пузы́рь m, волды́рь m.

**blithe** adj весёлый; (carefree) беспе́чный.

**blitz** n бомбёжка.

**blizzard** n мете́ль.

**bloated** adj взду́тый.

**blob** n (liquid) ка́пля; (colour) кля́кса.

**bloc** n блок.

**block** n (wood) чурба́н; (stone) глы́ба; (flats) жило́й дом; vt прегражда́ть impf, прегради́ть pf; ~ **up** забива́ть impf, заби́ть pf.

**blockade** n блока́да; vt блоки́ровать impf & pf.

**blockage** n затор.

**bloke** n па́рень m.

**blond** n блонди́н, ~ка, adj белоку́рый.

**blood** n кровь; ~ **donor** до́нор; ~-**poisoning** n зараже́ние кро́ви; ~ **pressure** кровяно́е давле́ние; ~ **relation** бли́зкий ро́дственник, -ая ро́дственница; ~ **transfusion** перелива́ние кро́ви. **bloodhound** n ище́йка. **bloodshed** n кровопроли́тие. **bloodshot** adj нали́тый кро́вью. **bloodthirsty** adj кровожа́дный. **bloody** adj крова́вый.

**bloom** n расцве́т; vi цвести́ impf.

**blossom** n цвет; **in** ~ в цвету́.

**blot** n кля́кса; пятно́; vt (dry) промока́ть impf, промокну́ть pf; (smudge) па́чкать impf, за~ pf.

**blotch** n пятно́.

**blotting-paper** n промока́тельная бума́га.

**blouse** n ко́фточка, блу́зка.

**blow**[1] n уда́р.

**blow**[2] vt & i дуть impf, по~ pf; ~ **away** сноси́ть impf, снести́ pf; ~ **down** вали́ть impf, по~ pf; ~ **one's nose** сморка́ться impf, сморкну́ться pf; ~ **out** задува́ть impf, заду́ть pf; ~ **over** (fig) проходи́ть impf, пройти́ pf; ~ **up** взрыва́ть impf, взорва́ть pf; (inflate) надува́ть impf, наду́ть pf. **blow-lamp** n пая́льная ла́мпа.

**blubber**[1] n во́рвань.

**blubber**[2] vi реве́ть impf.

**bludgeon** vt (compel) вынужда́ть impf, вы́нудить pf.

**blue** adj (dark) си́ний; (light) голубо́й; n си́ний, голубо́й, цвет. **bluebell** n колоко́льчик. **bluebottle** n си́няя му́ха. **blueprint** n си́нька, светоко́пия; (fig) прое́кт.

**bluff**[1] n блеф; vi блефова́ть impf.

**blunder** n опло́шность; vi оплоша́ть pf.

**blunt** adj тупо́й; (person) прямо́й; vt тупи́ть impf, за~, ис~.

**blur** vt затума́нивать impf, затума́нить pf. **blurred** adj расплы́вчатый.

**blurt** vt: ~ out выба́лтывать impf, вы́болтать pf.

**blush** vi красне́ть impf, по~ pf.

**bluster** vi бушева́ть impf; n пусты́е слова́ neut pl.

**boar** n бо́ров; (wild) каба́н.

**board** n доска́; (committee) правле́ние, сове́т; on ~ на борт(у́); vt сади́ться impf, сесть pf (на кора́бль, в по́езд и т.д.); ~ up заби́ть impf, забива́ть pf. **boarder** n пансионе́р. **boarding-house** n пансио́н. **boarding-school** n интерна́т.

**boast** vi хва́статься impf, по~ pf; vt горди́ться impf +instr. **boaster** n хвасту́н. **boastful** adj хвастли́вый.

**boat** n (small) ло́дка; (large) кора́бль m.

**bob** vi подпры́гивать impf, подпры́гнуть pf.

**bobbin** n кату́шка.

**bobsleigh** n бо́бслей.

**bode** vt: ~well/ill предвеща́ть impf хоро́шее/дурно́е.

**bodice** n лиф, корса́ж.

**bodily** adv целико́м; adj теле́сный.

**body** n те́ло, ту́ловище; (corpse) труп; (group) о́рган; (main part) основна́я часть. **bodyguard** n телохрани́тель m. **bodywork** n ку́зов.

**bog** n боло́то; get ~ged down увяза́ть impf, увя́знуть pf. **boggy** adj боло́тистый.

**bogus** adj подде́льный.

**boil**[1] n (med) furú́нкул.

**boil**[2] vi кипе́ть impf, вс~ pf; vt кипяти́ть impf, вс~ pf; (cook) вари́ть impf, с~ pf; ~ down to сходи́ться impf, сойти́сь pf к тому́, что; ~ over выкипа́ть impf, вы́кипеть pf; n кипе́ние; bring to the ~ доводи́ть impf, довести́ pf до кипе́ния. **boiled** adj варёный. **boiler** n котёл; ~ suit комбинезо́н. **boiling** adj кипя́щий; ~ point то́чка кипе́ния; ~ water кипято́к.

**boisterous** adj шумли́вый.

**bold** adj сме́лый; (type) жи́рный.

**bollard** n (in road) столб; (on quay) пал.

**bolster** n ва́лик; vt: ~ up подпира́ть impf, подпере́ть pf.

**bolt** n засо́в; (tech) болт; vt запира́ть impf, запере́ть pf на засо́в; скрепля́ть impf, скрепи́ть pf болта́ми; vi (flee) удира́ть impf, удра́ть pf; (horse) понести́ pf.

**bomb** n бо́мба; vt бомби́ть impf. **bombard** vt бомбарди́ровать impf. **bombardment** n бомбардиро́вка. **bomber** n бомбардиро́вщик.

**bombastic** adj напы́щенный.

**bond** n (econ) облига́ция; (link) связь; pl око́вы (-в) pl, (fig) у́зы (уз) pl.

**bone** n кость.

**bonfire** n костёр.

**bonnet** n ка́пор; (car) капо́т.

**bonus** n пре́мия.

**bony** adj кости́стый.

**boo** vt осви́стывать impf, освиста́ть pf; vi улюлю́кать impf.

**booby trap** n лову́шка.

**book** n кни́га; vt (order) зака́зывать impf, заказа́ть pf;

(*reserve*) брони́ровать *impf*, за~ *pf*. **bookbinder** *n* переплётчик. **bookcase** *n* кни́жный шкаф. **booking** *n* зака́з; ~ **office** ка́сса. **bookkeeper** *n* бухга́лтер. **bookmaker** *n* букме́кер. **bookshop** *n* кни́жный магази́н.

**boom**[1] *n* (*barrier*) бон.

**boom**[2] *n* (*sound*) гул; (*econ*) бум; *vi* гуде́ть *impf*; (*fig*) процвета́ть *impf*.

**boorish** *adj* ха́мский.

**boost** *n* содействие; *vt* увели́чивать *impf*, увели́чить *pf*.

**boot** *n* боти́нок; (*high*) сапо́г; (*football*) бу́тса; (*car*) бага́жник.

**booth** *n* кио́ск, бу́дка; (*polling*) каби́на.

**booty** *n* добы́ча.

**booze** *n* вы́пивка; *vi* выпива́ть *impf*.

**border** *n* (*frontier*) грани́ца; (*trim*) кайма́; (*gardening*) бордю́р; *vi* грани́чить *impf* (**on** с +*instr*). **borderline** *n* грани́ца.

**bore**[1] *n* (*calibre*) кана́л (ствола́); *vt* сверли́ть *impf*, про~ *pf*.

**bore**[2] *n* (*thing*) ску́ка; (*person*) ску́чный челове́к; *vt* надоеда́ть *impf*, надое́сть *pf*. **bored** *impers+dat+inst+с+gen*: **I'm** ~ мне ску́чно; **we were** ~ нам бы́ло ску́чно. **boredom** *n* ску́ка. **boring** *adj* ску́чный.

**born** *adj* прирождённый; **be** ~ роди́ться *impf & pf*.

**borough** *n* райо́н.

**borrow** *vt* одолжа́ть *impf*, одолжи́ть *pf* (**from** у+*gen*).

**Bosnia** *n* Бо́сния. **Bosnian** *n* босни́ец, -и́йка; *adj* босни́йский.

**bosom** *n* грудь.

**boss** *n* нача́льник; *vt* кома́ндовать *impf*, с~ *pf* +*instr*. **bossy** *adj* команди́рский.

**botanical** *adj* ботани́ческий. **botanist** *n* бота́ник. **botany** *n* бота́ника.

**botch** *vt* зала́тывать *impf*, залата́ть *pf*.

**both** *adj & pron* о́ба *m & neut*, о́бе *f*; ~ ... **and** и... и.

**bother** *n* доса́да; *vt* беспоко́ить *impf*.

**bottle** *n* буты́лка; *vt* разлива́ть *impf*, разли́ть *pf* по буты́лкам; ~ **up** сде́рживать *impf*, сдержа́ть *pf*.

**bottom** *n* (*of river, container, etc.*) дно; (*of mountain*) подно́жие; (*buttocks*) зад; **at the** ~ **of** (*stairs, page*) внизу́ +*gen*; **get to the** ~ **of** добира́ться *impf*, добра́ться *pf* до су́ти +*gen*; *adj* ни́жний. **bottomless** *adj* бездо́нный.

**bough** *n* сук.

**boulder** *n* валу́н.

**bounce** *vi* подпры́гивать *impf*, подпры́гнуть *pf*; (*cheque*) верну́ться *pf*.

**bound**[1] *n* (*limit*) преде́л; *vt* ограни́чивать *impf*, ограни́чить *pf*.

**bound**[2] *n* (*spring*) прыжо́к; *vi* пры́гать *impf*, пры́гнуть *pf*.

**bound**[3] *adj*: **he is** ~ **to be there** он обяза́тельно там бу́дет.

**bound**[4] *adj*: **to be** ~ **for** направля́ться *impf*, напра́виться *pf* в+*acc*.

**boundary** *n* грани́ца.

**boundless** *adj* безграни́чный.

**bountiful** *adj* (*generous*) ще́дрый; (*ample*) оби́льный.

**bounty** *n* ще́дрость; (*reward*) пре́мия.

**bouquet** *n* буке́т.

**bourgeois** *adj* буржуа́зный.

bourgeoisie *n* буржуази́я.

bout *n* (*med*) при́ступ; (*sport*) схва́тка.

bow¹ *n* (*weapon*) лук; (*knot*) бант; (*mus*) смычо́к.

bow² *n* (*obeisance*) покло́н; *vi* кла́няться *impf*, поклони́ться *pf*; *vt* склоня́ть *impf*, склони́ть *pf*.

bow³ *n* (*naut*) нос.

bowel *n* кишка́; (*depths*) не́дра (-р) *pl*.

bowl¹ *n* ми́ска.

bowl² *n* (*ball*) шар; *vi* подава́ть *impf*, пода́ть *pf* мяч. **bowler** *n* подаю́щий *sb* мяч; (*hat*) котело́к. **bowling-alley** *n* кегельба́н. **bowls** *n* игра́ в шары́.

box¹ *n* коро́бка, я́щик; (*theat*) ло́жа; ~ **office** ка́сса.

box² *vi* боксирова́ть *impf*. **boxer** *n* боксёр. **boxing** *n* бокс. **Boxing Day** *n* второ́й день Рождества́.

boy *n* ма́льчик. **boyfriend** *n* друг, молодо́й челове́к. **boyhood** *n* о́трочество. **boyish** *adj* мальчи́шеский.

boycott *n* бойко́т; *vt* бойкоти́ровать *impf* & *pf*.

bra *n* ли́фчик.

brace *n* (*clamp*) скре́па; *pl* подтя́жки *f pl*; (*dental*) ши́на; *vt* скрепля́ть *impf*, скрепи́ть *pf*; ~ **o.s.** собира́ться *impf*, собра́ться *pf* с си́лами.

bracelet *n* брасле́т.

bracing *adj* бодря́щий.

bracket *n* (*support*) кронште́йн; *pl* ско́бки *f pl*; (*category*) катего́рия.

brag *vi* хва́статься *impf*, по~ *pf*.

braid *n* тесьма́.

braille *n* шрифт Бра́йля.

brain *n* мозг. **brainstorm** *n*

припа́док безу́мия. **brainwash** *vt* промыва́ть *impf*, промы́ть *pf* мозги́+*dat*. **brainwave** *n* блестя́щая иде́я.

braise *vt* туши́ть *impf*, с~ *pf*.

brake *n* то́рмоз; *vt* тормози́ть *impf*, за~ *pf*.

bramble *n* ежеви́ка.

bran *n* о́труби (-бе́й) *pl*.

branch *n* ве́тка; (*fig*) о́трасль; (*comm*) филиа́л; *vi* разветвля́ться *impf*, разветви́ться *pf*; ~ **out** (*fig*) расширя́ть *impf*, расши́рить *pf* де́ятельность.

brand *n* (*mark*) клеймо́; (*make*) ма́рка; (*sort*) сорт; *vt* клейми́ть *impf*, за~ *pf*.

brandish *vt* разма́хивать *impf* +*instr*.

brandy *n* конья́к.

brash *adj* наха́льный.

brass *n* лату́нь, жёлтая медь; (*mus*) ме́дные инструме́нты *m pl*; *adj* лату́нный, ме́дный; ~ **band** ме́дный духово́й орке́стр; **top** ~ вы́сшее нача́льство.

brassière *n* бюстга́лтер.

brat *n* черте́нок.

bravado *n* брава́да.

brave *adj* хра́брый; *vt* покоря́ть *impf*, покори́ть *pf*. **bravery** *n* хра́брость.

bravo *int* бра́во.

brawl *n* сканда́л; *vi* дра́ться *impf*, по~ *pf*.

brawny *adj* му́скулистый.

bray *n* крик осла́; *vi* крича́ть *impf*.

brazen *adj* бессты́дный.

brazier *n* жаро́вня.

breach *n* наруше́ние; (*break*) проло́м; (*mil*) брешь; *vt* прорыва́ть *impf*, прорва́ть *pf*; (*rule*) наруша́ть *impf*, нару́шить *pf*.

**bread** n хлеб; (white) бу́лка. **breadcrumb** n кро́шка. **breadwinner** n корми́лец.

**breadth** n ширина́; (fig) широта́.

**break** n проло́м, разры́в; (pause) переры́в, па́уза; vt (& i) лома́ть(ся) impf, c~ pf; разбива́ть(ся) impf, разби́ть(ся) pf; vt (violate) наруша́ть impf, нару́шить pf; ~ away вырыва́ться impf, вы́рваться pf; ~ down (vi) (tech) лома́ться impf, c~ pf; (talks) срыва́ться impf, сорва́ться pf; (vt) (door) выла́мывать impf, вы́ломать pf; ~ in(to) вла́мываться impf, вломи́ться pf в+acc; ~ off (vt & i) отла́мывать(ся) impf, отломи́ть(ся) pf; (vi) (speaking) замолча́ть pf; (vt) (relations) порыва́ть impf, порва́ть pf; ~ out вырыва́ться impf, вы́рваться pf; (fire, war) вспы́хнуть pf; ~ through пробива́ться impf, проби́ться pf; ~ up (vi) (marriage) распада́ться impf, распа́сться pf; (meeting) прерыва́ться impf, прерва́ться pf; (vt) (disperse) разгоня́ть impf, разогна́ть pf; (vt & i) разбива́ть(ся) impf, разби́ть(ся) pf; ~ with порыва́ть impf, порва́ть pf c+instr. **breakage** n поло́мка. **breakdown** n поло́мка; (med) не́рвный срыв. **breaker** n буру́н. **breakfast** n за́втрак; vi за́втракать impf, по~ pf. **breakneck** adj: at ~ speed сломя́ го́лову. **breakthrough** n проры́в. **breakwater** n волноре́з.

**breast** n грудь; ~-feeding n кормле́ние гру́дью; ~ stroke n брасс.

**breath** n дыха́ние; be out of ~ запыха́ться impf & pf. **breathe** vi дыша́ть impf; ~ in вдыха́ть impf, вдохну́ть pf; ~ out выдыха́ть impf, вы́дохнуть pf. **breather** n переды́шка. **breathless** adj запыха́вшийся.

**breeches** n pl бри́джи (-жей) pl.

**breed** n поро́да; vi размножа́ться impf, размно́житься pf; vt разводи́ть impf, развести́ pf. **breeder** n -во́д: cattle ~ скотово́д. **breeding** n разведе́ние, -во́дство; (upbringing) воспи́танность.

**breeze** n ве́тер(о)к; (naut) бриз. **breezy** adj све́жий.

**brevity** n кра́ткость.

**brew** vt (beer) вари́ть impf, c~ pf; (tea) зава́ривать impf, завари́ть pf; (beer) ва́рка; (tea) зава́рка. **brewer** n пивова́р. **brewery** n пивова́ренный заво́д.

**bribe** n взя́тка; vt подкупа́ть impf, подкупи́ть pf. **bribery** n по́дкуп.

**brick** n кирпи́ч; adj кирпи́чный. **bricklayer** n ка́меньщик.

**bridal** adj сва́дебный. **bride** n неве́ста. **bridegroom** n жени́х. **bridesmaid** n подру́жка неве́сты.

**bridge**[1] n мост; (of nose) перено́сица; vt (gap) заполня́ть impf, запо́лнить pf; (overcome) преодолева́ть impf, преодоле́ть pf.

**bridge**[2] n (game) бридж.

**bridle** n узда́; vi возмуща́ться impf, возмути́ться pf.

**brief** adj недо́лгий; (concise) кра́ткий; n инстру́кция; vt инструкти́ровать impf & pf.

**briefcase** *n* портфе́ль *m*.
**briefing** *n* инструкта́ж.
**briefly** *adv* кра́тко. **briefs** *n pl* трусы́ (-со́в) *pl*.
**brigade** *n* брига́да. **brigadier** *n* генера́л-майо́р.
**bright** *adj* я́ркий. **brighten** (*also ~ up*) *vi* проясня́ться *impf*, проясни́ться *pf*; *vt* оживля́ть *impf*, оживи́ть *pf*. **brightness** *n* я́ркость.
**brilliant** *adj* блестя́щий.
**brim** *n* край; (*hat*) поля́ (-ле́й) *pl*.
**brine** *n* рассо́л.
**bring** *vt* (*carry*) приноси́ть *impf*, принести́ *pf* (*lead*) приводи́ть *impf*, привести́ *pf*; (*transport*) привози́ть *impf*, привезти́ *pf*; ~ **about** приноси́ть *impf*, принести́ *pf*; ~ **back** возвраща́ть *impf*, возврати́ть *pf*; ~ **down** сва́ливать *impf*, свали́ть *pf*; ~ **round** (*unconscious person*) приводи́ть *impf*, привести́ *pf* в себя́; (*deliver*) привози́ть *impf*, привезти́ *pf*; ~ **up** (*educate*) воспи́тывать *impf*, воспита́ть *pf*; (*question*) поднима́ть *impf*, подня́ть *pf*.
**brink** *n* край.
**brisk** *adj* (*lively*) оживлённый; (*air etc.*) све́жий; (*quick*) бы́стрый.
**bristle** *n* щети́на; *vi* щети́ниться *impf*, о~ *pf*.
**Britain** *n* Великобрита́ния, А́нглия. **British** *adj* брита́нский, англи́йский; ~ **Isles** Брита́нские острова́ *m pl*. **Briton** *n* брита́нец, -нка; англича́нин, -а́нка.
**brittle** *adj* хру́пкий.
**broach** *vt* затра́гивать *impf*, затро́нуть *pf*.
**broad** *adj* широ́кий; **in ~ day-**

**light** средь бе́ла дня; **in ~ outline** в о́бщих черта́х. **broad-minded** *adj* с широ́кими взгля́дами. **broadly** *adv*: ~ **speaking** вообще́ говоря́.
**broadcast** *n* переда́ча; *vt* передава́ть *impf*, переда́ть *pf* по ра́дио, по телеви́дению; (*seed*) се́ять *impf*, по~ *pf* вразбро́с. **broadcaster** *n* ди́ктор. **broadcasting** *n* ра́дио-, теле-, веща́ние.
**brocade** *n* парча́.
**broccoli** *n* бро́кколи *neut indecl*.
**brochure** *n* брошю́ра.
**broke** *predic* без гроша́. **broken** *adj* сло́манный; ~-**hearted** с разби́тым се́рдцем.
**broker** *n* комиссионе́р.
**bronchitis** *n* бронхи́т.
**bronze** *n* бро́нза; *adj* бро́нзовый.
**brooch** *n* брошь, бро́шка.
**brood** *n* вы́водок; *vi* мра́чно размышля́ть *impf*.
**brook**[1] *n* руче́й.
**brook**[2] *vt* терпе́ть *impf*.
**broom** *n* метла́. **broomstick** *n* (*witches'*) помело́.
**broth** *n* бульо́н.
**brothel** *n* публи́чный дом.
**brother** *n* брат; ~-**in-law** *n* (*sister's husband*) зять; (*husband's brother*) де́верь; (*wife's brother*) шу́рин; (*wife's sister's husband*) свояк. **brotherhood** *n* бра́тство. **brotherly** *adj* бра́тский.
**brow** *n* (*eyebrow*) бровь; (*forehead*) лоб; (*of hill*) гре́бень *m*. **browbeaten** *adj* запу́ганный.
**brown** *adj* кори́чневый; (*eyes*) ка́рий; *n* кори́чневый цвет; *vt* (*cul*) подрумя́нивать *impf*, подрумя́нить *pf*.

**browse** vi (look around) осма́триваться impf, осмотре́ться pf; (in book) просма́тривать impf просмотре́ть pf кни́гу.

**bruise** n синя́к; vt ушиба́ть impf, ушиби́ть pf.

**brunette** n брюне́тка.

**brunt** n основна́я тя́жесть.

**brush** n щётка; (paint) кисть; vt (clean) чи́стить impf, вы́~, по~ pf (щёткой); (touch) легко́ каса́ться impf, косну́ться pf +gen; (hair) расчёсывать impf, расчеса́ть pf щёткой; ~ aside отма́хиваться impf, отмахну́ться pf от+gen; ~ up сметать impf, смести pf; (renew) подчища́ть impf, подчи́стить pf.

**brushwood** n хво́рост.

**Brussels sprouts** n pl брюссе́льская капу́ста.

**brutal** adj жесто́кий. **brutality** n жесто́кость. **brutalize** vt ожесточа́ть impf, ожесточи́ть pf. **brute** n живо́тное sb; (person) ско́тина. **brutish** adj ха́мский.

**B.Sc.** abbr бакала́вр нау́к.

**bubble** n пузы́рь m; vi пузы́риться impf, кипе́ть impf, вс~ pf.

**buck** n саме́ц оле́ня, кро́лика etc.; vi брыка́ться impf.

**bucket** n ведро́.

**buckle** n пря́жка; vt застёгивать impf, застегну́ть pf (пря́жкой); vi (warp) коро́биться impf, по~, с~ pf.

**bud** n по́чка.

**Buddhism** n будди́зм. **Buddhist** n будди́ст; adj будди́йский.

**budge** vt & i шевели́ть(ся) impf, по~ pf.

**budget** n бюдже́т; vi: ~ for

предусма́тривать impf, предусмотре́ть pf в бюдже́те.

**buff** adj све́тло-кори́чневый.

**buffalo** n буйвол.

**buffet**[1] n буфе́т.

**buffet**[2] vt броса́ть impf (impers).

**buffoon** n шут.

**bug** n (insect) бука́шка; (germ) инфе́кция; (in computer) оши́бка в програ́мме; (microphone) потайно́й микрофо́н; vt (install ~) устана́вливать impf, установи́ть pf аппарату́ру для подслу́шивания в+prep; (listen) подслу́шивать impf.

**bugle** n горн.

**build** n (of person) телосложе́ние; vt стро́ить impf, по~ pf; ~ on пристра́ивать impf, пристро́ить pf (to k+dat); ~ up (vt) создава́ть impf, созда́ть pf; (vi) накопля́ться impf; накопи́ться pf. **builder** n строи́тель m. **building** n (edifice) зда́ние; (action) строи́тельство; ~ site стро́йка; ~ society жили́щно-строи́тельный кооперати́в.

**built-up area** n застро́енный райо́н.

**bulb** n лу́ковица; (electric) ла́мпочка. **bulbous** adj лу́ковичный.

**Bulgaria** n Болга́рия. **Bulgarian** n болга́рин, -га́рка; adj болга́рский.

**bulge** n вы́пуклость; vi вы́пя́чиваться impf, выпира́ть impf. **bulging** adj разбу́хший, оттопы́ривающийся.

**bulk** n (size) объём; (greater part) бо́льшая часть; **in** ~ гурто́м. **bulky** adj громо́здкий.

**bull** n бык; (male) саме́ц. **bulldog** n бульдо́г. **bulldozer**

*vt* расчища́ть *impf*, расчи́стить *pf* бульдо́зером. **bulldozer** *n* бульдо́зер. **bullfinch** *n* снеги́рь *m*. **bullock** *n* вол. **bull's-eye** *n* я́блоко.

**bullet** *n* пу́ля. **bullet-proof** *adj* пулесто́йкий.

**bulletin** *n* бюллете́нь *m*.

**bullion** *n*: gold ~ зо́лото в сли́тках.

**bully** *n* зади́ра *m* & *f*; *vt* запу́гивать *impf*, запуга́ть *pf*.

**bum** *n* зад.

**bumble-bee** *n* шмель *m*.

**bump** *n* (blow) уда́р, толчо́к; (swelling) ши́шка; (in road) уха́б; *vi* ударя́ться *impf*, уда́риться *pf*; ~ into ната́лкиваться *impf*, натолкну́ться *pf* на+*acc*. **bumper** *n* ба́мпер.

**bumpkin** *n* дереве́нщина *m* & *f*.

**bumptious** *adj* самоуве́ренный.

**bumpy** *adj* уха́бистый.

**bun** *n* сдо́бная бу́лка; (hair) пучо́к.

**bunch** *n* (of flowers) буке́т; (grapes) гроздь; (keys) свя́зка.

**bundle** *n* у́зел; *vt* свя́зывать *impf*, связа́ть *pf* в у́зел; ~ off спрова́живать *impf*, спрова́дить *pf*.

**bungalow** *n* бу́нгало *neut indecl*.

**bungle** *vt* по́ртить *impf*, ис~ *pf*.

**bunk** *n* ко́йка.

**bunker** *n* бу́нкер.

**buoy** *n* буй. **buoyancy** *n* плаву́честь; (fig) бо́дрость. **buoyant** *adj* плаву́чий; (fig) бо́дрый.

**burden** *n* бре́мя *neut*; *vt* обременя́ть *impf*, обремени́ть *pf*.

**bureau** *n* бюро́ *neut indecl*. **bureaucracy** *n* бюрокра́тия. **bureaucrat** *n* бюрокра́т. **bureaucratic** *adj* бюрократи́ческий.

**burger** *n* котле́та.

**burglar** *n* взло́мщик. **burglary** *n* кра́жа со взло́мом. **burgle** *vt* гра́бить *impf*, о~ *pf*.

**burial** *n* погребе́ние.

**burly** *adj* здорове́нный.

**burn** *vt* жечь *impf*, c~ *pf*; *vt* & *i* (injure) обжига́ть(ся) *impf*, обже́чь(ся) *pf*; *vi* горе́ть *impf*, c~ *pf*; (by sun) загора́ть *impf*, загоре́ть *pf*; *n* ожо́г. **burner** *n* горе́лка.

**burnish** *vt* полирова́ть *impf*, от~ *pf*.

**burp** *vi* рыга́ть *impf*, рыгну́ть *pf*.

**burrow** *n* нора́; *vi* рыть *impf*, вы́~ *pf* нору́; (fig) ры́ться *impf*.

**bursar** *n* казначе́й. **bursary** *n* стипе́ндия.

**burst** *n* разры́в, вспы́шка; *vi* разрыва́ться *impf*, разорва́ться *pf*; (bubble) ло́паться *impf*, ло́пнуть *pf*; *vt* разрыва́ть *impf*, разорва́ть *pf*; ~ into tears распла́каться *pf*.

**bury** *vt* (dead) хорони́ть *impf*, по~ *pf*; (hide) зарыва́ть *impf*, зары́ть *pf*.

**bus** *n* авто́бус; ~ stop авто́бусная остано́вка.

**bush** *n* куст. **bushy** *adj* густо́й.

**busily** *adv* энерги́чно.

**business** *n* (affair, dealings) де́ло; (firm) предприя́тие; mind your own ~ не ва́ше де́ло; on ~ по де́лу. **businesslike** *adj* делово́й. **businessman** *n* бизнесме́н.

**busker** n у́личный музыка́нт.
**bust** n бюст; (bosom) грудь.
**bustle** n суета́; vi суети́ться impf.
**busy** adj занято́й; vt: ~ o.s. занима́ться impf, за~ pf (with +instr). **busybody** n назо́йливый челове́к.
**but** conj но, а; ~ then зато́; prep кро́ме+gen.
**butcher** n мясни́к; vt ре́зать impf, за~ pf; ~'s shop мясна́я sb.
**butler** n дворе́цкий sb.
**butt**[1] n (cask) бо́чка.
**butt**[2] n (of gun) прикла́д; (cigarette) оку́рок.
**butt**[3] n (target) мише́нь.
**butt**[4] vt бода́ть impf, за~ pf; ~ in вме́шиваться impf, вмеша́ться pf.
**butter** n (сли́вочное) ма́сло; vt нама́зывать impf, нама́зать pf ма́слом; ~ up льстить impf, по~ pf +dat. **buttercup** n лю́тик. **butterfly** n ба́бочка.
**buttock** n я́годица.
**button** n пу́говица; (knob) кно́пка; vt застёгивать impf, застегну́ть pf. **buttonhole** n пе́тля.
**buttress** n контрфо́рс; vt подпира́ть impf, подпере́ть pf.
**buxom** adj полногру́дая.
**buy** n поку́пка; vt покупа́ть impf, купи́ть pf. **buyer** n поку́патель.
**buzz** n жужжа́ние; vi жужжа́ть impf.
**buzzard** n каню́к.
**buzzer** n зу́ммер.
**by** adv ми́мо; prep (near) о́коло+gen, у+gen; (beside) ря́дом с+instr; (past) ми́мо+gen; (time) к+dat; (means) instr without prep; ~ and large в це́лом.
**bye** int пока́!

**by-election** n дополни́тельные вы́боры m pl.
**Byelorussian** see **Belorussian**
**bygone** adj мину́вший; let ~s be ~s что прошло́, то прошло́. **by-law** n постановле́ние. **bypass** n обхо́д; vt обходи́ть impf, обойти́ pf. **by-product** n побо́чный проду́кт. **byroad** n небольша́я доро́га. **bystander** n свиде́тель m. **byway** n просёлочная доро́га. **byword** n олицетворе́ние (for +gen).
**Byzantine** adj византи́йский.

# C

**cab** n (taxi) такси́ neut indecl; (of lorry) каби́на.
**cabaret** n кабаре́ neut indecl.
**cabbage** n капу́ста.
**cabin** n (hut) хижина; (aeron) каби́на; (naut) каю́та.
**cabinet** n шкаф; (Cabinet) кабине́т; ~-maker краснодере́вец; ~-minister мини́стр-член кабине́та.
**cable** n (rope) кана́т; (electric) ка́бель m; (cablegram) телегра́мма; vt & i телеграфи́ровать impf & pf.
**cache** n потайно́й склад.
**cackle** n гого́тать impf.
**cactus** n ка́ктус.
**caddy** n (box) ча́йница.
**cadet** n новобра́нец.
**cadge** vi стреля́ть impf, стрельну́ть pf.
**cadres** n pl ка́дры m pl.
**Caesarean (section)** n ке́сарево-сече́ние.
**cafe** n кафе́ neut indecl. **cafeteria** n кафете́рий.
**caffeine** n кофеи́н.
**cage** n кле́тка.

**cajole** vt задáбривать impf, задóбрить pf.

**cake** n (large) торт, (small) пирóжное sb; (fruit~) кекс; vt: ~d облéпленный (in +instr).

**calamitous** adj бéдственный. **calamity** n бéдствие.

**calcium** n кáльций.

**calculate** vt вычислять impf, вычислить pf; vi рассчитывать impf, рассчитáть pf (on на+acc). **calculation** n вычислéние, расчёт. **calculator** n калькуля́тор.

**calendar** n календáрь m.

**calf**[1] n (cow) телёнок.

**calf**[2] n (leg) икрá.

**calibrate** vt калиброва́ть impf. **calibre** n калúбр.

**call** v звать impf, по~ pf; (name) называ́ть impf, назва́ть pf; (cry) крича́ть impf, крúкнуть pf; (wake) будúть impf, раз~ pf; (visit) заходúть impf, зайтú pf (on к+dat; at в+acc); (stop at) остана́вливаться impf, останови́ться pf (at в, на, +prep); (summon) вызыва́ть impf, вы́звать pf; (ring up) звонúть impf, по~ pf +dat; ~ for (require) трéбовать impf, по~ pf +gen; (fetch) заходúть impf, зайтú pf за+instr; ~ off отменя́ть impf, отменúть pf; ~ out вскрúкивать impf, вскрúкнуть pf; ~ up призыва́ть impf, призва́ть pf; n (cry) крик; (summons) зов, призы́в; (telephone) (телефóнный) вы́зов, разговóр; (visit) визúт; (signal) сигнáл; ~box телефóн-автомáт; ~up призы́в. **caller** n посетúтель m, ~ница; (tel) позвонúвший sb. **calling** n (voca-tion) призва́ние.

**callous** adj (person) чёрствый.

**callus** n мозóль.

**calm** adj спокóйный; n спокóйствие; vt & i (~ down) успока́ивать(ся) impf, успокóить(ся) pf.

**calorie** n калóрия.

**camber** n скат.

**camcorder** n камкóрдер.

**camel** n верблю́д.

**camera** n фотоаппарáт. **cameraman** n киноопера́тор.

**camouflage** n камуфля́ж; vt маскирова́ть impf, за~ pf.

**camp** n лáгерь m; vi (set up ~) располагáться impf, расположи́ться pf лáгерем; (go camping) жить impf в палáтках; ~-bed раскладýшка; ~-fire костёр.

**campaign** n кампáния; vi проводúть impf, провестú pf кампáнию.

**campsite** n лáгерь m, кéмпинг.

**campus** n университéтский городóк.

**can**[1] n бáнка; vt консервúровать impf, за~ pf.

**can**[2] n aux (be able) мочь impf, с~ pf +inf; (know how) умéть impf, с~ pf +inf.

**Canada** n Канáда. **Canadian** n канáдец, -дка; adj канáдский.

**canal** n канáл.

**canary** n канарéйка.

**cancel** vt (make void) аннулúровать impf & pf; (call off) отменя́ть impf, отменúть pf; (stamp) гасúть impf, по~ pf. **cancellation** n аннулúрование; отмéна.

**cancer** n рак; (C~) Рак. **cancerous** adj рáковый.

**candelabrum** n канделя́бр.

**candid** adj открове́нный.

**candidate** n кандида́т.

**candied** adj заса́харенный.

**candle** n свеча́. **candlestick** n подсве́чник.

**candour** n открове́нность.

**candy** n сла́дости f pl.

**cane** n (plant) тростни́к; (stick) трость, па́лка; vt бить impf, по~ pf па́лкой.

**canine** adj соба́чий; n (tooth) клык.

**canister** n ба́нка, коро́бка.

**canker** n рак.

**cannabis** n гаши́ш.

**cannibal** n людое́д. **cannibalism** n людое́дство.

**cannon** n пу́шка; ~-ball пу́шечное ядро́.

**canoe** n кано́э neut indecl; vi пла́вать indet, плыть det на кано́э.

**canon** n кано́н; (person) кано́ник. **canonize** vt канонизова́ть impf & pf.

**canopy** n балдахи́н.

**cant** n (hypocrisy) ха́нжество; (jargon) жарго́н.

**cantankerous** adj сварли́вый.

**cantata** n канта́та.

**canteen** n столо́вая sb.

**canter** n лёгкий гало́п; vi (rider) е́здить indet, е́хать det лёгким гало́пом; (horse) ходи́ть indet, идти́ det лёгким гало́пом.

**canvas** n (art) холст; (naut) паруси́на; (tent material) брезе́нт.

**canvass** vi агити́ровать impf, с~ pf (for за+acc); n собира́ние голосо́в; агита́ция. **canvasser** n собира́тель m голосо́в.

**canyon** n каньо́н.

**cap** n (of uniform) фура́жка; (cloth) ке́пка; (woman's) че-пе́ц; (lid) кры́шка; vt превосходи́ть impf, превзойти́ pf.

**capability** n спосо́бность. **capable** adj спосо́бный (of на+acc).

**capacious** adj вмести́тельный. **capacity** n ёмкость; (ability) спосо́бность; in the ~ of в ка́честве +gen.

**cape**[1] n (geog) мыс.

**cape**[2] n (cloak) наки́дка.

**caper** vi скака́ть impf.

**capers**[1] n pl (cul) ка́персы n pl.

**capillary** adj капилля́рный.

**capital** n (letter) пропи́сна́й; ~ **punishment** сме́ртная казнь; n (town) столи́ца; (letter) пропи́сная бу́ква; (econ) капита́л. **capitalism** n капитали́зм. **capitalist** n капитали́ст; adj капиталисти́ческий. **capitalize** vi извлека́ть impf, извле́чь pf вы́году (on из+gen).

**capitulate** vi капитули́ровать impf & pf. **capitulation** n капитуля́ция.

**caprice** n капри́з. **capricious** adj капри́зный.

**Capricorn** n Козеро́г.

**capsize** vt & i опроки́дывать(ся) impf, опроки́нуть(ся) pf.

**capsule** n ка́псула.

**captain** n капита́н; vt быть капита́ном +gen.

**caption** n по́дпись; (cin) титр.

**captious** adj приди́рчивый.

**captivate** vt пленя́ть impf, плени́ть pf. **captivating** adj плени́тельный. **captive** adj & n пле́нный. **captivity** n нево́ля; (esp mil) плен. **capture** n взя́тие, захва́т, пои́мка; vt (person) брать impf, взять pf в плен; (seize) захва́тывать *impf*, захвати́ть *pf*.

**car** *n* маши́на; автомоби́ль *m*; ~ **park** стоя́нка.

**carafe** *n* графи́н.

**caramel(s)** *n* караме́ль.

**carat** *n* кара́т.

**caravan** *n* фурго́н; (*convoy*) карава́н.

**caraway (seeds)** *n* тмин.

**carbohydrate** *n* углево́д. **carbon** *n* углеро́д; ~ **copy** ко́пия; ~ **dioxide** углекислота́; ~ **monoxide** о́кись углеро́да; ~ **paper** копирова́льная бума́га.

**carburettor** *n* карбюра́тор.

**carcass** *n* ту́ша.

**card** *n* (*stiff paper*) карто́н; (*visiting* ~) ка́рточка; (*playing* ~) ка́рта; (*greetings* ~) откры́тка; (*ticket*) биле́т. **cardboard** *n* карто́н; *adj* карто́нный.

**cardiac** *adj* серде́чный.

**cardigan** *n* кардига́н.

**cardinal** *adj* кардина́льный; ~ **number** коли́чественное числи́тельное *sb*; *n* кардина́л.

**care** *n* (*trouble*) забо́та; (*caution*) осторо́жность; (*tending*) ухо́д; in the ~ of на попече́нии +*gen*; **take** ~ осторо́жно!; смотри́(те)!; **take** ~ **of** уха́живать *impf*, по~ *pf* o+*prep*; *vi*: **I don't** ~ мне всё равно́; ~ **for** (*look after*) уха́живать *impf* за+*instr*; (*like*) нра́виться *impf*, по~ *pf impers* +*dat*.

**career** *n* карье́ра.

**carefree** *adj* беззабо́тный.

**careful** *adj* (*cautious*) осторо́жный; (*thorough*) тща́тельный; **careless** *adj* (*negligent*) небре́жный; (*incautious*) неосторо́жный.

**caress** *n* ла́ска; *vt* ласка́ть *impf*.

**caretaker** *n* смотри́тель *m*, ~ница; *attrib* вре́менный.

**cargo** *n* груз.

**caricature** *n* карикату́ра; *vt* изобража́ть *impf*, изобрази́ть *pf* в карикату́рном ви́де.

**carnage** *n* резня́.

**carnal** *adj* пло́тский.

**carnation** *n* гвозди́ка.

**carnival** *n* карнава́л.

**carnivorous** *adj* плотоя́дный.

**carol** *n* (рожде́ственский) гимн.

**carouse** *vi* кути́ть *impf*, кут-ну́ть *pf*.

**carp**[1] *n* карп.

**carp**[2] *vi* придира́ться *impf*, придра́ться *pf* (**at** к+*dat*).

**carpenter** *n* пло́тник. **carpentry** *n* пло́тничество.

**carpet** *n* ковёр; *vt* покрыва́ть *impf*, покры́ть *pf* ковро́м.

**carping** *adj* приди́рчивый.

**carriage** *n* (*vehicle*) каре́та; (*rly*) ваго́н; (*conveyance*) перево́зка; (*bearing*) оса́нка. **carriageway** *n* прое́зжая часть доро́ги. **carrier** *n* (*on bike*) бага́жник; (*firm*) тра́нспортная компа́ния; (*med*) баци́лоноси́тель *m*.

**carrot** *n* морко́вка; *pl* морко́вь (*collect*).

**carry** *vt* (*by hand*) носи́ть *indet*, нести́ *det*; переноси́ть *impf*, перенести́ *pf*; (*in vehicle*) вози́ть *indet*, везти́ *det*; (*sound*) передава́ть *impf*, переда́ть *pf*; *vi* (*sound*) быть слы́шен; **be carried away** увлека́ться *impf*, увле́чься *pf*; ~ **on** (*continue*) продолжа́ть *impf*; ~ **out** выполня́ть *impf*, вы́полнить *pf*; ~ **over** переноси́ть *impf*, перенести́ *pf*.

**cart** n теле́га; vt (lug) тащи́ть impf.

**cartilage** n хрящ.

**carton** n карто́нка.

**cartoon** n карикату́ра; (cin) мультфи́льм. **cartoonist** n карикатури́ст, ~ка.

**cartridge** n патро́н; (of record player) звукоснима́тель m.

**carve** vt ре́зать impf по+dat; (in wood) выреза́ть impf, вы́резать pf; (in stone) высека́ть impf, вы́сечь pf; (slice) нареза́ть impf, наре́зать pf. **carving** n резьба́; ~ knife нож для нареза́ния мя́са.

**cascade** n каска́д; vi па́дать impf.

**case**[1] n (instance) слу́чай; (law) де́ло; (med) больно́й sb; (gram) паде́ж; in ~ (в слу́чае) е́сли; in any ~ во вся́ком слу́чае; in no ~ ни в ко́ем слу́чае; just in ~ на вся́кий слу́чай.

**case**[2] n (box) я́щик; (suitcase) чемода́н; (small box) футля́р; (cover) чехо́л; (display ~) витри́на.

**cash** n нали́чные sb; (money) де́ньги pl; ~ on delivery нало́женным платежо́м; ~ desk, register ка́сса; vt: ~ a cheque получа́ть impf, получи́ть pf де́ньги по че́ку. **cashier** n касси́р.

**casing** n (tech) кожу́х.

**casino** n казино́ neut indecl.

**cask** n бо́чка.

**casket** n шкату́лка.

**casserole** n (pot) ла́тка; (stew) рагу́ neut indecl.

**cassette** n кассе́та; ~ recorder кассе́тный магнитофо́н.

**cassock** n ря́са.

**cast** vt (throw) броса́ть impf, бро́сить pf; (shed) сбра́сы-

вать impf, сбро́сить pf; (theat) распределя́ть impf, распредели́ть pf ро́ли +dat; (found) лить impf, с~ pf; ~ off (knitting) спуска́ть impf, спусти́ть pf пе́тли; (naut) отплыва́ть impf, отплы́ть pf; ~ on (knitting) набира́ть impf, набра́ть pf пе́тли; n (of mind etc.) склад; (mould) фо́рма; (moulded object) слепо́к; (med) ги́псовая повя́зка; (theat) де́йствующие ли́ца -(ц) pl. **castaway** n поте́рпевший sb кораблекруше́ние. **cast iron** n чугу́н. **cast-iron** adj чугу́нный. **cast-offs** n pl но́шеное пла́тье.

**castanet** n кастанье́та.

**caste** n ка́ста.

**castigate** vt бичева́ть impf.

**castle** n за́мок; (chess) ладья́.

**castor** n (wheel) ро́лик; ~ sugar са́харная пу́дра.

**castrate** vt кастри́ровать impf & pf. **castration** n кастра́ция.

**casual** adj (chance) случа́йный; (offhand) небре́жный; (clothes) обы́денный; (unofficial) неофициа́льный; (informal) лёгкий; (labour) подённый; ~ labourer подённщик, -ица. **casualty** n (wounded) ра́неный sb; (killed) уби́тый sb; pl поте́ри -(рь) pl; ~ ward пала́та ско́рой по́мощи.

**cat** n ко́шка; (tom) кот; ~'s-eye (on road) (доро́жный) рефле́ктор.

**catalogue** n катало́г; (price list) прейскура́нт; vt каталогизи́ровать impf & pf.

**catalyst** n катализа́тор. **catalytic** adj каталити́ческий.

**catapult** n (toy) рога́тка; (hist, aeron) катапу́льта; vt & i катапульти́ровать(ся) *impf* & *pf.*

**cataract** *n* (*med*) катара́кта.

**catarrh** *n* ката́р.

**catastrophe** *n* катастро́фа. **catastrophic** *adj* катастрофи́ческий.

**catch** *vt* (*ball, fish, thief*) лови́ть *impf*, пойма́ть *pf*; (*surprise*) застава́ть *impf*, заста́ть *pf*; (*disease*) зараза́ться *impf*, зарази́ться *pf* +*instr*; (*be in time for*) успева́ть *impf*, успе́ть *pf* на+*acc*; *vt* & *i* (*snag*) зацепля́ть(ся) *impf*, зацепи́ть(ся) *pf* (*on* за+*acc*); ~ **on** (*become popular*) прививáться *impf*, приви́ться *pf*; ~ **up with** догоня́ть *impf*, догна́ть *pf*; *n* (*of fish*) уло́в; (*trick*) уло́вка; (*on door etc.*) защёлка. **catching** *adj* зара́зный. **catchword** *n* мо́дное слове́чко. **catchy** *adj* прилипчивый.

**categorical** *adj* категори́ческий. **category** *n* катего́рия.

**cater** *vi*: ~ **for** поставля́ть *impf*, поста́вить *pf* прови́зию для+*gen*; (*satisfy*) удовлетворя́ть *impf*, удовлетвори́ть *pf*. **caterer** *n* поставщи́к (прови́зии).

**caterpillar** *n* гу́сеница.

**cathedral** *n* собо́р.

**catheter** *n* кате́тер.

**Catholic** *adj* католи́ческий; *n* като́лик, -и́чка. **Catholicism** *n* католи́чество.

**cattle** *n* скот.

**Caucasus** *n* Кавка́з.

**cauldron** *n* котёл.

**cauliflower** *n* цветна́я капу́ста.

**cause** *n* причи́на, по́вод; (*law etc.*) де́ло; *vt* причиня́ть *impf*, причини́ть *pf*; вызыва́ть *impf*, вы́звать *pf*; (*induce*) заста-

вля́ть *impf*, заста́вить *pf.*

**caustic** *adj* е́дкий.

**cauterize** *vt* прижига́ть *impf*, приже́чь *pf.*

**caution** *n* осторо́жность; (*warning*) предостереже́ние; *vt* предостерега́ть *impf*, предостере́чь *pf.* **cautious** *adj* осторо́жный. **cautionary** *adj* предостерега́ющий.

**cavalcade** *n* кавалька́да. **cavalier** *adj* бесцеремо́нный. **cavalry** *n* кавале́рия.

**cave** *n* пеще́ра; *vi*: ~ **in** обва́ливаться *impf*, обвали́ться *pf*; (*yield*) сдава́ться *impf*, сда́ться *pf.* **caveman** *n* пеще́рный челове́к. **cavern** *n* пеще́ра. **cavernous** *adj* пеще́ристый.

**caviare** *n* икра́.

**cavity** *n* впа́дина, по́лость; (*in tooth*) дупло́.

**cavort** *vi* скака́ть *impf.*

**caw** *vi* ка́ркать *impf*, ка́ркнуть *pf.*

**CD** *abbr* (*of compact disc*) компа́кт-ди́ск; ~ **player** прои́грыватель *m* компа́кт-ди́сков.

**cease** *vt* & *i* прекраща́ть(ся) *impf*, прекрати́ть(ся) *pf*; *vt* переставáть *impf*, переста́ть *pf* (+*inf*); ~ **fire** прекраще́ние огня́. **ceaseless** *adj* непреста́нный.

**cedar** *n* кедр.

**cede** *vt* уступа́ть *impf*, уступи́ть *pf.*

**ceiling** *n* потоло́к; (*fig*) макси́ма́льный у́ровень *m.*

**celebrate** *vt* & *i* пра́здновать *impf*, от~ *pf*; (*extol*) прославля́ть *impf*, просла́вить *pf.* **celebrated** *adj* знамени́тый. **celebration** *n* пра́зднование. **celebrity** *n* знамени́тость.

**celery** n сельдере́й.

**celestial** adj небе́сный.

**celibacy** n безбра́чие. **celibate** adj холосто́й; n холостя́к.

**cell** n (prison) ка́мера; (biol) кле́тка.

**cellar** n подва́л.

**cello** n виолонче́ль.

**cellophane** n целлофа́н. **cellular** adj кле́точный. **celluloid** n целлуло́ид.

**Celt** n кельт. **Celtic** adj ке́льтский.

**cement** n цеме́нт; vt цементи́ровать impf, за~ pf.

**cemetery** n кла́дбище.

**censor** n це́нзор; vt подверга́ть impf, подве́ргнуть pf цензу́ре. **censorious** adj сверхкрити́ческий. **censorship** n цензу́ра. **censure** n порица́ние; vt порица́ть impf.

**census** n пе́репись.

**cent** n цент; **per** ~ проце́нт.

**centenary** n столе́тие. **centennial** adj столе́тний. **centigrade** adj: 10° = 10° по Це́льсию. **centimetre** n сантиме́тр. **centipede** n сороконо́жка.

**central** adj центра́льный; ~ **heating** центра́льное отопле́ние. **centralization** n централиза́ция. **centralize** vt централизова́ть impf & pf. **centre** n центр; середи́на; ~ **forward** центр нападе́ния; vi & i: ~ **on** сосредото́чивать(ся) impf, сосредото́чить(ся) pf на+prep. **centrifugal** adj центробе́жный.

**century** n столе́тие, век.

**ceramic** adj керами́ческий. **ceramics** n pl кера́мика.

**cereals** n pl хле́бные зла́ки m pl; **breakfast** ~ зерновы́е

хло́пья (-ев) pl.

**cerebral** adj мозгово́й.

**ceremonial** adj церемониа́льный; n церемониа́л. **ceremonious** adj церемо́нный. **ceremony** n церемо́ния.

**certain** adj (confident) уве́рен (-нна); (undoubted) несомне́нный; (unspecified) изве́стный; (inevitable) ве́рный; **for** ~ наверняка́. **certainly** adv (of course) коне́чно, безусло́вно; (without doubt) несомне́нно; ~ **not!** ни в ко́ем слу́чае. **certainty** n (conviction) уве́ренность; (fact) несомне́нный факт.

**certificate** n свиде́тельство; сертифика́т. **certify** vt удостоверя́ть impf, удостове́рить pf.

**cervical** adj ше́йный. **cervix** n ше́йка ма́тки.

**cessation** n прекраще́ние.

**cf.** abbr ср., сравни́.

**CFCs** abbr (of chlorofluorocarbons) хлори́рованные фтороуглеро́ды m pl.

**chafe** vt (rub) тере́ть impf; (rub sore) натира́ть impf, натере́ть pf.

**chaff** n (husks) мяки́на; (straw) се́чка.

**chaffinch** n зя́блик.

**chagrin** n огорче́ние.

**chain** n цепь; ~ **reaction** цепна́я реа́кция; ~ **smoker** зая́длый кури́льщик.

**chair** n стул, (armchair) кре́сло; (univ) ка́федра; vt (preside) председа́тельствовать impf на+prep. **chairman, -woman** n председа́тель m, ~ница.

**chalice** n ча́ша.

**chalk** n мел. **chalky** adj мелово́й.

**challenge** n (summons, fig)

вы́зов; (*sentry's*) о́клик; (*law*) отво́д; *vt* вызыва́ть *impf*, вы́звать *pf*; (*sentry*) оклика́ть *impf*, окли́кнуть *pf*; (*law*) отводи́ть *impf*, отвести́ *pf*. **challenger** *n* претенде́нт. **challenging** *adj* интригу́ющий.

**chamber** *n* (*cavity*) ка́мера; (*hall*) зал; (*parl*) пала́та; *pl* (*law*) адвока́тская конто́ра; (*judge's*) кабине́т (судьи́); ~ music ка́мерная му́зыка; ~ pot ночно́й горшо́к. **chambermaid** *n* го́рничная *sb*.

**chameleon** *n* хамелео́н.

**chamois** *n* (*animal*) се́рна; (~-*leather*) за́мша.

**champagne** *n* шампа́нское *sb*.

**champion** *n* чемпио́н, ~ка; (*upholder*) побо́рник, -ица; *vt* боро́ться *impf* за +*acc*. **championship** *n* пе́рвенство, чемпиона́т.

**chance** *n* случа́йность; (*opportunity*) возмо́жность, (*favourable*) слу́чай; (*likelihood*) шанс (*usu pl*); by ~ случа́йно; *adj* случа́йный; *vi*: ~ it рискну́ть *pf*.

**chancellery** *n* канцеля́рия. **chancellor** *n* ка́нцлер; (*univ*) ре́ктор; C~ of the Exchequer ка́нцлер казначе́йства.

**chancy** *adj* риско́ванный.

**chandelier** *n* лю́стра.

**change** *n* измене́ние; (*of clothes etc.*) сме́на; (*money*) сда́ча; (*trains etc.*) переса́дка; for a ~ для разнообра́зия; *vt* & *i* меня́ть(ся) *impf*, изменя́ть(ся) *pf*, измени́ть(ся) *pf*, *vi* (*one's clothes*) переодева́ться *impf*, переоде́ться *pf*; (*trains etc.*) переса́живаться *impf*, пере-се́сть *pf*; *vt* (*a baby*) пере-пелёнывать *impf*, пере-

лена́ть *pf*; (*money*) обме́нивать *impf*, обменя́ть *pf*, (*give ~ for*) разме́нивать *impf*, разменя́ть *pf*; ~ into превраща́ться *impf*, преврати́ться *pf* в+*acc*; ~ over to переходи́ть *impf*, перейти́ *pf* на+*acc*. **changeable** *adj* изме́нчивый.

**channel** *n* (*water*) проли́в; (*also TV*) кана́л; (*fig*) путь *m*; the (English) C~ Ла-Ма́нш; *vt* (*fig*) направля́ть *impf*.

**chant** *n* (*eccl*) песнопе́ние; *vt* & *i* петь *impf*; (*slogans*) сканди́ровать *impf* & *pf*.

**chaos** *n* ха́ос. **chaotic** *adj* хаоти́чный.

**chap** *n* (*person*) па́рень *m*.

**chapel** *n* часо́вня; (*Catholic*) капе́лла.

**chaperone** *n* компаньо́нка.

**chaplain** *n* капелла́н.

**chapped** *adj* потре́скавшийся.

**chapter** *n* глава́.

**char** *vt* & *i* обу́гливать(ся) *impf*, обу́глить(ся) *pf*.

**character** *n* хара́ктер; (*theat*) де́йствующее лицо́; (*letter*) бу́ква; (*Chinese etc.*) иеро́глиф. **characteristic** *adj* характе́рный; *n* сво́йство; (*of person*) черта́ хара́ктера. **characterize** *vt* характеризова́ть *impf* & *pf*.

**charade** *n* шара́да.

**charcoal** *n* древе́сный у́голь *m*.

**charge** *n* (*for gun*; *electr*) заря́д; (*fee*) пла́та; (*person*) пито́мец, -мица; (*accusation*) обвине́ние; (*mil*) ата́ка; be in ~ of заве́довать *impf* +*instr*; in the ~ of на попече́нии +*gen*; *vt* (*gun*; *electr*) заря-жа́ть *impf*, заряди́ть *pf*; (*accuse*) обвиня́ть *impf*, обви-ни́ть *pf* (with в+*prep*); (*mil*)

атакова́ть *impf & pf*; *vi* броса́ться *impf*, бро́ситься *pf* в ата́ку; ~ **(for)** брать *impf*, взять *pf* (за+*acc*); ~ **to (the account of)** запи́сывать *impf*, записа́ть *pf* на счёт+*gen*.
**chariot** *n* колесни́ца.

**charisma** *n* обая́ние. **charismatic** *adj* обая́тельный.

**charitable** *adj* благотвори́тельный; (*kind, merciful*) милосе́рдный. **charity** *n* (*kindness*) милосе́рдие; (*organization*) благотвори́тельная организа́ция.

**charlatan** *n* шарлата́н.

**charm** *n* очарова́ние; пре́лесть; (*spell*) за́говор; *pl* ча́ры (чар) *pl*; (*amulet*) талисма́н; (*trinket*) брело́к; *vt* очаро́вывать *impf*, очарова́ть *pf*. **charming** *adj* очарова́тельный, преле́стный.

**chart** *n* (*naut*) морска́я ка́рта; (*table*) гра́фик; *vt* наноси́ть *impf*, нанести́ *pf* на гра́фик. **charter** *n* (*document*) ха́ртия; (*statutes*) уста́в; *vt* нанима́ть *impf*, наня́ть *pf*. **charwoman** *n* приходя́щая убо́рщица.

**chase** *vt* гоня́ться *indet*, гна́ться *det* за+*instr*; *n* пого́ня; (*hunting*) охо́та.

**chasm** *n* (*abyss*) бе́здна.

**chassis** *n* шасси́ *neut indecl*.

**chaste** *adj* целому́дренный.

**chastise** *vt* кара́ть *impf*, по~ *pf*.

**chastity** *n* целому́дрие.

**chat** *n* бесе́да; *vi* бесе́довать *impf*; ~ **show** телевизио́нная бесе́да-интервью́ *f*.

**chatter** *n* болтовня́; *vi* болта́ть *impf*; (*teeth*) стуча́ть *impf*. **chatterbox** *n* болту́н. **chatty** *adj* разгово́рчивый.

**chauffeur** *n* шофёр.

**chauvinism** *n* шовини́зм. **chauvinist** *n* шовини́ст; *adj* шовинисти́ческий.

**cheap** *adj* дешёвый. **cheapen** *vt* (*fig*) опошля́ть *impf*, опошли́ть *pf*. **cheaply** *adv* дёшево.

**cheat** *vt* обма́нывать *impf*, обману́ть *pf*; *vi* плутова́ть *impf*, на~, с~ *pf*; *n* (*person*) обма́нщик, -ица; плут; (*act*) обма́н.

**check**[1] *n* контро́ль *m*, прове́рка; (*chess*) шах; ~**mate** шах и мат; *vt* (*examine*) проверя́ть *impf*, прове́рить *pf*; контроли́ровать *impf*, про~ *pf*; (*restrain*) сде́рживать *impf*, сдержа́ть *pf*; ~ **in** регистри́роваться *impf*, за~ *pf*; ~ **out** выпи́сываться *impf*, вы́писаться *pf*; ~**out** ка́сса; ~**up** осмо́тр.

**check**[2] *n* (*pattern*) кле́тка. **check(ed)** *adj* кле́тчатый.

**cheek** *n* щека́; (*impertinence*) на́глость. **cheeky** *adj* на́глый.

**cheep** *vi* пища́ть *impf*, пи́скнуть *pf*.

**cheer** *n* ободря́ющий во́зглас; ~**s!** за (ва́ше) здоро́вье!; *vt* (*applaud*) приве́тствовать *impf & pf*; ~**up** ободря́ть(ся) *impf*, ободри́ть(ся) *pf*. **cheerful** *adj* весёлый. **cheerio** *int* пока́. **cheerless** *adj* уны́лый.

**cheese** *n* сыр; ~**cake** ва́трушка.

**cheetah** *n* гепа́рд.

**chef** *n* (шеф-)по́вар.

**chemical** *adj* хими́ческий; *n* хими́кат. **chemist** *n* хи́мик; (*druggist*) апте́карь *m*; ~**'s (shop)** апте́ка. **chemistry** *n* хи́мия.

**cheque** *n* чек; **~-book** чёковая кни́жка.

**cherish** *vt* (*foster*) леле́ять *impf*; (*hold dear*) дорожи́ть *impf* +*instr*; (*love*) не́жно люби́ть *impf*.

**cherry** *n* ви́шня; *adj* вишнё-вый.

**cherub** *n* херуви́м.

**chess** *n* ша́хматы (-т) *pl*; **~-board** ша́хматная доска́; **~-men** *n* ша́хматы (-т) *pl*.

**chest** *n* сунду́к; (*anat*) грудь; **~ of drawers** комо́д.

**chestnut** *n* кашта́н; (*horse*) гнедо́й *sb*.

**chew** *vt* жева́ть *impf*. **chewing-gum** *n* жева́тельная рези́нка.

**chic** *adj* элега́нтный.

**chick** *n* цыплёнок. **chicken** *n* ку́рица; цыплёнок; *adj* трусли́вый; **~ out** тру́сить *impf*, с~ *pf*. **chicken-pox** *n* ветря́нка.

**chicory** *n* цико́рий.

**chief** *n* глава́ *m* & *f*; (*boss*) нача́льник; (*of tribe*) вождь *m*; *adj* гла́вный. **chiefly** *adv* гла́вным о́бразом. **chieftain** *n* вождь *m*.

**chiffon** *n* шифо́н.

**child** *n* ребёнок; **~-birth** ро́ды (-дов) *pl*. **childhood** *n* де́тство. **childish** *adj* де́тский. **childless** *adj* безде́тный. **childlike** *adj* де́тский. **childrens'** *adj* де́тский.

**chili** *n* стручко́вый пе́рец.

**chill** *n* хо́лод; (*ailment*) просту́да; *vt* охлажда́ть *impf*, охлади́ть *pf*. **chilly** *adj* прохла́дный.

**chime** *n* (*set of bells*) набо́р колоколо́в; *pl* (*sound*) перезво́н; (*of clock*) бой; *vt* & *i* (*clock*) бить *impf*, про~ *pf*; *vi*

(*bell*) звони́ть *impf*, по~ *pf*.

**chimney** *n* труба́; **~-sweep** трубочи́ст.

**chimpanzee** *n* шимпанзе́ *m indecl*.

**chin** *n* подборо́док.

**china** *n* фарфо́р.

**China** *n* Кита́й. **Chinese** *n* кита́ец, -а́янка; *adj* кита́йский.

**chink¹** *n* (*sound*) звон; *vi* звене́ть *impf*, про~ *pf*.

**chink²** *n* (*crack*) щель.

**chintz** *n* си́тец.

**chip** *vt* & *i* отка́лывать(ся) *impf*, отколо́ть(ся) *pf*; *n* (*of wood*) ще́пка; (*in cup*) щерби́на; (*in game*) фи́шка; *pl* карто́фель-соло́мка (*collect*); (*electron*) чип, микросхе́ма.

**chiropodist** *n* челове́к, занима́ющийся педикю́ром. **chiropody** *n* педикю́р.

**chirp** *vi* чири́кать *impf*.

**chisel** *n* (*wood*) стаме́ска; (*masonry*) зуби́ло; *vt* высека́ть *impf*, вы́сечь *pf*.

**chit** *n* (*note*) запи́ска.

**chivalrous** *adj* ры́царский. **chivalry** *n* ры́царство.

**chlorine** *n* хлор. **chlorophyll** *n* хлорофи́лл.

**chock-full** *adj* битко́м наби́тый.

**chocolate** *n* шокола́д; (*sweet*) шокола́дная конфе́та; **~ bar** шокола́дка.

**choice** *n* вы́бор; *adj* отбо́рный.

**choir** *n* хор *m*; **~-boy** пе́вчий *sb*.

**choke** *n* (*valve*) дро́ссель *m*; *vi* дави́ться *impf*, по~ *pf*; (*with anger etc.*) задыха́ться *impf*, задохну́ться *pf* (*with* от+*gen*); *vt* (*suffocate*) души́ть *impf*, за~ *pf*; (*of plants*) заглуша́ть, глуши́ть *impf*, заглуши́ть *pf*.

**cholera** *n* холе́ра.

**cholesterol** *n* холестери́н.

**choose** *vt* (*select*) выбира́ть *impf*, вы́брать *pf*; (*decide*) реша́ть *impf*, реши́ть *pf*. **choosy** *adj* разбо́рчивый.

**chop** *vt* (*also* ~ *down*) руби́ть *impf*, рубну́ть *pf*; ~ **off** отруба́ть *impf*, отруби́ть *pf*; *n* (*cul*) отбивна́я котле́та.

**chopper** *n* топо́р. **choppy** *adj* бурли́вый.

**chop-sticks** *n* па́лочки *f pl* для еды́.

**choral** *adj* хорово́й. **chorale** *n* хора́л.

**chord** *n* (*mus*) акко́рд.

**chore** *n* обя́занность.

**choreographer** *n* хорео́граф. **choreography** *n* хореогра́фия.

**chorister** *n* пе́вчий *sb*.

**chortle** *vi* фы́ркать *impf*, фы́ркнуть *pf*.

**chorus** *n* хор; (*refrain*) припе́в.

**christen** *vt* крести́ть *impf* & *pf*. **Christian** *n* христиани́н, -а́нка; *adj* христиа́нский; ~ **name** и́мя *neut*. **Christianity** *n* христиа́нство. **Christmas** *n* Рождество́; ~ **Day** пе́рвый день Рождества́; ~ **Eve** соче́льник; ~ **tree** ёлка.

**chromatic** *adj* хромати́ческий. **chrome** *n* хром. **chromium** *n* хром. **chromosome** *n* хромосо́ма.

**chronic** *adj* хрони́ческий.

**chronicle** *n* хро́ника, ле́топись.

**chronological** *adj* хронологи́ческий.

**chrysalis** *n* ку́колка.

**chrysanthemum** *n* хризанте́ма.

**chubby** *adj* пу́хлый.

**chuck** *vt* броса́ть *impf*, бро́сить *pf*; ~ **out** вышиба́ть *impf*, вы́шибить *pf*.

**chuckle** *vi* посме́иваться *impf*.

**chum** *n* това́рищ.

**chunk** *n* ломо́ть *m*.

**church** *n* це́рковь. **churchyard** *n* кла́дбище.

**churlish** *adj* гру́бый.

**churn** *n* масло́бойка; *vt* сбива́ть *impf*, сбить *pf*; *vi* (*foam*) пе́ниться *impf*, вс~ *pf*; (*stomach*) крути́ть *impf*; ~ **out** выпека́ть *impf*, вы́печь *pf*; ~ **up** взбить *pf*.

**chute** *n* жёлоб.

**cider** *n* сидр.

**cigar** *n* сига́ра. **cigarette** *n* сигаре́та; папиро́са; ~ **lighter** зажига́лка.

**cinder** *n* шлак; *pl* зола́.

**cine-camera** *n* киноаппара́т. **cinema** *n* кино́ *neut indecl*.

**cinnamon** *n* кори́ца.

**cipher** *n* нуль *m*; (*code*) шифр.

**circle** *n* круг; (*theatre*) я́рус; *vi* кружи́ться *impf*; *vt* (*walking*) обходи́ть *impf*, обойти́ *pf*; (*flying*) облета́ть *impf*, облете́ть *pf*. **circuit** *n* кругооборо́т; (*by-pass*) объе́зд, обхо́д; (*electron*) схе́ма; (*electr*) цепь. **circuitous** *adj* окружно́й. **circular** *adj* кру́глый; (*moving in a circle*) кругово́й; *n* циркуля́р. **circulate** *vi* циркули́ровать *impf*; *vt* распространя́ть *impf*, распространи́ть *pf*. **circulation** *n* (*air*) циркуля́ция; (*distribution*) распростране́ние; (*of newspaper*) тира́ж; (*med*) кровообраще́ние.

**circumcise** *vt* обреза́ть *impf*, обре́зать *pf*. **circumcision** *n* обреза́ние.

**circumference** *n* окру́жность.

**circumspect** *adj* осмотри́тельный.

**circumstance** *n* обстоя́тельство; **under the ~s** при да́нных обстоя́тельствах, в тако́м слу́чае; **under no ~s** ни при каки́х обстоя́тельствах, ни в ко́ем слу́чае.

**circumvent** *vt* обходи́ть *impf*, обойти́ *pf*.

**circus** *n* цирк.

**cirrhosis** *n* цирро́з.

**CIS** *abbr* (*of* **Commonwealth of Independent States**) СНГ.

**cistern** *n* бачо́к.

**citadel** *n* цитаде́ль.

**cite** *vt* ссыла́ться *impf*, сосла́ться *pf* на+*acc*.

**citizen** *n* граждан|и́н, -а́нка.

**citizenship** *n* гражда́нство.

**citrus** *n* ци́трус; *adj* ци́трусовый.

**city** *n* го́род.

**civic** *adj* гражда́нский. **civil** *adj* гражда́нский; (*polite*) ве́жливый; **~ engineer** гражда́нский инжене́р; **~ engineering** гражда́нское строи́тельство; **C~ Servant** госуда́рственный слу́жащий *sb*; чино́вник; **C~ Service** госуда́рственная слу́жба. **civilian** *n* шта́тск|ий *sb*; *adj* шта́тский. **civility** *n* ве́жливость.

**civilization** *n* цивилиза́ция. **civilize** *vt* цивилизова́ть *impf* & *pf*. **civilized** *adj* цивилизо́ванный.

**clad** *adj* оде́тый.

**claim** *n* (*demand*) тре́бование, притяза́ние; (*assertion*) утвержде́ние; *vt* (*demand*) тре́бовать *impf* +*gen*; (*assert*) утвержда́ть *impf*, утверди́ть *pf*. **claimant** *n* претенде́нт.

**clairvoyant** *n* яснови́д|ец, -дица

*adj* яснови́дящий.

**clam** *n* моллю́ск; *vi*: **~ up** отка́зываться *impf*, отказа́ться *pf* разгова́ривать.

**clamber** *vi* кара́бкаться *impf*, вс-~*pf*.

**clammy** *adj* вла́жный.

**clamour** *n* шум; *vi*: **~ for** шу́мно тре́бовать *impf*, по-*pf* +*gen*.

**clamp** *n* зажи́м; *vt* скрепля́ть *impf*, скрепи́ть *pf*; **~ down on** прижа́ть *pf*.

**clan** *n* клан.

**clandestine** *adj* та́йный.

**clang, clank** *n* лязг; *vt* & *i* ля́згать *impf*, ля́згнуть *pf* (+*instr*).

**clap** *vt* & *i* хло́пать *impf*, хло́пнуть *pf* +*dat*; *n* хлопо́к; (*thunder*) уда́р.

**claret** *n* бордо́ *neut indecl*.

**clarification** *n* (*explanation*) разъясне́ние. **clarify** *vt* разъясня́ть *impf*, разъясни́ть *pf*.

**clarinet** *n* кларне́т.

**clarity** *n* я́сность.

**clash** *n* (*conflict*) столкнове́ние; (*disharmony*) дисгармо́ния; *vi* ста́лкиваться *impf*, столкну́ться *pf*; (*coincide*) совпада́ть *impf*, совпа́сть *pf*; не гармони́ровать *impf*.

**clasp** *n* застёжка; (*embrace*) объя́тие; *vt* обхва́тывать *impf*, обхвати́ть *pf*; **~ one's hands** сплести́ *pf* па́льцы рук.

**class** *n* класс; **~-room** класс; *vt* классифици́ровать *impf* & *pf*.

**classic** *adj* класси́ческий; *n* кла́ссик; *pl* (*literature*) кла́ссика; (*Latin and Greek*) класси́ческие языки́ *m pl*. **classical** *adj* класси́ческий.

**classification** *n* классифика́-

ция. **classified** adj засекре́-
ченный. **classify** vt класси-
фици́ровать impf & pf.
**classy** adj кла́ссный.
**clatter** n стук; vi стуча́ть impf,
по~ pf.
**clause** n статья́; (gram) пред-
ложе́ние.
**claustrophobia** n клаустро-
фо́бия.
**claw** n ко́готь; vt цара́пать
impf когтя́ми.
**clay** n гли́на; adj гли́няный.
**clean** adj чи́стый; adv (fully)
соверше́нно; ~-shaven гла́д-
ко вы́бритый; vt чи́стить
impf, вы́~, по~ pf. **cleaner**
n чи́стильщик, -ица. **cleaner's**
n химчи́стка. **clean(li)ness** n
чистота́. **cleanse** vt очи-
ща́ть impf, очи́стить pf.
**clear** adj я́сный; (transparent)
прозра́чный; (distinct) отчётливый; (free) свобо́дный (of
от+gen); (pure) чи́стый; vt & i
очища́ть(ся) impf, очи́стить-
(ся) pf; vt (jump over) пере-
пры́гивать impf, перепры́г-
нуть pf; (acquit) опра́в-
дывать impf, оправда́ть pf;
~ **away** убира́ть impf, уб-
ра́ть pf со стола́; ~ **off** (go
away) убира́ться impf, уб-
ра́ться pf; ~ **out** (vt) вы-
чища́ть impf, вы́чистить pf;
(vi) (make off) убира́ться
impf, убра́ться pf; ~ **up** (tidy
(away)) убира́ть impf, убра́ть
pf; проясня́ться impf, убра́ть
pf; (weather) проясня́ться
impf, проясни́ться pf; (explain) выясня́ть impf, вы́-
яснить pf. **clearance** n рас-
чи́стка; (permission) разре-
ше́ние. **clearing** n (glade)
поля́на. **clearly** adv я́сно.
**cleavage** n разре́з груди́.
**clef** n (mus) ключ.

**cleft** n тре́щина.
**clemency** n милосе́рдие.
**clench** vt (fist) сжима́ть impf,
сжа́ть pf; (teeth) сти́скивать
impf, сти́снуть pf.
**clergy** n духове́нство. **clergy-**
**man** n свяще́нник. **clerical**
adj (eccl) духо́вный; (of clerk)
канцеля́рский. **clerk** n кон-
то́рский слу́жащий sb.
**clever** adj у́мный. **cleverness**
n уме́ние.
**cliche** n клише́ neut indecl.
**click** vt щёлкать impf, щёлкнуть pf +instr.
**client** n клие́нт. **clientele** n
клиенту́ра.
**cliff** n утёс.
**climate** n кли́мат. **climatic**
adj климати́ческий.
**climax** n кульмина́ция.
**climb** vt & i ла́зить indet,
лезть det на+acc; влеза́ть
impf, влезть pf на+acc; под-
нима́ться impf, подня́ться pf
на+acc; ~ **down** (tree) сле-
за́ть impf, слезть pf (c+gen);
(mountain) спуска́ться impf,
спусти́ться pf (c+gen); (give
in) отступа́ть impf, отступи́ть
pf; n подъём. **climber** n аль-
пини́ст, ~ка; (plant) вью́-
щееся расте́ние. **climbing** n
альпини́зм.
**clinch** vt: ~ **a deal** закрепи́ть
pf сде́лку.
**cling** vi (stick) прилипа́ть impf,
прили́пнуть pf (to к+dat);
(grasp) цепля́ться impf, це-
пи́ться pf (to за+acc).
**clinic** n кли́ника. **clinical** adj
клини́ческий.
**clink** vt & i звене́ть impf,
про~ pf (+instr); **glasses**
чо́каться impf, чо́кнуться
pf; n звон.
**clip**[1] n скре́пка; зажи́м; vt

скрепля́ть *impf*, скрепи́ть *pf*.

**clip²** *vt* (*cut*) подстрига́ть *impf*, подстри́чь *pf*. **clippers** *n pl* но́жницы *f pl*. **clipping** *n* (*extract*) вы́резка.

**clique** *n* кли́ка.

**cloak** *n* плащ. **cloakroom** *n* гардеро́б; (*lavatory*) убо́рная *sb*.

**clock** *n* часы́ *m pl*; ~**wise** по часово́й стре́лке; ~-**work** *n* часово́й механи́зм; *vi*: ~ **in, out** отмеча́ться *impf*, отме́титься *pf* приходя́ на рабо́ту/уходя́ с рабо́ты.

**clod** *n* ком.

**clog** *vt*: ~ **up** засоря́ть *impf*, засори́ть *pf*.

**cloister** *n* арка́да.

**close** *adj* (*near*) бли́зкий; (*stuffy*) ду́шный; *vt & i* (*also* ~ **down**) закрыва́ть(ся) *impf*, закры́ть(ся) *pf*; (*conclude*) зака́нчивать *impf*, зако́нчить *pf*; *adv* бли́зко (*to* от+*gen*). **closed** *adj* закры́тый. **closeted** *adj*: be ~ **together** совеща́ться *impf* наедине́. **close-up** *n* фотогра́фия сня́тая кру́пным пла́ном. **closing** *n* закры́тие; *adj* заключи́тельный. **closure** *n* закры́тие.

**clot** *n* сгу́сток; *vi* сгуща́ться *impf*, сгусти́ться *pf*.

**cloth** *n* ткань; (*duster*) тря́пка; (*table-*~) ска́терть.

**clothe** *vt* одева́ть *impf*, оде́ть (**in** +*instr*, в+*acc*) *pf*. **clothes** *n pl* оде́жда, пла́тье.

**cloud** *n* о́блако, (*rain* ~) ту́ча; *vt* затемня́ть *impf*, затемни́ть *pf*; омрача́ть *impf*, омрачи́ть *pf*; ~ **over** покрыва́ться *impf*, покры́ться *pf* облака́ми, ту́чами. **cloudy** *adj* о́блачный; (*liquid*) му́тный.

**clout** *vt* ударя́ть *impf*, уда́рить *pf*; *n* затре́щина; (*fig*) влия́ние.

**clove** *n* гвозди́ка; (*of garlic*) зубо́к.

**cloven** *adj* раздво́енный.

**clover** *n* кле́вер.

**clown** *n* кло́ун.

**club** *n* (*stick*) дуби́нка; *pl* (*cards*) тре́фы (треф) *pl*; (*association*) клуб; *vt* колоти́ть *impf*, по~ *pf* дуби́нкой; *vi*: ~ **together** скла́дываться *impf*, сложи́ться *pf*.

**cluck** *vi* куда́хтать *impf*.

**clue** *n* (*evidence*) улика; (*to puzzle*) ключ; (*hint*) намёк.

**clump** *n* гру́ппа.

**clumsiness** *n* неуклю́жесть. **clumsy** *adj* неуклю́жий.

**cluster** *n* гру́ппа; *vi* собира́ться *impf*, собра́ться *pf* гру́ппами.

**clutch** *n* (*grasp*) хва́тка; ко́гти *m pl*; (*tech*) сцепле́ние; *vt* зажима́ть *impf*, зажа́ть *pf*; *vi*: ~ **at** хвата́ться *impf*, хвати́ться *pf* за+*acc*.

**clutter** *n* беспоря́док; *vt* загромажда́ть *impf*, загромозди́ть *pf*.

**c/o** *abbr* (*of* **care of**) по а́дресу +*gen*; че́рез+*acc*.

**coach** *n* (*horse-drawn*) каре́та; (*rly*) ваго́н; (*bus*) авто́бус; (*tutor*) репети́тор; (*sport*) тре́нер; *vt* репети́ровать *impf*, тренирова́ть *impf*, на~ *pf*.

**coagulate** *vi* сгуща́ться *impf*, сгусти́ться *pf*.

**coal** *n* у́голь *m*; ~**mine** у́гольная ша́хта.

**coalition** *n* коали́ция.

**coarse** *adj* гру́бый.

**coast** *n* побере́жье, бе́рег; ~**guard** берегова́я охра́на; *vi* (*move without power*) двигаться *impf*, двинуться *pf* по инерции. **coastal** *adj* береговой, прибрежный.

**coat** *n* пальто *neut indecl*; (*layer*) слой; (*animal*) шерсть, мех; ~ **of arms** покрывать *impf*, покрыть *pf*.

**coax** *vt* уговаривать *impf*, уговорить *pf*.

**cob** *n* (*corn-*~) початок кукурузы.

**cobble** *n* булыжник (*also* collect). **cobbled** *adj* булыжный.

**cobbler** *n* сапожник.

**cobweb** *n* паутина.

**Coca-Cola** *n* (*propr*) кока-кола.

**cocaine** *n* кокаин.

**cock** *n* (*bird*) петух; (*tap*) кран; (*of gun*) курок; *vt* (*gun*) взводить *impf*, взвести *pf* курок+*gen*.

**cockerel** *n* петушок.

**cockle** *n* сердцевидка.

**cockpit** *n* (*aeron*) кабина.

**cockroach** *n* таракан.

**cocktail** *n* коктейль *m*.

**cocky** *adj* чванный.

**cocoa** *n* какао *neut indecl*.

**coco(a)nut** *n* кокос.

**cocoon** *n* кокон.

**cod** *n* треска.

**code** *n* (*of laws*) кодекс; (*cipher*) код; *vt* шифровать *impf*, за~ *pf*. **codify** *vt* кодифицировать *impf & pf*.

**co-education** *n* совместное обучение.

**coefficient** *n* коэффициент.

**coerce** *vt* принуждать *impf*, принудить *pf*. **coercion** *n* принуждение.

**coexist** *vi* сосуществовать *impf*. **coexistence** *n* сосуществование.

**coffee** *n* кофе *m indecl*; ~-**mill** *n* кофейница; ~-**pot** *n* кофейник.

**coffer** *n pl* казна.

**coffin** *n* гроб.

**cog** *n* зубец. **cogwheel** *n* зубчатое колесо.

**cogent** *adj* убедительный.

**cohabit** *vi* сожительствовать *impf*.

**coherent** *adj* связный. **cohesion** *n* сплочённость. **cohesive** *adj* сплочённый.

**coil** *vt & i* свёртывать(ся) *impf*, свернуть(ся) *pf* кольцом; *n* кольцо; (*electr*) катушка.

**coin** *n* монета; *vt* чеканить *impf*, от~ *pf*.

**coincide** *vi* совпадать *impf*, совпасть *pf*. **coincidence** *n* совпадение. **coincidental** *adj* случайный.

**coke** *n* кокс.

**colander** *n* дуршлаг.

**cold** *n* холод; (*med*) простуда, насморк; *adj* холодный; ~-**blooded** *adj* жестокий; (*zool*) холоднокровный.

**colic** *n* колики *f pl*.

**collaborate** *vi* сотрудничать *impf*. **collaboration** *n* сотрудничество. **collaborator** *n* сотрудник, -ица; (*traitor*) коллаборационист, -истка.

**collapse** *vi* рухнуть *pf*; *n* падение; крушение.

**collar** *n* воротник; (*dog's*) ошейник; ~-**bone** ключица.

**colleague** *n* коллега *m & f*.

**collect** *vt* собирать *impf*, собрать *pf*; (*as hobby*) коллекционировать *impf*; (*fetch*) забирать *impf*, забрать *pf*. **collected** *adj* (*calm*) собранный; ~ **works** собрание сочинений. **collection** *n* (*stamps etc.*) коллекция; (*church etc.*) сбор; (*post*) выемка. **collective** *n* коллектив; *adj* коллекти́вный; ~ **farm** колхо́з; ~ **noun** собира́тельное существи́тельное *sb.* **collectivization** *n* коллективиза́ция. **collector** *n* сбо́рщик; колле́кционе́р.

**college** *n* колле́дж, учи́лище.

**collide** *vi* ста́лкиваться *impf*, столкну́ться *pf*. **collision** *n* столкнове́ние.

**colliery** *n* каменноуго́льная ша́хта.

**colloquial** *adj* разгово́рный. **colloquialism** *n* разгово́рное выраже́ние.

**collusion** *n* та́йный сго́вор.

**colon**[1] *n* (*anat*) то́лстая кишка́.

**colon**[2] *n* (*gram*) двоето́чие.

**colonel** *n* полко́вник.

**colonial** *adj* колониа́льный. **colonialism** *n* колониали́зм. **colonize** *vt* колонизова́ть *impf* & *pf.* **colony** *n* коло́ния.

**colossal** *adj* колосса́льный.

**colour** *n* цвет, кра́ска; (*pl*) (*flag*) зна́мя *neut*; ~**-blind** страда́ющий дальтони́змом; ~ **film** цветна́я плёнка; *vt* раскра́шивать *impf*, раскра́сить *pf*; *vi* красне́ть *impf*, по~ *pf.* **coloured** *adj* цветно́й. **colourful** *adj* я́ркий. **colourless** *adj* бесцве́тный.

**colt** *n* жеребёнок.

**column** *n* (*archit*, *mil*) коло́нна; (*of smoke etc.*) столб; (*of print*) столбе́ц. **columnist** *n* журнали́ст.

**coma** *n* ко́ма.

**comb** *n* гребёнка; *vt* причёсывать *impf*, причеса́ть *pf.*

**combat** *n* бой; *vt* боро́ться *impf* с+*instr*, про́тив+*gen*.

**combination** *n* сочета́ние, комбина́ция. **combine** *n* комбина́т; (~**-harvester**) комба́йн; *vt* & *i* совмеща́ть(ся)

*impf*, совмести́ть(ся) *pf.* **combined** *adj* совме́стный.

**combustion** *n* горе́ние.

**come** *vi* (*on foot*) приходи́ть *impf*, прийти́ *pf*; (*by transport*) приезжа́ть *impf*, прие́хать *pf*; ~ **about** случа́ться *impf*, случи́ться *pf*; ~ **across** случа́йно ната́лкиваться *impf*, натолкну́ться *pf* на+*acc*; ~ **back** возвраща́ться *impf*, возврати́ться *pf*; ~ **in** входи́ть *impf*, войти́ *pf*; ~ **out** выходи́ть *impf*, вы́йти *pf*; ~ **round** (*revive*) приходи́ть *impf*, прийти́ *pf* в себя́; (*visit*) заходи́ть *impf*, зайти́ *pf*; (*agree*) соглаша́ться *impf*, согласи́ться *pf*; ~ **up to** (*approach*) подходи́ть *impf*, подойти́ *pf* к+*dat*; (*reach*) доходи́ть *impf*, дойти́ *pf* до+*gen*. **come-back** *n* возвраще́ние. **come-down** *n* униже́ние.

**comedian** *n* комедиа́нт. **comedy** *n* коме́дия.

**comet** *n* коме́та.

**comfort** *n* комфо́рт; (*convenience*) удо́бство; (*consolation*) утеше́ние; *vt* утеша́ть *impf*, уте́шить *pf.* **comfortable** *adj* удо́бный.

**comic** *adj* коми́ческий; ко́мик; (*magazine*) ко́микс. **comical** *adj* смешно́й.

**coming** *adj* сле́дующий.

**comma** *n* запята́я *sb.*

**command** *n* (*order*) прика́з; (*order*, *authority*) кома́нда; **have** ~ **of** (*master*) владе́ть *impf* +*instr*; *vt* прика́зывать *impf*, приказа́ть *pf* +*dat*; (*mil*) кома́ндовать *impf*, с~ *pf* +*instr*. **commandant** *n* коменда́нт. **commandeer** *vt* реквизи́ровать *impf* & *pf.* **commander** *n* команди́р; ~**-in-**

**chief** главнокома́ндующий *sb.* **commandment** *n* за́поведь. **commando** *n* деса́нтник.

**commemorate** *vt* ознамено́вывать *impf*, ознаменова́ть *pf*. **commemoration** *n* ознаменова́ние. **commemorative** *adj* па́мятный.

**commence** *vt & i* начина́ть(ся) *impf*, нача́ть(ся) *pf*. **commencement** *n* нача́ло.

**commend** *vt* хвали́ть *impf*, по~ *pf*; (*recommend*) рекомендова́ть *impf & pf*. **commendable** *adj* похва́льный. **commendation** *n* похвала́.

**commensurate** *adj* соразме́рный.

**comment** *n* замеча́ние; *vi* де́лать *impf*, с~ *pf* замеча́ния; ~ **on** комменти́ровать *impf & pf*, про~ *pf*. **commentary** *n* коммента́рий. **commentator** *n* коммента́тор.

**commerce** *n* комме́рция. **commercial** *adj* торго́вый; *n* рекла́ма.

**commiserate** *vi*: ~ **with** соболе́зновать *impf +dat*. **commiseration** *n* соболе́знование.

**commission** *n* (*order for work*) зака́з; (*agent's fee*) комиссио́нные *sb*; (*of inquiry etc.*) коми́ссия; (*mil*) офице́рское зва́ние; *vt* зака́зывать *impf*, заказа́ть *pf*. **commissionaire** *n* швейца́р. **commissioner** *n* комисса́р.

**commit** *vt* соверша́ть *impf*, соверши́ть *pf*; ~ **o.s.** обя́зываться *impf*, обяза́ться *pf*. **commitment** *n* обяза́тельство.

**committee** *n* комите́т.

**commodity** *n* това́р.

**commodore** *n* (*officer*) командо́р.

**common** *adj* о́бщий; (*ordinary*) просто́й; *n* о́бщинная земля́; ~ **sense** здра́вый смысл. **commonly** *adv* обы́чно. **commonplace** *adj* бана́льный. **commonwealth** *n* содру́жество.

**commotion** *n* сумато́ха.

**communal** *adj* обще́ственный, коммуна́льный. **commune** *n* комму́на; *vi* обща́ться *impf*.

**communicate** *vt* передава́ть *impf*, переда́ть *pf*; сообща́ть *impf*, сообщи́ть *pf*. **communication** *n* сообще́ние; связь. **communicative** *adj* разгово́рчивый.

**communion** *n* (*eccl*) прича́стие.

**communiqué** *n* коммюнике́ *neut indecl*.

**Communism** *n* коммуни́зм. **Communist** *n* коммуни́ст, -ка; *adj* коммунисти́ческий.

**community** *n* общи́на.

**commute** *vt* заменя́ть *impf*, замени́ть *pf*; (*travel*) добира́ться *impf*, добра́ться *pf* тра́нспортом. **commuter** *n* регуля́рный пассажи́р.

**compact**[1] *n* (*agreement*) соглаше́ние.

**compact**[2] *adj* компа́ктный; ~ **disc** компа́кт-ди́ск; *n* пу́дреница.

**companion** *n* това́рищ; (*handbook*) спра́вочник. **companionable** *adj* общи́тельный. **companionship** *n* дру́жеское обще́ние. **company** *n* о́бщество, (*also firm*) компа́ния; (*theat*) тру́ппа; (*mil*) ро́та.

**comparable** *adj* сравни́мый. **comparative** *adj* сравни́

тельный; n сравни́тельная сте́пень. **compare** vt & i сра́внивать(ся) impf, сравни́ть(ся) pf (**to, with** c+instr).
**comparison** n сравне́ние.

**compartment** n отделе́ние; (rly) купе́ neut indecl.

**compass** n ко́мпас; pl ци́ркуль m.

**compassion** n сострада́ние. **compassionate** adj сострада́тельный.

**compatibility** n совмести́мость. **compatible** adj совмести́мый.

**compatriot** n соотече́ственник, -ица.

**compel** vt заставля́ть impf, заста́вить pf.

**compensate** vt компенси́ровать impf & pf (**for** за+acc). **compensation** n компенса́ция.

**compete** vi конкури́ровать impf; соревнова́ться impf.
**competence** n компете́нтность. **competent** adj компете́нтный.

**competition** n (contest) соревнова́ние, состяза́ние; (rivalry) конкуре́нция. **competitive** adj (comm) конкурентоспосо́бный. **competitor** n конкуре́нт, -ка.

**compilation** n (result) компиля́ция; (act) составле́ние. **compile** vt составля́ть impf, соста́вить pf. **compiler** n состави́тель m, -ница.

**complacency** n самодово́льство. **complacent** adj самодово́льный.

**complain** vi жа́ловаться impf, по~ pf. **complaint** n жа́лоба.

**complement** n дополне́ние; (full number) (ли́чный) со-

ста́в; vt дополня́ть impf, допо́лнить pf. **complementary** adj дополни́тельный.

**complete** vt заверша́ть impf, верши́ть pf; adj (entire, thorough) по́лный; (finished) зако́нченный. **completion** n заверше́ние.

**complex** adj сло́жный; n ко́мплекс. **complexity** n сло́жность.

**complexion** n цвет лица́.

**compliance** n усту́пчивость. **compliant** adj усту́пчивый.

**complicate** vt осложня́ть impf, осложни́ть pf. **complicated** adj сло́жный. **complication** n осложне́ние.

**complicity** n соуча́стие.

**compliment** n комплиме́нт; pl приве́т; vt говори́ть impf комплиме́нт(ы) +dat; хвали́ть impf, по~ pf. **complimentary** adj ле́стный; (free) беспла́тный.

**comply** vi: ~ **with** (fulfil) исполня́ть impf, испо́лнить pf; (submit to) подчиня́ться impf, подчини́ться pf +dat.

**component** n дета́ль; adj составно́й.

**compose** vt (music etc.) сочиня́ть impf, сочини́ть pf; (draft, constitute) составля́ть impf, соста́вить pf. **composed** adj споко́йный; **be ~ of** состоя́ть impf из+gen. **composer** n компози́тор. **composition** n сочине́ние; (make-up) соста́в.

**compost** n компо́ст.

**composure** n самооблада́ние.

**compound**[1] n (chem) соедине́ние; adj сло́жный.

**compound**[2] n (enclosure) огоро́женное ме́сто.

**comprehend** vt понима́ть impf,

поня́ть *pf*. **comprehensible** *adj* поня́тный. **comprehension** *n* понима́ние. **comprehensive** *adj* всеобъе́млющий; ~ **school** общеобразова́тельная шко́ла.

**compress** *vt* сжима́ть *impf*, сжать *pf*. **compressed** *adj* сжа́тый. **compression** *n* сжа́тие. **compressor** *n* компре́ссор.

**comprise** *vt* состоя́ть *impf* из+*gen*.

**compromise** *n* компроми́сс; *vt* компромети́ровать *impf*, с~ *pf*; *vi* идти́ *impf*, пойти́ *pf* на компроми́сс.

**compulsion** *n* принужде́ние. **compulsory** *adj* обяза́тельный.

**compunction** *n* угрызе́ние со́вести.

**computer** *n* компью́тер.

**comrade** *n* това́рищ. **comradeship** *n* това́рищество.

**con**¹ *see* **pro**¹

**con**² *vt* надува́ть *impf*, наду́ть *pf*.

**concave** *adj* во́гнутый.

**conceal** *vt* скрыва́ть *impf*, скрыть *pf*.

**concede** *vt* уступа́ть *impf*, уступи́ть *pf*; (*admit*) признава́ть *impf*, призна́ть *pf*; (*goal*) пропуска́ть *impf*, пропусти́ть *pf*.

**conceit** *n* самомне́ние. **conceited** *adj* самовлюблённый.

**conceivable** *adj* мы́слимый. **conceive** *vt* (*plan, imagine*) заду́мывать *impf*, заду́мать *pf*; (*biol*) зачина́ть *impf*, зача́ть *pf*; *vi* забере́менеть *pf*.

**concentrate** *vt* & *i* сосредото́чивать(ся) *impf*, сосредото́чить(ся) *pf* (**on** на+*prep*); *vt* (*also chem*) концентри-

ровать *impf*, с~ *pf*. **concentration** *n* сосредото́ченность, концентра́ция.

**concept** *n* поня́тие. **conception** *n* поня́тие; (*biol*) зача́тие.

**concern** *n* (*worry*) забо́та; (*comm*) предприя́тие; *vt* каса́ться *impf* +*gen*; ~ **o.s. with** занима́ться *impf*, заня́ться *pf* +*instr*. **concerned** *adj* озабо́ченный; **as far as I'm** ~ что каса́ется меня́. **concerning** *prep* относи́тельно+*gen*.

**concert** *n* конце́рт. **concerted** *adj* согласо́ванный.

**concertina** *n* гармо́ника.

**concession** *n* усту́пка; (*econ*) конце́ссия. **concessionary** *adj* конце́ссио́нный.

**conciliation** *n* примире́ние. **conciliatory** *adj* примири́тельный.

**concise** *adj* кра́ткий. **conciseness** *n* сжа́тость, кра́ткость.

**conclude** *vt* заключа́ть *impf*, заключи́ть *pf*. **concluding** *adj* заключи́тельный. **conclusion** *n* заключе́ние; (*deduction*) вы́вод. **conclusive** *adj* реша́ющий.

**concoct** *vt* стря́пать *impf*, со~ *pf*. **concoction** *n* стряпня́.

**concourse** *n* зал.

**concrete** *n* бето́н; *adj* бето́нный; (*fig*) конкре́тный.

**concur** *vi* соглаша́ться *impf*, согласи́ться *pf*. **concurrent** *adj* одновреме́нный.

**concussion** *n* сотрясе́ние.

**condemn** *vt* осужда́ть *impf*, осуди́ть *pf*; (*as unfit for use*) бракова́ть *impf*, за~ *pf*. **condemnation** *n* осужде́ние.

**condensation** *n* конденса́ция.

**condense** vt (liquid etc.) конденси́ровать impf & pf; (text etc.) сокраща́ть impf, сократи́ть pf. **condensed** adj сжа́тый; (milk) сгущённый. **condenser** n конденса́тор.

**condescend** vi снисходи́ть impf, снизойти́ pf. **condescending** adj снисходи́тельный. **condescension** n снисхожде́ние.

**condiment** n припра́ва.

**condition** n усло́вие; (state) состоя́ние; vt (determine) обусло́вливать impf, обусло́вить pf; (psych) приуча́ть impf, приучи́ть pf. **conditional** adj усло́вный.

**condolence** n: pl соболе́знование.

**condom** n презервати́в.

**condone** vt закрыва́ть impf, закры́ть pf глаза́ на+acc.

**conducive** adj спосо́бствующий (to +dat).

**conduct** n (behaviour) поведе́ние; vt вести́ impf, по~, про~ pf; (mus) дирижи́ровать impf +instr; (phys) проводи́ть impf. **conduction** n проводи́мость. **conductor** n (bus) конду́ктор; (mus) проводни́к; (mus) дирижёр.

**conduit** n трубопрово́д.

**cone** n ко́нус; (bot) ши́шка.

**confectioner** n конди́тер; ~'s (shop) конди́терская sb. **confectionery** n конди́терские изде́лия neut pl.

**confederation** n конфедера́ция.

**confer** vt присужда́ть impf, присуди́ть (on +dat) pf; vi совеща́ться impf. **conference** n совеща́ние; конфере́нция.

**confess** vt & i (acknowledge)

признава́ть(ся) impf, призна́ть(ся) pf (to в+prep); (eccl) испове́довать(ся) impf & pf. **confession** n призна́ние; и́споведь. **confessor** n духовни́к.

**confidant(e)** n бли́зкий собесе́дник. **confide** vt доверя́ть impf, дове́рить pf; ~ in дели́ться impf, по~ pf c+instr. **confidence** n (trust) дове́рие; (certainty) уве́ренность; (self-~) самоуве́ренность. **confident** adj уве́ренный. **confidential** adj секре́тный.

**confine** vt ограни́чивать impf, ограни́чить pf; (shut in) заключа́ть impf, заключи́ть pf. **confinement** n заключе́ние. **confines** n pl преде́лы m pl.

**confirm** vt подтвержда́ть impf, подтверди́ть pf. **confirmation** n подтвержде́ние; (eccl) конфирма́ция. **confirmed** adj закорене́лый.

**confiscate** vt конфискова́ть impf & pf. **confiscation** n конфиска́ция.

**conflict** n конфли́кт; противоре́чие; vi: ~ with противоре́чить impf +dat. **conflicting** adj противоречи́вый.

**conform** vi: ~ to подчиня́ться impf, подчини́ться pf +dat. **conformity** n соотве́тствие; (compliance) подчине́ние.

**confound** vt сбива́ть impf, сбить pf c то́лку. **confounded** adj прокля́тый.

**confront** vt стоя́ть impf лицо́м к лицу́ c+instr; ~ (person) with ста́вить impf, по~ pf лицо́м к лицу́ c+instr. **confrontation** n конфронта́ция.

**confuse** vt смущать impf, смутить pf; (also mix up) путать impf, за~, с~ pf.

**confusion** n смущение; путаница.

**congeal** vt густеть impf; (blood) свёртываться impf, свернуться pf.

**congenial** adj приятный.

**congenital** adj врождённый.

**congested** adj переполненный. **congestion** n (traffic) затор.

**congratulate** vt поздравлять impf, поздравить pf (on c+instr). **congratulation** n поздравление; ~s! поздравляю!

**congregate** vi собираться impf, собраться pf. **congregation** n (eccl) прихожане (-н) pl.

**congress** n съезд. **Congressman** n конгрессмен.

**conic(al)** adj конический.

**conifer** n хвойное дерево. **coniferous** adj хвойный.

**conjecture** n догадка; vt гадать impf.

**conjugal** adj супружеский.

**conjugate** vt спрягать impf, про~ pf. **conjugation** n спряжение.

**conjunction** n (gram) союз; in ~ with совместно с+instr.

**conjure** vi: ~ up (in mind) вызывать impf, вызвать pf в воображении. **conjurer** n фокусник. **conjuring trick** n фокус.

**connect** vt & i связывать(ся) impf, связать(ся) pf; соединять(ся) impf, соединить(ся) pf. **connected** adj связанный. **connection, -exion** n связь; (rly etc.) пересадка.

**connivance** n попустительство. **connive** vi: ~ at попу-

стительствовать impf +dat.

**connoisseur** n знаток.

**conquer** vt (country) завоёвывать impf, завоевать pf; (enemy) побеждать impf, победить pf; (habit) преодолевать impf, преодолеть pf. **conqueror** n завоеватель m. **conquest** n завоевание.

**conscience** n совесть. **conscientious** adj добросовестный. **conscious** adj сознательный; predic в сознании; be ~ of сознавать impf +acc. **consciousness** n сознание.

**conscript** vt призывать impf, призвать pf на военную службу; n призывник. **conscription** n воинская повинность.

**consecrate** vt освящать impf, освятить pf. **consecration** n освящение.

**consecutive** adj последовательный.

**consensus** n согласие.

**consent** vi соглашаться impf, согласиться pf (to +inf, на+acc); n согласие.

**consequence** n последствие; of great ~ большого значения; of some ~ довольно важный. **consequent** adj вытекающий. **consequential** adj важный. **consequently** adv следовательно.

**conservation** n сохранение; (of nature) охрана природы. **conservative** adj консервативный; n консерватор. **conservatory** n оранжерея. **conserve** vt сохранять impf, сохранить pf.

**consider** vt (think over) обдумывать impf, обдумать pf; (examine) рассматривать impf, рассмотреть pf; (regard *as, be of opinion that*) счита́ть *impf*, счесть *pf* +*instr*, за+*acc*, что; (*take into account*) счита́ться *impf* c+*instr*. **considerable** *adj* значи́тельный. **considerate** *adj* внима́тельный. **consideration** *n* рассмотре́ние; внима́ние; (*factor*) фа́ктор; **take into** ~ принима́ть *impf*, приня́ть *pf* во внима́ние. **considering** *prep* принима́я +*acc* во внима́ние.

**consign** *vt* передава́ть *impf*, переда́ть *pf*. **consignment** *n* (*goods*) па́ртия; (*consigning*) отпра́вка това́ров.

**consist** *vi*: ~ **of** состоя́ть *impf* из+*gen*. **consistency** *n* после́довательность; (*density*) консисте́нция. **consistent** *adj* после́довательный. **~ with** совмести́мый c+*instr*.

**consolation** *n* утеше́ние. **console**[1] *vt* утеша́ть *impf*, уте́шить *pf*.

**console**[2] *n* (*control panel*) пульт управле́ния.

**consolidate** *vt* укрепля́ть *impf*, укрепи́ть *pf*. **consolidation** *n* укрепле́ние.

**consonant** *n* согла́сный *sb*.

**consort** *n* супру́г, ~a.

**conspicuous** *adj* заме́тный.

**conspiracy** *n* за́говор. **conspirator** *n* заго́вщик, -ица. **conspiratorial** *adj* заго́вор-щицкий. **conspire** *vi* устра́ивать *impf*, устро́ить *pf* за́говор.

**constable** *n* полице́йский *sb*.

**constancy** *n* постоя́нство. **constant** *adj* постоя́нный. **constantly** *adv* постоя́нно.

**constellation** *n* созве́здие.

**consternation** *n* трево́га.

**constipation** *n* запо́р.

**constituency** *n* избира́тель-

ный о́круг. **constituent** *n* (*component*) составна́я часть; (*voter*) избира́тель *m*; *adj* составно́й. **constitute** *vt* составля́ть *impf*, соста́вить *pf*. **constitution** *n* (*polit, med*) конститу́ция; (*composition*) составле́ние. **constitutional** *adj* (*polit*) конституцио́нный.

**constrain** *vt* принужда́ть *impf*, прину́дить *pf*. **constrained** *adj* (*inhibited*) стеснённый. **constraint** *n* принужде́ние; (*inhibition*) стесне́ние.

**constrict** *vt* (*compress*) сжима́ть *impf*, сжать *pf*; (*narrow*) сужива́ть *impf*, су́зить *pf*. **constriction** *n* сжа́тие; суже́ние.

**construct** *vt* стро́ить *impf*, по~ *pf*. **construction** *n* строи́тельство; (*also gram*) констру́кция; (*interpretation*) истолкова́ние; ~ **site** стро́йка. **constructive** *adj* конструкти́вный.

**construe** *vt* истолко́вывать *impf*, истолкова́ть *pf*.

**consul** *n* ко́нсул. **consulate** *n* ко́нсульство.

**consult** *vt* сове́товаться *impf*, по~ *pf* c+*instr*. **consultant** *n* консульта́нт. **consultation** *n* консульта́ция.

**consume** *vt* потребля́ть *impf*, потреби́ть *pf*; (*eat or drink*) съеда́ть *impf*, съесть *pf*. **consumer** *n* потреби́тель *m*; ~ **goods** това́ры *m pl* широ́кого потребле́ния.

**consummate** *vt* заверша́ть *impf*, заверши́ть *pf*; ~ **a marriage** осуществля́ть *impf*, осуществи́ть *pf* бра́чные отноше́ния. **consummation** *n* заверше́ние; (*of marriage*) осуществле́ние.

**consumption** n потребле́ние.
**contact** n конта́кт; (person) связь; ~ **lens** конта́ктная ли́нза; vt свя́зываться impf, связа́ться pf c+instr.
**contagious** adj зара́зный.
**contain** vt содержа́ть impf; (restrain) сде́рживать impf, сдержа́ть pf. **container** n (vessel) сосу́д; (transport) конте́йнер.
**contaminate** vt загрязня́ть impf, загрязни́ть pf. **contamination** n загрязне́ние.
**contemplate** vt (gaze) созерца́ть impf; размышля́ть impf; (consider) предполага́ть impf, предположи́ть pf. **contemplation** n созерца́ние; размышле́ние. **contemplative** adj созерца́тельный.
**contemporary** n совреме́нник; adj совреме́нный.
**contempt** n презре́ние; ~ **of court** неуваже́ние к суду́; **hoid in** ~ презира́ть impf. **contemptible** adj презре́нный. **contemptuous** adj презри́тельный.
**contend** vi (compete) состяза́ться impf; ~ **for** оспа́ривать impf; ~ **with** справля́ться impf, спра́виться pf c+instr; vt утвержда́ть impf. **contender** n прете́нде́нт.
**content**[1] n содержа́ние; pl содержи́мое sb; (table of) ~**s** содержа́ние.
**content**[2] predic дово́лен (-льна); vt: ~ **o.s. with** дово́льствоваться impf, у~ pf +instr. **contented** adj дово́льный.
**contention** n (claim) утвержде́ние. **contentious** adj спо́рный.
**contest** n состяза́ние; vt (dispute) оспа́ривать impf, оспо-

рить pf. **contestant** n уча́стник, -ица, состяза́ния.
**context** n конте́кст.
**continent** n матери́к. **continental** adj материко́вый.
**contingency** n возмо́жный слу́чай; ~ **plan** вариа́нт пла́на. **contingent** adj случа́йный; n континге́нт.
**continual** adj непреста́нный. **continuation** n продолже́ние. **continue** vt & i продолжа́ть(ся) impf, продо́лжить(ся) pf. **continuous** adj непреры́вный.
**contort** vt искажа́ть impf, искази́ть pf. **contortion** n искаже́ние.
**contour** n ко́нтур; ~ **line** горизонта́ль.
**contraband** n контраба́нда.
**contraception** n предупрежде́ние зача́тия. **contraceptive** n противозача́точное сре́дство; adj противозача́точный.
**contract** n контра́кт, догово́р; vi (make a ~) заключа́ть impf, заключи́ть pf контра́кт; vt & i (shorten, reduce) сокраща́ть(ся) impf, сократи́ть(ся) pf; vt (illness) заболева́ть impf, заболе́ть pf +instr. **contraction** n сокраще́ние pf (med) схва́тки f pl. **contractor** n подря́дчик.
**contradict** vt противоре́чить impf +dat. **contradiction** n противоре́чие. **contradictory** adj противоречи́вый.
**contraflow** n встре́чное движе́ние.
**contralto** n контра́льто (voice) neut & (person) indecl.
**contraption** n приспособле́ние.
**contrary** adj (opposite) про-

тивополо́жный; (*perverse*) капри́зный; ~ to вопреки́ +*dat*; *n*: on the ~ наоборо́т.
**contrast** *n* контра́ст, противополо́жность; *vt* противопоставля́ть *impf*, противопоста́вить *pf* (with +*dat*); *vi* контрасти́ровать *impf*.
**contravene** *vt* наруша́ть *impf*, нару́шить *pf*. **contravention** *n* наруше́ние.
**contribute** *vt* (*to fund etc.*) же́ртвовать *impf*, по~ *pf* (to в+*acc*); ~ to (*further*) соде́йствовать *impf* & *pf*, по~ *pf* +*dat*; (*write for*) сотру́дничать *impf* в+*prep*. **contribution** *n* (*money*) поже́ртвование; (*fig*) вклад. **contributor** *n* (*donor*) же́ртвователь *m*; (*writer*) сотру́дник.
**contrite** *adj* ка́ющийся.
**contrivance** *n* приспособле́ние. **contrive** *vt* ухитря́ться *impf*, ухитри́ться *pf* +*inf*.
**control** *n* (*mastery*) контро́ль *m*; (*operation*) управле́ние; *pl* управле́ния *pl*; *vt* (*dominate*; *verify*) контроли́ровать *impf*, про~ *pf*; (*regulate*) управля́ть *impf* +*instr*; ~ o.s. сде́рживаться *impf*, сдержа́ться *pf*.
**controversial** *adj* спо́рный. **controversy** *n* спор.
**convalesce** *vi* выздора́вливать *impf*. **convalescence** *n* выздоровле́ние.
**convection** *n* конве́кция. **convector** *n* конве́ктор.
**convene** *vt* созыва́ть *impf*, созва́ть *pf*.
**convenience** *n* удо́бство; (*public* ~) убо́рная *sb*. **convenient** *adj* удо́бный.
**convent** *n* же́нский монасты́рь *m*.

**convention** *n* (*assembly*) съезд; (*agreement*) конве́нция; (*custom*) обы́чай; (*conventionality*) усло́вность. **conventional** *adj* общепри́нятый; (*of art*) усло́вный; (*also mil*) обы́чный.
**converge** *vi* сходи́ться *impf*, сойти́сь *pf*. **convergence** *n* сходи́мость.
**conversant** *predic*: ~ with знако́м с+*instr*.
**conversation** *n* разгово́р. **conversational** *adj* разгово́рный. **converse**[1] *vi* разгова́ривать *impf*.
**converse**[2] *n* обра́тное *sb*. **conversely** *adv* наоборо́т. **conversion** *n* (*change*) превраще́ние; (*of faith*) обраще́ние; (*of building*) перестро́йка.
**convert** *vt* (*change*) превраща́ть *impf*, преврати́ть *pf* (into в+*acc*); (*to faith*) обраща́ть *impf*, обрати́ть *pf* (to в+*acc*); (*a building*) перестра́ивать *impf*, перестро́ить *pf*. **convertible** *adj* обрати́мый; *n* автомоби́ль *m* со снима́ющейся кры́шей.
**convex** *adj* вы́пуклый.
**convey** *vt* (*transport*) перевози́ть *impf*, перевезти́ *pf*; (*communicate*) передава́ть *impf*, переда́ть *pf*. **conveyance** *n* перево́зка; переда́ча. **conveyancing** *n* нотариа́льная переда́ча. **conveyor belt** *n* транспортёрная ле́нта.
**convict** *n* осуждённый *sb*; *vt* осужда́ть *impf*, осуди́ть *pf*. **conviction** *n* (*law*) осужде́ние; (*belief*) убежде́ние. **convince** *vt* убежда́ть *impf*, убеди́ть *pf*. **convincing** *adj* убеди́тельный.

**convivial** *adj* весёлый.

**convoluted** adj изви́листый; (fig) запу́танный.

**convoy** n конво́й.

**convulse** vt: be ~d with содрога́ться impf, содрогну́ться pf от+gen. **convulsion** n (med) конву́льсия.

**cook** n куха́рка, по́вар; vt гото́вить impf; vi вари́ться impf; c~ pf. **cooker** n плита́, печь. **cookery** n кулина́рия.

**cool** adj прохла́дный; (calm) хладнокро́вный; (unfriendly) холо́дный; vt охлажда́ть impf, охлади́ть pf; ~ **down**, off остыва́ть impf, осты́(ну)ть pf. **coolness** n прохла́да; (calm) хладнокро́вие; (manner) хо́лодность.

**coop** n куря́тник; vt: ~ **up** держа́ть impf взаперти́.

**cooperate** vi сотру́дничать impf. **cooperation** n сотру́дничество. **cooperative** n коопера́тив; adj коoperatíвный; (helpful) услу́жливый.

**co-opt** vt коопти́ровать impf & pf.

**coordinate** vt координи́ровать impf & pf; n координа́та. **coordination** n координа́ция.

**cope** vi: ~ **with** справля́ться impf, спра́виться pf c+instr.

**copious** adj оби́льный.

**copper** n (metal) медь; adj ме́дный.

**coppice, copse** n ро́щица.

**copulate** vi совокупля́ться impf, совокупи́ться pf.

**copy** n ко́пия; (book) экземпля́р; vt (reproduce) копи́ровать impf, c~ pf; (transcribe) перепи́сывать impf, переписа́ть pf; (imitate) подража́ть impf +dat. **copyright** n а́вторское пра́во.

**coral** n кора́лл.

**cord** n (string) верёвка; (electr) шнур.

**cordial** adj серде́чный.

**corduroy** n ру́бчатый вельве́т.

**core** n сердцеви́на; (fig) суть.

**cork** n (material; stopper) про́бка; (float) поплаво́к. **corkscrew** n што́пор.

**corn**[1] n зерно́; (wheat) пшени́ца; (maize) кукуру́за. **cornflakes** n pl кукуру́зные хло́пья (-ьев) pl. **cornflour** n кукуру́зная мука́. **corny** adj (coll) бана́льный.

**corn**[2] n (med) мозо́ль.

**cornea** n рогова́я оболо́чка.

**corner** n у́гол; ~-**stone** n краеуго́льный ка́мень m; vt загна́ть pf, загна́ть pf в у́гол.

**cornet** n (mus) корне́т; (ice-cream) рожо́к.

**cornice** n карни́з.

**coronary (thrombosis)** n коронаротромбо́з. **coronation** n корона́ция. **coroner** n ме́дик суде́бной эксперти́зы.

**corporal**[1] n капра́л.

**corporal**[2] adj теле́сный; ~ **punishment** теле́сное наказа́ние.

**corporate** adj корпорати́вный. **corporation** n корпора́ция.

**corps** n ко́рпус.

**corpse** n труп.

**corpulent** adj ту́чный.

**corpuscle** n кровяно́й ша́рик.

**correct** adj пра́вильный; (conduct) корре́ктный; vt исправля́ть impf, испра́вить pf. **correction** n исправле́ние.

**correlation** n соотноше́ние.

**correspond** vi соотве́тствовать impf (**to, with** +dat); (by letter) перепи́сываться impf.

**correspondence** n соответствие; (letters) корреспонденция. **correspondent** n корреспондент. **corresponding** adj соответствующий (to +dat).

**corridor** n коридор.

**corroborate** vt подтверждать impf, подтвердить pf.

**corrode** vt разъедать impf, разъесть pf. **corrosion** n коррозия. **corrosive** adj едкий.

**corrugated iron** n рифлёное железо.

**corrupt** adj (person) развращённый; (government) продажный; vt развращать impf, развратить pf. **corruption** n развращение; коррупция.

**corset** n корсет.

**cortège** n кортеж.

**cortex** n кора.

**corundum** n корунд.

**cosmetic** adj косметический. **cosmetics** n pl косметика.

**cosmic** adj космический. **cosmonaut** n космонавт. **cosmopolitan** adj космополитический. **cosmos** n космос.

**Cossack** n казак, -ачка.

**cosset** vt нежить impf.

**cost** n стоимость, цена; vt стоить impf.

**costly** adj дорогой.

**costume** n костюм.

**cosy** adj уютный.

**cot** n детская кроватка.

**cottage** n коттедж; ~ cheese творог.

**cotton** n хлопок; (cloth) хлопчатобумажная ткань; (thread) нитка; ~ wool вата; adj хлопковый; хлопчатобумажный.

**couch** n диван.

**couchette** n спальное место.

**cough** n кашель m; vi кашлять impf.

**council** n совет; ~ tax местный налог; ~ house жильё из общественного фонда. **councillor** n член совета.

**counsel** n (advice) совет; (lawyer) адвокат; vt советовать impf, по~ pf +dat.

**count¹** vt считать impf, со~, счесть pf; со~; на рассчитывать impf на+acc; на счёт.

**countdown** n отсчёт времени.

**count²** n (title) граф.

**countenance** n лицо; vt одобрять impf, одобрить pf.

**counter** n прилавок; (token) фишка; adv: run ~ to идти impf вразрез с+instr; vt парировать impf, от~ pf. **counteract** vt противодействовать impf+dat. **counterbalance** n противовес; vt уравновешивать impf, уравновесить pf. **counterfeit** adj поддельный. **counterpart** n соответственная часть. **counterpoint** n контрапункт. **counter-revolutionary** n контрреволюционер; adj контрреволюционный. **countersign** vt ставить impf, по~ pf вторую подпись на+prep.

**countess** n графиня.

**countless** adj бесчисленный.

**country** n (nation) страна; (native land) родина; (rural areas) деревня; adj деревенский, сельский. **countryman** n (compatriot) соотечественник; сельский житель m. **countryside** n природный ландшафт.

**county** n графство.

**coup** n (polit) переворот.

**couple** n пápa; (a few) нéсколько +gen; vt сцепля́ть impf, сцепи́ть pf.

**coupon** n купóн; талóн; вáучер.

**courage** n хрáбрость. **courageous** adj хрáбрый.

**courier** n (messenger) курьéр; (guide) гид.

**course** n курс; (process) течéние; (of meal) блю́до; **of ~** конéчно.

**court** n двор; (sport) корт, площáдка; (law) суд; **~ martial** военный суд; vt уха́живать impf за+instr. **courteous** adj вéжливый. **courtesy** n вéжливость. **courtier** n придвóрный sb. **courtyard** n двор.

**cousin** n двою́родный брат, -ная сестрá.

**cove** n бухтóчка.

**covenant** n договóр.

**cover** n (covering; lid) покры́шка; (shelter) укры́тие; (chair ~, soft case) чехóл; (bed) покрывáло; (book) переплёт, облóжка; **under separate ~** в отдéльном конвéрте; vt покрывáть impf, покры́ть pf; (hide, protect) закрывáть impf, закры́ть pf. **coverage** n освещéние. **covert** adj скры́тый.

**covet** vt пожелáть pf +gen.

**cow**[1] n корóва. **cowboy** n ковбóй. **cowshed** n хлев.

**cow**[2] vt запу́гивать impf, запугáть pf.

**coward** n трус. **cowardice** n тру́сость. **cowardly** adj трусли́вый.

**cower** vi съёживаться impf, съёжиться pf.

**cox(swain)** n рулевóй m.

**coy** adj жемáнно стыдли́вый.

**crab** n краб.

**crack** n (in cup, ice) трéщина; (in wall) щель; (noise) треск; adj первоклáссный; vt (break) колóть impf, рас~ pf; (china) дéлать impf, с~ pf первоклáссный в+acc; vi трéснуть pf. **crackle** vi потрéскивать impf.

**cradle** n колыбéль.

**craft** n (trade) ремеслó; (boat) су́дно. **craftiness** n хи́трость. **craftsman** n ремéсленник. **crafty** adj хи́трый.

**crag** n утёс. **craggy** adj скали́стый.

**cram** vt (fill) набивáть impf, наби́ть pf; (stuff in) впи́хивать impf, впихну́ть pf; vi (study) зубри́ть impf.

**cramp**[1] n (med) су́дорога.

**cramp**[2] vt стесня́ть impf, стесни́ть pf. **cramped** adj тéсный.

**cranberry** n клю́ква.

**crane** n (bird) журáвль m; (machine) кран; vt (one's neck) вытя́гивать impf, вы́тянуть pf (шéю).

**crank**[1] n заводнáя ру́чка; **~-shaft** колéнчатый вал; **~** заводи́ть impf, завести́ pf.

**crank**[2] n (eccentric) чудáк. **cranky** adj чудáческий.

**cranny** n щель.

**crash** n (noise) грóхот, треск; (accident) авáрия; (financial) крах; **~ course** ускóренный курс; **~ helmet** защи́тный шлем; **~ landing** авари́йная посáдка; vi (~ into) врезáться impf, врéзаться pf в+acc; (aeron) разбивáться impf, разби́ться pf; (fall with ~) грóхнуться pf; vt (bang down) грóхнуть pf.

**crass** adj грубый.

**crate** n я́щик.

**crater** *n* кра́тер.

**crave** *vi*: ~ **for** жа́ждать *impf* +*gen*. **craving** *n* стра́стное жела́ние.

**crawl** *vi* по́лзать *indet*, ползти́ *det*; ~ **with** кише́ть+*instr*; *n* (*sport*) кроль *m*.

**crayon** *n* цветно́й каранда́ш.

**craze** *n* ма́ния. **crazy** *adj* поме́шанный (**about** на+*prep*).

**creak** *n* скрип; *vi* скрипе́ть *impf*.

**cream** *n* сли́вки (-вок) *pl*; (*cosmetic*; *cul*) крем; ~ **cheese** сли́вочный сыр; **soured** ~ смета́на; *vt* сбива́ть *impf*, сбить *pf*; *adj* (*of cream*) сли́вочный; (*colour*) кре́мовый. **creamy** *adj* сли́вочный, кре́мовый.

**crease** *n* скла́дка; *vt* мять *impf*, из~, с~ *pf*. **creased** *adj* мя́тый.

**create** *vt* создава́ть *impf*, созда́ть *pf*. **creation** *n* созда́ние. **creative** *adj* тво́рческий. **creator** *n* созда́тель *m*. **creature** *n* созда́ние.

**crèche** *n* (де́тские) я́сли (-лей) *pl*.

**credence** *n* ве́ра; **give** ~ ве́рить *impf* (**to** +*dat*). **credentials** *n pl* удостовере́ние; (*diplomacy*) вери́тельные гра́моты *f pl*. **credibility** *n* правдоподо́бие; (*of person*) спосо́бность вызыва́ть дове́рие. **credible** *adj* (*of thing*) правдоподо́бный; (*of person*) заслу́живающий дове́рия.

**credit** *n* дове́рие; (*comm*) креди́т; (*honour*) честь; **give** ~ кредитова́ть *impf* & *pf* +*acc*; отдава́ть *impf*, отда́ть до́лжное+*dat*; ~ **card** креди́тная ка́рточка; *vt*: ~ **with**

припи́сывать *impf*, приписа́ть *pf* +*dat*. **creditable** *adj* похва́льный. **creditor** *n* кредито́р.

**credulity** *n* легкове́рие. **credulous** *adj* легкове́рный.

**creed** *n* убежде́ние *neut pl*; (*eccl*) вероиспове́дание.

**creep** *vi* по́лзать *indet*, ползти́ *det*. **creeper** *n* (*plant*) ползу́чее расте́ние.

**cremate** *vt* кремирова́ть *impf* & *pf*. **cremation** *n* крема́ция.

**crematorium** *n* кремато́рий.

**crêpe** *n* креп.

**crescendo** *adv*, *adj*, & *n* креще́ндо *indecl*.

**crescent** *n* полуме́сяц.

**crest** *n* гре́бень *m*; (*heraldry*) герб.

**crevasse**, **crevice** *n* расще́лина, рассе́лина.

**crew** *n* брига́да; (*of ship, plane*) экипа́ж.

**crib**[1] *n* (*bed*) де́тская крова́тка; *vi* спи́сывать *impf*, списа́ть *pf*.

**crick** *n* растяже́ние мышц.

**cricket**[1] *n* (*insect*) сверчо́к.

**cricket**[2] *n* (*sport*) крике́т; ~ **bat** бита́.

**crime** *n* преступле́ние.

**Crimea** *n* Крым. **Crimean** *adj* кры́мский.

**criminal** *n* престу́пник; *adj* престу́пный; (*of crime*) уголо́вный.

**crimson** *adj* мали́новый.

**cringe** *vi* (*cower*) съёживаться *impf*, съёжиться *pf*.

**crinkle** *n* морщи́на; *vt* & *i* мо́рщить(ся) *impf*, на~, с~ *pf*.

**cripple** *n* кале́ка *m* & *f*; *vt* кале́чить *impf*, ис~ *pf*; (*fig*) расша́тывать *impf*, расша́тать *pf*.

**crisis** n кри́зис.
**crisp** adj (brittle) хрустя́щий; (fresh) све́жий. **crisps** n pl хрустя́щий карто́фель m.
**criss-cross** adv крест-на́крест.
**criterion** n крите́рий.
**critic** n кри́тик. **critical** adj крити́ческий. **critically** adv (ill) тяжело́; ~ critical. **criticism** n кри́тика. **criticize** vt критикова́ть impf. **critique** n кри́тика.
**croak** vi ква́кать impf, ква́кнуть pf; хрипе́ть impf.
**Croat** n хорва́т, ~ка. **Croatia** n Хорва́тия. **Croatian** adj хорва́тский.
**crochet** n вяза́ние крючко́м; vt вяза́ть impf, с~ pf (крючко́м).
**crockery** n посу́да.
**crocodile** n крокоди́л.
**crocus** n кро́кус.
**crony** n закады́чный друг.
**crook** n (staff) по́сох; (swindler) моше́нник. **crooked** adj криво́й; (dishonest) нече́стный.
**crop** n (yield) урожа́й; pl культу́ры f pl; (bird's) зоб; vt (cut) подстрига́ть impf, подстри́чь pf; ~ **up** возника́ть impf, возни́кнуть pf.
**croquet** n кроке́т.
**cross** n крест; (biol) по́месь; adj (angry) злой; vt (on foot) переходи́ть impf, перейти́ pf (че́рез) +acc; (by transport) переезжа́ть impf, перее́хать pf (че́рез) +acc; (biol) скре́щивать impf, скрести́ть pf; ~ **off, out** вычёркивать impf, вы́черкнуть pf; ~ **o.s.** крести́ться impf, пере~ pf; ~ **over** переходи́ть impf, перейти́ pf (че́рез) +acc. ~**bar** попере́чина. ~**breed** по́месь. ~**country race** кросс; ~**examination** перекрёстный до-

про́с; ~**examine**, ~**question** подверга́ть impf, подве́ргнуть pf перекрёстному допро́су; ~**eyed** косогла́зый; ~**legged: sit** ~ сиде́ть impf по-туре́цки; ~**reference** перекрёстная ссы́лка; ~**road(s)** перекрёсток; ~**section** перекрёстное сече́ние; ~**word (puzzle)** кроссво́рд. **crossing** n (intersection) перекрёсток; (foot) перехо́д; (transport; rly) перее́зд.
**crotch** n (anat) проме́жность.
**crotchet** n (mus) четвертна́я но́та.
**crotchety** adj раздражи́тельный.
**crouch** vi приседа́ть impf, присе́сть pf.
**crow** n воро́на; **as the** ~ **flies** по прямо́й ли́нии; vi кукаре́кать impf. **crowbar** n лом.
**crowd** n толпа́; vi тесни́ться impf, с~ pf; ~ **into** вти́скиваться impf, вти́снуться pf. **crowded** adj перепо́лненный.
**crown** n коро́на; (tooth) коро́нка; (head) те́мя; (hat) тулья́; vt корони́ровать impf & pf.
**crucial** adj (important) о́чень ва́жный; (decisive) реша́ющий; (critical) крити́ческий.
**crucifix, crucifixion** n распя́тие. **crucify** vt распина́ть impf, распя́ть pf.
**crude** adj (rude) гру́бый; (raw) сыро́й. **crudity** n гру́бость.
**cruel** adj жесто́кий. **cruelty** n жесто́кость.
**cruise** n круи́з; vi крейси́ровать impf. **cruiser** n кре́йсер.
**crumb** n кро́шка.
**crumble** vt кроши́ть impf, рас~ pf; vi обва́ливаться impf, обвали́ться pf. **crumbly** adj рассы́пчатый.

**crumple** vt мять impf, c~ pf; (intentionally) ко́мкать impf, c~ pf.

**crunch** n (fig) реша́ющий моме́нт; vt грызть impf, раз~ pf; vi хрусте́ть impf, хру́стнуть pf.

**crusade** n кресто́вый похо́д; (fig) кампа́ния. **crusader** n крестоно́сец; (fig) боре́ц (for за+acc).

**crush** n да́вка; (infatuation) си́льное увлече́ние; vt дави́ть impf, за~, раз~ pf; (crease) мять impf, c~ pf; (fig) подавля́ть impf, подави́ть pf.

**crust** n (of earth) кора́; (bread etc.) ко́рка.

**crutch** n косты́ль m.

**crux** n: ~ of the matter суть де́ла.

**cry** n крик; a far ~ from далеко́ от+gen; vi (weep) пла́кать impf; (shout) крича́ть impf, кри́кнуть pf.

**crypt** n склеп. **cryptic** adj зага́дочный.

**crystal** n криста́лл; (glass) хруста́ль m. **crystallize** vt & i кристаллизова́ть(ся) impf & pf.

**cub** n детёныш; bear ~ медвежо́нок; fox ~ лисёнок; lion ~ львёнок; wolf ~ волчо́нок.

**cube** n куб. **cubic** adj куби́ческий.

**cubicle** n каби́на.

**cuckoo** n куку́шка.

**cucumber** n огуре́ц.

**cuddle** vt обнима́ть impf, обня́ть pf; vi обнима́ться impf, обня́ться pf; ~ up прижима́ться impf, прижа́ться pf (to к+ dat).

**cudgel** n дуби́нка.

**cue**¹ n (theat) ре́плика.

**cue**² n (billiards) кий.

**cuff**¹ n манже́та; off the ~ экспро́мтом; ~-link за́понка.

**cuff**² vt (hit) шлёпать impf, шлёпнуть pf.

**cul-de-sac** n тупи́к.

**culinary** adj кулина́рный.

**cull** vt (select) отбира́ть impf, отобра́ть pf; (slaughter) бить impf.

**culminate** vi конча́ться impf, ко́нчиться pf (in +instr). **culmination** n кульминацио́нный пункт.

**culpability** n вино́вность. **culpable** adj вино́вный. **culprit** n вино́вник.

**cult** n культ.

**cultivate** vt (land) обраба́тывать impf, обрабо́тать pf; (crops) выра́щивать impf, вы́растить impf; (develop) развива́ть impf, разви́ть pf.

**cultural** adj культу́рный. **culture** n культу́ра. **cultured** adj культу́рный.

**cumbersome** adj громо́здкий.

**cumulative** adj кумуляти́вный.

**cunning** n хи́трость; adj хи́трый.

**cup** n ча́шка; (prize) ку́бок.

**cupboard** n шкаф.

**cupola** n ку́пол.

**curable** adj излечи́мый.

**curative** adj целе́бный.

**curator** храни́тель m.

**curb** vt обу́здывать impf, обузда́ть pf.

**curd** (cheese) n творо́г. **curdle** vt & i свёртывать(ся) impf, сверну́ть(ся) pf.

**cure** n сре́дство (for про́тив+gen); vt выле́чивать impf, вы́лечить pf; (smoke) копти́ть impf, за~ pf; (salt) соли́ть impf, по~ pf.

**curfew** n комендантский час.

**curiosity** n любопы́тство.

curious *adj* любопы́тный.

curl *n* ло́кон; *vt* завива́ть *impf*, зави́ть *pf*; ~ up сверты́ваться *impf*, сверну́ться *pf*.

curly *adj* кудря́вый.

currants *n pl* (dried) изю́м (collect).

currency *n* (prevalence) хожде́ние. current *adj* теку́щий; *n* тече́ние; (air) струя́; (water; electr) ток.

curriculum *n* курс обуче́ния; ~ vitae автобиогра́фия.

curry¹ *n* ка́рри neut indecl.

curry² *vt*: ~ favour with sb йскивать *impf* пе́ред+instr, у+gen.

curse *n* прокля́тие; (oath) руга́тельство; *vt* проклина́ть *impf*, прокля́сть *pf*; *vi* руга́ться *impf*, по~ *pf*.

cursory *adj* бе́глый.

curt *adj* ре́зкий.

curtail *vt* сокраща́ть *impf*, сократи́ть *pf*.

curtain *n* занаве́ска.

curts(e)y *n* реверанс; *vi* де́лать *impf*, с~ *pf* реверанс.

curve *n* изги́б; (line) крива́я; *vi* изгиба́ться *impf*, изогну́ться *pf*.

cushion *n* поду́шка; *vt* смягча́ть *impf*, смягчи́ть *pf*.

custard *n* сла́дкий заварно́й крем.

custodian *n* храни́тель *m*.

custody *n* опе́ка; (of police) аре́ст; to take into ~ арестова́ть *pf*.

custom *n* обы́чай; (comm) клиенту́ра; *pl* (duty) тамо́женные по́шлины *f pl*; go through ~s проходи́ть *impf*, пройти́ *pf* тамо́женный осмо́тр; ~-house тамо́жня; ~ officer тамо́женник.

customary *adj* обы́чный.

customer *n* клие́нт; покупа́тель *m*.

cut *vt* ре́зать *impf*, по~ *pf*; (hair) стричь *impf*, о~ *pf*; (mow) коси́ть *impf*, с~ *pf*; (price) снижа́ть *impf*, сни́зить *pf*; (cards) снима́ть *impf*, снять *pf* коло́ду; ~ back (prune) подреза́ть *impf*, подреза́ть *pf*; (reduce) сокраща́ть *impf*, сократи́ть *pf*; ~ down сруба́ть *impf*, сруби́ть *pf*; ~ off отреза́ть *impf*, отре́зать *pf*; (interrupt) прерыва́ть *impf*, прерва́ть *pf*; (disconnect) отключа́ть *impf*, отключи́ть *pf*; ~ out вырезывать *impf*, вы́резать *pf*; ~ out for со́зданный для+gen; ~ up разреза́ть *impf*, разре́зать *pf*; (gash) поре́з; (clothes) покро́й; (reduction) сниже́ние; ~ glass хруста́ль *m*.

cute *adj* симпати́чный.

cutlery *n* ножи́, ви́лки и ло́жки *pl*.

cutlet *n* отбивна́я котле́та.

cutting *n* (press) вы́резка; (plant) черено́к; *adj* ре́зкий.

CV *abbr* (of curriculum vitae) автобиогра́фия.

cycle *n* цикл; (bicycle) велосипе́д; *vi* е́здить *impf* на велосипе́де. cyclic(al) *adj* цикли́ческий. cyclist *n* велосипеди́ст.

cylinder *n* цили́ндр. cylindrical *adj* цилиндри́ческий.

cymbals *n pl* таре́лки *f pl*.

cynic *n* ци́ник. cynical *adj* цини́чный. cynicism *n* цини́зм.

cypress *n* кипари́с.

Cyrillic *n* кири́ллица.

cyst *n* киста́.

Czech *n* чех, че́шка; *adj* че́шский; ~ Republic Че́шская Респу́блика.

# D

**dab** n мазо́к; vt (eyes etc.) прикла́дывать impf платок к+dat; ~ **on** накла́дывать impf, наложи́ть pf мазка́ми.

**dabble** vi: ~ **in** пове́рхностно занима́ться impf, заня́ться pf +instr.

**dachshund** n та́кса.

**dad, daddy** n па́па; ~**-long-legs** n долгоно́жка.

**daffodil** n жёлтый нарци́сс.

**daft** adj глу́пый.

**dagger** n кинжа́л.

**dahlia** n георги́н.

**daily** adv ежедне́вно; adj ежедне́вный; n (charwoman) приходя́щая убо́рщица; (newspaper) ежедне́вная газе́та.

**dainty** adj изя́щный.

**dairy** n масло́дельня; (shop) моло́чная sb; adj моло́чный.

**dais** n помо́ст.

**daisy** n маргари́тка.

**dale** n доли́на.

**dally** vi (dawdle) ме́шкать impf; (toy) игра́ть impf +instr; (flirt) флиртова́ть impf.

**dam** n (barrier) плоти́на; vt запру́живать impf, запруди́ть pf.

**damage** n поврежде́ние; pl убы́тки m pl; vt поврежда́ть impf, повреди́ть pf.

**damn** vt (curse) проклина́ть impf, прокля́сть pf; (censure) осужда́ть impf, осуди́ть pf; int чёрт возьми́!; **I don't give a ~** мне наплева́ть. **damnation** n прокля́тие. **damned** adj прокля́тый.

**damp** n сы́рость; adj сыро́й; vt (also **dampen**) сма́чивать impf, смочи́ть pf; (fig) охла-

жда́ть impf, охлади́ть pf.

**dance** vi танцева́ть impf; n та́нец; (party) танцева́льный ве́чер. **dancer** n танцо́р, -ка; (ballet) танцо́вщик, -ица; балери́на.

**dandelion** n одува́нчик.

**dandruff** n пе́рхоть.

**Dane** n датча́нин, -а́нка; **Great ~** дог. **Danish** adj да́тский.

**danger** n опа́сность. **dangerous** adj опа́сный.

**dangle** vt &i пока́чивать(ся) impf.

**dank** adj промо́зглый.

**dapper** adj вы́холенный.

**dare** vi (have courage) осме́ливаться impf, осме́литься pf; (have impudence) сметь impf, по~ pf; vt вызыва́ть impf, вы́звать pf; n вы́зов. **daredevil** n лиха́ч; adj отча́янный. **daring** n отва́га; adj отча́янный.

**dark** adj тёмный; ~ **blue** тёмно-си́ний; n темнота́. **darken** vt затемня́ть impf, затемни́ть pf; vi темне́ть impf, по~ pf. **darkly** adv мра́чно. **darkness** n темнота́.

**darling** n дорого́й sb, ми́лый sb; adj дорого́й.

**darn** vt што́пать impf, за~ pf.

**dart** n (arrow) стрела́; (for game) мета́тельная стрела́; (tuck) вы́тачка; vi броси́ться pf.

**dash** n (hyphen) тире́ neut indecl; (admixture) при́месь; vt швыря́ть impf, швырну́ть pf; vi броса́ться impf, бро́ситься pf. **dashboard** n прибо́рная доска́. **dashing** adj лихо́й.

**data** n pl да́нные sb pl. **database** n ба́за да́нных.

**date**[1] n (fruit) фи́ник.

**date**[2] n число́, да́та; (engage-

*ment*) свида́ние; out of ~ устаре́лый; up to ~ совреме́нный; в ку́рсе де́ла; *vt* дати́ровать *impf & pf*; (*go out with*) встреча́ться *impf* c+*instr*; *vi* (*originate*) относи́ться *impf* (from к+*instr*).

**dative** *adj* (*n*) да́тельный (паде́ж).

**daub** *vt* ма́зать *impf*, на~ *pf* (with +*instr*).

**daughter** *n* дочь; ~-in-law неве́стка (*in relation to mother*), сноха́ (*in relation to father*).

**daunting** *adj* угрожа́ющий.

**dawdle** *vi* ме́шкать *impf*.

**dawn** *n* рассве́т; (*also fig*) заря́; *vi* (*day*) рассвета́ть *impf*, рассвести́ *pf impers*; (*up*)on осеня́ть *impf*, осени́ть *pf*; it ~ed on me меня́ осени́ло.

**day** *n* день *m*; (*24 hours*) су́тки *pl*; *pl* (*period*) пери́од, вре́мя *neut*; the ~ after ~ изо дня́ в день; the ~ after to-morrow послеза́втра; the ~ before накану́не; the ~ before yesterday позавчера́; the other ~ на дня́х; by ~ днём; every other ~ че́рез день; ~ off выходно́й день *m*; one ~ одна́жды; these ~s в на́ши дни. **daybreak** *n* рассве́т. **day-dreams** *n pl* мечты́ *f pl*. **daylight** *n* дневно́й свет; in broad ~ средь бе́ла дня́. **daytime** *n*: in the ~ днём.

**daze** *n*: in a ~, dazed *adj* оглушён (-ена́).

**dazzle** *vt* ослепля́ть *impf*, ослепи́ть *pf*.

**deacon** *n* дья́кон.

**dead** *adj* мёртвый; (*animals*) до́хлый; (*plants*) увя́дший; (*numb*) онеме́вший; *n*: the ~ мёртвые *sb pl*; at ~ of night

глубо́кой но́чью; *adv* соверше́нно; ~ end тупи́к; ~ heat одновреме́нный фи́ниш; ~line преде́льный срок; ~lock тупи́к.

**deaden** *vt* заглуша́ть *impf*, заглуши́ть *pf*.

**deadly** *adj* смерте́льный.

**deaf** *adj* глухо́й; ~ and dumb глухонемо́й. **deafen** *vt* оглуша́ть *impf*, оглуши́ть *pf*. **deafness** *n* глухота́.

**deal**[1] *n*: a great, good, ~ мно́го (+*gen*); (*with comp*) гора́здо.

**deal**[2] *n* (*bargain*) сде́лка; (*cards*) сда́ча; *vt* (*cards*) сдава́ть *impf*, сдать *pf*; (*blow*) наноси́ть *impf*, нанести́ *pf*; ~ in торгова́ть *impf* +*instr*; ~ out распределя́ть *impf*, распредели́ть *pf*; ~ with (*take care of*) занима́ться *impf*, заня́ться *pf* +*instr*; (*handle a person*) поступа́ть *impf*, поступи́ть *pf* c+*instr*; (*treat a subject*) рассма́тривать *impf*, рассмотре́ть *pf*; (*cope with*) справля́ться *impf*, спра́виться *pf* c+*instr*. **dealer** *n* торго́вец (in +*instr*).

**dean** *n* дека́н.

**dear** *adj* дорого́й; (*also n*) ми́лый (*sb*).

**dearth** *n* недоста́ток.

**death** *n* смерть; put to ~ казни́ть *impf & pf*; ~bed *n* сме́ртное ло́же; ~ certificate свиде́тельство о сме́рти; ~ penalty сме́ртная казнь. **deathly** *adj* сме́ртельный.

**debar** *vt*: ~ from не допуска́ть *impf* до+*gen*.

**debase** *vt* унижа́ть *impf*, уни́зить *pf*; (*coinage*) понижа́ть *impf*, пони́зить *pf* ка́чество +*gen*.

**debatable** adj спо́рный. **debate** n пре́ния (-ий) pl; vt обсужда́ть impf, обсуди́ть pf.

**debauched** adj развра́щенный. **debauchery** n разврат.

**debilitate** vt ослабля́ть impf, осла́бить pf. **debility** n сла́бость.

**debit** n де́бет; vt дебетова́ть impf & pf.

**debris** n обло́мки m pl.

**debt** n долг. **debtor** n должни́к.

**début** n дебю́т; **make one's** ~ дебюти́ровать impf & pf.

**decade** n десятиле́тие.

**decadence** n декаде́нтство. **decadent** adj декаде́нтский.

**decaffeinated** adj без кофеи́на.

**decant** vt перелива́ть impf, перели́ть pf. **decanter** n графи́н.

**decapitate** vt обезгла́вливать impf, обезгла́вить pf.

**decay** vi гнить impf, с~ pf; (tooth) разруша́ться impf, разру́шиться pf; n гние́ние; (tooth) разруше́ние.

**decease** n кончи́на. **deceased** adj поко́йный; n поко́йник, -ица.

**deceit** n обма́н. **deceitful** adj лжи́вый. **deceive** vt обма́нывать impf, обману́ть pf.

**deceleration** n замедле́ние.

**December** n дека́брь m; adj дека́брьский.

**decency** n прили́чие. **decent** adj прили́чный.

**decentralization** n децентрализа́ция. **decentralize** vt децентрализова́ть impf & pf.

**deception** n обма́н. **deceptive** adj обма́нчивый.

**decibel** n дециби́л.

**decide** vt реша́ть impf, ре-

ши́ть pf. **decided** adj реши́тельный.

**deciduous** adj листопа́дный.

**decimal** n десяти́чная дробь; adj десяти́чный; ~ **point** запята́я sb.

**decimate** vt (fig) коси́ть impf, с~ pf.

**decipher** vt расшифро́вывать impf, расшифрова́ть pf.

**decision** n реше́ние. **decisive** adj (firm) реши́тельный, (deciding) реша́ющий.

**deck** n па́луба; (bus etc.) эта́ж; ~**chair** n шезло́нг; vt: ~ **out** украша́ть impf, укра́сить pf.

**declaim** vt деклами́ровать impf, про~ pf.

**declaration** n объявле́ние; (document) деклара́ция. **declare** vt (proclaim) объявля́ть impf, объяви́ть pf; (assert) заявля́ть impf, заяви́ть pf.

**declension** n склоне́ние. **decline** n упа́док; vi приходи́ть impf, прийти́ pf в упа́док; vt отклоня́ть impf, отклони́ть pf; (gram) склоня́ть impf, про~ pf.

**decode** vt расшифро́вывать impf, расшифрова́ть pf.

**decompose** vi разлага́ться impf, разложи́ться pf.

**décor** n эстети́ческое оформле́ние. **decorate** vt украша́ть impf, укра́сить pf; (room) ремонти́ровать impf, от~ pf; (with medal) награжда́ть impf, награди́ть pf. **decoration** n украше́ние; (medal) о́рден. **decorative** adj декорати́вный. **decorator** n маля́р.

**decorous** adj прили́чный. **decorum** n прили́чие.

**decoy** n (bait) прима́нка; vt зама́нивать impf, зама́нить pf.

**decrease** *vt & i* уменьша́ть(ся) *impf*, уме́ньшить(ся) *pf*, *n* уменьше́ние.

**decree** *n* ука́з; *vt* постановля́ть *impf*, постанови́ть *pf*.

**decrepit** *adj* дря́хлый.

**dedicate** *vt* посвяща́ть *impf*, посвяти́ть *pf*. **dedication** *n* посвяще́ние.

**deduce** *vt* заключа́ть *impf*, заключи́ть *pf*.

**deduct** *vt* вычита́ть *impf*, вы́честь *pf*. **deduction** *n* (*subtraction*) вы́чет; (*inference*) вы́вод.

**deed** *n* посту́пок; (*heroic*) по́двиг; (*law*) акт.

**deem** *vt* счита́ть *impf*, счесть *pf* +*acc & instr*.

**deep** *adj* глубо́кий; (*colour*) тёмный; (*sound*) ни́зкий; ~ freeze морози́льник. **deepen** *vt & i* углубля́ть(ся) *impf*, углуби́ть(ся) *pf*.

**deer** *n* оле́нь *m*.

**deface** *vt* обезобра́живать *impf*, обезобра́зить *pf*.

**defamation** *n* диффама́ция. **defamatory** *adj* клеветни́ческий.

**default** *n* (*failure to pay*) неупла́та; (*failure to appear*) нея́вка; (*comput*) автомати́ческий вы́бор; *vi* не выполня́ть *impf* обяза́тельств.

**defeat** *n* пораже́ние; *vt* побежда́ть *impf*, победи́ть *pf*. **defeatism** *n* пораже́нчество. **defeatist** *n* пораже́нец; *adj* пораже́нческий.

**defecate** *vi* испражня́ться *impf*, испражни́ться *pf*.

**defect** *n* дефе́кт; *vi* перебега́ть *impf*, перебежа́ть *pf*. **defective** *adj* неиспра́вный. **defector** *n* перебе́жчик. **defence** *n* защи́та. **defence**less *adj* беззащи́тный. **defend** *vt* защища́ть *impf*, защити́ть *pf*. **defendant** *n* подсуди́мый *sb*. **defender** *n* защи́тник. **defensive** *adj* оборони́тельный.

**defer**[1] *vt* (*postpone*) отсро́чивать *impf*, отсро́чить *pf*.

**defer**[2] *vi*: ~ to подчиня́ться *impf* +*dat*. **deference** *n* уваже́ние. **deferential** *adj* почти́тельный.

**defiance** *n* неповинове́ние; in ~ of вопреки́+*dat*. **defiant** *adj* вызыва́ющий.

**deficiency** *n* недоста́ток. **deficient** *adj* недоста́точный. **deficit** *n* дефици́т.

**defile** *vt* оскверня́ть *impf*, оскверни́ть *pf*.

**define** *vt* определя́ть *impf*, определи́ть *pf*. **definite** *adj* определённый **definitely** *adv* несомне́нно. **definition** *n* определе́ние. **definitive** *adj* оконча́тельный.

**deflate** *vt & i* спуска́ть *impf*, спусти́ть *pf*; *vt* (*person*) сбива́ть *impf*, сбить *pf* спесь с+*gen*. **deflation** *n* дефля́ция.

**deflect** *vt* отклоня́ть *impf*, отклони́ть *pf*.

**deforestation** *n* обезле́сение.

**deformed** *adj* уро́дливый. **deformity** *n* уро́дство.

**defraud** *vt* обма́нывать *impf*, обману́ть *pf*; ~ of выма́нивать *impf*, вы́манить *pf* +*acc & у+gen* (*of person*).

**defray** *vt* опла́чивать *impf*, оплати́ть *pf*.

**defrost** *vt* размора́живать *impf*, разморо́зить *pf*.

**deft** *adj* ло́вкий.

**defunct** *adj* бо́льше не существу́ющий.

**defy** *vt* (*challenge*) вызыва́ть

*impf*, вы́звать *pf*; (*disobey*)
идти́ *impf*, по~ *pf* про́-
тив+*acc*; (*fig*) не поддава́ть-
ся *impf*+*dat*.
**degenerate** *vi* вырожда́ться
*impf*, вы́родиться *pf*; *adj*
вы́родившийся.
**degradation** *n* униже́ние. **de-
grade** *vt* унижа́ть *impf*, уни-
зи́ть *pf*. **degrading** *adj* уни-
зи́тельный.
**degree** *n* сте́пень; (*math etc.*)
гра́дус; (*univ*) учёная сте́пень.
**dehydrate** *vt* обезво́живать
*impf*, обезво́дить *pf*. **dehy-
dration** *n* обезво́живание.
**deign** *vi* снисходи́ть *impf*,
снизойти́ *pf*.
**deity** *n* божество́.
**dejected** *adj* удручённый.
**delay** *n* заде́ржка; **without ~**
неме́дленно; *vt* заде́рживать
*impf*, задержа́ть *pf*.
**delegate** *n* делега́т; *vt* делеги́-
ровать *impf* & *pf*. **delegation** *n* делега́ция.
**delete** *vt* вычёркивать *impf*,
вы́черкнуть *pf*.
**deliberate** *adj* (*intentional*)
преднаме́ренный; (*careful*)
осторо́жный; *vt* & *i* размы́-
шля́ть *impf*, размы́слить
*pf* (o+*prep*); (*discuss*) сове-
ща́ться *impf* (o+*prep*). **de-
liberation** *n* размышле́ние;
(*discussion*) совеща́ние.
**delicacy** *n* (*tact*) делика́т-
ность; (*dainty*) ла́комство.
**delicate** *adj* то́нкий; (*tactful,
needing tact*) делика́тный;
(*health*) боле́зненный.
**delicatessen** *n* гастроно́м.
**delicious** *adj* о́чень вку́сный.
**delight** *n* наслажде́ние; (*delightful thing*) пре́лесть. **delightful** *adj* преле́стный.
**delinquency** *n* престу́пность.

**delinquent** *n* правонаруши́-
тель *m*, ~ница; *adj* вино́в-
ный.
**delirious** *adj*: **be ~** бре́дить
*impf*. **delirium** *n* бред.
**deliver** *vt* (*goods*) доставля́ть
*impf*, доста́вить *pf*; (*save*)
избавля́ть *impf*, изба́вить *pf*
(*from* от+*gen*); (*lecture*) про-
чита́ть *impf*, проче́сть *pf*;
(*letters*) разноси́ть *impf*, раз-
нести́ *pf*; (*speech*) произно-
си́ть *impf*, произнести́ *pf*;
(*blow*) наноси́ть *impf*, нане-
сти́ *pf*. **deliverance** *n* изба-
вле́ние. **delivery** *n* доста́вка.
**delta** *n* де́льта.
**delude** *vt* вводи́ть *impf*, вве-
сти́ *pf* в заблужде́ние.
**deluge** *n* (*flood*) пото́п; (*rain*)
ли́вень *m*; (*fig*) пото́к.
**delusion** *n* заблужде́ние; **~s
of grandeur** ма́ния вели́чия.
**de luxe** *adj* -люкс (*added to
noun*).
**delve** *vi* углубля́ться *impf*,
углуби́ться *pf* (*into* в+*acc*).
**demand** *n* тре́бование; (*econ*)
спрос (**for** на+*acc*); *vt* тре́-
бовать *impf*, по~ *pf* +*gen*.
**demanding** *adj* тре́бова-
тельный.
**demarcation** *n* демарка́ция.
**demean** *vt*: ~ **o.s.** унижа́ться
*impf*, уни́зиться *pf*.
**demeanour** *n* мане́ра вести́
себя́.
**demented** *adj* сумасше́дший.
**dementia** *n* слабоу́мие.
**demise** *n* кончи́на.
**demobilize** *vt* демобилизо-
ва́ть *impf* & *pf*.
**democracy** *n* демокра́тия.
**democrat** *n* демокра́т. **democratic** *adj* демократи́ческий.
**democratization** *n* демокра-
тиза́ция.

**demolish** vt (destroy) разрушать impf, разрушить pf; (building) сносить impf, снести pf; (refute) опровергать impf, опровергнуть pf. **demolition** n разрушение; снос.

**demon** n демон.

**demonstrable** adj доказуемый. **demonstrably** adv наглядно. **demonstrate** vt демонстрировать impf & pf, vi участвовать impf в демонстрации. **demonstration** n демонстрация. **demonstrative** adj экспансивный; (gram) указательный. **demonstrator** n демонстратор; (polit) демонстрант.

**demoralize** vt деморализовать impf & pf.

**demote** vt понижать impf, понизить pf в должности.

**demure** adj скромный.

**den** n берлога.

**denial** n отрицание; (refusal) отказ.

**denigrate** vt чернить impf, о~ pf.

**denim** adj джинсовый; n джинсовая ткань.

**Denmark** n Дания.

**denomination** n (money) достоинство; (relig) вероисповедание. **denominator** n знаменатель.

**denote** vt означать impf, означить pf.

**denounce** vt (condemn) осуждать impf, осудить pf; (inform on) доносить impf, донести pf на+acc.

**dense** adj густой; (stupid) тупой. **density** n плотность.

**dent** n вмятина; v делать impf, с~ pf вмятину в+prep.

**dental** adj зубной. **dentist** n зубной врач. **dentures** n pl

зубной протез.

**denunciation** n (condemnation) осуждение; (informing) донос.

**deny** vt отрицать impf; (refuse) отказывать impf, отказать pf+dat (person) в+prep.

**deodorant** n дезодорант.

**depart** vi отбывать impf, отбыть pf; (deviate) отклоняться impf, отклониться pf (from от+gen).

**department** n отдел; (univ) кафедра; ~ store универмаг. **departure** n отбытие; (deviation) отклонение.

**depend** vi зависеть impf (on от+gen); (rely) полагаться impf, положиться pf (on на+acc). **dependable** adj надёжный. **dependant** n иждивенец. **dependence** n зависимость. **dependent** adj зависимый.

**depict** vt изображать impf, изобразить pf.

**deplete** vt истощать impf, истощить pf. **depleted** adj истощённый. **depletion** n истощение.

**deplorable** adj плачевный. **deplore** vt сожалеть impf о+prep.

**deploy** vt развёртывать impf, развернуть pf. **deployment** n развёртывание.

**deport** vt депортировать impf & pf, высылать impf, выслать pf. **deportation** n депортация; высылка.

**deportment** n осанка.

**depose** vt свергать impf, свергнуть pf. **deposit** n (econ) вклад; (advance) задаток; (sediment) осадок; (coal etc.) месторождение; vt (econ) вносить impf, внести pf.

**depot** n (transport) депо neut

*indecl*; (*store*) склад.

**deprave** *vt* развраща́ть *impf*, разврати́ть *pf*. **depraved** *adj* развращённый. **depravity** *n* развра́т.

**deprecate** *vt* осужда́ть *impf*, осуди́ть *pf*.

**depreciate** *vt & i* (*econ*) обесце́нивать(ся) *impf*, обесце́нить(ся) *pf*. **depreciation** *n* обесце́нение.

**depress** *vt* (*dispirit*) удруча́ть *impf*, удручи́ть *pf*. **depressed** *adj* удручённый. **depressing** *adj* угнета́ющий. **depression** *n* (*hollow*) впа́дина; (*econ, med, meteorol, etc.*) депре́ссия.

**deprivation** *n* лише́ние. **deprive** *vt* лиша́ть *impf*, лиши́ть *pf* (of +gen).

**depth** *n* глубина́; **in the ~ of winter** в разга́ре зимы́.

**deputation** *n* депута́ция. **deputize** *vi* замеща́ть *impf*, замести́ть *pf* (for +acc); **deputy** *n* замести́тель *m*; (*parl*) депута́т.

**derail** *vt*: **be derailed** сходи́ть *impf*, сойти́ *pf* с ре́льсов. **derailment** *n* сход с ре́льсов.

**deranged** *adj* сумасше́дший.

**derelict** *adj* забро́шенный.

**deride** *vt* высме́ивать *impf*, вы́смеять *pf*. **derision** *n* высме́ивание. **derisive** *adj* (*mocking*) насме́шливый. **derisory** *adj* (*ridiculous*) смехотво́рный.

**derivation** *n* происхожде́ние. **derivative** *n* произво́дное *sb*; *adj* произво́дный. **derive** *vt* извлека́ть *impf*, извле́чь *pf*; *vi*: **~ from** происходи́ть *impf*, произойти́ *pf* от+gen.

**derogatory** *adj* отрица́тельный.

**descend** *vi* (*& t*) (*go down*)

спуска́ться *impf*, спусти́ться *pf* (c+gen); **be descended from** происходи́ть *impf*, произойти́ *pf* из, от, +gen. **descendant** *n* пото́мок. **descent** *n* спуск; (*lineage*) происхожде́ние.

**describe** *vt* опи́сывать *impf*, описа́ть *pf*. **description** *n* описа́ние. **descriptive** *adj* описа́тельный.

**desecrate** *vt* оскверня́ть *impf*, оскверни́ть *pf*. **desecration** *n* оскверне́ние.

**desert**¹ *n* (*waste*) пусты́ня.

**desert**² *vt* покида́ть *impf*, поки́нуть *pf*; (*mil*) дезерти́ровать *impf & pf*. **deserter** *n* дезерти́р. **desertion** *n* дезерти́рство.

**deserts** *n pl* заслу́ги *f pl*. **deserve** *vt* заслу́живать *impf*, заслужи́ть *pf*. **deserving** *adj* досто́йный (of +gen).

**design** *n* (*pattern*) узо́р; (*of car etc.*) констру́кция, прое́кт; (*industrial*) диза́йн; (*aim*) у́мысел; *vt* проекти́ровать *impf*, с~ *pf*; (*intend*) предназнача́ть *impf*, предназна́чить *pf*.

**designate** *vt* (*indicate*) обознача́ть *impf*, обозна́чить *pf*; (*appoint*) назнача́ть *impf*, назна́чить *pf*.

**designer** *n* (*tech*) констру́ктор; (*industrial*) диза́йнер; (*of clothes*) модель́ер.

**desirable** *adj* жела́тельный. **desire** *n* жела́ние; *vt* жела́ть *impf*, по~ *pf* +gen.

**desist** *vi* (*refrain*) возде́рживаться *impf*, воздержа́ться *pf* (from от+gen).

**desk** *n* пи́сьменный стол; (*school*) па́рта.

**desolate** *adj* забро́шенный

**desolation** n заброшенность.
**despair** n отчаяние; vi отчаиваться impf, отчаяться pf.
**desperate** adj отчаянный.
**desperation** n отчаяние.
**despicable** adj презренный.
**despise** vt презирать impf, презреть pf.
**despite** prep несмотря на+acc.
**despondency** n уныние. **despondent** adj унылый.
**despot** n деспот.
**dessert** n десерт.
**destination** n (of goods) место назначения; (of journey) цель. **destiny** n судьба.
**destitute** adj без всяких средств.
**destroy** vt разрушать impf, разрушить pf. **destroyer** n (naut) эсминец. **destruction** n разрушение. **destructive** adj разрушительный.
**detach** vt отделять impf, отделить pf. **detached** adj отдельный; (objective) беспристрастный; ~ house особняк. **detachment** n (objectivity) беспристрастие; (mil) отряд.
**detail** n деталь, подробность; **in detail** подробно; vt подробно рассказывать impf, рассказать pf. **detailed** adj подробный.
**detain** vt задерживать impf, задержать pf. **detainee** n задержанный sb.
**detect** vt обнаруживать impf, обнаружить pf. **detection** n расследование. **detective** n детектив; ~ film, story, etc. детектив. **detector** n детектор.
**detention** n задержание; (school) задержка в наказание.
**deter** vt удерживать impf,

удержать pf (from от+gen).
**detergent** n моющее средство.
**deteriorate** vi ухудшаться impf, ухудшиться pf. **deterioration** n ухудшение.
**determination** n решимость. **determine** vt (ascertain) устанавливать impf, установить pf; (be decisive factor) определять impf, определить pf; (decide) решать impf, решить pf. **determined** adj решительный.
**deterrent** n средство устрашения.
**detest** vt ненавидеть impf. **detestable** adj отвратительный.
**detonate** vt & i взрывать(ся) impf, взорвать(ся) pf. **detonator** n детонатор.
**detour** n объезд.
**detract** vi: ~ from умалять impf, умалить pf+acc.
**detriment** n ущерб. **detrimental** adj вредный.
**deuce** n (tennis) равный счёт.
**devaluation** n девальвация. **devalue** vt девальвировать impf & pf.
**devastate** vt опустошать impf, опустошить pf. **devastated** adj потрясённый. **devastating** adj уничтожающий. **devastation** n опустошение.
**develop** vt & i развивать(ся) impf, развить(ся) pf; vt (phot) проявлять impf, проявить pf. **developer** n (of land etc.) застройщик. **development** n развитие.
**deviant** adj ненормальный. **deviate** vi отклоняться impf, отклониться pf (from от+gen). **deviation** n отклонение.
**device** n прибор.

**devil** n чёрт. **devilish** adj чертóвский.

**devious** adj (circuitous) окружнóй; (person) непорядочный.

**devise** vt придýмывать impf, придýмать pf.

**devoid** adj лишённый (of +gen).

**devolution** n передáча (влáсти).

**devote** vt посвящáть impf, посвятить pf. **devoted** adj прéданный. **devotee** n поклóнник. **devotion** n прéданность.

**devour** vt пожирáть impf, пожрáть pf.

**devout** adj нáбожный.

**dew** n росá.

**dexterity** n лóвкость. **dext(e)rous** adj лóвкий.

**diabetes** n диабéт. **diabetic** n диабéтик; adj диабетический.

**diabolic(al)** adj дьявольский.

**diagnose** vt диагности́ровать impf & pf. **diagnosis** n диагноз.

**diagonal** n диагонáль; adj диагонáльный. **diagonally** adv по диагонáли.

**diagram** n диаграмма.

**dial** n (clock) циферблáт; (tech) шкалá; vt набирáть impf, набрáть pf.

**dialect** n диалéкт.

**dialogue** n диалóг.

**diameter** n диáметр. **diametric(al)** adj диаметрáльный; ~ly opposed диаметрáльно противополóжный.

**diamond** n алмáз; (shape) ромб; pl (cards) бýбны (-бён, -бáм) pl.

**diaper** n пелёнка.

**diaphragm** n диафрáгма.

**diarrhoea** n понóс.

**diary** n дневни́к.

**dice** see **die**[1]

**dicey** adj рискóванный.

**dictate** vt диктовáть impf, про~ pf. **dictation** n диктóвка. **dictator** n диктáтор. **dictatorial** adj диктáторский. **dictatorship** n диктатýра.

**diction** n ди́кция.

**dictionary** n словáрь m.

**didactic** adj дидакти́ческий.

**die**[1] n (pl dice) игрáльная кость; (pl dies) (stamp) штамп.

**die**[2] vi (person) умирáть impf, умерéть pf; (animal) дóхнуть impf, из~, по~ pf; (plant) вя́нуть impf, за~ pf; **be dying to** óчень хотéть impf; ~ **down** (fire, sound) угасáть impf, угáснуть pf; ~ **out** вымирáть impf, вы́мереть pf.

**diesel** n (engine) ди́зель m; attrib ди́зельный.

**diet** n диéта; (habitual food) пи́ща; vi быть на диéте. **dietary** adj диети́ческий.

**differ** vi отличáться impf; различáться impf; (disagree) расходи́ться impf, разойти́сь pf. **difference** n рáзница; (disagreement) разноглáсие. **different** adj разли́чный, рáзный. **differential** n (math, tech) дифференциáл; (difference) рáзница. **differentiate** vt различáть impf, различи́ть pf.

**difficult** adj трýдный. **difficulty** n трýдность; (difficult situation) затруднéние; **without** ~ без трудá.

**diffidence** n неувéренность в себé. **diffident** adj неувéренный в себé.

**diffused** adj рассе́янный.

**dig** n (archaeol) раско́пки f pl; (poke) тычо́к; (gibe) шпи́лька; pl (lodgings) кварти́ра; **give a ~ in the ribs** ткнуть pf ло́ктем под рёбра; ~ out копа́ть impf, вы́~ pf, рыть impf, вы́~ pf; ~ **up** (bone) выка́пывать impf, вы́копать pf; (land) вска́пывать impf, вскопа́ть pf.

**digest** vt перева́ривать impf, перевари́ть pf. **digestible** adj удобовари́мый. **digestion** n пищеваре́ние.

**digger** n (tech) экскава́тор.

**digit** n (math) знак.

**dignified** adj велича́вый. **dignitary** n сано́вник. **dignity** n досто́инство.

**digress** vi отклоня́ться impf, отклони́ться pf. **digression** n отклоне́ние.

**dike** n да́мба; (ditch) ров.

**dilapidated** adj ве́тхий.

**dilate** vt & i расширя́ть(ся) impf, расши́рить(ся) pf.

**dilemma** n диле́мма.

**dilettante** n дилета́нт.

**diligence** n прилежа́ние. **diligent** adj приле́жный.

**dilute** vt разбавля́ть impf, разба́вить pf.

**dim** adj (not bright) ту́склый; (vague) сму́тный; (stupid) тупо́й.

**dimension** n (pl) разме́ры m pl; (math) измере́ние. **-dimensional** in comb -ме́рный; **three-~** трёхме́рный.

**diminish** vt & i уменьша́ть(ся) impf, уме́ньшить(ся) pf. **diminutive** adj ма́ленький; n уменьши́тельное sb.

**dimness** n ту́склость.

**dimple** n я́мочка.

**din** n гро́хот; (voices) гам.

**dine** vi обе́дать impf, по~ pf. **diner** n обе́дающий sb.

**dinghy** n шлю́пка; (rubber ~) надувна́я ло́дка.

**dingy** adj (drab) ту́склый; (dirty) гря́зный.

**dining-car** n ваго́н-рестора́н. **dining-room** n столо́вая sb. **dinner** n обе́д; **~-jacket** смо́кинг.

**dinosaur** n диноза́вр.

**diocese** n епа́рхия.

**dip** vt (immerse) окуна́ть impf, окуну́ть pf; (partially) обма́кивать impf, обмакну́ть pf; vi (slope) понижа́ться impf, пони́зиться pf; n (depression) впа́дина; (slope) укло́н; **have a ~** (bathe) купа́ться impf, вы́~ pf.

**diphtheria** n дифтери́я.

**diphthong** n дифто́нг.

**diploma** n дипло́м. **diplomacy** n диплома́тия. **diplomat** n диплома́т. **diplomatic** adj дипломати́ческий.

**dire** adj стра́шный; (ominous) злове́щий.

**direct** adj прямо́й; **~ current** постоя́нный ток; vt направля́ть impf, напра́вить pf; (guide, manage) руководи́ть impf +instr; (film) режисси́ровать impf. **direction** n направле́ние; (guidance) руково́дство; (instruction) указа́ние; (film) режиссу́ра; **stage ~** рема́рка. **directive** n директи́ва. **directly** adv прямо́; (at once) сра́зу. **director** n дире́ктор; (film etc.) режиссёр (-постано́вщик). **directory** n спра́вочник, указа́тель m; (tel) телефо́нная кни́га.

**dirt** n грязь. **dirty** adj гря́зный; vt па́чкать impf, за~ pf.

**disability** n физи́ческий/психи́ческий недоста́ток; (*disablement*) инвали́дность. **disabled** *adj*: he is ~ он инвали́д.

**disadvantage** n невы́годное положе́ние; (*defect*) недоста́ток. **disadvantageous** *adj* невы́годный.

**disaffected** *adj* недово́льный.

**disagree** vi не соглаша́ться *impf*, согласи́ться *pf*; (*not correspond*) не соотве́тствовать *impf* +dat. **disagreeable** *adj* неприя́тный. **disagreement** n разногла́сие; (*quarrel*) ссо́ра.

**disappear** vi исчеза́ть *impf*, исче́знуть *pf*. **disappearance** n исчезнове́ние.

**disappoint** vt разочаро́вывать *impf*, разочарова́ть *pf*. **disappointed** *adj* разочаро́ванный. **disappointing** *adj* разочаро́вывающий. **disappointment** n разочарова́ние.

**disapproval** n неодобре́ние. **disapprove** vt & i не одобря́ть *impf*.

**disarm** vt (*mil*) разоружа́ть *impf*, разоружи́ть *pf*; (*criminal*; *also fig*) обезору́живать *impf*, обезору́жить *pf*. **disarmament** n разоруже́ние.

**disarray** n беспоря́док.

**disaster** n бе́дствие. **disastrous** *adj* катастрофи́ческий.

**disband** vt распуска́ть *impf*, распусти́ть *pf*; vi расходи́ться *impf*, разойти́сь *pf*.

**disbelief** n неве́рие.

**disc, disk** n диск; — **jockey** веду́щий sb переда́чу.

**discard** vt отбра́сывать *impf*, отбро́сить *pf*.

**discern** vt различа́ть *impf*, различи́ть *pf*. **discernible** *adj* различи́мый. **discerning**

*adj* проница́тельный.

**discharge** vt (*ship etc.*) разгружа́ть *impf*, разгрузи́ть *pf* (*gun*; *electr*) разряжа́ть *impf*, разряди́ть *pf*; (*dismiss*) увольня́ть *impf*, уво́лить *pf*; (*prisoner*) освобожда́ть *impf*, освободи́ть *pf*; (*debt*; *duty*) выполня́ть *impf*, вы́полнить *pf*; (*from hospital*) выпи́сывать *impf*, вы́писать *pf*; n разгру́зка; (*electr*) разря́д; увольне́ние; освобожде́ние; выполне́ние; (*matter discharged*) выделе́ния neut pl.

**disciple** n учени́к.

**disciplinarian** n сторо́нник дисципли́ны. **disciplinary** *adj* дисциплина́рный. **discipline** n дисципли́на; vt дисциплини́ровать *impf* & *pf*.

**disclaim** vt (*deny*) отрица́ть *impf*; ~ **responsibility** слага́ть *impf*, сложи́ть *pf* с себя́ отве́тственность.

**disclose** vt обнару́живать *impf*, обнару́жить *pf*. **disclosure** n обнаруже́ние.

**discoloured** *adj* обесцве́ченный.

**discomfit** vt смуща́ть *impf*, смути́ть *pf*. **discomfiture** n смуще́ние.

**discomfort** n неудо́бство.

**disconcert** vt смуща́ть *impf*, смути́ть *pf*.

**disconnect** vt разъединя́ть *impf*, разъедини́ть *pf*; (*switch off*) выключа́ть *impf*, вы́ключить *pf*. **disconnected** *adj* (*incoherent*) бессвя́зный.

**disconsolate** *adj* неуте́шный.

**discontent** n недово́льство. **discontented** *adj* недово́льный.

**discontinue** vt прекраща́ть *impf*, прекрати́ть *pf*.

**discord** n разногла́сие; (mus) диссона́нс. **discordant** adj несогласу́ющийся; диссони́рующий.

**discotheque** n дискоте́ка.

**discount** n ски́дка; vt (disregard) не принима́ть impf, приня́ть pf в расчёт.

**discourage** vt обескура́живать impf, обескура́жить pf; (dissuade) отгова́ривать impf, отговори́ть pf.

**discourse** n речь.

**discourteous** adj неве́жливый.

**discover** vt открыва́ть impf, откры́ть pf; (find out) обнару́живать impf, обнару́жить pf. **discovery** n откры́тие.

**discredit** n позо́р; vt дискреди́тировать impf & pf.

**discreet** adj такти́чный. **discretion** n (judgement) усмотре́ние; (prudence) благоразу́мие; **at one's ~** по своему́ усмотре́нию.

**discrepancy** n несоотве́тствие.

**discriminate** vt различа́ть impf, различи́ть pf; **~ against** дискримини́ровать impf & pf. **discrimination** n (taste) разбо́рчивость; (bias) дискримина́ция.

**discus** n диск.

**discuss** vt обсужда́ть impf, обсуди́ть pf. **discussion** n обсужде́ние.

**disdain** n презре́ние. **disdainful** adj презри́тельный.

**disease** n боле́знь. **diseased** adj больно́й.

**disembark** vi выса́живаться impf, вы́садиться pf.

**disenchantment** n разочарова́ние.

**disengage** vt освобожда́ть

impf, освободи́ть pf; (clutch) отпуска́ть impf, отпусти́ть pf.

**disentangle** vt распу́тывать impf, распу́тать pf.

**disfavour** n неми́лость.

**disfigure** vt уро́довать impf, из~ pf.

**disgrace** n позо́р; (disfavour) неми́лость; vt позо́рить impf, о~ pf. **disgraceful** adj позо́рный.

**disgruntled** adj недово́льный.

**disguise** n маскиро́вка; vt маскирова́ть impf, за~ pf; (conceal) скрыва́ть impf, скрыть pf. **disguised** adj замаскиро́ванный.

**disgust** n отвраще́ние; vt внуша́ть impf, внуши́ть pf отвраще́ние +dat. **disgusting** adj отврати́тельный.

**dish** n блю́до; pl посу́да collect; **~-washer** (person) мо́ечная маши́на; vt: **~ up** подава́ть impf, пода́ть pf.

**dishearten** vt обескура́живать impf, обескура́жить pf.

**dishevelled** adj растрёпанный.

**dishonest** adj нече́стный. **dishonesty** n нече́стность. **dishonour** n бесче́стье; vt бесче́стить impf, о~ pf. **dishonourable** adj бесче́стный.

**disillusion** vt разочаро́вывать impf, разочарова́ть pf. **disillusionment** n разочаро́ванность.

**disinclination** n несклонность, неохо́та. **disinclined** adj **be ~** не хоте́ться impers +dat.

**disinfect** vt дезинфици́ровать impf & pf. **disinfectant** n дезинфици́рующее сре́дство.

**disingenuous** adj нейскре́нный.

**disinherit** vt лиша́ть impf, лиши́ть pf насле́дства.

**disintegrate** vi распада́ться impf, распа́сться pf. **disintegration** n распа́д.

**disinterested** adj бескоры́стный.

**disjointed** adj бессвя́зный.

**disk** see **disc**

**dislike** n нелюбо́вь (for k+dat); vt не люби́ть impf.

**dislocate** vt (med) вы́вихнуть pf.

**dislodge** vt смеща́ть impf, смести́ть pf.

**disloyal** adj нелоя́льный. **disloyalty** n нелоя́льность.

**dismal** adj мра́чный.

**dismantle** vt разбира́ть impf, разобра́ть pf.

**dismay** vt смуща́ть impf, смути́ть pf; n смуще́ние.

**dismiss** vt (sack) увольня́ть impf, уво́лить pf; (disband) распуска́ть impf, распусти́ть pf. **dismissal** n увольне́ние; ро́спуск.

**dismount** vi спе́шиваться impf, спе́шиться pf.

**disobedience** n непослуша́ние. **disobedient** adj непослу́шный. **disobey** vt не слу́шаться impf +gen.

**disorder** n беспоря́док. **disorderly** adj (untidy) беспоря́дочный; (unruly) бу́йный.

**disorganized** adj неорганизо́ванный.

**disorientation** n дезориента́ция. **disoriented** adj: **I am/was** ~ я потеря́л(а) направле́ние.

**disown** vt отка́зываться impf, отказа́ться pf от+gen.

**disparaging** adj оскорби́тельный.

**disparity** n нера́венство.

**dispassionate** adj беспристра́стный.

**dispatch** vt (send) отправля́ть impf, отпра́вить pf; (deal with) распра́вля́ться impf, распра́виться pf c+instr; n отпра́вка; (message) донесе́ние; (rapidity) быстрота́; ~rider мотоцикли́ст свя́зи.

**dispel** vt рассе́ивать impf, рассе́ять pf.

**dispensable** adj необяза́тельный.

**dispensary** n апте́ка.

**dispensation** n (exemption) освобожде́ние (от обяза́тельства). **dispense** vt (distribute) раздава́ть impf, разда́ть pf; ~ with обходи́ться impf, обойти́сь pf без+gen.

**dispersal** n распростране́ние. **disperse** vt (drive away) разгоня́ть impf, разогна́ть pf; (scatter) рассе́ивать impf, рассе́ять pf; vi расходи́ться impf, разойти́сь pf.

**dispirited** adj удручённый.

**displaced** adj: ~ **persons** переме́щённые ли́ца neut pl.

**display** n пока́з; vt пока́зывать impf, показа́ть pf.

**displeased** predic недово́лен (-льна). **displeasure** n недово́льство.

**disposable** adj однора́зовый.

**disposal** n удале́ние; **at your** ~ в ва́шем распоряже́нии.

**dispose** vi: ~ **of** избавля́ться impf, изба́виться pf от+gen. **disposed** predic: ~ **to** располо́жен (-ена) k+dat или +inf. **disposition** n расположе́ние; (temperament) нрав.

**disproportionate** adj непропорциона́льный.

**disprove** vt опроверга́ть impf, опрове́ргнуть pf.

**dispute** n (*debate*) спор; (*quarrel*) ссóра; vt оспáривать *impf*, оспóрить *pf.*

**disqualification** n дисквалификáция. **disqualify** vt дисквалифици́ровать *impf* & *pf.*

**disquieting** adj тревóжный.

**disregard** n пренебрежéние +*instr*; vt игнори́ровать *impf* & *pf*; пренебрегáть *impf*, пренебрéчь *pf* +*instr*.

**disrepair** n неиспрáвность.

**disreputable** adj пóльзующийся дурнóй слáвой. **disrepute** n дурнáя слáва.

**disrespect** n неуважéние. **disrespectful** adj непочти́тельный.

**disrupt** vt срывáть *impf*, сорвáть *pf*. **disruptive** adj подрывнóй.

**dissatisfaction** n недовóльство. **dissatisfied** adj недовóльный.

**dissect** vt разрезáть *impf*, разрéзать *pf*; (*med*) вскрывáть *impf*, вскрыть *pf.*

**disseminate** vt распространя́ть *impf*, распространи́ть *pf*; **dissemination** n распространéние.

**dissension** n раздóр. **dissent** n расхождéние; (*eccl*) раскóл.

**dissertation** n диссертáция.

**disservice** n плохáя услýга.

**dissident** n диссидéнт.

**dissimilar** adj несхóдный.

**dissipate** vt (*dispel*) рассéивать *impf*, рассéять *pf*; (*squander*) промáтывать *impf*, промотáть *pf*. **dissipated** adj распýтный.

**dissociate** vt: ~ **o.s.** отмежёвываться *impf*, отмежевáться *pf* (**from** от+*gen*).

**dissolute** adj распýтный. **dissolution** n расторжéние;

(*parl*) рóспуск. **dissolve** vt & i (in liquid) растворя́ть(ся) *impf*, раствори́ть(ся) *pf*; vt (*annul*) расторгáть *impf*, расторгнуть *pf*; (*parl*) распускáть *impf*, распусти́ть *pf.*

**dissonance** n диссонáнс. **dissonant** adj диссони́рующий.

**dissuade** vt отговáривать *impf*, отговори́ть *pf.*

**distance** n расстоя́ние; **from a ~** издали; **in the ~** вдалекé. **distant** adj далёкий, (*also of relative*) дáльний; (*reserved*) сдéржанный.

**distaste** n отвращéние. **distasteful** adj проти́вный.

**distended** adj надýтый.

**distil** vt (*whisky*) перегоня́ть *impf*, перегнáть *pf*; (*water*) дистилли́ровать *impf* & *pf*. **distillation** n перегóнка; дистилля́ция. **distillery** n перегóнный завóд.

**distinct** adj (*different*) отли́чный; (*clear*) отчётливый; (*evident*) замéтный. **distinction** n (*difference*; *excellence*) отли́чие; (*discrimination*) разли́чие. **distinctive** adj отличи́тельный. **distinctly** adv я́сно.

**distinguish** vt различáть *impf*, различи́ть *pf*; ~ **o.s.** отличáться *impf*, отличи́ться *pf*. **distinguished** adj выдаю́щийся.

**distort** vt искажáть *impf*, искази́ть *pf*; (*misrepresent*) извращáть *impf*, изврати́ть *pf*. **distortion** n искажéние; извращéние.

**distract** vt отвлекáть *impf*, отвлéчь *pf*. **distraction** n (*amusement*) развлечéние; (*madness*) безýмие. **distraught** adj обезýмевший.

**distress** n (suffering) огорче́ние; (danger) бе́дствие; vt огорча́ть impf, огорчи́ть pf.
**distribute** vt (hand out) раздава́ть impf, разда́ть pf; (allocate) распределя́ть impf, распредели́ть pf. **distribution** n распределе́ние. **distributor** n распредели́тель m.
**district** n райо́н.
**distrust** n недове́рие; vt не доверя́ть impf. **distrustful** adj недове́рчивый.
**disturb** vt беспоко́ить impf, о~ pf. **disturbance** n наруше́ние поко́я; pl (polit etc.) беспоря́дки m pl.
**disuse** n неупотребле́ние; **fall into** ~ выходи́ть impf, вы́йти pf из употребле́ния. **disused** adj забро́шенный.
**ditch** n кана́ва, ров.
**dither** vi колеба́ться impf.
**ditto** n то же са́мое; adv так же.
**divan** n дива́н.
**dive** n ныря́ть impf, нырну́ть pf; (aeron) пики́ровать impf & pf; n ныро́к, прыжо́к в во́ду. **diver** n водола́з.
**diverge** vi расходи́ться impf, разойти́сь pf. **divergent** adj расходя́щийся.
**diverse** adj разнообра́зный. **diversification** n расшире́ние ассортиме́нта. **diversify** vt разнообра́зить impf. **diversion** n (detour) объе́зд; (amusement) развлече́ние. **diversity** n разнообра́зие.
**divert** vt отклоня́ть impf, отклони́ть pf; (amuse) развлека́ть impf, развле́чь pf. **diverting** adj заба́вный.
**divest** vt (deprive) лиша́ть impf, лиши́ть pf (of +gen); ~ **o.s.** отка́зываться impf, от-

каза́ться pf (of от+gen).
**divide** vt (share; math) дели́ть impf, по~ pf; (separate) разделя́ть impf, раздели́ть pf. **dividend** n дивиде́нд.
**divine** adj боже́ственный.
**diving** n ныря́ние; ~**-board** трампли́н.
**divinity** n (quality) боже́ственность; (deity) божество́; (theology) богосло́вие.
**divisible** adj дели́мый. **division** n (dividing) деле́ние, разделе́ние; (section) отде́л; (mil) диви́зия.
**divorce** n разво́д; vi разводи́ться impf, развести́сь pf. **divorced** adj разведённый.
**divulge** vt разглаша́ть impf, разгласи́ть pf.
**DIY** abbr (of do-it-yourself): he **is good at** ~ у него́ золоты́е ру́ки; ~ **shop** магази́н «сде́лай сам».
**dizziness** n головокруже́ние.
**dizzy** adj (causing dizziness) головокружи́тельный; **I am** ~ у меня́ кру́жится голова́.
**DNA** abbr (of deoxyribonucleic acid) ДНК.
**do** vt де́лать impf, с~ pf; vi (be suitable) годи́ться impf; (suffice) быть доста́точным; ~**-it-yourself** see DIY; that will ~! хва́тит!; how ~ you ~? здра́вствуйте!; как вы пожива́ете?; ~ **away with** (abolish) уничтожа́ть impf, уничто́жить pf; ~ in (kill) убива́ть impf, уби́ть pf; ~ **up** (restore) ремонти́ровать impf, от~ pf; (wrap up) завёртывать impf, заверну́ть pf; (fasten) застёгивать impf, застегну́ть pf; ~ **without** обходи́ться impf, обойти́сь pf без+gen.

**docile** adj поко́рный. **docility** n поко́рность.

**dock**[1] n (naut) док; vt ста́вить impf, по~ pf в док; vi вводи́ть impf, войти́ pf в док; vi (spacecraft) стыкова́ться impf, со~ pf. **docker** n до́кер. **dockyard** n верфь.

**dock**[2] n (law) скамья́ подсуди́мых. **docket** n квита́нция; (label) ярлы́к.

**doctor** n врач; (also univ) до́ктор; vt (castrate) кастри́ровать impf & pf, (spay) удаля́ть impf, удали́ть pf яи́чники y+gen; (falsify) фальсифици́ровать impf & pf. **doctorate** n сте́пень до́ктора.

**doctrine** n доктри́на.

**document** n докуме́нт; vt документи́ровать impf & pf. **documentary** n документа́льный фильм. **documentation** n документа́ция.

**doddery** adj дря́хлый.

**dodge** n увёртка; vt уклоня́ться impf, уклони́ться pf от+gen; (jump to avoid) отска́кивать impf, отскочи́ть pf (от+gen). **dodgy** adj ка́верзный.

**doe** n са́мка.

**dog** n соба́ка, пёс; (fig) пресле́довать impf. **dog-eared** adj захва́танный.

**dogged** adj упо́рный.

**dogma** n до́гма. **dogmatic** adj догмати́ческий.

**doings** n pl дела́ neut pl.

**doldrums** n: be in the ~ хандри́ть impf.

**dole** n посо́бие по безрабо́тице; vt (~ out) выдава́ть impf, вы́дать pf.

**doleful** adj скорбный.

**doll** n ку́кла.

**dollar** n до́ллар.

**dollop** n соли́дная по́рция.

**dolphin** n дельфи́н.

**domain** n (estate) владе́ние; (field) о́бласть.

**dome** n ку́пол.

**domestic** adj (of household; animals) дома́шний; (of family) семе́йный; (polit) вну́тренний; n прислу́га. **domesticate** vt приручи́ть impf, приручи́ть pf. **domesticity** n дома́шняя, семе́йная, жизнь.

**domicile** n местожи́тельство.

**dominance** n госпо́дство. **dominant** adj преоблада́ющий; госпо́дствующий. **dominate** vt госпо́дствовать impf над+instr. **domineering** adj вла́стный.

**dominion** n влады́чество; (realm) владе́ние.

**domino** n кость домино́; pl (game) домино́ neut indecl.

**don** vt надева́ть impf, наде́ть pf.

**donate** vt же́ртвовать impf, по~ pf. **donation** n поже́ртвование.

**donkey** n осёл.

**donor** n же́ртвователь m; (med) до́нор.

**doom** n (ruin) ги́бель; vt обрека́ть impf, обре́чь pf.

**door** n дверь. **doorbell** n (дверно́й) звоно́к. **doorman** n швейца́р. **doormat** n полови́к. **doorstep** n поро́г. **doorway** n дверно́й проём.

**dope** n (drug) нарко́тик; vt дурма́нить impf, о~ pf.

**dormant** adj (sleeping) спя́щий; (inactive) безде́йствующий.

**dormer window** n слухово́е окно́.

**dormitory** n о́бщая спа́льня.

**dormouse** n со́ня.

**dorsal** adj спинно́й.

**dosage** n дозиро́вка. **dose** n до́за.

**dossier** n досье́ neut indecl.

**dot** n то́чка; vt ста́вить impf, по~ pf то́чки на+acc; (scatter) усе́ивать impf, усе́ять pf (with +instr); ~ted line пункти́р.

**dote** vi: ~ on обожа́ть impf.

**double** adj двойно́й; (doubled) удво́енный; ~-bass контраба́с; ~ bed двуспа́льная крова́ть; ~-breasted двубо́ртный; ~-cross обма́нывать impf, обману́ть pf; ~-dealer двуру́шник; ~-dealing двуру́шничество; ~-decker двухэта́жный авто́бус; ~-edged обоюдо́стрый; ~ glazing двойны́е ра́мы f pl; ~ room ко́мната на двои́х; adv вдвое; (two together) вдвоём; n двойно́е коли́чество; (person's) двойни́к; pl (sport) па́рная игра́; vt & i удва́ивать(ся) impf, удво́ить(ся) pf; ~ back возвраща́ться impf, верну́ться pf наза́д; ~ up (in pain) скрю́чиваться impf, скрю́читься pf; (share a room) помеща́ться impf, помести́ться pf вдвоём в одно́й ко́мнате; (~ up as) рабо́тать impf + instr по совмести́тельству.

**doubt** n сомне́ние; vt сомнева́ться impf в+prep. **doubtful** adj сомни́тельный. **doubtless** adv несомне́нно.

**dough** n те́сто. **doughnut** n по́нчик.

**douse** vt (drench) залива́ть impf, зали́ть pf.

**dove** n го́лубь m. **dovetail** n ла́сточкин хвост.

**dowdy** adj неэлега́нтный.

**down**[1] n (fluff) пух.

**down**[2] adv (motion) вниз; (position) внизу́; be ~ with (ill) боле́ть impf +instr; prep вниз с+gen, по+dat; (along) вдоль по+dat; vt (gulp) опроки́дывать impf, опроки́нуть pf; ~-and-out бродя́га m; ~-cast, ~-hearted уны́лый. **downfall** n ги́бель. **downhill** adv под го́ру. **downpour** n ли́вень m. **downright** adj я́вный; adv соверше́нно. **downstairs** adv (motion) вниз; (position) внизу́. **downstream** adv вниз по тече́нию. **down-to-earth** adj реалисти́ческий. **downtrodden** adj угнетённый.

**dowry** n прида́ное sb.

**doze** vi дрема́ть impf.

**dozen** n дю́жина.

**drab** adj бесцве́тный; (boring) ску́чный.

**draft** n (outline, rough copy) набро́сок; (document) прое́кт; (econ) тра́тта; see also **draught**; vt составля́ть impf, соста́вить pf план, прое́кт, +gen.

**drag** vt тащи́ть impf; (river etc.) драги́ровать impf & pf; ~ on (vi) затя́гиваться impf, затяну́ться pf; n (burden) обу́за; (on cigarette) затя́жка; in ~ в же́нской оде́жде.

**dragon** n драко́н. **dragonfly** n стрекоза́.

**drain** n водосто́к; (leakage, fig) уте́чка; vt осуша́ть impf, осуши́ть pf; vi спуска́ться impf, спусти́ться pf. **drainage** n дрена́ж; (system) канализа́ция.

**drake** n се́лезень m.

**drama** n дра́ма; (quality) драмати́зм. **dramatic** adj

драмати́ческий. **dramatist** *n* драмату́рг. **dramatize** *vt* драматизи́ровать *impf* & *pf*.

**drape** *vt* драпирова́ть *impf*, за~ *pf*; *n* драпиро́вка.

**drastic** *adj* радика́льный.

**draught** *n* (*air*) сквозня́к; (*traction*) тя́га; *pl* (*game*) ша́шки *f pl*; *see also* **draft**; **there is a** ~ сквози́т; ~ **beer** пи́во из бо́чки. **draughtsman** *n* чертёжник. **draughty** *adj*: **it is** ~ **here** здесь ду́ет.

**draw** *n* (*in lottery*) ро́зыгрыш; (*attraction*) прима́нка; (*drawn game*) ничья́; *vt* (*pull*) тащи́ть *impf*, по~ *pf*; таска́ть *indet*, тащи́ть *det*; (*curtains*) задёргивать *impf*, задёрнуть *pf* (*занаве́ски*); (*attract*) привлека́ть *impf*, привле́чь *pf*; (*pull out*) выта́скивать *impf*, вы́тащить *pf*; (*sword*) обнажа́ть *impf*, обнажи́ть *pf*; (*lots*) броса́ть *impf*, бро́сить *pf* (*жре́бий*); (*water; inspiration*) че́рпать *impf*, черпну́ть *pf*; (*evoke*) вызыва́ть *impf*, вы́звать *pf*; (*conclusion*) выводи́ть *impf*, вы́вести *pf* (*заключе́ние*); (*diagram*) черти́ть *impf*, на~ *pf*; (*picture*) рисова́ть *impf*, на~ *pf*; *vi* (*sport*) сыгра́ть *pf* вничью́; ~ **aside** отводи́ть *impf*, отвести́ *pf* в сто́рону; ~ **back** (*withdraw*) отступа́ть *impf*, отступи́ть *pf*; ~ **in** втя́гивать *impf*, втяну́ть *pf*; (*train*) входи́ть *impf*, войти́ *pf* на ста́нцию; (*car*) подходи́ть *impf*, подойти́ *pf* (**to** к + *dat*); (*days*) станови́ться *impf* коро́че; ~ **out** вытя́гивать *impf*, вы́тянуть *pf*; (*money*) выпи́сывать *impf*, вы́писать *pf*; (*train/car*) выходи́ть *impf*,

вы́йти *pf* (*со* ста́нции/на доро́гу); ~ **up** (*car*) подходи́ть *impf*, подойти́ *pf* (**to** к + *dat*); (*document*) составля́ть *impf*, соста́вить *pf*. **drawback** *n* недоста́ток. **drawbridge** *n* подъёмный мост. **drawer** *n* я́щик. **drawing** *n* (*action*) рисова́ние, черче́ние; (*object*) рису́нок, чертёж; ~**board** чертёжная доска́; ~**pin** кно́пка; ~**room** гости́ная *sb*.

**drawl** *n* протя́жное произноше́ние.

**dread** *n* страх; *vt* боя́ться *impf* +*gen*. **dreadful** *adj* ужа́сный.

**dream** *n* сон; (*fantasy*) мечта́; *vi* ви́деть *impf*, у~ *pf* сон; ~ **of** ви́деть *impf*, у~ *pf* во сне́; (*fig*) мечта́ть *impf* о+*prep*.

**dreary** *adj* (*weather*) па́смурный; (*boring*) ску́чный.

**dredge** *vt* (*river etc.*) драги́ровать *impf* & *pf*. **dredger** *n* дра́га.

**dregs** *n pl* оса́дки (-ков) *pl*.

**drench** *vt* прома́чивать *impf*, промочи́ть *pf*; **get** ~**ed** промока́ть *impf*, промо́кнуть *pf*.

**dress** *n* пла́тье; (*apparel*) оде́жда; ~ **circle** бельэта́ж; ~**maker** портни́ха; ~ **rehearsal** генера́льная репети́ция; *vt* & *i* одева́ть(ся) *impf*, оде́ть(ся) *pf*; *vt* (*cul*) приправля́ть *impf*, припра́вить *pf*; (*med*) перевя́зывать *impf*, перевяза́ть *pf*; ~ **up** наряжа́ть(ся) *impf*, наряди́ть(ся) *pf* (**as** + *instr*).

**dresser** *n* ку́хонный шкаф.

**dressing** *n* (*cul*) припра́ва; (*med*) перевя́зка; ~**gown** хала́т; ~**room** убо́рная *sb*; ~**table** туале́тный сто́лик.

**dribble** *vi* (*person*) пуска́ть *impf*, пусти́ть *pf* слю́ни;

(sport) вести impf мяч.

**dried** adj сушёный. **drier** n
сушилка.

**drift** n (meaning) смысл; (snow)
сугроб; vi плыть impf по
течению; (naut) дрейфовать
impf; (snow etc.) скопляться
impf, скопиться pf; ~ apart
расходиться impf, разо-
йтись pf.

**drill**[1] n сверло; (dentist's) бур;
vt сверлить impf, про~ pf.

**drill**[2] vt (mil) обучать impf,
обучить pf строю; vi про-
ходить impf, пройти pf стро-
евую подготовку; n строевая
подготовка.

**drink** n напиток; vi пить impf,
вы~ pf; ~**-driving** вождение
в нетрезвом состоянии.
**drinking-water** n питьевая
вода.

**drip** n (action) капанье; (drop)
капля; vi капать impf, кап-
нуть pf.

**drive** n (journey) езда; (excursion) прогулка; (campaign)
поход, кампания; (energy)
энергия; (tech) привод; (drive-
way) подъездная дорога; vt
(urge; chase) гонять indet,
гнать det; (vehicle) водить
indet, вести det; управлять
impf +instr; (convey) возить
indet, везти det, по~ pf; vi
(travel) ездить indet, ехать
det, по~ pf; ~ at подразу-
мевать impf, довести pf (to до+gen);
(nail etc.) вбивать impf,
вбить pf (into в+acc); ~ away
vt прогонять impf, прогнать
pf; vi уезжать impf, уехать
pf; ~ up подъезжать impf,
подъехать pf (to к+dat).

**driver** n (of vehicle) водитель
m, шофёр. **driving** adj (force)
движущий; (rain) пролив-

ной; ~**-licence** водительские
права neut pl; ~**-test** экза-
мен на получение води-
тельских прав; ~**-wheel** ве-
дущее колесо.

**drizzle** n мелкий дождь m; vi
моросить impf.

**drone** n (bee; idler) трутень m;
(of voice) жужжание; (of engine) гул; vi (buzz) жужжать
impf; (~ on) бубнить impf.

**drool** vi пускать impf, пустить
pf слюни.

**droop** vi поникать impf, по-
никнуть pf.

**drop** n (of liquid) капля; (fall)
падение, понижение; vt & i
(price) снижать(ся) impf,
снизить(ся) pf, vi (fall) падать impf, упасть pf; vt (let
fall) ронять impf, уронить
pf; (abandon) бросать impf,
бросить pf; ~ behind от-
ставать impf, отстать pf; ~
in заходить impf, зайти pf
(on к+dat); ~ off (fall asleep)
засыпать impf, заснуть pf;
(from car) высаживать impf,
высадить pf; ~ out выбы-
вать impf, выбыть pf (of из
+gen). **droppings** n pl помёт.

**drought** n засуха.

**droves** n pl: in ~ толпами.

**drown** vt топить impf, у~ pf;
(sound) заглушать impf, за-
глушить pf; vi тонуть impf,
у~ pf.

**drowsy** adj сонливый.

**drudgery** n нудная работа.

**drug** n медикамент; (narcotic)
наркотик; ~ **addict** наркоман,
~ка; vt давать impf,
дать pf наркотик+dat.

**drum** n барабан; vi бить impf
в барабан; барабанить impf;
~ **sth into s.o.** вдалбливать
impf, вдолбить pf + dat of

*person* в го́лову. **drummer** *n* бараба́нщик.

**drunk** *adj* пья́ный. **drunkard** *n* пья́ница *m* & *f*. **drunken** *adj* пья́ный; ~ **driving** вожде́ние в нетре́звом состоя́нии. **drunkenness** *n* пья́нство.

**dry** *adj* сухо́й; ~ **land** су́ша; *vt* суши́ть *impf*, вы́~ *pf* (*wipe dry*) вытира́ть *impf*, вы́тереть *pf*; *vi* со́хнуть *impf*, вы́~, про~ *pf*. **dry-cleaning** *n* хими́чистка. **dryness** *n* су́хость.

**dual** *adj* двойно́й; (*joint*) совме́стный; ~**-purpose** двойно́го назначе́ния.

**dub**[1] *vt* (*nickname*) прозыва́ть *impf*, прозва́ть *pf*.

**dub**[2] *vt* (*cin*) дубли́ровать *impf* & *pf*.

**dubious** *adj* сомни́тельный.

**duchess** *n* герцоги́ня. **duchy** *n* ге́рцогство.

**duck**[1] *n* (*bird*) у́тка.

**duck**[2] *vt* (*immerse*) окуна́ть *impf*, окуну́ть *pf*; (*one's head*) нагну́ть *pf*; (*evade*) увёртываться *impf*, уверну́ться *pf* от+*gen*; *vi* (~ *down*) накло́няться *impf*, наклони́ться *pf*.

**duckling** *n* утёнок.

**duct** *n* прохо́д; (*anat*) прото́к.

**dud** *n* (*forgery*) подде́лка; (*shell*) неразорва́вшийся снаря́д; *adj* подде́льный; (*worthless*) него́дный.

**due** *n* (*credit*) до́лжное *sb*; *pl* взно́сы *m pl*; *adj* (*proper*) до́лжный, надлежа́щий; *predic* (*expected*) до́лжен (-жна́); **in ~ course** со вре́менем; ~ **south** пря́мо на юг; ~ **to** благодаря́+*dat*.

**duel** *n* дуэ́ль.

**duet** *n* дуэ́т.

**duke** *n* ге́рцог.

**dull** *adj* (*tedious*) ску́чный;

(*colour*) ту́склый; (*weather*) па́смурный; (*not sharp; stupid*) тупо́й; *vt* притупля́ть *impf*, притупи́ть *pf*.

**duly** *adv* надлежа́щим о́бразом; (*punctually*) своевре́менно.

**dumb** *adj* немо́й. **dumbfounded** *adj* ошара́шенный.

**dummy** *n* (*tailor's*) манеке́н; (*baby's*) со́ска; ~ **run** испыта́тельный рейс.

**dump** *n* сва́лка; *vt* сва́ливать *impf*, свали́ть *pf*.

**dumpling** *n* кле́цка.

**dumpy** *adj* призе́мистый.

**dune** *n* дю́на.

**dung** *n* наво́з.

**dungarees** *n pl* комбинезо́н.

**dungeon** *n* темни́ца.

**dunk** *vt* мака́ть *impf*, макну́ть *pf*.

**duo** *n* па́ра; (*mus*) дуэ́т.

**dupe** *vt* надува́ть *impf*, наду́ть *pf*; *n* простофи́ля *m* & *f*.

**duplicate** *n* ко́пия; **in** ~ в двух экземпля́рах; *adj* (*double*) двойно́й; (*identical*) иденти́чный; *vt* размножа́ть *impf*, размно́жить *pf* **duplicity** *n* двули́чность.

**durability** *n* про́чность. **durable** *adj* про́чный. **duration** *n* продолжи́тельность.

**duress** *n* принужде́ние; **under** ~ под давле́нием.

**during** *prep* во вре́мя +*gen*; (*throughout*) в тече́ние +*gen*.

**dusk** *n* су́мерки (-рек) *pl*.

**dust** *n* пыль; ~**bin** му́сорный я́щик; ~**jacket** суперобло́жка; ~**man** му́сорщик; ~**pan** сово́к; *vt* & *i* (*clean*) стира́ть *impf*, стере́ть *pf* пыль (с+*gen*); (*sprinkle*) посыпа́ть *impf*, посы́пать *pf* *sth* +*acc*, *with* +*instr*.

**duster** *n* пы́льная тря́пка.

**dusty** adj пы́льный.
**Dutch** adj голла́ндский; n: the ~ голла́ндцы m pl. **Dutchman** n голла́ндец. **Dutchwoman** n голла́ндка.
**dutiful** adj послу́шный.
**duty** n (obligation) долг; обя́занность; (office) дежу́рство; (tax) по́шлина; **be on** ~ дежу́рить impf; ~-**free** adj беспо́шлинный.
**duvet** n стёганое одея́ло.
**dwarf** n ка́рлик m; vt (tower above) возвыша́ться impf, возвы́ситься pf над+instr.
**dwell** vi обита́ть impf; ~ **upon** остана́вливаться impf на+prep. **dweller** n жи́тель m. **dwelling** n жили́ще.
**dwindle** vi убыва́ть impf, убы́ть pf.
**dye** n краси́тель m; vt окра́шивать impf, окра́сить pf.
**dynamic** adj динами́ческий. **dynamics** n pl дина́мика.
**dynamite** n динами́т.
**dynamo** n дина́мо neut indecl.
**dynasty** n дина́стия.
**dysentery** n дизентери́я.
**dyslexia** n дисле́ксия. **dyslexic** adj: he is ~ он дисле́ктик.

# E

**each** adj & pron ка́ждый; ~ **other** друг дру́га (dat -гу, etc.).
**eager** adj (pupil) усе́рдный; **I am** ~ **to** мне не те́рпится +inf; о́чень жела́ю +inf.
**eagerly** adv с нетерпе́нием; жа́дно. **eagerness** n си́льное жела́ние.
**eagle** n орёл.
**ear**[1] n (corn) ко́лос.
**ear**[2] n (anat) у́хо; (sense) слух; ~-**ache** боль в у́хе; ~**drum** ба-

раба́нная перепо́нка; ~**mark** (assign) предназнача́ть impf, предназна́чить pf; ~**phone** нау́шник; ~**ring** серьга́; (clipon) клипс; ~**shot**: **within/out of** ~ в преде́лах/вне преде́лов слы́шимости.
**earl** n граф.
**early** adj ра́нний; adv ра́но.
**earn** vt зараба́тывать impf, зарабо́тать pf; (deserve) заслу́живать impf, заслужи́ть pf. **earnings** n pl за́работок.
**earnest** adj серьёзный; n: **in** ~ всерьёз.
**earth** n земля́; (soil) по́чва; vt заземля́ть impf, заземли́ть pf. **earthenware** adj гли́няный. **earthly** adj земно́й. **earthquake** n землетрясе́ние. **earthy** adj земли́стый; (coarse) гру́бый.
**earwig** n уховёртка.
**ease** n (facility) лёгкость; (unconstraint) непринуждённость; **with** ~ легко́; vt облегча́ть impf, облегчи́ть pf; vi успока́иваться impf, успоко́иться pf.
**easel** n мольбе́рт.
**east** n восто́к; (naut) ост; adj восто́чный. **easterly** adj восто́чный. **eastern** adj восто́чный. **eastward(s)** adv на восто́к, к восто́ку.
**Easter** n Па́сха.
**easy** adj лёгкий; (unconstrained) непринуждённый; ~-**going** уживчивый.
**eat** vt есть impf, с~ pf; ку́шать impf, по~, с~ pf; ~ **away** разъеда́ть impf, разъе́сть pf; ~ **into** въеда́ться impf, въе́сться pf в+acc; ~ **up** доеда́ть impf, дое́сть pf. **eatable** adj съедо́бный.
**eaves** n pl стреха́. **eavesdrop**

*vi* подслу́шивать *impf*.

**ebb** *n* (*tide*) отли́в; (*fig*) упа́док.

**ebony** *n* чёрное де́рево.

**ebullient** *adj* кипу́чий.

**EC** *abbr* (*of* European Community) Европе́йское соо́бщество.

**eccentric** *n* чуда́к; *adj* экцентри́чный.

**ecclesiastical** *adj* церко́вный.

**echo** *n* э́хо; *vi* (*resound*) отража́ться *impf*, отрази́ться *pf*; *vt* (*repeat*) повторя́ть *impf*, повтори́ть *pf*.

**eclipse** *n* затме́ние; *vt* затмева́ть *impf*, затми́ть *pf*.

**ecological** *adj* экологи́ческий. **ecology** *n* эколо́гия.

**economic** *adj* экономи́ческий. **economical** *adj* эконо́мный. **economist** *n* экономи́ст. **economize** *vt & i* эконо́мить *impf*, с~ *pf*. **economy** *n* эконо́мика; (*saving*) эконо́мия.

**ecstasy** *n* экста́з. **ecstatic** *adj* экстати́ческий.

**eddy** *n* водоворо́т.

**edge** *n* край; (*blade*) ле́звие; **on** ~ **is** в не́рвном состоя́нии; **have the** ~ **on** име́ть *impf* преиму́щество над+*instr*; *vt* (*border*) окаймля́ть *impf*, окайми́ть *pf*; *vi* пробира́ться *impf*, пробра́ться *pf*. **edging** *n* кайма́. **edgy** *adj* раздражи́тельный.

**edible** *adj* съедо́бный.

**edict** *n* ука́з.

**edifice** *n* зда́ние. **edifying** *adj* назида́тельный.

**edit** *vt* редакти́ровать *impf*, от~ *pf*; (*cin*) монти́ровать *impf*, с~ *pf*. **edition** *n* изда́ние; (*number of copies*) тира́ж. **editor** *n* реда́ктор.

**editorial** *n* передова́я статья́; *adj* реда́кторский, редакцио́нный.

**educate** *vt* дава́ть *impf*, дать *pf* образова́ние +*dat*; **where was he educated?** где он получи́л образова́ние? **educated** *adj* образо́ванный. **education** *n* образова́ние. **educational** *adj* образова́тельный; (*instructive*) уче́бный.

**eel** *n* у́горь *m*.

**eerie** *adj* жу́ткий.

**effect** *n* (*result*) сле́дствие; (*validity*; *influence*) де́йствие; (*impression*; *theat*) эффе́кт; **in** ~ факти́чески; **take** ~ вступа́ть *impf*, вступи́ть *pf* в си́лу; (*medicine*) начина́ть *impf*, нача́ть *pf* де́йствовать; *vt* производи́ть *impf*, произвести́ *pf*. **effective** *adj* эффекти́вный; (*striking*) эффе́ктный; (*actual*) факти́ческий. **effectiveness** *n* эффекти́вность.

**effeminate** *adj* женоподо́бный.

**effervesce** *vi* пузы́риться *impf*. **effervescent** *adj* (*fig*) и́скря́щийся.

**efficiency** *n* эффекти́вность. **efficient** *adj* эффекти́вный; (*person*) организо́ванный.

**effigy** *n* изображе́ние.

**effort** *n* уси́лие.

**effrontery** *n* на́глость.

**effusive** *adj* экспанси́вный.

**e.g.** *abbr* напр.

**egalitarian** *adj* эгалита́рный.

**egg¹** *n* яйцо́; ~**cup** рю́мка для яйца́; ~**shell** яи́чная скорлупа́.

**egg²** *vt*: ~ **on** подстрека́ть *impf*, подстрекну́ть *pf*.

**ego** *n* «Я». **egocentric** *adj*

эгоцентри́ческий. **egoism** *n* эгои́зм. **ego(t)ist** *n* эгои́ст, ~ка. **ego(t)istical** *adj* эгоистри́ческий. **egotism** *n* эготи́зм.

**Egypt** *n* Еги́пет. **Egyptian** *n* египтя́нин, -я́нка; *adj* еги́петский.

**eiderdown** *n* пухо́вое одея́ло.

**eight** *adj* & *n* во́семь; (*number* 8) восьмёрка. **eighteen** *adj* & *n* восемна́дцать. **eighteenth** *adj* & *n* восемна́дцатый. **eighth** *adj* & *n* восьмо́й; (*fraction*) восьма́я *sb*. **eightieth** *adj* & *n* восьмидеся́тый. **eighty** *adj* & *n* во́семьдесят; (*decade*) восьмидеся́тые го́ды (-до́в) *m pl*.

**either** *adj* & *pron* (*one of two*) оди́н из двух, тот и́ли друго́й; (*both*) и тот, и друго́й; о́ба; (*one or other*) любо́й; *adv* & *conj*: ~ ... *or* и́ли... и́ли, либо... ли́бо.

**eject** *vt* выбра́сывать *impf*, вы́бросить *pf*; *vi* (*pilot*) катапульти́роваться *impf* & *pf*.

**eke** *vt*: ~ **out a living** перебива́ться *impf*, перби́ться *pf* ко́е-как.

**elaborate** *adj* (*ornate*) витиева́тый; (*detailed*) подро́бный; *vt* разраба́тывать *impf*, разрабо́тать *pf*; (*detail*) уточня́ть *impf*, уточни́ть *pf*.

**elapse** *vi* проходи́ть *impf*, пройти́ *pf*; (*expire*) истека́ть *impf*, исте́чь *pf*.

**elastic** *n* рези́нка; *adj* эласти́чный, ~ **band** рези́нка. **elasticity** *n* эласти́чность.

**elated** *adj* в восто́рге. **elation** *n* восто́рг.

**elbow** *n* ло́коть *m*; *vt*: ~ (**one's way**) **through** прота́лкиваться *impf*, протолкну́ться *pf*

че́рез+*acc*.

**elder**[1] *n* (*tree*) бузина́.

**elder**[2] *n* (*person*) ста́рец; *pl* ста́ршие *sb*; *adj* ста́рший. **elderly** *adj* пожило́й. **eldest** *adj* ста́рший.

**elect** *adj* и́збранный; *vt* избира́ть *impf*, избра́ть *pf*. **election** *n* вы́боры *m pl*. **elector** *n* избира́тель *m*. **electoral** *adj* избира́тельный. **electorate** *n* избира́тели *m pl*.

**electric(al)** *adj* электри́ческий; ~ **shock** уда́р электри́ческим то́ком. **electrician** *n* эле́ктрик. **electricity** *n* электри́чество. **electrify** *vt* (*convert to electricity*) электрифици́ровать *impf* & *pf*; (*charge with electricity*; *fig*) электризова́ть *impf*, на~ *pf*. **electrode** *n* электро́д. **electron** *n* электро́н. **electronic** *adj* электро́нный. **electronics** *n* электро́ника.

**electrocute** *vt* убива́ть *impf*, уби́ть *pf* электри́ческим то́ком; (*execute*) казни́ть *impf* & *pf* на электри́ческом сту́ле. **electrolysis** *n* электро́лиз.

**elegance** *n* элега́нтность. **elegant** *adj* элега́нтный.

**elegy** *n* эле́гия.

**element** *n* элеме́нт; (*earth, wind, etc.*) стихи́я; **be in one's** ~ быть в свое́й стихи́и. **elemental** *adj* стихи́йный. **elementary** *adj* элемента́рный; (*school etc.*) нача́льный.

**elephant** *n* слон.

**elevate** *vt* поднима́ть *impf*, подня́ть *pf*. **elevated** *adj* возвы́шенный. **elevation** *n* (*height*) высота́. **elevator** *n* (*lift*) лифт.

**eleven** *adj* & *n* оди́ннадцать. **eleventh** *adj* & *n* оди́ннадцатый; **at the ~ hour** в последнюю минуту.

**elf** n эльф.

**elicit** vt (obtain) выявля́ть impf, вы́явить pf; (evoke) вызыва́ть impf, вы́звать pf.

**eligible** adj име́ющий пра́во (for на+acc); (bachelor) подходя́щий.

**eliminate** vt (do away with) устраня́ть impf, устрани́ть pf; (rule out) исключа́ть impf, исключи́ть pf.

**élite** n эли́та.

**ellipse** n э́ллипс. **elliptic(al)** adj эллипти́ческий.

**elm** n вяз.

**elocution** n ора́торское иску́сство.

**elongate** vt удлиня́ть impf, удлини́ть pf.

**elope** vi бежа́ть det (с возлю́бленным).

**eloquence** n красноре́чие. **eloquent** adj красноречи́вый.

**else** adv (besides) ещё; (instead) друго́й; (with neg) бо́льше; **nobody ~** никто́ бо́льше; **or ~** и́на́че; **а́ля** не то; и́ли же; **s.o. ~** кто-нибу́дь друго́й; **something ~?** ещё что́-нибудь? **elsewhere** adv (place) в друго́м ме́сте; (direction) в друго́е ме́сто.

**elucidate** vt разъясня́ть impf, разъясни́ть pf.

**elude** vt избега́ть impf +gen.

**elusive** adj неулови́мый.

**emaciated** adj истощённый.

**email** n электро́нная по́чта.

**emanate** vi исходи́ть impf (from из, от, +gen).

**emancipate** vt эмансипи́ровать impf & pf. **emancipation** n эмансипа́ция.

**embankment** n (river) на́бережная sb; (rly) на́сыпь.

**embargo** n эмба́рго neut indecl.

**embark** vi сади́ться impf, сесть pf на кора́бль; **~ upon** предпринима́ть impf, предприня́ть pf. **embarkation** n поса́дка (на кора́бль).

**embarrass** vt смуща́ть impf, смути́ть pf; **be ~ed** чу́вствовать impf себя́ неудо́бно.

**embarrassing** adj неудо́бный. **embarrassment** n смуще́ние.

**embassy** n посо́льство.

**embedded** adj вре́занный.

**embellish** vt (adorn) украша́ть impf, укра́сить pf; (story) прикра́шивать impf, прикра́сить pf. **embellishment** n украше́ние.

**embers** n pl тле́ющие угольки́ m pl.

**embezzle** vt растра́чивать impf, растра́тить pf. **embezzlement** n растра́та.

**embittered** adj озло́бленный.

**emblem** n эмбле́ма.

**embodiment** n воплоще́ние.

**embody** vt воплоща́ть impf, воплоти́ть pf.

**emboss** vt чека́нить impf, вы́~, от~ pf.

**embrace** n объя́тие; vi обнима́ться impf, обня́ться pf; vt обнима́ть impf, обня́ть pf; (accept) принима́ть impf, приня́ть pf; (include) охва́тывать impf, охвати́ть pf.

**embroider** vt вышива́ть impf, вы́шить pf; (story) прикра́шивать impf, прикра́сить pf. **embroidery** n вы́шивка.

**embroil** vt впу́тывать impf, впу́тать pf.

**embryo** n эмбрио́н.

**emerald** n изумру́д.

**emerge** vi появля́ться impf, появи́ться pf. **emergence** n появле́ние. **emergency** *n* кра́йняя необходи́мость; **state of ~** чрезвыча́йное положе́ние; **~ exit** запасно́й вы́ход.

**emery paper** *n* нажда́чная бума́га.

**emigrant** *n* эмигра́нт, **~ка**.

**emigrate** *vt* эмигри́ровать *impf & pf*. **emigration** *n* эмигра́ция.

**eminence** *n* (*fame*) знамени́тость. **eminent** *adj* выдаю́щийся. **eminently** *adv* чрезвыча́йно.

**emission** *n* испуска́ние. **emit** *vt* испуска́ть *impf*, испусти́ть *pf*; (*light*) излуча́ть *impf*, излучи́ть *pf*; (*sound*) издава́ть *impf*, изда́ть *pf*.

**emotion** *n* эмо́ция, чу́вство. **emotional** *adj* эмоциона́льный.

**empathize** *vt* сопережива́ть *impf*, сопережи́ть *pf*. **empathy** *n* эмпа́тия.

**emperor** *n* импера́тор.

**emphasis** *n* ударе́ние. **emphasize** *vt* подчёркивать *impf*, подчеркну́ть *pf*. **emphatic** *adj* вырази́тельный; категори́ческий.

**empire** *n* импе́рия.

**empirical** *adj* эмпири́ческий.

**employ** *vt* (*use*) по́льзоваться *impf* +*instr*; (*person*) нанима́ть *impf*, наня́ть *pf*. **employee** *n* сотру́дник, рабо́чий *sb*. **employer** *n* работода́тель *m*. **employment** *n* рабо́та, слу́жба; (*use*) испо́льзование.

**empower** *vt* уполномо́чивать *impf*, уполномо́чить *pf* (**to** на+*acc*).

**empress** *n* императри́ца.

**emptiness** *n* пустота́. **empty** *adj* пусто́й; **~-headed** пустоголо́вый; *vt* (*container*) опорожня́ть *impf*, опорожни́ть *pf*; (*solid*) высыпа́ть *impf*, вы́сыпать *pf*; (*liquid*) вылива́ть *impf*, вы́лить *pf*; *vi* пусте́ть *impf*, о~ *pf*.

**emulate** *vt* достига́ть *impf*, дости́гнуть, дости́чь *pf* +*gen*; (*copy*) подража́ть *impf* +*dat*.

**emulsion** *n* эму́льсия.

**enable** *vt* дава́ть *impf*, дать *pf* возмо́жность *+dat & inf*.

**enact** *vt* (*law*) принима́ть *impf*, приня́ть *pf*; (*theat*) разы́грывать *impf*, разыгра́ть *pf*. **enactment** *n* (*law*) постановле́ние; (*theat*) игра́.

**enamel** *n* эма́ль; *adj* эма́левый; *vt* эмалирова́ть *impf & pf*.

**encampment** *n* ла́герь *m*.

**enchant** *vt* очаро́вывать *impf*, очарова́ть *pf*. **enchanting** *adj* очарова́тельный. **enchantment** *n* очарова́ние.

**encircle** *vt* окружа́ть *impf*, окружи́ть *pf*.

**enclave** *n* анкла́в.

**enclose** *vt* огора́живать *impf*, огороди́ть *pf*; (*in letter*) прикла́дывать *impf*, приложи́ть *pf*; **please find ~d** прилага́ется (-а́ются) +*nom*. **enclosure** *n* огоро́женное ме́сто; (*in letter*) приложе́ние.

**encode** *vt* шифрова́ть *impf*, за~ *pf*.

**encompass** *vt* (*encircle*) окружа́ть *impf*, окружи́ть *pf*; (*contain*) заключа́ть *impf*, заключи́ть *pf*.

**encore** *int* бис!; *n* вы́зов на бис.

**encounter** *n* встре́ча; (*in combat*) столкнове́ние; *vt* встреча́ть *impf*, встре́тить *pf*; (*fig*) ста́лкиваться *impf*, столкну́ться *pf* c+*instr*.

**encourage** *vt* ободря́ть *impf*, ободри́ть *pf*. **encouragement** *n* ободре́ние. **encouraging** *adj* ободри́тельный.

**encroach** *vi* вторга́ться *impf*, вто́ргнуться *pf* (**on** в+*acc*). **encroachment** *n* вторже́ние.

**encumber** *vt* обременя́ть *impf*, обремени́ть *pf*. **encumbrance** *n* обу́за.

**encyclopaedia** *n* энциклопе́дия. **encyclopaedic** *adj* энциклопеди́ческий.

**end** *n* коне́ц; (*death*) смерть; (*purpose*) цель; **an ~ in itself** самоце́ль; **in the ~** в конце́ концо́в; **make ~s meet** своди́ть *impf*, свести́ *pf* концы́ с конца́ми; **no ~ of** ма́сса+*gen*; **on ~** (*upright*) стоймя́, дыбо́м; (*continuously*) подря́д; **put an ~to** класть *impf*, положи́ть *pf* коне́ц +*dat*; *vt* конча́ть *impf*, ко́нчить *pf*; (*halt*) прекраща́ть *impf*, прекрати́ть *pf*; *vi* конча́ться *impf*, ко́нчиться *pf*. **endanger** *vt* подверга́ть *impf*, подве́ргнуть *pf* опа́сности.

**endearing** *adj* привлека́тельный. **endearment** *n* ла́ска.

**endeavour** *n* попы́тка; (*exertion*) уси́лие; (*undertaking*) де́ло; *vi* стара́ться *impf*, по~ *pf*.

**endemic** *adj* эндеми́ческий.

**ending** *n* оконча́ние. **endless** *adj* бесконе́чный.

**endorse** *vt* (*document*) подпи́сывать *impf*, подписа́ть *pf*; (*support*) подде́рживать *impf*, поддержа́ть *pf*. **endorsement** *n* по́дпись; подде́ржка; (*on driving licence*) проко́л.

**endow** *vt* обеспе́чивать *impf*, обеспе́чить *pf* постоя́нным дохо́дом; (*fig*) одаря́ть *impf*, одари́ть *pf*. **endowment** *n* поже́ртвование; (*talent*) дарова́ние.

**endurance** *n* (*of person*) вы́носливость; (*of object*) про́чность. **endure** *vt* выноси́ть *impf*, вы́нести *pf*; терпе́ть *impf*, по~ *pf*; *vi* продолжа́ться *impf*, продолжи́ться *pf*.

**enemy** *n* враг; *adj* вра́жеский.

**energetic** *adj* энерги́чный. **energy** *n* эне́ргия; *pl* си́лы *f pl*.

**enforce** *vt* (*law etc.*) следи́ть *impf* за выполне́нием +*gen*. **enforcement** *n* наблюде́ние за выполне́нием +*gen*.

**engage** *vt* (*hire*) нанима́ть *impf*, наня́ть *pf*; (*tech*) зацепля́ть *impf*, зацепи́ть *pf*. **engaged** *adj* (*occupied*) за́нятый; **be ~ in** занима́ться *impf*, заня́ться *pf* +*instr*; **become ~** обруча́ться *impf*, обручи́ться *pf* (**to** c+*instr*). **engagement** *n* (*appointment*) свида́ние; (*betrothal*) обруче́ние; (*battle*) бой; **~ ring** обруча́льное кольцо́. **engaging** *adj* привлека́тельный.

**engender** *vt* порожда́ть *impf*, породи́ть *pf*.

**engine** *n* дви́гатель *m*; (*rly*) локомоти́в; **~-driver** (*rly*) маши́нист. **engineer** *n* инжене́р; *vt* (*fig*) организова́ть *impf* & *pf*. **engineering** *n* инжене́рное де́ло, те́хника.

**England** *n* А́нглия. **English** *adj* англи́йский; **n: the ~** (*pl*) англича́не (-н) *pl*. **Englishman, -woman** *n* англича́нин, -а́нка.

**engrave** vt гравирова́ть impf, вы́~ pf; (fig) вреза́ть impf, вре́зать pf. **engraver** n гравёр. **engraving** n гравю́ра.

**engross** vt поглоща́ть impf, поглоти́ть pf; **be ~ed** in быть поглощённым +instr.

**engulf** vt поглоща́ть impf, поглоти́ть pf.

**enhance** vt увели́чивать impf, увели́чить pf.

**enigma** n зага́дка. **enigmatic** adj зага́дочный.

**enjoy** vt получа́ть impf, получи́ть pf удово́льствие от+gen; наслажда́ться impf, наслади́ться pf +instr; (health etc.) облада́ть impf +instr; ~ o.s. хорошо́ проводи́ть impf, провести́ pf вре́мя. **enjoyable** adj прия́тный. **enjoyment** n удово́льствие.

**enlarge** vt увели́чивать impf, увели́чить pf; ~ **upon** распространя́ться impf, распространи́ться pf о+prep. **enlargement** n увеличе́ние.

**enlighten** vt просвеща́ть impf, просвети́ть pf. **enlightenment** n просвеще́ние.

**enlist** vi поступа́ть impf, поступи́ть pf на вое́нную слу́жбу; vt (mil) вербова́ть impf, за~ pf; (support etc.) заруча́ться impf, заручи́ться pf +instr.

**enliven** vt оживля́ть impf, оживи́ть pf.

**enmity** n вражда́.

**ennoble** vt облагора́живать impf, облагоро́дить pf.

**ennui** n тоска́.

**enormity** n чудо́вищность. **enormous** adj огро́мный. **enormously** adv чрезвы́чайно.

**enough** adj доста́точно +gen;

adv доста́точно, дово́льно; **be** ~ хвата́ть impf, хвати́ть pf impers+gen.

**enquire, enquiry** see inquire, inquiry

**enrage** vt беси́ть impf, вз~ pf.

**enrapture** vt восхища́ть impf, восхити́ть pf.

**enrich** vt обогаща́ть impf, обогати́ть pf.

**enrol** vt & i запи́сывать(ся) impf, записа́ть(ся) pf. **enrolment** n за́пись.

**en route** adv по пути́ (**to, for** в+acc).

**ensconce** vt: ~ **o.s.** заса́живаться impf, засе́сть pf (**with** за+acc).

**ensemble** n (mus) анса́мбль m.

**enshrine** vt (fig) охраня́ть impf, охрани́ть pf.

**ensign** n (flag) флаг.

**enslave** vt порабоща́ть impf, поработи́ть pf.

**ensue** vi сле́довать impf. **ensuing** adj после́дующий.

**ensure** vt обеспе́чивать impf, обеспе́чить pf.

**entail** vt (necessitate) влечь impf за собо́й.

**entangle** vt запу́тывать impf, запу́тать pf.

**enter** vt & i входи́ть impf, войти́ pf в+acc; (by transport) въезжа́ть impf, въе́хать pf в+acc; (vt (join) поступа́ть impf, поступи́ть pf в, на, +acc; (competition) вступа́ть impf, вступи́ть pf в+acc; (in list) вноси́ть impf, внести́ pf в+acc.

**enterprise** n (undertaking) предприя́тие; (initiative) предприи́мчивость. **enterprising** adj предприи́мчивый.

**entertain** vt (amuse) развлека́ть impf, развле́чь pf;

**enthral** vt порабоща́ть impf, поработи́ть pf.

**enthusiasm** n энтузиа́зм. **enthusiast** n энтузиа́ст, ~ка. **enthusiastic** adj восто́рженный; по́лный энтузиа́зма.

**entice** vt зама́нивать impf, замани́ть pf. **enticement** n прима́нка. **enticing** adj зама́нчивый.

**entire** adj по́лный, це́лый, весь; **entirely** adv вполне́, соверше́нно; (solely) исключи́тельно. **entirety** n: in its ~ полностью.

**entitle** vt (authorize) дава́ть impf, дать pf пра́во+dat (to на+acc); be ~d (book) называ́ться impf; be ~d to име́ть impf пра́во на+acc.

**entity** n объе́кт; феноме́н.

**entomology** n энтомоло́гия.

**entourage** n свита́.

**entrails** n pl вну́тренности (-тей) pl.

**entrance**[1] n вход, въезд; (theat) вы́ход; ~ **exam** вступи́тельный экза́мен; ~ **hall** вести-бю́ль m.

**entrance**[2] vt (charm) очаро́вывать impf, очарова́ть pf. **entrancing** adj очарова́тельный.

**entrant** n уча́стник (for +gen).

**entreat** vt умоля́ть impf, умоли́ть pf. **entreaty** n мольба́.

**entrench** vt be, become ~ed (fig) укореня́ться impf, укорени́ться pf.

**entrepreneur** n предприни-ма́тель m.

**entrust** vt (secret) вверя́ть impf, вве́рить pf (to +dat); (object; person) поруча́ть impf, поручи́ть pf (to +dat).

**entry** n вход, въезд; вступле́ние; (theat) вы́ход; (note) за́пись; (in reference book) статья́.

**entwine** vt (interweave) сплета́ть impf, сплести́ pf; (wreathe) обвива́ть impf, обви́ть pf.

**enumerate** vt перечисля́ть impf, перечи́слить pf.

**enunciate** vt (express) излага́ть impf, изложи́ть pf; (pronounce) произноси́ть impf, произнести́ pf. **enunciation** n изложе́ние; произноше́ние.

**envelop** vt оку́тывать impf, оку́тать pf. **envelope** n конве́рт.

**enviable** adj зави́дный. **envious** adj зави́стливый.

**environment** n среда́; (the ~) окружа́ющая среда́. **environs** n pl окре́стности f pl.

**envisage** vt предусма́тривать impf, предусмотре́ть pf.

**envoy** n посла́нник, аге́нт.

**envy** n за́висть; vt зави́довать impf, по~ pf +dat.

**enzyme** n энзи́м.

**ephemeral** adj эфеме́рный.

**epic** n эпопе́я; adj эпи́ческий.

**epidemic** n эпиде́мия.

**epilepsy** n эпиле́псия. **epileptic** n эпиле́птик; adj эпилепти́ческий.

**epilogue** n эпило́г.

**episode** n эпизо́д. **episodic** adj эпизоди́ческий.

**epistle** n посла́ние.

**epitaph** n эпита́фия.

**epithet** n эпи́тет.

**epitome** n воплоще́ние. **epitomize** vt воплоща́ть impf, во-

воплоти́ть *pf*.
**epoch** *n* эпо́ха.

**equal** *adj* ра́вный, одина́ковый; (*capable of*) спосо́бный (**to** на+*acc*, +*inf*); *n* ра́вный *sb*; *vt* равня́ться *impf* +*dat*. **equality** *n* ра́венство. **equalize** *vt* ура́внивать *impf*, уравня́ть *pf*; *vi* (*sport*) равня́ть *impf*, с~ *pf* счёт. **equally** *adv* равно́, ра́вным о́бразом.
**equanimity** *n* хладнокро́вие.
**equate** *vt* прира́внивать *impf*, приравня́ть *pf* (**with** к+*dat*). **equation** *n* (*math*) уравне́ние. **equator** *n* эква́тор. **equatorial** *adj* экваториа́льный.
**equestrian** *adj* ко́нный.
**equidistant** *adj* равностоя́щий. **equilibrium** *n* равнове́сие.
**equip** *vt* обору́довать *impf* & *pf*; (*person*) снаряжа́ть *impf*, снаряди́ть *pf*; (*fig*) вооружа́ть *impf*, вооружи́ть *pf*. **equipment** *n* обору́дование, снаряже́ние.
**equitable** *adj* справедли́вый. **equity** *n* справедли́вость; *pl* (*econ*) обыкнове́нные а́кции *f pl*.
**equivalent** *adj* эквивале́нтный; *n* эквивале́нт.
**equivocal** *adj* двусмы́сленный.
**era** *n* э́ра.
**eradicate** *vt* искореня́ть *impf*, искорени́ть *pf*.
**erase** *vt* стира́ть *impf*, стере́ть *pf*; (*from memory*) вычёркивать *impf*, вы́черкнуть *pf* (из па́мяти). **eraser** *n* ла́стик.
**erect** *adj* прямо́й; *vt* сооружа́ть *impf*, сооруди́ть *pf*. **erection** *n* сооруже́ние; (*biol*) эре́кция.

**erode** *vt* разруша́ть *impf*, разру́шить *pf*; (*fig*) разруша́ть. **erosion** *n* эро́зия.
**erotic** *adj* эроти́ческий.
**err** *vi* ошиба́ться *impf*, ошиби́ться *pf*; (*sin*) греши́ть *impf*, со~ *pf*.
**errand** *n* поруче́ние; **run ~s** быть на посы́лках (**for** y+*gen*).
**erratic** *adj* неро́вный.
**erroneous** *adj* оши́бочный. **error** *n* оши́бка.
**erudite** *adj* учёный. **erudition** *n* эруди́ция.
**erupt** *vi* взрыва́ться *impf*, взорва́ться *pf*; (*volcano*) изверга́ться *impf*, изве́ргнуться *pf*. **eruption** *n* изверже́ние.
**escalate** *vi* возраста́ть *impf*, возрасти́ *pf*; *vt* интенсифици́ровать *impf* & *pf*.
**escalator** *n* эскала́тор.
**escapade** *n* вы́ходка. **escape** *n* (*from prison*) побе́г; (*from danger*) спасе́ние; (*leak*) уте́чка; **have a narrow** ~ едва́ спасти́сь; *vi* (*flee*) бежа́ть *impf* & *pf*; (*from prison*) убежа́ть *pf*; (*save o.s.*) спаса́ться *impf*, спасти́сь *pf*; (*leak*) утека́ть *impf*, уте́чь *pf*; *vt* избега́ть *impf*, избежа́ть *pf* +*gen*; (*groan*) вырыва́ться *impf*, вы́рваться *pf* из, у, +*gen*.
**escort** *n* (*mil*) эско́рт; (*of lady*) кавале́р; *vt* сопровожда́ть *impf*, сопроводи́ть *pf*; (*mil*) эскорти́ровать *impf* & *pf*.

**Eskimo** *n* эскимо́с, ~ка.
**esoteric** *adj* эзотери́ческий.
**especially** *adv* особе́нно.
**espionage** *n* шпиона́ж.
**espousal** *n* подде́ржка. **espouse** *vt* (*fig*) подде́рживать

*impf*, поддержа́ть *pf*.

**essay** *n* о́черк; (*in school*) сочине́ние.

**essence** *n* (*philos*) су́щность; (*gist*) суть; (*extract*) эссе́нция. **essential** *adj* (*fundamental*) суще́ственный; (*necessary*) необходи́мый; *n pl* (*necessities*) необходи́мое *sb*; (*crux*) суть; (*fundamentals*) осно́вы *f pl*. **essentially** *adv* по существу́.

**establish** *vt* (*set up*) учрежда́ть *impf*, учреди́ть *pf*; (*fact etc.*) устана́вливать *impf*, установи́ть *pf*. **establishment** *n* (*action*) учрежде́ние, установле́ние; (*institution*) учрежде́ние.

**estate** *n* (*property*) име́ние; (*after death*) насле́дство; (*housing* ~) жило́й масси́в; ~ **agent** аге́нт по прода́же недви́жимости; ~ **car** автомоби́ль *m* с ку́зовом «универса́л».

**esteem** *n* уваже́ние; *vt* уважа́ть *impf*. **estimate** *n* (*of quality*) оце́нка; (*of cost*) сме́та; *vt* оце́нивать *impf*, оцени́ть *pf*. **estimation** *n* оце́нка, мне́ние.

**Estonia** *n* Эсто́ния. **Estonian** *n* эсто́нец, -нка; *adj* эсто́нский.

**estranged** *adj* отчуждённый. **estrangement** *n* отчужде́ние.

**estuary** *n* у́стье.

**etc.** *abbr* и т.д. **etcetera** и так да́лее.

**etch** *vt* трави́ть *impf*, вы́- *pf*. **etching** *n* (*action*) травле́ние; (*object*) офо́рт.

**eternal** *adj* ве́чный. **eternity** *n* ве́чность.

**ether** *n* эфи́р. **ethereal** *adj* эфи́рный.

**ethical** *adj* эти́ческий,

эти́чный. **ethics** *n* э́тика.

**ethnic** *adj* этни́ческий.

**etiquette** *n* этике́т.

**etymology** *n* этимоло́гия.

**EU** *abbr* (*of* **European Union**) ЕС.

**eucalyptus** *n* эвкали́пт.

**Eucharist** *n* прича́стие.

**eulogy** *n* похвала́.

**euphemism** *n* эвфеми́зм. **euphemistic** *adj* эвфемисти́ческий.

**Europe** *n* Евро́па. **European** *n* европе́ец; *adj* европе́йский; ~ **Community** Европе́йское соо́бщество; ~ **Union** Европе́йский сою́з.

**evacuate** *vt* (*person, place*) эвакуи́ровать *impf* & *pf*. **evacuation** *n* эвакуа́ция.

**evade** *vt* уклоня́ться *impf*, уклони́ться *pf* от+*gen*.

**evaluate** *vt* оце́нивать *impf*, оцени́ть *pf*. **evaluation** *n* оце́нка.

**evangelical** *adj* ева́нгельский. **evangelist** *n* еванге́ли́ст.

**evaporate** *vt* & *i* испаря́ть(ся) *impf*, испари́ть(ся) *pf*. **evaporation** *n* испаре́ние.

**evasion** *n* уклоне́ние *n* от+*gen*). **evasive** *adj* укло́нчивый.

**eve** *n* кану́н; **on the** ~ нака́нуне.

**even** *adj* ро́вный; (*number*) чётный; **get** ~ расквита́ться *pf* (**with** *c*+*instr*); *adv* да́же; (*just*) как раз; (*with comp*) ещё; ~ **if** да́же е́сли; ~ **though** хотя́; ~ **so** всё-таки; **not** ~ да́же не; *vt* выра́внивать *impf*, вы́ровнять *pf*.

**evening** *n* ве́чер; *adj* вече́рний; ~ **class** вече́рние ку́рсы *m pl*.

**evenly** *adv* по́ровну, ро́вно.

evenness n ро́вность.

event n собы́тие; происше́ствие; in the ~ of в слу́чае+gen; in any ~ во вся́ком слу́чае; in the ~ в коне́чном счёте. eventful adj по́лный собы́тий. eventual adj коне́чный. eventuality n возмо́жность. eventually adv в конце́ концо́в.

ever adv (at any time) когда́-либо, когда́-нибудь; (always) всегда́; (emph) же; ~ since с тех пор (как); ~ so о́чень; for ~ навсегда́; hardly ~ почти́ никогда́. evergreen adj вечнозелёный; ~ вечнозелёное расте́ние. everlasting adj ве́чный. evermore adv: for ~ навсегда́.

every adj ка́ждый, вся́кий, все (pl); ~ now and then вре́мя от вре́мени; ~ other ка́ждый второ́й; ~ other day че́рез день. everybody, everyone pron ка́ждый, все (pl). everyday adj (daily) ежедне́вный; (commonplace) повседне́вный. everything pron всё. everywhere adv всю́ду, везде́.

evict vt выселя́ть impf, вы́селить pf. eviction n выселе́ние.

evidence n свиде́тельство, доказа́тельство; give ~ свиде́тельствовать impf (o+prep; +acc; +что). evident adj очеви́дный.

evil n зло; adj злой.

evoke vt вызыва́ть impf, вы́звать pf.

evolution n эволю́ция. evolutionary adj эволюцио́нный. evolve vt & i развива́ть(ся) impf, разви́ть(ся) pf.

ewe n овца́.

ex- in comb бы́вший.

exacerbate vt обостря́ть impf, обостри́ть pf.

exact adj то́чный; vt взы́скивать impf, взыска́ть pf (from, of c+gen). exacting adj тре́бовательный. exactitude, exactness n то́чность. exactly adv то́чно; (just) как раз; (precisely) и́менно.

exaggerate vt преувели́чивать impf, преувели́чить pf. exaggeration n преувеличе́ние.

exalt vt возвыша́ть impf, возвы́сить pf; (extol) превозноси́ть impf, превознести́ pf.

examination n (inspection) осмо́тр; (exam) экза́мен; (law) допро́с. examine vt (inspect) осма́тривать impf, осмотре́ть pf; (test) экзаменова́ть impf, про~ pf; (law) допра́шивать impf, допроси́ть pf. examiner n экзамена́тор.

example n приме́р; for ~ наприме́р.

exasperate vt раздража́ть impf, раздражи́ть pf. exasperation n раздраже́ние.

excavate vt раска́пывать impf, раскопа́ть pf. excavations n pl раско́пки f pl. excavator n экскава́тор.

exceed vt превыша́ть impf, превы́сить pf. exceedingly adv чрезвыча́йно.

excel vt превосходи́ть impf, превзойти́ pf; vi отлича́ться impf, отличи́ться pf (at, in в+prep). excellence n превосхо́дство. excellency n превосходи́тельство. excellent adj отли́чный.

except vt исключа́ть impf, исключи́ть pf; prep кро́ме+gen. exception n исключе́ние; take ~ to возража́ть impf возразить *pf* против+*gen*. **exceptional** *adj* исключительный.

**excerpt** *n* отрывок.

**excess** *n* избыток. **excessive** *adj* чрезмерный.

**exchange** *n* обмен (of +*instr*); (*of currency*) размен; (*building*) биржа; (*telephone*) центральная телефонная станция; ~ **rate** курс; *vt* обменивать *impf*, обменять *pf* (**for** на+*acc*); обмениваться *impf*, обменяться *pf* +*instr*.

**Exchequer** *n* казначейство.

**excise**[1] *n* (*duty*) акциз(ный сбор).

**excise**[2] *vt* (*cut out*) вырезать *impf*, вырезать *pf*.

**excitable** *adj* возбудимый. **excite** *vt* (*cause, arouse*) возбуждать *impf*, возбудить *pf*; (*thrill, agitate*) волновать *impf*, вз~ *pf*. **excitement** *n* возбуждение; волнение.

**exclaim** *vi* восклицать *impf*, воскликнуть *pf*. **exclamation** *n* восклицание; ~ **mark** восклицательный знак.

**exclude** *vt* исключать *impf*, исключить *pf*. **exclusion** *n* исключение. **exclusive** *adj* исключительный.

**excommunicate** *vt* отлучать *impf*, отлучить *pf* (от церкви).

**excrement** *n* экскременты (-тов) *pl*.

**excrete** *vt* выделять *impf*, выделить *pf*. **excretion** *n* выделение.

**excruciating** *adj* мучительный.

**excursion** *n* экскурсия.

**excusable** *adj* простительный. **excuse** *n* оправдание; (*pretext*) отговорка; *vt* (*for-*

*give*) извинять *impf*, извинить *pf*; (*justify*) оправдывать *impf*, оправдать *pf*; (*release*) освобождать *impf*, освободить *pf* (**from** от+*gen*); ~ **me!** извините!; простите!

**execute** *vt* исполнять *impf*, исполнить *pf*; (*criminal*) казнить *impf* & *pf*. **execution** *n* исполнение; казнь. **executioner** *n* палач. **executive** *n* исполнительный орган; (*person*) руководитель *m*; *adj* исполнительный.

**exemplary** *adj* примерный. **exemplify** *vt* (*illustrate by example*) приводить *impf*, привести *pf* пример +*gen*; (*serve as example*) служить *impf*, по~ *pf* примером +*gen*.

**exempt** *adj* освобождённый; *vt* освобождать *impf*, освободить *pf* (**from** от+*gen*). **exemption** *n* освобождение.

**exercise** *n* применение; (*physical* ~; *task*) упражнение; **take** ~ упражняться *impf*; ~ **book** тетрадь; *vt* (*use*) применять *impf*, применить *pf*; (*dog*) прогуливать *impf*; (*train*) упражнять *impf*.

**exert** *vt* оказывать *impf*, оказать *pf*; ~ **o.s.** стараться *impf*, по~ *pf*. **exertion** *n* напряжение.

**exhale** *vt* выдыхать *impf*, выдохнуть *pf*.

**exhaust** *n* выхлоп; ~ **fumes** выхлопные газы *m pl*; ~ **pipe** выхлопная труба; *vt* (*use up*) истощать *impf*, истощить *pf*; (*person*) изнурять *impf*, изнурить *pf*; (*subject*) исчерпывать *impf*, исчерпать *pf*. **exhausted** *adj*: **be** ~ (*person*) быть изможденным. **exhausting** *adj* изнурительный.

**exhibit** 441 **explicit**

**exhaustion** *n* изнуре́ние; (*defension*) истоще́ние. **exhaustive** *adj* исче́рпывающий.

**exhibit** *n* экспона́т; (*law*) веще́ственное доказа́тельство; *vt* (*manifest*) проявля́ть *impf*, прояви́ть *pf*; (*publicly*) выставля́ть *impf*, вы́ставить *pf*. **exhibition** *n* вы́ставка. **exhibitor** *n* экспоне́нт.

**exhilarated** *adj* в припо́днятом настрое́нии. **exhilarating** *adj* возбужда́ющий. **exhilaration** *n* возбужде́ние.

**exhort** *vt* увещева́ть *impf*. **exhortation** *n* увеща́ние.

**exhume** *vt* выка́пывать *impf*, вы́копать *pf*.

**exile** *n* изгна́ние; (*person*) изгна́нник; *vt* изгоня́ть *impf*, изгна́ть *pf*.

**exist** *vi* существова́ть *impf*. **existence** *n* существова́ние. **existing** *adj* существу́ющий.

**exit** *n* вы́ход; (*for vehicles*) вы́езд; (*theat*) ухо́д (со сце́ны); ~ **visa** выездна́я ви́за; *vi* уходи́ть *impf*, уйти́ *pf*.

**exonerate** *vt* опра́вдывать *impf*, оправда́ть *pf*.

**exorbitant** *adj* непоме́рный.

**exorcize** *vt* (*spirits*) изгоня́ть *impf*, изгна́ть *pf*.

**exotic** *adj* экзоти́ческий.

**expand** *vt & i* расширя́ть(ся) *impf*, расши́рить(ся) *pf*; ~ **on** распространя́ться *impf*, распространи́ться *pf* o+*prep*. **expanse** *n* простра́нство. **expansion** *n* расшире́ние. **expansive** *adj* экспанси́вный.

**expatriate** *n* экспатриа́нт, ~ка.

**expect** *vt* (*await*) ожида́ть *impf* +*gen*; ждать *impf* +*gen*, что; (*suppose*) полага́ть *impf*; (*re-*

*quire*) тре́бовать *impf* +*gen*, что́бы. **expectant** *adj* вы́жидательный; ~ **mother** бере́менная же́нщина. **expectation** *n* ожида́ние.

**expediency** *n* целесообра́зность, (*advantage*) приём; *adj* целесообра́зный. **expedite** *vt* ускоря́ть *impf*, уско́рить *pf*. **expedition** *n* экспеди́ция. **expeditionary** *adj* экспедицио́нный.

**expel** *vt* (*drive out*) выгоня́ть *impf*, вы́гнать *pf*; (*from school etc.*) исключа́ть *impf*, исключи́ть *pf*; (*from country etc.*) изгоня́ть *impf*, изгна́ть *pf*.

**expend** *vt* тра́тить *impf*, из~, по~ *pf*. **expendable** *adj* необяза́тельный. **expenditure** *n* расхо́д. **expense** *n* расхо́д; *pl* расхо́ды *m pl*, at the ~ of за счёт+*gen*; (*fig*) цено́ю+*gen*. **expensive** *adj* дорого́й.

**experience** *n* о́пыт; (*incident*) пережива́ние; *vt* испы́тывать *impf*, испыта́ть *pf*; (*undergo*) пережива́ть *impf*, пережи́ть *pf*. **experienced** *adj* о́пытный.

**experiment** *n* экспериме́нт; *vi* эксперименти́ровать *impf* (on, with над, c+*instr*). **experimental** *adj* эксперимента́льный.

**expert** *n* экспе́рт; *adj* о́пытный. **expertise** *n* специа́льные зна́ния *neut pl*.

**expire** *vi* (*period*) истека́ть *impf*, исте́чь *pf*. **expiry** *n* истече́ние.

**explain** *vt* объясня́ть *impf*, объясни́ть *pf*. **explanation** *n* объясне́ние. **explanatory** *adj* объясни́тельный.

**expletive** *n* (*oath*) бра́нное сло́во.

**explicit** *adj* я́вный; (*of person*) прямо́й.

**explode** vt & i взрыва́ть(ся) impf, взорва́ть(ся) pf; vt (discredit) опроверга́ть impf, опрове́ргнуть pf; vi (with anger etc.) разража́ться impf, разрази́ться pf.

**exploit** n по́двиг; vt эксплуати́ровать impf; (use to advantage) испо́льзовать impf & pf. **exploitation** n эксплуата́ция. **exploiter** n эксплуата́тор.

**exploration** n иссле́дование. **exploratory** adj иссле́довательский. **explore** vt иссле́довать impf & pf. **explorer** n иссле́дователь m.

**explosion** n взрыв. **explosive** n взры́вчатое вещество́; adj взры́вчатый; (fig) взрывно́й.

**exponent** n (interpreter) истолкова́тель m; (advocate) сторо́нник.

**export** n вы́воз, э́кспорт; vt вы́возить impf, вы́везти pf; экспорти́ровать impf & pf. **exporter** n экспортёр.

**expose** vt (bare) раскрыва́ть impf, раскры́ть pf; (subject) подверга́ть impf, подве́ргнуть pf (to +dat); (discredit) разоблача́ть impf, разоблачи́ть pf; (phot) экспони́ровать impf & pf.

**exposition** n изложе́ние.

**exposure** n подверга́ние (to +dat); (phot) вы́держка; (unmasking) разоблаче́ние; (med) хо́лод.

**expound** vt излага́ть impf, изложи́ть pf.

**express** n (train) экспре́сс; adj (clear) то́чный; (purpose) специа́льный; (urgent) сро́чный; vt выража́ть impf, вы́разить pf. **expression** n выраже́ние; (expressiveness) вырази-

тельность. **expressive** adj вырази́тельный. **expressly** adv (clearly) я́сно; (specifically) специа́льно.

**expropriate** vt экспроприи́ровать impf & pf. **expropriation** n экспроприа́ция.

**expulsion** n (from school etc.) исключе́ние; (from country etc.) изгна́ние.

**exquisite** adj утончённый.

**extant** adj сохрани́вшийся.

**extempore** adv экспро́мптом.

**extemporize** vt & i импровизи́ровать impf, сымпровизи́ровать pf.

**extend** vt (stretch out) протя́гивать impf, протяну́ть pf; (enlarge) расширя́ть impf, расши́рить pf; (prolong) продлева́ть impf, продли́ть pf; vi простира́ться impf, простере́ться pf. **extension** n (enlarging) расшире́ние; (time) продле́ние; (to house) пристро́йка; (tel) доба́вочный. **extensive** adj обши́рный. **extent** n (degree) сте́пень.

**extenuating** adj: ~ circumstances смягча́ющие вину́ обстоя́тельства neut pl.

**exterior** n вне́шность; adj вне́шний.

**exterminate** vt истребля́ть impf, истреби́ть pf. **extermination** n истребле́ние.

**external** adj вне́шний.

**extinct** adj (volcano) поту́хший; (species) вы́мерший; **become** ~ вымира́ть impf, вы́мереть pf. **extinction** n вымира́ние.

**extinguish** vt гаси́ть impf, по~ pf. **extinguisher** n огнетуши́тель m.

**extol** vt превозноси́ть impf,

превознести́ *pf.*

**extort** *vt* вымога́ть *impf* (**from** y+*gen*). **extortion** *n* вымога́тельство. **extortionate** *adj* вымога́тельский.

**extra** *n* (*theat*) стати́ст, ~ка; (*payment*) припла́та; *adj* дополни́тельный; (*special*) осо́бый; *adv* осо́бенно.

**extract** *n* экстра́кт; (*from book etc.*) вы́держка; *vt* извлека́ть *impf*, извле́чь *pf*. **extraction** *n* извлече́ние; (*origin*) происхожде́ние. **extradite** *vt* выдава́ть *impf*, вы́дать *pf*. **extradition** *n* вы́дача.

**extramarital** *adj* внебра́чный. **extraneous** *adj* посторо́нний. **extraordinary** *adj* чрезвыча́йный.

**extrapolate** *vt* & *i* экстраполи́ровать *impf* & *pf*.

**extravagance** *n* расточи́тельность. **extravagant** *adj* расточи́тельный; (*fantastic*) сумасбро́дный.

**extreme** *n* кра́йность; *adj* кра́йний. **extremity** *n* (*end*) край; (*adversity*) кра́йность; *pl* (*hands & feet*) коне́чности *f pl.*

**extricate** *vt* выпу́тывать *impf*, вы́путать *pf.*

**exuberance** *n* жизнера́достность. **exuberant** *adj* жизнера́достный.

**exude** *vt* & *i* выделя́ть(ся) *impf*, вы́делить(ся) *pf*; (*fig*) излуча́ть(ся) *impf*, излучи́ть(ся) *pf.*

**exult** *vi* ликова́ть *impf*. **exultant** *adj* лику́ющий. **exultation** *n* ликова́ние.

**eye** *n* глаз; (*needle etc.*) ушко́; *vt* разгля́дывать *impf*, разгляде́ть *pf*. **eyeball** *n* глазно́е я́блоко. **eyebrow** *n* бровь.

**eyelash** *n* ресни́ца. **eyelid** *n* ве́ко. **eyeshadow** *n* те́ни *f pl* для век. **eyesight** *n* зре́ние. **eyewitness** *n* очеви́дец.

# F

**fable** *n* ба́сня.

**fabric** *n* (*structure*) структу́ра; (*cloth*) ткань. **fabricate** *vt* (*invent*) выду́мывать *impf*, вы́думать *pf*. **fabrication** *n* вы́думка.

**fabulous** *adj* ска́зочный.

**façade** *n* фаса́д.

**face** *n* лицо́; (*expression*) выраже́ние; (*grimace*) грима́са; (*side*) сторона́; (*surface*) пове́рхность; (*clock etc.*) цифербла́т; **make** ~s ко́рчить *impf* ро́жи; ~ **down** лицо́м вниз; ~ **to** ~ лицо́м к лицу́; **in the** ~ **of** пе́ред лицо́м+*gen*, вопреки́+*dat*; **on the** ~ **of it** на пе́рвый взгляд; *vt* (*be turned towards*) быть обращённым к+*dat*; (*of person*) стоя́ть *impf* лицо́м к+*dat*; (*meet firmly*) смотре́ть *impf* в лицо́+*dat*; (*cover*) облицо́вывать *impf*, облицева́ть *pf*; **I can't** ~ **it** я да́же ду́мать об э́том не могу́. **faceless** *adj* безли́чный.

**facet** *n* грань; (*fig*) аспе́кт. **facetious** *adj* шутли́вый.

**facial** *adj* лицево́й. **facilitate** *vt* облегча́ть *impf*, облегчи́ть *pf*. **facility** *n* (*ease*) лёгкость; (*ability*) спосо́бность; *pl* (*conveniences*) удо́бства *neut pl*, (*opportunities*) возмо́жности *f pl.*

**facing** *n* облицо́вка; (*of garment*) отде́лка.

**facsimile** n факси́миле neut indecl.

**fact** n факт; **the ~ is that ...** де́ло в том, что...; **as a matter of ~** со́бственно говоря́; **in ~** на са́мом де́ле.

**faction** n фра́кция.

**factor** n фа́ктор.

**factory** n фа́брика, заво́д.

**factual** adj факти́ческий.

**faculty** n спосо́бность; (univ) факульте́т.

**fade** vi (wither) вя́нуть impf, за~ pf; (colour) выцвета́ть impf, вы́цвести pf; (sound) замира́ть impf, замере́ть pf.

**faeces** n pl кал.

**fag** n (cigarette) сигаре́тка.

**fail** n: **without ~** обяза́тельно; vi (weaken) слабе́ть impf, (break down) отка́зывать impf, отказа́ть pf; (not succeed) терпе́ть impf, по~ pf неуда́чу; не удава́ться impf, уда́ться pf impers+dat; vt & i (exam) прова́ливать(ся) impf, провали́ть(ся) pf.; vt (disappoint) подводи́ть impf, подвести́ pf. **failing** n недоста́ток; prep за неиме́нием +gen. **failure** n неуда́ча; (person) неуда́чник, -ица.

**faint** n о́бморок; adj (weak) сла́бый; (pale) бле́дный; **I feel ~** мне ду́рно; **~-hearted** малоду́шный; vi па́дать impf, упа́сть pf в о́бморок.

**fair¹** n я́рмарка.

**fair²** adj (hair, skin) све́тлый; (weather) я́сный; (just) справедли́вый; (average) сно́сный; **a ~ amount** дово́льно мно́го +gen. **fairly** adv дово́льно.

**fairy** n фе́я; **~-tale** ска́зка.

**faith** n ве́ра; (trust) дове́рие. **faithful** adj ве́рный; **yours ~ly** с уваже́нием.

**fake** n подде́лка; vt подде́лывать impf, подде́лать pf.

**falcon** n со́кол.

**fall** n паде́ние; vi па́дать impf, (у)па́сть pf; **~ apart** распада́ться impf, распа́сться pf; **~ asleep** засыпа́ть impf, засну́ть pf; **~ back on** прибега́ть impf, прибе́гнуть pf к+dat; **~ down** упа́сть pf; (building) разва́ливаться impf, развали́ться pf; **~ in love with** влюбля́ться impf, влюби́ться pf в+acc; **~ off** отпада́ть impf, отпа́сть pf; **~ out** выпада́ть impf, вы́пасть pf; (quarrel) поссо́риться pf; **~ over** опроки́дываться impf, опроки́нуться pf; **~ through** прова́ливаться impf, провали́ться pf; **~-out** радиоакти́вные оса́дки (-ков) pl.

**fallacy** n оши́бка.

**fallible** adj подве́рженный оши́бкам.

**fallow** n: **lie ~** лежа́ть impf под па́ром.

**false** adj ло́жный; (teeth) иску́сственный; **~ start** неве́рный старт. **falsehood** n ложь. **falsification** n фальсифика́ция. **falsify** vt фальсифици́ровать impf & pf. **falsity** n ло́жность.

**falter** vi спотыка́ться impf, споткну́ться pf; (stammer) запина́ться impf, запну́ться pf.

**fame** n сла́ва. **famed** adj изве́стный.

**familiar** adj (well known) знако́мый; (usual) обы́чный; (informal) фамилья́рный. **familiarity** n знако́мство; фамилья́рность. **familiarize** vt ознакомля́ть impf, ознако́мить pf (with c+instr).

**family** *n* семья́; *attrib* семе́й-
ный; ~ **tree** родосло́вная *sb.*

**famine** *n* го́лод. **famished** *adj*:
be ~ голода́ть *impf*.

**famous** *adj* знамени́тый.

**fan**[1] *n* ве́ер; (*ventilator*) вентиля́-
тор; ~**-belt** реме́нь *m*
вентиля́тора; *vt* обма́хивать
*impf*, обмахну́ть *pf*; (*flame*)
раздува́ть *impf*, разду́ть *pf*.

**fan**[2] *n* покло́нник, -ица; (*sport*)
боле́льщик. **fanatic** *n* фана́-
тик. **fanatical** *adj* фанати́-
ческий.

**fanciful** *adj* причу́дливый.
**fancy** *n* фанта́зия; (*whim*)
причу́да; **take a ~ to** увле-
ка́ться *impf*, увле́чься *pf*
+*instr*; *adj* витиева́тый; *vt*
(*imagine*) представля́ть *impf*,
предста́вить *pf* себе́; (*suppose*) полага́ть *impf*; (*like*)
нра́виться *impf*, по~ *pf*
*impers*+*dat*; ~ **dress** маска-
ра́дный костю́м; ~**-dress**
костюми́рованный.

**fanfare** *n* фанфа́ра.

**fang** *n* клык; (*serpent's*) ядо-
ви́тый зуб.

**fantasize** *vi* фантази́ровать
*impf*. **fantastic** *adj* фантасти́-
ческий. **fantasy** *n* фанта́зия.

**far** *adj* да́льний; **Russia is ~
away** Росси́я о́чень далеко́;
*adv* далёко; (*fig*) намно́го;
**as ~ as** (*prep*) до+*gen*; (*conj*)
поско́льку; **by ~** намно́го;
**(in) so ~ as** поско́льку; **so
~** до сих пор; ~**-fetched**
притя́нутый за́ во́лосы; ~**-
reaching** далеко́ иду́щий; ~**-
sighted** дальнови́дный.

**farce** *n* фарс. **farcical** *adj*
смехотво́рный.

**fare** *n* (*price*) проездна́я пла́-
та; (*food*) пи́ща; *vi* пожи-
ва́ть *impf*. **farewell** *int* про-

ща́й(те)!; *n* проща́ние; *attrib*
проща́льный; **bid** ~ проща́-
ться *impf*, прости́ться *pf*
to c+*instr*).

**farm** *n* фе́рма. **farmer** *n* фе́р-
мер. **farming** *n* се́льское хо-
зя́йство.

**fart** (*vulg*) *n* пу́кание; *vi*
пу́кать *impf*, пу́кнуть *pf*.

**farther** *see* **further**. **farthest** *see*
**furthest**.

**fascinate** *vt* очаро́вывать *impf*,
очарова́ть *pf*. **fascinating**
*adj* очарова́тельный. **fascination** *n* очарова́ние.

**Fascism** *n* фаши́зм. **Fascist** *n*
фаши́ст, -ка; *adj* фаши́стский.

**fashion** *n* мо́да; (*manner*) ма-
не́ра; **after a ~** не́которым
о́бразом; *vt* придава́ть *impf*,
прида́ть *pf* фо́рму +*dat*. **fashionable** *adj* мо́дный.

**fast**[1] *n* пост; *vi* пости́ться *impf*.

**fast**[2] *adj* (*rapid*) ско́рый,
бы́стрый; (*colour*) сто́йкий;
(*shut*) пло́тно закры́тый; **be
~** (*timepiece*) спеши́ть *impf*.

**fasten** *vt* (*attach*) прикреп-
ля́ть *impf*, прикрепи́ть *pf* (**to**
к+*dat*); (*tie*) привя́зывать
*impf*, привяза́ть *pf* (**to** к+*dat*);
(*garment*) застёгивать *impf*,
застегну́ть *pf*. **fastener, fastening** *n* запо́р, задви́жка;
(*on garment*) застёжка.

**fastidious** *adj* брезгли́вый.

**fat** *n* жир; *adj* (*greasy*) жи́р-
ный; (*plump*) то́лстый; **get
~** толсте́ть *impf*, по~ *pf*.

**fatal** *adj* роково́й; (*deadly*)
смерте́льный. **fatalism** *n*
фатали́зм. **fatality** *n* (*death*)
смерте́льный слу́чай. **fate** *n*
судьба́. **fateful** *adj* роково́й.

**father** *n* оте́ц; ~**-in-law** (*husband's* ~) свёкор; (*wife's* ~)
тесть *m*. **fatherhood**

отцо́вство. **fatherland** n оте́-
чество. **fatherly** adj оте́че-
ский.

**fathom** n морска́я са́жень; vt
(fig) понима́ть impf, поня́ть
pf.

**fatigue** n утомле́ние; vt утом-
ля́ть impf, утоми́ть pf.

**fatten** vt отка́рмливать impf,
откорми́ть pf; vi толсте́ть
impf, по~ pf. **fatty** adj жи́р-
ный.

**fatuous** adj глу́пый.

**fault** n недоста́ток; (blame)
вина́; (geol) сброс. **faultless**
adj безупре́чный. **faulty** adj
дефе́ктный.

**fauna** n фа́уна.

**favour** n (kind act) любе́з-
ность; (goodwill) благоскло́н-
ность; in (s.o.'s) ~ в по́льзу
+gen; be in ~ of быть за+acc;
vt (support) благоприя́тство-
вать impf +dat; (treat with
partiality) ока́зывать impf,
оказа́ть pf предпочте́ние
+dat. **favourable** adj (propitious) благоприя́тный; (approving) благоскло́нный. **favourite** n люби́мец, -мица;
(also sport) фавори́т, ~ка;
adj люби́мый.

**fawn**¹ n олене́нок; adj желто-
ва́то-кори́чневый.

**fawn**² vi подли́зываться impf,
подлиза́ться pf (on к+dat).

**fax** n факс; vt посыла́ть impf,
посла́ть pf по фа́ксу.

**fear** n страх, боя́знь, опасе́-
ние; vt & i боя́ться impf
+gen; опаса́ться impf +gen.
**fearful** adj (terrible) стра́ш-
ный; (timid) пугли́вый. **fearless** adj бесстра́шный. **fear-
some** adj гро́зный.

**feasibility** n осуществи́мость.
**feasible** adj осуществи́мый.

**feast** n (meal) пир; (festival)
пра́здник; vi пирова́ть impf.

**feat** n по́двиг.

**feather** n перо́.

**feature** n черта́; (newspaper)
(темати́ческая) статья́; ~
film худо́жественный фильм;
vt помеща́ть impf, поме-
сти́ть pf на ви́дном ме́сте;
(in film) пока́зывать impf,
показа́ть pf; vi игра́ть impf
сыгра́ть pf роль. **February** n февра́ль m; adj
февра́льский.

**feckless** adj безала́берный.

**federal** adj федера́льный. **federation** n федера́ция.

**fee** n гонора́р; (entrance ~ etc.)
взнос; pl (regular payment,
school, etc.) пла́та.

**feeble** adj сла́бый.

**feed** n корм; vt корми́ть impf,
на~, по~ pf; vi корми́ться
impf, по~ pf; ~ up отка́рм-
ливать impf, откорми́ть pf;
**I am fed up with** мне надое́л
(-а, -о; -и) +nom. **feedback**
n обра́тная связь.

**feel** vt чу́вствовать impf, по~
pf; (think) счита́ть impf,
счесть pf; vi (~ bad etc.) чу́в-
ствовать impf, по~ pf себя́
+adv, +instr; ~ like хоте́ться
impf impers+dat. **feeling** n
(sense) ощуще́ние; (emotion)
чу́вство; (impression) впеча-
тле́ние; (mood) настрое́ние.

**feign** vt притворя́ться impf,
притвори́ться pf +instr.
**feigned** adj притво́рный.

**feline** adj коша́чий.

**fell** vt (tree) сруба́ть impf,
сруби́ть pf; (person) сбива́ть
impf, сбить pf с ног.

**fellow** n па́рень m; (of society
etc.) член; ~ **countryman** со-
оте́чественник. **fellowship**

това́рищество.

**felt** n фетр; adj фе́тровый; ~ **tip pen** флома́стер.

**female** n (animal) са́мка; (person) же́нщина; adj же́нский.

**feminine** adj же́нский, же́нственный; (gram) же́нского ро́да. **femininity** n же́нственность. **feminism** n feminíзм. **feminist** n feminíст, ~ка; adj feminíстский.

**fence** n забо́р; vt: ~ **in** огора́живать impf, огороди́ть pf; ~ **off** отгора́живать impf, отгороди́ть pf, vi (sport) фехтова́ть impf. **fencer** n фехтова́льщик, -ица. **fencing** n (enclosure) забо́р; (sport) фехтова́ние.

**fend** vt: ~ **off** отража́ть impf, отрази́ть pf; vi: ~ **for o.s.** забо́титься impf, по~ pf о себе́. **fender** n решётка.

**fennel** n фе́нхель m.

**ferment** n броже́ние; vi броди́ть impf, vt ква́сить impf, за~ pf; (excite) возбужда́ть impf, возбуди́ть pf. **fermentation** n броже́ние; (excitement) возбужде́ние.

**fern** n па́поротник.

**ferocious** adj свире́пый. **ferocity** n свире́пость.

**ferret** n хорёк; vt: ~ **out** (search out) разы́скивать impf, разню́хать pf; vi: ~ **about** (rummage) ры́ться impf.

**ferry** n паро́м; vt перевози́ть impf, перевезти́ pf.

**fertile** adj плодоро́дный. **fertility** n плодоро́дие. **fertilize** vt (soil) удобря́ть impf, удо́брить pf; (egg) оплодотворя́ть impf, оплодотвори́ть pf. **fertilizer** n удобре́ние.

**fervent** adj горя́чий. **fervour** n жар.

**fester** vi гнои́ться impf.

**festival** n пра́здник, (music etc.) фестива́ль m. **festive** adj пра́здничный. **festivities** n pl торжества́ neut pl.

**festoon** vt украша́ть impf.

**fetch** vt (carrying) приноси́ть impf, принести́ pf; (leading) приводи́ть impf, привести́ pf; (on foot) идти́ impf, по~ pf за+instr; (by vehicle) заезжа́ть impf, зае́хать pf за+instr; (price) выруча́ть impf, вы́ручить pf. **fetching** adj привлека́тельный.

**fetid** adj злово́нный.

**fetish** n фети́ш.

**fetter** vt ско́вывать impf, скова́ть pf; n pl канда́лы (-ло́в) pl; (fig) око́вы (-в) pl.

**fettle** n состоя́ние.

**feud** n кро́вная месть.

**feudal** adj феода́льный. **feudalism** n феодали́зм.

**fever** n лихора́дка. **feverish** adj лихора́дочный.

**few** adj & pron немно́гие pl; ма́ло+gen; **a** ~ не́сколько +gen; **quite a** ~ нема́ло +gen.

**fiancé** n жени́х. **fiancée** n неве́ста.

**fiasco** n прова́л.

**fib** n ложь; vi привира́ть impf, привра́ть pf.

**fibre** n воло́кно. **fibreglass** n стекловолокно́. **fibrous** adj волокни́стый.

**fickle** adj непостоя́нный.

**fiction** n худо́жественная литерату́ра; (invention) вы́думка. **fictional** adj беллетристи́ческий. **fictitious** adj вы́мышленный.

**fiddle** n (violin) скри́пка; (swindle) обма́н; vi: ~ **about**

безде́льничать *impf*; ~ with верте́ть *impf*; *vt* (*falsify*) подде́лывать *impf*, подде́лать *pf*; (*cheat*) жи́лить *impf*, у~ *pf*.

**fidelity** *n* ве́рность.

**fidget** *n* непосе́да *m* & *f*; *vi* ёрзать *impf*; не́рвничать *impf*. **fidgety** *adj* непосе́дливый.

**field** *n* по́ле; (*sport*) площа́дка; (*sphere*) о́бласть; ~ **glasses** полево́й бино́кль *m*. ~**work** полевы́е рабо́ты *f pl*.

**fiend** *n* дья́вол. **fiendish** *adj* дья́вольский.

**fierce** *adj* свире́пый; (*strong*) си́льный.

**fiery** *adj* о́гненный.

**fifteen** *adj* & *n* пятна́дцать. **fifteenth** *adj* & *n* пятна́дцатый. **fifth** *adj* & *n* пя́тый; (*fraction*) пя́тая *sb*. **fiftieth** *adj* & *n* пятидеся́тый. **fifty** *adj* & *n* пятьдеся́т; *pl* (*decade*) пятидеся́тые го́ды (-до́в) *m pl*.

**fig** *n* инжи́р.

**fight** *n* дра́ка; (*battle*) бой; (*fig*) борьба́; *vi* боро́ться *impf* *c+instr*; *vi* дра́ться *impf*; *vt* & *i* (*wage war*) воева́ть *impf* *c+instr*. **fighter** *n* бое́ц; (*aeron*) истреби́тель *m*. **fighting** *n* бой *m* pl.

**figment** *n* плод воображе́ния.

**figurative** *adj* перено́сный. **figure** *n* (*form, body, person*) фигу́ра; (*number*) ци́фра; (*diagram*) рису́нок; (*image*) изображе́ние; (*of speech*) оборо́т ре́чи; ~**head** (*naut*) носово́е украше́ние; (*person*) номина́льная глава́; *vt* (*think*) полага́ть *impf*; *vi* фигури́ровать *impf*; ~ **out** вычисля́ть *impf*, вы́числить *pf*.

**filament** *n* волокно́; (*electr*) нить.

**file**[1] *n* (*tool*) напи́льник; *vt* под-

пи́ливать *impf*, подпили́ть *pf*. **file**[2] *n* (*folder*) па́пка; (*comput*) файл; *vt* подшива́ть *impf*, подши́ть *pf*; (*complaint*) подава́ть *impf*, пода́ть *pf*. **file**[3] *n* (*row*) ряд; **in (single)** ~ гусько́м.

**filigree** *adj* филигра́нный.

**fill** *vt* & *i* (*also* ~ **up**) наполня́ть(ся) *impf*, напо́лнить(ся) *pf*; *vt* заполня́ть *impf*, запо́лнить *pf*; (*tooth*) пломбирова́ть *impf*, за~ *pf*; (*occupy*) занима́ть *impf*, заня́ть *pf*; (*satiate*) насыща́ть *impf*, насы́тить *pf*; ~ **in** (*vt*) заполня́ть *impf*, запо́лнить *pf*; (*vi*) замеща́ть *impf*, замести́ть *pf*.

**fillet** *n* (*cul*) филе́ *neut indecl*.

**filling** *n* (*tooth*) пло́мба; (*cul*) начи́нка.

**filly** *n* кобы́ла.

**film** *n* (*layer*; *phot*) плёнка; (*cin*) фильм; ~ **star** кинозвезда́; *vt* снима́ть *impf*, снять *pf*.

**filter** *n* фильтр; *vt* фильтрова́ть *impf*, про~ *pf*; ~ **through, out** проса́чиваться *impf*, просочи́ться *pf*.

**filth** *n* грязь. **filthy** *adj* гря́зный.

**fin** *n* плавни́к.

**final** *n* фина́л; *pl* выпускны́е экза́мены *m pl*; *adj* после́дний; (*decisive*) оконча́тельный. **finale** *n* фина́л. **finalist** *n* финали́ст. **finality** *n* зако́нченность. **finalize** *vt* (*complete*) заверша́ть *impf*, заверши́ть *pf*; (*settle*) ула́живать *impf*, ула́дить *pf*. **finally** *adv* (*at last*) наконе́ц; (*in the end*) в конце́ концо́в.

**finance** *n* фина́нсы (-сов) *pl*; *vt* финанси́ровать *impf* & *pf*. **financial** *adj* фина́нсовый.

**financier** n финанси́ст.

**finch** n see comb, e.g. bullfinch

**find** n нахо́дка; vt находи́ть impf, найти́ pf; (person) заставля́ть impf, заста́вить pf; ~ **out** узнава́ть impf, узна́ть pf; ~ **fault with** придира́ться impf, придра́ться pf к+dat. **finding** n pl (of inquiry) вы́воды m pl.

**fine**¹ n (penalty) штраф; vt штрафова́ть impf, о~ pf.

**fine**² adj (weather) я́сный; (excellent) прекра́сный; (delicate) то́нкий; (of sand etc.) ме́лкий; ~ **arts** изобрази́тельные иску́сства neut pl; adv хорошо́.

**finery** n наря́д. **finesse** n то́нкость.

**finger** n па́лец; ~-**nail** но́готь; ~-**print** отпеча́ток па́льца; ~-**tip** ко́нчик па́льца; **have at (one's) ~s** знать impf как свои́ пять па́льцев; vt щу́пать impf, по~ pf.

**finish** n коне́ц; (polish) отде́лка; (sport) фи́ниш; vt & i конча́ть(ся) impf, ко́нчить(ся) pf; vt ока́нчивать impf, око́нчить pf.

**finite** adj коне́чный.

**Finland** n Финля́ндия. **Finn** n финн, фи́нка. **Finnish** adj фи́нский.

**fir** n ель, пи́хта.

**fire** vt (bake) обжига́ть impf, обже́чь pf; (excite) воспламеня́ть impf, воспламени́ть pf; (gun) стреля́ть impf из+gen (**at** в+acc, по+dat); (dismiss) увольня́ть impf, уво́лить pf; n ого́нь m; (grate) ками́н; (conflagration) пожа́р; (bonfire) костёр; (fervour) пыл; **be on ~** горе́ть impf; **catch ~** загора́ться impf, загоре́ться pf; **set ~ to, set on ~** поджига́ть

impf, поджёчь pf; ~-**alarm** пожа́рная трево́га; ~-**arm(s)** огнестре́льное ору́жие; ~-**brigade** пожа́рная кома́нда; ~-**engine** пожа́рная маши́на; ~-**escape** пожа́рная ле́стница; ~ **extinguisher** огнетуши́тель m; ~-**guard** ками́нная решётка; ~-**man** пожа́рный sb; ~-**place** ками́н; ~-**side** ме́сто у ками́на; ~-**station** пожа́рное депо́ neut indecl; ~-**wood** дрова́ (-в) pl; ~-**work** фейерве́рк. **firing** n (shooting) стрельба́.

**firm**¹ n (business) фи́рма.

**firm**² adj твёрдый. **firmness** n твёрдость.

**first** adj пе́рвый; n пе́рвый sb; adv сперва́, снача́ла; (for the ~ time) впервы́е; **in the ~ place** во-пе́рвых; ~ **of all** пре́жде всего́; **at ~ sight** на пе́рвый взгляд; ~ **aid** пе́рвая по́мощь; ~-**class** первокла́ссный; ~-**hand** из пе́рвых рук; ~-**rate** первокла́ссный. **firstly** adv во-пе́рвых.

**fiscal** adj фина́нсовый.

**fish** n ры́ба; adj ры́бный; vi лови́ть impf ры́бу; ~ **out** выта́скивать impf, вы́таскать pf. **fisherman** n рыба́к. **fishery** n ры́бный про́мысел. **fishing** n ры́бная ло́вля; ~ **boat** рыболо́вное су́дно; ~ **line** ле́са; ~ **rod** у́дочка. **fishmonger** n торго́вец ры́бой. **fishmonger's** n ры́бный магази́н. **fishy** adj ры́бный; (dubious) подозри́тельный.

**fissure** n тре́щина.

**fist** n кула́к.

**fit**¹ n: **be a good ~** хорошо́ сиде́ть impf; adj (suitable) подходя́щий, го́дный; (healthy) здоро́вый; *vt* (*be suitable*) годи́ться *impf* +*dat*, на+*acc*, для+*gen*; *vt & i* (*be the right size (for)*) подходи́ть *impf*, подойти́ *pf* (+*dat*); (*adjust*) прила́живать *impf*, прила́дить *pf* (**to** к+*dat*); (*be small enough for*) входи́ть *impf*, войти́ *pf* в+*acc*; ~ **out** снабжа́ть *impf*, снабди́ть *pf*.

**fit**² *n* (*attack*) припа́док; (*fig*) поры́в. **fitful** *adj* поры́вистый.

**fitter** *n* монтёр. **fitting** *n* (*of clothes*) приме́рка; *pl* армату́ра; *adj* подходя́щий.

**five** *adj* & *n* пять; (*number 5*) пятёрка; **~-year plan** пятиле́тка.

**fix** *n* (*dilemma*) переде́лка; (*drugs*) уко́л; *vt* (*repair*) чини́ть *impf*, по~ *pf*; (*settle*) назнача́ть *impf*, назна́чить *pf*; (*fasten*) укрепля́ть *impf*, укрепи́ть *pf*; ~ **up** (*organize*) организова́ть *impf & pf*; (*install*) устана́вливать *impf*, установи́ть *pf*. **fixation** *n* фикса́ция. **fixed** *adj* устано́вленный. **fixture** *n* (*sport*) предстоя́щее спорти́вное мероприя́тие; (*fitting*) приспособле́ние.

**fizz, fizzle** *n* шипе́ть *impf*; **fizzle out** выдыха́ться *impf*, вы́дохнуться *pf*. **fizzy** *adj* шипу́чий.

**flabbergasted** *adj* ошеломлённый.

**flabby** *adj* дря́блый.

**flag**¹ *n* флаг, зна́мя *neut*; *vt*: ~ **down** остана́вливать *impf*, останови́ть *pf*.

**flag**² *vi* (*weaken*) ослабева́ть *impf*, ослабе́ть *pf*.

**flagon** *n* кувши́н.

**flagrant** *adj* вопию́щий.

**flagship** *n* фла́гман.

**flagstone** *n* плита́.

**flair** *n* чутьё.

**flake** *n* слой; *pl* хло́пья (-ьев) *pl*; *vi* шелуши́ться *impf*. **flaky** *adj* сло́истый.

**flamboyant** *adj* цвети́стый.

**flame** *n* пла́мя *neut*, ого́нь *m*; *vi* пыла́ть *impf*.

**flange** *n* фла́нец.

**flank** *n* (*of body*) бок; (*mil*) фланг; *vt* быть сбо́ку +*gen*.

**flannel** *n* флане́ль; (*for face*) моча́лка для лица́.

**flap** *n* (*board*) откидна́я доска́; (*pocket, tent* ~) кла́пан; (*panic*) па́ника; *vi* взма́хивать *impf*, взмахну́ть *pf* +*instr*; *vi* развева́ть *impf*.

**flare** *n* вспы́шка; (*signal*) сигна́льная раке́та; *vi* вспы́хивать *impf*, вспы́хнуть *pf*; ~ **up** (*fire*) возгора́ться *impf*, возгоре́ться *pf*; (*fig*) вспыли́ть *pf*.

**flash** *n* вспы́шка; **in a** ~ ми́гом; *vi* сверка́ть *impf*, сверкну́ть *pf*. **flashback** *n* ретроспе́кция. **flashy** *adj* показно́й.

**flask** *n* фля́жка.

**flat**¹ *n* (*dwelling*) кварти́ра.

**flat**² *n* (*mus*) бемо́ль *m*; (*tyre*) спу́щенная ши́на; **on the** ~ на пло́скости; *adj* пло́ский; **~-fish** ка́мбала. **flatly** *adv* наотре́з. **flatten** *vt & i* выра́внивать(ся) *impf*, вы́ровнять(ся) *pf*.

**flatmate** *n* сосе́д, ~ка по кварти́ре.

**flatter** *vt* льстить *impf*, по~ *pf* +*dat*. **flattering** *adj* льсти́вый. **flattery** *n* лесть.

**flaunt** *vi* щеголя́ть *impf*, щегольну́ть *pf* +*instr*.

**flautist** *n* флейти́ст.

**flavour** *n* вкус; (*fig*) при́вкус; *vt* приправля́ть *impf*, припра́вить *pf*.

**flaw** *n* изъя́н.

**flax** *n* лён. **flaxen** *adj* (*colour*) соло́менный.

**flea** *n* блоха́; ~ **market** барахо́лка.

**fleck** *n* кра́пинка.

**flee** *vi* бежа́ть *impf* & *pf* (**from** от+*gen*); *vt* бежа́ть *impf* из+*gen*.

**fleece** *n* руно́; *vt* (*fig*) обдира́ть *impf*, ободра́ть *pf*. **fleecy** *adj* шерсти́стый.

**fleet** *n* флот; (*vehicles*) парк.

**fleeting** *adj* мимолётный.

**flesh** *n* (*as opposed to mind*) плоть; (*meat*) мя́со; **in the** ~ во плоти́. **fleshy** *adj* мяси́стый.

**flex** *n* шнур; *vt* сгиба́ть *impf*, согну́ть *pf*. **flexibility** *n* ги́бкость. **flexible** *adj* ги́бкий.

**flick** *vt* & *i* щёлкать *impf*, щёлкнуть *pf* (+*instr*); ~ **through** пролиста́ть *pf*.

**flicker** *n* мерца́ние; *vi* мерца́ть *impf*.

**flier** *see* **flyer**

**flight¹** *n* (*fleeing*) бе́гство; **put (take) to** ~ обраща́ть(ся) *impf*, обрати́ть(ся) *pf* в бе́гство.

**flight²** *n* (*flying*) полёт; (*trip*) рейс; ~ **of stairs** ле́стничный марш. **flighty** *adj* ве́треный.

**flimsy** *adj* (*fragile*) непро́чный; (*dress*) лёгкий; (*excuse*) сла́бый.

**flinch** *vi* (*recoil*) отпря́дывать *impf*, отпря́нуть *pf*; (*fig*) уклоня́ться *impf*, уклони́ться *pf* от+*gen*.

**fling** *vt* швыря́ть *impf*, швырну́ть *pf*; *vi* (*also* ~ *o.s.*) броса́ться *impf*, бро́ситься *pf*.

**flint** *n* креме́нь *m*.

**flip** *vt* щёлкать *impf*, щёлкнуть *pf* +*instr*.

**flippant** *adj* легкомы́сленный.

**flipper** *n* ласт.

**flirt** *n* коке́тка; *vi* флиртова́ть *impf* (**with** с+*instr*). **flirtation** *n* флирт.

**flit** *vi* порха́ть *impf*, порхну́ть *pf*.

**float** *n* поплаво́к; *vi* пла́вать *indet*, плыть *det*; *vt* (*company*) пуска́ть *impf*, пусти́ть *pf* в ход.

**flock** *n* (*animals*) ста́до; (*birds*) ста́я; *vi* стека́ться *impf*, сте́чься *pf*.

**flog** *vt* сечь *impf*, вы́~ *pf*.

**flood** *n* наводне́ние; (*bibl*) пото́п; (*fig*) пото́к; *vi* (*river etc.*) выступа́ть *impf*, вы́ступить *pf* из берего́в; *vt* затопля́ть *impf*, затопи́ть *pf*. **floodgate** *n* шлюз. **floodlight** *n* проже́ктор.

**floor** *n* пол; (*storey*) эта́ж; ~**board** полови́ца; *vt* (*confound*) ста́вить *impf*, по~ *pf* в тупи́к.

**flop** *vi* (*fall*) плю́хаться *impf*, плю́хнуться *pf*; (*fail*) прова́ливаться *impf*, провали́ться *pf*.

**flora** *n* фло́ра. **floral** *adj* цвето́чный.

**florid** *adj* цвети́стый; (*ruddy*) румя́ный. **florist** *n* торго́вец цвета́ми.

**flounce¹** *vi* броса́ться *impf*, бро́ситься *pf*.

**flounce²** *n* (*of skirt*) обо́рка.

**flounder¹** *n* (*fish*) ка́мбала.

**flounder²** *vi* бара́хтаться *impf*.

**flour** *n* мука́.

**flourish** *n* (*movement*) разма́хивание (+*instr*); (*of pen*) ро́счерк; *vi* (*thrive*) процвета́ть *impf*, vt (*wave*) разма́хивать *impf*, размахну́ть *pf* +*instr*.

**flout** vt попира́ть *impf*, попра́ть *pf*.

**flow** vi течь *impf*; ли́ться *impf*; n тече́ние.

**flower** n цвето́к; ~-**bed** клу́мба; ~-**pot** цвето́чный горшо́к; vi цвести́ *impf*. **flowery** adj цвети́стый.

**flu** n грипп.

**fluctuate** vi колеба́ться *impf*, по~ *pf*. **fluctuation** n колеба́ние.

**flue** n дымохо́д.

**fluent** adj бе́глый. **fluently** adv свобо́дно.

**fluff** n пух. **fluffy** adj пуши́стый.

**fluid** n жи́дкость; adj жи́дкий.

**fluke** n случа́йная уда́ча.

**fluorescent** adj флюоресце́нтный.

**fluoride** n фтори́д.

**flurry** n (*squall*) шквал; (*fig*) волна́.

**flush** n (*redness*) румя́нец; vi (*redden*) красне́ть *impf*, по~ *pf*; vt спуска́ть *impf*, спусти́ть *pf* во́ду в+*acc*.

**flustered** adj сконфу́женный.

**flute** n фле́йта.

**flutter** vi (*flit*) порха́ть *impf*, порхну́ть *pf*; (*wave*) развева́ться *impf*.

**flux** n: **in a state of** ~ в состоя́нии измене́ния.

**fly**[1] n (*insect*) му́ха.

**fly**[2] vi лета́ть *indet*, лете́ть *det*, по~ *pf*; (*flag*) развева́ться *impf*; (*hasten*) нести́сь *impf*, по~ *pf*; vt (*aircraft*) управля́ть *impf* +*instr*; (*transport*) перевози́ть *impf*, перевезти́ *pf* (*самолётом*); (*flag*) поднима́ть *impf*, подня́ть *pf*. **flyer**, **flier** n лётчик. **flying** n полёт.

**foal** n (*horse*) жеребёнок.

**foam** n пе́на; ~ **plastic** пенопла́ст; ~ **rubber** пенорези́на; vi пе́ниться *impf*, вс~ *pf*. **foamy** adj пе́нистый.

**focal** adj фо́кусный. **focus** n фо́кус; (*fig*) центр; vt фокуси́ровать *impf*, с~ *pf*; (*concentrate*) сосредото́чивать *impf*, сосредото́чить *pf*.

**fodder** n корм.

**foe** n враг.

**foetus** n заро́дыш.

**fog** n тума́н. **foggy** adj тума́нный.

**foible** n сла́бость.

**foil**[1] n (*metal*) фольга́; (*contrast*) контра́ст.

**foil**[2] vt (*thwart*) расстра́ивать *impf*, расстро́ить *pf*.

**foil**[3] n (*sword*) рапи́ра.

**foist** vt навя́зывать *impf*, навяза́ть *pf* (**on** +*dat*).

**fold**[1] n (*sheep-*) овча́рня.

**fold**[2] n скла́дка, сгиб; vt скла́дывать *impf*, сложи́ть *pf*. **folder** n па́пка. **folding** adj складно́й.

**foliage** n листва́.

**folk** n наро́д, лю́ди pl; pl (*relatives*) родня́ collect; attrib наро́дный. **folklore** n фолькло́р.

**follow** vt сле́довать *impf*, по~ *pf* +*dat*, за+*instr*; (*walk behind*) идти́ *det* за+*instr*; (*fig*) следи́ть *impf* за+*instr*. **follower** n после́дователь m. **following** adj сле́дующий.

**folly** n глу́пость.

**fond** adj не́жный; **be** ~ **of** люби́ть *impf* +*acc*.

**fondle** vt ласка́ть *impf*.

**fondness** n любо́вь.

**font** n (*eccl*) купе́ль.

**food** n пи́ща, еда́. **foodstuff** n пищево́й проду́кт.

**fool** n дура́к, ду́ра; vt дура́чить

*impf*, о~ *pf*; *vi*: ~ about дурачиться *impf*. **foolhardy** *adj* безрассудно храбрый. **foolish** *adj* глупый. **foolishness** *n* глупость. **foolproof** *adj* абсолютно надёжный.

**foot** *n* нога; *(measure)* фут; *(of hill etc.)* подножие; **on ~** пешком; **put one's ~ in it** сесть *pf* в лужу. **football** *n* футбол; *attrib* футбольный. **footballer** *n* футболист. **foothills** *n pl* предгорье. **footing** *n (fig)* базис; **lose one's ~** оступиться *pf*; **on an equal ~** на равной ноге. **footlights** *n pl* рампа. **footman** *n* лакей. **footnote** *n* сноска. **footpath** *n (pavement)* тротуар; *(in country)* тропинка. **footprint** *n* след. **footstep** *n (sound)* шаг; *(footprint)* след. **footwear** *n* обувь.

**for** *prep (of time)* в течение +*gen*, на+*acc*; *(of purpose)* для+*gen*, за+*acc*, +*instr*; *(price)* за+*acc*; *(on account of)* из-за +*gen*; *(in place of)* вместо+*gen*; **~ the sake of** ради+*gen*; **as ~** что касается+*gen*; *conj* так как.

**forage** *n* фураж; *vi*: **~ for** разыскивать *impf*.

**foray** *n* набег.

**forbearance** *n* воздержанность.

**forbid** *vt* запрещать *impf*, запретить *pf* (+*dat* person) & *acc* (thing). **forbidding** *adj* грозный.

**force** *n (strength, validity)* сила; *(meaning)* смысл; *pl (armed ~)* вооружённые силы *f pl*; **by ~** силой; *vt (compel)* заставлять *impf*, заставить *pf*; *(lock etc.)* взламывать *impf*, взломать *pf*. **forceful** *adj* сильный; *(speech)* убеди-

тельный. **forcible** *adj* насильственный.

**forceps** *n* щипцы (-цов) *pl*.

**ford** *n* брод; *vt* переходить *impf*, перейти *pf* вброд+*acc*.

**fore** *n*: **come to the ~** выдвигаться *impf*, выдвинуться *pf* на передний план.

**forearm** *n* предплечье. **foreboding** *n* предчувствие. **forecast** *n* предсказание; *(of weather)* прогноз; *vt* предсказывать *impf*, предсказать *pf*. **forecourt** *n* передний двор. **forefather** *n* предок. **forefinger** *n* указательный палец. **forefront** *n (foreground)* передний план; *(leading position)* авангард. **foregone** *adj*: **~ conclusion** предрешённый исход. **foreground** *n* передний план. **forehead** *n* лоб.

**foreign** *adj (from abroad)* иностранный; *(alien)* чуждый; *(external)* внешний; **~ body** инородное тело; **~ currency** валюта. **foreigner** *n* иностранец, -нка.

**foreman** *n* мастер.

**foremost** *adj* выдающийся; **first and ~** прежде всего.

**forename** *n* имя.

**forensic** *adj* судебный.

**forerunner** *n* предвестник. **foresee** *vt* предвидеть *impf*. **foreshadow** *vt* предвещать *impf*. **foresight** *n* предвидение; *(caution)* предусмотрительность.

**forest** *n* лес. **forestall** *vt* предупреждать *impf*, предупредить *pf*. **forester** *n* лесничий *sb*. **forestry** *n* лесоводство.

**foretaste** *n* предвкушение; *vt* предвкушать *impf*

предвкуси́ть *pf*. **foretell** *vt* предска́зывать *impf*, предсказа́ть *pf*. **forethought** *n* предусмотри́тельность. **forewarn** *vt* предостерега́ть *impf*, предостере́чь *pf*. **foreword** *n* предисло́вие.

**forfeit** *n* (*in game*) фант; *vt* лиша́ться *impf*, лиши́ться *pf* +*gen*.

**forge**[1] *n* (*smithy*) ку́зница; (*furnace*) горн; *vt* кова́ть *impf*, вы́~ *pf*; (*fabricate*) подде́лывать *impf*, подде́лать *pf*.

**forge**[2] *vi*: ~ **ahead** продвига́ться *impf*, продви́нуться *pf* вперёд.

**forger** *n* фальшивомоне́тчик. **forgery** *n* подде́лка.

**forget** *vt* забыва́ть *impf*, забы́ть *pf*. **forgetful** *adj* забы́вчивый.

**forgive** *vt* проща́ть *impf*, прости́ть *pf*. **forgiveness** *n* проще́ние.

**forgo** *vt* возде́рживаться *impf*, воздержа́ться *pf* от+*gen*.

**fork** *n* (*eating*) ви́лка; (*digging*) ви́лы (-л) *pl*; (*in road*) разветвле́ние; *vi* (*road*) разветвля́ться *impf*, разветви́ться *pf*.

**forlorn** *adj* жа́лкий.

**form** *n* (*shape*; *kind*) фо́рма; (*class*) класс; (*document*) анке́та; *vt* (*make*, *create*) образо́вывать *impf*, образова́ть *pf*; (*develop*; *make up*) составля́ть *impf*, соста́вить *pf*; *vi* образо́вываться *impf*, образова́ться *pf*. **formal** *adj* форма́льный; (*official*) официа́льный. **formality** *n* форма́льность. **format** *n* форма́т. **formation** *n* образова́ние. **formative** *adj*: ~ **years** молоды́е го́ды (-до́в) *m pl*.

**former** *adj* (*earlier*) пре́жний; (*ex*) бы́вший; **the** ~ (*of two*) пе́рвый. **formerly** *adv* пре́жде.

**formidable** *adj* (*dread*) гро́зный; (*arduous*) тру́дный.

**formless** *adj* бесфо́рменный.

**formula** *n* фо́рмула. **formulate** *vt* формули́ровать *impf*, с~ *pf*. **formulation** *n* формулиро́вка.

**forsake** *vt* (*desert*) покида́ть *impf*, поки́нуть *pf*; (*renounce*) отка́зываться *impf*, отказа́ться *pf* от+*gen*.

**fort** *n* форт.

**forth** *adv* вперёд, да́льше; **back and** ~ взад и вперёд; **and so** ~ и так да́лее. **forthcoming** *adj* предстоя́щий; **be** ~ (*available*) поступа́ть *impf*, поступи́ть *pf*. **forthwith** *adv* неме́дленно.

**fortieth** *adj* & *n* сороково́й.

**fortification** *n* укрепле́ние. **fortify** *vt* укрепля́ть *impf*, укрепи́ть *pf*; (*fig*) подкрепля́ть *impf*, подкрепи́ть *pf*. **fortitude** *n* сто́йкость.

**fortnight** *n* две неде́ли *f pl*. **fortnightly** *adj* двухнеде́льный; *adv* раз в две неде́ли.

**fortress** *n* кре́пость.

**fortuitous** *adj* случа́йный.

**fortunate** *adj* счастли́вый. **fortunately** *adv* к сча́стью. **fortune** *n* (*destiny*) судьба́; (*good* ~) сча́стье; (*wealth*) состоя́ние.

**forty** *adj* & *n* со́рок; *pl* (*decade*) сороковы́е го́ды (-до́в) *m pl*.

**forward** *adj* пере́дний; (*presumptuous*) развя́зный; *n* (*sport*) напада́ющий *sb*; *adv* вперёд; *vt* (*letter*) пересыла́ть *impf*, пересла́ть *pf*.

**fossil** *n* ископа́емое *sb*; *adj*

ископа́емый. **fossilized** *adj* ископа́емый.

**foster** *vt* (*child*) приюти́ть *pf*; (*idea*) вына́шивать *impf*, вы́носить *pf*; (*create*) создава́ть *impf*, созда́ть *pf*; (*cherish*) леле́ять *impf*; ~**child** приёмыш.

**foul** *adj* (*dirty*) гря́зный; (*repulsive*) отврати́тельный; (*obscene*) непристо́йный; *n* (*sport*) наруше́ние пра́вил; *vt* (*dirty*) па́чкать *impf*, за~, ис~ *pf*; (*entangle*) запу́тывать *impf*, запу́тать *pf*.

**found** *vt* осно́вывать *impf*, основа́ть *pf*.

**foundation** *n* (*of building*) фунда́мент; (*basis*) осно́ва; (*institution*) учрежде́ние; (*fund*) фонд. **founder**¹ *n* основа́тель *m*.

**founder**² *vi* (*naut*, *fig*) тону́ть *impf*, по~ *pf*.

**foundry** *n* лите́йная *sb*.

**fountain** *n* фонта́н; ~**pen** авторру́чка.

**four** *adj* & *n* четы́ре; (*number 4*) четвёрка; **on all** ~**s** на четвере́ньках. **fourteen** *adj* & *n* четы́рнадцать. **fourteenth** *adj* & *n* четы́рнадцатый. **fourth** *adj* & *n* четвёртый; (*quarter*) че́тверть.

**fowl** *n* (*domestic*) дома́шняя пти́ца; (*wild*) дичь *collect*.

**fox** *n* лиса́, лиси́ца; *vt* озада́чивать *impf*, озада́чить *pf*.

**foyer** *n* фойе́ *neut indecl*.

**fraction** *n* (*math*) дробь; (*portion*) части́ца.

**fractious** *adj* раздражи́тельный.

**fracture** *n* перело́м; *vt* & *i* лома́ть(ся) *impf*, с~ *pf*.

**fragile** *adj* ло́мкий.

**fragment** *n* обло́мок; (*of conversation*) отры́вок; (*of writ-ing*) фрагме́нт. **fragmentary** *adj* отры́вочный.

**fragrance** *n* арома́т. **fragrant** *adj* арома́тный, души́стый.

**frail** *adj* хру́пкий.

**frame** *n* о́стов; (*build*) телосложе́ние; (*picture*) ра́ма; (*cin*) кадр; ~ **of mind** настрое́ние; *vt* (*devise*) создава́ть *impf*, созда́ть *pf*; (*formulate*) формули́ровать *impf*, с~ *pf*; (*picture*) вставля́ть *impf*, вста́вить в ра́му *pf*; (*incriminate*) фабрикова́ть *impf*, с~ *pf* обвине́ние про́тив+*gen*.

**framework** *n* о́стов; (*fig*) ра́мки *f pl*.

**franc** *n* франк.

**France** *n* Фра́нция.

**franchise** *n* (*comm*) привиле́гия; (*polit*) пра́во го́лоса.

**frank**¹ *adj* открове́нный.

**frank**² *vt* (*letter*) франки́ровать *impf*, за~ *pf*.

**frantic** *adj* неи́стовый.

**fraternal** *adj* бра́тский. **fraternity** *n* бра́тство.

**fraud** *n* обма́н; (*person*) обма́нщик. **fraudulent** *adj* обма́нный.

**fraught** *adj*: ~ **with** чрева́тый +*instr*.

**fray**¹ *vt* & *i* обтрёпывать(ся) *impf*, обтрепа́ть(ся) *pf*.

**fray**² *n* бой.

**freak** *n* уро́д; *attrib* необы́чный.

**freckle** *n* весну́шка. **freckled** *adj* весну́шчатый.

**free** *adj* свобо́дный; (*gratis*) беспла́тный; ~ **kick** штрафно́й уда́р; ~ **speech** свобо́да сло́ва; *vt* освобожда́ть *impf*, освободи́ть *pf*. **freedom** *n* свобо́да. **freehold** *n* неограни́ченное пра́во со́бственности на недви́жимость.

**freelance** adj внешта́тный.
**Freemason** n франкмасо́н.
**freeze** vi замерза́ть impf, мёрзнуть impf, замёрзнуть pf; vt замора́живать impf, заморо́зить pf. **freezer** n морози́льник; (compartment) морози́лка. **freezing** adj моро́зный; **below ~** ни́же нуля́.
**freight** n фрахт. **freighter** n (ship) грузово́е су́дно.
**French** adj францу́зский; **~ bean** фасо́ль; **~ horn** валто́рна; **~ windows** двуство́рчатое окно́ до по́ла. **Frenchman** n францу́з. **Frenchwoman** n францу́женка.
**frenetic** adj неи́стовый.
**frenzied** adj неи́стовый. **frenzy** n неи́стовство.
**frequency** n частота́. **frequent** adj ча́стый; vt ча́сто посеща́ть impf.
**fresco** n фре́ска.
**fresh** adj све́жий; (new) но́вый; **~ water** пре́сная вода́. **freshen** vt освежа́ть impf, освежи́ть pf; vi свеже́ть impf, по~ pf. **freshly** adv свежо́; (recently) неда́вно. **freshness** n све́жесть. **freshwater** adj пресново́дный.
**fret**[1] vi му́читься impf. **fretful** adj раздражи́тельный.
**fret**[2] n (mus) лад.
**fretsaw** n лобзи́к.
**friar** n мона́х.
**friction** n тре́ние; (fig) тре́ния neut pl.
**Friday** n пя́тница.
**fridge** n холоди́льник.
**fried** adj: **~ egg** яи́чница.
**friend** n друг, подру́га; прия́тель m, ~ница. **friendly** adj дру́жеский, ~ный. **friendship** n дру́жба.
**frieze** n фриз.

**frigate** n фрега́т.
**fright** n испу́г. **frighten** vt пуга́ть impf, ис~, на~ pf.
**frightful** adj стра́шный.
**frigid** adj холо́дный.
**frill** n обо́рка.
**fringe** n бахрома́; (of hair) чёлка; (edge) край.
**frisk** vi (frolic) резви́ться impf; vt (search) шмона́ть impf. **frisky** adj резвый.
**fritter** vt: **~ away** растра́чивать impf, растра́тить pf.
**frivolity** n легкомы́сленность. **frivolous** adj легкомы́сленный.
**fro** adv: **to and ~** взад и вперёд.
**frock** n пла́тье.
**frog** n лягу́шка.
**frolic** vi резви́ться impf.
**from** prep **off+gen**; (**~ off**, **down ~**; in time) **c+gen**; (out of) **из+gen**; (according to) **по+dat**; (because of) **из-за+gen**; **~ above** све́рху; **~ abroad** из-за грани́цы; **~ afar** и́здали; **~ among** из числа́+gen; **~ behind** из-за+gen; **~ day to day** изо дня в день; **~ everywhere** отовсю́ду; **~ here** отсю́да; **~ memory** по па́мяти; **~ now on** отны́не; **~ there** отту́да; **~ time to time** вре́мя от вре́мени; **~ under** из-под+gen.
**front** n фаса́д; пере́дняя сторона́; (mil) фронт; **in ~ of** впереди́+gen, пе́ред+instr; adj пере́дний; (first) пе́рвый.
**frontier** n грани́ца.
**frost** n моро́з; **~-bite** отмороже́ние; **~-bitten** отморо́женный. **frosted** adj: **~ glass** ма́товое стекло́. **frosty** adj моро́зный; (fig) ледяно́й.
**froth** n пе́на; vi пе́ниться impf,

вс~ pf. **frothy** adj пе́нистый.

**frown** n хму́рый взгляд; vi хму́риться impf, на~ pf.

**frugal** adj (careful) бережли́вый; (scanty) ску́дный.

**fruit** n плод; collect фру́кты m pl; adj фрукто́вый. **fruitful** adj плодотво́рный. **fruition** n: come to ~ осуществи́ться pf. **fruitless** adj бесплодный.

**frustrate** vt фрустри́ровать impf & pf. **frustrating** adj фрустри́рующий. **frustration** n фрустра́ция.

**fry**[1] n: small ~ мелюзга́.

**fry**[2] vt & i жа́рить(ся) impf, за~, из~ pf. **frying-pan** n сковорода́.

**fuel** n то́пливо.

**fugitive** n бегле́ц.

**fulcrum** n то́чка опо́ры.

**fulfil** vt (perform) выполня́ть impf, вы́полнить pf; (dreams) осуществля́ть impf, осуществи́ть pf. **fulfilling** adj удовлетворя́ющий. **fulfilment** n выполне́ние; осуществле́ние; удовлетворе́ние.

**full** adj по́лный (of +gen, instr); (replete) сы́тый; ~ stop то́чка; ~ time: I work ~ time я рабо́таю на по́лной ста́вку; n: in ~ по́лностью; to the ~ в по́лной ме́ре. **fullness** n полнота́. **fully** adv вполне́.

**fulsome** adj чрезме́рный.

**fumble** vi: ~ for нащу́пывать impf +acc; ~ with вози́ться impf c+instr.

**fume** vi (with anger) кипе́ть impf, вс~ pf гне́вом. **fumes** n pl пары́ neut pl. **fumigate** vt оку́ривать impf, окури́ть pf.

**fun** n заба́ва; it was ~ бы́ло

забáвно; have ~ забавля́ться impf, по~ pf над+instr.

**function** n фу́нкция; (event) ве́чер; vi функциони́ровать impf; де́йствовать impf. **functional** adj функциона́льный. **functionary** n чино́вник.

**fund** n фонд; (store) запа́с.

**fundamental** adj основно́й; n: pl осно́вы f pl.

**funeral** n по́хороны (-о́н, -она́м) pl.

**fungus** n гриб.

**funnel** n воро́нка; (chimney) дымова́я труба́.

**funny** adj смешно́й; (odd) стра́нный.

**fur** n мех; ~ coat шу́ба.

**furious** adj бе́шеный.

**furnace** n горн, печь.

**furnish** vt (provide) снабжа́ть impf, снабди́ть pf (with c+instr; (house) обставля́ть impf, обста́вить pf. **furniture** n ме́бель.

**furrow** n борозда́.

**furry** adj пуши́стый.

**further, farther** comp adj дальне́йший; adv да́льше; vt продвига́ть impf, продви́нуть pf. **furthermore** adv к тому́ же. **furthest, farthest** superl adj са́мый да́льний.

**furtive** adj скры́тый, та́йный.

**fury** n я́рость.

**fuse**[1] vt & i (of metal) сплавля́ть(ся) impf, спла́вить(ся) pf.

**fuse**[2] n (in bomb) запа́л; (detonating device) взрыва́тель m.

**fuse**[3] n (electr) про́бка; vi перегора́ть impf, перегоре́ть pf.

**fuselage** n фюзеля́ж.

**fusion** n пла́вка, слия́ние.

**fuss** n суета́; vi суети́ться

**futile** *impf.* **fussy** *adj* суетли́вый; *(fastidious)* разбо́рчивый.
**futile** *adj* тще́тный. **futility** *n* тще́тность.
**future** *n* бу́дущее *sb*; *(gram)* бу́дущее вре́мя *neut*; *adj* бу́дущий. **futuristic** *adj* футуристи́ческий.
**fuzzy** *adj (hair)* пуши́стый; *(blurred)* распльі́вчатый.

# G

**gabble** *vi* тарато́рить *impf.*
**gable** *n* щипе́ц.
**gad** *vi*: ~ **about** шата́ться *impf.*
**gadget** *n* приспособле́ние.
**gaffe** *n* опло́шность.
**gag** *n* кляп; *vt* засо́вывать *impf,* засу́нуть *pf* кляп в рот+*dat.*
**gaiety** *n* весёлость. **gaily** *adv* ве́село.
**gain** *n* при́быль; *pl* дохо́ды *m pl; (increase)* приро́ст; *vt (acquire)* получа́ть *impf,* получи́ть *pf;* ~ **on** нагоня́ть *impf,* нагна́ть *pf.*
**gait** *n* похо́дка.
**gala** *n* пра́зднество; *adj* пра́здничный.
**galaxy** *n* гала́ктика; *(fig)* плея́да.
**gale** *n* бу́ря, шторм.
**gall**[1] *n (bile)* жёлчь; *(cheek)* на́глость; ~**bladder** жёлчный пузы́рь *m.*
**gall**[2] *vt (vex)* раздража́ть *impf,* раздражи́ть *pf.*
**gallant** *adj (brave)* хра́брый; *(courtly)* гала́нтный. **gallantry** *n* хра́брость; гала́нтность.
**gallery** *n* галере́я.
**galley** *n (ship)* гале́ра; *(kitchen)* ка́мбуз.

**gallon** *n* галло́н.
**gallop** *n* гало́п; *vi* галопи́ровать *impf.*
**gallows** *n pl* ви́селица.
**gallstone** *n* жёлчный ка́мень *m.*
**galore** *adv* в изоби́лии.
**galvanize** *vt* гальванизи́ровать *impf & pf.*
**gambit** *n* гамби́т.
**gamble** *n (undertaking)* риско́ванное предприя́тие; *vi* игра́ть *impf* в аза́ртные и́гры; *(fig)* рискова́ть *impf* (with +*instr);* ~ **away** прои́грывать *impf,* проигра́ть *pf.* **gambler** *n* игро́к. **gambling** *n* аза́ртные и́гры *f pl.*
**game** *n* игра́; *(single* ~*)* па́ртия; *(collect, animals)* дичь; *adj (ready)* гото́вый. **gamekeeper** *n* лесни́к.
**gammon** *n* око́рок.
**gamut** *n* га́мма.
**gang** *n* ба́нда; *(workmen)* брига́да.
**gangrene** *n* гангре́на.
**gangster** *n* га́нгстер.
**gangway** *n (passage)* прохо́д; *(naut)* схо́дни *(-ней) pl.*
**gaol** *n* тюрьма́; *vt* заключа́ть *impf,* заключи́ть *pf* в тюрьму́. **gaoler** *n* тюре́мщик.
**gap** *n (empty space; deficiency)* пробе́л; *(in wall etc.)* брешь; *(fig)* разры́в.
**gape** *vi (person)* зева́ть *impf (at* на+*acc); (chasm)* зия́ть *impf.*
**garage** *n* гара́ж.
**garb** *n* одея́ние.
**garbage** *n* му́сор.
**garbled** *adj* искажённый.
**garden** *n* сад; *attrib* садо́вый. **gardener** *n* садо́вник. **gardening** *n* садово́дство.
**gargle** *vi* полоска́ть *impf,*

про~ *pf* го́рло.

**gargoyle** *n* горгу́лья.

**garish** *adj* крича́щий.

**garland** *n* гирля́нда.

**garlic** *n* чесно́к.

**garment** *n* предме́т оде́жды.

**garnish** *n* гарни́р; *vt* гарни́-
ровать *impf* & *pf*.

**garret** *n* манса́рда.

**garrison** *n* гарнизо́н.

**garrulous** *adj* болтли́вый.

**gas** *n* газ; *attrib* га́зовый; *vt*
отравля́ть *impf*, отрави́ть *pf*
га́зом. **gaseous** *adj* газо-
обра́зный.

**gash** *n* поре́з; *vt* поре́зать *pf*.

**gasket** *n* прокла́дка.

**gasp** *vi* задыха́ться *impf*, за-
дохну́ться *pf*.

**gastric** *adj* желу́дочный.

**gate** *n* (*large*) воро́та (-т) *pl*;
(*small*) кали́тка. **gateway** *n*
(*gate*) воро́та (-т) *pl*; (*entrance*) вход.

**gather** *vt* & *i* собира́ть(ся)
*impf*, собра́ть(ся) *pf*; *vt* за-
ключа́ть *impf*, заключи́ть
*pf*. **gathering** *n* (*assembly*)
собра́ние.

**gaudy** *adj* крича́щий.

**gauge** *n* (*measure*) ме́ра; (*instrument*) кали́бр, измери́-
тельный прибо́р; (*rly*) ко-
лея́; (*criterion*) крите́рий; *vt*
измеря́ть *impf*, изме́рить *pf*;
(*estimate*) оце́нивать *impf*,
оцени́ть *pf*.

**gaunt** *adj* то́щий.

**gauntlet** *n* рукави́ца.

**gauze** *n* ма́рля.

**gay** *adj* весёлый; (*bright*)
пёстрый; (*homosexual*) гомо-
сексуа́льный.

**gaze** *n* при́стальный взгляд;
*vt* при́стально гляде́ть *impf*
(*at* на+*acc*).

**gazelle** *n* газе́ль.

**GCSE** *abbr* (*of General Certificate of Secondary Education*)
аттеста́т о сре́днем образо-
ва́нии.

**gear** *n* (*equipment*) принад-
ле́жности *f pl*; (*in car*) ско́-
рость; ~ **lever** рыча́г; *vt*
приспособля́ть *impf*, при-
спосо́бить *pf* (**to** к+*dat*).
**gearbox** *n* коро́бка переда́ч.

**gel** *n* косме́ти́ческое желе́
*neut indecl*. **gelatine** *n*
желати́н.

**gelding** *n* ме́рин.

**gelignite** *n* гелигни́т.

**gem** *n* драгоце́нный ка́мень *m*.

**Gemini** *n* Близнецы́ *m pl*.

**gender** *n* род.

**gene** *n* ген.

**genealogy** *n* генеало́гия.

**general** *n* генера́л; *adj* о́б-
щий; (*nationwide*) всео́бщий;
**in** ~ вообще́. **generalization**
*n* обобще́ние. **generalize** *vi*
обобща́ть *impf*, обобщи́ть
*pf*. **generally** *adv* (*usually*)
обы́чно; (*in general*) вообще́.

**generate** *vt* порожда́ть *impf*,
породи́ть *pf*. **generation** *n*
(*in descent*) поколе́ние. **generator** *n* генера́тор.

**generic** *adj* родово́й; (*general*)
о́бщий.

**generosity** *n* (*magnanimity*)
великоду́шие; (*munificence*)
ще́дрость. **generous** *adj*
великоду́шный; ще́дрый.

**genesis** *n* происхожде́ние;
(G~) Кни́га Бытия́.

**genetic** *adj* генети́ческий.
**genetics** *n* гене́тика.

**genial** *adj* (*of person*) добро-
ду́шный.

**genital** *adj* полово́й. **genitals**
*n pl* полов́ые о́рганы *m pl*.

**genitive** *adj* (*n*) роди́тельный
(паде́ж).

**genius** n (*person*) ге́ний; (*ability*) гениа́льность.

**genocide** n геноци́д.

**genre** n жанр.

**genteel** adj благовоспи́тан-ный.

**gentile** adj невере́йский; n невере́й, ~ка.

**gentility** n благовоспи́тан-ность.

**gentle** adj (*mild*) мя́гкий; (*quiet*) ти́хий; (*light*) лёгкий.

**gentleman** n джентльме́н.

**gentleness** n мя́гкость. **gents** n pl мужска́я убо́рная sb.

**genuine** adj (*authentic*) по́длинный; (*sincere*) и́скренний.

**genus** n род.

**geographical** adj географи́-ческий. **geography** n геогра́фия. **geological** adj геоло́гический. **geologist** n гео́лог. **geology** n геоло́гия. **geometric(al)** adj геометри́-ческий. **geometry** n гео-ме́трия.

**Georgia** n Гру́зия. **Georgian** n грузи́н, ~ка; adj грузи́нский.

**geranium** n гера́нь.

**geriatric** adj гериатри́ческий.

**germ** m микро́б.

**German** n не́мец, не́мка; adj неме́цкий; ~ **measles** красну́ха.

**germane** adj уме́стный.

**Germanic** adj герма́нский.

**Germany** n Герма́ния.

**germinate** vi прораста́ть impf, прорасти́ pf.

**gesticulate** vi жестикули́-ровать impf. **gesture** n жест.

**get** vt (*obtain*) достава́ть impf, доста́ть pf; (*receive*) получа́ть impf, получи́ть pf; (*understand*) понима́ть impf, поня́ть pf; (*disease*) заража́ться impf, зарази́ться pf +instr;

(*induce*) угова́ривать impf, уговори́ть pf (**to do** +inf); (*fetch*) приноси́ть impf, при-нести́ pf; vi (*become*) стано-ви́ться impf, стать pf +instr; **have got** (*have*) име́ть impf; **have got to** быть до́лжен (-жна́) +inf; ~ **about** (*spread*) распространя́ться impf, рас-простра́ниться pf; (*move around*) передвига́ться impf, передви́нуться pf; (*travel*) разъезжа́ть impf; ~ **at** (*mean*) хоте́ть impf ска-за́ть; ~ **away** (*slip off*) уско-льза́ть impf, ускользну́ть pf; (*escape*) убега́ть impf, убе-жа́ть pf; (*leave*) уезжа́ть impf, уе́хать pf; ~ **away with** избега́ть impf, избежа́ть pf отве́тственности за+acc; ~ **back** (*recover*) получа́ть impf, получи́ть pf обра́тно; (*return*) возвраща́ться impf, верну́ться pf; ~ **by** (*manage*) справля́ться impf, спра́вить-ся pf; ~ **down** сходи́ть impf, сойти́ pf; ~ **down to** принима́ться impf, приня́ться pf за+acc; ~ **off** слеза́ть impf, слезть pf с+gen; ~ **on** сади́ться impf, сесть pf в, на, +acc; (*prosper*) преуспева́ть impf, преуспе́ть pf; ~ **on with** (*person*) ужива́ться impf, ужи́ться pf с+instr; ~ **out of** (*avoid*) избавля́ться impf, изба́виться pf от+gen; (*car*) выходи́ть impf, вы́йти pf из+gen; ~ **round to** успе-ва́ть impf, успе́ть pf to (*reach*) достига́ть impf, до-сти́гнуть & дости́чь pf+gen; ~ **up** (*from bed*) встава́ть impf, встать pf.

**geyser** n (*spring*) ге́йзер; (*water-heater*) коло́нка.

**ghastly** adj уга́сный.

**gherkin** *n* огуре́ц.

**ghetto** *n* ге́тто *neut indecl.*

**ghost** *n* привиде́ние. **ghostly** *adj* призра́чный.

**giant** *n* гига́нт; *adj* гига́нтский.

**gibberish** *n* тараба́рщина.

**gibbet** *n* ви́селица.

**gibe** *n* насме́шка; *vi* насме-ха́ться (**at** над+*instr*).

**giblets** *n pl* потроха́ (-хо́в) *pl.*

**giddiness** *n* головокруже́-ние. **giddy** *predic*: **I feel** ~ у меня́ кру́жится голова́.

**gift** *n* (*present*) пода́рок; (*donation*; *ability*) дар. **gifted** *adj* одарённый.

**gig** *n* (*theat*) выступле́ние.

**gigantic** *adj* гига́нтский.

**giggle** *n* хихи́канье; *vi* хихи́-кать *impf*, хихи́кнуть *pf*.

**gild** *vt* золоти́ть *impf*, вы́~, по~ *pf*.

**gill** *n* (*of fish*) жа́бра.

**gilt** *n* позоло́та; *adj* золочё-ный.

**gimmick** *n* трюк.

**gin** *n* (*spirit*) джин.

**ginger** *n* имби́рь *m*; *adj* (*colour*) ры́жий.

**gingerly** *adv* осторо́жно.

**gipsy** *n* цыга́н, ~ка.

**giraffe** *n* жира́ф.

**girder** *n* ба́лка. **girdle** *n* по́яс.

**girl** *n* (*child*) де́вочка; (*young woman*) де́вушка. **girlfriend** *n* подру́га. **girlish** *adj* де́вичий.

**girth** *n* обхва́т; (*on saddle*) подпру́га.

**gist** *n* суть.

**give** *vt* дава́ть *impf*, дать *pf*; ~ **away** выдава́ть *impf*, вы́-дать *pf*; ~ **back** возвраща́ть *impf*, возврати́ть *pf*; ~ **in** (*yield*, *vi*) уступа́ть *impf*, уступи́ть *pf* (**to** +*dat*); (*hand in*, *vt*) вруча́ть *impf*, вручи́ть *pf*; ~ **out** (*emit*) издава́ть

*impf*, изда́ть *pf*; (*distribute*) раздава́ть *impf*, разда́ть *pf*; ~ **up** отка́зываться *impf*, отказа́ться *pf* от+*gen*; (*habit etc.*) броса́ть *impf*, бро́сить *pf*; ~ **o.s. up** сдава́ться *impf*, сда́ться *pf*. **given** *predic* (*inclined*) скло́нен (-онна́, -о́нно) (**to** к+*dat*).

**glacier** *n* ледни́к.

**glad** *adj* ра́достный; *predic* рад. **gladden** *vt* ра́довать *impf*, об~ *pf*.

**glade** *n* поля́на.

**gladly** *adv* охо́тно.

**glamorous** *adj* я́ркий; (*attractive*) привлека́тельный.

**glamour** *n* я́ркость; привлека́тельность.

**glance** *n* (*look*) бе́глый взгляд; *vi*: ~ **at** взгля́дывать *impf*, взгляну́ть *pf* на+*acc*.

**gland** *n* железа́. **glandular** *adj* желе́зистый.

**glare** *n* (*light*) ослепи́тель-ный блеск; (*look*) свире́пый взгляд; *vi* свире́по смотре́ть *impf* (**at** на+*acc*). **glaring** *adj* (*dazzling*) ослепи́тельный; (*mistake*) гру́бый.

**glasnost** *n* гла́сность.

**glass** *n* (*substance*) стекло́; (*drinking vessel*) стака́н; (*wine* ~) рю́мка; (*mirror*) зе́ркало; *pl* (*spectacles*) очки́ (-ко́в) *pl*; *attrib* стекля́нный. **glassy** *adj* (*look*) ту́склый.

**glaze** *n* глазу́рь; *vt* (*with glass*) застекля́ть *impf*, застекли́ть *pf*; (*pottery*) глазурова́ть *impf* & *pf* (*cul*) глази́ровать *impf* & *pf*. **glazier** *n* стеко́ль-щик.

**gleam** *n* про́блеск; *vi* свети́ться *impf*.

**glean** *vt* собира́ть *impf*, со-бра́ть *pf* по крупи́цам.

**glee** n весе́лье. **gleeful** adj лику́ющий.

**glib** adj бо́йкий.

**glide** vi скользи́ть impf; (aeron) плани́ровать impf, с~ pf. **glider** n планёр.

**glimmer** n мерца́ние; vi мерца́ть impf.

**glimpse** vt мелько́м ви́деть impf, у~ pf.

**glint** n блеск; vi блесте́ть impf.

**glisten, glitter** vi блесте́ть impf.

**gloat** vi злора́дствовать impf.

**global** adj (world-wide) мирово́й; (total) всео́бщий. **globe** n (sphere) шар; (the earth) земно́й шар; (chart) гло́бус. **globule** n ша́рик.

**gloom** n мрак. **gloomy** adj мра́чный.

**glorify** vt прославля́ть impf, просла́вить pf. **glorious** adj сла́вный; (splendid) великоле́пный. **glory** n сла́ва; vi торжествова́ть impf.

**gloss** n лоск; vi: ~ **over** зама́зывать impf, зама́зать pf.

**glossary** n глосса́рий.

**glove** n перча́тка.

**glow** n за́рево; (of cheeks) румя́нец; vi (incandesce) накаля́ться impf, накали́ться pf; (shine) сия́ть impf.

**glucose** n глюко́за.

**glue** n клей; vt прикле́ивать impf, прикле́ить pf (**to** к+dat).

**glum** adj угрю́мый.

**glut** n избы́ток.

**glutton** n обжо́ра m & f. **gluttonous** adj обжо́рливый. **gluttony** n обжо́рство.

**gnarled** adj (hands) шишкова́тый; (tree) сучкова́тый.

**gnash** vt скрежета́ть impf +instr.

**gnat** n кома́р.

**gnaw** vt грызть impf.

**gnome** n гном.

**go** n (energy) эне́ргия; (attempt) попы́тка; **be on the ~** быть в движе́нии; **have a ~** пыта́ться impf, по~ pf; vi (on foot) ходи́ть indet, идти́ det, пойти́ pf; (by transport) е́здить indet, е́хать det, по~ pf; (work) рабо́тать impf; (become) станови́ться impf, стать pf +instr; (belong) идти́ impf; **be ~ing (to do)** собира́ться impf, собра́ться pf (+inf); ~ **about** (set to work at) бра́ться impf, взя́ться pf за+acc; (wander) броди́ть indet; ~ **away** (on foot) уходи́ть impf, уйти́ pf; (by transport) уезжа́ть impf, уе́хать pf; ~ **down** спуска́ться impf, спусти́ться pf (+gen); ~ **in(to)** (enter) входи́ть impf, войти́ pf (в+acc); (investigate) рассле́довать impf & pf; ~ **off** (go away) уходи́ть impf, уйти́ pf; (deteriorate) по́ртиться impf, ис~ pf; ~ **on** (continue) продолжа́ть(ся) impf, продо́лжить(ся) pf; ~ **out** выходи́ть impf, вы́йти pf; (flame etc.) га́снуть impf, по~ pf; ~ **over** (inspect) пересма́тривать impf, пересмотре́ть pf; (rehearse) повторя́ть impf, повтори́ть pf; (change allegiance etc.) переходи́ть impf, перейти́ pf (**to** в, на, к+dat); ~ **through** (scrutinize) разбира́ть impf, разобра́ть pf; ~ **through with** проводи́ть impf, довести́ pf до конца́; ~ **without** обходи́ться impf, обойти́сь pf без+gen; ~ **ahead** предприи́мчивый; ~ **between** посре́дник.

**goad** vt (*instigate*) подстрекáть *impf*, подстрекнýть *pf* (**into** к+*dat*); (*taunt*) раздражáть *impf*.

**goal** n (*aim*) цель; (*sport*) ворóта (-т) *pl*; (*point won*) гол.

**goalkeeper** n вратáрь *m*.

**goat** n козá; (*male*) козёл.

**gobble** vt (*eat*) жрать *impf*; ~ **up** пожирáть *impf*, пожрáть *pf*.

**goblet** n бокáл, кýбок.

**god** n бог; (G~) Бог. **godchild** n крéстник, -ица. **goddaughter** n крéстница. **goddess** n богúня. **godfather** n крёстный *sb*. **God-fearing** adj богобоя́зненный. **godless** adj безбóжный. **godly** adj набóжный. **godmother** n крёстная *sb*. **godparent** n крёстный *sb*. **godsend** n бóжий дар. **godson** n крéстник.

**goggle** vi тарáщить *impf* глазá (**at** на+*acc*); n: *pl* защúтные очкú (-кóв) *pl*.

**going** n *pl* дел á *neut pl*. **goings-on** n *pl* делá *neut pl*.

**gold** n зóлото; adj золотóй; ~-**plated** накладнóго зóлота; ~-**smith** золотых дел мáстер.

**golden** adj золотóй; ~ **eagle** бéркут. **goldfish** n золотáя рыбка.

**golf** n гольф; ~ **club** (*implement*) клюшка; ~ **course** площáдка для гóльфа. **golfer** n игрóк в гольф.

**gondola** n гóндола.

**gong** n гонг.

**gonorrhoea** n триппер.

**good** n добрó; *pl* (*wares*) товáр(ы); **do** ~ (*benefit*) идтú *impf*, пойтú *pf* на пóльзу +*dat*; adj хорóший, дóбрый; ~-**humoured** adj добродýшный. ~-**looking** adj красúвый; ~ **morn-**

**ing** дóброе ýтро!; ~ **night** спокóйной нóчи! **goodbye** int прощáй(те)!; до свидáния! **goodness** n добротá.

**goose** n гусь *m*; ~-**flesh** гусúная кóжа.

**gooseberry** n крыжóвник.

**gore**[1] n (*blood*) запёкшаяся кровь.

**gore**[2] vt (*pierce*) бодáть *impf*, за~ *pf*.

**gorge** n (*geog*) ущéлье; vi & t объедáться *impf*, объéсться *pf* (**on** +*instr*).

**gorgeous** adj великолéпный.

**gorilla** n горúлла.

**gorse** n утéсник.

**gory** adj кровáвый.

**gosh** int бóже мой!

**Gospel** n Евáнгелие.

**gossip** n сплéтня; (*person*) сплéтник, -ица; vi сплéтничать *impf*, на~ *pf*.

**Gothic** готúческий.

**gouge** vt: ~ **out** выдáлбливать *impf*, вы́долбить *pf*; (*eyes*) выкáлывать *impf*, вы́колоть *pf*.

**goulash** n гуля́ш.

**gourmet** n гурмáн.

**gout** n подáгра.

**govern** vt прáвить *impf* +*instr*; (*determine*) определя́ть *impf*, определúть *pf*. **governess** n гувернáнтка. **government** n правúтельство. **governmental** adj правúтельственный. **governor** n губернáтор; (*of school etc.*) член правлéния.

**gown** n плáтье; (*official's*) мáнтия.

**grab** vt хватáть *impf*, схватúть *pf*.

**grace** n (*gracefulness*) грáция; (*refinement*) изя́щество; (*favour*) мúлость; (*at meal*) молúтва); **have the** ~ **to** быть насто́лько такти́чен, что; **with bad ~** нелюбе́зно; **with good ~** с досто́инством; vt (adorn) украша́ть impf, укра́сить pf; (favour) удоста́ивать impf, удосто́ить pf (+gen). **graceful** adj грацио́зный.

**gracious** adj ми́лостивый.

**gradation** n града́ция.

**grade** n (level) сте́пень; (quality) сорт; vt сортирова́ть impf, рас~ pf.

**gradient** n укло́н.

**gradual** adj постепе́нный.

**graduate** n око́нчивший sb университе́т, вуз; vi конча́ть impf, ко́нчить pf (университе́т, вуз); vt градуи́ровать impf & pf.

**graffiti** n на́дписи f pl.

**graft** n (bot) черено́к; (med) переса́дка (живо́й тка́ни); vt (bot) привива́ть impf, приви́ть pf (to +dat); (med) переса́живать impf, пересади́ть pf.

**grain** n (seed; collect) зерно́; (particle) крупи́нка; (of sand) песчи́нка; (of wood) (древе́сное) волокно́; **against the ~** не по нутру́.

**gram(me)** n грамм.

**grammar** n грамма́тика; **~ school** гимна́зия. **grammatical** adj граммати́ческий.

**gramophone** n прои́грыватель m; **~ record** грампласти́нка.

**granary** n амба́р.

**grand** adj великоле́пный; **~ piano** роя́ль m. **grandchild** n внук, вну́чка. **granddaughter** n вну́чка. **grandfather** n де́душка m. **grandmother** n ба́бушка. **grandparents** n ба́бушка и де́душка. **grandson** n внук. **grandstand** n

трибу́на.

**grandeur** n вели́чие.

**grandiose** adj грандио́зный.

**granite** n грани́т.

**granny** n ба́бушка.

**grant** n (financial) дота́ция; (univ) стипе́ндия; vt дарова́ть impf & pf, (concede) допуска́ть impf, допусти́ть pf; **take for ~ed** (assume) счита́ть impf, счесть pf само́й собо́й разуме́ющимся; (not appreciate) принима́ть impf как до́лжное.

**granular** adj зерни́стый.

**granulated** adj: **~ sugar** са́харный песо́к.

**granule** n зёрнышко.

**grape** n (single grape) виногра́дина; collect виногра́д.

**grapefruit** n гре́йпфрут.

**graph** n гра́фик.

**graphic** adj графи́ческий; (vivid) я́ркий.

**graphite** n графи́т.

**grapple** vi (struggle) боро́ться impf (with c+instr).

**grasp** n (grip) хва́тка; (comprehension) понима́ние; vt (clutch) хвата́ть impf, схвати́ть pf; (comprehend) понима́ть impf, поня́ть pf. **grasping** adj жа́дный.

**grass** n трава́. **grasshopper** n кузне́чик. **grassy** adj травяни́стый.

**grate**[1] n (fireplace) решётка.

**grate**[2] vt (rub) тере́ть impf, на~ pf; vi (sound) скрежета́ть impf; **~ (up)on** (irritate) раздража́ть impf, раздражи́ть pf.

**grateful** adj благода́рный.

**grater** n тёрка.

**gratify** vt удовлетворя́ть impf, удовлетвори́ть pf.

**grating** n решётка.

**gratis** adv беспла́тно.

**gratitude** n благода́рность.

**gratuitous** adj (free) дарово́й; (motiveless) беспричи́нный.

**gratuity** n (tip) чаевы́е sb pl.

**grave**[1] n моги́ла. **gravedigger** n моги́льщик. **gravestone** n надгро́бный ка́мень m.

**graveyard** n кла́дбище.

**grave**[2] adj серьёзный.

**gravel** n гра́вий.

**gravitate** vi тяготе́ть impf (towards к+dat). **gravitational** adj гравитацио́нный. **gravity** n (seriousness) серьёзность; (force) тя́жесть.

**gravy** n (мясна́я) подли́вка.

**graze**[1] vi (feed) пасти́сь impf.

**graze**[2] n (abrasion) цара́пина; vt (touch) задева́ть impf, заде́ть pf; (abrade) цара́пать impf, o~ pf.

**grease** n жир; (lubricant) сма́зка; ~-paint грим; vt сма́зывать impf, сма́зать pf. **greasy** adj жи́рный.

**great** adj (large) большо́й; (eminent) вели́кий; (splendid) замеча́тельный; **to a ~ extent** в большо́й сте́пени; **a ~ deal** мно́го (+gen); **a ~ many** мно́гие; **~-aunt** двою́родная ба́бушка; **~-granddaughter** пра́внучка; **~-grandfather** пра́дед; **~-grandmother** праба́бка; **~-grandson** пра́внук; **~-uncle** двою́родный де́душка m. **greatly** adv о́чень.

**Great Britain** n Великобрита́ния.

**Greece** n Гре́ция.

**greed** n жа́дность (for k+dat).

**greedy** adj жа́дный (for k+dat).

**Greek** n грек, греча́нка; adj гре́ческий.

**green** n (colour) зелёный цвет; (grassy area) лужа́йка; pl зе́лень collect; adj зелёный. **greenery** n зе́лень. **greenfly** n тля. **greengrocer** n зеленщи́к. **greengrocer's** n овощно́й магази́н. **greenhouse** n тепли́ца; ~ **effect** парнико́вый эффе́кт.

**greet** vt здоро́ваться impf, по~ pf c+instr; (meet) встреча́ть impf, встре́тить pf. **greeting** n приве́т(ствие).

**gregarious** adj общи́тельный.

**grenade** n грана́та.

**grey** adj се́рый; (hair) седо́й. **greyhound** n борза́я sb.

**grid** n (grating) решётка; (electr) сеть; (map) координа́тная се́тка.

**grief** n го́ре; **come to ~** терпе́ть impf, по~ pf неуда́чу.

**grievance** n жа́лоба, оби́да. **grieve** vt огорча́ть impf, огорчи́ть pf; vi горева́ть impf (for o+prep). **grievous** adj тя́жкий.

**grill** n ра́шпер; vt (cook) жа́рить impf, за~, из~ pf (на ра́шпере); (question) допра́шивать impf, допроси́ть pf.

**grille** n (grating) решётка.

**grim** adj (stern) суро́вый; (unpleasant) неприя́тный.

**grimace** n грима́са; vi грима́сничать impf.

**grime** n грязь. **grimy** adj гря́зный.

**grin** n усме́шка; vi усмеха́ться impf, усмехну́ться pf.

**grind** vt (flour etc.) моло́ть impf, c~ pf; (axe) точи́ть impf, на~ pf; **one's teeth** скрежета́ть impf зуба́ми.

**grip** n хва́тка; vt схва́тывать impf, схвати́ть pf.

**gripe** vi ворча́ть impf.

**gripping** adj захва́тывающий.

**grisly** adj жу́ткий.
**gristle** n хрящ.
**grit** n песо́к; (for building) гра́вий; (firmness) вы́держка.
**grizzle** vi хны́кать impf.
**groan** n стон; vi стона́ть impf.
**grocer** n бакале́йщик; ~'s (shop) бакале́йная ла́вка, гастроно́м. **groceries** n pl бакале́я collect.
**groggy** adj разби́тый.
**groin** n (anat) пах.
**groom** n ко́нюх; (bridegroom) жени́х; vt (horse) чи́стить impf, по~ pf; (prepare) гото́вить impf, под~ pf (for к+dat); **well-groomed** хорошо́ вы́глядящий.
**groove** n желобо́к.
**grope** vi нащу́пывать impf (for, after +acc).
**gross**[1] n (12 dozen) гросс.
**gross**[2] adj (fat) ту́чный; (coarse) гру́бый; (total) валово́й; ~ weight вес бру́тто.
**grotesque** adj гроте́скный.
**grotto** n грот.
**ground** n земля́; (earth) по́чва; pl (dregs) гу́ща; (sport) площа́дка; pl (of house) парк; (reason) основа́ние; ~ floor пе́рвый эта́ж; vt (instruct) обуча́ть impf, обучи́ть pf осно́вам (in +gen); (aeron) запреща́ть impf, запрети́ть pf полёты +gen; vi (naut) сади́ться impf, сесть pf на мель. **groundless** adj необосно́ванный. **groundwork** n фунда́мент.
**group** n гру́ппа; vt & i группирова́ть(ся) impf, c~ pf.
**grouse**[1] n шотла́ндская куропа́тка.
**grouse**[2] vi (grumble) ворча́ть impf.
**grove** n ро́ща.

**grovel** vi пресмыка́ться impf (before пе́ред+instr).
**grow** vi расти́ impf; (become) станови́ться impf, стать pf +instr; vt (cultivate) выра́щивать impf, вы́растить pf; (hair) отра́щивать impf, отрасти́ть pf; ~ up (person) выраста́ть impf, вы́расти pf; (custom) возника́ть impf, возни́кнуть pf.
**growl** n ворча́ние; vi ворча́ть impf (at на+acc).
**grown-up** adj взро́слый sb.
**growth** n рост; (med) о́пухоль.
**grub** n (larva) личи́нка; (food) жратва́; vi: ~ about ры́ться impf. **grubby** adj запа́чканный.
**grudge** n зло́ба; have a ~ against име́ть impf зуб про́тив+gen; vt жале́ть impf, по~ pf +acc, +gen. **grudgingly** adv неохо́тно.
**gruelling** adj изнури́тельный.
**gruesome** adj жу́ткий.
**gruff** adj (surly) грубова́тый; (voice) хри́плый.
**grumble** vi ворча́ть impf (at на+acc).
**grumpy** adj брюзгли́вый.
**grunt** n хрю́канье; vi хрю́кать impf, хрю́кнуть pf.
**guarantee** n гара́нтия; vt гаранти́ровать impf & pf (against от+gen). **guarantor** n поручи́тель m.
**guard** n (device) предохрани́тель; (watch; soldiers) карау́л; (sentry) часово́й sb; (watchman) сто́рож; (rly) конду́ктор; pl (prison) надзира́тель m; vt охраня́ть impf, охрани́ть pf; vi: ~ against остерега́ться impf, остере́чься pf +gen, inf.
**guardian** n храни́тель m;

(law) опеку́н.

**guer(r)illa** n партиза́н; ~ **warfare** партиза́нская война́.

**guess** n дога́дка; vt & vi дога́дываться impf, догада́ться pf (о+prep); vt (~ correctly) уга́дывать impf, угада́ть pf.
**guesswork** n дога́дки f pl.

**guest** n гость m; ~ **house** ма́ленькая гости́ница.

**guffaw** n хо́хот; vi хохота́ть impf.

**guidance** n руково́дство.
**guide** n проводни́к, гид; (guidebook) путеводи́тель m; vt води́ть indet, вести́ det; (direct) руководи́ть impf +instr; ~ed **missile** управля́емая раке́та. **guidelines** n pl инстру́кции f pl; (advice) сове́т.

**guild** n ги́льдия, цех.

**guile** n кова́рство. **guileless** adj простоду́шный.

**guillotine** n гильоти́на.

**guilt** n вина́; (guiltiness) вино́вность. **guilty** adj (of crime) вино́вный (of в+prep); (of wrong) винова́тый.

**guinea-pig** n морска́я сви́нка; (fig) подо́пытный кро́лик.

**guise** n: under the ~ of под ви́дом+gen.

**guitar** n гита́ра. **guitarist** n гитари́ст.

**gulf** n (geog) зали́в; (chasm) про́пасть.

**gull** n ча́йка.

**gullet** n (oesophagus) пищево́д; (throat) го́рло.

**gullible** adj легкове́рный.

**gully** n (ravine) овра́г.

**gulp** n глото́к; vt жа́дно глота́ть impf.

**gum¹** n (anat) десна́.

**gum²** n каме́дь; (glue) клей; vt скле́ивать impf, скле́ить pf.

**gumption** n инициати́ва.

**gun** n (piece of ordnance) ору́дие, пу́шка; (rifle etc.) ружьё; (pistol) пистоле́т; vi: ~ **down** расстре́ливать impf, расстреля́ть pf. **gunner** n артиллери́ст. **gunpowder** n по́рох.

**gurgle** vi бу́лькать impf.

**gush** vi хлы́нуть pf.

**gusset** n клин.

**gust** n поры́в. **gusty** adj поры́вистый.

**gusto** n смак.

**gut** n кишка́; pl (entrails) кишки́ f pl; pl (bravery) му́жество; vt потроши́ть impf, вы́ pf; (devastate) опустоша́ть impf, опустоши́ть pf.

**gutter** n (of roof) (водосто́чный) жёлоб; (of road) сто́чная кана́ва.

**guttural** adj горта́нный.

**guy¹** n (rope) оття́жка.

**guy²** n (fellow) па́рень m.

**guzzle** vt (food) пожира́ть impf, пожра́ть pf; (liquid) хлеба́ть impf, хлебну́ть pf.

**gym** n (gymnasium) гимнасти́ческий зал; (gymnastics) гимна́стика. **gymnasium** n гимнасти́ческий зал. **gymnast** n гимна́ст. **gymnastic** adj гимнасти́ческий. **gymnastics** n гимна́стика.

**gynaecologist** n гинеко́лог. **gynaecology** n гинеколо́гия.

**gyrate** vi враща́ться impf.

# H

**haberdashery** n галантере́я; (shop) галантере́йный магази́н.

**habit** n привы́чка; (monk's) ря́са.

**habitable** adj приго́дный для

жилья́. **habitat** n есте́ственная среда́. **habitation** n: unfit for ~ непригóдный для жилья́.

**habitual** adj привы́чный.

**hack**[1] vt руби́ть impf; ~**saw** ножо́вка.

**hack**[2] n (hired horse) наёмная ло́шадь; (writer) халту́рщик.

**hackneyed** adj изби́тый.

**haddock** n пи́кша.

**haemophilia** n гемофили́я.
**haemorrhage** n кровотече́ние. **haemorrhoids** n pl геморро́й collect.

**hag** n карга́.

**haggard** adj измождённый.

**haggle** vi торгова́ться impf, c~ pf.

**hail**[1] n град; vi it is ~**ing** идёт град. **hailstone** n гра́дина.

**hail**[2] vt (greet) приве́тствовать impf (& pf in past); (taxi) подзыва́ть impf, подозва́ть pf.

**hair** n (single ~) во́лос; collect (human) во́лосы (-óс, -оса́м) pl; (animal) шерсть. **hairbrush** n щётка для воло́с. **haircut** n стри́жка; have a ~ постри́чься pf. **hair-do** n причёска. **hairdresser** n парикма́хер. **hairdresser's** n парикма́херская sb. **hairdryer** n фен. **hairstyle** n причёска. **hairy** adj волоса́тый.

**hale** n: ~ **and hearty** здоро́вый и бо́дрый.

**half** n полови́на; (sport) тайм; adj полови́нный; in ~ попола́м; one and a ~ полтора́; ~ **past** (one etc.) полови́на (второ́го и т.д.); ~**-hearted** равноду́шный; ~ **an hour** полчаса́; ~**-time** переры́в ме́жду та́ймами; ~**way** на полпути́; ~**-witted** слабоу́мный.

**hall** n (large room) зал; (entrance ~) холл, вестибю́ль m; (~ of residence) общежи́тие. **hallmark** n про́бное клеймо́; (fig) при́знак.

**hallo** int здра́сте, приве́т; (on telephone) алло́.

**hallucination** n галлюцина́ция.

**halo** n (around Saint) нимб; (fig) орео́л.

**halt** n остано́вка; vt & i остана́вливать(ся) impf, останови́ть(ся) pf; int (mil) стой(те)! **halting** adj запина́ющий.

**halve** vt дели́ть impf, раз~ pf попола́м.

**ham** n (cul) ветчина́.

**hamlet** n дереву́шка.

**hammer** n молото́к; vt бить impf молотко́м.

**hammock** n гама́к.

**hamper**[1] n (basket) корзи́на с кры́шкой.

**hamper**[2] vt (hinder) меша́ть impf, по~ pf +dat.

**hamster** n хомя́к.

**hand** n рука́; (worker) рабо́чий sb; (writing) по́черк; (clock) стре́лка; at ~ под руко́й; on ~s and knees на четвере́ньках; vt передава́ть impf, переда́ть pf; ~ **in** подава́ть impf, пода́ть pf; ~**out** раздава́ть impf, разда́ть pf. **handbag** n су́мка. **handbook** n руково́дство. **handcuffs** n pl нару́чники m pl. **handful** n горсть.

**handicap** n (sport) гандика́п; (hindrance) поме́ха. **handicapped** adj: ~ **person** инвали́д.

**handicraft** n ремесло́.

**handiwork** n ручна́я рабо́та.

**handkerchief** n носово́й плато́к.

**handle** n ру́чка, рукоя́тка; vt (people) обраща́ться impf c+instr; (situations) спра́виться impf, спра́виться pf c+instr; (touch) тро́гать impf, тро́нуть pf руко́й, рука́ми. **handlebar(s)** n руль m.

**handmade** adj ручно́й рабо́ты.

**handout** n пода́чка; (document) лифле́т.

**handrail** n пери́ла (-л) pl.

**handshake** n рукопожа́тие.

**handsome** adj краси́вый; (generous) ще́дрый.

**handwriting** n по́черк.

**handy** adj (convenient) удо́бный; (skilful) ло́вкий; **come in** ~ пригоди́ться pf.

**hang** vt ве́шать impf, пове́сить pf; vi висе́ть impf; ~ **about** слоня́ться impf; ~ **on** (cling) держа́ться impf; (tel) не ве́шать impf тру́бку; (persist) упо́рствовать impf; ~ **out** выве́шивать impf, вы́весить pf; (spend time) болта́ться impf; ~ **up** ве́шать impf, пове́сить pf; (tel) ве́шать impf, пове́сить pf тру́бку. **hanger** n ве́шалка. **hanger-on** n прилипа́ла m & f. **hangman** n пала́ч.

**hangar** n анга́р.

**hangover** n похме́лье.

**hang-up** n ко́мплекс.

**hanker** vi: ~ **after** мечта́ть impf o+prep.

**haphazard** adj случа́йный.

**happen** vi (occur) случа́ться impf, случи́ться pf; происходи́ть impf, произойти́ pf; ~ **upon** ната́лкиваться impf, натолкну́ться pf на+acc.

**happiness** n сча́стье. **happy** adj счастли́вый; ~-**go-lucky** беззабо́тный.

**harass** vt (pester) дёргать impf; (persecute) пресле́довать impf. **harassment** n тра́вля; пресле́дование.

**harbinger** n предве́стник.

**harbour** n га́вань, порт; vt (person) укрыва́ть impf, укры́ть pf; (thoughts) зата́ивать impf, затаи́ть pf.

**hard** adj твёрдый; (difficult) тру́дный; (difficult to bear) тяжёлый; (severe) суро́вый; adv (work) мно́го; (hit) си́льно; (try) о́чень; ~-**boiled egg** яйцо́ вкруту́ю; ~-**headed** практи́чный; ~-**hearted** жестокосерде́ный; ~-**up** стеснённый в сре́дствах; ~-**working** трудолюби́вый. **hardboard** n строи́тельный карто́н.

**harden** vt затвердева́ть impf, затверде́ть pf; (fig) ожесточа́ться impf, ожесточи́ться pf.

**hardly** adv едва́ (ли).

**hardship** n (privation) нужда́.

**hardware** n скобяны́е изде́лия neut pl; (comput) аппарату́ра.

**hardy** adj (robust) выно́сливый; (plant) морозосто́йкий.

**hare** n за́яц.

**hark** vi: ~ **back to** возвраща́ться impf, верну́ться pf к+dat; int слуша́й(те)!

**harm** n вред; vt вреди́ть impf, по~ pf +dat. **harmful** adj вре́дный. **harmless** adj безвре́дный.

**harmonic** adj гармони́ческий. **harmonica** n губна́я гармо́ника. **harmonious** adj гармони́чный. **harmonize** vi гармони́ровать (with c+instr). **harmony** n гармо́ния.

**harness** n у́пряжь; vt запря-

гáть *impf*, запря́чь *pf*; (fig) испо́льзовать *impf & pf*.
**harp** *n* áрфа; *vi*: ~ **on** тверди́ть *impf* о+*prep*.
**harpoon** *n* гарпу́н.
**harpsichord** *n* клавеси́н.
**harrow** *n* борона́. **harrowing** *adj* душераздира́ющий.
**harsh** *adj* (*sound, colour*) рéзкий; (*cruel*) суро́вый.
**harvest** *n* жа́тва, сбор (плодо́в); (*yield*) урожа́й; (*fig*) плоды́ *m pl*; *vt & abs* собира́ть *impf*, собра́ть (урожа́й).
**hash** *n*: **make a ~ of** напу́тать *pf* +*acc, prep*.
**hashish** *n* гаши́ш.
**hassle** *n* беспоко́йство.
**hassock** *n* поду́шечка.
**haste** *n* спе́шка. **hasten** *vi* спеши́ть *impf*, по~ *pf*; *vt & i* торопи́ть(ся) *impf*, по~ *pf*; *vt* уско́рять *impf*, уско́рить *pf*. **hasty** *adj* (*hurried*) поспе́шный; (*quick-tempered*) вспы́льчивый.
**hat** *n* шля́па; (*stylish*) шля́пка.
**hatch**[1] *n* люк; **~-back** маши́на-пика́п.
**hatch**[2] *vi* вылу́пливаться, вылупля́ться *impf*, вы́лупиться *pf*.
**hatchet** *n* топо́рик.
**hate** *n* нéнависть; *vt* ненави́деть *impf*. **hateful** *adj* ненави́стный. **hatred** *n* нéнависть.
**haughty** *adj* надмéнный.
**haul** *n* (*fish*) уло́в; (*loot*) добы́ча; (*distance*) езда́; *vt* (*drag*) тяну́ть *impf*; таска́ть *indet*, тащи́ть *det*. **haulage** *n* перево́зка.
**haunt** *n* люби́мое мéсто; *vt* (*ghost*) обита́ть *impf* в; (*memory*) преслéдовать *impf*. **haunted** *adj*: ~ **house** дом с приве-

дéниями. **haunting** *adj* навя́зчивый.
**have** *vt* имéть *impf*; I ~ (*possess*) у меня́ (есть; был, -á, -о) +*nom*; I ~ **not** у меня́ нет (*past* нé было) +*gen*; I ~ (*got*) **to** я до́лжен +*inf*; **you had better** вам лу́чше бы +*inf*; ~ (*on*) (*wear*) быть одéтым в +*prep*; (*be engaged in*) быть за́нятым +*instr*.
**haven** *n* (*refuge*) убéжище.
**haversack** *n* рюкза́к.
**havoc** *n* (*devastation*) опустошéние; (*disorder*) беспоря́док.
**hawk**[1] *n* (*bird*) я́стреб.
**hawk**[2] *vt* (*trade*) торгова́ть *impf* вразно́с+*instr*. **hawker** *n* разно́счик.
**hawser** *n* трос.
**hawthorn** *n* боя́рышник.
**hay** *n* сéно; **make** ~ коси́ть *impf*, с~ *pf* сéно; ~ **fever** сенна́я лихора́дка. **haystack** *n* стог.
**hazard** *n* риск; *vt* рискова́ть *impf* +*instr*. **hazardous** *adj* риско́ванный.
**haze** *n* ды́мка.
**hazel** *n* лещи́на. **hazelnut** *n* леснóй орéх.
**hazy** *adj* тума́нный; (*vague*) сму́тный.
**he** *pron* он.
**head** *n* голова́; (*mind*) ум; (~ *of coin*) лицева́я сторона́ монéты; **~s or tails?** орёл и́ли рéшка?; (*chief*) глава́ *m*, нача́льник; *attrib* гла́вный; *vt* (*lead*) возглавля́ть *impf*, возгла́вить *pf*; (*ball*) забива́ть *impf*, заби́ть *pf* голово́й; *vi*: ~ **for** напра́виться *pf* в, на, +*acc*, к+*dat*. **headache** *n* головна́я боль. **head-dress**

*n* головно́й убо́р. **header** *n* уда́р голово́й. **heading** *n* (*title*) заголо́вок. **headland** *n* мыс. **headline** *n* заголо́вок. **headlong** *adv* стремгла́в. **headmaster, -mistress** *n* дире́ктор шко́лы. **head-on** *adj* голово́й; *adv* в лоб. **headphone** *n* нау́шник. **headquarters** *n* штаб-кварти́ра. **headscarf** *n* косы́нка. **headstone** *n* надгро́бный ка́мень *m*. **headstrong** *adj* своево́льный. **headway** *n* движе́ние вперёд. **heady** *adj* опьяня́ющий.

**heal** *vt* изле́чивать *impf*, изле́чить *pf*; *vi* зажива́ть *impf*, зажи́ть *pf*. **healing** *adj* целе́бный.

**health** *n* здоро́вье; ~ **care** здравоохране́ние. **healthy** *adj* здоро́вый; (*beneficial*) поле́зный.

**heap** *n* ку́ча; *vt* нагроможда́ть *impf*, нагромозди́ть *pf*.

**hear** *vt* слы́шать *impf*, y~ *pf*; (*listen to*) слу́шать *impf*, по~ *pf*; ~ **out** выслу́шивать *impf*, вы́слушать *pf*. **hearing** *n* слух; (*law*) слу́шание. **hearsay** *n* слух.

**hearse** *n* катафа́лк.

**heart** *n* се́рдце; (*essence*) суть; *pl* (*cards*) че́рви (-ве́й) *pl*; **by** ~ наизу́сть; ~ **attack** серде́чный при́ступ. **heartburn** *n* изжо́га. **hearten** *vt* ободря́ть *impf*, ободри́ть *pf*. **heartfelt** *adj* серде́чный. **heartless** *adj* бессерде́чный. **heart-rending** *adj* душераздира́ющий. **hearty** *adj* (*cordial*) серде́чный; (*vigorous*) здоро́вый.

**hearth** *n* оча́г.

**heat** *n* жара́; (*phys*) теплота́; (*of feeling*) пыл; (*sport*) забе́г, зае́зд; *vt* & *i* (*heat up*) нагрева́ть(ся) *impf*, нагре́ть(ся) *pf*; *vt* (*house*) топи́ть *impf*. **heater** *n* нагрева́тель *m*. **heating** *n* отопле́ние.

**heath** *n* пу́стошь.

**heathen** *n* язы́чник; *adj* язы́ческий.

**heather** *n* ве́реск.

**heave** *vt* (*lift*) поднима́ть *impf*, подня́ть *pf*; (*pull*) тяну́ть *impf*, по~ *pf*.

**heaven** *n* (*sky*) не́бо; (*paradise*) рай; *pl* небеса́ *neut pl*. **heavenly** *adj* небе́сный; (*divine*) боже́ственный.

**heavy** *adj* тяжёлый; (*strong, intense*) си́льный. **heavyweight** *n* тяжелове́с.

**Hebrew** *adj* (дре́вне)евре́йский.

**heckle** *vt* пререка́ться *impf* c+*instr*.

**hectic** *adj* лихора́дочный.

**hedge** *n* жива́я и́згородь. **hedgerow** *n* шпале́ра.

**hedgehog** *n* ёж.

**heed** *vt* обраща́ть *impf*, обрати́ть *pf* внима́ние на+*acc*. **heedless** *adj* небре́жный.

**heel**[1] *n* (*of foot*) пята́; (*of foot, sock*) пя́тка; (*of shoe*) каблу́к. **heel**[2] *vi* крени́ться *impf*, на~ *pf*.

**hefty** *adj* дю́жий.

**heifer** *n* тёлка.

**height** *n* высота́; (*of person*) рост. **heighten** *vt* (*strengthen*) уси́ливать *impf*, уси́лить *pf*.

**heinous** *adj* гну́сный.

**heir** *n* насле́дник. **heiress** *n* насле́дница. **heirloom** *n* фами́льная вещь.

**helicopter** *n* вертолёт.

**helium** *n* ге́лий.

**hell** n ад. **hellish** adj áдский.

**hello** see **hallo**

**helm** n руль.

**helmet** n шлем.

**help** n пóмощь; vt помогáть impf, помóчь pf +dat; (can't ~) не мочь impf не +inf; ~ o.s. брать impf, взять pf себé; ~ yourself! бери́те! **helpful** adj полéзный; (obliging) услужливый. **helping** n (of food) пóрция. **helpless** adj беспóмощный.

**helter-skelter** adv как попáло.

**hem** n рубéц; vt подрубáть impf, подрубить pf; ~ in окружáть impf, окружить pf.

**hemisphere** n полушáрие.

**hemp** n (plant) конопля́; (fibre) пенька́.

**hen** n (female bird) сáмка; (domestic fowl) ку́рица.

**hence** adv (from here) отсю́да; (as a result) слéдовательно; **3 years** ~ чéрез три гóда. **henceforth** adv отны́не.

**henchman** n приспéшник.

**henna** n хна.

**hepatitis** n гепати́т.

**her** poss pron её; свой.

**herald** n вéстник; vt возвещáть impf, возвести́ть pf. **herb** n травá. **herbaceous** adj травяно́й; ~ border цветóчный бордю́р. **herbal** adj травяно́й.

**herd** n стáдо; (people) толпи́ться impf, с~ pf; vt (tend) пасти́ impf; (drive) загоня́ть impf, загнáть в стáдо.

**here** adv (position) здесь, тут; (direction) сюдá; ~ is ... вот (+nom); ~ and there там и сям; ~ you are! пожáлуйста. **hereabout(s)** adv поблизóсти. **hereafter** adv в бу́дущем. **hereby** adv э́тим. **here-**upon adv (in consequence) вслéдствие э́того; (after) пóсле э́того. **herewith** adv при сём.

**hereditary** adj наслéдственный. **heredity** n наслéдственность.

**heresy** n éресь. **heretic** n ерети́к. **heretical** adj ерети́ческий.

**heritage** n наслéдие.

**hermetic** adj герметический.

**hermit** n отшéльник.

**hernia** n грыжа.

**hero** n герóй. **heroic** adj герои́ческий.

**heroin** n герои́н.

**heroine** n геройня. **heroism** n герои́зм.

**heron** n цáпля.

**herpes** n лишáй.

**herring** n сельдь; (food) селёдка.

**hers** poss pron её; свой.

**herself** pron (emph) (онá) самá; (refl) себя́.

**hertz** n герц.

**hesitant** adj нереши́тельный. **hesitate** vi колебáться impf, по~ pf; (in speech) запинáться impf, запну́ться pf. **hesitation** n колебáние.

**hessian** n мешкови́на.

**heterogeneous** adj разнорóдный.

**heterosexual** adj гетеросексуáльный.

**hew** vt рубить impf.

**hexagon** n шестиугóльник.

**hey** int эй!

**heyday** n расцвéт.

**hi** int привéт!

**hiatus** n пробéл.

**hibernate** vi быть impf в спя́чке; впадáть impf, впасть pf в спя́чку. **hibernation** n спя́чка.

**hiccup** vi икáть impf, икнýть pf; n: pl икóта.

**hide¹** n (skin) шкýра.

**hide²** vt & i (conceal) прятать(ся) impf, c~ pf; скрывáть(ся) impf, скрыть(ся) pf.

**hideous** adj отвратительный.

**hideout** n укрытие.

**hiding** n (flogging) пóрка.

**hierarchy** n иерáрхия.

**hieroglyphics** n pl иероглифы m pl.

**hi-fi** n проигрыватель m с высококáчественным воспроизведéнием звýка зáписи.

**higgledy-piggledy** adv как придётся.

**high** adj высóкий; (wind) сильный; (on drugs) в наркотическом дурмáне; ~**er education** высшее образовáние; ~**-handed** своевóльный; ~**-heeled** на высóких каблукáх; ~ **jump** прыжóк в высотý; ~**-minded** благорóдный; идéйный; ~**-pitched** высóкий; ~**-rise** высóтный. **highbrow** adj интеллектуáльный. **highland(s)** n гóрная странá. **highlight** n (fig) высшая тóчка; vt обращáть impf, обратить pf внимáние на+acc. **highly** adv весьмá; ~**-strung** легкó возбуждáемый. **highness** n (title) высóчество. **highstreet** n глáвная ýлица. **highway** n магистрáль.

**hijack** vt похищáть impf, похитить pf. **hijacker** n похититель m.

**hike** n похóд.

**hilarious** adj уморительный. **hilarity** n весéлье.

**hill** n холм. **hillock** n хóлмик. **hillside** n склон холмá. **hilly** adj холмистый.

**hilt** n рукоятка.

**himself** pron (emph) (он) сам; (refl) себя.

**hind** adj (rear) зáдний.

**hinder** vt мешáть impf, по~ pf +dat. **hindrance** n помéха.

**Hindu** n индýс; adj индýсский.

**hinge** n шарнир; vi (fig) зависеть impf от+gen.

**hint** n намёк; vi намекáть impf, намекнýть pf (at на+acc)

**hip** n (anat) бедрó.

**hippie** n хиппи neut indecl.

**hippopotamus** n гиппопотáм.

**hire** n наём, прокáт; ~**-purchase** покýпка в рассрóчку; vt нанимáть impf, наня́ть pf; ~ **out** сдавáть impf, сдать pf напрокáт.

**his** poss pron егó; свой.

**hiss** n шипéние; vi шипéть impf; vt (performer) освистывать impf, освистáть pf.

**historian** n истóрик. **historic(al)** adj исторический. **history** n истóрия.

**histrionic** adj театрáльный.

**hit** n (blow) удáр; (on target) попадáние (в цель); (success) успéх; vt (strike) ударя́ть impf, удáрить pf; (target) попадáть impf, попáсть pf (в цель); ~ (up)on находить impf, найти pf.

**hitch** n (stoppage) задéржка; vt (fasten) привя́зывать impf, привязáть pf; ~ **up** подтягивать impf, подтянýть pf; ~**-hike** éздить indet, éхать impf, по~ pf автостóпом.

**hither** adv сюдá. **hitherto** adv до сих пор.

**HIV** abbr (of human immunodeficiency virus) ВИЧ.

**hive** n ýлей.

**hoard** n запáс; vt скáпливать impf, скопить pf.

**hoarding** n реклáмный щит.

**hoarse** *adj* хри́плый.

**hoax** *n* надува́тельство.

**hobble** *vi* ковыля́ть *impf.*

**hobby** *n* хо́бби *neut indecl.*

**hock** *n* (wine) рейнве́йн.

**hockey** *n* хокке́й.

**hoe** *n* моты́га; *vt* моты́жить *impf.*

**hog** *n* бо́ров.

**hoist** *n* подъёмник; *vt* поднима́ть *impf*, подня́ть *pf.*

**hold**¹ *n* (naut) трюм.

**hold**² *n* (grasp) захва́т; (influence) влия́ние (on на+acc); **catch ~ of** ухвати́ться *pf* за+acc; *vt* (grasp) держа́ть *impf*, вмести́ть *pf*; (possess) владе́ть *impf* +instr; (conduct) проводи́ть *impf*, провести́ *pf*; (consider) счита́ть *impf*, счесть *pf* (+acc & instr, за+acc); *vi* держа́ться *impf*; (weather) проде́рживаться *impf*, продержа́ться *pf*; **~ back** сде́рживать(ся) *impf*, сдержа́ть(ся) *pf*; **~ forth** разглаго́льствовать *impf*; **~ on** (wait) подожда́ть *pf*; (tel) не ве́шать *impf* тру́бку; (grip) держа́ться *impf* (to за+acc); **~ out** (stretch out) протя́гивать *impf*, протяну́ть *pf*; (resist) не сдава́ться *impf*; **~ up** (support) подде́рживать *impf*, поддержа́ть *pf*; (impede) заде́рживать *impf*, задержа́ть *pf*. **holdall** *n* су́мка. **hold-up** *n* (robbery) налёт; (delay) заде́ржка.

**hole** *n* дыра́; (animal's) нора́; (golf) лу́нка.

**holiday** *n* (day off) выходно́й день; (festival) пра́здник; (annual leave) о́тпуск; *pl* (school) кани́кулы (-л) *pl*; **~maker** тури́ст; **on ~** в о́тпуске.

**holiness** *n* свя́тость.

**Holland** *n* Голла́ндия.

**hollow** *n* впа́дина; (valley) лощи́на; *adj* пусто́й; (sunken) впа́лый; (sound) глухо́й; *vt* (~ out) выда́лбливать *impf*, вы́долбить *pf*.

**holly** *n* остроли́ст.

**holocaust** *n* ма́ссовое уничтоже́ние.

**holster** *n* кобура́.

**holy** *adj* свято́й, свяще́нный.

**homage** *n* почте́ние; **pay ~ to** преклоня́ться *impf*, преклони́ться *pf* пе́ред+instr.

**home** *n* дом; (native land) ро́дина; **at ~** до́ма; **feel at ~** чу́вствовать *impf* себя́ как до́ма; *adj* дома́шний; (native) родно́й; **H~ Affairs** вну́тренние дела́ *neut pl*; *adv* (direction) домо́й; (position) до́ма. **homeland** *n* ро́дина. **homeless** *adj* бездо́мный. **homemade** *adj* (food) дома́шний; (object) самоде́льный. **homesick** *adj*: **be ~** скуча́ть *impf* по до́му. **homewards** *adv* домо́й, восвоя́си.

**homely** *adj* просто́й.

**homicide** *n* (action) уби́йство.

**homogeneous** *adj* одноро́дный.

**homosexual** *n* гомосексуали́ст; *adj* гомосексуа́льный.

**honest** *n* че́стный. **honesty** *n* че́стность.

**honey** *n* мёд. **honeymoon** *n* медо́вый ме́сяц. **honeysuckle** *n* жи́молость.

**honk** *vi* гуде́ть *impf.*

**honorary** *adj* почётный.

**honour** *n* честь; *vt* (respect) почита́ть *impf*; (confer) удоста́ивать *impf*, удосто́ить *pf* (with +gen); (fulfil) выполня́ть *impf*, вы́полнить *pf*,

**honourable** *adj* че́стный.

**hood** *n* капюшо́н; (*tech*) капо́т.

**hoodwink** *vt* обма́нывать *impf*, обману́ть *pf*.

**hoof** *n* копы́то.

**hook** *n* крючо́к; *vt* (*hitch*) зацепля́ть *impf*, зацепи́ть *pf*; (*fasten*) застёгивать *impf*, застегну́ть *pf*.

**hooligan** *n* хулига́н.

**hoop** *n* о́бруч.

**hoot** *vi* (*owl*) у́хать *impf*, у́хнуть *pf*; (*horn*) гуде́ть *impf*. **hooter** *n* гудо́к.

**hop**[1] *n* (*plant; collect*) хмель *m*.

**hop**[2] *n* (*jump*) прыжо́к; *vi* пры́гать *impf*, пры́гнуть *pf* (на одно́й ноге́).

**hope** *n* наде́жда; *vi* наде́яться *impf*, по~ *pf* (*for* на+*acc*). **hopeful** *adj* (*promising*) обнадёживающий; **I am ~ я** наде́юсь. **hopefully** *adv* с наде́ждой; (*it is hoped*) на́до наде́яться. **hopeless** *adj* безнадёжный.

**horde** *n* (*hist; fig*) орда́.

**horizon** *n* горизо́нт. **horizontal** *adj* горизонта́льный.

**hormone** *n* гормо́н.

**horn** *n* рог; (*French horn*) валто́рна; (*car*) гудо́к.

**hornet** *n* ше́ршень *m*.

**horny** *adj* (*calloused*) мозо́листый.

**horoscope** *n* гороско́п.

**horrible, horrid** *adj* ужа́сный.

**horrify** *vt* ужаса́ть *impf*, ужасну́ть *pf*. **horror** *n* ужас.

**hors-d'oeuvre** *n* заку́ска.

**horse** *n* ло́шадь. **horse-chestnut** *n* ко́нский кашта́н. **horseman, -woman** *n* вса́дник, -ица. **horseplay** *n* возня́. **horsepower** *n* лошади́ная си́ла. **horse-racing** *n* ска́чки (-чек) *pl*. **horse-radish** *n*

хрен. **horseshoe** *n* подко́ва.

**horticulture** *n* садово́дство.

**hose** *n* (~*pipe*) шланг.

**hosiery** *n* чуло́чные изде́лия *neut pl*.

**hospitable** *adj* гостеприи́мный.

**hospital** *n* больни́ца.

**hospitality** *n* гостеприи́мство.

**host**[1] *n* (*multitude*) мно́жество.

**host**[2] *n* (*entertaining*) хозя́ин.

**hostage** *n* зало́жник.

**hostel** *n* общежи́тие.

**hostess** *n* хозя́йка; (*air ~*) стюарде́сса.

**hostile** *adj* вражде́бный. **hostility** *n* вражде́бность; *pl* вое́нные де́йствия *neut pl*.

**hot** *adj* горя́чий, жа́ркий; (*pungent*) о́стрый; **~-headed** вспы́льчивый; **~-water bottle** гре́лка. **hotbed** *n* (*fig*) оча́г. **hothouse** *n* тепли́ца. **hotplate** *n* пли́тка.

**hotel** *n* гости́ница.

**hound** *n* охо́тничья соба́ка; *vt* трави́ть *impf*, за~ *pf*.

**hour** *n* час. **hourly** *adj* ежеча́сный.

**house** *n* дом; (*parl*) пала́та; *attrib* дома́шний; *vt* помеща́ть *impf*, помести́ть *pf*. **household** *n* семья́; *adj* хозя́йственный; дома́шний. **housekeeper** *n* эконо́мка. **housewarming** *n* новосе́лье. **housewife** *n* хозя́йка. **housework** *n* дома́шняя рабо́та. **housing** *n* (*accommodation*) жильё; (*casing*) кожу́х; **~ estate** жило́й масси́в.

**hovel** *n* лачу́га.

**hover** *vi* (*bird*) пари́ть *impf*; (*helicopter*) висе́ть *impf*; (*person*) ма́ячить *impf*. **hovercraft** *n* су́дно на возду́шной поду́шке, СВП.

**how** adv как, каки́м о́бразом; ~ **do you do?** здра́вствуйте!; ~ **many,** ~ **much** ско́лько (+gen). **however** adv как бы ни (+past); conj одна́ко, тем не ме́нее; ~ **much** ско́лько бы ни (+gen & past).

**howl** n вой; vi выть impf.

**howler** n грубе́йшая оши́бка.

**hub** n (of wheel) ступи́ца; (fig) центр, средото́чие.

**hubbub** n шум, гам.

**huddle** vi: ~ **together** прижима́ться impf, прижа́ться pf друг к дру́гу.

**hue** n (tint) отте́нок.

**huff** n: **in a** ~ оскорблённый.

**hug** n (embrace) объя́тие; vt (embrace) обнима́ть impf, обня́ть pf.

**huge** adj огро́мный.

**hulk** n ко́рпус (корабля́). **hulking** adj (bulky) грома́дный; (clumsy) неуклю́жий.

**hull** n (of ship) ко́рпус.

**hum** n жужжа́ние; vi (buzz) жужжа́ть impf; vt & i (person) напева́ть impf.

**human** adj челове́ческий, людско́й; n челове́к. **humane, humanitarian** adj челове́чный. **humanity** n (human race) челове́чество; (humaneness) гума́нность; **the Humanities** гуманита́рные нау́ки f pl.

**humble** adj (person) смире́нный; (abode) скро́мный; vt унижа́ть impf, уни́зить pf.

**humdrum** adj однообра́зный.

**humid** adj вла́жный. **humidity** n вла́жность.

**humiliate** vt унижа́ть impf, уни́зить pf. **humiliation** n униже́ние.

**humility** n смире́ние.

**humorous** adj юмористи́ческий. **humour** n юмор; (mood) настрое́ние; vt пота-

ка́ть impf +dat.

**hump** n горб; (of earth) буго́р.

**humus** n перегно́й.

**hunch** n (idea) предчу́вствие; vt го́рбить impf, c~ pf. **hunchback** n (person) горбу́н, ~ья. **hunchbacked** adj горба́тый.

**hundred** adj & n сто; ~**s** of со́тни f pl +gen; **two** ~ две́сти; **three** ~ три́ста; **four** ~ четы́реста; **five** ~ пятьсо́т. **hundredth** adj & n со́тый. **hundredweight** n це́нтнер.

**Hungarian** n венгр, венге́рка; adj венге́рский. **Hungary** n Ве́нгрия.

**hunger** n го́лод; (fig) жа́жда (for +gen); ~ **strike** голодо́вка; vi голода́ть impf; ~ **for** жа́ждать impf +gen. **hungry** adj голо́дный.

**hunk** n ломо́ть m.

**hunt** n (also fig) по́иски pl (for +gen); vt охо́титься impf на+acc, за+instr, (persecute) трави́ть impf, за~ pf; ~ **down** вы́следить pf; ~ **for** иска́ть impf +acc or gen; ~ **out** отыска́ть pf. **hunter** n охо́тник. **hunting** n охо́та.

**hurdle** n (sport, fig) барье́р. **hurdler** n барьери́ст. **hurdles** n pl (sport) барье́рный бег.

**hurl** vt швыря́ть impf, швырну́ть pf.

**hurly-burly** n сумато́ха.

**hurrah, hurray** int ура́!

**hurricane** n урага́н.

**hurried** adj торопли́вый. **hurry** n спе́шка; **be in a** ~ спеши́ть impf; vt & i торопи́ть(ся) impf, по~ pf, vi спеши́ть impf, по~ pf.

**hurt** n уще́рб; vi боле́ть impf; vt поврежда́ть impf, повреди́ть pf; (offend) обижа́ть impf, оби́деть pf.

**hurtle** vi нестись impf, по~ pf.

**husband** n муж.

**hush** n тишина; vt: ~ up заминать impf, замять pf; int тише!

**husk** n шелуха.

**husky** adj (voice) хриплый.

**hustle** n толкотня; vt (push) затолкать impf, затолкнуть pf; (herd people) загонять impf, загнать pf; vt & i (hurry) торопить(ся) impf, по~ pf.

**hut** n хижина.

**hutch** n клетка.

**hyacinth** n гиацинт.

**hybrid** n гибрид; adj гибридный.

**hydrangea** n гортензия.

**hydrant** n гидрант.

**hydraulic** adj гидравлический.

**hydrochloric acid** n соляная кислота. **hydroelectric** adj гидроэлектрический; ~ **power station** гидроэлектростанция, ГЭС f indecl. **hydrofoil** n судно на подводных крыльях, СПК.

**hydrogen** n водород.

**hyena** n гиена.

**hygiene** n гигиена. **hygienic** adj гигиенический.

**hymn** n гимн.

**hyperbole** n гипербола.

**hyphen** n дефис. **hyphen(ate)** vt писать impf, на~ pf через дефис.

**hypnosis** n гипноз. **hypnotic** adj гипнотический. **hypnotism** n гипнотизм. **hypnotist** n гипнотизёр. **hypnotize** vt гипнотизировать impf, за~ pf.

**hypochondria** n ипохондрия. **hypochondriac** n ипохондрик.

**hypocrisy** n лицемерие. **hypo-**

**crite** n лицемер. **hypocritical** adj лицемерный.

**hypodermic** adj подкожный. **hypothesis** n гипотеза. **hypothesize** vi строить impf, по~ pf гипотезу. **hypothetical** adj гипотетический.

**hysterectomy** n гистерэктомия, удаление матки.

**hysteria** n истерия. **hysterical** adj истерический. **hysterics** n pl истерика.

# I

**I** pron я.

**ibid(em)** adv там же.

**ice** n лёд; ~**-age** ледниковый период; ~**-axe** ледоруб; ~**-cream** n мороженое sb; ~ **hockey** хоккей (с шайбой); ~ **rink** каток; ~ **skate** конёк; vi кататься impf на коньках; vt (chill) замораживать impf, заморозить pf; (cul) глазировать impf, ~ pf; vi: ~ **over, up** обледеневать impf, обледенеть pf. **iceberg** n айсберг. **icicle** n сосулька. **icing** n (cul) глазурь. **icy** adj ледяной.

**icon** n икона.

**ID** abbr (of **identification**) удостоверение личности.

**idea** n идея, мысль; (conception) понятие.

**ideal** n идеал; adj идеальный. **idealism** n идеализм. **idealist** n идеалист. **idealize** vt идеализировать impf & pf.

**identical** adj тождественный, одинаковый. **identification** n (recognition) опознание; (of person) установление личности. **identify** vt опознавать impf, опознать pf. **identity**

(*of person*) ли́чность; ~ **card** удостовере́ние ли́чности.

**ideological** *adj* идеологи́ческий. **ideology** *n* идеоло́гия.

**idiom** *n* идио́ма. **idiomatic** *adj* идиомати́ческий.

**idiosyncrasy** *n* идиосинкра́зия.

**idiot** *n* идио́т. **idiotic** *adj* идио́тский.

**idle** *adj* (*unoccupied; lazy; purposeless*) пра́здный; (*vain*) тще́тный; (*empty*) пусто́й; (*machine*) неде́йствующий; *vi* безде́льничать *impf*; (*engine*) рабо́тать *impf* вхолосту́ю; *vt*: ~ **away** пра́здно проводи́ть *impf*, провести́ *pf*. **idleness** *n* пра́здность.

**idol** *n* и́дол. **idolatry** *n* идолопокло́нство; (*fig*) обожа́ние. **idolize** *vt* боготвори́ть *impf*.

**idyll** *n* иди́ллия. **idyllic** *adj* идилли́ческий.

**i.e.** *abbr* т.е., то есть.

**if** *conj* е́сли, е́сли бы; (*whether*) ли; **as** ~ как бу́дто; **even** ~ да́же е́сли; ~ **only** е́сли бы то́лько.

**ignite** *vt* зажига́ть *impf*, заже́чь *pf*; *vi* загора́ться *impf*, загоре́ться *pf*. **ignition** *n* зажига́ние.

**ignoble** *adj* ни́зкий.

**ignominious** *adj* позо́рный.

**ignoramus** *n* неве́жда *m*. **ignorance** *n* неве́жество, (*of certain facts*) неве́дение. **ignorant** *adj* неве́жественный; (*uninformed*) несве́дущий (*of* в+*prep*).

**ignore** *vt* не обраща́ть *impf* внима́ния на+*acc*; игнори́ровать *impf* & *pf*.

**ilk** *n*: **of that** ~ тако́го ро́да.

**ill** *n* (*evil*) зло; (*harm*) вред; *pl* (*misfortunes*) несча́стья (-тий)

*pl*; *adj* (*sick*) больно́й; (*bad*) дурно́й; *adv* пло́хо, ду́рно; **fall** ~ заболева́ть *impf*, заболе́ть *pf*; ~-**advised** неблагоразу́мный; ~-**mannered** неве́жливый; ~-**treat** *vt* пло́хо обраща́ться *impf* с+*instr*.

**illegal** *adj* нелега́льный. **illegality** *n* незако́нность, нелега́льность.

**illegible** *adj* неразбо́рчивый.

**illegitimacy** *n* незако́нность, (*of child*) незаконноро́жденность. **illegitimate** *adj* незако́нный; незаконноро́жденный.

**illicit** *adj* незако́нный, недозво́ленный.

**illiteracy** *n* негра́мотность. **illiterate** *adj* негра́мотный.

**illness** *n* боле́знь.

**illogical** *adj* нелоги́чный.

**illuminate** *vt* освеща́ть *impf*, освети́ть *pf*. **illumination** *n* освеще́ние.

**illusion** *n* иллю́зия. **illusory** *adj* иллюзо́рный.

**illustrate** *vt* иллюстри́ровать *impf* & *pf*, про-~ *pf*. **illustration** *n* иллюстра́ция. **illustrative** *adj* иллюстрати́вный. **illustrious** *adj* знамени́тый.

**image** *n* (*phys; statue etc.*) изображе́ние; (*optical* ~) отраже́ние; (*likeness*) ко́пия; (*metaphor; conception*) о́браз; (*reputation*) репута́ция. **imagery** *n* о́бразность.

**imaginable** *adj* вообража́емый. **imaginary** *adj* вообража́емый. **imagination** *n* воображе́ние. **imagine** *vt* вообража́ть *impf*, вообрази́ть *pf*; (*conceive*) представля́ть *impf*, предста́вить *pf* себе́.

**imbecile** *n* слабоу́мный *sb*; (*fool*) глупе́ц.

imbibe *vt* (*absorb*) впи́тывать *impf*, впита́ть *pf*.

imbue *vt* внуша́ть *impf*, внуши́ть *pf* +*dat* (with +*acc*).

imitate *vt* подража́ть *impf* +*dat*. imitation *n* подража́ние (of +*dat*); *attrib* иску́сственный. imitative *adj* подража́тельный.

immaculate *adj* безупре́чный.

immaterial *adj* (*unimportant*) несуще́ственный.

immature *adj* незре́лый.

immeasurable *adj* неизмери́мый.

immediate *adj* (*direct*) непосре́дственный; (*swift*) неме́дленный. immediately *adv* то́тчас, сра́зу.

immemorial *adj*: from time ~ с незапа́мятных времён.

immense *adj* огро́мный.

immerse *vt* погружа́ть *impf*, погрузи́ть *pf*. immersion *n* погруже́ние.

immigrant *n* иммигра́нт, ~ка. immigration *n* имвигра́ция.

imminent *adj* надвига́ющийся; (*danger*) грозя́щий.

immobile *adj* неподви́жный. immobilize *vt* парализова́ть *impf* & *pf*.

immoderate *adj* неуме́ренный.

immodest *adj* нескро́мный.

immoral *adj* безнра́вственный. immorality *n* безнра́вственность.

immortal *adj* бессме́ртный. immortality *n* бессме́ртие. immortalize *vt* обессме́ртить *pf*.

immovable *adj* неподви́жный; (*fig*) непоколеби́мый.

immune *adj* (*to illness*) невоспри́мчивый (to к+*dat*); (*free from*) свобо́дный (from от+*gen*). immunity *n* имму-

нитéт (from к+*dat*); освобожде́ние (from от+*gen*). immunize *vt* иммунизи́ровать *impf* & *pf*.

immutable *adj* неизме́нный.

imp *n* бесёнок.

impact *n* уда́р; (*fig*) влия́ние.

impair *vt* вреди́ть *impf*, по~ *pf*.

impale *vt* протыка́ть *impf*, проткну́ть *pf*.

impart *vt* дели́ться *impf*, по~ *pf* +*instr* (to c+*instr*).

impartial *adj* беспристра́стный.

impassable *adj* непроходи́мый; (*for vehicles*) непрое́зжий.

impasse *n* тупи́к.

impassioned *adj* стра́стный.

impassive *adj* бесстра́стный.

impatience *n* нетерпе́ние. impatient *adj* нетерпели́вый.

impeach *vt* обвиня́ть *impf*, обвини́ть *pf* (for в+*prep*).

impeccable *adj* безупре́чный.

impecunious *adj* безде́нежный.

impedance *n* по́лное сопротивле́ние. impede *vt* препя́тствовать *impf*, вос~ *pf* +*dat*. impediment *n* препя́тствие; (*in speech*) заика́ние.

impel *vt* побужда́ть *impf*, побуди́ть *pf* (to +*inf*, к+*dat*).

impending *adj* предстоя́щий.

impenetrable *adj* непроница́емый.

imperative *adj* необходи́мый; *n* (*gram*) повели́тельное накло́нение.

imperceptible *adj* незаме́тный.

imperfect *n* имперфе́кт; *adj* несоверше́нный. imperfection *n* несоверше́нство; (*fault*) недоста́ток. imperfective (*n*) несоверше́нный (вид).

imperial *adj* импе́рский.

**imperialism** n империали́зм.
**imperialist** n империали́ст;
*attrib* империалисти́ческий.
**imperil** vt подверга́ть impf,
подве́ргнуть pf опа́сности.
**imperious** adj вла́стный.
**impersonal** adj безли́чный.
**impersonate** vt (*imitate*) подража́ть impf; (*pretend to be*)
выдава́ть impf, вы́дать pf
себя́ за+acc. **impersonation**
n подража́ние.
**impertinence** n де́рзость. **impertinent** adj де́рзкий.
**imperturbable** adj невозмути́мый.
**impervious** adj (*fig*) глухо́й
(**to** к+dat).
**impetuous** adj стреми́тельный.
**impetus** n дви́жущая си́ла.
**impinge** vi: ~ (**up**)**on** ока́зывать impf, оказа́ть pf (отрица́тельный) эффе́кт на+acc.
**implacable** adj неумоли́мый.
**implant** vt вводи́ть impf,
ввести́ pf; (*fig*) се́ять impf,
по~ pf.
**implement**¹ n ору́дие, инструме́нт.
**implement**² vt (*fulfil*) выполня́ть impf, вы́полнить pf.
**implicate** vt впу́тывать impf,
впу́тать pf. **implication** n (*inference*) намёк; pl значе́ние.
**implicit** adj подразумева́емый;
(*absolute*) безоговоро́чный.
**implore** vt умоля́ть impf.
**imply** vt подразумева́ть impf.
**impolite** adj неве́жливый.
**imponderable** adj неопределённый.
**import** n (*meaning*) значе́ние;
(*of goods*) и́мпорт; vt импорти́ровать impf & pf. **importer** n импортёр.
**importance** n ва́жность. **im-**

**portant** adj ва́жный.
**impose** vt (*tax*) облага́ть impf,
обложи́ть pf +instr (**on** +acc);
(*obligation*) налага́ть impf,
наложи́ть pf (**on** на+acc);
~ **on** налега́ть impf
на+acc. **imposing** adj внуши́тельный. **imposition** n
обложе́ние, наложе́ние.
**impossibility** n невозмо́жность. **impossible** adj невозмо́жный.
**impostor** n самозва́нец.
**impotence** n бесси́лие; (*med*)
импоте́нция. **impotent** adj
бесси́льный; (*med*) импоте́нтный.
**impound** vt (*confiscate*) конфискова́ть impf & pf.
**impoverished** adj обедне́вший.
**impracticable** adj невыполни́мый.
**imprecise** n нето́чный.
**impregnable** adj непристу́пный.
**impregnate** vt (*fertilize*) оплодотворя́ть impf, оплодотвори́ть pf; (*saturate*) пропи́тывать impf, пропита́ть pf.
**impresario** n аге́нт.
**impress** vt производи́ть impf,
произвести́ pf (како́е-либо)
впечатле́ние на+acc; ~ **upon**
(*s.o.*) внуша́ть impf, внуши́ть
pf (+dat). **impression** n впечатле́ние; (*imprint*) отпеча́ток; (*reprint*) (стереоти́пное) изда́ние.
**impressionism** n импрессиони́зм. **impressionist** n импрессиони́ст.
**impressive** adj впечатля́ющий.
**imprint** n отпеча́ток; vt отпеча́тывать impf, отпеча́тать
pf; (**on** *memory*) запеча́т-

вать *impf*, запечатлéть *pf*.

**imprison** *vt* заключáть *impf*, заключи́ть *pf* (в тюрьму́).
**imprisonment** *n* тюрéмное заключéние.

**improbable** *adj* невероя́тный.
**impromptu** *adj* импровизи́рованный; *adv* без подгото́вки, экспро́мтом.

**improper** *adj* (*incorrect*) непра́вильный; (*indecent*) неприли́чный. **impropriety** *n* неумéстность.

**improve** *vt & i* улучшáть(ся) *impf*, улу́чшить(ся) *pf*. **improvement** *n* улучшéние.

**improvisation** *n* импровизáция. **improvise** *vt & i* импровизи́ровать *impf*, сымпровизи́ровать *pf*.

**imprudent** *adj* неосторóжный.
**impudence** *n* нáглость. **impudent** *adj* нáглый.

**impulse** *n* толчóк, и́мпульс; (*sudden tendency*) порýв. **impulsive** *adj* импульси́вный.

**impunity** *n*: with ~ безнакáзанно.

**impure** *adj* нечи́стый.

**impute** *vt* припи́сывать *impf*, приписáть *pf* (**to** +*dat*).

**in** *prep* (*place*) в+*prep*, на+*prep*; (*into*) в+*acc*, на+*acc*; (*point in time*) в+*prep*, на+*prep*; **in the morning** (*etc.*) ýтром (*instr*); **in spring** (*etc.*) веснóй (*instr*); (*at some time*; *throughout*) во врéмя +*gen*; (*duration*) за+*acc*; (*after interval of*) чéрез+*acc*; (*during course of*) в течéние+*gen*; (*circumstance*) в+*prep*, при+*prep*; *adv* (*place*) внутри́; (*motion*) внутрь; (*at home*) дóма; (*in fashion*) в мóде; **in here, there** (*place*) здесь, там; (*motion*) сюдá, тудá; *adj* внýтренний; (*fash-*

*ionable*) мóдный; *n*: **the ins and outs** все ходы́ и вы́ходы.

**inability** *n* неспосóбность.
**inaccessible** *adj* недосту́пный.
**inaccurate** *adj* нетóчный.
**inaction** *n* бездéйствие. **inactive** *adj* бездéйственный. **inactivity** *n* бездéйственность.
**inadequate** *adj* недостáточный.
**inadmissible** *adj* недопусти́мый.
**inadvertent** *adj* нечáянный.
**inalienable** *adj* неотъéмлемый.
**inane** *adj* глýпый.
**inanimate** *adj* неодушевлённый.
**inappropriate** *adj* неумéстный.
**inarticulate** *adj* (*person*) косноязы́чный; (*indistinct*) невня́тный.
**inasmuch** *adv*: ~ **as** так как; ввидý тогó, что.
**inattentive** *adj* невнимáтельный.
**inaudible** *adj* неслы́шный.
**inaugural** *adj* вступи́тельный. **inaugurate** *vt* (*admit to office*) торжéственно вводи́ть *impf*, ввести́ *pf* в дóлжность; (*open*) открывáть *impf*, откры́ть *pf*; (*introduce*) вводи́ть *impf*, ввести́ *pf*. **inauguration** *n* введéние в дóлжность; откры́тие; начáло.
**inauspicious** *adj* неблагоприя́тный.
**inborn, inbred** *adj* врождённый.
**incalculable** *adj* неисчисли́мый.
**incandescent** *adj* накалённый.
**incantation** *n* заклинáние.
**incapability** *n* неспосóбность. **incapable** *adj* неспосóбный (**of** к+*dat*, на+*acc*).

incapacitate *vt* де́лать *impf*, с~ *pf* неспосо́бным. **incapacity** *n* неспосо́бность.

incarcerate *vt* заключа́ть *impf*, заключи́ть *pf* (в тюрьму́). **incarceration** *n* заключе́ние (в тюрьму́).

incarnate *adj* воплощённый. **incarnation** *n* воплоще́ние.

incendiary *adj* зажига́тельный.

incense¹ *n* фимиа́м, ла́дан.

incense² *vt* разгнева́ть *pf*.

incentive *n* побужде́ние.

inception *n* нача́ло.

incessant *adj* непреста́нный.

incest *n* кровосмеше́ние.

inch *n* дюйм; ~ by ~ ма́ло-пома́лу; *vi* ползти́ *impf*.

incidence *n* (*phys*) паде́ние; (*prevalence*) распростране́ние. **incident** *n* слу́чай, инциде́нт. **incidental** *adj* (*casual*) случа́йный; (*inessential*) несуще́ственный. **incidentally** *adv* ме́жду про́чим.

incinerate *vt* испепеля́ть *impf*, испепели́ть *pf*. **incinerator** *n* мусоросжига́тельная печь.

incipient *adj* начина́ющийся.

incision *n* надре́з (*in* на+*acc*). **incisive** *adj* (*fig*) о́стрый. **incisor** *n* резе́ц.

incite *vt* подстрека́ть *impf*, подстрекну́ть *pf* (to к+*dat*). **incitement** *n* подстрека́тельство.

inclement *adj* суро́вый.

inclination *n* (*slope*) накло́н; (*propensity*) скло́нность (for, to к+*dat*). **incline** *n* накло́н; *vt* & *i* склоня́ть(ся) *impf*, склони́ть(ся) *pf*. **inclined** *predic* (*disposed*) скло́нен (-о́нна́, -о́нно) (to к+*dat*).

include *vt* включа́ть *impf*, включи́ть *pf* (in в+*acc*); (*con-*

tain) заключа́ть *impf*, заключи́ть *pf* в себе́. **inclusion** *n* включе́ние. **inclusive** *adj* включа́ющий (в себе́); *adv* включи́тельно.

incognito *adv* инко́гнито.

incoherent *adj* бессвя́зный.

income *n* дохо́д; ~ tax подохо́дный нало́г.

incommensurate *adj* несоразме́рный.

incomparable *adj* несравни́мый (to, with с+*instr*); (*matchless*) несравне́нный.

incompatible *adj* несовмести́мый.

incompetence *n* некомпете́нтность. **incompetent** *adj* некомпете́нтный.

incomplete *adj* непо́лный, незако́нченный.

incomprehensible *adj* непоня́тный.

inconceivable *adj* невообрази́мый.

inconclusive *adj* (*evidence*) недоста́точный; (*results*) неопределённый.

incongruity *n* несоотве́тствие. **incongruous** *adj* несоотве́тствующий.

inconsequential *adj* незначи́тельный.

inconsiderable *adj* незначи́тельный.

inconsiderate *adj* невнима́тельный.

inconsistency *n* непосле́довательность. **inconsistent** *adj* непосле́довательный.

inconsolable *adj* безуте́шный.

inconspicuous *adj* незаме́тный.

incontinence *n* (*med*) недержа́ние. **incontinent** *adj*: be ~ страда́ть *impf* недержа́нием.

**incontrovertible** *adj* неопровержи́мый.

**inconvenience** *n* неудо́бство; *vt* затрудня́ть *impf*, затрудни́ть *pf*. **inconvenient** *adj* неудо́бный.

**incorporate** *vt* (*include*) включа́ть *impf*, включи́ть *pf*; (*unite*) объединя́ть *impf*, объедини́ть *pf*.

**incorrect** *adj* непра́вильный.

**incorrigible** *adj* неисправи́мый.

**incorruptible** *adj* неподку́пный.

**increase** *n* рост, увеличе́ние; (*in pay etc.*) приба́вка; *vt & i* увели́чивать(ся) *impf*, увели́чить(ся) *pf*.

**incredible** *adj* невероя́тный.

**incredulous** *adj* недове́рчивый.

**increment** *n* приба́вка.

**incriminate** *vt* изоблича́ть *impf*, изобличи́ть *pf*.

**incubate** *vt* (*eggs*) выводи́ть *impf*, вы́вести *pf* (в инкуба́торе). **incubator** *n* инкуба́тор.

**inculcate** *vt* внедря́ть *impf*, внедри́ть *pf*.

**incumbent** *adj* (*in office*) стоя́щий у вла́сти; **it is** ~ (**up**)**on you** вы обя́заны.

**incur** *vt* навлека́ть *impf*, навле́чь *pf* на себя́.

**incurable** *adj* неизлечи́мый.

**incursion** *n* (*invasion*) вторже́ние; (*attack*) набе́г.

**indebted** *predic* в долгу́ (**to** у+*gen*).

**indecency** *n* неприли́чие. **indecent** *adj* неприли́чный.

**indecision** *n* нереши́тельность. **indecisive** *adj* нереши́тельный.

**indeclinable** *adj* несклоня́емый.

**indeed** *adv* в са́мом де́ле, действи́тельно; (*interrog*) неуже́ли?

**indefatigable** *adj* неутоми́мый.

**indefensible** *adj* не име́ющий оправда́ния.

**indefinable** *adj* неопредели́мый. **indefinite** *adj* неопределённый.

**indelible** *adj* несмыва́емый.

**indemnify** *vt:* ~ **against** страхова́ть *impf*, за~ *pf* от+*gen*; ~ **for** (*compensate*) компенси́ровать *impf* & *pf*. **indemnity** *n* (*against loss*) гара́нтия от убы́тков; (*compensation*) компенса́ция.

**indent** *vt* (*printing*) писа́ть *impf*, с~ *pf* с отсту́пом. **indentation** *n* (*notch*) зубе́ц; (*printing*) о́тступ.

**independence** *n* незави́симость, самостоя́тельность. **independent** *adj* незави́симый, самостоя́тельный.

**indescribable** *adj* неопису́емый.

**indestructible** *adj* неразруши́мый.

**indeterminate** *adj* неопределённый.

**index** *n* (*alphabetical*) указа́тель *m*; (*econ*) и́ндекс; (*pointer*) стре́лка; ~ **finger** указа́тельный па́лец.

**India** *n* И́ндия. **Indian** *n* инди́ец, индиа́нка; (*American*) инде́ец, индиа́нка; *adj* инди́йский; (*American*) инде́йский; ~ **summer** ба́бье ле́то.

**indicate** *vt* ука́зывать *impf*, указа́ть *pf*; (*be a sign of*) свиде́тельствовать *impf* о+*prep*. **indication** *n* указа́ние; (*sign*) при́знак. **indicative** *adj* ука́зывающий; (*gram*) изъяви́тельный; *n* изъяви́тельное наклоне́ние. **indicator** *n* указа́тель *m*.

**indict** *vt* обвиня́ть *impf*, обвини́ть *pf* (**for** в+*prep*).

**indifference** *n* равноду́шие. **indifferent** *adj* равноду́шный; (*mediocre*) посре́дственный.

**indigenous** *adj* тузе́мный.

**indigestible** *adj* неудобовари́мый. **indigestion** *n* несваре́ние желу́дка.

**indignant** *adj* негоду́ющий; **be ~** негодова́ть *impf* (**with** на+*acc*). **indignation** *n* негодова́ние.

**indignity** *n* оскорбле́ние.

**indirect** *adj* непрямо́й; (*econ; gram*) ко́свенный.

**indiscreet** *adj* нескро́мный. **indiscretion** *n* нескро́мность. **indiscriminate** *adj* неразбо́рчивый. **indiscriminately** *adv* без разбо́ра.

**indispensible** *adj* необходи́мый.

**indisposed** *predic* (*unwell*) нездоро́в.

**indisputable** *adj* бесспо́рный.

**indistinct** *adj* нея́сный.

**indistinguishable** *adj* неразличи́мый.

**individual** *n* ли́чность; *adj* индивидуа́льный. **individualism** *n* индивидуали́зм. **individualist** *n* индивидуали́ст. **individualistic** *adj* индивидуалисти́ческий. **individuality** *n* индивидуа́льность.

**indivisible** *adj* недели́мый.

**indoctrinate** *vt* внуша́ть *impf*, внуши́ть *pf*+*dat* (**with** +*acc*).

**indolence** *n* ле́ность. **indolent** *adj* лени́вый.

**indomitable** *adj* неукроти́мый.

**Indonesia** *n* Индоне́зия.

**indoor** *adj* ко́мнатный. **indoors** *adv* (*position*) в до́ме; (*motion*) в дом.

**induce** *vt* (*prevail on*) убежда́ть *impf*, убеди́ть *pf*; (*bring about*) вызыва́ть *impf*, вы́звать *pf*. **inducement** *n* побужде́ние.

**induction** *n* (*logic, electr*) инду́кция; (*in post*) введе́ние в до́лжность.

**indulge** *vt* потво́рствовать *impf*+*dat*; *vi* предава́ться *impf*, преда́ться *pf* (**in** +*dat*). **indulgence** *n* потво́рство; (*tolerance*) снисходи́тельность. **indulgent** *adj* снисходи́тельный.

**industrial** *adj* промы́шленный. **industrialist** *n* промы́шленник. **industrious** *adj* трудолюби́вый. **industry** *n* промы́шленность; (*zeal*) трудолю́бие.

**inebriated** *adj* пья́ный.

**inedible** *adj* несъедо́бный.

**ineffective, ineffectual** *adj* безрезульта́тный; (*person*) неспосо́бный.

**inefficiency** *n* неэффекти́вность. **inefficient** *adj* неэффекти́вный.

**ineligible** *adj* не име́ющий пра́во (**for** на+*acc*).

**inept** *adj* неуме́лый.

**inequality** *n* нера́венство.

**inert** *adj* ине́ртный. **inertia** *adj* (*phys*) ине́рция; (*sluggishness*) ине́ртность.

**inescapable** *adj* неизбе́жный.

**inevitability** *n* неизбе́жность. **inevitable** *adj* неизбе́жный.

**inexact** *adj* нето́чный.

**inexcusable** *adj* непрости́тельный.

**inexhaustible** *adj* неистощи́мый.

inexorable *adj* неумоли́мый.

inexpensive *adj* недорого́й.

inexperience *n* нео́пытность. inexperienced *adj* нео́пытный.

inexplicable *adj* необъясни́мый.

infallible *adj* непогреши́мый.

infamous *adj* позо́рный. infamy *n* позо́р.

infancy *n* младе́нчество. infant *n* младе́нец. infantile *adj* де́тский.

infantry *n* пехо́та.

infatuate *vt* вскружи́ть *pf* го́лову +*dat*. infatuation *n* увлече́ние.

infect *vt* заража́ть *impf*, зарази́ть *pf* (with +*instr*). infection *n* зара́за, инфе́кция. infectious *adj* зара́зный; (*fig*) заразительный.

infer *vt* заключа́ть *impf*, заключи́ть *pf*. inference *n* заключе́ние.

inferior *adj* (in rank) ни́зший; (in quality) ху́дший, плохо́й; *n* подчинённый *sb*. inferiority *n* бо́лее ни́зкое ка́чество; ~ complex ко́мплекс неполноце́нности.

infernal *adj* а́дский. inferno *n* ад.

infertile *adj* неплодоро́дный.

infested *adj*: be ~ with кише́ть *impf* +*instr*.

infidelity *n* неве́рность.

infiltrate *vt* постепе́нно проника́ть *impf*, прони́кнуть *pf* в+*acc*.

infinite *adj* бесконе́чный. infinitesimal *adj* бесконе́чно ма́лый. infinitive *n* инфинити́в. infinity *n* бесконе́чность.

infirm *adj* не́мощный. infirmary *n* больни́ца. infirmity *n* не́мощь.

inflame *vt & i* (excite) возбужда́ть(ся) *impf*, возбуди́ть(ся) *pf*; (med) воспаля́ть(ся) *impf*, воспали́ть(ся) *pf*. inflammable *adj* огнеопа́сный. inflammation *n* воспале́ние. inflammatory *adj* подстрека́тельский.

inflate *vt* надува́ть *impf*, наду́ть *pf*. inflation *n* (econ) инфля́ция.

inflection *n* (gram) фле́ксия.

inflexible *adj* неги́бкий; (fig) непрекло́нный.

inflict *vt* (blow) наноси́ть *impf*, нанести́ *pf* ((up)on +*dat*); (suffering) причиня́ть *impf*, причини́ть *pf* ((up)on +*dat*); (penalty) налага́ть *impf*, наложи́ть *pf* ((up)on на+*acc*) ~ o.s. (up)on навя́зываться *impf*, навяза́ться *pf* +*dat*.

inflow *n* втека́ние, прито́к.

influence *n* влия́ние; *vt* влия́ть *impf*, по~ *pf* на+*acc*. influential *adj* влия́тельный.

influenza *n* грипп.

influx *n* (fig) напли́в.

inform *vt* сообща́ть *impf*, сообщи́ть *pf* +*dat* (about +*acc*, о+*prep*); *vi* доноси́ть *impf*, донести́ *pf* (against на+*acc*).

informal *adj* (unofficial) неофициа́льный; (casual) обы́денный.

informant *n* осведоми́тель *m*.

information *n* информа́ция. informative *adj* поучи́тельный. informer *n* доно́счик.

infra-red *adj* инфракра́сный.

infrequent *adj* ре́дкий.

infringe *vt* (violate) наруша́ть *impf*, нару́шить *pf*; *vi*: ~ (up)on посяга́ть *impf*, посягну́ть *pf* на+*acc*. infringement *n* наруше́ние; посяга́тельство.

**infuriate** vt разъяря́ть impf, разъяри́ть pf.

**infuse** vt (fig) внуша́ть impf, внуши́ть pf (into +dat). **infusion** n (fig) внуше́ние; (herbs etc) насто́й.

**ingenious** adj изобрета́тельный. **ingenuity** n изобрета́тельность.

**ingenuous** adj бесхи́тростный.

**ingot** n сли́ток.

**ingrained** adj закорене́лый.

**ingratiate** vt ~ o.s. вкра́дываться impf, вкра́сться pf в ми́лость (with +dat).

**ingratitude** n неблагода́рность.

**ingredient** n ингредие́нт, составля́ющее sb.

**inhabit** vt жить impf в, на, +prep; обита́ть impf в, на, +prep. **inhabitant** n жи́тель m, ~ница.

**inhalation** n вдыха́ние. **inhale** vt вдыха́ть impf, вдохну́ть pf.

**inherent** adj прису́щий (in +dat).

**inherit** vt насле́довать impf & pf, y~ pf. **inheritance** n насле́дство.

**inhibit** vt стесня́ть impf, стесни́ть pf. **inhibited** adj стесни́тельный. **inhibition** n стесне́ние.

**inhospitable** adj негостепри-и́мный; (fig) недружелю́бный.

**inhuman(e)** adj бесчелове́чный.

**inimical** adj вражде́бный; (harmful) вре́дный.

**inimitable** adj неподража́емый.

**iniquity** n несправедли́вость.

**initial** adj (перво)нача́льный; n нача́льная бу́ква; pl ини-циа́лы m pl; vt ста́вить impf, по~ pf инициа́лы на+acc.

**initially** adv в нача́ле.

**initiate** vt вводи́ть impf, ввести́ pf (into в+acc). **initiation** n введе́ние.

**initiative** n инициати́ва.

**inject** vt вводи́ть impf, ввести́ pf (person +dat, substance +acc). **injection** n уко́л; (fig) инъе́кция.

**injunction** n (law) суде́бный запре́т.

**injure** vt поврежда́ть impf, повреди́ть pf. **injury** n ра́на.

**injustice** n несправедли́вость.

**ink** n черни́ла (-л).

**inkling** n представле́ние.

**inland** adj вну́тренний; adv (motion) внутрь страны́; (place) внутри́ страны́; I-Revenue управле́ние нало́говых сбо́ров.

**in-laws** n pl ро́дственники m pl супру́га, -ги.

**inlay** n инкруста́ция; vt инкрусти́ровать impf & pf.

**inlet** n (of sea) у́зкий зали́в.

**inmate** n (prison) заключ-ённый sb; (hospital) больно́й sb.

**inn** n гости́ница.

**innate** adj врождённый.

**inner** adj вну́тренний. **innermost** adj глубоча́йший; (fig) сокрове́ннейший.

**innocence** n неви́нность; (guiltlessness) невино́вность. **innocent** adj неви́нный; (not guilty) невино́вный (of в+prep).

**innocuous** adj безвре́дный.

**innovate** vi вводи́ть impf, ввести́ pf но́вшества. **innovation** n нововведе́ние. **innovative** adj нова́торский. **innovator** n нова́тор.

**innuendo** *n* намёк, инсинуа́ция.

**innumerable** *adj* бесчи́сленный.

**inoculate** *vt* привива́ть *impf*, приви́ть *pf* +*dat* (**against** +*acc*). **inoculation** *n* приви́вка.

**inoffensive** *adj* безоби́дный.

**inopportune** *adj* несвоевре́менный.

**inordinate** *adj* чрезме́рный.

**inorganic** *adj* неоргани́ческий.

**in-patient** *n* стациона́рный больно́й *sb*.

**input** *n* ввод.

**inquest** *n* суде́бное сле́дствие, дозна́ние.

**inquire** *vt* спра́шивать *impf*, спроси́ть *pf*; *vi* справля́ться *impf*, спра́виться *pf* (**about** о+*prep*); рассле́довать *impf* & *pf* (**into** +*acc*). **inquiry** *n* вопро́с, спра́вка; (*investigation*) рассле́дование.

**inquisition** *n* инквизи́ция. **inquisitive** *adj* пытли́вый, любозна́тельный.

**inroad** *n* (*attack*) набе́г; (*fig*) посяга́тельство (**on**, **into** на+*acc*).

**insane** *adj* безу́мный. **insanity** *n* безу́мие.

**insatiable** *adj* ненасы́тный.

**inscribe** *vt* надпи́сывать *impf*, надписа́ть *pf*; (*engrave*) выреза́ть *impf*, вы́резать *pf*. **inscription** *n* на́дпись.

**inscrutable** *adj* непостижи́мый, непроница́емый.

**insect** *n* насеко́мое *sb*. **insecticide** *n* инсектици́д.

**insecure** *adj* (*unsafe*) небезопа́сный; (*not confident*) неуве́ренный (в себе́).

**insemination** *n* оплодотворе́ние.

**insensible** *adj* (*unconscious*) потеря́вший созна́ние.

**insensitive** *adj* нечувстви́тельный.

**inseparable** *adj* неотдели́мый; (*people*) неразлу́чный.

**insert** *vt* вставля́ть *impf*, вста́вить *pf*; вкла́дывать *impf*, вложи́ть *pf*; (*coin*) опуска́ть *impf*, опусти́ть *pf*. **insertion** *n* (*inserting*) вставле́ние, вкла́дывание; (*thing inserted*) вста́вка.

**inshore** *adj* прибре́жный; *adv* бли́зко к бе́регу.

**inside** *n* вну́тренняя часть; *pl* (*anat*) вну́тренности *f pl*; **turn ~ out** вывёртывать *impf*, вы́вернуть *pf* наизна́нку; *adj* вну́тренний; *adv* (*place*) внутри́; (*motion*) внутрь; *prep* (*place*) внутри́+*gen*, в+*prep*; (*motion*) внутрь+*gen*, в+*acc*.

**insidious** *adj* кова́рный.

**insight** *n* проница́тельность.

**insignia** *n* зна́ки *m pl* разли́чия.

**insignificant** *adj* незначи́тельный.

**insincere** *adj* нейскренний.

**insinuate** *vt* (*hint*) намека́ть *impf*, намекну́ть *pf* на+*acc*. **insinuation** *n* инсинуа́ция.

**insipid** *adj* пре́сный.

**insist** *vt* & *i* наста́ивать *impf*, настоя́ть *pf* (**on** на+*prep*). **insistence** *n* насто́йчивость. **insistent** *adj* насто́йчивый.

**insolence** *n* на́глость. **insolent** *adj* на́глый.

**insoluble** *adj* (*problem*) неразреши́мый; (*in liquid*) нераствори́мый.

**insolvent** *adj* несостоя́тельный.

**insomnia** *n* бессо́нница.

**inspect** *vt* инспекти́ровать *impf*, про– *pf*. **inspection** *n* инспе́кция. **inspector** n инспе́ктор; (ticket ~) контролёр.

**inspiration** n вдохнове́ние. **inspire** vt вдохновля́ть impf, вдохнови́ть pf; внуша́ть impf, внуши́ть pf +dat (with +acc).

**instability** n неусто́йчивость; (of character) неуравнове́шенность.

**install** vt (person in office) вводи́ть impf, ввести́ pf в до́лжность; (apparatus) устана́вливать impf, установи́ть pf. **installation** n введе́ние в до́лжность; установка; pl сооруже́ния neut pl.

**instalment** n (comm) взнос; (publication) вы́пуск; часть; by ~s в рассро́чку.

**instance** n (example) приме́р; (case) слу́чай; for ~ наприме́р.

**instant** n мгнове́ние, моме́нт; adj неме́дленный; (coffee etc.) раствори́мый. **instantaneous** adj мгнове́нный. **instantly** adv неме́дленно, то́тчас.

**instead** adv вме́сто (of +gen); ~ of going вме́сто того́, что́бы пойти́.

**instep** n подъём.

**instigate** vt подстрека́ть impf, подстрекну́ть pf (to к+dat). **instigation** n подстрека́тельство. **instigator** n подстрека́тель m, ~ница.

**instil** vt (ideas etc.) внуша́ть impf, внуши́ть pf (into +dat).

**instinct** n инсти́нкт. **instinctive** adj инстинкти́вный.

**institute** n институ́т; vt (establish) устана́вливать impf, установи́ть pf; (introduce) вводи́ть impf, ввести́ pf; (reforms) проводи́ть impf, про-

вести́ pf. **institution** n учрежде́ние.

**instruct** vt (teach) обуча́ть impf, обучи́ть pf (in +dat); (inform) сообща́ть impf, сообщи́ть pf +dat; (command) прика́зывать impf, приказа́ть pf +dat. **instruction** n (in pl) инстру́кция; (teaching) обуче́ние. **instructive** adj поучи́тельный. **instructor** n инстру́ктор.

**instrument** n ору́дие, инструме́нт. **instrumental** adj (mus) инструмента́льный; (gram) твори́тельный; be ~ in спосо́бствовать impf, по~ pf +dat; n (gram) твори́тельный паде́ж. **instrumentation** n (mus) инструменто́вка.

**insubordinate** adj неподчиня́ющийся.

**insufferable** adj невыноси́мый.

**insular** adj (fig) ограни́ченный.

**insulate** vt изоли́ровать impf & pf. **insulation** n изоля́ция. **insulator** n изоля́тор.

**insulin** n инсули́н.

**insult** n оскорбле́ние; vt оскорбля́ть impf, оскорби́ть pf. **insulting** adj оскорби́тельный.

**insuperable** adj непреодоли́мый.

**insurance** n страхова́ние; attrib страхово́й. **insure** vt страхова́ть impf, за~ pf (against от+gen).

**insurgent** n повста́нец.

**insurmountable** adj непреодоли́мый.

**insurrection** n восста́ние.

**intact** adj це́лый.

**intake** n (of persons) набо́р; (consumption) потребле́ние.

**intangible** adj неосязаемый.
**integral** adj неотъемлемый.
**integrate** vt & i интегрироваться impf & pf. **integration** n интеграция.
**integrity** n (honesty) честность.
**intellect** n интеллект. **intellectual** n интеллигент; adj интеллектуальный.
**intelligence** n (intellect) ум; (information) сведения neut pl; (~ service) разведка. **intelligent** adj умный.
**intelligentsia** n интеллигенция.
**intelligible** adj понятный.
**intemperate** adj невоздержанный.
**intend** vt собираться impf, собраться pf; (design) предназначать impf, предназначить pf (for для+gen, на+acc).
**intense** adj сильный. **intensify** vt & i усиливать(ся) impf, усилить(ся) pf. **intensity** n интенсивность, сила.
**intensive** adj интенсивный.
**intent** n намерение; adj (resolved) стремящийся (on к+dat); (occupied) погружённый (on в+acc); (earnest) внимательный. **intention** n намерение. **intentional** adj намеренный.
**inter** vt хоронить impf, по~ pf.
**interact** vi взаимодействовать impf. **interaction** n взаимодействие.
**intercede** vi ходатайствовать impf, по~ pf (for за+acc; with перед+instr).
**intercept** vt перехватывать impf, перехватить pf. **interception** n перехват.
**interchange** n обмен (of +instr); (junction) транспорт-

ная развязка; vt обмениваться impf, обменяться pf +instr. **interchangeable** adj взаимозаменяемый.
**inter-city** adj междугородный.
**intercom** n внутренняя телефонная связь.
**interconnected** adj взаимосвязанный. **interconnection** n взаимосвязь.
**intercourse** n (social) общение; (trade; sexual) сношения neut pl.
**interdisciplinary** adj межотраслевой.
**interest** n интерес (in к+dat); (econ) проценты m pl; vt интересовать impf; (~ person in) заинтересовывать impf, заинтересовать pf (in +instr); **be ~ed in** интересоваться impf +instr. **interesting** adj интересный.
**interfere** vi вмешиваться impf, вмешаться pf (in в+acc). **interference** n вмешательство; (radio) помехи f pl.
**interim** n: **in the ~** тем временем; adj промежуточный; (temporary) временный.
**interior** n (of building) интерьер; (of object) внутренность; adj внутренний.
**interjection** n восклицание; (gram) междометие.
**interlock** vt & i сцеплять(ся) impf, сцепить(ся) pf.
**interloper** n незваный гость m.
**interlude** n (theat) антракт; (mus, fig) интерлюдия.
**intermediary** n посредник.
**intermediate** adj промежуточный.
**interminable** adj бесконечный.
**intermission** n (theat) антракт.
**intermittent** adj прерывистый.

**intern** vt интерни́ровать impf & pf.

**internal** adj вну́тренний; ~ **combustion engine** дви́гатель m вну́треннего сгора́ния.

**international** adj междунаро́дный; n (contest) междунаро́дные состяза́ния neut pl.

**internment** n интерни́рование.

**interplay** n взаимоде́йствие.

**interpret** vt (explain) толкова́ть impf; (understand) истолко́вывать impf, истолкова́ть pf; vi переводи́ть impf, перевести́ pf. **interpretation** n толкова́ние. **interpreter** n перево́дчик, -ица.

**interrelated** adj взаимосвя́занный. **interrelationship** n взаи́мная связь.

**interrogate** vt допра́шивать impf, допроси́ть pf. **interrogation** n допро́с. **interrogative** adj вопроси́тельный.

**interrupt** vt прерыва́ть impf, прерва́ть pf. **interruption** n переры́в.

**intersect** vt & vi пересека́ть(ся) impf, пересе́чь(ся) pf. **intersection** n пересече́ние.

**intersperse** vt (scatter) рассыпа́ть impf, рассы́пать pf. (between, among ме́жду+instr, среди́+gen).

**intertwine** vt & i переплета́ть(ся) impf, переплести́(сь) pf.

**interval** n интерва́л; (theat) антра́кт.

**intervene** vi (occur) происходи́ть impf, произойти́ pf; ~ **in** вме́шиваться impf, вмеша́ться pf в+acc. **intervention** n вмеша́тельство; (polit) интерве́нция.

**interview** n интервью́ neut

indecl; vt интервьюи́ровать impf & pf, про~ pf. **interviewer** n интервьюе́р.

**interweave** vt вотка́ть pf.

**intestate** adj без завеща́ния.

**intestine** n кишка́; pl кише́чник.

**intimacy** n инти́мность. **intimate¹** adj инти́мный.

**intimate²** vt (hint) намека́ть impf, намекну́ть pf на+acc.

**intimation** n намёк.

**intimidate** vt запу́гивать impf, запуга́ть pf.

**into** prep в, во+acc, на+acc.

**intolerable** adj невыноси́мый.

**intolerance** n нетерпи́мость. **intolerant** adj нетерпи́мый.

**intonation** n интона́ция.

**intoxicated** adj пья́ный. **intoxication** n опьяне́ние.

**intractable** adj неподатли́вый.

**intransigent** adj непримири́мый.

**intransitive** adj непереходный.

**intrepid** adj неустраши́мый.

**intricacy** n запу́танность. **intricate** adj запу́танный.

**intrigue** n интри́га; vi интриго́вать impf; vt интригова́ть impf, за~ pf.

**intrinsic** adj прису́щий; (value) вну́тренний.

**introduce** vt вводи́ть impf, ввести́ pf; (person) представля́ть impf, предста́вить pf. **introduction** n введе́ние; представле́ние; (to book) предисло́вие. **introductory** adj вступи́тельный.

**introspection** n интроспе́кция.

**intrude** vi вторга́ться impf, вто́ргнуться pf (into в+acc); (disturb) меша́ть impf, по~ pf. **intruder** n (burglar) граби́тель m. **intrusion** n вторже́ние.

**intuition** *n* интуи́ция. **intuitive** *adj* интуити́вный.

**inundate** *vt* наводня́ть *impf*, наводни́ть *pf*. **inundation** *n* наводне́ние.

**invade** *vt* вторга́ться *impf*, вто́ргнуться *pf* в+*acc*. **invader** *n* захва́тчик.

**invalid**[1] *n* (person) инвали́д.

**invalid**[2] *adj* недействи́тельный. **invalidate** *vt* де́лать *impf*, с~ *pf* недействи́тельным.

**invaluable** *adj* неоцени́мый.

**invariable** *adj* неизме́нный.

**invasion** *n* вторже́ние.

**invective** *n* брань.

**invent** *vt* изобрета́ть *impf*, изобрести́ *pf*; (think up) выду́мывать *impf*, вы́думать *pf*. **invention** *n* изобрете́ние; вы́думка. **inventive** *adj* изобрета́тельный. **inventor** *n* изобрета́тель *m*.

**inventory** *n* инвента́рь *m*.

**inverse** *adj* обра́тный; *n* противополо́жность. **invert** *vt* перевора́чивать *impf*, переверну́ть *pf*. **inverted commas** *n pl* кавы́чки *f pl*.

**invest** *vt & i* (econ) вкла́дывать *impf*, вложи́ть *pf* (де́ньги) (in в+*acc*).

**investigate** *vt* иссле́довать *impf & pf*; (law) рассле́довать *impf & pf*. **investigation** *n* иссле́дование; рассле́дование.

**investment** *n* инвести́ция, вклад. **investor** *n* вкла́дчик.

**inveterate** *adj* закорене́лый.

**invidious** *adj* оскорби́тельный.

**invigorate** *vt* оживля́ть *impf*, оживи́ть *pf*.

**invincible** *adj* непобеди́мый.

**inviolable** *adj* неруши́мый.

**invisible** *adj* неви́димый.

**invitation** *n* приглаше́ние. **invite** *vt* приглаша́ть *impf*, пригласи́ть *pf*. **inviting** *adj* привлека́тельный.

**invoice** *n* факту́ра.

**invoke** *vt* обраща́ться *impf*, обрати́ться *pf* к+*dat*.

**involuntary** *adj* нево́льный.

**involve** *vt* (entangle) вовлека́ть *impf*, вовле́чь *pf*; (entail) влечь *impf* за собо́й. **involved** *adj* сло́жный.

**invulnerable** *adj* неуязви́мый.

**inward** *adj* вну́тренний. **inwardly** *adv* внутри́. **inwards** *adv* внутрь.

**iodine** *n* йод.

**iota** *n*: not an ~ ни на йо́ту.

**IOU** *n* долгова́я распи́ска.

**Iran** *n* Ира́н. **Iranian** *n* ира́нец, -нка; *adj* ира́нский.

**Iraq** *n* Ира́к. **Iraqi** *n* ира́кец; жи́тель *m*, ~ница Ира́ка; *adj* ира́кский.

**irascible** *adj* раздражи́тельный.

**irate** *adj* гне́вный.

**Ireland** *n* Ирла́ндия.

**iris** *n* (anat) ра́дужная оболо́чка; (bot) каса́тик.

**Irish** *adj* ирла́ндский. **Irishman** *n* ирла́ндец. **Irishwoman** *n* ирла́ндка.

**irk** *vt* раздража́ть *impf*, раздражи́ть *pf* +*dat*. **irksome** *adj* раздражи́тельный.

**iron** *n* желе́зо; (for clothes) утю́г; *adj* желе́зный; *vt* гла́дить *impf*, вы́~ *pf*.

**ironic(al)** *adj* ирони́ческий. **irony** *n* иро́ния.

**irradiate** *vt* (subject to radiation) облуча́ть *impf*, облучи́ть *pf*. **irradiation** *n* облуче́ние.

**irrational** *adj* неразу́мный.

**irreconcilable** *adj* непримири́мый.

**irrefutable** *adj* неопровержи́мый.

**irregular** *adj* нерегуля́рный; (*gram*) непра́вильный; (*not even*) неро́вный.

**irrelevant** *adj* неуме́стный.

**irreparable** *adj* непоправи́мый.

**irreplaceable** *adj* незамени́мый.

**irrepressible** *adj* неудержи́мый.

**irreproachable** *adj* безупре́чный.

**irresistible** *adj* неотрази́мый.

**irresolute** *adj* нереши́тельный.

**irrespective** *adj*: ~ of несмотря́ на+*acc*.

**irresponsible** *adj* безотве́тственный.

**irretrievable** *adj* непоправи́мый.

**irreverent** *adj* непочти́тельный.

**irreversible** *adj* необрати́мый.

**irrevocable** *adj* неотменя́емый.

**irrigate** *vt* ороша́ть *impf*, ороси́ть *pf*. **irrigation** *n* ороше́ние.

**irritable** *adj* раздражи́тельный. **irritate** *vt* раздража́ть *impf*, раздражи́ть *pf*. **irritation** *n* раздраже́ние.

**Islam** *n* исла́м. **Islamic** *adj* мусульма́нский.

**island, isle** *n* о́стров. **islander** *n* островитя́нин, -я́нка.

**isolate** *vt* изоли́ровать *impf* & *pf*. **isolation** *n* изоля́ция.

**Israel** *n* Изра́иль *m*. **Israeli** *n* израильтя́нин, -я́нка; *adj* изра́ильский.

**issue** *n* (*question*) спо́рный

вопро́с; (*of bonds etc.*) вы́пуск; (*of magazine*) но́мер; *vi* выходи́ть *impf*, вы́йти *pf*; (*flow*) вытека́ть *impf*, вы́течь *pf*; *vt* выпуска́ть *impf*, вы́пустить *pf*; (*give out*) выдава́ть *impf*, вы́дать *pf*.

**isthmus** *n* переше́ек.

**it** *pron* он, она́, оно́; *demonstrative* э́то.

**Italian** *n* италья́нец, -нка; *adj* италья́нский.

**italics** *n pl* курси́в; in ~ курси́вом. **italicize** *vt* выделя́ть *impf*, вы́делить *pf* курси́вом.

**Italy** *n* Ита́лия.

**ITAR-Tass** *abbr* ИТАР-ТА́СС.

**itch** *n* зуд; *vi* чеса́ться *impf*.

**item** *n* (*on list*) предме́т; (*on account*) статья́; (*on agenda*) пункт; (*in programme*) но́мер. **itemize** *vt* перечисля́ть *impf*, перечи́слить *pf*.

**itinerant** *adj* стра́нствующий. **itinerary** *n* маршру́т.

**its** *poss pron* его́, её; свой.

**itself** *pron* (*emph*) (он)(о) сам(о́), (она́) сама́; (*refl*) себя́, -ся (*suffixed to vt*).

**ivory** *n* слоно́вая кость.

**ivy** *n* плющ.

# J

**jab** *n* толчо́к; (*injection*) уко́л; *vt* ты́кать *impf*, ткнуть *pf*.

**jabber** *vi* тарато́рить *impf*.

**jack** *n* (*cards*) вале́т; (*lifting device*) домкра́т; *vt* (~ up) поднима́ть *impf*, подня́ть *pf* домкра́том.

**jackdaw** *n* га́лка.

**jacket** *n* (*tailored*) пиджа́к; (*anorak*) ку́ртка; (*on book*) (су́пер)обло́жка.

**jackpot** *n* банк.

**jade** n (mineral) нефри́т.
**jaded** adj утомлённый.
**jagged** adj зазу́бренный.
**jaguar** n ягуа́р.
**jail** see **gaol**
**jam**[1] n (crush) да́вка; (in traffic) про́бка; vt (thrust) впи́хивать, впихну́ть pf (into в+acc); (wedge open; block) закли́нивать impf, закли́нить pf; (radio) заглуша́ть impf, заглуши́ть pf; vi (machine) закли́ниваться impf, закли́ниться pf impers+acc.
**jam**[2] n (conserve) варе́нье, джем.
**jangle** vi (& t) звя́кать (+instr).
**janitor** n привра́тник.
**January** n янва́рь; adj янва́рский.
**Japan** n Япо́ния. **Japanese** n япо́нец, -нка; adj япо́нский.
**jar**[1] n (container) ба́нка.
**jar**[2] vi (irritate) раздража́ть impf, раздражи́ть pf (upon +acc).
**jargon** n жарго́н.
**jasmin(e)** n жасми́н.
**jaundice** n желту́ха. **jaundiced** adj (fig) цини́чный.
**jaunt** n прогу́лка.
**jaunty** adj бо́дрый.
**javelin** n копьё.
**jaw** n че́люсть; pl пасть, рот.
**jay** n со́йка.
**jazz** n джаз; adj джа́зовый.
**jealous** adj ревни́вый; (envious) зави́стливый; be ~ of (person) ревнова́ть impf; (thing) зави́довать impf, по~ pf+dat; (rights) ревни́во оберега́ть impf, обере́чь pf. **jealousy** n ре́вность; за́висть.
**jeans** n pl джи́нсы (-сов) pl.
**jeer** n насме́шка; vt & i насмеха́ться impf (at над+instr).
**jelly** n (sweet) желе́ neut

indecl; (aspic) сту́день m. **jellyfish** n меду́за.
**jeopardize** vt подверга́ть impf, подве́ргнуть pf опа́сности.
**jeopardy** n опа́сность.
**jerk** n рыво́к; vt (pull +instr) vi (twitch) дёргаться impf, дёрнуться pf. **jerky** adj неро́вный.
**jersey** n (garment) дже́мпер; (fabric) джерси́ neut indecl.
**jest** n шу́тка; in ~ в шу́тку; vi шути́ть impf, по~ pf. **jester** n шут.
**jet**[1] n (stream) струя́; (nozzle) сопло́; ~ engine реакти́вный дви́гатель m; ~ plane реакти́вный самолёт.
**jet**[2] n (mineralogy) гага́т; ~ black чёрный как смоль.
**jettison** vt выбра́сывать impf, вы́бросить pf за́ борт.
**jetty** n при́стань.
**Jew** n евре́й, евре́йка. **Jewish** adj евре́йский.
**jewel** n драгоце́нность, драгоце́нный ка́мень m. **jeweller** n ювели́р. **jewellery** n драгоце́нности f pl.
**jib** n (naut) кли́вер; vi: ~ at уклоня́ться impf от+gen.
**jigsaw** n (puzzle) моза́ика.
**jingle** n звя́канье; vi (& t) звя́кать impf, звя́кнуть pf (+instr).
**job** n (work) рабо́та; (task) зада́ние; (position) ме́сто. **jobless** adj безрабо́тный.
**jockey** n жоке́й; vi оттира́ть impf друг дру́га.
**ocular** adj шутли́вый.
**jog** n (push) толчо́к; vt подта́лкивать impf, подтолкну́ть pf; vi бе́гать impf трусцо́й. **jogger** n занима́ющийся оздорови́тельным бе́гом. **jogging** n оздорови́тельный бег.

**join** vt & i соединя́ть(ся) impf, соедини́ть(ся) pf; vt (a group of people) присоединя́ться impf, присоедини́ться pf к+dat; (as member) вступа́ть impf, вступи́ть pf в+acc; vi: ~ **in** принима́ть impf, приня́ть pf уча́стие (в+prep); ~ **up** вступа́ть impf, вступи́ть pf в а́рмию.

**joiner** n столя́р.

**joint** n соедине́ние; (anat) суста́в; (meat) кусо́к; adj совме́стный; (common) о́бщий.

**joist** n перекла́дина.

**joke** n шу́тка; vi шути́ть impf, по~ pf. **joker** n шутни́к; (cards) джо́кер.

**jollity** n весе́лье. **jolly** adj весёлый; adv о́чень.

**jolt** n толчо́к; vt & i трясти́(сь) impf.

**jostle** vt & i толка́ть(ся) impf, толкну́ть(ся) pf.

**jot** n йо́та; not a ~ ни на йо́ту; vt (~ **down**) запи́сывать impf, записа́ть pf.

**journal** n журна́л; (diary) дневни́к. **journalese** n газе́тный язы́к. **journalism** n журнали́стика. **journalist** n журнали́ст.

**journey** n путеше́ствие; vi путеше́ствовать impf.

**jovial** adj весёлый.

**joy** n ра́дость. **joyful, joyous** adj ра́достный. **joyless** adj безра́достный. **joystick** n рыча́г управле́ния; (comput) джо́йстик.

**jubilant** adj лику́ющий; **be ~** ликова́ть impf. **jubilation** n ликова́ние.

**jubilee** n юбиле́й.

**Judaism** n юдаи́зм.

**judge** n судья́ m; (connoisseur) цени́тель m; vt & i суди́ть

impf. **judgement** n (legal decision) реше́ние; (opinion) мне́ние; (discernment) рассуди́тельность.

**judicial** adj суде́бный. **judiciary** n суде́й m pl. **judicious** adj здравомы́слящий.

**judo** n дзюдо́ neut indecl.

**jug** n кувши́н.

**juggernaut** n (lorry) многото́нный грузови́к; (fig) неумоли́мая си́ла.

**juggle** vi жонгли́ровать impf. **juggler** n жонглёр.

**jugular** n яре́мная ве́на.

**juice** n сок. **juicy** adj со́чный.

**July** n ию́ль m; adj ию́льский.

**jumble** n (disorder) беспоря́док; (articles) барахло́; vt перепу́тывать impf, перепу́тать pf.

**jump** n прыжо́к, скачо́к; vi прыгать impf, пры́гнуть pf; скака́ть impf; (from shock) вздра́гивать impf, вздро́гнуть pf; vt (~ **over**) перепры́гивать impf, перепры́гнуть pf; ~ **at** (offer) ухва́тываться impf, ухвати́ться pf за+acc; ~ **up** вска́кивать impf, вскочи́ть pf.

**jumper** n дже́мпер.

**jumpy** adj не́рвный.

**junction** n (rly) у́зел; (roads) перекрёсток.

**juncture** n: **at this ~** в э́тот моме́нт.

**June** n ию́нь m; adj ию́ньский.

**jungle** n джу́нгли (-лей) pl.

**junior** adj мла́дший; ~ **school** нача́льная шко́ла.

**juniper** n можжеве́льник.

**junk** n (rubbish) барахло́.

**jurisdiction** n юрисди́кция.

**jurisprudence** n юриспруде́нция.

**juror** n прися́жный sb. **jury** n

прися́жные sb; (in competition) жюри́ neut indecl.

**just** adj (fair) справедли́вый; (deserved) заслу́женный; adv (exactly) как раз, и́менно; (simply) про́сто; (barely) едва́; (very recently) то́лько что; ~ **in case** на вся́кий слу́чай.

**justice** n (proceedings) правосу́дие; (fairness) справедли́вость; **do** ~ **to** отдава́ть impf, отда́ть pf до́лжное +dat.

**justify** vt опра́вдывать impf, оправда́ть pf. **justification** n оправда́ние.

**jut** vi (~ out) выдава́ться impf, вы́ступа́ть impf.

**juvenile** n & adj несовершенноле́тний sb & adj.

**juxtapose** vt помеща́ть impf, помести́ть pf ря́дом; (for comparison) сопоставля́ть impf, сопоста́вить pf (with c+instr).

# K

**kaleidoscope** n калейдоско́п.

**kangaroo** n кенгуру́ m indecl.

**Kazakhstan** n Казахста́н.

**keel** n киль m; vi: ~ **over** опроки́дываться impf, опроки́нуться pf.

**keen** adj (enthusiastic) по́лный энтузиа́зма; (sharp) о́стрый; (strong) си́льный; **be** ~ **on** увлека́ться impf, увле́чься pf +instr; (want to do) о́чень хоте́ть impf +inf.

**keep**[1] n (tower) гла́вная ба́шня; (maintenance) содержа́ние.

**keep**[2] vt (possess, maintain) держа́ть impf; (preserve) храни́ть impf; (observe) соблюда́ть impf, соблюсти́ pf (the law); сде́рживать impf, сдержа́ть pf

(one's word); (family) содержа́ть impf; (diary) вести́ impf; (detain) заде́рживать impf, задержа́ть pf; (retain, reserve) сохраня́ть impf, сохрани́ть pf; vi (of food) не по́ртиться impf; ~ **back** (vt) (hold back) уде́рживать impf, удержа́ть pf; (vi) выступа́ть impf сза́ди; ~ **doing sth** всё +verb: she ~s giggling она́ всё хихи́кает; ~ **from** уде́рживать impf, удержа́ть pf от+gen; ~ **on** продолжа́ть impf, продо́лжить pf (+inf); ~ **up (with)** (vi) не отстава́ть impf (от+gen).

**keepsake** n пода́рок на па́мять.

**keg** n бочо́нок.

**kennel** n конура́.

**kerb** n край тротуа́ра.

**kernel** n (nut) ядро́; (grain) зерно́; (fig) суть.

**kerosene** n кероси́н.

**kettle** n ча́йник.

**key** n ключ; (piano, typewriter) кла́виш(а); (mus) тона́льность; attrib веду́щий, ключево́й. **keyboard** n клавиату́ра. **keyhole** n замо́чная сква́жина.

**KGB** abbr КГБ.

**khaki** n & adj ха́ки neut, adj indecl.

**kick** n уда́р ного́й, пино́к; vt ударя́ть impf, уда́рить pf ного́й; пина́ть impf, пнуть pf; vi (of horse etc.) ляга́ться impf. **kick-off** n нача́ло (игры́).

**kid**[1] n (goat) козлёнок; (child) малы́ш.

**kid**[2] vt (deceive) обма́нывать impf, обману́ть pf; vi (joke) шути́ть impf, по~ pf.

**kidnap** vt похища́ть impf, похи́тить pf.

**kidney** n по́чка.

**kill** vt убива́ть impf, уби́ть pf. **killer** n уби́йца m & f. **killing** n уби́йство; adj (murderous, fig) уби́йственный; (amusing) умори́тельный.

**kiln** n о́бжиговая печь.

**kilo** n кило́ neut indecl. **kilohertz** n килоге́рц. **kilogram(me)** n килогра́мм. **kilometre** n киломе́тр. **kilowatt** n килова́тт.

**kilt** n шотла́ндская ю́бка.

**kimono** n кимоно́ neut indecl.

**kin** n (family) семья́; (collect, relatives) родня́.

**kind**[1] n сорт, род; a ~ of что́-то вро́де+gen; this ~ of тако́й; what ~ of что (э́то, он, etc.) за +nom; ~ of (adv) как бу́дто, ка́к-то.

**kind**[2] adj до́брый.

**kindergarten** n де́тский сад.

**kindle** vt зажига́ть impf, заже́чь pf. **kindling** n расто́пка.

**kindly** adj до́брый; adv любе́зно; (with imper) (request) бу́дьте добры́, +imper. **kindness** n доброта́.

**kindred** adj: ~ **spirit** родна́я душа́.

**kinetic** adj кинети́ческий.

**king** n коро́ль m (also chess, cards, fig); (draughts) да́мка. **kingdom** n короле́вство; (fig) ца́рство. **kingfisher** n зиморо́док.

**kink** n переги́б.

**kinship** n родство́; (similarity) схо́дство. **kinsman, -woman** n ро́дственник, -ица.

**kiosk** n кио́ск; (telephone) бу́дка.

**kip** n сон; vi дры́хнуть impf.

**kipper** n копчёная селёдка.

**Kirghizia** n Кирги́зия.

**kiss** n поцелу́й; vt & i целова́ть(ся) impf, по~ pf.

**kit** n (clothing) снаряже́ние; (tools) набо́р, компле́кт; vt: ~ **out** снаряжа́ть impf, снаряди́ть pf. **kitbag** n вещево́й мешо́к.

**kitchen** n ку́хня; attrib ку́хонный; ~ **garden** огоро́д.

**kite** n (toy) змей.

**kitsch** n дешёвка.

**kitten** n котёнок.

**knack** n сноро́вка.

**knapsack** n рюкза́к.

**knead** vt меси́ть impf, с~ pf.

**knee** n коле́но. **kneecap** n коле́нная ча́шка.

**kneel** vi стоя́ть impf на коле́нях; (~ down) станови́ться impf, стать pf на коле́ни.

**knickers** n pl тру́сики (-ов) pl.

**knick-knack** n безделу́шка.

**knife** n нож; vt коло́ть impf, за~ pf ножо́м.

**knight** n (hist) ры́царь m; (holder of order) кавале́р; (chess) конь m. **knighthood** n ры́царское зва́ние.

**knit** vt (garment) вяза́ть impf, с~ pf; vi (bones) сраста́ться impf, срасти́сь pf; ~ **one's brows** хму́рить impf, на~ pf бро́ви. **knitting** n (action) вяза́ние; (object) вяза́нье; ~ **needle** спи́ца. **knitwear** n трикота́ж.

**knob** n ши́шка, кно́пка; (door handle) ру́чка. **knob(b)ly** adj ши́шковатый.

**knock** n (noise) стук; (blow) уда́р; vt & i (strike) ударя́ть impf, уда́рить pf; (strike door etc.) стуча́ть impf, по~ pf (at в+acc); ~ **about** (treat roughly) колоти́ть impf, по~ pf;

(*wander*) шата́ться *impf*; **~ down** (*person*) сбива́ть *impf*, сбить *pf* с ног; (*building*) сноси́ть *impf*, снести́ *pf*; **~ off** сбива́ть *impf*, сбить *pf*; (*stop work*) шаба́шить *impf* (*работу*); (*deduct*) сбавля́ть *impf*, сба́вить *pf*; **~ out** выбива́ть *impf*, вы́бить *pf*; (*sport*) нокаути́ровать *impf* & *pf*; **~-out** нока́ут; **~ over** опроки́дывать *impf*, опроки́нуть *impf*. **knocker** *n* дверно́й молото́к.

**knoll** *n* буго́р.

**knot** *n* у́зел; *vt* завя́зывать *impf*, завяза́ть *pf* узло́м. **knotty** *adj* (*fig*) запу́танный.

**know** *vt* знать *impf*; (**~ how to**) уме́ть *impf*, *pf* +*inf*. **~how** уме́ние. **knowing** *adj* многозначи́тельный. **knowingly** *adv* созна́тельно. **knowledge** *n* зна́ние; **to my ~** наско́лько мне изве́стно.

**knuckle** *n* суста́в па́льца; *vi*: **~ down** впряга́ться *impf*, впря́чься *pf* в+*acc*; **~ under** уступа́ть *impf*, уступи́ть *pf* (**to** +*dat*).

**Korea** *n* Коре́я.

**ko(w)tow** *n* (*fig*) раболе́пствовать *impf* (**to** пе́ред+*instr*).

**Kremlin** *n* Кремль *m*.

**kudos** *n* сла́ва.

# L

**label** *n* этике́тка, ярлы́к; *vt* прикле́ивать *impf*, прикле́ить *pf* ярлы́к к+*dat*.

**laboratory** *n* лаборато́рия.

**laborious** *adj* кропотли́вый.

**labour** *n* труд; (*med*) ро́ды (-дов) *pl*; *attrib* трудово́й; **~ force** рабо́чая си́ла; **~-inten-**

**-sive** трудоёмкий; **L~ Party** лейбори́стская па́ртия; *vi* труди́ться *impf*; *vt*: **~ a point** входи́ть *impf*, войти́ *pf* в изли́шние подро́бности. **laboured** *adj* затруднённый; (*style*) вы́мученный. **labourer** *n* черноробо́чий *sb*. **labourite** *n* лейбори́ст.

**labyrinth** *n* лабири́нт.

**lace** *n* (*fabric*) кру́жево; (*cord*) шнуро́к; *vt* (**~ up**) шнурова́ть *impf*, за~ *pf*.

**lacerate** *vt* (*also fig*) терза́ть *impf*, ис~ *pf*. **laceration** *n* (*wound*) рва́ная ра́на.

**lack** *n* недоста́ток (**of** +*gen*, +*prep*), отсу́тствие; *vt* & *i* не хвата́ть *impf*, хвати́ть *pf impers* +*dat* (*person*), +*gen* (*object*).

**lackadaisical** *adj* то́мный.

**laconic** *adj* лакони́чный.

**lacquer** *n* лак; *vt* лакирова́ть *impf*, от~ *pf*.

**lad** *n* па́рень *m*.

**ladder** *n* ле́стница.

**laden** *adj* нагру́женный.

**ladle** *n* (*spoon*) поло́вник; *vt* че́рпать *impf*, черпну́ть *pf*.

**lady** *n* да́ма, ле́ди *f indecl*. **ladybird** *n* бо́жья коро́вка.

**lag**[1] *vi*: **~ behind** отстава́ть *impf*, отста́ть *pf* (**от** +*gen*).

**lag**[2] *vt* (*insulate*) изоли́ровать *impf* & *pf*.

**lagoon** *n* лагу́на.

**lair** *n* ло́говище.

**laity** *n* (*in religion*) миря́не (-н) *pl*.

**lake** *n* о́зеро.

**lamb** *n* ягнёнок; (*meat*) бара́нина.

**lame** *adj* хромо́й; **be ~** хрома́ть *impf*; **go ~** хроме́ть *impf*, о~ *pf*; *vt* кале́чить *impf*, о~ *pf*.

**lament** *n* плач; *vt* сожале́ть

*impf* o+*prep.* **lamentable** *adj* приско́рбный.

**laminated** *adj* сло́истый.

**lamp** *n* ла́мпа; (*in street*) фона́рь *m.* **lamp-post** *n* фона́рный столб. **lampshade** *n* абажу́р.

**lance** *n* пи́ка; *vt* (*med*) вскрыва́ть *impf*, вскрыть *pf* (ланце́том).

**land** *n* земля́; (*dry* ~) су́ша; (*country*) страна́; *vi* (*naut*) прича́ливать *impf*, прича́лить *pf*; *vt* & *i* (*aeron*) приземля́ть(ся) *impf*, приземли́ть(ся) *pf*; (*find o.s.*) попада́ть *impf*, попа́сть *pf*. **landing** *n* (*aeron*) поса́дка; (*on stairs*) площа́дка; ~**stage** при́стань. **landlady** *n* хозя́йка. **landlord** *n* хозя́ин. **landmark** *n* (*conspicuous object*) ориенти́р; (*fig*) ве́ха. **landowner** *n* землевладе́лец. **landscape** *n* ландша́фт; (*also picture*) пейза́ж. **landslide** *n* о́ползень *m.*

**lane** *n* (*in country*) доро́жка; (*street*) переу́лок; (*passage*) прохо́д; (*on road*) ряд; (*in race*) доро́жка.

**language** *n* язы́к; (*style, speech*) речь.

**languid** *adj* то́мный.

**languish** *vi* томи́ться *impf.*

**languor** *n* то́мность.

**lank** *adj* (*hair*) гла́дкий. **lanky** *adj* долговя́зый.

**lantern** *n* фона́рь *m.*

**lap¹** *n* (*of person*) коле́ни (-ней) *pl*; (*sport*) круг.

**lap²** *vt* (*drink*) лака́ть *impf*, вы~ *pf*; *vi* (*water*) плеска́ться *impf.*

**lapel** *n* отворо́т.

**lapse** *n* (*mistake*) оши́бка; (*interval*) промежу́ток; (*expiry*)

истече́ние; *vi* впада́ть *impf*, впасть *pf* (*into* в+*acc*); (*expire*) истека́ть *impf*, исте́чь *pf.*

**lapwing** *n* чи́бис.

**larch** *n* ли́ственница.

**lard** *n* свино́е са́ло.

**larder** *n* кладова́я *sb.*

**large** *adj* большо́й; *n*: at ~ (*free*) на свобо́де; by and ~ вообще́ говоря́. **largely** *adv* в значи́тельной сте́пени.

**largesse** *n* ще́дрость.

**lark¹** *n* (*bird*) жа́воронок.

**lark²** *n* прока́за; *vi* (~ *about*) резви́ться *impf.*

**larva** *n* личи́нка.

**laryngitis** *n* ларинги́т. **larynx** *n* горта́нь.

**lascivious** *adj* похотли́вый.

**laser** *n* ла́зер.

**lash** *n* (*blow*) уда́р плетью; (*eyelash*) ресни́ца; *vt* (*beat*) хлеста́ть *impf*, хлестну́ть *pf*; (*tie*) привя́зывать *impf*, привяза́ть *pf* (*to* к+*dat.*).

**last¹** *n* (*cobbler's*) коло́дка.

**last²** *adj* (*final*) после́дний; (*most recent*) про́шлый; **the year** (*etc.*) **before** ~ позапро́шлый год (и т.д.); ~ **but one** предпосле́дний; ~ **night** вчера́ ве́чером; **at** ~ наконе́ц; *adv* (*after all others*) по́сле всех; (*on the last occasion*) в после́дний раз; (*lastly*) наконе́ц.

**last³** *vi* (*go on*) продолжа́ться *impf*, продо́лжиться *pf*; дли́ться *impf*, про~ *pf*; (*be preserved*) сохраня́ться *impf*, сохрани́ться *pf*; (*suffice*) хвата́ть *impf*, хвати́ть *pf.* **lasting** *adj* (*permanent*) постоя́нный; (*durable*) про́чный.

**lastly** *adv* в заключе́ние; наконе́ц.

**latch** *n* щеко́лда.

**late** *adj* по́здний; (*recent*) неда́вний; (*dead*) поко́йный; be ~ for опа́здывать *impf*, опозда́ть *pf* на+*acc*; *adv* по́здно. **lately** *adv* в после́днее вре́мя. **later** *adv* (*after vv*) по́зже; ~ a year ~ год спустя́; see you ~! пока́!

**latent** *adj* скры́тый.

**lateral** *adj* боково́й.

**lath** *n* ре́йка.

**lathe** *n* тока́рный стано́к.

**lather** *n* (мы́льная) пе́на; *vt* & *i* мы́лить(ся) *impf*, на~ *pf*.

**Latin** *adj* лати́нский; ~ в лати́нский язы́к; ~-American лати́ноамерика́нский.

**latitude** *n* свобо́да; (*geog*) широта́.

**latter** *adj* после́дний; ~-day совреме́нный. **latterly** *adv* в после́днее вре́мя.

**lattice** *n* решётка.

**Latvia** *n* Ла́твия. **Latvian** *n* латви́ец, -и́йка; латы́ш, -ка; *adj* латви́йский, латы́шский.

**laud** *vt* хвали́ть *impf*, по~ *pf*. **laudable** *adj* похва́льный.

**laugh** *n* смех; *vi* смея́ться *impf* (at над+*instr*); ~ it off отшу́чиваться *impf*, отшути́ться *pf*; ~ing-stock посме́шище; **laughable** *adj* сме́шно́й. **laughter** *n* смех.

**launch**[1] *vt* (*ship*) спуска́ть *impf*, спусти́ть *pf* на́ воду; (*rocket*) запуска́ть *impf*, запусти́ть *pf*; (*undertake*) начина́ть *impf*, нача́ть *pf*; *n* спуск на́ воду; за́пуск. **launcher** *n* (*for rocket*) пусково́е устано́вка. **launching pad** *n* пускова́я площа́дка.

**launch**[2] *n* (*naut*) ка́тер.

**launder** *vt* стира́ть *impf*, вы́~ *pf*. **laund(e)rette** *n* пра́чеч-

ная *sb* самообслу́живания.

**laundry** *n* (*place*) пра́чечная *sb*; (*articles*) бельё.

**laurel** *n* лавр(о́вое де́рево).

**lava** *n* ла́ва.

**lavatory** *n* убо́рная *sb*.

**lavender** *n* лава́нда.

**lavish** *adj* ще́дрый; (*abundant*) оби́льный; *vt* расточа́ть *impf* (upon +*dat*).

**law** *n* зако́н; (*system*) пра́во; ~ and order правопоря́док. ~-court *n* суд. **lawful** *adj* зако́нный. **lawless** *adj* беззако́нный.

**lawn** *n* газо́н; ~-mower газонокоси́лка.

**lawsuit** *n* проце́сс.

**lawyer** *n* адвока́т, юри́ст.

**lax** *adj* сла́бый. **laxative** *n* слаби́тельное *sb*. **laxity** *n* сла́бость.

**lay**[1] *adj* (*non-clerical*) све́тский.

**lay**[2] *vt* (*place*) класть *impf*, положи́ть *pf*; (*cable, pipes*) прокла́дывать *impf*, проложи́ть *pf*; (*carpet*) стлать *impf*, по~ *pf*; (*trap etc.*) устра́ивать *impf*, устро́ить *pf*; (*eggs*) класть *impf*, положи́ть *pf*; *v abs* (*lay eggs*) нести́сь *impf*, с~ *pf*; ~ aside откла́дывать *impf*, отложи́ть *pf*; ~ bare раскрыва́ть *impf*, раскры́ть *pf*; ~ a bet держа́ть *impf* пари́ (on на+*acc*); ~ down (*relinquish*) отка́зываться *impf*, отказа́ться *pf* от+*gen*; (*rule etc.*) устана́вливать *impf*, установи́ть *pf*; ~ off (*workmen*) увольня́ть *impf*, уво́лить *pf*; ~ out (*spread*) выкла́дывать *impf*, вы́ложить *pf*; (*garden*) разбива́ть *impf*, разби́ть *pf*; ~ the table накрыва́ть *impf*, накры́ть *pf* стол (for (*meal*) k+*dat*); ~ **up** запаса́ть *impf*, запасти́ *pf* +*acc*, +*gen*; **be laid up** быть прико́ванным к посте́ли. **layabout** *n* безде́льник.

**layer** *n* слой, пласт.

**layman** *n* миря́нин; (*non-expert*) неспециали́ст.

**laze** *vi* безде́льничать *impf*.

**laziness** *n* лень. **lazy** *adj* лени́вый; ~**-bones** лентя́й, ~ка.

**lead**[1] *n* (*example*) приме́р; (*leadership*) руково́дство; (*position*) пе́рвое ме́сто; (*theat*) гла́вная роль; (*electr*) про́вод; (*dog's*) поводо́к; *vt* води́ть *indet*, вести́ *det*; (*be in charge of*) руководи́ть *impf* +*instr*; (*induce*) побужда́ть *impf*, побуди́ть *pf*; *vt* & *i* (*cards*) ходи́ть *impf* (с+*gen*); *vi* (*sport*) занима́ть *impf*, заня́ть *pf* пе́рвое ме́сто; ~ **away** уводи́ть *impf*, увести́ *pf*; ~ **to** (*result in*) приводи́ть *impf*, привести́ *pf* к+*dat*.

**lead**[2] *n* (*metal*) свине́ц. **leaden** *adj* свинцо́вый.

**leader** *n* руководи́тель *m*, ~ница, ли́дер; (*mus*) пе́рвая скри́пка; (*editorial*) передова́я статья́. **leadership** *n* руково́дство.

**leading** *adj* веду́щий, выдаю́щийся; ~ **article** передова́я статья́.

**leaf** *n* лист; (*of table*) откидна́я доска́; *vi*: ~ **through** перели́стывать *impf*, перелиста́ть *pf*. **leaflet** *n* листо́вка.

**league** *n* ли́га; **in** ~ **with** в сою́зе с +*instr*.

**leak** *n* течь, уте́чка; *vi* (*escape*) течь *impf*; (*allow water to* ~) пропуска́ть *impf* во́ду; ~ **out** проса́чиваться *impf*,

просочи́ться *pf*.

**lean**[1] *adj* (*thin*) худо́й; (*meat*) по́стный.

**lean**[2] *vt* & *i* прислоня́ть(ся) *impf*, прислони́ть(ся) *pf* (*against* к+*dat*); (*be inclined*) быть скло́нным (**to**(*wards*) к+*dat*); ~ **back** отки́дываться *impf*, откинуться *pf*; ~ **out** высо́вываться *impf*, вы́сунуться *pf* в +*acc*. **leaning** *n* скло́нность.

**leap** *n* прыжо́к, скачо́к; *vi* пры́гать *impf*, пры́гнуть *pf*; скака́ть *impf*, скакну́ть *pf*; ~ **year** високо́сный год.

**learn** *vt* (*a subject*) учи́ть *impf*, вы́~ *pf*; (*to do sth*) учи́ться *impf*, на~ *pf* +*inf*; (*find out*) узнава́ть *impf*, узна́ть *pf*. **learned** *adj* учёный. **learner** *n* учени́к, -и́ца. **learning** *n* (*studies*) уче́ние; (*erudition*) учёность.

**lease** *n* аре́нда; *vt* (*of owner*) сдава́ть *impf*, сдать *pf* в аре́нду; (*of tenant*) брать *impf*, взять *pf* в аре́нду. **leaseholder** *n* аренда́тор.

**leash** *n* при́вязь.

**least** *adj* наиме́ньший, мале́йший; *adv* ме́нее всего́; **at** ~ по кра́йней ме́ре; **not in the** ~ ничу́ть.

**leather** *n* ко́жа; *attrib* ко́жаный.

**leave**[1] *n* (*permission*) разреше́ние; (*holiday*) о́тпуск; **on** ~ в о́тпуске; **take** (**one's**) ~ проща́ться *impf*, прости́ться *pf* (*of* с+*instr*).

**leave**[2] *vt* & *i* оставля́ть *impf*, оста́вить *pf*; (*abandon*) покида́ть *impf*, поки́нуть *pf*; (*go away*) уходи́ть *impf*, уйти́ *pf* (**from** от+*gen*); уезжа́ть *impf*, уе́хать *pf* (**from** от+*gen*) (*go out of*) выходи́ть *impf*, вы́йти *pf* из+*gen*; (*entrust*) предоставля́ть *impf*, предоста́вить *pf* (**to** +*dat*); ~ **out** пропуска́ть *impf*, пропусти́ть *pf*.

**lecherous** *adj* развра́тный.

**lectern** *n* анало́й; (*in lecture room*) пюпи́тр.

**lecture** *n* (*discourse*) ле́кция; (*reproof*) нота́ция; *vi* (*deliver* ~(*s*)) чита́ть *impf*, про~ *pf* ле́кцию (-ии) (**on** +*dat*); *vt* (*admonish*) чита́ть *impf*, про~ *pf* нота́цию+*dat*; ~ **room** аудито́рия. **lecturer** *n* (*speaker*) ле́ктор; (*univ*) преподава́тель *m*, ~ница.

**ledge** *n* вы́ступ; (*shelf*) по́лочка.

**ledger** *n* гла́вная кни́га.

**lee** *n* защи́та; *adj* подве́тренный.

**leech** *n* (*worm*) пия́вка.

**leek** *n* лук-поре́й.

**leer** *vi* криви́ться *impf*, с~ *pf*.

**leeward** *n* подве́тренная сторона́; *adj* подве́тренный.

**leeway** *n* (*fig*) свобо́да де́йствий.

**left** *n* ле́вая сторона́; (**the L**~; *polit*) ле́вые *sb pl*; *adj* ле́вый; *adv* нале́во, сле́ва (**of** от+*gen*); ~**-hander** левша́ *m* & *f*; ~**wing** ле́вый.

**left-luggage office** *n* ка́мера хране́ния.

**leftovers** *n pl* оста́тки *m pl*; (*food*) объе́дки (-ков) *pl*.

**leg** *n* нога́; (*of furniture etc.*) но́жка; (*of journey etc.*) эта́п.

**legacy** *n* насле́дство.

**legal** *adj* (*of the law*) правово́й; (*lawful*) лега́льный. **legality** *n* лега́льность. **legalize** *vt* легализи́ровать *impf* & *pf*.

**legend** *n* леге́нда. **legendary** *adj* легенда́рный.

**leggings** *n pl* вя́заные рейту́зы (-з) *pl*.

**legible** *adj* разбо́рчивый.

**legion** *n* легио́н.

**legislate** *vi* издава́ть *impf*, изда́ть *pf* зако́ны. **legislation** *n* законода́тельство. **legislative** *adj* законода́тельный. **legislator** *n* законода́тель *m*. **legislature** *n* законода́тельные учрежде́ния *neut pl*.

**legitimacy** *n* зако́нность; (*of child*) законнорождённость. **legitimate** *adj* зако́нный; (*child*) законнорождённый. **legitimize** *vt* узако́нивать *impf*, узако́нить *pf*.

**leisure** *n* свобо́дное вре́мя, досу́г; **at** ~ на досу́ге. **leisurely** *adj* неторопли́вый.

**lemon** *n* лимо́н. **lemonade** *n* лимона́д.

**lend** *vt* дава́ть *impf*, дать *pf* взаймы́ (**to** +*dat*); ода́лживать *impf*, одолжи́ть *pf* (**to** +*dat*).

**length** *n* длина́; (*of time*) продолжи́тельность; (*of cloth*) отре́з; **at** ~ подро́бно. **lengthen** *vt* & *i* удлиня́ть(ся) *impf*, удлини́ть(ся) *pf*. **lengthways** *adv* в длину́, вдоль. **lengthy** *adj* дли́нный.

**leniency** *n* снисходи́тельность. **lenient** *adj* снисходи́тельный.

**lens** *n* ли́нза; (*phot*) объекти́в; (*anat*) хруста́лик.

**Lent** *n* вели́кий пост.

**lentil** *n* чечеви́ца.

**Leo** *n* Лев.

**leopard** *n* леопа́рд.

**leotard** *n* трико́ *neut indecl*.

**leper** *n* прокажённый *sb*. **leprosy** *n* прока́за.

**lesbian** n лесбия́нка; adj лес-
би́йский.
**lesion** n поврежде́ние.
**less** adj ме́ньший; adv ме́нь-
ше, ме́нее; prep за вы́четом
+gen.
**lessee** n аренда́тор.
**lessen** vt & i уменьша́ть(ся)
impf, уме́ньшить(ся) pf.
**lesser** adj ме́ньший.
**lesson** n уро́к.
**lest** conj (in order that not)
чтобы не; (that) как бы не.
**let** n (lease) сда́ча в наём; vt
(allow) позволя́ть impf, позво́-
лить pf +dat; разреша́ть
impf, разреши́ть pf +dat;
(rent out) сдава́ть impf, сдать
pf внаём (to +dat); v aux
(imperative) (1st person) да-
ва́й(те); (3rd person) пусть; ~
**alone** не говоря́ уже́ о+prep;
~ **down** (lower) опуска́ть
impf, опусти́ть pf; (fail) под-
води́ть impf, подвести́ pf;
(disappoint) разочаро́вывать
impf, разочарова́ть pf; ~ **go**
выпуска́ть impf, вы́пустить
pf; ~**'s go** пойдёмте!; по-
шли́!; поéхали!; ~ **in(to)** (admit) впуска́ть impf, впусти́ть
pf в+acc; (into secret) посвя-
ща́ть impf, посвяти́ть pf в+acc;
~ **know** дава́ть impf, дать pf
знать (to +dat); ~ **off** (gun) вы́-
стрелить pf из+gen; (not punish) отпуска́ть impf, отпу-
сти́ть pf без наказа́ния; ~
**out** (release, loosen) выпу-
ска́ть impf, вы́пустить pf;
**through** пропуска́ть impf,
пропусти́ть pf; ~ **up** зати-
ха́ть impf, зати́хнуть pf.
**lethal** adj (fatal) смерте́льный;
(weapon) смертоно́сный.
**lethargic** adj летарги́ческий.
**lethargy** n летарги́я.

**letter** n письмо́; (symbol)
бу́ква; (printing) ли́тера; ~-
**box** почто́вый я́щик. **letter-
ing** n шрифт.
**lettuce** n сала́т.
**leukaemia** n лейкеми́я.
**level** n у́ровень; adj ро́вный;
~ **crossing** (железнодоро́ж-
ный) перее́зд; ~-**headed** ура-
внове́шенный; vt (make) ~)
выра́внивать impf, вы́ровн-
ять pf; (sport) сра́внивать
impf, сравня́ть pf; (gun) на-
води́ть impf, навести́ pf (at
в, на, +acc); (criticism) на-
правля́ть impf, напра́вить pf
(at про́тив+gen).
**lever** n рыча́г. **leverage** n
де́йствие рычага́; (influence)
влия́ние.
**levity** n легкомы́слие.
**levy** n (tax) сбор; vt (tax) взи-
ма́ть impf (from c+gen).
**lewd** adj (lascivious) похот-
ли́вый; (indecent) са́льный.
**lexicon** n слова́рь m.
**liability** n (responsibility) от-
ве́тственность (for за+acc);
(burden) обу́за. **liable** adj
отве́тственный (for за+acc);
(susceptible) подве́рженный
(to +dat).
**liaise** vi подде́рживать impf
связь (c+instr). **liaison** n связь;
(affair) любо́вная связь.
**liar** n лгун, ~ья.
**libel** n клевета́; vt клевета́ть
impf, на+acc. **libel-
lous** adj клеветни́ческий.
**liberal** n либера́л; adj либе-
ра́льный; (generous) ще́дрый.
**liberate** vt освобожда́ть impf,
освободи́ть pf. **liberation** n
освобожде́ние. **liberator** n
освободи́тель m.
**libertine** n распу́тник.
**liberty** n свобо́да; **at ~** на

свобо́де.

**Libra** *n* Весы́ (-со́в) *pl*.

**librarian** *n* библиоте́карь *m*.
**library** *n* библиоте́ка.

**libretto** *n* либре́тто *neut indecl*.

**licence**[1] *n* (*permission, permit*) разреше́ние, лице́нзия; (*liberty*) (изли́шняя) во́льность.

**license, -ce**[2] *vt* (*allow*) разреша́ть *impf*, разреши́ть *pf* +dat; дава́ть *impf*, дать *pf* пра́во +dat.

**licentious** *adj* распу́щенный.

**lichen** *n* лиша́йник.

**lick** *n* лиза́ние; *vt* лиза́ть *impf*, лизну́ть *pf*.

**lid** *n* кры́шка; (*eyelid*) ве́ко.

**lie**[1] *n* (*untruth*) ложь; *vi* лгать *impf*, со∼ *pf*.

**lie**[2] *n*: ∼ **of the land** (*fig*) положе́ние веще́й; *vi* лежа́ть *impf*; (*be situated*) находи́ться *impf*; ∼ **down** ложи́ться *impf*, лечь *pf*; ∼ **in** остава́ться *impf* в посте́ли.

**lieu** *n*: **in** ∼ **of** вме́сто+gen.

**lieutenant** *n* лейтена́нт.

**life** *n* жизнь; (*way of* ∼) о́браз жи́зни; (*energy*) жи́вость. **lifebelt** *n* спаса́тельный по́яс. **lifeboat** *n* спаса́тельная ло́дка. **lifebuoy** *n* спаса́тельный круг. **lifeguard** *n* спаса́тель *m*, -ница. **life-jacket** *n* спаса́тельный жиле́т. **lifeless** *adj* безжи́зненный. **lifelike** *adj* реалисти́чный. **lifeline** *n* спаса́тельный коне́ц. **lifelong** *adj* пожи́зненный. **life-size(d)** *adj* в натура́льную величину́. **lifetime** *n* жизнь.

**lift** *n* (*machine*) лифт, подъёмник; (*force*) подъёмная си́ла; **give s.o. a** ∼ подвози́ть *impf*, подвезти́ *pf*; *vt & i* подни-ма́ть(ся) *impf*, подня́ть-(ся) *pf*.

**ligament** *n* свя́зка.

**light**[1] *n* свет, освеще́ние; (*source of* ∼) ого́нь *m*, ла́мпа, фона́рь *m*; *pl* (*traffic* ∼) светофо́р; **can I have a** ∼? мо́жно прикури́ть?; ∼**-bulb** ла́мпочка; *adj* (*bright*) све́тлый; (*pale*) бле́дный; *vt & i* (*ignite*) зажига́ть(ся) *impf*, заже́чь(ся) *pf*; *vt* (*illuminate*) освеща́ть *impf*, освети́ть *pf*; ∼ **up** освеща́ть(ся) *impf*, освети́ть(ся) *pf*; (*begin to smoke*) закури́ть *pf*.

**light**[2] *adj* (*not heavy*) лёгкий; ∼**-hearted** беззабо́тный.

**lighten**[1] *vt* (*make lighter*) облегча́ть *impf*, облегчи́ть *pf*; (*mitigate*) смягча́ть *impf*, смягчи́ть *pf*.

**lighten**[2] *vt* (*illuminate*) освеща́ть *impf*, освети́ть *pf*; *vi* (*grow bright*) светле́ть *impf*, по∼ *pf*.

**lighter** *n* зажига́лка.

**lighthouse** *n* мая́к.

**lighting** *n* освеще́ние.

**lightning** *n* мо́лния.

**lightweight** *n* (*sport*) легкове́с; *adj* легкове́сный.

**like**[1] *adj* (*similar*) похо́жий (на+acc); **what is he** ∼? что он за челове́к?

**like**[2] *vt* нра́виться *impf*, по∼ *pf impers*+dat: **I** ∼ **him** он мне нра́вится; люби́ть *impf*; *vi* (*wish*) хоте́ть *impf*; **if you** ∼ е́сли хоти́те; **I should** ∼ я хоте́л бы; мне хоте́лось бы. **likeable** *adj* симпати́чный.

**likelihood** *n* вероя́тность. **likely** *adj* (*probable*) вероя́т-ный; (*suitable*) подходя́щий.

**liken** *vt* уподобля́ть *impf*, уподо́бить *pf* (**to** +dat).

**likeness** *n* (*resemblance*) схо́д-ство; (*portrait*) портре́т.

**...e** adv (similarly) по-...

**...g** n вкус (for к+dat).

**...ь** n сирень; adj сире́невый.

**...и** n ли́лия; ~ of the valley ла́ндыш.

**limb** n член.

**limber** vi: ~ up размина́ться impf, размя́ться pf.

**limbo** n (fig) состоя́ние неопределённости.

**lime**[1] n (mineralogy) и́звесть. **limelight** n: in the ~ (fig) в це́нтре внима́ния. **limestone** n известня́к.

**lime**[2] n (fruit) лайм.

**lime**[3] n (~-tree) ли́па.

**limit** n грани́ца, преде́л; vt ограни́чивать impf, ограни́чить pf. **limitation** n ограниче́ние. **limitless** adj безграни́чный.

**limousine** n лимузи́н.

**limp**[1] n хромота́; vi хрома́ть impf.

**limp**[2] adj мя́гкий; (fig) вя́лый.

**limpid** adj прозра́чный.

**linchpin** n чека́.

**line**[1] n (long mark) ли́ния, черта́; (transport, tel) ли́ния; (cord) верёвка; (wrinkle) морщи́на; (limit) грани́ца; (row) ряд; (of words) строка́; (of verse) стих; vt (paper) линова́ть impf, раз~ pf; vt & i (~ up) выстра́ивать(ся) impf, вы́строить(ся) pf в ряд.

**line**[2] vt (clothes) класть impf, положи́ть pf на подкла́дку.

**lineage** n происхожде́ние.

**linear** adj лине́йный.

**lined**[1] adj (paper) линованный; (face) морщи́нистый.

**lined**[2] adj (garment) на подкла́дке.

**linen** n полотно́; collect бельё.

**liner** n ла́йнер.

**linesman** n боково́й судья́ m.

**linger** vi заде́рживаться impf, задержа́ться pf.

**lingerie** n да́мское бельё.

**lingering** adj (illness) затяжно́й.

**lingo** n жарго́н.

**linguist** n лингви́ст. **linguistic** adj лингвисти́ческий. **linguistics** n лингви́стика.

**lining** n (clothing etc.) подкла́дка; (tech) облицо́вка.

**link** n (of chain) звено́; (connection) связь; vt соединя́ть impf, соедини́ть pf; свя́зывать impf, связа́ть pf.

**lino(leum)** n линоле́ум.

**lintel** n перемы́чка.

**lion** n лев. **lioness** n льви́ца.

**lip** n губа́; (of vessel) край. **lipstick** n губна́я пома́да.

**liquefy** vt & i превраща́ть(ся) impf, преврати́ть(ся) pf в жи́дкое состоя́ние.

**liqueur** n ликёр.

**liquid** n жи́дкость; adj жи́дкий.

**liquidate** vt ликвиди́ровать impf & pf. **liquidation** n ликвида́ция; go into ~ ликвиди́роваться impf & pf.

**liquor** n (спиртно́й) напи́ток.

**liquorice** n лакри́ца.

**list**[1] n спи́сок; vt составля́ть impf, соста́вить pf спи́сок +gen; (enumerate) перечисля́ть impf, перечи́слить pf.

**list**[2] vi (naut) накреня́ться impf, крени́ться impf, накрени́ться pf.

**listen** vi слу́шать impf, по~ pf (to +acc). **listener** n слу́шатель m.

**listless** adj апати́чный.

**litany** n лита́ния.

**literacy** n гра́мотность.

**literal** adj буква́льный.

**literary** adj литературный.

**literate** adj грамотный.

**literature** n литература.

**lithe** adj гибкий.

**lithograph** n литография.

**Lithuania** n Литва. **Lithuanian** n литовец, -вка; adj литовский.

**litigation** n тяжба.

**litre** n литр.

**litter** n (rubbish) сор; (brood) помёт; vt (make untidy) сорить impf, на~ pf (with +instr).

**little** n немногое; ~ **by** ~ мало-помалу; a ~ немного +gen; adj маленький, небольшой; (in height) небольшого роста; (in distance, time) короткий; adv мало, немного.

**liturgy** n литургия.

**live**[1] adj живой; (coals) горящий; (mil) боевой; (electr) под напряжением; (broadcast) прямой.

**live**[2] vi жить impf; ~ **down** заглаживать impf, загладить pf; ~ **on** (feed on) питаться impf +instr; (through) переживать impf, пережить pf; ~ **until, to see** доживать impf, дожить pf до+gen; ~ **up to** жить impf согласно +dat.

**livelihood** n средства neut pl к жизни.

**lively** adj живой.

**liven (up)** vt & i оживлять(ся) impf, оживить(ся) pf.

**liver** n печень; (cul) печёнка.

**livery** n ливрея.

**livestock** n скот.

**livid** adj (angry) взбешённый.

**living** n средства neut pl к жизни; **earn a** ~ зарабатывать impf, заработать pf на жизнь; adj живой; ~**-room** гостиная sb.

**lizard** n ящерица.

**load** n груз; (also fig) бремя neut; (electr) нагрузка; pl (lots) куча; vt (goods) грузить impf, по~ pf; (vehicle) грузить impf, на~ pf; (fig) обременять impf, обременить pf; (gun, camera) заряжать impf, зарядить pf.

**loaf**[1] n буханка.

**loaf**[2] vi бездельничать impf.

**loafer** n бездельник.

**loan** n заём; vt давать impf, дать pf взаймы.

**loath, loth** predic: **be** ~ **to** не хотеть impf +inf.

**loathe** vt ненавидеть impf.

**loathing** n отвращение.

**loathsome** adj отвратительный.

**lob** vt высоко подбрасывать impf, подбросить pf.

**lobby** n вестибюль m; (parl) кулуары (-ров) pl.

**lobe** n (of ear) мочка.

**lobster** n омар.

**local** adj местный.

**locality** n местность.

**localized** adj локализованный.

**locate** vt (place) помещать impf, поместить pf; (find) находить impf, найти pf; **be** ~**d** находиться impf.

**location** n (position) местонахождение; **on** ~ (cin) на натуре.

**locative** adj (n) местный (падеж).

**lock**[1] n (of hair) локон; pl волосы (-ос, -осам) pl.

**lock**[2] n замок; (canal) шлюз; vt & i запирать(ся) impf, запереть(ся) pf; ~ **out** не впускать impf; (in imprison) сажать impf, посадить pf; (close) закрывать(ся) impf, закрыть(ся) pf.

**locker** *n* шка́фчик.
**locket** *n* медальо́н.
**locksmith** *n* сле́сарь *m*.
**locomotion** *n* передвиже́ние.
**locomotive** *n* локомоти́в.
**lodge** *n* (*hunting*) (охо́тничий) до́мик; (*porter's*) сторо́жка; (*Masonic*) ло́жа; *vt* (*accommodate*) помеща́ть *impf*, помести́ть *pf*; (*complaint*) подава́ть *impf*, пода́ть *pf*; *vi* (*reside*) жить *impf* with y+gen); (*stick*) заса́живать *impf*, засе́сть *pf*. **lodger** *n* жиле́ц, жили́ца. **lodging** *n* (*also pl*) кварти́ра, (снима́емая) ко́мната.
**loft** *n* (*attic*) черда́к.
**lofty** *adj* о́чень высо́кий; (*elevated*) возвы́шенный.
**log** *n* бревно́; (*for fire*) поле́но; ~-**book** (*naut*) ва́хтенный журна́л.
**logarithm** *n* логари́фм.
**loggerhead** *n*: be at ~s быть в ссо́ре.
**logic** *n* ло́гика. **logical** *adj* (*of logic*) логи́ческий; (*consistent*) логи́чный.
**logistics** *n pl* материа́льно-техни́ческое обеспе́чение; (*fig*) пробле́мы *f pl* организа́ции.
**logo** *n* эмбле́ма.
**loin** *n* (*pl*) поясни́ца; (*cul*) филе́йная часть.
**loiter** *vi* слоня́ться *impf*.
**lone, lonely** *adj* одино́кий. **loneliness** *n* одино́чество.
**long**[1] *vi* (*want*) стра́стно жела́ть *impf*, по~ *pf* (**for** +gen); (*miss*) тоскова́ть *impf* (**for** по+dat).
**long**[2] *adj* (*space*) дли́нный; (*time*) до́лгий; (*in measurements*) длино́й в+acc; **in the** ~ **run** в коне́чном счёте; ~-

**sighted** дальнозо́ркий; ~-**suffering** долготерпели́вый; ~-**term** долгосро́чный; ~-**winded** многоречи́вый; *adv* до́лго; ~ **ago** (*уже́*) давно́; **as** ~ **as** пока́; ~ **before** задо́лго до+gen.
**longevity** *n* долгове́чность.
**longing** *n* стра́стное жела́ние (**for** +gen); тоска́ (**for** по+dat); *adj* тоску́ющий.
**longitude** *n* долгота́.
**longways** *adv* в длину́.
**look** *n* (*glance*) взгляд; (*appearance*) вид; (*expression*) выраже́ние; *vi* смотре́ть *impf*, по~ *pf* (**at** на, в, +acc); (*appear*) вы́глядеть *impf* +instr; (*face*) выходи́ть *impf* (**towards, onto** на+acc); ~ **about** осма́триваться *impf*, осмотре́ться *pf*; ~ **after** (*attend to*) присма́тривать *impf*, присмотре́ть *pf* за+instr; ~ **down on** презира́ть *impf*; ~ **for** иска́ть *impf* +acc, +gen; ~ **forward to** предвкуша́ть *impf*, предвкуси́ть *pf*; ~ **in on** загля́дывать *impf*, загляну́ть *pf* к+dat; ~ **into** (*investigate*) рассма́тривать *impf*, рассмотре́ть *pf*; ~ **like** быть похо́жим на+acc; **it** ~s **like rain** похо́же на то, что бу́дет дождь; ~ **on** (*regard*) счита́ть *impf*, счесть *pf* (**as** +instr, за+instr); ~ **out** выгля́дывать *impf*, вы́гля-нуть *pf* (в окно́); быть насторо́же; *imper* осторо́жно!; ~ **over, through** просма́тривать *impf*, просмотре́ть *pf*; ~ **round** (*inspect*) осма́тривать *impf*, осмотре́ть *pf*; ~ **up** (*raise eyes*) поднима́ть *impf*, подня́ть *pf* глаза́; (*in dictionary etc.*) иска́ть *impf*; (*improve*) улучша́ться *impf*,

улу́чшиться *pf*; ~ **up to** уважа́ть *impf*.

**loom**[1] *n* тка́цкий стано́к.

**loom**[2] *vi* вырисо́вываться *impf*, вы́рисоваться *pf*, (*fig*) надвига́ться *impf*.

**loop** *n* пе́тля; *vt* образо́вывать *impf*, образова́ть *pf* пе́тлю; (*fasten with loop*) закрепля́ть *impf*, закрепи́ть *pf* пе́тлей; (*wind*) обма́тывать *impf*, обмота́ть *pf* (*around* вокру́г+*gen*).

**loophole** *n* бойни́ца; (*fig*) лазе́йка.

**loose** *adj* (*free; not tight*) свобо́дный; (*not fixed*) непрекреплённый; (*connection, screw*) сла́бый; (*lax*) распу́щенный; **at a ~ end** без де́ла.

**loosen** *vt & i* ослабля́ть(ся) *impf*, осла́бить(ся) *pf*.

**loot** *n* добы́ча; *vt* гра́бить *impf*, o~ *pf*.

**lop** *vt* (*tree*) подреза́ть *impf*, подре́зать *pf*; (~ *off*) отруба́ть *impf*, отруби́ть *pf*.

**lope** *vi* бежа́ть *indet*, бежа́ть *det* вприпры́жку.

**lopsided** *adj* кривобо́кий.

**loquacious** *adj* болтли́вый.

**lord** *n* (*master*) господи́н; (*eccl*) Госпо́дь; (*peer; title*) лорд; *vt*: ~ **it over** помыка́ть *impf* +*instr*. **lordship** *n* (*title*) све́тлость.

**lore** *n* зна́ния *neut pl*.

**lorry** *n* грузови́к.

**lose** *vt* теря́ть *impf*, по~ *pf*; *vt & i* (*game etc.*) прои́грывать *impf*, проигра́ть *pf*; *vi* (*clock*) отстава́ть *impf*, отста́ть *pf*. **loss** *n* поте́ря; (*monetary*) убы́ток; (*in game*) про́игрыш.

**lot** *n* жре́бий; (*destiny*) уча́сть; (*of goods*) па́ртия; **a ~, ~s**

мно́го; **the ~** всё, все *pl*.

**loth** *see* loath

**lotion** *n* лосьо́н.

**lottery** *n* лотере́я.

**loud** *adj* (*sound*) гро́мкий; (*noisy*) шу́мный; (*colour*) крича́щий; **out** ~ вслух. **loudspeaker** *n* громкоговори́тель *m*.

**lounge** *n* гости́ная *sb*; *vi* сиде́ть *impf* разва́лясь; (*idle*) безде́льничать *impf*.

**louse** *n* вошь. **lousy** *adj* (*coll*) парши́вый.

**lout** *n* балбе́с, у́вален *m*.

**lovable** *adj* ми́лый. **love** *n* любо́вь (**of, for** к+*dat*); **in ~ with** влюблённый в+*acc*; *vt* люби́ть *impf*. **lovely** *adj* прекра́сный; (*delightful*) преле́стный; **lover** *n* любо́вник, -ица.

**low** *adj* ни́зкий, невысо́кий; (*quiet*) ти́хий.

**lower**[1] *vt* опуска́ть *impf*, опусти́ть *pf*; (*price, voice, standard*) понижа́ть *impf*, пони́зить *pf*.

**lower**[2] *adj* ни́жний.

**lowland** *n* ни́зменность.

**lowly** *adj* скро́мный.

**loyal** *adj* ве́рный. **loyalty** *n* ве́рность.

**LP** *abbr* (**of long-playing record**) долгоигра́ющая пласти́нка.

**Ltd.** *abbr* (**of Limited**) с ограни́ченной отве́тственностью.

**lubricant** *n* сма́зка. **lubricate** *vt* сма́зывать *impf*, сма́зать *pf*. **lubrication** *n* сма́зка.

**lucid** *adj* я́сный. **lucidity** *n* я́сность.

**luck** *n* (*chance*) слу́чай; (*good*) сча́стье, уда́ча; (*bad*) неуда́ча. **luckily** *adv* к сча́стью. **lucky** *adj* счастли́вый; **be** ~ везти́ *imp*, по~ *pf impers* +*dat*: **I was** ~ мне повезло́.

lucrative adj при́быльный.
ludicrous adj смехотво́рный.
lug vt (drag) таска́ть indet, тащи́ть det.
luggage n бага́ж.
lugubrious adj печа́льный.
lukewarm adj теплова́тый; (fig) прохла́дный.
lull n (in storm) зати́шье; (interval) переры́в; vt (to sleep) убаю́кивать impf, убаю́кать pf; (suspicions) усыпля́ть impf, усыпи́ть pf.
lullaby n колыбе́льная пе́сня.
lumbar adj поясни́чный.
lumber¹ n (move) брести́ impf.
lumber² n (domestic) ру́хлядь; vt обременя́ть impf, обремени́ть pf. lumberjack n лесору́б.
luminary n свети́ло.
luminous adj светя́щийся.
lump n ком; (swelling) о́пухоль; vt: ~ together сме́шивать impf, смеша́ть pf (в одно́).
lunacy n безу́мие.
lunar adj лу́нный.
lunatic adj (n) сумасше́дший (sb).
lunch n обе́д; ~-hour, ~-time обе́денный переры́в; vi обе́дать impf, по~ pf.
lung n лёгкое sb.
lunge vi (move) де́лать impf, с~ pf вы́пад (at про́тив+gen).
lurch¹ n: leave in the ~ покида́ть impf, поки́нуть pf в беде́.
lurch² vi (stagger) ходи́ть indet, идти́ det шата́ясь.
lure n прима́нка; vt прима́нивать impf, примани́ть pf.
lurid adj (gaudy) крича́щий; (details) жу́ткий.
lurk vi зата́иваться impf, зата́иться pf.
luscious adj со́чный.

lush adj пы́шный, со́чный.
lust n по́хоть (of, for к+dat); vi стра́стно жела́ть impf, по~ pf (for +gen). lustful adj похотли́вый.
lustre n гля́нец. lustrous adj гля́нцеви́тый.
lusty adj (healthy) здоро́вый; (lively) живо́й.
lute n (mus) лю́тня.
luxuriant adj пы́шный.
luxuriate vi наслажда́ться impf, наслади́ться pf (in +instr).
luxurious adj роско́шный. luxury n ро́скошь.
lymph n лимфати́ческий.
lynch vt линчева́ть impf & pf.
lyric n ли́рика; pl слова́ neut pl пе́сни. lyrical adj лири́ческий.

# M

MA abbr (of Master of Arts) маги́стр гуманита́рных нау́к.
macabre adj жу́ткий.
macaroni n макаро́ны (-н) pl.
mace n (of office) жезл.
machination n махина́ция.
machine n маши́на; (state ~) аппара́т; attrib маши́нный; ~-gun пулемёт; ~ tool стано́к; vt обраба́тывать impf, обрабо́тать pf на станке́; (sew) шить impf, с~ pf (на маши́не). machinery n (machines) маши́ны f pl; (of state) аппара́т. machinist n маши́нист; (sewing) швей-ни́к, -и́ца, швея́.
mackerel n ску́мбрия, макре́ль.
mackintosh n плащ.
mad adj сумасше́дший. mad-

**den** vt беси́ть impf, вз~ pf.
**madhouse** n сумасше́дший дом. **madly** adv безу́мно. **madman** n сумасше́дший sb. **madness** n сумасше́ствие. **madwoman** n сумасше́дшая sb.

**madrigal** n мадрига́л.
**maestro** n ма́эстро m indecl.
**Mafia** n ма́фия.
**magazine** n журна́л; (of gun) магази́н.
**maggot** n личи́нка.
**magic** n ма́гия, волшебство́; adj (also **magical**) волше́бный. **magician** n волше́бник; (conjurer) фо́кусник.
**magisterial** adj авторите́тный.
**magistrate** n судья́ m.
**magnanimity** n великоду́шие.
**magnanimous** adj великоду́шный.
**magnate** n магна́т.
**magnesium** n ма́гний.
**magnet** n магни́т. **magnetic** adj магни́тный; (attractive) притяга́тельный. **magnetism** n магнети́зм; притяга́тельность. **magnetize** vt намагни́чивать impf, намагни́тить pf.
**magnification** n увеличе́ние.
**magnificence** n великоле́пие. **magnificent** adj великоле́пный.
**magnify** vt увели́чивать impf, увели́чить pf; (exaggerate) преувели́чивать impf, преувели́чить pf. **magnifying glass** n увеличи́тельное стекло́.
**magnitude** n величина́; (importance) ва́жность.
**magpie** n соро́ка.
**mahogany** n кра́сное де́рево.
**maid** n прислу́га. **maiden** adj (aunt etc.) незаму́жняя; (first)

пе́рвый; ~ **name** де́вичья фами́лия.
**mail** n (letters) по́чта; ~ **order** почто́вый зака́з; vt посыла́ть impf, посла́ть pf по по́чте.
**maim** vt кале́чить impf, ис~ pf.
**main** n (gas ~; pl) магистра́ль; **in the** ~ в основно́м; adj основно́й, гла́вный; (road) магистра́льный. **mainland** n матери́к. **mainly** adv в основно́м. **mainstay** n (fig) гла́вная опо́ра.
**maintain** vt (keep up) подде́рживать impf, поддержа́ть pf; (family) содержа́ть impf; (machine) обслу́живать impf, обслужи́ть pf; (assert) утвержда́ть impf. **maintenance** n подде́ржка; содержа́ние; обслу́живание.
**maize** n кукуру́за.
**majestic** adj вели́чественный. **majesty** n вели́чественность; (title) вели́чество.
**major**[1] n (mil) майо́р.
**major**[2] adj (greater) бо́льший; (more important) бо́лее ва́жный; (main) гла́вный; (mus) мажо́рный; n (mus) мажо́р. **majority** n большинство́; (full age) совершенноле́тие.
**make** vt де́лать impf, с~ pf; (produce) производи́ть impf, произвести́ pf; (prepare) гото́вить impf, при~ pf; (amount to) равня́ться impf +dat; зараба́тывать impf, зарабо́тать pf; (compel) заста́вить impf, заста́вить pf; (reach) добира́ться impf, добра́ться pf до+gen; (be in time for) успева́ть impf, успе́ть pf на+acc; **be made of** состоя́ть impf из+gen;

~ as if, though де́лать impf, с~ pf вид, что; ~ a bed стели́ть impf, по~ pf посте́ль; ~ believe притворя́ться impf, притвори́ться pf; ~-believe притво́рство; ~ do with дово́льствоваться impf, у~ pf +instr; ~ off удира́ть impf, удра́ть pf; ~ out (cheque) выпи́сывать impf, вы́писать pf; (assert) утвержда́ть impf, утверди́ть pf; (understand) разбира́ть impf, разобра́ть pf; ~ over передава́ть impf, переда́ть pf; ~ up (form, compose, complete) составля́ть impf, соста́вить pf; (invent) выду́мывать impf, вы́думать pf; (theat) гримирова́ть(ся) impf, за~ pf; ~ up (theat) грим; (cosmetics) косме́тика; (composition) соста́в; ~ it up мири́ться impf, по~ pf (with c+instr); ~ up for возмеща́ть impf, возмести́ть pf; ~ up one's mind реша́ться impf, реши́ться pf. **make** n ма́рка. **makeshift** adj вре́менный.

**malady** n боле́знь.

**malaise** n (fig) беспоко́йство.

**malaria** n маляри́я.

**male** n (animal) саме́ц; (person) мужчи́на m; adj мужско́й.

**malevolence** n недоброжела́тельность. **malevolent** adj недоброжела́тельный.

**malice** n зло́ба. **malicious** adj зло́бный.

**malign** vt клевета́ть impf, на~ pf+acc. **malignant** adj (harmful) зловре́дный; (malicious) зло́бный; (med) злока́чественный.

**malinger** vi притворя́ться impf, притвори́ться pf больны́м.

**malingerer** n симуля́нт.

**mallard** n кря́ква.

**malleable** adj ко́вкий; (fig) пода́тливый.

**mallet** n (деревя́нный) молото́к.

**malnutrition** n недоеда́ние.

**malpractice** n престу́пная небре́жность.

**malt** n со́лод.

**maltreat** vt пло́хо обраща́ться impf c+instr.

**mammal** n млекопита́ющее sb.

**mammoth** adj грома́дный.

**man** n (human, person) челове́к; (human race) челове́чество; (male) мужчи́на m; (labourer) рабо́чий sb; pl (soldiers) солда́ты m pl; vt (furnish with men) укомплекто́вывать impf, укомплектова́ть pf ли́чным соста́вом; ста́вить impf, по~ pf люде́й к+dat; (stall etc.) обслу́живать impf, обслужи́ть pf; (gate, checkpoint) стоя́ть impf на+prep.

**manacle** n нару́чник; vt надева́ть impf, наде́ть pf нару́чники на+acc.

**manage** vt (control) управля́ть impf +instr; vi(&t) (cope) справля́ться impf, спра́виться pf (c+instr); (succeed) суме́ть pf. **management** n управле́ние (of +instr); (the~) администра́ция. **manager** n управля́ющий sb (of +instr); ме́неджер. **managerial** adj администрати́вный. **managing director** n дире́ктор-распоряди́тель m.

**mandarin** n мандари́н.

**mandate** n манда́т. **mandated** adj подманда́тный. **mandatory** adj обяза́тельный.

**mane** *n* гри́ва.

**manful** *adj* му́жественный.

**manganese** *n* ма́рганец.

**manger** *n* я́сли (-лей) *pl*; **dog in the** ~ соба́ка на се́не.

**mangle** *vt* (*mutilate*) кале́чить *impf*, ис~ *pf*.

**mango** *n* ма́нго *neut indecl*.

**manhandle** *vt* гру́бо обраща́ться *impf* c+*instr*.

**manhole** *n* смотрово́й коло́дец.

**manhood** *n* возмужа́лость.

**mania** *n* ма́ния. **maniac** *n* манья́к, -я́чка. **manic** *adj* маниака́льный.

**manicure** *n* маникю́р; *vt* де́лать *impf*, c~ *pf* маникю́р +*dat*. **manicurist** *n* маникю́рша.

**manifest** *adj* очеви́дный; *vt* (*display*) проявля́ть *impf*, прояви́ть *pf*; *n* манифе́ст. **manifestation** *n* проявле́ние. **manifesto** *n* манифе́ст.

**manifold** *adj* разнообра́зный.

**manipulate** *vt* манипули́ровать *impf* +*instr*. **manipulation** *n* манипуля́ция.

**manly** *adj* му́жественный.

**mankind** *n* челове́чество.

**manner** *n* (*way*) о́браз; (*behaviour*) мане́ра; *pl* мане́ры *f pl*. **mannerism** *n* мане́ра.

**mannish** *adj* мужеподо́бный.

**manoeuvrable** *adj* мане́вренный. **manoeuvre** *n* манёвр; *vt* & *i* маневри́ровать *impf*.

**manor** *n* поме́стье; (*house*) поме́щичий дом.

**manpower** *n* челове́ческие ресу́рсы *m pl*.

**manservant** *n* слуга́ *m*.

**mansion** *n* особня́к.

**manslaughter** *n* непредумы́шленное уби́йство.

**mantelpiece** *n* ками́нная

доска́.

**manual** *adj* ручно́й; *n* руково́дство. **manually** *adv* вручну́ю.

**manufacture** *n* произво́дство; *vt* производи́ть *impf*, произвести́ *pf*. **manufacturer** *n* фабрика́нт.

**manure** *n* наво́з.

**manuscript** *n* ру́копись.

**many** *adj & n* мно́го +*gen*, мно́гие *pl*; **how** ~ ско́лько +*gen*.

**map** *n* ка́рта; (*of town*) план; *vt*: ~ **out** намеча́ть *impf*, наме́тить *pf*.

**maple** *n* клён.

**mar** *vt* по́ртить *impf*, ис~ *pf*.

**marathon** *n* марафо́н.

**marauder** *n* мароде́р. **marauding** *adj* мароде́рский.

**marble** *n* мра́мор; (*toy*) ша́рик; *attrib* мра́морный.

**March** *n* март; *adj* ма́ртовский.

**march** *vi* марширова́ть *impf*, про~ *pf*; *n* марш.

**mare** *n* кобы́ла.

**margarine** *n* маргари́н.

**margin** *n* (*on page*) по́ле; (*edge*) край; **profit** ~ при́быль; **safety** ~ запа́с про́чности.

**marigold** *n* ногото́к (-ко́в) *pl.*

**marijuana** *n* марихуа́на.

**marina** *n* мари́на.

**marinade** *n* марина́д; *vt* мелинова́ть *impf*, за~ *pf.*

**marine** *adj* морско́й; (*soldier*) солда́т морско́й пехо́ты; *pl* морска́я пехо́та. **mariner** *n* моря́к.

**marionette** *n* марионе́тка.

**marital** *adj* супру́жеский, бра́чный.

**maritime** *adj* морско́й; (*near sea*) примо́рский.

**mark**[1] *n* (*coin*) ма́рка.

**mark**[2] *n* (*for distinguishing*)

ме́тка; (sign) знак; (school) отме́тка; (trace) след; on your ~s на старт!; vt (indicate; celebrate) отмеча́ть impf, отме́тить pf; (school etc.) проверя́ть impf, прове́рить pf; (stain) па́чкать impf, за~ pf; (sport) закрыва́ть impf, закры́ть pf; ~ my words попо́мни(те) мои́ слова́!; ~ out размеча́ть impf, разме́тить pf. **marker** n знак; (in book) закла́дка.

**market** n ры́нок; (garden ~) огоро́д; ~-place база́рная пло́щадь; vt продава́ть impf, прода́ть pf.

**marksman** n стрело́к.

**marmalade** n апельси́новый джем.

**maroon**[1] adj (n) (colour) тёмно-бордо́вый (цвет).

**maroon**[2] vt (put ashore) выса́живать impf, вы́садить pf (на необита́емом о́строве); (cut off) отреза́ть impf, отре́зать pf.

**marquee** n тэнт.

**marquis** n марки́з.

**marriage** n брак; (wedding) сва́дьба; attrib бра́чный. **marriageable** adj: ~ age бра́чный во́зраст. **married** adj (man) жена́тый; (woman) заму́жняя, за́мужем; (to each other) жена́ты; (of ~ persons) супру́жеский.

**marrow** n ко́стный мозг; (vegetable) кабачо́к.

**marry** vt (of man) жени́ться impf & pf на +prep; (of woman) выходи́ть impf, вы́йти pf за́муж за +acc; vi (of couple) пожени́ться pf.

**marsh** n боло́то. **marshy** adj боло́тистый.

**marshal** n ма́ршал; vt вы-

стра́ивать impf, вы́строить pf; (fig) собира́ть impf, собра́ть pf.

**marsupial** n су́мчатое живо́тное sb.

**martial** adj вое́нный; ~ law вое́нное положе́ние.

**martyr** n му́ченик, -ица; vt му́чить impf, за~ pf. **martyrdom** n му́ченичество.

**marvel** n чу́до; vi изумля́ться impf, изуми́ться pf. **marvellous** adj чуде́сный.

**Marxist** n маркси́ст; adj маркси́стский. **Marxism** n маркси́зм.

**marzipan** n марципа́н.

**mascara** n тушь.

**mascot** n талисма́н.

**masculine** adj мужско́й; (gram) мужско́го ро́да; (of woman) мужеподо́бный.

**mash** n карто́фельное пюре́ neut indecl; vt размина́ть impf, размя́ть pf.

**mask** n ма́ска; vt маскирова́ть impf, за~ pf.

**masochism** n мазохи́зм. **masochist** n мазохи́ст. **masochistic** adj мазохи́стский.

**mason** n ка́менщик; (M~) масо́н. **Masonic** adj масо́нский. **masonry** n ка́менная кла́дка.

**masquerade** n маскара́д; vi: ~ as выдава́ть impf, вы́дать pf себя́ за+acc.

**Mass** n (eccl) ме́сса.

**mass** n ма́сса; (majority) большинство́; attrib ма́ссовый; ~ media сре́дства neut pl ма́ссовой информа́ции; ~-produced ма́ссового произво́дства; ~ production ма́ссовое произво́дство; vt масси́ровать impf & pf; vi собира́ться impf, собра́ться pf.

**massacre** n резня́; vt выреза́ть impf, вы́резать pf.

**massage** n масса́ж; vt масси́ровать impf & pf. **masseur, -euse** n массажи́ст, ~ка.

**massive** adj масси́вный; (huge) огро́мный.

**mast** n ма́чта.

**master** n (owner) хозя́ин; (of ship) капита́н; (teacher) учи́тель m; (M~, univ) маги́стр; (workman, artist) ма́стер; (original) по́длинник, оригина́л; be ~ of владе́ть impf +instr; ~key отмы́чка; vt (overcome) преодолева́ть impf, преодоле́ть pf; справля́ться impf, спра́виться pf с+instr; (a subject) овладева́ть impf, овладе́ть pf +instr. **masterful** adj вла́стный. **masterly** adj мастерско́й. **masterpiece** n шеде́вр. **mastery** n (of a subject) владе́ние (of +instr).

**masturbate** vi мастурби́ровать impf.

**mat** n (at door) полови́к; (on table) подста́вка.

**match¹** n спи́чка. **matchbox** n спи́чечная коро́бка.

**match²** n (equal) ро́вня m & f; (contest) матч, состяза́ние; (marriage) па́ртия; vi & t (go well (with)) гармони́ровать impf (c+instr); подходи́ть impf, подойти́ pf (к+dat).

**mate¹** n (chess) мат.

**mate²** n (one of pair) саме́ц, са́мка; (fellow worker) това́рищ; (naut) помо́щник капита́на; vi (of animals) спа́риваться impf, спа́риться pf.

**material** n материа́л; (cloth) мате́рия; pl (necessary articles) принадле́жности f pl. **materialism** n материали́зм. **materialistic** adj материалисти́ческий. **materialize** vi осуществля́ться impf, осу-

ществи́ться pf.

**maternal** adj матери́нский; ~ grandfather де́душка с матери́нской стороны́. **maternity** n матери́нство; ~ leave декре́тный о́тпуск; ~ ward роди́льное отделе́ние.

**mathematical** adj математи́ческий. **mathematician** n матема́тик. **mathematics, maths** n матема́тика.

**matinée** n дневно́й спекта́кль m.

**matriarchal** adj матриарха́льный. **matriarchy** n матриарха́т.

**matriculate** vi быть при́нятым в вуз. **matriculation** n зачисле́ние в вуз.

**matrimonial** adj супру́жеский. **matrimony** n брак.

**matrix** n ма́трица.

**matron** n ста́ршая сестра́.

**matt** adj ма́товый.

**matted** adj спу́танный.

**matter** n (affair) де́ло; (question) вопро́с; (substance) вещество́; (philos; med) мате́рия; (printed) материа́л; a ~ of life and death вопро́с жи́зни и сме́рти; a ~ of opinion спо́рное де́ло; a ~ of taste де́ло вку́са; as a ~ of fact факти́чески; со́бственно говоря́; what's the ~? в чём де́ло?; what's the ~ with him? что с ним?; ~-of-fact прозаи́чный; vi име́ть impf значе́ние; it doesn't ~ не име́ет значе́ния; it ~s a lot to me для меня́ э́то о́чень ва́жно.

**matting** n рого́жа.

**mattress** n матра́с.

**mature** adj зре́лый; vi зреть impf, co~ pf. **maturity** n зре́лость.

**maul** vt терза́ть impf.

**mausoleum** n мавзоле́й.

**mauve** adj (n) розова́то-лило́вый (цвет).

**maxim** n сенте́нция.

**maximum** n ма́ксимум; adj максима́льный.

**may** v aux (possibility, permission) мочь impf, c~ pf; (possibility) возмо́жно, что +indicative; (wish) пусть +indicative.

**May** n (month) май; adj ма́йский ~ **Day** Пе́рвое sb ма́я.

**maybe** adv мо́жет быть.

**mayonnaise** n майоне́з.

**mayor** n мэр. **mayoress** n жена́ мэ́ра; же́нщина-мэр.

**maze** n лабири́нт.

**meadow** n луг.

**meagre** adj ску́дный.

**meal**[1] n еда́; at ~times во вре́мя еды́.

**meal**[2] n (grain) мука́. **mealy** adj: ~-mouthed сладкоре́чивый.

**mean**[1] adj (average) сре́дний; n (middle point) середи́на; pl (method) сре́дство, спо́соб; pl (resources) сре́дства neut pl; by all ~s коне́чно, пожа́луйста; by ~s of при по́мощи +gen, посре́дством +gen; by no ~s совсе́м не; ~s test прове́рка нужда́емости.

**mean**[2] adj (ignoble) по́длый; (miserly) скупо́й; (poor) убо́гий.

**mean**[3] vt (have in mind) име́ть impf в виду́; (intend) намерева́ться impf +inf; (signify) зна́чить impf.

**meander** vi (stream) извива́ться impf; (person) броди́ть impf. **meandering** adj изви́листый.

**meaning** n значе́ние. **meaningful** adj (много)значи́тельный. **meaningless** adj бессмы́сленный.

**meantime**, **meanwhile** adv ме́жду тем.

**measles** n корь. **measly** adj ничто́жный.

**measurable** adj измери́мый.

**measure** n ме́ра; made to ~ сши́тый по ме́рке; сде́ланный на зака́з; vt измеря́ть impf, изме́рить pf; (for clothes) снима́ть impf, снять pf ме́рку c+gen; vi име́ть impf +acc: the room ~s 30 feet in length ко́мната име́ет три́дцать фу́тов в длину́; ~ off, out отмеря́ть impf, отме́рить pf; ~ up to соотве́тствовать impf +dat. **measured** adj (rhythmical) ме́рный. **measurement** n (action) измере́ние; pl (dimensions) разме́ры m pl.

**meat** n мя́со. **meatball** n котле́та. **meaty** adj мяси́стый; (fig) содержа́тельный.

**mechanic** n меха́ник. **mechanical** adj механи́ческий; (fig; automatic) машина́льный; ~ **engineer** инжене́р-меха́ник; ~ **engineering** машинострое́ние. **mechanics** n меха́ника. **mechanism** n механи́зм. **mechanization** n механиза́ция. **mechanize** vt механизи́ровать impf & pf.

**medal** n меда́ль. **medallion** n медальо́н. **medallist** n медали́ст.

**meddle** vi вме́шиваться impf, вмеша́ться pf (in, with в+acc).

**media** pl of **medium**

**mediate** vi посре́дничать impf. **mediation** n посре́дничество. **mediator** n посре́дник.

**medical** adj медици́нский; ~ **student** ме́дик, -и́чка. **med-**

**icated** adj (impregnated) пропи́танный лека́рством. **medicinal** adj (of medicine) лека́рственный; (healing) целе́бный. **medicine** n медици́на; (substance) лека́рство.

**medieval** adj средневеко́вый.

**mediocre** adj посре́дственный. **mediocrity** n посре́дственность.

**meditate** vi размышля́ть impf. **meditation** n размышле́ние. **meditative** adj заду́мчивый.

**Mediterranean** adj средиземномо́рский; n Средизе́мное мо́ре.

**medium** n (means) сре́дство; (phys) среда́; (person) ме́диум; pl (mass media) сре́дства neut pl ма́ссовой информа́ции; adj сре́дний; **happy** ~ золота́я середи́на.

**medley** n смесь; (mus) попурри́ neut indecl.

**meek** adj кро́ткий.

**meet** vt & i встреча́ть(ся) impf, встре́тить(ся) pf; vt (make acquaintance) знако́миться impf, по~ pf c+instr; vi (assemble) собира́ться impf, собра́ться pf. **meeting** n встре́ча; pf (of committee) заседа́ние, ми́тинг.

**megalomania** n мегалома́ния.

**megaphone** n мегафо́н.

**melancholic** adj меланхоли́ческий. **melancholy** n грусть; adj уны́лый, гру́стный.

**mellow** adj (colour, sound) со́чный; (person) доброду́шный; vi смягча́ться impf, смягчи́ться pf.

**melodic** adj мелоди́ческий. **melodious** adj мелоди́чный. **melody** n мело́дия.

**melodrama** n мелодра́ма.

**melodramatic** adj мелодрамати́ческий.

**melon** n ды́ня; (water-~) арбу́з.

**melt** vt & i раста́пливать(ся) impf, растопи́ть(ся) pf, (smelt) пла́вить(ся) impf, рас~ pf; (dissolve) растворя́ть(ся) impf, раствори́ть(ся) pf; vi (thaw) та́ять impf, рас~ pf; ~ing point то́чка плавле́ния.

**member** n член. **membership** n чле́нство; (number of ~) коли́чество чле́нов; attrib чле́нский.

**membrane** n перепо́нка.

**memento** n сувени́р. **memoir** n pl мемуа́ры (-ров) pl; воспомина́ния neut pl. **memorable** adj достопа́мятный. **memorandum** n запи́ска. **memorial** adj мемориа́льный; n па́мятник. **memorize** vt запомина́ть impf, запо́мнить pf. **memory** n па́мять; (recollection) воспомина́ние.

**menace** n угро́за; vt угрожа́ть impf +dat. **menacing** adj угрожа́ющий.

**menagerie** n звери́нец.

**mend** vt чини́ть impf, по~ pf; (clothes) што́пать impf, за~ pf; ~ **one's ways** исправля́ться impf, испра́виться pf.

**menial** adj ни́зкий, чёрный.

**meningitis** n менинги́т.

**menopause** n кли́макс.

**menstrual** adj менструа́льный. **menstruation** n менструа́ция.

**mental** adj у́мственный; (of illness) психи́ческий; ~ **arithmetic** счёт в уме́. **mentality** n ум; (character) склад ума́.

**mention** n упомина́ть impf, упомяну́ть pf; **don't** ~ **it** не́ за что!; **not to** ~ не говоря́ уже́ о+prep.

**menu** n меню́ neut indecl.
**mercantile** adj торго́вый.
**mercenary** adj коры́стный; (hired) наёмный; n наёмник.
**merchandise** n това́ры m pl.
**merchant** n купе́ц; торго́вец; ~ **navy** торго́вый флот.
**merciful** adj милосе́рдный. **mercifully** adv к сча́стью. **merciless** adj беспоща́дный.
**mercurial** adj (person) изме́нчивый. **mercury** n ртуть.
**mercy** n милосе́рдие; **at the** ~ **of** во вла́сти +gen.
**mere** adj просто́й; **a** ~ £40 всего́ лишь со́рок фу́нтов. **merely** adv то́лько, про́сто.
**merge** vt & i слива́ть(ся) impf, слить(ся) pf. **merger** n объедине́ние.
**meridian** n меридиа́н.
**meringue** n меренга.
**merit** n заслу́га, досто́инство; vt заслу́живать impf, заслужи́ть pf +gen.
**mermaid** n руса́лка.
**merrily** adv ве́село. **merriment** n весе́лье. **merry** adj весёлый; ~-**go-round** карусе́ль; ~-**making** весе́лье.
**mesh** n сеть; vi сцепля́ться impf, сцепи́ться pf.
**mesmerize** vt гипнотизи́ровать impf, за~ pf.
**mess** n (disorder) беспоря́док; (trouble) беда́; (eating-place) столо́вая sb; vi: ~ **about** вози́ться impf; ~ **up** по́ртить impf, ис~ pf.
**message** n сообще́ние. **messenger** n курье́р.
**Messiah** n месси́я m. **Messianic** adj месси́анский.
**Messrs** abbr господа́ (gen -д) m pl.
**messy** adj (untidy) беспоря́дочный; (dirty) гря́зный.

**metabolism** n обме́н веще́ств.
**metal** n мета́лл; adj металли́ческий. **metallic** adj металли́ческий. **metallurgy** n металлу́ргия.
**metamorphosis** n метаморфо́за.
**metaphor** n мета́фора. **metaphorical** adj метафори́ческий.
**metaphysical** adj метафизи́ческий. **metaphysics** n метафи́зика.
**meteor** n метео́р. **meteoric** adj метеори́ческий. **meteorite** n метеори́т. **meteorological** adj метеорологи́ческий. **meteorology** n метеороло́гия.
**meter** n счётчик; vt измеря́ть impf, изме́рить pf.
**methane** n мета́н.
**method** n ме́тод. **methodical** adj методи́чный.
**Methodist** n методи́ст; adj методи́стский.
**methodology** n методоло́гия.
**methylated** adj: ~ **spirit(s)** денатура́т.
**meticulous** adj тща́тельный.
**metre** n метр. **metric(al)** adj метри́ческий.
**metronome** n метроно́м.
**metropolis** n столи́ца. **metropolitan** adj столи́чный; n (eccl) митрополи́т.
**mettle** n хара́ктер.
**Mexican** adj мексика́нский; n мексика́нец, -а́нка. **Mexico** n Ме́ксика.
**mezzanine** n антресо́ли f pl.
**miaow** int мя́у; n мя́уканье; vi мяу́кать impf, мяу́кнуть pf.
**mica** n слюда́.
**microbe** n микро́б. **microchip** n чип, микросхе́ма. **microcomputer** n микрокомпью́тер. **microcosm** n микро-

косм. **microfilm** *n* микрофи́льм. **micro-organism** *n* микрооргани́зм. **microphone** *n* микрофо́н. **microscope** *n* микроско́п. **microscopic** *adj* микроскопи́ческий. **microwave** *n* микроволна́; ~ **oven** микроволно́вая печь.

**mid** *adj*: ~ **May** середи́на ма́я. **midday** *n* по́лдень *m*; *attrib* полуде́нный. **middle** *n* середи́на; *adj* сре́дний; ~-**aged** сре́дних лет; **M~ Ages** сре́дние века́ *m pl*; ~-**class** буржуа́зный; ~-**man** посре́дник; ~-**sized** сре́дней величины́. **middleweight** *n* сре́дний вес. **midge** *n* мо́шка. **midget** *n* ка́рлик, -ица. **midnight** *n* по́лночь; *attrib* полуно́чный. **midriff** *n* диафра́гма. **midst** *n* середи́на. **midsummer** *n* середи́на ле́та. **midway** *adv* на полпути́. **midweek** *n* середи́на неде́ли. **midwinter** *n* середи́на зимы́. **midwife** *n* акуше́рка. **midwifery** *n* акуше́рство.

**might** *n* мощь; **with all one's** ~ из всех сил. **mighty** *adj* мо́щный.

**migraine** *n* мигре́нь.

**migrant** *adj* кочу́ющий; (*bird*) перелётный; *n* (*person*) переселе́нец; (*bird*) перелётная пти́ца. **migrate** *vi* мигри́ровать *impf & pf*. **migration** *n* мигра́ция. **migratory** *adj* кочу́ющий; (*bird*) перелётный.

**mike** *n* микрофо́н.

**mild** *adj* мя́гкий.

**mildew** *n* пле́сень.

**mile** *n* ми́ля. **mileage** *n* расстоя́ние в ми́лях; (*of car*) пробе́г. **milestone** *n* верстово́й столб; (*fig*) ве́ха.

**militancy** *n* вой́нственность.

**militant** *adj* вой́нствующий; *n* активи́ст. **military** *adj* вое́нный; *n* вое́нные *sb pl*. **militate** *vi*: ~ **against** говори́ть *impf* про́тив+*gen*. **militia** *n* мили́ция. **militiaman** *n* милиционе́р.

**milk** *n* молоко́; *attrib* моло́чный; *vt* дои́ть *impf*, по~ *pf*. **milkman** *n* продаве́ц молока́. **milky** *adj* моло́чный; **M~ Way** Мле́чный Путь *m*.

**mill** *n* (*factory*) фа́брика; *vt* (*grain etc.*) моло́ть *impf*, с~ *pf*; (*metal*) фрезерова́ть *impf*, от~ *pf*; (*coin*) гурти́ть *impf*; *vi*: ~ **around** толпи́ться *impf*. **miller** *n* ме́льник.

**millennium** *n* тысячеле́тие.

**millet** *n* (*plant*) про́со; (*grain*) пшено́.

**milligram(me)** *n* миллигра́мм. **millimetre** *n* миллиме́тр. **million** *n* миллио́н. **millionaire** *n* миллионе́р. **millionth** *adj* миллио́нный.

**millstone** *n* жёрнов; (*fig*) ка́мень *m* на ше́е.

**mime** *n* (*dumb-show*) пантоми́ма; *vt* изобража́ть *impf*, изобрази́ть *pf* мими́чески. **mimic** *n* ми́мик; *vt* передра́знивать *impf*, передразни́ть *pf*. **mimicry** *n* имита́ция.

**minaret** *n* минаре́т.

**mince** *n* (*meat*) фарш; *vt* руби́ть *impf*; (*in machine*) пропуска́ть *impf*, пропусти́ть *pf* че́рез мясору́бку; *vi* (*walk*) семени́ть *impf*; **not** ~ **matters** говори́ть *impf* без обиняко́в. **mincemeat** *n* начи́нка из изю́ма, минда́ля и т.п. **mind** *n* ум; **bear in** ~ име́ть *impf* в виду́; **change one's**

передумывать *impf*, переду́мать *pf*; **make up one's** ~ реша́ться *impf*, реши́ться *pf*; **you're out of your** ~ вы с ума́ сошли́; *vt* (*give heed to*) обраща́ть *impf*, обрати́ть *pf* внима́ние на+*acc*; (*look after*) присма́тривать *impf*, присмотре́ть *pf* за+*instr*; **I don't** ~ я ничего́ не име́ю про́тив; **don't** ~ **me** не обраща́й(те) внима́ния на меня́!; ~ **you don't forget** смотри́ не забу́дь!; ~ **your own business** не вме́шивайтесь в чужи́е дела́!; **never** ~ ничего́! **mindful** *adj* по́мнящий. **mindless** *adj* бессмы́сленный.

**mine**[1] *poss pron* мой, свой.
**mine**[2] *n* ша́хта, рудни́к; (*fig*) исто́чник; (*mil*) ми́на; *vt* (*obtain from* ~) добыва́ть *impf*, добы́ть *pf*; (*mil*) мини́ровать *impf* & *pf*. **minefield** *n* ми́нное по́ле. **miner** *n* шахтёр.

**mineral** *n* минера́л; *adj* минера́льный; ~ **water** минера́льная вода́. **mineralogy** *n* минерало́гия.

**mingle** *vt* & *i* сме́шивать(ся) *impf*, смеша́ть(ся) *pf*.

**miniature** *n* миниатю́ра; *adj* миниатю́рный.

**minibus** *n* микроавто́бус.

**minim** *n* (*mus*) полови́нная но́та. **minimal** *adj* минима́льный. **minimize** *vt* (*reduce*) доводи́ть *impf*, довести́ *pf* до ми́нимума. **minimum** *n* ми́нимум; *adj* минима́льный.

**mining** *n* го́рное де́ло.

**minister** *n* мини́стр; (*eccl*) свяще́нник. **ministerial** *adj* министе́рский. **ministration** *n* по́мощь. **ministry** *n* (*polit*) министе́рство; (*eccl*) духове́нство.

**mink** *n* но́рка; *attrib* но́рковый.

**minor** *adj* (*unimportant*) незначи́тельный; (*less important*) второстепе́нный; *n* (*person under age*) несовершенноле́тний *n*; (*mus*) мино́р. **minority** *n* меньшинство́; (*age*) несовершенноле́тие.

**minstrel** *n* менестре́ль *m*.

**mint**[1] *n* (*plant*) мя́та; (*peppermint*) пе́речная мя́та.

**mint**[2] *n* (*econ*) моне́тный двор; **in** ~ **condition** но́венький; *vt* чека́нить *impf*, от-, вы́- *pf*.

**minuet** *n* менуэ́т.

**minus** *prep* ми́нус+*acc*; без+*gen*; *n* ми́нус.

**minuscule** *adj* малю́сенький.

**minute**[1] *n* мину́та; *pl* протоко́л.

**minute**[2] *adj* ме́лкий. **minutiae** *n pl* ме́лочи (-че́й) *pl*.

**miracle** *n* чу́до. **miraculous** *adj* чуде́сный.

**mirage** *n* мира́ж.

**mire** *n* (*mud*) грязь; (*swamp*) боло́то.

**mirror** *n* зе́ркало; *vt* отража́ть *impf*, отрази́ть *pf*.

**mirth** *n* весе́лье.

**misadventure** *n* несча́стный слу́чай.

**misapprehension** *n* недопонима́ние. **misappropriate** *vt* незако́нно присва́ивать *impf*, присво́ить *pf*. **misbehave** *vi* ду́рно вести́ *impf* себя́. **misbehaviour** *n* дурно́е поведе́ние.

**miscalculate** *vt* непра́вильно рассчи́тывать *impf*, рассчита́ть *pf*; (*fig, abs*) просчи́тываться *impf*, просчита́ться *pf*. **miscalculation** *n* просчёт. **miscarriage** *n* (*med*) вы́кидыш; ~ **of justice** су-

дéбная оши́бка. **miscarry** vi (med) имéть impf вы́кидыш.
**miscellaneous** adj рáзный, разнообрáзный. **miscellany** n смесь.
**mischief** n (harm) вред; (naughtiness) озорствó. **mischievous** adj озорнóй. **misconception** n непрáвильное представлéние. **misconduct** n дурнóе поведéние. **misconstrue** vt непрáвильно истолкóвывать impf, истолковáть pf.
**misdeed**, **misdemeanour** n простýпок. **misdirect** vt непрáвильно направля́ть impf, напрáвить pf; (letter) непрáвильно адресовáть impf & pf.
**miser** n скупéц. **miserable** adj (unhappy, wretched) несчáстный, жáлкий; (weather) сквéрный. **miserly** adj скупóй. **misery** n страдáние.
**misfire** vi давáть impf, дать pf осéчку. **misfit** n (person) неудáчник. **misfortune** n несчáстье. **misgiving** n опасéние. **misguided** adj обмáнутый.
**mishap** n неприя́тность. **misinform** vt непрáвильно информи́ровать impf & pf. **misinterpret** vt невéрно истолкóвывать impf, истолковáть pf. **misjudge** vt невéрно оцéнивать impf, оцени́ть pf. **misjudgement** n невéрная оцéнка. **mislay** vt затеря́ть pf. **mislead** vt вводи́ть impf, ввести́ pf в заблуждéние. **mismanage** vt плóхо управля́ть impf +instr. **mismanagement** n плóхое управлéние. **misnomer** n непрáвильное назвáние.
**misogynist** n женоненавист-

ник. **misogyny** n женоненави́стничество.
**misplaced** adj неумéстный. **misprint** n опечáтка. **misquote** vt непрáвильно цити́ровать impf, про~ pf. **misread** vt (fig) непрáвильно истолкóвывать impf, истолковáть pf. **misrepresent** vt искажáть impf, искази́ть pf. **misrepresentation** n искажéние.
**Miss** n (title) мисс.
**miss** n прóмах; vi промáхиваться impf, промахнýться pf; vt (fail to hit, see, hear) пропускáть impf, пропусти́ть pf; (train) опáздывать impf, опоздáть pf на+acc; (regret absence of) скучáть impf по+dat; ~ out пропускáть impf, пропусти́ть pf; ~ **the point** не понимáть impf, поня́ть pf сýти.
**misshapen** adj уродли́вый.
**missile** n снаря́д, ракéта.
**missing** adj отсýтствующий, недостáющий; (person) пропáвший без вéсти.
**mission** n ми́ссия; командирóвка. **missionary** n миссионéр. **missive** n послáние.
**misspell** vt непрáвильно писáть impf, на~ pf. **misspelling** n непрáвильное написáние.
**mist** n тумáн; vt & i затумáнивать(ся) impf, затумáнить(ся) pf.
**mistake** vt непрáвильно понимáть impf, поня́ть pf; ~ **for** принимáть impf, приня́ть pf за+acc; n оши́бка; **make a** ~ оши́бáться impf, оши́би́ться pf. **mistaken** adj оши́бочный; **be** ~ оши́бáться impf, оши́би́ться pf.

**mister** n ми́стер, господи́н.

**mistletoe** n оме́ла.

**mistress** n хозя́йка; (teacher) учи́тельница; (lover) любо́вница.

**mistrust** vt не доверя́ть impf +dat; n недове́рие. **mistrustful** adj недове́рчивый.

**misty** adj тума́нный.

**misunderstand** vt непра́вильно понима́ть impf, поня́ть pf. **misunderstanding** n недоразуме́ние.

**misuse** vt непра́вильно употребля́ть impf, употреби́ть pf; (ill treat) ду́рно обраща́ться impf c+instr; n непра́вильное употребле́ние.

**mite** n (insect) клещ.

**mitigate** vt смягча́ть impf, смягчи́ть pf. **mitigation** n смягче́ние.

**mitre** n ми́тра.

**mitten** n рукави́ца.

**mix** vt меша́ть impf, c~ pf; vi сме́шиваться impf, сме́шаться pf; (associate) обща́ться impf c+instr; ~ up (confuse) пу́тать impf, c~ pf; get ~ed up in заме́шиваться impf, замеша́ться pf в+acc; n смесь. **mixer** n смеси́тель m; (cul) ми́ксер. **mixture** n смесь; (medicine) миксту́ра.

**moan** n стон; vi стона́ть impf, про~ pf.

**moat** n (крепостно́й) ров.

**mob** n толпа́; vt (attack) напада́ть impf, напа́сть pf толпо́й на+acc. **mobster** n банди́т.

**mobile** adj подви́жный, передвижно́й; ~ phone порта́тивный телефо́н. **mobility** n подви́жность. **mobilization** n мобилиза́ция. **mobilize** vt & i мобилизова́ть(ся) impf & pf.

**moccasin** n мокаси́н (gen pl -н).

**mock** vt & i издева́ться impf над+instr; adj (sham) подде́льный; (pretended) мни́мый; ~-up n маке́т. **mockery** n издева́тельство; (travesty) паро́дия.

**mode** n (manner) о́браз; (method) ме́тод.

**model** n (representation) моде́ль; (pattern, ideal) образе́ц; (artist's) нату́рщик, -ица; (fashion) манеке́нщик, -ица; (make) моде́ль; adj образцо́вый; vt лепи́ть impf, вы́~, c~ pf; (clothes) демонстри́ровать impf & pf; vi (act as ~) быть нату́рщиком, -ицей; быть манеке́нщиком, -ицей; ~ after, on создава́ть impf, созда́ть pf по образцу́ +gen.

**moderate** adj (various senses; polit) уме́ренный; (medium) сре́дний; vt умеря́ть impf, уме́рить pf; vi стиха́ть impf, сти́хнуть pf. **moderation** n уме́ренность; in ~ уме́ренно.

**modern** adj совреме́нный; (language, history) но́вый. **modernization** n модерниза́ция. **modernize** vt модернизи́ровать impf & pf.

**modest** adj скро́мный. **modesty** n скро́мность.

**modification** n модифика́ция. **modify** vt модифици́ровать impf & pf.

**modish** adj мо́дный.

**modular** adj мо́дульный. **modulate** vt модули́ровать impf. **modulation** n модуля́ция. **module** n мо́дуль m.

**mohair** n мохе́р.

**moist** adj вла́жный. **moisten** vt & i увлажня́ть(ся) impf, увлажни́ть(ся) pf. **moisture** n вла́га.

**molar** n (tooth) коренно́й зуб.
**mole**[1] n (on skin) ро́динка.
**mole**[2] n (animal; agent) крот.
**molecular** adj молекуля́рный. **molecule** n моле́кула.
**molest** vt пристава́ть impf, приста́ть pf +dat.
**mollify** vt смягча́ть impf, смягчи́ть pf.
**mollusc** n моллю́ск.
**molten** adj распла́вленный.
**moment** n моме́нт, миг; **at the ~ сейча́с; at the last ~** в после́днюю мину́ту; **just a ~!** сейча́с! **momentarily** adv на мгнове́ние. **momentary** adj мгнове́нный. **momentous** adj ва́жный. **momentum** n коли́чество движе́ния; (impetus) дви́жущая си́ла; **gather ~** набира́ть impf, набра́ть pf ско́рость.
**monarch** n мона́рх. **monarchy** n мона́рхия.
**monastery** n монасты́рь m. **monastic** adj мона́шеский.
**Monday** n понеде́льник.
**money** n де́ньги (-нег, -нья́м) pl; **~-lender** ростовщи́к.
**mongrel** n дворня́жка.
**monitor** n (naut; TV) монито́р; vt проверя́ть impf, прове́рить pf.
**monk** n мона́х.
**monkey** n обезья́на.
**mono** n мо́но neut indecl. **monochrome** adj одноцве́тный. **monogamous** adj единобра́чный. **monogamy** n единобра́чие. **monogram** n моногра́мма. **monograph** n моногра́фия. **monolith** n моноли́т. **monolithic** adj моноли́тный. **monologue** n моноло́г. **monopolize** vt монополизи́ровать impf & pf. **monopoly** n

n монопо́лия. **monosyllabic** adj односло́жный. **monosyllable** n односло́жное сло́во.
**monotone** n моното́нность; **in a ~** моното́нно. **monotonous** adj моното́нный. **monotony** n моното́нность.
**monsoon** n (wind) муссо́н; (rainy season) дождли́вый сезо́н.
**monster** n чудо́вище. **monstrosity** n чудо́вище. **monstrous** adj чудо́вищный; (huge) грома́дный.
**montage** n монта́ж.
**month** n ме́сяц. **monthly** adj ме́сячный; n ежеме́сячник; adv ежеме́сячно.
**monument** n па́мятник. **monumental** adj монумента́льный.
**moo** vi мыча́ть impf.
**mood**[1] n (gram) наклоне́ние.
**mood**[2] n настрое́ние. **moody** adj капри́зный.
**moon** n луна́. **moonlight** n лу́нный свет; vi халту́рить. **moonlit** adj лу́нный.
**moor**[1] n ме́стность, поро́сшая ве́реском. **moorland** n ве́ресковая пу́стошь.
**moor**[2] vt & i швартова́ть(ся) impf, при~ pf. **mooring** n (place) прича́л; pl (cables) шварто́вы m pl.
**Moorish** adj маврита́нский.
**moose** n америка́нский лось m.
**moot** adj спо́рный.
**mop** n шва́бра; vt протира́ть impf, протере́ть pf (шва́брой); **~ one's brow** вытира́ть impf, вы́тереть pf лоб; **~ up** вытира́ть impf, вы́тереть pf.
**mope** vi хандри́ть impf.
**moped** n мопе́д.

**moraine** *n* море́на.
**moral** *adj* мора́льный; *n* мора́ль; *pl* нра́вы *m pl*. **morale** *n* мора́льное состоя́ние.
**morality** *n* нра́вственность, мора́ль. **moralize** *vi* морализи́ровать *impf*.
**morass** *n* боло́то.
**moratorium** *n* морато́рий.
**morbid** *adj* боле́зненный.
**more** *adj* (*greater quantity*) бо́льше +*gen*; (*additional*) ещё; *adv* бо́льше; (*forming comp*) бо́лее; **and what is** ~ и бо́льше того́; ~ **or less** бо́лее и́ли ме́нее; **once** ~ ещё раз; **moreover** *adv* сверх того́; кро́ме того́.
**morgue** *n* морг.
**moribund** *adj* умира́ющий.
**morning** *n* у́тро; *in the* ~ у́тром; *in the* ~s по утра́м; *attrib* у́тренний.
**moron** *n* слабоу́мный *sb*.
**morose** *adj* угрю́мый.
**morphine** *n* морфи́й.
**Morse (code)** *n* а́збука Мо́рзе.
**morsel** *n* кусо́чек.
**mortal** *adj* сме́ртный; (*fatal*) смерте́льный; *n* сме́ртный *sb*. **mortality** *n* сме́ртность.
**mortar** *n* (*vessel*) сту́п(к)а; (*cannon*) миномёт; (*cement*) (известко́вый) раство́р.
**mortgage** *n* ссу́да на поку́пку до́ма; *vt* закла́дывать *impf*, заложи́ть *pf*.
**mortify** *vt* унижа́ть *impf*, уни́зить *pf*.
**mortuary** *n* морг.
**mosaic** *n* моза́ика; *adj* моза́ичный.
**mosque** *n* мече́ть.
**mosquito** *n* комар.
**moss** *n* мох. **mossy** *adj* мши́стый.
**most** *adj* наибо́льший; *n* наи-

бо́льшее коли́чество; *adj & n* (*majority*) большинство́ +*gen*; бо́льшая часть +*gen*; *adv* бо́льше всего́, наибо́лее; (*forming superl*) са́мый. **most-ly** *adv* гла́вным о́бразом.
**MOT (test)** *n* техосмо́тр.
**motel** *n* моте́ль *m*.
**moth** *n* мотылёк; (*clothes-*~) моль.
**mother** *n* мать; *vt* относи́ться *impf* по-матери́нски к +*dat*; ~-**in-law** (*wife's* ~) тёща; (*husband's* ~) свекро́вь; ~-**of-pearl** перламу́тр; *adj* перламу́тровый; ~ **tongue** родно́й язы́к. **motherhood** *n* матери́нство. **motherland** *n* ро́дина. **motherly** *adj* матери́нский.
**motif** *n* моти́в.
**motion** *n* движе́ние; (*gesture*) жест; (*proposal*) предложе́ние; *vt* пока́зывать *impf*, показа́ть *pf* +*dat* же́стом, чтобы +*past*. **motionless** *adj* неподви́жный. **motivate** *vt* побужда́ть *impf*, побуди́ть *pf*. **motivation** *n* побужде́ние. **motive** *n* моти́в; *adj* дви́жущий.
**motley** *adj* пёстрый.
**motor** *n* дви́гатель *m*, мото́р; ~ **bike** мотоци́кл; ~ **boat** мото́рная ло́дка; ~ **car** автомоби́ль *m*; ~ **cycle** мотоци́кл; ~-**cyclist** мотоцикли́ст; ~ **racing** автомоби́льные го́нки *f pl*; ~ **scooter** мотороллер; ~ **vehicle** автомаши́на. **motoring** *n* автомобили́зм. **motorist** *n* автомобили́ст, ~ка. **motorize** *vt* моторизова́ть *impf & pf*. **motorway** *n* автостра́да.
**mottled** *adj* кра́пчатый.

**motto** n девиз.
**mould**¹ n (shape) фо́рма, фо́рмочка; vt формова́ть impf, c~ pf. **moulding** n (archit) лепно́е украше́ние.
**mould**² n (fungi) пле́сень. **mouldy** adj запле́сневелый.
**moulder** vi разлага́ться impf, разложи́ться pf.
**moult** vi линя́ть impf, вы́~ pf.
**mound** n холм; (heap) на́сыпь.
**Mount** n (in names) гора́.
**mount** vt (ascend) поднима́ться impf, подня́ться pf на+acc; (~ a horse etc.) сади́ться impf, сесть pf на+acc; (picture) накле́ивать impf, накле́ить pf на карто́н; (gun) устана́вливать impf, установи́ть pf; ~ up (accumulate) нака́пливаться impf, накопи́ться pf; n (for picture) карто́н; (horse) верхова́я ло́шадь.
**mountain** n гора́; attrib го́рный. **mountaineer** n альпини́ст, ~ка. **mountaineering** n альпини́зм. **mountainous** adj гори́стый.
**mourn** vt опла́кивать impf, опла́кать pf; vi скорбе́ть impf (over о+prep). **mournful** adj скорбный. **mourning** n тра́ур.
**mouse** n мышь.
**mousse** n мусс.
**moustache** n усы́ (усо́в) pl.
**mousy** adj мыши́ный; (timid) ро́бкий.
**mouth** n рот; (poetical) уста́ (-т) pl; (entrance) вход; (of river) у́стье; vi говори́ть impf, сказа́ть pf одни́ми губа́ми. **mouthful** n глото́к. **mouthorgan** n губна́я гармо́ника. **mouthpiece** n мундшту́к; (person) ру́пор.
**movable** adj подвижно́й.
**move** n (in game) ход; (change

of residence) перее́зд; (movement) движе́ние; (step) шаг; vt & i дви́гать(ся) impf, дви́нуть(ся) pf; vt (affect) тро́гать impf, тро́нуть pf; (propose) вноси́ть impf, внести́ pf; vi (develop) развива́ться impf, разви́ться pf; (~ house) переезжа́ть impf, перее́хать pf; ~ away (vt & i) удаля́ть(ся) impf, удали́ть(ся) pf; (vi) уезжа́ть impf, уе́хать pf; ~ in въезжа́ть impf, въе́хать pf; ~ on идти́ pf, пойти́ pf да́льше; ~ out съезжа́ть impf, съе́хать pf (of c+gen). **movement** n движе́ние; (mus) часть f. **moving** adj дви́жущийся; (touching) тро́гательный.
**mow** vt (also ~ down) коси́ть impf, c~ pf. **mower** n коси́лка.
**MP** abbr (of Member of Parliament) член парла́мента.
**Mr** abbr ми́стер, господи́н.
**Mrs** abbr ми́ссис f indecl, госпожа́.
**Ms** n миз, госпожа́.
**much** adj & n мно́го +gen; мно́гое sb; adv о́чень; (with comp adj) гора́здо.
**muck** n (dung) наво́з; (dirt) грязь; vt about вози́ться impf; ~ out чи́стить impf, вы́~ pf; ~ up изга́живать impf, изга́дить pf.
**mucous** adj сли́зистый. **mucus** n слизь.
**mud** n грязь. **mudguard** n крыло́.
**muddle** vt пу́тать impf, c~ pf; vi: ~ through ко́е-ка́к справля́ться impf, спра́виться pf в беспоря́дке.
**muddy** adj гря́зный; vt обры́згивать impf, обры́згать pf гря́зью.

**muff** *n* му́фта.

**muffle** *vt* (*for warmth*) заку́тывать *impf*, заку́тать *pf*; (*sound*) глуши́ть *impf*, за~ *pf*.

**mug** *n* (*vessel*) кру́жка; (*face*) мо́рда.

**muggy** *adj* сыро́й и тёплый.

**mulch** *n* му́льча; *vt* мульчи́ровать *impf & pf*.

**mule** *n* мул.

**mull** *vt*: ~ **over** обду́мывать *impf*, обду́мать *pf*. **mulled** *adj*: ~ **wine** глинтве́йн.

**mullet** *n* (*grey* ~) кефа́ль; (*red* ~) бараба́лька.

**multicoloured** *adj* многокра́сочный. **multifarious** *adj* разнообра́зный. **multilateral** *adj* многосторо́нний. **multimillionaire** *n* мультимиллионе́р. **multinational** *adj* многонациона́льный.

**multiple** *adj* составно́й; (*numerous*) многочи́сленный; ~ **sclerosis** рассе́янный склеро́з; *n* кра́тное число́; **least common** ~ о́бщее наиме́ньшее кра́тное *sb*. **multiplication** *n* умноже́ние. **multiplicity** *n* многочи́сленность. **multiply** *vt* (*math*) умножа́ть *impf*, умно́жить *pf*; *vi* размножа́ться *impf*, размно́житься *pf*.

**multi-storey** *adj* многоэта́жный.

**multitude** *n* мно́жество; (*crowd*) толпа́.

**mum**[1] *adj*: **keep** ~ молча́ть *impf*.

**mum**[2] *n* (*mother*) ма́ма.

**mumble** *vt & i* бормота́ть *impf*, про~ *pf*.

**mummy**[1] *n* (*archaeol*) му́мия.

**mummy**[2] *n* (*mother*) ма́ма, ма́мочка.

**mumps** *n* сви́нка.

**munch** *vt* жева́ть *impf*.

**mundane** *adj* земно́й.

**municipal** *adj* муниципа́льный. **municipality** *n* муниципалите́т.

**munitions** *n pl* вое́нное иму́щество.

**mural** *n* стенна́я ро́спись.

**murder** *n* уби́йство; *vt* убива́ть *impf*, уби́ть *pf*; (*language*) кове́ркать *impf*, ис~ *pf*. **murderer, murderess** *n* уби́йца *m & f*. **murderous** *adj* уби́йственный.

**murky** *adj* тёмный, мра́чный.

**murmur** *n* шёпот; *vt & i* шепта́ть *impf*, шепну́ть *pf*.

**muscle** *n* му́скул. **muscular** *adj* мы́шечный; (*person*) мускули́стый.

**Muscovite** *n* москви́ч, ~ка.

**muse** *vi* размышля́ть *impf*.

**museum** *n* музе́й.

**mush** *n* ка́ша.

**mushroom** *n* гриб.

**music** *n* му́зыка; (*sheet* ~) но́ты *f pl*; ~**hall** мю́зик-холл; ~ **stand** пюпи́тр. **musical** *adj* музыка́льный; *n* опере́тта. **musician** *n* музыка́нт.

**musk** *n* му́скус.

**musket** *n* мушке́т.

**Muslim** *n* мусульма́нин, -а́нка; *adj* мусульма́нский.

**muslin** *n* мусли́н.

**mussel** *n* ми́дия.

**must** *v aux* (*obligation*) до́лжен (-жна́) *predic+inf*; на́до *impers+dat & inf*; (*necessity*) ну́жно *impers+dat & inf*; ~ **not** (*prohibition*) нельзя́ *impers+dat & inf*.

**mustard** *n* горчи́ца.

**muster** *vt* собира́ть *impf*, собра́ть *pf*; (*courage etc.*) собира́ться *impf*, собра́ться *pf* с+*instr*.

**musty** adj затхлый.

**mutation** n мутация.

**mute** adj немой; n немой sb; (mus) сурдинка. **muted** adj приглушённый.

**mutilate** vt увечить impf, из~ pf. **mutilation** n увечье.

**mutineer** n мятежник. **mutinous** adj мятежный. **mutiny** n мятеж; vi бунтовать impf, взбунтовать pf.

**mutter** vi бормотать impf; impf; n бормотание.

**mutton** n баранина.

**mutual** adj взаимный; (common) общий.

**muzzle** n (animal's) мо́рда; (on animal) намордник; (of gun) дуло; vt надевать impf, надеть pf намордник на+acc; (fig) заставлять impf, заставить pf молчать.

**my** poss pron мой, свой.

**myopia** n близорукость. **myopic** adj близорукий.

**myriad** n мириады (-д) pl; adj бесчисленный.

**myrtle** n мирт; attrib миртовый.

**myself** pron (emph) (я) сам, сама; (refl) себя; -ся (suffixed to vt).

**mysterious** adj таинственный. **mystery** n тайна.

**mystic(al)** adj мистический; n мистик. **mysticism** n мистицизм. **mystification** n озадаченность. **mystify** vt озадачивать impf, озадачить pf.

**myth** n миф. **mythical** adj мифический. **mythological** adj мифологический. **mythology** n мифология.

# N

**nag**[1] n (horse) лошадь.

**nag**[2] vt (also ~ at) пилить impf +acc; vi (of pain) ныть impf.

**nail** n (finger-, toe-~) ноготь m; (metal spike) гвоздь m; ~ varnish лак для ногтей; vt прибивать impf, прибить pf (гвоздями).

**naïve** adj наивный. **naïvety** n наивность.

**naked** adj голый; ~ eye невооружённый глаз. **nakedness** n нагота.

**name** n название; (forename) имя neut; (surname) фамилия; (reputation) репутация; **what is his ~?** как его зовут?; ~ plate дощечка с фамилией; ~sake тёзка m & f; vt называть impf, назвать pf; (appoint) назначать impf, назначить pf. **nameless** adj безымянный. **namely** adv (а) именно; то есть.

**nanny** n няня.

**nap** n короткий сон; vi вздремнуть pf.

**nape** n загривок.

**napkin** n салфетка.

**nappy** n пелёнка.

**narcissus** n нарцисс.

**narcotic** adj наркотический; n наркотик.

**narrate** vt рассказывать impf, рассказать pf. **narration** n рассказ. **narrative** n рассказ; adj повествовательный. **narrator** n рассказчик.

**narrow** adj узкий; vt & i суживать(ся) impf, сузить(ся) pf. **narrowly** adv (hardly) чуть, еле-еле; **he ~ escaped drown-**

**ing** он чуть не утонýл. **narrow-minded** adj ограниченный. **narrowness** n ýзость.

**nasal** adj носовóй; (voice) гнусáвый.

**nasturtium** n настýрция.

**nasty** adj неприя́тный, противный; (person) злой.

**nation** n (people) нарóд; (country) странá. **national** adj национáльный; (of the state) госудáрственный; n пóдданный sb. **nationalism** n национали́зм. **nationalist** n национали́ст, -ка. **nationalistic** adj националисти́ческий. **nationality** n национáльность; (citizenship) граждáнство, пóдданство. **nationalization** n национализáция. **nationalize** vt национализи́ровать impf & pf.

**native** n (~ of) урожéнец, -нка (+gen); (aborigine) тузéмец, -мка; adj (innate) прирóдный; (indigenous) тузéмный; ~ **land** рóдина; ~ **language** роднóй язы́к; ~ **speaker** носи́тель m язы́ка.

**nativity** n Рождествó (Христóво).

**natter** vi болтáть impf.

**natural** adj естéственный, прирóдный; ~ **resources** прирóдные богáтства pl; ~ **selection** естéственный отбóр; n (mus) бекáр. **naturalism** n натурали́зм. **naturalist** n натурали́ст. **naturalistic** adj натуралисти́ческий. **naturalization** n натурализáция. **naturalize** vt натурализи́ровать impf & pf. **naturally** adv естéственно. **nature** n прирóда.

(character) харáктер; **by** ~ по прирóде.

**naught** n: **come to** ~ своди́ться impf, свести́сь pf к нулю́.

**naughty** adj шаловли́вый.

**nausea** n тошнотá. **nauseate** vt тошни́ть impf impers от +gen. **nauseating** adj тошнотвóрный. **nauseous** adj: **I feel** ~ меня́ тошни́т.

**nautical** n морскóй.

**naval** adj (воéнно-)морскóй.

**nave** n неф.

**navel** n пупóк.

**navigable** adj судохóдный. **navigate** vt (ship) вести́ impf; (sea) плáвать impf по+dat. **navigation** n навигáция. **navigator** n штýрман.

**navvy** n землекóп.

**navy** n воéнно-морскóй флот; ~ **blue** тёмно-си́ний.

**Nazi** n наци́ст, -ка; adj наци́стский. **Nazism** n наци́зм.

**NB** abbr нотабéне.

**near** adv бли́зко; ~ **at hand** под рукóй; ~ **by** adv ря́дом; prep вóзле+gen, óколо+gen, у+gen; adj бли́зкий; vt & i приближáться impf, прибли́зиться pf к+dat. **nearly** adv почти́.

**neat** adj (tidy) опря́тный, аккурáтный; (clear) чёткий; (undiluted) неразбáвленный. **nebulous** adj нея́сный.

**necessarily** adv обязáтельно. **necessary** adj необходи́мый; (inevitable) неизбéжный. **necessitate** vt дéлать impf, ~ pf необходи́мым. **necessity** n необходи́мость; неизбéжность; (object) предмéт пéрвой необходи́мости.

**neck** n шéя; (of garment) вы́рез; ~ **and** ~ головá в гóло-

ву. **necklace** *n* ожере́лье.
**neckline** *n* вы́рез.
**nectar** *n* некта́р.
**née** *adj* урождённая.
**need** *n* нужда́; *vt* нужда́ться
*impf* в+*prep*; I (*etc.*) ~ мне
(*dat*) ну́жен ( -жна́, -жно,
-жны́) +*nom*; I ~ five roubles
мне ну́жно пять рубле́й.
**needle** *n* игла́, иго́лка; (*knitting*) спи́ца; (*pointer*) стре́л-
ка; *vt* придира́ться *impf*,
придра́ться *pf* к+*dat*.
**needless** *adj* нену́жный; ~ to
say разуме́ется. **needy** *adj*
нужда́ющийся.
**negation** *n* отрица́ние. **negative** *adj* отрица́тельный; *n*
отрица́ние; (*phot*) негати́в.
**neglect** *vt* пренебрега́ть *impf*,
пренебре́чь *pf* +*instr*; не за-
бо́титься *impf* о+*prep*; *n*
пренебреже́ние; (*condition*)
забро́шенность. **neglectful**
*adj* небре́жный, невнима́-
тельный (**of** к+*dat*). **negligence** *n* небре́жность. **negligent** *adj* небре́жный. **neg-
ligible** *adj* незначи́тельный.
**negotiate** *vi* вести́ *impf* пере-
гово́ры; *vt* (*arrange*) заклю-
ча́ть *impf*, заключи́ть *pf*;
(*overcome*) преодолева́ть *impf*,
преодоле́ть *pf*. **negotiation** *n*
(*discussion*) перегово́ры *m pl*.
**Negro** *n* негр; *adj* негритя́н-
ский.
**neigh** *n* ржа́ние; *vi* ржать *impf*.
**neighbour** *n* сосе́д, ~ка.
**neighbourhood** *n* ме́стность;
in the ~ of о́коло+*gen*. **neighbouring** *adj* сосе́дний. **neigh-
bourly** *adj* добрососе́дский.
**neither** *adv* та́кже не, то́же
не; *pron* ни тот, ни друго́й;
~ ... nor ни... ни.
**neon** *n* нео́н; *attrib* нео́новый.

**nephew** *n* племя́нник.
**nepotism** *n* кумовство́.
**nerve** *n* нерв; (*courage*) сме́-
лость; (*impudence*) на́глость;
**get on the** ~**s of** де́йствовать
*impf*, по~ *pf* +*dat* на не́рвы.
**nervous** *adj* не́рвный; ~
**breakdown** не́рвное расстро́й-
ство. **nervy** *adj* нерво́зный.
**nest** *n* гнездо́; ~ **egg** сбе-
реже́ния *neut pl*; *vi* гнез-
ди́ться *impf*. **nestle** *vi* льнуть
*impf*, при~ *pf*.
**net**¹ *n* сеть, се́тка; *vt* (*catch*)
лови́ть *impf*, пойма́ть *pf*
се́тью.
**net**², **nett** *adj* чи́стый; *vt*
получа́ть *impf*, получи́ть *pf*
чи́стого дохо́да.
**Netherlands** *n* Нидерла́нды
(-ов) *pl*.
**nettle** *n* крапи́ва.
**network** *n* сеть.
**neurologist** *n* невро́лог.
**neurology** *n* невроло́гия.
**neurosis** *n* невро́з. **neurotic**
*adj* невроти́ческий.
**neuter** *adj* сре́дний, сре́днего
ро́да; *n* сре́дний род; *vt* ка-
стри́ровать *impf & pf*. **neutral** *adj* нейтра́льный; *n* (*gear*)
нейтра́льная ско́рость. **neutrality** *n* нейтралите́т. **neutralize** *vt* нейтрализова́ть *impf
& pf*. **neutron** *n* нейтро́н.
**never** *adv* никогда́ не; ~ **again**
никогда́ бо́льше; ~ **mind**
ничего́!; всё равно́!; ~ **once**
ни ра́зу. **nevertheless** *conj*,
*adv* тем не ме́нее.
**new** *adj* но́вый; (*moon*, *potatoes*) молодо́й. **new-born** *adj*
новорождённый. **newcomer**
*n* прише́лец. **newfangled** *adj*
новомо́дный. **newly** *adv*
то́лько что, неда́вно. **newness** *n* новизна́.

**news** n но́вость, -ти pl, изве́-
стие, -ия pl. **newsagent** n
продаве́ц газе́т. **newsletter**
n информацио́нный бюлле-
те́нь m. **newspaper** n газе́та.
**newsprint** n газе́тная бума́-
га. **newsreel** n кинохро́ника.

**newt** n трито́н.

**New Zealand** n Но́вая Зела́н-
дия; adj новозела́ндский.

**next** adj сле́дующий, бу́ду-
щий; adv (~ time) в сле́-
дующий раз; (then) пото́м,
зате́м; ~ **door** (house) в
сосе́днем до́ме; (flat) в со-
се́дней кварти́ре; ~ **of kin**
ближа́йший ро́дственник; ~
**to** ря́дом с+instr; (fig) почти́.
**next-door** adj сосе́дний; ~
**neighbour** ближа́йший сосе́д.

**nib** n перо́.

**nibble** vt & i грызть impf;
обгрыза́ть impf, обгры́зть
pf; (grass) щипа́ть impf; (fish)
клева́ть impf.

**nice** adj (pleasant) прия́тный,
хоро́ший; (person) ми́лый.
**nicety** n то́нкость.

**niche** n ни́ша; (fig) своё ме́сто.

**nick** n (scratch) цара́пина;
(notch) зару́бка; **in the ~ of
time** в са́мый после́дний мо-
ме́нт; vt (scratch) цара́пать
impf, о~ pf; (steal) стибри́ть
pf.

**nickel** n ни́кель m.

**nickname** n про́звище; vt про-
зыва́ть impf, прозва́ть pf.

**nicotine** n никоти́н.

**niece** n племя́нница.

**niggardly** adj скупо́й.

**niggling** adj ме́лочный.

**night** n ночь; (evening) ве́чер;
**at ~** но́чью; **last ~** вчера́
ве́чером; attrib ночно́й; ~
**club** ночно́й клуб. **nightcap**
n ночно́й колпа́к; (drink)

стака́нчик спиртно́го на́
ночь. **nightdress** n ночна́я
руба́шка. **nightfall** n наступ-
ле́ние но́чи. **nightingale** n
солове́й. **nightly** adj еже-
но́щный; adv ежено́щно.
**nightmare** n кошма́р. **nightmarish** adj кошма́рный.

**nil** n нуль m.

**nimble** adj прово́рный.

**nine** adj & n де́вять; (number
9) девя́тка. **nineteen** adj &
n девятна́дцать. **nineteenth**
adj & n девятна́дцатый. **ninetieth** adj & n девяно́стый. **ninety** adj & n девяно́сто; pl
(decade) девяно́стые го́ды
(-до́в) m pl. **ninth** adj & n
девя́тый.

**nip** vt (pinch) щипа́ть impf,
щипну́ть pf; (bite) куса́ть
impf, укуси́ть pf; ~ **in the
bud** пресека́ть impf, пресе́чь
pf в заро́дыше; n щипо́к;
уку́с; **there's a ~ in the air**
во́здух па́хнет моро́зцем.

**nipple** n сосо́к.

**nirvana** n нирва́на.

**nit** n гни́да.

**nitrate** n нитра́т. **nitrogen** n
азо́т.

**no** adj (not any) никако́й, не
оди́н; (not a fool etc.) (совсе́м) не; adv нет; (nischoly не
+compr; in отрица́ние,
отка́з; (in vote) го́лос
„про́тив"; ~ **doubt** коне́чно,
несомне́нно; ~ **longer** уже́
не, бо́льше не; **no one** никто́;
~ **wonder** не удиви́тельно.

**Noah's ark** n Но́ев ковче́г.

**nobility** n (class) дворя́нство;
(quality) благоро́дство. **noble**
adj дворя́нский; благоро́д-
ный. **nobleman** n дворяни́н.

**nobody** pron никто́; n ничто́-
жество.

**nocturnal** adj ночно́й.
**nod** vi кива́ть impf, кивну́ть pf голово́й; n киво́к.
**nodule** n узело́к.
**noise** n шум. **noiseless** adj бесшу́мный. **noisy** adj шу́мный.
**nomad** n коче́вник. **nomadic** adj коче́вой.
**nomenclature** n номенклату́ра. **nominal** adj номина́льный. **nominate** vt (propose) выдвига́ть impf, вы́двинуть pf; (appoint) назнача́ть impf, назна́чить pf. **nomination** n выдвиже́ние; назначе́ние. **nominative** adj (n) имени́тельный (паде́ж). **nominee** n кандида́т.
**non-alcoholic** adj безалко́гольный. **non-aligned** adj неприсоедини́вшийся.
**nonchalance** n беззабо́тность. **nonchalant** adj беззабо́тный.
**non-commissioned** adj: ~ officer у́нтер-офице́р. **non-committal** adj укло́нчивый. **non-conformist** n нонконформи́ст; adj нонконформи́стский.
**nondescript** adj неопределённый.
**none** pron (no one) никто́; (nothing) ничто́; (not one) не оди́н; adv ниско́лько не; ~ **the less** тем не ме́нее.
**nonentity** n ничто́жество.
**non-existent** adj несуществу́ющий. **non-fiction** n документа́льный. **non-intervention** n невмеша́тельство. **non-party** adj беспарти́йный. **non-payment** n непла́тёж.
**nonplus** vt ста́вить impf, по-pf в тупи́к.
**non-productive** adj непроизводи́тельный. **non-resident**

adj не прожива́ющий (где́-нибудь).
**nonsense** n ерунда́. **nonsensical** adj бессмы́сленный.
**non-smoker** n (person) некуря́щий sb; (compartment) купе́ neut indecl для некуря́щих.
**non-stop** adj безостано́вочный; (flight) беспоса́дочный; adv без остано́вок; без поса́дки. **non-violent** adj ненаси́льственный.
**noodles** n pl лапша́.
**nook** n уголо́к.
**noon** n по́лдень m.
**no one** see no
**noose** n петля́.
**nor** conj и не; то́же; **neither ... ~** ни... ни.
**norm** n но́рма. **normal** adj норма́льный. **normality** n норма́льность. **normalize** vt нормализова́ть impf & pf.
**north** n се́вер; (naut) норд; adj се́верный; adv к се́веру, на се́вер; ~**-east** се́веро-восто́к; ~**-easterly, -eastern** се́веро-восто́чный; ~**-west** се́веро-за́пад; ~**-westerly, -western** се́веро-за́падный. **northerly** adj се́верный. **northern** adj се́верный. **northerner** n северя́нин, -я́нка. **northward(s)** adv на се́вер, к се́веру.
**Norway** n Норве́гия. **Norwegian** n норве́жский; n норве́жец, -жка.
**nose** n нос; vt: ~ **about, out** разню́хивать impf, разню́хать pf. **nosebleed** n кровотече́ние и́з носу. **nosedive** n пике́ neut indecl.
**nostalgia** n ностальги́я. **nostalgic** adj ностальги́ческий.
**nostril** n ноздря́.
**not** adv не; нет; ни; ~ **at all** ниско́лько, ничу́ть; (reply to

*thanks*) не стóит (благодáрности); ~ once in a way ни рáзу; ~ that he то, чтóбы; ~ too довóльно +neg; to say чтóбы не сказáть; ~ to speak of не говорá ужé о+prep.

**notable** adj замéтный; (remarkable) замечáтельный. **notably** adv (especially) осóбенно; (perceptibly) замéтно.
**notary (public)** n нотáриус.
**notation** n нотáция; (mus) нóтное письмó.
**notch** n зарýбка; vt: ~ up выúгрывать impf, вúиграть pf.
**note** n (record) замéтка, зáпись; (annotation) примечáние; (letter) запúска; (banknote) банкнóт; (mus) нóта; (tone) тон; (attention) внимáние; vt отмечáть impf, отмéтить pf; ~ **down** запúсывать impf, записáть pf. **notebook** n запúсная книжка. **noted** adj знаменúтый; извéстный (for +instr). **notepaper** n почтóвая бумáга. **noteworthy** adj достóйный внимáния.
**nothing** n ничтó, ничегó; ~ **but** ничегó крóме+gen, тóлько; ~ **of the kind** ничегó подóбного; **come to** ~ кончáться impf, кóнчиться pf ничéм; **for** ~ (free) дáром; (in vain) зря, напрáсно; **have** ~ **to do with** не имéть impf никакóго отношéния к+dat; **there is** (was) ~ **for it** (but to) ничегó другóго не остаётся (остáвалось) (как); **to say** ~ **of** не говорá ужé о+prep.
**notice** n (sign) объявлéние; (warning) предупреждéние; (attention) внимáние; (review) óтзыв; **give (in) one's** ~ подавáть impf, подáть pf заявлéние об ухóде с рабó-

ты; **give s.o.** ~ предупреждáть impf, предупредúть pf об увольнéнии; **take** ~ **of** обращáть impf, обратúть pf внимáние на+acc; ~**-board** vt замечáть impf, замéтить pf. **noticeable** adj замéтный.
**notification** n извещéние.
**notify** vt извещáть impf, известúть pf (of o+prep).
**notion** n понáтие.
**notoriety** n дурнáя слáва. **notorious** adj преслóвутый.
**notwithstanding** prep несмотрá на+acc; adv тем не мéнее.
**nought** n (nothing) see **naught**; (zero) нуль m; (figure 0) ноль m.
**noun** n (úмя neut) существúтельное sb.
**nourish** vt питáть impf, напитáть pf. **nourishing** adj питáтельный. **nourishment** n питáние.
**novel** adj нóвый; (unusual) необыкновéнный; n ромáн. **novelist** n романúст. **novelty** n (newness) новизнá; (new thing) новúнка.
**November** n ноáбрь m; adj ноáбрьский.
**novice** n (eccl) послýшник, -ица; (beginner) новичóк.
**now** adv тепéрь, сейчáс; (immediately) тóтчас же; (next) тогдá же; conj: ~ (that) раз, когдá; (every) ~ **and again**, then врéмя от врéмени; by ~ ужé; from ~ **on** впредь. **nowadays** adv в нáше врéмя.
**nowhere** adv (place) нигдé; (direction) никудá; pron: I **have** ~ **to go** мне нéкуда пойтú.
**noxious** adj врéдный.
**nozzle** n соплó.
**nuance** n нюáнс.

**nuclear** adj ядерный. **nucleus** n ядро.

**nude** adj обнажённый, нагой; n обнажённая фигура.

**nudge** vt подталкивать impf, подтолкнуть pf локтем; n толчок локтем.

**nudity** n нагота.

**nugget** n самородок.

**nuisance** n досада; (person) раздражающий человек.

**null** adj: ~ **and void** недействительный. **nullify** vt аннулировать impf & pf. **nullity** n недействительность.

**numb** adj (from cold) окоченелый; **go** ~ онеметь pf; (from cold) окоченеть pf.

**number** n (total) количество; (total; symbol; math; group) число; (identifying numeral; item) номер; ~-**plate** номерная дощечка; vt (assign to) нумеровать impf, за~, про~ pf; (contain) насчитывать impf; ~ **among** причислять impf, причислить pf к+dat; **his days are** ~**ed** его дни сочтены.

**numeral** n цифра; (gram) (имя neut) числительное sb.

**numerical** adj числовой. **numerous** adj многочисленный; (many) много +gen m.

**nun** n монахиня. **nunnery** n (женский) монастырь m.

**nuptial** adj свадебный; n: ~s свадьба.

**nurse** n (child's) няня; (medical) медсестра; vt (suckle) кормить impf, на~, по~ pf; (tend sick) ухаживать impf за+instr; **nursing home** санаторий; дом престарелых.

**nursery** n (room) детская sb; (day) ясли (-лей) pl; (for plants) питомник; ~ **rhyme** детская прибаутка f pl; ~-**school** детский сад.

**nut** n орех; (for bolt etc.) гайка. **nutshell** n: **in a** ~ в двух словах.

**nutmeg** n мускатный орех.

**nutrient** n питательное вещество. **nutrition** n питание. **nutritious** adj питательный.

**nylon** n нейлон; pl нейлоновые чулки (-лок) pl.

**nymph** n нимфа.

# O

**O** int о!; ах!

**oaf** n неуклюжий человек.

**oak** n дуб; attrib дубовый.

**oar** n весло. **oarsman** n гребец.

**oasis** n оазис.

**oath** n присяга; (expletive) ругательство.

**oatmeal** n овсянка. **oats** n pl овёс (овса) collect.

**obdurate** adj упрямый.

**obedience** n послушание. **obedient** adj послушный.

**obese** adj тучный. **obesity** n тучность.

**obey** vt слушаться impf, по~ pf +gen; (law, order) подчиняться impf, подчиниться pf +dat.

**obituary** n некролог.

**object** n (thing) предмет; (aim) цель; (gram) дополнение; vi возражать impf, возразить pf (to против+gen); **I don't** ~ я не против. **objection** n возражение; **I have no** ~ я не возражаю. **objectionable** adj неприятный. **objective** adj объективный; n цель. **objectivity** n объективность.

**objector** n возража́ющий sb.
**obligation** n обяза́тельство;
I am under an ~ я обя́зан(а).
**obligatory** adj обяза́тельный.
**oblige** vt обя́зывать impf,
обяза́ть pf; be ~d to (grateful) быть обя́занным+dat.
**obliging** adj услу́жливый.
**oblique** adj косо́й; (fig; gram)
ко́свенный.
**obliterate** vt (efface) стира́ть
impf, стере́ть pf; (destroy)
уничтожа́ть impf, уничто-
жить pf. **obliteration** n стира́-
ние; уничтоже́ние.
**oblivion** n забве́ние. **oblivi-
ous** adj (forgetful) забы́вчи-
вый; to be ~ of не замеча́ть
impf+gen.
**oblong** adj продолгова́тый.
**obnoxious** adj проти́вный.
**oboe** n гобо́й.
**obscene** adj непристо́йный.
**obscenity** n непристо́йность.
**obscure** adj (unclear) нея́с-
ный; (little known) малоиз-
ве́стный; vt затемня́ть impf,
затемни́ть pf; де́лать impf,
с~ pf нея́сным. **obscurity** n
нея́сность; неизве́стность.
**obsequious** adj подобо-
стра́стный.
**observance** n соблюде́ние;
(rite) обря́д. **observant** adj
наблюда́тельный. **observation** n наблюде́ние; (remark)
замеча́ние. **observatory** n
обсервато́рия. **observe** vt
(law etc.) соблюда́ть impf,
соблюсти́ pf; (watch) наблю-
да́ть impf; (remark) заме-
ча́ть impf, заме́тить pf. **observer** n наблюда́тель m.
**obsess** vt пресле́довать impf;
**obsessed by** одержи́мый
+instr. **obsession** n одержи́-
мость; (idea) навя́зчивая

иде́я. **obsessive** adj навя́з-
чивый.
**obsolete** adj устаре́лый, вы́-
шедший из употребле́ния.
**obstacle** n препя́тствие.
**obstetrician** n акуше́р. **ob-
stetrics** n акуше́рство.
**obstinacy** n упря́мство. **obstinate** adj упря́мый.
**obstreperous** adj бу́йный.
**obstruct** vt загражда́ть impf,
загради́ть pf; (hinder) пре-
пя́тствовать impf, вос~ pf
+dat. **obstruction** n загра-
жде́ние; (obstacle) препя́т-
ствие. **obstructive** adj загра-
жда́ющий; препя́тствующий.
**obtain** vt получа́ть impf, по-
лучи́ть pf; доставля́ть impf,
доста́ть pf.
**obtrusive** adj навя́зчивый;
(thing) броса́ющийся в глаза́.
**obtuse** adj тупо́й.
**obviate** vt устраня́ть impf,
устрани́ть pf.
**obvious** adj очеви́дный.
**occasion** n слу́чай; (cause)
по́вод; (occurrence) собы́тие;
vt причиня́ть impf, причи-
ни́ть pf. **occasional** adj ре́д-
кий **occasionally** adv иногда́,
вре́мя от вре́мени.
**occult** adj оккульти́ный; n: the
~ окку́льт.
**occupancy** n заня́тие. **occu-
pant** n жи́тель m, ~ница.
**occupation** n заня́тие; (military ~) оккупа́ция; (profession) профе́ссия. **occupational** adj профессиона́ль-
ный; ~ **therapy** трудотера-
пи́я. **occupy** vt занима́ть
impf, заня́ть pf; (mil) окку-
пи́ровать impf & pf.
**occur** vi (happen) случа́ться
impf, случи́ться pf; (be
found) встреча́ться impf;

to приходи́ть *impf*, прийти́ *pf* в го́лову+*dat*. **occurrence** *n* слу́чай, происше́ствие.

**ocean** *n* океа́н. **oceanic** *adj* океа́нский.

**o'clock** *adv*: (at) six ~ (в) шесть часо́в.

**octagonal** *adj* восьмиуго́льный.

**octave** *n* (*mus*) окта́ва.

**October** *n* октя́брь *m*; *adj* октя́брьский.

**octopus** *n* осьмино́г.

**odd** *adj* (*strange*) стра́нный; (*not in a set*) разро́зненный; (*number*) нечётный; (*not paired*) непа́рный; (*casual*) случа́йный; five hundred ~ пятьсо́т с ли́шним; ~ job случа́йная рабо́та. **oddity** *n* стра́нность; (*person*) чуда́к, -а́чка. **oddly** *adv* стра́нно; ~ enough как э́то ни стра́нно. **oddment** *n* оста́ток. **odds** *n pl* ша́нсы *m pl*; be at ~ with (*person*) не ла́дить с+*instr*; (*things*) не соотве́тствовать *impf* +*dat*; long (short) ~ нера́вные (почти́ ра́вные) ша́нсы *m pl*; the ~ are that вероя́тнее всего́, что; ~ and ends обры́вки *m pl*.

**ode** *n* о́да.

**odious** *adj* ненави́стный.

**odour** *n* за́пах.

**oesophagus** *n* пищево́д.

**of** *prep expressing* **1.** *origin*: из-+*gen*: he comes ~ a working-class family он из рабо́чей семьи́; **2.** *cause*: от+*gen*: he died ~ hunger он у́мер от го́лода; **3.** *authorship*: *gen*: the works ~ Pushkin сочине́ния Пу́шкина, **4.** *material*: из+*gen*: made ~ wood сде́ланный из де́рева; **5.** *reference*: о+*prep*: he talked ~ Lenin он гово-

ри́л о Ле́нине; **6.** *partition*: *gen* (*often* in -у́(-ю́)): a glass ~ milk, tea стака́н молока́, ча́ю; *gen*+~ them оди́н из них; **7.** *belonging*: *gen*: the capital ~ England столи́ца А́нглии.

**off** *adv*: in phrasal *vv*, see *v*, e.g. clear ~ убира́ться *impf*; *prep* (*from surface of*) с+*gen*; (*away from*) от+*gen*; ~ and on вре́мя от вре́мени; ~-white не совсе́м бе́лый.

**offal** *n* требуха́.

**offence** *n* (*insult*) оби́да; (*against law*) преступле́ние; take ~ обижа́ться *impf*, оби́деться *pf* (at на+*acc*). **offend** *vt* обижа́ть *impf*, оби́деть *pf*; ~ against наруша́ть *impf*, нару́шить *pf*. **offender** *n* правонаруши́тель *m*, -ница. **offensive** *adj* (*attacking*) наступа́тельный; (*insulting*) оскорби́тельный; (*repulsive*) проти́вный; *n* нападе́ние.

**offer** *vt* предлага́ть *impf*, предложи́ть *pf*; *n* предложе́ние; on ~ в прода́же.

**offhand** *adj* бесцеремо́нный.

**office** *n* (*position*) до́лжность; (*place, room etc.*) бюро́ *neut indecl*, конто́ра, канцеля́рия. **officer** *n* должностно́е лицо́; (*mil*) офице́р. **official** *adj* служе́бный; (*authorized*) официа́льный; *n* должностно́е лицо́. **officiate** *vi* (*eccl*) соверша́ть *impf*, соверши́ть *pf* богослуже́ние. **officious** *adj* (*intrusive*) навя́зчивый.

**offing** *n*: be in the ~ предстоя́ть *impf*.

**off-licence** *n* ви́нный магази́н. **off-load** *vt* разгружа́ть *impf*, разгрузи́ть *pf*. **off-**

putting *adj* отта́лкивающий.
**offset** *vt* возмеща́ть *impf*,
возмести́ть *pf*. **offshoot** *n*
о́тпрыск. **offshore** *adj* при-
бре́жный. **offside** *adv* вне
игры́. **offspring** *n* пото́мок;
(collect) пото́мки *m pl*.
**often** *adv* ча́сто.
**ogle** *vt* & *i* смотре́ть *impf* с
вожделе́нием на+*acc*.
**ogre** *n* великáн-людоéд.
**oh** *int* о!; ах!
**ohm** *n* ом.
**oil** *n* (petroleum) нефть; (paint)
ма́сло, ма́сляные кра́-
ски *f pl*; *vt* сма́зывать *impf*,
сма́зать *pf*; ~**-painting** карти́-
на, напи́санная ма́сля-
ными кра́сками; ~ **rig** нефтя-
ная́я вы́шка; ~**-tanker** тáн-
кер; ~**-well** нефтяна́я сква́-
жина. **oilfield** *n* месторож-
де́ние не́фти. **oilskin** *n*
клеёнка; *pl* непромока́емый
костю́м. **oily** *adj* масляни́-
стый.
**ointment** *n* мазь.
**OK** *adv* & *adj* хорошо́, нор-
ма́льно; *int* ла́дно!; *vt* одоб-
ря́ть *impf*, одо́брить *pf*.
**old** *adj* ста́рый; (ancient; of
long standing) стари́нный;
(former) бы́вший; **how** ~ **are
you?** ско́лько тебе́, вам,
(dat) лет? ~ **age** ста́рость;
~**-age pension** пе́нсия по
ста́рости; **old-fashioned** ста-
ромо́дный; ~ **maid** ста́рая
де́ва; ~ **man** (also father, husband) стари́к; ~ **time** стари́н-
ный; ~ **woman** стару́ха; (coll)
стару́шка.
**olive** *n* (fruit) оли́вка; (colour)
оли́вковый цвет; *adj* оли́в-
ковый; ~ **oil** оли́вковое
ма́сло.
**Olympic** *adj* олимпи́йский; ~

**games** Олимпи́йские и́гры *f
pl*.
**omelette** *n* омле́т.
**omen** *n* предзнаменова́ние.
**ominous** *adj* злове́щий.
**omission** *n* про́пуск; (neglect)
упуще́ние. **omit** *vt* (leave out)
пропуска́ть *impf*, пропусти́ть
*pf*; (neglect) упуска́ть *impf*,
упусти́ть *pf*.
**omnibus** *n* (bus) авто́бус;
(collection) колле́кция.
**omnipotence** *n* всемогу́ще-
ство. **omnipotent** *adj* все-
могу́щий. **omnipresent** *adj*
вездесу́щий. **omniscient** *adj*
всеве́дущий.
**on** *prep* (position) на+*prep*;
(direction) на+*acc*; (time)
в+*acc*; ~ **the next day** на
сле́дующий день; ~ **Mon-
days** (repeated action) по
понеде́льникам (dat pl); ~
**the first of June** пе́рвого
ию́ня (gen); (concerning)
по+*prep*, о+*prep*, на+*acc*; *adv*
да́льше, вперёд; in phrasal
vv, see vv, e.g. **move** ~ идти́
да́льше; **and so** ~ и так
да́лее, и т.д.; **be** ~ (film etc.)
идти́ *impf*; **further** ~ да́льше;
**later** ~ по́зже.
**once** *adv* (оди́н) раз; (on past
occasion) одна́жды; (formerly)
не́когда; **at all** ~ неожи́дан-
но; **at** ~ сра́зу, неме́дленно;
(if, when) ~ как то́лько; ~
**again, more** ещё раз; ~ **and
for all** раз и навсегда́; ~ **or
twice** не́сколько раз; ~ **upon
a time there lived ...** жил-
был... .
**oncoming** *adj*: ~ **traffic**
встре́чное движе́ние.
**one** *adj* оди́н (одна́, -нó);
(only, single) еди́нственный;
*n* оди́н; *pron*: not usu trans-

lated; v translated in 2nd pers
sg or by impers construction:
~ never knows никогда́ не
зна́ешь; where can ~ buy
this book? где мо́жно ку-
пи́ть э́ту кни́гу?; ~ after another оди́н за други́м; ~ and
all все до одного́; все как
оди́н; ~ and only еди́нствен-
ный; ~ and the same оди́н и
тот же; ~ another друг дру́га
(dat -гу, etc.); ~ fine day в
оди́н прекра́сный день; ~
o'clock час; ~-parent family
семья́ с одни́м роди́телем;
~-sided, -track, -way одно-
сторо́нний; ~-time бы́вший;
~-way street у́лица односто-
ро́ннего движе́ния.

onerous adj тя́гостный.

oneself pron себя́; -ся (suffixed to vt).

onion n (plant; pl collect) лук;
(single ~) лу́ковица.

onlooker n наблюда́тель m.

only adj еди́нственный; adv
то́лько; if ~ е́сли бы то́лько;
~ just то́лько что; conj но.

onset n нача́ло.

onslaught n на́тиск.

onus n отве́тственность.

onward(s) adv вперёд.

ooze vt & i сочи́ться impf.

opal n опа́л.

opaque adj непрозра́чный.

open adj откры́тый; (frank)
открове́нный; in the ~ air на
откры́том во́здухе; ~-minded
adj непредупреждённый; vt
& i откры́ва(ть)ся impf, от-
кры́(ть)ся pf; vi (begin) начи-
на́ться impf, нача́ться pf;
(flowers) распуска́ться impf,
распусти́ться pf. opening n
откры́тие; (aperture) отве́р-
стие; (beginning) нача́ло; adj
нача́льный, пе́рвый; (intro-

ductory) вступи́тельный.

opera n о́пера; attrib о́пер-
ный; ~-house о́перный
теа́тр.

operate vi де́йствовать impf
(upon на+acc); (med) опери́-
ровать impf & pf (on +acc);
vt управля́ть impf +instr.

operatic adj о́перный.

operating-theatre n опера-
цио́нная sb. operation n де́й-
ствие; (med; mil) опера́ция.

operational adj (in use)
де́йствующий; (mil) опера-
ти́вный. operative adj де́й-
ствующий. operator n опе-
ра́тор; (telephone ~) теле-
фони́ст, -ка.

operetta n опере́тта.

ophthalmic adj глазно́й.

opinion n мне́ние; in my ~
по-мо́ему; ~ poll опро́с об-
ще́ственного мне́ния. opin-
ionated adj догмати́чный.

opium n о́пиум.

opponent n проти́вник.

opportune adj своевре́мен-
ный. opportunism n оппор-
туни́зм. opportunist n оп-
портуни́ст. opportunistic adj
оппортунисти́ческий. op-
portunity n слу́чай, возмо́ж-
ность.

oppose vt (resist) проти́вить-
ся impf, вос— pf +dat; (speak
etc. against) выступа́ть impf,
вы́ступить pf про́тив+gen.
opposed adj про́тив (to +gen);
as ~ to в противополо́ж-
ность+dat. opposing adj
проти́вный; (opposite) про-
тивополо́жный. opposite adj
противополо́жный; (reverse)
обра́тный; n противопо-
ло́жность; just the ~ как раз
наоборо́т; adv напро́тив; prep
(на)про́тив+gen. opposition

*n* (*resistance*) сопротивле́ние; (*polit*) оппози́ция.

**oppress** *vt* угнета́ть *impf.* **oppression** *n* угнете́ние. **oppressive** *adj* угнета́ющий. **oppressor** *n* угнета́тель *m.*

**opt** *vi* выбира́ть *impf,* вы́брать *pf* (for +*acc*); ~ **out** не принима́ть *impf* уча́стия (of в+*prep*).

**optic** *adj* зри́тельный. **optical** *adj* опти́ческий. **optician** *n* о́птик. **optics** *n* о́птика.

**optimism** *n* оптими́зм. **optimist** *n* оптими́ст. **optimistic** *adj* оптимисти́ческий. **optimum** *adj* оптима́льный.

**option** *n* вы́бор. **optional** *adj* необяза́тельный.

**opulence** *n* бога́тство. **opulent** *adj* бога́тый.

**opus** *n* о́пус.

**or** *conj* и́ли; ~ **else** ина́че; ~ **so** приблизи́тельно.

**oracle** *n* ора́кул.

**oral** *adj* у́стный; *n* у́стный экза́мен.

**orange** *n* (*fruit*) апельси́н; (*colour*) ора́нжевый цвет; *attrib* апельси́новый; (*colour*) ора́нжевый.

**oration** *n* речь. **orator** *n* ора́тор.

**oratorio** *n* орато́рия.

**oratory** *n* (*speech*) красноре́чие.

**orbit** *n* орби́та; *vt* враща́ться *impf* по орби́те вокру́г+*gen*. **orbital** *adj* орбита́льный.

**orchard** *n* фрукто́вый сад.

**orchestra** *n* орке́стр. **orchestral** *adj* орке́стровый. **orchestrate** *vt* оркестрова́ть *impf & pf.* **orchestration** *n* оркестро́вка.

**orchid** *n* орхиде́я.

**ordain** *vt* предпи́сывать *impf,* предписа́ть *pf;* (*eccl*) посвя-

ща́ть *impf,* посвяти́ть *pf* (в духо́вный сан).

**ordeal** *n* тяжёлое испыта́ние.

**order** *n* поря́док; (*command*) прика́з; (*for goods*) зака́з; (*insignia, medal; fraternity*) о́рден; (*archit*) о́рдер; *pl* (*holy* ~) духо́вный сан; **in ~ to** (для того́) что́бы +*inf,* *vt* (*command*) прика́зывать *impf,* приказа́ть *pf* +*dat;* (*goods etc.*) зака́зывать *impf,* заказа́ть *pf.* **orderly** *adj* аккура́тный; (*quiet*) ти́хий; *n* (*med*) санита́р; (*mil*) ордина́рец.

**ordinance** *n* декре́т.

**ordinary** *adj* обыкнове́нный, обы́чный.

**ordination** *n* посвяще́ние.

**ore** *n* руда́.

**organ** *n* о́рган; (*mus*) орга́н. **organic** *adj* органи́ческий. **organism** *n* органи́зм. **organist** *n* органи́ст. **organization** *n* организа́ция. **organize** *vt* организо́вывать *impf* (*pres not used*), организова́ть *impf* (*in pres*) *& pf;* устра́ивать *impf,* устро́ить *pf.* **organizer** *n* организа́тор.

**orgy** *n* о́ргия.

**Orient** *n* Восто́к. **oriental** *adj* восто́чный.

**orient, orientate** *vt* ориенти́ровать *impf & pf* (*o.s.* -ся). **orientation** *n* ориента́ция.

**orifice** *n* отве́рстие.

**origin** *n* происхожде́ние, нача́ло. **original** *adj* оригина́льный; (*initial*) первонача́льный; (*genuine*) по́длинный; *n* оригина́л. **originality** *n* оригина́льность. **originate** *vt* порожда́ть *impf,* породи́ть *pf;* *vi* брать *impf,* взять *pf* нача́ло (**from, in** в+*prep,* от+*gen*); (*arise*) возника́ть *impf*, возни́кнуть *pf*. **origin-ator** *n* а́втор, инициа́тор.

**ornament** *n* украше́ние; *vt* украша́ть *impf*, укра́сить *pf*. **ornamental** *adj* декорати́в-ный.

**ornate** *adj* витиева́тый.

**ornithologist** *n* орнито́лог. **ornithology** *n* орнитоло́гия.

**orphan** *n* сирота́ *m & f*; *vt*: be ~ed сироте́ть *impf*, о~ *pf*. **orphanage** *n* сиро́тский дом. **orphaned** *adj* осироте́лый.

**orthodox** *adj* ортодокса́ль-ный; (*eccl*, O~) правосла́в-ный. **orthodoxy** *n* ортодо́к-сия; (O~) правосла́вие.

**orthopaedic** *adj* ортопеди́-ческий.

**oscillate** *vi* колеба́ться *impf*, по~ *pf*. **oscillation** *n* колеба́-ние.

**osmosis** *n* о́смос.

**ostensible** *adj* мни́мый. **os-tensibly** *adv* я́кобы.

**ostentation** *n* выставле́ние напока́з. **ostentatious** *adj* показно́й.

**osteopath** *n* остеопа́т. **osteo-pathy** *n* остеопа́тия.

**ostracize** *vt* подверга́ть *impf*, подве́ргнуть *pf* остраки́зму. **ostrich** *n* стра́ус.

**other** *adj* друго́й, ино́й; тот; every ~ ка́ждый второ́й; every ~ day че́рез день; on the ~ hand с друго́й стороны́; on the ~ side на той стороне́, по ту сто́рону; one or the ~ тот и́ли ино́й; the ~ day на днях, неда́вно; the ~ way round наоборо́т; the ~s остальны́е *sb pl*. **other-wise** *adv* & *conj* и́наче, а то.

**otter** *n* вы́дра.

**ouch** *int* ой!, ай!

**ought** *v* *aux* до́лжен (-жна́)

(бы) +*inf*.

**ounce** *n* у́нция.

**our, ours** *poss pron* наш; свой. **ourselves** *pron* (*emph*) (мы) са́ми; (*refl*) себя́; -ся (*suffixed to vt*).

**oust** *vt* вытесня́ть *impf*, вы́-теснить *pf*.

**out** *adv* 1. *in phrasal vv* often rendered by pref вы-; 2.: to be ~ *in various senses*: he is ~ (*not at home*) его́ нет до́ма; (*not in office etc.*) он вы́шел; (*sport*) выходи́ть *impf*, вы́йти *pf* из игры́; (*of fashion*) вы́йти *pf* из мо́ды; (*be published*) вы́йти *pf* из печа́ти; (*of candle etc.*) по-ту́хнуть *pf*; (*be unconscious*) потеря́ть *pf* созна́ние; 3.: ~ and-~ отъя́вленный; 4.: ~ of из+*gen*, вне+*gen*; ~ of date устаре́лый, старомо́дный; ~ of doors на откры́том воз-ду́хе; ~ of flower безра́бот-ный; ~ of work безра́бот-ный.

**outbid** *vt* предлага́ть *impf*, предложи́ть *pf* бо́лее вы-со́кую це́ну, чем+*nom*. **out-board** *adj*: ~ motor подвесно́й мото́р *m*. **outbreak** *n* (*of anger, disease*) вспы́шка; (*of war*) нача́ло. **outbuilding** *n* надво́рная постро́йка. **out-burst** *n* взрыв. **outcast** *n* из-гна́нник. **outcome** *n* результа́т. **outcry** *n* (шу́мные) проте́сты *m pl*. **outdated** *adj* устаре́лый. **outdo** *vt* превос-ходи́ть *impf*, превзойти́ *pf*. **outdoor** *adj*, **outdoors** *adv* на откры́том во́здухе, на у́лице.

**outer** *adj* (*external*) вне́шний, нару́жный; (*far from centre*) да́льний. **outermost** *adj* са́-мый да́льний.

**outfit** n (equipment) снаряжёние; (set of things) набóр; (clothes) наря́д. **outgoing** adj уходя́щий; (sociable) общи́тельный. **outgoings** n pl изде́ржки f pl. **outgrow** vt выраста́ть impf, вы́расти pf из+gen. **outhouse** n надвóрная пострóйка.

**outing** n прогу́лка, экску́рсия.

**outlandish** adj дикóвинный. **outlaw** n лицó вне закóна, банди́т; vt объяви́ть impf, объяви́ть pf вне закóна. **outlay** n изде́ржки f pl. **outlet** n выходнóе отве́рстие; (fig) вы́ход; (market) ры́нок; (shop) торгóвая тóчка. **outline** n очерта́ние, контýр; (sketch, summary) набрóсок; vt оче́рчивать impf, очерти́ть pf; (plans etc.) набра́сывать impf, наброса́ть pf. **outlive** vt пережи́ть pf. **outlook** n перспекти́ва f pl; (attitude) кругозóр. **outlying** adj перифери́йный. **outmoded** adj старомóдный. **outnumber** vt чи́сленно превосходи́ть impf, превзойти́ pf. **out-patient** n амбулатóрный больнóй sb. **outpost** n форпóст. **output** n вы́пуск, продýкция.

**outrage** n безобрáзие; (indignation) возмущéние; vt оскорбля́ть impf, оскорби́ть pf. **outrageous** adj возмути́тельный.

**outright** adv (entirely) вполнé; (once for all) раз (и) навсегдá; (openly) открыто; adj прямóй. **outset** n начáло; at the ~ вначáле; from the ~ с сáмого начáла.

**outside** n нарýжная сторонá;

at the ~ сáмое бóльшее; from the ~ извнé; on the ~ снарýжи; adj нарýжный, внéшний; (sport) крáйний; adv (on the ~) снарýжи; (to the ~) нарýжу; (out of doors) на открытом вóздухе, на ýлице; prep внé+gen; за предéлами+gen. **outsider** n посторóнний sb; (sport) аутсáйдер.

**outsize** adj бóльше стандáртного размéра. **outskirts** n pl окрáина. **outspoken** adj прямóй. **outstanding** adj (remarkable) выдаю́щийся; (unpaid) неуплáченный. **outstay** vt: ~ one's welcome заси́живаться impf, засидéться pf. **outstretched** adj распрострётый. **outstrip** vt обгоня́ть impf, обогнáть pf. **outward** adj (external) внéшний, нарýжный. **outwardly** adv внéшне, на вид. **outwards** adv нарýжу. **outweigh** vt перевéшивать impf, перевéсить pf. **outwit** vt перехитри́ть pf.

**oval** adj овáльный; n овáл. **ovary** n яи́чник. **ovation** n овáция. **oven** n (industrial) печь; (domestic) духóвка.

**over** adv & prep with vv: see vv; prep (above) над+instr; (through; covering) по+dat; (concerning) o+prep; (across) чéрез+acc; (on the other side of) по ту стóрону+gen; (more than) свы́ше+gen; бóлее+gen; (with age) за+acc; all ~ (finished) всё кóнчено; (everywhere) повсю́ду; all ~ the country по всей странé; ~ again ещё раз; ~ against по сравнéнию c+instr; ~ and

**above** не говоря́ уже́ о+*prep*; ~ **the telephone** по телефо́ну; ~ **there** вон там.

**overall** *n* хала́т; *pl* комбинезо́н; *adj* о́бщий. **overawe** *vt* внуша́ть *impf*, внуши́ть *pf* благогове́йный страх+*dat*. **overbalance** *vi* теря́ть *impf*, по~ *pf* равнове́сие. **overbearing** *adj* вла́стный. **overboard** *adv* (*motion*) за́ борт; (*position*) за бо́ртом. **overcast** *adj* о́блачный. **overcoat** *n* пальто́ *neut indecl*. **overcome** *vt* преодолева́ть *impf*, преодоле́ть *pf*; *adj* охва́ченный. **overcrowded** *adj* переполненный. **overcrowding** *n* переполне́ние. **overdo** *vt* (*cook*) пережа́ривать *impf*, пережа́рить *pf*; ~ **it, things** (*work too hard*) переутомля́ться *impf*, переутоми́ться *pf*; (*go too far*) перебра́рщивать *impf*, переборщи́ть *pf*.

**overdose** *n* чрезме́рная до́за. **overdraft** *n* превыше́ние креди́та; (*amount*) долг ба́нку. **overdraw** *vi* превыша́ть *impf*, превы́сить *pf* креди́т (в ба́нке). **overdue** *adj* просро́ченный; **be** ~ (*late*) запа́здывать *impf*, запозда́ть *pf*. **overestimate** *vt* переоце́нивать *impf*, переоцени́ть *pf*. **overflow** *vi* перелива́ться *impf*, перели́ться *pf*; (*river etc.*) разлива́ться *impf*, разли́ться *pf*; (*outlet*) перели́в. **overgrown** *adj* заро́сший. **overhang** *vt* & *vi* выступа́ть *impf* над+*instr*; *n* свес, выступ. **overhaul** *vt* ремонти́ровать *impf* & *pf*; *n* ремо́нт. **overhead** *adv* наверху́, над голово́й; *adj* возду́шный, подвес-

но́й; *n*: *pl* накладны́е расхо́ды *m pl*. **overhear** *vt* неча́янно слы́шать *impf*, у~ *pf*. **overheat** *vt* & *i* перегрева́ть(ся) *impf*, перегре́ть(ся) *pf*. **overjoyed** *adj* (at от+*gen*). **overland** *adj* сухопу́тный; *adv* по су́ше. **overlap** *vt* части́чно покрыва́ть *impf*, покры́ть *pf*; *vi* части́чно совпада́ть *impf*, совпа́сть *pf*. **overleaf** *adv* на оборо́те. **overload** *vt* перегружа́ть *impf*, перегрузи́ть *pf*. **overlook** *vt* (*look down on*) смотре́ть *impf* све́рху на+*acc*; (*of window*) выходи́ть *impf* на, в, +*acc*; (*not notice*) не замеча́ть *impf*, заме́тить *pf* +*gen*; (~ *offence etc.*) проща́ть *impf*, прости́ть *pf*.

**overly** *adv* сли́шком. **overnight** *adv* (*during the night*) за́ ночь; (*suddenly*) неожи́данно; **stay** ~ ночева́ть *impf*, пере~ *pf*; *adj* ночно́й. **overpay** *vt* перепла́чивать *impf*, переплати́ть *pf*. **over-populated** *adj* перенаселённый. **over-population** *n* перенаселённость. **overpower** *vt* одолева́ть *impf*, одоле́ть *pf*. **overpriced** *adj* завы́шенный в цене́. **overproduction** *n* перепроизво́дство. **overrate** *vt* переоце́нивать *impf*, переоцени́ть *pf*. **override** *vt* (*fig*) отверга́ть *impf*, отве́ргнуть *pf*. **overriding** *adj* гла́вный, реша́ющий. **overrule** *vt* отверга́ть *impf*, отве́ргнуть *pf*. **overrun** *vt* (*conquer*) завоёвывать *impf*, завоева́ть *pf*; **be** ~ **with** кише́ть *impf* +*instr*.

**overseas** *adv* за мо́рем,

через мо́ре; *adj* замо́рский.

**oversee** *vt* надзира́ть *impf* за+*instr*. **overseer** *n* надзира́тель, -ница. **overshadow** *vt* затмева́ть *impf*, затми́ть *pf*. **overshoot** *vi* переходи́ть *impf*, перейти́ *pf* грани́цу. **oversight** *n* случа́йный недосмо́тр. **oversleep** *vi* просыпа́ть *impf*, проспа́ть *pf*. **overspend** *vi* тра́тить *impf* сли́шком мно́го. **overstate** *vt* преувели́чивать *impf*, преувели́чить *pf*. **overstep** *vt* переступа́ть *impf*, переступи́ть *pf*+*acc*, че́рез+*acc*.

**overt** *adj* я́вный, откры́тый.

**overtake** *vt* обгоня́ть *impf*, обогна́ть *pf*. **overthrow** *vt* сверга́ть *impf*, све́ргнуть *pf*. **overtime** *n* (*work*) сверхуро́чная рабо́та; (*payment*) сверхуро́чные *sb*; *adv* сверхуро́чно.

**overtone** *n* скры́тый намёк.

**overture** *n* предложе́ние; (*mus*) увертю́ра.

**overturn** *vt & i* опроки́дывать(ся) *impf*, опроки́нуть(ся) *pf*. **overwhelm** *vt* подавля́ть *impf*, подави́ть *pf*. **overwhelming** *adj* подавля́ющий. **overwork** *vt & i* переутомля́ть(ся) *impf*, переутоми́ть(ся) *pf*; (*cram*) набива́ть, наби́ть *pf*. **package** *n* посы́лка, паке́т; (*holiday*) организо́ванная туристи́ческая пое́здка. **packaging** *n* упако́вка. **packet** *n* паке́т; па́чка; (*large sum of money*) ку́ча де́нег. **packing-case** *n* я́щик.

**owe** *vt* (~ *money*) быть до́лжным +*acc & dat*; (*be indebted*) быть обя́занным +*instr & dat*; ~ **s.me three roubles** он до́лжен +*acc* три рубля́; ~ **s me** мне три рубля́; **she** ~ **s her life** она́ обя́зана ему́ жи́знью. **owing** *adj* ~ **be** причита́ться *impf* (**to** +*dat*); ~ **to** из-за+*gen*, по причи́не+*gen*.

**owl** *n* сова́.

**own** *adj* свой; (*свой*) со́бственный; **on one's** ~ самостоя́тельно; (*alone*) оди́н; *vt* (*possess*) владе́ть *impf* +*instr*; (*admit*) признава́ть *impf*, призна́ть *pf*; ~ **up** признава́ться *impf*, призна́ться *pf*. **owner** *n* владе́лец. **ownership** *n* владе́ние (**of** +*instr*), со́бственность.

**ox** *n* вол.

**oxidation** *n* окисле́ние. **oxide** *n* о́кись. **oxidize** *vt & i* окисля́ть(ся) *impf*, окисли́ть(ся) *pf*. **oxygen** *n* кислоро́д.

**oyster** *n* у́стрица.

**ozone** *n* озо́н.

# P

**pace** *n* шаг; (*fig*) темп; **keep** ~ **with** идти́ *impf* в но́гу c+*instr*; **set the** ~ задава́ть *impf*, зада́ть *pf* темп; *vi*: ~ **up and down** ходи́ть *indet* взад и вперёд. **pacemaker** *n* (*med*) электро́нный стимуля́тор.

**pacifism** *n* пацифи́зм. **pacifist** *n* пацифи́ст. **pacify** *vt* усмиря́ть *impf*, усмири́ть *pf*.

**pack** *n* у́зел, вьюк; (*soldier's*) ра́нец; (*hounds*) сво́ра; (*wolves*) ста́я; (*cards*) коло́да; *vt* (*& i*) упако́вывать(ся) *impf*, упакова́ть(ся) *pf*; (*cram*) набива́ть, наби́ть *pf*.

**pact** *n* пакт.

**pad** *n* (*cushion*) поду́шечка; (*shin- etc.*) щито́к; (*of paper*)

блокно́т; vt подбива́ть impf,
подби́ть pf. **padding** n наби́вка.

**paddle**[1] n (oar) весло́; vi (row) грести́ impf.

**paddle**[2] vi (wade) ходи́ть indet, идти́ det, пойти́ pf босико́м по воде́.

**paddock** n вы́гон.

**padlock** n вися́чий замо́к; vt запира́ть impf, запере́ть pf на вися́чий замо́к.

**paediatric** adj педиатри́ческий. **paediatrician** n педиа́тор.

**pagan** n язы́чник, -ица; adj язы́ческий. **paganism** n язы́чество.

**page**[1] n (~-boy) паж; vt (summon) вызыва́ть impf, вы́звать pf.

**page**[2] n (of book) страни́ца.

**pageant** n пы́шная проце́ссия. **pageantry** n пы́шность.

**pail** n ведро́.

**pain** n боль; pl (efforts) уси́лия neut pl; ~-killer болеутоля́ющее сре́дство; vt (fig) огорча́ть impf, огорчи́ть pf (part of body) боле́ть impf. **painless** adj безболе́зненный. **painstaking** adj стара́тельный.

**paint** n кра́ска; vt кра́сить impf, по~ pf; (portray) писа́ть impf, на~ pf кра́сками. **paintbrush** n кисть. **painter** n (artist) худо́жник, -ица; (decorator) маля́р. **painting** n (art) жи́вопись; (picture) карти́на.

**pair** n па́ра; often not translated when denoting a single object, e.g. a ~ of scissors но́жницы (-ц) pl; a ~ of trousers па́ра брюк; vt спари-

вать impf, спа́рить pf; ~ off разделя́ться impf, раздели́ться pf по па́рам.

**Pakistan** n Пакиста́н. **Pakistani** n пакиста́нец, -а́нка; adj пакиста́нский.

**pal** n прия́тель, ~ница.

**palace** n дворе́ц.

**palatable** adj вку́сный; (fig) прия́тный. **palate** n нёбо; (fig) вкус.

**palatial** adj великоле́пный.

**palaver** n (trouble) беспоко́йство; (nonsense) чепуха́.

**pale**[1] n (stake) кол; **beyond the ~** невообрази́мый.

**pale**[2] adj бле́дный; vi бледне́ть impf, по~ pf. **palette** n пали́тра.

**pall**[1] n покро́в.

**pall**[2] vi: ~ **on** надоеда́ть impf, надое́сть pf +dat.

**palliative** adj паллиати́вный; n паллиати́в.

**pallid** adj бле́дный. **pallor** n бле́дность.

**palm**[1] n (tree) па́льма; **P~ Sunday** Ве́рбное воскресе́нье.

**palm**[2] n (of hand) ладо́нь; vt: ~ **off** всу́чивать impf, всучи́ть pf (**on** +dat).

**palpable** adj осяза́емый.

**palpitations** n pl сердцебие́ние.

**paltry** adj ничто́жный.

**pamper** vt балова́ть impf, из~ pf.

**pamphlet** n брошю́ра.

**pan**[1] n (saucepan) кастрю́ля; (frying-) сковорода́; (of scales) ча́шка; vt: ~ **out** промыва́ть impf, промы́ть pf; (fig) выходи́ть impf, вы́йти pf.

**pan**[2] vi (cin) панорами́ровать impf & pf.

**panacea** n панаце́я.

**panache** n рисо́вка.

**pancake** n блин.

**pancreas** n поджелу́дочная железа́.

**panda** n па́нда.

**pandemonium** n гвалт.

**pander** vi: ~ **to** потво́рствовать impf +dat.

**pane** n око́нное стекло́.

**panel** n пане́ль; (control-~) щит управле́ния; (of experts) гру́ппа специали́стов; (of judges) жюри́ neut indecl. **panelling** n пане́льная обши́вка.

**pang** n pl му́ки (-к) pl.

**panic** n па́ника; ~**-stricken** охва́ченный па́никой; vi впада́ть impf, впасть pf в па́нику. **panicky** adj пани́ческий.

**pannier** n корзи́нка.

**panorama** n панора́ма. **panoramic** adj панора́мный.

**pansy** n аню́тины гла́зки (-зок) pl.

**pant** vi дыша́ть impf с одышкой.

**panther** n панте́ра.

**panties** n pl тру́сики (-ков) pl.

**pantomime** n рожде́ственское представле́ние; (dumb show) пантоми́ма.

**pantry** n кладова́я sb.

**pants** n pl трусы́ (-со́в) pl; (trousers) брю́ки (-к) pl.

**papal** adj па́пский.

**paper** n бума́га; pl докуме́нты m pl; (newspaper) газе́та; (wallpaper) обо́и (-ев) pl; (treatise) докла́д; adj бума́жный; vt окле́ивать impf, окле́ить pf обо́ями. **paperback** n кни́га в бума́жной обло́жке. **paperclip** n скре́пка. **paperwork** n канцеля́рская рабо́та.

**par** n: **feel below** ~ чу́вствовать impf себя́ нева́жно;

**on a** ~ **with** наравне́ c+instr.

**parable** n при́тча.

**parabola** n пара́бола.

**parachute** n парашю́т; vi спуска́ться impf, спусти́ться pf с парашю́том. **parachutist** n парашюти́ст.

**parade** n пара́д; vi шествова́ть impf; vt (show off) выставля́ть impf, вы́ставить pf напока́з.

**paradigm** n паради́гма.

**paradise** n рай.

**paradox** n парадо́кс. **paradoxical** adj парадокса́льный.

**paraffin** n (~ **oil**) кероси́н.

**paragon** n образе́ц.

**paragraph** n абза́ц.

**parallel** adj паралле́льный; n паралле́ль; vt соотве́тствовать impf +dat.

**paralyse** vt парализова́ть impf & pf. **paralysis** n парали́ч.

**parameter** n пара́метр.

**paramilitary** adj полувое́нный.

**paramount** adj первостепе́нный.

**paranoia** n парано́йя. **paranoid** adj: **he is** ~ он парано́ик.

**parapet** n (mil) бру́ствер.

**paraphernalia** n принадле́жности f pl.

**paraphrase** n переска́з; vt переска́зывать impf, пересказа́ть pf.

**parasite** n парази́т. **parasitic** adj паразити́ческий.

**parasol** n зо́нтик.

**paratrooper** n парашюти́ст-деса́нтник.

**parcel** n паке́т, посы́лка.

**parch** vt иссуша́ть impf, иссуши́ть pf; **become** ~**ed** пересыха́ть impf, пересо́хнуть pf.

**parchment** n перга́мент.

**pardon** n проще́ние; (law) поми́лование; vt проща́

*impf*, прости́ть *pf*; (*law*) поми́ловать *pf*.

**pare** *vt* (*fruit*) чи́стить *impf*, о~ *pf*; ~ **away, down** урéзывать *impf*, урéзать *pf*.

**parent** *n* роди́тель *m*, ~ница.

**parentage** *n* происхождéние.

**parental** *adj* роди́тельский.

**parentheses** *n pl* (*brackets*) ско́бки *f pl*.

**parish** *n* прихо́д. **parishioner** *n* прихожа́нин, ~áнка.

**parity** *n* рáвенство.

**park** *n* парк; (*for cars etc.*) стоя́нка; *vt & abs* стáвить *impf*, по~ *pf* (маши́ну). **parking** *n* стоя́нка.

**parliament** *n* парлáмент. **parliamentarian** *n* парламентáрий. **parliamentary** *adj* парлáментский.

**parlour** *n* гости́ная *sb*.

**parochial** *adj* прихо́дский; (*fig*) ограни́ченный. **parochialism** *n* ограни́ченность. **parody** *n* паро́дия; *vt* пароди́ровать *impf & pf*.

**parole** *n* чéстное сло́во; **on** ~ освобождённый под чéстное сло́во.

**paroxysm** *n* парокси́зм.

**parquet** *n* паркéт; *attrib* паркéтный.

**parrot** *n* попугáй.

**parry** *vt* пари́ровать *impf & pf*, от~ *pf*.

**parsimonious** *adj* скупо́й.

**parsley** *n* петру́шка.

**parsnip** *n* пастернáк.

**parson** *n* свящéнник.

**part** *n* часть; (*in play*) роль; (*mus*) пáртия; **for the most** ~ бо́льшей чáстью; **in** ~ чáстью; **for my** ~ что касáется меня; **take** ~ **in** учáствовать *impf* в+*prep*; ~**-time** (зáнятый) непо́лный рабо-

чий день; *vt & i* (*divide*) разделя́ть(ся) *impf*, раздели́ть(ся) *pf*; *vi* (*leave*) расставáться *impf*, расстáться *pf* (**from, with** *c+instr*); ~ **one's hair** дéлать *impf*, с~ *pf* себé пробо́р.

**partake** *vi* принимáть *impf*, приня́ть *pf* учáстие (**in, of** в+*prep*); (*eat*) есть *impf*, съ~ *pf* (**of** +*acc*).

**partial** *adj* части́чный; (*biased*) пристрáстный; ~ **to** неравноду́шный к+*dat*. **partiality** *n* (*bias*) пристрáстность. **partially** *adv* части́чно.

**participant** *n* учáстник, -ица (**in** +*gen*). **participate** *vi* учáствовать *impf* (**in** в+*prep*). **participation** *n* учáстие.

**participle** *n* причáстие.

**particle** *n* части́ца.

**particular** *adj* осо́бый, осо́бенный; (*fussy*) разбо́рчивый; *n* подро́бность; **in** ~ в чáстности.

**parting** *n* (*leave-taking*) прощáние; (*of hair*) пробо́р.

**partisan** *n* (*adherent*) сторо́нник; (*mil*) партизáн; *attrib* (*biased*) пристрáстный; партизáнский.

**partition** *n* (*wall*) перегоро́дка; (*polit*) раздéл; *vt* разделя́ть *impf*, раздели́ть *pf*; ~ **off** отгорáживать *impf*, отгороди́ть *pf*.

**partly** *adv* части́чно.

**partner** *n* (*in business*) компаньо́н; (*in dance, game*) партнёр, ~ша. **partnership** *n* товáрищество.

**partridge** *n* куропáтка.

**party** *n* (*polit*) пáртия; (*group*) гру́ппа; (*social gathering*) вечери́нка; (*law*) сторонá; **be a** ~ **to** принимáть *impf*,

приня́ть *pf* уча́стие в+*prep*; *attrib* парти́йный; ~ **line** (*polit*) ли́ния па́ртии; (*telephone*) о́бщий телефо́нный про́вод; ~ **wall** о́бщая стена́.
**pass** *vt & i* (*go past; of time*) проходи́ть *impf*, пройти́ *pf* (**by** ми́мо+*gen*); (*travel past*) проезжа́ть *impf*, прое́хать *pf* (**by** ми́мо+*gen*); (~ *examination*) сдать *pf* (экза́мен); *vt* (*sport*) пасова́ть *impf*; паснуть *pf*; (*overtake*) обгоня́ть *impf*, обогна́ть *pf*; (*time*) проводи́ть *impf*, провести́ *pf*; (*hand on*) передава́ть *impf*, переда́ть *pf*; (*law, resolution*) утвержда́ть *impf*, утверди́ть *pf*; (*sentence*) выноси́ть *impf*, вынести *pf* (**upon** +*dat*); ~ **as**, **for** слыть *impf*, про~ *pf* +*instr*, за+*acc*; ~ **away** (*die*) сконча́ться *pf*; ~ **o.s. off as** выдава́ть *impf*, вы́дать *pf* себя́ за+*acc*; ~ **out** теря́ть *impf*, по~ *pf* созна́ние; ~ **over** (*in silence*) обходи́ть *impf*, обойти́ *pf* молча́нием; ~ **round** передава́ть *impf*, переда́ть *pf*; ~ **up** (*miss*) пропуска́ть *impf*, пропусти́ть *pf*; *n* (*permit*) про́пуск; (*sport*) пас; (*geog*) перева́л; **come to** ~ случа́ться *impf*, случи́ться *pf*; **make a** ~ **at** пристава́ть *impf*, приста́ть *pf* к+*dat*.
**passable** *adj* проходи́мый, прое́зжий; (*not bad*) неплохо́й.
**passage** *n* прохо́д; (*of time*) тече́ние; (*sea trip*) рейс; (*in house*) коридо́р; (*in book*) отры́вок; (*mus*) пасса́ж.
**passenger** *n* пассажи́р.
**passer-by** *n* прохо́жий *sb*.

**passing** *adj* (*transient*) мимолётный; *n* ~ **in** ~ мимохо́дом.
**passion** *n* страсть (**for** к+*dat*).
**passionate** *adj* стра́стный.
**passive** *adj* пасси́вный; (*gram*) страда́тельный; *n* страда́тельный зало́г. **passivity** *n* пасси́вность.
**Passover** *n* евре́йская Па́сха.
**passport** *n* па́спорт.
**password** *n* паро́ль *m*.
**past** *adj* про́шлый; (*gram*) проше́дший; *n* про́шлое *sb*; (*gram*) проше́дшее вре́мя *neut*; *prep* ми́мо+*gen*; (*beyond*) за+*instr*; *adv* ми́мо.
**pasta** *n* макаро́нные изде́лия *neut pl*.
**paste** *n* (*of flour*) те́сто; (*creamy mixture*) па́ста; (*glue*) клей; (*jewellery*) страз; *vt* накле́ивать *impf*, накле́ить *pf*.
**pastel** *n* (*crayon*) пасте́ль; (*drawing*) рису́нок пасте́лью; *attrib* пасте́льный.
**pasteurize** *vt* пастеризова́ть *impf & pf*.
**pastime** *n* времяпрепровожде́ние.
**pastor** *n* па́стор. **pastoral** *adj* (*bucolic*) пастора́льный; (*of pastor*) па́сторский.
**pastry** *n* (*dough*) те́сто; (*cake*) пиро́жное *sb*.
**pasture** *n* (*land*) па́стбище.
**pasty**¹ *n* пирожо́к.
**pasty**² *adj* (~-*faced*) бле́дный.
**pat** *n* в шлепо́к; (*of butter etc.*) кусо́к; *vt* хло́пать *impf*, по~ *pf*.
**patch** *n* запла́та; (*over eye*) повя́зка (на глаз); (*spot*) пятно́; (*of land*) уча́сток земли́; *vt* ста́вить *impf*, по~ *pf* запла́ту на+*acc*; ~ **up** (*fig*) ула́живать *impf*, ула́дить *pf*.

**patchwork** n лоскутная работа; attrib лоскутный. **patchy** adj неровный.

**pâté** n паштет.

**patent** adj явный; ~ leather лакированная кожа; n патент; vt патентовать impf, за~ pf.

**paternal** adj отцовский. **paternity** n отцовство.

**path** n тропинка, тропа; (way) путь m.

**pathetic** adj жалкий.

**pathological** adj патологический. **pathologist** n патолог.

**pathos** n пафос.

**pathway** n тропинка, тропа.

**patience** n терпение; (cards) пасьянс. **patient** adj терпеливый; n больной sb, пациент, ~ка.

**patio** n терраса.

**patriarch** n патриарх. **patriarchal** adj патриархальный.

**patriot** n патриот, ~ка. **patriotic** adj патриотический. **patriotism** n патриотизм.

**patrol** n патруль m; on ~ на дозоре; vt & i патрулировать impf.

**patron** n покровитель m; (of shop) клиент. **patronage** n покровительство. **patroness** n покровительница. **patronize** vt (treat condescendingly) снисходительно относиться impf, к+dat. **patronizing** adj покровительственный.

**patronymic** n отчество.

**patter**[1] vi (sound) барабанить impf; по постукивать impf.

**patter**[2] n (speech) скороговорка.

**pattern** n (design) узор; (model sewing) выкройка.

**paunch** n брюшко.

**pauper** n бедняк.

**pause** n пауза, перерыв; (mus) фермата; vi останавливаться impf, остановиться pf.

**pave** vt мостить impf, вы~ pf; the way подготовить pf почву (for для+gen). **pavement** n тротуар.

**pavilion** n павильон.

**paw** n лапа; vt трогать impf лапой; (horse) бить impf копытом.

**pawn**[1] n (chess) пешка.

**pawn**[2] n: in ~ в закладе; vt закладывать impf, заложить pf. **pawnbroker** n ростовщик. **pawnshop** n ломбард.

**pay** vt платить impf, за~, у~ pf (for за+acc); (bill etc.) оплачивать impf, оплатить pf; vi (be profitable) окупаться impf, окупиться pf; n жалованье, зарплата; ~ packet получка; ~-roll платёжная ведомость. **payable** adj подлежащий уплате. **payee** n получатель m. **payload** n полезная нагрузка. **payment** n уплата, платёж.

**pea** n (also pl, collect) горох.

**peace** n мир; in ~ в покое; ~ and quiet мир и тишина. **peaceable**, **peaceful** adj мирный.

**peach** n персик.

**peacock** n павлин.

**peak** n (of cap) козырёк; (summit; fig) вершина; ~ hour часы m pl пик.

**peal** n (sound) звон, трезвон; (of laughter) взрыв.

**peanut** n арахис.

**pear** n груша.

**pearl** n (also fig) жемчужина; pl (collect) жемчуг.

**peasant** n крестьянин, -янка; attrib крестьянский.

**peat** n торф.
**pebble** n га́лька.
**peck** vt & i клева́ть impf, клю́нуть pf; n клево́к.
**pectoral** adj грудно́й.
**peculiar** adj (distinctive) своеобра́зный; (strange) стра́нный; ~ **to** сво́йственный +dat. **peculiarity** n осо́бенность; стра́нность.
**pecuniary** adj де́нежный.
**pedagogical** adj педагоги́ческий.
**pedal** n педа́ль; vi нажима́ть impf, нажа́ть pf педа́ль; (ride bicycle) е́хать impf, по~ pf на велосипе́де.
**pedant** n педа́нт. **pedantic** adj педанти́чный.
**peddle** vt торгова́ть impf вразно́с+instr.
**pedestal** n пьедеста́л.
**pedestrian** adj пешехо́дный; (prosaic) прозаи́ческий; n пешехо́д; ~ **crossing** перехо́д.
**pedigree** n родосло́вная sb; adj поро́дистый.
**pedlar** n разно́счик.
**pee** n пи-пи́ neut indecl; vi мочи́ться impf, по~ pf.
**peek** vi (~ **in**) загля́дывать impf, загляну́ть pf; (~ **out**) выгля́дывать impf, вы́глянуть pf.
**peel** n кожура́; vt очища́ть impf, очи́стить pf; vi (skin) шелуши́ться impf; (paint, off) сходи́ть impf, сойти́ pf. **peelings** n pl очи́стки (-ков) pl.
**peep** vi (~ **in**) загля́дывать impf, загляну́ть pf; (~ **out**) выгля́дывать impf, вы́глянуть pf; n (glance) бы́стрый взгляд; ~**hole** глазо́к.
**peer**[1] vi всма́триваться impf,

всмотре́ться pf (at в+acc).
**peer**[2] n (noble) пэр; (person one's age) све́рстник.
**peeved** adj раздражённый.
**peevish** adj раздражи́тельный.
**peg** n ко́лышек; (clothes ~) крючо́к; (for hat etc.) ве́шалка; **off the** ~ гото́вый; vt прикрепля́ть impf, прикрепи́ть pf ко́лышком, -ками.
**pejorative** adj уничижи́тельный.
**pelican** n пелика́н.
**pellet** n ша́рик; (shot) дроби́на.
**pelt**[1] n (skin) шку́ра.
**pelt**[2] vt забра́сывать impf, заброса́ть pf; vi (rain) бараба́нить impf.
**pelvis** n таз.
**pen**[1] n (for writing) ру́чка; ~**friend** друг по перепи́ске.
**pen**[2] n (enclosure) заго́н.
**penal** adj уголо́вный. **penalize** vt штрафова́ть impf, о~ pf; (sport) штраф; ~ **area** штрафна́я площа́дка; ~ **kick** штрафно́й уда́р. **penance** n епитимья́.
**penchant** n скло́нность (for к+dat).
**pencil** n каранда́ш; ~**-sharpener** точи́лка.
**pendant** n подве́ска.
**pending** adj (awaiting decision) ожида́ющий реше́ния; prep (until) в ожида́нии +gen, до+gen.
**pendulum** n ма́ятник.
**penetrate** vt проника́ть impf, прони́кнуть pf в+acc. **penetrating** adj проница́тельный; (sound) пронзи́тельный. **penetration** n проникнове́ние; (insight) проница́тельность.

**penguin** n пингви́н.

**penicillin** n пеницилли́н.

**peninsula** n полуо́стров.

**penis** n пе́нис.

**penitence** n раска́яние. **penitent** adj раска́ивающийся; n ка́ющийся гре́шник.

**penknife** n перо́чинный нож.

**pennant** n вы́мпел.

**penniless** adj без гроша́.

**penny** n пе́нни neut indecl, пенс.

**pension** n пе́нсия; vt: ~ off увольня́ть impf, уво́лить pf на пе́нсию. **pensionable** adj (age) пенсио́нный. **pensioner** n пенсионе́р, ~ка.

**pensive** adj заду́мчивый.

**pentagon** n пятиуго́льник; the P~ Пентаго́н.

**Pentecost** n Пятидеся́тница.

**penthouse** n шика́рная кварти́ра на ве́рхнем этаже́.

**pent-up** adj (anger etc.) сде́рживаемый.

**penultimate** adj предпосле́дний.

**penury** n нужда́.

**peony** n пио́н.

**people** n pl (persons) лю́ди m; sg (nation) наро́д; vt населя́ть impf, насели́ть pf.

**pepper** n пе́рец; vt перчи́ть impf, на~, по~ pf. **peppercorn** n перчи́нка.

**peppermint** n пе́речная мя́та; (sweet) мя́тная конфе́та.

**per** prep (for each) (person) на+acc; as ~ согла́сно+dat; ~ annum в год; ~ capita на челове́ка; ~ hour в час; ~ se сам по себе́.

**perceive** vt воспринима́ть impf, восприня́ть pf.

**per cent** adv n проце́нт. **percentage** n проце́нт; (part) часть.

**perceptible** adj заме́тный. **perception** n восприя́тие; (quality) понима́ние. **perceptive** adj то́нкий.

**perch**[1] n (fish) о́кунь m.

**perch**[2] n (roost) насе́ст; vi сади́ться impf, сесть pf. **perched** adj высоко́ сидя́щий, располо́женный.

**percussion** n (~ instruments) уда́рные инструме́нты m pl.

**peremptory** adj повели́тельный.

**perennial** adj (enduring) ве́чный; n (bot) многоле́тнее расте́ние.

**perestroika** n перестро́йка.

**perfect** adj соверше́нный; (gram) перфе́ктный; n перфе́кт; vt соверше́нствовать impf, y~ pf. **perfection** n соверше́нство. **perfective** adj (n) соверше́нный (вид).

**perforate** vt перфори́ровать impf & pf. **perforation** n перфора́ция.

**perform** vt (carry out) исполня́ть impf, испо́лнить pf; (theat, mus) игра́ть impf, сыгра́ть pf; vi выступа́ть impf, вы́ступить pf; (function) рабо́тать impf. **performance** n исполне́ние; (of person, device) де́йствие; (of play etc.) представле́ние, спекта́кль m; (of engine etc.) эксплуатацио́нные ка́чества neut pl. **performer** n исполни́тель m.

**perfume** n духи́ (-хо́в) pl; (smell) арома́т.

**perfunctory** adj пове́рхностный.

**perhaps** adv мо́жет быть.

**peril** n опа́сность, риск. **perilous** adj опа́сный, риско́ванный.

**perimeter** *n* вне́шняя грани́ца; (*geom*) периме́тр.

**period** *n* пери́од; (*epoch*) эпо́ха; (*menstrual*) ме́сячные *sb pl*.

**periodic** *adj* периоди́ческий.

**periodical** *adj* периоди́ческий; *n* периоди́ческое изда́ние.

**peripheral** *adj* перифери́йный. **periphery** *n* перифери́я.

**periscope** *n* периско́п.

**perish** *vi* погиба́ть *impf*, поги́бнуть *pf*; (*spoil*) по́ртиться *impf*, ис~ *pf*. **perishable** *adj* скоропо́ртящийся.

**perjure** *v*: ~ **o.s.** наруша́ть *impf*, нару́шить *pf* кля́тву. **perjury** *n* лжесвиде́тельство.

**perk**¹ *n* льго́та.

**perk**² *vi*: ~ **up** оживля́ться *impf*, оживи́ться *pf*. **perky** *adj* бо́йкий.

**perm** *n* пермане́нт. **permanence** *n* постоя́нство. **permanent** *adj* постоя́нный.

**permeable** *adj* проница́емый. **permeate** *vt* проника́ть *impf*, прони́кнуть *pf* в+*acc*.

**permissible** *adj* допусти́мый. **permission** *n* разреше́ние. **permissive** *adj* (*too*) либера́льный; ~ **society** о́бщество вседозво́ленности. **permissiveness** *n* вседозво́ленность. **permit** *vt* разреша́ть *impf*, разреши́ть *pf* +*dat*; *n* про́пуск.

**permutation** *n* перестано́вка.

**pernicious** *adj* па́губный.

**perpendicular** *adj* перпендикуля́рный; *n* перпендикуля́р.

**perpetrate** *vt* соверша́ть *impf*, соверши́ть *pf*. **perpetrator** *n* вино́вник.

**perpetual** *adj* ве́чный. **perpetuate** *vt* увекове́чивать *impf*, увекове́чить *pf*. **perpetuity** *n* ве́чность; **in** ~ навсегда́, наве́чно.

**perplex** *vt* озада́чивать *impf*, озада́чить *pf*. **perplexity** *n* озада́ченность.

**persecute** *vt* пресле́довать *impf*. **persecution** *n* пресле́дование.

**perseverance** *n* насто́йчивость. **persevere** *vi* насто́йчиво, продолжа́ть *impf* (**in**, **at** *etc*. +*acc*, *inf*).

**Persian** *n* перс, ~и́нка; *adj* перси́дский.

**persist** *vi* упо́рствовать *impf* (**in** в+*prep*); насто́йчиво продолжа́ть *impf* (**in** +*acc*, *inf*). **persistence** *n* упо́рство. **persistent** *adj* упо́рный.

**person** *n* челове́к; (*in play*; *gram*) лицо́; **in** ~ ли́чно. **personable** *adj* привлека́тельный. **personage** *n* ли́чность. **personal** *adj* ли́чный. **personality** *n* ли́чность. **personally** *adv* ли́чно. **personification** *n* олицетворе́ние. **personify** *vt* олицетворя́ть *impf*, олицетвори́ть *pf*.

**personnel** *n* ка́дры (-ров) *pl*, персона́л; ~ **department** отде́л ка́дров.

**perspective** *n* перспекти́ва.

**perspiration** *n* пот. **perspire** *vi* поте́ть *impf*, вс~ *pf*.

**persuade** *vt* (*convince*) убежда́ть *impf*, убеди́ть *pf* (**of** в+*prep*); (*induce*) угова́ривать *impf*, уговори́ть *pf*. **persuasion** *n* убежде́ние. **persuasive** *adj* убеди́тельный.

**pertain** *vi*: ~ **to** относи́ться *impf* отнести́сь *pf* к+*dat*.

**pertinent** *adj* уме́стный.

**perturb** *vt* трево́жить *impf*, вс~ *pf*.

**peruse** vt (read) внима́тельно чита́ть impf, про~ pf; (fig) рассма́тривать impf, рассмотре́ть pf.

**pervade** vt наполня́ть impf. **pervasive** adj распространённый.

**perverse** adj капри́зный. **perversion** n извраще́ние. **pervert** vt извраща́ть impf, изврати́ть pf; n извращённый челове́к.

**pessimism** n пессими́зм. **pessimist** n пессими́ст. **pessimistic** adj пессимисти́ческий.

**pest** n вреди́тель m; (fig) зану́да. **pester** vt пристава́ть impf, приста́ть pf к+dat. **pesticide** n пестици́д.

**pet** n (animal) дома́шнее живо́тное sb; (favourite) люби́мец, -мица; ~ **shop** зоомагази́н; vt ласка́ть impf.

**petal** n лепесто́к.

**peter** vi: ~ **out** (road) исчеза́ть impf, исче́знуть pf; (stream; enthusiasm) иссяка́ть impf, исся́кнуть pf.

**petite** adj ма́ленькая.

**petition** n пети́ция; vt подава́ть impf, пода́ть pf проше́ние +dat. **petitioner** n проси́тель m.

**petrified** adj окамене́лый; be ~ (fig) оцепене́ть pf (with от+gen).

**petrol** n бензи́н; ~ **pump** бензоколо́нка; ~ **station** бензозапра́вочная ста́нция; ~ **tank** бензоба́к. **petroleum** n нефть.

**petticoat** n ни́жняя ю́бка.

**petty** adj ме́лкий; ~ **cash** де́ньги (де́нег, -ньга́м) pl на ме́лкие расхо́ды.

**petulant** adj раздражи́тельный.

**pew** n (церко́вная) скамья́.

**phallic** adj фалли́ческий. **phallus** n фа́ллос.

**phantom** n фанто́м.

**pharmaceutical** adj фармацевти́ческий. **pharmacist** n фармаце́вт. **pharmacy** n фармаци́я; (shop) апте́ка.

**phase** n фа́за; vt: ~ **in**, **out** постепе́нно вводи́ть impf, упраздня́ть impf.

**Ph.D.** abbr (of Doctor of Philosophy) кандида́т нау́к.

**pheasant** n фаза́н.

**phenomenal** adj феномена́льный. **phenomenon** n фено́мен.

**phial** n пузырёк.

**philanderer** n волоки́та m.

**philanthropic** adj филантропи́ческий. **philanthropist** n филантро́п. **philanthropy** n филантро́пия.

**philately** n филатели́я.

**philharmonic** adj филармони́ческий.

**Philistine** n (fig) фили́стер.

**philosopher** n филосо́ф. **philosophical** adj филосо́фский. **philosophize** vi филосо́фствовать impf. **philosophy** n филосо́фия.

**phlegm** n мокрота́. **phlegmatic** adj флегмати́ческий.

**phobia** n фо́бия.

**phone** n телефо́н; vt & i звони́ть impf, по~ pf +dat. See also **telephone**

**phonetic** adj фонети́ческий. **phonetics** n фоне́тика.

**phoney** n подде́льный.

**phosphorus** n фо́сфор.

**photo** n фо́то neut indecl. **photocopier** n копирова́льная маши́на. **photocopy** n фотоко́пия; vt де́лать impf, с~ pf фотоко́пию +gen. **photogenic** adj фотогени́чный.

photograph *n* фотогра́фия; *vt* фотографи́ровать *impf*, с~ *pf*. photographer *n* фото́граф. **photographic** *adj* фотографи́ческий. photography *n* фотогра́фия.

phrase *n* фра́за; *vt* формули́ровать *impf*, с~ *pf*.

physical *adj* физи́ческий; ~ education физкульту́ра; ~ exercises заря́дка. physician *n* врач. physicist *n* фи́зик. physics *n* фи́зика.

physiological *adj* физиологи́ческий. physiologist *n* физио́лог. physiology *n* физиоло́гия. physiotherapist *n* физиотерапе́вт. physiotherapy *n* физиотерапия.

physique *n* телосложе́ние.

pianist *n* пиани́ст, ~ка. piano *n* фортепья́но *neut indecl*; (grand) роя́ль *m*; (upright) пиани́но *neut indecl*.

pick¹ *vt* (flower) срыва́ть *impf*, сорва́ть *pf*; (gather) собира́ть *impf*, собра́ть *pf*; (select) выбира́ть *impf*, вы́брать *pf*; ~ one's nose, teeth ковыря́ть *impf* в носу́, в зуба́х; ~ a quarrel иска́ть *impf* ссо́ры (with c+*instr*); ~ one's way пробира́ться *impf*, вы́браться *pf* доро́гу; ~ on (nag) придира́ться *impf* к+*dat*; ~ out отбира́ть *impf*, отобра́ть *pf*; ~ up (lift) поднима́ть *impf*, подня́ть *pf*; (acquire) приобрета́ть *impf*, приобрести́ *pf*; (fetch) (on foot) заходи́ть *impf*, зайти́ *pf* за+*instr*; (in vehicle) заезжа́ть *impf*, зае́хать *pf* за+*instr*; (a cold; a girl) подцепля́ть *impf*, подцепи́ть *pf*; ~ o.s. up поднима́ться *impf*, подня́ться *pf*;

~up (truck) пика́п; (electron) звукоснима́тель *m*.

pick² *n* вы́бор; (best part) лу́чшая часть; take your ~ выбира́й(те)!

pick³, pickaxe *n* кирка́.

picket *n* (person) пике́тчик, -ица; (collect) пике́т; *vt* пикети́ровать *impf*.

pickle *n* соле́нье; *vt* соли́ть *impf*, по~ *pf*. pickled *adj* солёный.

pickpocket *n* карма́нник.

picnic *n* пикни́к.

pictorial *adj* изобрази́тельный; (illustrated) иллюстри́рованный. picture *n* карти́на; (of health etc.) воплоще́ние; (film) фильм; the ~s кино́ *neut indecl*; *vt* (to o.s.) представля́ть *impf*, предста́вить *pf* себе́. picturesque *adj* живопи́сный.

pie *n* пиро́г.

piece *n* кусо́к, часть; (one of set) шту́ка; (of paper) листо́к; (mus, literature) произведе́ние; (chess) фигу́ра; (coin) моне́та; take to ~s разбира́ть *impf*, разобра́ть *pf* (на ча́сти); ~ of advice сове́т; ~ of information све́дение; ~ of news но́вость; ~-work сде́льщина; ~-worker сде́льщик; *vt*: ~ together создава́ть *impf*, воссозда́ть *pf* карти́ну +*gen*. piecemeal *adv* по частя́м.

pier *n* (mole) мол; (projecting into sea) пирс; (of bridge) бык; (between windows etc.) просте́нок.

pierce *vt* пронза́ть *impf*, пронзи́ть *pf*; (ears) прока́лывать *impf*, проколо́ть *pf*. piercing *adj* пронзи́тельный.

piety *n* на́божность.

**pig** n свинья́. **pigheaded** adj упря́мый. **piglet** n поросё-нок. **pigsty** n свина́рник. **pigtail** n коси́чка.

**pigeon** n го́лубь; **~-hole** отде́ление для бума́г.

**pigment** n пигме́нт. **pigmentation** n пигмента́ция.

**pike** n (fish) щу́ка.

**pilchard** n сарди́н(к)а.

**pile¹** n (heap) ку́ча, ки́па; vt: **~ up** сва́ливать impf, свали́ть pf в ку́чу; (load) нагружа́ть impf, нагрузи́ть pf (with +instr); vi: **~ in(to), on** забира́ться impf, забра́ться pf в+acc; **~ up** нака́пливаться, накопи́ться pf.

**pile²** n (on cloth etc.) ворс.

**piles** n pl геморро́й collect.

**pilfer** vt ворова́ть impf.

**pilgrim** n пилигри́м. **pilgrimage** n пало́мничество.

**pill** n пилю́ля; **the ~** противозача́точная пилю́ля.

**pillage** vt гра́бить impf, о~ pf; v abs мародёрствовать impf.

**pillar** n столб; **~-box** стоя́чий почто́вый я́щик.

**pillion** n за́днее сиде́нье (мотоци́кла).

**pillory** n позо́рный столб; vt (fig) пригвожда́ть impf, пригвозди́ть pf к позо́рному столбу́.

**pillow** n поду́шка. **pillowcase** n на́волочка.

**pilot** n (naut) ло́цман; (aeron) пило́т; adj о́пытный, про́бный; vt пилоти́ровать impf.

**pimp** n сво́дник.

**pimple** n прыщ.

**pin** n була́вка; (peg) па́лец; **~-point** то́чно определя́ть impf, определи́ть pf; **~-stripe**

то́нкая поло́ска; vt прика́лывать impf, приколо́ть pf; (press) прижима́ть impf, прижа́ть pf (against к+dat).

**pinafore** n пере́дник.

**pincers** n pl (tool) кле́щи (-ще́й) pl, пинце́т; (claw) клешня́ pl.

**pinch** vt щипа́ть impf, (у)щипну́ть pf; (finger in door etc.) прищемля́ть impf, прищеми́ть pf; (of shoe) жать impf; (steal) стяну́ть pf в щипо́к; (of salt) щепо́тка; **at a ~** в кра́йнем слу́чае.

**pine¹** vi томи́ться impf; **~ for** тоскова́ть impf по+dat, prep.

**pine²** n (tree) сосна́.

**pineapple** n анана́с.

**ping-pong** n пинг-по́нг.

**pink** n (colour) ро́зовый цвет; adj ро́зовый.

**pinnacle** n верши́на.

**pint** n пи́нта.

**pioneer** n пионе́р, **~ка**; vt прокла́дывать impf, проложи́ть pf путь к+dat.

**pious** adj набо́жный.

**pip¹** n (seed) зёрнышко.

**pip²** n (sound) бип.

**pipe** n труба́; (mus) ду́дка; (for smoking) тру́бка; **~-dream** пуста́я мечта́; vt пуска́ть impf, пусти́ть pf по труба́м; vi **~ down** затиха́ть impf, зати́хнуть pf. **pipeline** n трубопрово́д; (oil **~**) нефтепрово́д. **piper** n волы́нщик. **piping** adj: **~ hot** с па́ру.

**piquant** adj пика́нтный.

**pique** n: **in a fit of ~** в поры́ве раздраже́ния.

**pirate** n пира́т.

**pirouette** n пируэ́т; vi де́лать impf, с~ pf пируэ́т(ы).

**Pisces** n Ры́бы f pl.

**pistol** n пистоле́т.

**piston** n по́ршень m.

**pit** n я́ма; (mine) ша́хта; (orchestra ~) орке́стр; (motor-racing) заправочно-контро́льный пункт; vt: ~ **against** выставля́ть impf, вы́ставить pf про́тив+gen.

**pitch¹** n (resin) смола́; ~-**black** чёрный как смоль; ~-**dark** о́чень тёмный.

**pitch²** vt (camp, tent) разбива́ть impf, разби́ть pf; (throw) броса́ть impf, бро́сить pf; vi (fall) па́дать impf, (у)па́сть pf; (ship) кача́ть impf, n (football ~ etc.) по́ле; (degree) у́ровень m; (mus) высота́; (slope) укло́н.

**pitcher** n (vessel) кувши́н.

**pitchfork** n ви́лы (-л) pl.

**piteous** adj жа́лкий.

**pitfall** n западня́.

**pith** n сердцеви́на; (essence) суть. **pithy** adj (fig) содержа́тельный.

**pitiful** adj жа́лкий. **pitiless** adj безжа́лостный.

**pittance** n жа́лкие гроши́ (-ше́й) pl.

**pity** n жа́лость; it's a ~ жа́лко, жаль; take ~ **on** сжа́литься pf над+instr; what a ~ как жа́лко!; vt жале́ть impf, по~ pf; I ~ **you** мне жаль тебя́.

**pivot** n сте́ржень m; (fig) центр; vi враща́ться impf.

**pixie** n эльф.

**pizza** n пи́цца.

**placard** n афи́ша, плака́т.

**placate** vt умиротворя́ть impf, умиротвори́ть pf.

**place** n ме́сто; in ~ **of** вме́сто+gen; in the first, second, ~ во-пе́рвых, во-вторы́х; out of ~ не на ме́сте; (un-

suitable) неуме́стный; take ~ случа́ться impf, случи́ться pf; (pre-arranged event) состоя́ться pf; take the ~ **of** заменя́ть impf, замени́ть pf; vt (stand) ста́вить impf, по~ pf; (lay) класть impf, положи́ть pf; (an order etc.) помеща́ть impf, помести́ть pf.

**placenta** n плаце́нта.

**placid** adj споко́йный.

**plagiarism** n плагиа́т. **plagiarize** vt заи́мствовать impf & pf.

**plague** n чума́; vt му́чить impf, за~, из~ pf.

**plaice** n ка́мбала.

**plain** n равни́на; adj (clear) я́сный; (simple) просто́й; (ugly) некраси́вый; ~-**clothes policeman** переоде́тый полице́йский sb.

**plaintiff** n исте́ц, исти́ца.

**plaintive** adj жа́лобный.

**plait** n коса́; vt плести́ impf, с~ pf.

**plan** n план; vt плани́ровать impf, за~, с~ pf; (intend) намерева́ться impf +inf.

**plane¹** n (tree) плата́н.

**plane²** n (tool) руба́нок; vt строга́ть impf, вы́~ pf.

**plane³** n (surface) пло́скость; (level) у́ровень m; (aero-plane) самолёт.

**planet** n плане́та.

**plank** n доска́.

**plant** n расте́ние; (factory) заво́д; vt сажа́ть impf, посади́ть pf; (fix firmly) про́чно ста́вить impf, по~ pf; (garden etc.) заса́живать impf, засади́ть pf (with +instr).

**plantation** n (of trees) лесонасажде́ние; (of cotton etc.) планта́ция.

**plaque** n доще́чка.

**plasma** n пла́зма.

**plaster** n пла́стырь m; (for walls etc.) штукату́рка; (of Paris) гипс; vt (walls etc.) штукату́рить impf, от~, о~ pf; (cover) облепля́ть impf, облепи́ть pf. **plasterboard** n сухая штукату́рка. **plasterer** n штукату́р.

**plastic** n пластма́сса; adj (malleable) пласти́чный; (made of ~) пластма́ссовый; ~ surgery пласти́ческая хирурги́я. **plate** n таре́лка; (metal sheet) лист; (in book) (вкладна́я иллюстра́ция; (name ~ etc.) доще́чка. **plateau** n плато́ neut indecl. **platform** n платфо́рма; (rly) перро́н. **platinum** n пла́тина. **platitude** n бана́льность. **platoon** n взвод. **plausible** adj правдоподо́бный.

**play** vt & i игра́ть impf, сыгра́ть pf (game) в+acc, (instrument) на+prep, (record) ста́вить impf, по~ pf; ~ down преуменьша́ть impf, преуме́ньшить pf; ~ a joke, trick, on подшу́чивать impf, подшути́ть pf над+instr; ~ off игра́ть impf, сыгра́ть pf реша́ющую па́ртию; ~ safe де́йствовать impf наверняка́; n игра́; (theat) пье́са. **player** n игро́к; (actor) актёр, актри́са; (musician) музыка́нт. **playful** adj игри́вый. **playground** n площа́дка для игр. **playgroup, playschool** n де́тский ~-card игра́льная ка́рта; ~-field игрова́я площа́дка. **playmate** n друг де́тства. **play-**

**thing** n игру́шка. **playwright** n драмату́рг.

**plea** n (entreaty) мольба́; (law) заявле́ние. **plead** vi умоля́ть impf (with +acc; for o+prep); vt (offer as excuse) ссыла́ться impf, сосла́ться pf на+acc; ~ (not) guilty (не) признава́ть, призна́ть pf себя́ вино́вным.

**pleasant** adj прия́тный. **pleasantry** n любе́зность. **please** vt нра́виться impf, по~ pf +dat; imper пожа́луйста; бу́дьте добры́. **pleased** adj дово́льный; predic рад. **pleasing, pleasurable** adj прия́тный. **pleasure** n удово́льствие.

**pleat** n скла́дка; vt плиссиро́вать impf.

**plebiscite** n плебисци́т. **plectrum** n плектр. **pledge** n (security) зало́г; (promise) заро́к, обеща́ние; vt отдава́ть impf, отда́ть pf в зало́г; ~ o.s. обя́зываться impf, обяза́ться pf; ~ one's word дава́ть impf, дать pf сло́во.

**plentiful** adj оби́льный. **plenty** n изоби́лие; ~ of мно́го+gen. **plethora** n (fig) изоби́лие. **pleurisy** n плеври́т. **pliable** adj ги́бкий. **pliers** n pl плоскогу́бцы (-цев) pl.

**plight** n незави́дное положе́ние.

**plimsolls** n pl спорти́вные та́почки f pl.

**plinth** n плинтус.

**plod** vi тащи́ться impf.

**plonk** vt плю́хнуть pf.

**plot** n (of land) уча́сток; (of book etc.) фа́була; (conspiracy) за́говор; vt (on graph, map, *etc.*) наноси́ть *impf*, нанести́ на гра́фик, на ка́рту; *v abs* (*conspire*) составля́ть *impf*, соста́вить *pf* за́говор.

**plough** *n* плуг; *vt* паха́ть *impf*, вс~ *pf*; *vi*: ~ **through** проби́ваться *impf*, проби́ться *pf* сквозь+*acc*.

**ploy** *n* уло́вка.

**pluck** *n* (*courage*) сме́лость; *vt* (*chicken*) щипа́ть *impf*, об~ *pf*; (*mus*) щипа́ть *impf*, (*flower*) срыва́ть *impf*, сорва́ть *pf*; ~ **up courage** собира́ться *impf*, собра́ться *pf* с ду́хом; *vi*: ~ **at** дёргать *impf*, дёрнуть *pf*. **plucky** *adj* сме́лый.

**plug** *n* (*stopper*) про́бка; (*electr*) ви́лка; (*electr socket*) розе́тка; (~ **up**) затыка́ть *impf*, заткну́ть *pf*; ~ **in** включа́ть *impf*, включи́ть *pf*.

**plum** *n* сли́ва.

**plumage** *n* опере́ние.

**plumb** *n* лот; *adv* вертика́льно; (*fig*) то́чно; *vt* измеря́ть *impf*, изме́рить *pf* глубину́+*gen*; (*fig*) проника́ть *impf*, прони́кнуть *pf* в+*acc*; ~ **in** подключа́ть *impf*, подключи́ть *pf*. **plumber** *n* водопрово́дчик. **plumbing** *n* водопрово́д.

**plume** *n* (*feather*) перо́; (*on hat etc.*) султа́н.

**plummet** *vi* па́дать *impf*, (у)па́сть *pf*.

**plump**[1] *adj* пу́хлый.

**plump**[2] *vi*: ~ **for** выбира́ть *impf*, вы́брать *pf*.

**plunder** *vt* гра́бить *impf*, о~ *pf*; *n* добы́ча.

**plunge** *vt* & *i* (*immerse*) погружа́ть(ся) *impf*, погрузи́ть(ся) *pf* (**into** в+*acc*); *vi* (*dive*) ныря́ть *impf*, нырну́ть

*pf*; (*rush*) броса́ться *impf*, бро́ситься *pf*. **plunger** *n* плу́нжер.

**pluperfect** *n* давнопроше́дшее вре́мя *neut*.

**plural** *n* мно́жественное число́. **pluralism** *n* плюрали́зм. **pluralistic** *adj* плюралисти́ческий.

**plus** *prep* плюс+*acc*; *n* (знак) плюс.

**plushy** *adj* шика́рный.

**plutonium** *n* плуто́ний.

**ply** *vt* (*tool*) рабо́тать *impf* +*instr*; (*task*) занима́ться *impf* +*instr*; (*keep supplied*) по́тчевать *impf* (**with** +*instr*); ~ **with questions** засыпа́ть *impf*, засы́пать *pf* вопро́сами.

**plywood** *n* фане́ра.

**p.m.** *adv* по́сле полу́дня.

**pneumatic** *adj* пневмати́ческий; ~ **drill** отбо́йный молото́к.

**pneumonia** *n* воспале́ние лёгких.

**poach**[1] *vt* (*cook*) вари́ть *impf*; ~**ed egg** яйцо́-пашо́т.

**poach**[2] *vt* браконье́рствовать *impf*. **poacher** *n* браконье́р.

**pocket** *n* карма́н; **out of** ~ в убы́тке; ~ **money** карма́нные де́ньги (-нег, -нья́м) *pl*; *vt* класть *impf*, положи́ть *pf* в карма́н.

**pock-marked** *adj* рябо́й.

**pod** *n* стручо́к.

**podgy** *adj* то́лстенький.

**podium** *n* трибу́на; (*conductor's*) пульт.

**poem** *n* стихотворе́ние; (*longer* ~) поэ́ма. **poet** *n* поэ́т. **poetess** *n* поэте́сса. **poetic(al)** *adj* поэти́ческий. **poetry** *n* поэ́зия, стихи́ *m pl*.

**pogrom** *n* погро́м.

**poignancy** n острота́. **poignant** adj о́стрый.

**point**¹ n то́чка; (place; in list) пункт; (in score) очко́; (in time) моме́нт; (in space) ме́сто; (essence) суть; (sense) смысл; (sharp) о́стрие; (tip) ко́нчик; (power) ~ штепсель m; (rly) стре́лка; **to be on the ~ of** (doing) собира́ться impf, собра́ться pf +inf; **beside, off, the ~** не́кстати; **that is the ~** в э́том и де́ло; **the ~ is that** де́ло в том, что; **there is no ~** (in doing) не име́ет смы́сла (+inf); **to the ~** кста́ти; ~-**blank** прямо́й; ~ **of view** то́чка зре́ния.

**point**² vt (wall) расшива́ть impf, расши́ть pf швы+gen; (gun etc.) наводи́ть impf, навести́ pf (at на+acc); vi по-, у-, ка́зывать impf, по-, у-, каза́ть pf (at, to на+acc).

**pointed** adj (sharp) о́стрый. **pointer** n указа́тель m, стре́лка. **pointless** adj бессмы́сленный.

**poise** n уравнове́шенность. **poised** adj (composed) уравнове́шенный; (ready) гото́вый (to к+dat).

**poison** n яд; vt отравля́ть impf, отрави́ть pf. **poisonous** adj ядови́тый.

**poke** vt (prod) ты́кать impf, ткнуть pf; ~ **fun at** подшу́чивать impf, подшути́ть pf над+instr; (thrust) сова́ть impf, су́нуть pf; ~ **the fire** меша́ть impf, по- pf у́гли в ками́не; n тычо́к. **poker**¹ n (rod) кочерга́.

**poker**² n (cards) по́кер.

**poky** adj те́сный.

**Poland** n По́льша.

**polar** adj поля́рный; ~ **bear** бе́лый медве́дь m. **polarity** n поля́рность. **polarize** vt поляризова́ть impf & pf.

**pole**¹ n (geog; phys) по́люс; ~-**star** Поля́рная звезда́.

**pole**² n (rod) столб, шест; ~-**vaulting** прыжо́к с шесто́м.

**Pole** n поля́к, по́лька.

**polecat** n хорёк.

**polemic** adj полеми́ческий; n поле́мика.

**police** n поли́ция; (as pl) полице́йские; (in Russia) мили́ция; ~ **station** полице́йский уча́сток. **policeman** n полице́йский sb, полисме́н; (in Russia) милиционе́р. **policewoman** n же́нщина-полице́йский sb; (in Russia) же́нщина-милиционе́р.

**policy**¹ n поли́тика.

**policy**² n (insurance) по́лис.

**polio** n полиомиели́т.

**Polish** adj по́льский.

**polish** n (gloss, process) полиро́вка; (substance) политу́ра; (fig) лоск; vt полирова́ть impf, от- pf; ~ **off** расправля́ться impf, распра́виться pf c+instr.

**polished** adj отто́ченный.

**polite** adj ве́жливый. **politeness** n ве́жливость.

**politic** adj полити́чный. **political** adj полити́ческий; ~ **economy** политэконо́мика; ~ **prisoner** политзаключённый sb. **politician** n поли́тик. **politics** n поли́тика.

**poll** n (voting) голосова́ние; (opinion) ~ опро́с; **go to the** ~**s** голосова́ть impf, про- pf; vt получа́ть impf, получи́ть pf.

**pollen** n пыльца́. **pollinate** vt опыля́ть impf, опыли́ть pf.

**polling** attrib: ~ **booth** каби́на

для голосова́ния; ~ **station** избира́тельный уча́сток.

**pollutant** n загрязни́тель m.
**pollute** vt загрязня́ть impf, загрязни́ть pf. **pollution** n загрязне́ние.

**polo** n по́ло neut indecl; ~ **neck sweater** водола́зка.

**polyester** n полиэфи́р. **polyethylene** n полиэтиле́н. **polyglot** n полигло́т; adj многоязы́чный. **polygon** n многоуго́льник. **polymer** n полиме́р. **polystyrene** n полистиро́л. **polytechnic** n техни́ческий вуз. **polythene** n полиэтиле́н. **polyunsaturated** adj: ~ **fats** полиненасы́щенные жиры́ m pl. **polyurethane** n полиурета́н.

**pomp** n пы́шность. **pomposity** n напы́щенность. **pompous** adj напы́щенный.

**pond** n пруд.

**ponder** vt обду́мывать impf, обду́мать pf; vi размышля́ть impf, размы́слить pf.

**ponderous** adj тяжелове́сный.

**pony** n по́ни m indecl.

**poodle** n пу́дель m.

**pool**[1] n (of water) прудо́к; (puddle) лу́жа; (swimming ~) бассе́йн.

**pool**[2] n (collective stake) совоку́пность ста́вок; (common fund) о́бщий фонд; vt объединя́ть impf, объедини́ть pf.

**poor** adj бе́дный; (bad) плохо́й; n: the ~ бедняки́ m pl. **poorly** predic нездоро́в.

**pop**[1] vi хло́пать impf, хло́пнуть pf; vt (put) бы́стро всу́нуть (into в+acc); ~ **in** забега́ть impf, забежа́ть pf к+dat; n хлопо́к.

**pop**[2] adj поп-; ~ **concert** поп-

конце́рт; ~ **music** поп-му́зыка.

**pope** n Па́па m.

**poplar** n то́поль m.

**poppy** n мак.

**populace** n просто́й наро́д. **popular** adj наро́дный; (liked) популя́рный. **popularity** n популя́рность. **popularize** vt популяризи́ровать impf & pf. **populate** vt населя́ть impf, насели́ть pf. **population** n населе́ние. **populous** adj (мно́го)лю́дный.

**porcelain** n фарфо́р.

**porch** n крыльцо́.

**porcupine** n дикобра́з.

**pore**[1] n по́ра.

**pore**[2] vi: ~ **over** погружа́ться impf, погрузи́ться pf в+acc.

**pork** n свини́на.

**pornographic** adj порногра́фи́ческий. **pornography** n порногра́фия.

**porous** adj по́ристый.

**porpoise** n морска́я свинья́.

**porridge** n овся́ная ка́ша.

**port**[1] n (harbour) порт; (town) портово́й го́род.

**port**[2] n (naut) ле́вый борт.

**port**[3] n (wine) портве́йн.

**portable** adj порта́тивный.

**portend** vt предвеща́ть impf. **portent** n предзнаменова́ние. **portentous** adj злове́щий.

**porter**[1] n (at door) швейца́р.

**porter**[2] n (carrier) носи́льщик.

**portfolio** n портфе́ль m; (artist's) па́пка.

**porthole** n иллюмина́тор.

**portion** n часть, до́ля; (of food) по́рция.

**portly** adj доро́дный.

**portrait** n портре́т. **portray** vt изобража́ть impf, изобрази́ть pf. **portrayal** n изображе́ние.

**Portugal** n Португа́лия. **Portuguese** n португа́лец, -лка; adj португа́льский.

**pose** n по́за; vt (question) ста́вить impf, по~ pf; (a problem) представля́ть impf, предста́вить pf; vi пози́ровать impf; ~ **as** выдава́ть impf, вы́дать pf себя́ за+acc.

**posh** adj шика́рный.

**posit** vt постули́ровать impf & pf.

**position** n положе́ние, пози́ция; **in a** ~ **to** в состоя́нии +inf; vt ста́вить impf, по~ pf.

**positive** adj положи́тельный; (convinced) уве́ренный; (proof) несомне́нный; n (phot) позити́в.

**possess** vt облада́ть impf +instr; владе́ть impf +instr; (of feeling etc.) овладева́ть impf, овладе́ть pf +instr. **possessed** adj одержи́мый. **possession** n владе́ние (of +instr); pl со́бственность. **possessive** adj со́бственнический. **possessor** n облада́тель m.

**possibility** n возмо́жность. **possible** adj возмо́жный; **as much as** ~ ско́лько возмо́жно; **as soon as** ~ как мо́жно скоре́е. **possibly** adv возмо́жно, мо́жет (быть).

**post**[1] n (pole) столб; vt (~ up) выве́шивать impf, вы́весить pf.

**post**[2] n (station) пост; (job) до́лжность; vt (station) расставля́ть impf, расста́вить pf; (appoint) назнача́ть impf, назна́чить pf.

**post**[3] n (letters, or office) по́чта; **by** ~ по́чтой; attrib почто́вый; ~-**box** почто́вый я́щик; ~-**code** почто́вый и́ндекс; ~ **office** по́чта; vt (send by ~) отправля́ть impf, отпра́вить pf по по́чте; (put in ~-box) опуска́ть impf, опусти́ть pf в почто́вый я́щик. **postage** n почто́вый сбор, почто́вые расхо́ды n pl; ~ **stamp** почто́вая ма́рка. **postal** adj почто́вый; ~-**order** почто́вый перево́д. **postcard** n откры́тка.

**poster** n афи́ша, плака́т.

*poste restante* n до востре́бования.

**posterior** adj за́дний; n зад.

**posterity** n пото́мство.

**post-graduate** n аспира́нт.

**posthumous** adj посме́ртный.

**postman** n почтальо́н. **postmark** n почто́вый ште́мпель m.

**post-mortem** n вскры́тие тру́па.

**postpone** vt отсро́чивать impf, отсро́чить pf. **postponement** n отсро́чка.

**postscript** n постскри́птум.

**postulate** vt постули́ровать impf & pf.

**posture** n по́за, положе́ние.

**post-war** adj послевое́нный.

**posy** n буке́тик.

**pot** n горшо́к; (cooking ~) кастрю́ля; ~-**shot** вы́стрел науга́д; vt (food) консерви́ровать impf, за~ pf; (plant) сажа́ть impf, посади́ть pf в горшо́к; (billiards) загоня́ть impf, загна́ть pf в лу́зу.

**potash** n пота́ш. **potassium** n ка́лий.

**potato** n (also collect) карто́шка (no pl); (plant; also collect) карто́фель m (no pl).

**potency** n си́ла. **potent** adj си́льный.

**potential** *adj* потенциа́льный; *n* потенциа́л. **potentiality** *n* потенциа́льность.

**pot-hole** *n* (*in road*) вы́боина.

**potion** *n* зе́лье.

**potter**[1] *vi:* ~ **about** вози́ться *impf*.

**potter**[2] *n* гонча́р. **pottery** *n* (*goods*) гонча́рные изде́лия *neut pl*; (*place*) гонча́рная *sb*.

**potty**[1] *adj* (*crazy*) поме́шанный (**about** на+*prep*).

**potty**[2] *n* ночно́й горшо́к.

**pouch** *n* су́мка.

**poultry** *n* дома́шняя пти́ца.

**pounce** *vi:* ~ (**up**)**on** набра́сываться *impf*, набро́ситься *pf* на+*acc*.

**pound**[1] *n* (*measure*) фунт; ~ **sterling** фунт сте́рлингов.

**pound**[2] *vt* (*strike*) колоти́ть *impf*, по~ *pf* по+*dat*, в+*acc*; *vi* (*heart*) колоти́ться *impf*; ~ **along** (*run*) мча́ться *impf* с гро́хотом.

**pour** *vt* лить *impf*; ~ **out** налива́ть *impf*, нали́ть *pf*; *vi* ли́ться *impf*; **it is** ~**ing** (**with rain**) дождь льёт как из ведра́.

**pout** *vi* ду́ть(ся) *impf*, на~ *pf*.

**poverty** *n* бе́дность; ~ **stricken** убо́гий.

**POW** *abbr* военнопле́нный *sb.*

**powder** *n* порошо́к; (*cosmetic*) пу́дра; *vt* пу́дрить *impf*, на~ *pf*. **powdery** *adj* порошко́обра́зный.

**power** *n* (*vigour*) си́ла; (*might*) могу́щество; (*ability*) спосо́бность; (*control*) власть; (*authorization*) полномо́чие; (*State*) держа́ва; ~ **cut** переры́в электропита́ния; ~ **point** розе́тка; ~ **station** электроста́нция. **powerful** *adj* си́льный. **powerless** *adj* бесси́льный.

**practicable** *adj* осуществи́мый. **practical** *adj* (*help, activities*) практи́ческий; (*person, object*) практи́чный. **practically** *adv* практи́чески. **practice** *n* пра́ктика; (*custom*) обы́чай; (*mus*) заня́тия *neut pl*; **in** ~ на пра́ктике; **put into** ~ осуществля́ть *impf*, осуществи́ть *pf*. **practise** *vt* (*also abs of doctor etc.*) практикова́ть *impf*; упражня́ться *impf* в+*prep*; (*mus*) занима́ться *impf*, заня́ться *pf* на+*prep*. **practised** *adj* о́пытный. **practitioner** *n* (*doctor*) практику́ющий врач; **general** ~ врач о́бщей пра́ктики.

**pragmatic** *adj* прагмати́ческий. **pragmatism** *n* прагмати́зм. **pragmatist** *n* прагма́тик.

**prairie** *n* пре́рия.

**praise** *vt* хвали́ть *impf*, по~ *pf*; *n* похвала́. **praiseworthy** *adj* похва́льный.

**pram** *n* де́тская коля́ска.

**prance** *vi* гарцева́ть *impf*.

**prank** *n* вы́ходка.

**prattle** *vi* лепета́ть; *n* ле́пет.

**prawn** *n* креве́тка.

**pray** *vi* моли́ться *impf*, по~ *pf* (**to** +*dat*; **for** о+*prep*). **prayer** *n* моли́тва.

**preach** *vt* & *i* пропове́довать *impf*. **preacher** *n* пропове́дник.

**preamble** *n* преа́мбула.

**pre-arrange** *vt* зара́нее организо́вывать *impf*, организова́ть *pf*.

**precarious** *adj* опа́сный.

**precaution** *n* предосторо́жность. **precautionary** *adj:* ~ **measures** ме́ры предосторо́жности.

**precede** vt предше́ствовать impf +dat. **precedence** n предпочте́ние. **precedent** n прецеде́нт. **preceding** adj предыду́щий.

**precept** n наставле́ние.

**precinct** n двор; pl. окре́стности f pl. **pedestrian** ~ уча́сток для пешехо́дов; **shopping** ~ торго́вый пасса́ж.

**precious** adj драгоце́нный; (style) мане́рный; adv о́чень.

**precipice** n обры́в. **precipitate** adj (person) опроме́тчивый; vt (throw down) низверга́ть impf, низве́ргнуть pf; (hurry) ускоря́ть impf, ускоря́ть pf. **precipitation** n (meteorol) оса́дки m pl. **precipitous** adj обры́вистый.

**précis** n конспе́кт.

**precise** adj то́чный. **precisely** adv то́чно; (in answer) и́менно. **precision** n то́чность.

**preclude** vt предотвраща́ть impf, предотврати́ть pf.

**precocious** adj ра́но разви́вшийся.

**preconceived** adj предвзя́тый. **preconception** n предвзя́тое мне́ние.

**pre-condition** n предпосы́лка.

**precursor** n предше́ственник.

**predator** n хи́щник. **predatory** adj хи́щный.

**predecessor** n предше́ственник.

**predestination** n предопределе́ние.

**predetermine** vt предреша́ть impf, предреши́ть pf.

**predicament** n затрудни́тельное положе́ние.

**predicate** n (gram) сказу́емое sb. **predicative** adj предикати́вный.

**predict** vt предска́зывать impf, предсказа́ть pf. **predictable** adj предсказу́емый. **prediction** n предсказа́ние.

**predilection** n пристра́стие (for к+dat).

**predispose** vt предрасполага́ть impf, предрасположи́ть pf (to к+dat). **predisposition** n предрасположе́ние (to к+dat).

**predominance** n преоблада́ние. **predominant** adj преоблада́ющий. **predominate** vi преоблада́ть impf.

**pre-eminence** n превосхо́дство. **pre-eminent** adj выдаю́щийся.

**pre-empt** vt (fig) завладева́ть impf, завладе́ть pf +instr пре́жде други́х. **pre-emptive** adj (mil) упрежда́ющий.

**preen** vt (of bird) чи́стить impf, по~ pf клю́вом; ~ o.s. (be proud) горди́ться impf собо́й.

**pre-fab** n сбо́рный дом. **prefabricated** adj сбо́рный.

**preface** n предисло́вие.

**prefect** n префе́кт; (school) ста́роста m.

**prefer** vt предпочита́ть impf, предпоче́сть pf. **preferable** adj предпочти́тельный. **preference** n предпочте́ние. **preferential** adj предпочти́тельный.

**prefix** n приста́вка.

**pregnancy** n бере́менность. **pregnant** adj бере́менная.

**prehistoric** adj доистори́ческий.

**prejudice** n предубежде́ние; (detriment) уще́рб; vt наноси́ть impf, нанести́ pf уще́рб+dat; ~ against предубежда́ть impf, предубеди́ть pf про́тив+gen; be ~d against име́ть impf предубежде́ние про́тив +gen.

**preliminary** adj предвари́тельный.

**prelude** n прелю́дия.

**premarital** adj добра́чный.

**premature** adj преждевре́менный.

**premeditated** adj преднаме́ренный.

**premier** adj пе́рвый; n премье́р-мини́стр. **première** n премье́ра.

**premise, premiss** n (logic) (пред)посы́лка. **premises** n pl помеще́ние.

**premium** n пре́мия.

**premonition** n предчу́вствие.

**preoccupation** n озабо́ченность; (absorbing subject) забо́та. **preoccupied** adj озабо́ченный. **preoccupy** vt поглоща́ть impf, поглоти́ть pf.

**preparation** n приготовле́ние; pl подгото́вка (for к+dat); (substance) препара́т. **preparatory** adj подготови́тельный. **prepare** vt & i при-, под-, гота́вливать(ся) impf, при-, под-, гото́вить(ся) pf (for к+dat). **prepared** adj гото́вый.

**preponderance** n переве́с.

**preposition** n предло́г.

**prepossessing** adj привлека́тельный.

**preposterous** adj неле́пый.

**prerequisite** n предпосы́лка.

**prerogative** n прерогати́ва.

**presage** vt предвеща́ть impf.

**Presbyterian** n пресвитериа́нин, -а́нка; adj пресвитериа́нский.

**prescribe** vt предпи́сывать impf, предписа́ть pf; (med) прописа́ть pf. **prescription** n (med) реце́пт.

**presence** n прису́тствие; ~ of mind прису́тствие ду́ха. **present** adj прису́тствующий; (being dealt with) да́нный; (existing now) ны́нешний; (also gram) настоя́щий; predic налицо́; be ~ прису́тствовать impf (at на+prep); ~-day ны́нешний; n: the ~ настоя́щее sb; (gram) настоя́щее вре́мя neut; (gift) пода́рок; at ~ в настоя́щее вре́мя neut; for the ~ пока́; vt (introduce) представля́ть impf, предста́вить pf (to +dat); (award) вруча́ть impf, вручи́ть pf; (a play) ста́вить impf, по~ pf; (a gift) преподноси́ть impf, преподнести́ pf +dat (with +acc); o.s. явля́ться impf, яви́ться pf. **presentable** adj прили́чный. **presentation** n (introducing) представле́ние; (awarding) подноше́ние.

**presentiment** n предчу́вствие.

**presently** adv вско́ре.

**preservation** n сохране́ние. **preservative** n консерва́нт. **preserve** n (keep safe) сохраня́ть impf, сохрани́ть pf; (maintain) храни́ть impf; (food) консерви́ровать impf, за~ pf; n (for game etc) запове́дник; (jam) варе́нье.

**preside** vi председа́тельствовать impf (at на+prep). **presidency** n президе́нтство. **president** n президе́нт. **presidential** adj президе́нтский. **presidium** n прези́диум.

**press** n (machine) пресс; (printing firm) типогра́фия; (publishing house) изда́тельство; (the ~) пре́сса, печа́ть; ~ conference пресс-конфере́нция; vt (button etc) нажима́ть impf, нажа́ть pf; (clasp) прижима́ть impf, прижа́ть pf (to к+dat); (iron) гла́дить impf, вы́~ pf; (insist on) наста́ивать impf, насто́ять pf на+prep; угова́ривать impf; ~ on (make haste) потора́пливаться impf.

**pressing** adj неотло́жный. **pressure** n давле́ние; ~-**cooker** скорова́рка; ~ **group** инициати́вная гру́ппа. **pressurize** vt (fig) ока́зывать impf, оказа́ть pf давле́ние на+acc. **pressurized** adj гермети́ческий.

**prestige** n прести́ж. **prestigious** adj прести́жный.

**presumably** adv предположи́тельно. **presume** vt полага́ть impf; (venture) позволя́ть impf, позво́лить pf себе́. **presumption** n предположе́ние; (arrogance) самонаде́янность. **presumptuous** adj самонаде́янный.

**presuppose** vt предполага́ть impf.

**pretence** n притво́рство. **pretend** vt притворя́ться impf, притвори́ться pf (to be +instr); де́лать impf, с~ pf вид (что); vi: ~ to претендова́ть impf на+acc. **pretender** n претенде́нт. **pretension** n прете́нзия. **pretentious** adj претенцио́зный.

**pretext** n предло́г.

**prettiness** n милови́дность. **pretty** adj хоро́шенький; adv дово́льно.

**prevail** vi (predominate) преоблада́ть impf; ~ (up)on угова́ривать impf, уговори́ть pf. **prevalence** n распро-

стране́ние. **prevalent** adj распространённый.

**prevaricate** vi уви́ливать impf увильну́ть pf.

**prevent** vt (stop from happening) предупрежда́ть impf, предупреди́ть pf; (stop from doing) меша́ть impf, по~ pf +dat. **prevention** n предупрежде́ние. **preventive** adj предупреди́тельный.

**preview** n предвари́тельный просмо́тр.

**previous** adj предыду́щий; adv: ~ **to** до+gen; пре́жде чем +inf. **previously** adv ра́ньше.

**pre-war** adj довое́нный.

**prey** n (animal) добы́ча; (victim) же́ртва (**to** +gen); **bird of** ~ хи́щная пти́ца; vi: ~ **(up)on** (emotion etc.) му́чить impf.

**price** n цена́; ~-**list** прейскура́нт; vt назнача́ть impf, назна́чить pf це́ну +gen. **priceless** adj бесце́нный.

**prick** vt коло́ть impf, у~ pf; (conscience) му́чить impf; ~ **up one's ears** навостри́ть pf у́ши; n уко́л. **prickle** n (thorn) колю́чка; (spine) игла́. **prickly** adj колю́чий.

**pride** n го́рдость; ~ **o.s. on** горди́ться impf +instr.

**priest** n свяще́нник; (non-Christian) жрец.

**prig** n педа́нт.

**prim** adj чо́порный.

**primarily** adv первонача́льно; (above all) пре́жде всего́. **primary** adj основно́й; ~ **school** нача́льная шко́ла. **prime** n: **in one's** ~ в расцве́те сил; adj (chief) гла́вный; ~ **minister** премье́р-мини́стр; vt (engine) заправля́ть impf, запра́вить pf;

(*bomb*) активизировать *impf* & *pf*; (*with facts*) инструктировать *impf* & *pf*; (*with paint etc.*) грунтовать *impf*, за~ *pf*. **primer** *n* (*paint etc.*) грунт. **prim(a)eval** *adj* первобытный. **primitive** *adj* первобытный; (*crude*) примитивный. **primordial** *adj* исконный.

**primrose** *n* первоцвет; (*colour*) бледно-жёлтый цвет.

**prince** *n* принц; (*in Russia*) князь. **princely** *adj* княжеский; (*sum*) огромный. **princess** *n* принцесса; (*wife*) княгиня; (*daughter*) княжна.

**principal** *n* главный; *n* директор. **principality** *n* княжество. **principally** *adv* главным образом.

**principle** *n* принцип; in ~ в принципе; on ~ принципиально. **principled** *adj* принципиальный.

**print** *n* (*mark*) след; (*also phot*) отпечаток; (*printing*) печать; (*picture*) оттиск; in ~ в продаже; *vt* (*impress*) запечатлевать *impf*, запечатлеть *pf*; (*book etc.*) печатать *impf*, на~ *pf*; (*write*) писать *impf*, на~ *pf* печатными буквами; (*phot*; ~ out, off*) отпечатывать *impf*, отпечатать *pf*; ~ out (*of computer etc.*) распечатывать *impf*, распечатать *pf*; **~-out** распечатка. **printer** *n* (*person*) печатник, типограф; (*of computer*) принтер. **printing** *n* печатание; **~-press** печатный станок.

**prior** *adj* прежний; *adv*: ~ to до+*gen*. **priority** *n* приоритет. **priory** *n* монастырь *m*.

**prise** *vt*: ~ open взламывать

*impf*, взломать *pf*.

**prism** *n* призма.

**prison** *n* тюрьма; *attrib* тюремный; **~ camp** лагерь *m*. **prisoner** *n* заключённый *sb*; (~ of war*) (военно)пленный *sb*.

**pristine** *adj* нетронутый.

**privacy** *n* уединение; (*private life*) частная жизнь. **private** *adj* (*personal*) частный, личный; (*confidential*) конфиденциальный; in ~ наедине; в частной жизни; *n* рядовой *sb*.

**privation** *n* лишение.

**privilege** *n* привилегия. **privileged** *adj* привилегированный.

**privy** *adj*: ~ to посвящённый в+*acc*.

**prize** *n* премия, приз; **~-winner** призёр; *vt* высоко ценить *impf*.

**pro**[1] *n*: ~s and cons доводы *m pl* за и против.

**pro**[2] *n* (*professional*) профессионал.

**probability** *n* вероятность. **probable** *adj* вероятный. **probably** *adv* вероятно.

**probate** *n* утверждение завещания.

**probation** *n* испытательный срок; (*law*) условный приговор; **got two years ~** получил два года условно. **probationary** *adj* испытательный.

**probe** *n* (*med*) зонд; (*fig*) расследование; *vt* зондировать *impf*; (*fig*) расследовать *impf* & *pf*.

**probity** *n* честность.

**problem** *n* проблема, вопрос; (*math*) задача. **problematic** *adj* проблематичный.

**procedural** *adj* процеду́рный.
**procedure** *n* процеду́ра.
**proceed** *vi* (*go further*) идти́ *impf*, пойти́ *pf* да́льше; (*act*) поступа́ть *impf*, поступи́ть *pf*; (*abs*, ~ *to say*; *continue*) продолжа́ть *impf*, продо́лжить *pf*; (*of action*) продолжа́ться *impf*, продо́лжиться *pf*; ~ **from** исходи́ть *impf* из, от+*gen*; ~ **to** (*begin to*) принима́ться *impf*, приня́ться *pf* +*inf*. **proceedings** *n pl* (*activity*) де́ятельность; (*legal* ~) судопроизво́дство; (*published report*) труды́ *m pl*, запи́ски *f pl*. **proceeds** *n pl* вы́ручка. **process** *n* проце́сс; *vt* обраба́тывать *impf*, обрабо́тать *pf*. **procession** *n* проце́ссия, ше́ствие.
**proclaim** *vt* провозглаша́ть *impf*, провозгласи́ть *pf*. **proclamation** *n* провозглаше́ние.
**procure** *vt* достава́ть *impf*, доста́ть *pf*.
**prod** *vt* ты́кать *impf*, ткнуть *pf*; в тычо́к.
**prodigal** *adj* расточи́тельный.
**prodigious** *adj* огро́мный. **prodigy** *n*: **child** ~ вундерки́нд.
**produce** *vt* (*evidence etc.*) представля́ть *impf*, предста́вить *pf*; (*ticket etc.*) предъявля́ть *impf*, предъяви́ть *pf*; (*play etc.*) ста́вить *impf*, по~ *pf*; (*manufacture; cause*) производи́ть *impf*, произвести́ *pf*; (*collect*) проду́кты *m pl*. **producer** *n* (*econ*) производи́тель *m*; (*of play etc.*) режиссёр. **product** *n* проду́кт; (*result*) результа́т. **production** *n* произво́дство; (*of play etc.*) постано́вка. **productive** *adj* продукти́вный; (*fruitful*)

плодотво́рный. **productivity** *n* производи́тельность.
**profane** *adj* све́тский; (*blasphemous*) богоху́льный. **profanity** *n* богоху́льство.
**profess** *vt* (*pretend*) притворя́ться *impf*, притвори́ться *pf* (**to be** +*instr*); (*declare*) заявля́ть *impf*, заяви́ть *pf*; (*faith*) испове́довать *impf*. **profession** *n* (*job*) профе́ссия. **professional** *adj* профессиона́льный; *n* профессиона́л. **professor** *n* профе́ссор.
**proffer** *vt* предлага́ть *impf*, предложи́ть *pf*.
**proficiency** *n* уме́ние. **proficient** *adj* уме́лый.
**profile** *n* про́филь *m*.
**profit** *n* (*benefit*) по́льза; (*monetary*) при́быль; *vt* приноси́ть *impf*, принести́ *pf* по́льзу +*dat*; *vi*: ~ **from** по́льзоваться *impf*, вос~ *pf* +*instr*; (*financially*) получа́ть *impf*, получи́ть *pf* при́быль на +*prep*. **profitable** *adj* (*lucrative*) при́быльный; (*beneficial*) поле́зный. **profiteering** *n* спекуля́ция.
**profligate** *adj* распу́тный.
**profound** *adj* глубо́кий.
**profuse** *adj* оби́льный. **profusion** *n* изоби́лие.
**progeny** *n* пото́мство.
**prognosis** *n* прогно́з.
**program(m)e** *n* програ́мма; *vt* программи́ровать *impf*, за~ *pf*. **programmer** *n* программи́ст.
**progress** *n* прогре́сс; (*success*) успе́хи *m pl*; **make** ~ де́лать *impf*, с~ *pf* успе́хи; *vi* продвига́ться *impf*, продви́нуться *pf* вперёд. **progression** *n* продвиже́ние.

**progressive** adj прогресси́вный.

**prohibit** vt запреща́ть impf, запрети́ть pf. **prohibition** n запреще́ние; (on alcohol) сухо́й зако́н. **prohibitive** adj запрети́тельный; (price) недосту́пный.

**project** vt (plan) проекти́ровать impf, ~ pf; (a film) демонстри́ровать impf, про~ pf; vi (jut out) выступа́ть impf; n прое́кт. **projectile** n снаря́д. **projection** n (cin) прое́кция; (protrusion) вы́ступ; (forecast) прогно́з. **projector** n проє́ктор.

**proletarian** adj пролета́рский. **proletariat** n пролетариа́т.

**proliferate** vi распространя́ться impf, распространи́ться pf. **proliferation** n распростране́ние.

**prolific** adj плодови́тый.

**prologue** n проло́г.

**prolong** vt продлева́ть impf, продли́ть pf.

**promenade** n ме́сто для гуля́нья; (at seaside) на́бережная sb; vi прогу́ливаться impf, прогуля́ться pf.

**prominence** n изве́стность. **prominent** adj выступа́ющий; (distinguished) выдаю́щийся.

**promiscuity** n лёгкое поведе́ние. **promiscuous** adj лёгкого поведе́ния.

**promise** n обеща́ние; vt обеща́ть impf & pf. **promising** adj многообеща́ющий.

**promontory** n мыс.

**promote** vt (in rank) продвига́ть impf, продви́нуть pf; (assist) спосо́бствовать impf & pf +dat; (publicize) реклами́ровать impf. **promoter** n

(of event etc.) аге́нт. **promotion** n (in rank) продвиже́ние; (comm) рекла́ма.

**prompt** adj бы́стрый, неме́дленный; adv ро́вно; vt (incite) побужда́ть impf, побуди́ть pf (to k+dat; +inf); (speaker; also fig) подска́зывать impf, подсказа́ть pf +dat; (theat) суфли́ровать impf +dat; n подска́зка. **prompter** n суфлёр.

**prone** adj (лежа́щий) ничко́м; predic: ~ to скло́нен (-онна́, -о́нно) k+dat.

**prong** n зубе́ц.

**pronoun** n местоиме́ние.

**pronounce** vt (declare) объявля́ть impf, объяви́ть pf; (articulate) произноси́ть impf, произнести́ pf. **pronounced** adj я́вный; заме́тный. **pronouncement** n заявле́ние. **pronunciation** n произноше́ние.

**proof** n доказа́тельство; (printing) корректу́ра; ~-reader adj корре́ктор; adj (impenetrable) непроница́емый (**against** для+gen); (not yielding) неподдаю́щийся (**against** +dat).

**prop**[1] n (support) подпо́рка; (fig) опо́ра; vt (~ open, up) подпира́ть impf, подпере́ть pf; (fig) подде́рживать impf, поддержа́ть pf.

**prop**[2] n (theat) see props

**propaganda** n пропага́нда.

**propagate** vt & i размножа́ть(ся) impf, размно́жить(ся) pf; (disseminate) распространя́ть(ся) impf, распространи́ть(ся) pf. **propagation** n размноже́ние; распростране́ние.

**propel** vt приводи́ть impf, привести́ pf в движе́ние. **propeller** n винт.

**propensity** n наклóнность (to k+dat; +inf).

**proper** adj (correct) прáвильный; (suitable) подходя́щий; (decent) присто́йный; ~ noun и́мя со́бственное. **properly** adv как сле́дует.

**property** n (possessions) со́бственность, иму́щество; (attribute) сво́йство; pl (theat) реквизи́т.

**prophecy** n проро́чество. **prophesy** vt проро́чить impf, на~ pf. **prophet** n проро́к. **prophetic** adj проро́ческий.

**propitious** adj благоприя́тный.

**proponent** n сторо́нник.

**proportion** n пропо́рция; (due relation) соразме́рность; pl разме́ры pl. **proportional** adj пропорциона́льный. **proportionate** adj соразме́рный (to +dat; c+instr).

**proposal** n предложе́ние. **propose** vt предлага́ть impf, предложи́ть pf; (intend) предполага́ть impf; vi (~ marriage) де́лать impf, с~ pf предложе́ние (to +dat). **proposition** n предложе́ние.

**propound** vt предлага́ть impf, предложи́ть pf на обсужде́ние.

**proprietor** n со́бственник, хозя́ин.

**propriety** n прили́чие.

**props** n pl (theat) реквизи́т.

**propulsion** n движе́ние вперёд.

**prosaic** adj прозаи́ческий.

**proscribe** vt (forbid) запреща́ть impf, запрети́ть pf.

**prose** n про́за.

**prosecute** vt пресле́довать impf. **prosecution** n суде́бное пресле́дование; (pro-secuting party) обвине́ние. **prosecutor** n обвини́тель m.

**prospect** n вид; (fig) перспекти́ва; vi: ~ for иска́ть impf. **prospective** adj бу́дущий. **prospector** n разве́дчик. **prospectus** n проспе́кт.

**prosper** vi процвета́ть impf. **prosperity** n процвета́ние. **prosperous** adj процвета́ющий; (wealthy) зажи́точный.

**prostate (gland)** n проста́та.

**prostitute** n проститу́тка. **prostitution** n проститу́ция.

**prostrate** adj распростёртый, (лежа́щий) ничко́м; (exhausted) обесси́ленный; (with grief) уби́тый (with +instr).

**protagonist** n гла́вный геро́й; (in contest) протагони́ст.

**protect** vt защища́ть impf, защити́ть pf. **protection** n защи́та. **protective** adj защи́тный. **protector** n защи́тник.

**protégé(e)** n протеже́ m & f indecl.

**protein** n бело́к.

**protest** n проте́ст; vi проте́стовать impf; vt (affirm) утвержда́ть impf.

**Protestant** n протеста́нт, ~ка; adj протеста́нтский.

**protestation** n (торже́ственное) заявле́ние (о+prep; что); (protest) проте́ст.

**protocol** n протоко́л.

**proton** n прото́н.

**prototype** n прототи́п.

**protract** vt тяну́ть impf. **protracted** adj дли́тельный.

**protrude** vi выдава́ться impf, вы́даться pf.

**proud** adj го́рдый; be ~ of горди́ться impf +instr.

**prove** vt дока́зывать impf, доказа́ть pf; vi ока́зываться *impf,* оказа́ться *pf* (**to be** +*instr*). **proven** *adj* дока́занный.

**provenance** *n* происхожде́ние.

**proverb** *n* посло́вица. **proverbial** *adj* воше́дший в погово́рку; (*well-known*) общеизве́стный.

**provide** *vt* (*supply person*) снабжа́ть *impf,* снабди́ть *pf* (**with** +*instr*); (*supply thing*) предоставля́ть *impf,* предоста́вить *pf* (**to, for** +*dat*); дава́ть *impf,* дать *pf* (**to, for** +*dat*); *vi:* ~ **for** предусма́тривать *impf,* предусмотре́ть *pf* +*acc;* (~ **for family etc.**) содержа́ть *impf* +*acc.* **provided (that)** *conj* при усло́вии, что; е́сли то́лько. **providence** *n* провиде́ние; (*foresight*) предусмотри́тельность. **provident** *adj* предусмотри́тельный. **providential** *adj* счастли́вый. **providing** *see* **provided (that)**

**province** *n* о́бласть; *pl* (**the** ~) прови́нция. **provincial** *adj* провинциа́льный.

**provision** *n* снабже́ние; *pl* (*food*) прови́зия; (*in agreement etc.*) положе́ние; **make** ~ **against** принима́ть *impf,* приня́ть *pf* ме́ры про́тив+*gen.* **provisional** *adj* вре́менный. **proviso** *n* усло́вие.

**provocation** *n* провока́ция. **provocative** *adj* провокацио́нный. **provoke** *vt* провоци́ровать *impf,* с~ *pf;* (*call forth, cause*) вызыва́ть *impf,* вы́звать *pf.*

**prow** *n* нос.

**prowess** *n* уме́ние.

**prowl** *vi* ры́скать *impf.*

**proximity** *n* бли́зость.

**proxy** *n* полномо́чие; (*person*)

уполномо́ченный *sb,* замести́тель *m;* **by** ~ по дове́ренности; **stand** ~ **for** быть *impf* замести́телем +*gen.*

**prudence** *n* благоразу́мие. **prudent** *adj* благоразу́мный.

**prudery** *n* притво́рная стыдли́вость. **prudish** *adj* ни в ка́кую.

**prune**¹ *n* (*plum*) черносли́в.

**prune**² *vt* (*trim*) об-, под-, реза́ть *impf,* об-, под-, ре́зать *pf.*

**pry** *vi* сова́ть *impf* нос (**into** в+*acc*).

**PS** *abbr* (*of postscript*) постскри́птум.

**psalm** *n* псало́м.

**pseudonym** *n* псевдони́м.

**psyche** *n* пси́хика. **psychiatric** *adj* психиатри́ческий. **psychiatrist** *n* психиа́тр. **psychiatry** *n* психиатри́я. **psychic** *adj* яснови́дящий. **psychoanalysis** *n* психоана́лиз. **psychoanalyst** *n* психоанали́тик. **psychoanalytic(al)** *adj* психоаналити́ческий. **psychological** *adj* психологи́ческий. **psychologist** *n* психо́лог. **psychology** *n* психоло́гия. **psychopath** *n* психопа́т. **psychopathic** *adj* психопати́ческий. **psychosis** *n* психо́з. **psychotherapy** *n* психотерапи́я.

**PTO** *abbr* (*of please turn over*) см. на оборо́те, смотри́ на оборо́те.

**pub** *n* пивна́я *sb.*

**puberty** *n* полова́я зре́лость.

**public** *adj* обще́ственный; (*open*) публи́чный, откры́тый; ~ **school** ча́стная сре́дняя шко́ла; *n* пу́блика, обще́ственность; **in** ~ откры́то, публи́чно. **publication** *n* изда́ние. **publicity** n рекла́ма. **publicize** vt реклами́ровать impf & pf. **publicly** adv публи́чно, откры́то. **publish** vt публикова́ть impf, о~ pf; (book) издава́ть impf, изда́ть pf. **publisher** n изда́тель m. **publishing** n (business) изда́тельское де́ло; ~ **house** изда́тельство.

**pucker** vt & i мо́рщить(ся) impf, с~ pf.

**pudding** n пу́динг, запека́нка; (dessert) сла́дкое sb.

**puddle** n лу́жа.

**puff** n (of wind) поры́в; (of smoke) дымо́к; (of pastry) сло́ёное те́сто; vi пыхте́ть impf; ~ **at** (pipe etc.) попы́хивать impf +instr; vt: ~ **up**, **out** (inflate) надува́ть impf, наду́ть pf.

**pugnacious** adj драчли́вый.

**puke** vi рвать impf, вы́~ pf impers+acc.

**pull** vt тяну́ть impf, по~ pf; таска́ть indet, тащи́ть det, по~ pf; (a muscle) растя́гивать impf, растяну́ть pf; (vt & i) дёргать impf, дёрнуть pf (at (за)+acc); ~ **s.o.'s leg** разы́грывать impf, разыгра́ть pf; ~ **the trigger** спуска́ть impf, спусти́ть pf куро́к; ~ **apart**, **to pieces** разрыва́ть impf, разорва́ть pf; (fig) раскритикова́ть pf; ~ **down** (demolish) сноси́ть impf, снести́ pf; ~ **in** (of train) прибыва́ть impf, прибы́ть pf; (of vehicle) подъезжа́ть impf, подъе́хать pf к обо́чине (доро́ги); ~ **off** (garment) стя́гивать impf, стяну́ть pf; (achieve) успе́шно заверша́ть impf, заверши́ть pf; ~ **on** (garment) натя́гивать

impf, натяну́ть pf; ~ **out** (vt) (remove) выта́скивать impf, вы́тащить pf; (vi) (withdraw) отка́зываться impf, отказа́ться pf от уча́стия (**of** в+prep); (of vehicle) отъезжа́ть impf, отъе́хать pf от обо́чины (доро́ги); (of train) отходи́ть impf, отойти́ pf (от ста́нции); ~ **through** выжива́ть impf, вы́жить pf; ~ **o.s. together** брать impf, взять pf себя́ в ру́ки; ~ **up** (vt) подтя́гивать impf, подтяну́ть pf; (vt & i) (stop) остана́вливать(ся) impf, останови́ть(ся) pf; n тя́га; (fig) блат.

**pulley** n блок.

**pullover** n пуло́вер.

**pulp** n пу́льпа.

**pulpit** n ка́федра.

**pulsate** vi пульси́ровать impf.

**pulse** n пульс.

**pulses** n pl (food) бобо́вые sb.

**pulverize** vt размельча́ть impf, размельчи́ть pf.

**pummel** vt колоти́ть impf, по~ pf.

**pump** n насо́с; vt кача́ть impf; ~ **in(to)** вка́чивать impf, вкача́ть pf; ~ **out** выка́чивать impf, вы́качать pf; ~ **up** нака́чивать impf, накача́ть pf.

**pumpkin** n ты́ква.

**pun** n каламбу́р.

**punch**[1] vt (with fist) ударя́ть impf, уда́рить pf кулако́м; (hole) пробива́ть impf, проби́ть pf; (a ticket) компости́ровать impf, про~ pf; ~**up** дра́ка; n (blow) уда́р кулако́м; (for tickets) компо́стер; (for piercing) перфора́тор.

**punch**[2] n (drink) пунш.

**punctilious** adj щепети́льный.

**punctual** adj пунктуа́льный. **punctuality** n пунктуа́льность.

**punctuate** vt ста́вить impf, по~ pf зна́ки препина́ния в+acc; (fig) прерыва́ть impf, прерва́ть pf. **punctuation** n пунктуа́ция; ~ **marks** зна́ки m pl препина́ния.

**puncture** n проко́л; vt прока́лывать impf, проколо́ть pf.

**pundit** n (fig) знато́к.

**pungent** adj е́дкий.

**punish** vt нака́зывать impf, наказа́ть pf. **punishable** adj наказу́емый. **punishment** n наказа́ние. **punitive** adj кара́тельный.

**punter** n (gambler) игро́к; (client) клие́нт.

**puny** adj хи́лый.

**pupil** n учени́к, -и́ца; (of eye) зрачо́к.

**puppet** n марионе́тка, ку́кла.

**puppy** n щено́к.

**purchase** n поку́пка; (leverage) то́чка опо́ры; vt покупа́ть impf, купи́ть pf. **purchaser** n покупа́тель m.

**pure** adj чи́стый.

**purée** n пюре́ neut indecl.

**purely** adv чи́сто.

**purgatory** n чисти́лище; (fig) ад. **purge** vt очища́ть impf, очи́стить pf; n очище́ние; (polit) чи́стка.

**purification** n очи́стка. **purify** vt очища́ть impf, очи́стить pf.

**purist** n пури́ст.

**puritan, P.,** n пурита́нин, -а́нка. **puritanical** adj пурита́нский.

**purity** n чистота́.

**purple** adj (n) пу́рпурный, фиоле́товый (цвет).

**purport** vt претендова́ть impf.

**purpose** n цель, намере́ние;

on ~ наро́чно; **to no** ~ напра́сно. **purposeful** adj целеустремлённый. **purposeless** adj бесце́льный. **purposely** adv наро́чно.

**purr** vi мурлы́кать impf.

**purse** n кошелёк; vt поджима́ть impf, поджа́ть pf.

**pursue** vt пресле́довать impf. **pursuit** n пресле́дование; (pastime) заня́тие.

**purveyor** n поставщи́к.

**pus** n гной.

**push** vt толка́ть impf, толкну́ть pf; (press) нажима́ть impf, нажа́ть pf; (urge) подта́лкивать impf, подтолкну́ть pf; vi толка́ться impf; **be** ~**ed for** име́ть impf ма́ло+gen; **he is** ~**ing fifty** ему́ ско́ро сту́кнет пятьдеся́т; ~ **one's way** прота́лкиваться impf, протолкну́ться pf; ~ **around** (person) помыка́ть impf+instr; ~ **aside** (also fig) отстраня́ть impf, отстрани́ть pf; vt оття́лкивать impf, оттолкну́ть pf; ~ **off** (vi) (in boat) отта́лкиваться impf, оттолкну́ться pf (от бе́рега); (go away) убира́ться impf, убра́ться pf; ~ **on** (vi) продолжа́ть impf путь; (energy) эне́ргия. **pushchair** n коля́ска. **pusher** n (drugs) продаве́ц нарко́тиков. **pushing** adj напо́ристый.

**puss, pussy(-cat)** n ки́ска.

**put** vt класть impf, положи́ть pf; (upright) ста́вить impf, по~ pf; (place) помеща́ть impf, помести́ть pf; (into specified state) приводи́ть impf, привести́ pf; (express) выража́ть impf, вы́разить pf; (a question) задава́ть impf, зада́ть pf; ~ **an end, a stop, to**

класть *impf*, положи́ть *pf* коне́ц +*dat*; ~ **o.s. in another's place** ста́вить *impf*, по~ *pf* себя́ на ме́сто +*gen*; ~ **about** (*rumour etc.*) распространя́ть *impf*, распространи́ть *pf*; ~ **away** (*tidy*) убира́ть *impf*, убра́ть *pf*; (*save*) откла́дывать *impf*, отложи́ть *pf*; ~ **back** (*in place*) ста́вить *impf*, по~ *pf* на ме́сто; (*clock*) переводи́ть *impf*, перевести́ *pf* наза́д; ~ **by** (*money*) откла́дывать *impf*, отложи́ть *pf*; ~ **down** класть *impf*, положи́ть *pf*; (*suppress*) подавля́ть *impf*, подави́ть *pf*; (*write down*) запи́сывать *impf*, записа́ть *pf*; (*passengers*) выса́живать *impf*, вы́садить *pf*; (*attribute*) припи́сывать *impf*, приписа́ть *pf* (**to** +*dat*); ~ **forward** (*proposal*) предлага́ть *impf*, предложи́ть *pf*; (*clock*) переводи́ть *impf*, перевести́ *pf* вперёд; ~ **in** (*install*) устана́вливать *impf*, установи́ть *pf*; (*a claim*) предъявля́ть *impf*, предъяви́ть *pf*; (*interpose*) вставля́ть *impf*, вста́вить *pf*; ~ **in an appearance** появля́ться *impf*, появи́ться *pf*; ~ **off** (*postpone*) откла́дывать *impf*, отложи́ть *pf*; (*repel*) отта́лкивать *impf*, оттолкну́ть *pf*; (*dissuade*) отгова́ривать *impf*, отговори́ть *pf* от+*gen*, +*inf*; ~ **on** (*clothes*) надева́ть *impf*, наде́ть *pf*; (*kettle, a record, a play*) ста́вить *impf*, по~ *pf*; (*turn on*) включа́ть *impf*, включи́ть *pf*; (*add to*) прибавля́ть *impf*, приба́вить *pf*; ~ **on airs** ва́жничать *impf*; ~ **on weight** толсте́ть *impf*, по~ *pf*; ~ **out**

(*vex*) обижа́ть *impf*, оби́деть *pf*; (*inconvenience*) затрудня́ть *impf*, затрудни́ть *pf*; (*a fire etc.*) туши́ть *impf*, по~ *pf*; ~ **through** (*tel*) соединя́ть *impf*, соедини́ть *pf* по телефо́ну; ~ **up** (*building*) стро́ить *impf*, по~ *pf*; (*hang up*) ве́шать *impf*, пове́сить *pf*; (*price*) повыша́ть *impf*, повы́сить *pf*; (*a guest*) дава́ть *impf*, дать *pf* ночле́г +*dat*; (*as guest*) ночева́ть *impf*, пере~ *pf*; ~ **up to** (*instigate*) подбива́ть *impf*, подби́ть *pf* на+*acc*; ~ **up with** терпе́ть *impf*.

**putative** *adj* предполага́емый.
**putrefy** *vi* гнить *impf*, с~ *pf*.
**putrid** *adj* гнило́й.
**putty** *n* зама́зка.
**puzzle** *n* (*enigma*) зага́дка; (*toy etc.*) головоло́мка; (*jigsaw*) моза́ика; *vt* озада́чивать *impf*, озада́чить *pf*; ~ **out** разга́дывать *impf*, разгада́ть *pf*; *vi*: ~ **over** лома́ть *impf* себе́ го́лову над+*instr*.
**pygmy** *n* пигме́й.
**pyjamas** *n pl* пижа́ма.
**pylon** *n* пило́н.
**pyramid** *n* пирами́да.
**pyre** *n* погреба́льный костёр.
**python** *n* пито́н.

# Q

**quack**[1] *n* (*sound*) кря́канье; *vi* кря́кать *impf*, кря́кнуть *pf*.
**quack**[2] *n* шарлата́н.
**quad** *n* (*court*) четырёхуго́льный двор; *n* (*quadruplets*) че́тверо близнецо́в. **quadrangle** *n* (*figure*) четырёхуго́льник; (*court*) четырёхуго́льный двор. **quadrant** *n* квадра́нт.

**quadruped** *n* четвероно́гое живо́тное *sb.* **quadruple** *adj* четверно́й; *vt & i* учетверя́ть(ся) *impf*, учетвери́ть(ся) *pf.* **quadruplets** *n pl* че́тверо близнецо́в.

**quagmire** *n* боло́то.

**quail** *n* (*bird*) пе́репел.

**quaint** *adj* причу́дливый.

**quake** *vi* дрожа́ть *impf* (**with** от+*gen*).

**Quaker** *n* ква́кер, ~ка.

**qualification** *n* (*for post etc.*) квалифика́ция; (*reservation*) огово́рка. **qualified** *adj* компете́нтный; (*limited*) ограни́ченный. **qualify** *vt & i* (*prepare for job*) гото́вить(ся) *impf* (**for** к+*dat*; +*inf*); *vt* (*render fit*) де́лать *impf*, c~ *pf* приго́дным; (*entitle*) дава́ть *impf*, дать *pf* пра́во +*dat* (**to** на+*acc*); (*limit*): ~ **what one says** сде́лать *pf* огово́рку; *vi* получа́ть *impf*, получи́ть *pf* дипло́м; ~ **for** (*be entitled to*) име́ть *impf* пра́во на+*acc*.

**qualitative** *adj* ка́чественный. **quality** *n* ка́чество.

**qualm** *n* сомне́ние; (*of conscience*) угрызе́ние со́вести.

**quandary** *n* затрудни́тельное положе́ние.

**quantify** *vt* определя́ть *impf*, определи́ть *pf* коли́чество +*gen*. **quantitative** *adj* коли́чественный. **quantity** *n* коли́чество.

**quarantine** *n* каранти́н.

**quarrel** *n* ссо́ра; *vi* ссо́риться *impf*, по~ *pf* (**with** с+*instr*; **about, for** из-за+*gen*). **quarrelsome** *adj* вздо́рный.

**quarry**[1] *n* (*for stone etc.*) каменоло́мня; *vt* добыва́ть *impf*, добы́ть *pf.*

**quarry**[2] *n* (*prey*) добы́ча.

**quart** *n* ква́рта. **quarter** *n* че́тверть; (*of year*; *of town*) кварта́л; *pl* кварти́ры *f pl*; **a** ~ **to one** без че́тверти час; ~**-final** че́тверть-фина́л; *vt* (*divide*) дели́ть *impf*, раз~ *pf* на четы́ре ча́сти; (*lodge*) расквартиро́вывать *impf*, расквартирова́ть *pf.* **quarterly** *adj* кварта́льный; *adv* раз в кварта́л. **quartet** *n* кварте́т.

**quartz** *n* кварц.

**quash** *vt* (*annul*) аннули́ровать *impf & pf*; (*crush*) подавля́ть *impf*, подави́ть *pf.*

**quasi-** *in comb* квази-.

**quaver** *vi* дрожа́ть *impf*; *n* (*mus*) восьма́я *sb* но́ты.

**quay** *n* на́бережная *sb.*

**queasy** *adj*: **I feel** ~ меня́ тошни́т.

**queen** *n* короле́ва; (*cards*) да́ма; (*chess*) ферзь *m.*

**queer** *adj* стра́нный.

**quell** *vt* подавля́ть *impf*, подави́ть *pf.*

**quench** *vt* (*thirst*) утоля́ть *impf*, утоли́ть *pf*; (*fire, desire*) туши́ть *impf*, по~ *pf.*

**query** *n* вопро́с; *vt* (*express doubt*) выража́ть *impf* вы́разить *pf* сомне́ние в+*prep*.

**quest** *n* по́иски *m pl*; **in** ~ **of** в по́исках+*gen*. **question** *n* вопро́с; **beyond** ~ вне сомне́ния; **it is a** ~ **of** э́то вопро́с+*gen*; **it is out of the** ~ об э́том не мо́жет быть и ре́чи; **the person in** ~ челове́к, о кото́ром идёт речь; **the** ~ **is this** де́ло в э́том; **the** ~ **mark** вопроси́тельный знак; *vt* расспра́шивать *impf*, расспроси́ть *pf*; (*interrogate*) допра́шивать *impf* допроси́ть *pf*; (*doubt*) сомнева́ться *impf* в+*prep*. **questionable** *adj*

сомни́тельный. **questionnaire** n вопро́сник.

**queue** n о́чередь; vi стоя́ть
impf в о́череди.

**quibble** n софи́зм; (minor
criticism) придирка; vi приди-
ра́ться impf; (argue) спо́-
рить impf.

**quick** adj ско́рый, бы́стрый;
~-**tempered** вспы́льчивый;
~-**witted** нахо́дчивый; n: to
the ~ за живо́е; adv ско́ро,
бы́стро; as imper скоре́е!
**quicken** vt & i ускоря́ть(ся)
impf, уско́рить(ся) pf. **quickness** n быстрота́. **quicksand**
n зыбу́чий песо́к. **quicksil-
ver** n ртуть.

**quid** n фунт.

**quiet** n (silence) тишина́; (calm)
споко́йствие; adj ти́хий, спо-
ко́йный; int ти́ше!; vt & i
успока́ивать(ся) impf, успо-
ко́ить(ся) pf.

**quill** n перо́; (spine) игла́.

**quilt** n (стёганое) одея́ло; vt
стега́ть impf, вы́- pf. **quilted**
adj стёганый.

**quintessential** adj наибо́лее
суще́ственный.

**quintet** n квинте́т. **quins, quin-
tuplets** n pl пять близнецо́в.

**quip** n острота́; острить impf,
с~ pf.

**quirk** n причу́да. **quirky** adj с
причу́дами.

**quit** vi (leave) покида́ть impf,
поки́нуть pf; (stop) переста-
ва́ть impf, переста́ть pf;
(give up) броса́ть impf, бро́-
сить pf; (resign) уходи́ть impf,
уйти́ pf c+gen.

**quite** adv (wholly) совсе́м; (
rather) дово́льно; ~ **a few**
дово́льно мно́го.

**quits** predic: **we are** ~ мы с
тобо́й кви́ты; **I am** ~ **with him**

я расквита́лся (past) с ним.

**quiver** vi (tremble) трепета́ть
impf; n тре́пет.

**quiz** n викторина. **quizzical**
adj насме́шливый.

**quorum** n кво́рум.

**quota** n но́рма.

**quotation** n цита́та; (of price)
цена́; ~ **marks** кавы́чки (-чек)
pl. **quote** vt цити́ровать impf,
про~ pf; ссыла́ться impf, со-
сла́ться pf на+acc; (price) на-
знача́ть impf, назна́чить pf.

# R

**rabbi** n равви́н.

**rabbit** n кро́лик.

**rabble** n сброд.

**rabid** adj бе́шеный. **rabies** n
бе́шенство.

**race**[1] n (ethnic ~) ра́са; род.

**race**[2] n (contest) (on foot) бег;
(of cars etc.; fig) го́нка, го́нки
pl; (of horses) ска́чки f pl;
~-**track** трек; (for horse ~)
скакова́я доро́жка; vi (compete) состяза́ться impf в ско́-
рости; (rush) бежа́ть impf
наперегонки́; vt бежа́ть impf наперегонки́
c+instr. **racecourse** n иппо-
дро́м. **racehorse** n скакова́я
ло́шадь.

**racial** adj ра́совый. **rac(ial)-
ism** n раси́зм. **rac(ial)ist** n
раси́ст, ~ка; adj раси́стский.

**racing** n (horses) ска́чки f
pl; (cars) го́нки f pl; ~-**car**
го́ночный автомоби́ль m;
~ **driver** го́нщик.

**rack** n (for hats etc.) ве́шалка;
(for plates etc.) стелла́ж; (in
train etc.) се́тка; vt: ~ **one's
brains** лома́ть impf себе́
го́лову.

**racket**[1] n (bat) раке́тка.

**racket**[2] n (uproar) шум; (illegal activity) рэ́кет. **racketeer** n рэкети́р.

**racy** adj колори́тный.

**radar** n (system) радиолока́ция; (apparatus) радиолока́тор, рада́р; attrib рада́рный.

**radiance** n сия́ние. **radiant** adj сия́ющий. **radiate** vt & i излуча́ть(ся) impf, излучи́ть(ся) pf. **radiation** n излуче́ние. **radiator** n батаре́я; (in car) радиа́тор.

**radical** adj радика́льный; n радика́л.

**radio** n ра́дио neut indecl; (set) радиоприёмник; vt радирова́ть impf & pf +dat.

**radioactive** adj радиоакти́вный. **radioactivity** n радиоакти́вность. **radiologist** n радио́лог; рентгено́лог. **radiotherapy** n радиотерапи́я.

**radish** n реди́ска.

**radius** n ра́диус.

**raffle** n лотере́я; vt разы́грывать impf, разыгра́ть pf в лотере́е.

**raft** n плот.

**rafter** n (beam) стропи́ло.

**rag** n тря́пка; pl (clothes) лохмо́тья (-ьев) pl.

**rage** n я́рость; all the ~ после́дний крик мо́ды; vi беси́ться impf; (storm etc.) бушева́ть impf.

**ragged** adj (jagged) зазу́бренный; (of clothes) рва́ный.

**raid** n налёт; (by police) обла́ва; vt де́лать impf, с~ pf налёт на+acc.

**rail** n пери́ла (-л) pl; (rly) рельс; by ~ по́ездом. **railing** n пери́ла (-л) pl.

**railway** n желе́зная доро́га; attrib железнодоро́жный. **railwayman** n железно-

доро́жник.

**rain** n дождь m; v impers: it is (was) ~ing идёт (шёл) дождь; vt осыпа́ть impf, осыпа́ть pf +instr (upon +acc); vi осыпа́ться impf, осыпа́ться pf. **rainbow** n ра́дуга. **raincoat** n плащ. **raindrop** n дождева́я ка́пля. **rainfall** n (amount of rain) коли́чество оса́дков. **rainy** adj дождли́вый; ~ day чёрный день m.

**raise** vt (lift) поднима́ть impf, подня́ть pf; (heighten) повыша́ть impf, повы́сить pf; (provoke) вызыва́ть impf, вы́звать pf; (money) собира́ть impf, собра́ть pf; (children) расти́ть impf.

**raisin** n изю́минка; pl (collect) изю́м.

**rake** n (tool) гра́бли (-бель & -блей) pl; vt грести́ impf; (~ together, up) сгреба́ть impf, сгрести́ pf.

**rally** vt & i спла́чивать(ся) impf, сплоти́ть(ся) pf; vi (after illness etc.) оправля́ться impf, опра́виться pf; n (meeting) слёт; ми́тинг; (motoring ~) (авто)ра́лли neut indecl; (tennis) обме́н уда́рами.

**ram** n (sheep) бара́н; vt (beat down) трамбова́ть impf, у~ pf; (drive in) вбива́ть impf, вбить pf.

**ramble** vi (walk) прогу́ливаться impf, прогуля́ться pf; (speak) болта́ть impf; n прогу́лка. **rambling** adj (incoherent) бессвя́зный.

**ramification** n (fig) после́дствие.

**ramp** n скат.

**rampage** vi бу́йствовать impf.

**rampant** adj (plant) бу́йный; (unchecked) безу́держный.

**rampart** n вал.

**ramshackle** *adj* ве́тхий.

**ranch** *n* ра́нчо *neut indecl.*

**rancid** *adj* прого́рклый.

**rancour** *n* зло́ба.

**random** *adj* случа́йный; **at ~** науда́чу.

**range** *n* (of mountains) цепь; (artillery ~) полиго́н; (of voice) диапазо́н; (scope) круг, преде́лы *m pl*; (operating distance) да́льность; *vi* (vary) колеба́ться *impf*, по~ *pf*; (wander) броди́ть *impf*; **~ over** (include) охва́тывать *impf*, охвати́ть *pf*.

**rank**[1] *n* (row) ряд; (taxi ~) стоя́нка такси́; (grade) зва́ние, чин, ранг; *vt* (classify) классифици́ровать *impf & pf*; (consider) счита́ть *impf* (**as** +*instr*); *vi*: **~ with** быть в числе́+*gen*.

**rank**[2] *adj* (luxuriant) бу́йный; (in smell) злово́нный; (gross) я́вный.

**rankle** *vi* боле́ть *impf*.

**ransack** *vt* (search) обша́ривать *impf*, обша́рить *pf*; (plunder) гра́бить *impf*, о~ *pf*.

**ransom** *n* вы́куп; *vt* выкупа́ть *impf*, вы́купить *pf*.

**rant** *vi* вопи́ть *impf*.

**rap** *n* стук; *vt* (rezko) ударя́ть *impf*, уда́рить *pf*; *vi* стуча́ть *impf*, сту́кнуть *pf*.

**rape**[1] *vt* наси́ловать *impf*, из~ *pf*; *n* наси́лование.

**rape**[2] *n* (plant) рапс.

**rapid** *adj* бы́стрый; *n pl* поро́г, быстрина́. **rapidity** *n* быстрота́.

**rapt** *adj* восхищённый; (absorbed) поглощённый. **rapturous** *adj* восто́рг. **rapturous** *adj* восто́рженный.

**rare**[1] *adj* (of meat) недожа́ренный.

**rare**[2] *adj* ре́дкий. **rarity** *n* ре́дкость.

**rascal** *n* плут.

**rash**[1] *n* сыпь.

**rash**[2] *adj* опроме́тчивый.

**rasher** *n* ло́мтик (беко́на).

**rasp** *n* (file) ра́шпиль *m*; (sound) скре́жет; *vt*: **~ out** га́ркнуть *pf*.

**raspberry** *n* мали́на (*no pl*; *usu collect*).

**rasping** *adj* (sound) скрипу́чий.

**rat** *n* кры́са; **~ race** го́нка за успе́хом.

**ratchet** *n* храпови́к.

**rate** *n* но́рма, ста́вка; (speed) ско́рость; *pl* ме́стные нало́ги *m pl*; **at any ~** во вся́ком слу́чае; *vt* оце́нивать *impf*, оцени́ть *pf*; *vi* счита́ться *impf* (**as** +*instr*).

**rather** *adv* скоре́е; (somewhat) дово́льно; **he (she) had (would) ~** он (она́) предпочёл (-чла́) бы+*inf*.

**ratification** *n* ратифика́ция. **ratify** *vt* ратифици́ровать *impf & pf*.

**rating** *n* оце́нка.

**ratio** *n* пропо́рция.

**ration** *n* паёк, рацио́н; *vt* норми́ровать *impf & pf*; **be ~ed** выдава́ться *impf*, вы́даться *pf* по ка́рточкам.

**rational** *adj* разу́мный. **rationalism** *n* рационали́зм. **rationality** *n* разу́мность. **rationalize** *vt* обосно́вывать *impf*, обоснова́ть *pf*; (industry etc.) рационализи́ровать *impf & pf*.

**rattle** *vi & t* (sound) греме́ть *impf* (+*instr*); **~ along** (move) грохота́ть *impf*; **~ off** (utter) отбараба́нить *pf*; *n* (sound) треск, гро́хот; (toy) погрему́шка. **rattlesnake** n гремучая змея.

**raucous** adj ре́зкий.

**ravage** vt опустоша́ть impf, опустоши́ть pf; n: pl разруши́тельное де́йствие.

**rave** vi бре́дить impf; ~ about быть в восто́рге от+gen.

**raven** n во́рон.

**ravenous** adj голо́дный как волк.

**ravine** n уще́лье.

**ravishing** adj восхити́тельный.

**raw** adj сыро́й; (inexperienced) нео́пытный; ~ material(s) сырьё (no pl).

**ray** n луч.

**raze** vt: ~ to the ground ровня́ть impf, c~ pf с землёй.

**razor** n бри́тва; ~-blade ле́звие.

**reach** vt (attain, extend to, arrive at) достига́ть impf, дости́чь & дости́гнуть pf +gen, до+gen; доходи́ть impf, дойти́ pf до+gen; (with hand) дотя́гиваться impf, дотяну́ться pf до+gen; vi (extend) простира́ться impf; n досяга́емость; (pl, of river) тече́ние.

**react** vi реаги́ровать impf, от~, про~ pf (to на+acc). **reaction** n реа́кция. **reactionary** adj реакцио́нный; n реакционе́р. **reactor** n реа́ктор.

**read** vt чита́ть impf, про~, прочесть pf; (mus) разбира́ть impf, разобра́ть pf; (~ a meter etc.) снима́ть impf, снять pf показа́ния +gen; (univ) изуча́ть impf; (interpret) толкова́ть impf. **readable** adj интере́сный. **reader** n чита́тель m, ~ница; (book) хрестома́тия.

**readily** adv (willingly) охо́тно; (easily) легко́. **readiness** n гото́вность.

**reading** n чте́ние; (on meter) показа́ние.

**ready** adj гото́вый (for к+dat, на+acc); get ~ гото́виться impf; ~-made гото́вый; ~ money нали́чные де́ньги (-ег, -ньга́м) pl.

**real** adj настоя́щий, реа́льный; ~ estate недви́жимость. **realism** n реали́зм. **realist** n реали́ст. **realistic** adj реалисти́чный, -и́ческий. **reality** n действи́тельность; in ~ действи́тельно. **realization** n (of plan etc.) осуществле́ние; (of assets) реализа́ция; (understanding) осозна́ние. **realize** vt (plan etc.) осуществля́ть impf, осуществи́ть pf; (assets) реализова́ть impf & pf; (apprehend) осознава́ть impf, осозна́ть pf. **really** adv действи́тельно, в са́мом де́ле.

**realm** n (kingdom) короле́вство; (sphere) о́бласть.

**reap** vt жать impf, сжать pf; (fig) пожина́ть impf, пожа́ть pf.

**rear**[1] vt (lift) поднима́ть impf, подня́ть pf; (children) воспи́тывать impf, воспита́ть pf; vi (of horse) станови́ться impf, стать pf на дыбы́.

**rear**[2] n за́дняя часть; (mil) тыл; bring up the ~ замыка́ть impf, замкну́ть pf ше́ствие; adj за́дний; (also mil) ты́льный. **rearguard** n арьерга́рд; ~ action арьерга́рдный бой.

**rearmament** n перевооруже́ние.

**rearrange** vt меня́ть impf.

**reason** n (cause) причи́на, основа́ние; (intellect) ра́зум, рассу́док; vi рассужда́ть impf; ~ **with** (person) угова́ривать impf +acc. **reasonable** adj разу́мный; (inexpensive) недорого́й.

**reassurance** n успока́ивание. **reassure** vt успока́ивать impf, успоко́ить pf.

**rebate** n ски́дка.

**rebel** n повста́нец; vi восстава́ть impf, восста́ть pf. **rebellion** n восста́ние. **rebellious** adj мяте́жный.

**rebound** vi отска́кивать impf, отскочи́ть pf; n рикоше́т.

**rebuff** n отпо́р; vt дава́ть impf, дать pf +dat отпо́р.

**rebuild** vt перестра́ивать impf, перестро́ить pf.

**rebuke** vt упрека́ть impf, упрекну́ть pf; n упрёк.

**rebuttal** n опроверже́ние.

**recalcitrant** adj непоко́рный.

**recall** vt (an official) отзыва́ть impf, отозва́ть pf; (remember) вспомина́ть impf, вспо́мнить pf; n о́тзыв; (memory) па́мять.

**recant** vi отрека́ться impf, отре́чься pf.

**recapitulate** vt резюми́ровать impf & pf.

**recast** vt переде́лывать impf, переде́лать pf.

**recede** vi отходи́ть impf, отойти́ pf.

**receipt** n (receiving) получе́ние; pl (amount) вы́ручка; (written) квита́нция; (from till) чек. **receive** vt (admit, entertain) принима́ть impf, приня́ть pf; (get, be given) получа́ть impf, получи́ть pf. **receiver** n (radio, television) приёмник; (tel) тру́бка.

**recent** adj неда́вний; (new) но́вый. **recently** adv неда́вно.

**receptacle** n вмести́лище. **reception** n (parl) приём; ~ **room** приёмная sb. **receptionist** n секрета́рь m, -рша, в приёмной. **receptive** adj восприи́мчивый.

**recess** n (parl) кани́кулы (-л) pl; (niche) ни́ша. **recession** n спад.

**recipe** n реце́пт.

**recipient** n получа́тель m.

**reciprocal** adj взаи́мный. **reciprocate** vt отвеча́ть impf (взаи́мностью) на+acc.

**recital** n (sólnyj) конце́рт. **recitation** n публи́чное чте́ние. **recite** vt деклами́ровать impf, про— pf; (list) перечисля́ть impf, перечи́слить pf.

**reckless** adj (rash) опроме́тчивый; (careless) неосторо́жный.

**reckon** vt подсчи́тывать impf, подсчита́ть pf; (also regard as) счита́ть impf, счесть pf (to be +instr); vi: ~ **on** рассчи́тывать impf, рассчита́ть pf на+acc; ~ **with** счита́ться pf с+instr. **reckoning** n счёт; **day of** ~ час распла́ты.

**reclaim** vt тре́бовать impf, по— pf обра́тно; (land) осва́ивать impf, осво́ить pf.

**recline** vi полулежа́ть impf.

**recluse** n затво́рник.

**recognition** n узнава́ние; (acknowledgement) призна́ние. **recognize** vt узнава́ть impf, узна́ть pf; (acknowledge) признава́ть impf, призна́ть pf.

**recoil** vi отпря́дывать impf, отпря́нуть pf.

**recollect** vt вспомина́ть impf, вспо́мнить pf. **recollection** n воспомина́ние.

**recommend** vt рекомендова́ть impf & pf. **recommendation** n рекоменда́ция.

**recompense** n вознагражде́ние; vt вознагражда́ть impf, вознагради́ть pf.

**reconcile** vt примиря́ть impf, примири́ть pf; ~ **o.s.** примиря́ться impf, примири́ться pf (**to** c+instr). **reconciliation** n примире́ние.

**reconnaissance** n разве́дка.

**reconnoitre** vt разве́дывать impf, разве́дать pf.

**reconstruct** vt перестра́ивать impf, перестро́ить pf. **reconstruction** n перестро́йка.

**record** vt запи́сывать impf, записа́ть pf; n за́пись; (minutes) протоко́л; (gramophone ~) грампласти́нка; (sport etc.) реко́рд; **off the** ~ неофициа́льно; adj реко́рдный; ~-**breaker, -holder** рекордсме́н, ~ка; ~-**player** проигрыва́тель m. **recorder** n (mus) блок-фле́йта. **recording** n за́пись.

**recount**[1] vt (narrate) переска́зывать impf, пересказа́ть pf.

**re-count**[2] vt (count again) пересчи́тывать impf, пересчита́ть pf; n пересчёт.

**recoup** vt возвраща́ть impf, верну́ть pf (losses поте́рянное).

**recourse** n: **have** ~ **to** прибега́ть impf, прибе́гнуть pf к+dat.

**recover** vt (regain possession) получа́ть impf, получи́ть pf обра́тно, верну́ть pf; vi (~ health) поправля́ться impf, попра́виться pf (**from** по́сле+gen). **recovery** n возвраще́ние; выздоровле́ние.

**recreate** vt воссоздава́ть impf, воссозда́ть pf.

**recreation** n развлече́ние, о́тдых.

**recrimination** n взаи́мное обвине́ние.

**recruit** n новобра́нец; vt вербова́ть impf, за~ pf. **recruitment** n вербо́вка.

**rectangle** n прямоуго́льник. **rectangular** adj прямоуго́льный.

**rectify** vt исправля́ть impf, испра́вить pf.

**rector** n (priest) прихо́дский свяще́нник; (univ) ре́ктор. **rectory** n дом прихо́дского свяще́нника.

**rectum** n пряма́я кишка́.

**recuperate** vi поправля́ться impf, попра́виться pf. **recuperation** n выздоровле́ние.

**recur** vi повторя́ться impf, повтори́ться pf. **recurrence** n повторе́ние. **recurrent** adj повторя́ющийся.

**recycle** vt перераба́тывать impf, перерабо́тать pf.

**red** adj кра́сный; (of hair) ры́жий; n кра́сный цвет; (polit) кра́сный sb; **in the** ~ в долгу́; ~-**handed** с поли́чным; ~ **herring** ло́жный след; ~-**hot** раскалённый докрасна́; R~ **Indian** индее́ц, индиа́нка; ~ **tape** волоки́та. **redcurrant** n кра́сная сморо́дина (no pl; usu collect). **redden** vt окра́шивать impf, окра́сить pf в кра́сный цвет; vi красне́ть impf, по~ pf. **reddish** adj краснова́тый; (hair) рыжева́тый.

**redecorate** vt отде́лывать impf, отде́лать pf.

**redeem** vt (buy back) выкупа́ть impf, вы́купить pf.

(*from sin*) искупа́ть *impf*, искупи́ть *pf*. **redeemer** *n* искупи́тель *m*. **redemption** *n* вы́куп; искупле́ние.

**redeploy** *vt* передислоци́ровать *impf & pf*.

**redo** *vt* переде́лывать *impf*, переде́лать *pf*.

**redouble** *vt* удва́ивать *impf*, удво́ить *pf*.

**redress** *vt* исправля́ть *impf*, испра́вить *pf*; ~ **the balance** восстана́вливать *impf*, восстанови́ть *pf* равнове́сие; *n* возмеще́ние.

**reduce** *vt* (*decrease*) уменьша́ть *impf*, уме́ньшить *pf*; (*lower*) снижа́ть *impf*, сни́зить *pf*; (*shorten*) сокраща́ть *impf*, сократи́ть *pf*; (*bring to*) доводи́ть *impf*, довести́ *pf* (**to**+*acc*). **reduction** *n* уменьше́ние, сниже́ние, сокраще́ние; (*discount*) ски́дка.

**redundancy** *n* (*dismissal*) увольне́ние. **redundant** *adj* изли́шний; **make** ~ увольня́ть *impf*, уво́лить *pf*.

**reed** *n* (*plant*) тростни́к; (*in oboe etc.*) язычо́к.

**reef** *n* риф.

**reek** *n* вонь; *vi*: ~ (**of**) воня́ть *impf* (+*instr*).

**reel**[1] *n* кату́шка; *vt*: ~ **off** (*story etc.*) отбараба́нить *pf*.

**reel**[2] *vi* (*stagger*) пошату́ваться *impf*, пошатну́ться *pf*.

**refectory** *n* (*monastery*) тра́пезная *sb*; (*univ*) столо́вая *sb*.

**refer** *vt* (*direct*) отсыла́ть *impf*, отосла́ть *pf* (**to** к+*dat*); *vi*: ~ **to** (*cite*) ссыла́ться *impf*, сосла́ться *pf* на+*acc*; (*mention*) упомина́ть *impf*, упомяну́ть *pf* +*acc*. **referee** *n* судья́ *m*; *vt* суди́ть *impf*. **reference** *n* (*to book etc.*)

ссы́лка; (*mention*) упомина́ние; (*testimonial*) характери́стика; ~ **book** справочник.

**referendum** *n* рефере́ндум.

**refine** *vt* очища́ть *impf*, очи́стить *pf*. **refined** *adj* (*in style etc.*) утончённый; (*in manners*) культу́рный. **refinement** *n* утончённость. **refinery** *n* (*oil* ~) нефтеочисти́тельный заво́д.

**refit** *vt* переобору́довать *impf & pf*.

**reflect** *vt* отража́ть *impf*, отрази́ть *pf*; *vi* размышля́ть *impf*, размы́слить *pf* (**on** o+*prep*). **reflection** *n* отраже́ние; размышле́ние; **on** ~ поду́мав. **reflective** *adj* (*thoughtful*) серьёзный. **reflector** *n* рефле́ктор. **reflex** *n* рефле́кс; *adj* рефле́кторный. **reflexive** *adj* (*gram*) возвра́тный.

**reform** *vt* реформи́ровать *impf & pf*; *vt & i* (*of people*) исправля́ть(ся) *impf*, испра́вить(ся) *pf*; *n* рефо́рма; исправле́ние. **Reformation** *n* Реформа́ция.

**refract** *vt* преломля́ть *impf*, преломи́ть *pf*.

**refrain**[1] *n* припе́в.

**refrain**[2] *vi* возде́рживаться *impf*, воздержа́ться *pf* (**from** от+*gen*).

**refresh** *vt* освежа́ть *impf*, освежи́ть *pf*. **refreshments** *n pl* напи́тки *m pl*.

**refrigerate** *vt* охлажда́ть *impf*, охлади́ть *pf*. **refrigeration** *n* охлажде́ние. **refrigerator** *n* холоди́льник.

**refuge** *n* убе́жище; **take** ~ находи́ть *impf*, найти́ *pf* убе́жище. **refugee** *n* бе́женец, -нка.

**refund** *vt* возвраща́ть *impf*, возврати́ть *pf*, (*expenses*) возмеща́ть *impf*, возмести́ть *pf*; *n* возвраще́ние (де́нег) возмеще́ние.

**refusal** *n* отка́з. **refuse¹** *vt* (*decline to accept*) отка́зываться *impf*, отказа́ться *pf* от+*gen*; (*decline to do sth*) отка́зываться *impf*, отказа́ться *pf* +*inf*; (*deny s.o. sth*) отка́зывать *impf*, отказа́ть *pf* +*dat*+в+*prep*.

**refuse²** *n* му́сор.

**refute** *vt* опроверга́ть *impf*, опрове́ргнуть *pf*.

**regain** *vt* возвраща́ть *impf*, верну́ть *pf*.

**regal** *adj* короле́вский.

**regalia** *n pl* рега́лии *f pl*.

**regard** *vt* смотре́ть *impf*, по~ *pf* на+*acc*; (*take into account*) счита́ться *impf* с+*instr*; **as** счита́ть *impf* +*instr*, за+*instr*; **as ~s** что каса́ется+*gen*; *n* (*esteem*) уваже́ние; *pl* приве́т. **regarding** *prep* относи́тельно +*gen*. **regardless** *adv* не обраща́я внима́ния; **~ of** не счита́ясь с+*instr*.

**regatta** *n* рега́та.

**regenerate** *vt* перерожда́ть *impf*, перероди́ть *pf*.

**regent** *n* ре́гент.

**régime** *n* режи́м.

**regiment** *n* полк. **regimental** *adj* полково́й. **regimentation** *n* регламента́ция.

**region** *n* регио́н. **regional** *adj* региона́льный.

**register** *n* реэ́стр; (*also mus*) реги́стр; *vt* регистри́ровать *impf*, за~ *pf*; (*a letter*) отправля́ть *impf*, отпра́вить *pf* заказны́м. **registered** *adj* (*letter*) заказно́й. **registrar** *n* регистра́тор. **registration** *n*

регистра́ция; **~ number** но́мер маши́ны. **registry** *n* регистрату́ра; **~ office** загс.

**regret** *vt* сожале́ть *impf* о+*prep*; *n* сожале́ние. **regretful** *adj* по́лный сожале́ния. **regrettable** *adj* приско́рбный. **regrettably** *adv* к сожале́нию.

**regular** *adj* регуля́рный; (*also gram*) пра́вильный; *n* (*coll*) завсегда́тай. **regularity** *n* регуля́рность. **regulate** *vt* регули́ровать *impf*, y~ *pf*. **regulation** *n* регули́рование; *pl* пра́вила *neut pl*.

**rehabilitate** *vt* реабилити́ровать *impf* & *pf*. **rehabilitation** *n* реабилита́ция.

**rehearsal** *n* репети́ция. **rehearse** *vt* репети́ровать *impf*, от~ *pf*.

**reign** *n* ца́рствование; *vi* ца́рствовать *impf*; (*fig*) цари́ть *impf*.

**reimburse** *vt* возмеща́ть *impf*, возмести́ть *pf* (+*dat of person*). **reimbursement** *n* возмеще́ние.

**rein** *n* по́вод.

**reincarnation** *n* переволпоще́ние.

**reindeer** *n* се́верный оле́нь *m*.

**reinforce** *vt* подкрепля́ть *impf*, подкрепи́ть *pf*. **reinforcement** *n* (*also pl*) подкрепле́ние.

**reinstate** *vt* восстана́вливать *impf*, восстанови́ть *pf*. **reinstatement** *n* восстановле́ние.

**reiterate** *vt* повторя́ть *impf*, повтори́ть *pf*.

**reject** *vt* отверга́ть *impf*, отве́ргнуть *pf*; (*as defective*) бракова́ть *impf*, за~ *pf*; *n* брак. **rejection** *n* отка́з (*of* от+*gen*).

**rejoice** vi ра́доваться impf, об~ pf (in, at +dat). **rejoicing** n ра́дость.

**rejoin** vt (вновь) присоединя́ться impf, присоедини́ться pf к+dat.

**rejuvenate** vt омола́живать impf, омоloди́ть pf.

**relapse** n рециди́в; vi сно́ва впада́ть impf, впасть pf (into в+acc); (into illness) сно́ва забоlева́ть impf, заболе́ть pf. **relate** vt (tell) расска́зывать impf, рассказа́ть pf; (connect) свя́зывать impf, связа́ть pf; vi относи́ться impf (to к+dat). **related** adj ро́дственный. **relation** n отноше́ние; (person) ро́дственник, -ица. **relationship** n (connection; liaison) связь; (kinship) родство́. **relative** adj относи́тельный; n ро́дственник, -ица. **relativity** n относи́тельность.

**relax** vt ослабля́ть impf, осла́бить pf; vi (rest) рассла́бля́ться impf, рассла́биться pf. **relaxation** n ослабле́ние; (rest) о́тдых.

**relay** n (shift) сме́на; (sport) эстафе́та; (electr) реле́ neut indecl; vt передава́ть impf, переда́ть pf.

**release** vt (set free) освобожда́ть impf, освободи́ть pf; (unfasten, let go) отпуска́ть impf, отпусти́ть pf; (film etc.) выпуска́ть impf, вы́пустить pf; n освобожде́ние; вы́пуск.

**relegate** vt переводи́ть impf, перевести́ pf (в ни́зшую гру́ппу). **relegation** n перево́д (в ни́зшую гру́ппу).

**relent** vi смягча́ться impf, смягчи́ться pf. **relentless** adj непреста́нный.

**relevance** n уме́стность. **relevant** adj относя́щийся к де́лу; уме́стный.

**reliability** n надёжность. **reliable** adj надёжный. **reliance** n дове́рие. **reliant** adj: be ~ upon зави́сеть impf от+gen.

**relic** n оста́ток, рели́квия.

**relief**[1] n (art, geol) релье́ф.

**relief**[2] n (alleviation) облегче́ние; (assistance) по́мощь; (in duty) сме́на. **relieve** vt (alleviate) облегча́ть impf, облегчи́ть pf; (replace) сменя́ть impf, смени́ть pf; (unburden) освобожда́ть impf, освободи́ть pf (of от+gen).

**religion** n рели́гия. **religious** adj религио́зный.

**relinquish** vt оставля́ть impf, оста́вить pf; (right etc.) отка́зываться impf, отказа́ться pf от+gen.

**relish** n (enjoyment) смак; (cul) припра́ва; vt смакова́ть impf.

**relocate** vt & i переме́ща́ть impf, перемести́ть(ся) pf.

**reluctance** n неохо́та. **reluctant** adj неохо́тный; be ~ to не жела́ть impf +inf.

**rely** vi полага́ться impf, положи́ться pf (on на+acc).

**remain** vi остава́ться impf, оста́ться pf. **remainder** n оста́ток. **remains** n pl оста́тки m pl; (human ~) оста́нки (-ков) pl.

**remand** vt содержа́ть impf под стра́жей; be on ~ содержа́ться impf под стра́жей.

**remark** vt замеча́ть impf, заме́тить pf; n замеча́ние. **remarkable** adj замеча́тельный.

**remarry** vi вступа́ть impf, вступи́ть pf в но́вый брак.

**remedial** adj лече́бный. **remedy** n сре́дство (for от, про́тив+gen); vt исправля́ть impf, испра́вить pf.

**remember** vt по́мнить impf, вспомина́ть impf, вспо́мнить pf; (greet) передава́ть impf, переда́ть pf приве́т от+gen (to +dat). **remembrance** n па́мять.

**remind** vt напомина́ть impf, напо́мнить pf +dat (of +acc, o+prep). **reminder** n напомина́ние.

**reminiscence** n воспомина́ние. **reminiscent** adj напомина́ющий.

**remiss** predic adj небре́жный. **remission** n (pardon) отпуще́ние; (med) реми́ссия. **remit** vt пересыла́ть impf, пересла́ть pf. **remittance** n перево́д де́нег; (money) де́нежный перево́д.

**remnant** n оста́ток.

**remonstrate** vi: ~ with увеща́ть impf +acc.

**remorse** n угрызе́ния neut pl со́вести. **remorseful** adj по́лный раска́яния. **remorseless** adj безжа́лостный.

**remote** adj отдалённый; ~ control дистанцио́нное управле́ние.

**removal** n (taking away) удале́ние; (of obstacles) устране́ние. **remove** vt (take away) убира́ть impf, убра́ть pf; (get rid of) устраня́ть impf, устрани́ть pf.

**remuneration** n вознагражде́ние. **remunerative** adj вы́годный.

**renaissance** n возрожде́ние; **the R~** Возрожде́ние.

**render** vt воздава́ть impf, возда́ть pf; (help etc.) ока́зы-

вать impf, оказа́ть pf; (role etc.) исполня́ть impf, испо́лнить pf; (stone) штукату́рить impf, о~, от~ pf. **rendering** n исполне́ние.

**rendezvous** n (meeting) свида́ние.

**renegade** n ренега́т, ~ка.

**renew** vt (extend; continue) возобновля́ть impf, возобнови́ть pf; (replace) обновля́ть impf, обнови́ть pf. **renewal** n (воз)обновле́ние.

**renounce** vt отверга́ть impf, отве́ргнуть pf; (claim) отка́зываться impf, отказа́ться pf от+gen.

**renovate** vt ремонти́ровать impf, от~ pf. **renovation** n ремо́нт.

**renown** n сла́ва. **renowned** adj изве́стный; **be ~ for** сла́виться impf +instr.

**rent** n (for home) квартпла́та; (for premises) (аре́ндная) пла́та; vt (of tenant) аренд́овать impf & pf; (of owner) сдава́ть impf, сдать pf.

**renunciation** n (repudiation) отрица́ние; (of claim) отка́з.

**rep** n (comm) аге́нт.

**repair** vt ремонти́ровать impf, от~ pf. n (also pl) ремо́нт (only sg); (patch) почи́нка; **in good/bad** ~ в хоро́шем/плохо́м состоя́нии.

**reparations** n pl репара́ции f pl.

**repatriate** vt репатрии́ровать impf & pf. **repatriation** n репатриа́ция.

**repay** vt отпла́чивать impf, отплати́ть pf (person +dat). **repayment** n отпла́та.

**repeal** vt отменя́ть impf, отмени́ть pf. n отме́на.

**repeat** vt & i повторя́ть(ся)

*impf*, повтори́ть(ся) *pf*; *n* повторе́ние. **repeatedly** *adv* неоднокра́тно.

**repel** *vt* отта́лкивать *impf*, оттолкну́ть *pf*; (*enemy*) отража́ть *impf*, отрази́ть *pf*. **repent** *vi* раска́иваться *impf*, раска́яться *pf*. **repentance** *n* раска́яние. **repentant** *adj* раска́ивающийся.

**repercussion** *n* после́дствие. **repertoire** *n* репертуа́р. **repertory** *n* (*store*) запа́с; (*repertoire*) репертуа́р; ~ **company** постоя́нная тру́ппа.

**repetition** *n* повторе́ние. **repetitious**, **repetitive** *adj* повторя́ющийся.

**replace** *vt* (*put back*) класть *impf*, положи́ть *pf* обра́тно; (*substitute*) заменя́ть *impf*, замени́ть *pf* (**by** +*instr*). **replacement** *n* заме́на.

**replay** *n* переигро́вка. **replenish** *vt* пополня́ть *impf*, попо́лнить *pf*. **replete** *adj* насы́щенный; (*sated*) сы́тый. **replica** *n* ко́пия.

**reply** *vt* & *i* отвеча́ть *impf*, отве́тить *pf* (**to** на+*acc*); *n* отве́т.

**report** *vt* сообща́ть *impf*, сообщи́ть *pf*; *vi* докла́дывать *impf*, доложи́ть *pf*; (*present o.s.*) явля́ться *impf*, яви́ться *pf*; *n* сообще́ние; докла́д; (*school*) та́бель *m*; (*sound*) звук взры́ва, вы́стрела. **reporter** *n* корреспонде́нт.

**repose** *n* (*rest*) о́тдых; (*peace*) поко́й.

**repository** *n* храни́лище. **repossess** *vt* изыма́ть *impf*, изъя́ть *pf* за непла́тёж.

**reprehensible** *adj* предосуди́тельный.

**represent** *vt* представля́ть *impf*, (*portray*) изобража́ть *impf*, изобрази́ть *pf*. **representation** *n* (*being represented*) представи́тельство; (*statement of case*) представле́ние; (*portrayal*) изображе́ние. **representative** *adj* изобража́ющий (**of** +*acc*); (*typical*) типи́чный; *n* представи́тель *m*.

**repress** *vt* подавля́ть *impf*, подави́ть *pf*. **repression** *n* подавле́ние, репре́ссия. **repressive** *adj* репресси́вный.

**reprieve** *vt* отсро́чивать *impf*, отсро́чить *pf* +*dat* приведе́ние в исполне́ние (сме́ртного) пригово́ра; *n* отсро́чка приведе́ния в исполне́ние (сме́ртного) пригово́ра; (*fig*) переды́шка.

**reprimand** *n* вы́говор; *vt* де́лать *impf*, с~ *pf* вы́говор +*dat*.

**reprint** *vt* переиздава́ть *impf*, переизда́ть *pf*; *n* переизда́ние.

**reprisal** *n* отве́тная ме́ра.

**reproach** *n* упрека́ть *impf*, упрекну́ть *pf* (**with** в+*prep*). **reproachful** *adj* укори́зненный.

**reproduce** *vt* воспроизводи́ть *impf*, воспроизвести́ *pf*; *vi* размножа́ться *impf*, размножи́ться *pf*. **reproduction** *n* (*action*) воспроизведе́ние; (*object*) репроду́кция; (*of offspring*) размноже́ние. **reproductive** *adj* воспроизводи́тельный.

**reproof** *n* вы́говор. **reprove** *vt* де́лать *impf* с~ *pf* вы́говор +*dat*.

**reptile** *n* пресмыка́ющееся *sb*.

**republic** *n* респу́блика. **republican** *adj* республика́нский; *n* республика́нец, -нка.

**repudiate** vt (renounce) отка́зываться impf, отказа́ться pf от+gen; (reject) отверга́ть impf, отве́ргнуть pf. **repudiation** n отка́з (of от+gen).

**repugnance** n отвраще́ние. **repugnant** adj проти́вный.

**repulse** vt отража́ть impf, отрази́ть pf. **repulsion** n отвраще́ние. **repulsive** adj отврати́тельный.

**reputable** adj по́льзующийся хоро́шей репута́цией. **reputation, repute** n репута́ция. **reputed** adj предполага́емый. **reputedly** adv по о́бщему мне́нию.

**request** n про́сьба; by, on, ~ по про́сьбе; vt проси́ть impf, по~ pf +acc, +gen (person +acc).

**requiem** n ре́квием.

**require** vt (demand; need) тре́бовать impf, по~ pf +gen; (need) нужда́ться impf в+prep. **requirement** n тре́бование; (necessity) потре́бность. **requisite** adj необходи́мый; n необходи́мая вещь. **requisition** n реквизи́ция; vt реквизи́ровать impf & pf.

**resale** n перепрода́жа.

**rescind** vt отменя́ть impf, отмени́ть pf.

**rescue** vt спаса́ть impf, спасти́ pf; n спасе́ние. **rescuer** n спаси́тель m.

**research** n иссле́дование (+gen); (occupation) иссле́довательская рабо́та; vi: ~ into иссле́довать impf & pf +acc. **researcher** n иссле́дователь m.

**resemblance** n схо́дство. **resemble** vt походи́ть impf на+acc.

**resent** vt возмуща́ться impf, возмути́ться pf. **resentful** adj возмущённый. **resentment** n возмуще́ние.

**reservation** n (doubt) огово́рка; (booking) предвари́тельный зака́з; (land) резерва́ция.

**reserve** vt (keep) резерви́ровать impf & pf; (book) зака́зывать impf, заказа́ть pf; n (stock; mil) запа́с, резе́рв; (sport) запасно́й игро́к; (nature — etc.) запове́дник; (proviso) огово́рка; (self-restraint) сде́ржанность; attrib запасно́й. **reserved** adj (person) сде́ржанный. **reservist** n резерви́ст. **reservoir** n (for water) водохрани́лище; (for other fluids) резервуа́р.

**resettle** vt переселя́ть impf, пересели́ть pf. **resettlement** n переселе́ние.

**reshape** vt видоизменя́ть impf, видоизмени́ть pf.

**reshuffle** n перестано́вка.

**reside** vi прожива́ть impf. **residence** n (residing) прожива́ние; (abode) местожи́тельство; (official — etc.) резиде́нция. **resident** n постоя́нный жи́тель m, ~ница; adj прожива́ющий; (population) постоя́нный. **residential** adj жило́й.

**residual** adj оста́точный. **residue** n оста́ток.

**resign** vt отка́зываться impf, отказа́ться pf от+gen; vi уходи́ть impf, уйти́ pf в отста́вку; ~ o.s. to покоря́ться impf, покори́ться pf +dat. **resignation** n отста́вка, заявле́ние об отста́вке; (being resigned) поко́рность. **resigned** adj поко́рный.

**resilient** adj выно́сливый.

**resin** n смола́.

**resist** vt сопротивля́ться impf +dat; (temptation) устоя́ть pf пе́ред+instr. **resistance** n сопротивле́ние. **resistant** adj сто́йкий.

**resolute** adj реши́тельный. **resolution** n (character) реши́тельность; (vow) заро́к; (at meeting etc.) резолю́ция; (of problem) разреше́ние. **resolve** vt (decide) реша́ть impf, реши́ть pf; (settle) разреша́ть impf, разреши́ть pf; n реши́тельность; (decision) реше́ние.

**resonance** n резона́нс. **resonant** adj зву́чный.

**resort** vi: ~ to прибега́ть impf, прибе́гнуть pf к+dat; n (place) куро́рт; **in the last** ~ в кра́йнем слу́чае.

**resound** vi (of sound etc.) раздава́ться impf, разда́ться pf; (of place) оглаша́ться impf, огласи́ться pf (with +instr).

**resource** n (usu pl) ресу́рс. **resourceful** adj нахо́дчивый.

**respect** n (relation) отноше́ние; (esteem) уваже́ние; with ~ to что каса́ется+gen; vt уважа́ть impf. **respectability** n респекта́бельность. **respectable** adj прили́чный. **respectful** adj почти́тельный. **respective** adj свой. **respectively** adv соотве́тственно.

**respiration** n дыха́ние. **respirator** n респира́тор. **respiratory** adj дыха́тельный.

**respite** n переды́шка.

**resplendent** adj блиста́тельный.

**respond** vi: ~ to отвеча́ть impf, отве́тить pf на+acc; (react) реаги́ровать impf, про~, от~ pf на+acc. **response** n отве́т; (reaction)

о́тклик. **responsibility** n отве́тственность; (duty) обя́занность. **responsible** adj отве́тственный (to пе́ред+instr; for за+acc); (reliable) надёжный. **responsive** adj отзы́вчивый.

**rest**[1] vi отдыха́ть impf, отдохну́ть pf; vt (place) класть impf, положи́ть pf; (allow to ~) дава́ть impf, дать pf о́тдых+dat; (in repose) поко́иться impf; n (repose) поко́й; (mus) па́уза; (support) опо́ра.

**rest**[2] n (remainder) оста́ток; (the others) остальны́е sb pl.

**restaurant** n рестора́н.

**restful** adj успока́ивающий.

**restitution** n возвраще́ние.

**restive** adj беспоко́йный.

**restless** adj беспоко́йный.

**restoration** n реставра́ция; (return) восстановле́ние. **restore** vt реставри́ровать impf & pf; (return) восстана́вливать impf, восстанови́ть pf.

**restrain** vt уде́рживать impf, удержа́ть pf (from от+gen). **restraint** n сде́ржанность.

**restrict** vt ограни́чивать impf, ограни́чить pf. **restriction** n ограниче́ние. **restrictive** adj ограничи́тельный.

**result** vi сле́довать impf; происходи́ть impf (from из+gen); ~ **in** конча́ться impf, ко́нчиться pf +instr; n результа́т; **as a** ~ в результа́те (of +gen).

**resume** vt & i возобновля́ть(ся) impf, возобнови́ть(ся) pf.

**résumé** n резюме́ neut indecl.

**resumption** n возобновле́ние.

**resurrect** vt (fig) воскреша́ть impf, воскреси́ть pf. **resurrection** n (of the dead) воскресе́ние; (fig) воскреше́ние.

**resuscitate** vt приводи́ть impf, привести́ pf в созна́ние.

**retail** n ро́зничная прода́жа; attrib ро́зничный; adv в ро́зницу; vt продава́ть impf, прода́ть pf в ро́зницу; vi продава́ться impf в ро́зницу. **retailer** n ро́зничный торго́вец.

**retain** vt уде́рживать impf, удержа́ть pf.

**retaliate** vi отпла́чивать impf, отплати́ть pf тем же. **retaliation** n отпла́та, возме́здие.

**retard** vt замедля́ть impf, заме́длить pf. **retarded** adj отста́лый.

**retention** n удержа́ние. **retentive** adj (memory) хоро́ший.

**reticence** n сде́ржанность. **reticent** adj сде́ржанный.

**retina** n сетча́тка.

**retinue** n сви́та.

**retire** vi (withdraw) удаля́ться impf, удали́ться pf; (from office etc.) уходи́ть impf, уйти́ pf в отста́вку. **retired** adj в отста́вке. **retirement** n отста́вка. **retiring** adj скро́мный.

**retort**[1] vt отвеча́ть impf, отве́тить pf ре́зко; n возраже́ние.

**retort**[2] n (vessel) рето́рта.

**retrace** vt: ~ one's steps возвраща́ться impf, возврати́ться pf.

**retract** vt (draw in) втя́гивать impf, втяну́ть pf; (take back) брать impf, взять pf наза́д.

**retreat** vi отступа́ть impf, отступи́ть pf; n отступле́ние; (withdrawal) уедине́ние; (place) убе́жище.

**retrenchment** n сокраще́ние расхо́дов.

**retrial** n повто́рное слу́шание де́ла.

**retribution** n возме́здие.

**retrieval** n возвраще́ние; (comput) по́иск (информа́ции); vt брать impf, взять pf обра́тно.

**retrograde** adj (fig) реакцио́нный. **retrospect** n: in ~ ретроспекти́вно. **retrospective** adj (law) име́ющий обра́тную си́лу.

**return** vt & i (give back; come back) возвраща́ть(ся) impf, возврати́ть(ся) impf, верну́ть(ся) pf; vt (elect) избира́ть impf, избра́ть pf, n возвраще́ние; возвра́т; (profit) при́быль; by ~ обра́тной по́чтой; in ~ взаме́н (for +gen); many happy ~s! с днём рожде́ния!; ~ match отве́тный матч; ~ ticket обра́тный биле́т.

**reunion** n встре́ча (друзе́й и т. п.); family ~ сбор всей семьи́. **reunite** vt воссоединя́ть impf, воссоедини́ть pf.

**reuse** vt сно́ва испо́льзовать impf & pf.

**rev** n оборо́т; vt & i: ~ up рвану́ть(ся) pf.

**reveal** vt обнару́живать impf, обнару́жить pf. **revealing** adj показа́тельный.

**revel** vi пирова́ть impf; ~ in наслажда́ться impf +instr.

**revelation** n открове́ние.

**revenge** vt: ~ o.s. мстить impf, ото~ pf (for за+acc; on +dat); n месть.

**revenue** n дохо́д.

**reverberate** vi отража́ться impf. **reverberation** n отраже́ние; (fig) о́тзвук.

**revere** vt почита́ть impf. **reverence** n почте́ние. **Reverend** adj (in title) (его́) преподо́бие. **reverent(ial)**

почти́тельный.

**reverie** n мечта́ние.

**reversal** n (change) измене́ние; (of decision) отме́на. **reverse** adj обра́тный; ~ **gear** за́дний ход; vt (change) изменя́ть impf, измени́ть pf; (decision) отменя́ть impf, отмени́ть pf; vi дава́ть pf за́дний ход; n (the ~) обра́тное sb, противоположное sb; (~ gear) за́дний ход; (~ side) обра́тная сторона́. **reversible** adj обрати́мый; (cloth) двусторо́нний. **reversion** n возвраще́ние. **revert** vi возвраща́ться impf (to в+acc, к+dat); (law) переходи́ть impf, перейти́ pf (to к+dat).

**review** n (re-examination) пересмо́тр; (mil) пара́д; (survey) обзо́р; (criticism) реце́нзия; vt (re-examine) пересма́тривать impf, пересмотре́ть pf; (survey) обозрева́ть impf, обозре́ть pf; (troops etc.) принима́ть impf, приня́ть pf парад+gen; (book etc.) рецензи́ровать impf, про~ pf. **reviewer** n реце́нзент.

**revise** vt пересма́тривать impf, пересмотре́ть pf; исправля́ть impf, испра́вить pf; vi (for exam) гото́виться impf (for к+dat). **revision** n пересмо́тр, исправле́ние.

**revival** n возрожде́ние; (to life etc.) оживле́ние. **revive** vt возрожда́ть impf, возроди́ть pf; (resuscitate) оживля́ть impf, оживи́ть pf; vi ожива́ть impf, ожи́ть pf.

**revoke** vt отменя́ть impf, отмени́ть pf.

**revolt** n бунт; vt вызыва́ть impf, вы́звать pf отвраще́ние у+gen; vi бунтова́ть impf, взбунтова́ться pf. **revolting** adj отврати́тельный.

**revolution** n (single turn) оборо́т; (polit) револю́ция. **revolutionary** adj революцио́нный; n революционе́р. **revolutionize** vt революционизи́ровать impf & pf. **revolve** vt & i враща́ть(ся) impf. **revolver** n револьве́р.

**revue** n revю́ neut indecl.

**revulsion** n отвраще́ние.

**reward** n вознагражде́ние; vt (воз)награжда́ть impf, (воз)награди́ть pf.

**rewrite** vt переписывать impf, переписа́ть pf; (recast) переде́лывать impf, переде́лать pf.

**rhapsody** n рапсо́дия.

**rhetoric** n рито́рика. **rhetorical** adj ритори́ческий.

**rheumatic** adj ревмати́ческий. **rheumatism** n ревмати́зм.

**rhinoceros** n носоро́г.

**rhododendron** n рододе́ндрон.

**rhubarb** n реве́нь m.

**rhyme** n ри́фма; pl (verse) стихи́ m pl; vt & i рифмова́ть(ся) impf.

**rhythm** n ритм. **rhythmic(al)** adj ритми́ческий, -чный.

**rib** n ребро́.

**ribald** adj непристо́йный.

**ribbon** n ле́нта.

**rice** n рис.

**rich** adj бога́тый; (soil) ту́чный; (food) жи́рный. **riches** n pl бога́тство. **richly** adv (fully) вполне́.

**rickety** adj (shaky) расша́танный.

**ricochet** vi рикошети́ровать impf & pf.

**rid** vt освобожда́ть impf, освободи́ть pf (of от+gen);

get ~ of избавля́ться *impf*, изба́виться *pf* от+*gen.* **rid-dance** *n*: good ~! скате́ртью доро́га!

**riddle** *n* (*enigma*) зага́дка.

**riddled** *adj*: ~ with изреше́чённый; (*fig*) прони́занный.

**ride** *vi* е́здить *indet*, е́хать *det*, по~ *pf* (on horseback верхо́м); *vt* е́здить *indet*, е́хать *det*, по~ *pf* в, на+*prep*; *n* пое́здка, езда́. **rider** *n* вса́дник, -ица; (*clause*) дополне́ние.

**ridge** *n* хребе́т; (*on cloth*) рубчик; (*of roof*) конёк.

**ridicule** *n* насме́шка; *vt* осме́ивать *impf*, осмея́ть *pf*. **ri-diculous** *adj* смешно́й.

**riding** *n* (*horse-~*) (верхова́я) езда́.

**rife** *predic* распространённый.

**riff-raff** *n* подо́нки (-ков) *pl.*

**rifle** *n* винто́вка; *vt* (*search*) обы́скивать *impf*, обыска́ть *pf.*

**rift** *n* тре́щина (*also fig*).

**rig** *vt* оснаща́ть *impf*, оснасти́ть *pf*; ~ **out** наряжа́ть *impf*, наряди́ть *pf*; ~ **up** ско-ла́чивать *impf*, сколоти́ть *pf*; *n* бурова́я устано́вка. **rig-ging** *n* такела́ж.

**right** *adj* (*position; justified; polit*) пра́вый; (*correct*) пра́-вильный; (*the one wanted*) тот; (*suitable*) подходя́щий; ~ **angle** прямо́й у́гол; *vt* исправля́ть *impf*, испра́вить *pf*; *n* пра́во; (*what is just*) справедли́вость; (~ *side*) пра́вая сторона́; (*the R~*, *polit*) пра́вые *sb pl*; **be in the** ~ быть пра́вым; **by** ~**s** по пра́ву; ~ **of way** пра́во прохо́да, прое́зда; *adv* (*straight*) пря́мо; (*exactly*) то́чно, как

раз; (*to the full*) соверше́нно; (*correctly*) пра́вильно; **as follows:** (*on the* ~) спра́ва (of ~+*gen*); (*to the* ~) напра́во; ~ **away** сейча́с.

**righteous** *adj* (*person*) пра́-ведный; (*action*) справедли́вый.

**rightful** *adj* зако́нный.

**rigid** *adj* жёсткий; (*strict*) стро́гий. **rigidity** *n* жёст-кость; стро́гость.

**rigmarole** *n* кани́тель.

**rigorous** *adj* стро́гий. **rigour** *n* стро́гость.

**rim** *n* (*of wheel*) о́бод; (*specta-cles*) опра́ва. **rimless** *adj* без опра́вы.

**rind** *n* кожура́.

**ring**[1] *n* кольцо́; (*circle*) круг; (*boxing*) ринг; (*circus*) (цирко-ва́я) аре́на; ~ **road** кольце-ва́я доро́га; *vt* (*encircle*) окружа́ть *impf*, окружи́ть *pf.*

**ring**[2] *vi* (*sound*) звони́ть *impf*, по~ *pf* (ring out, of shot etc.) раздава́ться *impf*, разда́ться *pf*; (*of place*) оглаша́ться *impf*, огласи́ться *pf* (with +*instr*); *vt* звони́ть *impf*, по~ *pf* в+*acc*; ~ **back** перезва́-нивать *impf*, перезвони́ть *pf*; ~ **off** пове́сить *pf* тру́бку; ~ **up** звони́ть *impf*, по~ *pf* +*dat*; *n* звон, звоно́к.

**ringleader** *n* глава́рь *m.*

**rink** *n* като́к.

**rinse** *vt* полоска́ть *impf*, вы́-*pf*; *n* полоска́ние.

**riot** *n* бунт; **run** ~ бу́йство-вать *impf*; (*of plants*) бу́йно разраста́ться *impf*, разра-сти́сь *pf*; *vi* бунтова́ть *impf*, взбунтова́ться *pf*. **riotous** *adj* бу́йный.

**rip** *vt* & *i* рва́ть(ся) *impf*, разо-*pf*; ~ **up** разрыва́ть *impf*, разорва́ть *pf*; *n* проре́ха, разре́з.

**ripe** *adj* зре́лый, спе́лый.

**ripen** *vt* де́лать *impf*, с~ *pf* зре́лым; *vi* созрева́ть *impf*, созре́ть *pf*. **ripeness** *n* зре́лость.

**ripple** *n* рябь; *vt & i* покрыва́ть(ся) *impf*, покры́ть(ся) *pf* ря́бью.

**rise** *vi* поднима́ться *impf*, подня́ться *pf*; повыша́ться *impf*, повы́ситься *pf*; (*get up*) встава́ть *impf*, встать *pf*; (*rebel*) восстава́ть *impf*, восста́ть *pf*; (*sun etc.*) в(о)сходи́ть *impf*, взойти́; *n* подъём, подъём; (*in pay*) приба́вка; (*of sun etc.*) восхо́д. **riser** *n*: **he is an early** ~ он ра́но встаёт. **rising** *n* (*revolt*) восста́ние.

**risk** *n* риск; *vt* рискова́ть *impf*, рискну́ть *pf* +*instr*. **risky** *adj* риско́ванный.

*risqué* *adj* непристо́йный.

**rite** *n* обря́д. **ritual** *n* ритуа́л; *adj* ритуа́льный.

**rival** *n* сопе́рник, -ица; *adj* сопе́рничающий; *vt* сопе́рничать *impf* с+*instr*. **rivalry** *n* сопе́рничество.

**river** *n* река́. **riverside** *attrib* прибре́жный.

**rivet** *n* заклёпка; *vt* заклёпывать *impf*, заклепа́ть *pf*; (*fig*) прико́вывать *impf*, прикова́ть *pf* (**on** к+*dat*).

**road** *n* доро́га; (*street*) у́лица; ~**-block** загражде́ние на доро́ге; ~**-map** (доро́жная) ка́рта; ~ **sign** доро́жный знак. **roadside** *n* обо́чина; *attrib* придоро́жный. **roadway** *n* мостова́я *sb*.

**roam** *vt & i* броди́ть *impf* (по+*dat*).

**roar** *n* (*animal's*) рёв; *vi* реве́ть *impf*.

**roast** *vt & i* жа́рить(ся) *impf*, за~, из~ *pf*; *adj* жа́реный; ~ **beef** ро́стбиф; *n* жарко́е *sb*.

**rob** *vt* гра́бить *impf*, о~ *pf*; красть *impf*, у~ *pf* у+*gen* (**of** +*acc*); (*deprive*) лиша́ть *impf*, лиши́ть *pf* (**of** +*gen*). **robber** *n* граби́тель *m*. **robbery** *n* грабёж.

**robe** *n* (*also pl*) ма́нтия.

**robin** *n* малиновка.

**robot** *n* ро́бот.

**robust** *adj* кре́пкий.

**rock**[1] *n* (*geol*) (го́рная) поро́да; (*cliff etc.*) скала́; (*large stone*) большо́й ка́мень *m*; **on the** ~**s** (*in difficulty*) на мели́; (*drink*) со льдом.

**rock**[2] *vt & i* кача́ть(ся) *impf*, качну́ть(ся) *pf*; *n* (*mus*) рок; ~**ing-chair** ка́чалка; ~ **and roll** рок-н-ро́лл.

**rockery** *n* альпина́рий.

**rocket** *n* раке́та; *vi* подска́кивать *impf*, подскочи́ть *pf*.

**rocky** *adj* скали́стый; (*shaky*) ша́ткий.

**rod** *n* (*stick*) прут; (*bar*) сте́ржень *m*; (*fishing-*~) у́дочка.

**rodent** *n* грызу́н.

**roe**[1] *n* икра́; (*soft*) моло́ки (-о́к) *pl*.

**roe**[2] (**-deer**) *n* косу́ля.

**rogue** *n* плут.

**role** *n* роль.

**roll**[1] *n* (*cylinder*) руло́н; (*register*) спи́сок; (*bread*) бу́лочка; ~**-call** перекли́чка.

**roll**[2] *vt & i* ката́ть(ся) *indet*, кати́ть(ся) *det*, по~ *pf*; (~ **up**) свёртывать(ся) *impf*, сверну́ть(ся) *pf*; *vt* (~ **out**) (*dough*) раска́тывать *impf*, раската́ть *pf*; *vi* (*sound*) греме́ть *impf*; ~ **over**

перевора́чиваться *impf*, переверну́ться *pf*; *n* (*of drums*) бараба́нная дробь; (*of thunder*) раска́т.

**roller** *n* (*small*) ро́лик; (*large*) като́к; (*for hair*) бигуди́ *neut indecl*; ~**-skates** коньки́ *m pl* на ро́ликах.

**rolling** *adj* (*of land*) холми́стый; ~**-pin** ска́лка. ~**stock** подвижно́й соста́в.

**Roman** *n* ри́млянин, -я́нка; *adj* ри́мский; ~ **Catholic** (*n*) като́лик, -и́чка; (*adj*) ри́мско-католи́ческий.

**romance** *n* (*tale*; *love affair*) рома́н; (*quality*) рома́нтика.

**Romanesque** *adj* рома́нский.

**Romania** *n* Румы́ния. **Romanian** *n* румы́н, ~ка; *adj* румы́нский.

**romantic** *adj* романти́чный, -ческий. **romanticism** *n* романти́зм.

**romp** *vi* вози́ться *impf*.

**roof** *n* кры́ша; ~ **of the mouth** нёбо; *vt* крыть *impf*, покры́ть *pf*.

**rook**[1] *n* (*chess*) ладья́.

**rook**[2] *n* (*bird*) грач.

**room** *n* ко́мната; (*in hotel*) но́мер; (*space*) ме́сто. **roomy** *adj* просто́рный.

**roost** *n* насе́ст.

**root**[1] *n* ко́рень *m*; **take** ~ укореня́ться *impf*, укорени́ться *pf*; *vt* пуска́ть *impf*, пусти́ть *pf* ко́рни; ~ **out** вырыва́ть *impf*, вы́рвать *pf* с ко́рнем; **rooted to the spot** прико́ванный к ме́сту.

**root**[2] *vi* (*rummage*) ры́ться *impf*; ~ **for** боле́ть *impf* за +*acc*.

**rope** *n* верёвка; ~**-ladder** верёвочная ле́стница; *vt*: ~ **in** (*enlist*) втя́гивать *impf*,

втяну́ть *pf*; ~ **off** о(т)гора́живать *impf*, о(т)городи́ть *pf* верёвкой.

**rosary** *n* чётки (-ток) *pl*.

**rose** *n* ро́за; (*nozzle*) се́тка.

**rosemary** *n* розмари́н.

**rosette** *n* розе́тка.

**rosewood** *n* ро́зовое де́рево.

**roster** *n* расписа́ние дежу́рств.

**rostrum** *n* трибу́на.

**rosy** *adj* ро́зовый; (*cheeks*) румя́ный.

**rot** *n* гниль; (*nonsense*) вздор; *vi* гнить *impf*, с~ *pf*; *vt* гнои́ть *impf*, с~ *pf*.

**rota** *n* расписа́ние дежу́рств. **rotary** *adj* враща́тельный, ротацио́нный. **rotate** *vt & i* враща́ть(ся) *impf*. **rotation** *n* враще́ние; **in** ~ по о́череди.

**rote** *n*: **by** ~ наизу́сть.

**rotten** *adj* гнило́й; (*fig*) отврати́тельный.

**rotund** *adj* (*round*) кру́глый; (*plump*) по́лный.

**rouble** *n* рубль *m*.

**rough** *adj* (*uneven*) неро́вный; (*coarse*) грубый; (*sea*) бу́рный; (*approximate*) приблизи́тельный; ~ **copy** чернови́к; *n*: **the** ~ тру́дности *f pl*; *vt*: ~ **it** жить *impf* без удо́бств. **roughage** *n* грубая пи́ща. **roughly** *adv* (*approximately*) приблизи́тельно.

**roulette** *n* руле́тка.

**round** *adj* кру́глый; ~**-shouldered** суту́лый; *n* (~ *object*) круг; (*circuit*; *also pl*) обхо́д; (*sport*) тур, ра́унд; (*series*) ряд; (*ammunition*) патро́н; (*of applause*) взрыв; *adv* вокру́г; (*in a circle*) по кру́гу; **all** ~ круго́м; **all the year** ~ кру́глый год; *prep* вокру́г+*gen*; круго́м+*gen*; по+*dat*; ~ **the**

**corner** (*motion*) за́ угол, (*position*) за угло́м; *vt* (*go* ~) огиба́ть *impf*, обогну́ть *pf*; ~ **off** (*complete*) заверша́ть *impf*, заверши́ть *pf*; ~ **up** сгоня́ть *impf*, согна́ть *pf*; ~ **up** заго́н; (*raid*) обла́ва.

**roundabout** *n* (*merry-go-round*) карусе́ль; (*road junction*) кольцева́я тра́нспортная развя́зка; *adj* око́льный.

**rouse** *vt* буди́ть *impf*, разбуди́ть *pf*; (*to action etc.*) побужда́ть *impf*, побуди́ть *pf* (**to** +*dat*). **rousing** *adj* восто́рженный.

**rout** *n* (*defeat*) разгро́м.

**route** *n* маршру́т, путь *m*.

**routine** *n* заведённый поря́док, режи́м; *adj* устано́вленный; очередно́й.

**rove** *vi* скита́ться *impf*.

**row**[1] *n* (*line*) ряд.

**row**[2] *vi* (*in boat*) грести́ *impf*.

**row**[3] *n* (*dispute*) ссо́ра; (*noise*) шум; *vi* ссо́риться *impf*, по~ *pf*.

**rowdy** *adj* бу́йный.

**royal** *adj* короле́вский; (*majestic*) великоле́пный. **royalist** *n* роялист; *adj* роялисти́ческий. **royalty** *n* член, чле́ны *pl*, короле́вской семьи́; (*fee*) а́вторский гонора́р *pl*.

**rub** *vt* & *i* тере́ть(ся) *impf*; *vt* (*polish*, *chafe*) натира́ть *impf*, натере́ть *pf*; (~ **dry**) вытира́ть *impf*, вы́тереть *pf*; ~ **in, on** втира́ть *impf*, втере́ть *pf*; ~ **out** стира́ть *impf*, стере́ть *pf*; ~ **it** растра́вливать *impf*, растрави́ть *pf* ра́ну.

**rubber** *n* рези́на; (*eraser*, *also* ~ **band**) рези́нка; *attrib* рези́новый; **~-stamp** (*fig*) штампова́ть *impf*.

**rubbish** *n* му́сор; (*nonsense*) чепуха́.

**rubble** *n* ще́бень *m*.

**rubella** *n* красну́ха.

**ruby** *n* руби́н.

**ruck** *vt* (~ **up**) мять *impf*, из~, с~ *pf*.

**rucksack** *n* рюкза́к.

**rudder** *n* руль *m*.

**ruddy** *adj* (*face*) румя́ный; (*damned*) прокля́тый.

**rude** *adj* гру́бый. **rudeness** *n* гру́бость.

**rudimentary** *adj* рудимента́рный. **rudiments** *n* *pl* осно́вы *f* *pl*.

**rueful** *adj* печа́льный.

**ruff** *n* (*frill*) брыжи (-жей) *pl*; (*of feathers, hair*) кольцо́ (пе́рьев, ше́рсти) вокру́г ше́и.

**ruffian** *n* хулига́н.

**ruffle** *n* обо́рка; *vt* (*hair*) еро́шить *impf*, взъ~ *pf*; (*water*) ряби́ть *impf*; (*person*) смуща́ть *impf*, смути́ть *pf*.

**rug** *n* (*mat*) ковёр; (*wrap*) плед.

**rugby** *n* ре́гби *neut indecl*.

**rugged** *adj* (*rocky*) скали́стый.

**ruin** *n* (*downfall*) ги́бель; (*building*, *ruins*) разва́лины *f* *pl*, руи́ны *f* *pl*; *vt* губи́ть *impf*, по~ *pf*. **ruinous** *adj* губи́тельный.

**rule** *n* пра́вило; (*for measuring*) лине́йка; (*government*) правле́ние; **as a** ~ как пра́вило; *vt* & *i* пра́вить *impf* (+*instr*); (*decree*) постановля́ть *impf*, постанови́ть *pf*; ~ **out** исключа́ть *impf*, исключи́ть *pf*. **ruled** *adj* линёванный. **ruler** *n* (*person*) прави́тель *m*, ~ница; (*object*) лине́йка. **ruling** *n* (*of court etc.*) постановле́ние.

**rum** *n* (*drink*) ром.

**Rumania(n)** *see* **Romania(n)**

**rumble** *vi* громыха́ть *impf*; *n* громыха́ние.

**ruminant** *n* жва́чное (живо́тное) *sb*. **ruminate** *vi* (*fig*) размышля́ть *impf* (**over, on** o+*prep*).

**rummage** *vi* ры́ться *impf*.

**rumour** *n* слух; *vt*: **it is ~ed that** хо́дят слу́хи (*pl*), что.

**rump** *n* крестец; **~ steak** ромште́кс.

**rumple** *vt* мять *impf*, из~, с~ *pf*; (*hair*) еро́шить *impf*, взъ~ *pf*.

**run** *vi* бе́гать *indet*, бежа́ть *det*, по~ *pf*; (*work, of machines*) рабо́тать *impf*; (*ply, of bus etc.*) ходи́ть *indet*, идти́ *det*; (*seek election*) выставля́ть *impf*, вы́ставить *pf* свою́ кандидату́ру; (*of play etc.*) идти́ *impf*; (*of ink, dye etc.*) расплыва́ться *impf*, расплы́ться *pf*; (*flow*) течь *impf*; (*of document*) гласи́ть *impf*; *vt* (*manage; operate*) управля́ть *impf*+*instr*; (*a business etc.*) вести́ *impf*; **~ dry, low** исся́кнуть *impf*, исся́кнуть *pf*; **~ risks** рискова́ть *impf*; **~ across, into** (*meet*) встреча́ться *impf*, встре́титься *pf* c+*instr*; **~ away** (*flee*) убега́ть *impf*, убежа́ть *pf*; **~ down** (*knock down*) задави́ть *pf*; (*disparage*) принижа́ть *impf*, прини́зить *pf*; **be ~ down** (*of person*) переутомля́ться *pf* (*in past tense*); **~-down** (*decayed*) запу́щенный; **~ in** (*engine*) обка́тывать *impf*, обката́ть *pf*; **~ into** *see* **~ across**; **~ out** конча́ться *impf*, ко́нчиться *pf*; **~ out of** истоща́ть *impf*, истощи́ть *pf* свой запа́с +*gen*; **~ over** (*glance over*) бе́гло просма́тривать *impf*, просмотре́ть *pf*; (*injure*) задави́ть *pf*; **~ through** (*pierce*) прока́лывать *impf*, проколо́ть *pf*; (*money*) прома́тывать *impf*, промота́ть *pf*; (*review*) повторя́ть *impf*, повтори́ть *pf*; **~ to** (*reach*) (*of money*) хвата́ть *impf*, хвати́ть *pf impers*+*gen* на+*acc*; **the money won't ~ to a car** э́тих де́нег не хва́тит на маши́ну; **~ up against** ната́лкиваться *impf*, натолкну́ться *pf* на+*acc*; *n* бег; (*sport*) перебе́жка; (*journey*) пое́здка; (*period*) полоса́; **at a ~** бего́м; **on the ~** в бега́х; **~ on** большо́й спрос на+*acc*; **in the long ~** в конце́ концо́в.

**rung** *n* ступе́нька.

**runner** *n* (*also tech*) бегу́н; (*of sledge*) по́лоз; (*bot*) побе́г; **~ bean** фасо́ль; **~-up** уча́стник, заня́вший второ́е ме́сто. **running** *n* бег; (*management*) управле́ние (*of* +*instr*); **be in the ~** име́ть *impf* ша́нсы; *adj* бегу́щий; (*of* ~) бегово́й; (*after pl n, in succession*) подря́д; **~ commentary** репорта́ж; **~ water** водопрово́д. **runway** *n* взлётно-поса́дочная полоса́.

**rupee** *n* ру́пия.

**rupture** *n* разры́в; *vt & i* прорыва́ть(ся) *impf*, прорва́ть(ся) *pf*.

**rural** *adj* се́льский.

**ruse** *n* уло́вка.

**rush¹** *n* (*bot*) тростни́к.

**rush²** *vt & i* (*hurry*) торопи́ть(ся) *impf*, по~ *pf*; *vi* (*dash*) броса́ться *impf*, бро́ситься *pf*; (*of water*) нести́сь *impf*, по~ *pf*; *vt* (*to hospital etc.*) умча́ть *pf*; *n* (*of blood etc.*) прили́в; (*hurry*) спе́шка; **be**

in a ~ торопи́ться *impf*; ~-hour(s) часы́ *m pl* пик.

**Russia** *n* Росси́я. **Russian** *n* ру́сский *sb*; *adj* (*of nationality, culture*) ру́сский; (*of State*) росси́йский.

**rust** *n* ржа́вчина; *vi* ржаве́ть *impf*, за~, по~ *pf*.

**rustic** *adj* дереве́нский.

**rustle** *n* ше́лест, шо́рох, шурша́ние; *vi & t* шелесте́ть *impf* (+*instr*); ~ up раздобыва́ть *impf*; раздобы́ть *pf*.

**rusty** *adj* ржа́вый.

**rut** *n* колея́.

**ruthless** *adj* безжа́лостный.

**rye** *n* рожь; *attrib* ржано́й.

# S

**Sabbath** *n* (*Jewish*) суббо́та; (*Christian*) воскресе́нье.

**sabbatical** *n* годи́чный о́тпуск.

**sable** *n* со́боль.

**sabotage** *n* диве́рсия; *vt* саботи́ровать *impf & pf*. **saboteur** *n* диверса́нт.

**sabre** *n* са́бля.

**sachet** *n* упако́вка.

**sack**[1] *vt* (*plunder*) разгра́бить *pf*.

**sack**[2] *n* мешо́к; (*dismissal*): **get the** ~ быть уво́ленным; *vt* увольня́ть *impf*, уво́лить *pf*. **sacking** *n* (*hessian*) мешкови́на.

**sacrament** *n* та́инство; (*Eucharist*) прича́стие. **sacred** *adj* свяще́нный, свято́й. **sacrifice** *n* же́ртва; *vt* же́ртвовать *impf*, по~ *pf* +*instr*. **sacrilege** *n* святота́тство. **sacrosanct** *adj* свяще́нный.

**sad** *adj* печа́льный, гру́стный. **sadden** *vt* печа́лить *impf*, о~ *pf*.

**saddle** *n* седло́; *vt* седла́ть *impf*, о~ *pf*; (*burden*) обременя́ть *impf*, обремени́ть *pf* (**with** +*instr*).

**sadism** *n* сади́зм. **sadist** *n* сади́ст. **sadistic** *adj* сади́стский.

**sadness** *n* печа́ль, грусть.

**safe** *n* сейф; *adj* (*unharmed*) невреди́мый; (*out of danger*) в безопа́сности; (*secure*) безопа́сный; (*reliable*) наде́жный; ~ **and sound** цел и невреди́м. **safeguard** *n* предохрани́тельная ме́ра; *vt* предохраня́ть *impf*, предохрани́ть *pf*. **safety** *n* безопа́сность; ~-**belt** *n* реме́нь *m* безопа́сности; ~ **pin** англи́йская була́вка; ~-**valve** предохрани́тельный кла́пан.

**saga** *n* са́га.

**sage**[1] *n* (*herb*) шалфе́й.

**sage**[2] *n* (*person*) мудре́ц; *adj* му́дрый.

**Sagittarius** *n* Стреле́ц.

**sail** *n* па́рус; *vt* (*a ship*) управля́ть *impf* +*instr*; *vi* пла́вать *indet*, плыть *det*; (*depart*) отплыва́ть *impf*, отплы́ть *pf*. **sailing** *n* (*sport*) па́русный спорт; ~-**ship** па́русное су́дно. **sailor** *n* матро́с, моря́к.

**saint** *n* свято́й *sb*. **saintly** *adj* свято́й.

**sake** *n*: **for the** ~ **of** ра́ди+*gen*.

**salad** *n* сала́т; ~-**dressing** припра́ва к сала́ту.

**salami** *n* саля́ми *f indecl*.

**salary** *n* жа́лованье.

**sale** *n* прода́жа; (*also amount sold*) сбыт (*no pl*); (*with reduced prices*) распрода́жа; **be**

for ~ продава́ться *impf*. **saleable** *adj* хо́дкий. **salesman** *n* продаве́ц. **saleswoman** *n* продавщи́ца.

**salient** *adj* основно́й.

**saliva** *n* слюна́.

**sallow** *adj* желтова́тый.

**salmon** *n* ло́сось *m*.

**salon** *n* сало́н. **saloon** *n* (*on ship*) сало́н; (*car*) седа́н; (*bar*) бар.

**salt** *n* соль; ~**-cellar** соло́нка; ~ **water** морска́я вода́; ~-**water** морско́й; *adj* солёный; *vt* соли́ть *impf*, по~ *pf*. **salty** *adj* солёный.

**salutary** *adj* благотво́рный. **salute** *n* отда́ча че́сти; (*with guns*) салю́т; *vt* & *i* отдава́ть *impf*, отда́ть *pf* честь (+*dat*).

**salvage** *n* спасе́ние; *vt* спаса́ть *impf*, спасти́ *pf*.

**salvation** *n* спасе́ние; **S-Army** А́рмия спасе́ния.

**salve** *n* мазь; *vt*: ~ **one's conscience** успока́ивать *impf*, успоко́ить *pf* со́весть.

**salvo** *n* залп.

**same** *adj*: the ~ тот же (са́мый); (*applying to both or all*) оди́н; (*identical*) одина́ковый; *pron*: the ~ одно́ и то́ же, то же са́мое; *adv*: the ~ таки́м же о́бразом, так же; **all the** ~ всё-таки, тем не ме́нее. **sameness** *n* однообра́зие.

**samovar** *n* самова́р.

**sample** *n* образе́ц; *vt* про́бовать *impf*, по~ *pf*.

**sanatorium** *n* санато́рий.

**sanctify** *vt* освяща́ть *impf*, освяти́ть *pf*. **sanctimonious** *adj* ха́нжеский. **sanction** *n* са́нкция; *vt* санкциони́ровать *impf* & *pf*. **sanctity** *n* (*holiness*) свя́тость; (*sacred-*

*ness*) свяще́нность. **sanctuary** *n* святи́лище; (*refuge*) убе́жище; (*for wild life*) запове́дник.

**sand** *n* песо́к; *vt* (~ **down**) шкури́ть *impf*, по~ *pf*; ~-**dune** дю́на.

**sandal** *n* санда́лия.

**sandalwood** *n* санда́ловое де́рево.

**sandbank** *n* о́тмель.

**sandpaper** *n* шку́рка; *vt* шлифова́ть *impf*, от~ *pf* шку́ркой.

**sandstone** *n* песча́ник.

**sandwich** *n* бутербро́д; *vt*: ~ **between** вти́скивать *impf*, втисну́ть *pf* ме́жду+*instr*.

**sandy** *adj* (*of sand*) песча́ный; (*like sand*) песо́чный; (*hair*) рыжева́тый.

**sane** *adj* норма́льный; (*sensible*) разу́мный.

**sang-froid** *n* самооблада́ние.

**sanguine** *adj* оптимисти́ческий.

**sanitary** *adj* санита́рный, гигиени́ческий; ~ **towel** гигиени́ческая поду́шка. **sanitation** *n* (*conditions*) санита́рные усло́вия *neut pl*; (*system*) водопрово́д и канализа́ция.

**sanity** *n* психи́ческое здоро́вье; (*good sense*) здра́вый смысл.

**sap** *n* (*bot*) сок; *vt* (*exhaust*) истоща́ть *impf*, истощи́ть *pf*.

**sapling** *n* са́женец.

**sapphire** *n* сапфи́р.

**sarcasm** *n* сарка́зм. **sarcastic** *adj* саркасти́ческий.

**sardine** *n* сарди́на.

**sardonic** *adj* сардони́ческий.

**sash**[1] *n* (*scarf*) куша́к.

**sash**[2] *n* (*frame*) скользя́щая ра́ма; ~-**window** подъёмное окно́.

**satanic** *adj* сатани́нский.

**satchel** *n* ра́нец, су́мка.

**satellite** *n* спу́тник, сателли́т (*also fig*); ~ **dish** параболи́ческая анте́нна; таре́лка (*coll*); ~ **TV** спу́тниковое телеви́дение.

**satiate** *vt* насыща́ть *impf*, насы́тить *pf*.

**satin** *n* атла́с.

**satire** *n* сати́ра. **satirical** *adj* сатири́ческий. **satirist** *n* сати́рик. **satirize** *vt* высме́ивать *impf*, вы́смеять *pf*.

**satisfaction** *n* удовлетворе́ние. **satisfactory** *adj* удовлетвори́тельный. **satisfy** *vt* удовлетворя́ть *impf*, удовлетвори́ть *pf*; (*hunger, curiosity*) утоля́ть *impf*, утоли́ть *pf*.

**saturate** *vt* насыща́ть *impf*, насы́тить *pf*; **I got** ~**d** (*by rain*) я промо́к до ни́тки. **saturation** *n* насыще́ние.

**Saturday** *n* суббо́та.

**sauce** *n* со́ус; (*cheek*) на́глость. **saucepan** *n* кастрю́ля. **saucer** *n* блю́дце. **saucy** *adj* на́глый.

**Saudi** *n* сауди́вец, -вка; *adj* сауди́вский. **Saudi Arabia** *n* Сауди́вская Ара́вия.

**sauna** *n* фи́нская ба́ня.

**saunter** *vi* прогу́ливаться *impf*.

**sausage** *n* соси́ска; (*salami-type*) колбаса́.

**savage** *adj* ди́кий; (*fierce*) свире́пый; (*cruel*) жесто́кий; *n* дика́рь *m*; *vt* иску́са́ть *pf*. **savagery** *n* ди́кость; жесто́кость.

**save** *vt* (*rescue*) спаса́ть *impf*, спасти́ *pf*; (*money*) копи́ть *impf*, на~ *pf*; (*put aside, keep*) бере́чь *impf*; (*avoid using*) эконо́мить *impf*, с~ *pf*; *vi*: ~

**up** копи́ть *impf*, на~ *pf* де́ньги. **savings** *neut pl*; ~ **bank** сберега́тельная ка́сса. **saviour** *n* спаси́тель *m*.

**savour** *vt* смакова́ть *impf*.

**savoury** *adj* пика́нтный; (*fig*) поря́дочный.

**saw** *n* пила́; *vt* пили́ть *impf*; ~ **up** распи́ливать *impf*, распили́ть *pf*. **sawdust** *n* опи́лки (-лок) *pl*.

**saxophone** *n* саксофо́н.

**say** *vt* говори́ть *impf*, сказа́ть *pf*; **to** ~ **nothing of** не говоря́ уже́ о+*prep*; **that is to** ~ то есть; (*let us*) ~ ска́жем; **it is said** (**that**) говоря́т (что); *n* (*opinion*) мне́ние; (*influence*) влия́ние; **have one's** ~ вы́сказаться *pf*. **saying** *n* погово́рка.

**scab** *n* (*on wound*) струп; (*polit*) штрейкбре́хер.

**scabbard** *n* но́жны (*gen* -жен) *pl*.

**scaffold** *n* эшафо́т. **scaffolding** *n* леса́ (-со́в) *pl*.

**scald** *vt* обва́ривать *impf*, обвари́ть *pf*.

**scale** *n* (*ratio*) масшта́б; (*grading*) шкала́; (*mus*) га́мма; *vt* (*climb*) взбира́ться *impf*, взобра́ться *pf* на+*acc*; ~ **down** понижа́ть *impf*, пони́зить *pf*.

**scales**¹ *n pl* (*of fish*) чешуя́ (*collect*).

**scales**² *n pl* весы́ (-со́в) *pl*.

**scallop** *n* гребешо́к; (*decoration*) фесто́н.

**scalp** *n* ко́жа головы́.

**scalpel** *n* ска́льпель *m*.

**scaly** *adj* чешу́йчатый; (*of boiler etc.*) покры́тый на́кипью.

**scamper** *vi* бы́стро бе́гать *impf*; (*frolic*) резви́ться *impf*.

**scan** vt & i (verse) сканди́ровать(ся) impf; vt (intently) рассма́тривать impf; (quickly) просма́тривать impf, просмотре́ть pf; (med) просве́чивать impf, просвети́ть pf; n просве́чивание.

**scandal** n сканда́л; (gossip) спле́тни (-тен) pl. **scandalize** vt шоки́ровать impf & pf.

**scandalous** adj сканда́льный.

**Scandinavia** n Скандина́вия. **Scandinavian** adj скандина́вский.

**scanty** adj ску́дный.

**scapegoat** n козёл отпуще́ния.

**scar** n шрам; vt оставля́ть impf, оста́вить pf шрам на+prep.

**scarce** adj дефици́тный; (rare) ре́дкий. **scarcely** adv едва́. **scarcity** n дефици́т; ре́дкость.

**scare** vt пуга́ть impf, ис~, на~ pf; ~ away, off отпу́гивать impf, отпугну́ть pf; n па́ника. **scarecrow** n пу́гало.

**scarf** n шарф.

**scarlet** adj (n) а́лый (цвет).

**scathing** adj уничтожа́ющий.

**scatter** vt & i рассыпа́ть(ся) impf, рассы́пать(ся) pf; (disperse) рассе́ивать(ся) impf, рассе́ять(ся) pf; ~-brained ве́треный. **scattered** adj разбро́санный; (sporadic) отде́льный.

**scavenge** vi ры́ться impf в отбро́сах. **scavenger** n (person) му́сорщик; (animal) живо́тное sb, пита́ющееся па́далью.

**scenario** n сцена́рий. **scene** n (place of disaster etc.)

ме́сто; (place of action) ме́сто де́йствия; (view) вид, пейза́ж; (picture) карти́на; (theat) сце́на, явле́ние; (incident) сце́на; **behind the ~s** за кули́сами; **make a ~** устра́ивать impf, устро́ить pf сце́ну. **scenery** n (theat) декора́ции; (landscape) пейза́ж. **scenic** adj живопи́сный.

**scent** n (smell) арома́т; (perfume) духи́ (-хо́в) pl; (trail) след. **scented** adj души́стый.

**sceptic** n ске́птик. **sceptical** adj скепти́ческий. **scepticism** n скептици́зм.

**schedule** n (timetable) расписа́ние; vt составля́ть impf, соста́вить pf расписа́ние +gen.

**schematic** adj схемати́ческий.

**scheme** n (plan) прое́кт; (intrigue) махина́ция; vi интригова́ть impf.

**schism** n раско́л.

**schizophrenia** n шизофрени́я. **schizophrenic** adj шизофрени́ческий; n шизофре́ник.

**scholar** n учёный sb: **scholarly** adj учёный. **scholarship** n учёность; (payment) стипе́ндия.

**school** n шко́ла; attrib шко́льный; vt (train) приуча́ть impf, приучи́ть pf (to к+dat, +inf). **school-book** n уче́бник. **schoolboy** n шко́льник. **schoolgirl** n шко́льница. **schooling** n обуче́ние. **school-leaver** n выпускни́к, -и́ца. **school teacher** n учи́тель m, ~ница.

**schooner** n шху́на.

**sciatica** n и́шиас.

**science** n нау́ка; ~ **fiction** нау́чная фанта́стика. **scientific** adj нау́чный. **scientist**

*n* учёный *sb.*

**scintillating** *adj* блиста́тельный.

**scissors** *n pl* но́жницы (-ц) *pl.*

**scoff** *vi* (*mock*) смея́ться *impf* (**at** над+*instr*).

**scold** *vt* брани́ть *impf*, вы́~ *pf.*

**scoop** *n* (*large*) черпа́к; (*ice-cream ~*) ло́жка для моро́женого; *vt* (*~ out, up*) вычерпывать *impf*, вы́черпать *pf.*

**scooter** *n* (*motor ~*) мотороллер.

**scope** *n* (*range*) преде́лы *m pl*; (*chance*) возмо́жность.

**scorch** *vt* (*fingers*) обжига́ть *impf*, обже́чь *pf*; (*clothes*) сжига́ть *impf*, сже́чь *pf.*

**score** *n* (*of points etc.*) счёт; (*mus*) партиту́ра; *pl* (*great numbers*) мно́жество; *vt* (*notch*) де́лать *impf*, с~ *pf* зару́бки на+*prep*; (*points etc.*) получа́ть *impf*, получи́ть *pf*; (*mus*) оркестрова́ть *impf & pf*; *vi* (*keep ~*) вести́ *impf*, с~ *pf* счёт. **scorer** *n* счётчик.

**scorn** *n* презре́ние; *vt* презира́ть *impf*, презре́ть *pf*. **scornful** *adj* презри́тельный.

**Scorpio** *n* Скорпио́н.

**scorpion** *n* скорпио́н.

**Scot** *n* шотла́ндец, -дка. **Scotch** *n* (*whisky*) шотла́ндское ви́ски *neut indecl*. **Scotland** *n* Шотла́ндия. **Scots**, **Scottish** *adj* шотла́ндский.

**scoundrel** *n* негодя́й.

**scour**[1] *vt* (*cleanse*) отчища́ть *impf*, отчи́стить *pf.*

**scour**[2] *vt & i* (*rove*) ры́скать *impf* (по+*dat*).

**scourge** *n* бич.

**scout** *n* разве́дчик; (**S~**) бой-

скау́т; *vi*: ~ **about** разы́скивать *impf* (**for** +*acc*).

**scowl** *vi* хму́риться *impf*, на~ *pf*; *n* хму́рый взгляд.

**scrabble** *vi*: ~ **about** ры́ться *impf.*

**scramble** *vi* кара́бкаться *impf*, вс~ *pf*; (*struggle*) дра́ться *impf* (**for** за+*acc*); ~**d eggs** яи́чница-болту́нья.

**scrap**[1] *n* (*fragment*) кусо́чек; *pl* оста́тки *m pl*; *pl* (*of food*) объе́дки (-ков) *pl*; ~ **metal** металло́м; *vt* сдава́ть *impf*, сдать *pf* в ути́ль.

**scrap**[2] *n* (*fight*) дра́ка; *vi* дра́ться *impf.*

**scrape** *vt* скрести́ *impf*; (*graze*) цара́пать *impf*, о~ *pf*; ~ **off** отскреба́ть *impf*, отскрести́ *pf*; ~ **through** (*exam*) с трудо́м выде́рживать *impf*, вы́держать *pf*; ~ **together** наскреба́ть *impf*, наскрести́ *pf.*

**scratch** *vt* цара́пать *impf*, о~ *pf*; *vt & i* (*when itching*) чеса́ть(ся) *impf*, по~ *pf*; *n* цара́пина.

**scrawl** *n* кара́кули *f pl*; *vt* писа́ть *impf*, на~ *pf* кара́кулями.

**scrawny** *adj* сухопа́рый.

**scream** *n* крик; *vi* крича́ть *impf*, кри́кнуть *pf.*

**screech** *n* визг; *vi* визжа́ть *impf.*

**screen** *n* ши́рма; (*cin*, TV) экра́н; ~-**play** сцена́рий; *vt* (*protect*) защища́ть *impf*, защити́ть *pf*; (*hide*) укрыва́ть *impf*, укры́ть *pf*; (*show film etc.*) демонстри́ровать *impf & pf*; (*check on*) проверя́ть *impf*, прове́рить *pf*; ~ **off** отгора́живать *impf*, отгороди́ть *pf* ши́рмой.

**screw** n винт; vt (~ on) привинчивать impf, привинтить pf; (~ up) завинчивать impf, завинтить pf; (crumple) комкать impf, c~ pf; ~ up one's eyes щуриться impf, co~ pf. **screwdriver** n отвёртка.

**scribble** vt строчить impf, на~ pf; n каракули f pl.

**script** n (of film etc.) сценарий; (of speech etc.) текст; (writing system) письмо; ~ **writer** n сценарист.

**Scripture** n священное писание.

**scroll** n свиток; (design) завиток.

**scrounge** vt (cadge) стрелять impf, стрельнуть pf; vi попрошайничать impf.

**scrub**[1] n (brushwood) кустарник; (area) заросли f pl.

**scrub**[2] vt мыть impf, вы~ pf щёткой.

**scruff** n: by the ~ of the neck за шиворот.

**scruffy** adj обо́дранный.

**scrum** n схватка вокруг мяча.

**scruple** n (also pl) колебания neut pl; угрызения neut pl совести. **scrupulous** adj скрупулёзный.

**scrutinize** vt рассматривать impf. **scrutiny** n рассмотрение.

**scuffed** adj поцарапанный.

**scuffle** n потасовка.

**sculpt** vt ваять impf, из~ pf. **sculptor** n скульптор. **sculpture** n скульптура.

**scum** n накипь.

**scurrilous** adj непристойный.

**scurry** vi поспешно бегать indet, бежать det.

**scuttle**[1] n (coal) ведёрко для угля.

**scuttle**[2] vi (run away) удирать

impf, удрать pf.

**scythe** n коса.

**sea** n море; attrib морской; ~ **front** набережная sb; ~ **gull** чайка; ~-**level** уровень m моря; ~-**lion** морской лев; ~-**shore** побережье. **seaboard** n побережье. **seafood** n продукты m pl моря.

**seal**[1] n (on document etc.) печать; vt скреплять impf, скрепить pf печатью; (close) запечатывать impf, запечатать pf; ~ **up** заделывать impf, заделать pf.

**seal**[2] n (zool) тюлень m; (fur~) котик.

**seam** n шов; (geol) пласт.

**seaman** n моряк, матрос.

**seamless** adj без шва.

**seamstress** n швея.

**seance** n спиритический сеанс.

**seaplane** n гидросамолёт.

**searing** adj палящий.

**search** vt обыскивать impf, обыскать pf; vi искать impf (for +acc); n поиски m pl; обыск; ~-**party** поисковая группа. **searching** adj (look) испытующий. **searchlight** n прожектор.

**seasick** adj: I was ~ меня укачало. **seaside** n берег моря.

**season** n сезон; (one of four) время neut года; ~ **ticket** сезонный билет; vt (flavour) приправлять impf, приправить pf. **seasonable** adj по сезону; (timely) своевременный. **seasonal** adj сезонный. **seasoning** n приправа.

**seat** n (place) место; (of chair) сиденье; (chair) стул; (bench) скамейка; (of trousers) зад; ~ **belt** привязной ремень m

*vt* сажа́ть *impf*, посади́ть *pf*; (*of room etc.*) вмеща́ть *impf*, вмести́ть *pf*; be ~ed сади́ться *impf*, сесть *pf*.
**seaweed** *n* морска́я во́доросль.
**secateurs** *n pl* сека́тор.
**secede** *vi* отка́лываться *impf*, отколо́ться *pf*. **secession** *n* отко́л.
**secluded** *adj* укро́мный. **seclusion** *n* укро́мность.
**second**[1] *adj* второ́й; ~-**class** второкла́ссный; ~-**hand** поде́ржанный; (*of information*) из вторы́х рук; ~-**rate** второразря́дный; ~ **sight** ясновиде́ние; **on** ~ **thoughts** взве́сив всё ещё раз; **have** ~ **thoughts** переду́мывать *impf*, переду́мать *pf* (**about** +*acc*); *n* второ́й *sb*; (*date*) второ́е (число́) *sb*; (*time*) секу́нда; *pl* (*comm*) това́р второ́го со́рта; ~ (**hand** *of clock*) секу́ндная стре́лка; *vt* (*support*) подде́рживать *impf*, поддержа́ть *pf*; (*transfer*) откомандиро́вывать *impf* откомандирова́ть *pf*. **secondary** *adj* втори́чный, второстепе́нный; (*education*) сре́дний. **secondly** *adv* во-вторы́х.
**secrecy** *n* секре́тность. **secret** *n* та́йна, секре́т; *adj* та́йный, секре́тный; (*hidden*) потайно́й.
**secretarial** *adj* секрета́рский. **secretariat** *n* секретариа́т. **secretary** *n* секрета́рь *m*, -рша; (*minister*) мини́стр.
**secrete** *vt* (*conceal*) укрыва́ть *impf*, укры́ть *pf*; (*med*) выделя́ть *impf*, вы́делить *pf*. **secretion** *n* укрыва́ние; (*med*) выделе́ние.
**secretive** *adj* скры́тный.

**sect** *n* се́кта. **sectarian** *adj* секта́нтский.
**section** *n* се́кция; (*of book*) разде́л; (*geom*) сече́ние. **sector** *n* се́ктор.
**secular** *adj* све́тский. **secularization** *n* секуляриза́ция.
**secure** *adj* (*safe*) безопа́сный; (*firm*) надёжный; (*emotionally*) уве́ренный; *vt* (*fasten*) закрепля́ть *impf*, закрепи́ть *pf*; (*guarantee*) обеспе́чивать *impf*, обеспе́чить *pf*; (*obtain*) достава́ть *impf*, доста́ть *pf*. **security** *n* безопа́сность; (*guarantee*) зало́г; *pl* це́нные бума́ги *f pl*.
**sedate** *adj* степе́нный.
**sedation** *n* успокое́ние. **sedative** *n* успока́ивающее сре́дство.
**sedentary** *adj* сидя́чий.
**sediment** *n* оса́док.
**seduce** *vt* соблазня́ть *impf*, соблазни́ть *pf*. **seduction** *n* обольще́ние. **seductive** *adj* соблазни́тельный.
**see** *vt & i* ви́деть *impf*, у~ *pf*; *vt* (*watch, look*) смотре́ть *impf*, по~ *pf*; (*find out*) узнава́ть *impf*, узна́ть *pf*; (*understand*) понима́ть *impf*, поня́ть *pf*; (*meet*) ви́деться *impf*, у~ *pf* c+*instr*; (*imagine*) представля́ть *impf*, предста́вить *pf* себе́; (*escort*, ~ **off**) провожа́ть *impf*, проводи́ть *pf*; ~ **about** (*attend to*) забо́титься *impf*, по~ *pf* о+*prep*; ~ **through** (*fig*) ви́деть *impf* наскво́зь+*acc*.
**seed** *n* се́мя *neut*. **seedling** *n* се́янец; *pl* расса́да. **seedy** *adj* (*shabby*) потрёпанный.
**seeing (that)** *conj* ввиду́ того́, что.
**seek** *vt* иска́ть *impf* +*acc, gen*.

**seem** *vi* каза́ться *impf*, по~ *pf* (+*instr*). **seemingly** *adv* по-ви́димому.

**seemly** *adj* прили́чный.

**seep** *vi* проса́чиваться *impf*, просочи́ться *pf*.

**seethe** *vi* кипе́ть *impf*, вс~ *pf*.

**segment** *n* отре́зок; (*of orange etc.*) до́лька; (*geom*) сегме́нт.

**segregate** *vt* отделя́ть *impf*, отдели́ть *pf*. **segregation** *n* сегрега́ция.

**seismic** *adj* сейсми́ческий.

**seize** *vt* хвата́ть *impf*, схвати́ть *pf*; *vi*: ~ **up** заеда́ть *impf*, зае́сть *pf impers*+*acc*; ~ **upon** ухва́тываться *impf*, ухвати́ться *pf* за+*acc*. **seizure** *n* захва́т; (*med*) припа́док.

**seldom** *adv* ре́дко.

**select** *adj* и́збранный; *vt* отбира́ть *impf*, отобра́ть *pf*. **selection** *n* (*choice*) вы́бор. **selective** *adj* разбо́рчивый.

**self** *n* со́бственное «я» *neut indecl*.

**self-** *in comb* само-; ~**absorbed** эгоцентри́чный; ~**assured** самоуве́ренный; ~**catering (accommodation)** жилье́ с ку́хней; ~**centred** эгоцентри́чный; ~**confessed** открове́нный; ~**confidence** самоуве́ренность; ~**confident** самоуве́ренный; ~**conscious** засте́нчивый; ~**contained** (*person*) незави́симый; (*flat etc.*) отде́льный; ~**control** самооблада́ние; ~**defence** самозащи́та; ~**denial** самоотрече́ние; ~**determination** самоопределе́ние; ~**effacing** скро́мный; ~**employed person** незави́симый предпринима́тель *m*; ~**esteem**

самоуваже́ние; ~**evident** очеви́дный; ~**governing** самоуправля́ющий; ~**help** самопо́мощь; ~**importance** самомне́ние; ~**imposed** доброво́льный; ~**indulgent** изба́лованный; ~**interest** со́бственный интере́с; ~**pity** жа́лость к себе́; ~**portrait** автопортре́т; ~**preservation** самосохране́ние; ~**reliance** самостоя́тельность; ~**respect** самоуваже́ние; ~**righteous** *adj* ха́нжеский; ~**sacrifice** самопоже́ртвование; ~**satisfied** самодово́льный; ~**service** самообслу́живание (*attrib in gen after n*); ~**styled** самозва́ный; ~**sufficient** самостоя́тельный.

**selfish** *adj* эгоисти́чный. **selfless** *adj* самоотве́рженный.

**sell** *vt* & *i* продава́ть(ся) *impf*, прода́ть(ся) *pf*; *vt* (*deal in*) торгова́ть *impf* +*instr*; ~ **out of** распродава́ть *impf*, распрода́ть *pf*. **seller** *n* продаве́ц. **selling** *n* прода́жа. **sell-out** *n*: **the play was a** ~ пье́са прошла́ с аншла́гом.

**Sellotape** *n* (*propr*) ли́пкая ле́нта.

**semantic** *adj* семанти́ческий. **semantics** *n* сема́нтика.

**semblance** *n* ви́димость.

**semen** *n* се́мя *neut*.

**semi-** *in comb* полу-; ~**detached house** дом, разделённый о́бщей стено́й. **semibreve** *n* це́лая но́та. **semicircle** *n* полукру́г. **semicircular** *adj* полукру́глый. **semicolon** *n* то́чка с запято́й. **semiconductor** *n* полупроводни́к. **semifinal** *n* полуфина́л.

**seminar** *n* семина́р. **seminary**

*n* семина́рия.

**semiquaver** *n* шестна́дцатая но́та.

**semitone** *n* полуто́н.

**senate** *n* сена́т; (*univ*) сове́т. **senator** *n* сена́тор.

**send** *vt* посыла́ть *impf*, посла́ть *pf* (**for** за+*instr*); ~ off отправля́ть *impf*, отпра́вить *pf*; ~-off про́воды (-дов) *pl*. **sender** *n* отправи́тель *m*.

**senile** *adj* ста́рческий. **senility** *n* ста́рческое слабоу́мие.

**senior** *adj* (*n*) ста́рший (*sb*); ~ citizen стари́к, стару́ха. **seniority** *n* старшинство́.

**sensation** *n* сенса́ция; (*feeling*) ощуще́ние. **sensational** *adj* сенсацио́нный.

**sense** *n* чу́вство; (*good*) здра́вый смысл; (*meaning*) смысл; *pl* (*sanity*) ум; чу́вствовать *impf*. **senseless** *adj* бессмы́сленный.

**sensibility** *n* чувстви́тельность; *pl* самолю́бие. **sensible** *adj* благоразу́мный. **sensitive** *adj* чувстви́тельный; (*touchy*) оби́дчивый. **sensitivity** *n* чувстви́тельность.

**sensory** *adj* чувстви́тельный.

**sensual**, **sensuous** *adj* чу́вственный.

**sentence** *n* (*gram*) предложе́ние; (*law*) пригово́р; *vt* пригова́ривать *impf*, приговори́ть *pf* (**to** к+*dat*).

**sentiment** *n* (*feeling*) чу́вство; (*opinion*) мне́ние. **sentimental** *adj* сентимента́льный. **sentimentality** *n* сентимента́льность.

**sentry** *n* часово́й *sb*.

**separable** *adj* отдели́мый. **separate** *adj* отде́льный; *vt & i* отделя́ть(ся) *impf*, отде-

ли́ть(ся) *pf*. **separation** *n* отделе́ние. **separatism** *n* сепарати́зм. **separatist** *n* сепарати́ст.

**September** *n* сентя́брь *m*; *adj* сентя́брьский.

**septic** *adj* септи́ческий.

**sepulchre** *n* моги́ла.

**sequel** *n* (*result*) после́дствие; (*continuation*) продолже́ние.

**sequence** *n* после́довательность; ~ **of events** ход собы́тий.

**sequester** *vt* секвестрова́ть *impf* & *pf*.

**sequin** *n* блёстка.

**Serb(ian)** *adj* се́рбский; *n* серб, ~ка. **Serbia** *n* Се́рбия. **Serbo-Croat(ian)** *adj* сербскохорва́тский.

**serenade** *n* серена́да.

**serene** *adj* споко́йный. **serenity** *n* споко́йствие.

**serf** *n* крепостно́й *sb*. **serfdom** *n* крепостно́е пра́во.

**sergeant** *n* сержа́нт.

**serial** *adj*: ~ **number** сери́йный но́мер; *n* (*story*) рома́н с продолже́нием; (*broadcast*) сери́йная постано́вка. **serialize** *vt* ста́вить *impf*, по-~ *pf* в не́сколько частя́х.

**series** *n* (*succession*) ряд; (*broadcast*) се́рия переда́ч.

**serious** *adj* серьёзный. **seriousness** *n* серьёзность.

**sermon** *n* про́поведь.

**serpent** *n* змея́.

**serrated** *adj* зазу́бренный.

**serum** *n* сы́воротка.

**servant** *n* слуга́ *m*, служа́нка. **serve** *vt* служи́ть *impf*, по-~ *pf* +*dat* (**as, for** +*instr*); (*attend to*) обслу́живать *impf*, обслужи́ть *pf*; (*food; ball*) подава́ть *impf*, пода́ть *pf*; (*sentence*) отбыва́ть *impf*, отбы́ть *pf*;

(*writ etc.*) вруча́ть *impf*, вручи́ть *pf* (**on** +*dat*); *vi* (*be suitable*) годи́ться (**for** на +*acc*, для+*gen*); (*sport*) подава́ть *impf*, пода́ть *pf* мяч; **it ~s him right** подело́м ему́ (*dat*). **service** *n* (*act of serving*; *branch of public work*; *eccl*) слу́жба; (*quality of* ~) обслу́живание; (*of car etc.*) техобслу́живание; (*set of dishes*) серви́з; (*sport*) пода́ча; (*transport*) сообще́ние; **at your ~** к ва́шим услу́гам; *vt* (*car*) проводи́ть *impf*, провести́ *pf* техобслу́живание +*gen*; **~ charge** пла́та за обслу́живание; **~ station** ста́нция обслу́живания. **serviceable** *adj* (*useful*) поле́зный; (*durable*) про́чный. **serviceman** *n* военнослу́жащий *sb*.

**serviette** *n* салфе́тка.

**servile** *adj* рабо́лепный.

**session** *n* заседа́ние, се́ссия.

**set¹** *vt* (*put*; ~ *clock*, *trap*) ста́вить *impf*, по- *pf*; (*table*) накрыва́ть *impf*, накры́ть *pf*; (*bone*) вправля́ть *impf*, впра́вить *pf*; (*hair*) укла́дывать *impf*, уложи́ть *pf*; (*gem*) оправля́ть *impf*, опра́вить *pf*; (*bring into state*) приводи́ть *impf*, привести́ *pf* (**in, to** в+*acc*); (*example*) подава́ть *impf*, пода́ть *pf*; (*task*) задава́ть *impf*, зада́ть *pf*; *vi* (*solidify*) тверде́ть *impf*, за- *pf*; засты(ва́)ть *impf*, засты́(нуть) *pf*; (*sun etc.*) заходи́ть *impf*, зайти́ *pf*; сади́ться *impf*, сесть *pf*; **~ about** (*begin*) начина́ть *impf*, нача́ть *pf*; (*attack*) напада́ть *impf*, напа́сть *pf* на+*acc*; **~ back** (*impede*) препя́тствовать *impf*, вос- *pf* +*dat*; **~-back** неуда́-

ча; **~ in** наступа́ть *impf*, наступи́ть *pf*; **~ off** (*on journey*) отправля́ться *impf*, отпра́виться *pf*; (*enhance*) оттеня́ть *impf*, оттени́ть *pf*; **~ out** (*state*) излага́ть *impf*, изложи́ть *pf*; (*on journey*) *see* **~ off**; **~ up** (*business*) осно́вывать *impf*, основа́ть *pf*.

**set²** *n* набо́р, компле́кт; (*of dishes*) серви́з; (*radio*) приёмник; (*television*) телеви́зор; (*tennis*) сет; (*theat*) декора́ция; (*cin*) съёмочная площа́дка.

**set³** *adj* (*established*) устано́вленный.

**settee** *n* дива́н.

**setting** *n* (*frame*) опра́ва; (*surroundings*) обстано́вка; (*of mechanism etc.*) устано́вка; (*of sun etc.*) захо́д.

**settle** *vt* (*decide*) реша́ть *impf*, реши́ть *pf*; (*reconcile*) ула́живать *impf*, ула́дить *pf*; (*a bill etc.*) опла́чивать *impf*, оплати́ть *pf*; (*calm*) успока́ивать *impf*, успоко́ить *pf*; *vi* поселя́ться *impf*, посели́ться *pf*; (*subside*) оседа́ть *impf*, осе́сть *pf*; **~ down** уса́живаться *impf*, усе́сться *pf* (**to** за+*acc*). **settlement** *n* поселе́ние; (*agreement*) соглаше́ние; (*payment*) упла́та. **settler** *n* посе́ленец.

**seven** *adj* & *n* семь; (*number* 7) семёрка. **seventeen** *adj* & *n* семна́дцать. **seventeenth** *adj* & *n* семна́дцатый. **seventh** *adj* & *n* седьмо́й; (*fraction*) седьма́я *sb*. **seventieth** *adj* & *n* семидеся́тый. **seventy** *adj* & *n* се́мьдесят; *pl* (*decade*) семидеся́тые го́ды (-до́в) *m pl*.

**sever** *vt* (*cut off*) отреза́ть

*impf*, отрезать *pf*; *(relations)* разрывать *impf*, разорвать *pf*.

**several** *pron (adj)* несколько (+*gen*).

**severance** *n* разры́в; ~ **pay** выходно́е посо́бие.

**severe** *adj* стро́гий, суро́вый; *(pain, frost)* си́льный; *(illness)* тяжёлый. **severity** *n* стро́гость, суро́вость.

**sew** *vt* шить *impf*, с~ *pf*; ~ **on** пришива́ть *impf*, приши́ть *pf*; ~ **up** зашива́ть *impf*, заши́ть *pf*.

**sewage** *n* сто́чные во́ды *f pl*; ~-**farm** поля́ *neut pl* ороше́ния. **sewer** *n* сто́чная труба́. **sewerage** *n* канализа́ция.

**sewing** *n* шитьё; ~-**machine** шве́йная маши́на.

**sex** *n* *(gender)* пол; *(sexual activity)* секс; **have** ~ име́ть *impf* сноше́ние. **sexual** *adj* полово́й, сексуа́льный; ~ **intercourse** полово́е сноше́ние. **sexuality** *n* сексуа́льность. **sexy** *adj* эроти́ческий.

**sh** *int* ти́ше! тсс!

**shabby** *adj* ве́тхий.

**shack** *n* лачу́га.

**shackles** *n pl* око́вы (-в) *pl*.

**shade** *n* тень; *(of colour, meaning)* отте́нок; *(lamp~)* абажу́р; **a** ~ чуть-чу́ть; *vt* затеня́ть *impf*, затени́ть *pf*; *(eyes etc.)* заслоня́ть *impf* заслони́ть *pf*; *(drawing)* тушева́ть *impf*, за~ *pf*. **shadow** *n* тень; *vt (follow)* та́йно следи́ть *impf* за+*instr*. **shadowy** *adj* тёмный. **shady** *adj* тени́стый; *(suspicious)* подозри́тельный.

**shaft** *n (of spear)* дре́вко; *(arrow; fig)* стрела́; *(of light)* луч; *(of cart)* огло́бля; *(axle)*

вал; *(mine, lift)* ша́хта.

**shaggy** *adj* лохма́тый.

**shake** *vt & i* трясти́(сь) *impf*; *vi (tremble)* дрожа́ть *impf*; *vt (weaken)* колеба́ть *impf*, по~ *pf*; *(shock)* потряса́ть *impf* потрясти́ *pf*; ~ **hands** пожима́ть *impf*, пожа́ть *pf* ру́ку (**with** +*dat*); ~ **one's head** покача́ть *pf* голово́й; ~ **off** стря́хивать *impf*, стряхну́ть *pf*; *(fig)* избавля́ться *impf*, изба́виться *pf* от+*gen*. **shaky** *adj* ша́ткий.

**shallow** *adj* ме́лкий; *(fig)* пове́рхностный.

**sham** *vt & i* притворя́ться *impf*, притвори́ться *pf* +*instr*; *n* притво́рство; *(person)* притво́рщик, -ица; *adj* притво́рный.

**shambles** *n* хао́с.

**shame** *n (guilt)* стыд; *(disgrace)* позо́р; **what a** ~! как жаль!; *vt* стыди́ть *impf*, при~ *pf*. **shameful** *adj* позо́рный. **shameless** *adj* бессты́дный.

**shampoo** *n* шампу́нь *m*.

**shanty**¹ *n (hut)* хиба́рка; ~ **town** трущо́ба.

**shanty**² *n (song)* матро́сская пе́сня.

**shape** *n* фо́рма; *vt* придава́ть *impf*, прида́ть *pf* фо́рму+*dat*; *vi*: ~ **up** скла́дываться *impf*, сложи́ться *pf*. **shapeless** *adj* бесфо́рменный. **shapely** *adj* стро́йный.

**share** *n* до́ля; *(econ)* а́кция; *vt* дели́ть *impf*, по~ *pf*; *(opinion etc.)*; ~ **out** разделя́ть *impf*, раздели́ть *pf*. **shareholder** *n* акционе́р.

**shark** *n* аку́ла.

**sharp** *adj* о́стрый; *(steep)* круто́й; *(sudden; harsh)* ре́зкий; *n (mus)* дие́з; *adv (with time)* ро́вно; (of angle) кру́то. **sharpen** vt точи́ть impf, на~ pf.

**shatter** vt & i разбива́ть(ся) impf, разби́ть(ся) pf вдре́безги; (hopes etc.) разруша́ть impf, разру́шить pf.

**shave** vt & i бри́ть(ся) impf, по~ pf; n бритьё. **shaver** n электри́ческая бри́тва.

**shawl** n шаль.

**she** pron она́.

**sheaf** n сноп; (of papers) свя́зка.

**shear** vt стричь impf, о~ pf. **shears** n pl но́жницы (-ц) pl.

**sheath** n но́жны (gen -жен) pl.

**shed**[1] n сара́й.

**shed**[2] vt (tears, blood, light) пролива́ть impf, проли́ть pf; (skin, clothes) сбра́сывать impf, сбро́сить pf.

**sheen** n блеск.

**sheep** n овца́. **sheepish** adj сконфу́женный. **sheepskin** n овчи́на; ~ **coat** дублёнка.

**sheer** adj (utter) су́щий; (textile) прозра́чный; (rock etc.) отве́сный.

**sheet** n (on bed) простыня́; (of glass, paper, etc.) лист.

**sheikh** n шейх.

**shelf** n по́лка.

**shell** n (of mollusc) ра́ковина; (seashell) раку́шка; (of tortoise) щит; (of egg, nut) скорлупа́; (of building) о́стов; (explosive) снаря́д; vt (peas etc.) лущи́ть impf, об~ pf; (bombard) обстре́ливать impf, обстреля́ть pf. **shellfish** n (mollusc) моллю́ск; (crustacean) ракообра́зное sb.

**shelter** n убе́жище; vt (provide with refuge) приюти́ть pf, vt & i укрыва́ть(ся) impf, укры́ть(ся) pf.

**shelve**[1] vt (defer) откла́дывать impf, отложи́ть pf.

**shelve**[2] vi (slope) отло́го спуска́ться impf.

**shelving** n (shelves) стелла́ж.

**shepherd** n пасту́х; vt проводи́ть impf, провести́ pf.

**sherry** n хе́рес.

**shield** n щит; vt защища́ть impf, защити́ть pf.

**shift** vt & i (change position) перемеща́ть(ся) impf, перемести́ть(ся) pf; (change) меня́ть(ся) impf; n переме́на; (of workers) сме́на; ~ **work** сме́нная рабо́та. **shifty** adj ско́льзкий.

**shimmer** vi мерца́ть impf; n мерца́ние.

**shin** n го́лень.

**shine** vi свети́ть(ся) impf; (glitter) блесте́ть impf; (excel) блиста́ть impf; (sun, eyes) сия́ть impf; vt (a light) освеща́ть impf, освети́ть pf фонарём (on +acc); n гля́нец.

**shingle** n (pebbles) га́лька.

**shingles** n опоя́сывающий лиша́й.

**shiny** adj блестя́щий.

**ship** n кора́бль m; су́дно; (transport) перевози́ть impf, перевезти́ pf; (dispatch) отправля́ть impf, отпра́вить pf. **shipbuilding** n судостро́и́тельство. **shipment** n (dispatch) отпра́вка; (goods) па́ртия. **shipping** n суда́ (-до́в) pl. **shipshape** adv в по́лном поря́дке. **shipwreck** n кораблекруше́ние; **be** ~**ed** терпе́ть impf, по~ pf кораблекруше́ние. **shipyard** n верфь.

**shirk** vt уви́ливать impf, увильну́ть pf от+gen.

**shirt** n руба́шка.

**shit** (*vulg*) *n* говно́; *vi* срать *impf*, по~ *pf*.

**shiver** *vi* (*tremble*) дрожа́ть *impf*; *n* дрожь.

**shoal** *n* (*of fish*) ста́я.

**shock** *n* (*emotional*) потрясе́ние; (*impact*) уда́р, толчо́к; (*electr*) уда́р то́ком; (*med*) шок; *vt* шоки́ровать *impf*.

**shocking** *adj* (*outrageous*) сканда́льный; (*awful*) ужа́сный.

**shoddy** *adj* халту́рный.

**shoe** *n* ту́фля; *vt* подко́вывать *impf*, подкова́ть *pf*. **shoe-lace** *n* шнуро́к. **shoe-maker** *n* сапо́жник. **shoe-string** *n*: on a ~ с небольши́ми сре́дствами.

**shoo** *int* кш!; *vt* прогоня́ть *impf*, прогна́ть *pf*.

**shoot** *vt* & *i* стреля́ть *impf*, вы́стрелить *pf* (*a gun* за +*gen*; *at* в+*acc*); (*arrow*) пуска́ть *impf*, пусти́ть *pf*; (*kill*) застрели́ть *pf*; (*execute*) расстре́ливать *impf*, расстреля́ть *pf*; (*hunt*) охо́титься *impf* на+*acc*; (*football*) бить *impf* (по воро́там); (*cin*) снима́ть *impf*, снять *pf* (*фильм*); *vi* (*go swiftly*) проноси́ться *impf*, пронести́сь *pf*; ~ **down** (*aircraft*) сбива́ть *impf*, сбить *pf*; ~ **up** (*grow*) бы́стро расти́ *impf*, по~ *pf*; (*prices*) подска́кивать *impf*, подскочи́ть *pf*; *n* (*branch*) росто́к, побе́г; (*hunt*) охо́та. **shooting** *n* стрельба́; (*hunting*) охо́та; ~**-gallery** тир.

**shop** *n* магази́н, (*workshop*) мастерска́я *sb*, цех; ~ **assistant** продаве́ц, -вщи́ца; ~**-lifter** магази́нный вор; ~**-lifting** *n* воровство́ в магази́нах;

~ **steward** цехово́й ста́роста *m*; ~**-window** витри́на; *vi* де́лать *impf*, с~ *pf* поку́пки (*f pl*). **shopkeeper** *n* ла́вочник. **shopper** *n* покупа́тель *m*, ~ница. **shopping** *n* поку́пки *f pl*; go, do one's ~ де́лать *impf*, с~ *pf* поку́пки; ~ **centre** торго́вый центр.

**shore**[1] *n* бе́рег.

**shore**[2] *vt*: ~ **up** подпира́ть *impf*, подпере́ть *pf*.

**short** *adj* коро́ткий; (*not tall*) ни́зкого ро́ста; (*deficient*) недоста́точный; be ~ of испы́тывать *impf*, испыта́ть *pf* недоста́ток в+*prep*; (*curt*) ре́зкий; in ~ одни́м сло́вом; ~**-change** обсчи́тывать *impf*, обсчита́ть *pf*; ~ **circuit** коро́ткое замыка́ние; ~ **cut** коро́ткий путь *m*; ~ **list** оконча́тельный спи́сок; ~**-list** включа́ть *impf*, включи́ть *pf* в оконча́тельный спи́сок; ~**-lived** недолгове́чный; ~**-sighted** близору́кий; (*fig*) недальнови́дный; ~ **story** расска́з; in ~ **supply** дефици́тный; ~**-tempered** вспы́льчивый; ~ **term** краткосро́чный; ~**-wave** коротково́лновый. **shortage** *n* недоста́ток. **shortcoming** *n* недоста́ток. **shorten** *vt* & *i* укора́чивать(ся) *impf*, укороти́ть(ся) *pf*. **shortfall** *n* дефици́т. **shorthand** *n* стеногра́фия; ~ **typist** машини́стка-стенографи́стка. **shortly** *adv*: ~ **after** вско́ре (*по́сле*+*gen*); ~ **before** незадо́лго (*до*+*gen*).

**shorts** *n pl* шо́рты (-т) *pl*.

**shot** *n* (*discharge of gun*) вы́стрел; (*pellets*) дробь; (*person*) стрело́к; (*attempt*) попы́тка; (*phot*) сни́мок; (*cin*) кадр; (sport) (stroke) уда́р; (throw) бросо́к; like a ~ неме́дленно; ~-gun дробови́к.

**should** v aux (ought) до́лжен (бы) +inf: you ~ know that вы должны́ э́то знать; he ~ be here soon он до́лжен бы быть тут ско́ро; (conditional) бы +past: I ~ say я бы сказа́л(а); I ~ like я бы хоте́л(а).

**shoulder** n плечо́; vi крича́ть ~-blade лопа́тка; ~-strap брете́лька; взва́ливать impf, взвали́ть pf на пле́чи; (fig) брать impf, взять pf на себя́.

**shout** n крик; vi крича́ть impf, кри́кнуть pf; ~ down перекри́кивать impf, перекрича́ть pf.

**shove** n толчо́к; vt & i толка́ть(ся) impf, толкну́ть pf; ~ off (coll) убира́ться impf, убра́ться pf.

**shovel** n лопа́та; vt (~ up) сгреба́ть impf, сгрести́ pf.

**show** vt пока́зывать impf, показа́ть pf; (exhibit) выставля́ть impf, вы́ставить pf; (film etc.) демонстри́ровать impf, про~ pf; vi (also ~ up) быть ви́дным, заме́тным; ~ off (vi) привлека́ть impf, привле́чь pf к себе́ внима́ние; ~ up see vi; (appear) появля́ться impf, появи́ться pf; n (exhibition) вы́ставка; (theat) спекта́кль m; (effect) ви́димость; ~ of hands голосова́ние подня́тием руки́; ~-case витри́на; ~-jumping соревнова́ние по ска́чкам; ~-room сало́н. **showdown** n развя́зка.

**shower** n (rain) до́ждик; (hail, fig) град; (~-bath) душ; vt осыпа́ть impf, осы́пать pf +instr (on +acc); vi прини-

ма́ть impf, приня́ть pf душ.

**showery** adj дождли́вый.

**showpiece** n образе́ц. **showy** adj показно́й.

**shrapnel** n шрапне́ль.

**shred** n клочо́к; **not a ~** ни ка́пли; vt мельчи́ть impf, из~ pf.

**shrewd** adj проница́тельный.

**shriek** vi визжа́ть impf; взви́гнуть pf.

**shrill** adj пронзи́тельный.

**shrimp** n креве́тка.

**shrine** n святы́ня.

**shrink** vi сади́ться impf, сесть pf; (recoil) отпря́нуть pf; vt вызыва́ть impf, вы́звать pf уса́дку у+gen; ~ from избега́ть impf +gen. **shrinkage** n уса́дка.

**shrivel** vi смо́рщиваться impf, смо́рщиться pf.

**shroud** n са́ван; vt (fig) оку́тывать impf, оку́тать pf (in +instr).

**Shrove Tuesday** вто́рник на ма́сленой неде́ле.

**shrub** n куст. **shrubbery** n куста́рник.

**shrug** vt & i пожима́ть impf, пожа́ть pf (плеча́ми).

**shudder** n содрога́ние; vi дрога́ться impf, содрогну́ться pf.

**shuffle** vt & i (one's feet) ша́ркать impf (нога́ми); vt (cards) тасова́ть impf, с~ pf; n тасо́вка.

**shun** vt избега́ть impf +gen.

**shunt** vi (rly) маневри́ровать impf, с~ pf; vt (rly) переводи́ть impf, перевести́ pf на запасны́й путь.

**shut** vt & i (also ~ down) закрыва́ть(ся) impf, закры́ть(ся) pf; ~ out (exclude) исключа́ть impf, исключи́ть *pf;* (*fence off*) загора́живать *impf,* загороди́ть *pf;* (*keep out*) не пуска́ть *impf,* пусти́ть *pf,* ~ **up** (*vi*) замолча́ть *pf;* (*imper*) заткни́сь!

**shutter** *n* ста́вень *m;* (*phot*) затво́р.

**shuttle** *n* челно́к.

**shy**[1] *adj* засте́нчивый.

**shy**[2] *vi* (*in alarm*) отпря́дывать *impf,* отпря́нуть *pf.*

**Siberia** *n* Сиби́рь *f.* **Siberian** *adj* сиби́рский; *n* сибиря́к, -я́чка.

**sick** *adj* больно́й; **be** ~ (*vomit*) рвать *impf,* вы́~ *pf impers* +*acc:* **he was** ~ его́ вы́рвало; **feel** ~ тошни́ть *impf impers* +*acc;* **be** ~ **of** надоеда́ть *impf,* надое́сть *pf* +*nom* (*object*) & *dat* (*subject*): **I'm** ~ **of her** она́ мне надое́ла; ~-**leave** о́тпуск по боле́зни. **sicken** *vt* вызыва́ть *impf,* вы́звать *pf* тошноту́, (*disgust*) отвраще́ние, у+*gen; vi* заболева́ть *impf,* заболе́ть *pf.* **sickening** *adj* отврати́тельный.

**sickle** *n* серп.

**sickly** *adj* боле́зненный; (*nauseating*) тошнотво́рный. **sickness** *n* боле́знь; (*vomiting*) тошнота́.

**side** *n* сторона́; (*of body*) бок; ~ **by** ~ ря́дом (**with** c+*instr*); **on the** ~ на стороне́; *vi:* ~ **with** встава́ть *impf,* встать *pf* на сто́рону+*gen;* ~-**effect** побо́чное де́йствие; ~-**step** (*fig*) уклоня́ться *impf,* уклони́ться *pf* от+*gen;* ~-**track** (*distract*) отвлека́ть *impf,* отвле́чь *pf.* **sideboard** *n* буфе́т; *pl* ба́ки (-к) *pl.* **sidelight** *n* боково́й фона́рь *m.* **sideline** *n* (*work*) побо́чная рабо́та. **sidelong** *adj* (*glance*) косо́й.

**sideways** *adv* бо́ком.

**siding** *n* запасно́й путь *m.*

**sidle** *vi:* ~ **up to** подходи́ть *impf,* подойти́ *pf* к (+*dat*) бочко́м.

**siege** *n* оса́да; **lay** ~ **to** оса́ждать *impf,* осади́ть *pf;* **raise the** ~ **of** снима́ть *impf,* снять *pf* оса́ду c+*gen.*

**sieve** *n* си́то; *vt* просе́ивать *impf,* просе́ять *pf.*

**sift** *vt* просе́ивать *impf,* просе́ять *pf;* (*fig*) тща́тельно рассма́тривать *impf,* рассмотре́ть *pf.*

**sigh** *vi* вздыха́ть *impf,* вздохну́ть *pf; n* вздох.

**sight** *n* (*faculty*) зре́ние; (*view*) вид; (*spectacle*) зре́лище; *pl* достопримеча́тельности *f pl;* (*on gun*) прице́л; **at first** ~ с пе́рвого взгля́да; **catch** ~ **of** уви́деть *pf;* **know by** ~ знать *impf* в лицо́; **lose** ~ **of** теря́ть *impf,* по~ *pf* из ви́ду; (*fig*) упуска́ть *impf,* упусти́ть *pf* из ви́ду.

**sign** *n* знак; (*indication*) при́знак; (~*board*) вы́веска; *vt* & *abs* подпи́сывать(ся) *impf,* подписа́ть(ся) *pf; vi* (*give* ~) подава́ть *impf,* пода́ть *pf* знак; ~ **on** (*as unemployed*) запи́сываться *impf,* записа́ться *pf* в списки безрабо́тных; (~ **up**) нанима́ться *impf,* наня́ться *pf.*

**signal** *n* сигна́л; *vt* & *i* сигнализи́ровать *impf* & *pf.* **signal-box** *n* сигна́льная бу́дка.

**signalman** *n* сигна́льщик.

**signatory** *n* подписа́вший *sb;* (*of treaty*) сторона́, подписа́вшая догово́р.

**signature** *n* по́дпись.

**significance** *n* значе́ние. **significant** *adj* значи́тельный.

**signify** vt означа́ть impf.

**signpost** n указа́тельный столб.

**silage** n си́лос.

**silence** n молча́ние, тишина́; vt заста́вить pf замолча́ть.

**silencer** n глуши́тель m. **silent** adj (not speaking) безмо́лвный; (of film) немо́й; (without noise) ти́хий; be ~ молча́ть impf.

**silhouette** n силуэ́т; vt: be ~d выри́совываться impf, вы́рисоваться pf (against на фо́не+gen).

**silicon** n кре́мний. **silicone** n силико́н.

**silk** n шёлк; attrib шёлковый. **silky** adj шелкови́стый.

**sill** n подоко́нник.

**silly** adj глу́пый.

**silo** n си́лос.

**silt** n ил.

**silver** n серебро́; (cutlery) столо́вое серебро́; (of ~) сере́бряный; (silvery) сере́бристый; ~-plated посере́брённый. **silversmith** n сере́бряных дел ма́стер. **silverware** n столо́вое серебро́. **silvery** adj сере́бристый.

**similar** adj подо́бный (to +dat). **similarity** n схо́дство. **similarly** adv подо́бным о́бразом.

**simile** n сравне́ние.

**simmer** vt кипяти́ть impf на ме́дленном огне́; vi кипе́ть impf на ме́дленном огне́; ~ down успока́иваться impf, успоко́иться pf.

**simper** vi жема́нно улыба́ться impf, улыбну́ться pf.

**simple** adj просто́й; ~-minded тупова́тый. **simplicity** n простота́. **simplify** vt упроща́ть impf, упрости́ть pf. **simply** adv про́сто.

**simulate** vt притворя́ться impf, притвори́ться pf +instr; (conditions etc.) модели́ровать impf & pf. **simulated** adj (pearls etc.) иску́сственный.

**simultaneous** adj одновре́менный.

**sin** n грех; vi греши́ть impf, со~ pf.

**since** adv с тех пор; prep c+gen; conj с тех пор как; (reason) так как.

**sincere** adj и́скренний. **sincerely** adv и́скренне; yours ~ и́скренне Ваш. **sincerity** n и́скренность.

**sinew** n сухожи́лие.

**sinful** adj гре́шный.

**sing** vt & i петь impf, про~, с~ pf.

**singe** vt пали́ть impf, о~ pf.

**singer** n певе́ц, -ви́ца.

**single** adj оди́н; (unmarried) (of man) нежена́тый; (of woman) незаму́жняя; (bed) односпа́льный; ~-handed без посторо́нней по́мощи; ~-minded целеустремлённый; ~ parent мать/оте́ц-одино́чка; ~ room ко́мната на одного́; n (ticket) биле́т в оди́н коне́ц; pl (tennis etc.) одино́чная игра́ vt: ~ out выделя́ть impf, вы́делить pf. **singly** adv по-одному́.

**singular** n еди́нственное число́; adj еди́нственный; (unusual) необыча́йный. **singularly** adv необыча́йно.

**sinister** adj злове́щий.

**sink** vi (descend slowly) опуска́ться impf, опусти́ться pf; (in mud etc.) погружа́ться impf, погрузи́ться pf; (in water) тону́ть impf, по~ pf; vt (ship) топи́ть impf, по~ pf (*pipe*, *post*) вка́пывать *impf*, вкопа́ть *pf*; *n* ра́ковина.

**sinner** *n* гре́шник, -ица.

**sinus** *n* па́зуха.

**sip** *vt* пить *impf*, ма́ленькими глотка́ми; *n* ма́ленький глото́к.

**siphon** *n* сифо́н; ~ **off** (*also fig*) перека́чивать *impf*, перекача́ть *pf*.

**sir** *n* сэр.

**siren** *n* сире́на.

**sister** *n* сестра́; ~**-in-law** (*husband's sister*) золо́вка; (*wife's sister*) своя́ченица; (*brother's wife*) неве́стка.

**sit** *vi* (*be sitting*) сиде́ть *impf*; (~ **down**) сади́ться *impf*, сесть *pf*; (*parl*, *law*) заседа́ть *impf*; *vt* уса́живать *impf*, усади́ть *pf*; (*exam*) сдава́ть *impf*; ~ **back** отки́дываться *impf*, отки́нуться *pf*; ~ **down** сади́ться *impf*, сесть *pf*; ~ **up** приподнима́ться *impf*, приподня́ться *pf*; (*not go to bed*) не ложи́ться *impf* спать.

**site** *n* (*where a thing takes place*) ме́сто; (*where a thing is*) местоположе́ние.

**sitting** *n* (*parl etc.*) заседа́ние; (*for meal*) сме́на; ~**-room** гости́ная *sb*.

**situated** *adj*: **be** ~ находи́ться *impf*. **situation** *n* местоположе́ние; (*circumstances*) положе́ние; (*job*) ме́сто.

**six** *adj* & *n* шесть; (*number 6*) шестёрка. **sixteen** *adj* & *n* шестна́дцать. **sixteenth** *adj* & *n* шестна́дцатый. **sixth** *adj* & *n* шесто́й; (*fraction*) шеста́я *sb*. **sixtieth** *adj* & *n* шестидеся́тый. **sixty** *adj* & *n* шестьдеся́т; *pl* (*decade*) шестидеся́тые го́ды (-до́в) *m pl*.

**size** *n* разме́р; *vt*: ~ **up** оце́нивать *impf*, оцени́ть *pf*. **sizeable** *adj* значи́тельный.

**sizzle** *vi* шипе́ть *impf*.

**skate**[1] *n* (*fish*) скат.

**skate**[2] *n* (*ice*~) конёк; (*roller*~) конёк на ро́ликах; *vi* ката́ться *impf* на конька́х; **skating-rink** като́к.

**skeleton** *n* скеле́т.

**sketch** *n* зарисо́вка; (*theat*) скетч; *vt* & *i* зарисо́вывать *impf*, зарисова́ть *pf*. **sketchy** *adj* схемати́ческий; (*superficial*) пове́рхностный.

**skew** *adj* косо́й; **on the** ~ ко́со.

**skewer** *n* ве́ртел.

**ski** *n* лы́жа; ~**-jump** трампли́н; *vi* ходи́ть *impf* на лы́жах.

**skid** *n* зано́с; *vi* заноси́ть *impf*, занести́ *pf impers+acc*.

**skier** *n* лы́жник. **skiing** *n* лы́жный спорт.

**skilful** *adj* иску́сный. **skill** *n* мастерство́; (*countable*) поле́зный на́вык. **skilled** *adj* иску́сный; (*trained*) квалифици́рованный.

**skim** *vt* снима́ть *impf*, снять *pf* (*cream* сли́вки *pl*, *scum* на́кипь) c+*gen*; *vi* скользи́ть *impf* (**over**, **along** по+*dat*); ~ **through** бе́гло просма́тривать *impf*, посмотре́ть *pf*; *adj*: ~ **milk** снято́е молоко́.

**skimp** *vt* & *i* скупи́ться *impf* (**на**+*acc*). **skimpy** *adj* ску́дный.

**skin** *n* ко́жа; (*hide*) шку́ра; (*of fruit etc.*) кожура́; (*on milk*) пёнка; *vt* сдира́ть *impf*, содра́ть *pf* ко́жу, шку́ру, c+*gen*; (*fruit*) снима́ть *impf*, снять *pf* кожуру́ c+*gen*. **skinny** *adj* то́щий.

**skip**[1] *vi* скака́ть *impf*; (*with rope*) пры́гать *impf* че́рез

скака́лку; vt (omit) пропуска́ть impf, пропусти́ть pf.
**skip²** n (container) скип.
**skipper** n (naut) шки́пер.
**skirmish** n схва́тка.
**skirt** n ю́бка; vt (go round) обойти́ pf стороно́й; ~ing-board пли́нтус.
**skittle** n ке́гля; pl ке́гли f pl.
**skulk** vi (hide) скрыва́ться impf; (creep) кра́сться impf.
**skull** n че́реп.
**skunk** n скунс.
**sky** n не́бо. **skylark** n жа́воронок. **skylight** n окно́ в кры́ше. **skyline** n горизо́нт. **skyscraper** n небоскрёб.
**slab** n плита́; (of cake etc.) кусо́к.
**slack** adj (loose) сла́бый; (sluggish) вя́лый; (negligent) небре́жный; n (of rope) слабина́; pl брю́ки (-к) pl. **slacken** vt ослабля́ть impf, осла́бить pf; vt & i (slow down) замедля́ть(ся) impf, заме́длить(ся) pf; vi ослабева́ть impf, осла́беть pf.
**slag** n шлак.
**slam** vt & i захло́пывать(ся) impf, захло́пнуть(ся) pf.
**slander** n клевета́; vt клевета́ть impf, на~ pf на+acc. **slanderous** adj клеветни́ческий.
**slang** n жарго́н. **slangy** adj жарго́нный.
**slant** vt & i наклоня́ть(ся) impf, наклони́ть(ся) pf; n укло́н. **slanting** adj косо́й.
**slap** vt шлёпать impf, шлёпнуть pf, шлепо́к; adv пря́мо. **slapdash** adj небре́жный. **slapstick** n фарс.
**slash** vt (cut) поро́ть impf, рас~ pf; (fig) уре́зывать impf, уре́зать pf; n разре́з;

(sign) дробь.
**slat** n пла́нка.
**slate¹** n сла́нец; (for roofing) (кро́вельная) пли́тка.
**slate²** vt (criticize) разноси́ть impf, разнести́ pf.
**slaughter** n (of animals) убо́й; (massacre) резня́; vt (animals) ре́зать impf, за~ pf; (people) убива́ть impf, уби́ть pf. **slaughterhouse** n бо́йня.
**Slav** n славяни́н, -я́нка; adj славя́нский.
**slave** n раб, рабы́ня; vi рабо́тать impf как раб. **slavery** n ра́бство.
**Slavic** adj славя́нский.
**slavish** adj ра́бский.
**Slavonic** adj славя́нский.
**slay** vt убива́ть impf, уби́ть pf.
**sleazy** adj убо́гий.
**sledge** n са́ни (-не́й) pl.
**sledge-hammer** n кува́лда.
**sleek** adj гла́дкий.
**sleep** n сон; **go to ~** засыпа́ть impf, засну́ть pf; vi спать impf; (spend the night) ночева́ть impf, пере~ pf. **sleeper** n спя́щий sb; (on track) шпа́ла; (sleeping-car) спа́льный ваго́н. **sleeping** adj спя́щий; **~-bag** спа́льный мешо́к; **~-car** спа́льный ваго́н; **~-pill** снотво́рная табле́тка. **sleepless** adj бессо́нный. **sleepy** adj сонли́вый.
**sleet** n мо́крый снег.
**sleeve** n рука́в; (of record) конве́рт.
**sleigh** n са́ни (-не́й) pl.
**sleight-of-hand** n ло́вкость рук.
**slender** adj (slim) то́нкий; (meagre) ску́дный; (of hope etc.) сла́бый.
**sleuth** n сы́щик.

**slice** n кусо́к; vt (~ up) нареза́ть impf, наре́зать pf.
**slick** adj (dextrous) ло́вкий; (crafty) хи́трый; n нефтяна́я плёнка.
**slide** vi скользи́ть impf; vt (drawer etc.) задвига́ть impf, задви́нуть pf, n (children's ~) го́рка; (microscope ~) предме́тное стекло́; (phot) диапозити́в, слайд; (for hair) зако́лка. **sliding** adj (door) задвижно́й.
**slight**[1] adj (slender) то́нкий; (inconsiderable) небольшо́й; (light) лёгкий; not the ~est ни мале́йшего, ~шей (gen); not in the ~est ничу́ть.
**slight**[2] vt пренебрега́ть impf, пренебре́чь pf +instr; n оби́да.
**slightly** adv слегка́, немно́го.
**slim** adj то́нкий; (chance etc.) сла́бый; vi худе́ть impf, по—pf.
**slime** n слизь. **slimy** adj сли́зистый; (person) скользкий.
**sling** vt (throw) швыря́ть impf, швырну́ть pf; (suspend) подве́шивать impf, подве́сить pf; n (med) пе́ревязь.
**slink** vi кра́сться impf.
**slip** n (mistake) оши́бка; (garment) комбина́ция; (pillowcase) на́волочка; (paper) листо́чек; ~ of the tongue обмо́лвка; give the ~ ускользну́ть pf от+gen; vi скользи́ть impf, скользну́ть pf; (fall over) поскользну́ться pf; (from hands etc.) выска́льзывать impf, вы́скользнуть pf; vt (insert) сова́ть impf, су́нуть pf; ~ off (depart) ускольза́ть impf, ускользну́ть pf; ~ up (make mistake) ошиба́ться impf, ошиби́ться pf. **slipper** n та́пка. **slippery** adj ско́льзкий.

**slit** vt разреза́ть impf, разре́зать pf; (throat) перере́зать pf; n щель; (cut) разре́з.
**slither** vi скользи́ть impf.
**sliver** n ще́пка.
**slob** n неря́ха m & f.
**slobber** vi пуска́ть impf, пусти́ть pf слю́ни.
**slog** vt (hit) си́льно ударя́ть impf, уда́рить pf; (work) упо́рно рабо́тать impf.
**slogan** n ло́зунг.
**slop** n: pl помо́и (-о́ев) pl; vt & i выплёскивать(ся) impf, вы́плескать(ся) pf.
**slope** n (artificial) накло́н; (geog) склон; vi име́ть impf накло́н, **sloping** adj накло́нный.
**sloppy** adj (work) неря́шливый; (sentimental) сентимента́льный.
**slot** n отве́рстие; ~-machine автома́т; vt: ~ in вставля́ть impf, вста́вить pf.
**sloth** n лень.
**slouch** vi (stoop) суту́литься impf.
**slovenly** adj неря́шливый.
**slow** adj ме́дленный; (tardy) медли́тельный; (stupid) тупо́й; (business) вя́лый; be ~ (clock) отстава́ть impf, отста́ть pf; adv ме́дленно; vt & i (~ down, up) замедля́ть(ся) impf, заме́длить(ся) pf.
**sludge** n (mud) грязь; (sediment) отсто́й.
**slug** n (zool) слизня́к.
**sluggish** adj вя́лый.
**sluice** n шлюз.
**slum** n трущо́ба.
**slumber** n сон; vi спать impf.
**slump** n спад; vi ре́зко па́дать impf, (у)па́сть pf; (of person) сва́ливаться impf, свали́ться pf.

**slur** *vt* говори́ть *impf* невня́тно; *n* (*stigma*) пятно́.

**slush** *n* сля́коть.

**slut** *n* (*sloven*) неря́ха; (*trollop*) потаску́ха.

**sly** *adj* хи́трый; on the ~ тайко́м.

**smack**[1] *vi*: ~ of па́хнуть *impf* +*instr*.

**smack**[2] *n* (*slap*) шлепо́к; *vt* шлёпать *impf*, шлёпнуть *pf*.

**small** *adj* ма́ленький, небольшо́й, ма́лый; (*of agent, particles; petty*) ме́лкий; ~ change ме́лочь; ~-scale мелкомасшта́бный; ~ talk све́тская бесе́да.

**smart**[1] *vi* са́днить *impf impers.*

**smart**[2] *adj* элега́нтный; (*brisk*) бы́стрый; (*cunning*) ло́вкий; (*sharp*) смека́листый (*coll*).

**smash** *vt & i* разбива́ть(ся) *impf*, разби́ть(ся) *pf*; ~ into вреза́ться *impf*, вре́заться *pf* в+*acc*; *n* (*crash*) гро́хот; (*collision*) столкнове́ние; (*blow*) си́льный уда́р.

**smattering** *n* пове́рхностное зна́ние.

**smear** *vt* сма́зывать *impf*, сма́зать *pf*; (*dirty*) па́чкать *impf*, ис~ *pf*; (*discredit*) поро́чить *impf*, о~ *pf*; *n* (*spot*) пятно́; (*slander*) клевета́; (*med*) мазо́к.

**smell** *n* (*sense*) обоня́ние; (*odour*) за́пах; *vt* чу́вствовать *impf* за́пах+*gen*; (*sniff*) ню́хать *impf*, по~ *pf*; *vi* ~ of па́хнуть *impf* +*instr*. **smelly** *adj* воню́чий.

**smelt** *vt* (*ore*) пла́вить *impf*; (*metal*) выплавля́ть *impf*, вы́плавить *pf*.

**smile** *vi* улыба́ться *impf*, улыбну́ться *pf*; *n* улы́бка.

**smirk** *vi* ухмыля́ться *impf*,

ухмыльну́ться *pf*; *n* ухмы́лка.

**smith** *n* кузне́ц.

**smithereens** *n*: (in)to ~ вдре́безги.

**smithy** *n* ку́зница.

**smock** *n* блу́за.

**smog** *n* тума́н (с ды́мом).

**smoke** *n* дым; ~-screen ды́мовая заве́са; *vt & i* (*cigarette etc.*) кури́ть *impf*, по~ *pf*; *vt* (*cure; colour*) копти́ть *impf*, за~ *pf*; *vi* (*abnormally*) дыми́ть *impf*; (*of fire*) дыми́ться *impf*. **smoker** *n* кури́льщик, -ица, куря́щий *sb*. **smoky** *adj* ды́мный.

**smooth** *adj* (*surface etc.*) гла́дкий; (*movement etc.*) пла́вный; *vt* пригла́живать *impf*, пригла́дить *pf*; ~ over сгла́живать *impf*, сгла́дить *pf*.

**smother** *vt* (*stifle, also fig*) души́ть *impf*, за~ *pf*; (*cover*) покрыва́ть *impf*, покры́ть *pf*.

**smoulder** *vi* тлеть *impf*.

**smudge** *n* пятно́; *vt* сма́зывать *impf*, сма́зать *pf*.

**smug** *adj* самодово́льный.

**smuggle** *vt* провози́ть *impf*, провезти́ *pf* контраба́ндой; (*convey secretly*) проноси́ть *impf*, пронести́ *pf*. **smuggler** *n* контрабанди́ст. **smuggling** *n* контраба́нда.

**smut** *n* са́жа; (*indecency*) непристо́йность. **smutty** *adj* гря́зный; непристо́йный.

**snack** *n* заку́ска; ~ bar заку́сочная *sb*, (*within institution*) буфе́т.

**snag** *n* (*fig*) загво́здка; *vt* зацепля́ть *impf*, зацепи́ть *pf*.

**snail** *n* ули́тка.

**snake** *n* змея́.

**snap** *vi* (*of dog or person*)

огрыза́ться *impf*, огрызну́ться *pf* (at на+*acc*); *vt & i* (break) обрыва́ть(ся) *impf*, оборва́ть(ся) *pf*; *vt* (make sound) щёлкать *impf*, щёлкнуть *pf* +*instr*; ~ up (buy) расхва́тывать *impf*, расхвата́ть *pf*; *n* (sound) щёлк; (photo) сни́мок; *adj* (decision) скоропали́тельный. **snappy** *adj* (brisk) живо́й; (stylish) шика́рный. **snapshot** *n* сни́мок.

**snare** *n* лову́шка.

**snarl** *vi* рыча́ть *impf*, за~ *pf*; *n* рыча́ние.

**snatch** *vt* хвата́ть *impf*, (с)хвати́ть *pf*; *vi*: ~ at хвата́ться *impf*, (с)хвати́ться *pf* за+*acc*; *n* (fragment) обры́вок.

**sneak** *vi* (slink) кра́сться *impf*; *vt* (steal) стащи́ть *pf*; *n* я́бедник, -ица (coll). **sneaking** *adj* та́йный. **sneaky** *adj* лука́вый.

**sneer** *vi* насмеха́ться *impf* (at над+*instr*).

**sneeze** *vi* чиха́ть *impf*, чихну́ть *pf*; *n* чиха́нье.

**snide** *adj* еxи́дный.

**sniff** *vi* ню́хать *impf*, шмыгну́ть *pf* но́сом; *vt* ню́хать *impf*, по~ *pf*.

**snigger** *vi* хихи́кать *impf*, хихикнуть *pf*; *n* хихи́канье.

**snip** *vt* ре́зать *impf* (но́жницами); ~ off среза́ть *impf*, сре́зать *pf*.

**snipe** *vi* стреля́ть *impf* из укры́тия (at в+*acc*); (fig) напада́ть *impf*, напа́сть *pf* на+*acc*. **sniper** *n* сна́йпер.

**snippet** *n* отре́зок; *pl* (of news etc.) обры́вки *m pl*.

**snivel** *vi* (run at nose) распу́скать *impf*, распусти́ть *pf* со́пли; (whimper) хны́кать *impf*.

**snob** *n* сноб. **snobbery** *n* сно-

би́зм. **snobbish** *adj* сноби́стский.

**snoop** *vi* шпио́нить *impf*; ~ about разню́хивать *impf*, разню́хать *pf*.

**snooty** *adj* чва́нный.

**snooze** *vi* вздремну́ть *pf*; *n* коро́ткий сон.

**snorkel** *n* шно́ркель *m*.

**snort** *vi* фы́ркать *impf*, фы́ркнуть *pf*.

**snot** *n* со́пли (-ле́й) *pl*.

**snout** *n* ры́ло, мо́рда.

**snow** *n* снег; ~-white белосне́жный; *vi*: it ~ing, it snows идёт снег; ~ed under зава́ленный рабо́той; we were ~ed up, в нас занесло́ сне́гом. **snowball** *n* снежо́к. **snowdrop** *n* подсне́жник. **snowflake** *n* снежи́нка. **snowman** *n* сне́жная ба́ба. **snowstorm** *n* мете́ль. **snowy** *adj* сне́жный; (snow-white) белосне́жный.

**snub** *vt* игнори́ровать *impf & pf*.

**snuff**[1] *n* (tobacco) нюха́тельный таба́к.

**snuff**[2] *vt*: ~ out туши́ть *impf*, по~ *pf*.

**snuffle** *vi* сопе́ть *impf*.

**snug** *adj* ую́тный.

**snuggle** *vi*: ~ up to прижима́ться *impf*, прижа́ться *pf* к+*dat*.

**so** *adv* так; (in this way) так; (thus, at beginning of sentence) ита́к; (also) та́кже, то́же; *conj* (therefore) так что, поэ́тому; **and ~ on** и так да́лее; **if ~** в тако́м слу́чае; **~ ... as** так(о́й) ... как; **~ as to** с тем что́бы; **~-called** так называ́емый; (in) **~ far as** насто́лько;

long! пока́!; ~ long as поско́льку; ~ much настолько; ~ much до тако́й сте́пени; ~ much the better тем лу́чше; ~ that что́бы; ... that так... что; ~ to say, speak что́ сказа́ть; ~ what? ну и что?

soak vt мочи́ть impf, на~ pf; (drench) прома́чивать impf, промочи́ть pf; ~ up впи́тывать impf, впита́ть pf; vi: ~ through проса́чиваться impf, просочи́ться pf; get ~ed промока́ть impf, промо́кнуть pf.

soap n мы́ло; vt мы́лить impf, на~ pf; ~ opera многосери́йная переда́ча; ~ powder стира́льный порошо́к. soapy adj мы́льный.

soar vi пари́ть impf; (prices) подска́кивать impf, подскочи́ть pf.

sob vi рыда́ть impf; n рыда́ние.

sober adj тре́звый; vt & i: ~ up отрезвля́ть(ся) impf, отрезви́ть(ся) pf. sobriety n тре́звость.

soccer n футбо́л.

sociable adj общи́тельный. social adj обще́ственный, социа́льный; S~ Democrat социа́л-демокра́т; ~ sciences обще́ственные нау́ки f pl; ~ security социа́льное обеспе́чение. socialism n социали́зм. socialist n социали́ст; adj социалисти́ческий. socialize vt обща́ться impf. society n о́бщество. sociological adj социологи́ческий. sociologist n социо́лог. sociology n социоло́гия.

sock n носо́к.

socket n (eye) впа́дина; (electr)

штѐпсель m; (for bulb) патро́н.

soda n со́да; ~-water содо́вая вода́.

sodden adj промо́кший.

sodium n на́трий.

sodomy n педера́стия.

sofa n дива́н.

soft adj мя́гкий; (sound) ти́хий; (colour) нея́ркий; (malleable) ко́вкий; (tender) не́жный; ~ drink безалкого́льный напи́ток. soften vt & i смягча́ть(ся) impf, смягчи́ть(ся) pf. softness n мя́гкость. software n програ́ммное обеспе́чение.

soggy adj сыро́й.

soil¹ n по́чва.

soil² vt па́чкать impf, за~, ис~ pf.

solace n утеше́ние.

solar adj со́лнечный.

solder n припо́й; vt пая́ть impf; (~ together) спа́ивать impf, спая́ть pf. soldering iron n пая́льник.

soldier n солда́т.

sole¹ n (of foot, shoe) подо́шва.

sole² n (fish) морско́й язы́к.

sole³ adj еди́нственный.

solemn adj торже́ственный. solemnity n торже́ственность.

solicit vt проси́ть impf, по~ pf +acc, gen, o+prep; vi (of prostitute) пристава́ть impf к мужчи́нам. solicitor n адвока́т. solicitous adj забо́тливый.

solid adj (not liquid) твёрдый; (not hollow; continuous) сплошно́й; (firm) про́чный; (pure) чи́стый; n твёрдое те́ло; pl твёрдая пи́ща. solidarity n солида́рность. solidify vi затвердева́ть impf, затверде́-

**pf. solidity** n твёрдость; про́чность.

**soliloquy** n моноло́г.

**solitary** adj одино́кий, уединённый; ~ **confinement** одино́чное заключе́ние. **solitude** n одино́чество, уедине́ние.

**solo** n со́ло neut indecl; adj со́льный; adv со́ло. **soloist** n соли́ст, ~а.

**solstice** n солнцестоя́ние.

**soluble** adj раствори́мый. **solution** n раство́р; (of puzzle etc.) реше́ние. **solve** vt реша́ть impf, реши́ть pf. **solvent** adj растворя́ющий; (financially) платёжеспосо́бный; n раствори́тель m.

**sombre** adj мра́чный.

**some** adj & pron (any) како́й-нибудь; (a certain) како́й-то; (a certain amount or number of) не́который, or often expressed by noun in (partitive) gen; (several) не́сколько+gen; (~ people, things) не́которые pl; ~ **day** когда́-нибудь; ~ **more** ещё; ~ ... others ... други́е. **somebody, someone** n, pron (def) кто-то; (indef) кто́-нибудь. **somehow** adv ка́к-то; ка́к-нибудь; (for some reason) почему́-то; ~ **or other** так и́ли ина́че. **somersault** n са́льто neut indecl; vi кувыркаться impf, кувыр(к)ну́ться pf. **something** n & pron (def) что́-то; (indef) что́-нибудь; ~ **like** (approximately) приблизи́тельно; (a thing like) что́-то вро́де+gen. **sometime** adv не́когда; adj бы́вший. **sometimes** adv иногда́. **somewhat** adv не́сколько, дово́льно. **somewhere** adv (po-

sition) (def) где́-то; (indef) где́-нибудь; (motion) куда́-то; куда́-нибудь.

**son** n сын; ~-**in-law** зять m.

**sonata** n сона́та.

**song** n пе́сня.

**sonic** adj звуково́й.

**sonnet** n соне́т.

**soon** adv ско́ро; (early) ра́но; **as** ~ **as** как то́лько; **as** ~ **as possible** как мо́жно скоре́е; ~**er or later** ра́но и́ли по́здно; the ~**er the better** чем ра́ньше, тем лу́чше.

**soot** n са́жа, ко́поть.

**soothe** vt успока́ивать impf, успоко́ить pf; (pain) облегча́ть impf, облегчи́ть pf.

**sophisticated** adj (person) иску́шённый; (equipment) сло́жный.

**soporific** adj снотво́рный.

**soprano** n сопра́но (voice) neut & (person) f indecl.

**sorcerer** n колду́н. **sorcery** n колдовство́.

**sordid** adj гря́зный.

**sore** n боля́чка; adj больно́й; **my throat is** ~ у меня́ боли́т го́рло.

**sorrow** n печа́ль. **sorrowful** adj печа́льный. **sorry** adj жа́лкий; predic: **be** ~ жале́ть impf (about o+prep); жаль impers+dat (for +gen); ~! извини́(те)!

**sort** n род, вид, сорт; vt (also ~ **out**) сортирова́ть impf, рас~ pf; (also fig) разбира́ть impf, разобра́ть pf.

**sortie** n вы́лазка.

**SOS** n (ра́дио)сигна́л бе́дствия.

**soul** n душа́.

**sound**[1] adj (healthy, thorough) здоро́вый; (in good condition) испра́вный; (logical) здра́вый, разу́мный; (of sleep) кре́пкий.

**sound²** n (noise) звук, шум; attrib звуково́й; ~ effects звуковы́е эффе́кты m pl; vi звуча́ть impf, про~ pf.

**sound³** vt (naut) измеря́ть impf, изме́рить pf глубину́ +gen; ~ out выпы́тывать impf, по~ pf; n зонд.

**sound⁴** n (strait) проли́в.

**soup** n суп; vt: ~ed up форси́рованный.

**sour** adj ки́слый; ~ cream смета́на; vt & i (fig) озлобля́ть(ся) impf, озло́бить(ся) pf.

**source** n исто́чник; (of river) исто́к.

**south** n юг; (naut) зюйд; adj ю́жный; adv к ю́гу, на юг; ~-east юго-восто́к; ~-west юго-за́пад. **southerly** adj ю́жный. **southern** adj ю́жный. **southerner** n южа́нин, -а́нка. **southward(s)** adv на юг, к ю́гу.

**souvenir** n сувени́р.

**sovereign** adj сувере́нный; n мона́рх. **sovereignty** n сувере́нитет.

**soviet** n сове́т; S~ Union Сове́тский Сою́з; adj (S~) сове́тский.

**sow¹** n свинья́.

**sow²** vt (seed) се́ять impf, по~ pf; (field) засе́ивать impf, засе́ять pf.

**soya** n: ~ bean со́евый боб.

**spa** n куро́рт.

**space** n (place, room) ме́сто; (expanse) простра́нство; (interval) промежу́ток; (outer ~) ко́смос; attrib косми́ческий; vt расставля́ть impf, расста́вить pf с промежу́тками. **spacecraft**, **-ship** n

косми́ческий кора́бль m. **spacious** adj просто́рный.

**spade** n (tool) лопа́та; pl (cards) пи́ки (пик) pl.

**spaghetti** n спаге́тти neut indecl.

**Spain** n Испа́ния.

**span** n (of bridge) пролёт; (aeron) разма́х; vt (of bridge) соединя́ть impf, соедини́ть pf сто́роны +gen; (river) берега́ +gen; (fig) охва́тывать impf, охвати́ть pf.

**Spaniard** n испа́нец, -нка. **Spanish** adj испа́нский.

**spank** vt шлёпать impf, шлёпнуть pf.

**spanner** n га́ечный ключ.

**spar¹** n (aeron) лонжеро́н.

**spar²** vi бокси́ровать impf; (fig) препира́ться impf.

**spare** adj (in reserve) запасно́й; (extra, to ~) ли́шний; (of seat, time) свобо́дный; ~ parts запасны́е ча́сти f pl; ~ room ко́мната для госте́й; n: pl запча́сти f pl; vt (grudge) жале́ть impf, по~ pf +acc, gen; he ~d no pains он не жале́л трудо́в; (do without) обходи́ться impf, обойти́сь pf без+gen; (time) уделя́ть impf, удели́ть pf; (show mercy towards) щади́ть impf, по~ pf; (save from) избавля́ть impf, изба́вить pf от+gen: **me the details** изба́вьте меня́ от подро́бностей.

**spark** n и́скра; ~-plug запа́льная свеча́; vt (~ off) вызыва́ть impf, вы́звать pf.

**sparkle** vi сверка́ть impf.

**sparrow** n воробе́й.

**sparse** adj ре́дкий.

**Spartan** adj спарта́нский.

**spasm** n спазм. **spasmodic** adj спазмоди́ческий.

**spastic** *n* парали́тик.

**spate** *n* разли́в; (*fig*) пото́к.

**spatial** *adj* простра́нственный.

**spatter, splatter** *vt* (*liquid*) бры́згать *impf* +*instr*; (*person etc.*) забры́згивать *impf*, забры́згать *pf* (**with** +*instr*); *vi* плеска́ть(ся) *impf*, плесну́ть *pf*.

**spatula** *n* шпа́тель *m*.

**spawn** *vt* & *i* мета́ть *impf* (икру́); *vt* (*fig*) порожда́ть *impf*, породи́ть *pf*.

**speak** *vt* & *i* говори́ть *impf*, сказа́ть *pf*; *vi* (*make speech*) выступа́ть *impf*, вы́ступить *pf* (с ре́чью); (~ **out**) выска́зываться *impf*, вы́сказаться *pf* (**for** за+*acc*; **against** про́тив+*gen*). **speaker** *n* говоря́щий *sb*; (*giving speech*) выступа́ющий *sb*; (*orator*) ора́тор; (S~, *parl*) спи́кер; (*loud*-~) громкоговори́тель *m*.

**spear** *n* копьё; *vt* пронза́ть *impf*, пронзи́ть *pf* копьём. **spearhead** *vt* возглавля́ть *impf*, возгла́вить *pf*.

**special** *adj* осо́бый, специа́льный. **specialist** *n* специали́ст, -ка. **speciality** *n* (*dish*) фи́рменное блю́до; (*subject*) специа́льность. **specialization** *n* специализа́ция. **specialize** *vi* & *t* специализи́ровать(ся) *impf* & *pf*. **specially** *adv* осо́бенно.

**species** *n* вид.

**specific** *adj* осо́бенный. **specification(s)** *n* специфика́ция. **specify** *vt* уточня́ть *impf*, уточни́ть *pf*.

**specimen** *n* образе́ц, экземпля́р.

**speck** *n* кра́пинка, пя́тнышко. **speckled** *adj* кра́пчатый.

**spectacle** *n* зре́лище; *pl* очки́ (-ко́в) *pl*.

**spectacular** *adj* эффе́ктный; (*amazing*) потряса́ющий.

**spectator** *n* зри́тель *m*.

**spectre** *n* при́зрак.

**spectrum** *n* спектр.

**speculate** *vi* (*meditate*) размышля́ть *impf*, размы́слить *pf* (**on** о+*prep*); (*conjecture*) гада́ть *impf*; (*comm*) спекули́ровать *impf*. **speculation** *n* (*conjecture*) дога́дка; (*comm*) спекуля́ция. **speculative** *adj* гипотети́ческий; спекуляти́вный. **speculator** *n* спекуля́нт.

**speech** *n* речь. **speechless** *adj* (*fig*) онеме́вший.

**speed** *n* ско́рость; *vi* мча́ться *impf*, про~ *pf*; (*illegally*) превыша́ть *impf*, превы́сить *pf* ско́рость; ~ **up** ускоря́ть(ся *impf*, уско́рить(ся *pf*. **speedboat** *n* быстрохо́дный ка́тер. **speedometer** *n* спидо́метр. **speedy** *adj* бы́стрый.

**spell**[1] *n* (*charm*) заго́вор.

**spell**[2] *vt* (*say*) произноси́ть *impf*, произнести́ *pf* по бу́квам; (*write*) пра́вильно писа́ть *impf*, на~ *pf*; **how do you ~ that word?** как пи́шется э́то сло́во?

**spell**[3] *n* (*period*) пери́од.

**spellbound** *adj* зачаро́ванный.

**spelling** *n* правописа́ние.

**spend** *vt* (*money; effort*) тра́тить *impf*, ис~, по~ *pf*; (*time*) проводи́ть *impf*, провести́ *pf*.

**sperm** *n* спе́рма.

**sphere** *n* сфе́ра; (*ball*) шар. **spherical** *adj* сфери́ческий.

**spice** *n* пря́ность; *vt* приправля́ть *impf*, припра́вить *pf*.

**spicy** adj пря́ный; (fig) пика́нтный.

**spider** n пау́к.

**spike** n (point) остриё; (on fence) зубе́ц; (on shoes) шип.

**spill** vt & i (liquid) пролива́ть(ся) impf, проли́ть(ся) pf; (dry substance) рассыпа́ть(ся) impf, рассы́пать(ся) pf.

**spin** vt (thread etc.) прясть impf, с~ pf; (coin) подбра́сывать impf, подбро́сить pf; vt & i (turn) кружи́ть(ся) impf; ~ out (prolong) затя́гивать impf, затяну́ть pf.

**spinach** n шпина́т.

**spinal** adj спинно́й; ~ column спинно́й хребе́т; ~ cord спинно́й мозг.

**spindle** n ось m. **spindly** adj дли́нный и то́нкий.

**spine** n (anat) позвоно́чник, хребе́т; (prickle) игла́; (of book) корешо́к. **spineless** adj (fig) бесхара́ктерный.

**spinning** n пряде́ние; ~ wheel пря́лка.

**spinster** n незаму́жняя же́нщина.

**spiral** adj спира́льный; (staircase) винтово́й; n спира́ль; vi (rise sharply) ре́зко возраста́ть impf, возрасти́ pf.

**spire** n шпиль m.

**spirit** n дух, душа́; pl (mood) настрое́ние; pl (drinks) спиртно́е sb; ~-level ватерпа́с; vt: ~ away та́йно уноси́ть impf, унести́ pf. **spirited** adj живо́й. **spiritual** adj духо́вный. **spiritualism** n спирити́зм. **spiritualist** n спири́т.

**spit**¹ n (skewer) ве́ртел.

**spit**² vi плева́ть impf, плю́нуть pf; (of rain) мороси́ть impf; (of fire) разбры́згивать impf, разбры́згать pf и́скры; (sizzle) шипе́ть impf; vt: ~ out выплёвывать impf, вы́плюнуть pf; ~ing image то́чная ко́пия; n слюна́.

**spite** n зло́ба; in ~ of несмотря́ на+acc. **spiteful** adj зло́бный.

**spittle** n слюна́.

**splash** vt (person) забры́згивать impf, забры́згать pf (with +instr); (liquid) бры́згать impf +instr; vi плеска́ть(ся) impf, плесну́ть pf; (move) шлёпать impf, шлёпнуть pf (through по+dat); n (act, sound) плеск; (mark made) пятно́.

**splatter** see spatter

**spleen** n селезёнка.

**splendid** adj великоле́пный. **splendour** n великоле́пие.

**splice** vt (ropes etc.) сра́щивать impf, срасти́ть pf; (film, tape) скле́ивать impf, скле́ить pf концы́+gen.

**splint** n ши́на.

**splinter** n оско́лок; (in skin) зано́за; vt & i расщепля́ть(ся) impf, расщепи́ть(ся) pf.

**split** n расще́лина, расще́п; (schism) раско́л; pl шпага́т; vt & i расщепля́ть(ся) impf, расщепи́ть(ся) pf; раска́лывать(ся) impf, расколо́ть(ся) pf; vt (divide) дели́ть impf, раз~ pf; ~ second мгнове́ние pf; ~ up (part company) расходи́ться impf, разойти́сь pf.

**splutter** vi бры́згать impf слюно́й; vt (utter) говори́ть impf захлёбываясь.

**spoil** n (booty) добы́ча; vt & i (damage, decay) по́ртить(ся) impf, ис~ pf; vt (indulge) балова́ть impf, из~ pf.

**spoke** n спи́ца.

**spokesman, -woman** n предстáвитель m, ~ница.

**sponge** n гýбка; ~ **cake** бисквѝт; vt (wash) мыть impf, вы~, по~ гýбкой; vi: ~ **on** жить impf на счёт+gen.

**sponger** n приживáльщик.

**spongy** adj гýбчатый.

**sponsor** n спóнсор; vt финансѝровать impf & pf.

**spontaneity** n спонтáнность.

**spontaneous** adj спонтáнный.

**spoof** n парóдия.

**spooky** adj жýткий.

**spool** n катýшка.

**spoon** n лóжка; vt чéрпать impf, черпнýть pf лóжкой.

**spoonful** n лóжка.

**sporadic** adj спорадѝческий.

**sport** n спорт; ~**s car** спортѝвный автомобѝль m; vt щеголя́ть impf, щегольнýть pf +instr. **sportsman** n спортсмéн. **sporty** adj спортѝвный.

**spot** n (place) мéсто; (mark) пятнó; (pimple) прыщик; **on the** ~ (at once) срáзу; ~ **check** выборочная провéрка; vt (notice) замéчать impf, замéтить pf; n (tube) нóсик; (jet) струя́.

**spotless** adj абсолю́тно чѝстый. **spotlight** n прожéктор; (fig) внимáние. **spotty** adj прыщевáтый.

**spouse** n супрýг, ~а.

**spout** vi бить impf струёй, хлынуть pf; (pontificate) орáторствовать impf; vt извергáть impf, извéргнуть pf; (verses etc.) деклами́ровать impf, про~ pf; n (tube) нóсик; (jet) струя́.

**sprain** vt растя́гивать impf, растянýть pf; n растяжéние.

**sprawl** vi (of person) развáли-

ваться impf, развалѝться pf; (of town) раскѝдываться impf, раскѝнуться pf.

**spray**[1] n (flowers) вéт(оч)ка.

**spray**[2] n брызги (-г) pl; (atomizer) пульверизáтор; vt опры́скивать impf, опры́скать pf (**with** +instr); (cause to scatter) распыля́ть impf, распылѝть pf.

**spread** vt & i (news, disease, etc.) распространя́ть(ся) impf, распространѝть(ся) pf; vt (~ out) расстилáть impf, разостлáть pf; (unfurl, unroll) развёртывать impf, развернýть pf; (bread etc. +acc; butter etc. +instr) намáзывать impf, намáзать pf; n (expansion) распространéние; (span) размáх; (feast) пир; (paste) пáста.

**spree** n кутёж; **go on a** ~ кутѝть impf, кутнýть pf.

**sprig** n вéточка.

**sprightly** adj бóдрый.

**spring** vi (jump) пры́гать impf, пры́гнуть pf; vt (tell unexpectedly) неожи́данно сообщáть impf, сообщи́ть pf (**on** +dat); ~ **a leak** давáть impf, дать pf течь; ~ **from** (originate) происходи́ть impf, произойти́ pf из+gen; n (jump) прыжóк; (season) веснá, attrib весéнний; (water) истóчник; (elasticity) упрýгость; (coil) пружи́на; ~**-clean** генерáльная убóрка. **springboard** n трамплѝн.

**sprinkle** vt (with liquid) опры́скивать impf, опры́скать pf (**with** +instr); (with solid) посыпáть impf, посы́пать pf (**with** +instr). **sprinkler** n разбры́згиватель m.

**sprint** vi бежáть impf на

коро́ткую диста́нцию; (rush)
рвану́ться pf; n спринт.
**sprinter** n спри́нтер.
**sprout** vi пуска́ть impf, пусти́ть pf ростки́; n росто́к;
pl брюссе́льская капу́ста.
**spruce**¹ adj наря́дный, элега́нтный; vt: ~ o.s. up приводи́ть impf, привести́ pf себя́ в поря́док.
**spruce**² n ель.
**spur** n шпо́ра; (fig) сти́мул;
on the ~ of the moment под
влия́нием мину́ты; vt: ~ on
подхлёстывать impf, подхлестну́ть pf.
**spurious** adj подде́льный.
**spurn** vt отверга́ть impf, отве́ргнуть pf.
**spurt** n (jet) струя́; (effort)
рыво́к; vi бить impf струёй;
(make an effort) де́лать impf,
с~ pf рыво́к.
**spy** n шпио́н; vi шпио́нить
impf (on за+instr). **spying** n
шпиона́ж.
**squabble** n перебра́нка; vi
вздо́рить impf, по~ pf.
**squad** n кома́нда, гру́ппа.
**squadron** n (mil) эскадро́н;
(naut) эска́дра; (aeron) эскадри́лья.
**squalid** adj убо́гий.
**squall** n шквал.
**squalor** n убо́жество.
**squander** vt растра́чивать
impf, растра́тить pf.
**square** n (shape) квадра́т; (in
town) пло́щадь; (on paper,
material) кле́тка; (instrument)
науго́льник; adj квадра́тный; (meal) пло́тный; ~ root
квадра́тный ко́рень m; vt
(accounts) своди́ть impf, свести́ pf; (math) возводи́ть
impf, возвести́ pf в квадра́т;
vi (correspond) соотве́тство-

вать impf (with +dat).
**squash** n (crowd) толку́чка;
(drink) сок; vt разда́вливать
impf, раздави́ть pf; (suppress)
подавля́ть impf, подави́ть pf;
vi вти́скиваться impf,
вти́снуться pf.
**squat** adj призе́мистый; vi
сиде́ть impf на ко́рточках;
~ down сади́ться impf, сесть
pf на ко́рточки.
**squatter** n незако́нный жиле́ц.
**squawk** n клёкот; vi клекота́ть impf.
**squeak** n писк; (of object)
скрип; vi пища́ть impf, пи́скнуть pf; (of object) скрипе́ть
impf, скри́пнуть pf. **squeaky**
adj пискли́вый, скрипу́чий.
**squeal** n визг; vi визжа́ть
impf, ви́згнуть pf.
**squeamish** adj брезгли́вый.
**squeeze** n (crush) да́вка;
(pressure) сжа́тие; (hand) пожа́тие; vt дави́ть impf; сжима́ть impf, сжать pf; ~ in
впи́хивать(ся) impf, впихну́ть(ся) pf; вти́скивать(ся)
impf, вти́снуть(ся) pf; ~ out
выжима́ть impf, вы́жать pf;
~ through проти́скивать(ся)
impf, проти́снуть(ся) pf.
**squelch** vi хлю́пать impf,
хлю́пнуть pf.
**squid** n кальма́р.
**squint** n косогла́зие; vi коси́ть impf; (screw up eyes)
щу́риться impf.
**squire** n сквайр, поме́щик.
**squirm** vi (wriggle) извива́ться impf, изви́ться pf.
**squirrel** n бе́лка.
**squirt** n струя́; vi бить impf
струёй; vt пуска́ть impf, пусти́ть pf струю́ (substance
+gen; at на+acc).

(*of* **Saint**) св., Свято́й, -а́я.
**stab** *n* уда́р (ножо́м *etc.*); (*pain*) внеза́пная о́страя боль; *vt* наноси́ть *impf*, нанести́ *pf* уда́р (ножо́м *etc.*) (*person* +*dat*).
**stability** *n* усто́йчивость, стаби́льность. **stabilize** *vt* стабилизи́ровать *impf & pf.*
**stable** *adj* усто́йчивый, стаби́льный; (*psych*) уравнове́шенный; *n* коню́шня.
**staccato** *n* стакка́то *neut indecl; adv* стакка́то; *adj* отры́вистый.
**stack** *n* ку́ча; *vt* скла́дывать *impf*, сложи́ть *pf* в ку́чу.
**stadium** *n* стадио́н.
**staff** *n* (*personnel*) штат, сотру́дники *m pl*; (*stick*) по́сох, жезл; *adj* шта́тный; (*mil*) штабно́й.
**stag** *n* саме́ц-оле́нь *m.*
**stage** *n* (*theat*) сце́на; (*period*) ста́дия; *vt* (*theat*) ста́вить *impf*, по~ *pf*; (*organize*) организо́вывать *impf & pf*; **~-manager** режиссёр.
**stagger** *vi* шата́ться *impf*, шатну́ться *pf*; *vt* (*hours of work etc.*) распределя́ть *impf*, распредели́ть *pf*. **be staggered** *vi* поража́ться *impf*, порази́ться *pf*. **staggering** *adj* потряса́ющий.
**stagnant** *adj* (*water*) стоя́чий; (*fig*) засто́йный. **stagnate** *vi* заста́иваться *impf*, застоя́ться *pf*; (*fig*) косне́ть *impf*, за~ *pf.*
**staid** *adj* сте́пенный.
**stain** *n* пятно́; (*dye*) кра́ска; *vt* па́чкать *impf*, за~, ис~ *pf*; (*dye*) окра́шивать *impf*, окра́сить *pf*; **~ed glass** цветно́е стекло́. **stainless** *adj*: ~ **steel** нержаве́ющая сталь.

**stair** *n* ступе́нька. **staircase**, **stairs** *n pl* ле́стница.
**stake** *n* (*stick*) кол; (*bet*) ста́вка; (*comm*) до́ля; **be at ~** быть поста́вленным на ка́рту; *vt* (*mark out*) огора́живать *impf*, огороди́ть *pf* ко́льями; (*support*) укрепля́ть *impf*, укрепи́ть *pf* колом; (*risk*) ста́вить *impf*, по~ *pf* на ка́рту.
**stale** *adj* несве́жий; (*musty, damp*) за́тхлый; (*hackneyed*) изби́тый.
**stalemate** *n* пат; (*fig*) тупи́к.
**stalk** *n* сте́бель *m; vt* высле́живать *impf; vi* (& *t*) (*stride*) ше́ствовать *impf* (по+*dat*).
**stall** *n* сто́йло; (*booth*) ларёк, *pl* (*theat*) парте́р; *vi* (*of engine*) гло́хнуть *impf*, за~ *pf*; (*play for time*) оття́гивать *impf*, оттяну́ть *pf* вре́мя; *vt* (*engine*) неча́янно заглуша́ть *impf*, заглуши́ть *pf.*
**stallion** *n* жеребе́ц.
**stalwart** *adj* сто́йкий; *n* сто́йкий приве́рженец.
**stamina** *n* выно́сливость.
**stammer** *vi* заика́ться *impf; n* заика́ние.
**stamp** *n* печа́ть; (*postage*) (почто́вая) ма́рка; *vt* штампова́ть *impf; vi* то́пать *impf*, то́пнуть *pf* (нога́ми); **~ out** поборо́ть *pf.*
**stampede** *n* пани́ческое бе́гство; *vi* обраща́ться *impf* в пани́ческое бе́гство.
**stance** *n* пози́ция.
**stand** *n* (*hat, coat*) ве́шалка; (*music*) пюпи́тр; (*umbrella, support*) подста́вка; (*booth*) ларёк; (*taxi*) стоя́нка; (*at stadium*) трибу́на; (*position*) пози́ция; (*resistance*) сопротивле́ние; *vi* стоя́ть *impf*; (~ *up*)

вставать *impf*, встать *pf*; (*remain in force*) оставаться *impf*, остаться в силе; *vt* (*put*) ставить *impf*, по~ *pf*; (*endure*) терпеть *impf*, по~ *pf*; ~ **back** отходить *impf*, отойти *pf* (**from** от+*gen*); (*not go forward*) держаться *impf* позади; ~ **by** (*vi*) (*not interfere*) не вмешиваться *impf*, вмешаться *pf*; (*be ready*) быть *impf* на-готове; (*vt*) (*support*) поддерживать *impf*, поддержать *pf*; (*stick to*) придерживаться *impf* +*gen*; ~ **down** (*resign*) уходить *impf*, уйти *pf* с поста (**as** +*gen*); ~ **for** (*signify*) означать *impf*; (*tolerate*) **I shall not** ~ **for it** я не потерплю; ~-**in** заместитель *m*; ~ **in** (**for**) замещать *impf*, заместить *pf*; ~ **out** выделяться *impf*, выделиться *pf*; ~ **up** вставать *impf*, встать *pf*; ~ **up for** (*defend*) отстаивать *impf*, отстоять *pf*; ~ **up to** (*endure*) выдерживать *impf*, выдержать *pf*; (*not give in to*) противостоять *impf* +*dat*. **standard** *n* (*norm*) стандарт, норм; (*flag*) знамя *neut*; ~ **of living** жизненный уровень *m*; *adj* нормальный, стандартный. **standardization** *n* нормализация, стандартизация. **standardize** *vt* стандартизировать *impf* & *pf*; нормализовать *impf* & *pf*. **standing** *n* положение; *adj* (*upright*) стоячий; (*permanent*) постоянный. **standpoint** *n* точка зрения. **standstill** *n* остановка, застой, пауза; **be at a** ~ стоять *impf* на мёртвой точке; **bring (come) to a** ~ останавли-

вать(ся) *impf*, остановить-(ся) *pf*. **stanza** *n* строфа. **staple**[1] *n* (*metal bar*) скоба; (*for paper*) скрепка; *vt* скреплять *impf*, скрепить *pf*. **staple**[2] *n* (*product*) главный продукт; *adj* основной. **star** *n* звезда; (*asterisk*) звёздочка; *vi* играть *impf*, сыграть *pf* главную роль. **starfish** *n* морская звезда. **starboard** *n* правый борт. **starch** *n* крахмал; *vt* крахмалить *impf*, на~ *pf*. **starchy** *adj* крахмалистый; (*prim*) чопорный. **stare** *n* пристальный взгляд; *vi* пристально смотреть *impf* (**at** на+*acc*). **stark** *adj* (*bare*) голый; (*desolate*) пустынный; (*sharp*) резкий; *adv* совершенно. **starling** *n* скворец. **starry** *adj* звёздный. **start** *n* начало; (*sport*) старт; *vi* начинаться *impf*, начаться *pf*; (*engine*) заводиться *impf*, завестись *pf*; (*set out*) отправляться *impf*, отправиться *pf*; (*shudder*) вздрагивать *impf*, вздрогнуть *pf*; (*sport*) стартовать *impf* & *pf*; *vt* начинать *impf*, начать *pf* (*gerund, inf* +*inf*; **by**, +*gerund* с того, что...; **with** +*instr*, с+*gen*); (*car, engine*) заводить *impf*, завести *pf*; (*fire, rumour*) пускать *impf*, пустить *pf*; (*found*) основывать *impf*, основать *pf*. **starter** *n* (*tech*) стартёр; (*cul*) закуска. **starting-point** *n* отправной пункт. **startle** *vt* испугать *pf*. **starvation** *n* голод. **starve** *vi* голодать *impf*; (*to death*) умирать *impf*, умереть с го́лоду; *vt* мори́ть *impf*, по~, у~ *pf* го́лодом. **starving** *adj* голода́ющий; (*hungry*) о́чень голо́дный.

**state** *n* (*condition*) состоя́ние; (*polit*) госуда́рство, штат; *adj* (*ceremonial*) торже́ственный; пара́дный; (*polit*) госуда́рственный; *vt* (*announce*) заявля́ть *impf*, заяви́ть *pf*; (*expound*) излага́ть *impf*, изложи́ть *pf*. **stateless** *adj* не име́ющий гражда́нства.

**stately** *adj* вели́чественный.

**statement** *n* заявле́ние; (*comm*) отчёт. **statesman** *n* госуда́рственный де́ятель *m*.

**static** *adj* неподви́жный.

**station** *n* (*rly*) вокза́л, ста́нция; (*social*) обще́ственное положе́ние; (*meteorological, hydro-electric power, radio etc.*) ста́нция; (*post*) пост, *vt* размеща́ть *impf*, размести́ть *pf*.

**stationary** *adj* неподви́жный.

**stationery** *n* канцеля́рские принадле́жности *f pl*; (*writing-paper*) почто́вая бума́га; ~ **shop** канцеля́рский магази́н.

**statistic** *n* статисти́ческое да́нное. **statistical** *adj* статисти́ческий. **statistician** *n* стати́стик. **statistics** *n* стати́стика.

**statue** *n* ста́туя. **statuette** *n* статуэ́тка. **stature** *n* рост; (*merit*) кали́бр. **status** *n* ста́тус. **status quo** *n* ста́тус-кво́ *neut indecl*. **statute** *n* стату́т. **statutory** *adj* устано́вленный зако́ном.

**staunch** *adj* ве́рный.

**stave** *vt*: ~ **off** предотвраща́ть *impf*, предотврати́ть *pf*.

**stay** *n* (*time spent*) пребыва́ние; *vi* (*remain*) остава́ть-

ся *impf*, оста́ться *pf* (**to dinner** обе́дать); (*put up*) остана́вливаться *impf*, останови́ться *pf* (**at** (*place*) в+*prep*; **at** (*friends' etc.*) у+*gen*); (*live*) жить; ~ **behind** остава́ться *impf*, оста́ться *pf*; ~ **in** остава́ться *impf*, оста́ться *pf* до́ма; ~ **up** не ложи́ться *impf* спать; (*trousers*) держа́ться *impf*. **staying-power** *n* выно́сливость.

**stead** *n*: **stand s.o. in good** ~ ока́зываться *impf*, оказа́ться *pf* поле́зным кому́-л. **steadfast** *adj* сто́йкий, непоколеби́мый.

**steady** *adj* (*firm*) усто́йчивый; (*continuous*) непреры́вный; (*wind, temperature*) ро́вный; (*speed*) постоя́нный; (*unshakeable*) непоколеби́мый; *vt* (*boat etc.*) приводи́ть *impf*, привести́ *pf* в равнове́сие.

**steak** *n* бифште́кс.

**steal** *vt* & *abs* ворова́ть *impf*, с~ *pf*; красть *impf*, у~ *pf*; *vi* (*creep*) кра́сться *impf*; подкра́дываться *impf*, подкра́сться *pf*. **stealth** *n*: **by** ~ укра́дкой. **stealthy** *adj* ворова́тый, та́йный, скры́тый.

**steam** *n* пар; **at full** ~ на всех пара́х; **let off** ~ (*fig*) дава́ть *impf*, дать *pf* вы́ход свои́м чу́вствам; *vt* па́рить *impf*; *vi* па́риться *impf*, по~ *pf*; (*vessel*) ходи́ть *indet*, идти́ *det* на пара́х; ~ **up** (*mist over*) запотева́ть *impf*, запоте́ть *pf*; поте́ть *impf*, за~, от~ *pf*; **engine** парова́я маши́на. **steamer**, **steamship** *n* парохо́д. **steamy** *adj* напо́лненный па́ром; (*passionate*) горя́чий.

**steed** n конь m.
**steel** n сталь f; adj стально́й; vt:
~ **o.s.** ожесточа́ться impf,
ожесточи́ться pf; ~ **works**
сталелите́йный заво́д. **steely**
adj стально́й.
**steep**[1] adj круто́й; (excessive)
чрезме́рный.
**steep**[2] vt (immerse) погру-
жа́ть impf, погрузи́ть pf (in
в+acc); (saturate) пропи́ты-
вать impf, пропита́ть pf (in
+instr).
**steeple** n шпиль m. **steeple-
chase** n ска́чки f pl с пре-
пя́тствиями.
**steer** vt управля́ть impf, пра́-
вить impf +instr; v abs ру-
ли́ть impf; ~ **clear of** избе-
га́ть impf, избежа́ть pf +gen.
**steering-wheel** n руль m.
**stem**[1] n сте́бель m; (of wineglass) но́жка; (ling) осно́ва;
vi: ~ **from** происходи́ть impf,
произойти́ pf от+gen.
**stem**[2] vt (stop) остана́вли-
вать impf, останови́ть pf.
**stench** n злово́ние.
**stencil** n трафаре́т; (tech)
шабло́н; vt наноси́ть impf,
нанести́ pf по трафаре́ту.
**stencilled** adj трафаре́тный.
**step** n (pace, action) шаг;
(dance) pа neut indecl; (of
stairs, ladder) ступе́нь; ~ **by**
~ шаг за ша́гом; **in** ~ в но́гу;
**out of** ~ не в но́гу; **take** ~**s**
принима́ть impf, приня́ть pf
ме́ры и шага́ть impf, шаг-
ну́ть pf; ступа́ть impf, сту-
пи́ть pf; ~ **aside** сторо-
ни́ться impf, по~ pf; ~ **back**
отступа́ть impf, отступи́ть
pf; ~ **down** (resign) уходи́ть
impf, уйти́ pf в отста́вку; ~
**forward** выступа́ть impf, вы́-
ступить pf; ~ **in** (intervene)

вме́шиваться impf, вме-
ша́ться pf; ~ **on** наступа́ть
impf, наступи́ть pf на+acc
(s.o.'s foot кому́-л. на́ ногу); ~
**over** перешага́ть impf,
перешагну́ть pf +acc, че́-
рез+acc; ~ **up** (increase) по-
выша́ть impf, повы́сить pf.
**step-ladder** n стремя́нка.
**stepping-stone** n ка́мень m
для перехо́да; (fig) сре́д-
ство. **steps** n pl ле́стница.
**stepbrother** n сво́дный брат.
**stepdaughter** n па́дчерица.
**stepfather** n о́тчим. **stepmother** n ма́чеха. **stepsister**
n сво́дная сестра́. **stepson**
n па́сынок.
**steppe** n степь f.
**stereo** n (system) стереофо-
ни́ческая систе́ма; (stereo-
phony) стереофо́ния; adj (re-
corded in ~) сте́рео indecl.
**stereophonic** adj стерео-
фони́ческий. **stereotype** n
стереоти́п. **stereotyped** adj
стереоти́пный.
**sterile** adj стери́льный. **sterility** n стери́льность. **steri-
lization** n стерилиза́ция. **sterilize** vt стерилизова́ть impf &
pf.
**sterling** n сте́рлинг; **pound** ~
фунт сте́рлингов; adj сте́р-
линговый.
**stern**[1] n корма́.
**stern**[2] adj суро́вый, стро́гий.
**stethoscope** n стетоско́п.
**stew** n (cul) мя́со туше́ное
вме́сте с овоща́ми; vt & i
(cul) туши́ть(ся) impf, с~ pf;
(fig) томи́ть(ся) impf.
**steward** n бортпроводни́к.
**stewardess** n стюарде́сса.
**stick**[1] n па́лка; (of chalk etc.)
па́лочка; (hockey) клюшка́.
**stick**[2] (spear) зака́лывать

*impf,* заколо́ть *pf; (make adhere)* прикле́ивать *impf,* прикле́ить *pf* **(to** к+*dat); (coll) (put)* ста́вить *impf,* по~ *pf; (lay)* класть *impf,* положи́ть *pf; (endure)* терпе́ть *impf,* вы~ *pf; vi (adhere)* ли́пнуть *impf* **(to** к+*dat),* прилипа́ть *impf,* прили́пнуть *pf* **(to** к+*dat);* ~ **in** *(thrust in)* втыка́ть *impf,* воткну́ть *pf; (into opening)* всо́вывать *impf,* всу́нуть *pf;* ~ **on** *(glue on)* накле́ивать *impf,* накле́ить *pf;* ~ **out** *(thrust out)* высо́вывать *impf,* вы́сунуть *pf* **(from** из+*gen); (project)* торча́ть *impf;* ~ **to** *(keep to)* приде́рживаться *impf,* придержа́ться *pf*+*gen; (remain at)* не отвлека́ться *impf* от+*gen;* ~ **together** держа́ться *impf* вме́сте; ~ **up for** защища́ть *impf,* защити́ть *pf;* **be, get, stuck** застрева́ть *impf,* застря́ть *pf.* **sticker** *n* накле́йка.
**sticky** *adj* ли́пкий.
**stiff** *adj* жёсткий, неги́бкий; *(prim)* чо́порный; *(difficult)* тру́дный; *(penalty)* суро́вый; **be** ~ *(ache)* боле́ть *impf.* **stiffen** *vt* де́лать *impf,* с~ *pf* жёстким; *vi* станови́ться *impf,* стать *pf* жёстким. **stiffness** *n* жёсткость; *(primness)* чо́порность.
**stifle** *vt* души́ть *impf,* за~ *pf; (suppress)* подавля́ть *impf,* подави́ть *pf; (sound)* заглуша́ть *impf,* заглуши́ть *pf; vi* задыха́ться *impf,* задохну́ться *pf.* **stifling** *adj* удуши́вый.
**stigma** *n* клеймо́.
**stile** *n* перела́з *(coll).*
**stilettos** *n pl* ту́фли *f pl* на шпи́льках.

**still** *adv* (всё) ещё; *(nevertheless)* тем не ме́нее; *(motionless)* неподви́жно; **stand** ~ не дви́гаться *impf,* дви́нуться *pf; n (quiet)* тишина́; *adj* ти́хий; *(immobile)* неподви́жный. **still-born** *adj* мертворождённый. **still life** *n* натюрмо́рт. **stillness** *n* тишина́.
**stilted** *adj* ходу́льный.
**stimulant** *n* возбужда́ющее сре́дство. **stimulate** *vt* возбужда́ть *impf,* возбуди́ть *pf.* **stimulating** *adj* возбуди́тельный. **stimulation** *n* возбужде́ние. **stimulus** *n* сти́мул.
**sting** *n (wound)* уку́с; *(stinger, fig)* жа́ло; *vt* жа́лить *impf,* у~ *pf; vi (burn)* жечь *impf.* **stinging** *adj (caustic)* язви́тельный.
**stingy** *adj* скупо́й.
**stink** *n* вонь; *vi* воня́ть *impf* **(of** +*instr).* **stinking** *adj* воню́чий.
**stint** *n* срок; *vi:* ~**on** скупи́ться *impf,* по~ *pf* на+*acc.*
**stipend** *n (salary)* жа́лование; *(grant)* стипе́ндия.
**stipulate** *vt* обусло́вливать *impf,* обусло́вить *pf.* **stipulation** *n* усло́вие.
**stir** *n (commotion)* шум; *(mix)* меша́ть *impf,* по~ *pf; (excite)* волнова́ть *impf,* вз~ *pf; vi (move)* шевели́ться *impf,* шевельну́ться *pf;* ~ **up** возбужда́ть *impf,* возбуди́ть *pf.* **stirring** *adj* волну́ющий.
**stirrup** *n* стре́мя *neut.*
**stitch** *n* стежо́к; *(knitting)* пе́тля; *(med)* шов; *(pain)* ко́лики *f pl* в боку́; *vt (embroider, make line of ~es)* строчи́ть *impf,* про~ *pf; (join by sewing, make, suture)* сшива́ть

*impf*, сшить *pf*; ~ **up** заши-
ва́ть *impf*, заши́ть *pf*. **stitch-**
**ing** *n* (*stitches*) стро́чка.

**stoat** *n* горноста́й.

**stock** *n* (*store*) запа́с; (*of shop*)
ассортиме́нт; (*live*~) скот;
(*cul*) бульо́н; (*lineage*) семья́;
(*fin*) а́кции *pl*; **in** ~ в нали́-
чии; **out of** ~ распро́дан;
**take** ~ **of** крити́чески оце́-
нивать *impf*, оцени́ть *pf*; *adj*
станда́ртный; *vt* име́ть в на-
ли́чии; ~ **up** запаса́ться *impf*,
запасти́сь *pf* (**with** +*instr*).
**stockbroker** *n* биржево́й
ма́клер. **stock-exchange** *n*
би́ржа. **stockpile** *n* запа́с; *vt*
нака́пливать *impf*, накопи́ть
*pf*. **stock-taking** *n* переучёт.

**stocking** *n* чуло́к.

**stocky** *adj* призе́мистый.

**stodgy** *adj* тяжёлый.

**stoic(al)** *adj* сто́ический. **sto-**
**icism** *n* стоици́зм.

**stoke** *vt* топи́ть *impf*.

**stolid** *adj* флегмати́чный.

**stomach** *n* желу́док, (*also sur-*
*face of body*) живо́т; *vt* тер-
пе́ть *impf*, по~ *pf*. **stomach**
**ache** *n* боль в животе́.

**stone** *n* ка́мень *m*; (*of fruit*)
ко́сточка; *adj* ка́менный; *vt*
побива́ть *impf*, поби́ть *pf*
камня́ми; (*fruit*) вынима́ть
*impf*, вы́нуть *pf* ко́сточки
из+*gen*. **Stone Age** *n* ка́мен-
ный век. **stone-deaf** *adj* со-
верше́нно глухо́й. **stone-ma-**
**son** *n* ка́менщик. **stonily** *adv*
с ка́менным выраже́нием,
хо́лодно. **stony** *adj* камени́-
стый; (*fig*) ка́менный.

**stool** *n* табуре́т, табуре́тка.

**stoop** *n* суту́лость; *vt* & *i* су-
ту́лить(ся) *impf*, с~ *pf*; (*bend*
*down*) наклоня́ть(ся) *impf*,
наклони́ть(ся) *pf*; ~ **to**

(*abase o.s.*) унижа́ться *impf*,
уни́зиться *pf* до+*gen*; (*conde-*
*scend*) снисходи́ть *impf*, сни-
зойти́ *pf* до+*gen*. **stooped**,
**stooping** *adj* суту́лый.

**stop** *n* остано́вка; **put a** ~ **to**
положи́ть *pf* коне́ц +*dat*; *vt*
остана́вливать *impf*, остано-
ви́ть *pf*; (*discontinue*) пре-
краща́ть *impf*, прекрати́ть
*pf*; (*restrain*) уде́рживать
*impf*, удержа́ть *pf* (**from**
от+*gen*); *vi* остана́вливаться
*impf*, останови́ться *pf*; (*dis-*
*continue*) прекраща́ться *impf*,
прекрати́ться *pf*; (*cease*)
перестава́ть *impf*, переста́ть
*pf* (+*inf*); ~ **up** затыка́ть
*impf*, заткну́ть *pf*. **stoppage**
*n* остано́вка; (*strike*) заба-
сто́вка. **stopper** *n* про́бка.
**stop-press** *n* э́кстренное со-
обще́ние в газе́те. **stop-**
**watch** *n* секундоме́р.

**storage** *n* хране́ние. **store** *n*
запа́с; (*storehouse*) склад;
(*shop*) магази́н; **set** ~ **by**
цени́ть *impf*; **what is in** ~ **for**
**me?** что ждёт меня́ впе-
реди́?; *vt* запаса́ть *impf*, за-
пасти́ *pf*; (*put into storage*)
сдава́ть *impf*, сдать *pf* на
хране́ние. **storehouse** *n* склад.
**store-room** *n* кладова́я *sb*.

**storey** *n* эта́ж.

**stork** *n* а́ист.

**storm** *n* бу́ря, (*thunder* ~)
гроза́; *vt* (*mil*) штурмова́ть
*impf*; *vi* бушева́ть *impf*. **stormy**
*adj* бу́рный.

**story** *n* расска́з, по́весть; (*an-*
*ecdote*) анекдо́т; (*plot*) фа́-
була; ~**-teller** *n* расска́зчик.

**stout** *adj* (*strong*) кре́пкий;
(*staunch*) сто́йкий; (*portly*)
доро́дный.

**stove** *n* (*with fire inside*) печь;

(cooker) плита́.

**stow** vt укла́дывать impf, уложи́ть pf. **stowaway** n безбиле́тный пассажи́р.

**straddle** vt (sit astride) сиде́ть impf верхо́м на+prep; (stand astride) стоя́ть impf, рас-ста́вив но́ги над+instr.

**straggle** vi отстава́ть impf, отста́ть pf. **straggler** n отста́вший sb. **straggling** adj разбро́санный. **straggly** adj растрёпанный.

**straight** adj прямо́й; (undiluted) неразба́вленный; predic (in order) в поря́дке; adv пря́мо; ~ **away** сра́зу. **straighten** vt & i выпрямля́ть(ся) impf, вы́прямить(ся) pf; vt (put in order) поправля́ть impf, по-пра́вить pf. **straightforward** adj прямо́й; (simple) просто́й.

**strain**[1] n (tension) натяже́ние; (sprain) растяже́ние; (effort, exertion) напряже́ние; (tendency) скло́нность; (sound) звук; vt (stretch) натя́гивать impf, натяну́ть pf; (sprain) растя́гивать impf, растяну́ть pf; (exert) напря́чь pf; (filter) проце́живать impf, проце́дить pf; vi (also exert o.s.) напряга́ться impf, напря́чься pf. **strained** adj натя́нутый. **strainer** n (tea ~) си́течко; (sieve) си́то.

**strain**[2] n (breed) поро́да.

**strait(s)** n (geog) проли́в. **strait-jacket** n смири́тельная руба́шка. **straits** n pl (difficulties) затрудни́тельное поло-же́ние.

**strand**[1] n (hair, rope) прядь; (thread, also fig) нить.

**strand**[2] vt сажа́ть impf, поса-ди́ть pf на мель. **stranded** adj на мели́.

**strange** adj стра́нный; (unfamiliar) незнако́мый; (alien) чужо́й. **strangely** adv стра́н-но. **strangeness** n стра́н-ность. **stranger** n незнако́-мец.

**strangle** vt души́ть impf, за-pf. **stranglehold** n мёртвая хва́тка. **strangulation** n удуше́ние.

**strap** n реме́нь m; vt (tie up) стя́гивать impf, стяну́ть pf ремнём. **strapping** adj ро́с-лый.

**stratagem** n хи́трость. **strategic** adj стратеги́ческий. **strategist** n страте́г. **strategy** n страте́гия.

**stratum** n слой.

**straw** n соло́ма; (drinking) соло́минка; **the last** ~ после́д-няя ка́пля; adj соло́менный.

**strawberry** n клубни́ка (no pl; usu collect); (wild) ~ земляни́ка (no pl; usu collect).

**stray** vi сбива́ться impf, сби́ть-ся pf; (digress) отклоня́ться impf, отклони́ться pf; adj (lost) заблуди́вшийся; (homeless) бездо́мный; n (from flock) отби́вшееся от ста́да живо́тное sb; ~ **bullet** шальна́я пу́ля.

**streak** n полоса́ (of luck везе́ния); (tendency) жи́лка; vi (rush) проноси́ться impf, про-нести́сь pf. **streaked** adj c полоса́ми (with +gen). **streaky** adj полоса́тый; (meat) c про-сло́йками жи́ра.

**stream** n (brook, tears) руче́й; (brook, flood, tears, people etc.) пото́к; (current) тече́-ние; **up/down** ~ вверх/вниз по тече́нию; vi течь impf; струи́ться impf; (rush) про-носи́ться impf, пронести́сь

*pf;* (*blow*) развева́ться *impf.*
**streamer** *n* вы́мпел. **stream-**
**lined** *adj* обтека́емый; (*fig*)
хорошо́ нала́женный.
**street** *n* у́лица; *adj* у́личный;
~ **lamp** у́личный фона́рь *m.*
**strength** *n* си́ла; (*numbers*)
чи́сленность; **on the** ~ **of** в
си́лу+*gen.* **strengthen** *vt* уси-
ливать *impf,* уси́лить *pf.*
**strenuous** *adj* (*work*) тру́д-
ный; (*effort*) напряжённый.
**stress** *n* напряже́ние; (*men-*
*tal*) стресс; (*emphasis*) ударе́-
ние; *vt* (*accent*) ста́вить *impf,*
по~ *pf* ударе́ние на+*acc;*
(*emphasize*) подчёркивать
*impf* подчеркну́ть *pf.* **stress-**
**ful** *adj* стре́ссовый.
**stretch** *n* (*expanse*) отре́зок;
**at a** ~ (*in succession*) подря́д;
*vt* & *i* (*widen, spread out*)
растя́гивать(ся) *impf,* рас-
тяну́ть(ся) *pf;* (*in length, ~ out*
*limbs*) вытя́гивать(ся) *impf,*
вы́тянуть(ся) *pf;* (*tauten*) на-
тя́гивать(ся) *impf,* натяну́ть-
(ся) *pf;* (*extend, e.g. rope, ~*
*forth limbs*) протя́гивать(ся)
*impf,* протяну́ть(ся) *pf;* *vi*
(*material, land*) тяну́ться *impf;*
~ **one's legs** (*coll*) размя-
на́ть *impf,* размя́ть *pf* но́ги.
**stretcher** *n* носи́лки (-лок) *pl.*
**strew** *vt* разбра́сывать *impf,*
разброса́ть *pf;* ~ **with** посы-
па́ть *impf,* посы́пать *pf* +*instr.*
**stricken** *adj* поражённый.
**strict** *adj* стро́гий. **stricture(s)**
*n* (*строгая*) кри́тика.
**stride** *n* (*большой*) шаг; *n*
(*fig*) успе́хи *m pl;* **to take sth**
**in one's** ~ преодолева́ть
*impf,* преодоле́ть *pf* что-л.
без уси́лий; *vi* шага́ть *impf.*
**strident** *adj* ре́зкий.
**strife** *n* раздо́р.

**strike** *n* (*refusal to work*)
забасто́вка; (*mil*) уда́р; *vi* (*be*
*on* ~) бастова́ть *impf;* (*go on*
~) забастова́ть *pf;* (*attack*)
ударя́ть *impf,* уда́рить *pf;* (*hit*
*the hour*) бить *impf,* про~
*pf; vt* (*hit*) ударя́ть *impf,* уда́-
рить *pf;* (*impress*) поража́ть
*impf,* порази́ть *pf;* (*discover*)
открыва́ть *impf,* откры́ть
*pf;* (*match*) зажига́ть *impf,*
заже́чь *pf;* (*the hour*) бить
*impf,* про~ *pf;* (*occur to*)
приходи́ть *impf,* прийти́ *pf* в
го́лову+*dat;* ~ **off** вычёркивать *impf,* вы́черк-
нуть *pf;* ~ **up** начина́ть *impf,*
нача́ть *pf.* **striker** *n* заба-
сто́вщик. **striking** *adj* пора-
зи́тельный.
**string** *n* бечёвка; (*mus*)
струна́; (*series*) ряд; *pl* (*mus*)
стру́нные инструме́нты *m*
*pl;* ~ **bag,** ~ **vest** се́тка; *vt*
(*thread*) низа́ть *impf,* на~ *pf;*
~ **along** (*coll*) води́ть *impf* за
нос; ~ **out** (*prolong*) растя́-
гивать *impf,* растяну́ть *pf;*
**strung up** (*tense*) напряжённый. **stringed** *adj* стру́нный.
**stringy** *adj* (*fibrous*) воло́к-
ни́стый; (*meat*) жи́листый.
**stringent** *adj* стро́гий.
**strip¹** *n* полоса́, поло́ска.
**strip²** *vt* (*undress*) раздева́ть
*impf,* разде́ть *pf;* (*deprive*)
лиша́ть *impf,* лиши́ть *pf* +
*gen;* ~ **off** (*tear off*) сди-
ра́ть *impf,* содра́ть *pf; vi* разде-
ва́ться *impf,* разде́ться *pf.*
**strip-tease** *n* стриптиз.
**stripe** *n* полоса́. **striped** *adj*
полоса́тый.
**strive** *vi* (*endeavour*) стре-
ми́ться *impf* (**for** к+*dat*);
(*struggle*) боро́ться *impf* (**for**
за+*acc;* **against** про́тив+*gen*).

**stroke** n (blow, med) уда́р; (of oar) взмах; (swimming) стиль m; (of pen etc.) штрих; (piston) ход; vt гла́дить impf, по~ pf.

**stroll** n прогу́лка; vi прогу́ливаться impf, прогуля́ться pf.

**strong** adj си́льный; (stout, of drinks) кре́пкий; (healthy) здоро́вый; (opinion etc.) твёрдый. **stronghold** n кре́пость. **strong-minded, strong-willed** adj реши́тельный.

**structural** adj структу́рный. **structure** n структу́ра; (building) сооруже́ние; vt организова́ть impf & pf.

**struggle** n борьба́; vi боро́ться impf (**for** за+acc; **against** про́тив+gen); (writhe, ~ **with** (fig)) би́ться (**with** над+instr).

**strum** vi бренча́ть impf (**on** на+prep).

**strut**[1] n (vertical) сто́йка; (horizontal) распо́рка.

**strut**[2] vi ходи́ть indet, идти́ det го́голем.

**stub** n (cigarette) оку́рок; (counterfoil) коре-шо́к; vt: ~ **one's toe** ударя́ться impf, уда́риться pf ного́й (**of** на+acc); ~ **out** гаси́ть impf, по~ pf.

**stubble** n жнивьё; (hair) щети́на.

**stubborn** adj упря́мый. **stubbornness** n упря́мство.

**stucco** n штукату́рка.

**stud**[1] n (collar, cuff) за́понка; (nail) гвоздь m с большо́й шля́пкой; vt (bestrew) усе́ивать impf, усе́ять pf (**with** +instr).

**stud**[2] n (horses) ко́нный заво́д.

**student** n студе́нт, ~ка.

**studied** adj напускно́й.

**studio** n сту́дия.

**studious** adj лю́бящий нау́ку; (diligent) стара́тельный.

**study** n изуче́ние; pl заня́тия neut pl; (investigation) иссле́дование; (art, mus) этю́д; (room) кабине́т; vt изуча́ть impf, изучи́ть pf, учи́ться impf, об~ pf +dat; (scrutinize) рассма́тривать impf, рассмотре́ть pf; vi (take lessons) учи́ться impf, об~ pf; (do one's studies) занима́ться impf.

**stuff** n (material) материа́л; (things) ве́щи f pl; vt на-бива́ть impf, наби́ть pf; (cul) начиня́ть impf, начини́ть pf; (cram into) запи́хивать impf, запиха́ть pf (**into** в+acc); (shove into) сова́ть impf, су́нуть pf (**into** в+acc); vi (overeat) объеда́ться impf, объе́сться pf. **stuffiness** n духота́. **stuffing** n наби́вка; (cul) начи́нка. **stuffy** adj ду́шный.

**stumble** vi (also fig) спотыка́ться impf, споткну́ться pf (**over** о+acc); ~ **upon** натыка́ться impf, наткну́ться pf на+acc. **stumbling-block** n ка́мень m преткнове́ния.

**stump** n (tree) пень m; (pencil) огры́зок; (limb) культя́; vt (perplex) ста́вить impf, по~ pf в тупи́к.

**stun** vt (also fig) оглуша́ть impf, оглуши́ть pf. **stunning** adj потряса́ющий.

**stunt**[1] n трюк.

**stunt**[2] vt заде́рживать impf, заде́ржать pf рост+gen. **stunted** adj низкоро́слый.

**stupefy** vt оглуша́ть impf, оглуши́ть pf. **stupendous** adj колосса́льный. **stupid** adj глу́пый. **stupidity** n глу́пость. **stupor** n оцепене́ние.

**sturdy** adj кре́пкий.

**stutter** n заика́ние; vi заика́ться impf.

**sty**¹ n (pig~) свина́рник.

**sty**² n (on eye) ячме́нь m.

**style** n стиль m; (taste) вкус; (fashion) мо́да; (sort) род; (of hair) причёска. **stylish** adj мо́дный. **stylist** n (of hair) парикма́хер. **stylistic** adj стилисти́ческий. **stylize** vt стилизова́ть impf & pf.

**stylus** n игла́ звукоснима́теля.

**suave** adj обходи́тельный.

**subconscious** adj подсозна́тельный; n подсозна́ние.

**subcontract** vt дава́ть impf, дать pf подря́дчику. **subcontractor** n подря́дчик. **subdivide** vt подразделя́ть impf, подраздели́ть pf. **subdivision** n подразделе́ние. **subdue** n vt покоря́ть impf, покори́ть pf. **subdued** adj (suppressed, dispirited) пода́вленный; (soft) мя́гкий; (indistinct) приглушённый. **sub-editor** n помо́щник реда́ктора.

**subject** n (theme) те́ма; (discipline, theme) предме́т; (question) вопро́с; (thing on to which action is directed) объе́кт; (gram) подлежа́щее sb; (national) по́дданный sb; adj: ~ to (susceptible to) подве́рженный+dat; (on condition that) при усло́вии, что…; е́сли; be ~ to (change etc.) подлежа́ть impf +dat; vt: ~ to подверга́ть impf, подве́ргнуть pf+dat. **subjection** n подчине́ние. **subjective** adj субъекти́вный. **subjectivity** n субъекти́вность. **subject-matter** n (of book, lecture) содержа́ние, те́ма; (of discussion) предме́т.

**subjugate** vt покоря́ть impf, покори́ть pf. **subjugation** n покоре́ние.

**subjunctive (mood)** n сослага́тельное наклоне́ние.

**sublet** vt передава́ть impf, переда́ть pf в субаре́нду.

**sublimate** vt сублими́ровать impf & pf. **sublimation** n сублима́ция. **sublime** adj возвы́шенный.

**subliminal** adj подсозна́тельный. **sub-machine-gun** n автома́т. **submarine** n подво́дная ло́дка. **submerge** vt погружа́ть impf, погрузи́ть pf. **submission** n подчине́ние; (for inspection) представле́ние. **submissive** adj поко́рный. **submit** vt подчиня́ться impf, подчини́ться pf (to +dat); vt представля́ть impf, предста́вить pf. **subordinate** n подчинённый sb; adj подчинённый; (secondary) второстепе́нный; (gram) прида́точный; vt подчиня́ть impf, подчини́ть pf. **subscribe** vi подпи́сываться impf, подписа́ться pf (to на+acc); ~ to (opinion) присоединя́ться impf, присоедини́ться pf к+dat. **subscriber** n подпи́счик; абоне́нт. **subscription** n подпи́ска, абонеме́нт; (fee) взнос. **subsection** n подразде́л. **subsequent** adj после́дующий. **subsequently** adv впосле́дствии. **subservient** adj раболе́пный. **subside** vi убыва́ть impf, убы́ть pf; (soil) оседа́ть impf, осе́сть pf. **subsidence** n (soil) оседа́ние. **subsidiary** adj вспомога́тельный; (secondary) второстепе́нный; n филиа́л. **subsidize** vt субсиди́ровать *impf* & *pf.* **subsidy** *n* субси́дия. **subsist** *vi* (*live*) жить *impf* (**on** +*instr*). **substance** *n* вещество́; (*essence*) су́щность, суть; (*content*) содержа́ние. **substantial** *adj* (*durable*) про́чный; (*considerable*) значи́тельный; (*food*) пло́тный. **substantially** *adv* (*basically*) в основно́м; (*considerably*) значи́тельно. **substantiate** *vt* обосно́вывать *impf*, обоснова́ть *pf.* **substitute** *n* (*person*) замести́тель *m*; (*thing*) заме́на; *vt* заменя́ть *impf*, замени́ть *pf* (**for** +*acc*); **I ~ water for milk** заменя́ю молоко́ водо́й. **substitution** *n* заме́на. **subsume** *vt* относи́ть *impf*, отнести́ *pf* к какой-л. катего́рии. **subterfuge** *n* уве́ртка. **subterranean** *adj* подзе́мный. **subtitle** *n* подзаголо́вок; (*cin*) субти́тр.

**subtle** *adj* то́нкий. **subtlety** *n* то́нкость.

**subtract** *vt* вычита́ть *impf*, вы́честь *pf.* **subtraction** *n* вычита́ние. **suburb** *n* при́город. **suburban** *adj* при́городный. **subversion** *n* подрывна́я де́ятельность. **subversive** *adj* подрывно́й. **subway** *n* подзе́мный перехо́д.

**succeed** *vi* удава́ться *impf*, уда́ться *pf*; **the plan will ~** план уда́стся; **he ~ed in buying the book** ему́ удало́сь купи́ть кни́гу; (*be successful*) преуспева́ть *impf*, преуспе́ть *pf* (**in** в+*prep*); (*follow*) сменя́ть *impf*, смени́ть *pf*; (*be heir*) насле́довать *impf* & *pf* (**to** +*dat*). **succeeding** *adj* после́дующий. **success** *n* успе́х. **successful** *adj* успе́шный.

**succession** *n* (*series*) ряд; (*to throne*) престолонасле́дие; **right of ~** пра́во насле́дования; **in ~** подря́д, оди́н за други́м. **successive** *adj* (*consecutive*) после́довательный. **successor** *n* прее́мник.

**succinct** *adj* сжа́тый.

**succulent** *adj* со́чный.

**succumb** *vi* (*to pressure*) уступа́ть *impf*, уступи́ть *pf* (**to** +*dat*); (*to temptation*) поддава́ться *impf*, подда́ться *pf* (**to** +*dat*).

**such** *adj* тако́й; **~ people** таки́е лю́ди; **~ as** (*for example*) так наприме́р; (*of a kind as*) тако́й как; **~ beauty as yours** така́я красота́ как ва́ша; (*that which*) тот, кото́рый; **I shall read ~ books as I like** я бу́ду чита́ть те кни́ги, кото́рые мне нра́вятся; **~ as to** тако́й, что́бы; **his illness was not ~ as to cause anxiety** его́ боле́знь была́ не тако́й (серьёзной), что́бы вы́звать беспоко́йство; **~ and ~** тако́й-то; *pron* тако́в; **~ was his character** тако́в был его́ хара́ктер; **as ~** сам по себе́; **~ is not the case** э́то не так. **suchlike** *pron* (*inanimate*) тому́ подо́бное; (*people*) таки́е лю́ди *pl*.

**suck** *vt* соса́ть *impf*; **~ in** вса́сывать *impf*, всоса́ть *pf*; (*engulf*) заса́сывать *impf*, засоса́ть *pf*; **~ out** выса́сывать *impf*, вы́сосать *pf*; **~ up to** (*coll*) подли́зываться *impf*, подлиза́ться *pf* к+*dat*. **sucker** *n* (*biol, rubber device*) присо́ска; (*bot*) корнево́й побе́г. **suckle** *vt* корми́ть *impf*, на~ *pf* гру́дью. **suction** *n* вса́сывание.

**sudden** adj внеза́пный. **suddenly** adv вдруг. **suddenness** n внеза́пность.

**sue** vt & i подава́ть impf, пода́ть pf в суд (на+acc); ~ s.o. for damages предъявля́ть impf, предъяви́ть pf (к) кому́-л. иск о возмеще́нии уще́рба.

**suede** n за́мша; adj за́мшевый.

**suet** n нутряно́е са́ло.

**suffer** vt страда́ть impf, по~ pf +instr, от+gen; (loss, defeat) терпе́ть impf, по~ pf; (tolerate) терпе́ть impf; vi страда́ть impf, по~ pf (from +instr, от+gen). **sufferance** n: he is here on ~ его́ здесь те́рпят. **suffering** n страда́ние.

**suffice** vi & t быть доста́точным (для+gen); хвата́ть impf, хвати́ть pf impers+gen (+dat). **sufficient** adj доста́точный.

**suffix** n су́ффикс.

**suffocate** vt удуша́ть impf, удуши́ть pf; vi задыха́ться impf, задохну́ться pf. **suffocating** adj уду́шливый. **suffocation** n удуше́ние.

**suffrage** n избира́тельное пра́во.

**suffuse** vt залива́ть impf, зали́ть pf (with +instr).

**sugar** n са́хар; adj са́харный; vt подсла́щивать impf, подсласти́ть pf; ~ basin са́харница; ~ beet са́харная свёкла; ~ cane са́харный тро́стник. **sugary** adj са́харный; (fig) сла́щавый.

**suggest** vt предлага́ть impf, предложи́ть pf; (evoke) напомина́ть impf, напо́мнить pf; (imply) намека́ть impf,

намекну́ть pf на+acc; (indicate) говори́ть impf о+prep. **suggestion** n предложе́ние; (psych) внуше́ние. **suggestive** adj вызыва́ющий мы́сли (of o+prep); (indecent) собла́знительный.

**suicidal** adj самоуби́йственный; (fig) губи́тельный. **suicide** n самоуби́йство; **commit** ~ соверша́ть impf, соверши́ть pf самоуби́йство.

**suit** n (clothing) костю́м; (law) иск; (cards) масть; **follow** ~ (fig) сле́довать impf, по~ pf приме́ру; vt (be convenient for) устра́ивать impf, устро́ить pf; (adapt) приспоса́бливать impf, приспосо́бить pf; (be ~able for, match) подходи́ть impf, подойти́ pf (+dat); (look attractive on) идти́ impf +dat. **suitability** n приго́дность. **suitable** adj (fitting) подходя́щий; (convenient) удо́бный. **suitably** adv соотве́тственно. **suitcase** n чемода́н.

**suite** n (retinue) сви́та; (furniture) гарниту́р; (rooms) апарта́менты m pl; (mus) сюи́та.

**suitor** n покло́нник.

**sulk** vi ду́ться impf. **sulky** adj наду́тый.

**sullen** adj угрю́мый.

**sully** vt пятна́ть impf, за~ pf.

**sulphur** n се́ра. **sulphuric** adj: ~ **acid** се́рная кислота́.

**sultana** n (raisin) изю́минка, pl кишми́ш (collect).

**sultry** adj зно́йный.

**sum** n су́мма; (arithmetical problem) арифмети́ческая зада́ча; v: ~ **up** vi & t (summarize) подводи́ть impf, подвести́ pf ито́ги (+gen); vt (appraise) оце́нивать impf, оцени́ть *pf*.

**summarize** *vt* сумми́ровать *impf* & *pf*. **summary** *n* резюме́ *neut indecl*, сво́дка; *adj* сумма́рный; (*dismissal*) бесцеремо́нный.

**summer** *n* ле́то; *attrib* ле́тний. **summer-house** *n* бесе́дка.

**summit** *n* верши́на; ~ **meeting** встре́ча на верха́х.

**summon** *vt* вызыва́ть *impf*, вы́звать *pf*; ~ **up one's courage** собира́ться *impf*, собра́ться *pf* с ду́хом. **summons** *n* вы́зов; (*law*) пове́стка в суд; *vt* вызыва́ть *impf*, вы́звать *pf* в суд.

**sumptuous** *adj* роско́шный.

**sun** *n* со́лнце; **in the ~** на со́лнце. **sunbathe** *vi* загора́ть *impf*. **sunbeam** *n* со́лнечный луч. **sunburn** *n* зага́р; (*inflammation*) со́лнечный ожо́г. **sunburnt** *adj* заго́релый; **become ~** загора́ть *impf*, загоре́ть *pf*.

**Sunday** *n* воскресе́нье.

**sundry** *adj* ра́зный; **all and ~** всё и вся.

**sunflower** *n* подсо́лнечник. **sun-glasses** *n pl* очки́ (-ко́в) *pl* от со́лнца.

**sunken** *adj* (*cheeks, eyes*) впа́лый; (*submerged*) погру-жённый; (*ship*) затоплен-ный; (*below certain level*) ни́же (како́го-л. у́ровня).

**sunlight** *n* со́лнечный свет. **sunny** *adj* со́лнечный. **sunrise** *n* восхо́д со́лнца. **sunset** *n* зака́т. **sunshade** *n* (*parasol*) зо́нтик; (*awning*) наве́с. **sunshine** *n* со́лнечный свет. **sunstroke** *n* со́лнечный уда́р. **suntan** *n* зага́р. **sun-tanned** *adj* заго́релый.

**super** *adj* замеча́тельный.

**superb** *adj* превосхо́дный.

**supercilious** *adj* высоко-ме́рный. **superficial** *adj* пове́рхностный. **superficiality** *n* пове́рхностность. **superfluous** *adj* ли́шний. **superhuman** *adj* сверхчелове́ческий. **superintendent** *n* заве́дующий *sb* (*of* +*instr*); (*police*) ста́рший полице́йский офице́р. **superior** *n* ста́рший *sb*; *adj* (*better*) превосхо́дный; (*in rank*) ста́рший; (*haughty*) высокоме́рный. **superiority** *n* превосхо́дство. **superlative** *adj* превосхо́дный; *n* (*gram*) превосхо́дная сте́пень. **superman** *n* сверхчелове́к. **supermarket** *n* универса́м. **supernatural** *adj* сверхъесте́ственный. **superpower** *n* сверхдержа́ва. **supersede** *vt* заменя́ть *impf*, замени́ть *pf*. **supersonic** *adj* сверхзвуково́й. **superstition** *n* суеве́рие. **superstitious** *adj* суеве́рный. **superstructure** *n* надстро́йка. **supervise** *vt* наблюда́ть *impf* за+*instr*. **supervision** *n* надзо́р. **supervisor** *n* нача́льник; (*of studies*) руководи́тель *m*.

**supper** *n* у́жин; **have ~** у́жинать *impf*, по~ *pf*.

**supple** *adj* ги́бкий. **suppleness** *n* ги́бкость.

**supplement** *n* (*to book*) дополне́ние; (*to periodical*) приложе́ние; *vt* дополня́ть *impf*, допо́лнить *pf*. **supplementary** *adj* дополни́тельный.

**supplier** *n* поставщи́к. **supply** *n* (*stock*) запа́с; (*econ*) предложе́ние; *pl* (*mil*) припа́сы (-ов) *pl*, *vt* снабжа́ть *impf*, снабди́ть *pf* (**with** +*instr*

**support** *n* подде́ржка; *vt* подде́рживать *impf*, поддержа́ть *pf*; (*family*) содержа́ть *impf*. **supporter** *n* сторо́нник; (*sport*) боле́льщик. **supportive** *adj* уча́стливый.

**suppose** *vt* (*think*) полага́ть *impf*; (*presuppose*) предполага́ть *impf*, предположи́ть *pf*; (*assume*) допуска́ть *impf*, допусти́ть *pf*. **supposed** *adj* (*assumed*) предполага́емый. **supposition** *n* предположе́ние.

**suppress** *vt* подавля́ть *impf*, подави́ть *pf*. **suppression** *n* подавле́ние.

**supremacy** *n* госпо́дство. **supreme** *adj* верхо́вный.

**surcharge** *n* наце́нка.

**sure** *adj* уве́ренный (*of* в+*prep*; *that* что); (*reliable*) ве́рный; ~ **enough** действи́тельно; **he is** ~ **to come** он обяза́тельно придёт; **make** ~ **of** (*convince o.s.*) убежда́ться *impf*, убеди́ться *pf* в+*prep*; **make** ~ **that** (*check up*) проверя́ть *impf*, прове́рить *pf* что. **surely** *adv* наверняка́. **surety** *n* пору́ка; **stand** ~ **for** руча́ться *impf*, поручи́ться *pf* за+*acc*.

**surf** *n* прибо́й; *vi* занима́ться *impf*, заня́ться *pf* сёрфингом.

**surface** *n* пове́рхность; (*exterior*) вне́шность; **on the** ~ (*fig*) вне́шне; **under the** ~ (*fig*) по существу́; *adj* пове́рхностный; *vi* всплыва́ть *impf*, всплыть *pf*.

**surfeit** *n* (*surplus*) изли́шек.

**surge** *n* волна́; *vi* (*rise, heave*) вздыма́ться *impf*; (*emotions*) нахлы́нуть *pf*; ~ **forward** ри́нуться *pf* вперёд.

**surgeon** *n* хиру́рг. **surgery** *n* (*treatment*) хирурги́я; (*place*)

кабине́т; (~ *hours*) приёмные часы́ *m pl* (врача́). **surgical** *adj* хирурги́ческий.

**surly** *adj* (*morose*) угрю́мый; (*rude*) гру́бый.

**surmise** *vt* & *i* предполага́ть *impf*, предположи́ть *pf*.

**surmount** *vt* преодолева́ть *impf*, преодоле́ть *pf*.

**surname** *n* фами́лия.

**surpass** *vt* превосходи́ть *impf*, превзойти́ *pf*.

**surplus** *n* изли́шек; *adj* изли́шний.

**surprise** *n* (*astonishment*) удивле́ние; (*surprising thing*) сюрпри́з; *vt* удивля́ть *impf*, удиви́ть *pf*; (*come upon suddenly*) застава́ть *impf*, заста́ть *pf* враспло́х; **be** ~**d** (*at*) удивля́ться *impf*, удиви́ться *pf* (+*dat*). **surprising** *adj* удиви́тельный.

**surreal** *adj* сюрреалисти́ческий. **surrealism** *n* сюрреали́зм. **surrealist** *n* сюрреали́ст; *adj* сюрреалисти́ческий.

**surrender** *n* сда́ча; (*renunciation*) отка́з; *vt* сдава́ть *impf*, сдать *pf*; (*give up*) отка́зываться *impf*, отказа́ться *pf* от+*gen*; *vi* сдава́ться *impf*, сда́ться *pf*; ~ **o.s. to** предава́ться *impf*, преда́ться *pf* +*dat*.

**surreptitious** *adj* та́йный.

**surrogate** *n* замени́тель *m*.

**surround** *vt* окружа́ть *impf*, окружи́ть *pf* (*with* +*instr*). **surrounding** *adj* окружа́ющий. **surroundings** *n* (*environs*) окре́стность *f pl*; (*milieu*) среда́.

**surveillance** *n* надзо́р.

**survey** *n* (*review*) обзо́р; (*inspection*) инспе́кция; (*poll*) опро́с; *vt* (*review*) обозревать *impf*, обозре́ть *pf*: (*inspect*) инспекти́ровать *impf*, про~ *pf*; (*poll*) опра́шивать *impf*, опроси́ть *pf*. **surveyor** *n* инспе́ктор.

**survival** *n* (*surviving*) выжива́ние; (*relic*) пережи́ток. **survive** *vt* пережива́ть *impf*, пережи́ть *pf*; *vi* выжива́ть *impf*, вы́жить *pf*. **survivor** *n* уцеле́вший *sb*; (*fig*) боре́ц.

**susceptible** *adj* подве́рженный (**to** влия́нию +*gen*); (*sensitive*) чувстви́тельный (**to** к+*dat*); (*impressionable*) впечатли́тельный.

**suspect** *n* подозрева́емый *sb*; *adj* подозри́тельный; *vt* подозрева́ть *impf* (**of** в+*prep*); (*assume*) полага́ть *impf*.

**suspend** *vt* (*hang*) подве́шивать *impf*, подве́сить *pf*; (*delay*) приостана́вливать *impf*, приостанови́ть *pf*; (*debar temporarily*) вре́менно отстраня́ть *impf*, отстрани́ть *pf*; ~**ed sentence** усло́вный пригово́р. **suspender** *n* (*stocking*) подвя́зка. **suspense** *n* неизве́стность. **suspension** *n* (*halt*) приостано́вка; (*of car*) рессо́ры *f pl*; ~ **bridge** вися́чий мост.

**suspicion** *n* подозре́ние; **on** ~ по подозре́нию (**of** в+*loc*); (*trace*) отте́нок. **suspicious** *adj* подозри́тельный.

**sustain** *vt* (*support*) подде́рживать *impf*, поддержа́ть *pf*; (*suffer*) потерпе́ть *pf*. **sustained** *adj* непреры́вный. **sustenance** *n* пи́ща.

**swab** *n* (*mop*) шва́бра; (*med*) тампо́н; (*specimen*) мазо́к.

**swagger** *vi* расха́живать *impf* с ва́жным ви́дом.

**swallow**[1] *n* глото́к; *vt* про-

гла́тывать *impf*, проглоти́ть *pf*; ~ **up** поглоща́ть *impf*, поглоти́ть *pf*.

**swallow**[2] *n* (*bird*) ла́сточка.

**swamp** *n* боло́та; *vt* залива́ть *impf*, зали́ть *pf*; (*fig*) зава́ливать *impf*, завали́ть *pf* (**with** +*instr*). **swampy** *adj* боло́тистый.

**swan** *n* ле́бедь *m*.

**swap** *n* обме́н; *vt* (*for different thing*) меня́ть *impf*, об~, по~ *pf* (**for** на+*acc*); (*for similar thing*) обме́ниваться *impf*, обменя́ться *pf* +*instr*.

**swarm** *n* рой; (*crowd*) толпа́; *vi* рои́ться *impf*; толпи́ться *impf*; (*teem*) кише́ть *impf* (**with** +*instr*).

**swarthy** *adj* сму́глый.

**swastika** *n* сва́стика.

**swat** *vt* прихло́пывать *impf*, прихло́пнуть *pf*.

**swathe** *n* (*expanse*) простра́нство; *vt* (*wrap*) заку́тывать *impf*, заку́тать *pf*.

**sway** *n* (*influence*) влия́ние; (*power*) власть *n* & *i* кача́ть(ся) *impf*, качну́ть(ся) *pf*; *vt* (*influence*) име́ть *impf* влия́ние на+*acc*.

**swear** *vi* (*vow*) кля́сться *impf*, по~ *pf*; (*curse*) руга́ться *impf*, ругну́ться *pf*; ~**-word** руга́тельство.

**sweat** *n* пот; *vi* поте́ть *impf*, вс~ *pf*. **sweater** *n* сви́тер. **sweatshirt** *n* тёплая футбо́лка с дли́нными рукава́ми. **sweaty** *adj* по́тный.

**swede** *n* брю́ква.

**Swede** *n* швед, ~дка. **Sweden** *n* Шве́ция. **Swedish** *adj* шве́дский.

**sweep** *n* (*span*) разма́х; (*chimney*~) трубочи́ст; *vt* подмета́ть *impf*, подмести́ *pf*; *vi* *(go majestically)* ходи́ть *indet,* идти́ *det,* пойти́ *pf* велича́во; *(move swiftly)* мча́ться *impf;* ~ **away** смета́ть *impf,* смести́ *pf.* **sweeping** *adj (changes)* радика́льный; *(statement)* огу́льный.

**sweet** *n (sweetmeat)* конфе́та; *(dessert)* сла́дкое *sb; adj* сла́дкий; *(fragrant)* души́стый; *(dear)* ми́лый. **sweeten** *vt* подсла́щивать *impf,* подсласти́ть *pf.* **sweetheart** *n* возлюбленный, -нная *sb.* **sweetness** *n* сла́дость.

**swell** *vi (up)* опуха́ть *impf,* опу́хнуть *pf; vt & i (a sail)* надува́ть(ся) *impf,* наду́ть(ся) *pf; vt (increase)* увеличи́вать *impf,* увели́чить *pf (of sea)* зыбь. **swelling** *n* о́пухоль.

**swelter** *vi* изнемога́ть *impf* от жары́. **sweltering** *adj* зно́йный.

**swerve** *vi* ре́зко свёртывать, свора́чивать *impf,* сверну́ть *pf.*

**swift** *adj* бы́стрый.

**swig** *n* глото́к; *vt* хлеба́ть *impf.*

**swill** *n* по́йло; *vt (rinse)* полоска́ть *impf,* вы́~ *pf.*

**swim** *vi* пла́вать *indet,* плыть *det; vt (across)* переплыва́ть *impf,* переплы́ть *pf +acc,* че́рез+*acc.* **swimmer** *n* плове́ц, пловчи́ха. **swimming** *n* пла́вание. **swimming-pool** *n* бассе́йн для пла́вания. **swimsuit** *n* купа́льный костю́м.

**swindle** *vt* обма́нывать *impf,* обману́ть *pf; n* обма́н. **swindler** *n* моше́нник.

**swine** *n* свинья́.

**swing** *vi* кача́ться *impf,* качну́ться *pf; vt* кача́ть *impf,* качну́ть *pf +acc, instr; (arms)* разма́хивать *impf +instr; n*

кача́ние; *(shift)* крен; *(seat)* каче́ли (-лей) *pl;* **in full** ~ **b** по́лном разга́ре.

**swingeing** *adj (huge)* грома́дный; *(forcible)* си́льный.

**swipe** *n* си́льный уда́р; *vt* c си́лой ударя́ть *impf,* уда́рить *pf.*

**swirl** *vi* крути́ться *impf; n (of snow)* вихрь *m.*

**swish** *vi (cut the air)* рассека́ть *impf,* рассе́чь *pf* во́здух со сви́стом; *vt (tail)* взма́хивать *impf,* взмахну́ть *pf +instr; (brandish)* разма́хивать *impf +instr; n (of whip)* свист; *(rustle)* ше́лест.

**Swiss** *n* швейца́рец, -ца́рка; *adj* швейца́рский.

**switch** *n (electr)* выключа́тель *m; (change)* измене́ние; *vt & i (also ~ over)* переключа́ть(ся) *impf,* переключи́ть(ся) *pf; vt (swap)* меня́ть(ся) *impf,* об~, по~ *pf +instr;* ~ **off** выключа́ть *impf,* вы́ключить *pf;* ~ **on** включа́ть *impf,* включи́ть *pf.* **switchboard** *n* коммута́тор.

**Switzerland** *n* Швейца́рия.

**swivel** *vt & i* враща́ть(ся) *impf.*

**swollen** *adj* взду́тый.

**swoon** *n* о́бморок; *vi* па́дать *impf,* упа́сть *pf* в о́бморок.

**swoop** *vi:* ~ **down** налета́ть *impf,* налете́ть *pf (on* на+*acc); n* налёт; **at one fell** ~ одни́м уда́ром.

**sword** *n* меч.

**sycophantic** *adj* льсти́вый.

**syllable** *n* слог.

**syllabus** *n* програ́мма.

**symbol** *n* си́мвол. **symbolic(al)** *adj* символи́ческий. **symbolism** *n* символи́зм. **symbolize** *vt* символизи́ровать *impf.*

**symmetrical** *adj* симметри́ческий. **symmetry** *n* симме́трия.

**sympathetic** *adj* сочу́вственный. **sympathize** *vi* сочу́вствовать *impf* (**with** +*dat*).

**sympathizer** *n* сторо́нник. **sympathy** *n* сочу́вствие.

**symphony** *n* симфо́ния.

**symposium** *n* симпо́зиум.

**symptom** *n* симпто́м. **symptomatic** *adj* симптомати́чный.

**synagogue** *n* синаго́га.

**synchronization** *n* синхрониза́ция. **synchronize** *vt* синхронизи́ровать *impf* & *pf*.

**syndicate** *n* синдика́т.

**syndrome** *n* синдро́м.

**synonym** *n* сино́ним. **synonymous** *adj* синоними́чный.

**synopsis** *n* конспе́кт.

**syntax** *n* си́нтаксис.

**synthesis** *n* си́нтез. **synthetic** *adj* синтети́ческий.

**syphilis** *n* си́филис.

**Syria** *n* Си́рия. **Syrian** *n* сири́ец, сири́йка; *adj* сири́йский.

**syringe** *n* шприц; *vt* спринцева́ть *impf*.

**syrup** *n* сиро́п; (*treacle*) па́тока.

**system** *n* систе́ма; (*network*) сеть; (*organism*) органи́зм. **systematic** *adj* системати́ческий. **systematize** *vt* систематизи́ровать *impf* & *pf*.

# T

**tab** *n* (*loop*) пе́телька; (*on uniform*) петли́ца; (*of boot*) ушко́; **keep ~s on** следи́ть *impf* за+*instr*.

**table** *n* стол; (*chart*) табли́ца; **~cloth** ска́терть; **~spoon** столо́вая ло́жка; **~ tennis** насто́льный те́ннис; *vt* (*for*

*discussion*) предлага́ть *impf*, предложи́ть *pf* на обсужде́ние.

**tableau** *n* жива́я карти́на.

**tablet** *n* (*pill*) табле́тка; (*of stone*) плита́; (*memorial* ~) мемориа́льная доска́; (*name plate*) доще́чка.

**tabloid** *n* (*newspaper*) малоформа́тная газе́та; (*derog*) бульва́рная газе́та.

**taboo** *n* табу́ *neut indecl*; *adj* запрещённый.

**tacit** *adj* молчали́вый. **taciturn** *adj* неразгово́рчивый.

**tack¹** *n* (*nail*) гвоздик; (*stitch*) намётка; (*naut*) галс; (*fig*) курс; *vt* (*fasten*) прикрепля́ть *impf*, прикрепи́ть *pf* гво́здиками; (*stitch*) смётывать *impf*, смета́ть *pf* на живу́ю ни́тку; (*fig*) добавля́ть *impf*, доба́вить *pf* ((**on)to** +*dat*); *vi* (*naut*; *fig*) лави́ровать *impf*.

**tack²** *n* (*riding*) сбру́я (*collect*).

**tackle** *n* (*requisites*) снасть (*collect*); (*sport*) блокиро́вка; *vt* (*problem*) бра́ться *impf*, взя́ться *pf* за+*acc*; (*sport*) блоки́ровать *impf* & *pf*.

**tacky** *adj* ли́пкий.

**tact** *n* такт(и́чность). **tactful** *adj* такти́чный.

**tactical** *adj* такти́ческий. **tactics** *n pl* та́ктика.

**tactless** *adj* беста́ктный.

**tadpole** *n* голова́стик.

**Tadzhikistan** *n* Таджикиста́н.

**tag** *n* (*label*) ярлы́к; (*of lace*) наконе́чник; *vt* (*label*) прикрепля́ть *impf*, прикрепи́ть *pf* ярлы́к на+*acc*; *vi*: **~ along** (*follow*) тащи́ться *impf* сзади; **may I ~ along?** мо́жно с ва́ми?

**tail** *n* хвост; (*of shirt*) ни́жний

коне́ц; (of coat) фа́лда; (of coin) обра́тная сторона́ моне́ты; **heads or ~s?** орёл и́ли ре́шка?; pl (of coat) фрак; vt (shadow) высле́живать impf, vi: **~ away, off** постепе́нно уменьша́ться impf, (grow silent, abate) затиха́ть impf. **tailback** n хвост. **tailcoat** n фрак.

**tailor** n портно́й sb; **~-made** сши́тый на зака́з; (fig) сде́ланный индивидуа́льно.

**taint** vt по́ртить impf, ис~ pf.

**Taiwan** n Тайва́нь m.

**take** vt (various senses) брать impf, взять pf; (also seize, capture) захва́тывать impf, захвати́ть pf; (receive, accept; ~ breakfast; ~ medicine; ~ steps) принима́ть impf, приня́ть pf; (convey, escort) провожа́ть impf, проводи́ть pf; (public transport) е́здить indet, е́хать det, по~ pf +instr, на+prep; (photograph) снима́ть impf, снять pf; (occupy; ~ time) занима́ть impf, заня́ть pf; (impers) **how long does it ~?** ско́лько вре́мени ну́жно?; (size in clothing) носи́ть impf; (exam) сдава́ть impf, vi (be successful) име́ть impf успе́х (of injection) привива́ть impf, приви́ться pf; **~ after** походи́ть impf на+acc; **~ away** (remove) убира́ть impf, убра́ть pf; (subtract) вычита́ть impf, вы́честь pf; **~ away** магази́н, где продаю́т на вы́нос; **~ back** (return) возвраща́ть impf, возврати́ть pf; (retrieve, retract) брать impf, взять pf наза́д; **~ down** (in writing) запи́сывать impf, записа́ть pf; (remove) снима́ть impf, снять

pf; **~ s.o., sth for, to be** принима́ть impf, приня́ть pf за+acc; **~ from** отнима́ть impf, отня́ть pf у, от+gen; **~ in** (carry in) вноси́ть impf, внести́ pf; (lodgers; work) брать impf, взять pf; (clothing) ушива́ть impf, уши́ть pf; (understand) понима́ть impf, поня́ть pf; (deceive) обма́нывать impf, обману́ть pf; **~ off** (clothing) снима́ть impf, снять pf; (mimic) передра́знивать impf, передразни́ть pf; (aeroplane) взлета́ть impf, взлете́ть pf; **~-off** (imitation) подража́ние; (aeron) взлёт; **~ on** (undertake; hire) брать impf, взять pf на себя́; (acquire) приобрета́ть impf, приобрести́ pf; (at game) сража́ться impf, срази́ться pf с+instr (at в+acc); **~ out** вынима́ть impf, вы́нуть pf; (dog) выводи́ть impf, вы́вести pf (for a walk на прогу́лку); (to theatre, restaurant etc.) приглаша́ть impf, пригласи́ть pf (to в+acc); **we took them out every night** мы приглаша́ли их куда́-нибудь ка́ждый ве́чер; **~ it out on** срыва́ть impf, сорва́ть pf всё на+prep; **~ over** принима́ть impf, приня́ть pf руково́дство +instr; **~ to** (thing) пристрасти́ться pf к+dat; (person) привя́зываться impf, привяза́ться pf к+dat; (begin) станови́ться impf, стать pf +inf; **~ up** (interest oneself in) занима́ться impf, заня́ться pf; (with an official etc.) обраща́ться impf, обрати́ться pf с+instr, к+dat; (challenge) принима́ть impf, приня́ть pf; (time, space) занима́ть *impf*, заня́ть *pf*; ~ **up with** (*person*) свя́зываться *impf*, связа́ться *pf* c+*instr*; (*cin*) дубль *m*.

**taking** *adj* привлека́тельный.

**takings** *n pl* сбор.

**talcum powder** *n* тальк.

**tale** *n* расска́з.

**talent** *n* тала́нт. **talented** *adj* тала́нтливый.

**talk** *vi* разгова́ривать *impf* (**to**, **with** c+*instr*); (*gossip*) спле́тничать *impf*, на~ *pf*; *vt & i* говори́ть *impf*, по~ *pf*; ~ **down to** говори́ть *impf* свысока́ c+*instr*; ~ **into** угова́ривать *impf*, уговори́ть *pf* +*inf*; ~ **out of** отгова́ривать *impf*, отговори́ть *pf* +*inf*, от+*gen*; ~ **over** (*discuss*) обсужда́ть *impf*, обсуди́ть *pf*; ~ **round** (*persuade*) переубежда́ть *impf*, переубеди́ть *pf*; *n* (*conversation*) разгово́р; (*lecture*) бесе́да; *pl* перегово́ры (-ров) *pl*. **talkative** *adj* разгово́рчивый; (*derog*) болтли́вый. **talker** *n* говоря́щий *sb*; (*chatterer*) болту́н (*coll*); (*orator*) ора́тор. **talking-to** *n* (*coll*) вы́говор.

**tall** *adj* высо́кий; (*in measurements*) ро́стом в+*acc*.

**tally** *n* (*score*) счёт; *vi* соотве́тствовать (**with** +*dat*).

**talon** *n* ко́готь *m*.

**tambourine** *n* бу́бен.

**tame** *adj* ручно́й; (*insipid*) пре́сный; *vt* прируча́ть *impf*, приручи́ть *pf*. **tamer** *n* укроти́тель *m*.

**tamper** *vi*: ~ **with** (*meddle*) тро́гать *impf*, тро́нуть *pf*; (*forge*) подде́лывать *impf*, подде́лать *pf*.

**tampon** *n* тампо́н.

**tan** *n* (*sun*~) зага́р; *adj* жел-

това́то-кори́чневый; *vt* (*hide*) дуби́ть *impf*, вы́~ *pf*; (*beat*) (*coll*) дуба́сить *impf*, от~ *pf*; *vi* загора́ть *impf*, загоре́ть *pf*; (*of sun*): **tanned** загоре́лый.

**tang** *n* (*taste*) ре́зкий при́вкус; (*smell*) о́стрый за́пах.

**tangent** *n* (*math*) каса́тельная *sb*; (*trigonometry*) та́нгенс; **go off at a** ~ отклоня́ться *impf*, отклони́ться *pf* от те́мы.

**tangerine** *n* мандари́н.

**tangible** *adj* осяза́емый.

**tangle** *vt & i* запу́тывать(ся) *impf*, запу́таться *pf*; *n* пу́таница.

**tango** *n* та́нго *neut indecl*.

**tangy** *adj* о́стрый; ре́зкий.

**tank** *n* бак; (*mil*) танк.

**tankard** *n* кру́жка.

**tanker** *n* (*sea*) та́нкер; (*road*) автоцисте́рна.

**tantalize** *vt* дразни́ть *impf*.

**tantamount** *predic* равноси́лен (-льна) (**to** +*dat*).

**tantrum** *n* при́ступ раздраже́ния.

**tap**[1] *n* кран; *vt* (*resources*) испо́льзовать *impf & pf*; (*telephone conversation*) подслу́шивать *impf*.

**tap**[2] *n* (*knock*) стук; *vt* стуча́ть *impf*, по~ *pf* в+*acc*, по+*dat*; ~-**dance** (*vi*) отбива́ть *impf*, отби́ть *pf* чечётку; (*n*) чечётка; ~-**dancer** чечёточник, -ица.

**tape** *n* (*cotton strip*) тесьма́; (*adhesive, magnetic, measuring, etc.*) ле́нта; ~-**measure** руле́тка; ~ **recorder** магнитофо́н; ~ **recording** за́пись; *vt* (*seal*) закле́ивать *impf*, закле́ить *pf*; (*record*) запи́сывать *impf*, записа́ть *pf* на ле́нту.

**taper** vt & i су́живать(ся) impf, су́зить(ся) pf.

**tapestry** n гобеле́н.

**tar** n дёготь m.

**tardy** adj (slow) медли́тельный; (late) запозда́лый.

**target** n мише́нь, цель.

**tariff** n тари́ф.

**tarmac** n (material) гудро́н; (road) гудрони́рованное шоссе́ neut indecl; (runway) бетони́рованная площа́дка; vt гудрони́ровать impf & pf.

**tarnish** vt де́лать impf, c~ pf ту́склым; (fig) пятна́ть impf, за~ pf; vi тускне́ть impf, по~ pf.

**tarpaulin** n брезе́нт.

**tarragon** n эстраго́н.

**tart**[1] adj (taste) ки́слый; (fig) ко́лкий.

**tart**[2] n (pie) сла́дкий пиро́г.

**tart**[3] n (prostitute) шлю́ха.

**tartan** n шотла́ндка.

**tartar** n ви́нный ка́мень m.

**task** n зада́ча; **take to** ~ де́лать impf, c~ pf вы́говор+dat; ~ **force** операти́вная гру́ппа.

**Tass** abbr ТАСС, Телегра́фное аге́нтство Сове́тского Сою́за.

**tassel** n ки́сточка.

**taste** n (also fig) вкус; **take a ~ of** про́бовать impf, по~ pf; vt испро́бовать impf, по~ pf вкус+gen; (sample) про́бовать impf, по~ pf; (fig) вкуша́ть impf, вкуси́ть pf; (wine etc.) дегусти́ровать impf & pf; vi име́ть вкус, привку́с (**of** +gen). **tasteful** adj (сде́ланный) со вку́сом. **tasteless** adj безвку́сный. **tasting** n дегуста́ция. **tasty** adj вку́сный.

**tatter** n pl лохмо́тья (-ьев) pl. **tattered** adj обо́рванный.

**tattoo** n (design) татуиро́вка; vt татуи́ровать impf & pf.

**taunt** n насме́шка; vt насмеха́ться impf над+instr.

**Taurus** n Теле́ц.

**taut** adj ту́го натя́нутый; туго́й.

**tavern** n таве́рна.

**tawdry** adj мишу́рный.

**tawny** adj рыжева́то-кори́чневый.

**tax** n нало́г; ~-**free** освобождённый от нало́га; vt облага́ть impf, обложи́ть pf нало́гом; (strain) напряга́ть impf, напря́чь pf; (patience) испы́тывать impf, испыта́ть pf. **taxable** adj подлежа́щий обложе́нию нало́гом. **taxation** n обложе́ние нало́гом. **taxing** adj утоми́тельный. **taxpayer** n налогоплате́льщик.

**taxi** n такси́ neut indecl; ~-**driver** води́тель m такси́; ~-**rank** стоя́нка такси́; vi (aeron) рули́ть impf.

**tea** n чай impf, impf, ~ **bag** паке́тик с сухи́м ча́ем; ~ **cloth**, ~ **towel** полоте́нце для посу́ды; ~ **cosy** чехо́льчик (для ча́йника); ~-**cup** ча́йная ча́шка; ~-**leaf** ча́йный лист; ~-**pot** ча́йник; ~-**spoon** ча́йная ло́жка; ~-**strainer** ча́йное си́течко.

**teach** vt учи́ть impf, на~ pf (person +acc; subject +dat, inf); преподава́ть impf (subject +acc); (coll) проучи́ть impf, проучи́ть pf. **teacher** n учи́тель m, ~ница; преподава́тель m, ~ница. ~-**training college** педагоги́ческий институ́т. **teaching** n (instruction) обуче́ние; (doctrine) уче́ние.

**teak** n тик; attrib ти́ковый.

**team** n (sport) кома́нда; (of people) брига́да; (of horses etc.) упря́жка; ~-mate член той же кома́нды; ~work сотру́дничество; vi (~ up) объединя́ться impf, объедини́ться pf.

**tear**[1] n (rent) проре́ха; vt (also ~ up) рвать impf, (also ~ up) разрыва́ть impf, разорва́ть pf; vi рва́ться impf; (rush) мча́ться impf; ~ down, off срыва́ть impf, сорва́ть pf; ~ out вырыва́ть impf, вы́рвать pf.

**tear**[2] n (~-drop) слеза́; ~-gas слезоточи́вый газ. **tearful** adj слезли́вый.

**tease** vt дразни́ть impf.

**teat** n сосо́к.

**technical** adj техни́ческий; ~ college техни́ческое учи́лище. **technicality** n форма́льность. **technically** adv (strictly) форма́льно. **technician** n те́хник. **technique** n те́хника; (method) ме́тод. **technology** n техноло́гия, те́хника. **technological** adj техноло́гический. **technologist** n техно́лог.

**teddy-bear** n медвежо́нок.

**tedious** adj ску́чный. **tedium** n ску́ка.

**teem**[1] vi (swarm) кише́ть impf (with +instr).

**teem**[2] vi: it is ~ing (with rain) дождь льёт как из ведра́.

**teenage** adj ю́ношеский. **teenager** n подро́сток. **teens** n pl во́зраст от трина́дцати до девятна́дцати лет.

**teeter** vi кача́ться impf, качну́ться pf.

**teethe** vi: the child is teething у ребёнка проре́зываются

зу́бы; **teething troubles** (fig) нача́льные пробле́мы f pl.

**teetotal** adj тре́звый. **teetotaller** n тре́звенник.

**telecommunication(s)** n да́льняя связь. **telegram** n телегра́мма. **telegraph** n телегра́ф; ~ pole телегра́фный столб. **telepathic** adj телепати́ческий. **telepathy** n телепа́тия. **telephone** n телефо́н; vt (message) телефони́ровать impf & pf +acc, o+prep; (person) звони́ть impf, по~ pf (по телефо́ну) +dat; ~ box телефо́нная бу́дка; ~ directory телефо́нная кни́га; ~ exchange телефо́нная ста́нция; ~ number но́мер телефо́на. **telephonist** n телефони́ст, ~ка. **telephoto lens** n телеобъекти́в. **telescope** n телеско́п. **telescopic** adj телескопи́ческий. **televise** vt пока́зывать impf по телеви́дению. **television** n телеви́дение; (set) телеви́зор; attrib телевизио́нный. **telex** n те́лекс.

**tell** vt & i (relate) расска́зывать impf, рассказа́ть pf (thing told +acc, o+prep; person told +dat); vt (utter, inform) говори́ть impf, сказа́ть pf (thing uttered +acc; thing informed about o+prep; person informed +dat); (order) веле́ть impf & pf +dat; ~ one thing from another отлича́ть impf, отличи́ть pf +acc от+gen; vi (have an effect) ска́зываться impf, сказа́ться pf (on на+prep); ~ off отчи́тывать impf, отчита́ть pf; ~ on, ~ tales about я́бедничать impf, на~ pf на+acc.

**teller** n (of story) расска́зчик; (of votes) счётчик; (in bank) касси́р. **telling** adj (effective) эффекти́вный; (significant) многозначи́тельный. **telltale** n спле́тник; adj преда́тельский.

**temerity** n де́рзость.

**temp** n рабо́тающий sb вре́менно; vi рабо́тать impf вре́менно.

**temper** n (character) нрав; (mood) настрое́ние; (anger) гнев; **lose one's ~** выходи́ть impf, вы́йти pf из себя́; vt (fig) смягча́ть impf, смягчи́ть pf.

**temperament** n темпера́мент. **temperamental** adj темпера́ментный.

**temperance** n (moderation) уме́ренность; (sobriety) тре́звенность.

**temperate** adj уме́ренный.

**temperature** n температу́ра; (high ~) повы́шенная температу́ра; **take s.o.'s ~** изме́рять impf, изме́рить pf температу́ру +dat.

**tempest** n бу́ря. **tempestuous** adj бу́рный.

**template** n шабло́н.

**temple**[1] n (religion) храм.

**temple**[2] n (anat) висо́к.

**tempo** n темп.

**temporal** adj (of time) вре́менно́й; (secular) мирско́й.

**temporary** adj вре́менный.

**tempt** vt соблазня́ть impf, соблазни́ть pf; **~ fate** испы́тывать impf, испыта́ть pf судьбу́. **temptation** n собла́зн. **tempting** adj соблазни́тельный.

**ten** adj & n де́сять; (number 10) деся́тка. **tenth** adj & n деся́тый.

**tenable** adj (logical) разу́мный.

**tenacious** adj це́пкий. **tenacity** n це́пкость.

**tenancy** n (renting) наём помеще́ния; (period) срок аре́нды. **tenant** n аренда́тор.

**tend**[1] vi (be apt) име́ть скло́нность (to k+dat, +inf).

**tend**[2] vt (look after) уха́живать impf за+instr.

**tendency** n тенде́нция. **tendentious** adj тенденцио́зный.

**tender**[1] vt (offer) предлага́ть impf, предложи́ть pf; vi (make ~ for) подава́ть impf, пода́ть pf заявку (на торга́х.); **~ резиgnation** (на торга́х.); legal **~** зако́нное платёжное сре́дство.

**tender**[2] adj (delicate, affectionate) не́жный. **tenderness** n не́жность.

**tendon** n сухожи́лие.

**tendril** n у́сик.

**tenement** n (dwelling-house) жило́й дом; **~-house** многокварти́рный дом.

**tenet** n до́гмат, при́нцип.

**tennis** n те́ннис.

**tenor** n (direction) направле́ние; (purport) смысл; (mus) те́нор.

**tense**[1] n вре́мя neut.

**tense**[2] vt напряга́ть impf, напря́чь pf; adj напряжённый. **tension** n напряже́ние.

**tent** n пала́тка.

**tentacle** n щу́пальце.

**tentative** adj (experimental) про́бный; (preliminary) предвари́тельный.

**tenterhooks** n pl: **be on ~** сиде́ть как на иго́лках.

**tenth** see ten

**tenuous** adj (fig) неубеди́тельный.

**tenure** n (of property) владе́ние; (of office) пребыва́ние в до́лжности; (period) срок; (guaranteed employment) несменя́емость.

**tepid** adj теплова́тый.

**term** n (period) срок; (univ) семе́стр; (school) че́тверть; (technical word) те́рмин; (expression) выраже́ние; pl (conditions) усло́вия neut pl; (relations) отноше́ния neut pl; on good ~s в хоро́ших отноше́ниях; come to ~s with (resign o.s. to) покоря́ться impf, покори́ться pf k+dat; vt называ́ть impf, назва́ть pf.

**terminal** adj коне́чный; (med) сме́ртельный; n (electr) зажи́м; (computer, aeron) термина́л; (terminus) коне́чная остано́вка.

**terminate** vt & i конча́ть(ся) impf, ко́нчить(ся) pf (in +instr). **termination** n прекраще́ние.

**terminology** n терминоло́гия.

**terminus** n коне́чная остано́вка.

**termite** n терми́т.

**terrace** n терра́са; (houses) ряд домо́в.

**terracotta** n терракота.

**terrain** n ме́стность.

**terrestrial** adj земно́й.

**terrible** adj ужа́сный. **terribly** adv ужа́сно.

**terrier** n терье́р.

**terrific** adj (huge) огро́мный; (splendid) потряса́ющий. **terrify** vt ужаса́ть impf, ужасну́ть pf.

**territorial** adj территориа́льный. **territory** n терри́тория.

**terror** n у́жас; (person; polit) терро́р. **terrorism** n терро́ризм. **terrorist** n террори́ст,

~ка. **terrorize** vt терроризи́ровать impf & pf.

**terse** adj кра́ткий.

**tertiary** adj тре́тичный; (education) вы́сший.

**test** n испыта́ние, про́ба; (exam) экза́мен; контро́льная рабо́та; (analysis) ана́лиз; ~tube проби́рка; vt (try out) испы́тывать impf, испыта́ть pf; (check up on) проверя́ть impf, прове́рить pf; (give exam to) экзаменова́ть impf, про~ pf.

**testament** n завеща́ние; Old, New T~ Ве́тхий, Но́вый заве́т.

**testicle** n яи́чко.

**testify** vi свиде́тельствовать impf (to в по́льзу+gen; against про́тив+gen); vt (declare) заявля́ть impf, заяви́ть pf; (be evidence of) свиде́тельствовать o+prep.

**testimonial** n рекоменда́ция, характери́стика. **testimony** n свиде́тельство.

**tetanus** n столбня́к.

**tetchy** adj раздражи́тельный.

**tête-à-tête** n & adv тет-а-те́т.

**tether** n: be at, come to the end of one's ~ дойти́ pf до то́чки; vt привя́зывать impf, привяза́ть pf.

**text** n текст. **textbook** n уче́бник.

**textile** n текст́ильный; n ткань; pl тексти́ль m (collect).

**textual** adj тексто́вой.

**texture** n тексту́ра.

**than** conj (comparison) чем; other ~ (except) кро́ме+gen.

**thank** vt благодари́ть impf, по~ pf (for за+acc); ~ God сла́ва Бо́гу; ~ you спаси́бо; благодарю́ вас; n pl благода́рность; ~s to (good result) благодаря́ +dat; (bad result) из-за+gen. **thankless** adj неблагода́рный. **thankful** adj неблагода́рный. **thanksgiving** n благодаре́ние.

**that** demonstrative adj & pron тот; ~ **which** тот кото́рый; rel pron кото́рый; conj что; (purpose) что́бы; adv так, до тако́й сте́пени.

**thatched** adj соло́менный.

**thaw** vt раста́пливать impf, растопи́ть pf; vi та́ять impf, рас~ pf; n о́ттепель.

**the** def article, not translated; adv тем; the ... the ... чем...тем; ~ **more** ~ **better** чем бо́льше, тем лу́чше.

**theatre** n теа́тр; (lecture ~) аудито́рия; (operating ~) операцио́нная sb; ~**-goer** театра́л. **theatrical** adj театра́льный.

**theft** n кра́жа.

**their**, **theirs** poss pron их; свой.

**theme** n те́ма.

**themselves** pron (emph) (они́) са́ми; (refl) себя́; -ся (suffixed to vt).

**then** adv (at that time) тогда́; (after that) пото́м; **now and** ~ вре́мя от вре́мени; conj в тако́м слу́чае, тогда́; adj тогда́шний; **by** ~ к тому́ вре́мени; **since** ~ с тех пор.

**thence** adv отту́да. **thenceforth**, **-forward** adv с того́/э́того вре́мени.

**theologian** n тео́лог. **theological** adj теологи́ческий. **theology** n теоло́гия.

**theorem** n теоре́ма. **theoretical** adj теорети́ческий. **theorize** vi теоретизи́ровать impf. **theory** n тео́рия.

**therapeutic** adj терапевти́ческий. **therapist** n (psychotherapist) психотерапе́вт. **therapy** n терапи́я.

**there** adv (place) там; (direction) туда́; int вот!; ну!; ~s, **are** есть, име́ется (-е́ются); ~ **you are** (on giving sth) пожа́луйста. **thereabouts** adv (near) побли́зости; (approximately) приблизи́тельно. **thereafter** adv по́сле э́того. **thereby** adv таки́м о́бразом. **therefore** adv поэ́тому. **therein** adv в э́том. **thereupon** adv зате́м.

**thermal** adj теплово́й, терми́ческий; (underwear) тёплый.

**thermometer** n термо́метр, гра́дусник. **thermos** n те́рмос. **thermostat** n термоста́т.

**thesis** n (proposition) те́зис; (dissertation) диссерта́ция.

**they** pron они́.

**thick** adj то́лстый, (in measurements) толщино́й в+acc; (dense) густо́й; (stupid) тупо́й; ~**-skinned** толстоко́жий. **thicken** vt & i утолща́ть(ся) impf, утолсти́ть(ся) pf; (make, become denser) сгуща́ть(ся) impf, сгусти́ть(ся) pf; vi (become more intricate) усложня́ться impf, усложни́ться pf. **thicket** n ча́ща. **thickness** n (also dimension) толщина́; (density) густота́; (layer) слой. **thickset** adj корена́стый.

**thief** n вор. **thieve** vi ворова́ть impf. **thievery** n воровство́.

**thigh** n бедро́.

**thimble** n напёрсток.

**thin** adj (slender; not thick) то́нкий; (lean) худо́й; (too liquid) жи́дкий; (sparse) редкий; *vt* & *i* де́лать(ся) *impf*, с~ *pf* то́нким, жи́дким; *vi* (*also* ~ *out*) реде́ть *impf*, по~ *pf*; *vt*: ~ *out* проре́живать *impf*, прореди́ть *pf*.

**thing** *n* вещь; (*object*) предме́т; (*matter*) де́ло.

**think** *vt* & *i* ду́мать *impf*, по~ *pf* (**about,** *of* о+*prep*); (*consider*) счита́ть *impf*, счесть *pf* (**to be** +*instr*, за+*acc*; **that** что); *vi* (*reflect, reason*) мы́слить *impf*; (*intend*) намерева́ться *impf* (*of doing* +*inf*); ~ **out** проду́мывать *impf*, проду́мать *pf*; ~ **over** обду́мывать *impf*, обду́мать *pf*; ~ **up,** *of* приду́мывать *impf*, приду́мать *pf*. **thinker** *n* мысли́тель *m*. **thinking** *adj* мы́слящий; *n* (*reflection*) размышле́ние; **to my way of** ~ по моему́ мне́нию.

**third** *adj* & *n* тре́тий; (*fraction*) треть; **T**~ **World** стра́ны *f pl* тре́тьего ми́ра.

**thirst** *n* жа́жда (**for** +*gen* (*fig*)); *vi* (*fig*) жа́ждать *impf* (**for** +*gen*). **thirsty** *adj*: **be** ~ хоте́ть *impf* пить.

**thirteen** *adj* & *n* трина́дцать. **thirteenth** *adj* & *n* трина́дцатый.

**thirtieth** *adj* & *n* тридца́тый. **thirty** *adj* & *n* три́дцать; *pl* (*decade*) тридца́тые го́ды (-до́в) *m pl*.

**this** *demonstrative adj* & *pron* э́тот; **like** ~ вот так; ~ **morning** сего́дня у́тром.

**thistle** *n* чертополо́х.

**thither** *adv* туда́.

**thorn** *n* шип. **thorny** *adj* колю́чий; (*fig*) терни́стый.

**thorough** *adj* основа́тельный; (*complete*) соверше́нный. **thoroughbred** *adj*

чистокро́вный. **thoroughfare** *n* прое́зд; (*walking*) прохо́д. **thoroughgoing** *adj* радика́льный. **thoroughly** *adv* (*completely*) соверше́нно. **thoroughness** *n* основа́тельность.

**though** *conj* хотя́; несмотря́ на то, что; **as** ~ как бу́дто; *adv* одна́ко.

**thought** *n* мысль; (*meditation*) размышле́ние; (*intention*) наме́рение; *pl* (*opinion*) мне́ние. **thoughtful** *adj* заду́мчивый; (*considerate*) внима́тельный. **thoughtless** *adj* необду́манный; (*inconsiderate*) невнима́тельный.

**thousand** *adj* & *n* ты́сяча. **thousandth** *adj* & *n* ты́сячный.

**thrash** *vt* бить *impf*, по~ *pf*; ~ **out** (*discuss*) обстоя́тельно обсужда́ть *impf*, обсуди́ть *pf*; *vi*: ~ **about** мета́ться *impf*. **thrashing** *n* (*beating*) взбу́чка (*coll*).

**thread** *n* ни́тка, нить (*also fig*); (*of screw etc.*) резьба́; *vt* (*needle*) продева́ть *impf*, проде́ть *pf* ни́тку в+*acc*; (*beads*) нани́зывать *impf*, низа́ть *pf*; ~ **one's way** пробира́ться *impf*, пробра́ться *pf* (**through** че́рез+*acc*). **threadbare** *adj* потёртый.

**threat** *n* угро́за. **threaten** *vt* угрожа́ть *impf*, грози́ть *impf*, при~ *pf* (**person** +*dat*; **with** +*instr*; **to do** +*inf*).

**three** *adj* & *n* три; (*number 3*) тро́йка; ~-**dimensional** трёхме́рный; ~-**quarters** три че́тверти. **threefold** *adj* тройно́й; *adv* втройне́. **threesome** *n* тро́йка.

**thresh** *vt* молоти́ть *impf*.

**threshold** *n* порог.

**thrice** *adv* трижды.

**thrift** *n* бережливость. **thrifty** *adj* бережливый.

**thrill** *n* трепет; *vt* восхищать *impf*, восхитить *pf*; **be thrilled** быть в востороге. **thriller** *n* приключенческий, детективный (*novel*) роман, (*film*) фильм. **thrilling** *adj* захватывающий.

**thrive** *vi* процветать *impf*.

**throat** *n* горло.

**throb** *vi* (*heart*) сильно биться *impf*; пульсировать *impf*; *n* биение; пульсация.

**throes** *n pl*: **in the ~** в мучительных попытках.

**thrombosis** *n* тромбоз.

**throne** *n* трон, престол; **come to the ~** вступать *impf*, вступить *pf* на престол.

**throng** *n* толпа; *vi* толпиться *impf*; *vt* заполнять *impf*, заполнить *pf*.

**throttle** *n* (*tech*) дроссель *m*; *vt* (*strangle*) душить *impf*, за~ *pf*; (*tech*) дросселировать *impf* & *pf*; **~ down** сбавлять *impf*, сбавить *pf* газ.

**through** *prep* (*across, via, opening*) через+*acc*; (*esp thick of*) сквозь+*acc*; (*air, streets etc.*) по+*dat*; (*agency*) посредством+*gen*; (*reason*) из-за+*gen*; *adv* насквозь; (*from beginning to end*) до конца; **be ~ with** (*sth*) оканчивать *impf*, окончить *pf*; (*s.o.*) порывать *impf*, порвать *pf* с+*instr*; **put ~** (*on telephone*) соединять *impf*, соединить *pf*; **~ and ~** совершенно; *adj* (*train*) прямой; (*traffic*) сквозной. **throughout** *adv* повсюду, во всех отношениях; *prep* по всему (всей, всему; *pl* всем)+*dat*; (*from beginning to end*) с начала до конца+*gen*.

**throw** *n* бросок; *vt* бросать *impf*, бросить *pf*; (*confuse*) смущать *impf*, смутить *pf*; (*rider*) сбрасывать *impf*, сбросить *pf*; (*party*) устраивать *impf*, устроить *pf*; **~ o.s. into** бросаться *impf*, броситься *pf* в+*acc*; **~ away, out** выбрасывать *impf*, выбросить *pf*; **~ down** сбрасывать *impf*, сбросить *pf*; **~ in** (*add*) добавлять *impf*, добавить *pf*; (*sport*) вбрасывать *impf*, вбросить *pf*; **~-in** вбрасывание мяча; **~ off** сбрасывать *impf*, сбросить *pf*; **~ open** распахивать *impf*, распахнуть *pf*; **~ out** (*see also ~ away*) (*expel*) выгонять *impf*, выгнать *pf*; (*reject*) отвергать *impf*, отвергнуть *pf*; **~ over, up** (*abandon*) бросать *impf*, бросить *pf*; **~ up** подбрасывать *impf*, подбросить *pf*; (*vomit*) рвать *impf impers*; **he threw up** его вырвало.

**thrush** *n* (*bird*) дрозд.

**thrust** *n* (*shove*) толчок; (*tech*) тяга; *vt* (*shove*) толкать *impf*, толкнуть *pf*; (*~ into, out of*) give quickly, carelessly) совать *impf*, сунуть *pf*.

**thud** *n* глухой звук; *vi* падать *impf*, пасть *pf* с глухим стуком.

**thug** *n* головорез (*coll*).

**thumb** *n* большой палец; **under the ~ of** под башмаком у+*gen*; *vt*: **~ through** перелистывать *impf*, перелистать *pf*; **~ a lift** голосовать *impf*, про~ *pf*.

**thump** *n* (*blow*) тяжёлый

уда́р; (*thud*) глухо́й звук,
стук; *vi* колоти́ть *impf*, по-
*pf* в+*acc*, по+*dat*; *vi* колоти́ться *impf*.

**thunder** *n* гром; *vi* греме́ть *impf*; **it thunders** гром греми́т. **thunderbolt** *n* уда́р мо́лнии. **thunderous** *adj* громово́й. **thunderstorm** *n* гроза́. **thundery** *adj* грозово́й.

**Thursday** *n* четве́рг.

**thus** *adv* так, таки́м о́бразом.

**thwart** *vt* меша́ть *impf*, по-
*pf*+*dat*; (*plans*) расстра́ивать *impf*, расстро́ить *pf*.

**thyme** *n* тимья́н.

**thyroid** *n* (~ **gland**) щитови́дная железа́.

**tiara** *n* тиа́ра.

**tick** *n* (*noise*) ти́канье; (*mark*) пти́чка; *vi* ти́кать *impf*, ти́кнуть *pf*; *vt* отмеча́ть *impf*, отме́тить *pf* пти́чкой; ~ **off** (*scold*) отде́лывать *impf*, отде́лать *pf*.

**ticket** *n* биле́т; (*label*) ярлы́к; (*season* ~) ка́рточка; (*cloakroom* ~) номеро́к; (*receipt*) квита́нция; ~ **collector** контролёр; ~ **office** (биле́тная) ка́сса.

**tickle** *n* щеко́тка; *vt* щекота́ть *impf*, по- *pf*; (*amuse*) весели́ть *impf*, по-, раз- *pf*; *vi* щекота́ть *impf*, по- *impers*; **my throat** ~**s** у меня́ щеко́чет в го́рле. **ticklish** *adj* (*fig*) щекотли́вый; **to be** ~ боя́ться *impf* щеко́тки.

**tidal** *adj* прили́во-отли́вный; ~ **wave** прили́вная волна́.

**tide** *n* прили́в и отли́в; (*high* ~) прили́в; (*low* ~) отли́в; (*current, tendency*) тече́ние; **the** ~ **turns** (*fig*) собы́тия принима́ют друго́й оборо́т; *vt*: ~ **over** помога́ть *impf*,

помо́чь *pf* +*dat of person* справля́ться (*difficulty* c+*instr*); **will this money** ~ **you over?** вы протя́нете с э́тими деньга́ми?

**tidiness** *n* аккура́тность. **tidy** *adj* аккура́тный; (*considerable*) поря́дочный; *vt* убира́ть *impf*, убра́ть *pf*; приводи́ть *impf*, привести́ *pf* в поря́док.

**tie** *n* (*garment*) га́лстук; (*cord*) завя́зка; (*link, tech*) связь; (*equal points etc.*) ра́вный счёт; **end in a** ~ зака́нчиваться *impf*, зако́нчиться *pf* вничью́; (*burden*) обу́за; *pl* (*bonds*) у́зы (уз) *pl*; *vt* свя́зывать *impf*, связа́ть *pf* (*also fig*); (~ **up**) завя́зывать *impf*, завяза́ть *pf*; (*restrict*) ограни́чивать *impf*, ограни́чить *pf*; ~ **down** (*fasten*) привя́зывать *impf*, привяза́ть *pf*; ~ **up** (*tether*) привя́зывать *impf*, привяза́ть *pf*; (*parcel*) перевя́зывать *impf*, перевяза́ть *pf*; (*be* ~**d**) завя́зываться *impf*, завяза́ться *pf*; (*sport*) сыгра́ть *pf* вничью́; ~ **in, up, with** совпада́ть *impf*, совпа́сть *pf* c+*instr*.

**tier** *n* ряд, я́рус.

**tiff** *n* размо́лвка.

**tiger** *n* тигр.

**tight** *adj* (*cramped*) те́сный; у́зкий; (*strict*) стро́гий; (*taut*) туго́й; ~ **corner** (*fig*) тру́дное положе́ние. **tighten** *vt* & *i* натя́гивать(ся) *impf*, натяну́ть(ся) *pf*; (*clench, contract*) сжима́ть(ся) *impf*, сжа́ть(ся) *pf*; ~ **one's belt** потуже затя́гивать *impf*, затяну́ть *pf* по́яс (*also fig*); ~ **up** (*discipline etc.*) подтя́гивать *impf*, подтяну́ть *pf* (*coll*). **tightly** *adv* *(strongly)* про́чно; *(closely, cramped)* те́сно. **tightrope** *n* натя́нутый кана́т. **tights** *n pl* колго́тки (-ток) *pl*.

**tile** *n (roof)* черепи́ца *(also collect)*; *(decorative)* ка́фель *m (also collect)*; *vt* черепи́цей, по~ *pf* черепи́цей, ка́фелем, по~ *pf*. **tiled** *adj (roof)* черепи́чный; *(floor)* ка́фельный.

**till**¹ *prep* до+*gen*; **not** ~ то́лько *(Friday* в пя́тницу; **the next day** на сле́дующий день); *conj* пока́ не; **not** ~ то́лько когда́.

**till**² *n* ка́сса.

**till**³ *vt* возде́лывать *impf*, возде́лать *pf*.

**tiller** *n (naut)* ру́мпель *m*.

**tilt** *n* накло́н; **at full** ~ по́лным хо́дом; *vt & i* накло-ня́ть(ся) *impf*, наклони́ть(ся) *pf*; *(heel (over))* кре-ни́ть(ся) *impf*, на~ *pf*.

**timber** *n* лесоматериа́л.

**time** *n* вре́мя *neut*; *(occasion)* раз; *(mus)* такт; *(sport)* тайм; *pl (period)* времена́ *pl*; *(in comparison)* раз; **five** ~**s as big** в пять раз бо́льше; *(multiplication)* **four** ~ **four** четы́режды четы́ре; ~ **and again,** ~ **after** ~ не раз, ты́сячу раз; **at a** ~ ра́зом, одновреме́нно; **at the** ~ в э́то вре́мя; **at** ~**s** времена́ми; **at the same** ~ в то же вре́мя; **before my** ~ до меня́; **for a long** ~ до́лго; *(up to now)* пока́; **for the** ~ **being** пока́; **from** ~ **to** ~ вре́мя от вре́мени; **in** *(early enough)* во́-время; *(with)* со вре́менем; **in good** ~ забла́говре́менно; **in** ~ **with** в такт +*dat*; **in no** ~ момента́льно; **on** ~ во́-время; **one** **at a** ~ по одному́; **be in** ~ успева́ть *impf*, успе́ть *pf* для к+*dat*, на+*acc*); **have** ~ **to** *(manage)* успева́ть *impf*, успе́ть *pf* +*inf*; **have a good** ~ хорошо́ проводи́ть *impf*, провести́ *pf* вре́мя; **it is** ~ пора́ (**to** +*inf*); **what is the** ~? кото́рый час?; ~ **bomb** бо́мба заме́дленного де́йствия; ~-**consuming** отнима́ющий мно́го вре́мени; ~ **difference** ра́зница во вре́мени; ~-**lag** отстава́ние во вре́мени; ~ **zone** часово́й по́яс; *vt (choose* ~) выбира́ть *impf*, вы́брать *pf* вре́мя +*gen*; *(ascertain* ~ *of)* измеря́ть *impf*, изме́рить *pf* вре́мя +*gen*. **timeless** *adj* ве́чный. **timely** *adj* своевре́менный. **timetable** *n* расписа́ние; гра́фик.

**timid** *adj* ро́бкий.

**tin** *n (metal)* о́лово; *(container)* ба́нка; *(cake—)* фо́рма; *(baking* ~) про́тивень *m*; ~ **foil** оловя́нная фольга́; ~-**opener** консе́рвный нож; ~**ned food** консе́рвы (-вов) *pl*.

**tinge** *n* отте́нок; *vt (also fig)* слегка́ окра́шивать *impf*, окра́сить *pf*.

**tingle** *vi (sting)* коло́ть *impf impers*; **my fingers** ~ у меня́ ко́лет па́льцы; **his nose** ~**d with the cold** моро́з пощи́-пывал ему́ нос; *(burn)* горе́ть *impf*.

**tinker** *vi:* ~ **with** вози́ться *impf* с+*instr*.

**tinkle** *n* звон, звя́канье; *vi (& t)* звене́ть *impf* (+*instr*).

**tinsel** *n* мишура́.

**tint** *n* отте́нок; *vt* подкра́шивать *impf*, подкра́сить *pf*.

**tiny** *adj* кро́шечный.

**tip**¹ *n (end)* ко́нчик.

**tip²** n (money) чаевы́е (-ы́х) pl; (advice) сове́т; (dump) сва́лка; vt & i (tilt) наклоня́ть(ся) impf, наклони́ть(ся) pf; (give ~) дава́ть impf, дать pf (person +dat; money де́ньги на чай, information ча́стную информа́цию); ~ out выва́ливать impf, вы́валить pf; ~ over, up (vt & i) опроки́дывать(ся) impf, опроки́нуть(ся) pf.

**Tippex** n (propr) бели́ла.

**tipple** n напи́ток.

**tipsy** adj подвы́пивший.

**tiptoe** n: on ~ на цы́почках.

**tip-top** adj превосхо́дный.

**tirade** n тира́да.

**tire** vt (weary) утомля́ть impf, утоми́ть pf; vi утомля́ться impf, утоми́ться pf. **tired** adj уста́лый; be ~ of: I am ~ of him мне на надое́л; I am ~ of playing мне надое́ло игра́ть; ~ out изму́ченный; ~ out pf за здоро́вье +gen. **tiredness** n уста́лость. **tireless** adj неутоми́мый. **tiresome** adj надое́дливый. **tiring** adj утоми́тельный.

**tissue** n ткань; (handkerchief) бума́жная салфе́тка; **tissue-paper** n папиро́сная бума́га.

**tit¹** n (bird) сини́ца.

**tit²** n: ~ for tat зуб за́ зуб.

**titbit** n ла́комый кусо́к; (news) пика́нтная но́вость.

**titillate** vt щекота́ть impf, по~ pf.

**title** n (of book etc.) загла́вие; (rank) зва́ние; (sport) зва́ние чемпио́на; ~-holder чемпио́н; ~-page ти́тульный лист; ~-role загла́вная роль. **titled** adj титуло́ванный.

**titter** n хихи́канье; vi хихи́кать impf, хихи́кнуть pf.

**to** prep (town, a country,

theatre, school, etc.) в+acc; (the sea, the moon, the ground, post-office, meeting, concert, north, etc.) на+acc; (the doctor; towards, up ~) one's surprise etc.) к+dat; (with accompaniment of) под+acc; (in toast) за+acc; (time): ten minutes ~ three без десяти́ три; (compared with) в сравне́нии с+instr; it is ten ~ one that déвять из десяти́ за то, что; ~ the left (right) нале́во (напра́во); (in order to) что́бы +inf; adv: shut the door ~ закро́йте дверь; come ~ приходи́ть impf, прийти́ pf в созна́ние; ~ and fro взад и вперёд.

**toad** n жа́ба. **toadstool** n пога́нка.

**toast** n (bread) поджа́ренный хлеб; (drink) тост; vt (bread) поджа́ривать impf, поджа́рить pf; (drink) пить impf, вы́~ pf за здоро́вье +gen. **toaster** n то́стер.

**tobacco** n таба́к. **tobacconist's** n (shop) таба́чный магази́н.

**toboggan** n сани (-не́й) pl; vi ката́ться impf на саня́х.

**today** adv сего́дня; (nowadays) в на́ши дни; n сего́дняшний день m; ~'s newspaper сего́дняшняя газе́та.

**toddler** n малы́ш.

**toe** n па́лец ноги́; (of sock etc.) носо́к; vt: ~ the line (fig) ходи́ть indet по стру́нке.

**toffee** n (substance) ири́с; (a single ~) ири́ска.

**together** adv вме́сте; (simultaneously) одновреме́нно.

**toil** n тяжёлый труд; vi труди́ться impf.

**toilet** n туале́т; ~ paper туале́тная бума́га. **toiletries** n *pl* туале́тные принадле́жности *f pl*.

**token** *n* (*sign*) знак; (*coin substitute*) жето́н; **as a ~** в знак +*gen*; *attrib* символи́ческий.

**tolerable** *adj* терпи́мый; (*satisfactory*) удовлетвори́тельный. **tolerance** *n* терпи́мость. **tolerant** *adj* терпи́мый. **tolerate** *vt* терпе́ть *impf*, по~ *pf*; (*allow*) допуска́ть *impf*, допусти́ть *pf*. **toleration** *n* терпи́мость.

**toll¹** *n* (*duty*) по́шлина; **take its ~** сказа́ться *impf*, сказа́ться *pf* (**on** на+*prep*).

**toll²** *vi* звони́ть *impf*, по~ *pf*.

**tom(-cat)** *n* кот.

**tomato** *n* помидо́р; *attrib* тома́тный.

**tomb** *n* моги́ла. **tombstone** *n* надгро́бный ка́мень *m*.

**tomboy** *n* сорване́ц.

**tome** *n* том.

**tomorrow** *adv* за́втра; *n* за́втрашний день *m*; **~ morning** за́втра у́тром; **the day after ~** послеза́втра; **see you ~** до за́втра.

**ton** *n* то́нна; (*pl, lots*) ма́сса.

**tone** *n* тон; *vt*: **~ down** смягча́ть *impf*, смягчи́ть *pf*; **~ up** тонизи́ровать *impf & pf*.

**tongs** *n* щипцы́ (-цо́в) *pl*.

**tongue** *n* язы́к; **~-in-cheek** с насме́шкой, ирони́чески; **~-tied** косноязы́чный; **~-twister** скорогово́рка.

**tonic** *n* (*med*) тонизи́рующее сре́дство; (*mus*) то́ника; (*drink*) напи́ток «то́ник».

**tonight** *adv* сего́дня ве́чером.

**tonnage** *n* тонна́ж.

**tonsil** *n* минда́лина. **tonsillitis** *n* тонзилли́т.

**too** *adv* сли́шком; (*also*) та́к-

же, то́же; (*very*) о́чень; (*moreover*) к тому́ же; **none ~** не сли́шком.

**tool** *n* инструме́нт; (*fig*) ору́дие.

**toot** *n* гудо́к; *vi* гуде́ть *impf*.

**tooth** *n* зуб; (*tech*) зубе́ц; *attrib* зубно́й; **~-brush** зубна́я щётка. **toothache** *n* зубна́я боль. **toothless** *adj* беззу́бый. **toothpaste** *n* зубна́я па́ста. **toothpick** *n* зубочи́стка. **toothy** *adj* зуба́стый (*coll*).

**top¹** *n* (*toy*) волчо́к.

**top²** *n* (*of object; fig*) верх; (*of hill etc.*) верши́на; (*of tree*) верху́шка; (*of head*) маку́шка; (*lid*) кры́шка; (*upper part*) ве́рхняя часть; **~ hat** цили́ндр; **~-heavy** переве́шивающий в свое́й ве́рхней ча́сти; **~-secret** соверше́нно секре́тный; **on ~ of** (*position*) на+*prep*, сверх+*gen*; (*on to*) на+*acc*; **~ of everything** сверх всего́; **from ~ to bottom** све́рху до́низу; **at the ~ of** one's voice во весь го́лос; **at ~ speed** во весь опо́р; *adj* ве́рхний, вы́сший, са́мый высо́кий; (*foremost*) пе́рвый; *vt* (*cover*) покрыва́ть *impf*, покры́ть *pf*; (*exceed*) превосходи́ть *impf*, превзойти́ *pf*; (*cut ~ off*) обреза́ть *impf*, обре́зать *pf* верху́шку +*gen*; **~ up** (*with liquid*) долива́ть *impf*, доли́ть *pf*.

**topic** *n* те́ма, предме́т. **topical** *adj* актуа́льный.

**topless** *adj* с обнажённой гру́дью.

**topmost** *adj* са́мый ве́рхний, са́мый ва́жный.

**topographical** *adj* топографи́ческий. **topography** *n* топогра́фия.

**topple** vt & i опроки́дывать(ся) impf, опроки́нуть(ся) pf.

**topsy-turvy** adj пове́рнутый вверх дном; (disorderly) беспоря́дочный; adv вверх дном.

**torch** n электри́ческий фона́рь m; (flaming) фа́кел.

**torment** n муче́ние, му́ка; vt му́чить impf, за-, из- pf.

**tornado** n торна́до neut indecl.

**torpedo** n торпе́да; vt торпеди́ровать impf & pf.

**torrent** n пото́к. **torrential** adj (rain) проливно́й.

**torso** n ту́ловище; (art) торс.

**tortoise** n черепа́ха. **tortoiseshell** n черепа́ха.

**tortuous** adj изви́листый.

**torture** n пы́тка; (fig) му́ка; vt пыта́ть impf; (torment) му́чить impf, за-, из- pf.

**toss** n бросо́к; **win (lose) the ~** (не) выпада́ть impf, вы́пасть pf жре́бий impers (**I won the ~** мне вы́пал жре́бий); vt броса́ть impf, бро́сить pf; (coin) подбра́сывать impf, подбро́сить pf; (head) вски́дывать impf, вски́нуть pf; (salad) переме́шивать impf, переме́шать pf; vi (in bed) мета́ться impf; **~ aside, away** отбра́сывать impf, отбро́сить pf; **~ up** броса́ть impf, бро́сить pf жре́бий.

**tot**[1] n (child) малы́ш; (of liquor) глото́к.

**tot**[2]: **~ up** (vt) скла́дывать impf, сложи́ть pf; (vi) равня́ться impf (**to** +dat).

**total** n ито́г, су́мма; adj о́бщий; (complete) по́лный; **in ~** в це́лом, вме́сте; vt подсчи́тывать impf, подсчита́ть pf; vi равня́ться impf +dat.

**totalitarian** adj тоталита́рный. **totality** n вся су́мма целико́м; **the ~ of** весь. **totally** adv соверше́нно.

**totter** vi шата́ться impf.

**touch** n прикоснове́ние; (sense) осяза́ние; (shade) отте́нок; (taste) при́вкус; (small amount) чу́точка; (of illness) лёгкий при́ступ; **get in ~ with** свя́зываться impf, связа́ться pf c+instr; **keep in ~ with** подде́рживать impf, поддержа́ть pf (теря́ть impf, по-, pf) связь, конта́кт c+instr; **put the finishing ~es to** отде́лывать impf, отде́лать pf; vt (lightly) прика́саться impf, прикосну́ться pf к+dat; каса́ться, косну́ться pf +gen; (also disturb; affect) тро́гать impf, тро́нуть pf; (be comparable with) идти́ impf в сравне́нии с+instr; vi (be contiguous; come into contact) соприкаса́ться impf, соприкосну́ться pf; **~ down** приземля́ться impf, приземли́ться pf; **~down** поса́дка; **~ (up)on** (fig) каса́ться impf, косну́ться pf +gen; **~ up** поправля́ть impf, попра́вить pf. **touched** adj тро́нутый.

**touchiness** n оби́дчивость.

**touching** adj тро́гательный.

**touchstone** n про́бный ка́мень m. **touchy** adj оби́дчивый.

**tough** adj жёсткий; (durable) про́чный; (hard) тру́дный; (hardy) выно́сливый. **toughen** vt & i де́лать(ся) impf, с-pf жёстким.

**tour** n (journey) путеше́ствие, пое́здка; (excursion) экску́рсия; (of artistes) гастро́ли f pl; (of duty) объе́зд; vi (& t) путеше́ствовать *impf* (по +*dat*); (*theat*) гастроли́ровать *impf*. **tourism** *n* тури́зм. **tourist** *n* тури́ст, ~ка.

**tournament** *n* турни́р.

**tousle** *vt* взъеро́шивать *impf*, взъеро́шить *pf* (*coll*).

**tout** *n* зазыва́ла *m*; (*ticket* ~) жучо́к.

**tow** *vt* букси́ровать *impf*; *n*: on ~ на букси́ре.

**towards** *prep* к+*dat*.

**towel** *n* полоте́нце.

**tower** *n* ба́шня; *vi* вы́ситься *impf*, возвыша́ться *impf* (**above** над+*instr*).

**town** *n* го́род; *attrib* городско́й; ~ **hall** ра́туша. **townsman** *n* горожа́нин.

**toxic** *adj* токси́ческий.

**toy** *n* игру́шка; *vi*: ~ **with** (*sth in hands*) верте́ть *impf* в рука́х; (*trifle with*) игра́ть *impf* (c)+*instr*.

**trace** *n* след; *vt* (*track* (*down*)) высле́живать *impf*, вы́следить *pf*; (*copy*) кальки́ровать *impf*, c~ *pf*; ~ **out** (*plan*) набра́сывать *impf*, наброса́ть *pf*; (*map, diagram*) черти́ть *impf*, на~ *pf*.

**tracing-paper** *n* ка́лька.

**track** *n* (*path*) доро́жка; (*mark*) след; (*rly*) путь *m*; (*sport, on tape*) доро́жка; (*on record*) за́пись; ~ **suit** трениро́вочный костю́м; off the beaten ~ в глуши́; **go off the** ~ (*fig*) отклоня́ться *impf*, отклони́ться *pf* от те́мы; **keep** ~ **of** следи́ть *impf* за+*instr*; **lose** ~ **of** теря́ть *impf*, по~ *pf* след+*gen*; *vt* просле́живать *impf*, проследи́ть *pf*; ~ **down** высле́живать *impf*, вы́следить *pf*.

**tract**[1] *n* (*land*) простра́нство.

**tract**[2] *n* (*pamphlet*) брошю́ра.

**tractor** *n* тра́ктор.

**trade** *n* торго́вля; (*occupation*) профе́ссия, ремесло́; ~ **mark** фабри́чная ма́рка; ~ **union** профсою́з; ~-**unionist** член профсою́за; *vi* торгова́ть *impf* (**in** +*instr*); *vt* (*swap like things*) обме́ниваться *impf*, обменя́ться *pf*+*instr*; (~ **for sth different**) обме́нивать *impf*, обменя́ть *pf* (**for** на+*acc*); ~ **in** сдава́ть *impf*, сдать *pf* в счёт поку́пки но́вого. **trader, tradesman** *n* торго́вец. **trading** *n* торго́вля.

**tradition** *n* тради́ция. **traditional** *adj* традицио́нный. **traditionally** *adv* по тради́ции.

**traffic** *n* движе́ние; (*trade*) торго́вля; ~ **jam** про́бка; *vi* торгова́ть *impf* (**in** +*instr*). **trafficker** *n* торго́вец (**in** +*instr*). **traffic-lights** *n pl* светофо́р.

**tragedy** *n* траге́дия. **tragic** *adj* траги́ческий.

**trail** *n* (*trace, track*) след; (*path*) тропи́нка; *vt* (*track*) высле́живать *impf*, вы́следить *pf*; *vt* & *i* (*drag*) таска́ть(ся) *indet*, тащи́ть(ся) *det*. **trailer** *n* (*on vehicle*) прице́п; (*cin*) (ки́но)ро́лик.

**train** *n* по́езд; (*of dress*) шлейф; *vt* (*instruct*) обуча́ть *impf*, обучи́ть *pf* (**in** +*dat*); (*prepare*) гото́вить *impf* (**for** к+*dat*); (*sport*) тренирова́ть *impf*, на~ *pf*; (*animals*) дрессирова́ть *impf*, вы́~ *pf*; (*aim*) наводи́ть *impf*, навести́ *pf*; (*plant*) направля́ть *impf*, напра́вить *pf* рост+*gen*; *vi* приготавливаться *impf*, приготовиться *pf* (**for** к+*dat*); (*sport*) тренироваться *impf*, на~ *pf*. **trainee** *n* стажёр, практикант. **trainer** *n* (*sport*) тренер; (*of animals*) дрессировщик; (*shoe*) кроссовка.

**training** *n* обучение; (*sport*) тренировка; (*of animals*) дрессировка; ~**-college** (*teachers'*) педагогический институт.

**traipse** *vi* таскаться *indet*, тащиться *pf*.

**trait** *n* черта.

**traitor** *n* предатель *m*, ~ница.

**trajectory** *n* траектория.

**tram** *n* трамвай.

**tramp** *n* (*vagrant*) бродяга *m*; *vi* (*walk heavily*) топать *impf*.

**trample** *vt* топтать *impf*, по~, ис~ *pf*; ~ **down** вытаптывать *impf*, вытоптать *pf*; ~ **on** (*fig*) попирать *impf*, попрать *pf*.

**trampoline** *n* батут.

**trance** *n* транс.

**tranquil** *adj* спокойный. **tranquillity** *n* спокойствие. **tranquillize** *vt* успокаивать *impf*, успокоить *pf*. **tranquillizer** *n* транквилизатор.

**transact** *vt* (*business*) вести *impf*; (*a deal*) заключать *impf*, заключить *pf*. **transaction** *n* дело, сделка; *pl* (*publications*) труды *m pl*.

**transatlantic** *adj* трансатлантический.

**transcend** *vt* превосходить *impf*, превзойти *pf*. **transcendental** *adj* (*philos.*) трансцендентальный.

**transcribe** *vt* (*copy out*) переписывать *impf*, переписать *pf*. **transcript** *n* копия. **transcription** *n* (*copy*) копия.

**transfer** *n* (*of objects*) перенос, перемещение; (*of money*;

of people) перевод; (*of property*) передача; (*design*) переводная картинка; *vt* (*objects*) переносить *impf*, перенести *pf*; перемещать *impf*, переместить *pf*; (*money; people; design*) переводить *impf*, перевести *pf*; (*property*) передавать *impf*, передать *pf*; *vi* (**to** *different job*) переходить *impf*, перейти *pf*; (*change trains etc.*) пересаживаться *impf*, пересесть *pf*. **transferable** *adj* допускающий передачу.

**transfix** *vt* (*fig*) приковывать *impf*, приковать *pf* к месту.

**transform** *vt* & *i* преобразовывать(ся) *impf*, преобразовать(ся) *pf*; ~ **into** *vt* (*i*) превращать(ся) *impf*, превратить(ся) *pf* в+*acc*. **transformation** *n* преобразование; превращение. **transformer** *n* трансформатор.

**transfusion** *n* переливание (крови).

**transgress** *vt* нарушать *impf*, нарушить *pf*; *vi* (*sin*) грешить *impf*, за~ *pf*. **transgression** *n* нарушение; (*sin*) грех.

**transience** *n* мимолётность. **transient** *adj* мимолётный.

**transistor** *n* транзистор; ~-**radio** транзисторный приёмник.

**transit** *n* транзит; **in** ~ (*goods*) при перевозке; (*person*) по пути; ~ **camp** транзитный лагерь *m*. **transition** *n* переход. **transitional** *adj* переходный. **transitive** *adj* переходный. **transitory** *adj* мимолётный.

**translate** *vt* переводить *impf*, перевести *pf*. **translation** *n* перево́д. **translator** n перево́дчик.

**translucent** adj полупрозра́чный.

**transmission** n переда́ча. **transmit** vt передава́ть impf, переда́ть pf. **transmitter** n (ра́дио)переда́тчик.

**transparency** n (phot) диапозити́в. **transparent** adj прозра́чный.

**transpire** vi (become known) обнару́живаться impf, обнару́житься pf; (occur) случа́ться impf, случи́ться pf.

**transplant** vt переса́живать impf, пересади́ть pf; (med) де́лать pf (occur) переса́дку+gen; n (med) переса́дка.

**transport** n (various senses) тра́нспорт; (conveyance) перево́зка; attrib тра́нспортный; vt перевози́ть impf, перевезти́ pf. **transportation** n тра́нспорт, перево́зка.

**transpose** vt переставля́ть impf, переста́вить pf; (mus) транспони́ровать impf & pf. **transposition** n перестано́вка; (mus) транспони́ровка.

**transverse** adj попере́чный.

**transvestite** n трансвести́т.

**trap** n лову́шка (also fig), западня́; vt (catch) лови́ть impf, пойма́ть pf (в лову́шку); (jam) защемля́ть impf, защеми́ть pf. **trapdoor** n люк.

**trapeze** n трапе́ция.

**trapper** n звероло́в.

**trappings** n pl (fig) (exterior attributes) вне́шние атрибу́ты m pl; (adornments) украше́ния neut pl.

**trash** n дрянь (coll). **trashy** adj дрянно́й.

**trauma** n тра́вма. **traumatic**

adj травмати́ческий.

**travel** n путеше́ствие; ~ **agency** бюро́ neut indecl путеше́ствий; ~ **sick: be** ~ **sick** ука́чивать impf, укача́ть pf impers +acc; **I am** ~ **sick in cars** меня́ в маши́не ука́чивает; vi путеше́ствовать impf, vt объезжа́ть impf, объе́хать pf. **traveller** n путеше́ственник; (salesman) коммивояжёр; ~'s **cheque** тури́стский чек.

**traverse** vt пересека́ть impf, пересе́чь pf.

**travesty** n паро́дия.

**trawler** n тра́улер.

**tray** n подно́с; **in-** (**out-**)~ корзи́нка для входя́щих (исходя́щих) бума́г.

**treacherous** adj преда́тельский; (unsafe) ненадёжный. **treachery** n преда́тельство.

**treacle** n па́тока.

**tread** n похо́дка; (stair) ступе́нька; (of tyre) проте́ктор; vi ступа́ть impf, ступи́ть pf; ~ **on** наступа́ть impf, наступи́ть pf на+acc; vt топта́ть impf.

**treason** n изме́на.

**treasure** n сокро́вище; vt высоко́ цени́ть impf. **treasurer** n казначе́й. **treasury** n (also fig) сокро́вищница; the T~ госуда́рственное казначе́йство.

**treat** n (pleasure) удово́льствие; (entertainment) угоще́ние; vt (have as guest) угоща́ть impf, угости́ть pf (**to** +instr); (med) лечи́ть impf (**for** от+gen; **with** +instr); (behave towards) обраща́ться impf с+instr; (process) обраба́тывать impf, обрабо́тать pf (**with** +instr); (discuss) трактова́ть *impf* o+*prep*; (*regard*) относи́ться *impf*, отнести́сь *pf* к+*dat* (as как к+*dat*). **treatise** *n* тракта́т. **treatment** *n* (*behaviour*) обраще́ние; (*med*) лече́ние; (*processing*) обрабо́тка; (*discussion*) тракто́вка. **treaty** *n* догово́р.

**treble** *adj* тройно́й; (*trebled*) утро́енный; *adv* втро́е; *n* (*mus*) ди́ска́нт; *vt* & *i* утра́ивать(ся) *impf*, утро́ить(ся) *pf*.

**tree** *n* де́рево.

**trek** *n* (*migration*) переселе́ние; (*journey*) путеше́ствие; *vi* (*migrate*) переселя́ться *impf*, перели́ться *pf*; (*journey*) путеше́ствовать *impf*.

**trellis** *n* шпале́ра; (*for creepers*) решётка.

**tremble** *vi* дрожа́ть *impf* (with от+*gen*); **trembling** *n* дрожь; **in fear and ~** трепеща́.

**tremendous** *adj* (*huge*) огро́мный; (*excellent*) потряса́ющий.

**tremor** *n* дрожь; (*earthquake*) толчо́к. **tremulous** *adj* дрожа́щий.

**trench** *n* кана́ва, ров; (*mil*) око́п.

**trend** *n* направле́ние, тенде́нция. **trendy** *adj* мо́дный.

**trepidation** *n* тре́пет.

**trespass** *vi* (*on property*) наруше́ние грани́ц; *vi* наруша́ть *impf*, нару́шить *pf* грани́цу (**on** +*gen*); (*fig*) вторга́ться *impf*, вто́ргнуться *pf* (**on** в+*acc*). **trespasser** *n* нару́шитель *m*.

**trestle** *n* ко́злы (-зел, -злам) *pl*; **~ table** стол на ко́злах.

**trial** *n* (*test*) испыта́ние (*also ordeal*), про́ба; (*law*) проце́сс, суд; (*sport*) попы́тка;

**on ~** (*probation*) на испыта́нии; (*of objects*) взя́тый на про́бу; (*law*) под судо́м; **~ and error** ме́тод проб и оши́бок.

**triangle** *n* треуго́льник. **triangular** *adj* треуго́льный.

**tribal** *adj* племенно́й. **tribe** *n* пле́мя *neut*.

**tribulation** *n* го́ре, несча́стье.

**tribunal** *n* трибуна́л.

**tributary** *n* прито́к. **tribute** *n* дань; **pay ~** (*fig*) отдава́ть *impf*, отда́ть *pf* дань (уваже́ния) (**to** +*dat*).

**trice** *n*: **in a ~** мгнове́нно.

**trick** *n* (*ruse*) хи́трость; (*deception*) обма́н; (*conjuring*) фо́кус; (*stunt*) трюк; (*joke*) шу́тка; (*habit*) привы́чка; (*cards*) взя́тка; **play a ~ on** игра́ть *impf*, сыгра́ть *pf* шу́тку с+*instr*; *vt* обма́нывать *impf*, обману́ть *pf*. **trickery** *n* обма́н.

**trickle** *vi* сочи́ться *impf*.

**trickster** *n* обма́нщик. **tricky** *adj* сло́жный.

**tricycle** *n* трёхколёсный велосипе́д.

**trifle** *n* пустя́к; **a ~** (*adv*) немно́го +*gen*; *vi* шути́ть *impf*, по~ *pf* (with с+*instr*). **trifling** *adj* пустяко́вый.

**trigger** *n* (*of gun*) куро́к; *vt*: **~ off** вызыва́ть *impf*, вы́звать *pf*.

**trill** *n* трель.

**trilogy** *n* трило́гия.

**trim** *n* поря́док, гото́вность; **in fighting ~** в боево́й гото́вности; **in good ~** (*sport*) в хоро́шей фо́рме; (*haircut*) подстри́жка; *adj* опря́тный; *vt* (*cut, clip, cut off*) подреза́ть *impf*, подре́зать *pf*; (*hair*) подстрига́ть *impf*, подстри́чь *pf*; (*a dress etc.*) отде́лывать *impf*, отде́лать *pf*. **trimming** *n* (*on dress*) отде́лка; (*to food*) гарни́р.

**Trinity** *n* Тро́ица.

**trinket** *n* безделу́шка.

**trio** *n* три́о *neut indecl*; (*of people*) тро́йка.

**trip** *n* пое́здка, путеше́ствие, экску́рсия; (*business ~*) командиро́вка; *vi* (*stumble*) спотыка́ться *impf*, споткну́ться *pf* (*over* o+*acc*); *vt* (*also ~ up*) подставля́ть *impf*, подста́вить *pf* но́жку +*dat* (*also fig*); (*confuse*) запу́тывать *impf*, запу́тать *pf*.

**triple** *adj* тройно́й; (*tripled*) утро́енный; *vt & i* утра́ивать(ся) *impf*, утро́ить(ся) *pf*. **triplet** *n* (*mus*) трио́ль; (*one of* ~s) близне́ц (из тро́йни); *pl* тро́йня.

**tripod** *n* трено́жник.

**trite** *adj* бана́льный.

**triumph** *n* торжество́, побе́да; *vi* торжествова́ть *impf*, вос~ *pf* (*over* над+*instr*). **triumphal** *adj* триумфа́льный. **triumphant** *adj* (*exultant*) торжеству́ющий; (*victorious*) победоно́сный.

**trivia** *n pl* ме́лочи (-че́й) *pl*.

**trivial** *adj* незначи́тельный.

**triviality** *n* тривиа́льность.

**trivialize** *vt* опошля́ть *impf*, опо́шлить *pf*.

**trolley** *n* теле́жка; (*table on wheels*) сто́лик на колёсиках. **trolley-bus** *n* тролле́йбус.

**trombone** *n* тромбо́н.

**troop** *n* гру́ппа, отря́д; (*mil*) войска́ *neut pl*; *vi* идти́ *impf*, по~ *pf* стро́ем.

**trophy** *n* трофе́й; (*prize*) приз.

**tropic** *n* тро́пик. **tropical** *adj* тропи́ческий.

**trot** *n* рысь; *vi* рыси́ть *impf*; (*rider*) е́здить *indet*, е́хать *det*, по~ *pf* ры́сью; (*horse*) ходи́ть *indet*, идти́ *det*, пойти́ *pf* ры́сью.

**trouble** *n* (*worry*) беспоко́йство, трево́га; (*misfortune*) беда́; (*unpleasantness*) неприя́тность *f pl*; (*effort, pains*) труд; (*care*) забо́та; (*disrepair*) неиспра́вность (*with* +*prep*); (*illness*) боле́знь; **heart ~** больно́е се́рдце; **~-maker** наруши́тель *m*, ~ница споко́йствия; **ask for ~** напра́шиваться *impf*, напроси́ться *pf* на неприя́тности; **be in ~** име́ть *impf* неприя́тности; **get into ~** попа́сть *pf* в беду́; **take ~** стара́ться *impf*, по~ *pf*; **take the ~** труди́ться *impf*, по~ *pf* (*to* +*inf*); **the ~ is** (*that*) беда́ в том, что; *vt* (*make anxious, disturb, give pain*) беспоко́ить *impf*; **may I ~ you for ...?** мо́жно попроси́ть у вас +*acc*?; *vi* (*take the ~*) труди́ться *impf*. **troubled** *adj* беспоко́йный. **troublesome** *adj* (*restless, fidgety*) беспоко́йный; (*capricious*) капри́зный; (*difficult*) тру́дный.

**trough** *n* (*for food*) корму́шка.

**trounce** *vt* (*beat*) поро́ть *impf*, вы~ *pf*; (*defeat*) разбива́ть *impf*, разби́ть *pf*.

**troupe** *n* тру́ппа.

**trouser-leg** *n* штани́на (*coll*). **trousers** *n pl* брю́ки (-к) *pl*, штаны́ (-но́в) *pl*.

**trout** *n* форе́ль.

**trowel** *n* (*for building*) мастеро́к; (*garden ~*) садо́вый сово́к.

**truancy** *n* прогу́л. **truant**

прогу́льщик; **play** ~ прогу́-
ливать *impf*, прогуля́ть *pf*.
**truce** *n* переми́рие.
**truck**[1] *n*: **have no** ~ with не
име́ть никаки́х дел с+*instr*.
**truck**[2] *n* (*lorry*) грузови́к;
(*rly*) вагон-платфо́рма.
**truculent** *adj* свире́пый.
**trudge** *vi* уста́ло тащи́ться
*impf*.
**true** *adj* (*faithful, correct*) ве́р-
ный; (*correct*) пра́вильный;
(*story*) правди́вый; (*real*) на-
стоя́щий; **come** ~ сбыва́ть-
ся *impf*, сбы́ться *pf*.
**truism** *n* трюи́зм. **truly** *adv*
(*sincerely*) и́скренне; (*really,
indeed*) действи́тельно; **yours**
~ пре́данный Вам.
**trump** *n* ко́зырь *m*; *vt* бить
*impf*, по~ *pf* ко́зырем; ~ **up**
фабрикова́ть *impf*, с~ *pf*.
**trumpet** *n* труба́; *vt* (*proclaim*)
труби́ть *impf* о+*prep*. **trumpeter** *n* труба́ч.
**truncate** *vt* усека́ть *impf*,
усе́чь *pf*.
**truncheon** *n* дуби́нка.
**trundle** *vt & i* ката́ть(ся) *indet*,
кати́ть(ся) *det*, по~ *pf*.
**trunk** *n* (*stem*) ствол; (*anat*)
ту́ловище; (*elephant's*) хо́бот;
(*box*) сунду́к; *pl* (*swimming*)
пла́вки (-вок) *pl*; (*boxing etc.*)
трусы́ (-со́в) *pl*; ~ **call** вы́-
зов по междугоро́дному те-
лефо́ну; ~ **road** магистра́ль-
ная доро́га.
**truss** *n* (*girder*) фе́рма; (*med*)
грыжево́й банда́ж; *vt* (*tie
up, bird*) свя́зывать *impf*,
связа́ть *pf*; (*reinforce*) укреп-
ля́ть *impf*, укрепи́ть *pf*
**trust** *n* дове́рие; (*body of trus-
tees*) опе́ка; (*property held in*
~) довери́тельная со́бствен-
ность; (*econ*) трест; **take on**

~ принима́ть *impf*, приня́ть
*pf* на ве́ру; *vt* доверя́ть *impf*,
дове́рить *pf* +*dat* (**with** +*acc*:
**to** +*inf*); *vi* (*hope*) наде́яться
*impf*, по~. **trustee** *n*
опеку́н. **trustful, trusting** *adj*
дове́рчивый. **trustworthy,
trusty** *adj* надёжный, ве́рный.
**truth** *n* пра́вда; **tell the** ~
говори́ть *impf*, сказа́ть *pf*
пра́вду; **to tell you the** ~ по
пра́вде говоря́. **truthful** *adj*
правди́вый.
**try** *n* (*attempt*) попы́тка; (*test,
trial*) испыта́ние, про́ба; *vt*
(*taste; sample*) про́бовать *impf*,
по~ *pf*; (*patience*) испы́ты-
вать *impf*, испыта́ть *pf*; (*law*)
суди́ть *impf*; (*for* за+*acc*); *vi*
(*endeavour*) стара́ться *impf*,
по~; ~ **on** (*clothes*) приме-
ря́ть *impf*, приме́рить *pf*.
**trying** *adj* тру́дный.
**tsar** *n* царь *m*. **tsarina** *n*
цари́ца.
**T-shirt** *n* футбо́лка.
**tub** *n* ка́дка; (*bath*) ва́нна; (*of
margarine etc.*) упако́вка.
**tubby** *adj* то́лстенький.
**tube** *n* тру́бка, труба́; (*toothpaste etc.*) тю́бик; (*underground*) метро́ *neut indecl*.
**tuber** *n* клу́бень *m*. **tuberculosis** *n* туберкулёз.
**tubing** *n* тру́бы *m pl*. **tubular**
*adj* тру́бчатый.
**tuck** *n* (*in garment*) скла́дка;
*vt* (*thrust into*, ~ **away**) за-
со́вывать *impf*, засу́нуть *pf*;
(*hide away*) пря́тать *impf*, с~
*pf*, ~ **in** (*shirt etc.*) заправ-
ля́ть *impf*, запра́вить *pf*; ~
**in, up** (*blanket, skirt*) под-
ты́ка́ть *impf*, подоткну́ть *pf*;
~ **up** (*sleeves*) засу́чивать
*impf*, засучи́ть *pf*; (*in bed*)
укрыва́ть *impf*, укры́ть *pf*.

**Tuesday** n вто́рник.

**tuft** n пучо́к.

**tug** vt тяну́ть impf, по~ pf; vi (sharply) дёргать impf, дёрнуть pf (at за+acc); n рыво́к; (tugboat) букси́р.

**tuition** n обуче́ние (in +dat).

**tulip** n тюльпа́н.

**tumble** vi (fall) па́дать impf, (у)па́сть pf; n паде́ние. **tumbledown** adj полуразру́шенный. **tumbler** n стака́н.

**tumour** n о́пухоль.

**tumult** n (uproar) сумато́ха; (agitation) волне́ние. **tumultuous** adj шу́мный.

**tuna** n туне́ц.

**tundra** n ту́ндра.

**tune** n мело́дия; **in ~** в тон, (of instrument) настро́енный; **out of ~** не в тон, фальши́вый, (of instrument) расстро́енный; **change one's ~** (пере)меня́ть impf, переме́нить pf тон; vt (instrument; radio) настра́ивать impf, настро́ить pf; (engine etc.) регули́ровать impf, от~ pf; **~ in** настра́ивать impf, настро́ить pf (radio) ра́дио (to на+acc); vi: **~ up** настра́ивать impf, настро́ить pf инструме́нт(ы). **tuneful** adj мелоди́чный. **tuner** n (mus) настро́йщик; (receiver) приёмник.

**tunic** n ту́ника; (of uniform) ки́тель m.

**tuning** n настро́йка; (of engine) регулиро́вка; **~-fork** камерто́н.

**tunnel** n тунне́ль m; vi прокла́дывать impf, проложи́ть pf тунне́ль.

**turban** n тюрба́н.

**turbine** n турби́на.

**turbulence** n бу́рность; (aeron) турбуле́нтность. **turbulent** adj бу́рный.

**tureen** n су́пник.

**turf** n дёрн.

**turgid** adj (pompous) напы́щенный.

**Turk** n ту́рок, турча́нка. **Turkey** n Ту́рция.

**turkey** n индю́к, f инде́йка; (dish) индю́шка.

**Turkish** adj туре́цкий. **Turkmenistan** n Туркмениста́н.

**turmoil** n (disorder) беспоря́док; (uproar) сумато́ха.

**turn** n (change of direction) поворо́т; (revolution) оборо́т; (service) услу́га; (change) измене́ние; (one's ~ to do sth) о́чередь; (theat) но́мер; **~ of phrase** оборо́т ре́чи; **at every ~** на ка́ждом шагу́; **by, in turn(s)** по о́череди; vt (handle, key, car around, etc.) пова́рачивать impf, поверну́ть pf; (revolve, rotate) враща́ть impf; (page; on its face) перевёртывать impf, переверну́ть pf; (direct) направля́ть impf, напра́вить pf; (cause to become) де́лать impf, с~ pf +instr; (on lathe) точи́ть impf; vi (change direction) пова́рачивать impf, поверну́ть pf; (rotate) враща́ться impf; (~ round) пова́рачиваться impf, поверну́ться pf; (become) станови́ться impf, стать pf +instr; **~ against** ополча́ться impf, ополчи́ться pf на+acc, про́тив+gen; **~ around** see **~ round**; **~ away** (vt & i) отвора́чивать(ся) impf, отверну́ть(ся) pf; (refuse admittance) прогоня́ть impf, прогна́ть pf; **~ back** (vi) пова́рачивать impf, поверну́ть pf наза́д; (vt) (bend

*back)* отгиба́ть *impf*, ото-
гну́ть *pf*; ~ **down** *(refuse)*
отклоня́ть *impf*, отклони́ть
*pf*; *(collar)* отгиба́ть *impf*,
отогну́ть *pf*; *(make quieter)*
де́лать *impf*, с~ *pf* ти́ше; ~
**grey** *(vi)* седе́ть *impf*, по~
*pf*; ~ **in** *(so as to face inwards)*
повора́чивать *impf*, поверну́ть *pf* вовну́трь; ~ **inside
out** выора́чивать *impf*,
вы́вернуть *pf* наизна́нку; ~
**into** *(change into)* *(vt & i)*
превраща́ть(ся) *impf*, пре-
врати́ть(ся) *pf* в+*acc*; *(street)*
свора́чивать *impf*, сверну́ть
*pf* на+*acc*; ~ **off** *(light, radio
etc.)* выключа́ть *impf*, вы-
ключить *pf*; *(tap)* закрыва́ть
*impf*, закры́ть *pf*; *(vi)* *(branch
off)* свора́чивать *impf*, свер-
ну́ть *pf*; ~ **on** *(light, radio
etc.)* включа́ть *impf*, вклю-
чи́ть *pf*; *(tap)* открыва́ть
*impf*, откры́ть *pf*; *(attack)*
напада́ть *impf*, напа́сть *pf*
на+*acc*; ~ **out** *(light etc.):* see
~ **off**; *(prove to be)* оказы-
ваться *impf*, оказа́ться *pf* (**to
be** +*instr*); *(drive out)* вы-
гоня́ть *impf*, вы́гнать *pf*;
*(pockets)* выёртывать *impf*,
вы́вернуть *pf*; *(be present)*
приходи́ть *impf*, прийти́ *pf*;
*(product)* выпуска́ть *impf*,
вы́пустить *pf*; ~ **over** *(page,
on its back, roll over)* *(vt & i)*
переёртывать(ся) *impf*,
переверну́ть(ся) *pf*; *(hand
over)* передава́ть *impf*, пере-
да́ть *pf*; *(think about)* обду́-
мывать *impf*, обду́мать *pf*;
*(overturn)* *(vt & i)* опроки́-
дывать(ся) *impf*, опроки́-
нуть(ся) *pf*; ~ **pale** бледне́ть
*impf*, по~ *pf*; ~ **red** красне́ть
*impf*, по~ *pf*; ~ **round** *(vi)*

*(rotate*; ~ **one's back**; ~ **to
face sth)** поёртываться *impf*,
поверну́ться *pf*; *(~ to face)*
обора́чиваться *impf*, обер-
ну́ться *pf*; *(vt)* поёртывать
*impf*, поверну́ть *pf*; ~ **sour**
скиса́ть *impf*, ски́снуть *pf*; ~
**to** обраща́ться *impf*, обра-
ти́ться *pf* к+*dat* (**for** за+*instr*);
~ **up** *(appear)* появля́ться
*impf*, появи́ться *pf*; *(be found)*
находи́ться *impf*, найти́сь *pf*;
*(shorten garment)* подшива́ть
*impf*, подши́ть *pf*; *(crop up)*
подвёртываться *impf*, под-
верну́ться *pf*; *(bend up; stick
up)* *(vt & i)* загиба́ть(ся)
*impf*, загну́ть(ся) *pf*; *(make
louder)* де́лать *impf*, с~ *pf*
гро́мче; ~ **up one's nose** во-
роти́ть *impf* нос (**at** от+*gen*)
*(coll)*; ~ **upside down** пере-
ёрачивать *impf*, переверну́ть *pf* вверх дном. **turn-out**
*n* коли́чество приходя́щих.
**turn-up** *n* *(on trousers)* об-
шла́г.

**turner** *n* то́карь *m*.
**turning** *n* *(road)* поворо́т.
**turning-point** *n* поворо́тный
пункт.
**turnip** *n* ре́па.
**turnover** *n* *(econ)* оборо́т; *(of
staff)* теку́честь рабо́чей си́лы.
**turnpike** *n* доро́жная заста́ва.
**turnstile** *n* турнике́т.
**turntable** *n* *(rly)* поворо́тный
круг; *(gramophone)* диск.
**turpentine** *n* скипида́р.
**turquoise** *n* *(material, stone)*
бирюза́; *adj* бирюзо́вый.
**turret** *n* ба́шенка.
**turtle** *n* черепа́ха.
**turtle-dove** *n* го́рлица.
**tusk** *n* би́вень *m*, клык.
**tussle** *n* дра́ка; *vi* дра́ться
*impf* (**for** за+*acc*).

**tutor** n (private teacher) ча́стный дома́шний учи́тель m, ~ница; (univ) преподава́тель m, ~ница; (primer) уче́бник; vt (instruct) обуча́ть impf, обучи́ть pf (in +dat); (give lessons to) дава́ть impf, дать pf уро́ки+dat; (guide) руководи́ть impf +instr. **tutorial** n консульта́ция.

**tutu** n (ballet) па́чка.

**TV** abbr (of television) ТВ, телеви́дение; (set) телеви́зор.

**twang** n (of string) ре́зкий звук (натя́нутой струны́); (voice) гнуса́вый го́лос.

**tweak** n щипо́к; vt щипа́ть impf, (у)щипну́ть pf.

**tweed** n твид.

**tweezers** n pl пинце́т.

**twelfth** adj & n двена́дцатый.

**twelve** adj & n двена́дцать.

**twentieth** adj & n двадца́тый. **twenty** adj & n два́дцать; pl (decade) двадца́тые го́ды (-до́в) pl.

**twice** adv два́жды; ~ as вдво́е, в два ра́за +comp.

**twiddle** vt (turn) верте́ть impf +acc, instr; (toy with) игра́ть impf +instr; ~ one's thumbs (fig) безде́льничать impf.

**twig** n ве́точка, прут.

**twilight** n су́мерки (-рек) pl.

**twin** n близне́ц; pl (Gemini) Близнецы́ m pl; in ~ beds па́ра односпа́льных крова́тей; ~ brother брат-близне́ц; ~ town го́род-побрати́м.

**twine** n бечёвка, шпага́т; vt (twist, weave) вить impf, с~ pf; vt & i (~ round) обвива́ть(ся) impf, обви́ть(ся) pf.

**twinge** n при́ступ (бо́ли) (of conscience) угрызе́ние.

**twinkle** n мерца́ние; (of eyes) огонёк; vi мерца́ть impf,

сверка́ть impf. **twinkling** n мерца́ние; in the ~ of an eye в мгнове́ние о́ка.

**twirl** vt & i (twist, turn) верте́ть(ся) impf; (whirl, spin) кружи́ть(ся) impf.

**twist** n (bend) изги́б, поворо́т; (~ing) круче́ние; (in story) поворо́т фа́булы; vt скру́чивать impf, крути́ть impf, с~ pf; (distort) искажа́ть impf, искази́ть pf; (sprain) подвёртывать impf, подверну́ть pf; vi (climb, meander, twine) ви́ться impf. **twisted** adj искривлённый (also fig).

**twit** n дура́к.

**twitch** n подёргивание; vt & i дёргать(ся) impf, дёрнуть(ся) pf (at за+acc).

**twitter** n щебет; vi щебета́ть impf, чири́кать impf.

**two** adj & n два, две (f); (collect; 2 pairs) дво́е; (number 2) дво́йка; in ~ (in half) надвое, попола́м; ~-seater двухме́стный (автомоби́ль); ~way двусторо́нний. **twofold** adj двойно́й; adv вдво́йне.

**twosome** n па́ра.

**tycoon** n магна́т.

**type** n тип, род; (printing) шрифт; vt писа́ть impf, на~ pf на маши́нке. **typescript** n маши́нопись. **typewriter** n пи́шущая маши́нка. **typewritten** adj машинопи́сный.

**typhoid** n брюшно́й тиф.

**typical** adj типи́чный. **typify** vt служи́ть impf, по~ pf типи́чным приме́ром +gen.

**typist** n машини́стка.

**typography** n книгопеча́тание; (style) оформле́ние.

**tyrannical** adj тирани́ческий. **tyrant** n тира́н.

**tyre** n ши́на.

# U

**ubiquitous** *adj* вездесу́щий.

**udder** *n* вы́мя *neut*.

**UFO** *abbr* (of unidentified flying object) НЛО, неопо́знанный лета́ющий объе́кт.

**ugh** *int* тьфу!

**ugliness** *n* уро́дство. **ugly** *adj* некраси́вый, уро́дливый; (*unpleasant*) неприя́тный.

**UK** *abbr* (of United Kingdom) Соединённое Короле́вство.

**Ukraine** *n* Украи́на. **Ukrainian** *n* украи́нец, -нка; *adj* украи́нский.

**ulcer** *n* я́зва.

**ulterior** *adj* скры́тый.

**ultimate** *adj* (*final*) после́дний, оконча́тельный; (*purpose*) коне́чный. **ultimately** *adv* в коне́чном счёте, в конце́ концо́в. **ultimatum** *n* ультима́тум.

**ultrasound** *n* ультразву́к. **ultra-violet** *adj* ультрафиоле́товый.

**umbilical** *adj*: ~ **cord** пупови́на.

**umbrella** *n* зо́нтик, зонт.

**umpire** *n* судья́ *m*; *vt & i* суди́ть *impf*.

**umpteenth** *adj*: for the ~ **time** в кото́рый раз.

**unabashed** *adj* без вся́кого смуще́ния. **unabated** *adj* неосла́бленный. **unable** *adj*: be ~ **to** не мочь *impf*, c~ *pf*; быть не в состоя́нии; (*not know how to*) не уме́ть *impf*, c~ *pf*. **unabridged** *adj* несокращённый. **unaccompanied** *adj* без сопровожде́ния; (*mus*) без аккомпанеме́нта. **unaccountable** *adj*

необъясни́мый. **unaccustomed** *adj* (*not accustomed*) непривы́кший (**to** к+*dat*); (*unusual*) непривы́чный. **unadulterated** *adj* настоя́щий; (*utter*) чисте́йший. **unaffected** *adj* непринуждённый. **unaided** *adj* без по́мощи, самостоя́тельный. **unambiguous** *adj* недвусмы́сленный. **unanimity** *n* единоду́шие. **unanimous** *adj* единоду́шный. **unanswerable** *adj* (*irrefutable*) неопровержи́мый. **unarmed** *adj* невооружённый. **unashamed** *adj* бессо́вестный. **unassailable** *adj* непристу́пный; (*irrefutable*) неопровержи́мый. **unassuming** *adj* скро́мный. **unattainable** *adj* недосяга́емый. **unattended** *adj* без присмо́тра. **unattractive** *adj* непривлека́тельный. **unauthorized** *adj* неразрешённый. **unavailable** *adj* не име́ющийся в нали́чии, недосту́пный. **unavoidable** *adj* неизбе́жный. **unaware** *predic*: **be ~ of** не сознава́ть *impf* +*acc*; не знать *impf* о+*prep*. **unawares** *adv* враспло́х.

**unbalanced** *adj* (*psych*) неуравнове́шенный. **unbearable** *adj* невыноси́мый. **unbeatable** *adj* (*unsurpassable*) не могу́щий быть превзойдённым; (*invincible*) непобеди́мый. **unbeaten** *adj* (*undefeated*) непокорённый; (*unsurpassed*) непревзойдённый. **unbelief** *n* неве́рие. **unbelievable** *adj* невероя́тный. **unbeliever** *n* неве́рующий *sb*. **unbiased** *adj* беспристра́стный. **unblemished** *adj* незапя́тнанный. **unblock** *vt* прочища́ть *impf*, прочи́стить *pf*. **unbolt** *vt* отпира́ть *impf*, отпере́ть *pf*. **unborn** *adj* ещё не рождённый. **unbounded** *adj* неограни́ченный. **unbreakable** *adj* небью́щийся. **unbridled** *adj* разну́зданный. **unbroken** *adj* (*intact*) неразби́тый, це́лый; (*continuous*) непреры́вный; (*unsurpassed*) непоби́тый; (*horse*) необъе́зженный. **unbuckle** *vt* расстёгивать *impf*, расстегну́ть *pf*. **unburden** *vt*: ~ **o.s.** отводи́ть *impf*, отвести́ *pf* ду́шу. **unbutton** *vt* расстёгивать *impf*, расстегну́ть *pf*.

**uncalled-for** *adj* неуме́стный. **uncanny** *adj* жу́ткий, сверхъесте́ственный. **unceasing** *adj* непреры́вный. **unceremonious** *adj* бесцеремо́нный. **uncertain** *adj* (*not sure, hesitating*) неуве́ренный; (*indeterminate*) неопределённый, нея́сный; **be** ~ (*not know for certain*) то́чно не знать *impf*; **in no** ~ **terms** недвусмы́сленно. **uncertainty** *n* неизве́стность; неопределённость. **unchallenged** *adj* не вызыва́ющий возраже́ний. **unchanged** *adj* неизмени́вшийся. **unchanging** *adj* неизменя́ющийся. **uncharacteristic** *adj* нетипи́чный. **uncharitable** *adj* немилосе́рдный, жесто́кий. **uncharted** *adj* неиссле́дованный. **unchecked** *adj* (*unrestrained*) необу́зданный. **uncivilized** *adj* нецивилизо́ванный. **unclaimed** *adj* невостре́бованный.

**uncle** *n* дя́дя *m*.
**unclean** *adj* нечи́стый. **un-**

clear *adj* нея́сный. **uncomfortable** *adj* неудо́бный. **uncommon** *adj* необыкнове́нный; (*rare*) ре́дкий. **uncommunicative** *adj* неразгово́рчивый, сде́ржанный. **uncomplaining** *adj* безро́потный. **uncomplicated** *adj* несло́жный. **uncompromising** *adj* бескомпроми́ссный. **unconcealed** *adj* нескрыва́емый. **unconcerned** *adj* (*unworried*) беззабо́тный; (*indifferent*) равноду́шный. **unconditional** *adj* безогово́рочный, безусло́вный. **unconfirmed** *adj* неподтверждённый. **unconnected** *adj* ~ **with** не свя́занный с+*instr*. **unconscious** *adj* (*also unintentional*) бессозна́тельный; (*predic*) без созна́ния; **be** ~ **of** не сознава́ть *impf* +*gen*; *n* подсозна́тельное *sb*. **unconsciousness** *n* бессозна́тельное состоя́ние. **unconstitutional** *adj* неконституцио́нный. **uncontrollable** *adj* неуде́ржимый. **uncontrolled** *adj* бесконтро́льный. **unconventional** *adj* необы́чный; оригина́льный. **unconvincing** *adj* неубеди́тельный. **uncooked** *adj* сыро́й. **uncooperative** *adj* неотзы́вчивый. **uncouth** *adj* гру́бый. **uncover** *vt* раскрыва́ть *impf*, раскры́ть *pf*. **uncritical** *adj* некрити́чный.

**unctuous** *adj* еле́йный.
**uncut** *adj* неразре́занный; (*unabridged*) несокращённый.
**undamaged** *adj* неповреждённый. **undaunted** *adj* бесстра́шный. **undecided** *adj* (*not settled*) нерешённый; (*irresolute*) нереши́тельный.

**undefeated** adj непокорённый. **undemanding** adj нетре́бовательный. **undemocratic** adj недемократи́ческий. **undeniable** adj неоспори́мый.

**under** prep (position) под+instr; (direction) под+acc; (fig) под +instr, (less than) ме́ньше+gen; (in view of, in the reign, time of) при+prep; ~**age** несовершенноле́тний; ~ **way** на ходу́; adv (position) внизу́; (direction) вниз; (less) ме́ньше.

**undercarriage** n шасси́ neut indecl. **underclothes** n pl ни́жнее бельё. **undercoat** n (of paint) грунто́вка. **undercover** adj та́йный. **undercurrent** n подво́дное тече́ние; (fig) скры́тая тенде́нция. **undercut** vt (price) назнача́ть impf, назна́чить pf бо́лее ни́зкую це́ну чем+nom. **underdeveloped** adj слаборазви́тый. **underdog** n неуда́чник. **underdone** adj недожа́ренный. **underemployment** n непо́лная за́нятость. **underestimate** vt недооце́нивать impf, недооцени́ть pf; n недооце́нка. **underfoot** adv под нога́ми.

**undergo** vt подверга́ться impf, подве́ргнуться pf +dat; (endure) переноси́ть impf, перенести́ pf. **undergraduate** n студе́нт, ~ка. **underground** n (rly) метро́ neut indecl; (fig) подпо́лье; adj (fig) подпо́льный; adv под землёй; (fig) подпо́льно. **undergrowth** n подле́сок. **underhand** adj заку́лисный. **underlie** vt (fig) лежа́ть impf в осно́ве +gen. **underline** vt подчёркивать impf, под-

черкну́ть pf. **underlying** adj лежа́щий в осно́ве. **underling** n подчинённый sb.

**undermine** vt (authority) подрыва́ть impf, подорва́ть pf; (health) разруша́ть impf, разру́шить pf.

**underneath** adv (position) внизу́; (direction) вниз; prep (position) под+instr; (direction) под+acc, n ни́жняя часть; adj ни́жний.

**undernourished** adj исхуда́лый; be ~ недоеда́ть impf.

**underpaid** adj низкоопла́чиваемый. **underpants** n pl трусы́ (-со́в) pl. **underpass** n прое́зд под полотно́м доро́ги; тонне́ль m. **underpin** vt подводи́ть impf, подвести́ pf фунда́мент под+acc; (fig) подде́рживать impf, поддержа́ть pf. **underprivileged** adj обделённый; (poor) бе́дный. **underrate** vt недооце́нивать impf, недооцени́ть pf. **underscore** vt подчёркивать impf, подчеркну́ть pf. **undersecretary** n замести́тель m мини́стра. **underside** n ни́жняя сторона́, низ. **undersized** adj малоро́слый. **understaffed** adj неукомплекто́ванный.

**understand** vt понима́ть impf, поня́ть pf; (have heard say) слы́шать impf. **understandable** adj поня́тный. **understanding** n понима́ние; (agreement) соглаше́ние; adj (sympathetic) отзы́вчивый. **understate** vt преуменьша́ть impf, преуме́ньшить pf. **understatement** n преуменьше́ние.

**understudy** n дублёр.

**undertake** vt (enter upon)

предпринима́ть *impf*, предприня́ть *pf*; (*responsibility*) брать *impf*, взять *pf* на себя́; (+*inf*) обя́зываться *impf*, обяза́ться *pf*. **undertaker** *n* гробо́вщик. **undertaking** *n* предприя́тие; (*pledge*) обяза́тельство.

**undertone** *n* (*fig*) подте́кст; **in an ~** вполго́лоса. **underwater** *adj* подво́дный. **underwear** *n* ни́жнее бельё. **underweight** *adj* исхуда́лый. **underworld** *n* (*mythology*) преиспо́дняя; (*criminals*) престу́пный мир. **underwrite** *vt* (*guarantee*) гаранти́ровать *impf* & *pf*. **underwriter** *n* страхо́вщик.

**undeserved** *adj* незаслу́женный. **undesirable** *adj* нежела́тельный; *n* нежела́тельное лицо́. **undeveloped** *adj* нера́звитый; (*land*) незастро́енный. **undignified** *adj* недосто́йный. **undiluted** *adj* неразба́вленный. **undisciplined** *adj* недисциплини́рованный. **undiscovered** *adj* неоткры́тый. **undisguised** *adj* я́вный. **undisputed** *adj* бесспо́рный. **undistinguished** *adj* заура́дный. **undisturbed** *adj* (*untouched*) нетро́нутый; (*peaceful*) споко́йный. **undivided** *adj*: **~ attention** по́лное внима́ние **undo** *vt* (*open*) открыва́ть *impf*, откры́ть *pf*; (*untie*) развя́зывать *impf*, развяза́ть *pf*; (*unbutton, unhook, unbuckle*) расстёгивать *impf*, расстегну́ть *pf*; (*destroy, cancel*) уничтожа́ть *impf*, уничто́жить *pf*. **undoubted** *adj* несомне́нный. **undoubtedly** *adv* несомне́нно. **undress** *vt* & *i* раздева́ть(ся) *impf*, разде́ть(ся)

*pf*. **undue** *adj* чрезме́рный. **unduly** *adv* чрезме́рно. **undulating** *adj* волни́стый; (*landscape*) холми́стый. **undying** *adj* (*eternal*) ве́чный. **unearth** *vt* (*dig up*) выка́пывать *impf*, вы́копать *pf* из земли́; (*fig*) раска́пывать *impf*, раскопа́ть *pf*. **uneasiness** *n* (*anxiety*) беспоко́йство; (*awkwardness*) нело́вкость. **uneasy** *adj* беспоко́йный; нело́вкий. **uneconomic** *adj* нерента́бельный. **uneconomical** *adj* (*car etc.*) неэкономи́чный; (*person*) неэконо́мный. **uneducated** *adj* необразо́ванный. **unemployed** *adj* безрабо́тный. **unemployment** *n* безрабо́тица; **~ benefit** посо́бие по безрабо́тице. **unending** *adj* бесконе́чный. **unenviable** *adj* незави́дный. **unequal** *adj* нера́вный. **unequalled** *adj* непревзойдённый. **unequivocal** *adj* недвусмы́сленный. **unerring** *adj* безоши́бочный. **uneven** *adj* неро́вный. **uneventful** *adj* непримеча́тельный. **unexceptional** *adj* обы́чный. **unexpected** *adj* неожи́данный. **unexplored** *adj* неиссле́дованный.

**unfailing** *adj* неизме́нный; (*inexhaustible*) неисчерпа́емый. **unfair** *adj* несправедли́вый. **unfaithful** *adj* неве́рный. **unfamiliar** *adj* незнако́мый; (*unknown*) неве́домый. **unfashionable** *adj* немо́дный. **unfasten** *vt* (*detach, untie*) открепля́ть *impf*, открепи́ть *pf*; (*undo, unbutton, unhook*) расстёгивать *impf*, расстегну́ть *pf*; (*open*) открыва́ть *impf*, откры́ть *pf*. **unfavour-**

able *adj* неблагоприя́тный. unfeeling *adj* бесчу́вственный. unfinished *adj* незако́нченный. unfit *adj* него́дный; (*unhealthy*) нездоро́вый. unflagging *adj* неослабева́ющий. unflattering *adj* неле́стный. unflinching *adj* непоколеби́мый. unfold *vt & i* развёртывать(ся) *impf*, разверну́ть(ся) *pf*; *vi* (*fig*) раскрыва́ться *impf*, раскры́ться *pf*. unforeseen *adj* непредви́денный. unforgettable *adj* незабыва́емый. unforgivable *adj* непрости́тельный. unforgiving *adj* непроща́ющий. unfortunate *adj* несча́стный; (*regrettable*) неуда́чный; *n* неуда́чник. unfortunately *adv* к сожале́нию. unfounded *adj* необосно́ванный. unfriendly *adj* недружелю́бный. unfulfilled *adj* (*hopes etc.*) неосуществлённый; (*person*) неудовлетворённый. unfurl *vt & i* развёртывать(ся) *impf*, разверну́ть(ся) *pf*. unfurnished *adj* немеблиро́ванный.

ungainly *adj* неуклю́жий. ungovernable *adj* неуправля́емый. ungracious *adj* нелюбе́зный. ungrateful *adj* неблагода́рный. unguarded *adj* (*incautious*) неосторо́жный.

unhappiness *n* несча́стье. unhappy *adj* несча́стливый. unharmed *adj* невреди́мый. unhealthy *adj* нездоро́вый; (*harmful*) вре́дный. unheard-of *adj* неслы́ханный. unheeded *adj* незаме́ченный. unheeding *adj* невнима́тельный. unhelpful *adj* беспле́зный; (*person*) неотзы́вчивый. unhesitating *adj* ре-

ши́тельный. unhesitatingly *adv* без колеба́ний. unhindered *adj* беспрепя́тственный. unhinge *vt* (*fig*) расстра́ивать *impf*, расстро́ить *pf*. unholy *adj* (*impious*) нечести́вый; (*awful*) ужа́сный. unhook *vt* (*undo hooks of*) расстёгивать *impf*, расстегну́ть *pf*; (*uncouple*) расцепля́ть *impf*, расцепи́ть *pf*. unhurt *adj* невреди́мый.

unicorn *n* единоро́г. unification *n* объедине́ние. uniform *n* фо́рма; *adj* единообра́зный; (*unchanging*) постоя́нный. uniformity *n* единообра́зие. unify *vt* объединя́ть *impf*, объедини́ть *pf*.

unilateral *adj* односторо́нний. unimaginable *adj* невообрази́мый. unimaginative *adj* лишённый воображе́ния, проза́ичный. unimportant *adj* нева́жный. uninformed *adj* (*ignorant*) несве́дущий (**about** в+*prep*); (*ill-informed*) неосведомлённый. uninhabited *adj* необита́емый. uninhibited *adj* нестеснённый. uninspired *adj* бана́льный. unintelligible *adj* непоня́тный. unintentional *adj* неча́янный. unintentionally *adv* неча́янно. uninterested *adj* незаинтересо́ванный. uninteresting *adj* неинтере́сный. uninterrupted *adj* непреры́вный.

union *n* (*alliance*) сою́з; (*joining together, alliance*) объедине́ние; (*trade* ~) профсою́з. unionist *n* член профсою́за; (*polit*) униони́ст. unique *adj* уника́льный. unison *n*: in ~ (*mus*) в унисо́н; (*fig*) в согла́сии.

unit n единица; (mil) часть.

unite vt & i соединя́ть(ся) impf, соедини́ть(ся) pf; объединя́ть(ся) impf, объедини́ть(ся) pf. united adj соединённый, объединённый; U~ Kingdom Соединённое Короле́вство; U~ Nations Организа́ция Объединённых На́ций; U~ States Соединённые Шта́ты m pl Аме́рики. unity n еди́нство.

universal adj всео́бщий; (many-sided) универса́льный. universe n вселе́нная sb; (world) мир. university n университе́т; attrib университе́тский.

unjust adj несправедли́вый. unjustifiable adj непрости́тельный. unjustified adj необра́кованный.

unkempt adj нечёсаный. unkind adj недо́брый, злой. unknown adj неизве́стный.

unlawful adj незако́нный. unleaded adj неэтили́рованный. unleash vt (also fig) развя́зывать impf, развяза́ть pf. unless conj е́сли… не.

unlike adj непохо́жий (на+acc); (in contradistinction to) в отли́чие от+gen. unlikely adj маловероя́тный; it is ~ that вряд ли. unlimited adj неограни́ченный. unlit adj неосвещённый. unload vt (a vehicle etc.) разгружа́ть impf, разгрузи́ть pf; (goods etc.) выгружа́ть impf, вы́грузить pf. unlock vt отпира́ть impf, отпере́ть pf; открыва́ть impf, откры́ть pf. unlucky adj (number etc.) несчастли́вый; (unsuccessful) неуда́чный.

unmanageable adj тру́дный, непоко́рный. unmanned adj автомати́ческий. unmarried adj холосто́й; (of man) жена́тый; (of woman) незаму́жняя. unmask vt (fig) разоблача́ть impf, разоблачи́ть pf. unmentionable adj неупомина́емый. unmistakable adj несомне́нный, я́сный. unmitigated adj (thorough) отъя́вленный. unmoved adj: be ~ остава́ться impf, оста́ться pf равноду́шен, -шна.

unnatural adj неесте́ственный. unnecessary adj нену́жный. unnerve vt лиша́ть impf, лиши́ть pf му́жества; (upset) расстра́ивать impf, расстро́ить pf. unnoticed adj незаме́ченный.

unobserved adj незаме́ченный. unobtainable adj недосту́пный. unobtrusive adj скро́мный, ненавя́зчивый. unoccupied adj незаня́тый, свобо́дный; (house) пусто́й. unofficial adj неофициа́льный. unopposed adj не встре́тивший сопротивле́ния. unorthodox adj неортодокса́льный.

unpack vt распако́вывать impf, распакова́ть pf. unpaid adj (bill) неупла́ченный; (person) не получа́ющий пла́ты; (work) беспла́тный. unpalatable adj невку́сный; (unpleasant) неприя́тный. unparalleled adj несравни́мый. unpleasant adj неприя́тный. unpleasantness n неприя́тность. unpopular adj непопуля́рный. unprecedented adj беспрецеде́нтный. unpredictable adj непредсказу́емый. unprejudiced adj беспристра́стный. unprepared adj неподгото́вленный, неготóвый. **unprepossessing** *adj* непривлекáтельный. **unpretentious** *adj* простóй, без претéнзий. **unprincipled** *adj* беспринцúпный. **unproductive** *adj* непродуктúвный. **unprofitable** *adj* невýгодный. **unpromising** *adj* малообещáющий. **unprotected** *adj* незащищённый. **unproven** *adj* недокáзанный. **unprovoked** *adj* непровоцúрованный. **unpublished** *adj* неопубликóванный, неúзданный. **unpunished** *adj* безнакáзанный.

**unqualified** *adj* неквалифицúрованный; (*unconditional*) безоговóрочный. **unquestionable** *adj* несомнéнный, неоспорúмый. **unquestionably** *adv* несомнéнно, бесспóрно.

**unravel** *vt & i* распýтывать(ся) *impf*, распутáть(ся) *pf*; *vt* (*solve*) разгáдывать *impf*, разгадáть *pf*. **unread** *adj* (*book etc.*) непрочúтанный. **unreadable** *adj* (*illegible*) неразбóрчивый; (*boring*) неудобочитáемый. **unreal** *adj* нереáльный. **unrealistic** *adj* нереáльный. **unreasonable** *adj* (*person*) неразýмный; (*behaviour, demand, price*) необоснóванный. **unrecognizable** *adj* неузнавáемый. **unrecognized** *adj* непрúзнанный. **unrefined** *adj* неочúщенный; (*manners etc.*) грýбый. **unrelated** *adj* не имéющий отношéния (**to** к+*dat*), несвя́занный (**to** с+*instr*); **we are ~** мы не в родствé. **unrelenting** *adj* (*ruthless*) безжáлостный; (*unremitting*) неослáбный. **unreliable** *adj* не-

надёжный. **unremarkable** *adj* невыдаю́щийся. **unremitting** *adj* неослáбный; (*incessant*) непрестáнный. **unrepentant** *adj* нераскáявшийся. **unrepresentative** *adj* нетипúчный. **unrequited** *adj:* ~ **love** неразделённая любóвь. **unreserved** *adj* (*full*) пóлный; (*open*) откровéнный; (*unconditional*) безоговóрочный; (*seat*) незабронúрованный. **unresolved** *adj* нерешённый. **unrest** *n* беспокóйство; (*polit*) волнéния *neut pl*. **unrestrained** *adj* несдéржанный. **unrestricted** *adj* неогранúченный. **unripe** *adj* незрéлый. **unrivalled** *adj* бесподóбный. **unroll** *vt & i* развёртывать(ся) *impf*, развернýть(ся) *pf*. **unruffled** *adj* (*smooth*) глáдкий; (*calm*) спокóйный. **unruly** *adj* непокóрный.

**unsafe** *adj* опáсный; (*insecure*) ненадёжный. **unsaid** *adj:* **leave** ~ молчáть *impf* о+*prep*. **unsaleable** *adj* нехóдкий. **unsalted** *adj* несолёный. **unsatisfactory** *adj* неудовлетворúтельный. **unsatisfied** *adj* неудовлетворённый. **unsavoury** *adj* (*unpleasant*) неприя́тный; (*disreputable*) сомнúтельный. **unscathed** *adj* невредúмый; (*predic*) цел и невредúм. **unscheduled** *adj* (*transport*) внеочереднóй; (*event*) незапланúрованный. **unscientific** *adj* ненаýчный. **unscrew** *vt & i* отвúнчивать(ся) *impf*, отвинтúть(ся) *pf*. **unscrupulous** *adj* беспринцúпный. **unseat** *vt* (*of horse*) сбрáсывать *impf*, сбро́сить *pf* с седлá; (*parl* лиша́ть *impf*, лиши́ть *pf* парла́ментского манда́та.

**unseemly** *adj* неподоба́ющий. **unseen** *adj* неви́данный. **unselfconscious** *adj* непосре́дственный. **unselfish** *adj* бескоры́стный. **unsettle** *vt* выбива́ть *impf*, вы́бить *pf* из колеи́; (*upset*) расстра́ивать *impf*, расстро́ить *pf*. **unsettled** *adj* (*weather*) неусто́йчивый; (*unresolved*) нерешённый. **unsettling** *adj* волну́ющий. **unshakeable** *adj* непоколеби́мый. **unshaven** *adj* небри́тый. **unsightly** *adj* непригля́дный, уро́дливый. **unsigned** *adj* неподпи́санный. **unskilful** *adj* неуме́лый. **unskilled** *adj* неквалифици́рованный. **unsociable** *adj* необщи́тельный. **unsold** *adj* непро́данный. **unsolicited** *adj* непро́шеный. **unsolved** *adj* нерешённый. **unsophisticated** *adj* просто́й. **unsound** *adj* (*unhealthy, unwholesome*) нездоро́вый; (*not solid*) непро́чный; (*unfounded*) необосно́ванный; **of ~ mind** душевнобольно́й. **unspeakable** *adj* (*inexpressible*) несказа́нный; (*very bad*) отврати́тельный. **unspecified** *adj* то́чно не ука́занный, неопределённый. **unspoilt** *adj* неиспо́рченный. **unspoken** *adj* невы́сказанный. **unstable** *adj* неусто́йчивый; (*mentally*) неуравнове́шенный. **unsteady** *adj* неусто́йчивый. **unstuck** *adj*: **come ~** откле́иваться *impf*, откле́иться *pf*; (*fig*) прова́ливаться *impf*, провали́ться *pf*. **unsuccessful** *adj* неуда́чный, безуспе́шный. **unsuitable** *adj* непод-

ходя́щий. **unsuited** *adj* неприго́дный. **unsung** *adj* невоспе́тый. **unsupported** *adj* неподдёржанный. **unsure** *adj* неуве́ренный (**of o.s.** в себе́). **unsurpassed** *adj* непревзойдённый. **unsurprising** *adj* неудиви́тельный. **unsuspected** *adj* (*unforeseen*) непредви́денный. **unsuspecting** *adj* неподозрева́ющий. **unsweetened** *adj* неподсла́щенный. **unswerving** *adj* непоколеби́мый. **unsympathetic** *adj* несочу́вствующий. **unsystematic** *adj* несистемати́чный.

**untainted** *adj* неиспо́рченный. **untangle** *vt* распу́тывать *impf*, распу́тать *pf*. **untapped** *adj*: **~ resources** неиспо́льзованные ресу́рсы *m pl*. **untenable** *adj* несостоя́тельный. **untested** *adj* неиспы́танный. **unthinkable** *adj* невообрази́мый. **unthinking** *adj* безду́мный. **untidiness** *n* неопря́тность; (*disorder*) беспоря́док. **untidy** *adj* неопря́тный; (*in disorder*) в беспоря́дке. **untie** *vt* развя́зывать *impf*, развяза́ть *pf*; (*set free*) освобожда́ть *impf*, освободи́ть *pf*.

**until** *prep* до+*gen*; **not ~** не ра́ньше+*gen*; **~ then** до тех пор; *conj* пока́, пока́... не; **not ~** то́лько когда́.

**untimely** *adj* (*premature*) безвре́менный; (*inappropriate*) неуме́стный. **untiring** *adj* неутоми́мый. **untold** *adj* (*incalculable*) бессчётный, несме́тный; (*inexpressible*) невырази́мый. **untouched** *adj* нетро́нутый; (*indifferent*) равноду́шный. **untoward**

неблагоприя́тный. **untrained** *adj* необу́ченный. **untried** *adj* неиспы́танный. **untroubled** *adj* споко́йный. **untrue** *adj* неве́рный. **untrustworthy** *adj* ненадёжный. **untruth** *n* непра́вда, ложь. **untruthful** *adj* лжи́вый.

**unusable** *adj* непригóдный. **unused** *adj* неиспóльзованный; (*unaccustomed*) непривы́кший (to к+*dat*); **I am ~ to this** я к э́тому не привы́к. **unusual** *adj* необыкновéнный, необы́чный. **unusually** *adv* необыкновéнно. **unutterable** *adj* невырази́мый.

**unveil** *vt* (*statue*) торжéственно открыва́ть *impf*, откры́ть *pf*; (*disclose*) обнарóдовать *impf & pf*.

**unwanted** *adj* нежела́нный. **unwarranted** *adj* неопра́вданный. **unwary** *adj* неосторо́жный. **unwavering** *adj* непоколеби́мый. **unwelcome** *adj* нежела́тельный; (*unpleasant*) неприя́тный. **unwell** *adj* нездорóвый. **unwieldy** *adj* громóздкий. **unwilling** *adj* несклóнный; **be ~ to** не хотéть *impf*, за~ *pf* (to +*inf*). **unwillingly** *adv* неохóтно. **unwillingness** *n* неохóта. **unwind** *vt & i* разма́тывать(ся) *impf*, размота́ть(ся) *pf*; (*rest*) отдыха́ть *impf*, отдохну́ть *pf*. **unwise** *adj* не(благо)разу́мный. **unwitting** *adj* нево́льный. **unwittingly** *adv* нево́льно. **unworkable** *adj* непримени́мый. **unworldly** *adj* не от ми́ра сегó. **unworthy** *adj* недостóйный. **unwrap** *vt* развёртывать *impf*, разверну́ть *pf*. **unwritten** *adj*: **~ law** непи́саный

закóн.

**unyielding** *adj* упóрный, неподáтливый.

**unzip** *vt* расстёгивать *impf*, расстегну́ть *pf* (мóлнию)+*gen*).

**up** *adv* (*motion*) наве́рх, вверх; (*position*) наверху́, вверху́; **~ and down** вверх и вниз; (*back and forth*) взад и вперёд; **~ to** (*towards*) к+*dat*; (*as far as, until*) до+*gen*; **~ to now** до сих пор; **be ~ against** имéть *impf* дéло с+*instr*; **it is ~ to you**+*inf*, э́то вам+*inf*, вы должны́+*inf*; **what's ~?** что случи́лось?; **в чём дéло?**; **your time is ~** ва́ше врéмя истеклó; **~ and about** на ногáх; **he isn't ~ yet** он ещё не встал; **he isn't ~ to this job** он не годи́тся для э́той рабóты; *prep* вверх по+*dat*; (*along*) (вдоль) по+*dat*; **~** повыша́ть *impf*, повы́сить; *vi* (*leap up*) взять *pf*; *adj*: **~-to-date** совремéнный; (*fashionable*) мóдный; **~-and-coming** многообещáющий; *n*: **~s and downs** (*fig*) превра́тности *f pl* судьбы́.

**upbringing** *n* воспита́ние.

**update** *vt* модернизи́ровать *impf & pf*; (*a book etc.*) дополня́ть *impf*, допóлнить *pf*.

**upgrade** *vt* повыша́ть *impf*, повы́сить *pf* (по слу́жбе).

**upheaval** *n* потрясéние.

**uphill** *adj* (*fig*) тяжёлый; *adv* в гóру.

**uphold** *vt* подде́рживать *impf*, поддержа́ть *pf*.

**upholster** *vt* обива́ть *impf*, оби́ть *pf*. **upholsterer** *n* обóйщик. **upholstery** *n* оби́вка.

**upkeep** *n* содержáние.

**upland** *n* гори́стая часть страны́; *adj* нагóрный.

**uplift** vt поднима́ть impf, подня́ть pf.

**up-market** adj дорого́й.

**upon** prep (position) на+prep, (motion) на+acc; see **on**

**upper** adj ве́рхний; (socially, in rank) вы́сший; **gain the ~ hand** одержа́ть impf, одержа́ть pf верх (over над+instr); n передо́к. **uppermost** adj са́мый ве́рхний, вы́сший; be **~ in person's mind** бо́льше всего́ занима́ть impf, заня́ть pf мы́сли кого́-л.

**upright** n сто́йка; adj вертика́льный; (honest) че́стный; **~ piano** пиани́но neut indecl.

**uprising** n восста́ние.

**uproar** n шум, гам.

**uproot** vt вырыва́ть impf, вы́рвать pf с ко́рнем; (people) выселя́ть impf, вы́селить pf.

**upset** n расстро́йство; vt расстра́ивать impf, расстро́ить pf; (overturn) опроки́дывать impf, опроки́нуть pf; adj (miserable) расстро́енный; **~ stomach** расстро́йство желу́дка.

**upshot** n развя́зка, результа́т.

**upside-down** adj переве́рнутый вверх дном; adv вверх дном; (in disorder) в беспоря́дке.

**upstairs** adv (position) наверху́; (motion) наве́рх; n ве́рхний эта́ж; adj находя́щийся в ве́рхнем этаже́.

**upstart** n вы́скочка m & f.

**upstream** adv про́тив тече́ния; (situation) вверх по тече́нию.

**upsurge** n подъём, волна́.

**uptake** n: **be quick on the ~** бы́стро сообража́ть impf, сообрази́ть pf.

**upturn** n (fig) улучше́ние. **up-**

**turned** adj (face etc.) по́днятый кве́рху; (inverted) переёрнутый.

**upward** adj напра́вленный вверх. **upwards** adv вверх; **~ of** свы́ше+gen.

**uranium** n ура́н.

**urban** adj городско́й.

**urbane** adj ве́жливый.

**urchin** n мальчи́шка m.

**urge** n (incitement) побужде́ние; (desire) жела́ние; vt (impel, ~ on) подгоня́ть impf, подогна́ть pf; (warn) предупрежда́ть impf, предупреди́ть pf; (try to persuade) убежда́ть impf. **urgency** n сро́чность, ва́жность; **a matter of great ~** сро́чное де́ло. **urgent** adj сро́чный; (insistent) настоя́тельный. **urgently** adv сро́чно.

**urinate** vi мочи́ться impf, по-~ pf. **urine** n моча́.

**urn** n у́рна.

**US(A)** abbr (of United States of America) США, Соединённые Шта́ты Аме́рики.

**usable** adj го́дный к употребле́нию. **usage** n употребле́ние; (treatment) обраще́ние. **use** n (utilization) употребле́ние, по́льзование; (benefit) по́льза; (application) примене́ние; **it is no ~ (-ing)** бесполе́зно (+inf); **make ~ of** испо́льзовать impf & pf; по́льзоваться impf +instr; vt употребля́ть impf, употреби́ть pf; по́льзоваться impf +instr; (apply) применя́ть impf, примени́ть pf; обраща́ться impf с+instr; **~d to see him often** я ча́сто его́ встреча́л; **be, get ~d to** привыка́ть impf, привы́кнуть pf (to к+dat); **~ up** расхо́довать *impf*, из~ *pf*. **used** *adj* (*second-hand*) ста́рый.

**useful** *adj* поле́зный; **come in ~**, **prove ~** пригоди́ться *pf* (to +*dat*). **useless** *adj* бесполе́зный. **user** *n* потреби́тель *m*.

**usher** *n* (*theat*) билетёр; *vt* (*lead in*) вводи́ть *impf*, ввести́ *pf*; (*proclaim*, **~ in**) возвеща́ть *impf*, возвести́ть *pf*. **usherette** *n* билетёрша.

**USSR** *abbr* (*of* Union of Soviet Socialist Republics) СССР, Сою́з Сове́тских Социалисти́ческих Респу́блик.

**usual** *adj* обыкнове́нный, обы́чный; **as ~** как обы́чно. **usually** *adv* обыкнове́нно, обы́чно.

**usurp** *vt* узурпи́ровать *impf* & *pf*. **usurper** *n* узурпа́тор. **usury** *n* ростовщи́чество.

**utensil** *n* инструме́нт; *pl* у́тварь, посу́да.

**uterus** *n* ма́тка.

**utilitarian** *adj* утилита́рный. **utilitarianism** *n* утилитари́зм. **utility** *n* поле́зность; *pl*: **public utilities** комму́нальные услу́ги *f pl*. **utilize** *vt* испо́льзовать *impf* & *pf*.

**utmost** *adj* (*extreme*) кра́йний; **this is of the importance to me** э́то для меня́ кра́йне ва́жно; *n*: **do one's ~** де́лать *impf*, с~ *pf* всё возмо́жное.

**Utopia** *n* уто́пия. **utopian** *adj* утопи́ческий.

**utter** *attrib* по́лный, абсолю́тный; (*out-and-out*) отъя́вленный; (*coll*) vt произноси́ть *impf*, произнести́ *pf*; (*let out*) издава́ть *impf*, изда́ть *pf*. **utterance** *n* (*uttering*) произнесе́ние; (*pronouncement*)

выска́зывание. **utterly** *adv* соверше́нно.

**Uzbek** *n* узбе́к, -е́чка. **Uzbekistan** *n* Узбекиста́н.

# V

**vacancy** *n* (*for job*) вака́нсия, свобо́дное ме́сто; (*at hotel*) свобо́дный но́мер. **vacant** *adj* (*post*) вака́нтный; (*post: not engaged, free*) свобо́дный; (*empty*) пусто́й; (*look*) отсу́тствующий. **vacate** *vt* освобожда́ть *impf*, освободи́ть *pf*. **vacation** *n* кани́кулы (-л) *pl*; (*leave*) о́тпуск.

**vaccinate** *vt* вакцини́ровать *impf* & *pf*. **vaccination** *n* приви́вка (**against** от, про́тив +*gen*). **vaccine** *n* вакци́на.

**vacillate** *vi* колеба́ться *impf*. **vacillation** *n* колеба́ние.

**vacuous** *adj* пусто́й. **vacuum** *n* ва́куум; (*fig*) пустота́; *vt* пылесо́сить *impf*, про~ *pf*; **~ cleaner** пылесо́с; **~ flask** те́рмос.

**vagabond** *n* бродя́га *m*.

**vagary** *n* капри́з.

**vagina** *n* влага́лище.

**vagrant** *n* бродя́га *m*.

**vague** *adj* (*indeterminate, uncertain*) неопределённый; (*unclear*) нея́сный; (*dim*) сму́тный; (*absent-minded*) рассе́янный. **vagueness** *n* неопределённость, нея́сность; (*absent-mindedness*) рассе́янность.

**vain** *adj* (*futile*) тще́тный, напра́сный; (*empty*) пусто́й; (*conceited*) тщесла́вный; **in ~** напра́сно.

**vale** *n* дол, доли́на.

**valentine** *n* (*card*) поздрави́тельная ка́рточка с днём свято́го Валенти́на.

**valet** *n* камерди́нер.

**valiant** *adj* хра́брый.

**valid** *adj* действи́тельный; (*weighty*) ве́ский. **validate** *vt* (*ratify*) утвержда́ть *impf*, утверди́ть *pf*. **validity** *n* действи́тельность; (*weightiness*) ве́скость.

**valley** *n* доли́на.

**valour** *n* до́блесть.

**valuable** *adj* це́нный; *n pl* це́нности *f pl*. **valuation** *n* оце́нка. **value** *n* це́нность; (*math*) величина́; *pl* це́нности *f pl*; ~-added tax нало́г на доба́вленную сто́имость; ~ judgement субъекти́вная оце́нка; *vt* (*estimate*) оце́нивать *impf*, оцени́ть *pf*; (*hold dear*) цени́ть *impf*.

**valve** *n* (*tech, med, mus*) кла́пан; (*tech*) ве́нтиль *m*; (*radio*) электро́нная ла́мпа.

**vampire** *n* вампи́р.

**van** *n* фурго́н.

**vandal** *n* ванда́л. **vandalism** *n* вандали́зм. **vandalize** *vt* разруша́ть *impf*, разру́шить *pf*.

**vanguard** *n* аванга́рд.

**vanilla** *n* вани́ль.

**vanish** *vi* исчеза́ть *impf*, исче́знуть *pf*.

**vanity** *n* (*futility*) тщета́; (*conceit*) тщесла́вие.

**vanquish** *vt* побежда́ть *impf*, победи́ть *pf*.

**vantage-point** *n* (*mil*) наблюда́тельный пункт; (*fig*) вы́годная пози́ция.

**vapour** *n* пар.

**variable** *adj* изме́нчивый; (*weather*) неусто́йчивый, переме́нный; (*math*) переме́нная (величина́). **variance** *n*: be at ~ with (*contradict*) противоре́чить *impf* +dat; (*disa-*

*gree*) расходи́ться *impf*, разойти́сь *pf* во мне́ниях с+*instr*.

**variant** *n* вариа́нт. **variation** *n* (*varying*) измене́ние; (*variant*) вариа́нт; (*variety*) разнови́дность; (*mus*) вариа́ция.

**varicose** *adj*: ~ veins расшире́ние вен.

**varied** *adj* разнообра́зный. **variegated** *adj* разноцве́тный. **variety** *n* разнообра́зие; (*sort*) разнови́дность; (*a number*) ряд; ~ show варьете́ *neut indecl*. **various** *adj* ра́зный.

**varnish** *n* лак; *vt* лакирова́ть *impf*, от~ *pf*.

**vary** *vt* разнообра́зить *impf*, меня́ть *impf*; *vi* (*change*) меня́ться *impf*; (*differ*) ра́зниться *impf*.

**vase** *n* ва́за.

**Vaseline** *n* (*propr*) вазели́н.

**vast** *adj* грома́дный. **vastly** *adv* значи́тельно.

**VAT** *abbr* (*of* value-added tax) нало́г на доба́вленную сто́имость.

**vat** *n* чан, бак.

**vaudeville** *n* водеви́ль *m*.

**vault**[1] *n* (*leap*) прыжо́к; *vt* перепры́гивать *impf*, перепры́гнуть *pf*; *vi* пры́гать *impf*, пры́гнуть *pf*.

**vault**[2] *n* (*arch, covering*) свод; (*cellar*) по́греб; (*tomb*) склеп. **vaulted** *adj* сво́дчатый.

**VDU** *abbr* (*of* visual display unit) монито́р.

**veal** *n* теля́тина.

**vector** *n* (*math*) ве́ктор.

**veer** *vi* (*change direction*) изменя́ть *impf*, измени́ть *pf* направле́ние; (*turn*) повора́чивать *impf*, повороти́ть *pf*.

**vegetable** *n* о́вощ; *adj* овощно́й. **vegetarian** *n* вегетари-

а́нец, -нка; *attrib* вегетари-
а́нский. **vegetate** *vi (fig)*
прозяба́ть *impf*. **vegetation**
*n* расти́тельность.

**vehemence** *n (force)* си́ла;
*(passion)* стра́стность. **vehem-
ent** *adj (forceful)* си́льный;
*(passionate)* стра́стный.

**vehicle** *n* тра́нспортное сре́д-
ство; *(motor ~)* автомоби́ль
*m; (medium)* сре́дство.

**veil** *n* вуа́ль; *(fig)* заве́са.
**veiled** *adj* скры́тый.

**vein** *n* ве́на; *(of leaf, streak)*
жи́лка; **in the same ~** в том
же ду́хе.

**velocity** *n* ско́рость.

**velvet** *n* ба́рхат; *(adj)* ба́рхат-
ный. **velvety** *adj* бархати́-
стый.

**vending-machine** *n* торго́вый
автома́т. **vendor** *n* продаве́ц,
-вщи́ца.

**vendetta** *n* венде́тта.

**veneer** *n* фане́ра; *(fig)* лоск.

**venerable** *adj* почте́нный.
**venerate** *vt* благогове́ть *impf*
пе́ред+*instr*. **veneration** *n*
благогове́ние.

**venereal** *adj* венери́ческий.

**venetian blind** *n* жалюзи́ *neut
indecl*.

**vengeance** *n* месть; **take ~**
мстить *impf*, ото~ *pf* (**on**
+*dat*; **for** за+*acc*); **with a ~**
вовсю́. **vengeful** *adj* мсти́-
тельный.

**venison** *n* оле́нина.

**venom** *n* яд. **venomous** *adj*
ядови́тый.

**vent**[1] *n (opening)* вы́ход *(also
fig)*, отве́рстие; *vt (feelings)*
дава́ть *impf*, дать *pf* вы́-
ход+*dat*; излива́ть *impf*, из-
ли́ть *pf* (**on** на+*acc*).

**vent**[2] *n (slit)* разре́з.

**ventilate** *vt* прове́тривать *impf*,

прове́трить *pf*. **ventilation** *n*
вентиля́ция. **ventilator** *n*
вентиля́тор.

**ventriloquist** *n* чревовеща́-
тель *m*.

**venture** *n* предприя́тие; *vi
(dare)* осме́ливаться *impf*,
осме́литься *pf*; *vt (risk)*
рискова́ть *impf* +*instr*.

**venue** *n* ме́сто.

**veranda** *n* вера́нда.

**verb** *n* глаго́л. **verbal** *adj
(oral)* у́стный; *(relating to
words)* слове́сный; *(gram)*
отглаго́льный. **verbatim** *adj*
досло́вный; *adv* досло́вно.

**verbose** *adj* многосло́вный.

**verdict** *n* пригово́р.

**verge** *n (also fig)* край; *(of
road)* обо́чина; *(fig)* грань;
**on the ~ of** на гра́ни+*gen*; **he
was on the ~ of telling all** он
чуть не рассказа́л всё; *vi: ~*
**on** грани́чить *impf* с+*instr*.

**verification** *n* прове́рка; *(confirmation)* подтвержде́ние.
**verify** *vt* проверя́ть *impf*,
прове́рить *pf; (confirm)* под-
твержда́ть *impf*, подтвер-
ди́ть *pf*.

**vermin** *n* вреди́тели *m pl*.

**vernacular** *n* родно́й язы́к;
ме́стный диале́кт; *(homely
language)* разгово́рный язы́к.

**versatile** *adj* многосторо́нний.

**verse** *n (also bibl)* стих; *(stanza)*
строфа́; *(poetry)* стихи́ *m pl*.
**versed** *adj* о́пытный, све́ду-
щий *(in* в+*prep)*.

**version** *n (variant)* вариа́нт;
*(interpretation)* ве́рсия; *(text)*
текст.

**versus** *prep* про́тив+*gen*.

**vertebra** *n* позвоно́к; *pl* позво-
но́чник. **vertebrate** *n* позво-
но́чное живо́тное *sb*.

**vertical** *adj* вертика́льный; *n*

вертика́ль.
**vertigo** n головокруже́ние.
**verve** n жи́вость, энтузиа́зм.
**very** adj (that ~ same) тот са́мый; (this ~ same) э́тот са́мый; **at that ~ moment** в тот са́мый моме́нт; (precisely) как раз; **you are the ~ person I was looking for** как раз вас я иска́л; the ~ (even the) да́же, оди́н; the ~ thought frightens me одна́, да́же, мысль об э́том меня́ пуга́ет; (the extreme) са́мый; **at the ~ end** в са́мом конце́; adv ~ much о́чень; ~ much +comp гора́здо +comp; ~+superl, superl; ~ first са́мый пе́рвый; ~ well (agreement) хорошо́, ла́дно; not ~ не о́чень, дово́льно +neg.
**vessel** n сосу́д; (ship) су́дно.
**vest**[1] n ма́йка; (waistcoat) жиле́т.
**vest**[2] vt (with power) облека́ть impf, обле́чь pf (with +instr). **vested** adj: ~ **interest** ли́чная заинтересо́ванность; ~ **interests** (entrepreneurs) кру́пные предпринима́тели m pl.
**vestibule** n вестибю́ль m.
**vestige** n (trace) след; (sign) при́знак.
**vestments** n pl (eccl) облаче́ние. **vestry** n ри́зница.
**vet** n ветерина́р; vt (fig) проверя́ть impf, прове́рить pf.
**veteran** n ветера́н; adj ста́рый.
**veterinary** adj ветерина́рный; n ветерина́р.
**veto** n ве́то neut indecl; vt налага́ть impf, наложи́ть pf ве́то на+acc.
**vex** vt досажда́ть impf, досади́ть pf +dat. **vexation** n доса́да. **vexed** adj (annoyed)

серди́тый; (question) спо́рный. **vexatious**, **vexing** adj доса́дный.
**via** prep че́рез+acc.
**viable** adj (able to survive) жизнеспосо́бный; (feasible) осуществи́мый.
**viaduct** n виаду́к.
**vibrant** adj (lively) живо́й. **vibrate** vi вибри́ровать impf; vt (make) ~ заставля́ть impf, заста́вить pf вибри́ровать. **vibration** n вибра́ция. **vibrato** n вибра́то neut indecl.
**vicar** n прихо́дский свяще́нник. **vicarage** n дом свяще́нника.
**vicarious** adj чужо́й.
**vice**[1] n (evil) поро́к.
**vice**[2] n (tech) тиски́ (-ко́в) pl.
**vice-** in comb ви́це-, замести́тель m; ~**chairman** замести́тель m председа́теля; ~**chancellor** (univ) проре́ктор; ~**president** ви́це-президе́нт.
**viceroy** n ви́це-коро́ль m.
**vice versa** adv наоборо́т.
**vicinity** n окре́стность; **in the ~** побли́зости; (of ot+gen).
**vicious** adj зло́бный; ~ **circle** поро́чный круг.
**vicissitude** n превра́тность.
**victim** n же́ртва; (of accident) пострада́вший sb. **victimization** n пресле́дование. **victimize** vt пресле́довать impf.
**victor** n победи́тель m. ~**ница.**
**Victorian** adj викториа́нский.
**victorious** adj победоно́сный. **victory** n побе́да.
**video** n (~ recorder, ~ cassette, ~ film) ви́део neut indecl; ~ **camera** видеока́мера; ~ **cassette** видеокассе́та; ~ **cassette) recorder** видеомагнитофо́н; ~ **game** видеоигра́; vt запи́сывать impf,

записа́ть *pf* на ви́део.

**vie** *vi* сопе́рничать *impf* (with с+*instr*; for в+*prep*).

**Vietnam** *n* Вьетна́м. **Vietnamese** *n* вьетна́мец, -мка; *adj* вьетна́мский.

**view** *n* (*prospect, picture*) вид; (*opinion*) взгляд; (*viewing*) просмо́тр; (*inspection*) осмо́тр; in ~ of ввиду́+*gen*; on ~ вы́ставленный для обозре́ния; with a ~ to с це́лью+*gen*, +*inf*; *vt* (*pictures etc*.) рассма́тривать *impf*; (*inspect*) осма́тривать *impf*, осмотре́ть *pf*; (*mentally*) смотре́ть *impf* на+*acc*. **viewer** *n* зри́тель *m*, ~ница. **viewfinder** *n* видоиска́тель *m*. **viewpoint** *n* то́чка зре́ния.

**vigil** *n* бо́дрствование; keep ~ бо́дрствовать *impf*, дежу́рить *impf*. **vigilance** *n* бди́тельность. **vigilant** *adj* бди́тельный. **vigilante** *n* дружи́нник.

**vigorous** *adj* си́льный, энерги́чный. **vigour** *n* си́ла, эне́ргия.

**vile** *adj* гну́сный. **vilify** *vt* черни́ть *impf*, о~ *pf*.

**villa** *n* ви́лла.

**village** *n* дере́вня; *attrib* дереве́нский. **villager** *n* жи́тель *m* дере́вни.

**villain** *n* злоде́й.

**vinaigrette** *n* припра́ва из у́ксуса и оли́вкового ма́сла.

**vindicate** *vt* опра́вдывать *impf*, оправда́ть *pf*. **vindication** *n* оправда́ние.

**vindictive** *adj* мсти́тельный.

**vine** *n* виногра́дная лоза́.

**vinegar** *n* у́ксус.

**vineyard** *n* виногра́дник.

**vintage** *n* (*year*) год; (*fig*) вы́пуск; *attrib* (*wine*) ма́роч-

ный; (*car*) архаи́ческий.

**viola** *n* (*mus*) альт.

**violate** *vt* (*treaty, privacy*) наруша́ть *impf*, нару́шить *pf*; (*grave*) оскверня́ть *impf*, оскверни́ть *pf*. **violation** *n* наруше́ние; оскверне́ние.

**violence** *n* (*physical coercion, force*) наси́лие; (*strength, force*) си́ла. **violent** *adj* (*person, storm, argument*) свире́пый; (*pain*) си́льный; (*death*) наси́льственный. **violently** *adv* си́льно, очень.

**violet** *n* (*bot*) фиа́лка; (*colour*) фиоле́товый цвет; *adj* фиоле́товый.

**violin** *n* скри́пка. **violinist** *n* скрипа́ч, ~ка.

**VIP** *abbr* (*of* **very important person**) о́чень ва́жное лицо́.

**viper** *n* гадю́ка.

**virgin** *n* де́вственница, (*male*) де́вственник; V~ Mary де́ва Мари́я. **virginal** *adj* де́вственный. **virginity** *n* де́вственность. **Virgo** *n* Де́ва.

**virile** *adj* му́жественный. **virility** *n* му́жество.

**virtual** *adj* факти́ческий. **virtually** *adv* факти́чески. **virtue** *n* (*excellence*) доброде́тель; (*merit*) досто́инство; by ~ of на основа́нии+*gen*. **virtuosity** *n* виртуо́зность. **virtuoso** *n* виртуо́з. **virtuous** *adj* доброде́тельный.

**virulent** *adj* (*med*) вируле́нтный; (*fig*) зло́бный.

**virus** *n* ви́рус.

**visa** *n* ви́за.

**vis-à-vis** *prep* (*with regard to*) по отноше́нию к+*dat*.

**viscount** *n* вико́нт. **viscountess** *n* вико́нтесса.

**viscous** *adj* вя́зкий.

**visibility** *n* ви́димость. **visible**

*adj* ви́димый. **visibly** *adv* я́вно, заме́тно.

**vision** *n* (*sense*) зре́ние; (*apparition*) виде́ние; (*dream*) мечта́; (*insight*) проница́тельность. **visionary** *adj* (*unreal*) при́зрачный; (*impracticable*) неосуществи́мый; (*insightful*) проница́тельный; *n* (*dreamer*) мечта́тель *m*.

**visit** *n* посеще́ние, визи́т; *vt* посеща́ть *impf*, посети́ть *pf*; (*call on*) заходи́ть *impf*, зайти́ *pf* к+*dat*. **visitation** *n* официа́льное посеще́ние. **visitor** *n* гость *m*, посети́тель *m*.

**visor** *n* (*of cap*) козырёк; (*in car*) солнцезащи́тный щито́к; (*of helmet*) забра́ло.

**vista** *n* перспекти́ва, вид.

**visual** *adj* (*of vision*) зри́тельный; (*graphic*) нагля́дный; ~ **aids** нагля́дные посо́бия *neut pl*. **visualize** *vt* представля́ть *impf*, предста́вить *pf* себе́.

**vital** *adj* абсолю́тно необходи́мый (**to, for** для+*gen*) (*essential to life*) жи́зненный; *of* ~ **importance** первостепе́нной ва́жности. **vitality** *n* (*liveliness*) эне́ргия. **vitally** *adv* жи́зненно.

**vitamin** *n* витами́н.

**vitreous** *adj* стекля́нный.

**vitriolic** *adj* (*fig*) е́дкий.

**vivacious** *adj* живо́й. **vivacity** *n* жи́вость.

**viva (voce)** *n* у́стный экза́мен.

**vivid** *adj* (*bright*) я́ркий; (*lively*) живо́й. **vividness** *n* я́ркость; жи́вость.

**vivisection** *n* вивисе́кция.

**vixen** *n* лиси́ца-са́мка.

**viz.** *adv* то есть, а и́менно.

**vocabulary** *n* (*range, list, of words*) слова́рь *m*; (*range of words*) запа́с слов; (*of a lan-*

*guage*) слова́рный соста́в.

**vocal** *adj* голосово́й; (*mus*) вока́льный; (*noisy*) шу́мный; ~ **chord** голосова́я свя́зка. **vocalist** *n* певе́ц, -ви́ца.

**vocation** *n* призва́ние. **vocational** *adj* профессиона́льный.

**vociferous** *adj* шу́мный.

**vodka** *n* во́дка.

**vogue** *n* мо́да; **in** ~ в мо́де.

**voice** *n* го́лос; *vt* выража́ть *impf*, вы́разить *pf*.

**void** *n* пустота́; *adj* пусто́й; (*invalid*) недействи́тельный; *of* лишённый +*gen*.

**volatile** *adj* (*chem*) лету́чий; (*person*) непостоя́нный, неусто́йчивый.

**volcanic** *adj* вулкани́ческий. **volcano** *n* вулка́н.

**vole** *n* (*zool*) полёвка.

**volition** *n* во́ля; **by one's own** ~ по свое́й во́ле.

**volley** *n* (*missiles*) залп; (*fig*) град; (*sport*) уда́р с лёта; *vt* (*sport*) ударя́ть *impf*, уда́рить *pf* с лёта. **volleyball** *n* волейбо́л.

**volt** *n* вольт. **voltage** *n* напряже́ние.

**voluble** *adj* говорли́вый.

**volume** *n* (*book*) том; (*capacity, size*) объём; (*loudness*) гро́мкость. **voluminous** *adj* обши́рный.

**voluntary** *adj* доброво́льный. **volunteer** *n* доброво́лец; *vt* предлага́ть *impf*, предложи́ть *pf*; *vi* (*offer*) вызыва́ться *impf*, вы́зваться *pf* (*inf*, +*inf*; **for** в+*acc*); (*mil*) идти́ *impf*, пойти́ *pf* доброво́льцем.

**voluptuous** *adj* сластолюби́вый.

**vomit** *n* рво́та; *vt* (& *i*) рвать

*impf*, вы́рвать *pf impers*
(+*instr*); he was ~ing blood
его́ рва́ло кро́вью.

**voracious** *adj* прожо́рливый;
(*fig*) ненасы́тный.

**vortex** *n* (*also fig*) водоворо́т,
вихрь *m*.

**vote** *n* (*poll*) голосова́ние;
(*individual*) го́лос; the ~
(*suffrage*) пра́во го́лоса; (*resolution*) во́тум *no pl*; ~ of no
confidence во́тум недове́рия
(in +*dat*); ~ of thanks выра-
же́ние благода́рности; *vi* голо-
сова́ть *impf*, про~ *pf* (for
за+*acc*; against про́тив+*gen*);
*vt* (*allocate by*) ~ ассигно-
ва́ть *impf* & *pf*; (*deem*) при-
знава́ть *impf*, призна́ть *pf*;
the film was ~d a failure
фильм был при́знан неуда́ч-
ным; ~ in избира́ть *impf*,
избра́ть *pf* голосова́нием.
**voter** *n* избира́тель *m*.

**vouch** *vi*: ~ for руча́ться
*impf*, поручи́ться *pf* за+*acc*.
**voucher** *n* (*receipt*) распи́с-
ка; (*coupon*) тало́н.

**vow** *n* обе́т; *vi* кля́сться *impf*,
по~ *pf* в+*prep*.

**vowel** *n* гла́сный *sb*.

**voyage** *n* путеше́ствие.

**vulgar** *adj* вульга́рный, гру́-
бый, по́шлый. **vulgarity** *n*
вульга́рность, по́шлость.

**vulnerable** *adj* уязви́мый.

**vulture** *n* гриф; (*fig*) хи́щник.

# W

**wad** *n* комо́к; (*bundle*) па́чка.
**wadding** ва́та; (*padding*) наби́-
вка.
**waddle** *vi* ходи́ть *indet*, идти́
*det*, пойти́ *pf* вперева́лку
(*coll*).

**wade** *vt* & *i* (*river*) переходи́ть
*impf*, перейти́ *pf* вброд; *vi*:
~ through (*mud etc.*) про-
бира́ться *impf*, пробра́ться
*pf* по+*dat*; (*sth boring etc.*)
одолева́ть *impf*, одоле́ть *pf*.

**wafer** *n* ва́фля.

**waffle**[1] *n* (*dish*) ва́фля.
**waffle**[2] *vi* трепа́ться *impf*.

**waft** *vt* & *i* нести́(сь) *impf*,
по~ *pf*.

**wag** *vt* & *i* (*tail*) виля́ть *impf*,
вильну́ть *pf* (+*instr*); *vt* (*finger*) грози́ть *impf*, по~ *pf*
+*instr*.

**wage**[1] *n* (*pay*) see wages
**wage**[2] *vt*: ~ war вести́ *impf*,
про~ *pf* войну́.

**wager** *n* пари́ *neut indecl*; *vi*
держа́ть *impf* пари́ (that
что); *vt* ста́вить *impf*, по~
*pf*.

**wages** *n pl* за́работная пла́та.

**waggle** *vt* & *i* пома́хивать
*impf*, помаха́ть *pf* (+*instr*).

**wag(g)on** *n* (*carriage*) пово́з-
ка; (*cart*) теле́га; (*rly*) ваго́н-
платфо́рма.

**wail** *n* вопль *m*; *vi* вопи́ть *impf*.

**waist** *n* та́лия; (*level of* ~)
по́яс; ~-deep, high (*adv*) по
по́яс. **waistband** *n* по́яс.
**waistcoat** *n* жиле́т. **waistline**
*n* та́лия.

**wait** *n* ожида́ние; lie in ~ (for)
подстерега́ть *impf*, подсте-
ре́чь *pf*; *vi* (& *t*) (*also* ~ for)
ждать *impf* (+*gen*); *vi* (*be a
waiter, waitress*) быть офи-
циа́нтом, -ткой; ~ on обслу́-
живать *impf*, обслужи́ть *pf*.
**waiter** *n* официа́нт. **waiting**
*n*: ~-list спи́сок; ~-room
приёмная *sb*; (*rly*) зал ожи-
да́ния. **waitress** *n* официа́-
нтка.

**waive** *vt* отка́зываться *impf*,
отказа́ться *pf* от+*gen*.

**wake**[1] n (at funeral) помѝнки (-нок) pl.

**wake**[2] n (naut) кильва́тер; **in the ~ of** по слѐду +gen, за+instr.

**wake**[3] vt (also ~ up) буди́ть impf, раз~ pf; vi (also ~ up) просыпа́ться impf, просну́ться pf.

**Wales** n Уэ́льс.

**walk** n (walking) ходьба́; (gait) похо́дка; (stroll) прогу́лка; (path) тропа́; **~-out** (strike) забасто́вка; (as protest) демонстрати́вный ухо́д; **~-over** лёгкая побе́да; **ten minutes' ~ from here** де́сять мину́т ходьбы́ отсю́да; **go for a ~** идти́ impf, пойти́ pf гуля́ть; **from all ~s of life** всех слоёв о́бщества; vi ходи́ть indet, идти́ det, пойти́ pf гуля́ть impf, по~ pf; **~ away, off** уходи́ть impf, уйти́ pf; **in** входи́ть impf, войти́ pf; **~ out** выходи́ть impf, вы́йти pf; **~ out on** броса́ть impf, бро́сить pf; vt (traverse) обходи́ть impf, обойти́ pf; (take for ~) выводи́ть impf, вы́вести pf гуля́ть. **walker** n ходо́к. **walkie-talkie** n ра́ция. **walking** n; **~-stick** трость.

**Walkman** n (propr) во́кмен.

**wall** n стена́; vt обноси́ть impf, обнести́ pf стено́й; **~ up** (door, window) заде́лывать impf, заде́лать pf; (brick up) замуро́вывать impf, замурова́ть pf.

**wallet** n бума́жник.

**wallflower** n желтофио́ль.

**wallop** n си́льный уда́р; vt си́льно ударя́ть impf, уда́рить pf.

**wallow** vi валя́ться impf; **~ in**

(give o.s. up to) погружа́ться impf, погрузи́ться pf в+acc.

**wallpaper** n обо́и (обо́ев) pl.

**walnut** n гре́цкий оре́х; (wood, tree) оре́ховое де́рево, оре́х.

**walrus** n морж.

**waltz** n вальс; vi вальси́ровать impf.

**wan** adj бле́дный.

**wand** n па́лочка.

**wander** vi броди́ть impf; (also of thoughts etc.) блужда́ть impf; **~ from the point** отклоня́ться impf, отклони́ться pf от те́мы. **wanderer** n стра́нник.

**wane** n: **be on the ~** убыва́ть impf, vi убыва́ть impf, убы́ть pf; (weaken) ослабева́ть impf, ослабе́ть pf.

**wangle** vt заполуча́ть impf, заполучи́ть pf.

**want** n (lack) недоста́ток; (requirement) потре́бность; (desire) жела́ние; **for ~ of** за недоста́тком +gen; vt хоте́ть impf, за~ pf +gen, acc; (need) нужда́ться impf в+prep; **I ~ you to come at six** я хочу́, что́бы ты пришёл в шесть. **wanting** adj: **be ~** недостава́ть impf (impers+gen); **experience is ~** недостаёт о́пыта.

**wanton** adj (licentious) распу́тный; (senseless) бессмы́сленный.

**war** n война́; (attrib) вое́нный; **at ~** в состоя́нии войны́; **~ memorial** па́мятник па́вшим в войне́.

**ward** n (hospital) пала́та; (child etc.) подопе́чный sb; (district) райо́н; vt: **~ off** отража́ть impf, отрази́ть pf.

**warden** n (prison) нача́льник; (college) ре́ктор; (hostel) коменда́нт.

**warder** n тюре́мщик.

**wardrobe** n платяно́й шкаф.

**warehouse** n склад. **wares** n pl изде́лия neut pl, това́ры m pl.

**warfare** n война́.

**warhead** n боева́я голо́вка.

**warily** adv осторо́жно.

**warlike** adj вои́нственный.

**warm** n тепло́; adj (also fig) тёплый; ~-**hearted** серде́чный; vt & i греть(ся) impf, согре́ть(ся) impf, согре́ть(ся) pf; ~ **up** (food etc.) подогрева́ть(ся) impf, подогре́ть(ся) pf; (liven up) оживля́ть(ся) impf, оживи́ть(ся) pf; (sport) размина́ться impf, размя́ться pf; (mus) разы́грываться impf, разыгра́ться pf. **warmth** n тепло́; (cordiality) серде́чность.

**warn** vt предупрежда́ть impf, предупреди́ть pf (about o+prep). **warning** n предупрежде́ние.

**warp** vt & i (wood) коро́бить(ся) impf, по~, с~ pf; vt (pervert) извраща́ть impf, изврати́ть pf.

**warrant** n (for arrest etc.) о́рдер; vt (justify) опра́вдывать impf, оправда́ть pf; (guarantee) гаранти́ровать impf & pf. **warranty** n гара́нтия.

**warrior** n во́ин.

**warship** n вое́нный кора́бль m.

**wart** n борода́вка.

**wartime** n: in ~ во вре́мя войны́.

**wary** adj осторо́жный.

**wash** n мытьё; (thin layer) то́нкий слой; (lotion) примо́чка; (surf) прибо́й; (back-

wash) попу́тная волна́; **at the** ~ в сти́рке; **have a** ~ мы́ться impf, по~ pf; ~-**basin** умыва́льник; ~-**out** (fiasco) прова́л; ~-**room** умыва́льная sb; vt & i мыть(ся) impf, вы́~, по~ pf; vt (clothes) стира́ть impf, вы́~ pf; (of sea) омыва́ть impf; ~ **away, off, out** смыва́ть(ся) impf; ~ (carry away) сноси́ть impf, снести́ pf; ~ **out** (rinse) спола́скивать impf, сполосну́ть pf; ~ **up** (dishes) мыть impf, вы́~, по~ pf (посу́ду); ~ **one's hands (of it)** умыва́ть impf, умы́ть pf ру́ки. **washed-out** adj (exhausted) утомлённый. **washer** n (tech) ша́йба. **washing** n (of clothes) мытьё; (clothes) бельё; ~-**machine** стира́льная маши́на; ~-**powder** стира́льный порошо́к; ~-**up** (action) мытьё посу́ды; (dishes) гря́зная посу́да; ~-**up liquid** жи́дкое мы́ло для мытья́ посу́ды.

**wasp** n оса́.

**wastage** n уте́чка. **waste** n (desert) пусты́ня; (refuse) отбро́сы m pl; (of time, money, etc.) тра́та; **go to** ~ пропада́ть impf, пропа́сть pf да́ром; adj (desert) пусты́нный; (superfluous) нену́жный; (uncultivated) невозде́ланный; **lay** ~ опустоша́ть impf, опусто́шить pf; ~-**land** пусты́рь m; ~ **paper** нену́жные бума́ги f pl; (for recycling) макулату́ра; ~ **products** отхо́ды m pl; ~-**paper basket** корзи́на для бума́ги; vt тра́тить impf, ис~, по~ pf; (time) теря́ть impf, по~ pf; vi: ~ **away** ча́хнуть impf, за~ pf.

**wasteful** adj расточи́тель-
ный.

**watch** n (timepiece) часы́ (-со́в)
pl; (duty) дежу́рство; (naut)
ва́хта; keep ~ over наблю-
да́ть impf за+instr; ~-dog
сторожево́й пёс; ~-tower
сторожева́я ба́шня; vt (observe) наблюда́ть impf; (keep
an eye on) следи́ть impf
за+instr; (look after) смо-
тре́ть impf, по~ pf за+instr;
~ television, a film смотре́ть
impf, по~ pf телеви́зор,
фильм; vi смотре́ть impf; ~
out (be careful) бере́чься impf
(for +gen); ~ out for ждать
impf +gen; ~ out! осторо́ж-
но! **watchful** adj бди́тель-
ный. **watchman** n (ночно́й)
сто́рож. **watchword** n ло́зунг.

**water** n вода́; ~-colour аква-
ре́ль; ~-heater кипяти́ль-
ник; ~-main водопрово́дная
магистра́ль; ~ melon арбу́з;
~-pipe водопрово́дная труба́;
~-ski (n) во́дная лы́жа; ~-
skiing водолы́жный спорт;
~-supply водоснабже́ние;
~-way во́дный путь m; vt
(flowers etc.) полива́ть impf,
поли́ть pf, (animals) пои́ть
impf, на~ pf, (irrigate) оро-
ша́ть impf, ороси́ть pf; vi
(eyes) слези́ться impf; (mouth):
my mouth ~s у меня́ слю́нки
теку́т; ~ down разбавля́ть
impf, разба́вить pf. **water-
course** n ру́сло. **watercress**
n кресс водяно́й. **waterfall** n
водопа́д. **waterfront** n часть
го́рода примыка́ющая к бе́-
регу. **watering-can** n ле́йка.
**waterlogged** adj заболо́чен-
ный. **watermark** n водяно́й
знак. **waterproof** adj непро-
мока́емый; n непромока́е-

мый плащ. **watershed** n
водоразде́л. **waterside** n бе́-
рег. **watertight** adj водоне-
проница́емый; (fig) неопро-
верж́имый. **waterworks** n pl
водопрово́дные сооруже́ния
neut pl. **watery** adj водяни́-
стый.

**watt** n ватт.

**wave** vt (hand etc.) маха́ть
impf, махну́ть pf +instr; (flag)
разма́хивать impf +instr; vi
(~ hand) маха́ть impf, по~
pf (at +dat); (flutter) разве-
ва́ться impf; ~ aside отма́-
хиваться impf, отмахну́ться
pf от+gen; ~ down остана́-
вливать impf, останови́ть
pf; n (in various senses)
волна́; (of hand) взмах; (in
hair) зави́вка. **wavelength** n
длина́ волны́. **waver** vi
колеба́ться impf. **wavy** adj
волни́стый.

**wax** n воск; (in ear) се́ра; vt
вощи́ть impf, на~ pf. **wax-
work** n восковая фигу́ра; pl
музе́й восковых фигу́р.

**way** n (road, path, route; fig)
доро́га, путь m; (direction)
сторона́; (manner) о́браз;
(method) спо́соб; (respect)
отноше́ние; (habit) привы́ч-
ка; by the ~ (fig) кста́ти,
ме́жду про́чим; on the ~ по
доро́ге, по пути́; this ~ (direction) сюда́; (in this ~) та-
ки́м о́бразом; the other ~
round наоборо́т; under ~ на
ходу́; be in the ~ меша́ть
impf; get out of the ~ ухо-
ди́ть impf, уйти́ pf с доро́ги;
give ~ (yield) поддава́ться
impf, подда́ться pf (to +dat);
(collapse) обру́шиваться impf,
обру́шиться pf; go out of
one's ~ to стара́ться impf,

по~ *pf* изо всех сил +*inf*; **get, have, one's own** ~ добиваться *impf*, добиться *pf* своего; **make** ~ дорогу *impf*, уступить *pf* дорогу (for +*dat*). **waylay** *vt* (*lie in wait for*) подстерегать *impf*, подстеречь *pf*; (*stop*) перехватывать *impf*, перехватить *pf* по пути. **wayside** *adj* придорожный; *n*: **fall by the** ~ выбывать *impf*, выбыть *pf* из строя.

**wayward** *adj* своенравый.

**WC** *abbr* (*of* water-closet) уборная *sb*.

**we** *pron* мы.

**weak** *adj* слабый. **weaken** *vt* ослаблять *impf*, ослабить *pf*; *vi* слабеть *impf*, о~ *pf*. **weakling** *n* (*person*) слабый человек; (*plant*) слабое растение. **weakness** *n* слабость.

**weal** *n* (*mark*) рубец.

**wealth** *n* богатство; (*abundance*) изобилие. **wealthy** *adj* богатый.

**wean** *vt* отнимать *impf*, отнять *pf* от груди; (*fig*) отучать *impf*, отучить *pf* (of, from от+*gen*).

**weapon** *n* оружие. **weaponry** *n* вооружение.

**wear** *n* (*wearing*) носка; (*clothing*) одежда; (~ *and tear*) износ; *vt* носить *impf*, быть в+*prep*; **what shall I** ~ что мне надеть?; *vi* носиться *impf*, ~ **off** (*pain, novelty*) проходить *impf*, пройти *pf*; (*cease to have effect*) переставать *impf*, перестать *pf* действовать; ~ **out** (*clothes*) изнашивать(ся) *impf*, износить(ся) *pf*; (*exhaust*) изматывать *impf*, измучить *pf*.

**weariness** *n* усталость. **wearing, wearisome** *adj* утомительный. **weary** *adj* усталый; *vt* & *i* утомлять(ся) *impf*, утомить(ся) *pf*.

**weasel** *n* ласка.

**weather** *n* погода; **be under the** ~ неважно себя чувствовать *impf*; ~**-beaten** обветренный; ~**-forecast** прогноз погоды; *vt* (*storm etc.*) выдерживать *impf*, выдержать *pf*; (*expose to atmosphere*) подвергать *impf*, подвергнуть *pf* атмосферным влияниям. **weathercock, weathervane** *n* флюгер. **weatherman** *n* метеоролог.

**weave**¹ *vt* & *i* (*fabric*) ткать *impf*, co~ *pf*; *vt* (*fig; also wreath etc.*) плести *impf*, c~ *pf*. **weaver** *n* ткач, ~иха.

**weave**² *vi* (*wind*) виться *impf*.

**web** *n* (*cobweb; fig*) паутина; (*fig*) сплетение. **webbed** *adj* перепончатый. **webbing** *n* тканая лента.

**wed** *vt* (*of man*) жениться *impf* & *pf* на+*prep*; (*of woman*) выходить *impf*, выйти *pf* замуж за+*acc*; (*unite*) сочетать *impf* & *pf*; (*fig*) пожениться *pf*. **wedded** *adj* супружеский; ~ **to** (*fig*) преданный +*dat*. **wedding** *n* свадьба, бракосочетание; ~**-cake** свадебный торт; ~**-day** день *m* свадьбы; ~**-dress** подвенечное платье; ~**-ring** обручальное кольцо.

**wedge** *n* клин; *vt* (~ *open*) заклинивать *impf*, заклинить *pf*; *vt* & *i*: ~ **in(to)** вклинивать(ся) *impf*, вклинить(ся) *pf* (в+*acc*).

**wedlock** *n* брак; **born out of** ~ рождённый вне брака, внебрачный.

**Wednesday** *n* среда.

**weed** n сорня́к; ~-killer герби́ци(д; vt поло́ть impf, вы́- pf; ~ out удаля́ть impf, удали́ть pf. **weedy** adj (person) то́щий.

**week** n неде́ля; ~-end суббо́та и воскресе́нье, выходны́е sb pl. **weekday** n бу́дний день m. **weekly** adj еженеде́льный; (wage) неде́льный; adv еженеде́льно; n еженеде́льник.

**weep** vi пла́кать impf. **weeping willow** n плаку́чая и́ва.

**weigh** vt (also fig) взве́шивать impf, взве́сить pf; (consider) обду́мывать impf, обду́мать pf; vt & i (so much) ве́сить impf; ~ down отягоща́ть impf, отяготи́ть pf; ~ on тяготи́ть impf; ~ out отве́шивать impf, отве́сить pf; ~ up (appraise) оце́нивать impf, оцени́ть pf. **weight** n (also authority) вес; (load, also fig) тя́жесть; (sport) шта́нга; (influence) влия́ние; lose ~ худе́ть impf, по~ pf; put on ~ толсте́ть impf, по~ pf; ~-lifter штанги́ст; ~-lifting подня́тие тя́жестей; vt (make heavier) утяжеля́ть impf, утяжели́ть pf. **weightless** adj невесо́мый. **weighty** adj ве́ский.

**weir** n плоти́на.

**weird** adj (strange) стра́нный.

**welcome** n приём; adj жела́нный; (pleasant) прия́тный; you are ~ (don't mention it) пожа́луйста; you are ~ to use my bicycle мой велосипе́д к ва́шим услу́гам; you are ~ to stay the night вы мо́жете переночева́ть у меня/нас; vt приве́тствовать impf (& pf in past tense); int добро́ пожа́ловать!

**weld** vt сва́ривать impf, свари́ть pf. **welder** n сва́рщик.

**welfare** n благосостоя́ние; W~ State госуда́рство все́общего благосостоя́ния.

**well**[1] n коло́дец; (for stairs) ле́стничная кле́тка.

**well**[2] vi: ~ up (anger etc.) вскипа́ть impf, вскипе́ть pf; tears ~ed up глаза́ напо́лнились слеза́ми.

**well**[3] adj (healthy) здоро́вый; feel ~ чу́вствовать impf, по~ pf себя́ хорошо́, здоро́вым; get ~ поправля́ться impf, попра́виться pf; look ~ хорошо́ вы́глядеть impf; all is ~ всё в поря́дке; int ну(!); adv хорошо́; (very much) о́чень; as ~ то́же; as ~ as (in addition to) кро́ме+gen; it may ~ be true вполне́ возмо́жно, что э́то так; very ~! хорошо́!; ~ done! молоде́ц!; ~-balanced уравнове́шенный; ~-behaved (благо)воспи́танный; ~-being благополу́чие; ~-bred благовоспи́танный; ~-built кре́пкий; ~-defined чёткий; ~-disposed благоскло́нный; ~-done (cooked) (хорошо́) прожа́ренный; ~-fed отко́рмленный; ~-founded обосно́ванный; ~-groomed (person) хо́леный; ~-heeled состоя́тельный; ~-informed (хорошо́) осведомлённый (about в+prep); ~-known изве́стный; ~-meaning де́йствующий из лу́чших побужде́ний; ~-nigh почти́; ~-off состоя́тельный; ~-paid хорошо́ опла́чиваемый; ~-preserved хорошо́ сохрани́вшийся; ~-to-do состоя́тельный; ~-wisher доброжела́тель m.

**wellington (boot)** n рези́новый сапо́г.
**Welsh** adj уэ́льский. **Welshman** n валли́ец. **Welshwoman** n валли́йка.
**welter** n пу́таница.
**wend** vt: ~ one's way держа́ть impf путь.
**west** n за́пад; (naut) вест; adj за́падный; adv на за́пад, к за́паду. **westerly** adj за́падный. **western** adj за́падный; n (film) ве́стерн. **westward(s)** adv на за́пад, к за́паду.
**wet** adj мо́крый; (paint) непросо́хший; (rainy) дождли́вый; ~ through промо́кший до ни́тки; n (dampness) вла́жность; (rain) дождь m; vt мочи́ть impf, на~ pf.
**whack** n (blow) уда́р; vt колоти́ть impf, по~ pf. **whacked** adj разби́тый.
**whale** n кит.
**wharf** n при́стань.
**what** pron (interrog, int) что; (how much) ско́лько; (rel) (то,) что; ~ (...) for заче́м; ~ if а что е́сли; ~ is your name как вас зову́т?; adj (interrog, int) како́й; ~ kind of како́й. **whatever**, **whatsoever** pron что бы ни+past (~ you think что бы вы ни ду́мали), всё, что (take ~ you want возьми́те всё, что хоти́те); adj како́й бы ни+past (~ books he read(s) каки́е бы кни́ги он ни прочита́л); at all): there is no chance ~ нет никако́й возмо́жности; is there any chance ~? есть ли хоть кака́я-нибудь возмо́жность?
**wheat** n пшени́ца.
**wheedle** vt (coax into doing) угова́ривать impf, угово-

ри́ть pf с по́мощью ле́сти; ~ out of выма́нивать impf, вы́манить pf y+gen.
**wheel** n колесо́; (steering, helm) руль m; (potter's) гонча́рный круг; vt (push) ката́ть indet, кати́ть det, по~ pf; vt & i (turn) повёртывать(ся) impf, поверну́ть(ся) pf; vi (circle) кружи́ться impf. **wheelbarrow** n та́чка. **wheelchair** n инвали́дное кре́сло.
**wheeze** vi сопе́ть impf.
**when** adv когда́; conj когда́, в то вре́мя как; (whereas) тогда́ как; (if) е́сли; (although) хотя́. **whence** adv отку́да. **whenever** adv когда́ же; conj (every time) вся́кий раз когда́; (at any time) когда́; (no matter when) когда́ бы ни+past; we shall have dinner ~ you arrive во ско́лько бы вы ни прие́хали, мы пообе́даем.
**where** adv & conj (place) где; (whither) куда́; from ~ отку́да. **whereabouts** adv где; n местонахожде́ние. **whereas** conj тогда́ как; хотя́. **whereby** adv & conj посре́дством чего́. **wherein** adv & conj в чём. **wherever** adv & conj (place) где бы ни+past; (whither) куда́ бы ни+past; ~ he goes куда́ бы он ни пошёл; ~ you like где/куда́ хоти́те. **wherewithal** n сре́дства neut pl.
**whet** vt точи́ть impf, на~ pf; (fig) возбужда́ть impf, возбуди́ть pf.
**whether** conj ли; I don't know ~ he will come я не зна́ю, придёт ли он; ~ he comes or not придёт (ли) он и́ли нет.

**which** adj (interrog, rel)
какóй; pron (interrog) какóй;
(person) кто; (rel) котóрый;
(rel to whole sentence) что;
~ **is** ~? (persons) кто из них
кто?; (things) что-что? **whichever** adj & pron какóй бы
ни+past (~ **book you choose**
какýю бы кнúгу ты ни вы-
брал); любóй (take ~ **book
you want** возьмúте любýю
кнúгу).

**whiff** n зáпах.

**while** n врéмя neut; **a little** ~
недóлго; **a long** ~ дóлго; **for
a long** ~ (up to now) давнó;
**for a** ~ на врéмя; **in a little**
~ скóро; **it is worth** ~
э́то сдéлать; vt: ~ **away** проводúть impf, провестú pf;
conj покá; (although) хотя́; (contrast) а;
**we went to the cinema — they
went to the theatre** мы ходú-
ли в кинó, а онú в теáтр.

**whilst** see while

**whim** n прúхоть, капрúз.

**whimper** vt хны́кать impf;
(dog) скулúть impf.

**whimsical** adj капрúзный;
(odd) причýдливый.

**whine** n (wail) вой; (whimper)
хны́канье; vi (dog) скулúть
impf; (wail) выть impf; (whimper)
хны́кать impf.

**whinny** vi тúхо ржать impf.

**whip** n кнут, хлыст; vt (lash)
хлестáть impf, хлестнýть pf;
(cream) сбивáть impf, сбить
pf; ~ **off** скúдывать impf,
скúнуть pf; ~ **out** выхвáты-
вать impf, вы́хватить pf; ~
**round** бы́стро повёртывать-
ся impf, повернýться pf; ~
**round** сбор дéнег; ~ **up** (stir
up) разжигáть impf, раз-
жéчь pf.

**whirl** n кружéние; (of dust,
fig) вихрь m; (turmoil) суе-
тóха; vt & i кружúть(ся) impf,
за-, про- pf. **whirlpool** n водо-
ворóт. **whirlwind** n вихрь m.

**whirr** vi жужжáть impf.

**whisk** n (of twigs etc.) вé-
ничек; (utensil) мутóвка; (movement) помáхивание; (of cream
etc.) сбивáть impf, сбить pf;
~ **away, off** (brush off) смá-
хивать impf, смахнýть pf;
(take away) бы́стро уносúть
impf, унестú pf.

**whisker** n (human) вóлос на
лицé; (animal) ус; pl (human)
бакенбáрды f pl.

**whisky** n вúски neut indecl.

**whisper** n шёпот; vt & i шеп-
тáть impf, шепнýть pf.

**whistle** n (sound) свист; (instrument) свистóк; vi сви-
стéть impf, свúстнуть pf; vt
насвúстывать impf.

**white** adj бéлый; (hair) седóй;
(pale) блéдный; (with milk)
с молокóм; **paint** ~ крáсить
impf, по- pf в бéлый свет;
~**collar worker** служáщий
sb; ~ **lie** невúнная ложь; n
(colour) бéлый цвет; (egg,
eye) белóк; (~ person) бéлый sb. **whiten** vt белúть
impf, на-, по-, вы́- pf; vi
белéть impf, по- pf. **whiteness** n белизнá. **whitewash**
n побéлка; vt белúть impf,
по- pf; (fig) обеля́ть impf,
обелúть pf.

**whither** adv & conj кудá.

**Whitsun** n Трóица.

**whittle** vt: ~ **down** уменьшáть
impf, умéньшить pf.

**whiz(z)** vi: ~ **past** просвистéть
pf.

**who** pron (interrog) кто; (rel)
котóрый.

**whoever** 683 **will**

**whoever** pron кто бы ни+past; (he who) тот, кто.
**whole** adj (entire) весь, це́лый; (intact, of number) це́лый; n (thing complete) це́лое sb; (all there is) весь sb; (sum) су́мма; **on the** ~ в о́бщем. **whole-hearted** adj беззаве́тный. **whole-heartedly** adv от всего́ се́рдца. **wholemeal** adj из непросе́янной муки́. **wholesale** adj опто́вый; (fig) ма́ссовый; adv о́птом. **wholesaler** n опто́вый торго́вец. **wholesome** adj здоро́вый. **wholly** adv по́лностью.
**whom** pron (interrog) кого́ etc.; (rel) кото́рого etc.
**whoop** n крик; vi крича́ть impf, кри́кнуть pf; **~ it up** бу́рно весели́ться impf; **~ing cough** коклю́ш.
**whore** n проститу́тка.
**whose** pron (interrog, rel) чей; (rel) кото́рого.
**why** adv почему́; int да ведь!
**wick** n фити́ль m.
**wicked** adj ди́кий. **wickedness** n ди́кость.
**wicker** attrib плетёный.
**wicket** n (cricket) воро́тца.
**wide** adj широ́кий; (extensive) обши́рный; (in measurements) в+acc ширино́й; **~ awake** по́лный внима́ния; **~ open** широко́ откры́тый; adv (off target) ми́мо це́ли. **widely** adv широко́. **widen** vt & i расширя́ть(ся) impf, расши́рить(ся) pf. **widespread** adj распространённый.
**widow** n вдова́. **widowed** adj овдове́вший. **widower** n вдове́ц.
**width** n ширина́; (fig) широта́; (of cloth) полотни́ще.
**wield** vt (brandish) разма́хи-

вать impf +instr; (power) по́льзоваться impf +instr.
**wife** n жена́.
**wig** n пари́к.
**wiggle** vt & i (move) шевели́ть(ся) impf, по~, шевельну́ть(ся) pf (+instr).
**wigwam** n вигва́м.
**wild** adj ди́кий; (flower) полево́й; (uncultivated) невозде́ланный; (tempestuous) бу́йный; (furious) нейстовый; (ill-considered) необду́манный; **be ~ about** быть без ума́ от+gen; **~-goose chase** сумасбро́дная зате́я; n: pl де́бри (-рей) pl. **wildcat** adj (unofficial) неофициа́льный.
**wilderness** n пусты́ня. **wildfire** n: **spread like ~** распространя́ться impf, распространи́ться pf с молниено́сной быстрото́й. **wildlife** n жива́я приро́да. **wildness** n ди́кость.
**wile** n хи́трость.
**wilful** adj (obstinate) упря́мый; (deliberate) преднаме́ренный.
**will** n во́ля; (~-power) си́ла во́ли; (at death) завеща́ние; **against one's ~** про́тив во́ли; **of one's own free ~** до́бровольно; **with a ~** с энтузиа́змом; **good ~** до́брая во́ля; **make one's ~** писа́ть impf, на~ pf завеща́ние; vt (want) хоте́ть impf, за~ pf +gen, acc; v aux: **he ~ be president** он бу́дет президе́нтом; **he ~ return tomorrow** он вернётся за́втра; **~ you open the window?** откро́йте окно́, пожа́луйста.
**willing** adj гото́вый; (eager) стара́тельный. **willingly** adv охо́тно. **willingness** n гото́вность.

**willow** *n* и́ва.

**willy-nilly** *adv* во́лей-нево́лей.

**wilt** *vi* поника́ть *impf*, пони́кнуть *pf*.

**wily** *adj* хи́трый.

**win** *n* побе́да; *vt & vi* выи́грывать *impf*, вы́играть *impf*; *vt* (*obtain*) добива́ться *impf*, доби́ться *pf* +*gen*; ~ over угова́ривать *impf*, уговори́ть *pf*; (*charm*) располага́ть *impf*, расположи́ть *pf* к себе́.

**wince** *vi* вздра́гивать *impf*, вздро́гнуть *pf*.

**winch** *n* лебёдка; поднима́ть *impf*, подня́ть *pf* с по́мощью лебёдки.

**wind**[1] *n* (*air*) ве́тер; (*breath*) дыха́ние; (*flatulence*) ве́тры *m pl*; ~ **instrument** духово́й инструме́нт; ~**-swept** откры́тый ветра́м; **get** ~ **of** прон̄ю́хивать *impf*, проню́хать *pf*; *vt* (*make gasp*) заставля́ть *impf*, заста́вить *pf* задохну́ться.

**wind**[2] *vi* (*meander*) ви́ться *impf*, извива́ться *impf*; *vt* (*coil*) нама́тывать *impf*, намота́ть *pf*; (*watch*) заводи́ть *impf*, завести́ *pf* (*wrap*) уку́тывать *impf*, уку́тать *pf*; ~ **up** (*vt*) (*reel*) сма́тывать *impf*, смота́ть *pf*; (*watch*) *see* **wind**[2]; (*vt & i*) (*end*) конча́ть(ся) *impf*, ко́нчить(ся) *pf*; ~ **winding** *adj* (*meandering*) изви́листый; (*staircase*) винтово́й.

**windfall** *n* па́далица; (*fig*) золото́й дождь.

**windmill** *n* ветряна́я ме́льница.

**window** *n* окно́; (*of shop*) витри́на; ~**-box** нару́жный я́щик для цвето́в; ~**-cleaner** мо́йщик око́н; ~**-dressing** оформле́ние витри́н; (*fig*)

показу́ха; ~**-frame** око́нная ра́ма; ~**-ledge** подоко́нник; ~**-pane** око́нное стекло́; ~**-shopping** рассма́тривание витри́н; ~**-sill** подоко́нник.

**windpipe** *n* дыха́тельное го́рло. **windscreen** *n* ветрово́е стекло́; ~ **wiper** дво́рник. **windsurfer** *n* виндсёрфинѓист. **windsurfing** *n* виндсёрфинг. **windward** *adj* наве́тренный. **windy** *adj* ве́треный.

**wine** *n* вино́; ~ **bar** ви́нный погребо́к; ~ **bottle** ви́нная буты́лка; ~ **list** ка́рта вин; ~**-tasting** дегуста́ция вин. **wineglass** *n* рю́мка. **winery** *n* ви́нный заво́д. **winy** *adj* ви́нный.

**wing** *n* (*also polit*) крыло́; (*archit*) фли́гель *m*; (*sport*) фланг; *pl* (*theat*) кули́сы *f pl*. **winged** *adj* крыла́тый.

**wink** *n* (*blink*) морга́ние; (*as sign*) подми́гивание; *vi* морга́ть *impf*, мигну́ть *pf*; ~ **at** подми́гивать *impf*, подмигну́ть *pf* +*dat*; (*fig*) смотре́ть *impf*, по~ *pf* сквозь па́льцы на+*acc*.

**winkle** *vt*: ~ **out** выко́вы́ривать *impf*, вы́ковырять *pf*.

**winner** *n* победи́тель *m*, ~ница. **winning** *adj* (*victorious*) вы́игравший; (*shot etc.*) реша́ющий; (*charming*) обая́тельный; *n*: *pl* вы́игрыш; ~**-post** фи́нишный столб.

**winter** *n* зима́; *attrib* зи́мний. **wintry** *adj* зи́мний; (*cold*) холо́дный.

**wipe** *vt* (*also* ~ **out inside of**) вытира́ть *impf*, вы́тереть *pf*; ~ **away, off** стира́ть *impf*, стере́ть *pf*; ~ **out** (*exterminate*) уничтожа́ть *impf*, уни-

что́жить *pf*; (*cancel*) смыва́ть *impf*, смыть *pf*.
**wire** *n* про́волока; (*carrying current*) про́вод; ~ **netting** про́волочная се́тка. **wireless** *n* ра́дио *neut indecl.* **wiring** *n* электропрово́дка. **wiry** *adj* жи́листый.
**wisdom** *n* му́дрость; ~ **tooth** зуб му́дрости. **wise** *adj* му́дрый; (*prudent*) благоразу́мный.
**wish** *n* жела́ние; **with best** ~**es** всего́ хоро́шего, с наилу́чшими пожела́ниями; *vt* хоте́ть *impf*, за~ *pf* (I ~ **I could see him** мне хоте́лось бы его́ ви́деть; I ~ **to go** я хочу́ пойти́; I ~ **you to come early** я хочу́, что́бы вы ра́но пришли́; I ~ **the day were over** хорошо́ бы день уже́ ко́нчился); жела́ть *impf* +*gen* (I ~ **you luck** желаю вам уда́чи); (*congratulate on*) поздравля́ть *impf*, поздра́вить *pf* (I ~ **you a happy birthday** поздравля́ю тебя́ с днём рожде́ния); *vi*: ~ **for** жела́ть *impf* +*gen*; мечта́ть *impf* о+*prep*. **wishful** *adj*: ~ **thinking** самообольще́ние; приня́тие жела́емого за действи́тельное.
**wisp** *n* (*of straw*) пучо́к; (*hair*) клочо́к; (*smoke*) стру́йка.
**wisteria** *n* глици́ния.
**wistful** *adj* тоскли́вый.
**wit** *n* (*mind*) ум; (*wittiness*) остроу́мие; (*person*) остря́к; **be at one's** ~'s **end** не знать *impf* что де́лать.
**witch** *n* ве́дьма; ~-**hunt** охо́та за ве́дьмами. **witchcraft** *n* колдовство́.
**with** *prep* (*in company of, together* ~) (вме́сте) с+*instr*;

(*as a result of*) от+*gen*; (*at house of, in keeping of*) у+*gen*; (*by means of*) +*instr*; (*in spite of*) несмотря́ на+*acc*; (*including*) включа́я+*acc*; ~ **each/ one another** друг с дру́гом.
**withdraw** *vt* (*retract*) брать *impf*, взять *pf* наза́д; (*hand*) отдёргивать *impf*, отдёрнуть *pf*; (*cancel*) снима́ть *impf*, снять *pf*; (*mil*) выводи́ть *impf*, вы́вести *pf*; (*money from circulation*) изыма́ть *impf*, изъя́ть *pf* из обраще́ния; (*diplomat etc.*) отзыва́ть *impf*, отозва́ть *pf*; (*from bank*) брать *impf*, взять *pf*; *vi* удаля́ться *impf*, удали́ться *pf*; (*drop out*) выбыва́ть *impf*, вы́быть *pf*; (*mil*) отходи́ть *impf*, отойти́ *pf*. **withdrawal** *n* (*retraction*) взя́тие наза́д; (*cancellation*) (*mil*) отхо́д; (*money from circulation*) изъя́тие; (*departure*) ухо́д. **withdrawn** *adj* за́мкнутый.
**wither** *vi* вя́нуть *impf*, за~ *pf*. **withering** *adj* (*fig*) уничтожа́ющий.
**withhold** *vt* (*refuse to grant*) не дава́ть *impf*, дать *pf* +*gen*; (*payment*) уде́рживать *impf*, удержа́ть *pf*; (*information*) ута́ивать *impf*, утаи́ть *pf*.
**within** *prep* (*inside*) внутри́+*gen*, в+*prep*; (~ **the limits of**) в преде́лах +*gen*; (*time*) в тече́ние +*gen*; *adv* внутри́; **from** ~ изнутри́.
**without** *prep* без+*gen*; ~ **saying good-bye** не проща́ясь; **do** ~ обходи́ться *impf*, обойти́сь *pf* без+*gen*.
**withstand** *vt* выде́рживать *impf*, вы́держать *pf*.
**witness** *n* (*person*) свиде́тель *m*; (*eye-*~) очеви́дец; (*to sig-*

*nature etc.*) завери́тель *m*; **bear ~ to** свиде́тельствовать *impf*, за~ *pf*. **~box** ме́сто для свиде́тельских показа́ний; *vt* быть свиде́телем+*gen*; (*document etc.*) заверя́ть *impf*, заве́рить *pf*. **witticism** *n* остро́та. **witty** *adj* остроу́мный.

**wizard** *n* волше́бник, колду́н.

**wizened** *adj* морщи́нистый.

**wobble** *vt & i* шата́ть(ся) *impf*, шатну́ть(ся) *pf*; *vi* (*voice*) дрожа́ть *impf*. **wobbly** *adj* ша́ткий.

**woe** *n* го́ре; **~ is me!** го́ре мне! **woeful** *adj* жа́лкий.

**wolf** *n* волк; *vt* пожира́ть *impf*, пожра́ть *pf*.

**woman** *n* же́нщина. **womanizer** *n* волоки́та. **womanly** *adj* же́нственный.

**womb** *n* ма́тка.

**wonder** *n* чу́до; (*amazement*) изумле́ние; (**it's no**) ~ неудиви́тельно; *vt* интересова́ться *impf* (**I ~ who will come** интересно, кто придёт); *vi*: **I shouldn't ~ if** неудиви́тельно бу́дет, е́сли; **I ~ if you could help me** не могли́ бы вы мне помо́чь; **~ at** удивля́ться *impf*, удиви́ться *pf* +*dat*. **wonderful, wondrous** *adj* замеча́тельный.

**wont** *n*: **as is his ~** по своему́ обыкнове́нию; *predic*: **be ~ to** име́ть привы́чку+*inf*.

**woo** *vt* уха́живать *impf* за +*instr*.

**wood** *n* (*forest*) лес; (*material*) де́рево; (*firewood*) дрова́ *pl*. **woodcut** *n* гравю́ра на де́реве. **wooded** *adj* леси́стый. **wooden** *adj* (*also fig*) деревя́нный. **woodland** *n* леси́-

стая ме́стность; *attrib* лесно́й. **woodpecker** *n* дя́тел. **woodwind** *n* деревя́нные духовы́е инструме́нты *m pl*. **woodwork** *n* столя́рная рабо́та; (*wooden parts*) деревя́нные ча́сти (-те́й) *pl*. **woodworm** *n* жучо́к. **woody** *adj* (*plant etc.*) деревяни́стый; (*wooded*) леси́стый.

**wool** *n* шерсть. **woollen** *adj* шерстяно́й. **woolly** *adj* шерсти́стый; (*indistinct*) нея́сный.

**word** *n* сло́во; (*news*) изве́стие; **by ~ of mouth** у́стно; **have a ~ with** поговори́ть *pf* с+*instr*; **in a ~** одни́м сло́вом; **in other ~s** други́ми слова́ми; **~ for ~** сло́во в сло́во; **~ processor** компью́тер(-изда́тель) *m*; *vt* выража́ть *impf*, вы́разить *pf*; формули́ровать *impf*, с~ *pf*. **wording** *n* формулиро́вка.

**work** *n* рабо́та; (*labour*; *toil*; *scholarly* ~) труд; (*occupation*) заня́тие; (*studies*) заня́тия *neut pl*; (*of art*) произведе́ние; (*book*) сочине́ние; *pl* (*factory*) заво́д; (*mechanism*) механи́зм; **at ~** (*doing* ~) за рабо́той; (*at place of* ~) на рабо́те; **out of ~** безрабо́тный; **~force** рабо́чая си́ла; **~load** нагру́зка; *vi* (*also function*) рабо́тать *impf* (**at, on** над+*instr*); (*study*) занима́ться *impf*, заня́ться *pf*; (*also toil*, *labour*) труди́ться *impf*; (*have effect*, *function*) де́йствовать *impf*; (*succeed*) удава́ться *impf*, уда́ться *pf*; *vt* (*operate*) управля́ть *impf* +*instr*; обраща́ться *impf* с+*instr*; (*wonders*) творить *impf*, со~ *pf*; (*soil*) обрабатывать *impf*, обработать *pf*; (*compel to* ~) заставлять *impf*, заставить *pf*; ~ **in** вставлять *impf*, вставить *pf*; ~ **off** (*debt*) отрабатывать *impf*, отработать *pf*; (*weight*) сгонять *impf*, согнать *pf*; (*energy*) давать *impf*, дать *pf* выход +*dat*; ~ **out** (*solve*) находить *impf*, найти *pf* решение +*gen*; (*plans etc.*) разрабатывать *impf*, разработать *pf*; (*sport*) тренироваться *impf*; **everything** ~ **ed out well** всё кончилось хорошо; ~ **out at** (*amount to*) составлять *impf*, составить *pf*; ~ **up** (*perfect*) вырабатывать *impf*, выработать *pf*; (*excite*) возбуждать *impf*, возбудить *pf*; (*appetite*) нагуливать *impf*, нагулять *pf*. **workable** *adj* осуществимый, реальный. **workaday** *n* будничный. **workaholic** *n* труженик *n* работник; (*manual*) рабочий *sb*. **working** *adj*: ~ **class** рабочий класс; ~ **hours** рабочее время *neut*; ~ **party** комиссия. **workman** *n* работник. **workmanlike** *adj* искусный. **workmanship** *n* искусство, мастерство. **workshop** *n* мастерская *sb*.

**world** *n* мир, свет; *attrib* мировой; ~**famous** всемирно известный; ~ **war** мировая война; ~**wide** всемирный. **worldly** *adj* мирской; (*person*) опытный.

**worm** *n* червь *m*; (*intestinal*) глист; *vt*: ~ **o.s. into** вкрадываться *impf*, вкрасться *pf* в+*acc*; ~ **out** выведывать

*impf*, выведать *pf* (*of* у+*gen*); ~ **one's way** пробираться *impf*, пробраться *pf*.

**worry** *n* (*anxiety*) беспокойство; (*care*) забота; *vt* беспокоить *impf*, о~ *pf*; *vi* беспокоиться *impf*, о~ *pf* (*about* о+*prep*).

**worse** *adj* худший; *adv* хуже; *n*: **from bad to** ~ всё хуже и хуже. **worsen** *vt* & *i* ухудшать(ся) *impf*, ухудшить(ся) *pf*.

**worship** *n* поклонение (*of* +*dat*); (*service*) богослужение; *vt* поклоняться *impf* +*dat*; (*adore*) обожать *impf*. **worshipper** *n* поклонник, -ица.

**worst** *adj* наихудший, самый плохой; *adv* хуже всего; *n* самое плохое.

**worth** *n* (*value*) цена, ценность; (*merit*) достоинство; **give me a pound's** ~ **of petrol** дайте мне бензина на фунт; *adj*: **be** ~ (*of equal value to*) стоить *impf* (**what is it** ~? сколько это стоит?); (*deserve*) стоить *impf* +*gen* (**is this film** ~ **seeing?** стоит посмотреть этот фильм?). **worthless** *adj* ничего не стоящий; (*useless*) бесполезный. **worthwhile** *adj* стоящий. **worthy** *adj* достойный.

**would** *v aux* (*conditional*): **he** ~ **be angry if he found out** он бы рассердился, если бы узнал; (*expressing wish*) **she** ~ **like to know** она бы хотела знать; **I** ~ **rather** я бы предпочёл; (*expressing indirect speech*): **he said he** ~ **be late** он сказал, что придёт поздно.

**would-be** *adj*: ~ **actor** человек мечтающий стать актёром.

**wound** n ра́на; vt ра́нить impf & pf. **wounded** adj ра́неный.

**wrangle** n пререка́ние; vi пререка́ться impf.

**wrap** n (shawl) шаль; vt (also ~ up) завёртывать impf, заверну́ть pf; ~ up (in wraps) заку́тывать(ся) impf, заку́тать(ся) pf; ~ped up (in fig) поглощённый +instr. **wrapper** n обёртка. **wrapping** n обёртка; ~ **paper** обёрточная бума́га.

**wrath** n гнев.

**wreak** vt: ~ havoc on разоря́ть impf, разори́ть pf.

**wreath** n вено́к.

**wreck** n (ship) оста́нки (-ов) корабля́; (vehicle, person, building, etc.) разва́лина; vt (destroy, also fig) разруша́ть impf, разру́шить pf; **be ~ed** терпе́ть impf, по~ pf круше́ние; (of plans etc.) ру́хнуть pf. **wreckage** n обло́мки m pl круше́ния.

**wren** n крапи́вник.

**wrench** n (jerk) дёрганье; (tech) га́ечный ключ; (fig) боль; vt (snatch, pull out) вырыва́ть impf, вы́рвать pf (from y+gen); ~ **open** взла́мывать impf, взлома́ть pf.

**wrest** vt (wrench) вырыва́ть impf, вы́рвать pf (from y+gen).

**wrestle** vi боро́ться impf. **wrestler** n боре́ц. **wrestling** n борьба́.

**wretch** n несча́стный sb; (scoundrel) него́дяй. **wretched** adj жа́лкий; (unpleasant) скве́рный.

**wriggle** vi извива́ться impf, изви́ться pf; (fidget) ёрзать impf; ~ **out of** увили́вать impf, увильну́ть от+gen.

**wring** vt (also ~ out) выжи-

ма́ть impf, вы́жать pf; (extort) исторга́ть impf, исто́ргнуть pf (from y+gen); (neck) свёртывать impf, сверну́ть pf (of +dat); ~ **one's hands** лома́ть impf, с~ pf ру́ки.

**wrinkle** n морщи́на; vt & i мо́рщить(ся) impf, с~ pf.

**wrist** n запя́стье; ~**watch** нару́чные часы́ (-со́в) pl.

**writ** n пове́стка.

**write** vt & i писа́ть impf, на~ pf; ~ **down** запи́сывать impf, записа́ть pf; ~ **off** (cancel) спи́сывать impf, списа́ть pf; **the car was a ~off** маши́на была́ соверше́нно испо́рчена; ~ **out** выпи́сывать impf, вы́писать pf (in full по́лностью); ~ **up** (account of) подро́бно опи́сывать impf, описа́ть pf; (notes) перепи́сывать impf, переписа́ть pf; ~**up** (report) отчёт. **writer** n писа́тель m, ~ница.

**writhe** vi ко́рчиться impf, с~ pf.

**writing** n (handwriting) по́черк; (work) произведе́ние; **in** ~ в пи́сьменной фо́рме; ~**paper** почто́вая бума́га.

**wrong** adj (incorrect) непра́вильный, неве́рный; (the wrong ...) не тот (**I have bought the** ~ **book** я купи́л не ту кни́гу; **you've got the** ~ **number** (tel) вы не туда́ попа́ли); (mistaken) непра́в (**you are** ~ ты непра́в); (unjust) несправедли́вый; (sinful) дурно́й; (out of order) нела́дный; (side of cloth) ле́вый; ~ **side out** наизна́нку; ~ **way round** наоборо́т; в зло; (injustice) несправедли́вость; **be in the** ~ быть непра́вым; **do** ~ греши́ть

*impf,* со— *pf; adv* неправильно, неверно; **go** ~ не получаться *impf,* получиться *pf; vt* обидеть *impf,* (*be unjust to*) быть несправедливым к+*dat.* **wrongdoer** *n* преступник, грешник, -ица. **wrongful** *adj* несправедливый. **wrongly** *adv* неправильно; (*unjustly*) несправедливо.
**wrought** *adj:* ~ **iron** сварочное железо.
**wry** *adj* (*smile*) кривой; (*humour*) сухой, иронический.

# X

**xenophobia** *n* ксенофобия.
**X-ray** *n* (*picture*) рентгеновский снимок); *pl* (*radiation*) рентгеновы лучи *m pl; vt* (*photograph*) делать *impf,* с— *pf* рентген +*gen.*

# Y

**yacht** *n* яхта. **yachting** *n* парусный спорт. **yachtsman** *n* яхтсмен.
**yank** *vt* рвануть *pf.*
**yap** *vi* тявкать *impf,* тявкнуть *pf.*
**yard**[1] *n* (*piece of ground*) двор.
**yard**[2] *n* (*measure*) ярд. **yardstick** *n* (*fig*) мерило.
**yarn** *n* пряжа; (*story*) рассказ.
**yawn** *n* зевок; *vi* зевать *impf,* зевнуть *pf;* (*chasm etc.*) зиять *impf.*
**year** *n* год; ~ **in,** ~ **out** из года́ в год. **yearbook** *n* ежегодник. **yearly** *adj* ежегодный, годовой; *adv* ежегодно.
**yearn** *vi* тосковать *impf* (**for**

по+*dat*). **yearning** *n* тоска (**for** по+*dat*).
**yeast** *n* дрожжи (-жей) *pl.*
**yell** *n* крик; *vi* кричать *impf,* крикнуть *pf.*
**yellow** *adj* жёлтый; *n* жёлтый цвет. **yellowish** *adj* желтоватый.
**yelp** *n* визг; *vi* визжать *impf,* взвизгнуть *pf.*
**yes** *adv* да; *n* утверждение, согласие; (*in vote*) голос «за».
**yesterday** *adv* вчера; *n* вчерашний день *m;* ~ **morning** вчера утром; **the day before** ~ позавчера; ~**'s newspaper** вчерашняя газета.
**yet** *adv* (*still yet*) ещё; (*so far*) до сих пор; (*in questions*) уже; (*nevertheless*) тем не менее; ~ пока; до сих пор; **not** ~ ещё не; *conj* однако, но.
**yew** *n* тис.
**Yiddish** *n* идиш.
**yield** *n* (*harvest*) урожай; (*econ*) доход; *vt* (*fruit, revenue, etc.*) приносить *impf,* принести *pf;* (*give up*) сдавать *impf,* сдать *pf, vi* (*give in*) (*to enemy etc.*) уступать *impf,* уступить *pf* (**to** +*dat*); (*give way*) поддаваться *impf,* поддаться *pf* (**to** +*dat*).
**yoga** *n* йога.
**yoghurt** *n* кефир.
**yoke** *n* (*also fig*) ярмо; (*fig*) иго; (*of dress*) кокетка; *vt* впрягать *impf,* впрячь *pf* в ярмо.
**yolk** *n* желток.
**yonder** *adv* вон там; *adj* вон тот.
**you** *pron* (*familiar sg*) ты; (*familiar sg, polite sg & pl*) вы; (*one*) *not usu translated; v translated in 2nd pers sg or by impers construction:* ~ **never**

know никогда́ не зна́ешь.

**young** *adj* молодо́й; **the ~** молодёжь; *n* (*collect*) детёныши *m pl*. **youngster** *n* ма́льчик, де́вочка.

**your(s)** *poss pron* (*familiar sg*; *also in letter*) твой; (*familiar pl*, *polite sg & pl*; *also in letter*) ваш; свой. **yourself** *pron* (*emph*) (*familiar sg*) (ты) сам (*m*), сама́ (*f*); (*familiar pl*, *polite sg & pl*) (вы) са́ми; (*refl*) себя́, -ся (*suffixed to vt*); **by ~** (*independently*) самостоя́тельно, сам; (*alone*) оди́н.

**youth** *n* (*age*) мо́лодость; (*young man*) ю́ноша *m*; (*collect*, *as pl*) молодёжь; **~ club** молодёжный клуб; **~ hostel** молодёжная турба́за. **youthful** *adj* ю́ношеский.

**Yugoslavia** *n* Югосла́вия.

# Z

**zany** *adj* смешно́й.

**zeal** *n* рве́ние, усе́рдие. **zealot** *n* фана́тик. **zealous** *adj* ре́вностный, усе́рдный.

**zebra** *n* зе́бра.

**zenith** *n* зени́т.

**zero** *n* нуль *m*, ноль *m*.

**zest** *n* (*piquancy*) пика́нтность; (*ardour*) энтузиа́зм; **~ for life** жизнера́достность.

**zigzag** *n* зигза́г; *adj* зигзаго-обра́зный; *vi* де́лать *impf*, c~ *pf* зигза́ги; идти́ *det* зигза́гами.

**zinc** *n* цинк.

**Zionism** *n* сиони́зм. **Zionist** *n* сиони́ст.

**zip** *n* (*~ fastener*) (застёжка-)мо́лния; *vt & i*: **~ up** застёгивать(ся) *impf*, застегну́ть(ся) *pf* на мо́лнию.

**zodiac** *n* зодиа́к; **sign of the ~** знак зодиа́ка.

**zombie** *n* челове́к спя́щий на ходу́.

**zone** *n* зо́на; (*geog*) по́яс.

**zoo** *n* зоопа́рк. **zoological** *adj* зоологи́ческий; **~ garden(s)** зоологи́ческий сад. **zoologist** *n* зоо́лог. **zoology** *n* зооло́гия.

**zoom** *vi* (*rush*) мча́ться *impf*; **~ in** (*phot*) де́лать *impf*, c~ *pf* наплы́в; **~ lens** объекти́в с переме́нным фо́кусным расстоя́нием.

**Zulu** *adj* зулу́сский; *n* зулу́с, ~ка.

# Appendix I  Spelling Rules

It is assumed that the user is acquainted with the following spelling rules which affect Russian declension and conjugation.

1.  **ы**, **ю**, and **я** do not follow **г**, **к**, **х**, **ж**, **ч**, **ш**, and **щ**; instead, **и**, **у**, and **а** are used, e.g. **ма́льчики**, **кричу́**, **лежа́т**, **ноча́ми**; similarly, **ю** and **я** do not follow **ц**; instead, **у** or **а** are used.

2.  Unstressed **о** does not follow **ж**, **ц**, **ч**, **ш**, or **щ**; instead, **е** is used, e.g. **му́жем**, **ме́сяцев**, **хоро́шее**.

# Appendix II  Declension of Russian Adjectives

The following patterns are regarded as regular and are not shown in the dictionary entries.

| Singular | nom | acc | gen | dat | instr | prep |
|---|---|---|---|---|---|---|
| *Masculine* | тёпл\|ый | ~ый | ~ого | ~ому | ~ым | ~ом |
| *Feminine* | тёпл\|ая | ~ую | ~ой | ~ой | ~ой | ~ой |
| *Neuter* | тёпл\|ое | ~ое | ~ого | ~ому | ~ым | ~ом |

| Plural | nom | acc | gen | dat | instr | prep |
|---|---|---|---|---|---|---|
| *Masculine* | тёпл\|ые | ~ые | ~ых | ~ым | ~ыми | ~ых |
| *Feminine* | тёпл\|ые | ~ые | ~ых | ~ым | ~ыми | ~ых |
| *Neuter* | тёпл\|ые | ~ые | ~ых | ~ым | ~ыми | ~ых |

## Appendix III  Declension of Russian Nouns

The following patterns are regarded as regular and are
not shown in the dictionary entries. Forms marked *
should be particularly noted.

### 1  *Masculine*

| Singular nom | acc | gen | dat | instr | prep |
|---|---|---|---|---|---|
| обе́\|д | ~ | ~а | ~у | ~ом | ~е |
| слу́ча\|й | ~й | ~я | ~ю | ~ем | ~е |
| марш | ~ | ~а | ~у | ~ем | ~е |
| каранда́ш | ~ | ~а́ | ~у́ | ~о́м* | ~е́ |
| сцена́ри\|й | ~й | ~я | ~ю | ~ем | ~и* |
| портфе́л\|ь | ~ь | ~я | ~ю | ~ем | ~е |

| Plural nom | acc | gen | dat | instr | prep |
|---|---|---|---|---|---|
| обе́д\|ы | ~ы | ~ов | ~ам | ~ами | ~ах |
| слу́ча\|и | ~и | ~ев | ~ям | ~ями | ~ях |
| ма́рш\|и | ~и | ~ей* | ~ам | ~ами | ~ах |
| карандаш\|и́ | ~и́ | ~е́й* | ~а́м | ~а́ми | ~а́х |
| сцена́ри\|и | ~и | ~ев* | ~ям | ~ями | ~ях |
| портфе́л\|и | ~и | ~ей* | ~ям | ~ями | ~ях |

### 2  *Feminine*

| Singular nom | acc | gen | dat | instr | prep |
|---|---|---|---|---|---|
| газе́т\|а | ~у | ~ы | ~е | ~ой | ~е |
| ба́н\|я | ~ю | ~и | ~е | ~ей | ~е |
| ли́ни\|я | ~ю | ~и | ~и* | ~ей | ~и* |
| ста́ту\|я | ~ю | ~и | ~е* | ~ей | ~е* |
| бол\|ь | ~ь | ~и | ~и* | ~ью* | ~и* |

| Plural | nom | acc | gen | dat | instr | prep |
|--------|-----|-----|-----|-----|-------|------|
| газе́т\|ы | ~ы | ~ | ~ам | ~ами | ~ах |
| ба́н\|и | ~и | ~ь* | ~ям | ~ями | ~ях |
| ли́ни\|и | ~и | ~й* | ~ям | ~ями | ~ях |
| ста́ту\|и | ~и | ~й* | ~ям | ~ями | ~ях |
| бо́л\|и | ~и | ~ей* | ~ям | ~ями | ~ях |

## 3 Neuter

| Singular | nom | acc | gen | dat | instr | prep |
|----------|-----|-----|-----|-----|-------|------|
| чу́вств\|о | ~о | ~а | ~у | ~ом | ~е |
| учи́лищ\|е | ~е | ~а | ~у | ~ем | ~е |
| зда́ни\|е | ~е | ~я | ~ю | ~ем | ~и* |
| уще́л\|ье | ~ье | ~ья | ~ью | ~ьем | ~ье |

| Plural | nom | acc | gen | dat | instr | prep |
|--------|-----|-----|-----|-----|-------|------|
| чу́вств\|а | ~а | ~ | ~ам | ~ами | ~ах |
| учи́лищ\|а | ~а | ~ | ~ам | ~ами | ~ах |
| зда́ни\|я | ~я | ~й* | ~ям | ~ями | ~ях |
| уще́л\|ья | ~ья | ~ий* | ~ьям | ~ьями | ~ьях |

# Appendix IV Conjugation of Russian Verbs

The following patterns are regarded as regular and are not shown in the dictionary entries.

## 1. -e- conjugation

| | | | | | | |
|---|---|---|---|---|---|---|
| (a) **чита́\|ть** | ~ю | ~ешь | ~ет | ~ем | ~ете | ~ют |
| (b) **сия́\|ть** | ~ю | ~ешь | ~ет | ~ем | ~ете | ~ют |
| (c) **про́б\|овать** | ~ую | ~уешь | ~ует | ~уем | ~уете | ~уют |
| (d) **рис\|ова́ть** | ~у́ю | ~у́ешь | ~у́ет | ~у́ем | ~у́ете | ~у́ют |

## 2. -и- conjugation

| | | | | | | |
|---|---|---|---|---|---|---|
| (a) **говор\|и́ть** | ~ю́ | ~и́шь | ~и́т | ~и́м | ~и́те | ~я́т |
| (b) **стро́\|ить** | ~ю | ~ишь | ~ит | ~им | ~ите | ~ят |

## Notes

1. Also belonging to the **-e-** conjugation are:

   i) most other verbs in **-ать** (but see Note 2(v) below), e.g. **жа́ждать** (жа́жду, -ждешь); **пря́тать** (пря́чу, -чешь), **колеба́ть** (коле́блю, -блешь).

   ii) verbs in **-еть** for which the 1st pers sing **-ею** is given, e.g. **жале́ть.**

   iii) verbs in **-нуть** for which the 1st pers sing **-ну** is given (e.g. **вя́нуть**), **ю** becoming **у** in the 1st pers sing and 3rd pers pl.

   iv) verbs in **-ять** which drop the **я** in conjugation, e.g. **ла́ять** (ла́ю, ла́ешь); **се́ять** (се́ю, се́ешь).

2. Also belonging to the **-и-** conjugation are:

    i) verbs in consonant + **-ить** which change the consonant in the first person singular, e.g. **досади́ть** (-ажу́, -ади́шь), or insert an **-л-**, e.g. **доба́вить** (доба́влю, -вишь).

    ii) other verbs in vowel + **-ить**, e.g. **затаи́ть, кле́ить** (as 2b above).

    iii) verbs in **-еть** for which the 1st pers sing is given as consonant + **ю** or **у**, e.g. **звене́ть** (-ню́, -ни́шь), **ви́деть** (ви́жу, ви́дишь).

    iv) two verbs in **-ять (стоя́ть, боя́ться).**

    v) verbs in **-ать** whose stem ends in **ч, ж, щ,** or **ш,** not changing between the infinitive and conjugation, e.g. **крича́ть** (-чу́, -чи́шь). Cf. Note 1(i).

# Key to the Russian Alphabet

| Capital | Lower-case | Approx. English Sound |
|---------|------------|----------------------|
| А | а | a |
| Б | б | b |
| В | в | v |
| Г | г | g |
| Д | д | d |
| Е | е | ye |
| Ё | ё | yo |
| Ж | ж | zh (as in measure) |
| З | з | z |
| И | и | i |
| Й | й | y |
| К | к | k |
| Л | л | l |
| М | м | m |
| Н | н | n |
| О | о | o |
| П | п | p |
| Р | р | r |
| С | с | s |
| Т | т | t |
| У | у | oo |
| Ф | ф | f |
| Х | х | kh (as in loch) |
| Ц | ц | ts |
| Ч | ч | ch |
| Ш | ш | sh |
| Щ | щ | shch |
| Ъ | ъ | ″ ('hard sign'; not pronounced as separate sound) |
| Ы | ы | y |
| Ь | ь | ′ ('soft sign'; not pronounced as separate sound) |
| Э | э | e |
| Ю | ю | yu |
| Я | я | ya |